CLYMER® MANUALS

HARLEY-DAVIDSON

FXD EVOLUTION • 1991-1998

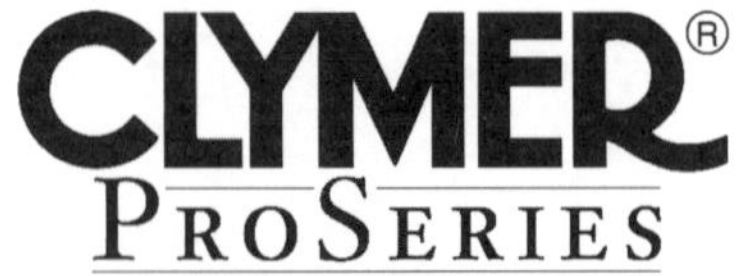

More information available at Clymer.com
Phone: 805-498-6703

Haynes Publishing Group
Sparkford Nr Yeovil
Somerset BA22 7JJ England

Haynes North America, Inc
859 Lawrence Drive
Newbury Park
California 91320 USA

ISBN-10: 0-89287-871-1
ISBN-13: 978-0-89287-871-0
Library of Congress: 2003109486

Author: *Ron Wright*
Technical Photography: *Ed Scott*
Technical Illustrations: *Steve Amos*
Cover: *Mark Clifford Photography, Los Angeles, California (www.markclifford.com)*

Printed in Malaysia

M424-2, 11R1, 13-552 **ABCDEFGHIJKLMN**

Common spark plug conditions

NORMAL

Symptoms: Brown to grayish-tan color and slight electrode wear. Correct heat range for engine and operating conditions.
Recommendation: When new spark plugs are installed, replace with plugs of the same heat range.

WORN

Symptoms: Rounded electrodes with a small amount of deposits on the firing end. Normal color. Causes hard starting in damp or cold weather and poor fuel economy.
Recommendation: Plugs have been left in the engine too long. Replace with new plugs of the same heat range. Follow the recommended maintenance schedule.

CARBON DEPOSITS

Symptoms: Dry sooty deposits indicate a rich mixture or weak ignition. Causes misfiring, hard starting and hesitation.
Recommendation: Make sure the plug has the correct heat range. Check for a clogged air filter or problem in the fuel system or engine management system. Also check for ignition system problems.

ASH DEPOSITS

Symptoms: Light brown deposits encrusted on the side or center electrodes or both. Derived from oil and/ or fuel additives. Excessive amounts may mask the spark, causing misfiring and hesitation during acceleration.
Recommendation: If excessive deposits accumulate over a short time or low mileage, install new valve guide seals to prevent seepage of oil into the combustion chambers. Also try changing gasoline brands.

OIL DEPOSITS

Symptoms: Oily coating caused by poor oil control. Oil is leaking past worn valve guides or piston rings into the combustion chamber. Causes hard starting, misfiring and hesitation.
Recommendation: Correct the mechanical condition with necessary repairs and install new plugs.

GAP BRIDGING

Symptoms: Combustion deposits lodge between the electrodes. Heavy deposits accumulate and bridge the electrode gap. The plug ceases to fire, resulting in a dead cylinder.
Recommendation: Locate the faulty plug and remove the deposits from between the electrodes.

TOO HOT

Symptoms: Blistered, white insulator, eroded electrode and absence of deposits. Results in shortened plug life.
Recommendation: Check for the correct plug heat range, over-advanced ignition timing, lean fuel mixture, intake manifold vacuum leaks, sticking valves and insufficient engine cooling.

PREIGNITION

Symptoms: Melted electrodes. Insulators are white, but may be dirty due to misfiring or flying debris in the combustion chamber. Can lead to engine damage.
Recommendation: Check for the correct plug heat range, over-advanced ignition timing, lean fuel mixture, insufficient engine cooling and lack of lubrication.

HIGH SPEED GLAZING

Symptoms: Insulator has yellowish, glazed appearance. Indicates that combustion chamber temperatures have risen suddenly during hard acceleration. Normal deposits melt to form a conductive coating. Causes misfiring at high speeds.
Recommendation: Install new plugs. Consider using a colder plug if driving habits warrant.

DETONATION

Symptoms: Insulators may be cracked or chipped. Improper gap setting techniques can also result in a fractured insulator tip. Can lead to piston damage.
Recommendation: Make sure the fuel anti-knock values meet engine requirements. Use care when setting the gaps on new plugs. Avoid lugging the engine.

MECHANICAL DAMAGE

Symptoms: May be caused by a foreign object in the combustion chamber or the piston striking an incorrect reach (too long) plug. Causes a dead cylinder and could result in piston damage.
Recommendation: Repair the mechanical damage. Remove the foreign object from the engine and/or install the correct reach plug.

CONTENTS

CHAPTER EIGHT

CHAPTER NINE

CHAPTER TEN

CHAPTER ELEVEN

CHAPTER TWELVE

QUICK REFERENCE DATA

MOTORCYCLE INFORMATION

MODEL:______________________________ YEAR:______________
VIN NUMBER:______________________________
ENGINE SERIAL NUMBER:______________________________
CARBURETOR SERIAL NUMBER OR I.D. MARK:______________________________

TIRE PRESSURE

	psi	kg/cm²
Up to 300 lb. (136 kg) load		
Front	30	2.1
Rear	36	2.5
Up to GVWR maximum load		
Front	30	2.1
Rear	40	2.8

ENGINE OIL

Type	HD rating	Viscosity	Lowest ambient operating temperature
HD Multigrade	HD 240	SAE10W/40	Below 40° F
HD Multigrade	HD 240	SAE 20W/50	Above 40° F
HD Regular Heavy	HD 240	SAE 50	Above 60° F
HD Extra Heavy	HD 240	SAE 60	Above 80° F

RECOMMENDED LUBRICANTS AND FLUIDS

Battery	Distilled water
Brake fluid	DOT 5
Front fork oil	HD Type E or equivalent
Fuel	87 pump octane or higher leaded or unleaded
Transmission	HD Sport Trans Fluid or equivalent
Primary chaincase	HD Primary Chaincase Lubricant

ENGINE AND PRIMARY DRIVE/TRANSMISSION OIL CAPACITIES

Oil tank refill capacity	
With oil filter	3 U.S. qts. (2.8 L, 2.5 Imp. qts.)
Without oil filter	2 U.S. qts. and 14 oz. (2.3 L)
Primary chaincase	
1991-1997	30-36 U.S. oz. (890-1065 ml, 31-37 Imp. Oz.)
1998	26 U.S. oz. (770 ml)
Transmission	
1991-1998	16 U.S. oz. (473 ml, 16.7 Imp. Oz.)

TUNE-UP SPECIFICATIONS

Engine compression	90 psi (6.2 kg/cm^2)
Spark plugs	
Type	
Autolite	4265
Champion	RN12YC
Harley-Davidson	5R6A
Gap	0.038-0.043 in. (0.97-1.09 mm)
Igniton timing	
Range	0-35° BTDC
Start	0° BTDC
Idle speed	1000-1050 rpm

MAINTENANCE TIGHTENING TORQUES

	ft.-lb.	N•m
Air filter		
Backplate screws	3-5	4-7
Cover screw	3-5	4-7
Cylinder head screws	10-12	14-16
Clutch adjusting screw locknut	6-10	8-14
Clutch inspection cover screws	4-6	5-8
Primary chain inspection cover screws	9-10	12-14
Primary chain adjuster shoe nut	25	34
Rear axle nut	60-65	81-88
Spark plugs	18-22	24-30
Lifter screen plug	7-10	10-14
Transmission drain plug	14-21	19-28
Upper and lower fork bracket pinch bolts		
FXDWG	30-35	41-47
All other models	25-30	34-41

FUEL TANK CAPACITY

	U.S. gal.	Liters	Imp. Gal
1991-1992			
Total	4.9	18.5	4.1
Reserve	4.1	4.2	0.9
1993-1994			
Total	5.2	19.7	4.3
Reserve	1.1	4.2	0.9
1995-1998			
FXDWG			
Total	5.2	19.7	4.3
Reserve	1.1	4.2	0.9
All other models			
Total	4.9	18.5	4.1
Reserve	1.1	4.2	0.9

1

CHAPTER ONE

GENERAL INFORMATION

This Clymer shop manual covers the Harley-Davidson Dyna Glide produced from 1991-1998.

Procedures unique to 1996-1998 models are covered in the supplement at the end of the manual.

Troubleshooting, tune-up, maintenance and repair are not difficult, if you know what tools and equipment to use and what steps to follow. Step-by-step instructions guide you through jobs ranging from simple maintenance to engine and suspension repair.

Anyone from a first time do-it yourselfer to a professional mechanic can use this manual. Detailed drawings and clear photographs give you the information you need to work on your Dyna Glide correctly.

Table 1 lists model coverage.

Table 2 lists general specifications.

Table 3 lists overall vehicle weight specifications.

Table 4 lists gross vehicle weight ratings.

Table 5 lists fuel capacity.

Table 6 lists U.S. to metric conversion. Metric and U.S. standards are used throughout this manual.

Table 7 lists general torque specifications. Critical torque specifications are found in table form at the end of each chapter (as required). Use the general torque specifications in **Table 7** if a chapter table does not list a torque specific tightening.

Table 8 lists conversion tables.

Table 9 lists tap drill sizes.

Tables 1-9 are at the end of the chapter.

MANUAL ORGANIZATION

This chapter provides general information useful to Dyna Glide owners and mechanics. In addition, information in this chapter discusses the tools and techniques for preventive maintenance, troubleshooting and repair.

Chapter Two provides methods and suggestions for quick and accurate diagnosis of problems. Troubleshooting procedures discuss typical symptoms and logical methods to pinpoint the cause of the trouble.

Chapter Three explains all periodic lubrication and routine maintenance necessary to keep your Dyna Glide operating well.

Chapter Three also includes recommended tune-up procedures, eliminating the need to consult other chapters on the various assemblies.

Subsequent chapters describe specific systems, providing disassemby, repair, assembly and adjustment procedures in simple step-by-step form. If a repair is impractical for a home mechanic, the text will suggest that you have the service done at a dealership or repair shop. Doing so will save you time and money. Service specifications and tightening torques are listed at the end of the appropriate chapter.

NOTES, CAUTIONS AND WARNINGS

The terms NOTE, CAUTION and WARNING have specific meanings in this manual. A NOTE provides additional information to make a step or procedure easier or clearer. Disregarding a NOTE could cause inconvenience, but would not cause damage or personal injury.

A CAUTION emphasizes areas where equipment damage could occur. Disregarding a CAUTION could cause permanent mechanical damage; however, personal injury is unlikely.

A WARNING emphasizes areas where personal injury or even death could result from negligence. Mechanical damage may also occur. WARNINGS *must be taken seriously*. Sometimes, serious injury and death have resulted from disregarding similar warnings.

SAFETY FIRST

Professional mechanics can work for years and never sustain a serious injury. If you observe a few rules of common sense and safety, you can enjoy many safe hours servicing your own machine. If you ignore these rules you can hurt yourself or damage the equipment.

1. Never use gasoline as a cleaning solvent.

WARNING
Store gasoline in an approved gasoline storage container, properly labeled. Wipe spilled gasoline up immediately.

2. Never smoke or use a torch near flammable liquids, such as cleaning solvent in an open container.
3. Before welding or brazing on the machine, remove the fuel tank to a safe distance, at least 50 ft. (15m) away.
4. Use the proper sized wrenches to avoid damage to fasteners and injury to yourself.
5. When loosening a tight or stuck fastener, protect yourself should the wrench slip or the fastener break.
6. When replacing a fastener, make sure to use one with the same measurements and strength as the old one. Incorrect or mismatched fasteners can result in damage to your motorcycle and possible personal injury. Beware of fastener kits filled with cheap and poorly-made nuts, bolts, washers and cotter pins. Refer to *Fasteners* in this chapter for additional information.
7. Keep all hand and power tools in good condition. Wipe greasy and oily tools after using them. They are difficult to hold and can cause injury. Repair or replace worn or damaged tools.
8. Keep your work area clean and uncluttered.
9. Wear safety goggles during all operations involving drilling, grinding, the use of a cold chisel or whenever you feel unsure about the safety of your eyes. Also, wear safety goggles (**Figure 1**) when using solvent and compressed air to clean parts.

WARNING
*The improper use of compressed air is very dangerous. Using compressed air to dust off your clothes, bike or workbench can cause flying particles to blow into your eyes or skin. **Never** direct compressed air directly at your skin or into body openings (including cuts) as this can cause severe injury or death. Use compressed air carefully. Never allow children to use or play with compressed air.*

10. Keep an approved fire extinguisher nearby (**Figure 2**). The correct ratings are Class B for gasoline fires and Class C for electrical fires.
11. When drying bearings or other rotating parts with compressed air, never allow the air jet to rotate

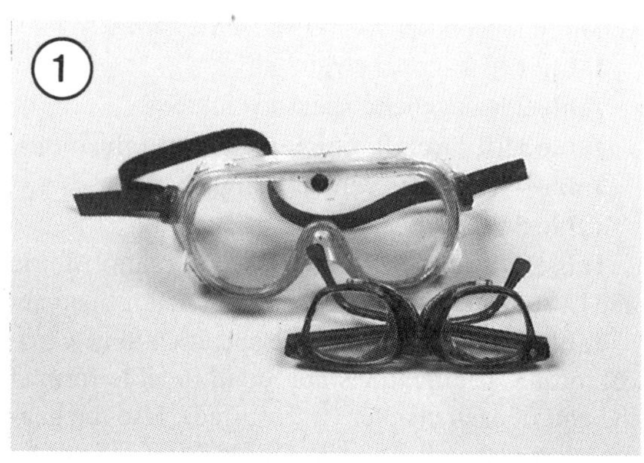

the bearing or part. The air jet can rotate a bearing at excessive speeds. When this happens, the bearing or rotating part is very likely to disintegrate and cause serious injury and damage. Hold the inner bearing race (**Figure 3**) by hand when drying it with compressed air.

12. Never work on the upper part of the bike while someone is working underneath it.
13. Do not carry sharp tools or objects in your pockets when working on your bike.
14. When working on your bike, learn to use tools correctly.

SERVICE HINTS

Most of the service procedures covered are straightforward and can be performed by anyone handy with tools. However, always consider your own capabilities carefully before attempting any operation involving major disassembly.

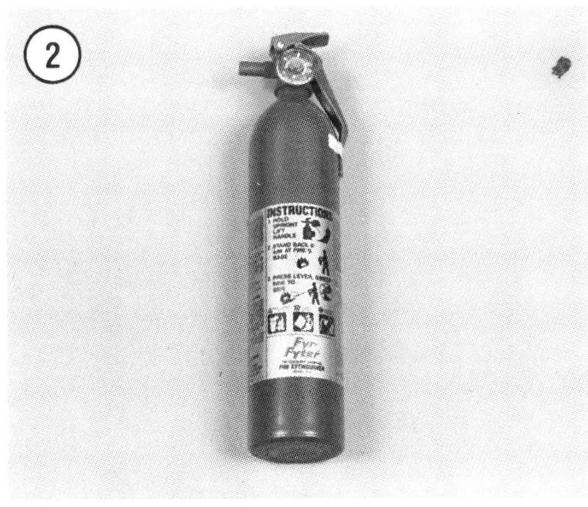

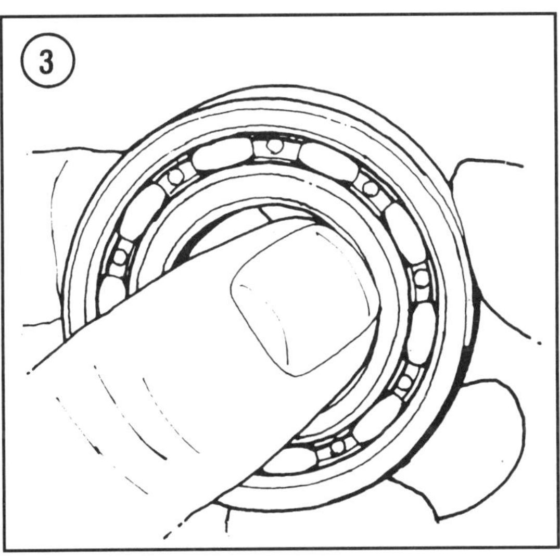

1. "Front," as used in this manual, refers to the front of the motorcycle; the front of any component is the end closest to the front of the motorcycle. The "left" and "right" side refer to the position of the parts as viewed by a rider sitting on the seat and facing forward. For example, the throttle control is on the right-hand side. These rules are simple, but confusion can cause a major inconvenience during service.

2. Whenever servicing the engine or a suspension component, secure the bike properly. When you park your bike on its jiffy stand or on a commercial stand, check the bike before walking away from it. Block the front and rear wheels if they remain on the ground. Because of the motorcycle's weight, use a commercial stand that can safely lift and hold it.

3. Repairs go much faster and easier if the bike is clean before you begin work. Select the proper chemical for washing the engine and related parts. Spray or brush on the cleaning solution, following the manufacturer's directions. Rinse parts with a garden hose. Clean all oily or greasy parts with cleaning solvent as you remove them.

WARNING

***Never** use gasoline as a cleaning agent. It presents an extreme fire hazard. Work in a well-ventilated area when using cleaning solvent. Keep a fire extinguisher, rated for gasoline fires, handy in any case.*

4. Much of the labor charged for by mechanics is to remove and disassemble other parts to reach the defective unit. Performing the preliminary operations yourself is usually possible. Then, take the defective unit to a dealership for repair.

5. Once you have decided to tackle the job yourself, read the entire section *completely* while looking at the actual parts before starting the job. Make sure you have identified the proper procedure. Study the illustrations and text until you have a good idea of what is involved in completing the job satisfactorily. If the service job requires a special tool or replacement parts, arrange to get them before you start. It is frustrating to get partly into a job and then be unable to complete it.

NOTE
Some of the procedures or service specifications listed in this manual may not be applicable if you modified or installed aftermarket equipment on your bike. When modifying or installing aftermarket equipment, file the manufacturer's instructions in a book for future reference.

6. You can make simple wiring checks at home, but a basic knowledge of electricity is almost a necessity when performing tests with complicated test gear.

CAUTION
Improper testing can sometimes damage an electrical component.

7. Disconnect the negative battery cable (**Figure 4**) when working on or near electrical, clutch or starter systems. On all models covered in this manual, the negative terminal is marked with a minus (–) sign. The positive terminal is marked with a plus (+) sign.

WARNING
Disconnecting the positive cable while the negative cable is still connected may cause a spark. This could ignite the hydrogen gas given off by the battery, causing an explosion.

8. During disassembly, keep a few general cautions in mind. You rarely need to apply force during disassembly. If parts are a tight fit, such as a bearing in a case, there is usually a tool designed to separate them. Never use a screwdriver to pry parts with machined surfaces such as crankcase halves. You will mar the surfaces and end up with leaks.
9. Make diagrams (or take a Polaroid picture) wherever similar-appearing parts are found. You may think you can remember where everything came from—but mistakes are costly.
10. Tag all similar internal parts for location and mark all mating parts for position (**Figure 5**). Record the number and thickness of any shims as they are removed; measure them with a vernier caliper or micrometer. Place small parts in plastic sandwich bags (**Figure 5**). Seal and label them with masking tape.
11. Place parts from a specific area of the engine (such as cylinder heads, cylinders, clutch and transmission) into plastic boxes (**Figure 5**) to keep them separated.

12. When disassembling assemblies with many parts, use an egg flat (type that restaurants get their eggs in) (**Figure 5**) and set the parts in the depressions in the same order in which you removed them.

13. Identify wires and connectors with a marking pen and masking tape. Again, do not rely on memory alone, especially if a previous owner changed the wiring.

14. Protect finished surfaces from physical damage or corrosion. Keep gasoline off painted surfaces.

15. Use penetrating oil on frozen or tight bolts, then strike the bolt head a few times with a hammer and punch. Avoid the use of heat where possible, as it can warp, melt or affect the temper of parts. Heat will also ruin painted and plastic surfaces.

16. Many parts will require the use of a puller or press during disassembly and reassembly. If a part is difficult to remove or install, find out why before proceeding.

17. Cover all openings after removing parts or components to prevent dirt, small tools or other contamination from falling in.

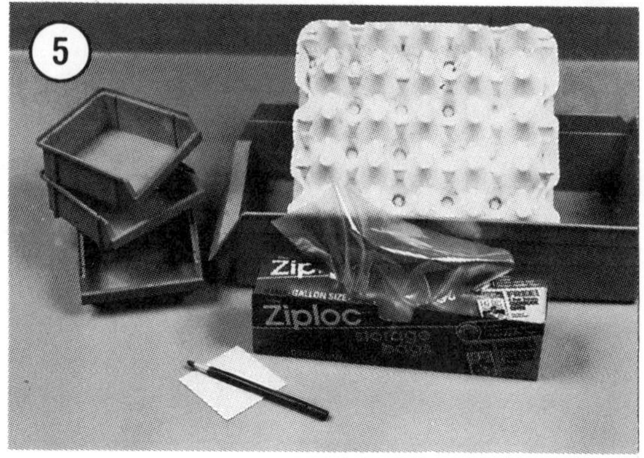

18. The text makes occasional recommendations to refer certain service or maintenance jobs to a Harley-Davidson dealership. In these cases, the dealership can probably do the work more quickly and economically than if you performed the job yourself.
19. In procedural steps, the word "replace" means to discard a defective part and replace it with a new or exchange unit. "Overhaul" means to remove, disassemble, inspect, measure, repair or replace defective parts, reassemble and install major systems or parts.
20. Some operations require the use of a hydraulic press. If you do not have a press, refer the job to a dealership or machine shop.
21. When assembling parts, install all shims and washers in their original mounting position and order.
22. Whenever a rotating part butts against a stationary part, look for a shim or washer.
23. Always use new gaskets and O-rings during reassembly.
24. If it becomes necessary to purchase gasket material to make a gasket, measure the thickness of the old gasket (at an uncompressed point) and purchase gasket material with the same approximate thickness.
25. Use heavy grease to hold small parts in place if they tend fall out during assembly. However, keep grease and oil away from electrical and brake components.
26. Never use wire to clean out jets and air passages. Use compressed air to blow out the carburetor only if you removed the diaphragm first.
27. Take your time and do the job right. Do not forget that a newly rebuilt engine must be broken in just like a new one.

6

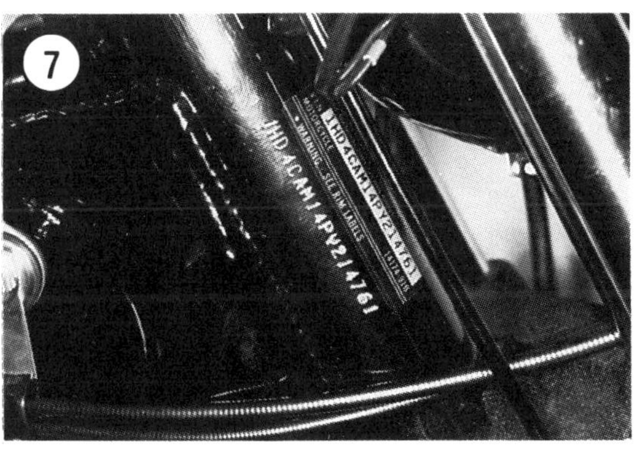

7

SERIAL NUMBERS

You must know the model serial number and VIN number for registration purposes and when ordering replacement parts. The serial number locations are as follows:

a. The engine serial number is on the rear right-hand side of the engine case (**Figure 6**).
b. The frame serial number is stamped on the steering head (**Figure 7**).

PARTS REPLACEMENT

Always order parts by the frame and engine serial numbers.

Compare new parts and old parts. If they are not alike, have the parts manager explain the difference to you.

TORQUE SPECIFICATIONS

This manual lists torque specifications in foot-pounds (ft-lb.) and newton-meters (N•m).

Table 7 lists general torque specifications for nuts and bolts that are not listed in the respective chapters. To use the table, first determine the size of the bolt or nut. Use a vernier caliper and measure the inside diameter of the threads of the nut (**Figure 8**) and outer diameter of the threads for a bolt (**Figure 9**).

FASTENERS

Fasteners (screws, bolts, nuts, studs, pins, clips, etc.) are used to secure various pieces of the engine, frame and suspension together. Proper selection and installation of fasteners are important to ensure that the motorcycle operates satisfactorily; otherwise, failure is possible.

Threaded Fasteners

Most of the components on your motorcycle are held together by threaded fasteners such as screws, bolts, nuts and studs. Most fasteners are tightened by turning clockwise (right-hand threads), although some fasteners may have left-hand threads if rotating parts can cause loosening.

Two dimensions are needed to match threaded fasteners: the number of threads in a given distance and the outside diameter of the threads. Two standards are currently used in the United States to specify the dimensions of threaded fasteners, the U.S. common system and the metric system. Pay particular attention when working with unidentified fasteners; mismatching thread types can damage threads.

NOTE
Threaded fasteners must be hand tightened during initial assembly to be sure mismatched fasteners are not being used and cross-threading is not occurring. If fasteners are hard to turn, determine the cause before using a tool for final tightening.

Screws and bolts built to U.S. common system standard are classified by length (L, **Figure 10**), diameter (D) and threads per inch (TPI). A typical bolt might be identified by the numbers 7/16—14 × 1 1/2, which would show that the bolt has a diameter of 7/16 in., 14 threads per inch and a length of 1 1/2 in.

U.S. screws and bolts are graded according to Society of Automotive Engineers (SAE) specifications to indicate their strength. Slash marks are on top of the screw or bolt as shown in **Figure 10**. These marks show the strength grade with a greater number of slashes indicating greater strength (**Figure 11**). Ungraded screws and bolts (no slash marks on head) are the weakest.

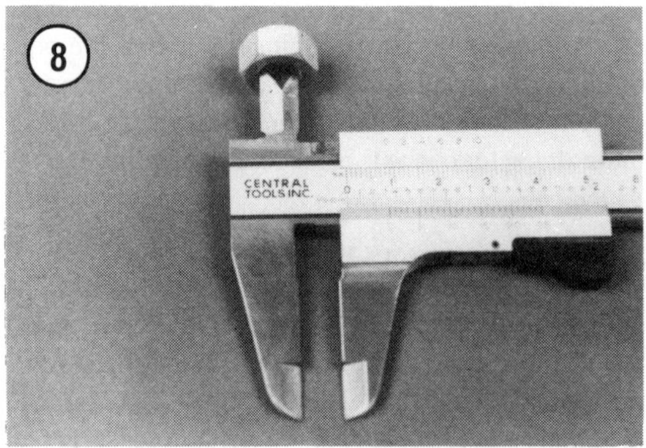

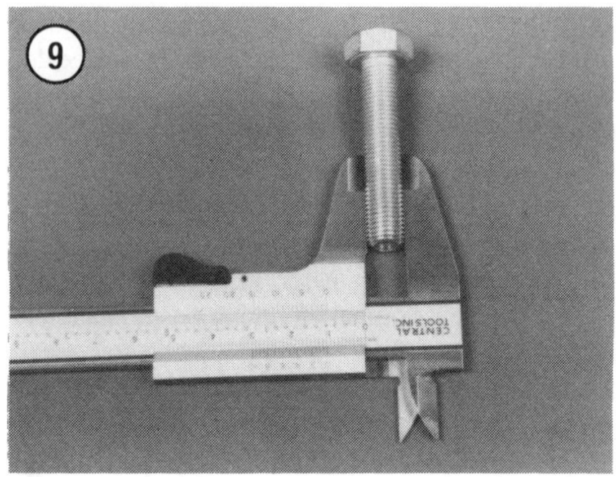

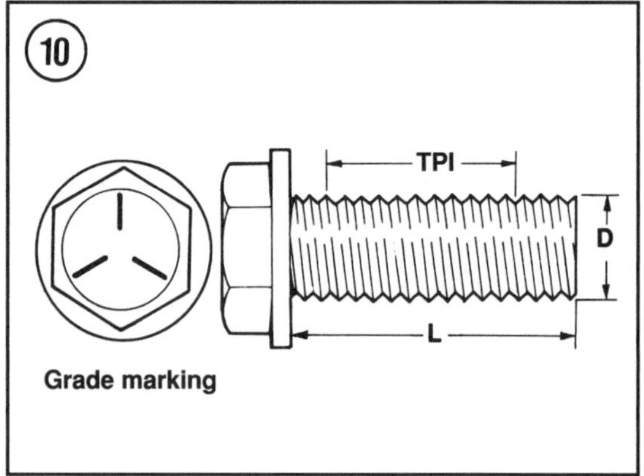

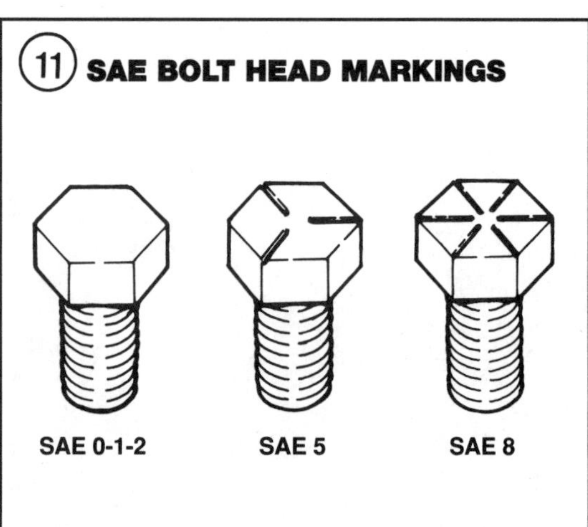

Metric screws and bolts are classified by length (L, **Figure 12**), diameter (D) and distance between thread crests (T). A typical bolt might be identified by the numbers 8 × 1.25—130, which indicates that the bolt has a diameter of 8 mm, the distance between threads crests is 1.25 mm and bolt length is 130 mm.

The strength of metric screws and bolts is indicated by numbers located on top of the screw or bolt as shown in **Figure 12**. The higher the number the stronger the screw or bolt. Unnumbered screws and bolts are the weakest.

CAUTION
***Do not** install screws or bolts with a lower strength grade classification than installed originally by the manufacturer. Doing so may cause vehicle failure and possible injury.*

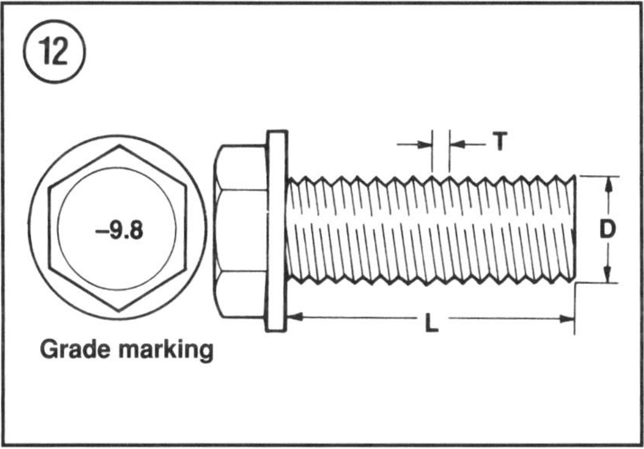

Tightening a screw or bolt increases the clamping force it exerts. The stronger the screw or bolt, the greater the possible clamping force. Critical torque specifications are listed in a table at the end of the appropriate chapter. If not, use the torque specifications listed in **Table 7**.

Machine screw is a numbering system used to identify screws smaller than 1/4 in. Machine screws are identified by gauge size (diameter) and threads per inch. For example, 12-28 indicates a 12 gauge screw with 28 threads per inch.

Screws and bolts are manufactured with a variety of head shapes to fit specific design requirements. Your motorcycle is equipped with the common hex and slotted head types, but other types, like those shown in **Figure 13** and **Figure 14** will also be encountered.

The most common nut used is the hex nut (**Figure 15**). The hex nut is often used with a lockwasher. Self-locking nuts have a nylon insert that prevents loosening; no lockwasher is required. Wing nuts, designed for fast removal by hand, are used for convenience in non-critical locations. Nuts are sized using the same system as screws and bolts. On hex-type nuts, the distance between two opposing flats indicates the proper wrench size to use.

Self-locking screws, bolts and nuts may use a locking mechanism that uses an interference fit between mating threads. Manufacturers achieve Interference in various ways: by distorting threads, coating threads with dry adhesive or nylon, distort-

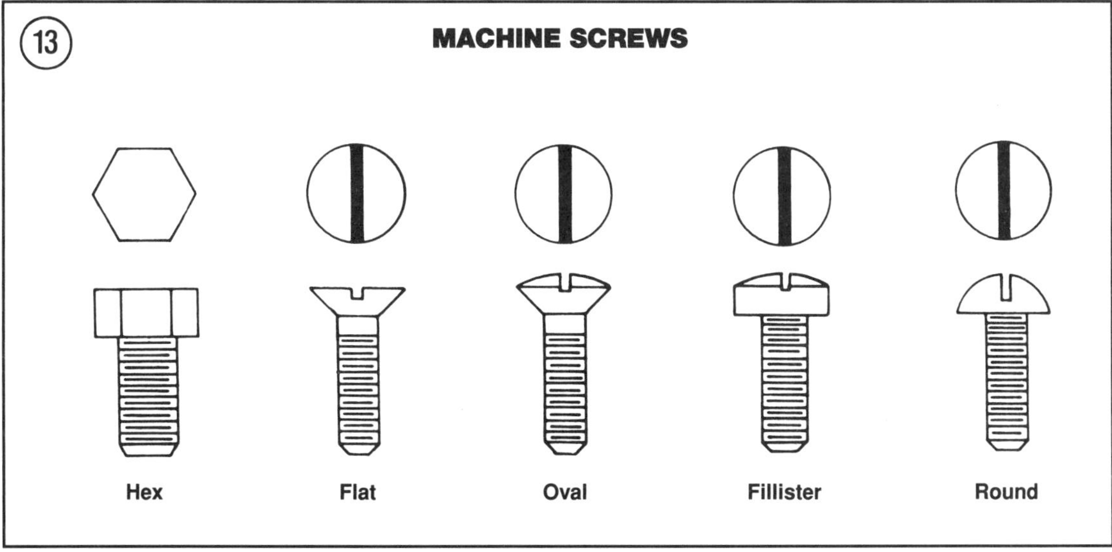

ing the top of an all-metal nut or using a nylon insert in the center or at the top of a nut. Self-locking fasteners offer greater holding strength and better vibration resistance than standard fasteners. For greatest safety, install new self-locking fasteners during reassembly.

Washers

There are 2 basic types of washers: flat washers and lockwashers. Flat washers are simple discs with a hole to fit a screw or bolt. Manufacturers design lockwashers to prevent a fastener from working loose due to vibration, expansion and contraction. Install lockwashers between a bolt head or nut and a flat washer. **Figure 16** shows several types of washers. Washers are also used in the following functions:

a. As spacers.

b. To prevent galling or damage of the equipment by the fastener.

c. To help distribute fastener load during torquing.

d. As fluid seals (copper or laminated washers).

Note that flat washers are often used between a lockwasher and a fastener to provide a smooth bear-

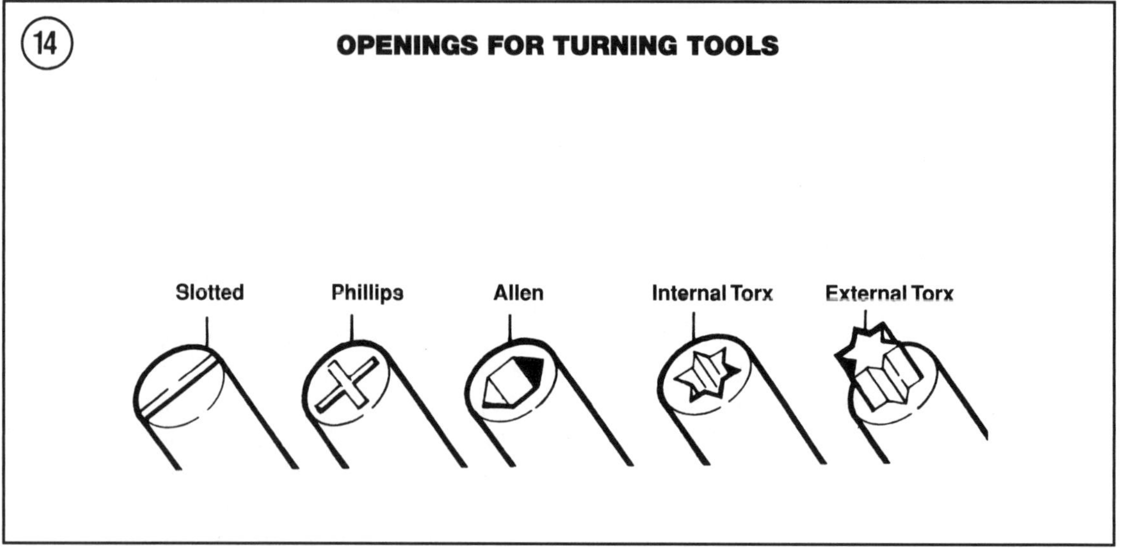

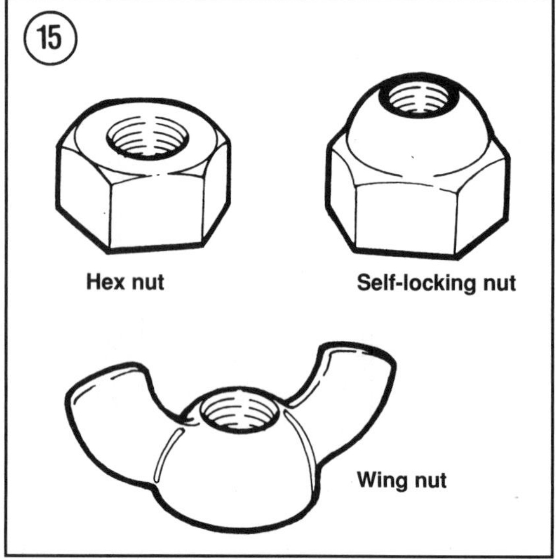

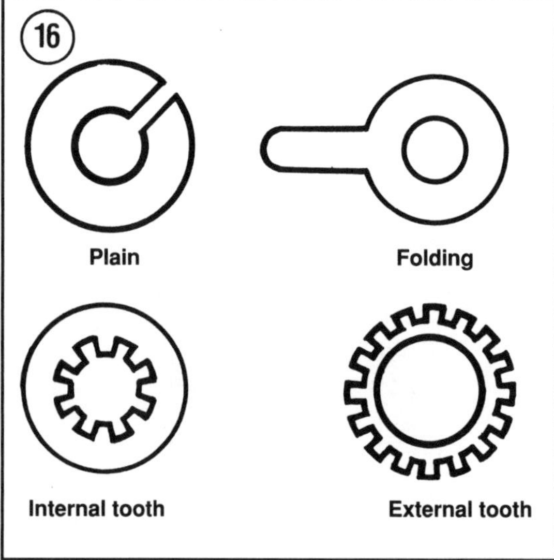

ing surface. This allows the fastener to be turned easily with a tool.

NOTE

As much care must be given to the selection and purchase of washers as that given to bolts, nuts and other fasteners. Beware of washers made of a thin and weak material. These will deform and crush the first time they are used in a high torque application.

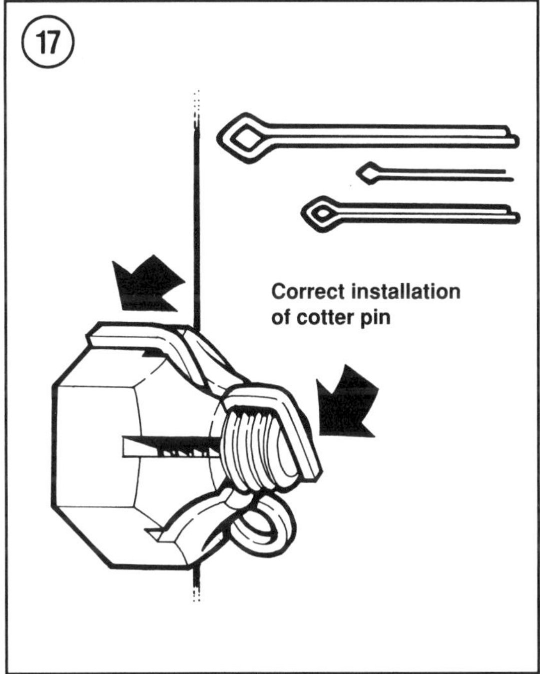

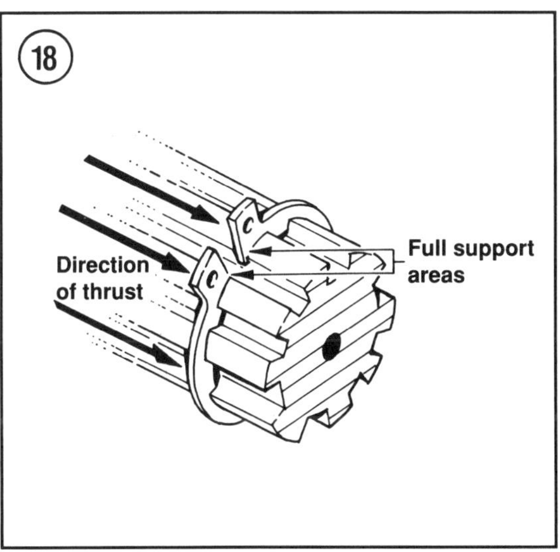

Cotter Pins

Cotter pins (**Figure 17**) secure fasteners in special locations. The threaded stud, bolt or axle must have a hole in it. Its nut or nut lock piece has castellations around its upper edge into which the cotter pin fits to keep it from loosening. When *properly* installed, a cotter pin is a positive locking device.

The first step in properly installing a cotter pin is to purchase one that will fit snugly when inserted through the nut and the mating thread part. This is not a problem when purchasing cotter pins through a dealer; you can order them by their respective part number. However, when you stop off at your local hardware or automotive store, keep this in mind. The cotter pin must not be so tight that you have to drive it in and out. However, you do not want it so loose that it can move or float after you install it.

Before installing a cotter pin, tighten the nut to the recommended torque specification. If the castellations in the nut do not align with the hole in the bolt or axle, tighten the nut until the slot and hole align. Do not loosen the nut to make alignment. Insert a *new* cotter pin through the nut and hole, then tap the head lightly to seat it. Bend one arm over the flat on the nut and the other against the top of the axle or bolt (**Figure 17**). Cut the arms to a suitable length to prevent them from snagging on clothing, or worse, your hands, arms or legs. When the cotter pin is bent and its arms cut to length, it must be tight. If you can wiggle the cotter pin, you have improperly installed it. Do not reuse cotter pins.

Circlips

Circlips can be of internal or external design. Circlips retain items on shafts (external type) or within tubes (internal type). In some applications, circlips of varying thickness are used to control the end play of assembled parts. These are often called selective circlips. You must replace circlips during reassembly as removal weakens and deforms them.

Two basic styles of circlips are available: machined and stamped circlips. Machined circlips (**Figure 18**) can be installed in either direction (shaft or housing) because both faces are machined, thus creating two sharp edges. Stamped circlips (**Figure 19**) are manufactured with one sharp edge and one rounded edge. When installing stamped circlips in a thrust situation, the sharp edge must face away from the part producing the thrust. When installing circlips, observe the following:

a. Remove and install circlips with circlip pliers. See *Circlip Pliers* in this chapter.
b. Compress or expand circlips only enough to install them.
c. After installing a circlip, make sure it seats in its groove completely.

Transmission circlips can become worn with use and increase side play. For this reason, always use new circlips whenever rebuilding a transmission.

LUBRICANTS

Periodic lubrication helps ensure long life for any type of equipment. The *type* of lubricant used is just as important as the lubrication service itself, although in an emergency the wrong type of lubricant is better than none at all. The following paragraphs describe the types of lubricants most often used on motorcycle equipment. Follow the manufacturer's recommendations for lubricant types and use.

If Harley-Davidson recommends any unique lubricant, it is specified in the service procedure.

Generally, all liquid lubricants are called oil. They may be mineral-based (including petroleum bases), natural-based (vegetable and animal bases), synthetic-based or emulsions (mixtures). Grease is an oil to which a thickening base has been added so that the end product is semi-solid. Grease is often classified by the type of thickener added; lithium soap is commonly used.

Engine Oil

Four-cycle oil for motorcycle and automotive engines is classified by the American Petroleum Institute (API) and the Society of Automotive Engineers (SAE) in several categories. Oil containers display these classifications on the top or label (**Figure 20**).

Letters indicate API oil classification; oil for gasoline engines is identified by an S.

Viscosity is an indication of the oil's thickness. The SAE uses numbers to indicate viscosity; thin oil has low numbers while thick oil has high numbers. A W after the number indicates that the viscosity testing was done at low temperature to simulate cold-weather operation. Engine oil falls into the 5W-30 and 20W-50 range.

Multigrade oil (for example 10W-40) is less viscous (thinner) at low temperatures and more viscous (thicker) at high temperatures. This allows the oil to perform efficiently across a wide range of engine operating conditions. The lower the number, the better the engine will start in cold climates. Higher numbers are usually recommended for engine running in hot weather conditions.

Grease

Grease is graded by the National Lubricating Grease Institute (NLGI). Grease is graded by number according to the consistency of the grease; these range from No. 000 to No. 6, with No. 6 being the most solid. A typical multipurpose grease is NLGI No. 2. For specific applications, equipment manufacturers may require grease with an additive such as molybdenum disulfide (MOS2).

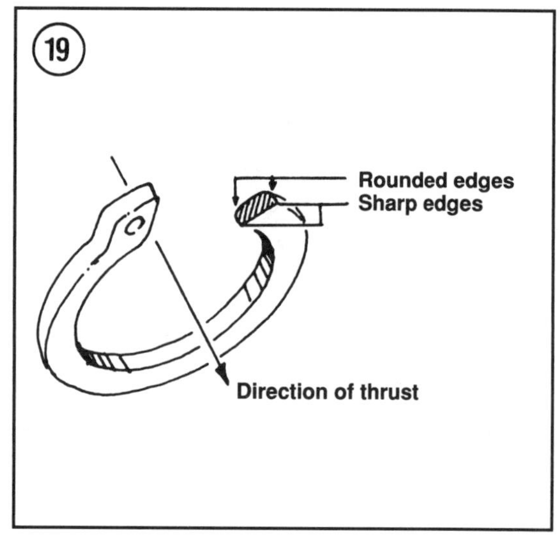

Antiseize Lubricant

An antiseize lubricant may be specified in some assembly applications. The antiseize lubricant prevents the formation of corrosion that may lock parts together.

SEALANT, CEMENTS AND CLEANERS

Sealants and Adhesives

Many mating surfaces of an engine require a gasket or seal between them to prevent fluids and gases from passing through the joint. At times, the gasket or seal is installed as is. However, some times a sealer is applied to enhance the sealing capability of the gasket or seal. Note, however, that a sealing compound may be added to the gasket or seal during manufacturing and adding a sealant may cause premature failure of the gasket or seal.

RTV Sealants

One of the most common sealants is RTV (room temperature vulcanizing) sealant (**Figure 21**). This sealant hardens (cures) at room temperature over a period of several hours, which allows sufficient time to reposition parts if necessary without damaging the gaskets. RTV sealant is designed for different uses, including high temperatures. If in doubt as to the correct type to use, ask a vendor or read the manufacturers literature.

Cements and Adhesives

A variety of cements and adhesives is available (**Figure 22**), their use dependent on the type of materials to be sealed, and to some extent, the personal preference of the mechanic. Automotive parts stores offer cements and adhesives in a wide selection. Some points to consider when selecting cements or adhesives are the type of material being sealed (metal, rubber, plastic), the type of fluid contacting the seal (gasoline, oil, water) and whether the seal is permanent or must be broken periodically, in which case a pliable sealant might be desirable. Unless you are experienced in the selection of cements and adhesives, follow the recommendation if the text specifies a particular sealant.

Thread Locking Compound

A thread locking compound is a fluid applied to fastener threads. After tightening the fastener, the fluid dries to a solid filler between the mating threads, thereby preventing loosening due to vibration.

Thread locking compound is available in different strengths, so make sure to follow the manufacturers recommendation when using their particular compound. Two manufacturers of thread locking compound are ThreeBond of America and the Loctite Corporation.

Before applying a thread locking compound, clean the contacting threads with an aerosol electrical contact cleaner. Use only as much compound as necessary, usually one or two drops depending on the size of the fastener. Excess fluid can work its way into adjoining parts.

Cleaners and Solvents

Cleaners and solvents are helpful in removing oil, grease and other residue when maintaining and overhauling your motorcycle. Before purchasing cleaners and solvents, consider how they will be used and disposed of, particularly if they are not water soluble. Local ordinances may require special procedures for the disposal of certain cleaners and solvents.

WARNING
Some cleaners and solvents are harmful and may be flammable. Follow any safety precautions noted on the container or in the manufacturers literature. Use petroleum-resistant gloves to protect hands and arms from the harmful effect of cleaners and solvents.

Figure 23 shows a variety of cleaners and solvents. Cleaners designed for ignition contact cleaning are excellent for removing light oil from a part without leaving a residue. Cleaners designed to remove heavy oil and grease residues, called degreasers, contain a solvent that usually must "work" awhile. Some degreasers will wash off with water. Ease the removal of stubborn gaskets with a gasket remover.

One of the more powerful cleaning solutions is carburetor cleaner. It is designed to dissolve the varnish that may build up in carburetor jets and orifices. Good carburetor cleaner is usually expensive and requires special disposal. Carefully read directions before purchase; do not immerse non-metallic parts in carburetor cleaner.

Gasket Remover

Stubborn gaskets can present a problem during engine service as they can take a long time to remove. Consequently, there is the added problem of secondary damage occurring to the gasket mating surfaces from the incorrect use of gasket scraping tools. To remove stubborn gaskets, use a spray gasket remover. Spray gasket remover can be purchased through automotive parts houses. Follow the manufacturer's directions for use.

EXPENDABLE SUPPLIES

Certain expendable supplies are required during maintenance and repair work. These include grease, oil, gasket cement, wiping rags and cleaning solvent. Ask your dealer for the silicone lubricants, contact cleaner and other products which make maintenance simpler and easier. Cleaning solvent or kerosene is available at some service stations or hardware stores.

BASIC HAND TOOLS

You can perform many tuning and maintenance procedures in this manual with hand tools and test equipment familiar to the average home mechanic. Keep your tools clean and in a tool box. Keep your tools organized with related tools stored together. After using a tool, wipe off dirt and grease with a clean cloth and return the tool to its correct place.

Top quality tools are essential; they are also more economical over time. If you are now starting to build your tool collection, stay away from the advertised specials featured at some parts houses, discount stores and chain drug stores. These are usually poor grade tools that can be sold cheaply and that is exactly what they are—*cheap*. They are usually made of inferior material, and are thick, heavy and clumsy. Their rough finish makes them difficult to clean and they usually don't last very long. If it is ever your misfortune to use such tools, you will probably find out that the wrenches do not fit the heads of bolts and nuts correctly and can damage the fastener.

Quality tools are made of alloy steel and are heat treated for greater strength. They are lighter and better balanced than cheap ones. Their surface is smooth, making them a pleasure to work with and

easy to clean. The initial cost of good quality tools may be higher but they are less expensive over time. Don't try to buy everything in all sizes at first; do it a little at a time until you have the necessary tools.

The following tools are required to perform virtually any repair job. Each tool is described and the recommended size given for starting a tool collection. Additional tools and some duplicates may be added as you become familiar with your Harley-Davidson.

Screwdrivers

The screwdriver is a very basic tool, but if used improperly it will do more damage than good. The slot on a screw has a definite dimension and shape. Select a screwdriver to conform to the shape of the screw head used. Through improper use or selection, a screwdriver can damage the screw head, making removal of the screw difficult. Two basic types of screwdrivers are required: standard (flat- or slot-blade) screwdrivers (**Figure 24**) and Phillips screwdrivers (**Figure 25**).

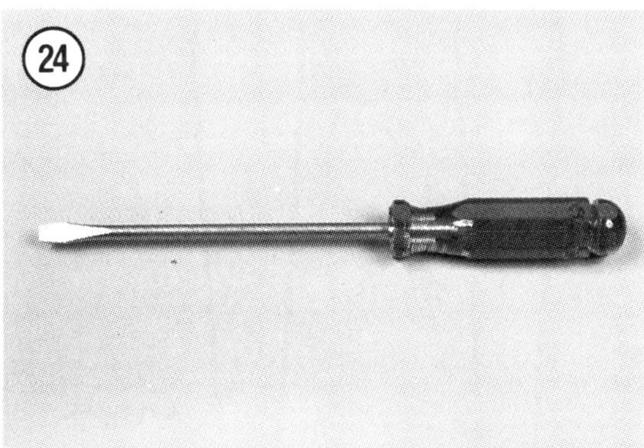

24

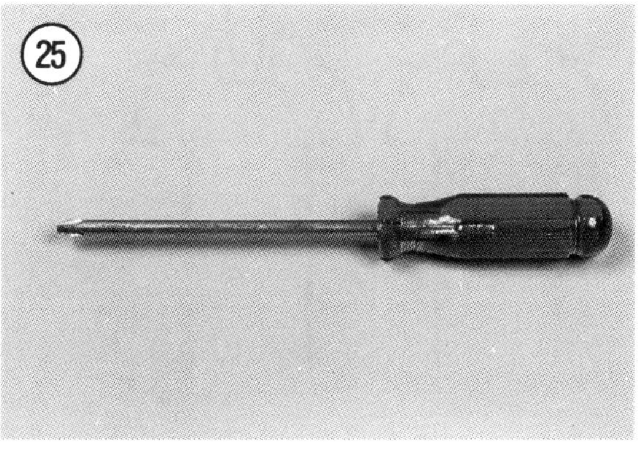

25

Note the following when selecting and using screwdrivers:

a. The screwdriver must always fit the screw head. If the screwdriver blade is too small for the screw slot, damage may occur to the screw slot and screwdriver. If the blade is too large, it cannot engage the slot properly and will result in damage to the screw head.
b. Standard screwdrivers are identified by the length of their blade. A 6-in. screwdriver has a six in. blade. The width of the screwdriver blade will vary, so make sure that the blade engages the screw slot the complete width of the screw.
c. Phillips screwdrivers are sized according to their point size. They are numbered 1, 2, 3 and 4. The degree of taper determines the point size; the No. 1 Phillips screwdriver is the most pointed. The points become more blunt as their number increases.
d. When selecting a screwdriver, note that you can apply more power using less effort with a longer screwdriver than with a short one. Of course, there will be situations where only a short handle screwdriver can be used. Keep this in mind though, when removing tight screws.
e. Because the working end of a screwdriver receives quite a bit of abuse, purchase screwdrivers with hardened tips. The extra money will be well spent.

Screwdrivers are available in sets which often include an assortment of common and Phillips blades. If you buy them individually, buy at least the following:

a. Common screwdriver—5/16 × 6 in. blade.
b. Common screwdriver—3/8 × 12 in. blade.
c. Phillips screwdriver—size 2 tip, 6 in. blade.
d. Phillips screwdriver—size 3 tip, 6 and 8 in. blade.

Use screwdrivers only for driving screws. Never use a screwdriver for prying or chiseling metal. Do not try to remove a Phillips, Torx or Allen head screw with a standard screwdriver (unless the screw has a combination head that will accept either type); you can damage the head so that even the proper tool will be unable to remove it.

Keep screwdrivers in the proper condition and they will last longer and perform better. Always keep the tip of a standard screwdriver in good condition. **Figure 26** shows how to grind the tip to the proper shape if it becomes damaged. Note the symmetrical sides of the tip.

Pliers

Pliers come in a wide range of types and sizes. Pliers are useful for cutting, bending and crimping. Do not use them to cut hardened objects or to turn bolts or nuts. **Figure 27** shows several pliers useful in repairing your motorcycle.

Each type of pliers has a specialized function. Slip-joint pliers are general purpose pliers used mainly for holding things and for bending. Needlenose pliers are used to hold or bend small objects. Adjustable pliers can be adjusted to hold various sizes of objects; the jaws remain parallel to grip around objects such as pipe or tubing. There are many more types of pliers.

CAUTION
Do not use pliers for loosening or tightening nuts or bolts. The pliers sharp teeth will grind off the nut or bolt corners and damage it.

CAUTION
When using a slip-joint or adjustable pliers to hold an object with a finished surface, wrap the object with tape or cardboard for protection.

Locking Pliers

Locking pliers (**Figure 28**) are used to hold objects tightly. While locking pliers work well, you must use them carefully. Because locking pliers exert more force than regular pliers, their sharp jaws can permanently scar the object. In addition, when you lock them into position, they can crush or deform thin wall material.

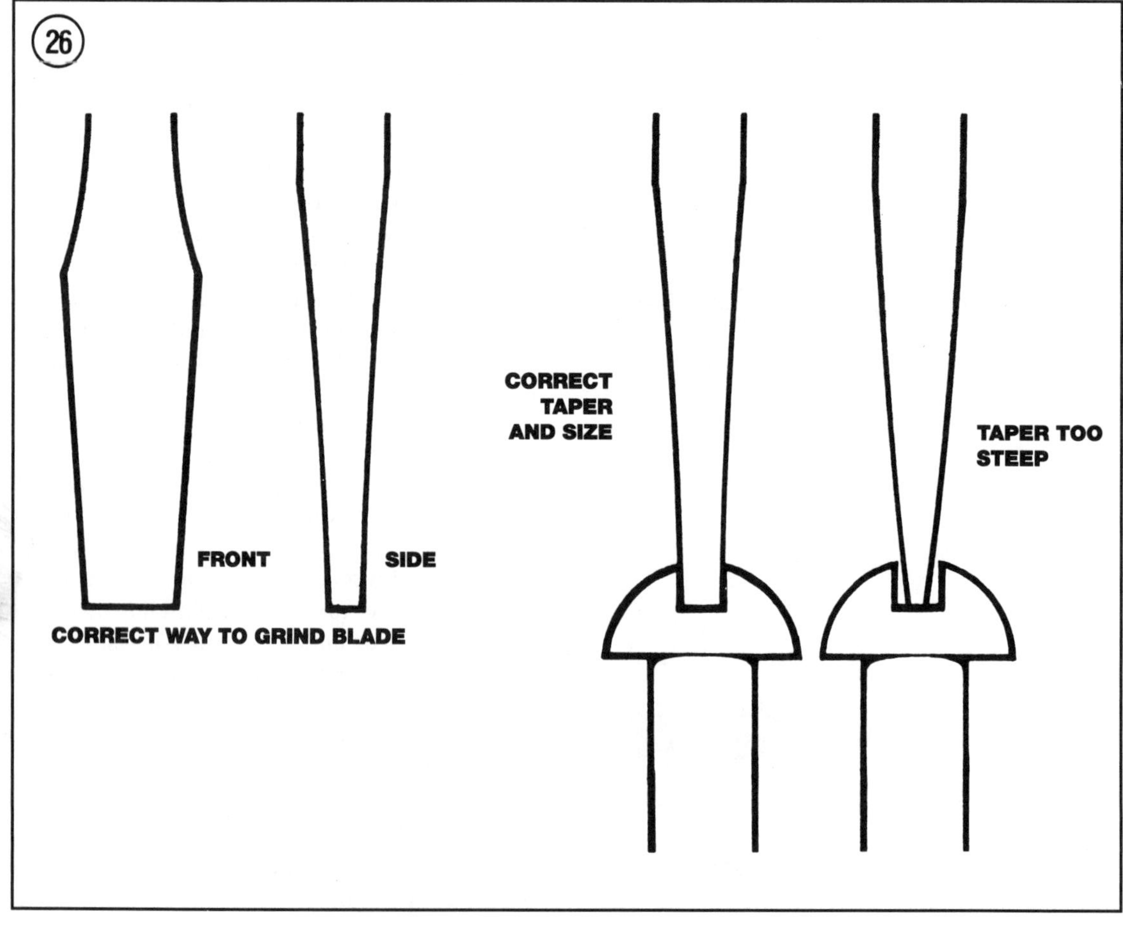

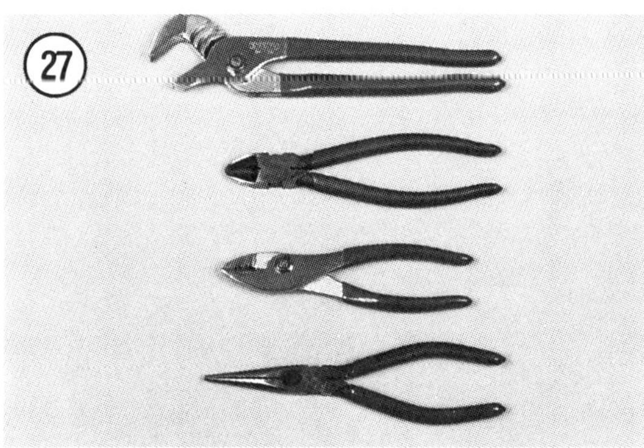

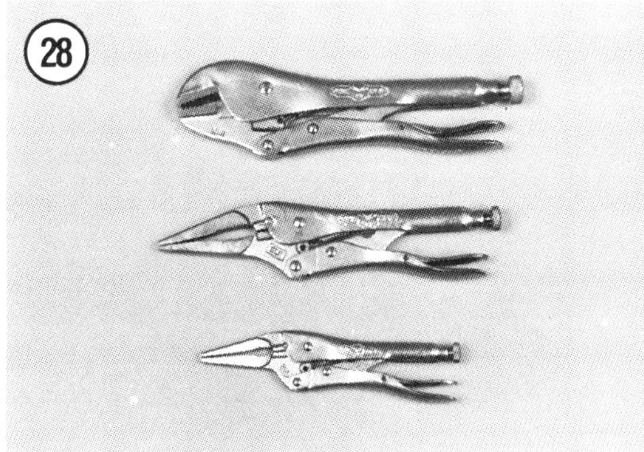

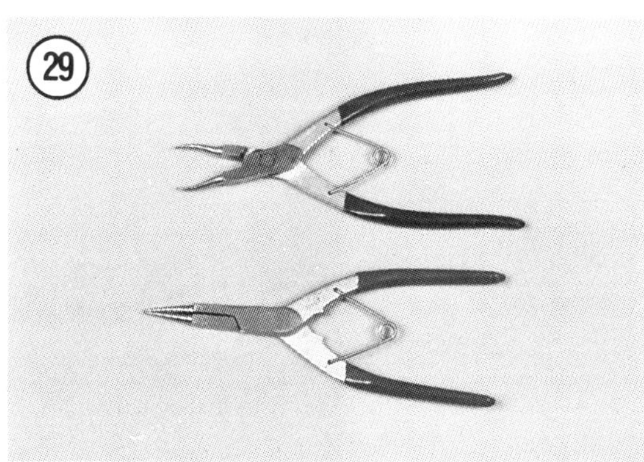

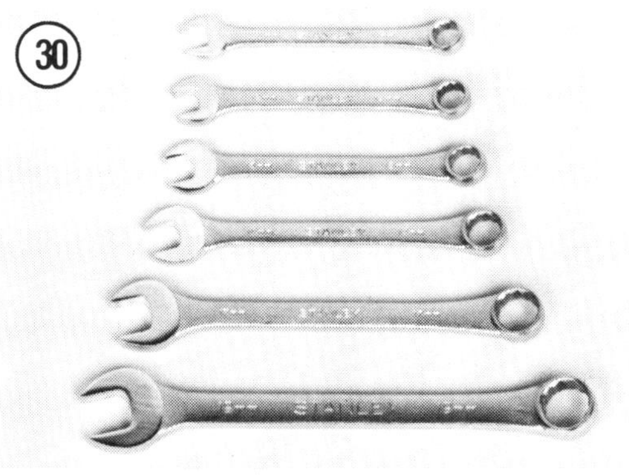

Locking pliers are available in many types for more specific tasks.

Circlip Pliers

Circlip pliers (**Figure 29**) are special in that they are only used to remove or install circlips. When purchasing circlip pliers, there are 2 kinds to distinguish from. External pliers (spreading) are used to remove circlips that fit on the outside of a shaft. Internal pliers (squeezing) are used to remove circlips which fit inside a housing.

WARNING
Because circlips can sometimes slip and fly off during removal and installation, always wear safety glasses when servicing them.

Box end, Open-end and Combination Wrenches

Box end and open-end wrenches (**Figure 30**) are available in sets or separately in a variety of sizes. The size number stamped near the end refers to the distance between 2 parallel flats on the hex head bolt or nut.

Box end wrenches are usually superior to open-end wrenches. Open-end wrenches grip the fastener on only 2 flats. Unless a wrench fits well, it may slip and round off the points on the fastener. The box end wrench grips on all 6 flats. Both 6-point and 12-point openings on box wrenches are available. The 6-point gives superior holding power; the 12-point allows a shorter swinging radius when working in a confined area.

Combination wrenches which are open on one side and boxed on the other are also available. Both ends are the same size.

No matter what style of wrench you choose, proper use is important to prevent personal injury. When using a wrench, get into the habit of pulling the wrench toward you. This technique will reduce the risk of injuring your hand should the wrench slips. If you have to push the wrench away from you to loosen or tighten a fastener, open and push with the palm of your hand; your fingers and knuckles will be out of the way if the wrench slips. Before using a wrench, always think ahead as to what could happen if the wrench slips or if the fastener strips or breaks.

Adjustable Wrenches

An adjustable wrench can be adjusted to fit nearly any nut or bolt head which has clear access around its entire perimeter. Adjustable wrenches are best used as a backup wrench to keep a large nut or bolt from turning while the other end is being loosened or tightened using a proper wrench. See **Figure 31**.

Adjustable wrenches have only two gripping surfaces which makes them more subject to slipping off the fastener and damaging the part and possibly your hand. See *Box-end, Open-end and Combination Wrenches* in this chapter.

These wrenches are directional; the solid jaw must be the one transmitting the force. If you use the adjustable jaw to transmit the force, it will loosen and possibly slip off. Adjustable wrenches come in all sizes but something in the 6 to 8 in. range is recommended as an all-purpose wrench.

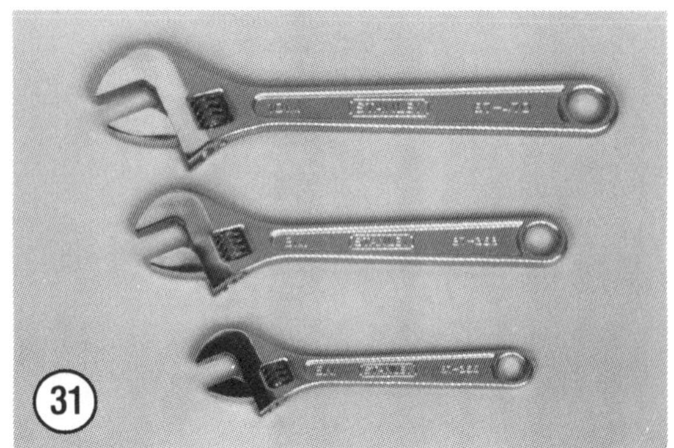

31

Socket Wrenches

This type is undoubtedly the fastest, safest and most convenient to use. Sockets which attach to a ratchet handle (**Figure 32**) are available with 6-point or 12-point openings and 1/4, 3/8, 1/2 and 3/4 in. drives. The drive size indicates the size of the square hole which mates with the ratchet handle.

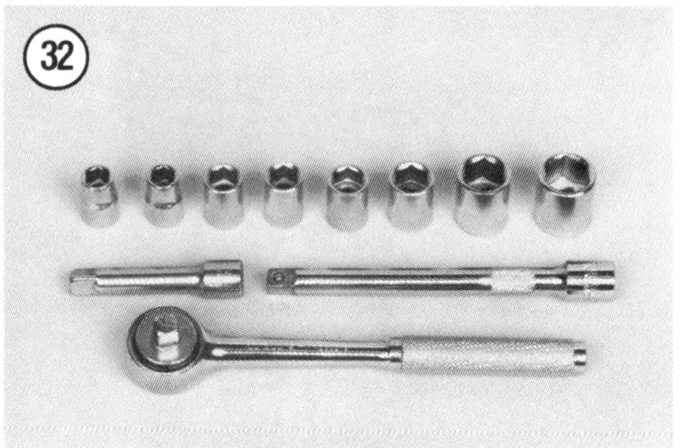

32

Torque Wrench

A torque wrench (**Figure 33**) is used with a socket to measure how tightly a nut or bolt is installed. They come in a wide price range and with either 3/8 or 1/2 in. square drive. The drive size indicates the size of the square drive which mates with the socket.

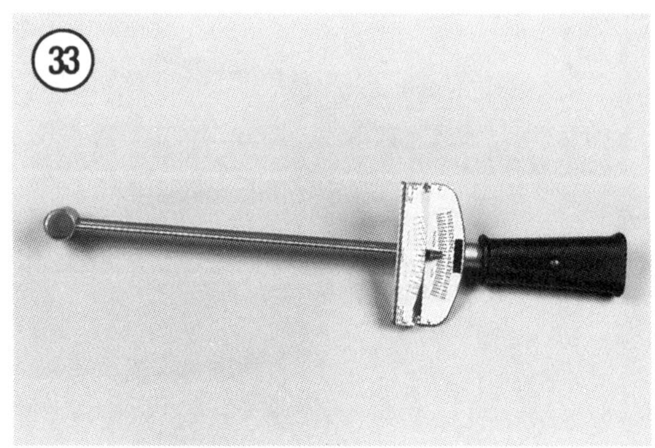

33

Impact Driver

This tool makes removal of tight fasteners easy and eliminates damage to bolts and screw slots. Impact drivers and interchangeable bits (**Figure 34**) are available at most large hardware and motorcycle dealers. Do not purchase a cheap one as they do not work as well and require more force than a moderately priced one. Sockets can also be used with a hand impact driver. However, make sure the socket is designed for use with an impact driver. Do not use regular hand type sockets, as they may shatter during use.

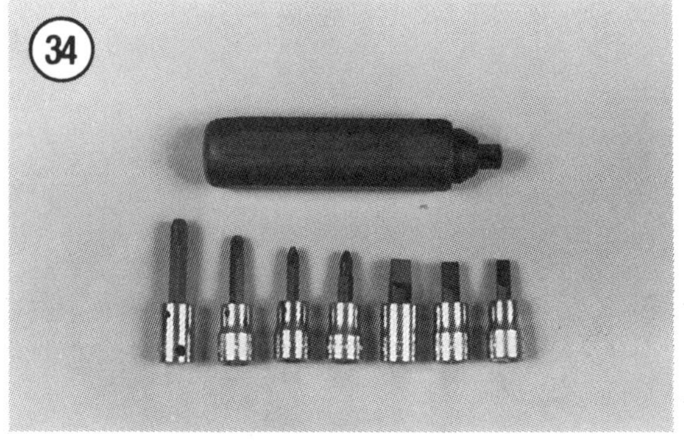

34

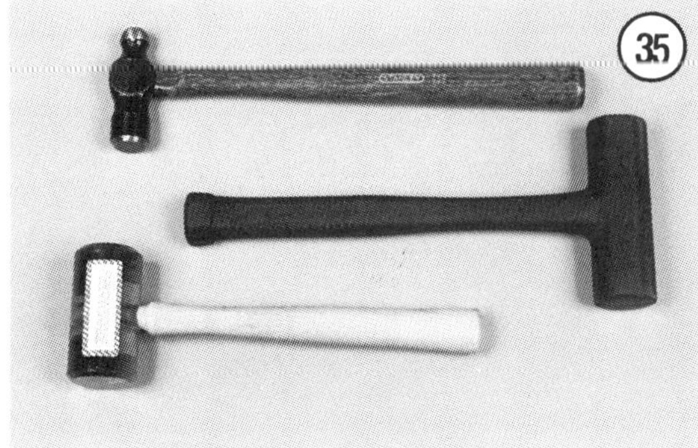

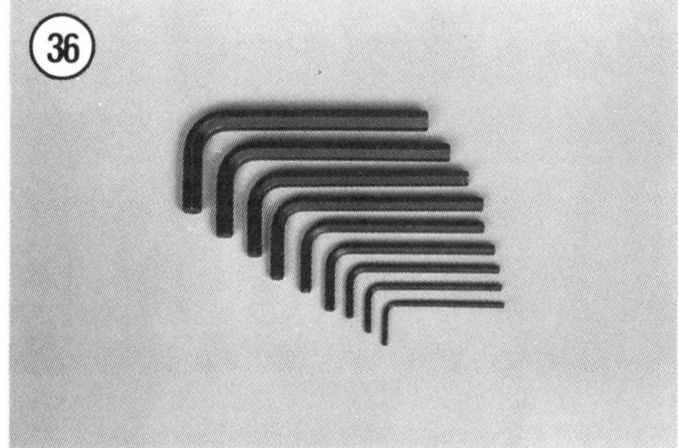

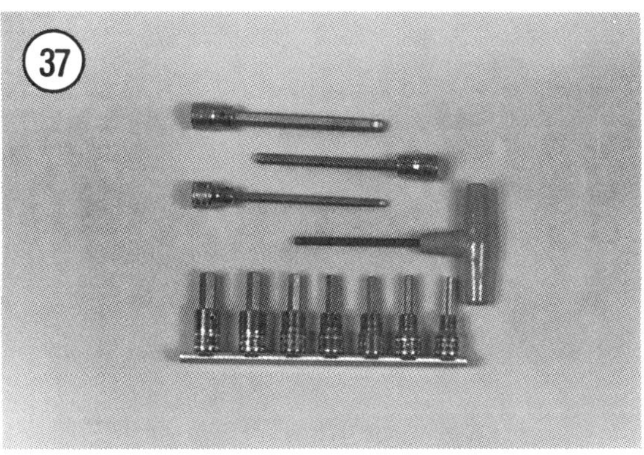

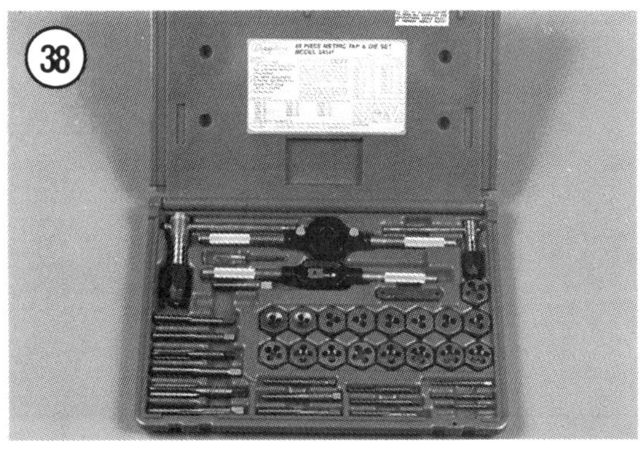

Hammers

The correct hammer (**Figure 35**) is necessary for certain repairs. Use only a hammer with a face (or head) of rubber or plastic or the soft-faced type that is filled with lead shot. These are sometimes necessary during engine disassembly. *Never* use a metal-faced hammer on engine or suspension parts, as severe damage will result in most cases. Ball-peen or machinist's hammers are required when striking another tool, such as a punch or impact driver. When striking a hammer against a punch, cold chisel or similar tool, the face of the hammer must be at least 1/2 in. larger than the head of the tool. When it is necessary to strike hard against a steel part without damaging it, use a brass hammer. A brass hammer can be used because brass is softer than steel.

When using a hammer, note the following:

a. *Always* wear safety glasses when using a hammer.
b. Inspect the hammer for damaged or broken parts. Repair or replace the hammer as required. Do *not* use a hammer with a taped handle.
c. Always wipe oil or grease off of the hammer *before* using it.
d. The head of the hammer must always strike the object squarely. Do not use the side of the hammer or the handle to strike an object.
e. Always use the correct hammer for the job.

Allen Wrenches

Allen wrenches (**Figure 36**) are available in sets or separately in a variety of sizes. These sets come in metric and U.S. Standard size. Allen bolts are sometimes called socket bolts.

Sometimes the bolts are difficult to reach and it is suggested that a variety of Allen wrenches be purchased such as socket driven, T-handle and extension type, as shown in **Figure 37**.

Tap and Die Set

A complete tap and die set (**Figure 38**) is a relatively expensive tool. However, when you need a tap or die to repair a damaged thread, there is really no substitute.

Tire Levers

When changing tires, use a good set of tire levers (**Figure 39**). Never use a screwdriver in place of a tire lever; refer to Chapter Ten for tire changing procedures using these tools. Before using the tire levers, check the working ends of the tool and remove any burrs. Don't use a tire lever for prying anything but tires. **Figure 39** shows a regular pair of 10 in. long tire levers. However, for better leverage when changing tires on your Dyna Glide, you may

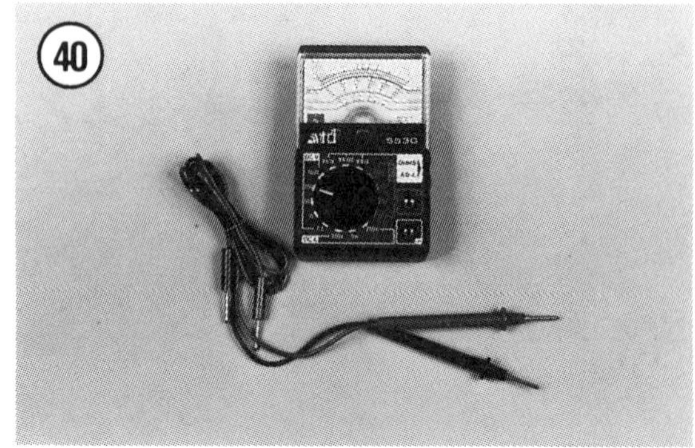
40

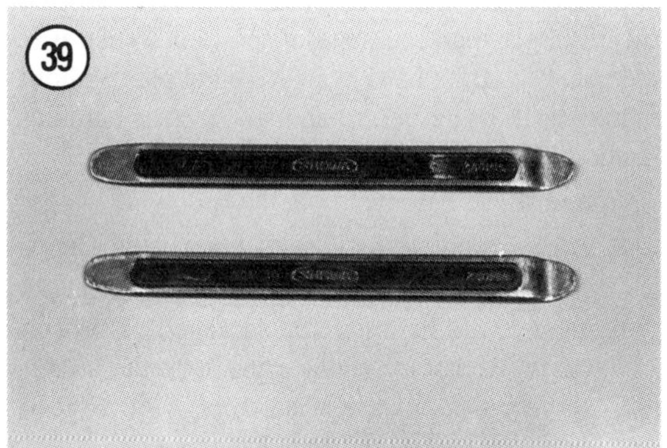
39

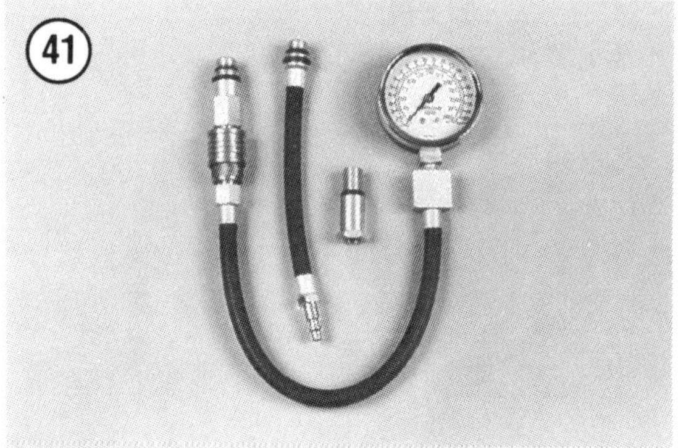
41

42

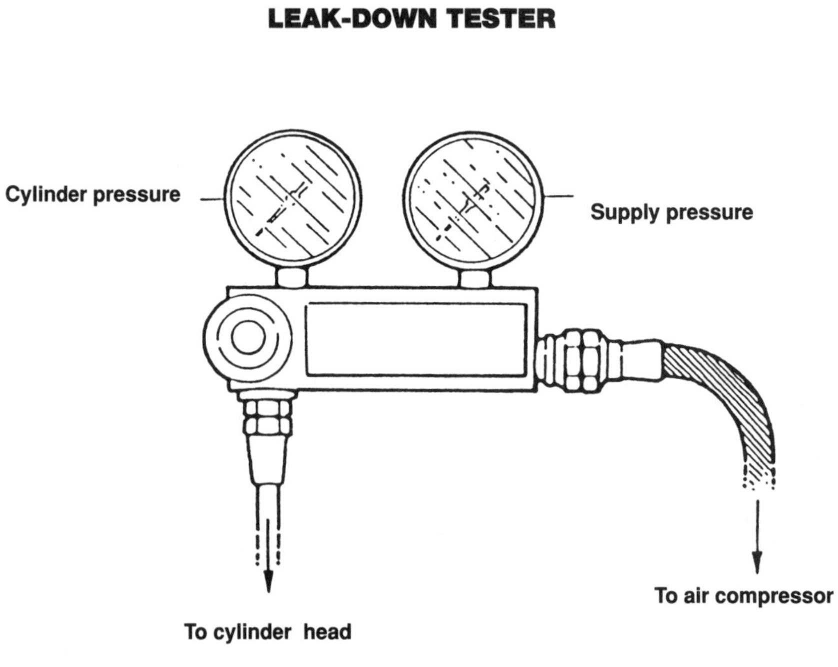

LEAK-DOWN TESTER

Cylinder pressure

Supply pressure

To air compressor

To cylinder head

want to invest in a set of 16 in. long tire irons. These can be ordered through your dealer.

Drivers and Pullers

These tools are used to remove and install oil seals, bushings, bearings and gears. They are called out during service procedures in later chapters as required.

Bike Stand

Because your Dyna Glide is not equipped with a centerstand, you will need some safe means of raising the bike when servicing the wheels and other components as described in this manual.

There are a number of commercial bike stands that can be used to raise and support your Dyna Glide safely during service. When selecting a bike stand, make sure it can support your bike. When using a bike stand, check the stability of the bike before walking away from it or when working on it.

TEST EQUIPMENT

Multimeter or Volt-ohm Meter

A multimeter (**Figure 40**) is invaluable for electrical system troubleshooting and service. It combines a voltmeter, and ohmmeter and an ammeter into one unit, so it is often called a VOM.

Two types of multimeter are commonly available, analog and digital. Analog meters have a moving needle with marked bands indicated the volt, ohm and amperage scales. The digital meter (DVOM) is ideally suited for troubleshooting because it is easy to read, more accurate than analog, contains internal overload protection, is auto-ranging (analog meters must be calibrated each time the scale is changed) and has automatic polarity compensation.

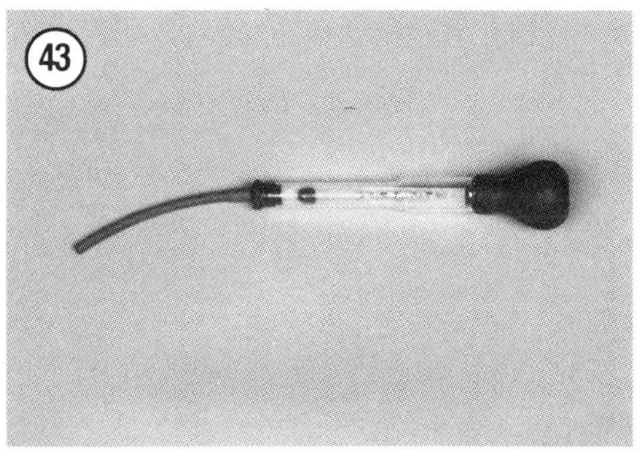
43

Compression Gauge

An engine with low compression cannot be properly tuned and will not develop full power. A compression gauge measures engine compression. The one shown in **Figure 41** has a flexible stem with an extension that allows you to hold it while cranking the engine. Open the throttle all the way when checking engine compression. See Chapter Three.

Cylinder Leak Down Tester

Certain engine problems (leaking valve, broken, worn or stuck piston rings) can be isolated by performing a cylinder leak-down test. An air compressor and a cylinder leak-down tester are required. To leak-down test a cylinder, position the piston on its compression stroke (both valves closed), then pressurize the cylinder and listen for air escaping from the exhaust system, carburetor or cylinder head mating surface. This procedure is described in Chapter Three. A cylinder leak-down tester (**Figure 42**) can be purchased through accessory tool manufacturers and automotive tool suppliers.

Battery Hydrometer

A hydrometer (**Figure 43**) is the best way to check a battery's state of charge. A hydrometer measures the weight or density of the battery's electrolyte. Specific gravity is the density of the electrolyte as compared to pure water. This tool and its use is described in Chapter Three.

Portable Tachometer

A portable tachometer is necessary for tuning (**Figure 44**). Ignition timing and carburetor adjustments must be performed at specified engine speeds. The best instrument for this purpose is one with a low range of 0-1,000 or 0-2,000 rpm and a high range of 0-4,000. Extended range (0-6,000 or 0-8,000 rpm) instruments lack accuracy at lower speeds. The instrument must be capable of detecting a 25 rpm variation on the low range.

Timing Light

Suitable timing lights range from inexpensive neon bulb types (**Figure 45**) to powerful xenon strobe lights. A light with an inductive pickup is recommended to prevent any possible damage to ignition wiring.

PRECISION MEASURING TOOLS

Measurement is an important part of motorcycle service. When performing many of the service procedures in this manual, you will be required to make a number of measurements. These include basic checks such as engine compression and spark plug gap. As you become more involved with engine disassembly and service, measurements will be required to determine the condition of the piston and cylinder bore, crankshaft runout and so on. When making these measurements, the degree of accuracy will dictate which tool is required. Precision measuring tools are expensive. If this is your first experience at engine service, it may be worthwhile to have the checks made at a dealership. However, as your skills and enthusiasm increase for doing your own service work, you may want to begin purchasing some of these specialized tools. The following is a description of the measuring tools required during engine overhaul.

Feeler Gauge

The feeler gauge (**Figure 46**) is made of either a piece of a flat or round hardened steel of a specified thickness. Wire gauges are used to measure spark plug gap. Flat gauges are used for all other measurements.

Vernier Caliper

This tool (**Figure 47**) is invaluable when it is necessary to measure inside, outside and depth measurements with close precision. It can be used to measure the thickness of shims and thrust washers. It is perhaps the most often used measuring tool in the motorcycle service shop. Vernier calipers are available in a wide assortment of styles and price ranges.

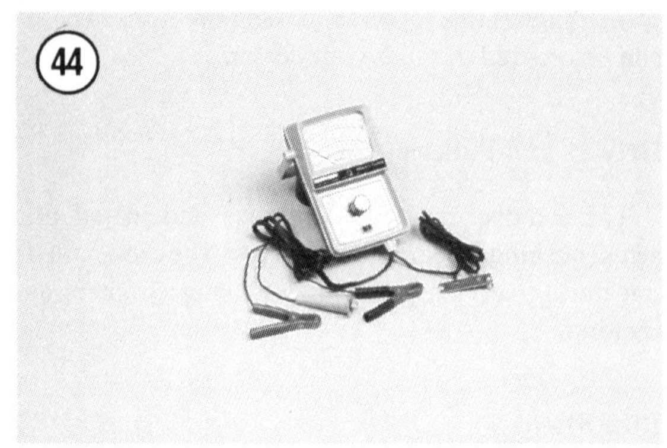
44

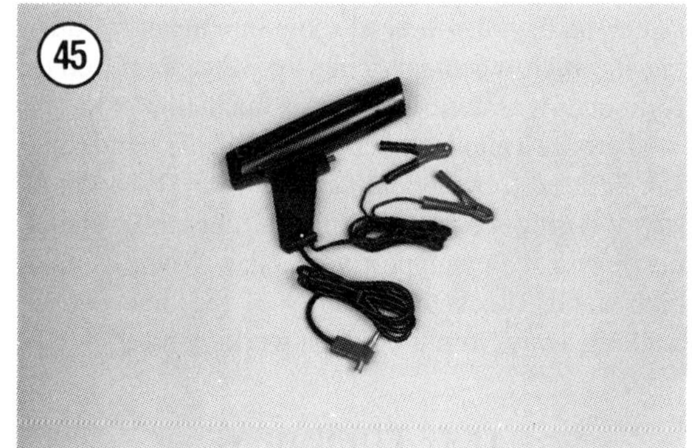
45

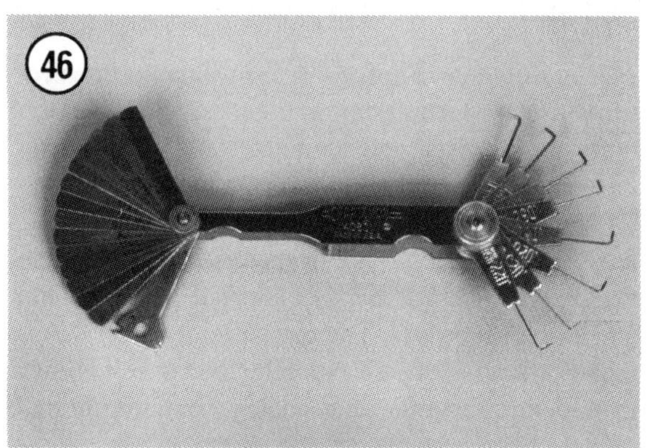
46

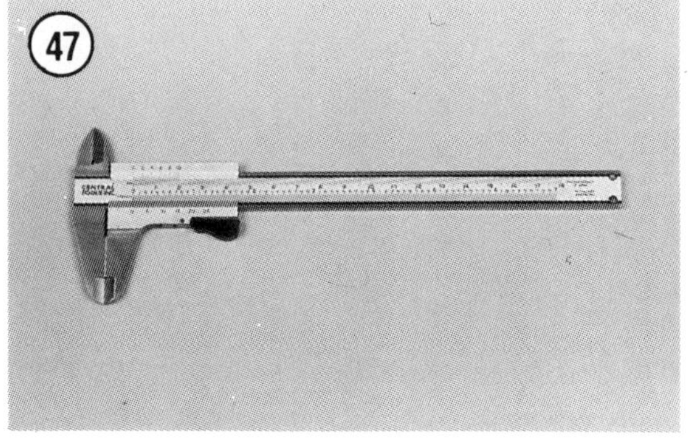
47

Outside Micrometers

An outside micrometer (**Figure 48**) is one of the most reliable instruments for precision measurement. Outside micrometers are typically accurate to 0.0001 in. (0.0025 mm). An outside micrometer is required to precisely measure piston diameter, piston pin diameter, crankshaft journal and crankpin diameter. Used with a telescoping gauge, an outside micrometer can be used to measure cylinder bore size and to determine cylinder taper and out-of-round. Outside micrometers are delicate instruments; if dropped to the floor, they most certainly will be knocked out of calibration. Always handle and use micrometers carefully to ensure accuracy. Store micrometers in their padded case when not in use to prevent damage.

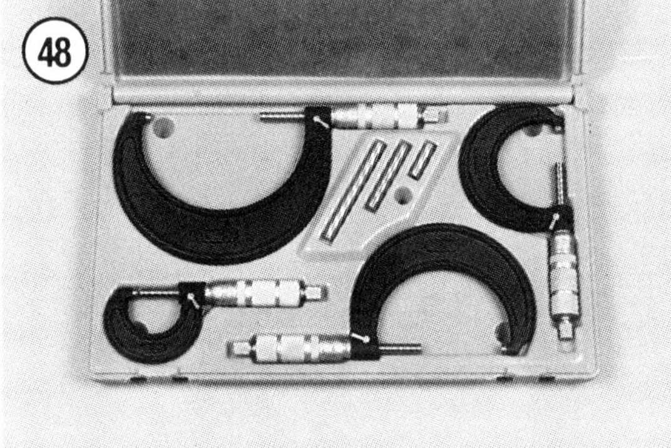

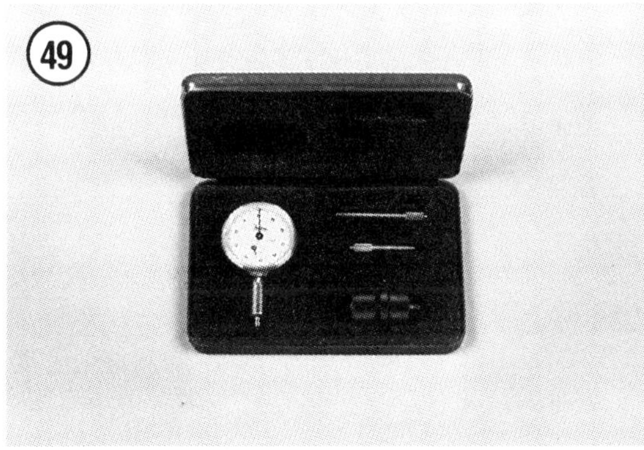

Dial Indicator

Dial indicators (**Figure 49**) are precision tools used to check crankshaft and drive shaft runout, lash between gears and end play of shaft assemblies. For motorcycle repair, select a dial indicator with a continuous dial (**Figure 50**).

Cylinder Bore Gauge

The cylinder bore gauge is a very specialized precision tool. The gauge set shown in **Figure 51** is comprised of a dial indicator, handle and a number of length adapters to adapt the gauge to different bore sizes. The bore gauge can be used to make cylinder bore measurements such as bore size, taper and out-of-round. An outside micrometer must be used to calibrate the bore gauge to the specific bore diameter.

Small Hole Gauges

A set of small hole gauges (**Figure 52**) allows you to measure a hole, groove or slot ranging in size up

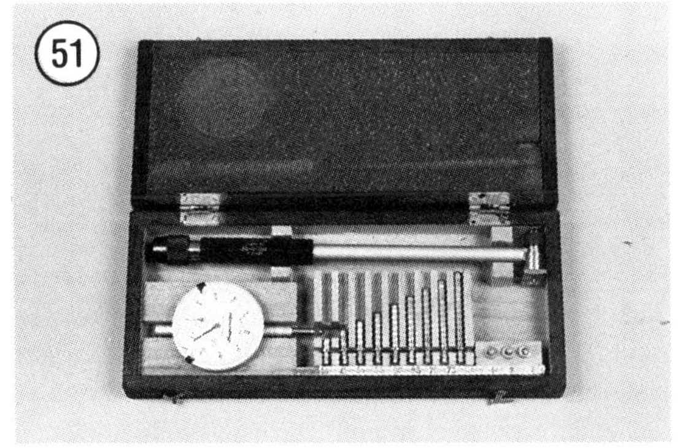

to 1/2 in. An outside micrometer must be used to measure the small hole gauge after fitting it to the hole, groove or slot.

Telescoping Gauges

Telescoping gauges (**Figure 53**) can be used to measure hole diameters. Like the small hole gauge, the telescoping gauge does not have a scale gauge for direct readings. An outside micrometer is required to measure the telescoping gauge after it fitted to the hole or bore.

Screw Pitch Gauge

A screw pitch gauge (**Figure 54**) determines the thread pitch of bolts, screws and studs. The gauge is made up of a number of thin plates. Each plate has a thread shape cut on one edge to match one thread pitch. When using a screw pitch gauge to determine a thread pitch size, try to fit different blade sizes onto the bolt thread until both threads match exactly.

Surface Plate

A surface plate is used to check the flatness of parts or to provide a perfectly flat surface for minor resurfacing of cylinder head or other critical gasket surfaces. While industrial quality surface plates are quite expensive, the home mechanic can improvise. A thick metal plate can be put to use as a surface plate. The metal surface plate shown in **Figure 55** has a piece of sandpaper glued to its surface that is used for cleaning and smoothing cylinder head and crankcase mating surfaces.

NOTE
Check with a local machine shop on the availability and cost of having a metal plate resurfaced for use as a surface plate.

OTHER SPECIAL TOOLS

A few other special tools may be required for major service. These are described in the appropriate chapters and are available from Harley-Davidson dealerships or other manufacturers as indicated.

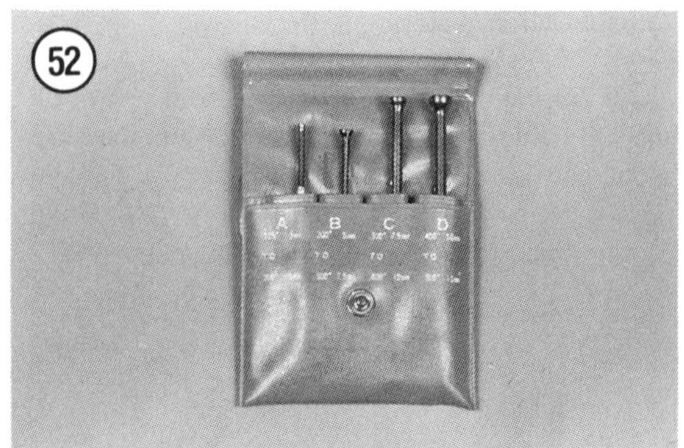

52

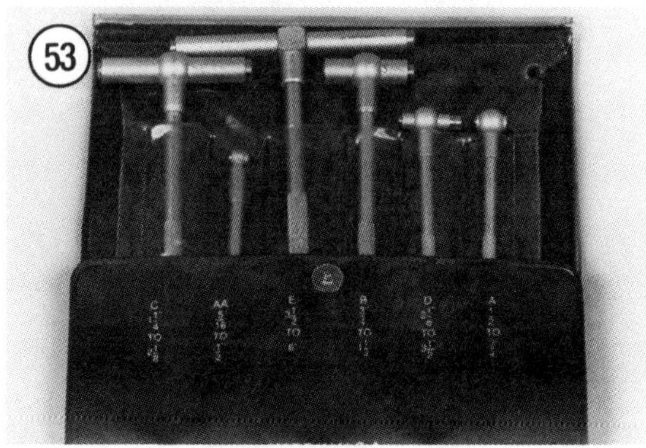
53

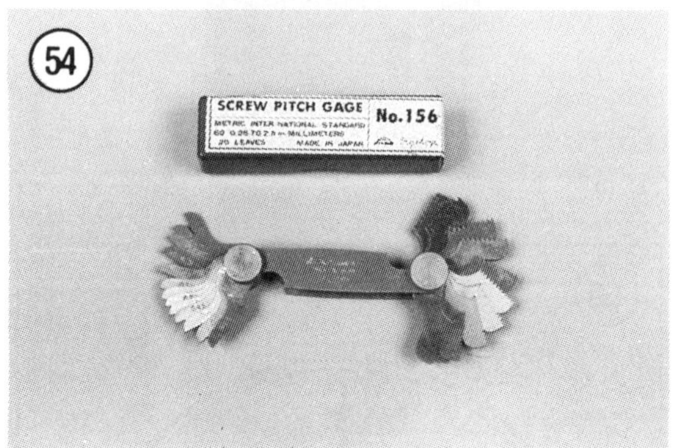

54

55

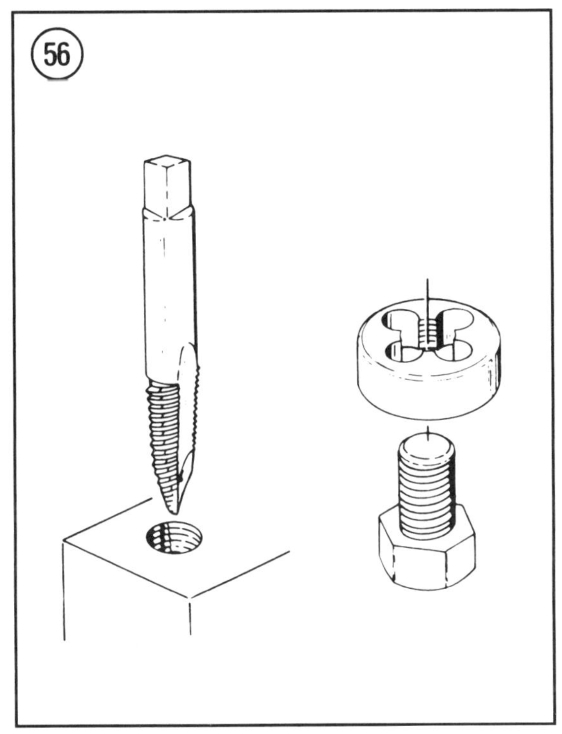

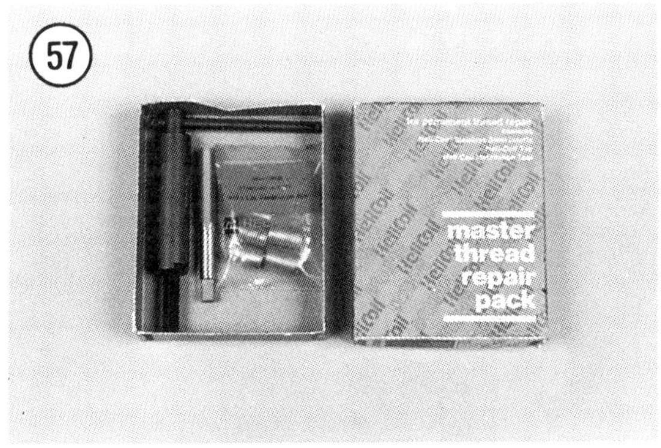

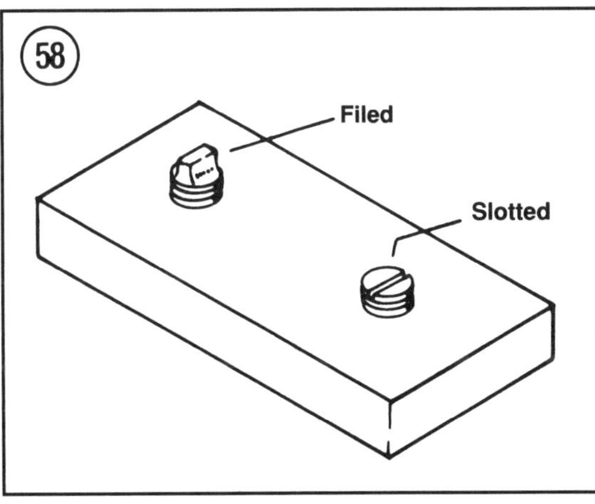

MECHANIC'S TIPS

Removing Frozen Nuts and Screws

When a fastener rusts and cannot be removed, several methods may be used to loosen it. First, apply penetrating oil such as Liquid Wrench or WD-40 (available at hardware or auto supply stores). Apply it liberally and let it penetrate for 10-15 minutes. Rap the fastener several times with a small hammer, but do not hit it hard enough to cause damage. Reapply the penetrating oil if necessary.

For frozen screws, apply penetrating oil as described, then insert a screwdriver in the slot and rap the top of the screwdriver with a hammer. This loosens the rust so the screw can be removed in the normal way. If the screw head is too damaged to use this method, grip the head with locking pliers and twist the screw out.

Avoid applying heat unless specifically instructed, as it may melt, warp or remove the temper from parts.

Remedying Stripped Threads

Occasionally, threads are stripped through carelessness or impact damage. Often the threads can be repaired by running a tap (for internal threads on nuts) or die (for external threads on bolts) through the threads. See **Figure 56**. To clean or repair spark plug threads, a spark plug tap can be used.

If an internal thread is damaged, it may be necessary to install a Helicoil (**Figure 57**) or some other type of thread insert. These kits have all of the necessary parts to repair a damaged internal thread.

If it is necessary to drill and tap a hole, refer to **Table 9** for SAE tap drill sizes.

Removing Broken Screws or Bolts

If the head breaks off a screw or bolt, several methods are available to remove the remaining portion.

If a large portion of the remainder projects out, try gripping it with locking pliers. If the projecting portion is too small, file it to fit a wrench or cut a slot in it to fit a screwdriver. See **Figure 58**.

If the head breaks off flush, use a screw extractor. To do this, centerpunch the exact center of the remaining portion of the screw or bolt. Drill a small hole in the screw and tap the extractor into the hole. Back the screw out using a wrench on the extractor. See **Figure 59**.

Removing Broken or Damaged Studs

If a stud is broken or the threads severely damaged, perform the following. A stud remover, tube of

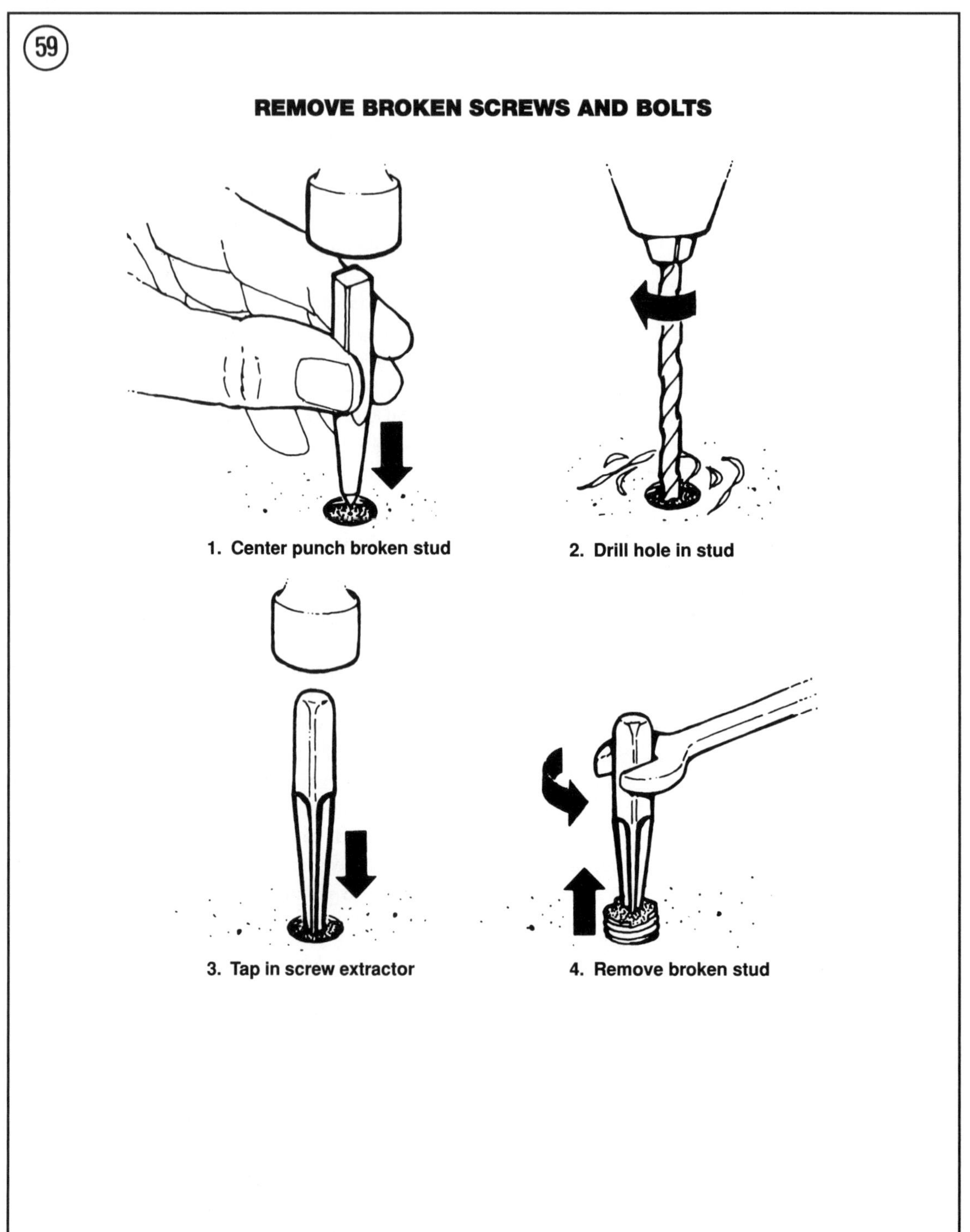

threadlock, 2 nuts, 2 wrenches and a new stud are required during this procedure.

NOTE
*The following steps describe general procedures for replacing a typical stud. However, if you are replacing cylinder studs, refer to **Cylinder Stud Replacement** in Chapter Four. Do **not** use the following steps to replace cylinder studs. The improper installation of cylinder studs can cause cylinder head leakage.*

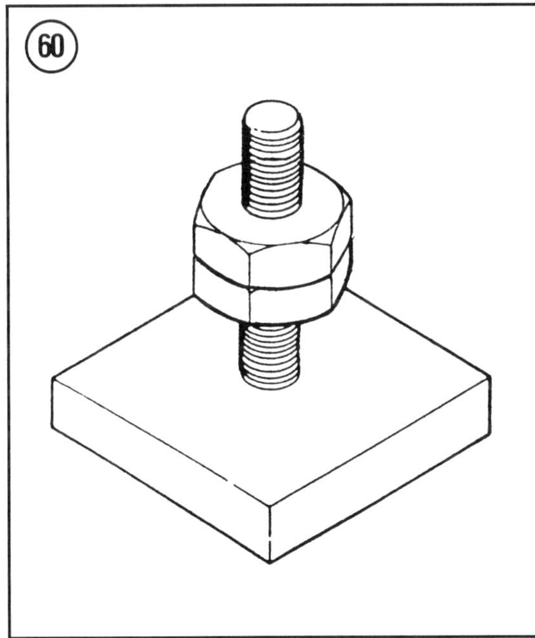

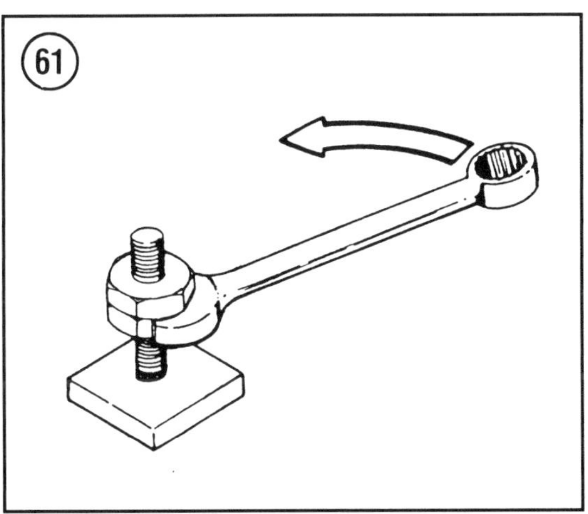

1. Thread two nuts onto the damaged stud (**Figure 60**). Then tighten the 2 nuts against each other so that they are locked.

NOTE
If the threads on the damaged stud do not allow installation of the 2 nuts, remove the stud with a stud remover.

2. Turn the bottom nut counterclockwise and unscrew the stud.
3. Threaded holes with a bottom surface must be blown out with compressed air as dirt buildup in the bottom of the hole may prevent the stud from being installed completely. If necessary, use a bottoming tap to true up the threads and to remove any deposits.
4. Install 2 nuts on the top half of the new stud as in Step 1. Make sure they are locked securely.
5. Apply a few drops of a threadlock to the bottom stud threads.
6. Turn the top nut clockwise (**Figure 61**) and tighten the new stud securely.
7. Remove the nuts and repeat for each stud as required.
8. Follow threadlock manufacturers directions regarding cure time before assembling the component.

BALL BEARING REPLACEMENT

Bearings are used throughout your motorcycles engine and chassis to reduce power loss, heat and noise resulting from friction. Because ball bearings are precision made parts, they must be maintained by proper lubrication and maintenance. If a bearing is found to be damaged, it must be replaced immediately. However, when installing a new bearing, care must be taken to prevent damage to the new bearing. While bearing replacement is described in the individual chapters where applicable, the following can be used as a guideline.

NOTE
Unless otherwise specified, install bearings with their manufacturer's mark or number on the bearing facing outward.

Bearing Removal

While bearings are normally removed only when damaged, there may be times when it is necessary to remove a bearing that is in good condition. Depending on the situation, you may be able to remove the bearing without damaging it. However, bearing removal in some situations, no matter how careful you are, will cause bearing damage. Care must be given to bearings during their removal to prevent secondary damage to the shaft or housing. Note the following when removing bearings.

1. When using a puller to remove a bearing on a shaft, care must be taken so that shaft damage does not occur. Always place a piece of metal between the end of the shaft and the puller screw. In addition, place the puller arms next to the inner bearing race. See **Figure 62**.
2. When using a hammer to remove a bearing on a shaft, do not strike the hammer directly against the shaft. Instead, use a brass or aluminum spacer between the hammer and shaft (**Figure 63**). In addition, make sure to support *both* bearing races with wooden blocks as shown in **Figure 63**.
3. The most ideal method of bearing removal is with a hydraulic press. However, certain procedures must be followed or damage may occur to the bearing, shaft or case half. Note the following when using a press:
   a. Always support the inner and outer bearing races with a suitable size wood or aluminum spacer ring (**Figure 64**). If only the outer race is supported, the balls and/or the inner race will be damaged.

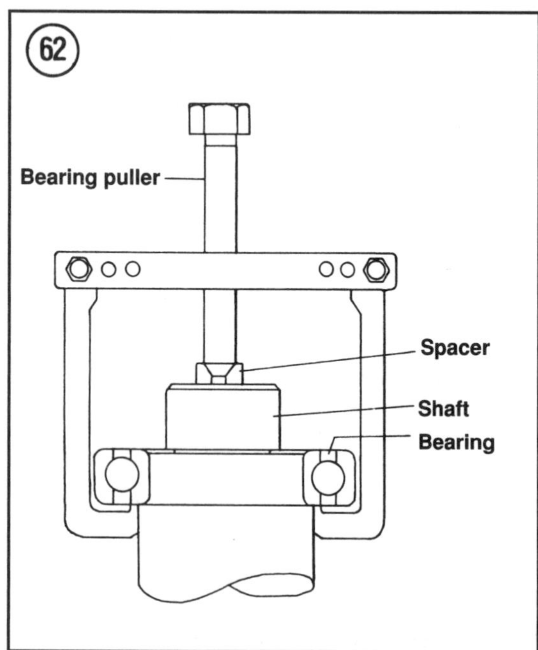

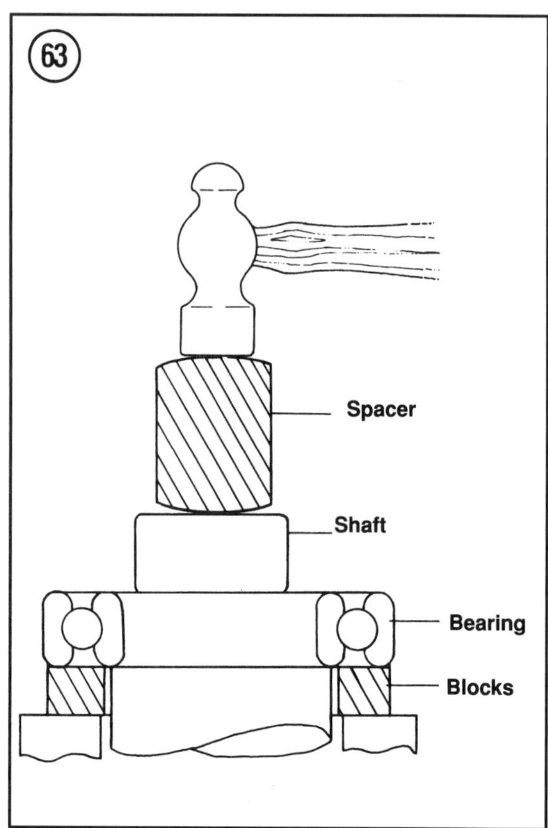

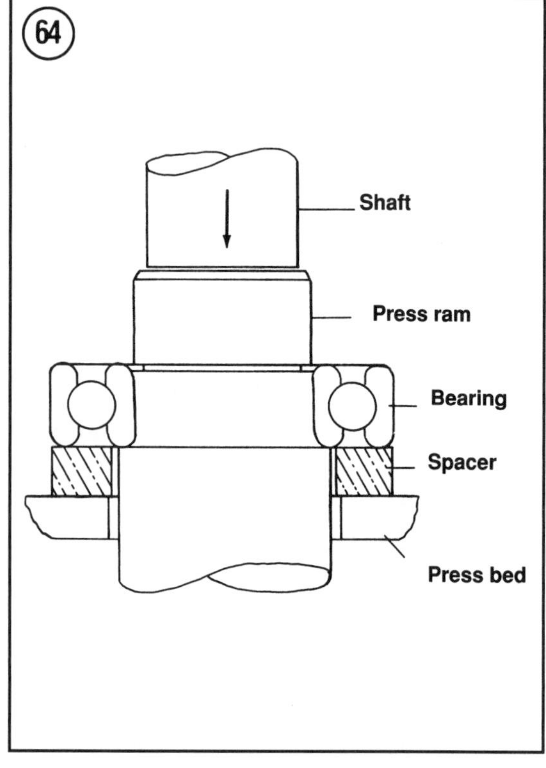

b. Always make sure the press ram (**Figure 64**) aligns with the center of the shaft. If the ram is not centered, it may damage the bearing and/or shaft.

c. The moment the shaft is free of the bearing, it will drop to the floor. Secure or hold the shaft to prevent it from falling.

Bearing Installation

1. When installing a bearing in a housing, apply pressure to the *outer* bearing race (**Figure 65**). When installing a bearing on a shaft, apply pressure to the *inner* bearing race (**Figure 66**).

2. When installing a bearing as described in Step 1, some type of driver will be required. Never strike the bearing directly with a hammer or the bearing will be damaged. When installing a bearing, a piece of pipe or a socket with an outer diameter that matches the bearing race will be required. **Figure 67** shows the correct way to use a socket and hammer when installing a bearing over a shaft.

3. Step 1 describes how to install a bearing in a case half or over a shaft. However, when installing a bearing over a shaft and into a housing at the same time, a snug fit is required for both outer and inner bearing races. In this situation, a spacer must be installed underneath the driver tool so that pressure is applied evenly across *both* races. See **Figure 68**. If the outer race is not supported as shown in **Figure 68**, the balls will push against the outer bearing track and damage it.

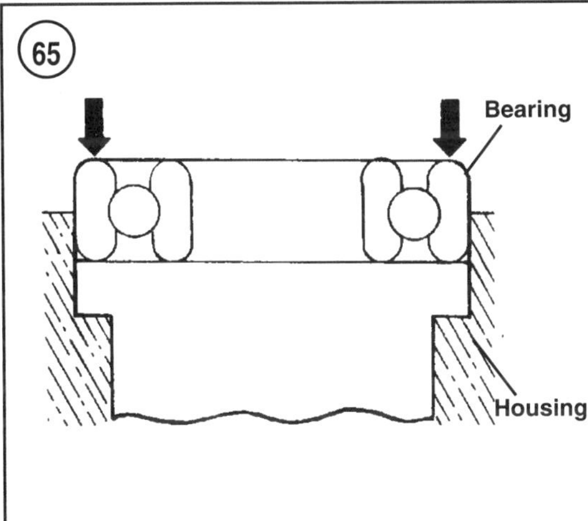

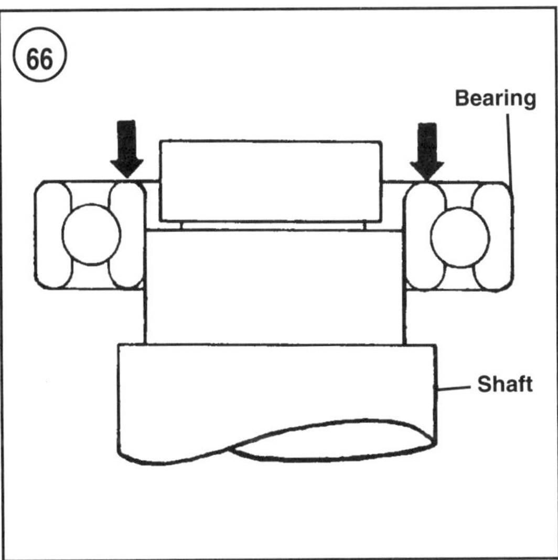

Shrink Fit

1. *Installing a bearing over a shaft*: When a tight fit is required, the bearing inside diameter is smaller than the shaft. In this case, driving the bearing on the shaft may cause bearing damage. Instead, the bearing must be heated before installation. Note the following:

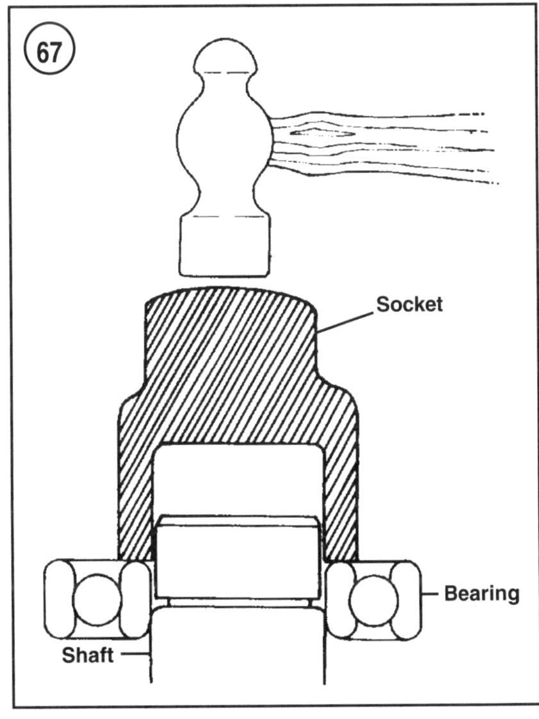

1

a. Secure the shaft so that it can be ready for bearing installation.
b. Clean the bearing surface on the shaft of all residue. Remove burrs with a file or sandpaper.
c. Fill a suitable pot or beaker with clean mineral oil. Place a thermometer (rated higher than 248° F [120° C]) in the oil. Support the thermometer so that it does not rest on the bottom or side of the pot.
d. Secure the bearing with a piece of heavy wire bent to hold it in the pot. Hang the bearing in the pot so that it does not touch the bottom or sides of the pot.
e. Turn the heat on and monitor the thermometer. When the oil temperature rises to approximately 248° F (120° C), remove the bearing from the pot and quickly install it. If necessary, place a socket on the inner bearing race and tap the bearing into place. As the bearing chills, it will tighten on the shaft so you must work quickly when installing it. Make sure the bearing is installed all the way.

2. *Installing a bearing in a housing*: Bearings are generally installed in a housing with a slight interference fit. Driving the bearing into the housing may damage the housing or bearing. Instead, heat the housing before installing the bearing. Note the following:

CAUTION
Before heating the housing in this procedure to remove the bearings, wash the housing thoroughly with detergent and water. Rinse and rewash the housing as required to remove all traces of oil and other chemical deposits.

a. The housing must be heated to a temperature of about 212° F (100° C) in a shop oven. An easy way to determine if it is at the proper temperature is to drop tiny drops of water on the housing as it heats up; if they sizzle and evaporate immediately, the temperature is correct. Heat only one housing at a time.

CAUTION
Do not heat the housing with a torch (propane or acetylene)—never bring a flame into contact with the bearing or housing. The direct heat will destroy the case hardening of the bearing and will likely warp the housing.

b. Remove the housing from the oven or hot plate. Hold onto the housing with a kitchen pot holder, heavy gloves, or heavy shop cloths—*it is hot.*

NOTE
A suitable size socket and extension works well for removing and installing bearings.

c. Hold the housing with the bearing side down and tap the bearing out. Repeat for all bearings in the housing.
d. While heating the housing halves, place the new bearings in a freezer if possible. Chilling them will slightly reduce their overall diameter while the hot housing assembly is slightly larger due to heat expansion. This makes installation much easier.

NOTE
Always install bearings with their manufacturer's mark or number facing outward.

e. While the housing is still hot, install the new bearing(s) into the housing. Install the bearings by hand, if possible. If necessary, lightly tap the bearing(s) into the housing with a socket placed on the outer bearing race. *Do not* install new bearings by driving on the inner

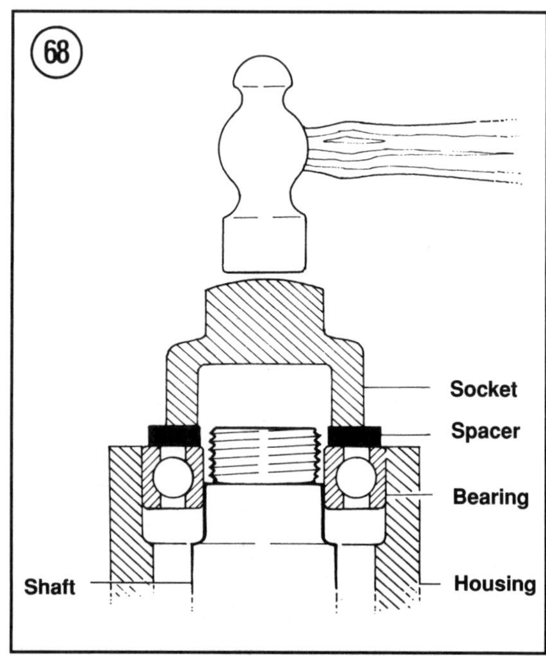

bearing race. Install the bearing(s) until it seats completely.

OIL SEALS

Oil seals (**Figure 69**) are used to contain oil, water, grease or combustion gasses in a housing or shaft. Improper removal of a seal can damage the housing or shaft. Improper installation of the seal can damage the seal. Note the following:

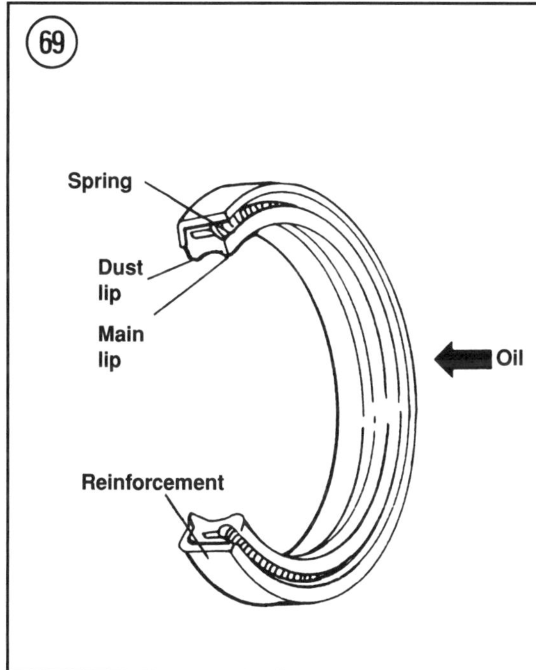

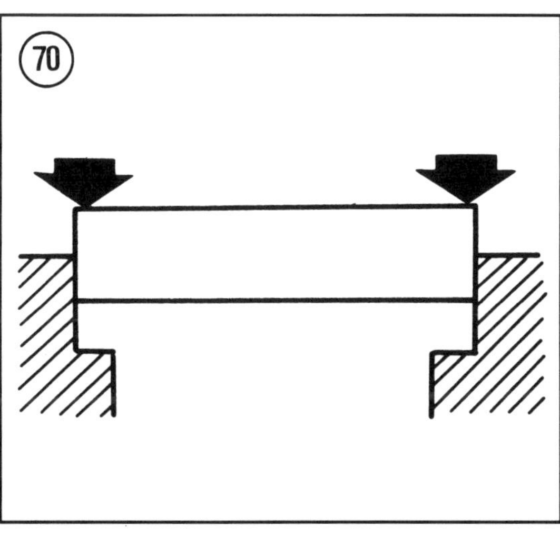

a. Prying is generally the easiest and most effective method to remove a seal from a housing. However, always place a rag underneath the pry tool to prevent damage to the housing.
b. Pack grease in the seal lips before installing the seal.
c. Unless specified otherwise in the text, install oil seals with their manufacturer's numbers or marks facing out.
d. Install oil seals with a driver placed on the outside of the seal as shown in **Figure 70**. Make sure the seal is driven squarely into the housing. Never install a seal by hitting against the top of the seal with a hammer.

1

RIDING SAFETY

General Tips

1. Read your owner's manual and know your machine.
2. Check the throttle and brake controls before starting the engine.
3. Know how to make an emergency stop.
4. Never add fuel while anyone is smoking in the area or when the engine is running.
5. Never wear loose scarves, belts or boot laces that could catch on moving parts.
6. Always wear eye and head protection and protective clothing to protect your *entire* body. Today's riding apparel is very stylish and you will be ready for action as well as being well protected.
7. Riding in the winter months requires a good set of clothes to keep your body dry and warm; otherwise your entire trip may be miserable. If you dress properly, perspiration will evaporate from your body. If your clothes trap the perspiration, you will become cold. Even mild temperatures can be very uncomfortable and dangerous when combined with a strong wind or traveling at high speed. See **Table 10** for windchill factors. Always dress according to what the windchill factor is, not the ambient temperature.
8. Never allow anyone to operate the bike without proper instruction. This is for their bodily protection and to keep your machine from damage or destruction.
9. Use the "buddy system" for long trips, just in case you have a problem or run out of gasoline.

10. Never attempt to repair your machine with the engine running except when necessary for certain tune-up procedures.
11. Check all of the machine components and hardware as described in Chapter Three, especially the wheels and the steering.

Operating Tips

1. Avoid dangerous terrain.
2. Keep the headlight, turn signal lights and taillight free of dirt.
3. Always steer with both hands.
4. Be aware of the terrain and avoid operating the bike at excessive speed.
5. Do not panic if the throttle sticks. Turn the engine stop switch to the OFF position.
6. Do not tailgate. Rear end collisions can cause injury and machine damage.
7. Do not mix alcoholic beverages or drugs with riding—*ride straight.*
8. Check your fuel supply regularly. Make certain your fuel supply will permit you to arrive at the next fuel stop.

Table 1 MODEL DESIGNATION

1991
FXDB Sturgis
1992
FXDB Dyna Daytona
FXDC Dyna Glide Custom
1993
FXDL Dyna Low Rider
FXDWG Dyna Glide Anniversary Edition
FXDWG Dyna Wide Glide (Accessorized edition)
1994
FXDL Dyna Low Rider
FXDWG Dyna Wide Glide
1995-1998
FXDL Dyna Low Rider
FXDWG Dyna Wide Glide
FXD Dyna Super Glide
FXDS-CONV Dyna Convertible

Table 2 GENERAL SPECIFICATIONS

	in.	mm
Wheelbase		
1991-1992	65.50	1,663
1993-1994		
FXDWG	66.10	1,679
FXDL	65.60	1,666
1995-1998		
FXDWG	66.10	1,664
FXDL	65.60	1,679
FXD	62.50	1,588
FXD-CONV	63.88	1,623
Overall length		
1991-1994	94.00	2,388
1995-1998		
FXDWG	95.50	2,426
FXDL	94.00	2,388
FXD	91.00	2,311
FXD-CONV	92.88	2,359
Overall width		
1991-1994	28.50	724
1995-1998		
FXDWG	31.70	805
All other models	28.50	724
Overall height	47.50	1,206
Saddle height		
1991-1992	26.62	676
1993-1994		
FXDWG	26.60	675.6
FXDL	26.62	676
1995-1998		
FXDWG	27.80	706
FXDL	27.00	686
FXD	27.00	686
FXD-CONV	28.75	730

(continued)

Table 2 GENERAL SPECIFICATIONS (continued)

	in.	mm
Road clearance		
1991-1994	5.62	143
1995-1998		
FXD-CONV	6.25	159
All other models	5.62	143

Table 3 OVERALL VEHICLE WEIGHT*

Model	lb.	kg.
1991-1994	598	272
1995-1998		
FXDWG	598	272
FXDL	598	272
FXD	593	269
FXD-CONV	621	282

* Dry weight as shipped from factory.

Table 4 GROSS VEHICLE WEIGHT RATINGS

	lb.	kg
Gross vehicle weight rating (GVWR)	1,085	493
Gross axle weight ratings (GAWR)		
Front	390	177
Rear	695	316

* GVWR is the maximum allowable vehicle weight. This weight includes combined vehicle, rider(s) and accessory weight.

Table 5 FUEL TANK CAPACITY

	U.S. gal.	Liters	Imp. gal
1991-1992			
Total	4.9	18.5	4.1
Reserve	1.1	4.2	0.9
1993-1994			
Total	5.2	19.7	4.3
Reserve	1.1	4.2	0.9
1995			
FXDWG			
Total	5.2	19.7	4.3
Reserve	1.1	4.2	0.9
All other models			
Total	4.9	18.5	4.1
Reserve	1.1	4.2	0.9

Table 6 DECIMAL AND METRIC EQUIVALENTS

Fractions	Decimal in.	Metric mm	Fractions	Decimal in.	Metric mm
1/64	0.015625	0.39688	33/64	0.515625	13.09687
1/32	0.03125	0.79375	17/32	0.53125	13.49375
3/64	0.046875	1.19062	35/64	0.546875	13.89062
1/16	0.0625	1.58750	9/16	0.5625	14.28750
5/64	0.078125	1.98437	37/64	0.578125	14.68437
3/32	0.09375	2.38125	19/32	0.59375	15.08125
7/64	0.109375	2.77812	39/64	0.609375	15.47812
1/8	0.125	3.1750	5/8	0.625	15.87500
9/64	0.140625	3.57187	41/64	0.640625	16.27187
5/32	0.15625	3.96875	21/32	0.65625	16.66875
11/64	0.171875	4.36562	43/64	0.671875	17.06562
3/16	0.1875	4.76250	11/16	0.6875	17.46250
13/64	0.203125	5.15937	45/64	0.703125	17.85937
7/32	0.21875	5.55625	23/32	0.71875	18.25625
15/64	0.234375	5.95312	47/64	0.734375	18.65312
1/4	0.250	6.35000	3/4	0.750	19.05000
17/64	0.265625	6.74687	49/64	0.765625	19.44687
9/32	0.28125	7.14375	25/32	0.78125	19.84375
19/64	0.296875	7.54062	51/64	0.796875	20.24062
5/16	0.3125	7.93750	13/16	0.8125	20.63750
21/64	0.328125	8.33437	53/64	0.828125	21.03437
11/32	0.34375	8.73125	27/32	0.84375	21.43125
23/64	0.359375	9.12812	55/64	0.859375	22.82812
3/8	0.375	9.52500	7/8	0.875	22.22500
25/64	0.390625	9.92187	57/64	0.890625	22.62187
13/32	0.40625	10.31875	29/32	0.90625	23.01875
27/64	0.421875	10.71562	59/64	0.921875	23.41562
7/16	0.4375	11.11250	15/16	0.9375	23.81250
29/64	0.453125	11.50937	61/64	0.953125	24.20937
15/32	0.46875	11.90625	31/32	0.96875	24.60625
31/64	0.484375	12.30312	63/64	0.984375	25.00312
1/2	0.500	12.70000	1	1.00	25.40000

Table 7 GENERAL TORQUE SPECIFICATIONS (FT.-LB.)*

	Body Size or Outside Diameter									
Type**	1/4	5/16	3/8	7/16	1/2	9/16	5/8	3/4	7/8	1
SAE 2	6	12	20	32	47	69	96	155	206	310
SAE 5	10	19	33	54	78	114	154	257	382	587
SAE 7	13	25	44	71	110	154	215	360	570	840
SAE 8	14	29	47	78	119	169	230	380	600	700

* Convert ft.-lb. specification to N•m by multiplying by 1.3558.

** Fastener strength of SAE bolts can be determined by the bolt head grade markings. Unmarked bolt heads and cap screws are usually mild steel. More grade markings indicate higher fastener quality.

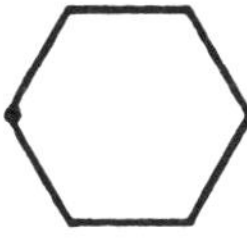

SAE 2

SAE 5

SAE 7

SAE 8

Table 8 CONVERSION TABLES

Multiply	By	To get equivalent of
Length		
Inches	25.4	Millimeter
Inches	2.54	Centimeter
Miles	1.609	Kilometer
Feet	0.3048	Meter
Millimeter	0.03937	Inches
Centimeter	0.3937	Inches
Kilometer	0.6214	Mile
Meter	3.281	Mile
Fluid volume		
U.S. quarts	0.9463	Liters
U.S. gallons	3.785	Liters
U.S. ounces	29.573529	Milliliters
Imperial gallons	4.54609	Liters
Imperial quarts	1.1365	Liters
Liters	0.2641721	U.S. gallons
Liters	1.0566882	U.S. quarts
Liters	33.814023	U.S. ounces
Liters	0.22	Imperial gallons
Liters	0.8799	Imperial quarts
Milliliters	0.033814	U.S. ounces
Milliliters	1.0	Cubic centimeters
Milliliters	0.001	Liters
Torque		
Foot-pounds	1.3558	Newton-meters
Foot-pounds	0.138255	Meters-kilograms
Inch-pounds	0.11299	Newton-meters
Newton-meters	0.7375622	Foot-pounds
Newton-meters	8.8507	Inch-pounds
Meters-kilograms	7.2330139	Foot-pounds
Volume		
Cubic inches	16.387064	Cubic centimeters
Cubic centimeters	0.0610237	Cubic inches
Temperature		
Fahrenheit	$(F - 32°) \times 0.556$	Centigrade
Centigrade	$(C \times 1.8) + 32$	Fahrenheit
Weight		
Ounces	28.3495	Grams
Pounds	0.4535924	Kilograms
Grams	0.035274	Ounces
Kilograms	2.2046224	Pounds
Pressure		
Pounds per square inch	0.070307	Kilograms per square centimeter
Kilograms per square centimeter	14.223343	Pounds per square inch
Speed		
Miles per hour	1.609344	Kilometers per hour
Kilometers per hour	0.6213712	Miles per hour

TABLE 9 AMERICAN TAP DRILL SIZES

Tap thread	Drill size	Tap thread	Drill size
#0-80	3/64	1/4-28	No. 3
#1-64	No. 53	5/16-18	F
#1-72	No. 53	5/16-24	I

(continued)

TABLE 9 AMERICAN TAP DRILL SIZES (continued)

Tap thread	Drill size	Tap thread	Drill size
#2-56	No. 51	3/8-16	5/16
#2-64	No. 50	3/8-24	Q
#3-48	5/64	7/16-14	U
#3-56	No. 46	7/16-20	W
#4-40	No. 43	1/2-13	27/64
#4-48	No. 42	1/2-20	29/64
#5-40	No. 39	9/16-12	31/64
#5-44	No. 37	9/16-18	33/64
#6-32	No. 36	5/8-11	17/32
#6-40	No. 33	5/18-18	37/64
#8-32	No. 29	3/4-10	21/32
#8-36	No. 29	3/4-16	11/16
#10-24	No. 25	7/8-9	49-64
#10.32	No. 21	7/8-14	13/16
#12-24	No. 17	1-8	7/8
#12-28	No. 15	1-14	15/16
1/4-20	No. 8		

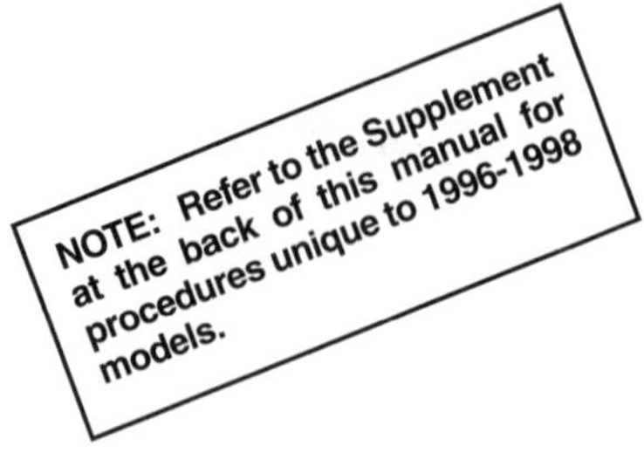

CHAPTER TWO

TROUBLESHOOTING

Every motorcycle engine requires an uninterrupted supply of fuel and air, proper ignition and adequate compression. If any of these are lacking, the engine will not run.

Diagnosing electrical and mechanical problems is simple if you use orderly procedures and keep a few basic principles in mind.

The troubleshooting procedures in this chapter analyze typical symptoms and show logical methods of isolating causes. These are not the only methods, but to save time and work more efficiently when troubleshooting a problem, follow a systematic approach.

Never assume anything or overlook obvious problem areas. If you are riding along and the bike suddenly quits, check the easiest, most accessible areas first. Is there gasoline in the tank? Has a spark plug wire broken or fallen off?

If nothing obvious turns up in a quick check, look a little farther. Learning to recognize and describe symptoms will help you or a mechanic to solve the problem fast. When working with a mechanic, describe problems accurately and fully. Saying that "it won't run" isn't the same thing as saying "it quit at high speed and won't start," or that "it sat in my garage for 3 months and then wouldn't start."

Gather as many symptoms as possible to aid in diagnosis. Note whether the engine lost power gradually or all at once. Remember that the more complicated a machine is, the easier it is to troubleshoot because symptoms point to specific problems.

After defining the symptoms, test and analyze areas which could cause the problem. Guessing at the cause of a problem may eventually provide the solution, but it can easily lead to frustration, wasted time and a series of expensive, unnecessary parts replacements.

You do not need expensive equipment or complicated test gear to determine if you can fix the problem at home. A few simple checks could save a large repair bill and lost time while the bike sits in a dealer's service department. On the other hand, do not attempt repairs beyond your abilities. Service departments tend to charge heavily for putting together a disassembled engine. Some won't even take on such a job—so use common sense and don't get overwhelmed.

Table 1 and **Table 2** (end of chapter) list electrical specifications.

OPERATING REQUIREMENTS

An engine needs 3 basics to run properly: correct fuel/air mixture, adequate compression and a spark at the correct time (**Figure 1**). If one or more are missing, the engine will not run. If all three engine basics are present, but one or more is not working properly, the engine may start, but it will not run properly.

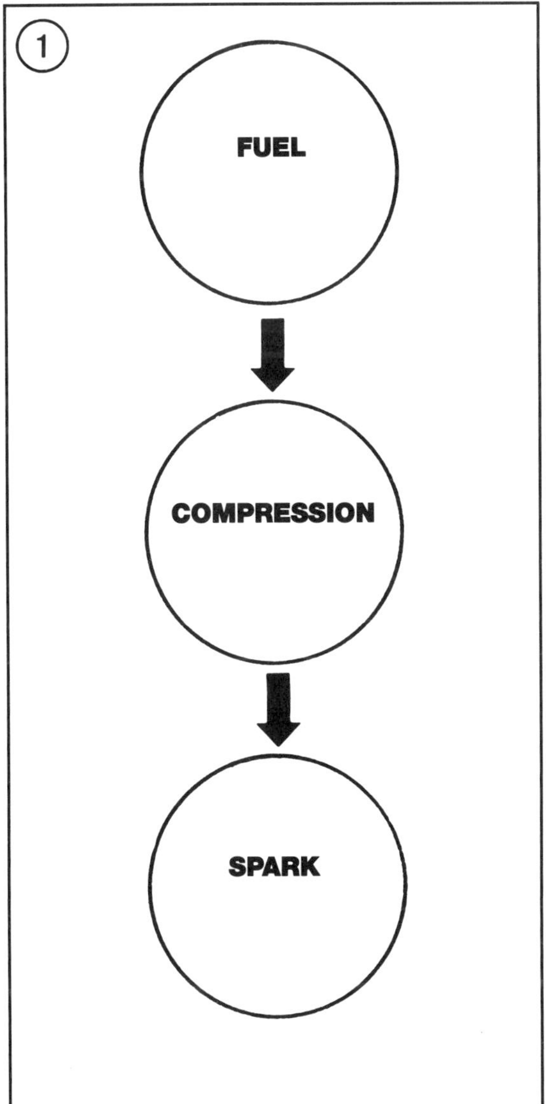

The electrical system is the weakest link of the 3 basics. More problems result from electrical breakdowns than from any other source. Keep that in mind before you begin tampering with carburetor and engine adjustments.

If you haven't ridden the machine for some time and it will not start, first check and clean the spark plugs. Then look to the gasoline delivery system. This includes the fuel tank, fuel shutoff valve and fuel line to the carburetor. Gasoline deposits may have formed and gummed up the carburetor jets and air passages.

TROUBLESHOOTING INSTRUMENTS

Chapter One describes some tools required for troubleshooting.

TESTING ELECTRICAL COMPONENTS

Most dealerships will not accept returns on electrical parts purchased from them. When testing electrical components, perform the test procedures as described in this chapter and know how to operate your test equipment. If a test result shows that a component is defective, but only slightly out of specification, have the parts tested at a dealership. They can verify the test result before you purchase a new electrical component.

EMERGENCY TROUBLESHOOTING

If the bike is difficult to start, or won't start at all, it doesn't help to wear down the battery by using the electric starter. Check for obvious problems even before getting out your tools. Go down the following list in order. If the bike still will not start, refer to the appropriate troubleshooting procedures in this chapter. As described under *Operating Requirements*, the engine requires 3 basics before it will start and run properly. The following procedure illustrates steps for checking each of the 3 basic engine principles.

1. Visually inspect the bike for gas or oil leakage, loose wires or other abnormal conditions. If you do not find anything that could cause a starting problem continue with the following.
2. Check that the engine stop switch is not in the OFF position (**Figure 2**).

WARNING
*Do **not** use an open flame to check for fuel in the tank. A serious explosion is certain to result.*

3. Is there fuel in the tank? Open the filler cap and rock the bike. Listen for fuel sloshing around.

NOTE
If you have not run the engine for some time, gasoline deposits may have gummed up carburetor jets and air passages. In addition, gasoline tends to lose its potency after standing for a long period. You may even find water in the tank. Drain the old gasoline and try starting with a fresh tankful.

NOTE
If you notice dirt, rust or other debris draining out of the fuel tank, bits of the same material are clogging the carburetor jets and fuel passages.

4. Is the fuel supply valve (**Figure 3**) in the ON position? If the fuel level in the tanks is low, turn the valve to RESERVE.
5. Is the enrichener knob (**Figure 4**) in the correct position? Pull the enrichener knob out when starting a cold engine and push it in when starting a warm or hot engine. If the enrichener system is not operating correctly, adjust it as described in Chapter Three.

NOTE
Unlike a choke, the enrichener system does not use detent positions on the enrichener shaft. The enrichener operates in any position from closed to full out. The position required generally depends on the engine's temperature—cold, warm or hot. Just remember that the engine's speed increases when the knob is pulled out.

NOTE
The condition of your engine's spark plugs is a deciding factor in its performance and an important reference point during troubleshooting and general maintenance.

6. After attempting to start the engine, immediately remove the spark plugs (**Figure 5**) and check their firing tips. Refer to Chapter Three for information on reading spark plugs. If fuel is present on both

spark plug firing tips, there is sufficient fuel to start the engine. If there is no sign of fuel on the plugs, suspect a fuel delivery problem. Refer to*Fuel System* in this chapter. If there is water on the plugs, the fuel tank is contaminated or there is water in the crankcase.

7. Perform a spark test as described under *Engine Fails to Start (Spark Test)* in this chapter. If there is a strong spark, perform Step 8.

8. Check engine compression as described in Chapter Three. Low compression indicates a problem with one or both cylinders. Worn piston rings and a damaged piston will reduce compression. Refer to *Engine* in this chapter.

Engine Fails to Start (Spark Test)

Perform the following spark test to find out if the ignition system is capable of producing sufficient spark.

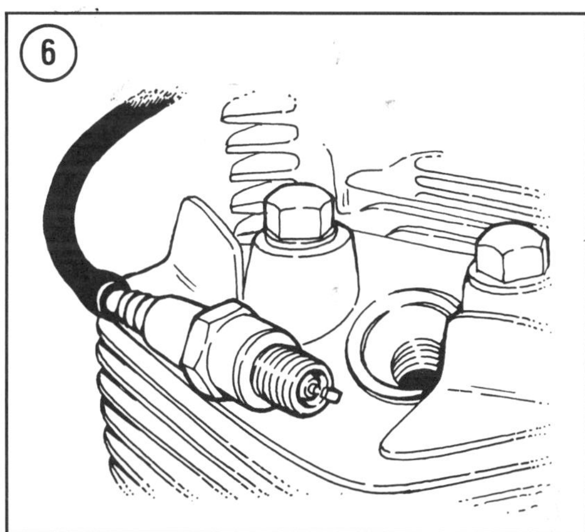
6

7

1. Remove the spark plugs.
2. Connect the spark plug wire to the spark plug and touch the spark plug base to a good ground like the engine cylinder head. Position the spark plug so you can see the electrodes. See **Figure 6**. Repeat for the other spark plug.

WARNING
Cranking the engine with the spark plugs removed will eject fuel through the spark plug holes. When making a spark test, place the spark plugs away from the open spark plug holes or fuel may ignite and cause a fire or explosion to occur.

3. Crank the engine with the starter. A fat blue spark firing across both spark plug electrodes indicates that the ignition system is working properly.

WARNING
You can receive a serious electrical shock if you hold the spark plug wire or connector with your hand when making a spark test. If you cannot see the plug tip, hold the spark plug or wire with a pair of insulated pliers. The high voltage generated by the ignition system could produce serious or fatal shocks.

4. If the spark is good, check for one or more of the following possible malfunctions:
   a. Obstructed fuel line or fuel filter.
   b. Leaking head gasket(s).
   c. Low compression.
5. If the spark is not good, check for one or more of the following:
   a. Loose electrical connections at the ignition coil (**Figure 7**).
   b. Dirty electrical connections.
   c. Loose or broken ignition coil ground wire.
   d. Loose or damaged high tension leads.
   e. Discharged battery.
   f. Disconnected or damaged battery connection.
   g. Damaged ignition system component (ignition coil, ignition module or ignition sensor).

Engine is Difficult to Start

Check for one or more of the following possible malfunctions:
   a. Fouled spark plug(s).
   b. Improperly adjusted enrichener valve.

c. Intake manifold air leak.
d. A plugged fuel tank filler cap.
e. Clogged carburetor fuel line.
f. Contaminated fuel system.
g. An improperly adjusted carburetor.
h. A faulty ignition unit.
i. Faulty ignition coil.
j. Damaged ignition coil wires (**Figure 7**).
k. Incorrect ignition timing.
l. Low engine compression.
m. Engine oil too heavy (winter temperatures).
n. Discharged battery.
o. A faulty starter motor.
p. Loose or corroded starter and/or battery cables.
q. A loose ignition sensor and module electrical connector.
r. Incorrect pushrod length (consider this if you just removed and installed the pushrods).

Engine Will Not Crank

Check for one or more of the following possible malfunctions:

a. Ignition switch turned OFF.
b. A faulty ignition switch.
c. Engine run switch in OFF position.
d. A faulty engine run switch.
e. Loose or corroded starter and battery cables (solenoid chatters).
f. Discharged or defective battery.
g. A defective starter motor.
h. A faulty starter solenoid.
i. A faulty starter shaft pinion gear.
j. Slipping overrunning clutch assembly.
k. A seized piston(s).
l. Seized crankshaft bearings.
m. A broken connecting rod.

ENGINE PERFORMANCE

In the following check list, it is assumed that the engine runs, but is not operating at peak performance. This will serve as a starting point from which to isolate a performance malfunction.

Fouled Spark Plugs

If the spark plugs continually foul, note the following:

a. Air filter element severely contaminated.
b. An incorrect heat range spark plug. See Chapter Three for correct heat range spark plugs to use in your model.
c. Fuel mixture too rich.
d. Worn or damaged piston rings.
e. Worn or damaged valve guide oil seals.
f. Excessive valve stem-to-guide clearance.
g. Incorrect carburetor float level.

Engine Runs but Misfires

a. Fouled or improperly gapped spark plugs.
b. Damaged spark plug cables.
c. Incorrect ignition timing.
d. Faulty ignition components.
e. An obstructed fuel line or fuel shutoff valve.
f. Obstructed fuel filter.
g. Clogged carburetor jets.
h. Battery nearly discharged.
i. Loose battery connection.
j. Wiring or connector damage.
k. Water in fuel.
l. Weak or damaged valve springs.
m. Incorrect valve timing.
n. A damaged valve.
o. Dirty electrical connections.
p. Intake manifold or carburetor filter air leak.
q. A plugged carburetor vent hose.
r. Plugged fuel tank vent system.

Engine Overheating

a. Incorrect carburetor adjustment or jet selection.
b. Ignition timing retarded. Incorrect ignition timing or defective ignition system components.
c. Improper spark plugs.
d. Damaged or blocked cooling fins.
e. Oil level too low.
f. Oil not circulating properly.
g. Leaking valves.
h. Heavy engine carbon deposit.

Smoky Exhaust and Engine Runs Roughly

a. Clogged air filter element.
b. Incorrect carburetor adjustment—mixture too rich.
c. Choke not operating correctly.
d. Water or other contaminants in fuel.
e. Clogged fuel line.
f. Spark plugs fouled.
g. A defective ignition coil.
h. A defective ignition module or sensor.
i. Loose or defective ignition circuit wire.
j. Short circuits from damaged wire insulation.
k. Loose battery cable connection.
l. Incorrect cam timing.
m. Intake manifold or air filter air leaks.

Engine Loses Power

a. Incorrect carburetor adjustment.
b. Engine overheating.
c. Incorrect ignition timing.
d. Incorrectly gapped spark plugs.
e. An obstructed muffler.
f. Dragging brake(s).

Engine Lacks Acceleration

a. Carburetor mixture too lean.
b. Clogged fuel line.
c. Incorrect ignition timing.
d. Dragging brake(s).

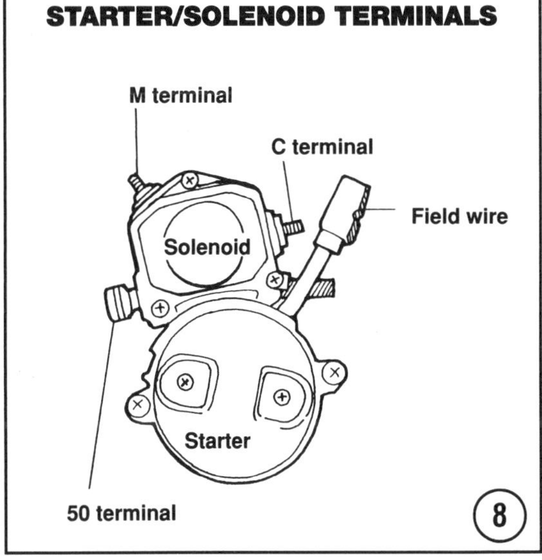

Valve Train Noise

a. Bent pushrod(s).
b. A faulty hydraulic lifter.
c. A bent valve.
d. Rocker arm seizure or damage (binding on shaft).
e. Worn or damaged cam gear bushing(s).
f. Worn or damaged cam gear(s).

ELECTRIC STARTING SYSTEM

The starting system consists of the battery, starter motor, starter relay, solenoid, start switch, starter mechanism and related wiring.

When the ignition switch is turned on and the start button pushed in, current is transmitted from the battery to the starter relay. When the relay is activated, it in turn activates the starter solenoid which mechanically engages the starter with the engine.

Starting system problems are easy to find. Most often, the trouble is a loose or corroded electrical connection.

Figure 8 identifies the starter motor and solenoid assembly and its terminal numbers. Refer to **Figure 8** when troubleshooting the starting system.

When troubleshooting the starting system, refer to the starting system diagram for your model:

a. **Figure 9**: All 1991-1992 models and 1993 FXDL.
b. **Figure 10**: 1993 FXDWG.
c. **Figure 11**: 1994 FXDL.
d. **Figure 12**: 1994 FXDWG.
e. **Figure 13**: 1995 FXDL.
f. **Figure 14**: 1995 FXDWG.

Troubleshooting Preparation

Before troubleshooting the starting system, check that:

a. The battery is fully charged.
b. Battery cables are the proper size and length. Replace damaged or undersize cables.
c. All electrical connections are clean and tight. High resistance caused from dirty or loose connectors can affect voltage and current levels.

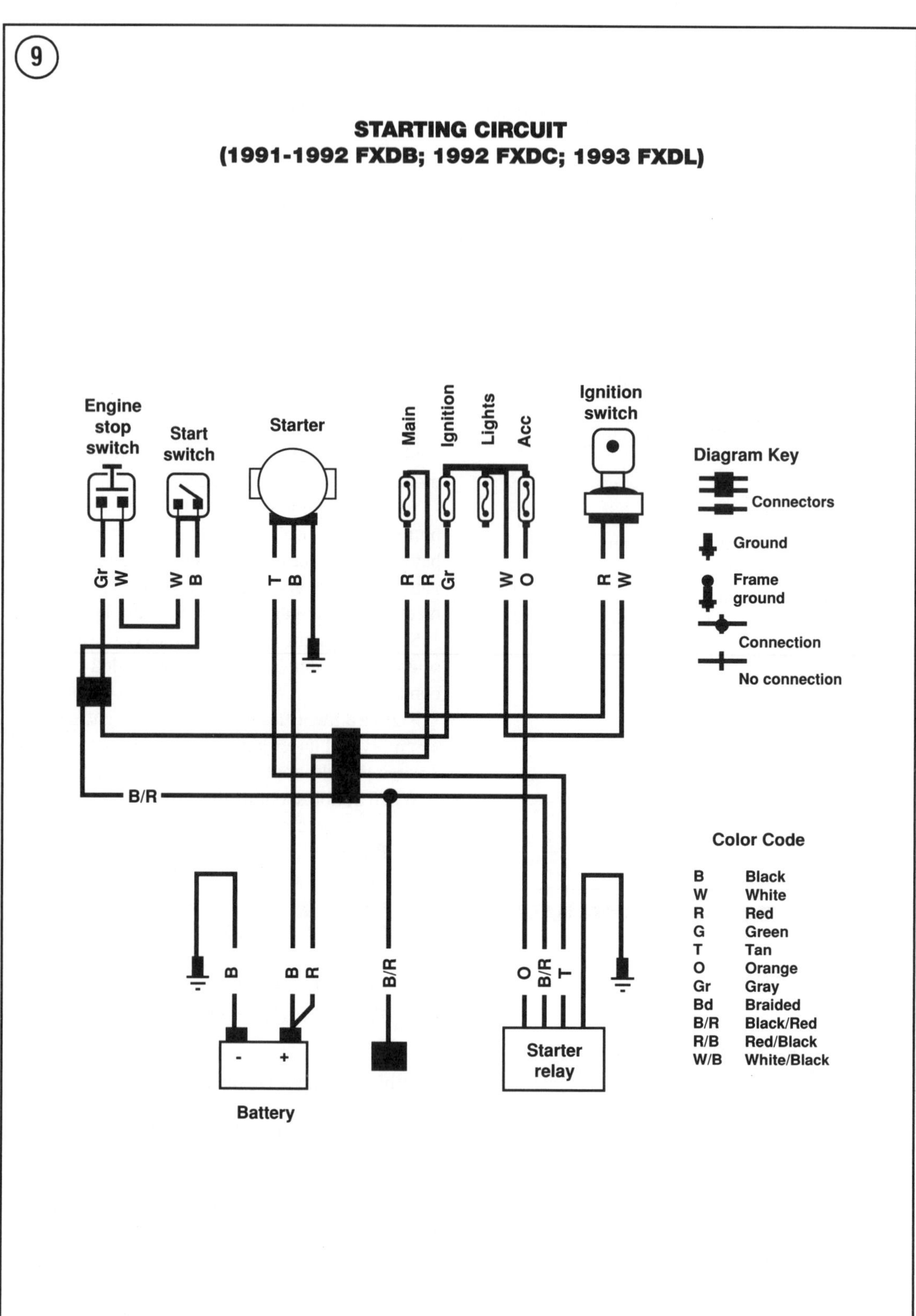
9
STARTING CIRCUIT
(1991-1992 FXDB; 1992 FXDC; 1993 FXDL)
Engine stop switch
Start switch
Starter
Main
Ignition
Lights
Acc
Ignition switch
Diagram Key
Connectors
Ground
Frame ground
Connection
No connection
Gr W
W B
T B
R R Gr
W O
R W
B/R
B
B R
B/R
O B/R T
Battery
Starter relay
Color Code
B Black
W White
R Red
G Green
T Tan
O Orange
Gr Gray
Bd Braided
B/R Black/Red
R/B Red/Black
W/B White/Black

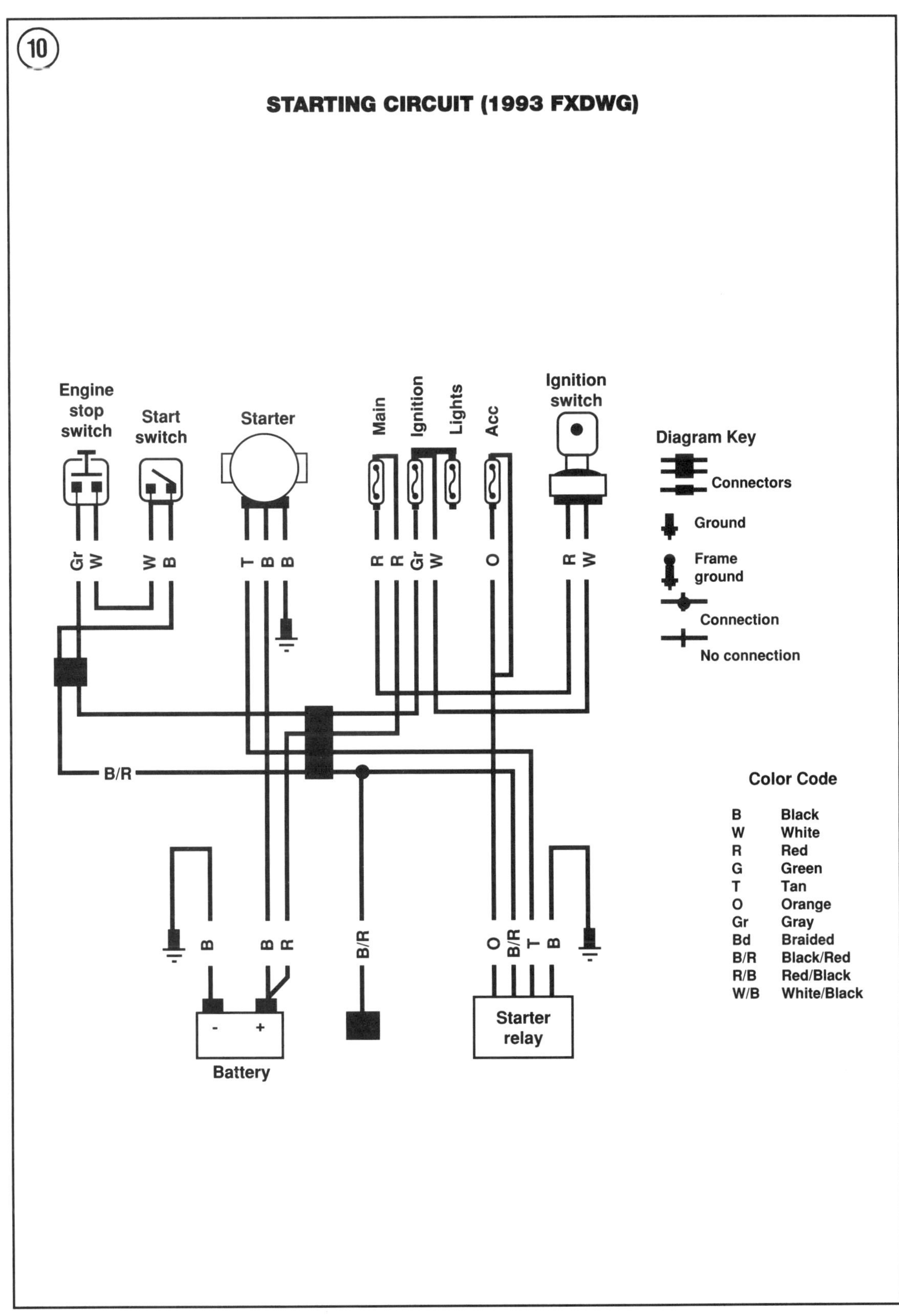
10
STARTING CIRCUIT (1993 FXDWG)
Engine stop switch
Start switch
Starter
Main
Ignition
Lights
Acc
Ignition switch
Diagram Key
Connectors
Ground
Frame ground
Connection
No connection
Gr W
W B
T B B
R R Gr W
O
R W
B/R
B
B R
B/R
O B/R T B
Battery
Starter relay
Color Code
B Black
W White
R Red
G Green
T Tan
O Orange
Gr Gray
Bd Braided
B/R Black/Red
R/B Red/Black
W/B White/Black

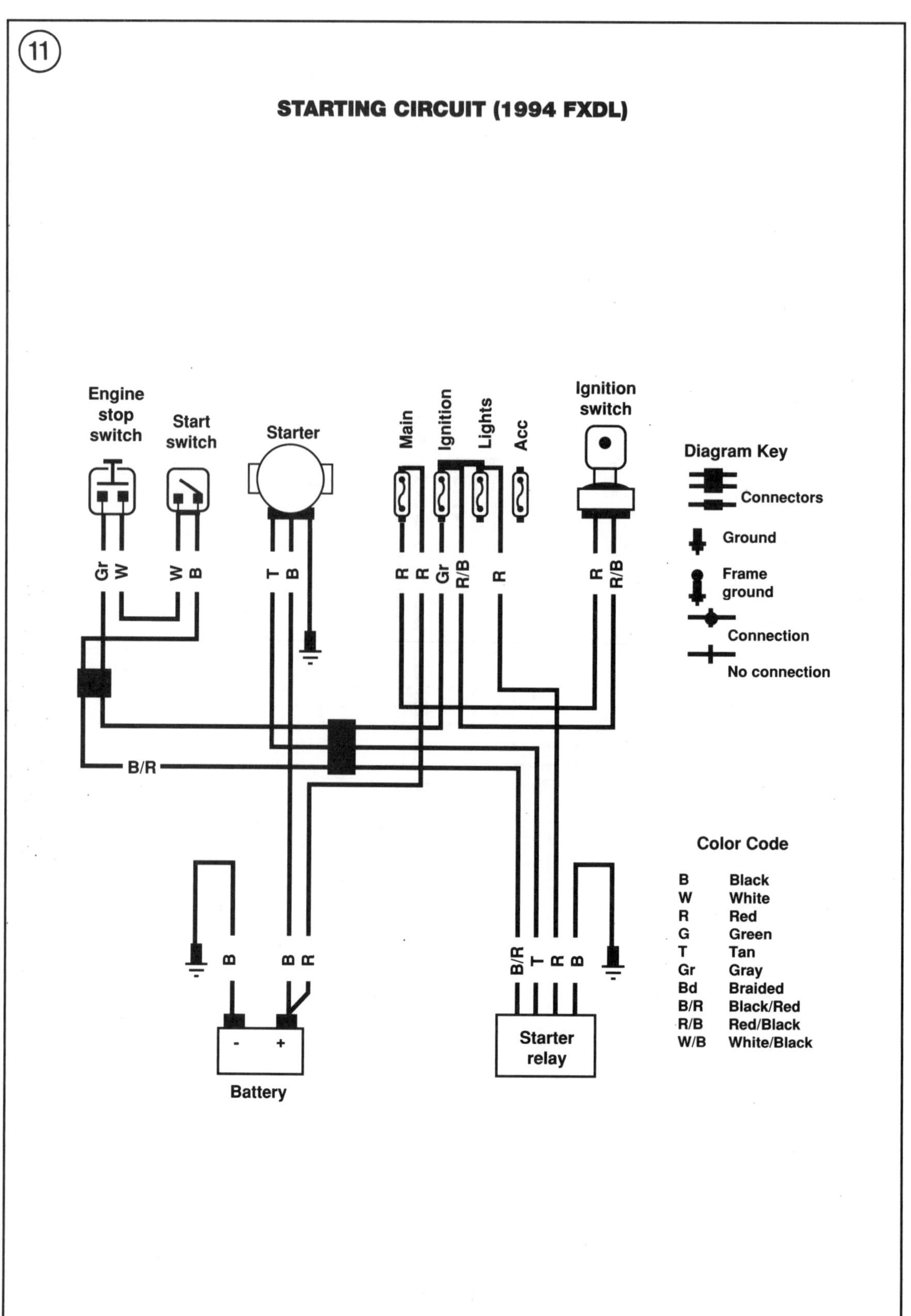
11
STARTING CIRCUIT (1994 FXDL)
Engine stop switch
Start switch
Starter
Main
Ignition
Lights
Acc
Ignition switch
Gr W
W B
T B
R R Gr R/B R
R R/B
B/R
B
B R
B/R T R B
Battery
Starter relay
Diagram Key
Connectors
Ground
Frame ground
Connection
No connection
Color Code
B Black
W White
R Red
G Green
T Tan
Gr Gray
Bd Braided
B/R Black/Red
R/B Red/Black
W/B White/Black

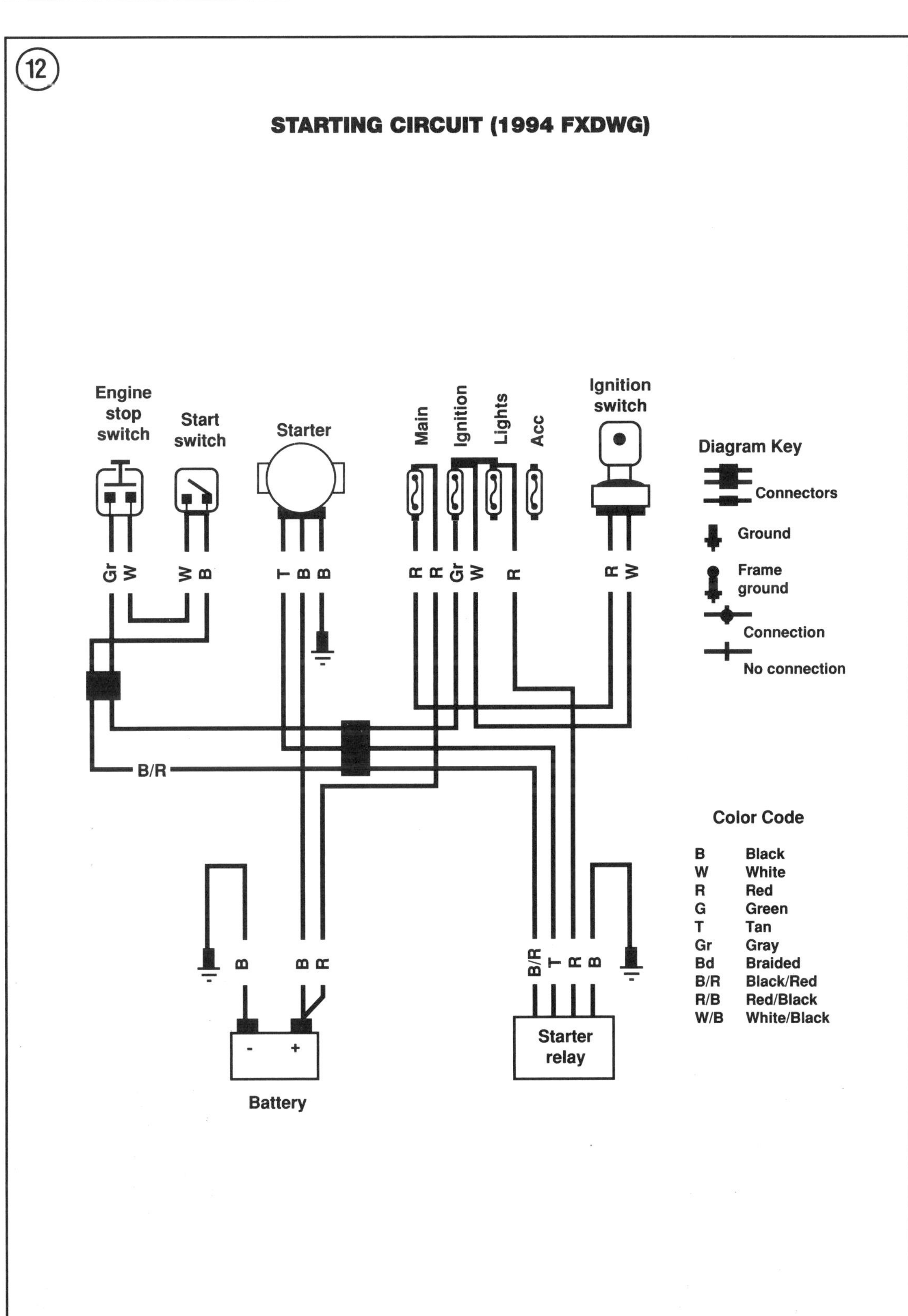
12
STARTING CIRCUIT (1994 FXDWG)
Engine stop switch
Start switch
Starter
Main
Ignition
Lights
Acc
Ignition switch
Diagram Key
Connectors
Ground
Frame ground
Connection
No connection
Gr W
W B
T B B
R R Gr W
R
R W
B/R
B
B R
Battery
B/R T R B
Starter relay
Color Code
B Black
W White
R Red
G Green
T Tan
Gr Gray
Bd Braided
B/R Black/Red
R/B Red/Black
W/B White/Black

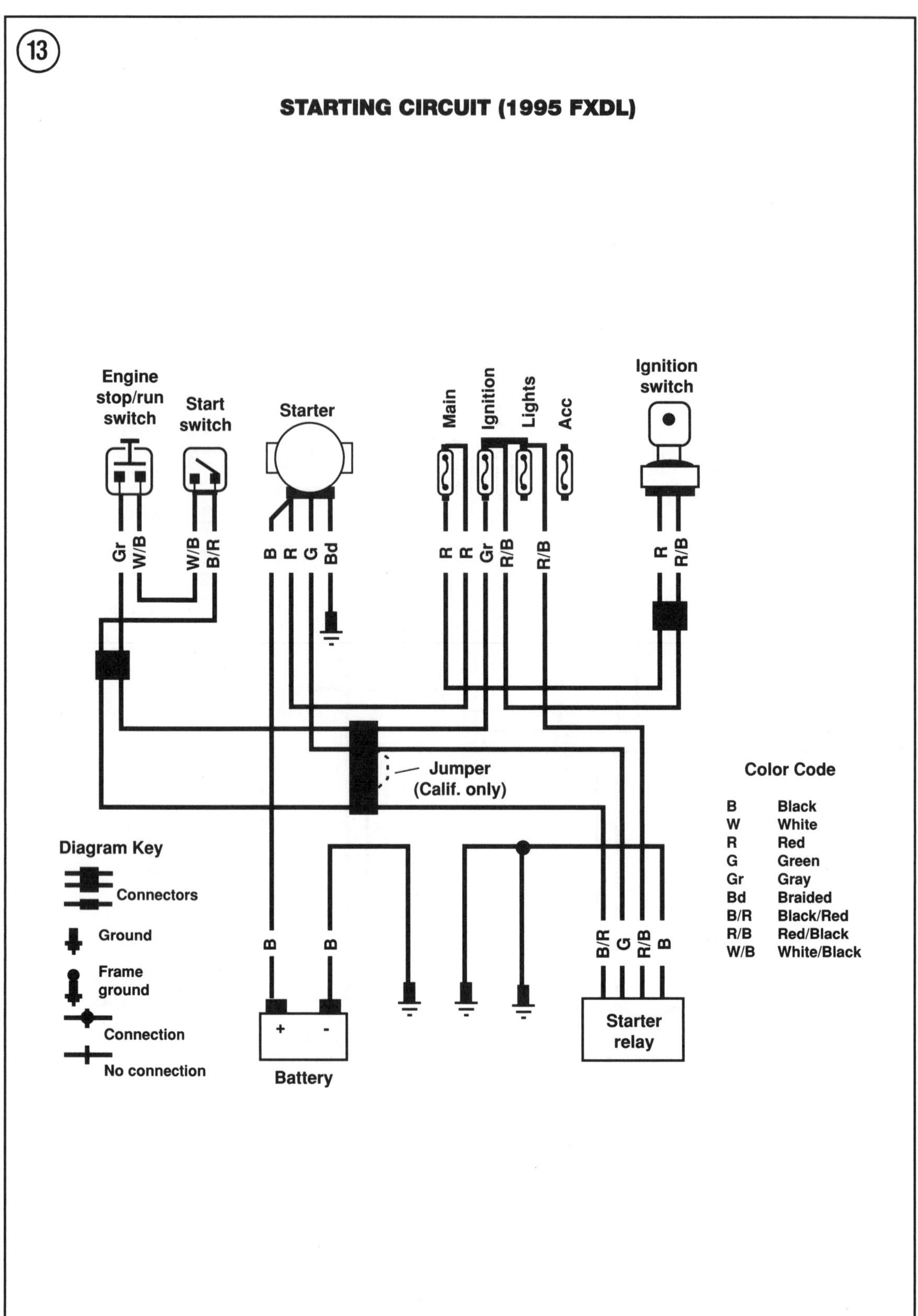
13
STARTING CIRCUIT (1995 FXDL)
Engine stop/run switch
Start switch
Starter
Main
Ignition
Lights
Acc
Ignition switch
Gr
W/B
W/B
B/R
B
R
G
Bd
R
R
Gr
R/B
R/B
R
R/B
Jumper (Calif. only)
Color Code
B Black
W White
R Red
G Green
Gr Gray
Bd Braided
B/R Black/Red
R/B Red/Black
W/B White/Black
Diagram Key
Connectors
Ground
Frame ground
Connection
No connection
B
B
+
-
Battery
B/R
G
R/B
B
Starter relay

14

STARTING CIRCUIT (1995 FXDWG)
Engine stop/run switch
Start switch
Starter
Main
Ignition
Lights
Acc
Ignition switch
Color Code
B Black
W White
R Red
G Green
Gr Gray
Bd Braided
B/R Black/Red
R/B Red/Black
W/B White/Black
Gr
W/B
W/B
B/R
B
R
G
Bd
R
R
Gr
R/B
R/B
R
R/B
Jumper (Calif. only)
Diagram Key
Connectors
Ground
Frame ground
Connection
No connection
B
B
B/R
G
R/B
B
-
+
Battery
Starter relay

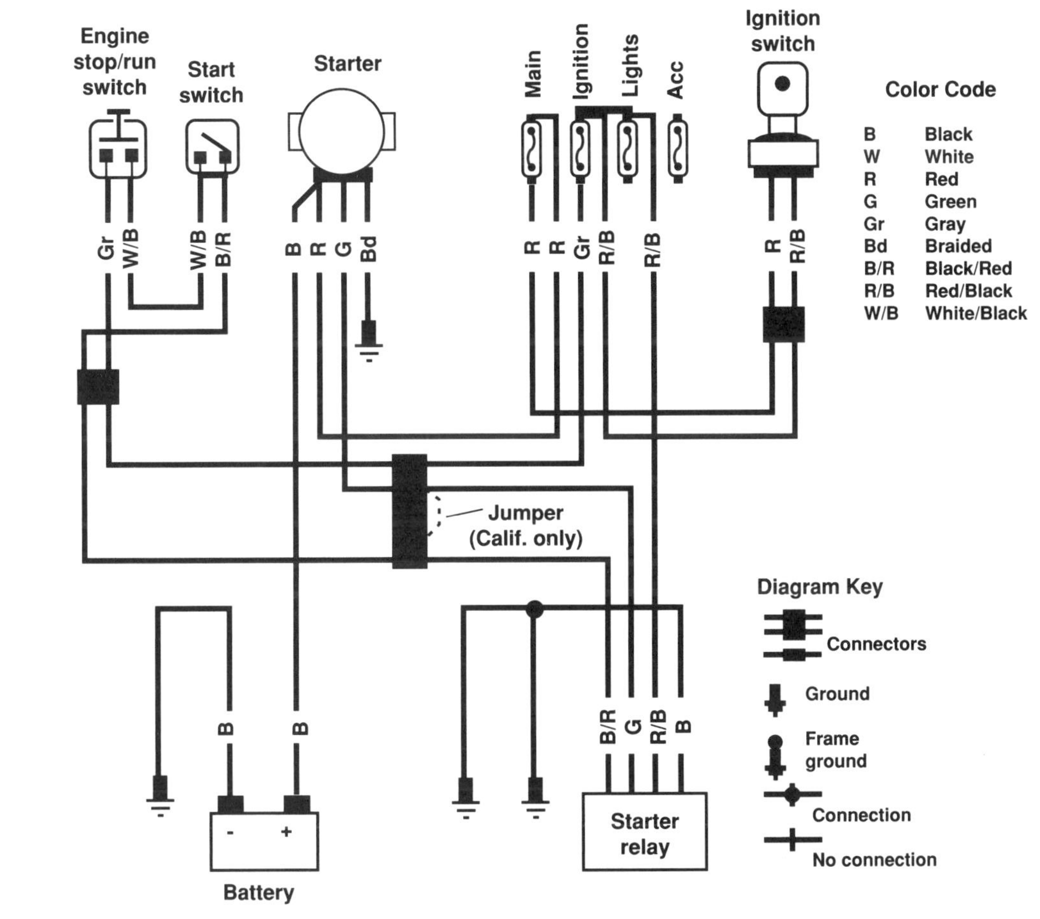

d. The wiring harness is in good condition, with no worn or frayed insulation or loose harness sockets.
e. The fuel tank is filled with an adequate supply of fresh gasoline.
f. The spark plugs are in good condition and properly gapped.
g. The ignition system is correctly timed and adjusted.

Troubleshooting helps you isolate a malfunction to a certain component. If bench testing is required, remove the suspect component and test it further.

Voltage Drop Test

Before performing the steps listed under *Troubleshooting*, perform the voltage drop tests listed here. These steps will help you find weak or damaged electrical components that may be causing the starting system problem. You need a voltmeter to test voltage drop.

1. To check voltage drop in the solenoid circuit, connect the positive voltmeter lead to the positive battery terminal; connect the negative voltmeter lead to the solenoid. See **Figure 15**.

NOTE
The voltmeter lead must not touch the starter-to-solenoid terminal. ***Figure 16*** *shows the solenoid terminal with the starter/solenoid removed for clarity.*

2. Turn the ignition switch on and push the starter button while reading the voltmeter scale. Note the following:
   a. The circuit is operating correctly if the voltmeter reading is 2 volts or less. A voltmeter reading of 12 volts indicates an open circuit.
   b. A voltage drop of more than 2 volts shows a problem in the solenoid circuit.
   c. If the voltage drop reading is correct, continue with Step 3.
3. To check the starter motor ground circuit, connect the negative voltmeter lead to the negative battery terminal; connect the positive voltmeter lead to the starter motor housing. See **Figure 17**.
4. Turn the ignition switch on and push the starter button while reading the voltmeter scale. The voltage drop must not exceed 0.2 volts. If it does, check the ground connections between the meter leads.
5. If you did not find the problem, refer to *Troubleshooting* in this section.

NOTE
Steps 3 and 4 check the voltage drop across the starter motor ground circuit. You can repeat this test to check any ground circuit in the starting circuit. To do so, leave the negative voltmeter lead

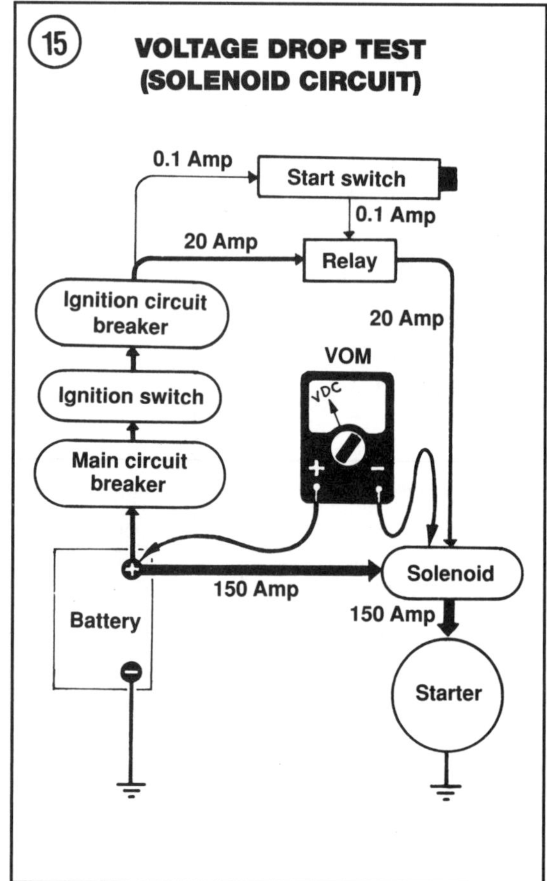

connected to the battery and connect the positive voltmeter lead to the ground in question.

Troubleshooting

The basic starter related troubles are:

a. Starter does not spin.

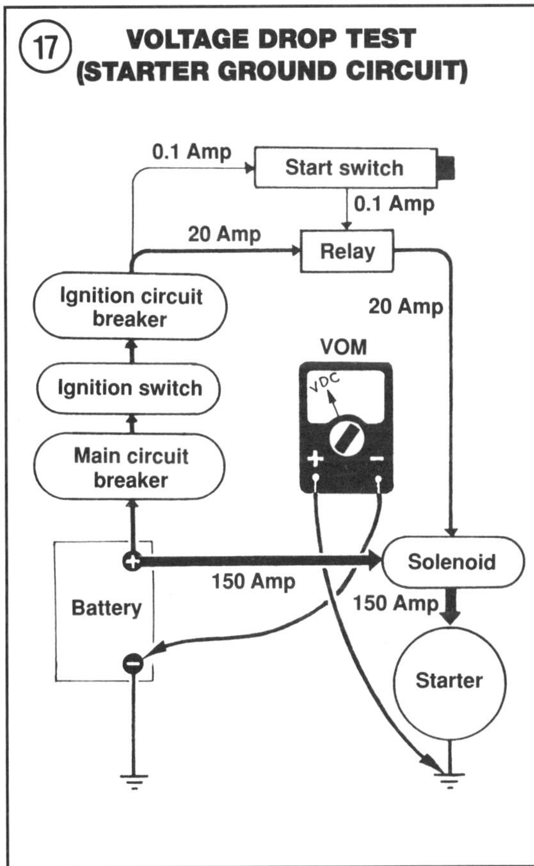

b. Starter spins but does not engage.

c. The starter will not disengage after the start button is released.

d. Loud grinding noises when starter turns.

e. Starter stalls or spins too slowly.

Perform the steps listed under *Troubleshooting Preparation*. The following test results must be within 1/2 volt of battery voltage.

CAUTION
Never operate the starter motor for more than 30 seconds at a time. Allow the starter to cool before reusing it. Failing to allow the starter motor to cool after continuous starting attempts can damage the starter.

Starter does not spin

1. Turn the ignition switch on and push the starter button while listening for a click at the starter relay (**Figure 18**). Turn the ignition switch off and note the following:
   a. If the starter relay clicks, test the starter relay as described under *Component Testing* in this section. If the starter relay test readings are correct, continue with Step 2.
   b. If the solenoid clicks, go to Step 3.
   c. If there was no click, go to Step 6.
2. Check the wiring connectors between the starter relay and solenoid. Note the following:
   a. Repair any dirty, loose-fitting or damaged connectors or wiring.
   b. If the wiring is okay, remove the starter motor (Chapter Eight) and perform the solenoid and starter motor bench tests described in this section.
3. Perform a voltage drop test between the battery and solenoid terminals as described under *Voltage Drop Tests* in this section. The normal voltage drop is less than 2 volts. Note the following:
   a. If the voltage drop is less than 2 volts, perform Step 4.
   b. If the voltage drop is more than 2 volts, check the solenoid and battery wires and connections for dirty or loose-fitting terminals; clean and repair as required.
4. Remove the starter motor as described under *Starter Removal* in Chapter Eight. Momentarily connect a fully charged 12-volt battery to the starter motor as shown in **Figure 19**. If the starter motor is

operational, it will turn when connected to the battery. Disconnect the battery and note the following:

a. If the starter motor turns, perform the solenoid pull-in and hold-in tests as described under *Solenoid Testing (Bench Tests)* in this section.
b. If the starter motor does not turn, disassemble the starter motor (Chapter Eight) and check it for opens, shorts and grounds.

5. If the problem is not evident after performing Steps 3 and 4, check the starter shaft to see if it is binding at the jackshaft. **Figure 20** shows the jackshaft and coupling with the inner primary housing removed. Check the jackshaft for binding or damage. Refer to *Starter Jackshaft* in Chapter Five.

6. If there is no click when performing Step 1, measure voltage between the starter button and the starter relay (**Figure 18**). The voltmeter must read battery voltage. Note the following:

a. If battery voltage is noted, continue with Step 7.
b. If there is no voltage, go to Step 8.

7. Check the starter relay ground at the starter relay (**Figure 18**). Note the following:

a. If the starter relay is properly grounded, test the starter relay as described in this section.
b. If the starter relay is not grounded, check the ground connection. Repair the ground connection, then restest.

8. Check for voltage at the starter button. Note the following:

a. If there is voltage at the starter button, test the starter relay as described in this section.
b. If there is no voltage at the starter button, check continuity across the starter button. If there is voltage leading to the starter button but no voltage leaving the starter button, replace the button switch and retest. If there is no voltage leading to the starter button, check the starter button wiring for dirty or loose-fitting terminals or damaged wiring; clean and/or repair as required.

Starter spins but does not engage

If the starter spins but the pinion gear does not engage the ring gear, perform the following:

1. Remove the outer primary cover as described in Chapter Five.
2. Check the pinion gear (**A, Figure 21**) mounted on the end of the jackshaft. If the teeth are chipped

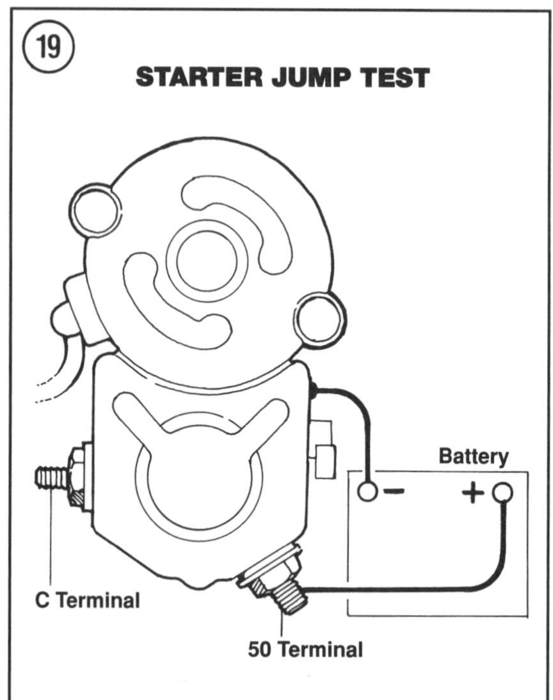

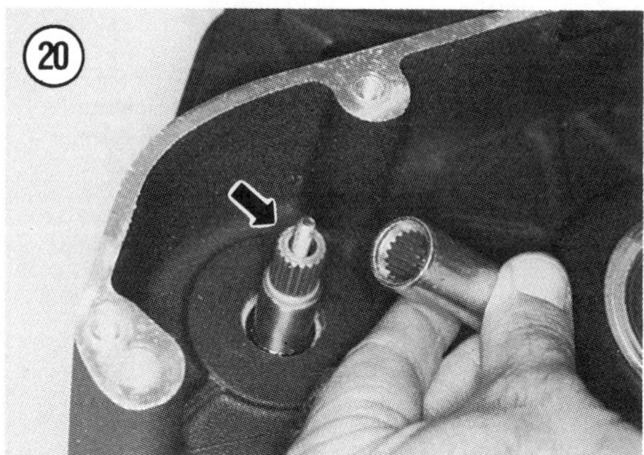

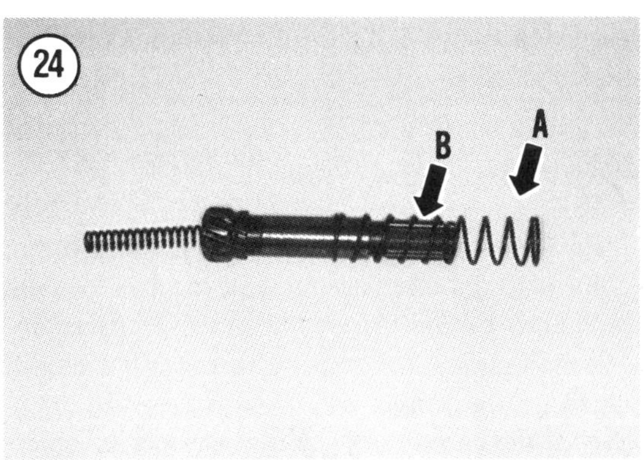

or worn, inspect the clutch ring gear (**B, Figure 21**) for the same problems. Note the following:

a. If the pinion gear and ring gear are damaged, service these parts as described in Chapter Five.
b. If the pinion gear and ring gear are not damaged, continue with Step 3.

3. Remove and disassemble the starter motor as described in Chapter Eight. Then check the overrunning clutch assembly (**Figure 22**) for:

a. Roller damage (**Figure 23**).
b. Compression spring damage (**A, Figure 24**).
c. Excessively worn or damaged pinion teeth.
d. Pinion does not run in overrunning direction.
e. Damaged clutch shaft splines (**B, Figure 24**).
f. Damaged overrunning clutch assembly (**Figure 25**).

4. Replace worn or damaged parts as required.

Starter will not disengage after the start button is released

1. A sticking solenoid, caused by a worn solenoid compression spring (**A, Figure 24**), can cause this problem. Replace the solenoid if damaged.
2. On high-mileage models, the pinion gear (A, **Figure 21**) can jam on a worn clutch ring gear (B, **Figure 21**). Unable to return, the starter will continue to run. This condition usually requires ring gear replacement.
3. Check the start switch and starter relay (**Figure 18**) for internal damage. Test the start switch as described under *Switches* in Chapter Eight. Test the starter relay as described in this chapter.

Loud grinding noises when the starter runs

Incorrect pinion gear and clutch ring gear engagement (**Figure 21**) or a broken overrunning clutch mechanism (**Figure 25**) can cause this problem. Remove and inspect the starter as described in Chapter Eight.

Starter stalls or spins too slowly

1. Perform a voltage drop test between the battery and solenoid terminals as described under *Voltage Drop Tests* in this section. The normal voltage drop is less than 2 volts. Note the following:

a. If the voltage drop is less than 2 volts, continue with Step 2.
b. If the voltage drop exceeds 2 volts, check the solenoid and battery wires and connections for dirty or loose-fitting terminals; clean and repair as required.

2. Perform a voltage drop test between the solenoid terminals and the starter motor as described under *Voltage Drop Tests* in this section. The normal voltage drop is less than 2 volts. Note the following:
a. If the voltage drop is less than 2 volts, continue with Step 3.
b. If the voltage drop exceeds 2 volts, check the solenoid and starter motor wires and connections for dirty or loose-fitting terminals; clean and repair as required.

3. Perform a voltage drop test between the battery ground wire and the starter motor as described under *Voltage Drop Tests* in this section. The normal voltage drop is less than 2 volts. Note the following:
a. If the voltage drop is less than 2 volts, continue with Step 4.
b. If the voltage drop exceeds 2 volts, check the battery ground wire connections for dirty or loose-fitting terminals; clean and repair as required.

4. Perform the *Starter Current Draw Test* in this section. Note the following:
a. If the current draw is excessive, check for a damaged starter or starter drive assembly. Remove the starter motor (Chapter Eight) and perform the *Free Running Current Draw Test* in this section.
b. If the current draw reading is correct, continue with Step 5.

5. Remove the outer primary cover as described in Chapter Five. Check the pinion gear (A, **Figure 21**). If the teeth are chipped or worn, inspect the clutch ring gear (B, **Figure 21**) for the same problem.
a. If the pinion gear and ring gear are damaged, service these parts as described in Chapter Five.
b. If the pinion gear and ring gear are not damaged, continue with Step 6.

6. Remove and disassemble the starter motor as described in Chapter Eight. Then bench check the starter motor, checking for opens, shorts and grounds.

Component Testing

The following sections describe how to test individual starting system components. Refer to Chapter Eight for starter service.

Starter Relay Testing

You can check starter relay operation with an ohmmeter, jumper wires and a fully charged 12-volt battery.

1. Remove the electric panel cover screws and washers and remove the cover.
2. Remove the electric panel (**Figure 26**) mounting screws and pull the panel away from the frame. Do not disconnect the ignition module wire connectors.
3. Disconnect and remove the starter relay (**Figure 18**) from the starting circuit on the bike. See **Figure 27**.
4. Connect an ohmmeter and 12-volt battery between the relay terminals shown in **Figure 28**. This setup will energize the relay for testing.
5. Measure continuity through the relay contacts using an ohmmeter while the relay coil is energized. The correct reading is 0 ohms (continuity). If resistance is excessive or if there is no continuity, replace the relay.

Starter Current Draw Tests

The following current draw test measures current (amperage) that the starter circuit requires to crank the engine. **Table 1** lists current draw specifications.

A short circuit in the starter motor or a damaged pinion gear assembly can cause excessive current draw. If the current draw is low, suspect an undercharged battery or an open circuit in the starting circuit.

Current draw test with the starter mounted on the engine

NOTE
This test requires a fully charged battery.

1. Shift the transmission into NEUTRAL.
2. Disconnect the 2 spark plug caps from the spark plugs. Then ground the plug caps with 2 extra spark

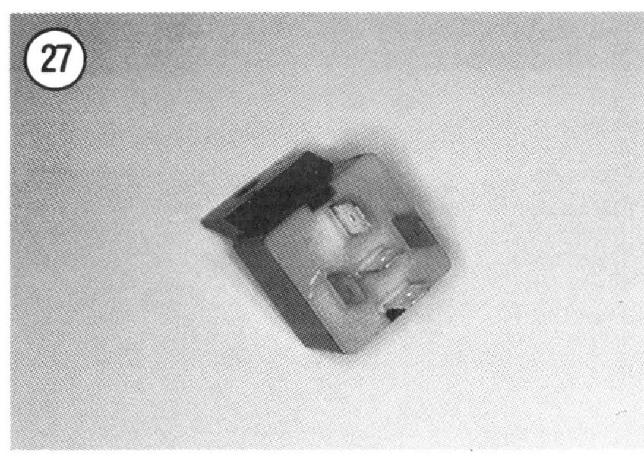

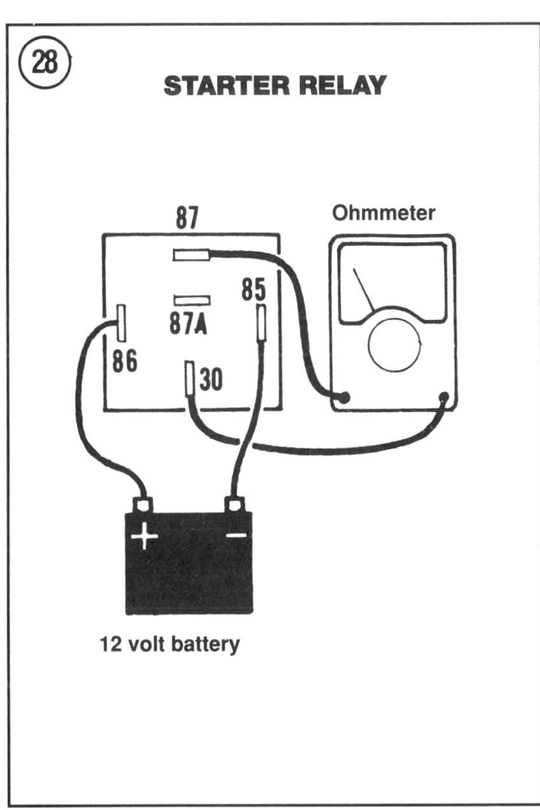

plugs. Do not remove the spark plugs from the cylinder heads.

3. Connect an induction ammeter between the starter motor terminal and positive battery terminal (**Figure 29**). Connect a jumper cable from the negative battery terminal to ground (**Figure 29**).

4. Turn the ignition switch ON and press the start button for approximately 10 seconds. Note the ammeter reading.

NOTE
The current draw is high when the start button is first pressed, then it will drop and stabilize at a lower reading. Refer to the lower stabilized reading during this test.

5. If the current draw exceeds the current draw specification listed in **Table 1**, check for a faulty starter or starter drive mechanism. Remove and service these components as described in Chapter Eight.

6. Disconnect the ammeter and jumper cables.

No-load current draw test (starter motor removed from the engine)

This test requires a fully charged 12-volt battery, an induction ammeter, a jumper wire (14 gauge minimum) and 3 jumper cables (6 gauge minimum).

1. Remove the starter motor as described in Chapter Eight.

NOTE
The solenoid must be installed on the starter during the following tests.

2. Mount the starter motor in a vise with soft jaws.

3. Connect the 14 gauge jumper cable between the positive battery terminal and the solenoid 50 terminal (**Figure 30**).

4. Connect a jumper cable (6 gauge minimum) between the positive battery terminal and the ammeter (**Figure 30**).

5. Connect the second jumper cable between the ammeter and the M terminal on the starter solenoid (**Figure 30**).

6. Connect the third jumper cable between the battery ground terminal and the starter motor mounting flange (**Figure 30**).

7. Read the current indicated on the ammeter. The correct ammeter reading is 90 amps. A damaged pinion gear assembly will cause an excessively high current draw reading. If the current draw reading is

low, check for an undercharged battery or an open field winding or armature in the starter motor.

Solenoid Testing (Bench Tests)

This test requires a fully charged 12-volt battery and 3 jumper wires.

1. Remove the starter motor (A, **Figure 31**) as described in Chapter Nine.

NOTE

*The solenoid (B, **Figure 31**) must be installed on the starter motor during the following tests. Do not remove it.*

2. Disconnect the C field wire terminal (C, **Figure 31**) from the solenoid before performing the following tests. Insulate the end of the wire terminal so that it cannot short out on any of the test connectors.

CAUTION

Because you apply battery voltage directly to the solenoid and starter in the following tests, do not leave the jumper cables connected to the solenoid for more than 3-5 seconds; otherwise, the voltage will damage the solenoid.

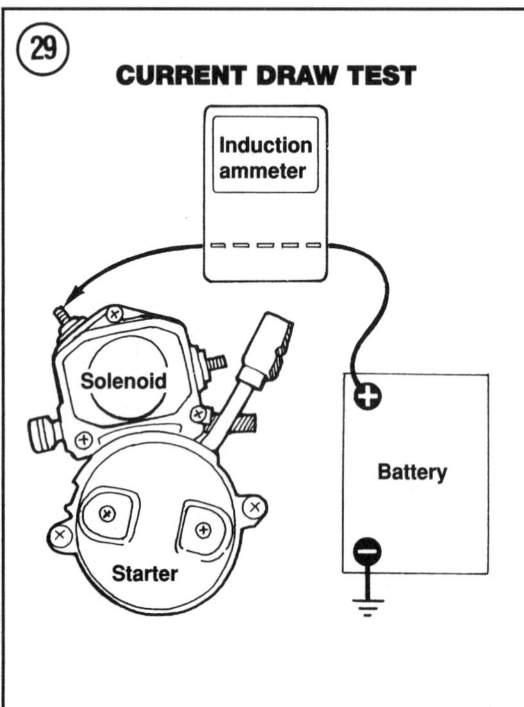

NOTE

Read the following procedure through to familiarize yourself with the procedures and test connections, then perform the tests in order and without interruption.

3. Perform the solenoid pull-in test as follows:

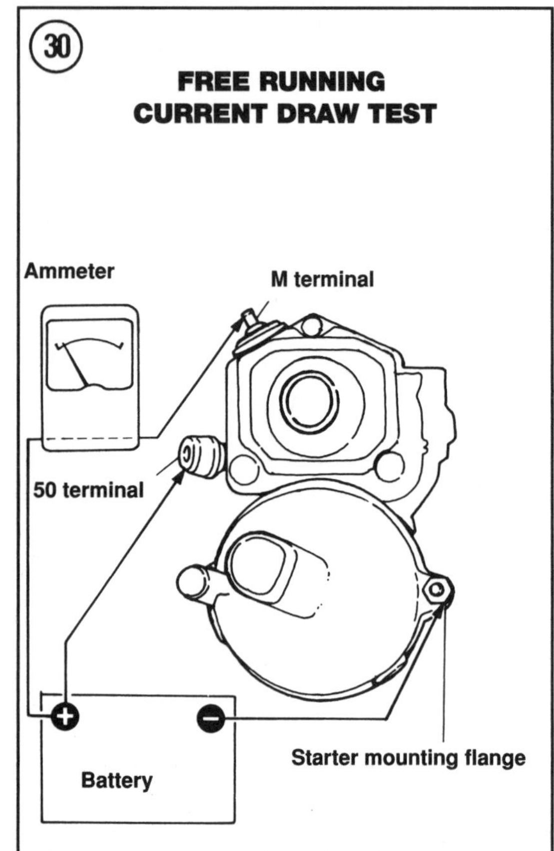

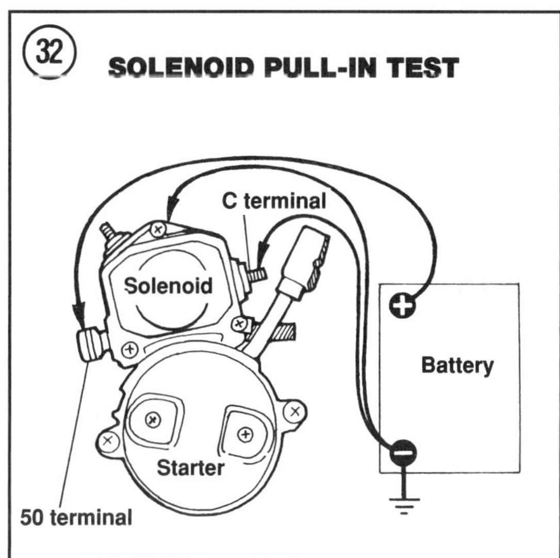

32 SOLENOID PULL-IN TEST

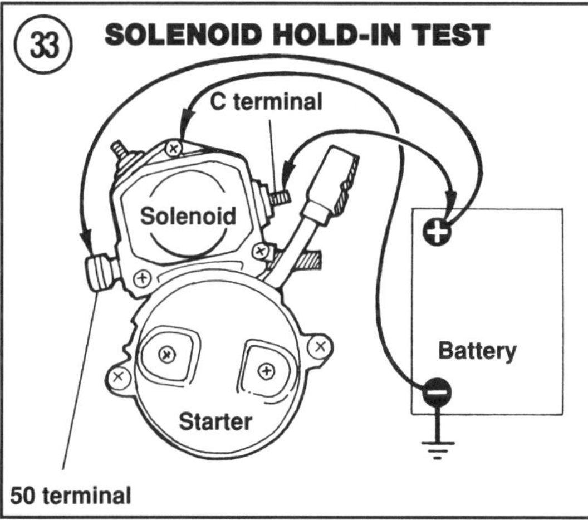

33 SOLENOID HOLD-IN TEST

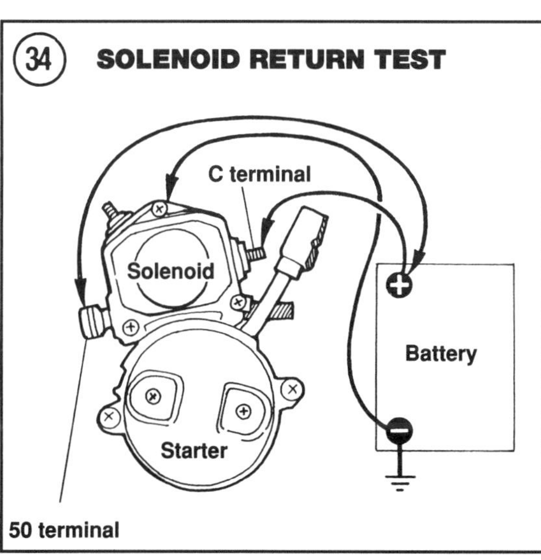

34 SOLENOID RETURN TEST

a. Connect 1 jumper wire from the negative battery terminal to the solenoid C terminal (**Figure 32**).

b. Connect 1 jumper wire from the negative battery terminal to the solenoid housing (ground) (**Figure 32**).

c. Touch a jumper wire from the positive battery terminal to the starter 50 terminal (**Figure 32**). The pinion shaft (D, **Figure 31**) must pull into the housing.

d. Leave the jumper wires connected and continue with Step 4.

4. To perform the solenoid hold-in test, perform the following:

a. With the pinion shaft extended (Step 3), disconnect the C terminal jumper wire from the negative battery terminal and connect it to the positive battery terminal (**Figure 33**). The pinion shaft will *remain* in the housing. If the pinion shaft returns to its normal position, replace the solenoid.

b. Leave the jumper wires connected and continue with Step 5.

5. To perform the solenoid return test, perform the following:

a. Disconnect the jumper wire from the starter 50 terminal (**Figure 34**); the pinion shaft must *return* to its original position.

b. Disconnect all of the jumper wires from the solenoid and battery.

6. Replace the solenoid if the starter shaft failed to operate as described in Steps 3-5. See *Solenoid Replacement* in Chapter Nine.

CHARGING SYSTEM

The charging system consists of the battery, alternator and a solid state rectifier/voltage regulator.

The alternator generates alternating current (AC) which the rectifier converts to direct current (DC). The regulator maintains the voltage to the battery and load (lights, ignition and accessories) at a constant voltage despite variations in engine speed and load.

A malfunction in the charging system generally causes the battery to remain undercharged.

When troubleshooting the charging system, refer to the charging system diagram for your model:

a. **Figure 35**: 1991-1993.

b. **Figure 36**: 1994.

c. **Figure 37**: 1995.

Service Precautions

Before servicing the charging system, observe the following precautions to prevent damage to any charging system component.

1. Never reverse battery connections. Instantaneous damage will occur.
2. Do not short across any connection.
3. Never attempt to polarize an alternator.
4. Never start the engine with the alternator disconnected from the voltage regulator/rectifier, unless instructed to do during testing.
5. Never attempt to start or run the engine with the battery disconnected.
6. Never attempt to use a high-output battery charger to help start the engine.
7. Before charging the battery, remove it from the motorcycle as described in Chapter Eight.
8. Never disconnect the voltage regulator/rectifier connector with the engine running. The voltage regulator/rectifier (**Figure 38**) is mounted on the front frame down tubes.
9. Do not mount the voltage regulator/rectifier unit at another location.
10. Make sure the negative battery terminal is connected to the engine and frame.

Troubleshooting

If the battery is discharged, perform the following procedure.

1. Test the battery as described in Chapter Eight. Charge the battery if required. If the battery will hold a charge, continue with Step 2.
2. Perform the regulator ground test.

Testing

If charging system trouble is suspected, first check the battery charge. Clean and test the battery as described in Chapter Eight. If the battery is fully charged and in acceptable condition, test the charging system as follows.

If the battery discharges while riding the motorcycle, perform the *Voltage Regulator/Rectifier Test.* Also refer to *Current Drain Test (Battery Discharges While Riding the Motorcycle).*

If the battery discharges while the motorcycle is not running, perform the *Current Drain Test (Battery Discharges While the Motorcycle is Not Running).*

Voltage Regulator Ground Test

The voltage regulator base (**Figure 38**) must be grounded to the frame for proper operation.

1. Switch an ohmmeter to the R × 1 scale. Then touch the leads together and zero the meter.
2. Connect one ohmmeter lead to a good engine or frame ground and the other ohmmeter lead to the regulator base. Read the ohmmeter scale. The correct reading is 0 ohms. Note the following:
   a. If there is low resistance (0 ohms), the voltage regulator is properly grounded.
   b. If there is high resistance or no continuity, remove the voltage regulator and clean its frame mounting points.
3. Check that the voltage regulator connector plug (**Figure 39**) is clean and tightly connected.

Voltage Regulator Bleed Test

This test requires a 12-volt test lamp. This tool relies on the vehicles battery to supply power to the component being tested.

1. Disconnect the voltage regulator connector from the engine crankcase (**Figure 40**).

NOTE

Do not disconnect the wire connecting the voltage regulator to the 30 amp circuit breaker.

2. Connect one test lamp probe to a good frame or engine ground.
3. Connect the other test lamp probe to one of the voltage regulator pins, then to the other pin.
4. If the test lamp lights, replace the voltage regulator.
5. Reconnect the voltage regulator connector at the engine crankcase.

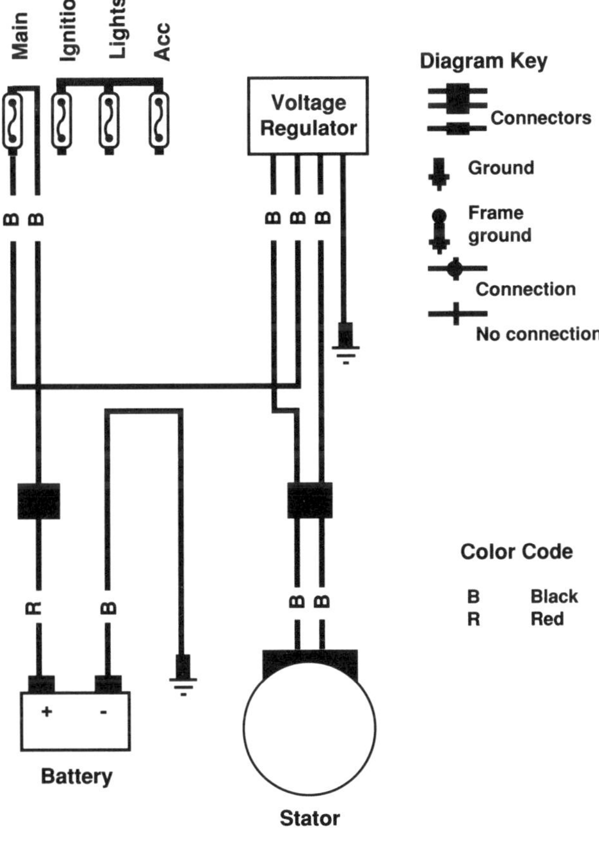
CHARGING SYSTEM (1991-1993)
Main
Ignition
Lights
Acc
Voltage Regulator
B B
B B B
R
B
B B
Battery
+
-
Stator
Diagram Key
Connectors
Ground
Frame ground
Connection
No connection
Color Code
B Black
R Red

CHARGING SYSTEM (1994)

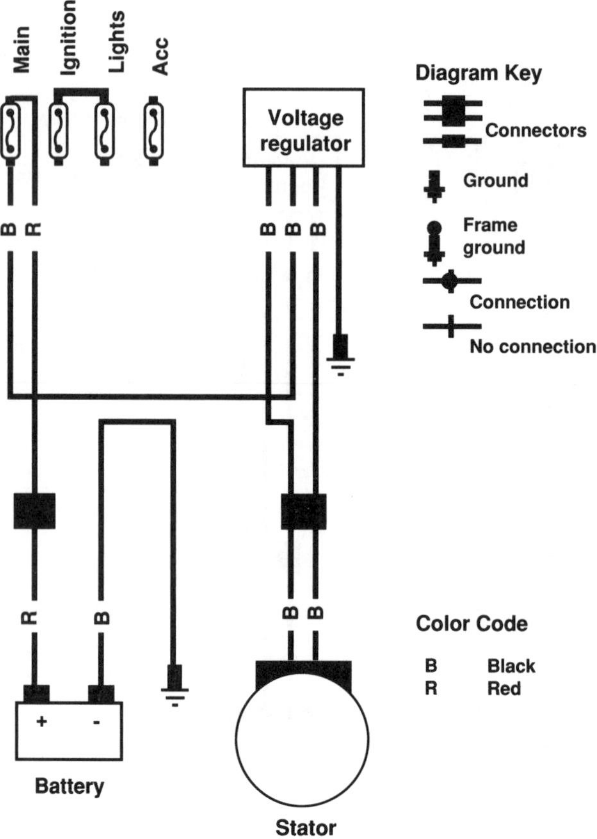

(37)

CHARGING SYSTEM (1995)

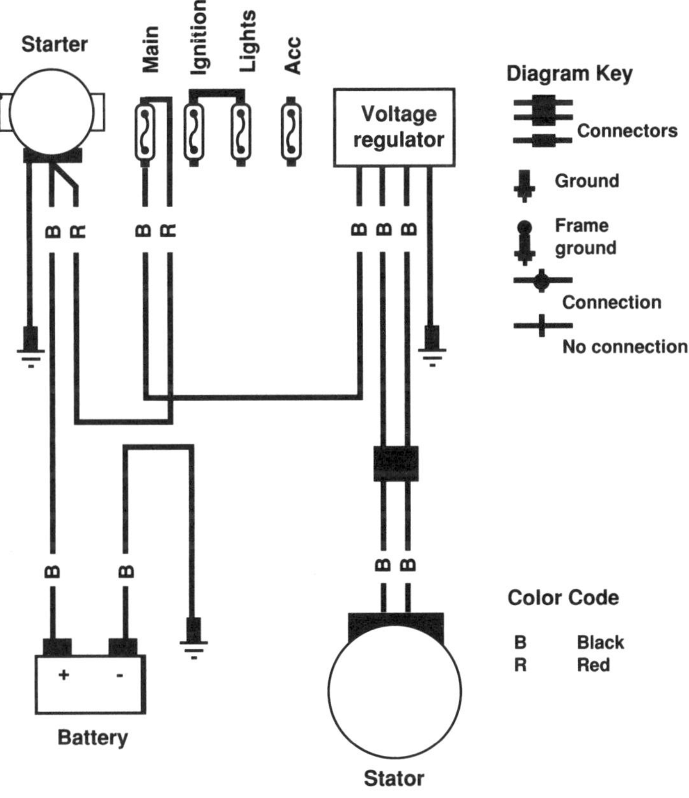

2

Current Drain Test (Battery Discharges While the Motorcycle is Not Running)

Accessory items that are wired to stay on all the time will eventually drain the battery. Perform the following steps to check a factory or accessory part. When testing, there must be no more than 3 milliamperes (mA) of current drain when the ignition switch and all of the lights are turned off. If the measured load exceeds 3 mA, the drain is excessive and will leave the battery dead. This test requires a fully charged 12-volt battery.

1. Disconnect the negative battery cable from the battery.

2. Connect an ammeter between the negative battery terminal and the battery ground cable as shown in **Figure 41**.

3. With the ignition switch, lights and all accessories turned off, read the ammeter. If the current drain exceeds 3 mA, continue with Step 4.

4. Refer to the wiring diagram for your model and check the charging system wires and connectors for shorts or other damage.

5. Unplug each electrical connector separately and check for a change in the meter reading. If the meter reading changes after disconnecting a connector, you have found the damaged component. Check the electrical connectors carefully before testing the individual component.

6. After completing the test, disconnect the ammeter and reconnect the negative battery cable.

Current Drain Test (Battery Discharges While Riding the Motorcycle)

If the battery runs down while riding the vehicle, the combined current draw of the stock or any add-

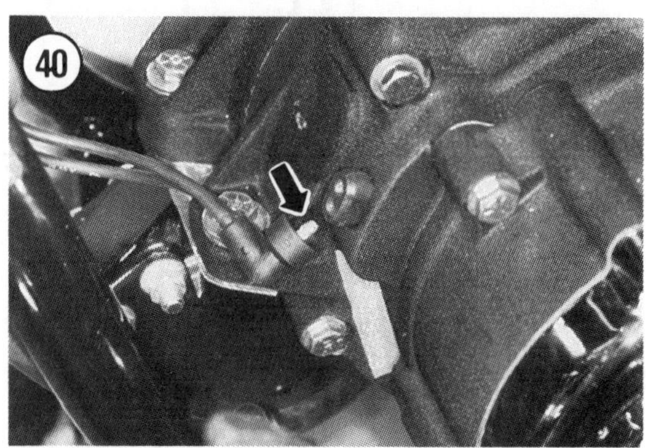

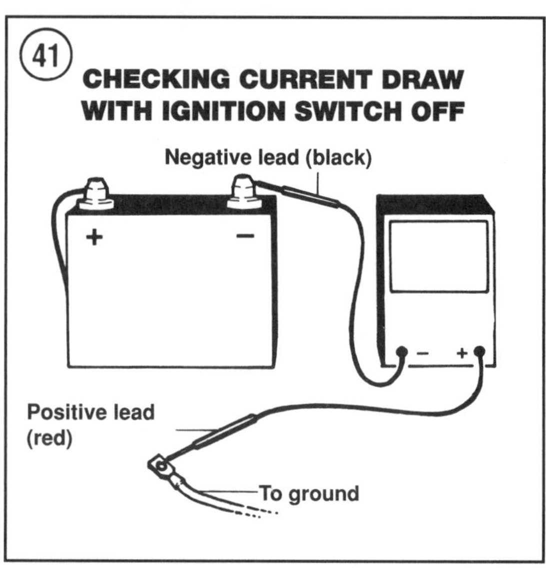

on accessories may be exceeding the charging system output.

This test measures the current draw on the vehicles electrical system. A load tester is required for this test. Perform this test when you know the charging system is working correctly but the battery is still going dead. The battery must be fully charged when performing this test.

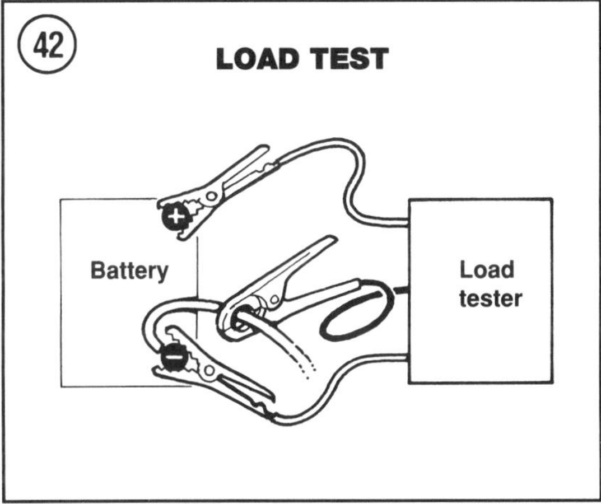

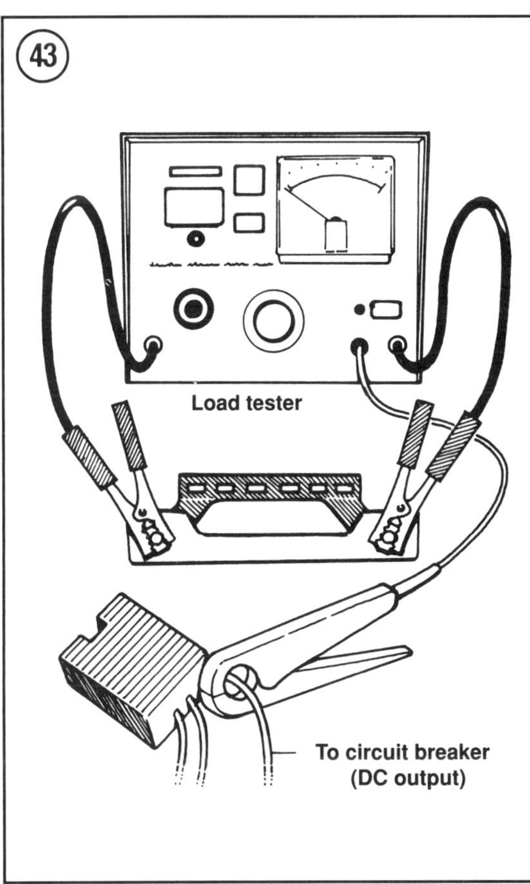

NOTE
When using a load tester, read and follow its manufacturer's instructions. To prevent tester damage from overheating, do not leave the load switch ON for more than 20 seconds at a time.

1. Connect a load tester to the battery as shown in **Figure 42**.
2. Turn the ignition switch ON (but do not start the engine). Then turn on all electrical accessories and switch the headlight beam to HIGH.
3. Read the ampere reading (current draw) on the load tester and compare it to the test results obtained in the *Charging System Output Test* in this chapter. The charging system output test results (current reading) must exceed the current draw by 3.5 amps.
4. Owner-installed accessories can increase the current draw and drain the battery. The combined current draw of both stock and aftermarket electrical components may be exceeding the charging system limit. You can check this by disconnecting all of the aftermarket equipment and repeating this test; if the current draw is now within specification, you have found the problem. However, if you have not added any electrical aftermarket accessories to your bike, a short circuit may be causing the battery to discharge.

Charging System Output Test

This test requires a load tester.

1. To perform this test, the battery must be fully charged. Use a hydrometer to check the battery specific gravity as described in Chapter Eight. Charge the battery if required.

NOTE
When using a load tester, read and follow its manufacturer's instructions. To prevent tester damage from overheating, do not leave the load switch ON for more than 20 seconds at a time.

2. Connect the load tester negative and positive leads to the battery terminals. Then place the tester's load test induction pickup between the wire connecting the 30 amp circuit breaker to the voltage regulator. See **Figure 43**.

3. Start the engine and slowly bring its speed up to 2,000 rpm while reading the load tester scale. With the engine running at 3,000 rpm, operate the load tester switch until the voltage scale reads 13.0 volts. The tester must show an alternator current output reading of 26-32 amps.

4. With the engine still running at 3,000 rpm, turn the load switch off and read the load tester voltage scale. Battery voltage must not exceed 15 volts. Turn the engine off and disconnect the load tester from the bike.

5. An incorrect reading in Steps 3 and 4 suggests that:

   a. The voltage regulator/rectifier unit (**Figure 38**) is damaged.

   b. There is a short circuit in the wiring system.

Stator Check

1. With the ignition switch turned off, disconnect the regulator/rectifier connector from the crankcase (**Figure 40**).

2. Switch an ohmmeter to its R × 1 scale. Then connect it between either stator socket (at the crankcase) and ground (**Figure 44**). The correct ohmmeter reading is infinity (no continuity). Any other reading (continuity) suggests a grounded stator. Repeat this test for the other stator socket.

3. Switch an ohmmeter to its R × 1 scale. Then connect it between both stator sockets (at the crankcase). The correct ohmmeter reading is 0.2-0.4 ohms. If resistance is not as specified, replace the stator.

4. Check stator AC voltage output as follows:

   a. Connect an AC voltmeter across the stator pins as shown in **Figure 45**.

   c. Start the engine and slowly increase engine speed. The correct voltmeter reading is 16-20 volts AC per each 1,000 rpm. For example, if the engine is running at 2,000 rpm, the correct AC output reading is 32-40 volts AC.

   d. If the AC voltage output reading is below the specified range, the trouble is probably a faulty stator (**Figure 46**) or rotor. If these parts are not damaged, perform the *Charging System Output Test* in this section.

5. Reconnect the regulator/rectifier connector.

IGNITION SYSTEM

All models use an electronic ignition system. This system provides a longer life for the components and delivers a more efficient spark throughout the speed range of the engine than breaker-point systems.

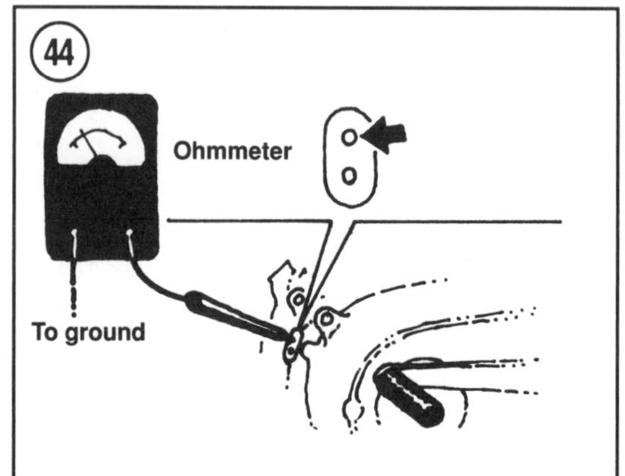

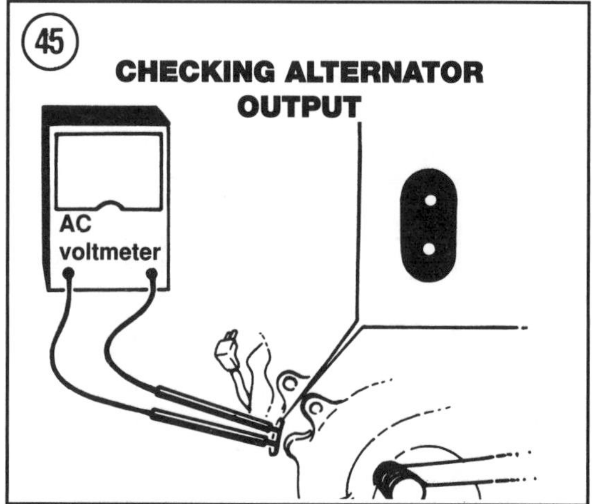

When troubleshooting the ignition system, refer to the system diagram for your model:

a.All 1991-1992 models and 1993-1994 FXDL: **Figure 47**.

b. 1993-1994 FXDWG: **Figure 48.**

c. 1995: **Figure 49**.

Most problems involving failure to start, poor driveability or rough running are caused by trouble in the ignition system.

Note the following symptoms:

a. An engine misfire.

b. Stumbles on acceleration (misfiring).

c. Loss of power at high speed (misfiring).

d. Hard starting or failure to start.

e. Rough idle.

Precautions

When testing the ignition system, observe the following precautions to prevent damage to the system or one of its components.

1. Do not reverse the battery connections. This reverses polarity and can damage the ignition components.

2. Do not "spark" the battery terminals with the battery cable connections to check polarity.

3. Do not disconnect the battery cables with the engine running. A voltage surge will occur which will damage the ignition components and possibly burn out the lights. A spark may occur which can cause the battery to explode.

4. Do not crank the engine if the ignition module (**Figure 50**) is not securely grounded to the frame. The black wire leading from the ignition module wiring harness is the ground wire. Check the end of the wire for corrosion or damage.

5. Whenever working on any part of the ignition system, first turn the ignition switch off, then disconnect the negative battery lead. This will prevent damage to the ignition system components from an accidental short circuit.

6. Keep all connections between the various units clean and tight. Push the wiring connections together firmly to keep out moisture.

7. Check that all ground wires are attached and free of all oil and corrosion residues.

Troubleshooting Preparation

If you suspect a problem with the ignition system, perform the following procedures in order.

1. Check the wiring harness and all plug-in connections to make sure that all terminals are free of corrosion, all connectors are tight and the wiring insulation is in good condition.

2. Check all electrical components grounded to the engine for a good ground. For ground locations, see **Figure 47**, **Figure 48** or **Figure 49** for your model. These includes the ignition module, battery-to-frame, and engine-to-frame ground wires and straps.

3. Check that all ground wires are properly connected and that the connections are clean and tight. Clean connectors with electrical contact cleaner.

4. Check all other wiring and connectors for disconnected wires and short or open circuits.

5. Check for a damaged ignition circuit breaker (**Figure 51**).

NOTE
The ignition circuit breaker mounts behind the electric panel.

6. The fuel tank must have an adequate supply of fuel that is reaching the carburetor.

7. Check spark plug cable routing and their connections at the spark plugs. If cable routing is correct, perform the *Engine Fails to Start (Spark Test)* in this chapter. If there is no spark or only a weak one, repeat the test with new spark plugs. If the condition remains the same with new spark plugs and if all external wiring connections are good, the problem is most likely in the ignition system; perform the following tests. If a strong spark is noted, the problem is probably not in the ignition system. Check the fuel system.

Ignition Test (No Spark at Spark Plug)

Refer to **Figure 47**, **Figure 48** or **Figure 49** when performing these procedures.

1. This test requires a fully charged 12-volt battery.

2. The black ignition module ground lead must be fastened securely. Check also that the battery ground lead is fastened and in good condition.

2

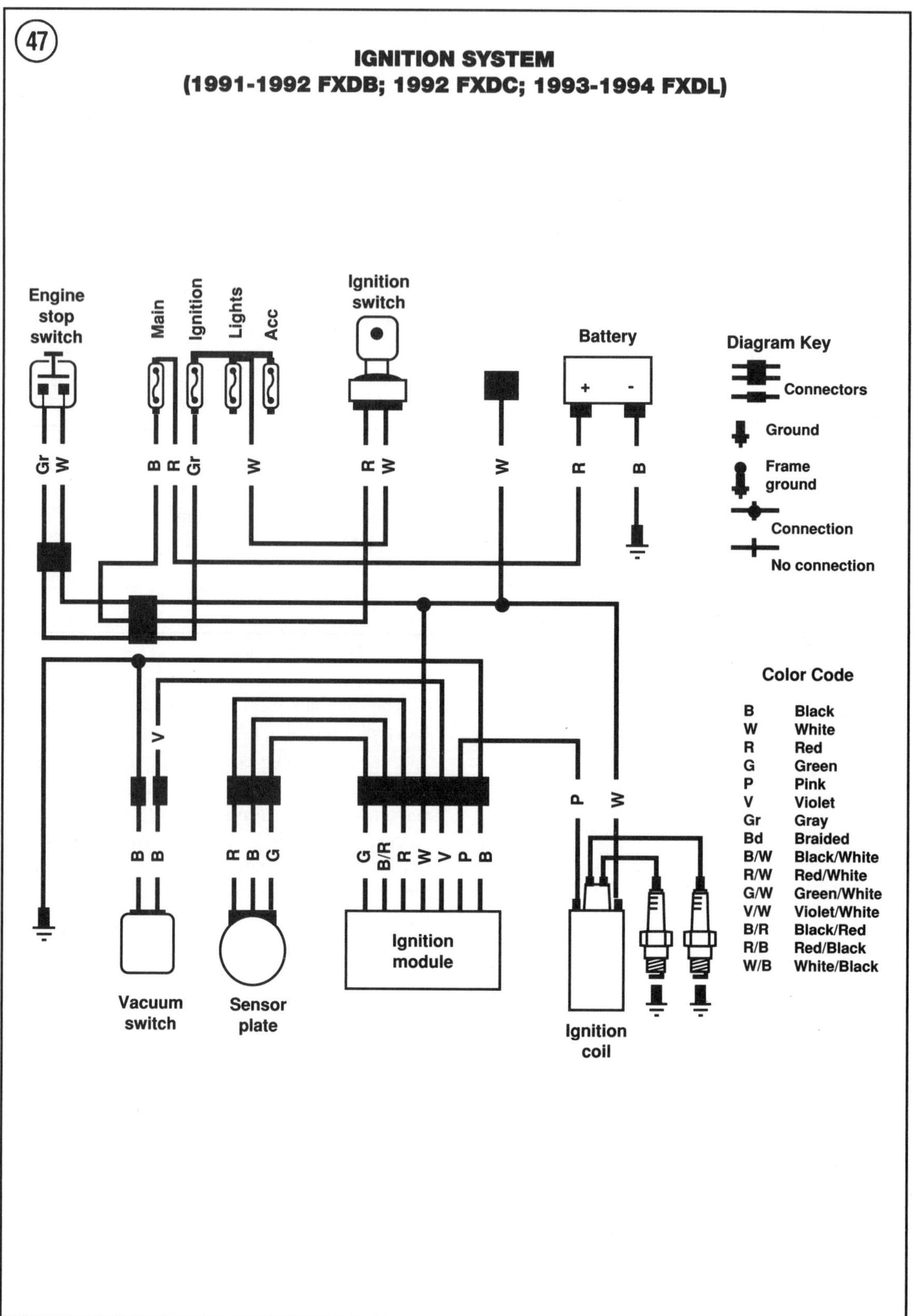
47
IGNITION SYSTEM
(1991-1992 FXDB; 1992 FXDC; 1993-1994 FXDL)
Engine stop switch
Main
Ignition
Lights
Acc
Ignition switch
Battery
Diagram Key
Connectors
Ground
Frame ground
Connection
No connection
Color Code
B Black
W White
R Red
G Green
P Pink
V Violet
Gr Gray
Bd Braided
B/W Black/White
R/W Red/White
G/W Green/White
V/W Violet/White
B/R Black/Red
R/B Red/Black
W/B White/Black
Vacuum switch
Sensor plate
Ignition module
Ignition coil

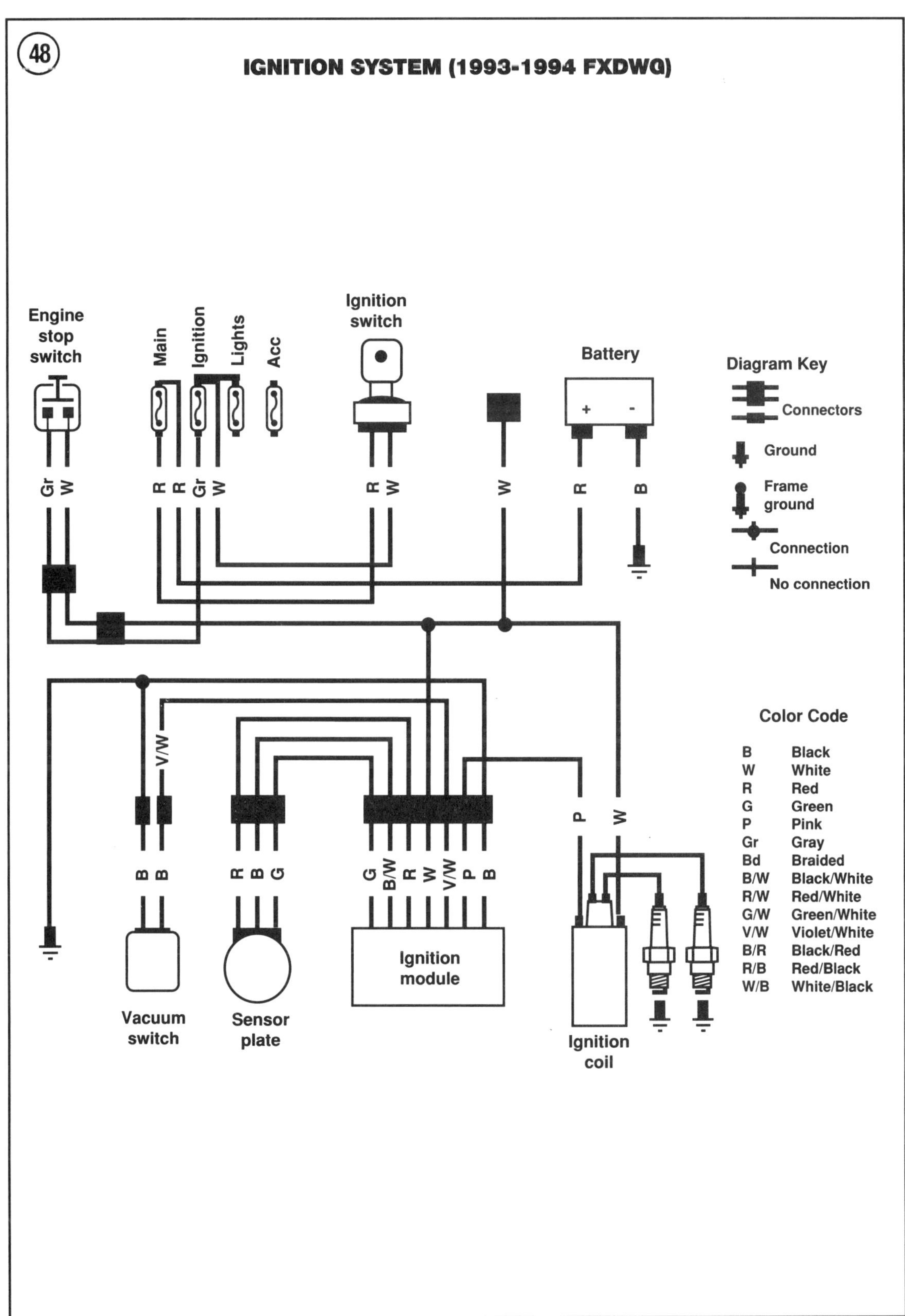
48
IGNITION SYSTEM (1993-1994 FXDWG)
Engine stop switch
Main
Ignition
Lights
Acc
Ignition switch
Battery
+
-
Diagram Key
Connectors
Ground
Frame ground
Connection
No connection
Gr W
R R Gr W
R W
W
R
B
V/W
P
W
B B
R B G
G B/W R W V/W P B
Color Code
B Black
W White
R Red
G Green
P Pink
Gr Gray
Bd Braided
B/W Black/White
R/W Red/White
G/W Green/White
V/W Violet/White
B/R Black/Red
R/B Red/Black
W/B White/Black
Vacuum switch
Sensor plate
Ignition module
Ignition coil

2

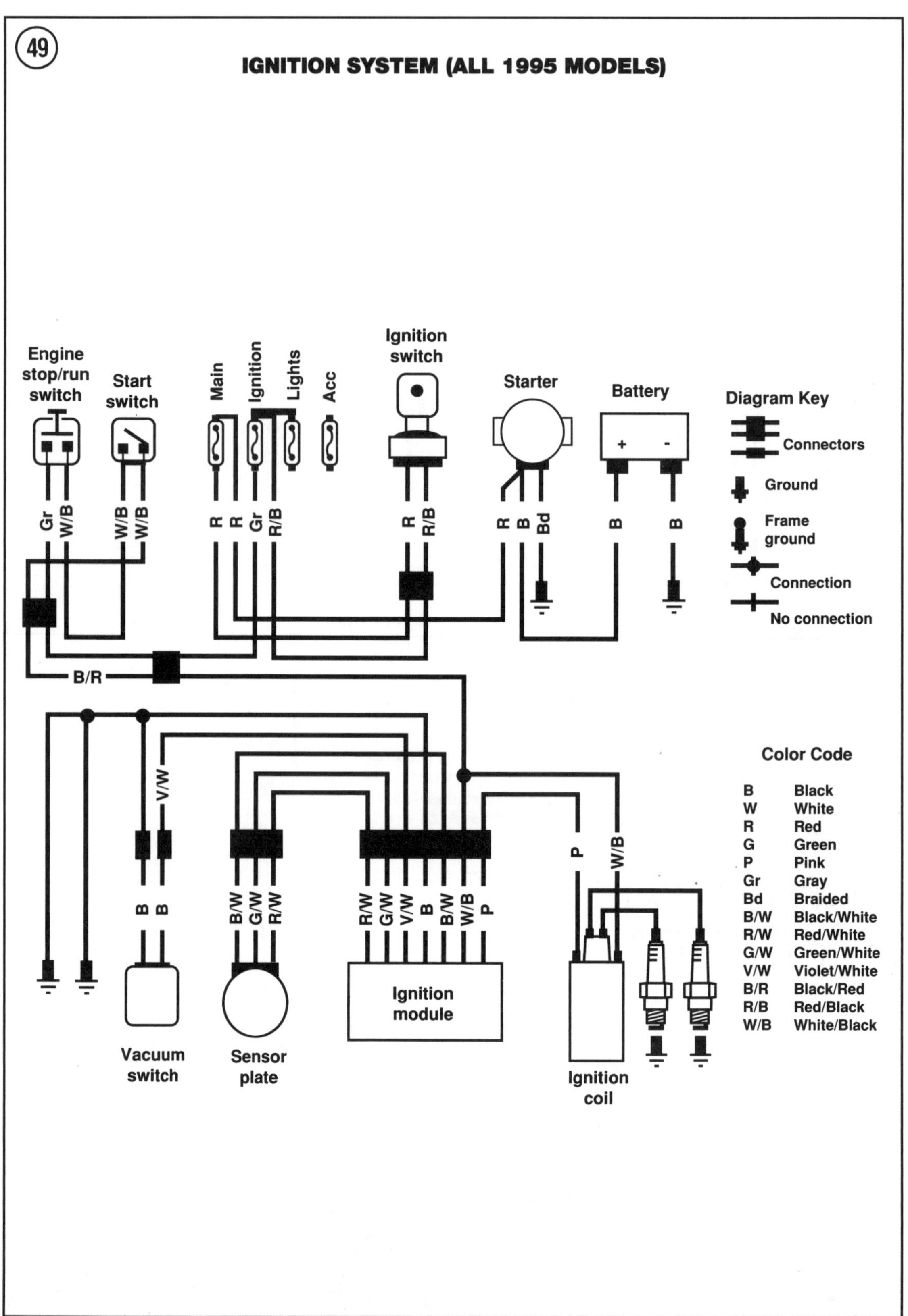
49
IGNITION SYSTEM (ALL 1995 MODELS)
Engine stop/run switch
Start switch
Main
Ignition
Lights
Acc
Ignition switch
Starter
Battery
Diagram Key
Connectors
Ground
Frame ground
Connection
No connection
Gr
W/B
W/B
W/B
R
R
Gr
R/B
R
R/B
R
B
Bd
B
B
B/R
V/W
B
B
B/W
G/W
R/W
R/W
G/W
V/W
B
B/W
W/B
P
P
W/B
Color Code
B Black
W White
R Red
G Green
P Pink
Gr Gray
Bd Braided
B/W Black/White
R/W Red/White
G/W Green/White
V/W Violet/White
B/R Black/Red
R/B Red/Black
W/B White/Black
Vacuum switch
Sensor plate
Ignition module
Ignition coil

NOTE
*Before making the following tests, fabricate a test jumper from 2 lengths of 16 gauge wire, 3 clips and a 0.33 mfd capacitor as shown in **Figure 52**. The test jumper must reach from the ignition coil to a good engine ground.*

NOTE
This test requires a voltmeter.

3. Connect the red voltmeter lead to the white (1991-1994) or white/black (1995) ignition coil wire and the black voltmeter lead to ground (**Figure 53**). Turn the ignition switch ON. The voltmeter must read 11-13 volts. Turn the ignition switch OFF and note the following.

a. If the voltage is correct, continue with Step 4.
b. If the voltage is not as specified, check ignition coil wiring for dirty or loose-fitting terminals. Then check the main and ignition circuit breakers (Chapter Eight). If these are okay, check the ignition switch and engine stop/run switch (Chapter Eight).

4. Disconnect the pink wire from the ignition coil terminal (**Figure 54**). Then slide the rubber cover away from the coil white (1991-1994) or white/black (1995) wire to expose the terminal.

2

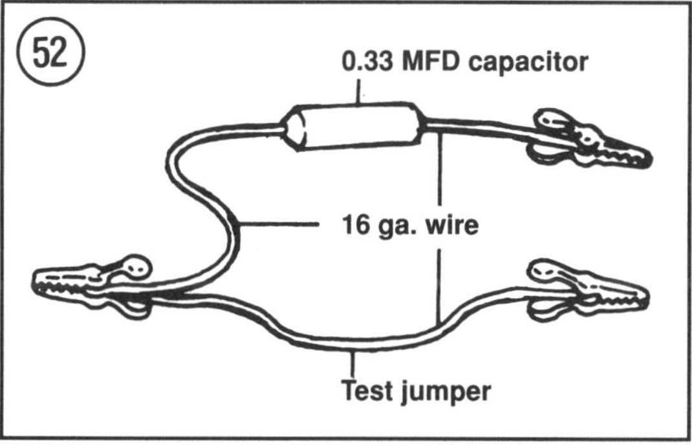

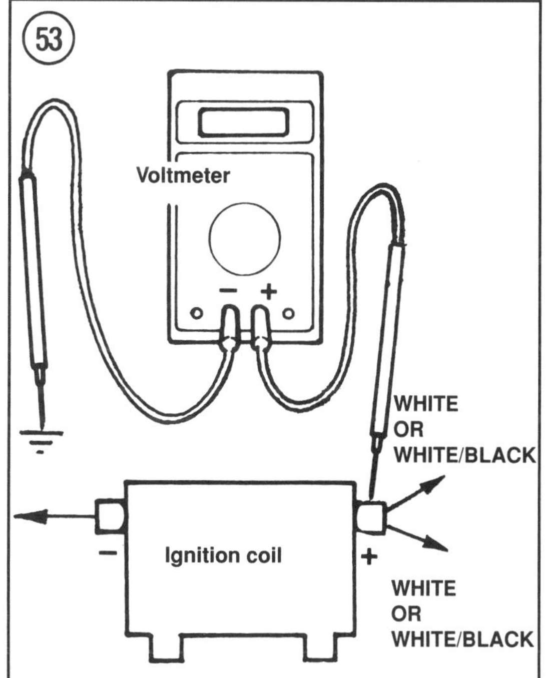

However, do not disconnect this wire. Turn the ignition switch ON.

5. Connect the black voltmeter lead to ground. Then momentarily touch the red voltmeter lead to the ignition coil pink wire terminal and then to the white or white/black terminal (**Figure 55**). The correct voltmeter reading at each terminal is 12 volts. Turn the ignition switch off and note the following:

a. If the voltage is correct, continue with Step 6.

b. If the voltmeter shows no reading or an incorrect reading, check the ignition coil resistance as described in this chapter. If the resistance readings are correct, continue with Step 6.

NOTE
Do not reconnect the pink ignition coil wire. It must remain disconnected when performing Step 6 and Step 7.

6. Remove 1 spark plug. Then connect the spark plug wire and connector to the spark plug and touch the spark plug base to a good ground like the engine cylinder head (**Figure 56**). Position the spark plug so you can see the electrodes. Turn the ignition switch ON.

7. Connect the jumper wire (**Figure 52**) with the capacitor between the pink wire terminal at the ignition coil and a good ground. Then momentarily touch the jumper wire (without the capacitor) to the pink wire terminal at the ignition coil while observing the spark plug firing tip, then remove it (**Figure 57**). The spark plug must fire when you remove the jumper wire. Turn the ignition switch OFF and remove the jumper wire assembly. Note the following.

a. If there is a spark at the spark plug, continue with Step 8.

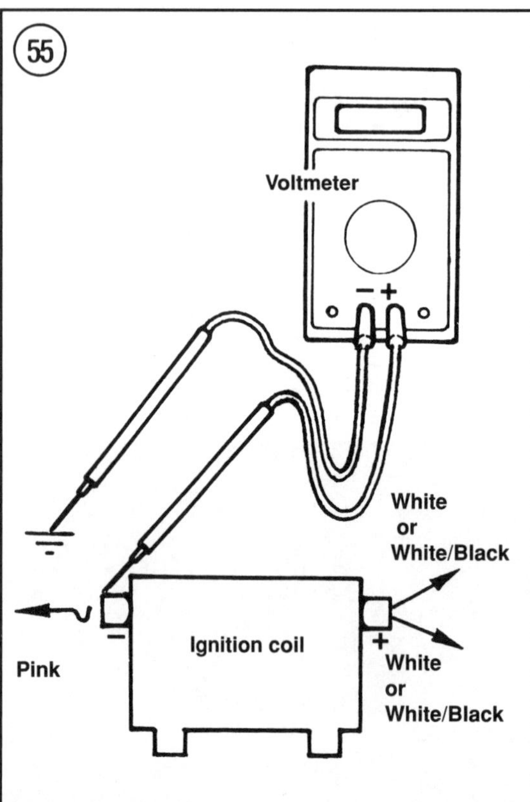

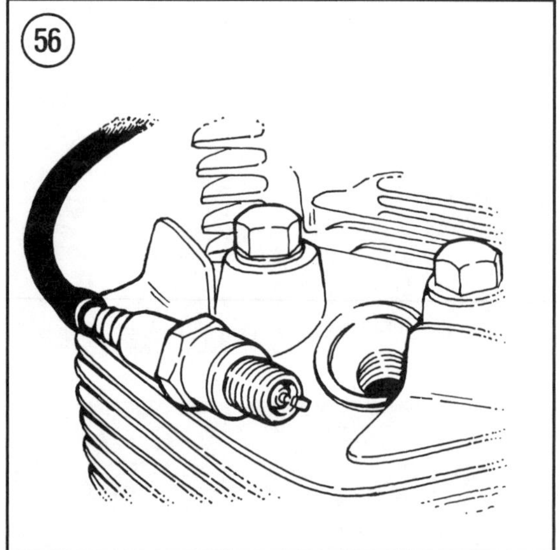

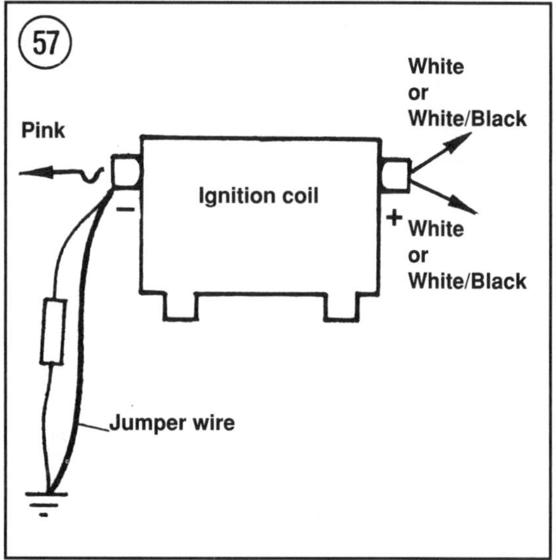

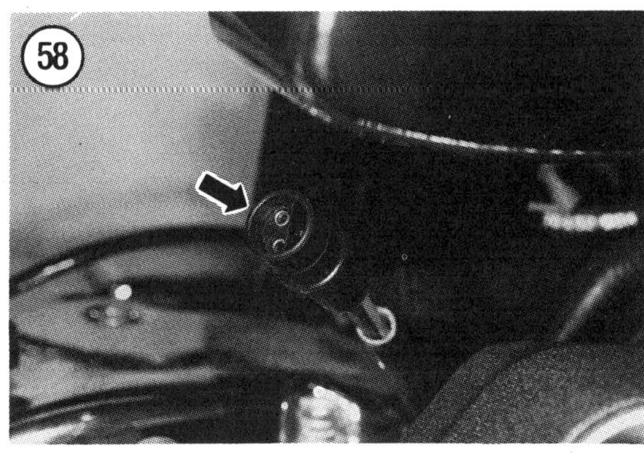

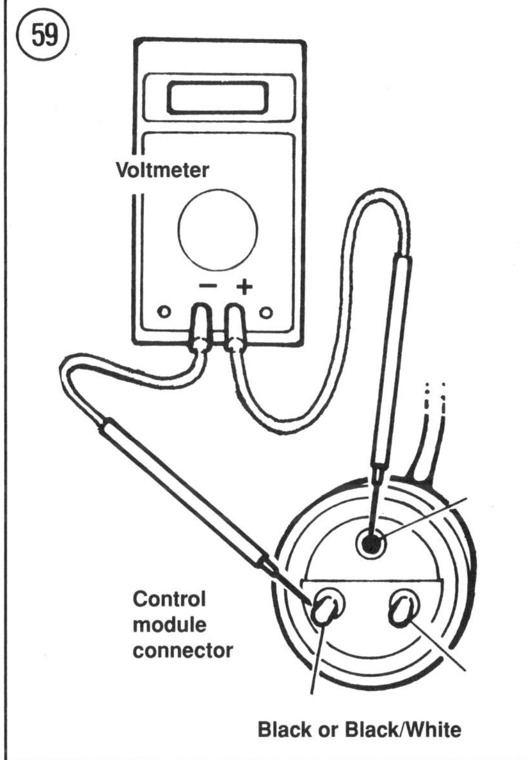

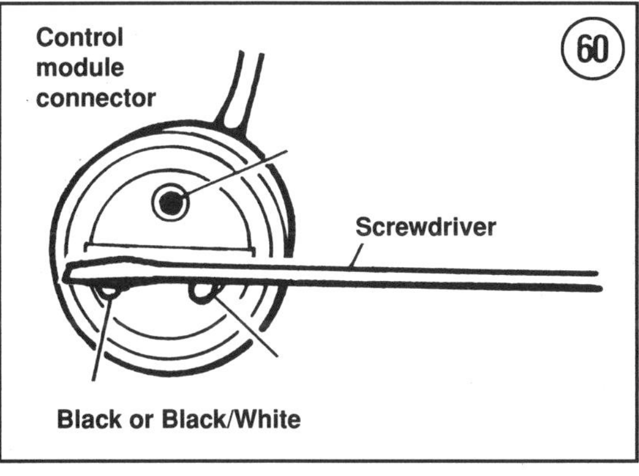

b. If there is no spark at the spark plug, replace the ignition coil and retest.

8. Reconnect the pink wire (**Figure 54**) to the ignition coil.

9. Disconnect the sensor plate-to-ignition module electrical connector (**Figure 58**).

NOTE
Perform the tests in Step 10 on the ignition module side of the connector.

10. Turn the ignition switch ON. Then connect the red voltmeter lead to the ignition module red wire pin and the black voltmeter lead to the ignition module black or black/white pin as shown in **Figure 59**. The correct voltmeter reading is 12 ±0.5 volts. Disconnect the voltmeter and turn the ignition switch OFF. Note the following.

a. If the voltage reading is correct, continue with Step 11.

b. If the voltage is not as specified, check the ignition module electrical connectors and ground wire for dirty or loose-fitting terminals. If these are okay, continue with Step 11.

NOTE
Do not reconnect the sensor plate-to-ignition module electrical connector. It must remain disconnected when performing the test in Step 11.

NOTE
Because the ignition module ignores the first 4 sensor inputs, ground the screwdriver against the ignition module connector pins 6 to 10 times in Step 11.

11. Turn the ignition switch on. Then momentarily ground a screwdriver across the ignition module green and black or black/white connector pins (**Figure 60**) while observing the spark plug firing tip. Repeat this step 6-10 times. Because the ignition module ignores the first 4 sensor inputs, the spark plug will fire on the 5th and all subsequent attempts. Turn the ignition switch OFF and note the following.

a. If the spark plug fires on the 5th and all subsequent attempts, the ignition system is working properly. However, this test may not find an intermittent problem. To confirm these test results, perform the *Ignition Testing (Intermittent Problems)* procedure in this section.

b. If the spark plug does not fire on the 5th and subsequent attempts, or if the spark is weak,

2

check the ignition module resistance as described under *Ignition Module and Sensor Resistance Testing* in this section.

12. If you have not isolated the problem, look for an intermittent problem; refer to *Ignition Testing Intermittent Problems)* in this section.

Ignition Testing (Intermittent Problems)

Troubleshooting an intermittent problem is both difficult and frustrating. When troubleshooting, try to duplicate the condition under which the problem occurs. Then use normal troubleshooting methods to identify the damaged component.

Temperature tests

NOTE
Perform Steps 1-3 on a cold engine.

1. Remove the outer timing cover, inner timing cover and gasket to expose the sensor plate (**Figure 61**). Refer to Chapter Eight.
2. Start the engine and allow to idle.
3. Spray the sensor (**Figure 61**) with a spray refrigerant (available at electronic supply stores). If the engine dies, replace the sensor as described in Chapter Eight.
4. Allow the engine to warm to normal operating temperature. Then apply heat to the sensor with a hair dryer or heat gun. If the engine dies, replace the sensor as described in Chapter Eight.
5. Turn the engine off.
6. Remove the electric panel cover.
7. Start the engine and allow to idle.
8. Apply heat to the ignition module (**Figure 50**) with a hair dryer or heat gun. If the engine dies, replace the ignition module as described in Chapter Eight.
9. Install the inner timing cover, gasket and outer timing cover as described in Chapter Eight.
10. Install the electric panel cover.

Vibration tests

Read this procedure completely through before starting.

1. Check the battery connections.
2. Check the ignition module (**Figure 50**) ground wire connection. If necessary, remove the ground wire from the frame and scrape all paint from the mounting point. Using a star washer, reinstall the ground wire.
3. Start the engine and retest. If there is still an intermittent problem, continue with Step 4.
4. Disconnect the white (1991-1994) or white/black (1995) wire from the ignition coil (**Figure 54**).
5. Connect a 16 gauge jumper wire from the ignition coil white (1991-1994) or white/black (1995) terminal to the positive battery terminal (**Figure 62**).

WARNING
Steps 4 and 5 have bypassed the engine stop switch. After starting the engine, stop it by removing the jumper wire installed in Step 5. Before test riding the bike, check your electrical hookups by starting and then disconnecting the jumper wire. When performing Step 6, test ride the bike on a paved surface in a secluded area away from all traffic. If you do not feel that you can perform this test safely, or if you do not have access to a safe riding area, refer testing to a Harley-Davidson dealership.

6. Test ride the bike. If the intermittent problem stopped, the engine stop switch is faulty. If the problem continues, look for loose connections in the starter circuit safety switches.
7. Stop the bike and then shift it into NEUTRAL. Disconnect the jumper wire and reconnect the white (1991-1994) or white/black (1995) wire to the ignition coil terminal.

Ignition Coil Testing

Use an ohmmeter to check the ignition coil secondary and primary resistance. Test the coil twice: first when it is cold (room temperature) and then at its normal operating temperature. If the engine will not start, heat the coil with a hair dryer, then test with the ohmmeter.

1. Disconnect the secondary and primary wires from the ignition coil (**Figure 54**).

NOTE
When switching between ohmmeter scales in the following tests, always cross the test leads and zero the needle to assure a correct reading (analog meter only).

2. Set an ohmmeter on R × 1. Measure the ignition coil primary resistance between the coil primary terminals (**Figure 63**). Compare reading to the specification listed in **Table 2**. Replace the ignition coil if the reading is not within specification.
3. Set the ohmmeter on its highest scale. Measure the ignition coil secondary resistance between the secondary terminals (**Figure 63**). Compare reading to specification listed in **Table 2**. Replace the ignition coil if the reading is not within specification.

Ignition Coil Cables and Caps Inspection

All Dyna Glide models are equipped with high-resistance (resistor-core) spark plug cables (**Figure 64**). High-resistance plug cables are used to reduce interferences with CB radios, stereos and electronic ignitions. The conductor used in the factory cables consists of a carbon impregnated fabric core material instead of solid wire. These cables are often called suppression cables.

If a plug cable becomes damaged, either due to corrosion or conductor breaks, its resistance increases. Excessive cable resistance will cause engine misfire and other ignition or driveability problems.

When troubleshooting the ignition system, inspect the spark plug cables (**Figure 65**) for:

a. Corroded or damaged connector ends.
b. Breaks in the cable insulation that could allow arcing.

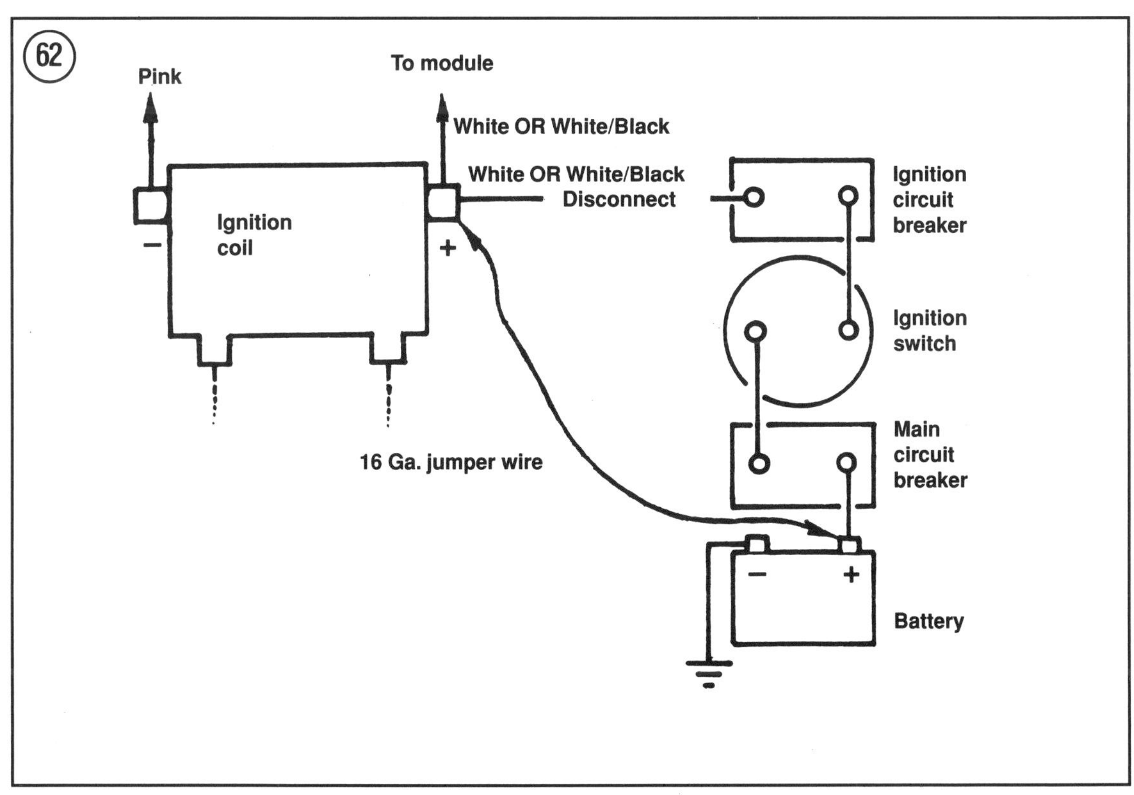

c. Split or damaged plug caps that could allow arcing to the cylinder heads.

Replace damaged or questionable spark plug cables.

Ignition Module and Sensor Plate Resistance Testing

An ohmmeter is required for the following tests.

NOTE
In the following tests, the red ohmmeter lead is the positive lead and the black ohmmeter lead is the negative lead.

Ignition module ground test

1. Disconnect the negative battery cable from the battery.
2. Disconnect the ignition module-to-sensor plate 3-pin electrical connector. See **Figure 47**, **Figure 48** or **Figure 49**.

NOTE
Perform the tests in Step 3 on the ignition module side of the connector.

3. Connect the red ohmmeter lead to the black or black/white module pin and the black ohmmeter lead to ground (**Figure 66**). Read the resistance shown on the ohmmeter. The correct reading is 0-1 ohm. Note the following:

a. If the reading is correct, continue with Step 4.

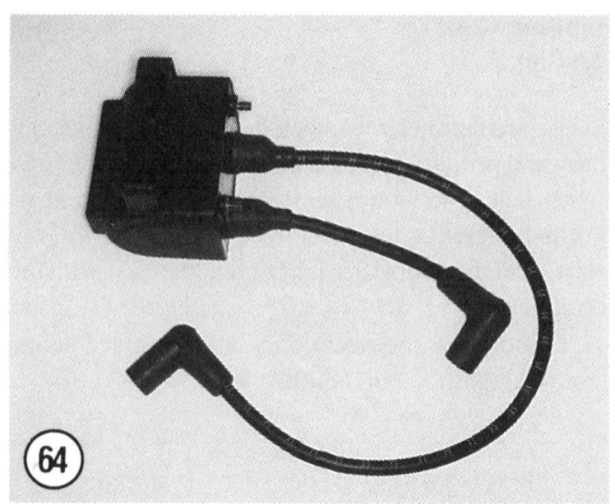
64

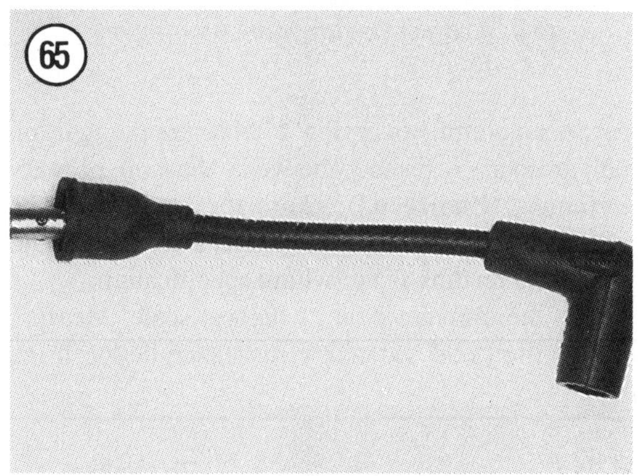
65

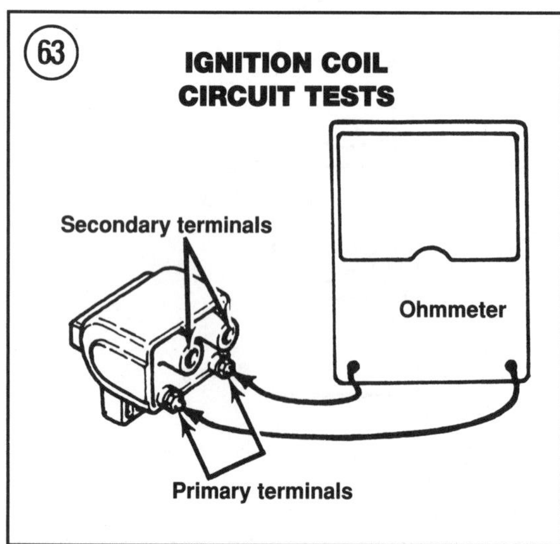
63 IGNITION COIL CIRCUIT TESTS

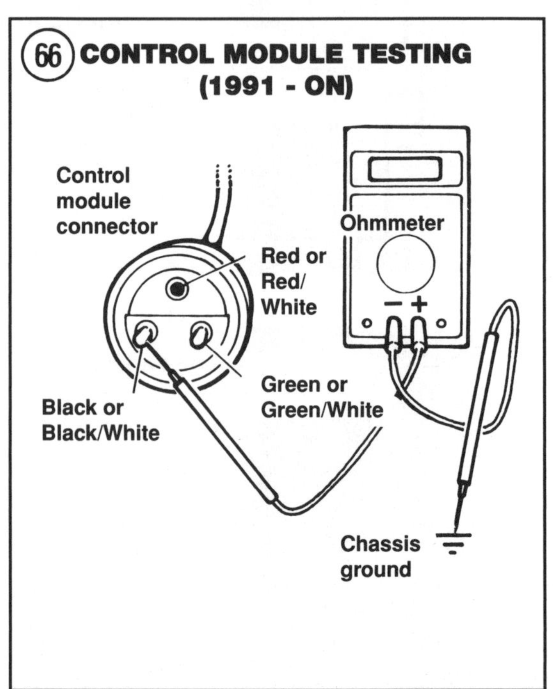
66 CONTROL MODULE TESTING (1991 - ON)

b. If the ohmmeter reading is not as specified, refer to *Ignition Module Resistance Test* in this section.

4. Reconnect the ignition module-to-sensor plate connector.

5. Reconnect the negative battery cable to the battery.

Ignition module resistance test

1. Disconnect the negative battery cable from the battery.

2. Turn the engine stop switch (**Figure 67**) to the OFF position.

3. Disconnect the ignition module to sensor plate 3-pin electrical connector. See **Figure 47**, **Figure 48** or **Figure 49**.

4. To disconnect the ignition module 7-pin connector:

   a. Remove the electric panel cover (**Figure 68**).

   b. Remove the nuts securing the electric panel (**Figure 69**) to its mounting studs. Do not remove the ignition module (A, **Figure 70**) from the electric panel.

   c. Disconnect the ignition module 7-pin connector (B, **Figure 70**).

5. Set the ohmmeter to the R × 1 scale. On an analog ohmmeter, cross the test leads and zero the needle to ensure an accurate reading.

NOTE

Perform the tests in Step 6 on the wiring harness connector side, not on the ignition module connector side.

6. See **Figure 71**. Connect the red ohmmeter lead to the No. 4 ignition module connector pin. Connect the black ohmmeter lead to a good engine ground. Wiggle the wiring harness and read the resistance shown on the ohmmeter. The correct ohmmeter reading is 0-1 ohm. Note the following:

   a. If the resistance reading is correct, continue with Step 7.

   b. If a high resistance reading is obtained (over 1 ohm), check for dirty or loose-fitting terminals or a bare or damaged wire; clean and repair as required.

7. Connect the red ohmmeter lead to the No. 1 ignition module connector pin. Connect the black ohmmeter lead to a good engine ground. Wiggle the wiring harness when reading the ohmmeter. The

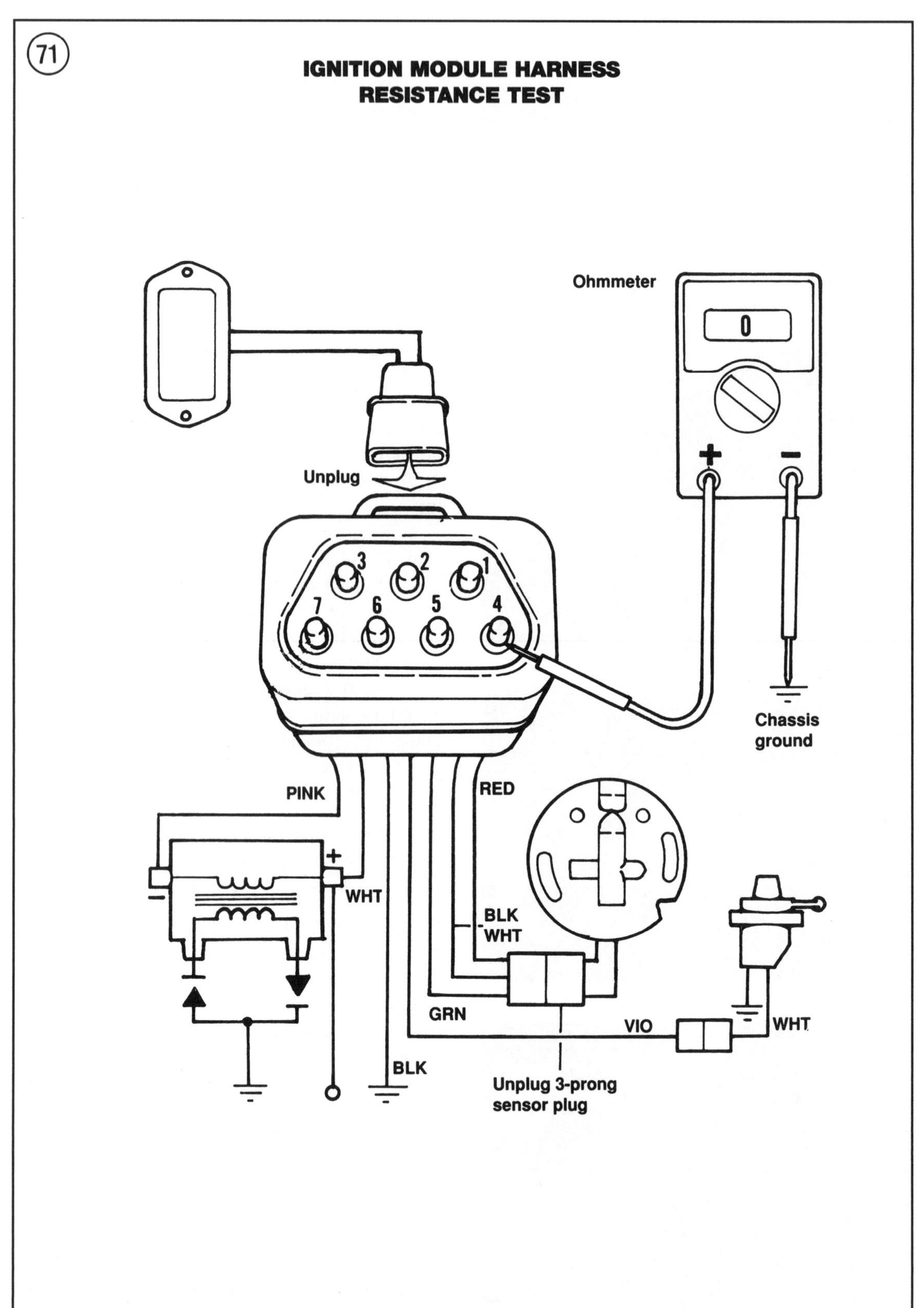
71
IGNITION MODULE HARNESS
RESISTANCE TEST
Ohmmeter
0
+
−
Unplug
3
2
1
7
6
5
4
Chassis
ground
PINK
RED
+
WHT
BLK
WHT
GRN
VIO
WHT
BLK
Unplug 3-prong
sensor plug

correct ohmmeter reading is infinity (high resistance). Repeat this test for the No. 2, 3, 5, 6 and 7 ignition module connector sockets. Note the following:

a. If the reading is infinity at each module pin, continue with Step 8.

b. If the meter shows a reading, the wire is shorting out to ground. Repair the wire and retest.

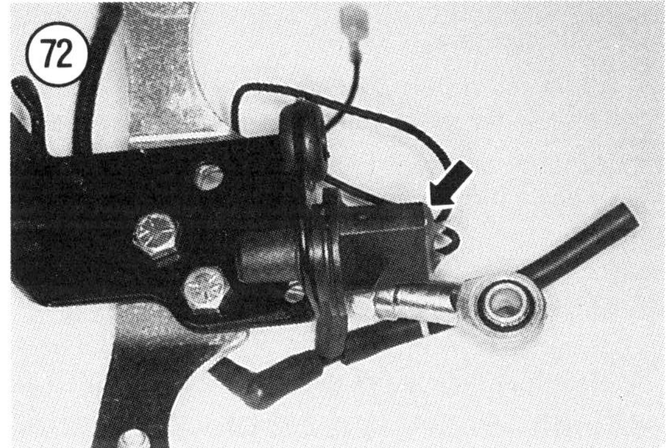

72

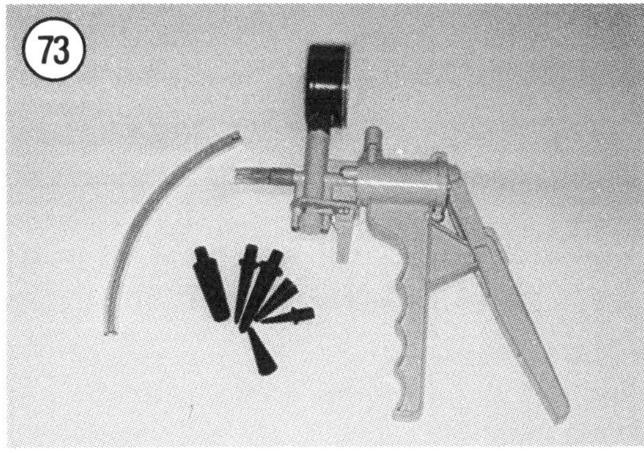

73

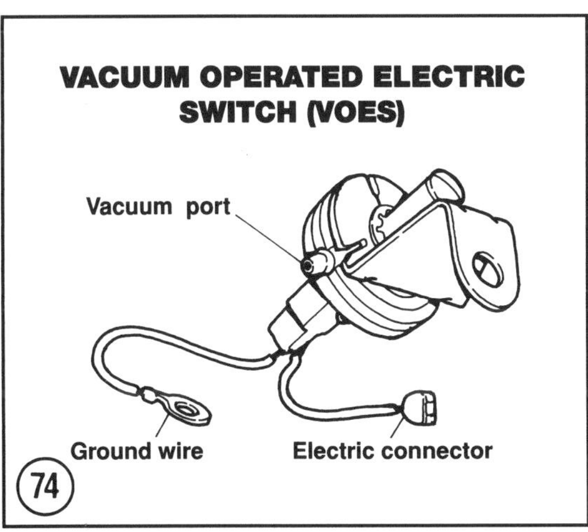

74

8. Check each of the ignition module wires (except No. 4) for continuity with an ohmmeter set on R × 1. Check between the connector pin and the opposite end of the wire (at its connector). The correct ohmmeter reading for each wire is 0-1 ohm. An infinity reading indicates an open in the wire; check for a dirty, loose-fitting or a damaged connector or wire.

2

Vacuum Operated Electric Switch Bench Testing

To provide the correct spark curve (advance or retard) to match all engine load requirements, the ignition system is equipped with a vacuum operated electric switch (VOES). See **Figure 72**. The VOES switch is connected to the carburetor (vacuum hose) and to the ignition module (wires and connectors). The VOES switch sends an electric signal to the ignition module according to the amount of vacuum that exists at the carburetor. The ignition module then selects one of two different vacuum spark curves to advance or retard the ignition timing. When a high vacuum is present (small throttle opening and low speed), the ignition timing is advanced. When no vacuum exists (large throttle opening and high speed), the ignition timing is retarded.

The VOES switch is not adjustable. A faulty VOES switch can cause the engine to run roughly and misfire, will cause spark knock or pinging, and engine overheating.

Perform an operational check of the vacuum operated electric switch (VOES) after checking and setting the ignition timing. See *Ignition Timing* in Chapter Three. If the VOES fails this operational check, check the VOES wires (ignition module and ground wires) for loose or damaged connections. If the wires are in good condition, remove the VOES switch (Chapter Eight) and bench test as follows. An ohmmeter and a hand-operated vacuum pump (**Figure 73**) are required to test the VOES switch.

1. With the VOES switch removed from the vehicle, connect an ohmmeter (set at R × 1) across the 2 switch leads (**Figure 74**). Note the following:

a. If the ohmmeter shows no reading (open circuit), leave the ohmmeter leads attached and continue with Step 2.

b. If the ohmmeter shows a resistance reading, the switch is faulty. Replace the switch and retest.

NOTE
When no vacuum exists at the VOES, the switch is normally open. In Step 2, you will be applying vacuum to the switch and testing it in its closed position.

2. Connect a vacuum pump to the VOES switch vacuum port (**Figure 74**). Slowly operate the pump handle while reading the ohmmeter and vacuum pump scales. When the VOES valve closes, the ohmmeter will show continuity (less than 1 ohm) and the vacuum pump will show 3.5-4.5 in. (89-114 mm) Hg vacuum. If either reading is incorrect, replace the VOES switch and repeat the test.
3. Disconnect the test equipment and install the VOES switch as described in Chapter Eight.

FUEL SYSTEM

The fuel system consists of the fuel tank, fuel valve, fuel line and carburetor (**Figure 75**).

During engine operation, fuel will flow from the fuel tank, through the fuel valve into the carburetor where it is mixed with air before entering the engine. If fuel flow is entering the carburetor incorrectly (too much or too little), the engine will not run properly.

Many owners automatically assume that the carburetor is at fault if the engine does not run properly. While fuel system problems are not uncommon, carburetor adjustment is seldom the answer. In many cases, adjusting the carburetor only compounds the problem by making the engine run worse.

When troubleshooting the fuel system, start at the fuel tank and work through the system, reserving the carburetor as the final point. Most fuel system problems result from an empty fuel tank, sour fuel, a dirty air filter or clogged carburetor jets.

Identifying Carburetor Conditions

Use the following list to identify rich and lean carburetor conditions.

If the engine is running too rich, one or more of the following conditions may be present:

a. The spark plugs foul.
b. The engine misfires and runs rough when under a load.
c. As the throttle is increased, the exhaust smoke becomes more excessive.
d. With the throttle open, the exhaust will sound choked or dull. Bringing the motorcycle to a dead stop and trying to clear the exhaust with the throttle held wide open does not clear up the sound.

If the engine is running too lean, one or more of the following conditions may be present:

a. The spark plug firing end becomes very white or blistered in appearance.
b. The engine overheats.
c. Acceleration is slower.
d. Flat spots are felt during operation that feel much like the engine is trying to run out of gas.
e. Engine power is reduced.
f. At full throttle, engine speed fluctuates.

Troubleshooting

Isolate fuel system problems to the fuel tank, fuel valve and filter, fuel hoses, external fuel filter (if used) or carburetor. The following procedures assume that the ignition system is working properly and is correctly adjusted. A hand-operated vacuum pump (**Figure 73**) is required to test the vacuum operated fuel valve on 1995 models.

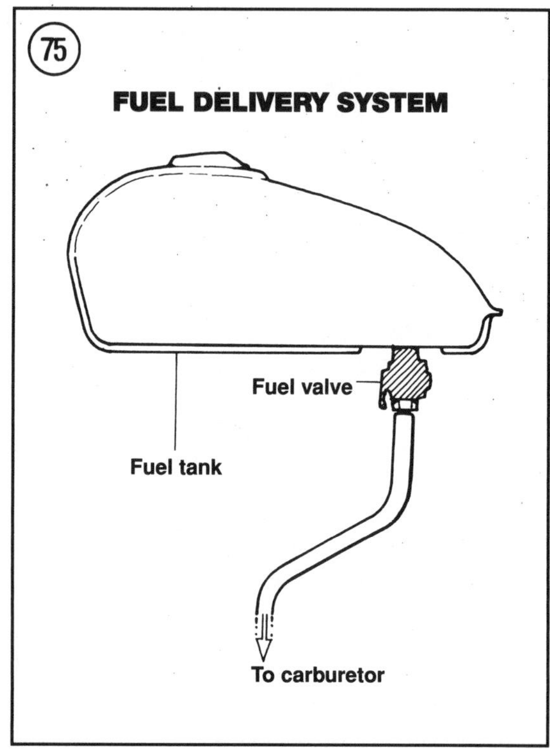

Fuel Delivery System (1991-1994)

To check fuel flow, you need a gas can, drain hose (long enough to reach from the fuel valve to the gas can) and hose clamp.

WARNING
Gasoline is highly flammable. When servicing the fuel system in the following sections, work in a well-ventilated area. Do not expose gasoline and fumes to sparks or other ignition sources.

1. Disconnect the negative battery cable from the battery.
2. Check the level of fuel in the tank. Add fuel if required.
3. Turn the fuel valve OFF (**Figure 76**) and disconnect the fuel hose from the fuel valve. Plug the open end of the hose.
4. Connect the drain hose to the fuel valve and secure it with a hose clamp. Insert the end of the drain hose into a gas can.

WARNING
There must be no open flames in the area when performing the following steps.

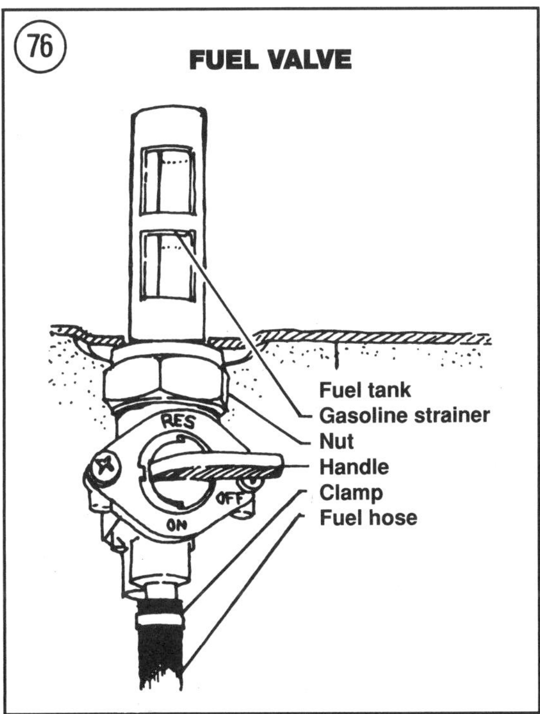

5. The fuel valve controls fuel flow from the fuel tank to the carburetor. A 3-position fuel valve (**Figure 76**) is used on these models. Because this system is gravity-fed, fuel is always present at the fuel valve when there is fuel in the tank. Turn the fuel valve so that the end of the handle faces down (valve is normal operating position). Fuel must flow into the gas can. Turn the fuel valve so that the end of the handle faces up (valve is in RESERVE). Fuel must flow into the can. If there is no fuel from the hose:
   a. Look for a plugged fuel valve. If fuel flows in the RESERVE but not in the ON position, the fuel level in the tank is too low. If the fuel level is high enough to flow in the ON position, the ON side of the valve is clogged. This also holds true if the RESERVE side failed to work properly.
   b. The fuel tank is not properly vented. Check by opening the fuel tank cap. If fuel flows with the cap open, check for a plugged vent.
6. If a good fuel flow is present, fuel is reaching the carburetor. Examine the fuel in the container for rust or dirt that could clog or restrict the fuel hose and carburetor jets. If there is evidence of contamination, remove, flush and clean the fuel tank, fuel valve assembly, fuel hose and carburetor. Refer to Chapter Seven for fuel system service.
7. If fuel is flowing through the fuel valve and the fuel is not contaminated with dirt or rust, refer to the troubleshooting chart in **Figure 77** for additional information.
8. Disconnect the drain hose and reconnect the fuel hose. Secure it with a hose clamp.

WARNING
When reconnecting the fuel hose, the fuel hose must be inserted through the nylon hose insulator. Do not operate the engine without the insulator properly installed.

Fuel Delivery System (1995)

A vacuum operated fuel valve is installed on all 1995 models. A damaged fuel valve or disconnected vacuum hose will prevent fuel flow. Refer to *Vacuum Operated Fuel Valve Testing* in this section.

2

77

CV CARBURETOR TROUBLESHOOTING

Hard starting	Check: • Fuel overflow from float assembly • Enrichener system inoperative • Plugged pilot jet and/or passage • Fuel overflow
Fuel overflows	Check: • Incorrect fuel level • Damaged float assembly • Worn float needle valve or dirty seat • Incorrect float alignment • Damaged float bowl O-ring or loose float bowl mounting screws • Plugged vent in fuel tank cap (1991-1994) • Incorrect fuel tank cap installed
Poor idling	Check: • Incorrect idle speed • Plugged pilot jet system • Loose pilot jet • Air leak at carburetor mounting • Enrichener valve nut loose or damaged
Poor acceleration	Check: • Fuel level too low • Clogged fuel passages • Clogged jets • Plugged vent in fuel tank cap (1991-1994) • Incorrect fuel tank cap installed (non-vent type) • Enrichener valve nut loose or damaged • Worn or damaged needle jet or needle • Throttle cable misadjusted • Air leak at carburetor mounting • Damaged vacuum piston

(continued)

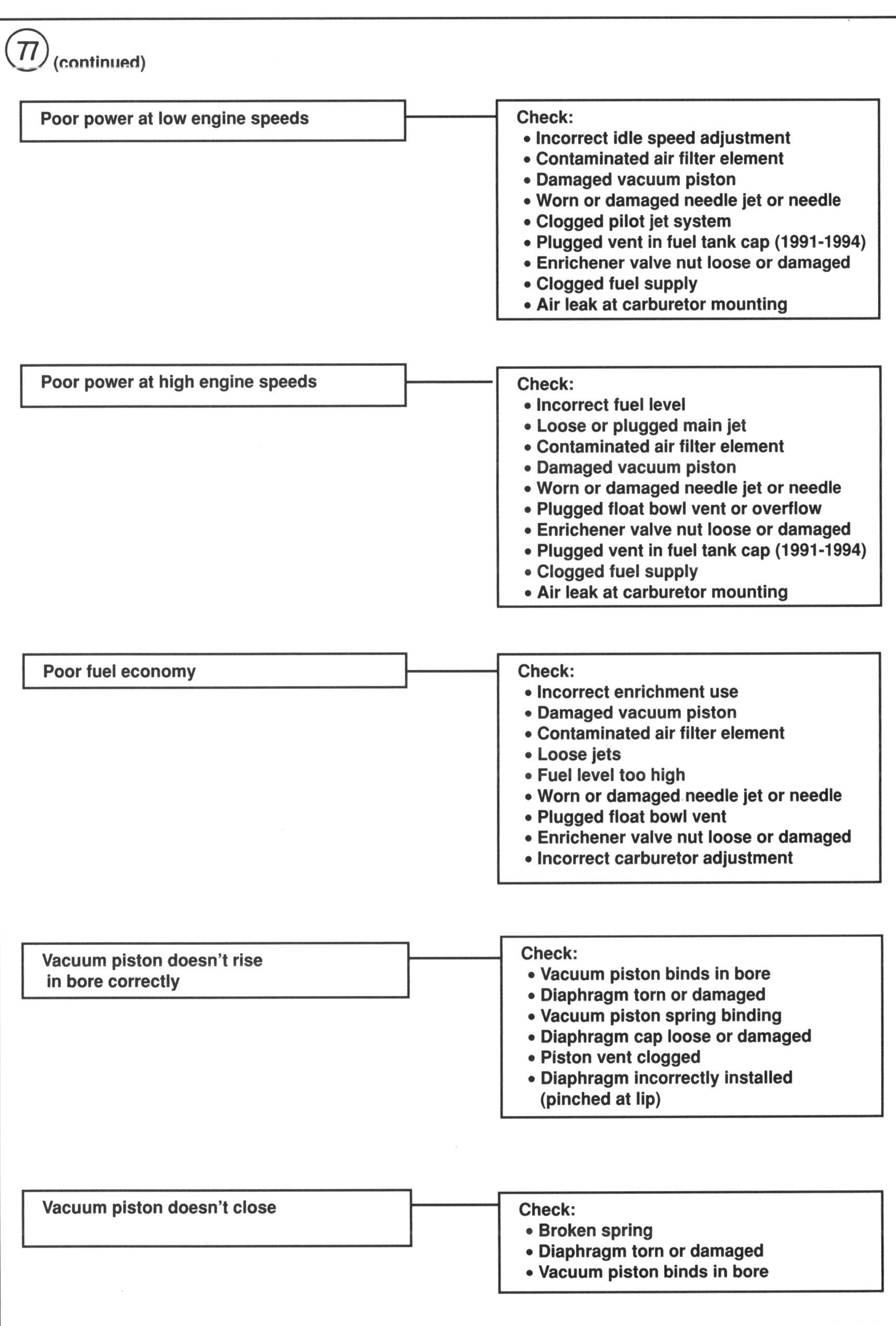
77 (continued)
Poor power at low engine speeds
Check:
• Incorrect idle speed adjustment
• Contaminated air filter element
• Damaged vacuum piston
• Worn or damaged needle jet or needle
• Clogged pilot jet system
• Plugged vent in fuel tank cap (1991-1994)
• Enrichener valve nut loose or damaged
• Clogged fuel supply
• Air leak at carburetor mounting
Poor power at high engine speeds
Check:
• Incorrect fuel level
• Loose or plugged main jet
• Contaminated air filter element
• Damaged vacuum piston
• Worn or damaged needle jet or needle
• Plugged float bowl vent or overflow
• Enrichener valve nut loose or damaged
• Plugged vent in fuel tank cap (1991-1994)
• Clogged fuel supply
• Air leak at carburetor mounting
Poor fuel economy
Check:
• Incorrect enrichment use
• Damaged vacuum piston
• Contaminated air filter element
• Loose jets
• Fuel level too high
• Worn or damaged needle jet or needle
• Plugged float bowl vent
• Enrichener valve nut loose or damaged
• Incorrect carburetor adjustment
Vacuum piston doesn't rise in bore correctly
Check:
• Vacuum piston binds in bore
• Diaphragm torn or damaged
• Vacuum piston spring binding
• Diaphragm cap loose or damaged
• Piston vent clogged
• Diaphragm incorrectly installed (pinched at lip)
Vacuum piston doesn't close
Check:
• Broken spring
• Diaphragm torn or damaged
• Vacuum piston binds in bore

2

Fuel Level System

The fuel level system is shown in **Figure 78**. Proper carburetor operation depends on a constant and correct carburetor fuel level. As fuel is drawn from the float bowl during engine operation, the float level in the bowl drops. As the float drops, the fuel valve moves away from its seat and allows fuel to flow through the seat into the float bowl. Fuel entering the float bowl will cause the float to rise and push against the fuel valve. When the fuel level reaches a predetermined level, the fuel valve is pushed against the seat to prevent the float bowl from overfilling.

If the fuel valve doesn't close, the engine will run too rich or flood with fuel. Symptoms of this problem are rough running, excessive black smoke and poor acceleration. This condition will sometimes clear up when the engine is run at wide-open throttle, as the fuel is being used up before the float bowl can overfill. As the engine speed is reduced, however, the rich running condition repeats itself.

Figure 77 lists several things that can cause fuel overflow. In most instances, it can be as simple a small piece of dirt trapped between the fuel valve and seat or an incorrect float level. If you see fuel flowing out of the overflow tube connected to the bottom of the float bowl, the fuel valve inside the carburetor is being held open. First check the position of the fuel valve lever. Turn the fuel valve lever OFF. Then tap on the carburetor (not too hard) and turn the fuel valve lever back ON. If the fuel flow stops running out of the overflow tube, you may have dislodged whatever was holding the fuel valve off of its seat. If fuel continues to flow from the overflow tube, remove and service the carburetor. See Chapter Seven.

NOTE

On 1995 models, fuel will not flow from the vacuum operated fuel valve until the engine is running.

Starter or Choke System

A cold engine requires a very rich mixture to start and run properly. On all models, a cable actuated enrichener valve is used for cold-starting.

The carburetor choke can also present a problem by causing difficult cold starting. If the engine is difficult to start when cold, check the choke cable adjustment described in Chapter Three. If the choke cable adjustment is correct, refer to the possible causes listed under *Hard Starting* in **Figure 77**.

Accelerator Pump System

Because the carburetor cannot supply enough fuel during sudden throttle openings (quick acceleration), a lean air/fuel mixture will cause hesitation and poor acceleration. To prevent this condition, factory installed carburetors are equipped with a diaphragm type accelerator pump system. See **Figure 79**. A spring-loaded neoprene diaphragm is installed in a pump chamber at the bottom of the float

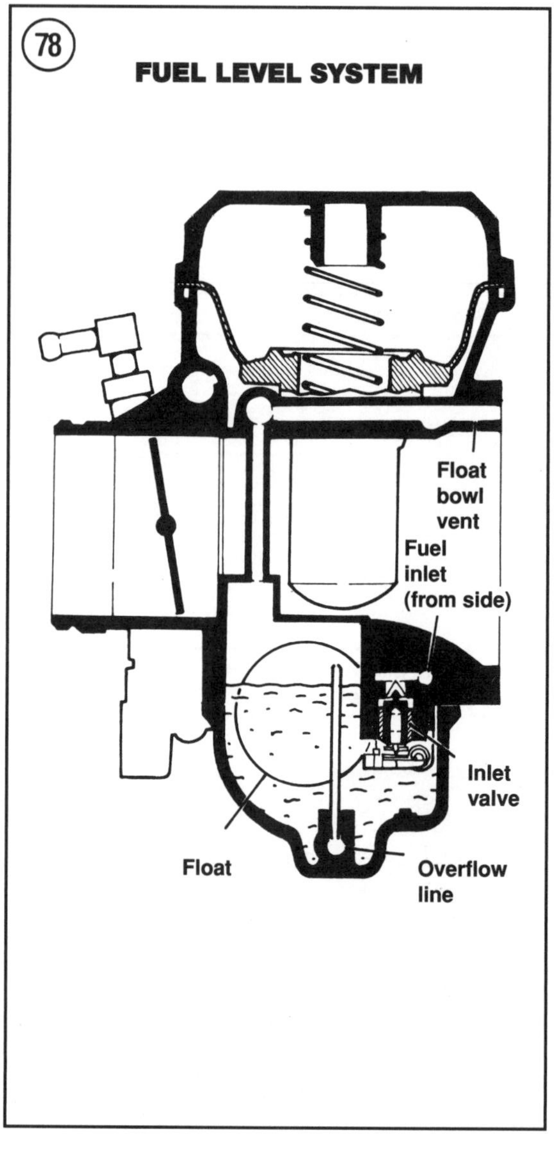

bowl. During sudden acceleration, the diaphragm is compressed by the pump lever, forcing fuel out of the pump chamber through a check valve and into the carburetor venturi. This additional fuel richens the existing air/fuel mixture to prevent engine hesitation. The diaphragm spring returns the diaphragm to its uncompressed position, allowing the chamber to refill with fuel for its next use. The check valve prevents fuel from back flowing into the chamber during pump operation.

If your bike hesitates during sudden acceleration or if it suffers from overall poor acceleration, perform the checks listed under *Poor Acceleration* in **Figure 77**. If the accelerator pump system is faulty, service the carburetor as described in Chapter Seven. 2

ACCELERATOR PUMP SYSTEM

Throttle rod
Pump lever
Throttle shaft
Spring
Venturi
Pump nozzle
Check valve
Diaphragm
Pump rod
Spring

79

80

Vacuum Operated Fuel Valve Testing (1995)

All 1995 models are equipped with a vacuum operated fuel valve (**Figure 80**). A vacuum hose is connected between the fuel valve and the vacuum operated electric switch (VOES). When the engine is running, vacuum is applied to the fuel valve through this hose. For fuel to flow through the fuel valve, a vacuum must be present with the fuel valve handle in the ON or RES position. The following steps troubleshoot the fuel valve by applying vacuum from a separate source. A hand-operated vacuum pump (**Figure 73**), gas can, drain hose (long enough to reach from the fuel valve to the gas can) and hose clamp are required for this test.

WARNING
Gasoline is highly flammable. When servicing the fuel system in the following sections, work in a well-ventilated area. Do not expose gasoline and fumes to sparks or other ignition sources.

1. Disconnect the negative battery cable from the battery.
2. Visually check the amount of fuel in the tank. Add fuel if necessary.
3. Turn the fuel valve OFF and disconnect the fuel hose (A, **Figure 81**) from the fuel valve. Plug the open end of the hose.
4. Connect the drain hose (**Figure 82**) to the fuel valve and secure it with a hose clamp. Insert the end of the drain hose into a gas can.

WARNING
Do not perform this test if there are open flames or sparks in the area.

6. Disconnect the vacuum hose (B, **Figure 81**) from the fuel valve.
7. Connect a hand-operated vacuum pump to the fuel valve vacuum hose nozzle (B, **Figure 81**). See **Figure 83**.

8. Turn the fuel valve lever (**Figure 80**) to the ON position.

CAUTION
In Step 9, do not apply more than 10 in. (254 mm) Hg vacuum or you will damage the fuel valve diaphragm.

9. Operate the vacuum pump handle to apply 1-10 in. (25.4-254 mm) Hg vacuum. Fuel must flow through the fuel valve when the vacuum is applied.
10. With the vacuum still applied, turn the fuel valve lever (**Figure 80**) to the RES position. Fuel will continue to flow through the valve.
11. Turn the fuel valve OFF and release the vacuum. Disconnect the vacuum pump and drain hoses.
12. If fuel does not flow through the valve when vacuum was applied, refer to **Figure 84** for possible causes.

Vacuum Piston Inspection

A malfunctioning vacuum piston (**Figure 85**) can cause the following conditions:

a. Poor fuel economy.
b. Poor acceleration.
c. Poor road and high speed performance.

If you suspect that the vacuum piston is not operating properly (failing to rise or close properly), perform the following procedures before removing the carburetor.

1. Check vacuum piston rise as follows:
   a. Remove the air filter and its backplate (Chapter Three) so that you can see the vacuum piston.

WARNING
Never stand close to the carburetor when checking vacuum piston operation with the engine running. A backfire could cause eye injury or facial burns. Protect your eyes by wearing safety glasses and standing a safe distance away from the carburetor. Have an assistant operate the throttle for you.

   b. With the engine running and properly warmed up, have an assistant open and close the throttle several times while you watch vacuum piston operation (**Figure 85**). The vacuum piston must rise and lower as the throttle is opened and closed. Turn the engine off.
   c. With the engine off, lift the vacuum piston all the way up the carburetor bore with your finger, then release it. Note how the piston traveled upward in the bore. The piston must move smoothly with no sign of roughness or binding.
2. Check piston closing as follows:
   a. With the engine off, lift the vacuum piston all the way up the carburetor bore with your finger and release it. Note how the piston drops

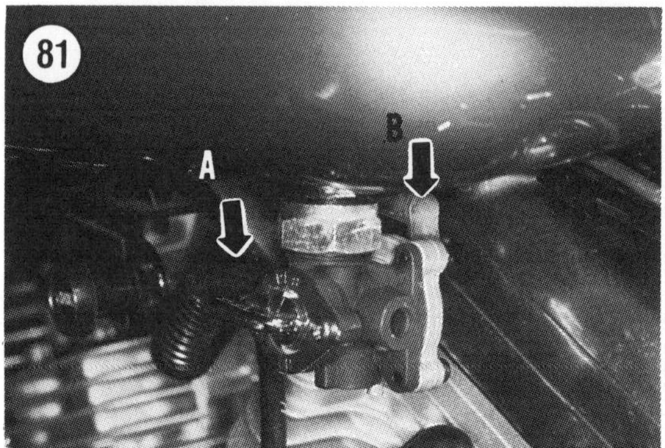

in the bore. It must drop smoothly and come to a stop at the bottom of the bore.

b. Without touching the vacuum piston, observe the bottom of the vacuum piston in relation to the carburetor piston bore. The lower edge of the vacuum piston must align with the horizontal groove (**Figure 86**) at the bottom of the piston track.

3. If the vacuum piston fails to operate as described in these steps, remove the carburetor (Chapter Seven) and inspect the vacuum piston diaphragm for damage.

ENGINE NOISES

Often the first evidence of an internal engine problem is a strange noise. That knocking, clicking or tapping sound which you never heard before is warning you of impending trouble.

While engine noises can indicate problems, they can be difficult to interpret.

Professional mechanics often use a special stethoscope for isolating engine noises. See **Figure 87**. You can also use a "sounding stick," which can be an ordinary piece of doweling or a section of small hose. By placing one end in contact with the area in which you want to listen and the other end near your ear, you can hear sounds emanating from that area. If you can, have an experienced friend or mechanic help you sort out the noises.

Consider the following when troubleshooting engine noises:

1. *Knocking or pinging during acceleration*—Caused by using a lower octane fuel than recommended or old fuel or a too hot heat range spark plug. Refer to *Correct Spark Plug Heat Range* in Chapter Three.

2

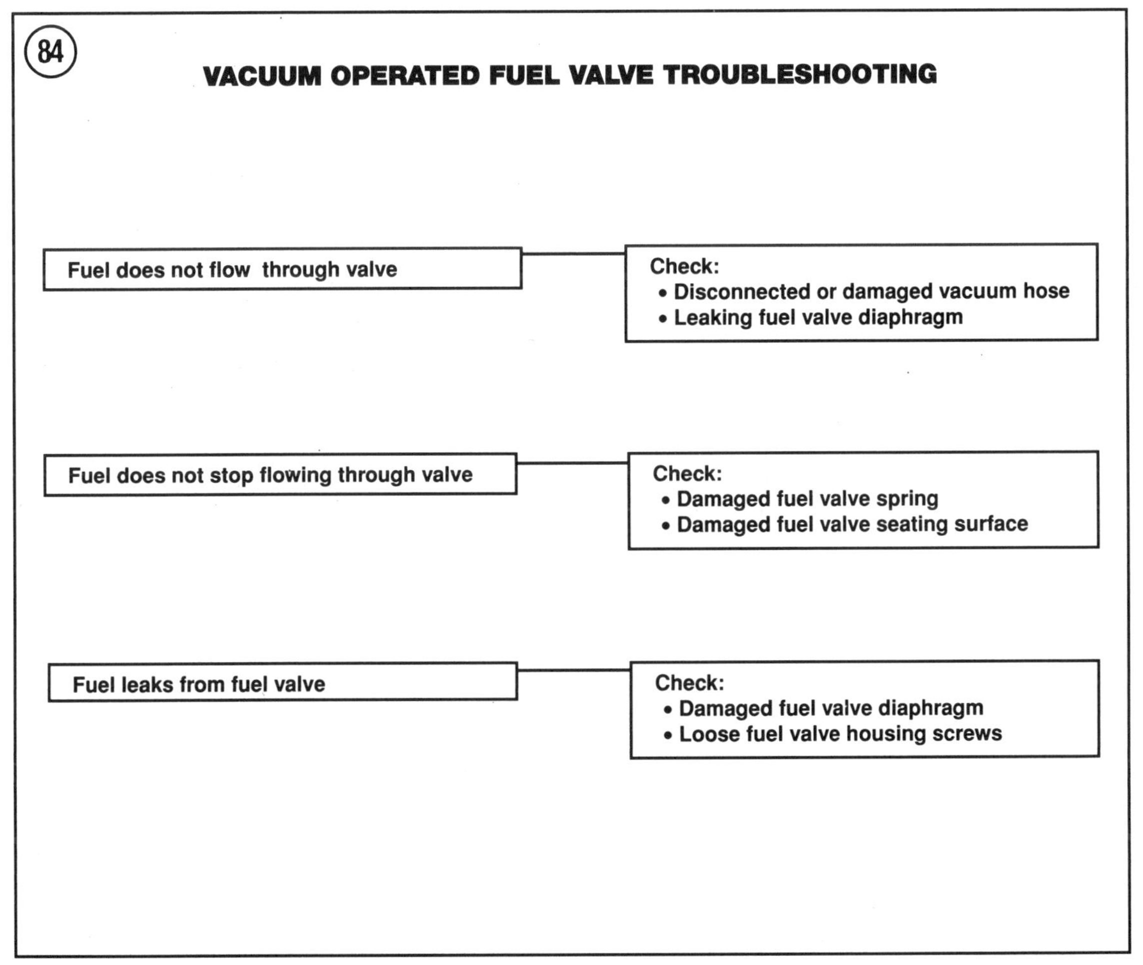

2. *Slapping or rattling noises at low speed or during acceleration*—May be caused by piston slap (excessive piston-cylinder wall clearance).
3. *Knocking or rapping while decelerating*— Usually caused by excessive rod bearing clearance.
4. *Persistent knocking and vibration*— Usually caused by worn main bearing(s).
5. *Rapid on-off squeal*— Compression leak around cylinder head gasket(s) or spark plugs.
6. *Valve train noise*— Check for the following:
   a. Bent pushrod(s).
   b. Defective lifters.
   c. Valve sticking in guide.
   d. Worn cam gears and/or cam.
   e. Damaged rocker arm or shaft. Rocker arm may be binding on shaft.

ENGINE LUBRICATION

An improperly operating engine lubrication system will quickly lead to serious engine damage. Check the engine oil level weekly as described in Chapter Three. Oil pump service is covered in Chapter Four.

Oil Light

The oil light, mounted on the indicator light panel (**Figure 88**), will come on when the ignition switch is turned to ON before starting the engine. After the engine is started, the oil light will turn off when the engine speed is above idle.

If the oil light does not come on when the ignition switch is turned to ON and the engine is not running, check for a burned out oil light bulb as described in Chapter Nine. If the bulb is okay, check the oil pressure switch (**Figure 89**) as described in Chapter Eight.

If the oil light remains on when the engine speed is above idle, turn the engine off and check the oil level in the oil tank. If the oil level is satisfactory, check the following:

a. Oil may not be returning to the tank from the return line. Check for a clogged or damaged return line or a damaged oil pump.
b. Check for a plugged tappet screen (**Figure 90**). Remove and service the screen as described in Chapter Three.
c. If you are operating your motorcycle in conditions where the ambient temperature is be-

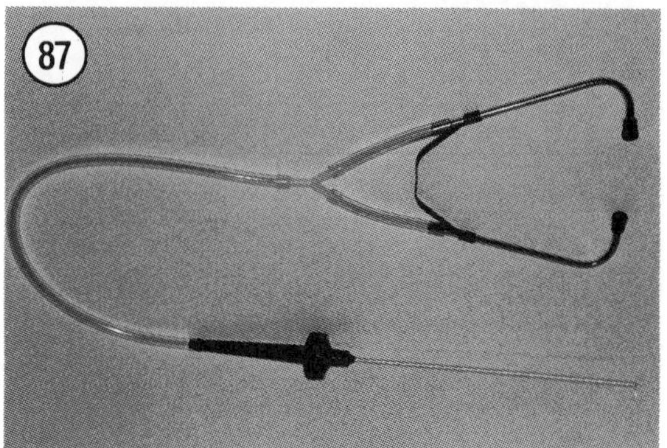

low freezing, ice and sludge may be blocking the oil feed pipe. This condition will prevent the oil from circulating properly.

Oil Consumption High or Engine Smokes Excessively

Check engine compression and perform a cylinder leakage test as described in Chapter Three. Causes can be one or more of the following:

89

90

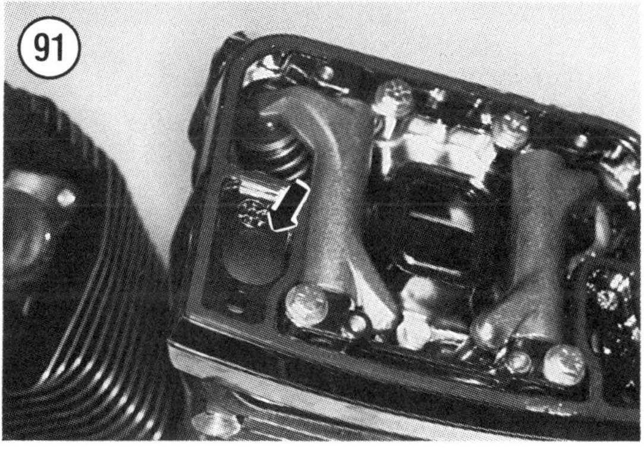

91

a. Worn valve guides.
b. Worn valve guide seals.
c. Worn or damaged piston rings.
d. Restricted oil tank return line.
e. Oil tank overfilled.
f. Oil filter restricted.
g. Leaking cylinder head surfaces.
h. Incorrectly timed breather valve.

Oil Fails to Return to Oil Tank

a. Oil lines or fittings restricted or damaged.
b. Oil pump damaged or operating incorrectly.
c. Oil tank empty.
d. Oil filter restricted.
e. Damaged oil feed pump.
f. Sheared scavenger pump gear key.

Engine Oil Leaks

a. Clogged air filter breather hose.
b. Restricted or damaged oil return line to oil tank.
c. Loose engine parts.
d. Damaged gasket sealing surfaces.
e. Oil tank overfilled.
f. Incorrectly timed breather valve.
g. Restricted oil filter.
h. Plugged air filter-to-breather system hose.
i. Umbrella valve(s) incorrectly installed in the middle rocker cover (**Figure 91**).

CLUTCH

All clutch troubles, except adjustments, require partial clutch disassembly to identify and cure the problem. Refer to Chapter Five for clutch service procedures.

Clutch Chatter or Noise

This problem is generally caused by worn or warped friction and steel plates. Also check for worn or damaged bearings.

Clutch Slippage

a. Incorrect clutch adjustment.
b. Worn friction plates.

c. Weak or damaged diaphragm spring.
d. Damaged pressure plate.

Clutch Dragging

a. Incorrect clutch adjustment.
b. Warped clutch plates.
c. Worn or damaged clutch shell or clutch hub.
d. Worn or incorrectly assembled clutch ball and ramp mechanism.
e. Incorrect primary chain alignment.
f. Weak or damaged diaphragm spring.

TRANSMISSION

Transmission symptoms are sometimes hard to distinguish from clutch symptoms. Refer to Chapter Six for transmission service procedures.

Jumping Out of Gear

a. Worn or damaged shifter parts.
b. Incorrect shifter rod adjustment.
c. Incorrect shifter drum adjustment.
d. Severely worn or damaged gears and/or shifter forks.

Difficult Shifting

a. Worn or damaged shifter forks.
b. Worn or damaged shifter clutch dogs.
c. Weak or damaged shifter return spring.
e. Clutch drag.

Excessive Gear Noise

a. Worn or damaged bearings.
b. Worn or damaged gears.
c. Excessive gear backlash.

ELECTRICAL PROBLEMS

If bulbs burn out frequently, check for excessive vibration, loose connections that permit sudden current surges, or the installation of the wrong type of bulb.

Most light and ignition problems are caused by loose or corroded ground connections. Check these prior to replacing a bulb or electrical component.

EXCESSIVE VIBRATION

Excessive vibration is usually caused by loose engine mounting hardware. A bent axle shaft or loose suspension component will cause high-speed vibration problems. Vibration can also be caused by the following conditions:

a. Broken frame.
b. Severely worn primary chain.
c. Tight primary chain links.
d. Loose, worn or damaged engine stabilizer link.
e. Loose or damaged rubber mounts.
f. Improperly balanced wheel(s).
g. Defective or damaged wheel(s).
h. Defective or damaged tire(s).
i. Internal engine wear or damage.
j. Loose or worn steering head bearings.
k. Loose swing arm pivot shaft nut.

FRONT SUSPENSION AND STEERING

Poor handling may be caused by improper pressure, a damaged or bent frame or front steering components, worn wheel bearings or dragging brakes. Possible causes for suspension and steering malfunctions are listed below.

Irregular or Wobbly Steering

a. Loose wheel axle nut(s).
b. Loose or worn steering head bearings.
c. Excessive wheel hub bearing play.
d. Damaged cast wheel.
e. Spoke wheel out of alignment.
f. Unbalanced wheel assembly.
g. Worn hub bearings.
h. Incorrect wheel alignment.
i. Bent or damaged steering stem or frame (at steering neck).
j. Tire incorrectly seated on rim.
k. Excessive front end loading from non-standard equipment.

Stiff Steering

a. Low front tire air pressure.
b. Bent or damaged steering stem or frame (at steering neck).
c. Loose or worn steering head bearings.

Stiff or Heavy Fork Operation

a. Incorrect fork springs.
b. Incorrect fork oil viscosity.
c. Excessive amount of fork oil.
d. Bent fork tubes.

Poor Fork Operation

a. Worn or damage fork tubes.
b. Fork oil capacity low due to leaking fork seals.
c. Bent or damaged fork tubes.
d. Contaminated fork oil.
e. Incorrect fork springs.
f. Heavy front end loading from non-standard equipment.

Poor Rear Shock Absorber Operation

a. Weak or worn springs.
b. Damper unit leaking.
c. Shock shaft worn or bent.
d. Incorrect rear shock springs.
e. Rear shocks adjusted incorrectly.
f. Heavy rear end loading from non-standard equipment.
g. Incorrect loading.

BRAKE PROBLEMS

All models are equipped with front and rear disc brakes. Good brakes are vital to the safe operation of any vehicle. Perform the maintenance specified in Chapter Three to minimize brake system problems. Brake system service is covered in Chapter Twelve. When refilling the front and rear master cylinders, use only DOT 5 silicone-based brake fluid.

Insufficient Braking Power

Worn brake pads or disc, air in the hydraulic system, glazed or contaminated pads, low brake fluid level, or a leaking brake line or hose can cause this problem. Visually check for leaks. Check for worn brake pads. Check also for a leaking or damaged primary cup seal in the master cylinder. Bleed and adjust the brakes. Rebuild a leaking master cylinder or brake caliper. Brake drag will result in excessive heat and brake fade. See *Brake Drag* in this section.

Spongy Brake Feel

This problem is generally caused by air in the hydraulic system. Bleed and adjust the brakes.

Brake Drag

Check brake adjustment, looking for insufficient brake pedal and/or hand lever free play. Also check for worn, loose or missing parts in the brake calipers. Check the brake disc for warpage or excessive runout.

Brakes Squeal or Chatter

Check brake pad thickness and disc condition. Check that the anti-rattle springs are properly installed and in good condition. Clean off any dirt on the pads. Loose components can also cause this. Check for:

a. Warped brake disc.
b. Loose brake disc.
c. Loose caliper mounting bolts.
d. Loose front axle nut.
e. Worn wheel bearings.
f. Damaged hub.

Table 1 STARTER MOTOR TEST SPECIFICATIONS

Minimum no-load speed @ 11.5 volts	3,000 rpm
Maximum no-load current @ 11.5 volts	90 amps
Current draw	
Normal	160-180 amps
Maximum	200 amps

Table 2 ELECTRICAL SPECIFICATIONS

Battery capacity	12 volt, 19 amp hour
Alternator	
AC voltage output	16-20 VAC per 1,000 rpm
Stator coil resistance	0.1-0.2 ohms
Voltage regulator	
Voltage output @ 3,600 rpm	13.8-15 volts
Amps @ 3,600 rpm	32 amps
Ignition coil resistance	
Primary	2.5-3.1 ohms
Secondary	10,000-12,500 rpm

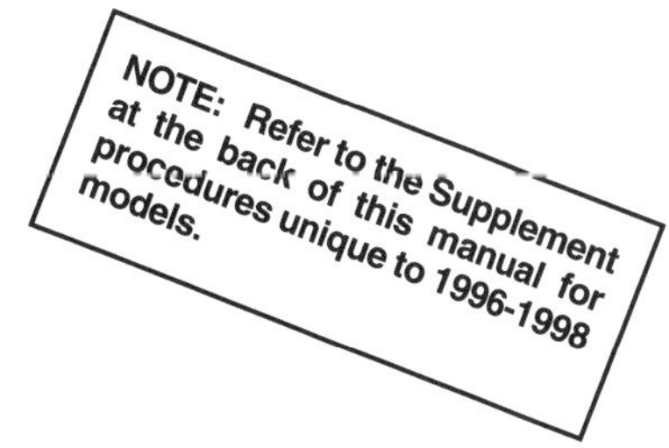

CHAPTER THREE

PERIODIC LUBRICATION, MAINTENANCE AND TUNE-UP

The service life and operation of your Harley-Davidson depends on the maintenance it receives. This is easy to understand, once you realize that a motorcycle, even in normal use, is subjected to tremendous heat, stress and vibration. When neglected, any bike becomes unreliable and dangerous to ride.

All motorcycles require attention before and after riding them. The time spent on basic maintenance and lubrication will give you the utmost in safety and performance. Minor problems found during these inspections are simple and inexpensive to correct. If they are not found and corrected at this time they can lead to major and more expensive problems.

If this is your first bike, start by doing simple tune-up, lubrication and maintenance procedures. Tackle more involved jobs as you become more acquainted with the bike.

Perform critical maintenance tasks and checks weekly. Perform others at specific time or mileage intervals or if certain symptoms appear. The *Tune-up* section at the end of this chapter lists procedures which affect driveability and performance. When procedures are too detailed to be performed in this chapter, references will refer you to the specific chapter.

Harley-Davidson recommends the service procedures and intervals shown in **Table 1**. **Tables 1-8** are at the end of the chapter.

ROUTINE SAFETY CHECKS

Perform the following safety checks before the first ride of the day.

General Inspection

1. Inspect the engine for oil or fuel leakage.
2. Check the tires for embedded stones. Pry them out with a suitable tool.
3. Make sure all lights work.

NOTE
Check brake light operation frequently. It can burn out anytime. Cars can't stop

as quickly as you and need all the warning you can give.

4. Inspect the fuel lines and fittings for leakage.
5. Check the fuel level in the fuel tank. Top off, if required.
6. Check the operation of the front and rear brakes. Add DOT 5 brake fluid to the front and rear master cylinders as required.
7. Check clutch operation. If necessary, adjust the clutch as described in this chapter.
8. Check the throttle operation. The hand throttle must move smoothly with no roughness, sticking or tightness. The throttle must snap back when released. Adjust throttle free play, if necessary, as described in this chapter.
9. Check the rear brake pedal. It must move smoothly. If necessary, adjust free play as described in this chapter.
10. Inspect the front and rear suspension. Make sure they have a good solid feel with no looseness.
11. Check the exhaust system for leakage or damage.

CAUTION
*When checking the tightness of the exposed fasteners on your Dyna Glide, do **not** check the cylinder head bolts in this process. Harley-Davidson lists a specific cylinder head tightening sequence to prevent warpage, head gasket leakage and stud failure. When tightening the cylinder head bolts, follow the procedure described in Chapter Four.*

Engine Oil Tank Level

Refer to *Periodic Lubrication* in this chapter.

Tire Pressure

Check tire pressure when the tires are cold. The tire pressures listed in **Table 2** vary according to your vehicles load. Refer to *Tire Pressure* in this chapter.

Battery

Remove the battery and check the battery electrolyte level. Maintain the electrolyte level within the MIN and MAX battery markings (**Figure 1**).

For complete details, see *Battery* in Chapter Eight.

Lights and Horn

With the engine running, check the following.

1. Pull the front brake lever and check that the brake light comes on.
2. Push the rear brake pedal down and check that the brake light comes on soon after you have begun depressing the pedal.
3. Make sure the headlight and taillight are on.
4. Move the dimmer switch up and down between the high and low positions, and make sure both headlight elements are working.
5. Push the turn signal switch to the left and right positions and make sure all 4 turn signal lights are working.
6. Check that all accessory lights work properly, if so equipped.
7. Push the horn button and make sure that it blows loudly.
8. If the horn or any light fails to work properly, refer to Chapter Eight.

MAINTENANCE INTERVALS

The factory recommends the services and intervals shown in **Table 1**. Strict adherence to these recommendations will go a long way toward ensuring long service from your motorcycle. To prevent rust damage when operating the bike in areas of high humidity or when riding near the ocean, increase the lubrication service intervals.

For convenient maintenance, this chapter describes most of the services shown in **Table 1**. The remaining chapters cover those procedures which require more than minor disassembly or adjustment. Use the *Table of Contents* and *Index* to find a particular service procedure.

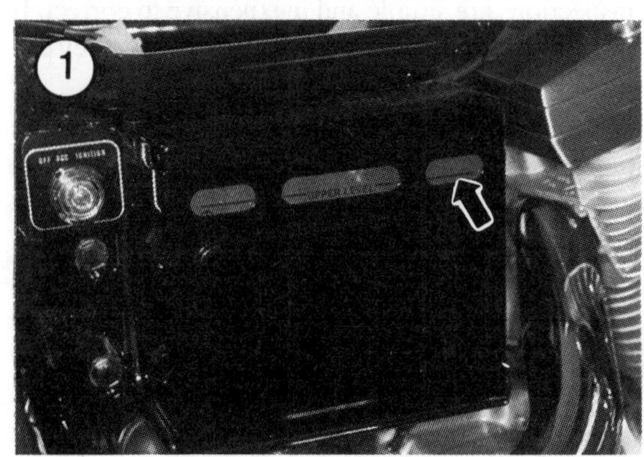

CLEANING YOUR MOTORCYCLE

Regular cleaning of your motorcycle is important. It makes routine maintenance a lot easier by not having to work your way through built-up dirt and oil to get to a component for adjustment or replacement. It also makes the bike look like new though it may have many thousands of miles on it.

If you ride in rural areas, clean the bike more often. This will maintain the painted, plated and polished surfaces. Keep a good coat of wax on the bike during the winter to prevent premature weathering of all finishes.

Wash the bike carefully to avoid damage to the painted and plated finishes and to components that cannot withstand high-pressure water. Try to avoid using the coin-operated car wash systems as the cleaning agents may be harmful to the plastic parts on the bike. Also the high water pressure in these systems will force water into areas that must be kept dry.

Use a mild detergent (mild liquid dish washing detergent) or a commercial car washing detergent available at most auto parts outlets. These detergents may remove some wax that you have applied to the finish. Follow the manufacturer's instructions for the correct detergent-to-water mixture.

When the lower end of the engine and frame are covered with oil, grease or road dirt, spray the area with a commercial cleaner. Follow the manufacturer's instructions and rinse with *plenty of cold water*. Do not allow any of this cleaner residue to settle in any pockets as it will stain or destroy the finish of most painted parts.

Use a commercial tar-stain remover to remove any severe road dirt and tar stains. Then rinse thoroughly to remove the chemical residue.

Prior to washing plastic and painted surfaces, make sure the surfaces are cool. Do not wash a hot bike as the soap can dry and streak the finish before being rinsed off.

CAUTION

Do not allow water to enter the air intake, brake assemblies, electrical switches and connectors, instrument cluster, wheel bearing areas, swing arm bearings or any other moisture sensitive areas of the bike.

After all of the heavily soiled areas are cleaned, use a soft natural sponge and carefully wash down the entire bike, including the wheels and tires. Always wet the bike down *before* washing with your detergent soaked sponge or rag. This will remove dirt from sensitive areas and prevent scratching. Don't use too much detergent as the soap can be difficult to rinse off. After washing the bike, rinse with *low-pressure cold water*. Make sure you rinse the bike thoroughly.

3

NOTE

Before washing the fuel tank, check for small pebbles, metal shavings or dirt stuck to or partially hidden in your sponge and rags. These objects may scratch and mar the tank's finish. As you wash your bike, rinse the sponge or rag frequently to remove accumulated dirt.

If you have access to compressed air, *gently* blow excess water from areas where the water may have collected. Do not force the water into any of the sensitive areas mentioned in the previous *CAUTION*. Gently dry off the bike with a chamois, a clean soft turkish towel or an old plain T-shirt (transfers or hand-painted designs may scratch the tank). If your bike has a windshield, clean it carefully. Windshields can be easily scratched or damaged. Do not use a cleaner with an abrasive or a combination cleaner and wax. Never use gasoline or cleaning solvent. These products will destroy the surface finish of the windshield.

Clean the windshield with a soft cloth or natural sponge and plenty of water. Dry thoroughly with a soft cloth or chamois—do not press hard.

WARNING

Damp or wet brake pads will reduce braking effectiveness. If you are going to ride the bike soon after washing it, make the ride a slow one while lightly applying the brakes to dry the pads.

Start the engine and let it reach normal operating temperature. Take the bike out for a *slow and careful* ride around to blow off any residual water. Bring the bike back to the wash area and dry off any residual water streaks from the painted and plated surfaces.

When the bike is dry, wax all painted, plated and polished surfaces.

TIRES AND WHEELS

Tire Pressure

Check the tire pressure often to maintain tire profile, traction, and handling and to get the maximum life out of the tire. Carry a tire gauge (**Figure 2**) in your bikes tool kit. **Table 2** lists the appropriate tire pressures for the factory equipped tires.

NOTE

*After checking and adjusting the air pressure, make sure to reinstall the air valve caps (**Figure 3**). These caps prevent small pebbles and dirt from collecting in the valve stems and causing air leakage or incorrect tire pressure readings.*

Tire Inspection

The tires take a lot of punishment so inspect them periodically for excessive wear, deep cuts and imbedded objects such as stones or nails. If you find a nail or other object in a tire, mark its location with a light crayon prior to removing it. This will help you find the hole for repair. Refer to Chapter Nine for tire changing and repair information. Check local traffic regulations concerning minimum tread depth. Measure with a tread depth gauge (**Figure 4**) or a small ruler. As a guideline, replace tires when the tread depth is 5/16 in. (8.0 mm.) or less.

Wire Spoke Tension

Check wire spoke wheels for loose or damaged spokes. Refer to Chapter Nine for spoke service.

Rim Inspection

On both cast and wire spoked wheels, check the wheel rims for cracks and other damage. If damaged, a rim can make the bike steer and handle poorly. Refer to Chapter Nine for wheel service.

PERIODIC LUBRICATION

Oil

Oil is graded according to its viscosity, which is an indication of how thick it is. The Society of Automotive Engineers (SAE) system distinguishes oil viscosity by numbers. Thick oil has higher viscosity numbers than thin oil. For example, a SAE 5 oil is a thin oil while a SAE 90 oil is thick.

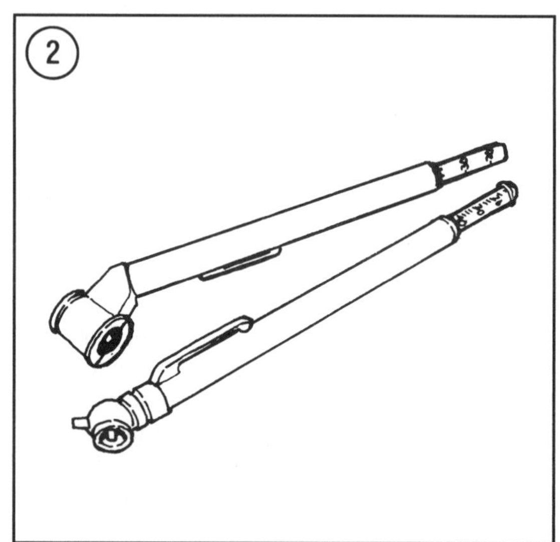

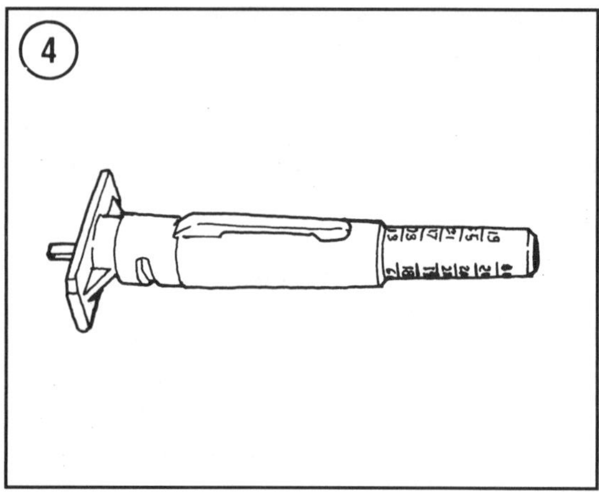

Grease

Use a good quality waterproof grease (**Figure 5**). Water does not wash grease off parts as easily as it washes oil off. In addition, grease maintains its lubricating qualities better than oil on long and strenuous rides.

Oil Tank Inspection

Before checking the oil level, inspect the oil tank for cracks or other damage. Repair any oil leaks. Check the oil tank for loose or missing fasteners; replace or tighten fasteners as required. Secure each hose with a hose clamp. Check each hose for swelling, cracks or damage and replace immediately; otherwise, oil leakage may occur and cause engine damage. Check each hose connection at the tank, engine and transmission.

On all Dyna Glide models, the oil tank mounts to the bottom of the transmission housing (**Figure 6**). Refer to **Figure 7** (1991) or **Figure 8** (1992-on) for oil hose routing diagrams.

Oil Tank Level Check

Check the engine oil level using the dipstick mounted on the oil filler cap. The oil filler cap (**Figure 9**) mounts onto the front-right corner of the transmission housing. **Figure 10** shows the filler cap and dipstick assembly.

1. Start and run the engine for approximately 10 minutes or until the engine has reached normal operating temperature. Then turn the engine off and allow the oil to settle in the tank.
2. Roll the bike on a level surface and park it on its jiffy stand.

CAUTION
Holding the bike straight up will result with an incorrect oil level reading.

3. Wipe the oil tank filler cap and the area around the cap with a clean rag. Then pull the filler cap and dipstick (**Figure 9**) out of the oil tank. Wipe the dipstick off with a clean rag and reinsert the filler cap all the way into the oil tank. Withdraw the filler cap again and check the oil level on the dipstick. The oil level is okay when it is above the ADD QUART mark on the dipstick (**Figure 11**). If the oil level is even with or below the ADD QUART mark, continue with Step 4. If the oil level is correct, go to Step 5.
4. To correct the oil level, add the recommended engine oil listed in **Table 3**.

CAUTION
Do not overfill the oil tank or the oil filler cap will pop out of the oil tank when the oil gets hot.

5. Check the O-ring (**Figure 12**) for cracks or other damage. Replace the O-ring if necessary.
6. Reinstall the oil filler cap.

Engine Oil and Filter Change

Table 1 lists the factory-recommended oil and filter change interval. This assumes that you operate the motorcycle in moderate climates. In extreme climates, change the oil more often. The time interval is more important than the mileage interval. This is because combustion acids, formed by gasoline and water vapor, will contaminate the oil even if you do not run the motorcycle for several months. If you operate your motorcycle under dusty conditions, the oil will get dirty more quickly. Under these condi-

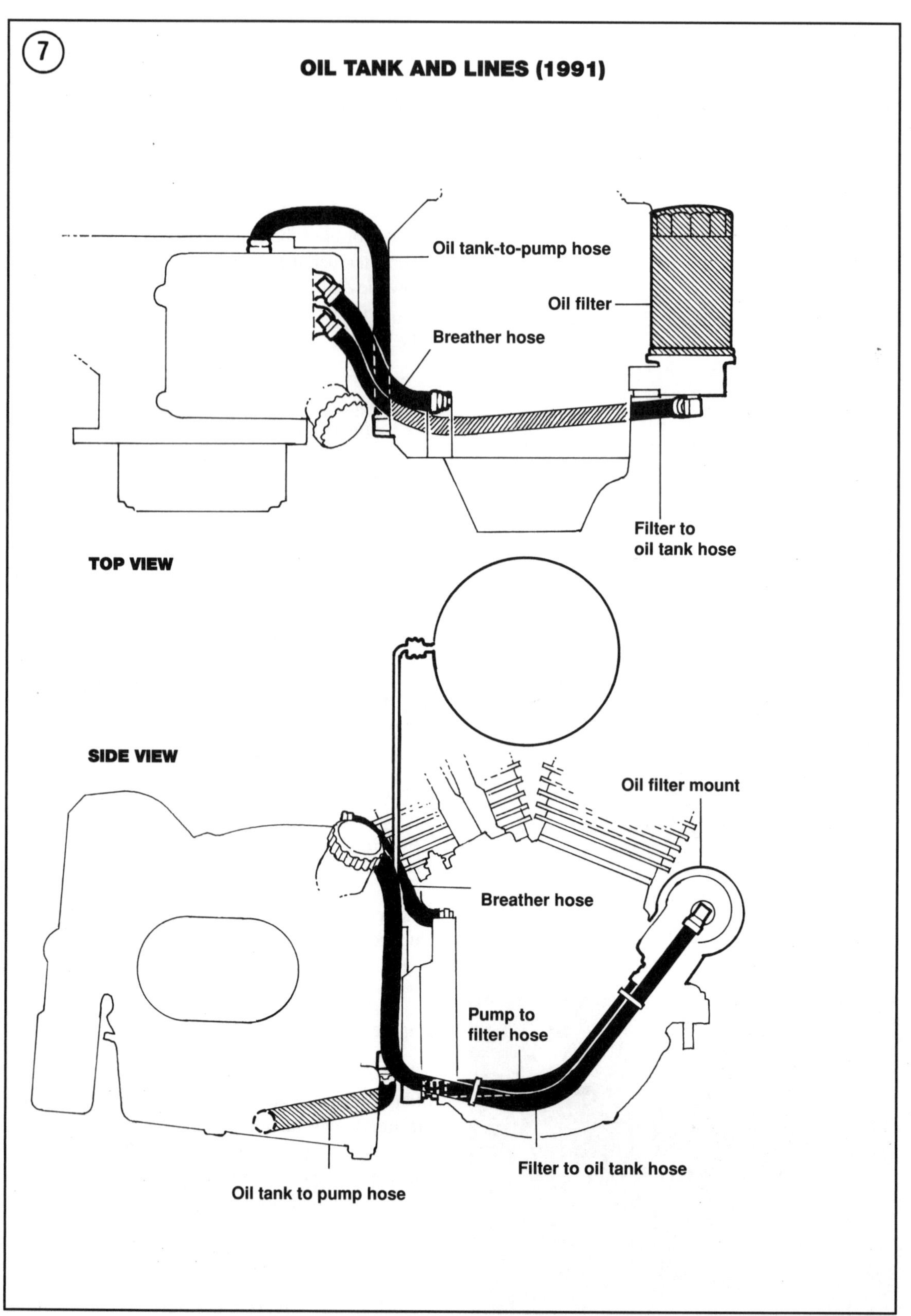
7
OIL TANK AND LINES (1991)
Oil tank-to-pump hose
Oil filter
Breather hose
Filter to
oil tank hose
TOP VIEW
SIDE VIEW
Oil filter mount
Breather hose
Pump to
filter hose
Filter to oil tank hose
Oil tank to pump hose

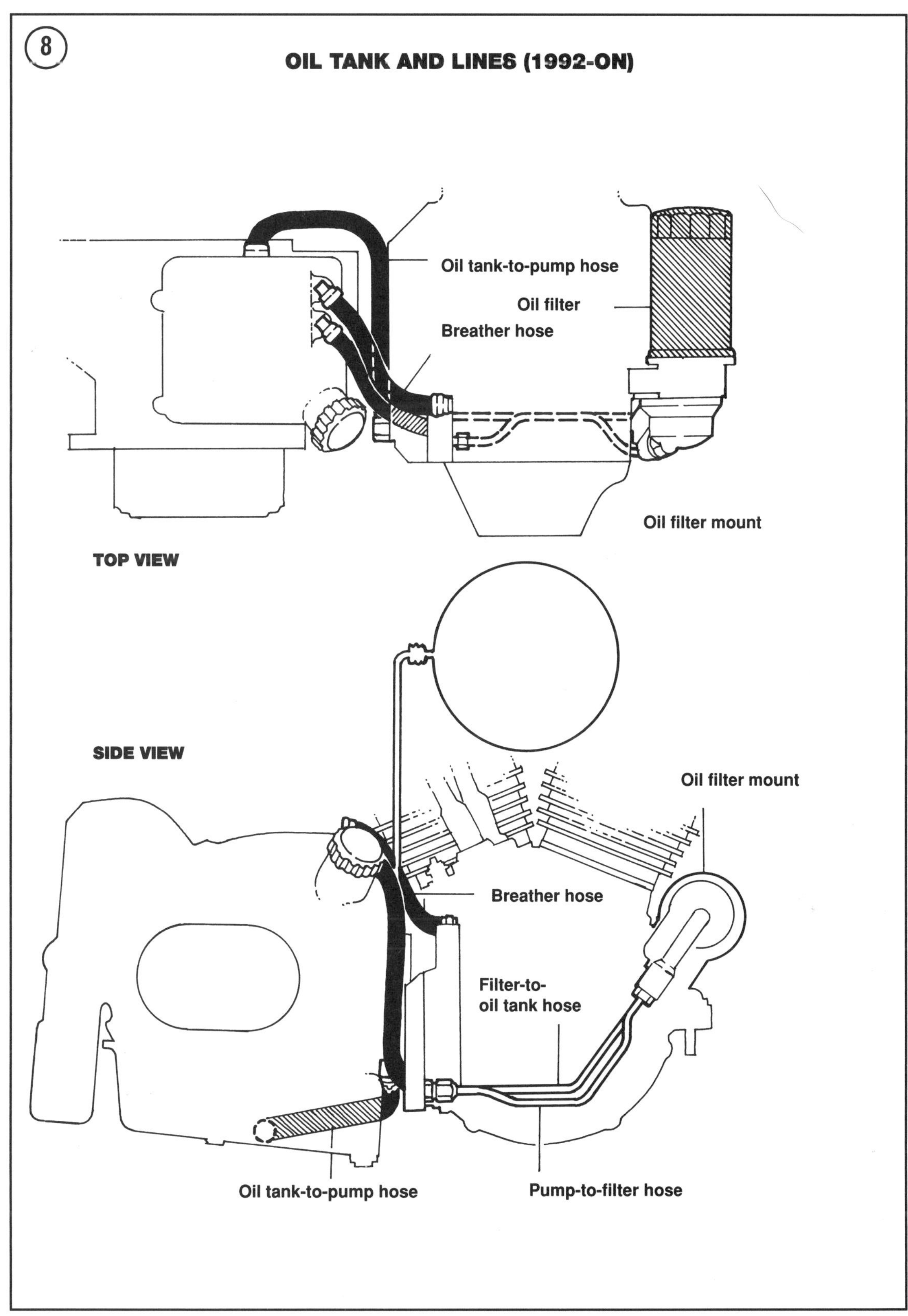
8
OIL TANK AND LINES (1992-ON)
Oil tank-to-pump hose
Oil filter
Breather hose
Oil filter mount
TOP VIEW
SIDE VIEW
Oil filter mount
Breather hose
Filter-to-
oil tank hose
Oil tank-to-pump hose
Pump-to-filter hose

tions, change the oil more frequently than recommended.

The American Petroleum Institute and the Society of Automotive Engineers (SAE) classify oil for motorcycle and automotive engines. Oil containers display these classifications on the top of the oil can or on the bottle label (**Figure 13**).

Use only a detergent oil with an API classification of SF or SG. Try to use the same brand of oil at each change. Refer to **Table 3** for correct oil viscosity to use under anticipated ambient temperatures (not engine oil temperature).

Never dispose of motor oil in the trash, on the ground or down a storm drain. Many service stations and oil retailers accept used oil for recycling. Do not combine othe fluids with motor oil for recycling. To locate a recycler, contract the American Petroleum Institute (API) at www.recycleoil.com.

1. Start and run the engine for approximately 10 minutes or until the engine has reached normal operating temperature. Then turn the engine off and allow the oil to settle in the tank. Support the bike so

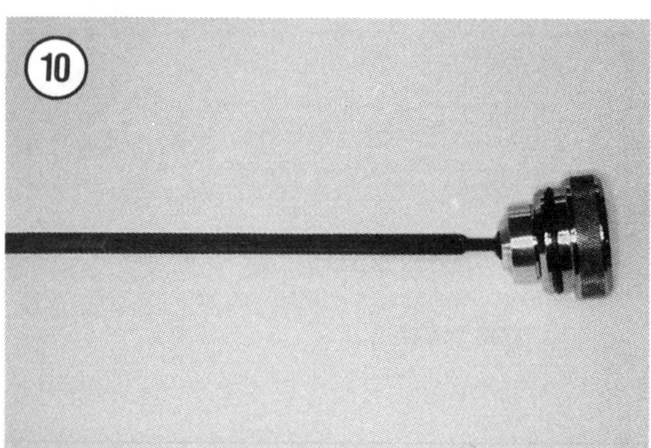

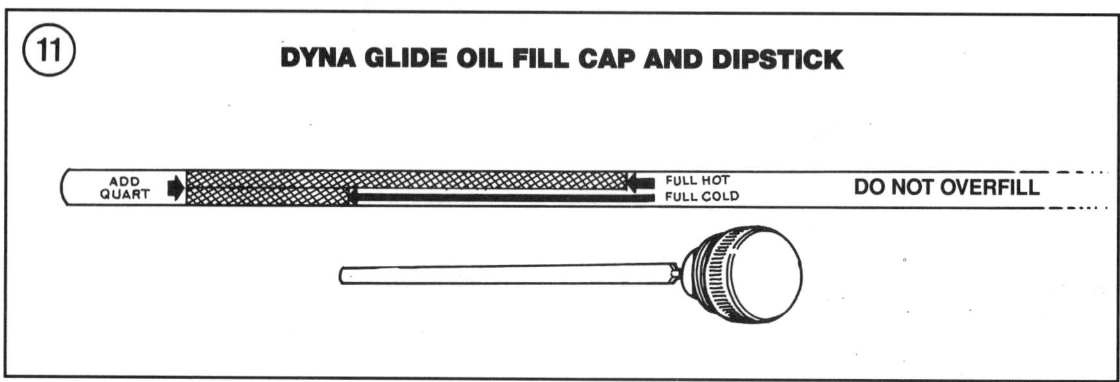

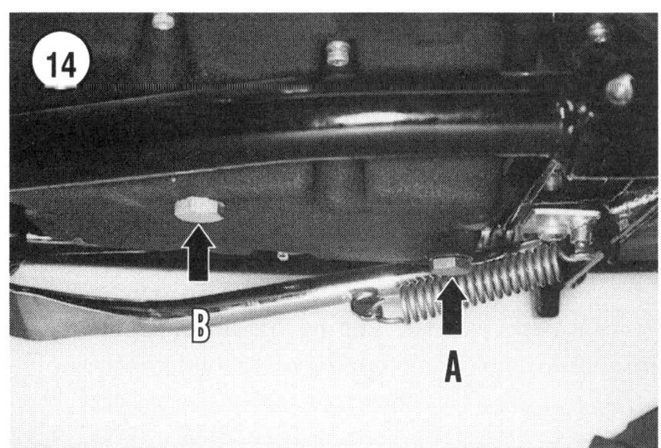

that the oil can drain completely.

NOTE
Before removing the oil tank cap, clean off all dirt and oil around it.

NOTE
The oil tank is equipped with 2 drain plugs. Make sure you remove the engine oil drain plug (A, ***Figure 14****) and not the transmission oil drain plug (B,* ***Figure 14****).*

2. Place a drain pan underneath the oil tank and remove the engine oil drain plug and O-ring (A, **Figure 14**).

3. To replace the oil filter, perform the following:

   a. Remove the oil filter (**Figure 15**) with a filter wrench.

   b. Pour any trapped oil out of the oil filter and discard it.

   c. Wipe the crankcase gasket surface with a clean, lint-free cloth.

   d. Coat the neoprene gasket (**Figure 16**) on the new filter with clean oil.

   e. Screw the oil filter onto its mount *by hand* until the filter gasket just touches the base; that is, until you feel the slightest resistance when turning the filter. Then tighten the filter *by hand* 3/4 to 1 turn more.

CAUTION
Do not overtighten and do not use a filter wrench or the filter may leak.

4. Replace the engine oil drain plug O-ring (**Figure 17**) if leaking or damaged.

5. Lubricate the O-ring with clean engine oil before installing it. Then screw in the drain plug and O-ring and tighten securely (A, **Figure 14**).

6. Clean the lifter oil screen as described in this section.

CAUTION
Do not overfill the oil tank in Step 7. ***Table 4*** *lists 2 oil tank refill capacities. If you add too much oil, the oil filler cap will pop out of the oil tank when the oil gets hot.*

7. Remove the oil filler cap (**Figure 9**) and add the correct viscosity (**Table 3**) and quantity (**Table 4**) of oil to the oil tank. Insert the oil filler cap into the oil tank.

NOTE
*After you add oil to the oil tank, the oil level will register above the FULL HOT dipstick mark (**Figure 11**) until the engine runs and the filter fills with oil. To obtain a correct reading after adding oil and installing a new oil filter, follow the procedure in Step 8.*

8. After changing the engine oil (and filter), check the oil level as follows:
   a. Start and run the engine for 1 minute, then shut it off.
   b. Check the oil level on the dipstick as described in this chapter.
   c. If the oil level is correct, it will register in the dipsticks safe operating level range. If so, do not top off or add oil to bring it to the FULL HOT level on the dipstick.
9. Check the oil filter and drain plug for leaks.

Lifter Oil Screen Cleaning

Clean the lifter oil screen at each oil change. The lifter oil screen (**Figure 18**) is mounted in the right crankcase above the oil pump.

1. Remove the lifter screen plug and O-ring (**Figure 19**) from the crankcase.
2. Remove the oil screen and spring (**Figure 20**).
3. Clean the screen and spring in solvent and dry with compressed air.
4. Replace the screen if damaged.
5. If removed, install the spring over the oil screen (**Figure 18**).
6. Install the oil screen (**Figure 20**) into the crankcase with its open side facing down.
7. Screw on the lifter screen plug and its O-ring and tighten to the torque specification in **Table 6**.

Transmission Oil Level Check

Table 1 lists the factory-recommended transmission oil inspection intervals. When checking the transmission oil level, do not allow any dirt or foreign matter to enter the housing opening.

1. Start and run the engine for approximately 10 minutes or until the engine has reached normal operating temperature. Park the bike on a level surface and have an assistant support it so that it is standing

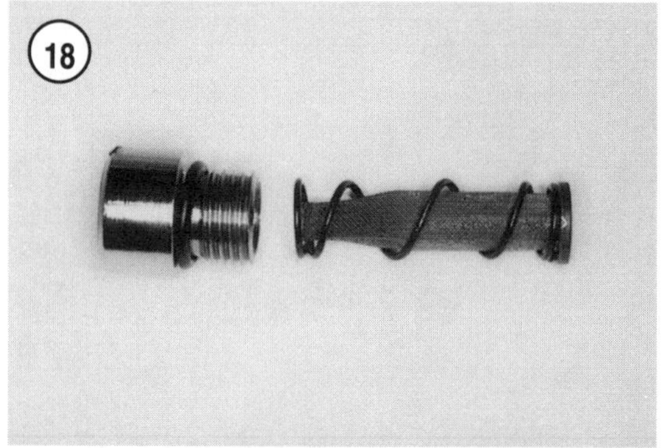

straight up. Turn the engine off and allow the oil to settle in the tank.

CAUTION
Do not check the oil level with the motorcycle supported on its jiffy stand or the reading will be incorrect.

2. Wipe the area around the transmission filler cap (**Figure 21**), then remove the filler cap and dipstick (**Figure 22**).

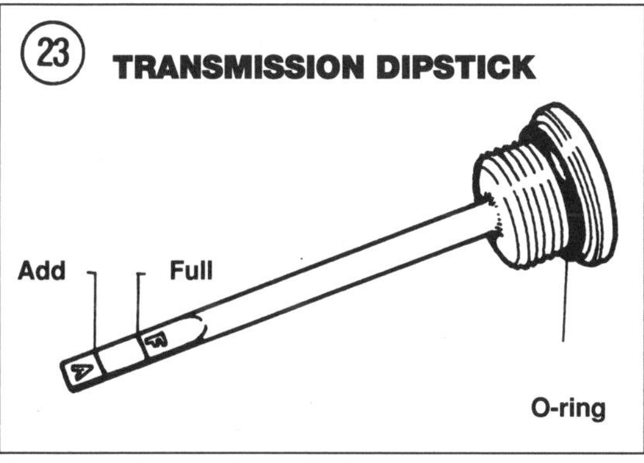

3. Wipe the dipstick and reinsert it back into the transmission housing; do not screw the cap in place. Rest it on the housing and then withdraw it. The oil level is correct when it registers between the 2 dipstick marks (**Figure 23**).
4. If the oil level is low, add the recommended type of oil listed in **Table 5**. Do not overfill.
5. Inspect the filler cap O-ring. Replace if worn or damaged.
6. Install the oil filler cap and its O-ring.
7. Wipe spilled oil off the transmission case.

3

Transmission Oil Change

Table 1 lists the factory-recommended transmission oil change intervals. To change the transmission oil, you need the following:

a. Drain pan.
b. Funnel.
c. Wrench for drain plug.
d. Transmission oil; see **Table 4** for quantity.

1. Start and run the engine for approximately 10 minutes or until the engine has reached normal operating temperature, then turn the engine off. Support the bike so that it is standing straight up. Do not support it on its jiffy stand.
2. Wipe the area around the filler cap and unscrew the filler cap and O-ring (**Figure 22**).

NOTE
*The oil tank is equipped with 2 drain plugs. Make sure you remove the transmission oil drain plug (B, **Figure 14**) and not the engine oil drain plug (A, **Figure 14**).*

3. Place a drain pan underneath the oil tank and remove the transmission oil drain plug and O-ring (B, **Figure 14**).

WARNING
If some oil spills onto the ground, wipe it up immediately so that it cannot contact the rear tire.

4. Check the drain plug O-ring (**Figure 17**) for damage and replace if necessary.
5. The drain plug is magnetic. Check the plug (**Figure 17**) for metal debris that may suggest transmission damage, then wipe the plug off. Replace the plug if damaged.

6. Screw in the transmission drain plug and its gasket (B, **Figure 14**) and tighten to the torque specification in **Table 6**.

7. Refill the transmission through the oil filler hole (**Figure 22**) with the recommended quantity (**Table 4**) and type (**Table 5**) transmission oil.

> *CAUTION*
> *Make sure you add transmission oil (**Figure 24**) into the transmission housing.*

8. Install the oil filler cap and O-ring (**Figure 21**) and tighten securely.

9. Remove the oil drain pan from underneath the transmission and dispose of the oil as outlined under *Engine Oil and Filter Change* in this chapter.

10. Ride the bike until the transmission oil reaches normal operating temperature. Then shut the engine off.

11. Check the transmission oil level as described in this chapter. Readjust the level if necessary.

Primary Chaincase Oil Level Check

The primary chaincase oil lubricates the clutch, primary chain and sprockets.

Table 1 lists the chaincase oil level check intervals. When checking the primary chaincase oil level, do not allow any dirt or foreign matter to enter the housing.

1. Park the bike on a level surface and support it so that it is standing straight up. Do not support it on its jiffy stand.

> *CAUTION*
> *Do not check the oil level with the motorcycle supported on its jiffy stand or the reading will be incorrect.*

2. Remove the clutch inspection cover and O-ring (**Figure 25**).

3. The oil level is correct if it is even with the bottom of the clutch opening or at the bottom of the clutch diaphragm spring (**Figure 26**).

4. If necessary, add Harley-Davidson Primary Chaincase Lubricant (or equivalent) through the opening (**Figure 26**) to correct the level.

5. Install the clutch inspection cover and its O-ring (**Figure 25**). Tighten the cover screws to the torque specification in **Table 6**.

Primary Chaincase Oil Replacement

Table 1 lists the factory-recommended primary chaincase lubricant replacement intervals. To change the primary chaincase lubricant, you need the following:

a. Drain pan.
b. Wrench for drain plug.
c. Primary chaincase oil; see **Table 4** for quantity.

1. Start and run the engine for approximately 10 minutes or until the engine has reached normal operating temperature and turn the engine off. Support the bike so that it is standing straight up. Do not support it with its jiffy stand.
2. Place a drain pan under the chaincase and remove the drain plug (**Figure 27**).
3. Allow the oil to drain for at least 10 minutes.
4. Reinstall the drain plug, making sure you do not overtighten it.

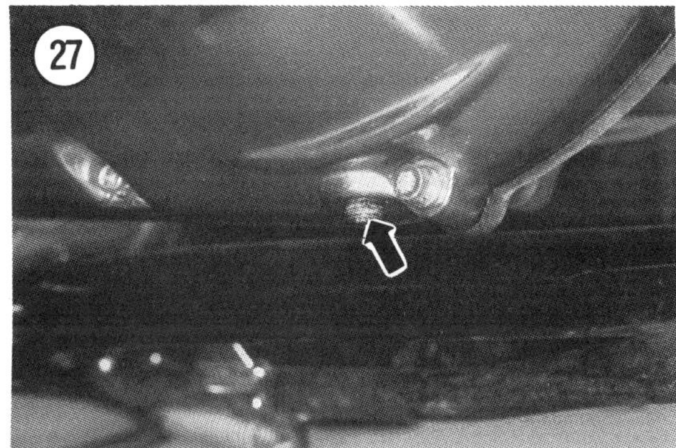

5. Remove the clutch inspection cover and O-ring (**Figure 25**)
6. Refill the primary chaincase through the clutch opening (**Figure 26**) with the recommended quantity (**Table 4**) and type (**Table 5**) primary chaincase oil. Do not overfill. The oil level must be even with the bottom of the clutch opening or at the bottom of the clutch diaphragm spring (**Figure 26**).

CAUTION
*Make sure you add primary chaincase oil (**Figure 28**), not engine or transmission oil, into the chaincase.*

7. Install the clutch inspection cover and its O-ring (**Figure 25**). Tighten the cover screws to the torque specification in **Table 6**.

Front Fork Oil Change

Table 1 lists the factory-recommended fork oil change intervals.
1. Place a drain pan beside one fork tube, then remove the drain screw and washer (**Figure 29**) from the slider.

CAUTION
Do not remove the Allen bolt installed in the bottom of the slider.

2. Straddle the bike and apply the front brake lever. Push down on the forks and release. Repeat to force as much oil out of the fork tube as possible.

CAUTION
Do not allow the fork oil to come in contact any of the brake components.

3. Replace the drain screw washer if damaged.
4. Install the drain screw and its washer. Tighten securely.
5. Repeat Steps 1-4 for the opposite fork tube.
6. Raise and secure the front end so that the front tire clears the ground. Make sure both fork tubes are fully extended.
7A. On fork caps with a center plug, remove the center plug and its gasket (**Figure 30**). Do not remove the fork cap.

NOTE
If the handlebars interfere with fork cap removal in Step 7B, remove the handlebars as described in Chapter Ten.

7B. On all other models, loosen the upper fork bracket pinch bolt (A, **Figure 31**). Then loosen and remove the fork cap (B, **Figure 31**).

8. Insert a small funnel into the fork tube opening.

NOTE
*If you disassembled the fork tube, refer to the "dry" specification to determine the correct amount of oil to refill the fork. Otherwise, refer to the "wet" specification. See **Table** 7.*

9. Fill the fork tube with the correct viscosity and quantity of fork oil. Refer to **Table 5** and **Table 7**. Remove the small funnel.

10. Replace the center plug gasket or fork cap O-ring if damaged.

11A. Screw on the center plug and its gasket (**Figure 30**) and tighten securely.

11B. If you removed the fork cap, install it as follows:

   a. Install the fork cap (B, **Figure 31**) and tighten securely.
   b. Tighten the upper fork bracket pinch bolt (A, **Figure 31**) to the torque specification in **Table 6**.

12. Repeat for the opposite fork tube.
13. Install all parts previously removed.
14. Road test the bike and check for leaks.

Control Cables

Lubricate the control cables at the intervals specified in **Table 1**. Also, inspect each cable for fraying and cable sheath damage. Replace damaged cables.

Lubricate the control cables using a suitable cable lubricant and lubricator tool.

CAUTION
Do not use chain lube to lubricate control cables.

CAUTION
The enrichener (choke) cable is designed to operate with a certain amount of cable resistance. Do not lubricate the enrichener cable or its conduit.

1A. Disconnect both clutch cable ends as described under *Clutch Cable Replacement* in Chapter Five.

1B. Disconnect the throttle cable ends as described under *Throttle and Idle Cable Replacement* in Chapter Seven.

2. Attach a lubricator tool to the cable following its manufacturer's instructions (**Figure 32**).

NOTE
Place a shop cloth at the end of the cable to catch all excess lubricant.

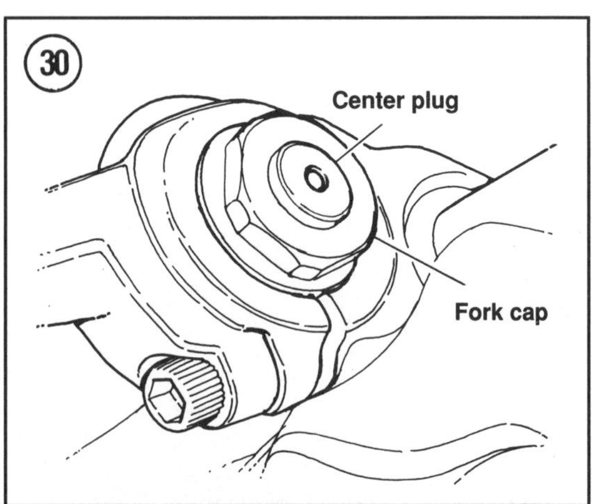

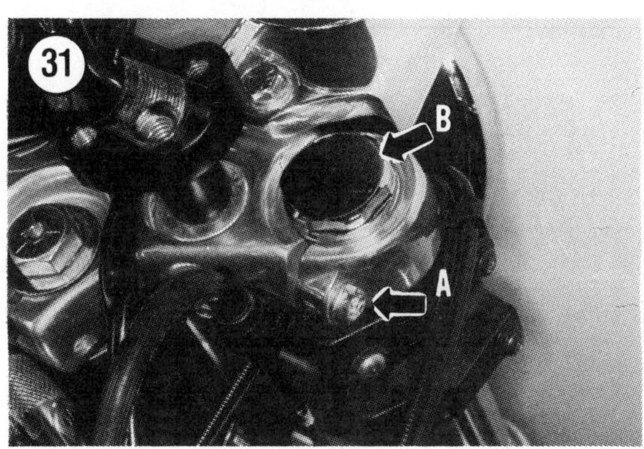

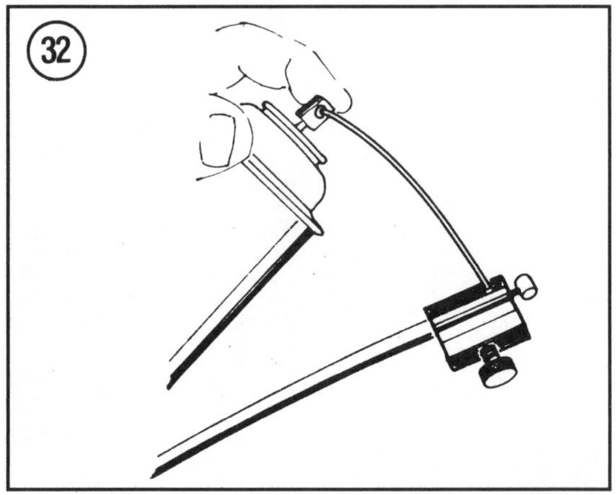

3. Insert the lubricant nozzle tube into the lubricator, press the button on the can and hold it down until the lubricant begins to flow out of the other end of the cable. If the lubricant squirts out from around the lubricator, you have not clamped it to the cable properly. Loosen and reposition the cable lubricator.

NOTE
If the lubricant does not flow out of the other end of the cable, check the cable for fraying, bending or other damage. Replace damaged cables.

4. Remove the lubricator tool and wipe off both ends of the cable.
5A. Reconnect both clutch cable ends as described under *Clutch Cable Replacement* in Chapter Five.
5B. Reconnect both the throttle cable ends as described under *Throttle and Idle Cable Replacement* in Chapter Seven.
6. Adjust the cables as described in this chapter.

Throttle Control Grip Lubrication

Table 1 lists the factory recommended throttle control grip lubrication intervals. To remove and install the throttle grip (**Figure 33**), refer to *Throttle and Idle Cable Replacement* in Chapter Seven. Lubricate the throttle control grip (where it contacts the handlebar) with graphite.

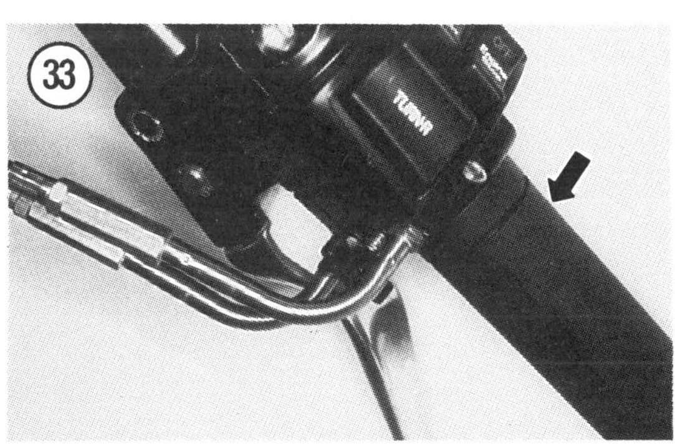

Speedometer Cable Lubrication (1991-1994)

Table 1 lists the factory recommended speedometer cable lubrication intervals.

1. Disconnect the speedometer cable from underneath the speedometer.
2. Pull the cable from the sheath.
3. If the grease is contaminated, thoroughly clean off all old grease.
4. Thoroughly coat the cable with multipurpose grease and reinstall into the sheath.
5. Make sure you seated the cable into the drive unit. If not, disconnect the cable from its lower connection and reattach it.

Steering Head Lubrication

Lubricate the steering head bearings at the intervals specified in **Table 1**. Complete lubrication requires removal of the steering head assembly. Refer to Chapter Ten.

Wheel Bearings

Lubricate the wheel bearings (**Figure 34**) at the intervals specified in **Table 1**. Complete lubrication requires removal of the wheel bearing assemblies. Refer to Chapter Nine.

Rear Brake Caliper Pin Bolts and Boots Lubrication and Inspection

Remove, inspect and lubricate the rear brake caliper pin bolts (**Figure 35**) at the intervals specified in **Table 1**. Remove any rust or corrosion from the pin bolt shoulders (**Figure 36**). While you have the pins out, inspect the pin boots (**Figure 37**), installed in the caliper mounting bracket, for cuts and other damage. Replace damaged pin boots. See Chapter Twelve for service procedures.

Front Brake Lever Pivot Pin Lubrication

Inspect the front brake lever pivot pin (**Figure 38**) for lubrication at the intervals specified in **Table 1**. If the pin is dry, lubricate it with a light-weight oil. To service the pivot pin, refer to *Front Master Cylinder* in Chapter Twelve.

Clutch Lever Pivot Pin Lubrication

Inspect the clutch lever pivot pin (**Figure 39**) for adequate lubrication at the intervals specified in **Table 1**. If the pin is dry, lubricate it with a light-weight oil. To service the pivot pin, refer to *Clutch Cable Replacement* in Chapter Five.

PERIODIC MAINTENANCE

This section describes the periodic inspection, adjustment and replacement of various operational items on your Dyna Glide. Perform the procedures at the intervals listed in **Table 1**, or earlier, if necessary.

Primary Chain Adjustment

As the primary chain stretches and wears, its free play movement increases. Excessive free play will cause premature chain and sprocket wear and increase chain noise.

1. Disconnect the negative battery cable from the battery.
2. Support the bike with the rear wheel off the ground.
3. Remove the gearshift lever (**Figure 40**).
4. Remove the left footpeg assembly.
5. Remove the primary chain inspection cover and gasket (**Figure 41**). Replace a leaking or damaged gasket.

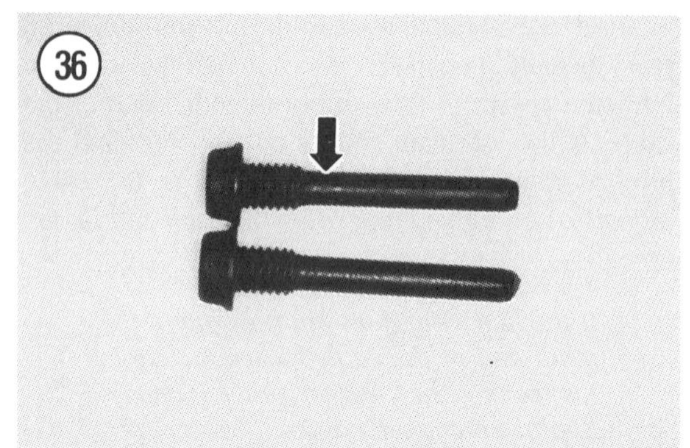

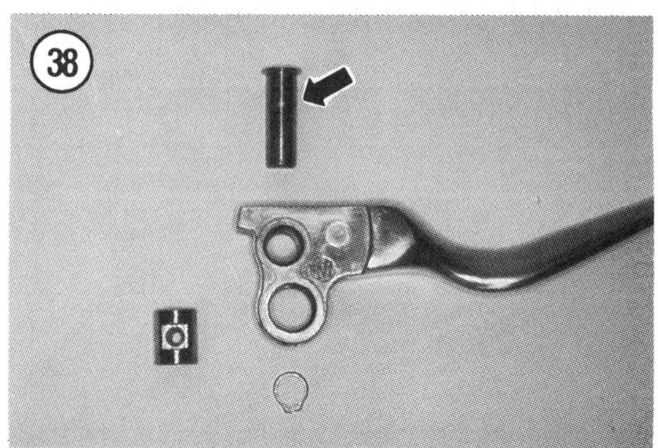

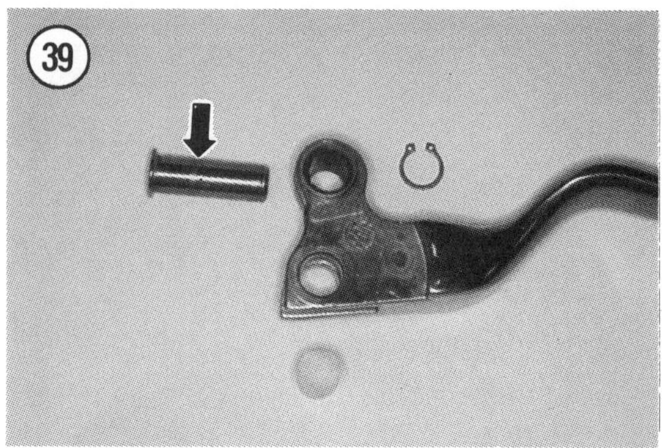

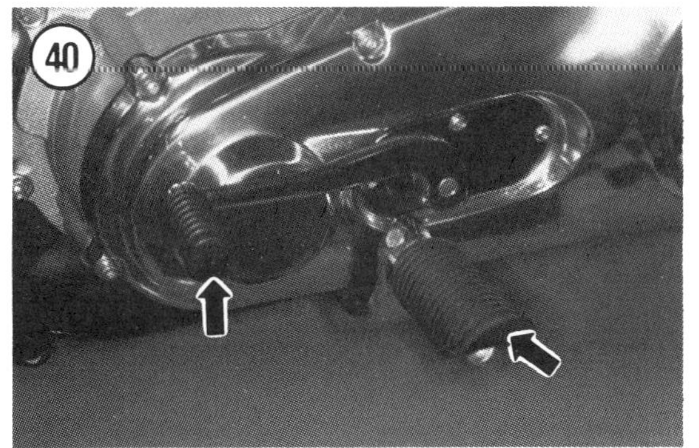

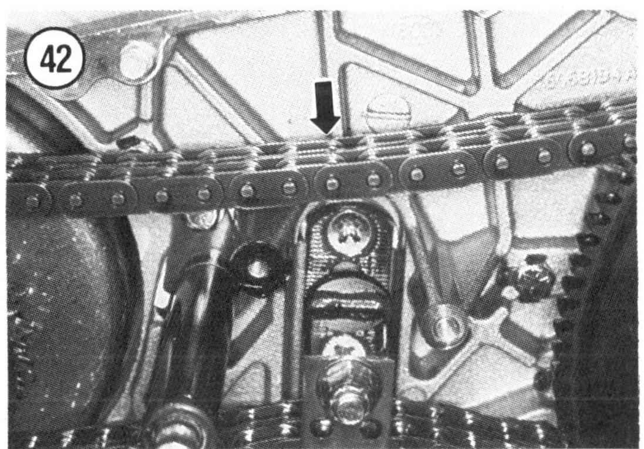

6. Turn the primary chain to find the tightest point on the chain. Measure chain free play at this point.
7. Check primary chain free play at the upper chain run midway between the sprockets (**Figure 42**). The correct primary chain free play specifications are:
   a. Cold engine: 5/8 to 7/8 in. (15.9-22.3 mm).
   b. Hot engine: 3/8 to 5/8 in. (9.5-15.9 mm).

If the primary chain free play is incorrect, continue with Step 8. If the free play is correct, go to Step 11.
8. Loosen the primary chain adjuster shoe nut (**Figure 43**).
9. Move the shoe assembly up or down to correct free play.
10. Tighten the primary chain adjuster shoe nut (**Figure 43**) to the torque specification in **Table 6**, then recheck free play.
11. Install the primary chain inspection cover and gasket (**Figure 41**). Tighten the cover screws to the torque specification in **Table 6**.
12. Install the shift lever and left footpeg assembly.

Final Drive Belt Deflection and Alignment

Inspect drive belt deflection and rear axle alignment at the intervals specified in **Table 1**. If the drive belt (**Figure 44**) is severely worn, or if it is wearing incorrectly, refer to Chapter Eleven for inspection and replacement procedures.

NOTE
Check drive belt deflection and axle alignment when the belt is cold.

1. Support the bike with the rear wheel off the ground. Then turn the rear wheel and check the drive belt for its tightest point. When you find this point,

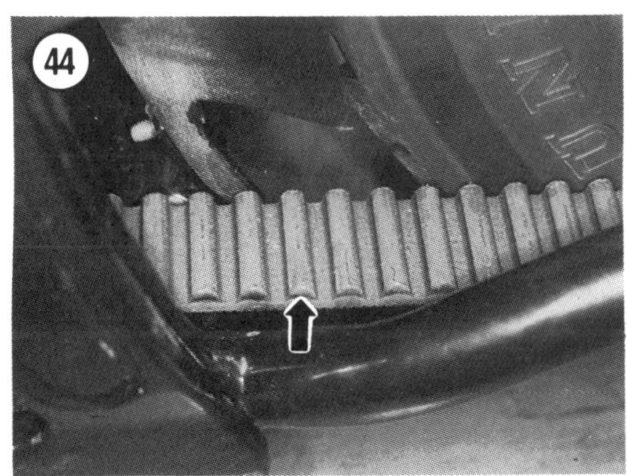

turn the wheel so that the belts tight spot is on the lower belt run, midway between the front and rear sprockets.

2. Position the bike so that both wheels are on the ground. When checking and adjusting drive belt deflection in the following steps, a rider must be sitting on the motorcycles seat facing in the normal riding position.

NOTE
Use the Harley-Davidson belt tension gauge (part No. HD-35381) or equivalent to apply pressure against the drive belt in Step 3.

3. Apply a force of 10 lb. (4.5 kg) to the middle of the lower belt strand while measuring the belts deflection measurement at the same point. See **Figure 45** and **Figure 46**. The correct belt deflection measurement is 5/16-3/8 in. (7.9-9.5 mm). If the belt deflection measurement is incorrect, continue with Step 4. If the deflection measurement is correct, go to Step 6.

4. Remove the cotter pin and loosen the rear axle nut (A, **Figure 47**).

5. Turn each axle adjuster (B, **Figure 47**) in equal amounts to adjust belt deflection while maintaining rear wheel alignment. Recheck drive belt deflection as described in Step 3.

6. When the drive belt deflection measurement is correct, check axle alignment as follows:
   a. To make the alignment tool shown in **Figure 48**, refer to *Special Tools* under *Vehicle Alignment* in Chapter Nine.
   b. Support the bike with the rear wheel off the ground.
   c. See **Figure 49**. Insert the alignment tool into one of the swing arm index holes. Then hold it parallel to the rear axle and slide the grommet along the tool until it aligns with the axle center point.
   d. Without repositioning the grommet, remove the tool and check the opposite side of the swing arm, comparing this position with the opposite side. Axle alignment is correct if the 2 measurements are identical or within 1/32 in. (0.8 mm) of each other.
   e. If the axle alignment is incorrect, adjust the axle with the axle adjusters (B, **Figure 47**) while maintaining the correct drive belt deflection measurement.

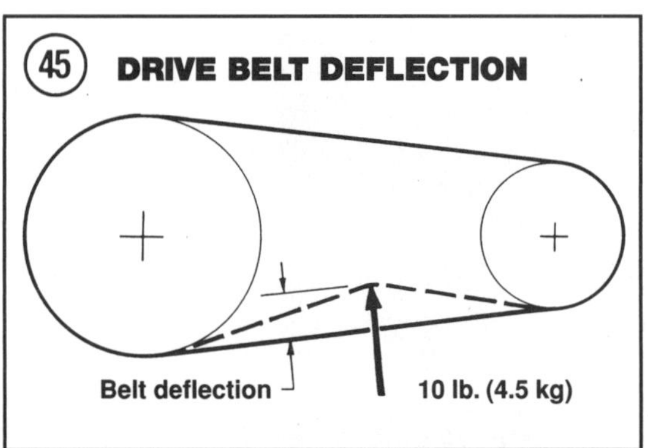

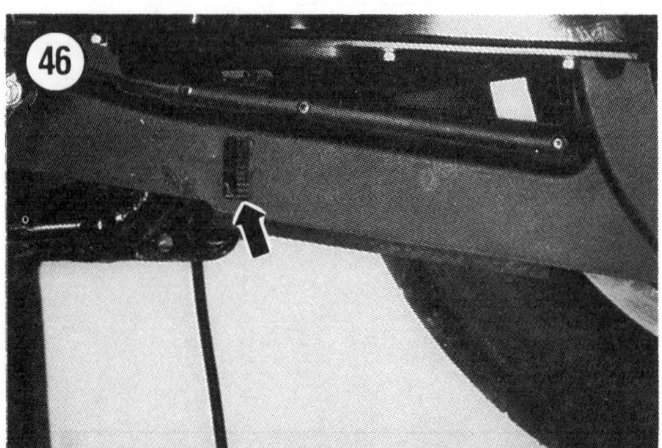

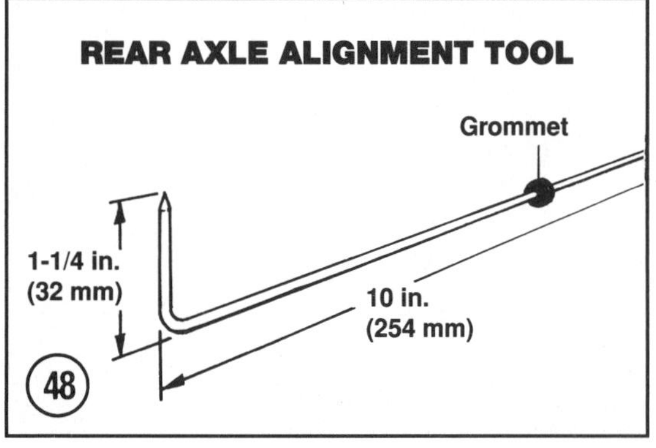

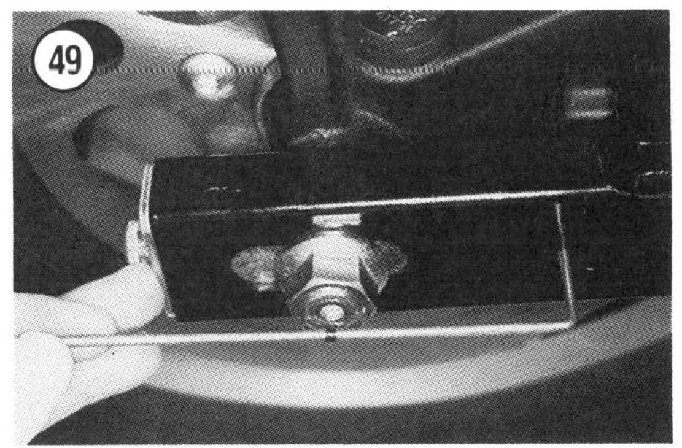
49

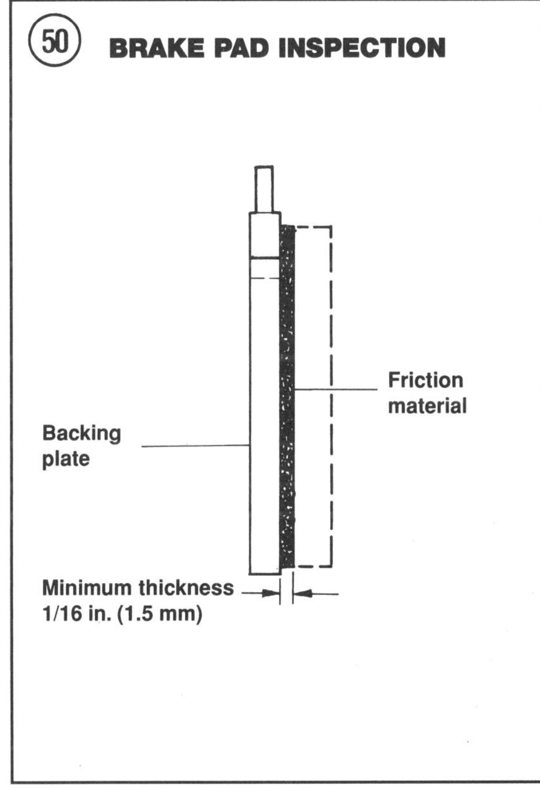

51

7. When the drive belt deflection and axle alignment adjustments are correct, tighten the rear axle nut (A, **Figure 47**) to the torque specification in **Table 6**.

8. Lower the rear wheel to the ground.

Front and Rear Brake Pad Inspection

1. Without removing the front or rear brake calipers, inspect the brake pads for damage.

2. Measure the thickness of each brake pad lining with a ruler. Replace the brake pad if its thickness is 1/16 in. (1.6 mm) or less (**Figure 50**) or if it is damaged. Replace the brake pads as described in Chapter Twelve.

Disc Brake Fluid Level

1A. *Front brake:* Turn the handlebar to level the master cylinder. The brake fluid level is correct if you can see brake fluid through the inspection window on the side of the master cylinder reservoir (**Figure 51**).

1B. *Rear brake:* Support the bike so that the rear master cylinder is level. The brake fluid level is correct if you can see brake fluid through the inspection window on the side of the master cylinder reservoir (**Figure 52**).

2. If the brake fluid level is low, perform the following:

   a. Wipe the master cylinder cover with a clean shop cloth.
   b. Remove the cover and lift the diaphragm or gasket out of the housing.
   c. Add fresh DOT 5 brake fluid to correct the level.

WARNING

Only use brake fluid clearly marked DOT 5 and specified for disc brakes. Others may vaporize and cause brake failure.

   d. Reinstall all parts.

NOTE

If the brake fluid level is low enough to allow air in the hydraulic system, bleed the brakes as described in Chapter Twelve.

Front and Rear Brake Disc Inspection

Visually inspect the front and rear brake discs (**Figure 53**) for scoring, cracks or other damage. Measure brake disc thickness and service the brake discs as described in Chapter Twelve.

Disc Brake Lines and Seals

Check the brake lines between the master cylinder and the brake caliper. If there is any leakage, tighten the connections and bleed the brakes as described in Chapter Twelve.

Disc Brake Fluid Change

Every time you remove the reservoir cap, a small amount of dirt and moisture enters the brake fluid. The same thing happens if a leak occurs or if any part of the hydraulic system is loosened or disconnected. Dirt can clog the system and cause unnecessary wear. Water in the fluid vaporizes at high temperatures, impairing the hydraulic action and reducing brake performance.

To change brake fluid, follow the brake bleeding procedure in Chapter Twelve. Continue adding new fluid to the master cylinder until the fluid leaving the calipers is clean and free of contaminants and air bubbles.

WARNING
Only use brake fluid clearly marked DOT 5. Others may vaporize and cause brake failure.

Front Disc Brake Adjustment

The front disc brake does not require periodic adjustment.

Rear Brake Adjustment (All Models)

WARNING
After adjusting the rear brake, make sure the brake is operating properly before riding the motorcycle.

FXDWG

The rear brake pedal on these models is not adjustable. When you properly assemble and mount the rear brake master cylinder on the bike, the brake pedal assembly is properly adjusted.

All other models

Adjusting the rear brake on these models consists of measuring and adjusting the brake pedal height. Because free play is built into the master cylinder, there is no free play adjustment. To check free play, push the rear brake pedal down while noticing its initial movement. The pedal will move a small distance before taking hold. This initial distance is free play. If you do not feel any free play, service the rear master cylinder as described in Chapter Twelve. If there is noticeable free play, go to Step 1.

1. Park the bike on level ground so it is sitting straight up.
2. Check that the brake pedal is in the at-rest position.
3. Determine brake pedal height as follows:

a. Place a ruler on the ground and measure the distance from the ground to the top of the right footpeg assembly (**Figure 54**). Record the height measurement.

b. Measure from the ground to the top of the brake pedal. Record the height measurement.

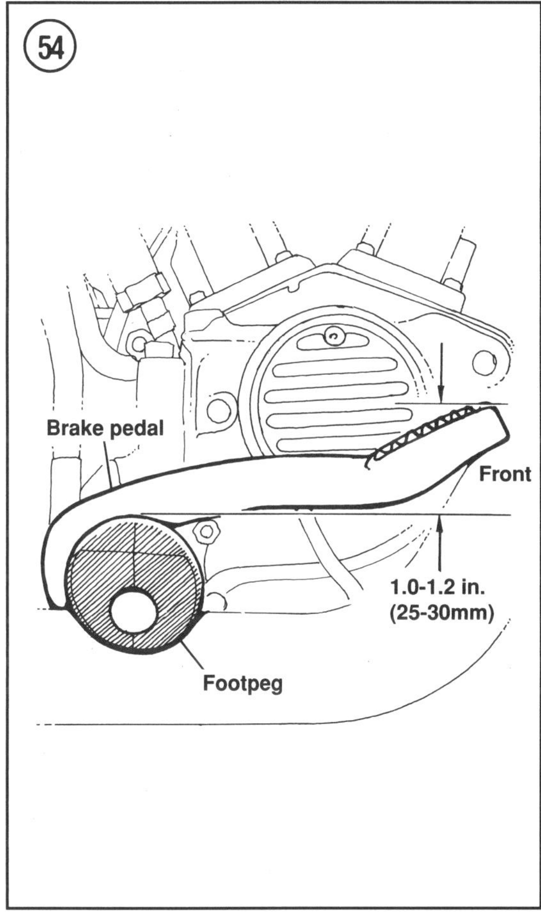

c. Subtract substep a from substep b. The difference is brake pedal height. The correct height is 1.0-1.2 in. (25-30 mm). If the brake pedal height distance is incorrect, continue with Step 4.

WARNING

When adjusting the rear master cylinder pushrod in Step 4, do not turn the pushrod so far that it disengages or almost disengages at either end. If this happens, the pushrod could disengage when you apply the rear brake. This could cause you to lose control of the motorcycle. If you are unsure about this adjustment or the position of the pushrod, take your bike to a dealership for rear brake inspection and adjustment.

4. Loosen the locknuts at the rear master cylinder pushrod and turn the pushrod to adjust the rear brake pedal height. Tighten the locknuts and recheck the measurement.
5. Support the bike with the rear wheel off the ground.
6. Turn the rear wheel while applying the rear brake. Check for brake drag or other abnormal conditions. Lower the rear wheel to the ground.

WARNING

Do not ride the motorcycle until you are sure the rear brake pedal and rear brake are operating correctly.

Clutch Adjustment

CAUTION

Because the clutch adjuster screw clearance increases with engine temperature, adjust the clutch when the engine is cold. If the clutch is adjusted when the engine is hot, insufficient pushrod clearance can cause the clutch to slip.

1. Remove the clutch inspection cover and O-ring (**Figure 55**).
2. Slide the cover away from the clutch cable adjuster. Then loosen the adjuster locknut (**Figure 56**) and turn the adjuster to provide maximum cable slack.
3. Check that the clutch cable seats squarely in its perch (**Figure 57**) at the handlebar.

4. Loosen the clutch adjusting screw locknut (**Figure 58**) and then turn the adjusting screw (**Figure 59**) clockwise (inward) until it is tight (no slack between the pushrods).

5. Turn the adjusting screw counterclockwise (outward) 1/2 to 1 turn. Then hold the adjusting screw (**Figure 59**)and tighten the locknut to the torque specification in **Table 6**.

6. Squeeze the clutch lever 3 times to set the clutch ball and ramp release mechanism (installed behind the transmission side cover).

7. Turn the clutch cable adjuster (**Figure 56**) to obtain a 1/16-1/8 in. (1.6-3.2 mm) gap at the clutch lever as shown in **Figure 60.** Pull on the clutch cable sheath (at the clutch lever) when adjusting the cable.

8. When the adjustment is correct, tighten the clutch cable locknut (**Figure 56**) and slide the rubber boot over the cable adjuster.

9. Install the clutch inspection cover and its O-ring (**Figure 55**). Tighten the cover screws to the torque specification in **Table 6**.

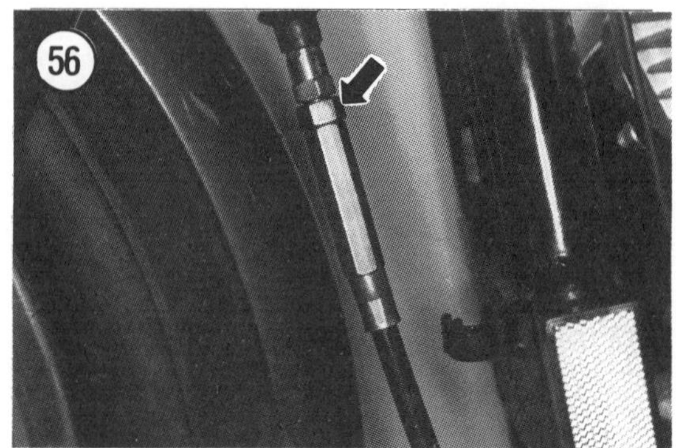

56

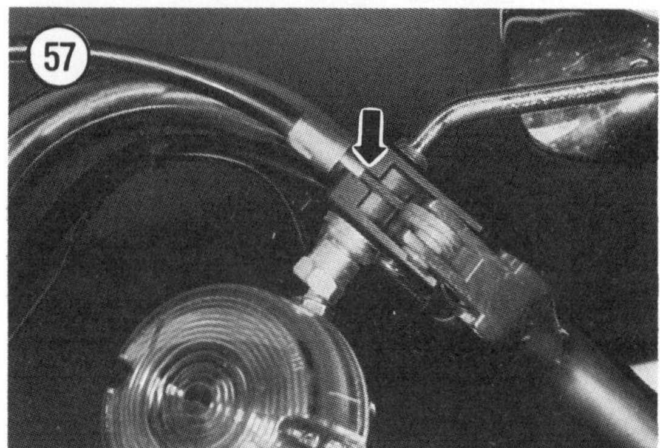

57

58

59

Throttle Cable(s)

Check the throttle cable from grip to carburetor. Make sure they have not been kinked or chafed. Replace it if necessary.

Make sure that the throttle grip rotates smoothly from fully closed to fully open. Check with the handlebar at center, full left and full right positions.

Throttle Cable Adjustment

Figure 61 and **Figure 62** identify the throttle cables:

a. Throttle cable: A, **Figure 61** and A, **Figure 62**.
b. Idle cable: B, **Figure 61** and B, **Figure 62**.

NOTE
You can also identify the throttle and idle cables by checking the size of the threads used on the cable's threaded adjusters. The throttle cable uses a 5/16-18 threaded adjuster. The idle cable uses a 1/4-20 threaded adjuster.

1. Loosen both cable adjuster locknuts (A and B, **Figure 61**), then turn the cable adjusters clockwise as far as possible to increase cable slack.

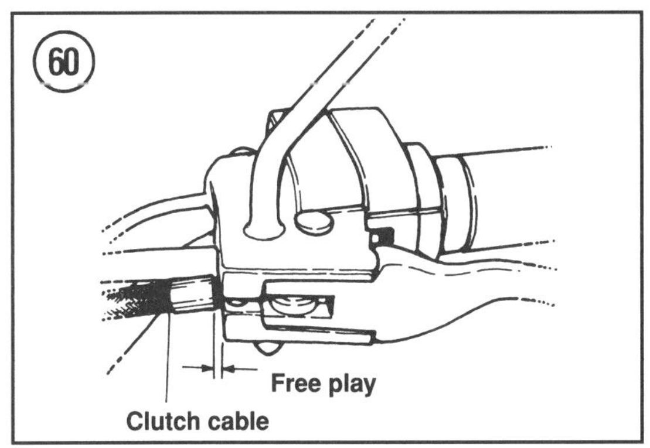

60

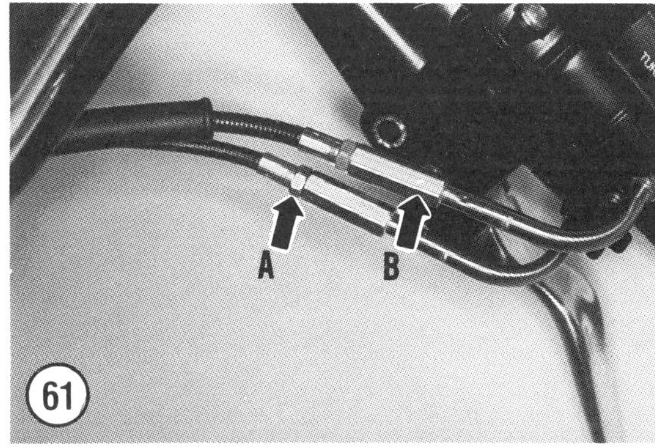

61

62

63

2. Turn the handlebars so that the front wheel points straight ahead. Then turn the throttle grip to open the throttle completely and hold it in this position.

3. Turn the throttle cable adjuster (A, **Figure 61**) counterclockwise until the throttle cam (A, **Figure 63**) stop just touches the stop boss (B, **Figure 63**) on the carburetor body. Then tighten the throttle cable adjuster locknut (A, **Figure 61**) and release the throttle grip.

4. Turn the front wheel all the way to the right (full lock).

5. Lengthen the idle cable adjuster (B, **Figure 61**) until the lower end of the idle cable just contacts the spring in the carburetor cable guide (C, **Figure 63**). Tighten the cable locknut (B, **Figure 61**).

6. Start the engine and accelerate it several times. Release the throttle and make sure engine speed returns to idle. If engine speed does not return to idle, loosen the idle cable adjuster locknut (B, **Figure 61**) and turn the cable adjuster (B, **Figure 61**) clockwise as required. Tighten the cable adjuster (B, **Figure 61**).

7. Start the engine and allow it to idle in NEUTRAL. Then turn the handlebar from side to side. Do not operate the throttle. If the engine speed increases when you turn the handlebar assembly, the throttle cables are routed incorrectly or damaged. Recheck cable routing and adjustment.

WARNING

Do not ride the motorcycle until you properly adjust the throttle cables. Likewise, the cables must not catch or pull when you turn the handlebars. Improper cable routing and adjustment can cause the throttle to stick open. This could cause you to lose control and crash. Recheck this adjustment before riding the bike.

Enrichener/Choke Cable Adjustment

The enrichener knob (**Figure 64**) must move from fully open to fully closed without any sign of binding. The knob must also stay in its fully closed or fully open position without creeping. If the knob does not stay in position, adjust tension on the cable by turning the knurled plastic nut behind the enrichener knob (**Figure 65**) as follows:

3

NOTE
The enrichener cable must have sufficient cable resistance to work properly. Do not lubricate the enrichener cable or its conduit.

1. Loosen the hex nut behind the mounting bracket. Then move the cable to free it from its mounting bracket slot.
2. Hold the cable across its flats with a wrench and turn the knurled plastic nut counterclockwise to reduce cable resistance. The knob must slide inward freely.
3. Turn the knurled plastic nut (**Figure 65**) clockwise to increase cable resistance. Continue adjustment until the knob remains stationary when pulled all the way out. The knob must move without any roughness or binding.
4. Reinstall the cable into the slot in its mounting bracket. Tighten the hex nut to secure the cable to the mounting bracket.

Fuel Shutoff Valve/Filter

Refer to Chapter Seven for fuel shutoff valve service.

Fuel Line Inspection

Inspect the fuel lines from the fuel tank to the carburetor. Replace leaking or damaged fuel lines. Make sure the small hose clamps are in place and holding securely. Check the hose fittings for looseness.

WARNING
A damaged or deteriorated fuel line can cause a fire or explosion if fuel spills onto a hot engine or exhaust pipe.

Exhaust System

Check all fittings for exhaust leakage. Do not forget the crossover pipe connections. Tighten all bolts and nuts. Replace any gaskets as necessary. See Chapter Seven for removal and installation procedures.

Air Filter Removal/Installation

A clogged air filter can decrease the efficiency and life of the engine. Never run the bike without the air filter installed; even minute particles of dust can cause severe internal engine wear.

Follow the service intervals in **Table 1**. If you live in a rural or agricultural area, service the air filter more often.

Refer to **Figure 66** or **Figure 67** when servicing the air filter.

1. Remove the air filter cover screw and washer (A, **Figure 68**) and remove the cover (B, **Figure 68**).

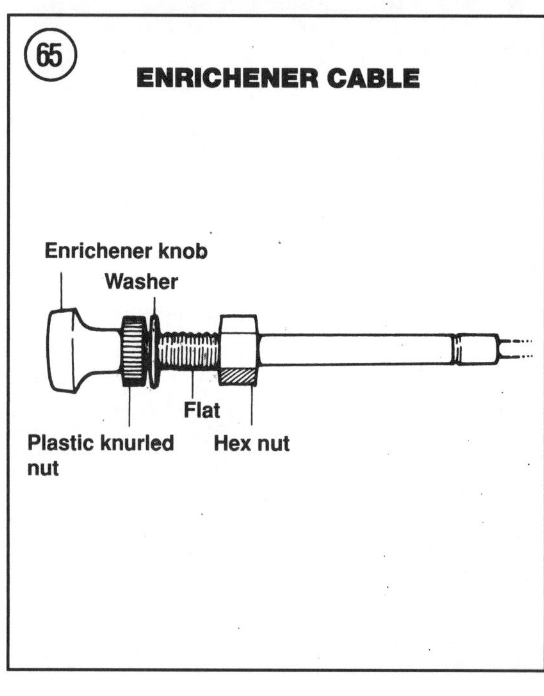

66

AIR FILTER
(1991-1992)

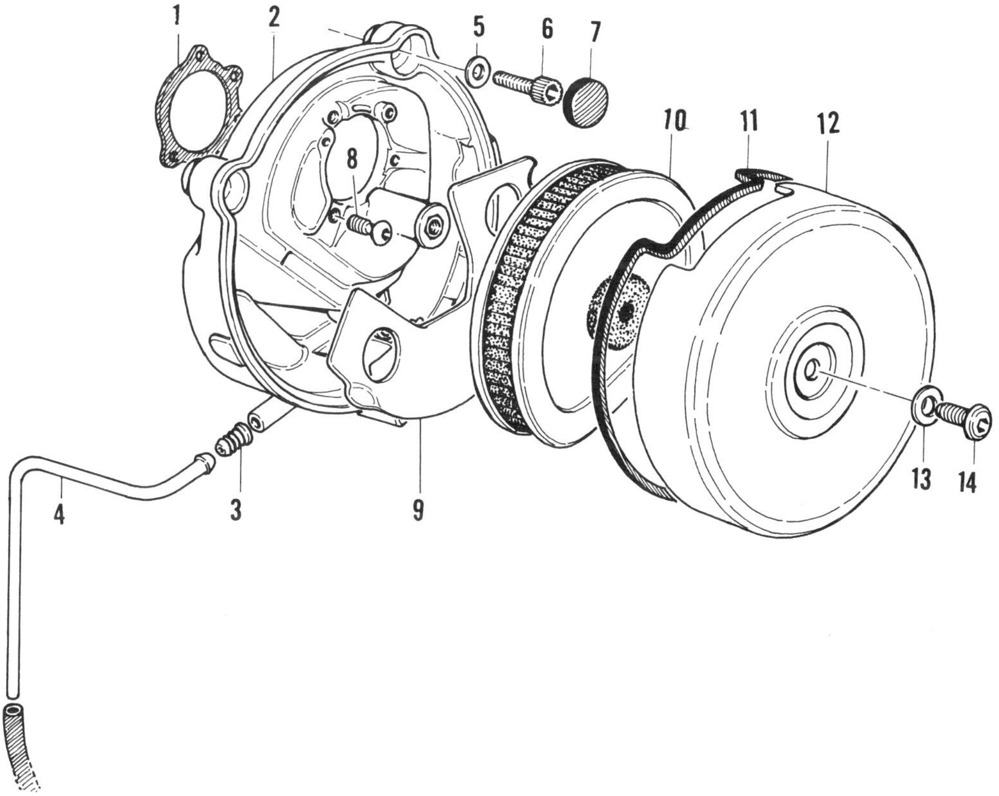

1. Gasket
2. Backplate
3. Fitting
4. Hose
5. Washer
6. Bolt
7. Plug
8. Bolt
9. Baffle
10. Air filter
11. Gasket
12. Cover
13. Washer
14. Screw

AIR FILTER (1993-ON)

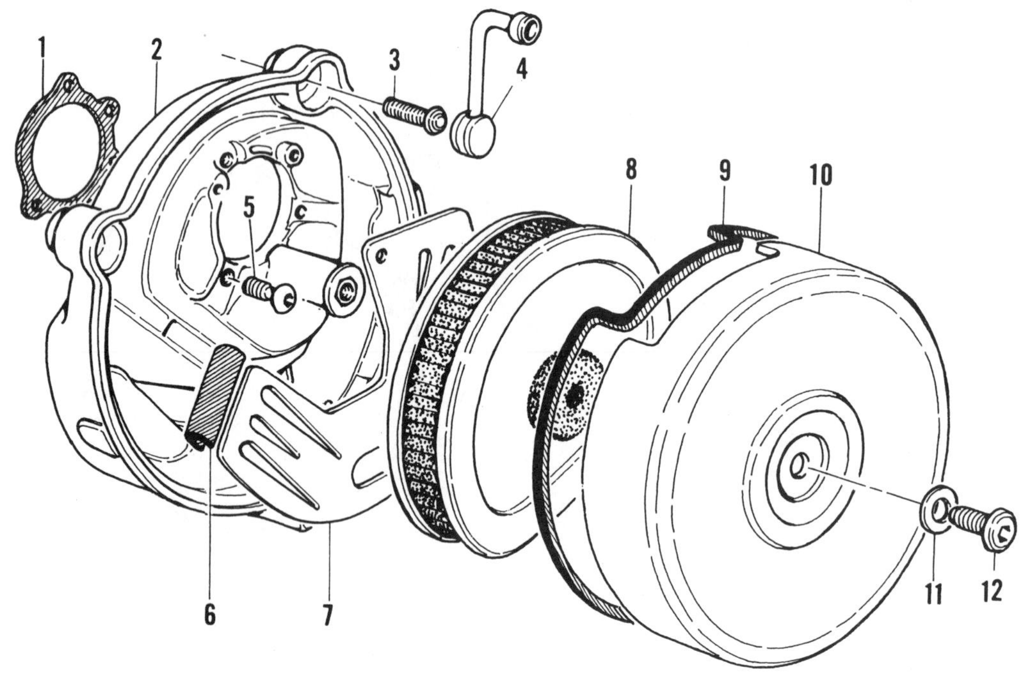

1. Gasket
2. Backplate
3. Bolt
4. Breather connector
5. Screw
6. Tab
7. Baffle
8. Air filter
9. Gasket
10. Cover
11. Washer
12. Screw

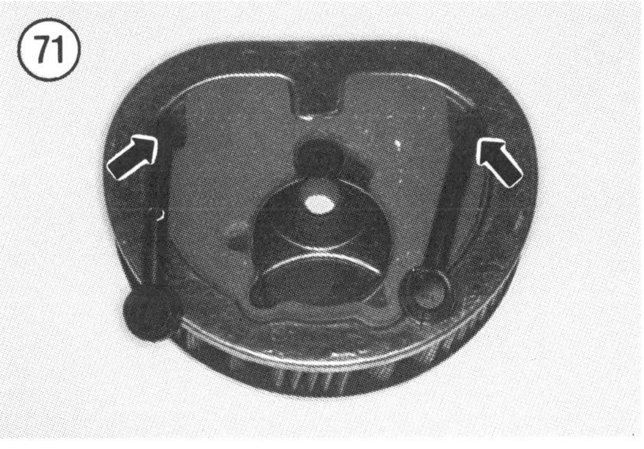

2A. On 1991-1992 models, remove the air filter (**Figure 69**).

2B. On 1993 and later models, disconnect the breather connectors (**Figure 70**), then remove the air filter.

3. Clean the air filter as described in this chapter. If you cannot satisfactorily clean the air filter, replace it.

4. To remove the air filter housing, refer to *Air Filter Backplate* in Chapter Seven.

5. Installation is the reverse of these steps, noting the following.

6. If removed, install the 2 breather connectors into the air filter element as shown in **Figure 71**.

7. Install the stock air filter so the 2 arrow marks on its outer filter plate (**Figure 72**) point down. See **Figure 69**.

8. Tighten the air filter cover screw to the torque specification in **Table 6**.

Air Filter Cleaning

A paper/wire mesh air filter element (**Figure 73**) is installed on all models.

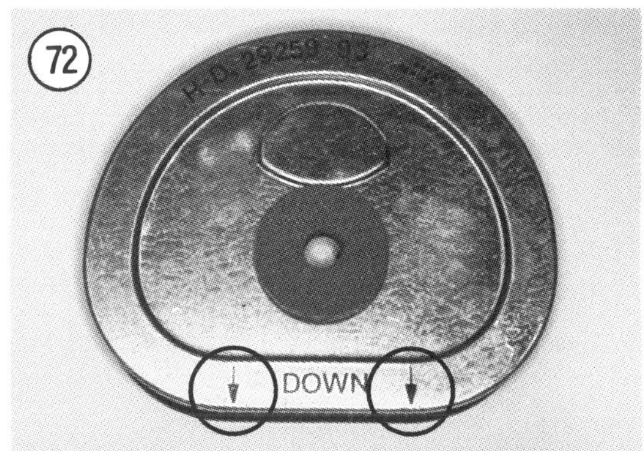

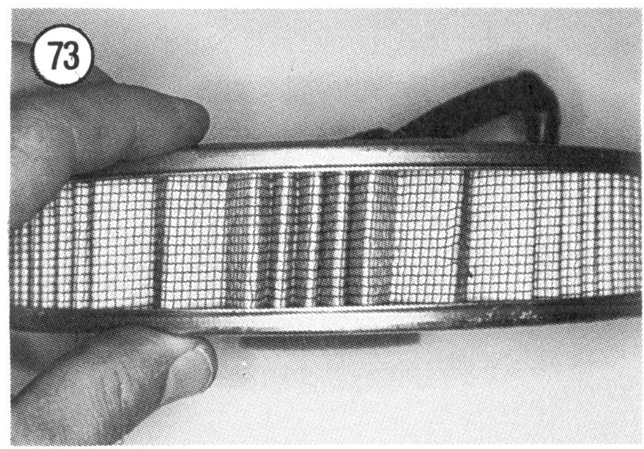

1. Remove the air filter as described in this chapter.
2. Replace the air filter if damaged.

WARNING
Never clean the air filter in gasoline or any type of low flash point solvent. The residual solvent or vapors left by these chemicals may cause a fire or explosion after the filter is reinstalled. Do not clean the air filter in any type of solvent.

3. Place the air filter in a pan filled with hot soapy water. Move the air filter back and forth to help dislodge trapped dirt. If the filter is saturated with oil or other chemicals, replace it.
4. Remove the air filter and hold it up to a strong light. Check the filter pores for dirt and oil. Repeat Step 3 until you can no longer see dirt and oil in the filter pores. If the air filter will not come clean, replace it.

CAUTION
*Do **not** use high air pressure to dry the filter, as this will damage it.*

CAUTION
In the next step, do not blow compressed air through the outer air filter element surface. Doing so can imbed dirt trapped on the outer filter surface deeper into the filter element, restricting air flow and damaging the air filter.

5. *Gently* apply compressed air through the inside of the air filter element to remove loosened dirt and dust trapped in the filter.
6. Inspect the filter. Replace if torn or damaged. Do *not* ride your Dyna Glide with a damaged filter as it may allow dirt to enter the engine. If you do, study Chapter Four to familiarize yourself with engine overhaul procedures.
7. Wipe the backplate with a clean shop rag.
8. Allow the filter to dry completely, then reinstall it as described in this chapter.

CAUTION
Air will not pass through a wet or damp filter. Make sure the filter is dry before installing it.

Steering Play

Check the steering head play at the intervals specified in **Table 1**. To adjust, refer to *Steering Play Adjustment* in Chapter Ten.

Rear Swing Arm Pivot Bolt

Check the rear swing arm pivot bolt (**Figure 74**) tightness at the intervals specified in **Table 1**. Refer to *Rear Swing Arm* in Chapter Eleven for procedures and the required tightening torque.

Rear Shock Absorbers

Check the rear shock absorbers (**Figure 75**) for oil leakage or damaged bushings. Check the shock absorber mounting bolts and nuts for tightness. Refer to *Shock Absorbers* in Chapter Eleven for the correct service procedures and tightening torques.

Engine Mounts and Stabilizer

Check the stabilizer and the engine and frame mounts for loose or damaged parts. Refer to Chapter Four for procedures and tightening torques.

Nuts, Bolts, and Other Fasteners

Constant vibration can loosen many fasteners on a motorcycle. Check the tightness of all fasteners, especially those on:

CAUTION
You must follow special procedures when tightening the cylinder head mounting bolts. To accurately check these bolts for tightness, refer to ***Cylinder Head Installation*** *in Chapter Four. Tightening these bolts incorrectly can cause an oil leak or cylinder head warpage.*

a. Engine mounting hardware.
b. Engine and primary covers.
c. Handlebar and front forks.
d. Gearshift lever.
e. Sprocket bolts and nuts.
f. Brake pedal and lever.
g. Exhaust system.
h. Lighting equipment.

Electrical Equipment and Switches

Check all of the electrical equipment and switches for proper operation.

TUNE-UP

A complete tune-up restores performance and power lost due to normal wear and deterioration of engine parts. Because engine wear occurs over a combined period of time and mileage, perform the engine tune-up every 5,000 miles (8,000 km). The bike will require more frequent tune-ups if operated primarily in stop-and-go traffic.

Replace the spark plugs at every other tune-up or if the electrodes show signs of wear, fouling or erosion. In addition, this is a good time to clean the air filter element. Have the new parts on hand before you begin.

Table 8 summarizes tune-up specifications.

Because different systems in an engine interact, perform the procedures in the following order:

a. Clean or replace the air filter element.
b. Check engine compression.
c. Check or replace the spark plugs.
d. Check the ignition timing.
e. Adjust carburetor idle speed.

To perform a tune-up on your Dyna Glide, you need the following tools:

a. Spark plug wrench.
b. Socket wrench and assorted sockets.
c. Compression gauge.
d. Spark plug wire feeler gauge and gapper tool.
e. Ignition timing light.

Air Filter

Clean the air filter element before performing other tune-up procedures. Refer to *Air Filter* in this chapter.

Compression Test

Check cylinder compression at every tune-up. Record the results and compare them to the next check.

The results, when properly interpreted can show general cylinder, piston ring and valve condition.

1. Warm the engine to normal operating temperature, then turn it off.
2. Remove the spark plugs (**Figure 76**) and reinstall them in their caps. Place the spark plugs against the cylinder to ground them.
3. Connect the compression tester to one cylinder following its manufacturer's instructions (**Figure 77**).

3

4. Place the throttle in the wide-open position. Make sure the choke (enrichener valve) is in the fully OFF position.
5. Crank the engine over until there is no further rise in pressure.
6. Record the reading and remove the tester.
7. Repeat Steps 3-6 for the other cylinder.

When interpreting the results, actual readings are not as important as the difference between the readings. **Table 8** lists the standard engine compression reading. Pressure must not vary between the cylinders by more than 10 percent. Greater differences indicate worn or broken rings, leaky or sticky valves, blown head gasket or a combination of all.

If compression readings do not differ between cylinders by more than 10 percent, the rings and valves are in good condition. A low reading (10 percent or more) on one cylinder indicates valve or ring trouble. To decide which, pour about a teaspoon of engine oil through the spark plug hole onto the top of the piston. Turn the engine over once to clear some of the excess oil, then take another compression test and record the reading. If the compression increases significantly, the valves are good but the rings are defective on that cylinder. If compression does not increase, the valves require servicing.

NOTE
An engine cannot be tuned to maximum performance with low compression.

8. Reinstall the spark plugs and reconnect their caps.

Cylinder Leakage Test

A cylinder leakage test can determine engine problems from leaking valves, blown head gaskets or broken, worn or stuck piston rings. A cylinder leakage test is performed by applying compressed air to the cylinder and then measuring the percent of leakage. This test requires a cylinder leakage tester and air compressor.

Follow the tester manufacturer's directions along with the following information when performing a cylinder leakage test.

1. Start and run the engine until it reaches normal operating temperature.
2. Remove the air filter assembly. Place the throttle in the wide-open position and the choke (enrichener valve) fully OFF.
3. Remove the ignition timing inspection plug from the crankcase (**Figure 78**).
4. Set the piston for the cylinder being tested to TDC on its compression stroke.
5. Remove the spark plug (**Figure 76**) for that cylinder.

NOTE
To prevent the engine from turning over when applying air pressure to the cylinder, shift the transmission into 5th gear and position the rear brake pedal to lock the rear brake.

6. Make a cylinder leakage test following the tester manufacturer's instructions. Listen for leaking air while noting the following:
   a. Air leaking through the exhaust pipe indicates a leaking exhaust valve.
   b. Air leaking through the carburetor indicates a leaking intake valve.

NOTE
Pushrods that are too long can also cause air to leak through the valves.

   c. Air leaking through the ignition timing inspection hole indicates worn or broken piston rings, a leaking cylinder head gasket or a worn piston.
7. Repeat for the other cylinder.
8. A cylinder with a leakdown of 12% or more requires further service.

Correct Spark Plug Heat Range

Spark plugs are available in various heat ranges that are hotter or colder than the spark plugs originally installed at the factory.

Select plugs in a heat range designed for the loads and temperature conditions under which the engine will operate. Using an incorrect heat range can cause piston seizure, scored cylinder walls or damaged piston crowns.

Overall, use a hotter plug for low speeds, low loads and low temperatures. Use a colder plug for high speeds, high engine loads and high temperatures.

The reach (length) of a plug is also important. A longer than normal plug could interfere with the valves and pistons, causing severe damage. A plug that is too short will cause hard starting and allow carbon to buildup on the exposed plug threads in the cylinder head. **Figure 79** compares long and short reach plugs.

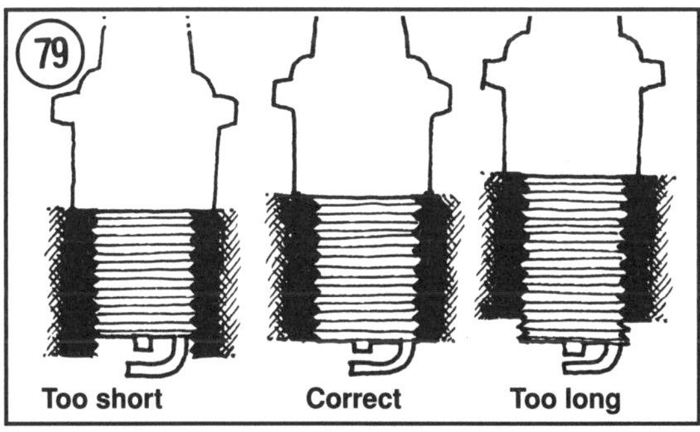

Table 8 lists the recommended heat range spark plugs.

Spark Plug Cleaning/Replacement

1. Grasp the spark plug leads as near to the plug as possible and pull them off the plugs.
2. Blow away any dirt that has accumulated around the base of the spark plugs (**Figure 76**).

CAUTION
Dirt that falls into the cylinder will increase engine wear.

NOTE
Mark the front and rear spark plugs after removing them. If one spark plug shows signs of abnormal engine operation, it is a good idea to know its cylinder position.

3. Remove the spark plugs with a spark plug wrench.

NOTE
If plugs are difficult to remove, apply penetrating oil such as WD-40 or Liquid Wrench around base of plugs and let it soak in about 10-20 minutes.

4. Inspect the spark plug carefully (**Figure 80**). Look for plugs with broken center porcelain, excessively eroded electrodes and excessive carbon or oil fouling (**Figure 81**). Replace worn or fouled spark plugs.

NOTE
For optimum performance, replace both spark plugs at the same time.

Spark Plug Gapping and Installation

Gap new spark plugs to ensure a reliable, consistent spark.

1. Screw on the small terminal that may be loose in the box (**Figure 82**).
2. Insert a wire gauge between the center and the side electrode of each plug (**Figure 83**). **Table 8** lists the correct spark plug gap. If the gap is correct, you will feel a slight drag as you pull the wire through. If there is no drag, or the gauge won't pass through,

81

SPARK PLUG CONDITIONS

NORMAL

GAP BRIDGED

CARBON FOULED

OVERHEATED

OIL FOULED

SUSTAINED PREIGNITION

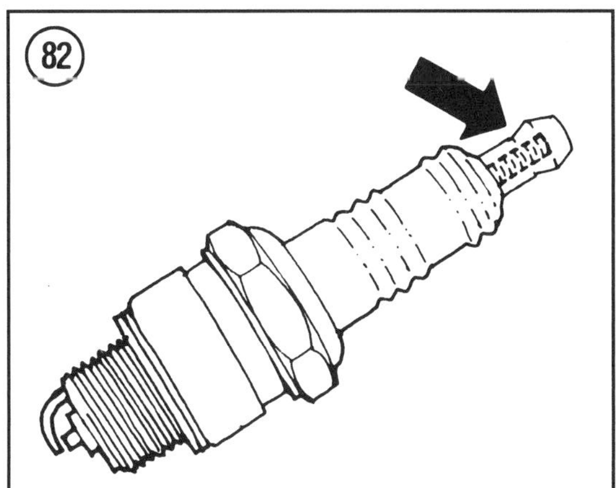

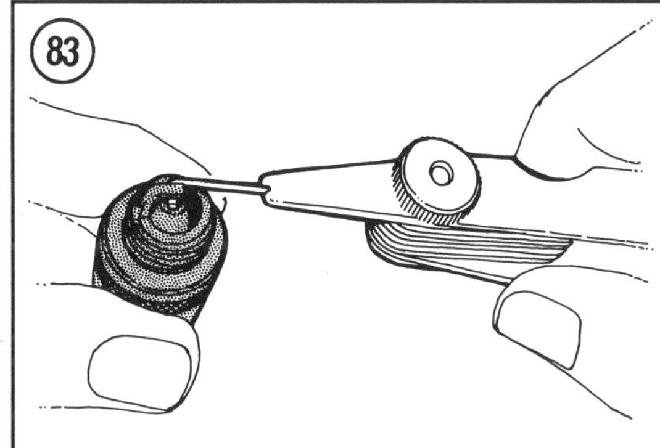

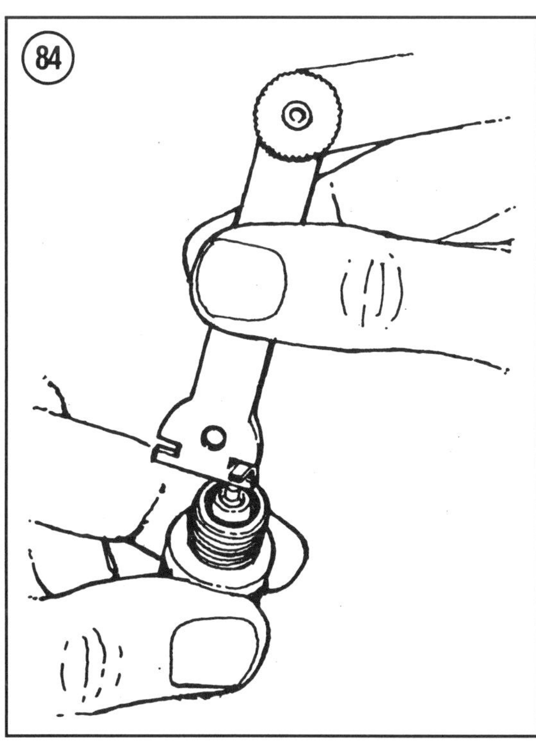

bend the side electrode *with the gapping tool* (**Figure 84**) to set the proper gap (**Table 8**).

3. Put a small drop of antiseize compound on the threads of each spark plug.

4. Screw each spark plug in by hand until it seats. If force is necessary, you may have cross-threaded the plug or damaged the cylinder head threads. Unscrew it and try again.

5. Tighten the spark plugs to the torque specification in **Table 6**. If you don't have a torque wrench, turn the plug an additional 1/4 to 1/2 turn after the gasket contacts the head. If you are reinstalling old spark plugs and are reusing the old gaskets, tighten the plug an additional 1/4 turn after the gasket contacts the cylinder head.

NOTE

Do not overtighten. This will only crush the gasket and destroy its sealing ability. Overtightening may also cause thread damage in the cylinder head.

6. Install each spark plug wire. Make sure it it is connected to the correct spark plug.

Reading Spark Plugs

You can determine engine and spark plug performance by reading the spark plugs. This information is more valid after performing the following steps.

1. Ride the bike a short distance at full throttle in third or fourth gear.

2. Turn off the kill switch before closing the throttle and simultaneously pull in clutch. Coast and brake to a stop. *Do not* downshift the transmission while stopping.

3. Remove one spark plug at a time and examine it. Compare the firing tip to **Figure 81** and the following:

   a. If the plug has a light tan or gray colored deposit and no abnormal gap wear or electrode erosion is evident, the plug and the engine are running properly.
   b. If the plug is covered with soft, dry soot deposits, the engine is running too rich.
   c. If the plug is brightly colored from overheating, the engine is running too lean.
   d. If the plug exhibits a black insulator tip, a damp and oily film over the firing end and a

carbon layer over the entire nose, it is oil fouled.

NOTE
If a spark plug is fouled, refer to Chapter Two for information on troubleshooting engine and fuel systems.

4. If the existing spark plug is okay, reinstall it. If not, replace it with a new one.
5. Repeat for the other spark plug. Replace both plugs as a set for maximum performance.

IGNITION SERVICE

Ignition Timing Inspection and Adjustment

1. Remove the plug from the timing hole on the left side of the engine (**Figure 78**). A clear plastic viewing plug is available from Harley-Davidson dealers that will contain oil spray when the engine is running. If you use a viewing plug, make sure it doesn't contact the flywheel.
2. Connect an inductive clamp-on timing light to the front cylinder spark plug wire following its manufacturer's instructions.
3. Check that the vacuum hose (**Figure 85**) is connected between the carburetor and the vacuum operated electric switch (VOES).
4. Start the engine and allow to run at 1,300-1,500 rpm. If necessary, adjust the engine speed as described in this chapter.
5. Aim the timing light at the timing inspection hole. At 1,300-1,500 rpm, the ignition timing is correct if the front cylinder's advance timing mark is centered in the inspection window as shown in **Figure 86** or **Figure 87**. Turn the engine off and note the following:
   a. If the ignition timing is incorrect, continue with Step 6.
   b. If the ignition timing is correct, go to Step 7.
6. If the ignition timing is incorrect, perform the following:
   a. Remove the sensor plate outer cover (**Figure 88**), gasket and inner cover as described under *Sensor Plate Removal* in Chapter Eight.
   b. Loosen the sensor plate screws (**Figure 89**) just enough to allow the plate to rotate.
   c. Start the engine and run it at 1,300-1,500 rpm.

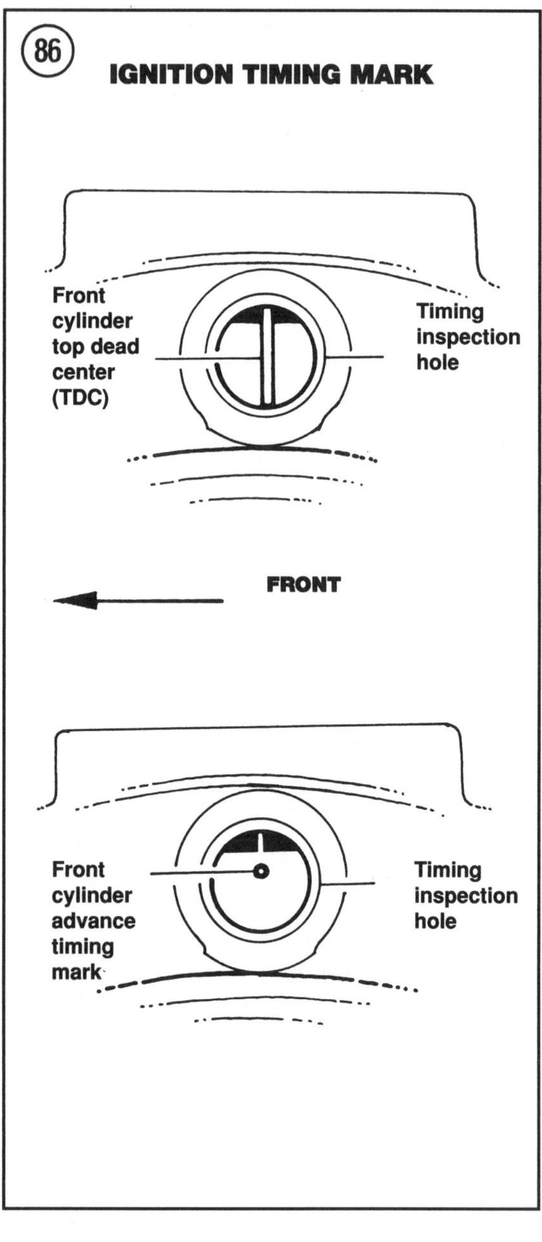

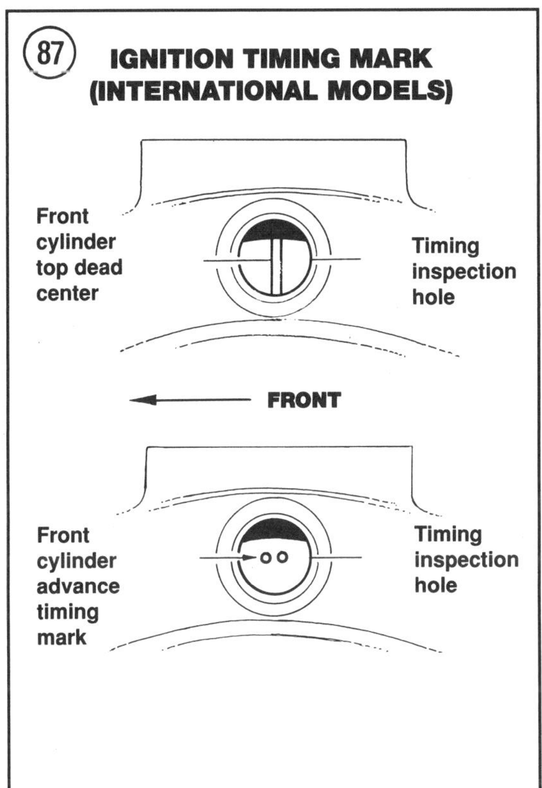

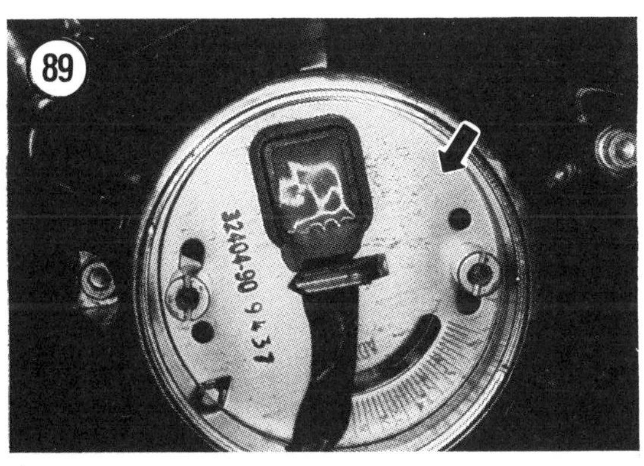

   d. Turn the sensor plate (**Figure 89**) until the advanced timing mark aligns with the center of the inspection window as shown in **Figure 86** or **Figure 87**. Tighten the sensor plate screws and recheck the ignition timing.
   e. Install the inner cover, gasket and outer cover (**Figure 88**) as described under *Sensor Plate Installation* in Chapter Eight.

7. Check the vacuum operated electric switch (VOES) as follows:
   a. Start the engine and allow to idle.
   b. Disconnect the vacuum hose (**Figure 85**) from the carburetor VOES port.
   c. Plug the carburetor VOES port with your finger. With the port blocked, the engine speed will decrease and the ignition timing will retard (the ignition timing mark is not visible in the inspection window). When you reconnect the vacuum hose, the engine speed will increase and the ignition timing will advance. Turn the engine off.
   d. If the engine failed to operate as described in sub-step c, check the VOES wire connection at the ignition module. Also, check for a loose or damaged VOES ground wire. If the wire and its connectors are okay, test the VOES switch as described under *Vacuum Operated Electric Switch Bench Testing* in Chapter Two.

CAUTION

Test the Vacuum Operated Electric Switch (VOES) at each tune-up. The VOES switch is non-adjustable. A faulty VOES switch will cause the engine to run roughly and misfire, cause spark knock or pinging, and engine overheating.

IDLE SPEED ADJUSTMENT

1. On models without a tachometer, connect a handheld tachometer to the engine following its manufacturers instructions.
2. Start the engine and warm it to normal operating temperature. Make sure the enrichener valve (**Figure 90**) is closed (pushed all the way in).
3. With the engine idling, compare the tachometer reading to the idle speed specification listed in **Table 8**. If the tachometer reading is incorrect, set the idle speed with the carburetor throttle stop screw (**Figure 91**).

4. The idle mixture is set and sealed at the factory and is not adjustable.
5. Accelerate the engine a couple of times and release the throttle. The idle speed must return to the speed set in Step 3. If necessary, readjust the idle speed by turning the throttle stop screw (**Figure 91**).
6. If installed, disconnect and remove the tachometer.

Table 1 PERIODIC MAINTENANCE

Pre-ride inspection
Check tires for correct tire pressure and for excessive wear or damage
Check engine oil level
Check throttle and choke (enrichener) cable operation
Check engine idle
Check drive belt tension
Check electrical switches and equipment for proper operation
Initial 500 miles (800 km); thereafter every 2,500 miles (4,000 km)
Check front and rear brake pads for wear or damage
Check front and rear brake disc for excessive wear or damage
Check throttle cable operation
Check choke (enrichener) cable operation
Check fuel valve, fuel line and all fittings for leaks or damage
Check engine idle speed; adjust if necessary
Check battery fluid level; refill with distilled water
Check battery condition; clean cables if required
Check electrical switches and equipment for proper operation
Check tires for correct tire pressure and for excessive wear or damage
Road test vehicle
Initial 500 miles (800 km); thereafter every 5,000 miles (8,000 km)
Change engine oil and filter
Change primary chaincase lubricant
Change transmission lubricant
Remove, inspect and clean tappet oil screen
Check condition of front and rear brake fluid
Check front and rear brake fluid level
Check rear brake pedal height adjustment
Lubricate the front brake and clutch lever pivot pin, if necessary
Lubricate clutch cable if necessary
Check rear swing arm pivot bolt tightness; retighten if necessary
Check rear shock absorbers for a leaking damper or other damage
Inspect and clean air filter element; replace if necessary
Inspect rear drive belt; adjust if necessary
Check primary chain adjustment; adjust if necessary
Check and adjust the clutch
Check the stabilizer link and engine mounts for looseness or damage
Check all fasteners for tightness; retighten if necessary**
(continued)

Table 1 PERIODIC MAINTENANCE (continued)

Initial 500 miles (800 km) and first 5,000 miles (8,000 km); thereafter every 10,000 miles (16,000 km)
  Check steering bearing adjustment
Initial 5,000 miles (8,000 km); thereafter every 10,000 miles (16,000 km)
  Inspect spark plugs
Every 5,000 miles (8,000 km)
  Check primary chaincase lubricant level
  Check transmission lubricant level
  Inspect and lubricate the rear brake caliper pin bolts
  Check the rear brake pedal adjustment; adjust if necessary
  Check the shifter linkage adjustment; adjust if necessary
  Lubricate the throttle grip sleeve
  Lubricate the speedometer cable (1991-1994)
  Check the vacuum operated electric switch (VOES)
  Check ignition timing
Every 10,000 miles (16,000 km)
  Replace spark plugs
  Replace the fork oil
  Inspect and lubricate the wheel bearings

* Consider this maintenance schedule a guide to general maintenance and lubrication intervals. Harder than normal use and exposure to mud, water, high humidity, etc., will naturally dictate more frequent attention to most maintenance items.

** Except cylinder head bolts. Cylinder head bolts must be tightened by following the procedure listed in Chapter Four. Improper tightening of the cylinder head bolts may cause cylinder head gasket damage and/or cylinder head leakage.

Table 2 TIRE PRESSURE

	PSi	kg/cm2
Up to 300 lb. (136 kg) load		
Front	30	2.1
Rear	36	2.5
Up to GVWR maximum load		
Front	30	2.1
Rear	40	2.8

Table 3 ENGINE OIL

Type	HD rating	Viscosity	Lowest ambient operating temperature
HD Multigrade	HD 240	SAE 10W/40	Below 40° F
HD Multigrade	HD 240	SAE 20W/50	Above 40° F
HD Regular Heavy	HD 240	SAE 50	Above 60° F
HD Extra Heavy	HD 240	SAE 60	Above 80° F

Table 4 ENGINE AND PRIMARY DRIVE/TRANSMISSION OIL CAPACITIES

Oil tank refill capacity	
With oil filter	3 U.S. qts. (2.8 L, 2.5 imp. qts.)
Without oil filter	2 U.S. qts. and 14 oz. (2.3 L)
Primary chaincase	30-36 U.S. oz. (890-1,065 ml, 31-37 imp. oz.)
Transmission	
1991-1994	16 U.S. oz. (473 ml, 16.7 imp. oz.)

Table 5 RECOMMENDED LUBRICANTS AND FLUIDS

Battery	Distilled water
Brake fluid	DOT 5
Front fork oil	HD Type E or equivalent
Fuel	87 pump octane or higher leaded or unleaded
Transmission	HD Sport Trans Fluid or equivalent
Primary chain case	HD Primary Chain Case Lubricant

Table 6 TIGHTENING TORQUES

	ft.-lb.	N•m
Air filter		
Backplate screws	3-5	4-7
Cover screw	3-5	4-7
Cylinder head screws	10-12	14-16
Clutch adjusting screw locknut	6-10	8-14
Clutch inspection cover screws	4-6	5-8
Primary chain inspection cover screws	9-10	12-14
Primary chain adjuster shoe nut	25	34
Rear axle nut	60-65	81-88
Spark plugs	18-22	24-30
Lifter screen plug	7-10	10-14
Transmission drain plug	14-21	19-28
Upper and lower fork bracket pinch bolts		
FXDWG	30-35	41-47
All other models	25-30	34-41

Table 7 FRONT FORK OIL CAPACITY

	Wet		Dry	
	U.S. oz.	ml	U.S. oz.	ml
1991-1992	9.2	272	10.2	302
1993-1994				
FXDL	9.2	272	10.2	302
FXDWG	10.2	302	11.2	331
1995-1998				
FXDWG	10.2	302	11.2	331
All other models	9.2	272	10.2	302

Table 8 TUNE-UP SPECIFICATIONS

Engine compression	90 psi (6.2 kg/cm^2)
Spark plugs	
Type	
Autolite	4265
Champion	RN12YC
Harley-Davidson	5R6A
Gap	0.038-0.043 in. (0.97-1.09 mm)
Ignition timing	
Range	0-35° BTDC
Start	0° BTDC
Idle speed	1,000-1,050 rpm

CHAPTER FOUR

ENGINE

All models are equipped with the V2 Evolution engine, an air-cooled 4-stroke, overhead-valve V-twin engine. The engine consists of three major assemblies: engine, crankcase and gearcase. Viewed from the engine's right side, engine rotation is clockwise.

Both cylinders fire once in 720° of crankshaft rotation. The rear cylinder fires 315° after the front cylinder. The front cylinder fires again in another 405°. Note that one cylinder is always on its exhaust stroke when the other fires on its compression stroke.

This chapter provides complete service and overhaul procedures, including information for disassembly, removal, inspection, service and engine reassembly.

Work on the engine requires considerable mechanical ability. You must carefully consider your own capabilities before attempting any operation involving major engine disassembly.

Much of the labor charge for dealer repairs involves the removal and disassembly of other parts to reach the defective component. Even if you decide not to overhaul the engine, it may be less expensive to perform some of the work yourself, then take the engine to a dealer. Since dealers have lengthy waiting lists for service (especially during the spring and summer seasons), this practice can reduce the time your unit is in the shop.

Table 1 lists general engine specifications. **Tables 1-5** are found at the end of the chapter.

SERVICE PRECAUTIONS

Before servicing the engine, note the following:

1. Read Chapter One of this manual. You will do a better job with this information fresh in your mind.
2. The text mentions the left and right side of the engine. This refers to the engine's mounting position in the frame, not as it sits on your workbench.
3. Always replace a worn or damaged fastener with one of the same size, type and torque requirements. Make sure to identify each bolt before replacing it. Lubricate bolt threads with engine oil, unless otherwise specified, before tightening. If **Table 4** does not list a torque specification, refer to the torque and fastener information in Chapter One.

NOTE
The engine is assembled with hardened fasteners. Do not install fasteners with a lower strength grade classification.

4. Use special tools where noted.
5. Store parts in boxes, plastic bags and containers (**Figure 1**). Use masking tape and a permanent, waterproof marking pen to label parts.
6. Use a vise with protective jaws to hold parts.
7. Use a press or special tools when force is required to remove and install parts. **Do not** try to pry, hammer or otherwise force them on or off.
8. Refer to **Table 4** for torque specifications.
9. Discard all O-rings and oil seals during disassembly. Apply a small amount of grease to the inner lips of each new oil seal to prevent damage when the engine is first started.
10. Keep a record of all shims and where they came from.

SPECIAL TOOLS

When a procedure requires a special tool, the text will list the tool's part number. Harley-Davidson tool numbers have a "HD" prefix. You can purchase special tools through Harley-Davidson and aftermarket dealers.

SERVICING ENGINE IN FRAME

Many components can be serviced while the engine is mounted in the frame:

a. Rocker arm cover.

NOTE
On some models you may have to lower the engine in the frame before you can remove both rocker arm covers.

b. Cylinder head.
c. Cylinder and pistons.
d. Camshaft.
e. Gearshift mechanism.
f. Clutch.
g. Transmission.
h. Carburetor.
i. Starter motor and gears.
j. Alternator and electrical systems.

ENGINE

This section describes removal and installation of the complete engine assembly.

WARNING
Because of the explosive and flammable conditions that exist around gasoline, observe the following precautions.

1. Disconnect the negative battery cable from the battery before doing any service work.
2. Gasoline dripping onto a hot engine component may cause a fire. Always allow the engine to cool completely before working on any fuel system component.
3. Wipe up spilled gasoline with dry rags. Then store the rags in a suitable metal container until they can be cleaned or disposed. Do not store gas or solvent soaked rags in an open container.
4. Do not service any fuel system component while near open flames, sparks or while anyone is smoking.
5. Always have a fire extinguisher nearby when working on the engine.

Removal

1. Thoroughly clean the engine exterior of dirt, oil and foreign material.
2. Before disassembly check engine compression and perform a leak down test as described in Chapter Three. Record the measurements for future reference.
3. Disconnect the negative battery cable from the battery.
4. Support the bike on a stand.

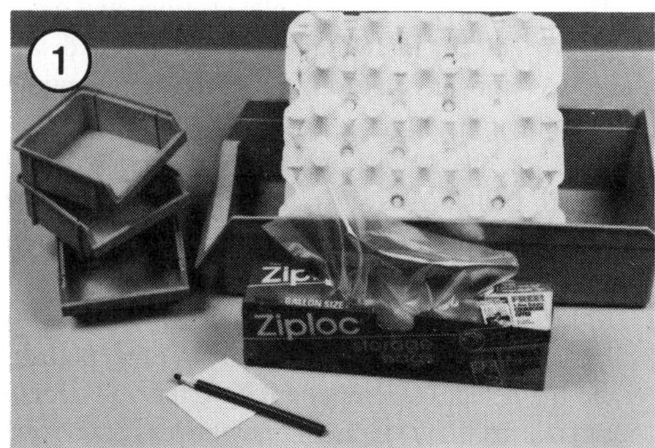

5. Remove the fuel tank as described in Chapter Eight.
6. Remove the air filter backplate as described in Chapter Seven.
7. Remove the carburetor as described in Chapter Seven.
8. Remove the right footpeg assembly.
9. Remove the rear brake pedal and master cylinder assembly as described in Chapter Twelve.
10. Remove the exhaust system as described in Chapter Seven.
11. Drain the engine oil as described in Chapter Three.
12. Disconnect the oil lines from the oil pump. Plug the oil lines to prevent dirt from entering the hoses. See **Figure 2** or **Figure 3**.
13. Disconnect the wire from the oil pressure switch (**Figure 4**).
14. Disconnect the alternator connector from the engine (**Figure 5**).
15. Disconnect the sensor plate electrical connector.
16. Disconnect the spark plug caps from the spark plugs.
17. Remove the inner primary chaincase as described in Chapter Five.
18. Remove the rotor as described in Chapter Eight.
19. Remove the clutch cable mounting bracket.
20. Remove the upper cylinder head mounting bracket (**Figure 6**).
21. Remove the front (**Figure 7**) and rear (**Figure 8**) engine mount bolts and washers.
22. Check the engine to make sure you have disconnected or removed all wiring, hoses and other related components.
23. Support the transmission housing with a jack or wooden blocks before removing the engine from the frame.

NOTE
Engine removal requires a minimum of 2 people or an engine lift.

24. Remove the engine from the right side of the frame.
25. Mount the engine in an engine stand (**Figure 9**) or take it to a workbench for further disassembly.
26. Service the front engine mount (**Figure 10**), if necessary.
27. Clean the front and rear engine mount bolts and washers in solvent and dry thoroughly.
28. Replace leaking or damaged oil hoses.

Installation

1. Install the engine from the right side of the frame.
2. Install the front (**Figure 7**) and rear (**Figure 8**) engine mount bolts and washers. Do not tighten the bolts at this time.
3. Install the stator and rotor as described in Chapter Eight.
4. Install the O-ring onto the engine crankcase shoulder (**Figure 11**).
5. If removed, install the starter jackshaft assembly and the inner primary housing as described under *Starter Jackshaft* in Chapter Five.

NOTE
*Before installing the coupling in Step 6, note the circlip (**Figure 12**) installed inside the coupling. The coupling side with the circlip closest to its end slides over the jackshaft.*

6. Install the coupling (**Figure 13**) onto the end of the starter jackshaft.
7. If removed, install the drive belt over the drive sprocket (**Figure 14**).
8. Wrap the mainshaft splines with tape.
9. Insert the shift shaft (**Figure 14**) through the collar when installing the inner primary housing.

CAUTION
The following steps describe how to align the engine and transmission with the inner primary housing. Improper alignment may cause premature primary chain wear and transmission damage.

10. Align the inner primary housing with the engine and transmission and install it. See **Figure 15**.
11. Apply a bead of RTV sealant around the 2 bottom inner primary housing bolt holes (**Figure 16**).
12. Install the inner primary housing bolts and washers. Install lockwashers (**Figure 17**) on the bolts installed inside the housing. Tighten the bolts finger-tight.
13. Tighten the engine mounting bolts in the following order:
   a. Tighten the rear engine mount bolts (**Figure 8**) to the torque specification in **Table 4**.
   b. Tighten the front engine mount bolts (**Figure 7**) to the torque specification in **Table 4**.

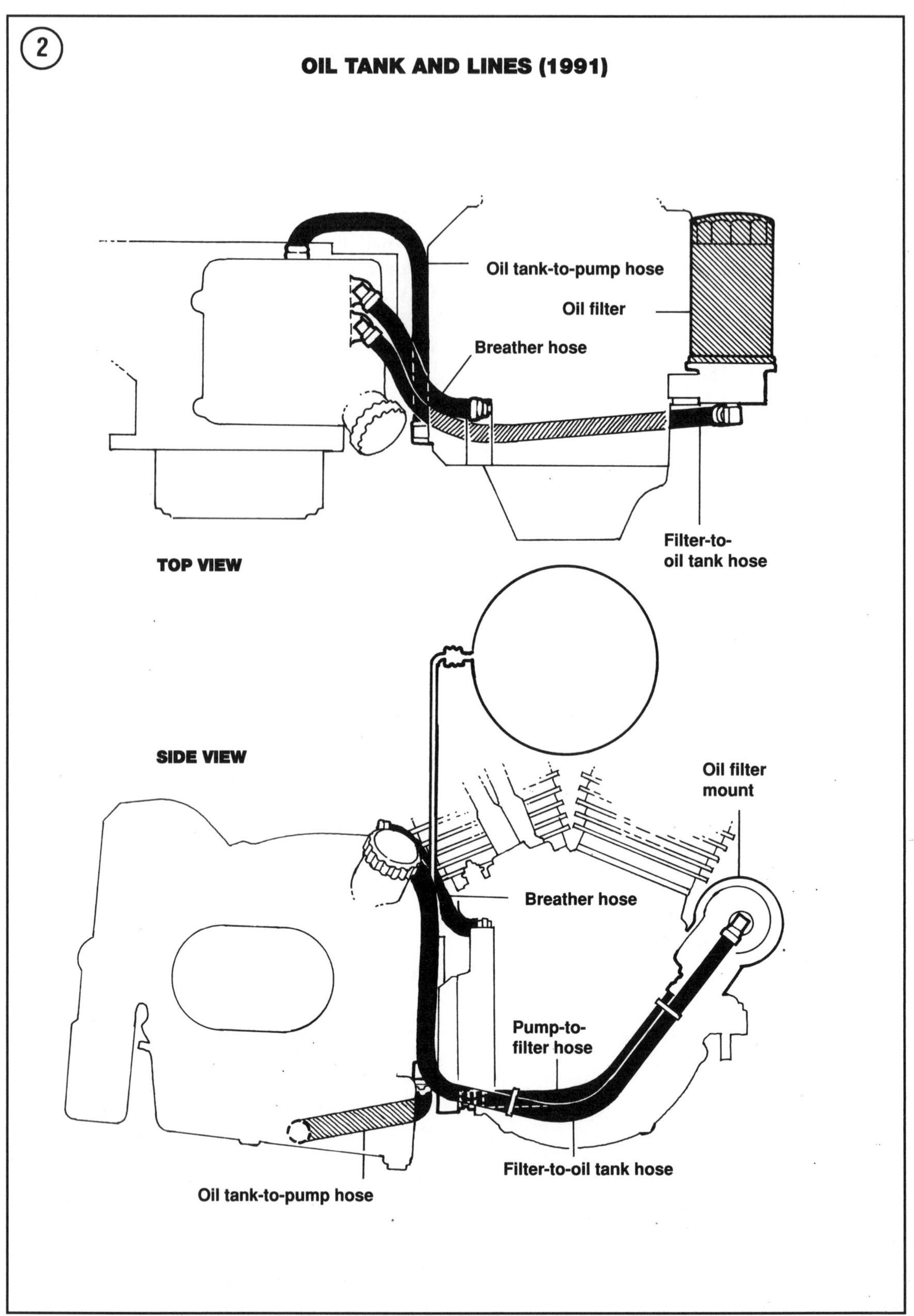
2
OIL TANK AND LINES (1991)
Oil tank-to-pump hose
Oil filter
Breather hose
Filter-to-
oil tank hose
TOP VIEW
SIDE VIEW
Oil filter
mount
Breather hose
Pump-to-
filter hose
Filter-to-oil tank hose
Oil tank-to-pump hose

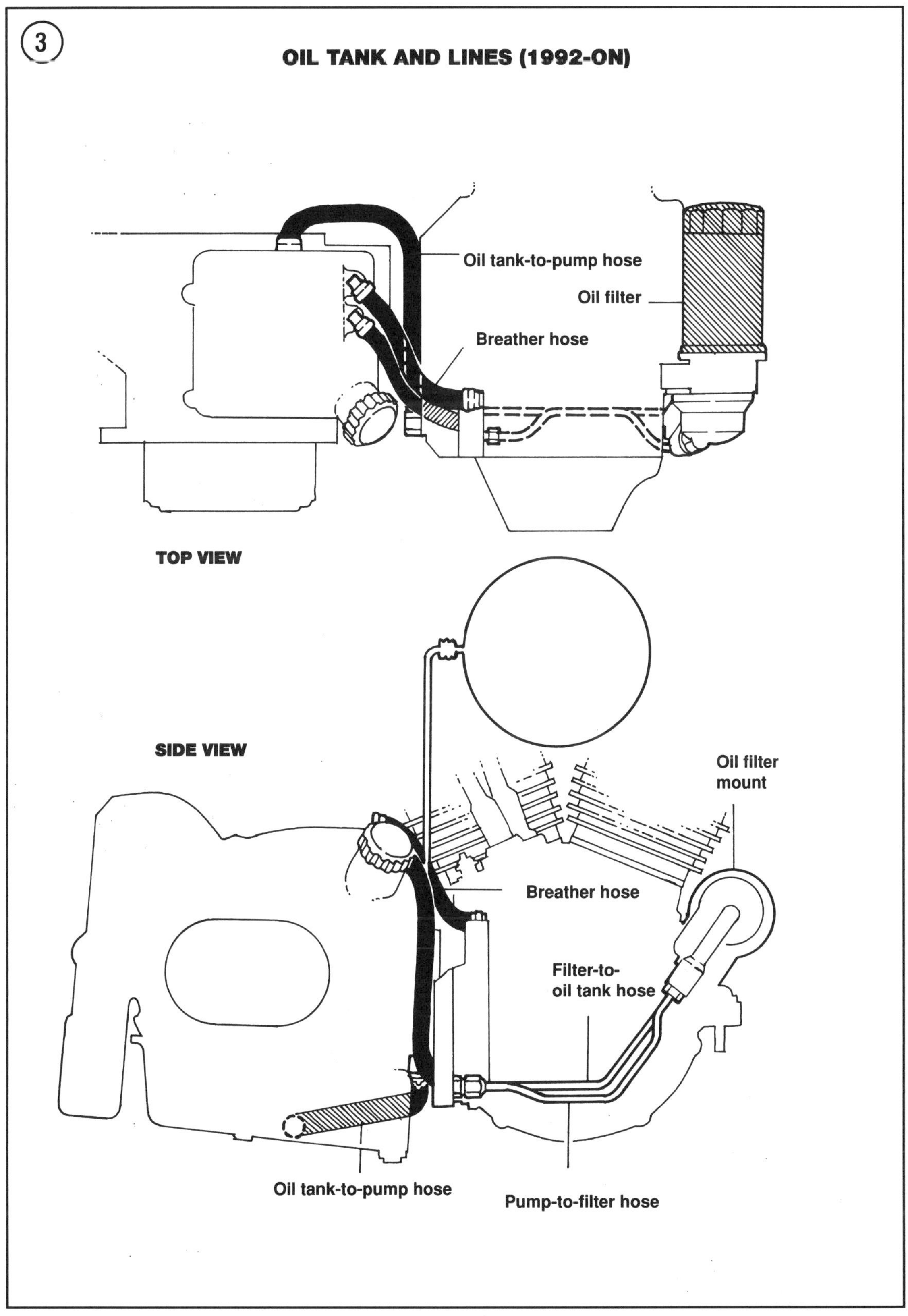
3
OIL TANK AND LINES (1992-ON)
Oil tank-to-pump hose
Oil filter
Breather hose
TOP VIEW
SIDE VIEW
Oil filter
mount
Breather hose
Filter-to-
oil tank hose
Oil tank-to-pump hose
Pump-to-filter hose

4
8
5
9
6
10
7
11

14. Tighten the inner primary housing mounting bolts in the following order:

a. Tighten the inner primary housing-to-transmission housing mounting bolts to the torque specification in **Table 4**. Bend the lockwasher tabs against the bolt heads.
b. Tighten the inner primary housing-to-engine crankcase mounting bolts to the torque specification in **Table 4**. Bend the lockwasher tabs against the bolt heads.

15. If disassembled, install the top end assembly (pistons, cylinder heads and rocker arm covers) as described in this chapter.

16. Install the upper engine mounting bracket onto the engine and frame (**Figure 10**). Then tighten the mounting bracket bolts in the following order:

a. Tighten the engine mounting bracket-to-cylinder head mounting bolts to the torque specification in **Table 4**.

12

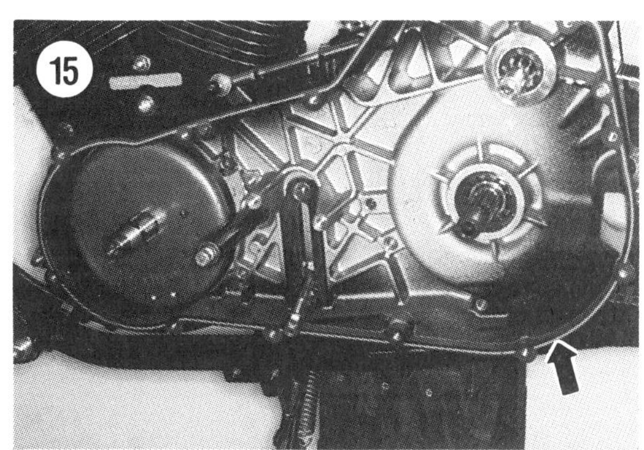
15

13

16

14

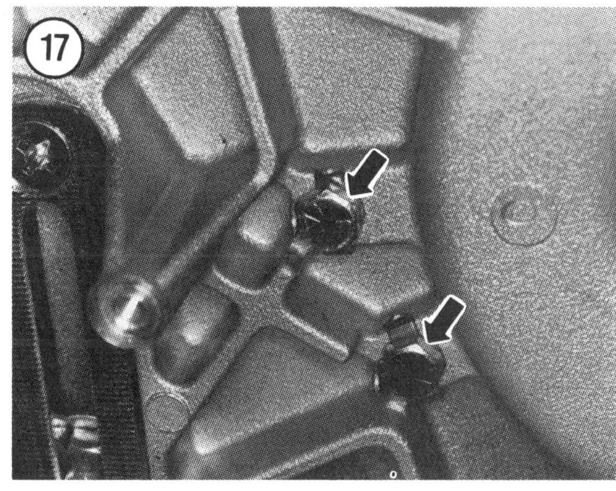
17

b. Tighten the engine mounting bracket-to-frame mounting bolts to the torque specification in **Table 4**.

17. Install the compensating sprocket, clutch and primary drive chain as described in Chapter Five.
18. Install the outer primary cover as described in Chapter Five.
19. Reconnect the alternator connector to the engine (**Figure 5**).
20. Reconnect the wire to the oil pressure switch (**Figure 4**).
21. Reconnect the sensor plate electrical connector.
22. Reconnect the spark plug caps to the spark plugs.
23. Install the clutch cable mounting bracket.
24. Reconnect the oil lines to the oil pump. Secure the oil lines with new hose clamps. See **Figure 2** or **Figure 3**.
25. Install a new oil filter and refill the engine oil as described in Chapter Seven.
26. Install the exhaust system as described in Chapter Seven.
27. Install the rear brake pedal and master cylinder assembly as described in Chapter Twelve. Bleed the brake system as described in Chapter Twelve.
28. Install the right footpeg assembly.
29. Install the carburetor as described in Chapter Seven.
30. Install the air filter backplate as described in Chapter Seven.
31. Install the fuel tank as described in Chapter Eight.
32. Reconnect the negative battery cable to the battery.
33. Adjust the clutch as described in Chapter Five.
34. Check vehicle alignment as described in Chapter Nine.

ROCKER ARM COVER AND CYLINDER HEAD

Refer to **Figure 18** and **Figure 19** when performing procedures in this section.

Removal

This procedure describes rocker arm and cylinder head removal.

1. If the engine is mounted in the frame, perform the following:
   a. Perform Steps 1-7 under *Engine Removal* in this chapter.
   b. Remove the upper cylinder head mounting bracket (**Figure 6**).
2. Remove the spark plugs.
3. Remove the 4 upper rocker arm cover bolts and washers.
4. Remove the upper rocker arm cover (**Figure 20**).
5. Remove the middle rocker arm cover. Discard the gaskets.
6. Rotate the engine until both valves are closed on the cylinder head being removed.

NOTE
You can determine valve position by watching the rocker arms as you turn the engine over.

7. Using a screwdriver, pry the spring cap retainer (**Figure 21**) out from between the cylinder head and spring cap. Repeat for the opposite pushrod (**Figure 22**).

NOTE
When removing the rocker arm and pushrod assemblies in the following steps, do not intermix the parts from each set. Install the parts in their original mounting positions.

8. Remove the lower cover mounting bolts and remove the lower cover (**Figure 23**) along with the rocker arms. See **Figure 24**.
9. Mark each pushrod (**Figure 25**) as to its top and bottom position and then its operating position in the cylinder head.

NOTE
The pushrods must be reinstalled in their original positions and facing in the same direction.

10. Remove the 2 pushrods (**Figure 25**).
11. Remove the pushrod cover assembly (**Figure 26**). Then remove the upper O-ring (1, **Figure 26**) and the lower O-ring and spacer (10 and 11, **Figure 26**).
12. Loosen the cylinder head bolts (**Figure 27**) 1/8 turn at a time in the pattern shown in **Figure 28**.
13. Tap the cylinder head with a rubber mallet to free it, then lift it off the cylinder (**Figure 29**).
14. Remove and discard the cylinder head gasket.

ROCKER ARM ASSEMBLY

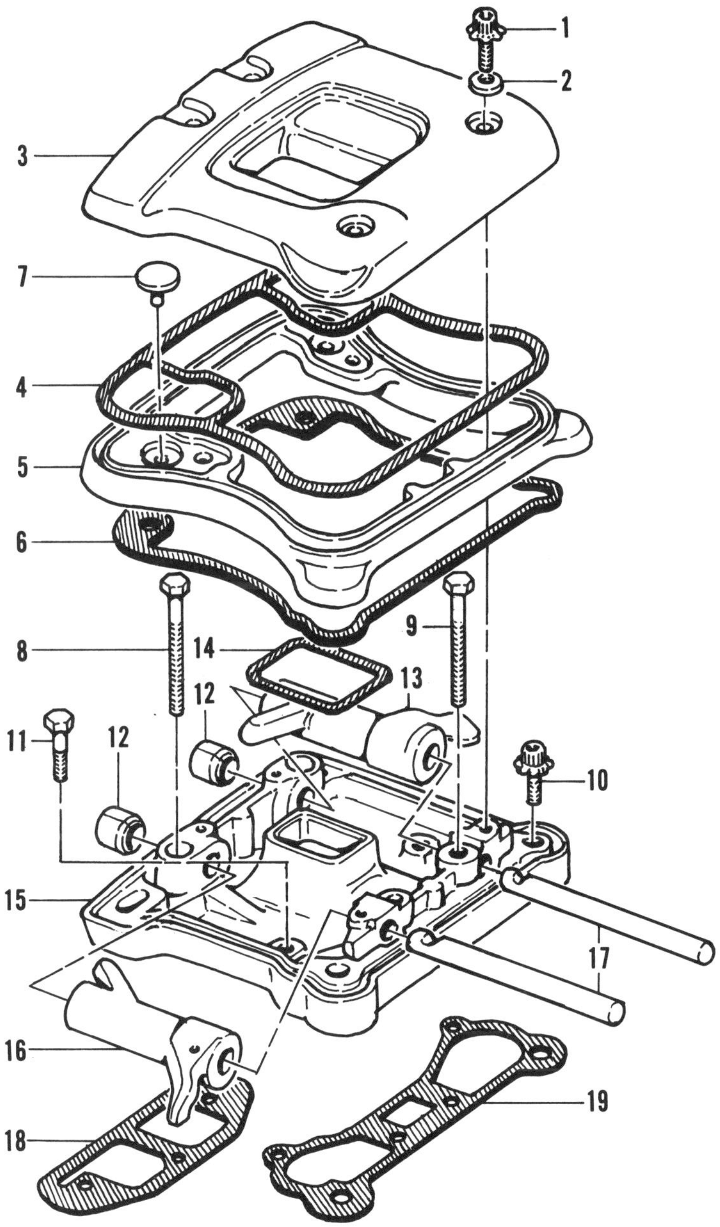

1. Bolt
2. Washer
3. Upper rocker cover
4. Gasket
5. Middle rocker cover
6. Gasket
7. Umbrella valve
8. Bolt
9. Bolt
10. Bolt and washer
11. Bolt
12. Bushing
13. Rocker arm
14. Gasket
15. Lower rocker cover
16. Rocker arm
17. Rocker arm shafts
18. Gasket
19. Gasket

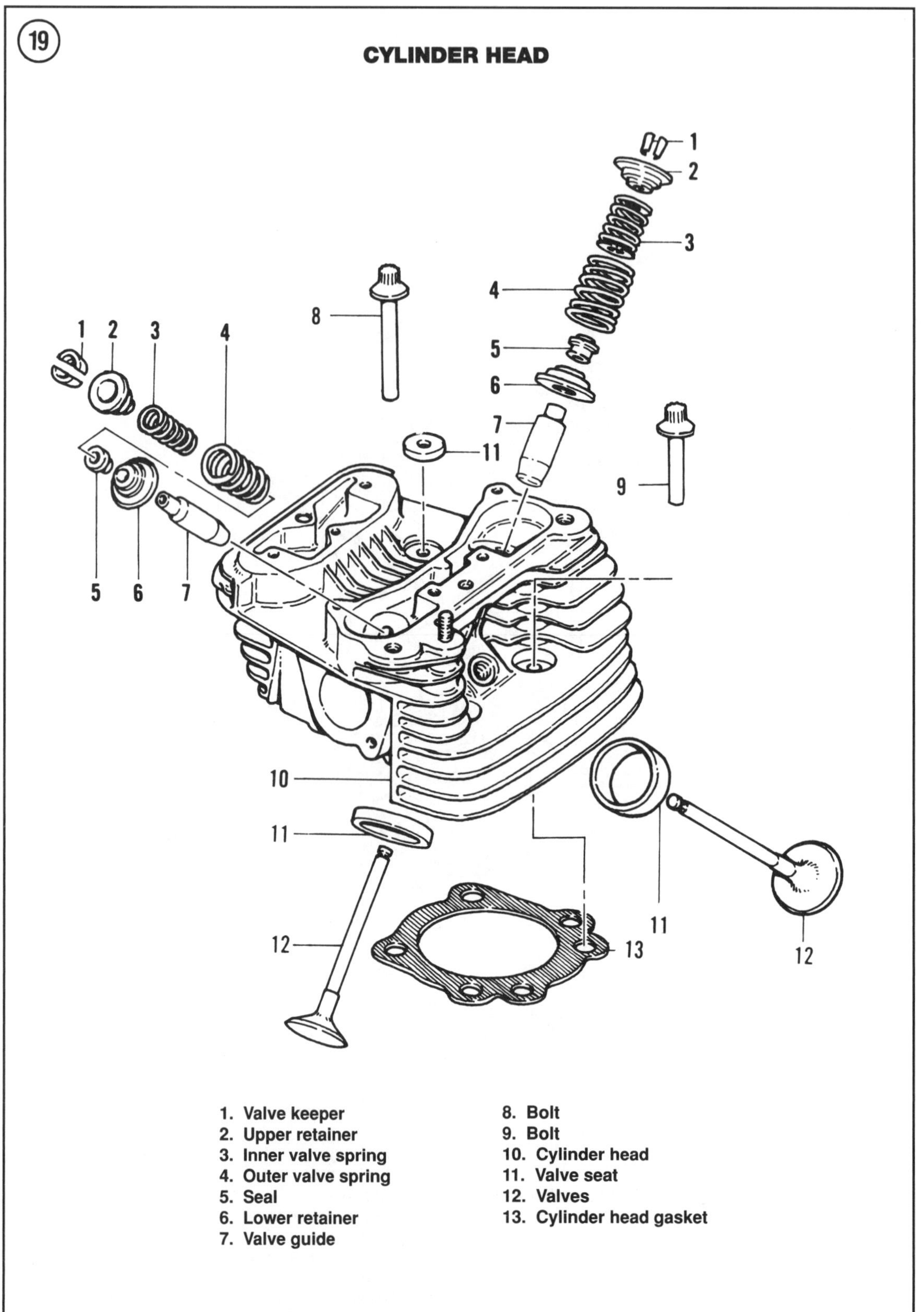

1. Valve keeper
2. Upper retainer
3. Inner valve spring
4. Outer valve spring
5. Seal
6. Lower retainer
7. Valve guide
8. Bolt
9. Bolt
10. Cylinder head
11. Valve seat
12. Valves
13. Cylinder head gasket

15. Remove the 2 O-rings and the cylinder head dowel pins (**Figure 30**).

16. Repeat these steps to remove the opposite cylinder head.

17. Disassemble and inspect the rocker arm and cylinder head assemblies as described in this chapter.

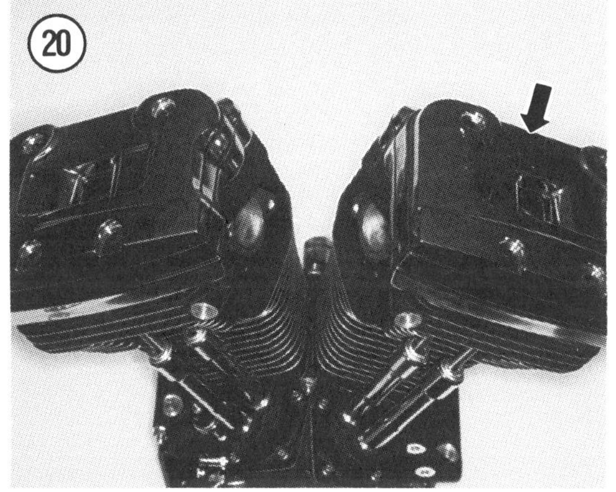

Rocker Arm Removal/Inspection/Installation

Do not intermix the rocker arm sets. Label all parts so that you can reinstall them in their original mounting positions. Refer to **Figure 18**.

1. Before removing the rocker arms, measure rocker arm end clearance as follows:
   a. Insert a feeler gauge between the rocker arm and the inside rocker arm cover boss as shown in **Figure 31**.
   b. Record the measurement.

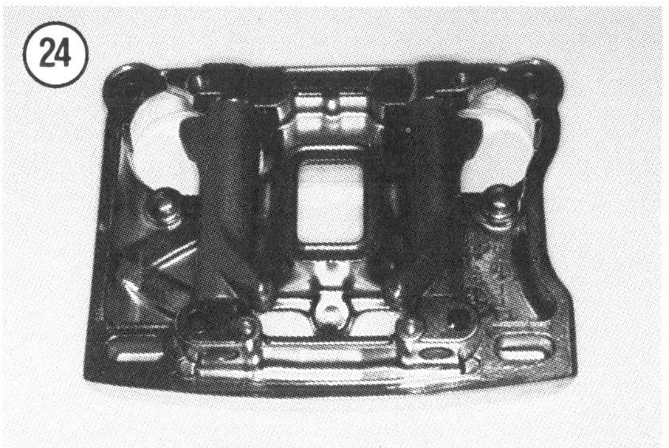

c. Repeat for each rocker arm.

d. Replace the rocker arm or the lower rocker arm cover if the end clearance exceeds the service limit in **Table 2**.

2. See **Figure 32**. Remove the rocker arm shafts (A) and rocker arms (B).

3. Clean all parts in solvent. Blow compressed air through all oil passages.

4. Inspect the rocker arm pads and ball sockets (**Figure 33**) for pitting and excessive wear. Replace the rocker arms if necessary.

26

PUSHROD ASSEMBLY

1. O-ring
2. Pushrod
3. Upper pushrod cover
4. Spring cap retainer
5. Cap
6. Spring
7. Spacer
8. O-ring
9. Lower pushrod cover
10. O-ring
11. Spacer
12. Tappet
13. Bolt
14. Tappet guide
15. Gasket

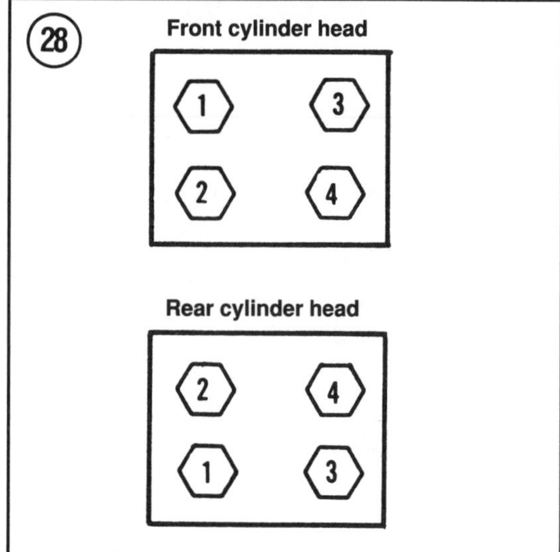

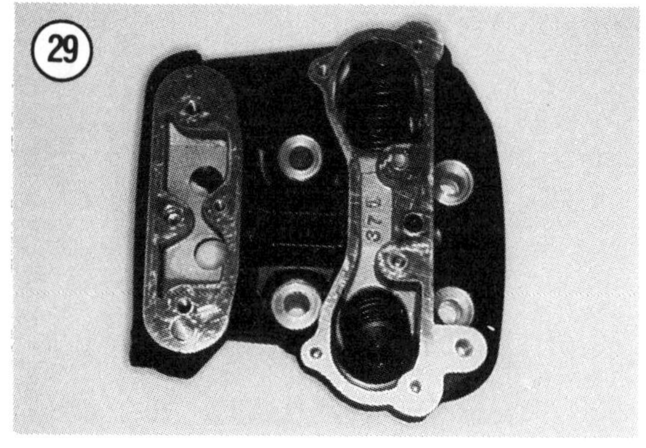

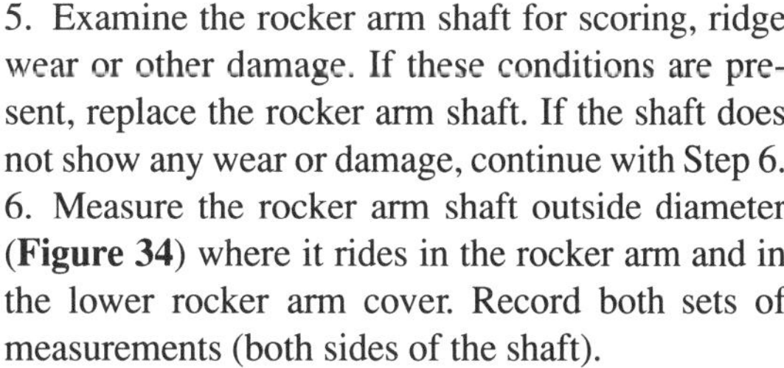

5. Examine the rocker arm shaft for scoring, ridge wear or other damage. If these conditions are present, replace the rocker arm shaft. If the shaft does not show any wear or damage, continue with Step 6.
6. Measure the rocker arm shaft outside diameter (**Figure 34**) where it rides in the rocker arm and in the lower rocker arm cover. Record both sets of measurements (both sides of the shaft).
7. Measure the rocker arm bushing inside diameter (**Figure 35**) and the lower rocker arm cover bore diameter where the shaft rides (**Figure 36**). Record each measurement.

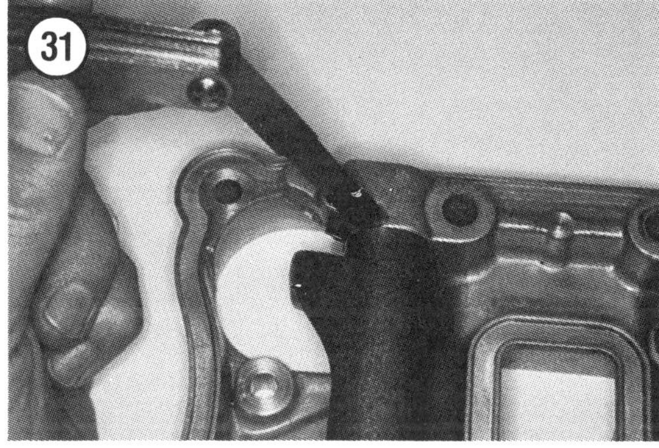

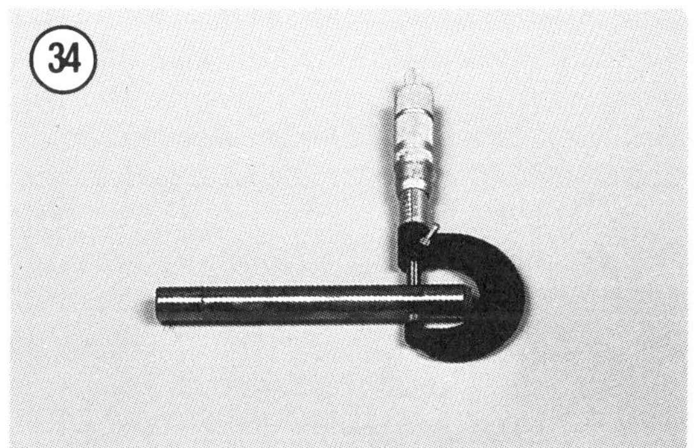

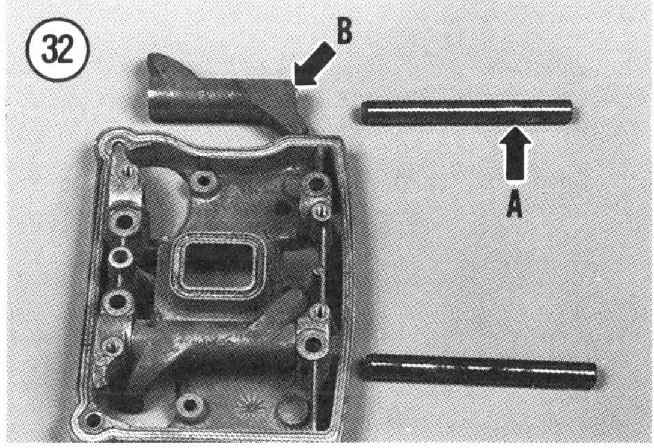

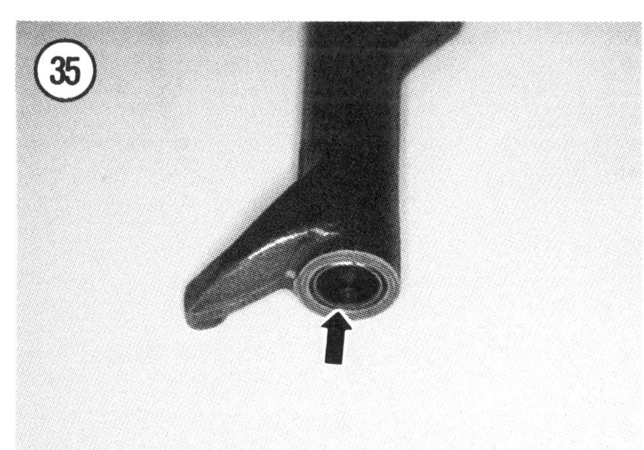

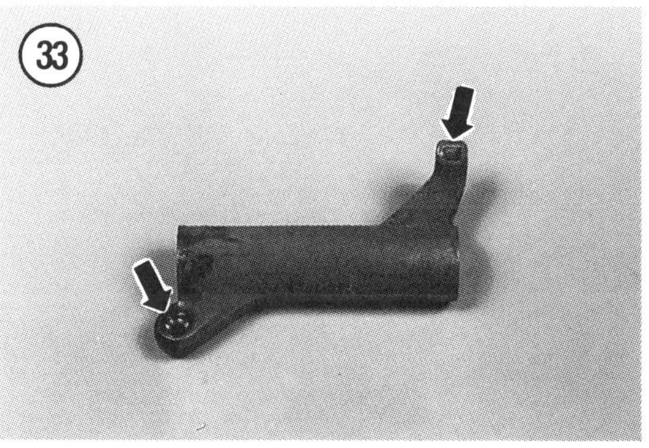

8. Subtract the measurements taken in Step 6 from those taken in Step 7 to obtain the following rocker arm shaft measurements:
   a. Shaft fit in rocker cover.
   b. Shaft fit in rocker arm bushing.

9. Replace the rocker arm bushings or the lower rocker arm cover if the clearance exceeds the specifications in **Table 2**. Rocker arm bushing replacement is described in this chapter.

10. Install the rocker arms into their original positions (**Figure 37**).

11. Install a rocker arm shaft partway through its original rocker arm.

12. Align the notch in the rocker arm shaft (**Figure 38**) with the mating bolt hole in the cover and install the shaft all the way. Repeat for the other rocker arm.

13. Inspect the upper and middle cover gasket surfaces for damage or warpage. Replace parts as necessary.

14. Inspect the umbrella valve installed in each middle cover (**Figure 39**). Replace the umbrella valve if damaged.

Rocker Arm Bushing Replacement

Each rocker arm is equipped with 2 bushings (**Figure 35**). Replacement bushings require reaming after installation. If you are doing this work yourself, use the Harley-Davidson rocker arm bushing reamer (part No. HD-94804-57). If you do not have the correct size reamer, refer bushing replacement to a Harley-Davidson dealership.

NOTE

Because you must ream the new bushings, remove one bushing at a time. You will then use the opposite bushing as a guide when reaming the first bushing.

1. Press one bushing (**Figure 35**) out of the rocker arm. Do not remove the second bushing. If the bushing is difficult to remove, perform the following:
   a. Thread a 9/16-18 tap into the bushing.
   b. Support the rocker arm in a press so that the tap is at the bottom.
   c. Insert a mandrel through the top of the rocker arm and seat it on top of the tap.
   d. Press on the mandrel to force the bushing and tap out of the rocker arm. Dont let the tap fall to the floor or the impact may shatter it.
   e. Remove the tap from the bushing and discard the bushing.

2. Press the new bushing (with its split portion facing toward the top of the rocker arm) into the rocker arm. Continue until the bushing's outer surface is flush with the end of rocker arm bore (**Figure 35**).

3. Ream the new bushing with the bushing reamer (part No. HD-94804-57) as follows:
   a. Mount the rocker arm in a vise with soft jaws so that the new bushing is at the bottom.

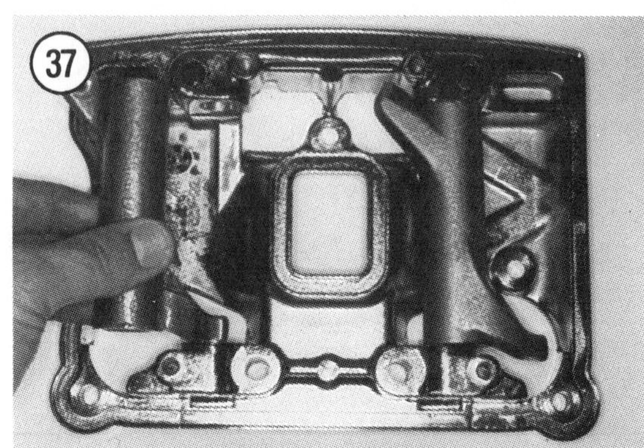

37

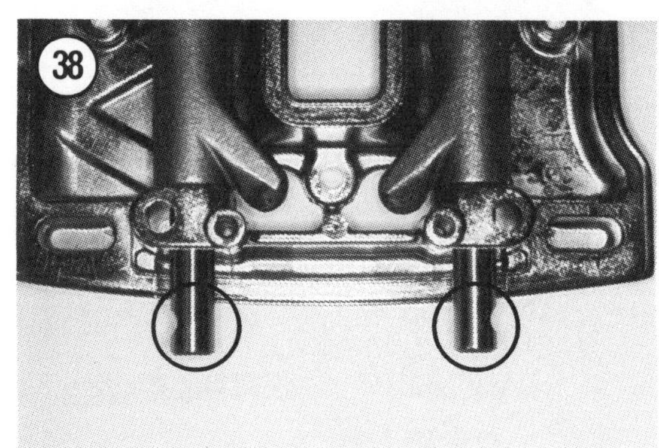

38

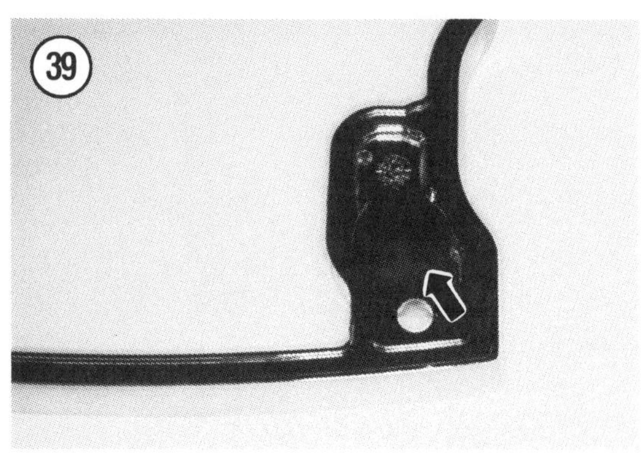

39

CAUTION
Turn the reamer clockwise only. Do not turn the reamer backward (counterclockwise) or you may damage the reamer.

b. Mount a tap handle on top of the reamer and insert the reamer into the bushing. Turn the reamer clockwise until it passes through the new bushing, remove it from the bottom side.

4. Remove the rocker arm from the vise and repeat Steps 1-3 to replace the opposite bushing. The first bushing will now serve as a guide while reaming the second bushing.

5. After installing and reaming both bushings, clean the rocker arm assembly in solvent. Then clean with hot, soapy water and rinse with clear, cold water. Dry with compressed air.

6. Measure the inside diameter of each bushing. When properly reamed, the bushings must provide a shaft clearance of 0.0007-0.0022 in. (0.013-0.050 mm). The shaft clearance service limit is 0.0035 in. (0.089 mm).

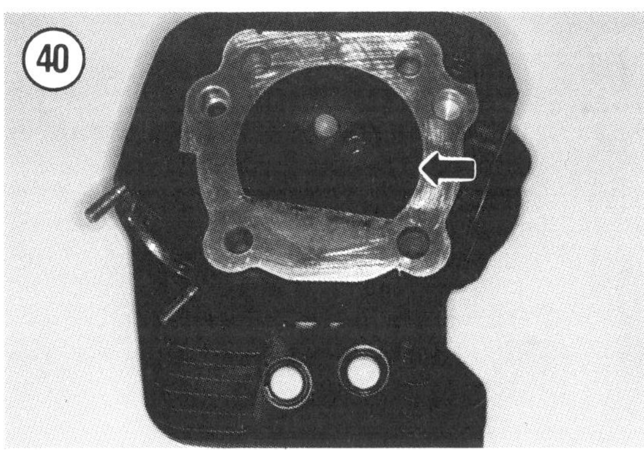
40

41

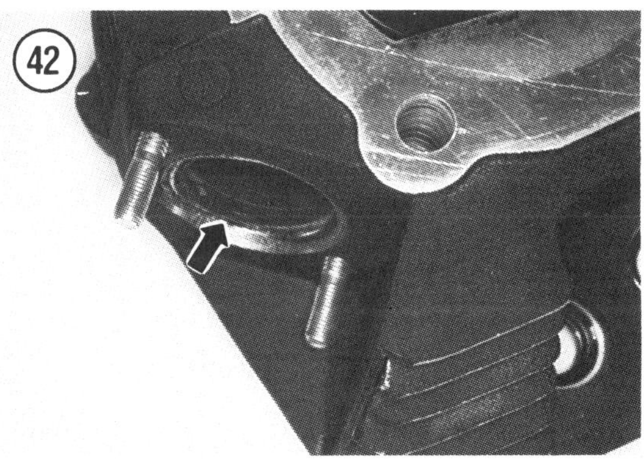
42

Cylinder Head Inspection

Refer to **Figure 19** for this procedure.

1. Without removing the valves, use a wire brush to remove all carbon deposits from the combustion chambers (**Figure 40**).

CAUTION
If you clean the combustion chambers after removing the valves, keep the scraper or wire brush away from the valve seats. Otherwise, the tool will damage the seat surface.

2. Examine the spark plug threads (**Figure 41**) for damage. If necessary, clean or repair thread damage with a spark plug tap.

3. After cleaning the combustion chambers and valve ports and repairing the spark plug holes, clean the cylinder head in solvent. Use compressed air, if available, to thoroughly dry the head and to remove small debris from passages.

4. Remove all carbon residue from the piston crown. Do not remove the carbon ridge from the top of the cylinder bore.

5. Check for cracks in the combustion chamber (**Figure 40**) and exhaust port (**Figure 42**). Repair or replace a cracked head.

6. Place a straightedge across the gasket surface at several points (**Figure 43**). Insert a flat feeler gauge between the straightedge and cylinder head at several locations. **Table 2** lists the maximum allowable warpage. If warpage exceeds this limit, refer service to your dealership.

7. Check the rocker arm cover mating surface using the procedure in Step 6.

8. Check the valves and valve guides as described under *Valves and Valve Components* in this chapter.

Pushrod Inspection and Replacement

1. Clean the pushrods in fresh solvent. Dry with compressed air.
2. Check pushrods (**Figure 44**) for bending, cracks and excessively worn or damaged ball heads.
3. Each pushrod is a different length. You can identify each pushrod by its color-coded stripes (**Figure 45**):
   a. Purple: rear exhaust (A, **Figure 46**).
   b. Blue: rear intake (B, **Figure 46**).
   c. Yellow: front intake (C, **Figure 46**).
   d. Green: front exhaust (D, **Figure 46**).

Installation

You need the following items to install the cylinder heads:

a. New gaskets and O-rings.
b. New engine oil.
c. Torque wrench.
d. Marking pen.

Refer to **Figure 18** and **Figure 19** when performing this procedure.

1. Lubricate the cylinder studs and cylinder head bolts as follows:
   a. Clean the cylinder head bolts (**Figure 47**) in solvent and dry with compressed air.
   b. Apply clean engine oil to the cylinder head bolt threads and to the flat shoulder surface on each bolt (**Figure 47**). Wipe off any excess oil from the bolts. You only want to leave an oil film on these surfaces.
2. Install the pistons, rings and cylinders as described in this chapter.
3. Install the 2 dowel pins (**Figure 48**) into the top of the cylinder block.

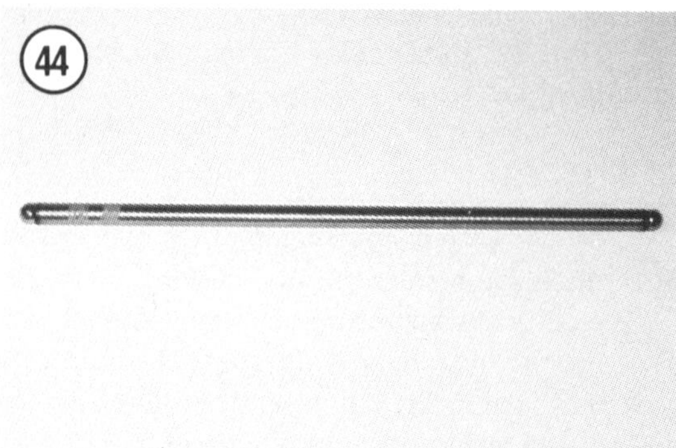

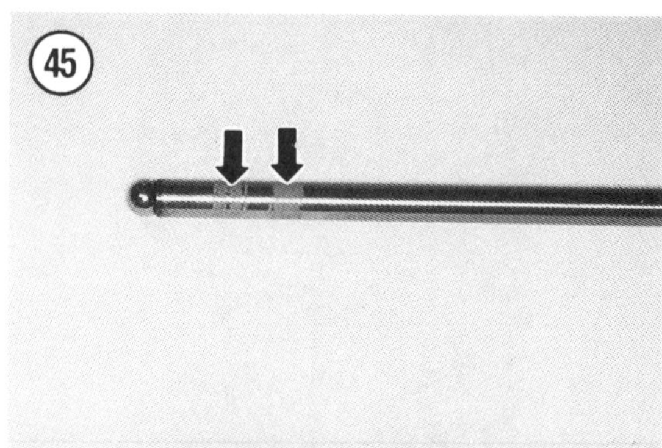

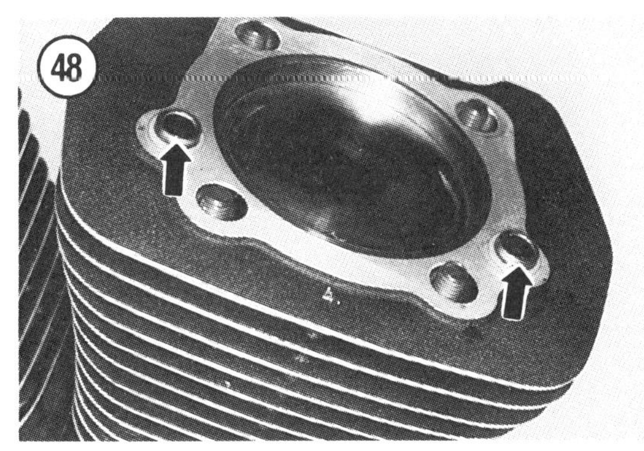

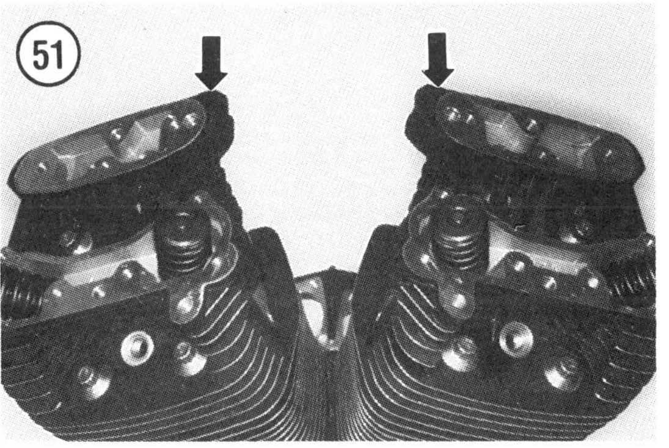

4. Install a new O-ring over each dowel pin; see **Figure 19**.

CAUTION
Because the O-rings center the head gasket on the cylinder block, install them before installing the head gasket.

5. Install a new head gasket (**Figure 19**) onto the cylinder block.

CAUTION
Do not use sealer on stock head gaskets. If you are using an aftermarket head gasket, follow the manufacturer's instructions for gasket installation.

NOTE
*Identify the cylinder heads by the "Front" or "Rear" mark cast into the bottom side of the head (**Figure 49**).*

6. Install the cylinder head (**Figure 50**) onto the cylinder dowel pins. Position the head carefully so that you don't knock the head gasket out of alignment. **Figure 51** shows the front and rear cylinder heads properly installed.
7. Install the cylinder head bolts (**Figure 50**) and run them down finger-tight. Install the long bolts in the center bolt holes; install the short bolts in the outer bolt holes (next to the spark plug hole).

CAUTION
Failure to follow the torque pattern and sequence in Step 8 may cause cylinder head distortion and gasket leakage.

8. Torque the cylinder head bolts as follows:
   a. **Figure 52** identifies the front and rear cylinder head bolt numbers.

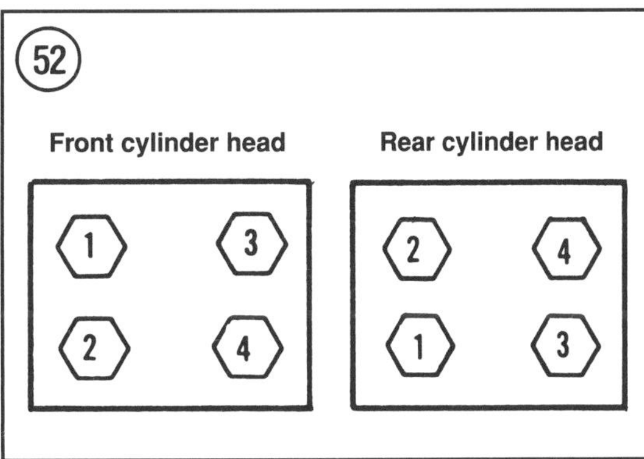

b. Using a torque wrench, tighten bolt No. 1 to 7-9 ft.-lb. (9-12 N·m). Then continue and tighten bolts No. 2, 3 and 4 in numerical order.
c. Tighten bolt No. 1 to 12-14 ft.-lb. (16-19 N·m). Then continue and tighten bolts No. 2, 3 and 4 in numerical order.
d. Using a pen (**Figure 53**), make a vertical mark on the No. 1 bolt head and a matching mark

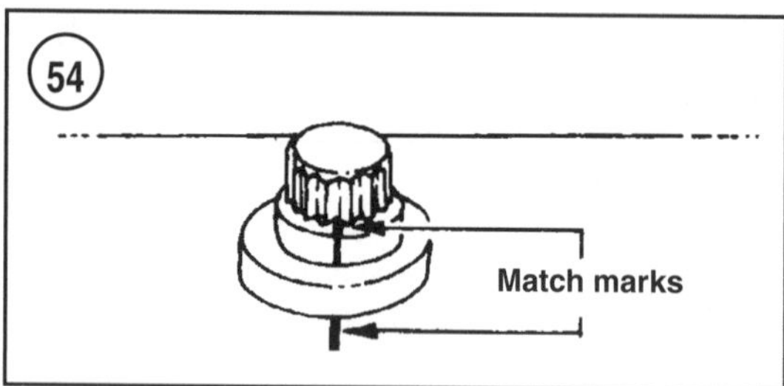

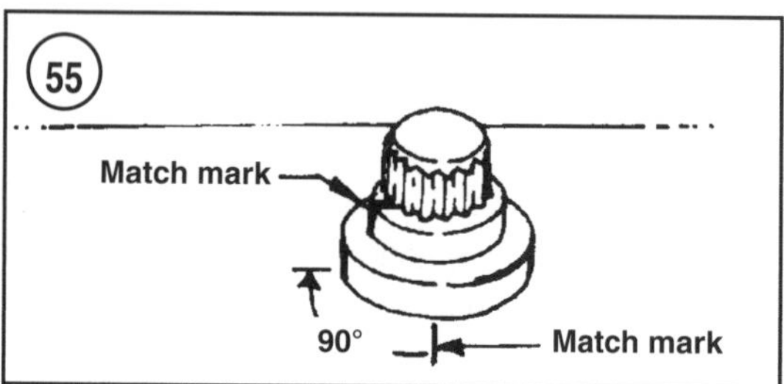

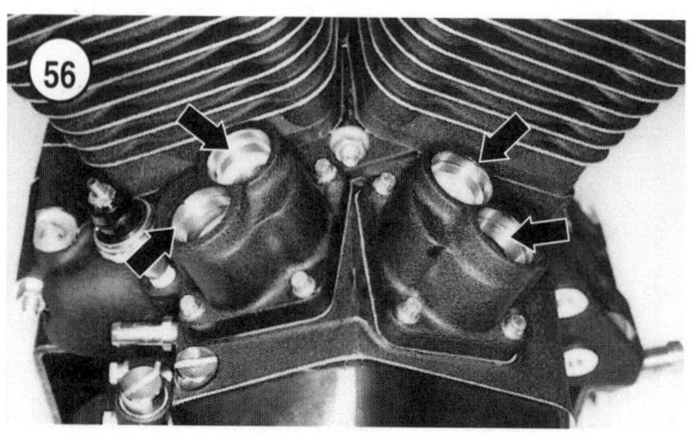

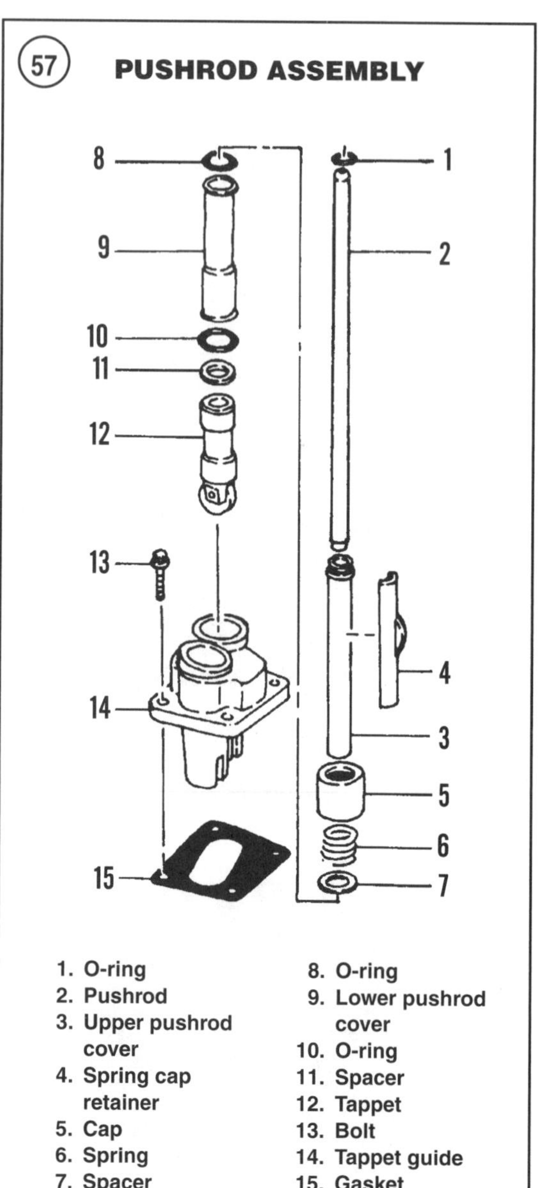

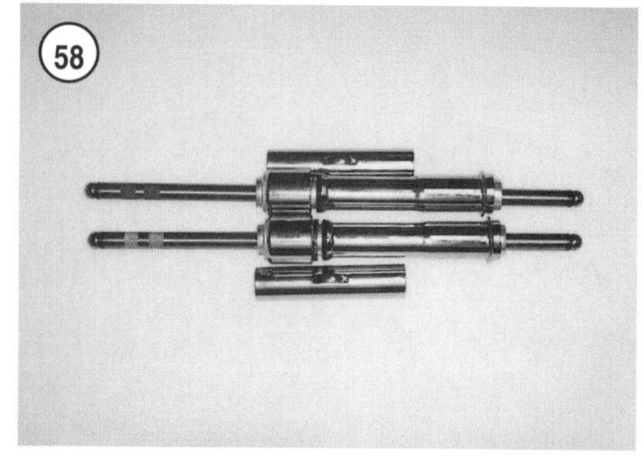

on the cylinder head. Repeat for each bolt. See **Figure 54**.

e. Following the torque sequence in **Figure 52**, use the match marks as a guide (**Figure 54**) and turn each bolt head 1/4 turn (90°) clockwise (**Figure 55**).

f. Repeat for the opposite cylinder head.

9. If you removed the valve lifters, install them as described under *Valve Lifters* in this chapter.

10. Rotate the engine until both lifters (**Figure 56**) for the cylinder head being serviced seat onto the cams lowest position (base circle).

11. Install the pushrod covers (**Figure 57**) as follows:

a. Replace worn or damaged O-rings in the following steps.

b. Identify the pushrod sets (**Figure 58**) prior to installation. Refer to your disassembly notes and to *Pushrod Inspection and Replacement* in this chapter.

c. Install a spacer then an O-ring (**Figure 59**) into one lifter block as shown in **Figure 60**.

d. Install the second O-ring into the pushrod cutout in the bottom of the cylinder head (**Figure 61**).

e. If you disassembled the pushrod cover assembly, reassemble it as described under *Pushrods* in this chapter.

f. Install the pushrod cover assembly (**Figure 62**) into the lifter block. Then seat its bottom shoulder into the spacer and O-ring.

g. Repeat these steps to install the opposite pushrod cover assembly.

12. Install the pushrods as follows:

CAUTION

Four different length pushrods are used in the Dyna Glides engine. Make sure you correctly identify the pushrods before installing them. In addition, when reinstalling the original pushrods, install them so that each end faces in its original operating position. These pushrod ends have developed a set wear pattern and installing them upside down may cause rapid wear to the pushrod, lifter and rocker arm.

a. If you labeled the pushrods during removal, install each pushrod in its original position (**Figure 63**).

b. If you did not label the pushrods, or if you are installing new pushrods, identify them as de-

4

scribed under *Pushrod Inspection and Replacement* in this chapter.

NOTE
Because new pushrods are symmetrical, you can install them with either end facing up.

c. Make sure that you center each pushrod in its respective lifter.

13. Install new lower rocker arm cover gaskets with the sealer bead on each gasket facing up.

14. Place the lower rocker cover into position (A, **Figure 64**, while guiding the pushrod ends into the rocker arm sockets (B, **Figure 64**).

15. Install the lower rocker arm cover bolts and washers in their respective bolt holes but do not tighten them. Note how the rocker cover is sitting above the cylinder head surface.

NOTE
*Before tightening the lower rocker cover mounting bolts, note the gap between the rocker cover and cylinder head surfaces. This gap is normal. Tightening the mounting bolts forces the rocker cover against the cylinder head while the pushrods bleed the lifters. To avoid damaging a pushrod, rocker arm or valve, tighten the rocker cover mounting bolts evenly and in a crisscross pattern. When tightening the mounting bolts, spin each pushrod with your fingers (**Figure 65**). This will let you know that you are tightening the rocker cover (**Figure 66**) evenly and that the pressure applied against the pushrods is correct. If you cannot spin one or both pushrods, back off on the mounting bolts to distribute*

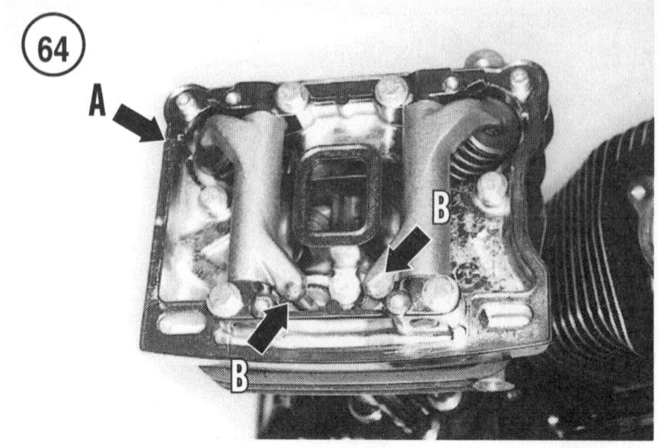

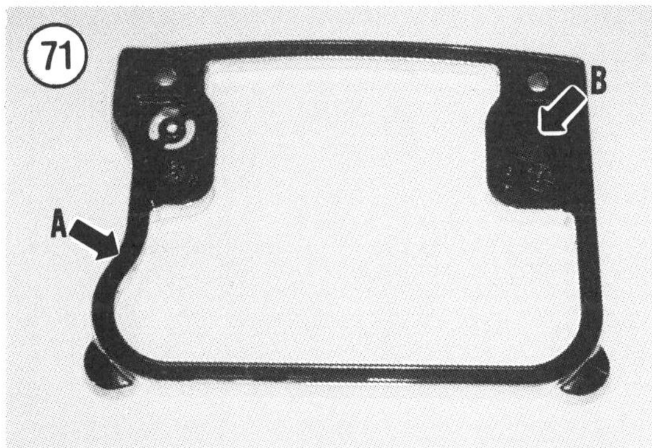

the pressure evenly between the bolts and rocker cover.

16. Starting with the 5/16 in. rocker cover bolts, finger-tighten each bolt 1 turn at a time. When you can no longer turn the bolts by hand, tighten the bolts gradually in a crisscross pattern to the torque specification in **Figure 4**.

CAUTION
Do not turn the engine crankshaft until you can turn both pushrods by hand. Otherwise, you may damage the rocker arms or pushrods.

17. Check that you can turn each pushrod by hand (**Figure 65**).
18. Lift the inner pushrod cover (**Figure 67**) up and seat it into the cylinder head with a screwdriver (**Figure 68**). Then position the spring cap retainer between the cap and cylinder head and pry it into position with a screwdriver (**Figure 69**).
19. Repeat Step 18 for the other pushrod (**Figure 70**).
20. Install the middle rocker cover (A, **Figure 71**) as follows:
    a. Install new center and outer gaskets onto the lower rocker arm cover.
    b. If removed, install a new umbrella valve (B, **Figure 71**) into the cover.
    c. Install the middle rocker cover so that its umbrella valve faces toward the intake side of the engine as shown in **Figure 72.**
21. Install the upper rocker cover as follows:
    a. Install a new gasket onto the middle rocker cover.
    b. Install the upper rocker cover onto the middle rocker cover.
    c. Slide a steel washer and fiber seal onto each upper rocker cover mounting bolt (**Figure 73**).

4

d. Install the upper rocker cover mounting bolts and tighten to the torque specification in **Table 4**.

22. Repeat Steps 1-21 for the other cylinder head and rocker box assembly.
23. Reverse Steps 1 and 2 under *Removal* to complete assembly.
24. If you installed new top end components, perform the *Engine Break-in* procedure in this chapter.

VALVES AND VALVE COMPONENTS

This section describes complete cylinder head and valve service. If you do not have the equipment or experience to perform accurate cylinder head work, refer all service to a dealership.

Refer to **Figure 74** when servicing the cylinder head and valves in the following sections.

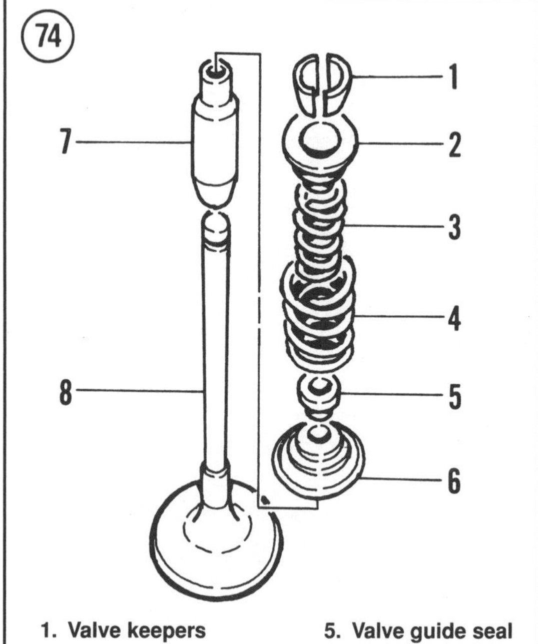

1. Valve keepers
2. Upper spring seat
3. Inner valve spring
4. Outer valve spring
5. Valve guide seal
6. Lower spring seat
7. Valve guide
8. Valve

Valve Removal

NOTE
Do not intermix the valve assemblies when removing them in the following steps.

1. Remove the cylinder head(s) as described in this chapter.
2. Install a valve spring compressor squarely over the valve retainer with the other end of the tool placed against the valve head (**Figure 75**).
3. Tighten the valve spring compressor until the split valve keepers separate. Remove the split valve keepers.
4. Gradually loosen the valve spring compressor and remove it from the cylinder head. Lift off the upper spring seat and both valve springs (**Figure 76**).

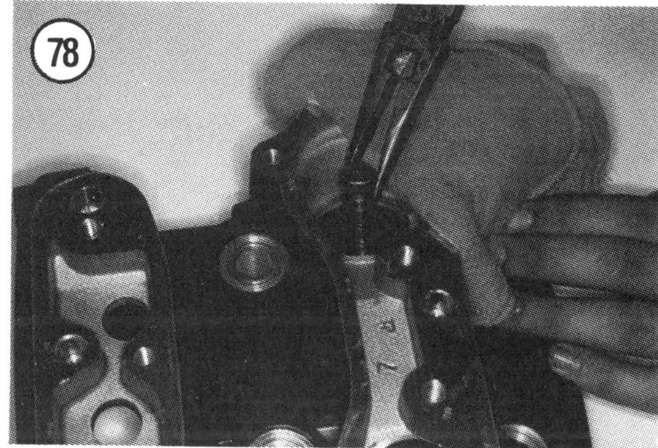

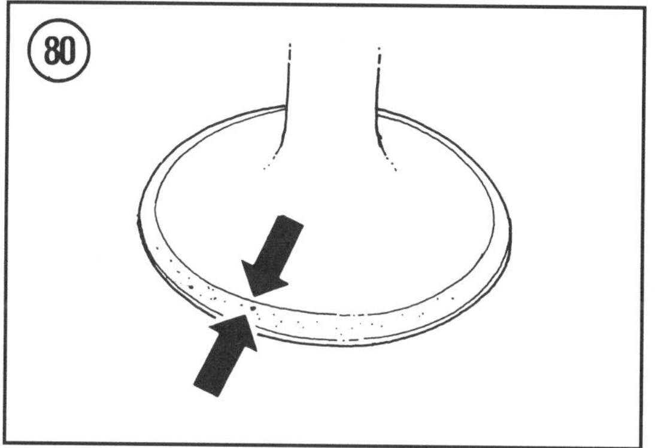

CAUTION

*Remove any burrs from the valve stem grooves (**Figure 77**) before removing the valve; otherwise, you will damage the valve guide as the valve stem passes through.*

5. Remove the valve.
6. Pry the valve guide oil seal off the guide using a screwdriver as shown in **Figure 78**.
7. Remove the lower spring seat (**Figure 79**).
8. Repeat Steps 2-7 to remove the opposite valve assembly.

Inspection

1. Clean valves with a wire brush and solvent.
2. Inspect the contact surface of each valve for burning (**Figure 80**). You can remove minor roughness and pitting by lapping the valve as described in this chapter. Excessive unevenness at the seating surface is an indication that the valve is not serviceable.

NOTE

While you may grind a valve on a valve grinding machine, you will get better results by replacing burned and damaged valves.

3. Inspect the valve stems for wear and roughness.
4. Measure each valve stem diameter using a micrometer (**Figure 81**). Record the diameter for each valve.
5. To clean the valve guides, perform the following:
   a. Lightly hone the valve guide with the Harley-Davidson valve guide hone (part No. HD-34723). Lubricate the hone with honing oil—do not use motor oil. Drive the hone with an electric drill (500-1,200 rpm).
   b. Soak the head in hot, soapy water and clean the guides with a valve guide brush. Use the

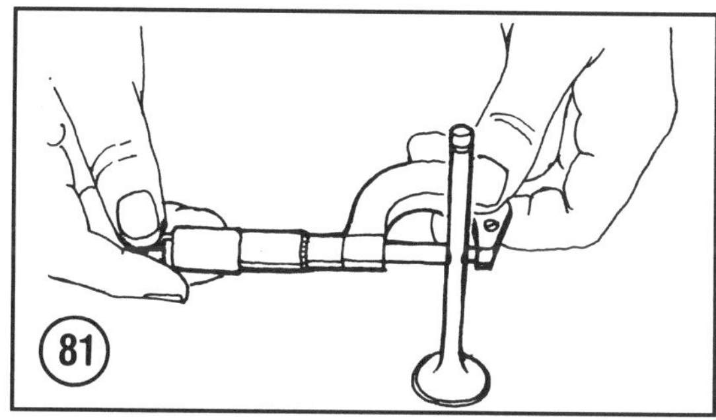

Harley-Davidson valve guide brush (part No. HD-34751) or equivalent.

c. Repeat for each valve guide.

d. Rinse the cylinder head in cold water and dry with compressed air.

6. Measure each valve guide (A, **Figure 82**) at the top, center and bottom with a bore gauge or small hole gauge. Record the inside diameter for each valve guide.

7. Subtract the measurement made in Step 4 from the measurement made in Step 6 above. The difference is the valve guide-to-valve stem clearance. See specifications in **Table 2** for the specified clearance. Replace any guide and valve that are not within tolerance.

NOTE

Harley-Davidson does not list valve guide and valve stem diameter specifications. The valve stem clearance measurement determines service wear.

8. Place a valve spring on a flat surface and check it for tilt with a square as shown in **Figure 83**. The spring must be parallel to the square. If not, replace the spring.

9. Measure the valve spring free length with a vernier caliper (**Figure 84**). Replace the spring if sagged to the service limit in **Table 2**.

10. Measure valve spring compression pressure with a compression tool (**Figure 85**) and compare to specifications in **Table 3**. Replace weak or damaged springs.

11. If any one valve spring is worn or damaged as determined in Steps 8-10, replace all the valve springs as a set.

12. Check the valve spring retainers and split keepers (**Figure 86**). Replace worn or damaged parts as required.

13. Inspect the valve seats (B, **Figure 82**). If worn or burned, you must recondition them. Refer this service to your dealership or local machine shop. If the valve seats are in serviceable condition (not burned, pitted or cracked), recondition them using a suitable valve lapping compound.

Valve Guide Replacement

When guides are worn so that there is excessive stem-to-guide clearance or valve tipping, you must

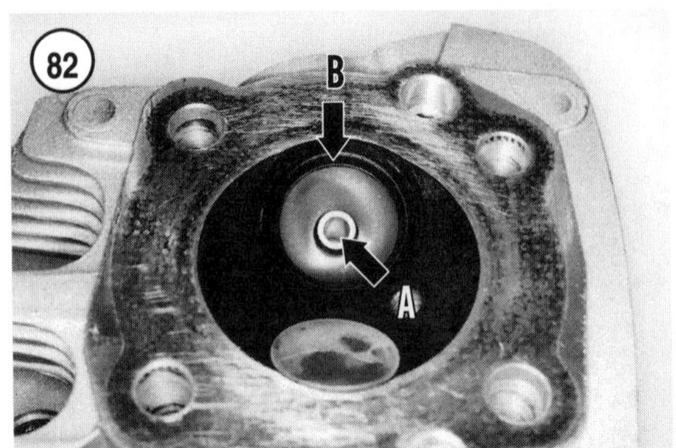

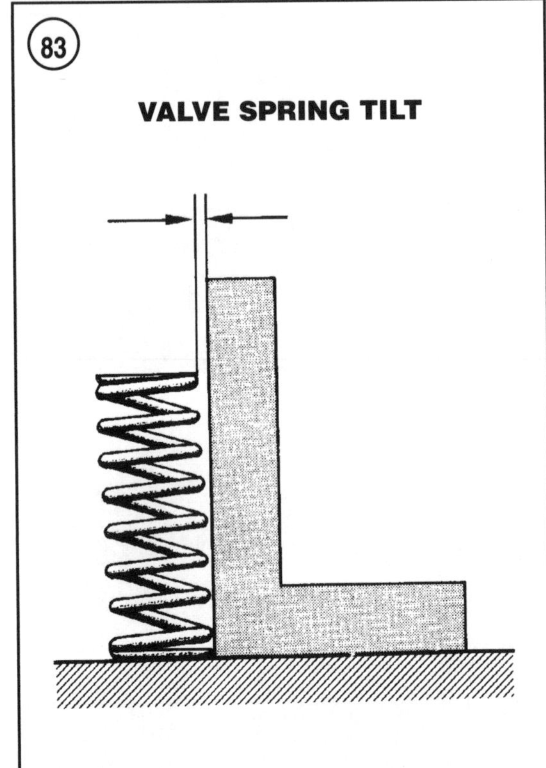

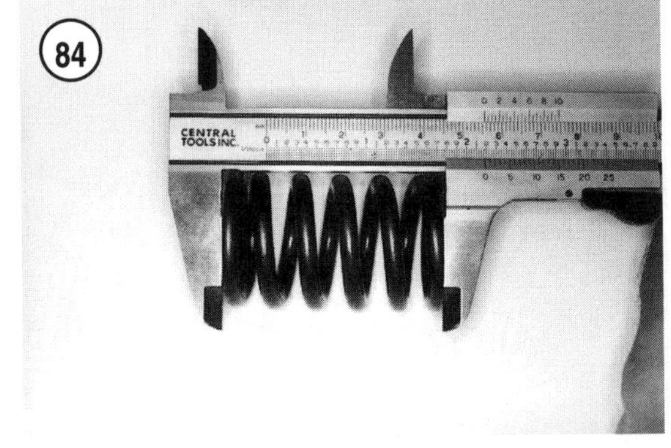

replace them. Replace all of the guides at the same time.

You need the following tools to replace the valve guides:

NOTE
The following part numbers are all factory Harley-Davidson numbers.

a. Driver Handle and Remover (part No. HD-34740) or equivalent. This tool, along with the Valve Guide Installation Tool, is used to remove and install the valve guides.

b. Valve Guide Installation Tool (part No. HD-34731) or equivalent.

c. Valve Guide Reamer (part No. HD-39932) or equivalent. This tool is used to ream the valve guides after installing them in the cylinder head.

d. Valve Guide Hone (part No. HD-34723). This tool is used to hone the valve guides after reaming them to size.

e. Valve Guide Brush (part No. HD-34751). This tool is used to clean the valve guides after honing them.

f. Honing oil.

1. Place the cylinder head on a wooden surface with the combustion chamber side facing down.

2. Shoulderless valve guides are used. Before you remove the valve guides, note and record the shape of the guide that projects into the combustion chamber. If you are not going to use the valve guide installation tool, measure the distance from the face of the guide to the cylinder head surface with a vernier caliper (**Figure 87**). Record the distance for each valve guide. You must install the valve guides to this height dimension.

3. Remove the valve guides as follows:

CAUTION
Use the correct size valve guide removal tool when removing the valve guides; otherwise, the tool may expand the end of the guide. An expanded guide will widen the guide bore in the cylinder head as it passes through it.

a. Support the cylinder head so that the combustion chamber faces down. If you are driving the guides out, place the cylinder on a piece of

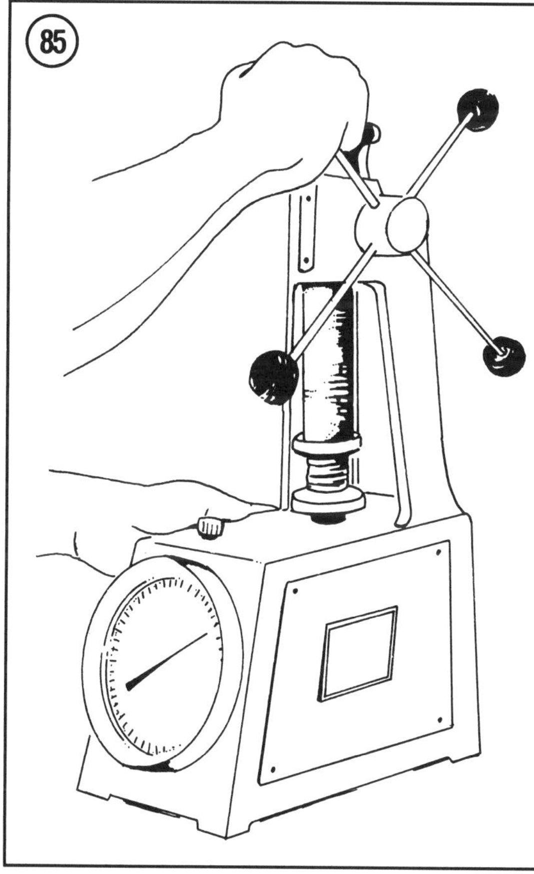

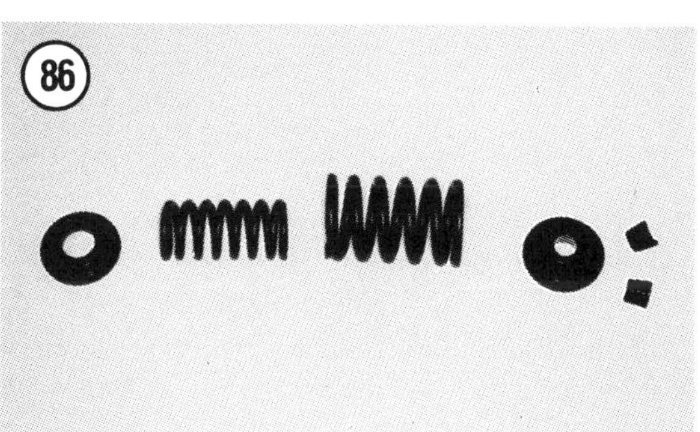

wood. If you are pressing the guides out, support the cylinder head in a press so that the valve guide is perpendicular to the press table.

b. Insert the driver handle and remover into the top of the valve guide.

c. Press or drive the valve guide out through the combustion chamber.

d. Repeat to remove the remaining valve guides.

4. Clean the valve guide bores in the cylinder head.

5. Because the valve guide bores in the cylinder head may have enlarged when you removed the old guides, measure each valve guide bore prior to purchasing the new guides. Then purchase the new valve guides to match its respective bore diameter. Determine the bore diameter as follows:

a. Measure the valve guide bore diameter in the cylinder head with a bore gauge or snap gauge. Record the bore diameter

b. The new valve guide outside diameter must be 0.0020-0.0033 in. (0.050-0.083 mm) larger than the guide bore in the cylinder head. When purchasing new valve guides, measure the new guide's outside diameter with a micrometer. If the new guide's outside diameter is not within this specification, you must install oversize valve guide(s). See your dealer for available sizes.

6. Apply a thin coating of molylube or white grease to the outer valve guide surface before installing it in the cylinder head.

CAUTION

When installing oversize valve guides, make sure to match each guide to its respective bore in the cylinder head.

7. Install the new guide using the Harley-Davidson driver handle and valve guide installation tools or equivalent aftermarket tools. Press or drive the guide into the cylinder head until the valve guide installation tool bottoms out on the cylinder head surface. When the tool bottoms out, you have installed the valve guide to the correct height. If you don't have the driver handle tool, install the valve to the same height recorded prior to removing the valve guide; measure the valve guide's installed height using a vernier caliper (**Figure 87**) when installing it.

NOTE

Because replacement valve guides are sold with a smaller inside diameter than the valve stem, you must ream the guide to fit the valve stem. Use the Harley-Davidson valve guide reamer. Use cutting oil on the reamer when reaming the guide.

8. Ream the guide to within 0.0005-0.0010 in. (0.013-0.025 mm) of the finished valve guide inside diameter. See **Table 2** for valve stem clearances and service limits.

CAUTION

When honing the valve guides, you only have 0.0015-0.0033 in. (0.038-0.084 mm) (exhaust) and 0.0008-0.0026 in. (0.020-0.066 mm) (intake) valve stem clearance to work with. Excessive valve stem clearance reduces engine performance while increasing oil blowby and consumption.

9. Lightly hone the valve guide using the Harley-Davidson Valve Guide Hone (part No. HD-34723) or equivalent. Lubricate the hone with honing oil—do not use motor oil. Drive the hone with an electric drill (500-1,200 rpm). Hone the guide until you obtain the valve stem clearance specified in **Table 2** and with a crosshatch pattern of 60°.

10. Repeat for each valve guide.

11. Soak the cylinder head in a container filled with hot, soapy water. Then clean the valve guides using the Harley-Davidson valve guide brush or an equivalent bristle brush—do not use a steel brush. Do not use cleaning solvent, kerosene or gasoline as these chemicals will not remove all of the abrasive particles produced during the honing operation. Repeat this step until you have cleaned all of the valve guides thoroughly. Then rinse the cylinder head and valve guides in clear, cold water and dry with compressed air.

12. After cleaning and drying the valve guides, apply clean engine oil to the guides to prevent rust.

13. Reface the valve seats to make them concentric with the new valve guides. Refer to *Valve Seat Reconditioning* in this chapter.

Valve Seat Inspection

1. Remove all of the carbon residue from each valve seat. Then clean the cylinder head as described under *Valve Inspection* in this chapter.

NOTE
The most accurate method of checking the valve seat width and position is with machinist's dye.

2. Check the valve seat with machinist's dye as follows:

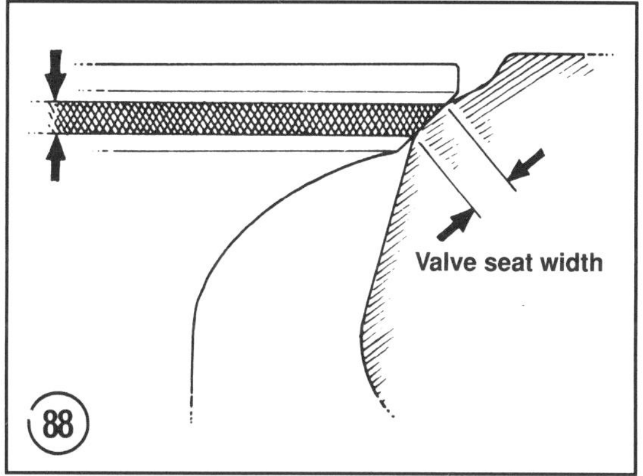

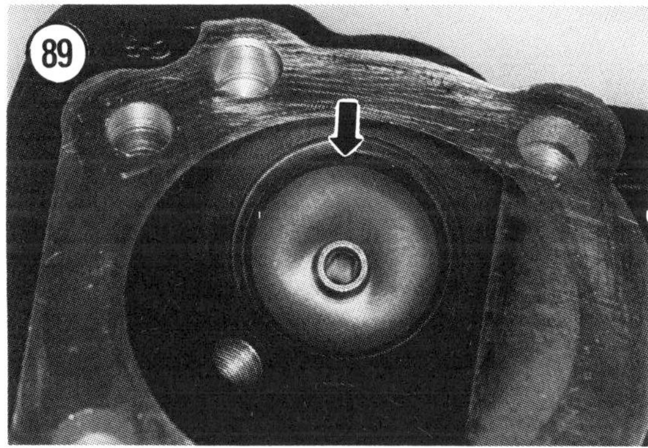

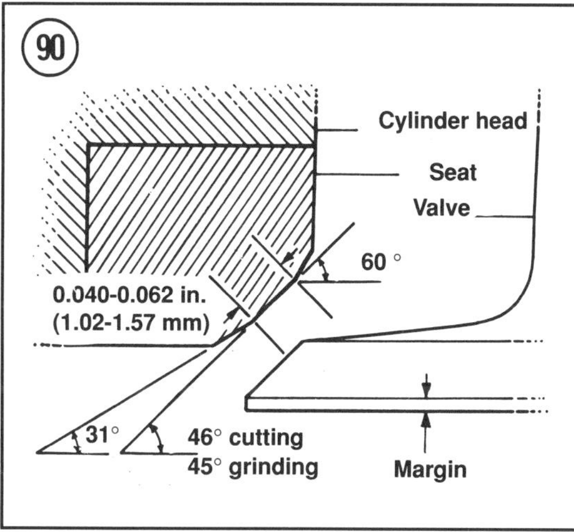

NOTE
Install the valves in their original locations when performing the following.

a. Thoroughly clean the valve face and valve seat with contact cleaner.
b. Spread a thin layer of Prussian blue or machinist's dye evenly on the valve face.
c. Insert the valve into its guide and turn it with a valve lapping tool.
d. Remove the valve and examine the impression left by the machinist's dye. If the impression left in the dye (on the valve or in the cylinder head) is not even and continuous and the valve seat width (**Figure 88**) is not even and continuous within the specified tolerance in **Table 2**, you must recondition the cylinder head valve seat.

3. Closely examine the valve seat in the cylinder head (**Figure 89**). It must be smooth and even with a polished seating surface.
4. If the valve seat is okay, install the valve as described in this chapter.
5. If the valve seat is not correct, recondition the valve seat as described in this chapter.

4

Valve Seat Reconditioning

Special valve seat cutter tools and considerable experience are required to recondition the valve seats in the cylinder head properly. You can save considerable money by removing the cylinder head and taking both cylinders to a dealership or machine shop and have the valve seats ground.

The following procedure is provided should you choose to perform this task yourself.

While the valve seat for both intake valves and exhaust valves are machined to the same angle, different cutter sizes are required. Use the Neway Valve Seat Cutter Set (part No. HD-35758) to cut the valve seats.

NOTE
Follow the manufacturer's instructions with using valve facing equipment.

Figure 90 shows the valve seat angles. Note that Harley-Davidson specifies a 45-degree seat angle when grinding seats and a 46-degree seat angle when cutting seats.

1. Clean the valve guides as described under *Inspection* in this chapter.

2. Carefully rotate and insert the solid pilot into the valve guide. Make sure you correctly seat the pilot.

CAUTION
Valve seat accuracy will depend on a correctly sized and installed pilot.

3. Using the 45-degree (stone) or 46-degree (cutter), descale and clean the valve seat with one or two turns.

CAUTION
*Measure the valve seat contact area in the cylinder head (**Figure 88**) after each cut to make sure its size and area are correct. Overgrinding will sink the valves too far into the cylinder head, requiring replacement of the valve seat.*

4. If the seat is still pitted or burned, turn the cutter until the surface is clean. Refer to the previous CAUTION to avoid removing too much material from the valve seat.
5. Remove the pilot from the valve guide.
6. Apply a small amount of valve lapping compound to the valve face and install the valve. Rotate the valve against the valve seat using a valve lapping tool. Remove the valve.
7. Measure the valve seat with a vernier caliper (**Figure 88** and **Figure 90**). Record the measurement to use as a reference point when performing the following.

CAUTION
The 31-degree cutter removes material quickly. Work carefully and check your progress often.

8. Reinsert the solid pilot into the valve guide. Be certain the pilot is properly seated. Install the 31-degree cutter onto the solid pilot and lightly cut the seat to remove 1/4 of the existing valve seat.
9. Install the 60-degree cutter onto the solid pilot and lightly cut the seat to remove the lower 1/4 of the existing valve seat.
10. Measure the valve seat with a vernier caliper. Then fit the 45-degree grinding stone or 46-degree cutter onto the solid pilot and cut the valve seat to the specified seat width listed in **Table 2**.
11. When the valve seat width is correct, check valve seating as follows.
12. Remove the solid pilot from the cylinder head.
13. Inspect the valve seat-to-valve face impression as follows:
    a. Clean the valve seat with contact cleaner.
    b. Spread a thin layer of Prussian Blue or machinist's dye evenly on the valve face.
    c. Insert the valve into its guide.
    d. Support the valve with your fingers and turn it with a valve lapping tool.
    e. Remove the valve and examine the impression left by the Prussian blue or machinist's dye.
    f. Measure the valve seat width (**Figure 88** and **Figure 90**). Refer to **Table 2** for the correct seat width.
    g. The valve seat contact area must be in the center of the valve face area.
14. If the contact area is too high on the valve, or if it is too wide, cut the seat with the 31-degree cutter. This will remove part of the top valve seat area to lower or narrow the contact area.
15. If the contact area is too low on the valve, or if it is too wide, use the 60-degree cutter and remove part of the lower area to raise and widen the contact area.
16. After obtaining the desired valve seat position and angle, use the 45° grinding stone or the 46° cutter and very lightly clean off any burrs caused by the previous cuts.
17. When the contact area is correct, lap the valve as described in this chapter.
18. Repeat Steps 1-17 for all remaining valve seats.
19. Thoroughly clean the cylinder head and all valve components in solvent, then clean with detergent and hot water and rinse in cold water. Dry with compressed air. Then apply a light coat of engine oil to all non-aluminum metal surfaces to prevent any rust formation.

Valve Lapping

Valve lapping is a simple operation which can restore the valve seal without machining if wear or distortion is not too great.

1. Smear a light coating of fine grade valve lapping compound on the seating surface of the valve.
2. Insert the valve into the head.
3. Wet the suction cup of the lapping tool and stick it onto the head of the valve. Lap the valve to the seat by spinning tool between your hands while lifting and moving the valve around the seat 1/4 turn at a time.

4. Wipe off the valve and seat frequently to check progress of lapping. Lap only enough to achieve a precise seating ring around valve head.

5. Closely examine the valve seat in the cylinder head. The seat must be smooth and even with a polished seating ring.

6. Thoroughly clean the valves and cylinder head in solvent to remove all of the grinding compound residue. Compound left on the valves or the cylinder head will cause rapid engine wear.

7. After installing the valves into the cylinder head, test each valve for proper seating. Check by pouring solvent into the intake and exhaust ports. Solvent must not leak past the valve seats. If leakage occurs, the combustion chamber will appear wet. If solvent leaks past any of the seats, disassemble that valve assembly and repeat the lapping procedure until there is no leakage.

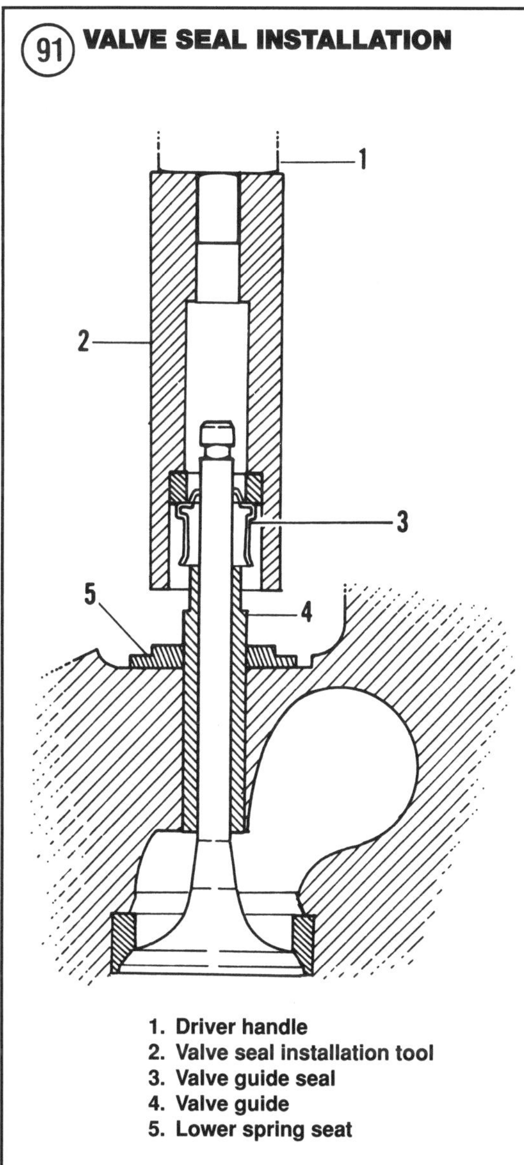

1. Driver handle
2. Valve seal installation tool
3. Valve guide seal
4. Valve guide
5. Lower spring seat

Valve Seat Replacement

Valve seat replacement requires considerable experience and equipment. Refer this work to a Harley-Davidson dealership or machine shop.

Valve Installation

You need the following tools to install the valves:

a. Valve spring compressor.
b. Harley-Davidson Valve Seal Installation Tool (part No. HD-34643A) or equivalent.
c. Harley-Davidson Driver Handle (part No. HD-34740) or equivalent.

1. Lap valves as described in this chapter.

CAUTION
The cylinder heads, valve seats and valves must be thoroughly cleaned of all abrasive lapping compound before reassembly. Any lapping compound left in the engine will result in excessive engine wear.

2. Coat a valve stem with oil and insert the valve into its valve guide in cylinder head.
3. Install the lower spring seat so that its flat side faces down. See **Figure 79** and **(5, Figure 91)**.
4. Install new valve guide seals as follows:
   a. Place a protective cover over the end of the valve stem (covering the valve keeper groove on the valve stem).

   CAUTION
   The protective cover used in sub-step b prevents the valve stem keeper groove from tearing the valve stem seal.

   b. Wipe the protective cover with new engine oil and place a new valve guide seal on the cover.
   c. Tap the seal into place with the Harley-Davidson valve seal installation tool and driver handle; see **Figure 91**. When the installation tool bottoms out on the lower spring seat, the oil seal is properly installed. If you do not have the special tools, use a socket and hammer and

tap the seal into place until it bottoms out against the lower spring seat. See **Figure 92**.

d. If you have to remove an oil seal after installing it, discard the seal and install a new one.

5. Install the valve springs and the upper spring seat (**Figure 76**).
6. Push down on the upper spring seat with the valve spring compressor (**Figure 75**) and install the valve keepers. After releasing tension from the compressor, lightly tap the upper spring seat with a plastic hammer to make sure the keepers (**Figure 93**) are seated.
7. Repeat to install the remaining valve guide seals and valves.

CAUTION
If you remove the valve after installing it the valve seal will be damaged. If you must remove the valve, install a new seal.

CYLINDERS

Refer to **Figure 94** when servicing the cylinders in the following sections.

Removal

1. Remove the cylinder head as described in this chapter.
2. Remove all dirt and foreign material from the cylinder base.
3. Remove the 2 dowel pins and O-rings (**Figure 95**) from the top of the cylinder.
4. Turn the crankshaft until the piston is at bottom dead center (BDC).
5. Loosen the cylinder by tapping around the perimeter with a rubber or plastic mallet.

NOTE
*The front and rear cylinders (**Figure 96**) are identical (same part number). Mark each cylinder so that you can reinstall it in its original position.*

6. Pull the cylinder straight up and off the piston and cylinder studs.
7. Place clean shop rags into the crankcase opening to prevent objects from falling undetected into the crankcase.
8. Install a rubber hose over each stud. This will protect both the piston and studs from damage.

CAUTION
After removing the cylinder, use care when working around the cylinder studs to prevent bending or damaging them. The slightest bend could cause a stud failure during engine operation.

9. Repeat Steps 1-8 for the other cylinder.

Inspection

Because of the factory pistons' complex shape and design, you cannot accurately measure piston diameter using standard measuring tools. Check piston-to-cylinder clearance by measuring the cylinder bore diameter. If a cylinder is worn, have the cylinder bored by a dealer to the factory oversize specification—not to match a particular piston size as with conventional methods.

The following procedure requires the use of highly specialized and expensive measuring tools. If you do not have the special tools described in this section, refer service to a dealership.

NOTE
Harley-Davidson recommends clamping the cylinder between torque plates

94

PISTON/CYLINDER ASSEMBLY

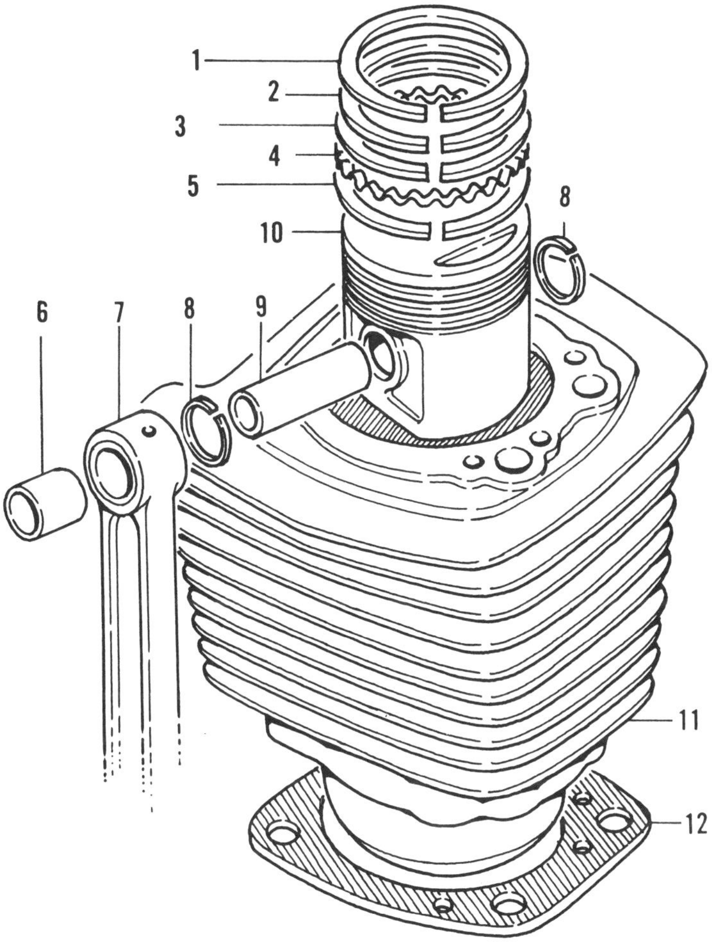

1. Upper compression ring
2. Lower compression ring
3. Upper oil ring
4. Spacer
5. Lower oil ring
6. Bushing
7. Connecting rod
8. Retaining rings
9. Piston pin
10. Piston
11. Cylinder
12. Base gasket

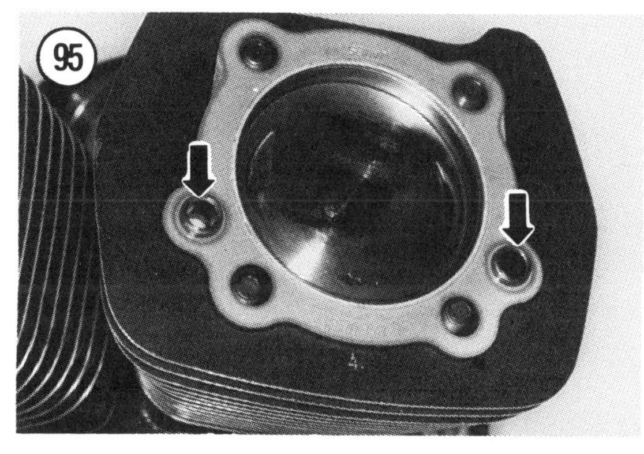

*(part No. HD-33446) (**Figure 97**) when making cylinder measurements and when boring and honing the cylinder. This arrangement simulates the dforce applied to the cylinder when properly installed on the engine. Measurements made without the engine torque plate can vary by 0.001 in. (0.025 mm). If you do not have access to the torque plates, refer service to a dealership.*

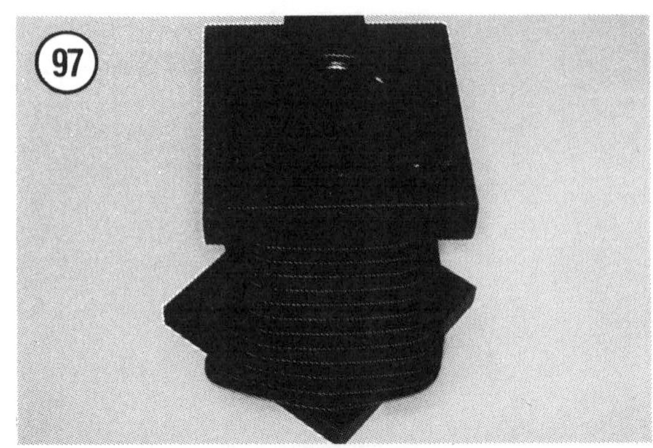

1. Carefully remove all gasket residue from both cylinder gasket surfaces.
2. Thoroughly clean the cylinder with solvent and dry with compressed air. Lightly oil the cylinder bore to prevent rust after performing Step 3.
3. Check the top (**Figure 98**) and bottom cylinder block gasket surfaces with a straightedge and feeler gauge. Replace the cylinder and piston if the following warpage limits are exceeded:
   a. Top cylinder surface: 0.006 in. (0.152 mm).
   b. Bottom cylinder surface: 0.008 in. (0.203 mm).

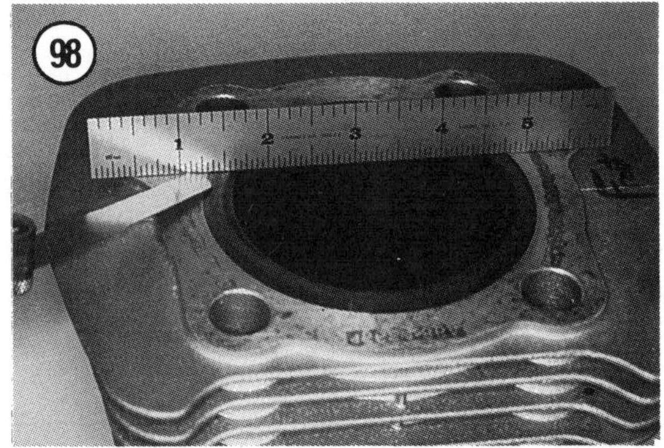

4. Install a new cylinder head and base gasket onto the cylinder and clamp the cylinder between the torque plates (**Figure 97**). Install the torque plate bolts, making sure they engage the gaskets properly. Tighten the torque plate bolts following the procedure and torque specification given for the cylinder heads as described in this chapter.
5. Measure the cylinder bore, with a bore gauge or inside micrometer at the points shown in **Figure 99**. Make the initial measurement 0.500 in. (12.7 mm) below the top (**Figure 100**) of the cylinder. The 0.500 in. (12.7 mm) depth represents the start of the ring path area; do not take readings that are out of the ring path area.

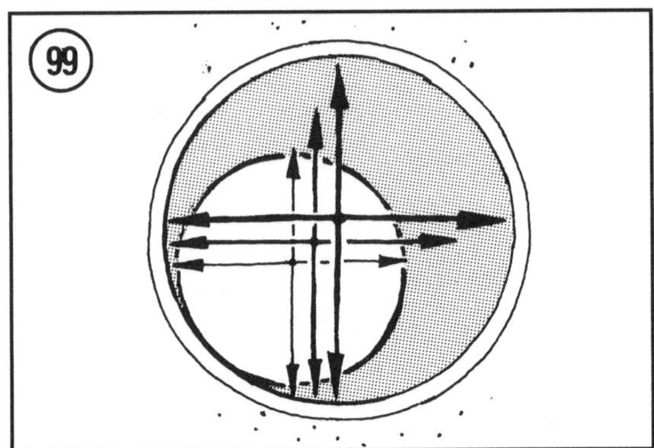

6. Measure in 2 axes—aligned with the piston pin and at 90° to the pin. If the taper or out-of-round measurements exceed the service limits in **Table 2**, bore the cylinders to the next oversize and install oversize pistons and rings. Rebore both cylinders though only one may be worn.
7. Check the cylinder walls for scuffing, scratches or other damage.
8. Confirm all cylinder measurements with your dealer before ordering replacement parts or having the cylinders serviced.
9. After servicing the cylinders, wash each cylinder in hot, soapy water. This is the only way to clean the

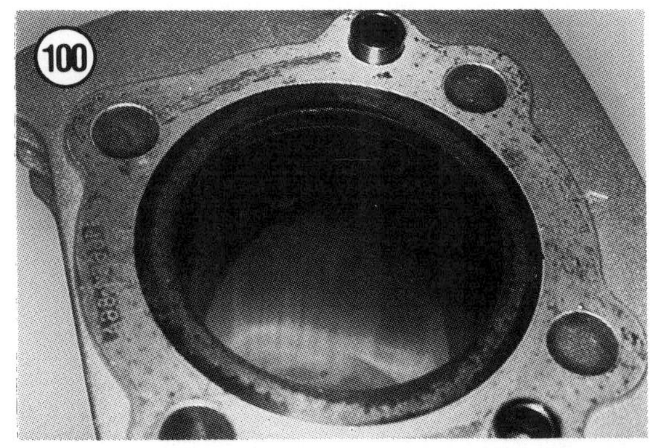

cylinder walls of the fine grit material left from the boring or honing process. After washing the cylinder bore, run a clean white cloth through it. If the cloth shows traces of grit or oil, the cylinder is not clean enough. Repeat until the cloth comes out clean. When the cylinder wall is clean, dry with compressed air then lubricate with clean engine oil to prevent the cylinder wall from rusting. Repeat for the other cylinder.

CAUTION
The hot soapy water described in Step 9 is the only solution that will completely clean the cylinder walls. Solvent and kerosene cannot wash fine grit out of the cylinder crevices. Grit left in the cylinder will act as an abrasive grinding compound and cause premature wear to the engine components.

Installing New Pistons

Because you cannot accurately measure the pisons, the actual bore size determines piston selection. See *Inspection* in this section.

101

102

Cylinder Studs and Cylinder Head Bolts Inspection and Cleaning

The cylinder studs and cylinder head bolts must be in good condition and properly cleaned prior to installing the cylinders and cylinder heads. Otherwise, damaged or dirty studs may cause cylinder head distortion and gasket leakage.

1. Replace damaged cylinder head bolts (**Figure 101**).
2. Examine the cylinder studs for bending, looseness or damage. Replace studs as described under *Cylinder Stud Replacement* in this chapter. If the studs are in good condition, perform Step 3.

CAUTION
The cylinder studs, cylinder head bolts and washers consist of hardened material. Do not substitute these items with a part made of a lower grade material. If they require replacement, purchase new parts from a Harley-Davidson dealership.

3. Cover both crankcase openings with shop rags to prevent abrasive dust from falling into the engine.
4. Remove all carbon residue from the cylinder studs and cylinder head bolts as follows:
   a. Apply solvent to the cylinder stud and mating cylinder head bolt threads and thread the bolt onto the stud.
   b. Turn the cylinder head bolt back and forth to loosen and remove the carbon residue from the threads. Remove the bolt from the stud. Blow both thread sets with compressed air.
   c. Repeat until both thread sets are free of all carbon residues.
   d. Spray the cylinder stud and cylinder head bolt with electrical contact cleaner and allow to dry.
   e. Set the cleaned bolt aside and install it on the same stud when installing the cylinder head.
5. Repeat Step 4 for each cylinder stud and cylinder head bolt set.

Installation

1. Install the pistons and rings as described in this chapter.

NOTE
*Be certain that you have installed all of the piston pin retaining rings (***Figure 102***).*

2. Remove all gasket residue and clean the cylinders as described under *Inspection* in this chapter.
3. Install the dowel pin (A, **Figure 103**), if removed.
4. Install a new base gasket (B, **Figure 103**) onto the crankcase.
5. Turn the crankshaft until the piston is at top dead center (TDC).
6. Lubricate the cylinder bore and piston liberally with engine oil.
7. Slide the protective hoses off the cylinder studs.
8. Stagger the piston ring end gaps so that they are 180° apart (**Figure 104**).
9. Compress the rings with a ring compressor (**Figure 105**).

NOTE
Install the cylinder in its original position.

10. Carefully align the cylinder (front facing forward) with the cylinder studs and slide it down until it is over the top of the piston. Then continue sliding the cylinder down and past the rings. Remove the ring compressor once the piston rings enter the cylinder (**Figure 106**).
11. Continue to slide the cylinder down until it bottoms out on the crankcase (**Figure 107**).
12. Repeat to install the opposite cylinder.
13. Install the cylinder heads as described in this chapter.

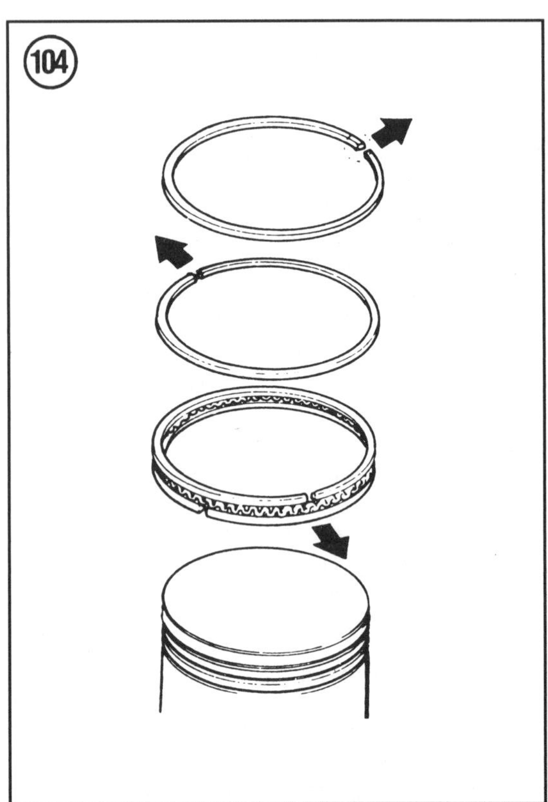

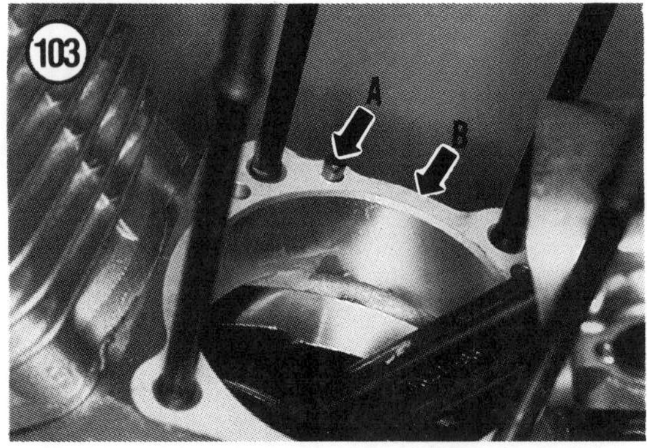

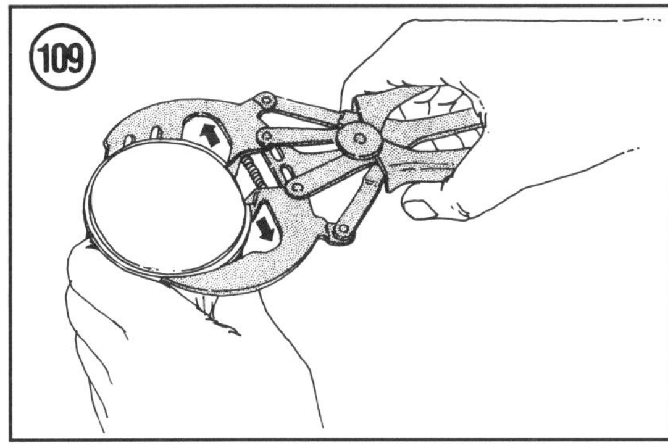

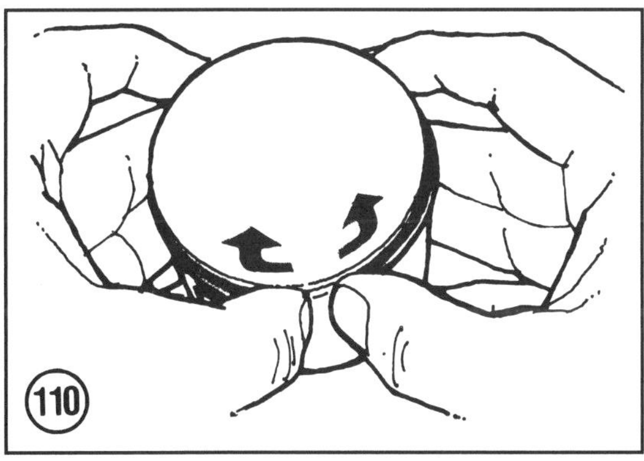

PISTONS AND PISTON RINGS

Refer to **Figure 94** when servicing the pistons and rings in this section.

Piston and Piston Rings Removal

1. Remove the cylinder as described in this chapter.
2. Stuff the crankcase with clean shop rags.
3. Lightly mark the pistons with an F (front) or R (rear).

WARNING
The piston pin retaining rings are highly compressed in the piston. Wear safety glasses when removing them in Step 4.

4. Using an awl, pry the piston pin retaining rings (**Figure 102**) out of the piston. Place your thumb over the hole to help prevent the rings from flying out during removal.

NOTE
Mark the piston pins so you can reinstall them into their original positions.

5. Support the piston and push out the piston pin. If the piston is difficult to remove, use a piston pin removal tool (**Figure 108**).

NOTE
If you intend to reuse the piston rings, identify the rings so that they can be reinstalled in their original ring grooves.

6. Remove the piston rings using a ring expander tool (**Figure 109**) or spread them with your fingers (**Figure 110**) and remove them.
7. Inspect the pistons, piston pins and pistons rings as described in this chapter.

Piston Inspection

1. Carefully clean the carbon from the piston crown (**Figure 111**) using a soft scraper. Do not remove or damage the carbon ridge around the circumference of the piston above the top ring.

CAUTION
Do not wire brush piston skirts.

4

2. Using a broken piston ring, remove all carbon deposits from the piston ring grooves (**Figure 112**). Do not remove metal from the piston ring grooves when cleaning them.
3. Examine each ring groove for burrs, dented edges and wear. Pay particular attention to the top compression ring groove, as it usually wears more than the others.
4. Measure cylinder bore diameter as described in this chapter. Replace worn or damaged parts as required.

Piston Pin Inspection

1. Clean the piston pin in solvent and dry thoroughly.
2. Replace the piston pin if cracked, pitted or scored.
3. Check piston pin clearance as described *Piston Pin Bushing Inspection and Replacement* in this chapter.

Piston Pin Bushing Inspection and Replacement

A piston pin bushing (**Figure 94**) is installed in the small end of each connecting rod. These bushings are reamed to provide correct piston pin clearance (clearance between piston pin and bushing). This clearance is critical in preventing pin knock and severe top end damage.

1. Inspect the piston pin bushings (**Figure 94**) for excessive wear or damage (pit marks, scoring or wear grooves). Then check for loose bushings. The bushings must be a tight fit in the connecting rods.
2. Measure the piston pin diameter using a micrometer (**Figure 113**) where it rides in the bushing. Then measure the piston pin bushing diameter using

111

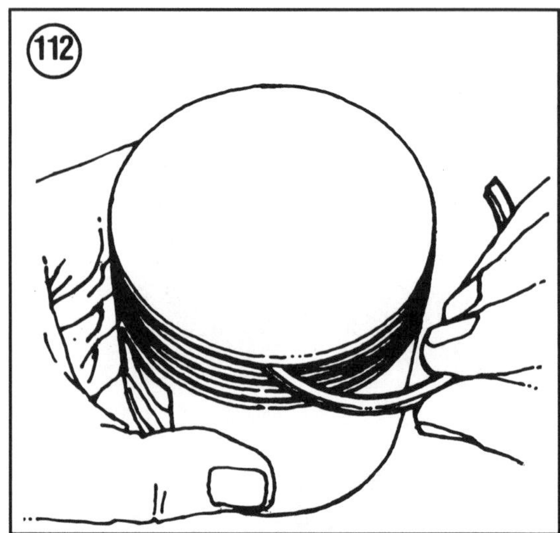
112

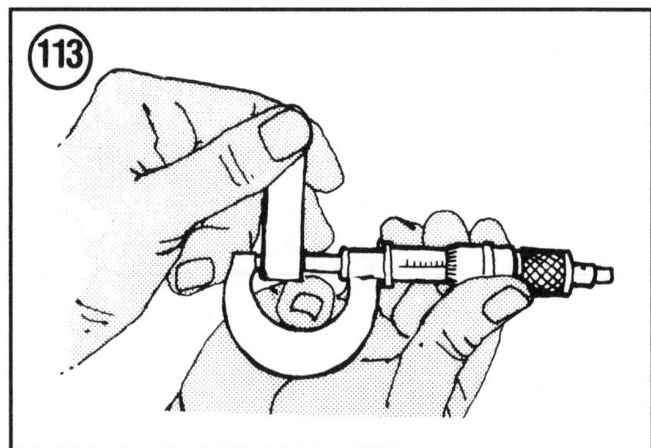
113

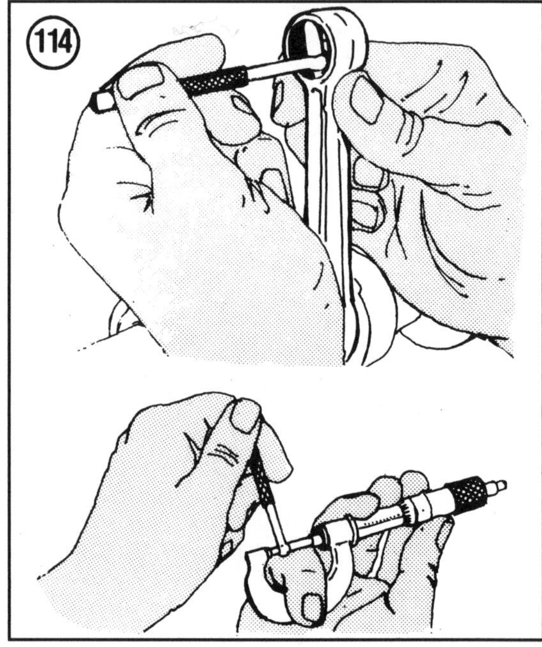
114

a snap gauge or bore gauge (**Figure 114**). Subtract the pin outer diameter from bushing inner diameter to determine piston pin clearance. Replace the pin and bushing if the clearance meets or exceeds the service limit in **Table 2**.

Piston Pin Bushing Replacement

You can replace the piston pin bushings with the engine cases assembled and installed on the bike.

You need the following special tools to replace and ream the piston pin bushings. If you do not have these tools, refer bushing replacement to a Harley-Davidson mechanic.

NOTE
All of the following part numbers are factory Harley-Davidson part numbers. Aftermarket tools are also available.

a. Rod clamping fixture (part No. HD-95952-33A). This tool is required if you are going to replace the bushings with the engine cases assembled.
b. Piston pin bushing tool (part No. HD-95970-32B).
c. Piston pin bushing reamer (part No. HD-94800-26A).
d. Connecting rod bushing hone (part No. HD-35102).

1. Remove 2 of the plastic hoses protecting the cylinder studs and slide the rod clamping fixture over the studs. Reinstall the 2 hoses.

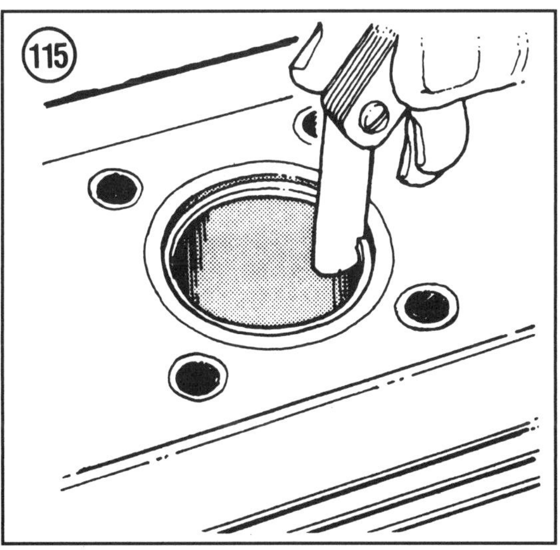

2. Stuff some clean shop rags into the crankcase opening to keep bushing particles and abrasive dust from falling into the engine.
3. Wrap some brass shim stock around the rod and then tighten the 2 thumb screws against the rod to hold it in place.

NOTE
When installing the new bushing, align the oil hole in the bushing with the oil hole in the connecting rod.

4. Replace the bushing using the piston pin bushing tool, following the tool manufacturer's instructions. The bushing must be flush with both sides of the rod.

CAUTION
Be certain the bushing and connecting rod oil holes align.

5. Turning the reamer clockwise, undercut the new bushing so that the piston pin clearance is 0.0005 in. (0.031 mm).
6. Hone the new bushing to obtain the piston pin clearance specified in **Table 2**. Use honing oil—not engine oil—when honing the bushing to size.
7. Install the piston pin through the bushing. The pin must move through the bushing smoothly with no binding or roughness. Confirm pin clearance using a micrometer and bore gauge.
8. Carefully remove the shop rags from the crankcase openings and replace them with clean rags.

Piston Ring Inspection

1. Clean the piston ring grooves as described under *Piston Inspection* in this chapter.
2. Inspect the ring grooves for burrs, nicks, or broken or cracked lands. Replace the piston if necessary.
3. Insert one piston ring into the top of its cylinder and tap it down about 1/2 in. (12.7 mm) using the piston to square it in the bore. Measure the ring end gap (**Figure 115**) with a feeler gauge and compare with the specification in **Table 2**. Replace the piston rings as a set if any one ring end gap measurement is excessive. Repeat for each ring.
4. Roll each compression ring around its piston groove as shown in **Figure 116**. The ring must move smoothly with no binding. If a ring binds in its groove, check the groove for damage. Replace the piston if necessary.

Piston Ring Installation

Each piston is equipped with 3 piston rings: 2 compression rings and 1 oil ring (**Figure 117**). The top compression ring is not marked. The second compression is marked with a dot (**Figure 118**).

You must install used piston rings on their original piston and in their original groove.

NOTE

When installing oversize compression rings, check them to make sure you are installing the correct size rings. The ring numbers must be the same as the piston oversize number.

1. Wash the piston in hot, soapy water. Then rinse with cold water and dry with compressed air. Make sure the oil control holes in the lower ring groove are clear and open.
2. Clean the piston rings carefully and dry with compressed air.
3. Install the oil ring assembly as follows:
   a. The oil ring consists of 3 rings: a ribbed spacer ring and 2 steel rings (C, **Figure 117**).
   b. Install the spacer ring into the lower ring groove. Butt the spacer ring ends together. Do *not* overlap the ring ends.
   c. Insert one end of the first steel ring into the lower groove so that it is below the spacer ring. Then spiral the other end over the piston crown and into the lower groove. To protect the ring end from scratching the side of the piston, place a piece of shim stock or a thin, flat feeler gauge between the ring and piston.
   d. Repeat sub-step c to install the other steel ring above the spacer ring.

NOTE

*When installing the compression rings, use a ring expander as shown in **Figure 109**. Do not expand the rings any more than necessary to install them.*

4. Install the second compression ring as follows:
   a. A dot mark is installed on one side of the second compression ring (B, **Figure 117**).
   b. Install the second compression ring with the dot mark facing up (**Figure 118**).
5. Install the top compression ring as follows:
   a. Harley-Davidson does not mark the top compression ring (A, **Figure 117**).

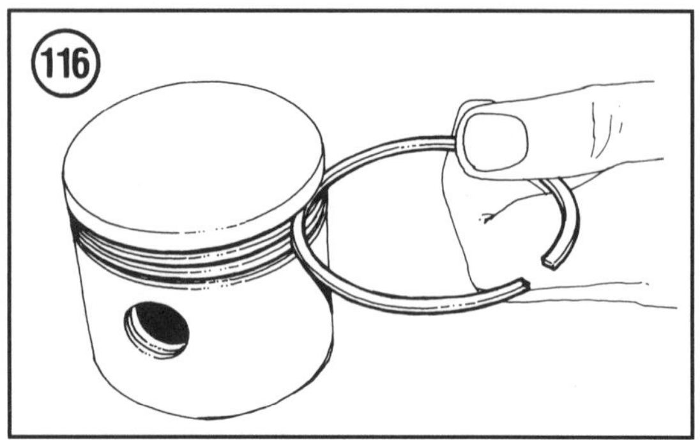

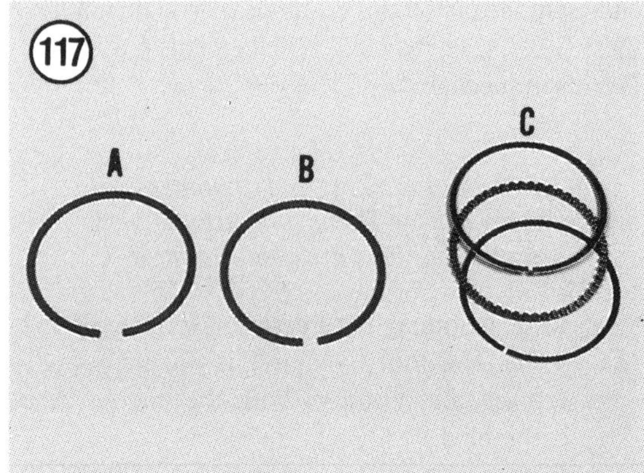

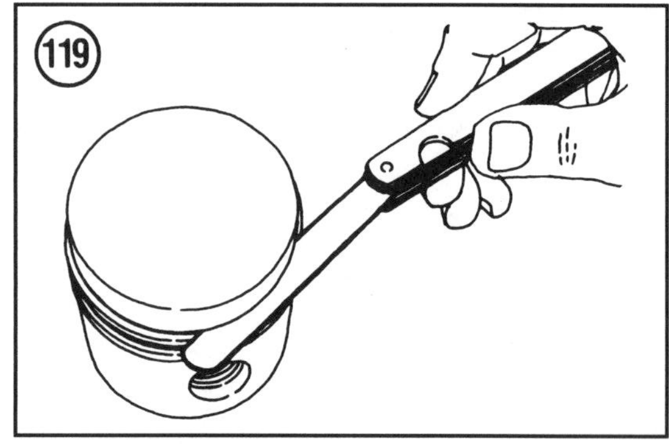

b. You can install new upper compression rings with either side facing up. If the original upper compression rings are used, install them with their original upper side facing up.

6. Check ring side clearance with a feeler gauge as shown in **Figure 119**. Check side clearance in several spots around the piston. If the clearance meets or exceeds the service limit in **Table 2**, note the following:

a. If the ring grooves are not clean, remove the rings and clean the grooves. Then reinstall the rings and recheck clearance.

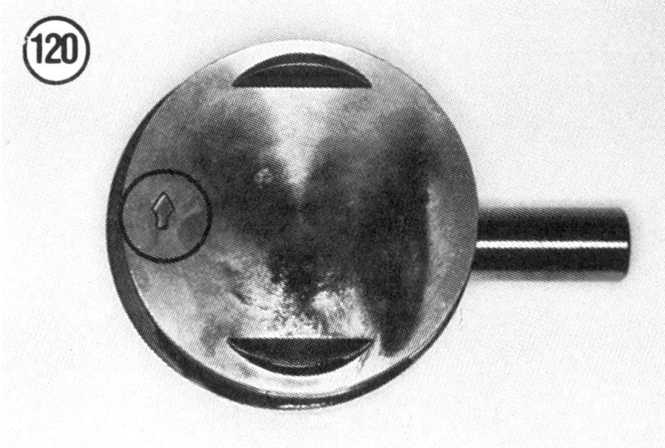

b. If installing the old rings, replace the rings and recheck side clearance.

c. If installing new rings, replace the piston.

7. Stagger the ring gaps around the piston as shown in **Figure 104**.

Piston Installation

1. Cover both crankcase openings to avoid dropping a retaining ring into the engine.
2. Install a *new* piston pin retaining ring into one groove in the piston. Make sure the ring seats in the groove completely.
3. Coat the connecting rod bushing and piston pin with assembly oil.

NOTE

The piston markings described in Step 4 are for factory Harley-Davidson pistons. If you are using aftermarket pistons, follow their manufacturer's directions for piston alignment and installation.

4. Place the piston over the connecting rod with its arrow mark facing *forward*. See **Figure 120**. Install used pistons on their original connecting rods; refer to the marks you made on the piston during removal. Install oversize pistons into the cylinder they were fitted to during the boring process.
5. Insert the piston pin (**Figure 121**) through the piston.
6. Install the other new piston pin retaining ring (**Figure 122**) into the piston groove.
7. Repeat for the other piston.
8. Install the cylinders as described in this chapter.

PUSHRODS

Refer to **Figure 123** when servicing the pushrods in this section.

Pushrod Identification

Each pushrod is a different length. You can identify each pushrod by its color-coded stripes (**Figure 124**):

a. Purple: rear exhaust (A, **Figure 125**).
b. Blue: rear intake (B, **Figure 125**).
c. Yellow: front intake (C, **Figure 125**).
d. Green: front exhaust (D, **Figure 125**).

4

Removal/Installation

Remove and install the pushrods as described under *Rocker Arm Cover and Cylinder Head Removal* in this chapter.

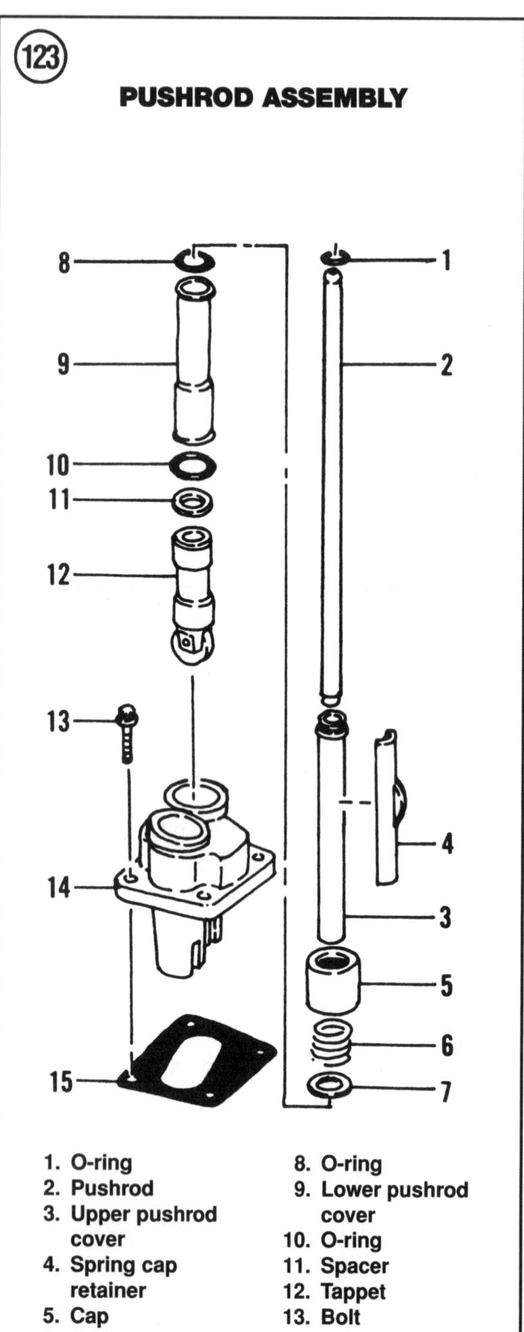

1. O-ring
2. Pushrod
3. Upper pushrod cover
4. Spring cap retainer
5. Cap
6. Spring
7. Spacer
8. O-ring
9. Lower pushrod cover
10. O-ring
11. Spacer
12. Tappet
13. Bolt
14. Tappet guide
15. Gasket

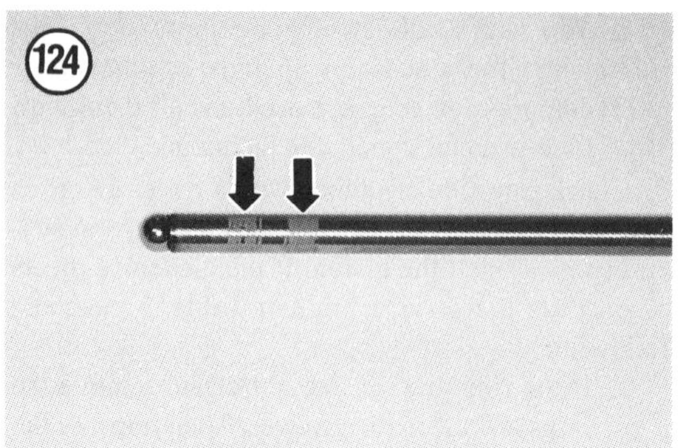

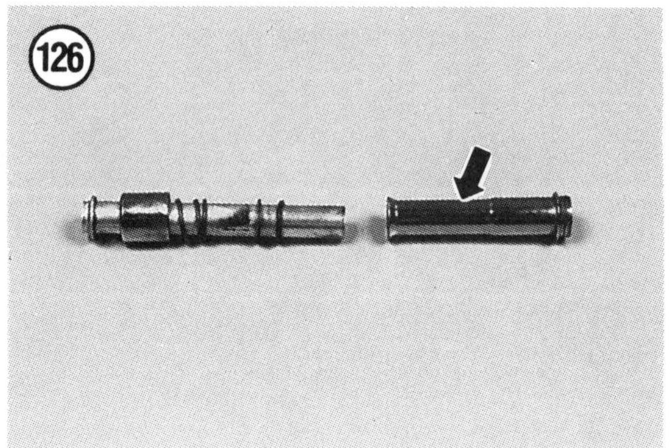

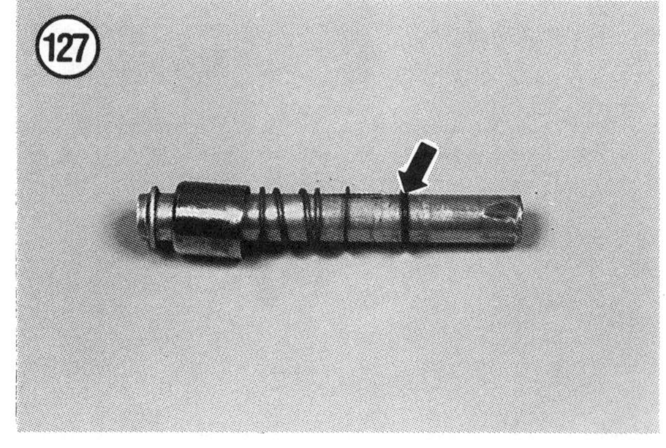

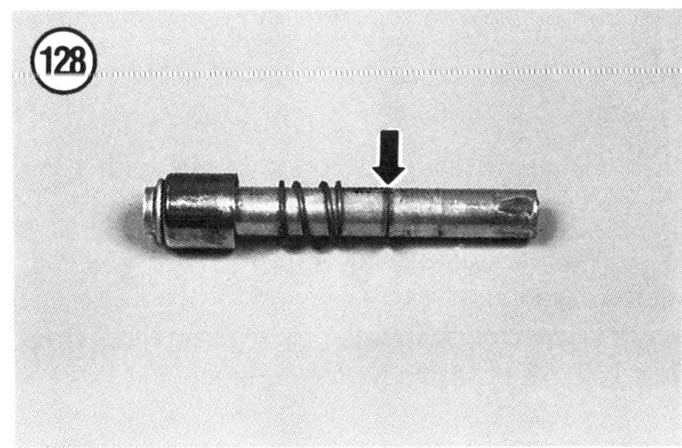

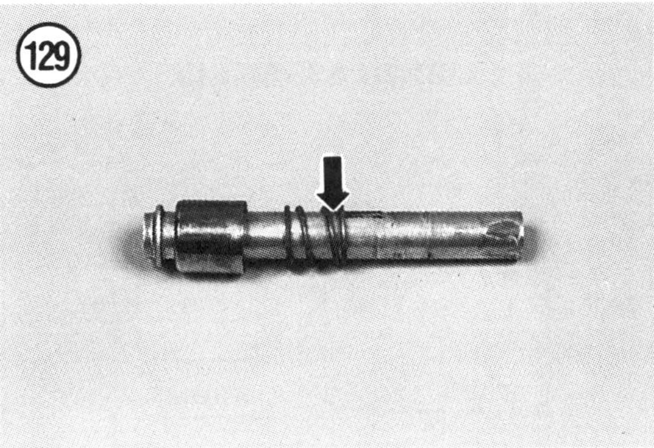

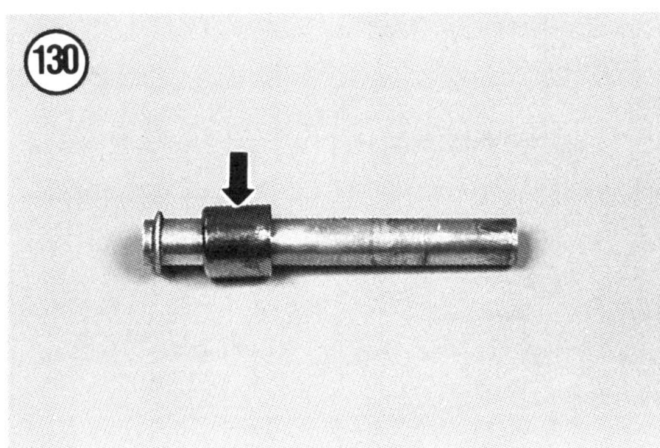

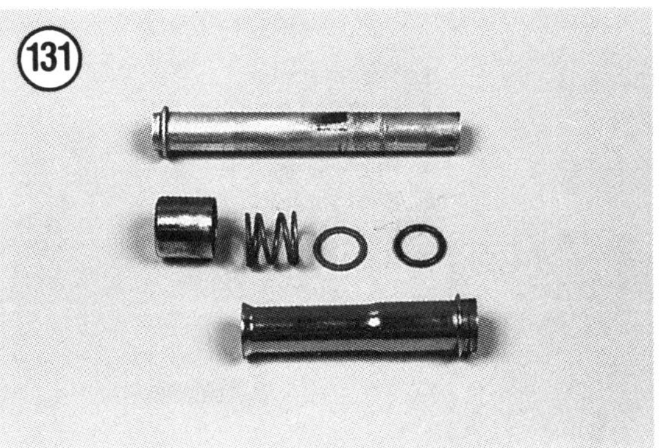

Inspection

1. Disassemble the pushrod cover as follows:
   a. Remove the lower pushrod cover (**Figure 126**).
   b. Remove the O-ring (**Figure 127**).
   c. Remove the spacer (**Figure 128**).
   d. Remove the spring (**Figure 129**).
   e. Remove the cap (**Figure 130**).
2. Check the pushrod cover assembly (**Figure 131**) as follows:
   a. Check the spring for sagging or cracking.
   b. Check the spacer for deformation or damage.
   c. Check the O-ring for cracking or wear.
   d. Check the pushrod covers for cracking or damage.
3. Check the pushrod ends (**Figure 124**) for wear.
4. Roll the pushrods on a flat surface, such as a piece of glass, and check for bending.
5. Replace all worn or damaged parts.
6. Reverse Step 1 to assemble the pushrod cover assembly. Push the lower pushrod cover into the cap to seat the O-ring. See **Figure 132**.

LIFTERS AND LIFTER GUIDES

Figure 123 shows a lifter in relation to its pushrod and lifter guide. The valve lifters and guides are installed on the right side of the engine. **Figure 133** shows the lifter assembly. During engine operation, the lifters pump themselves full of engine oil, thus taking up all play in the valve train. When you turn the engine off, the lifters leak down after a period of time as the oil drains out of each lifter. When you start the engine, the lifters will click until they refill with oil. The lifters are working properly when they stop clicking after the engine is run for a few minutes.

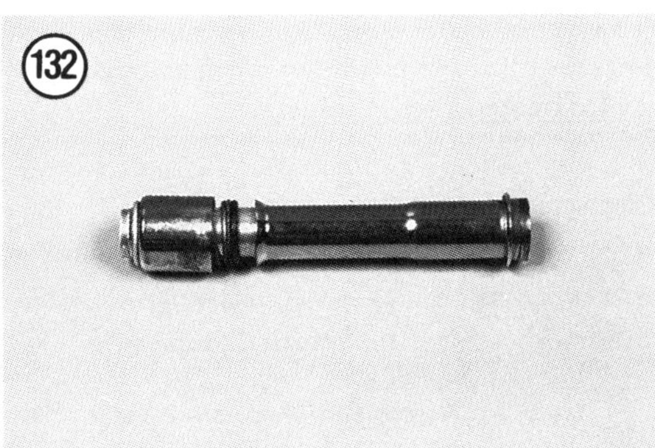

Special Tool

You need the Harley-Davidson lifter guide alignment tool (part No. HD-33442) to install the lifter guides. This tool is described later in this section.

Removal

During removal, store lifters in proper sequence for installation in their original position.

1. Remove the pushrods as described under *Rocker Arm Cover and Cylinder Head Removal* in this chapter.
2. Remove the lifter guide (**Figure 134**) mounting bolts .

3A. To remove the lifter guide and lifters with the gearcase installed on the engine, perform the following:

a. Bend a piece of stiff wire into a U-shape, then insert its ends into the holes in the top of each lifter as shown in **Figure 135**.

b. Pull the wire back to bind the lifters in the guide and then remove the guide and lifters from the engine. See **Figure 136**.

3B. If the gearcase is removed from the engine, perform the following:

a. Push the lifters against the side of the lifter guide to hold it in position.

b. Then lift the lifter guide away from the gearcase while still holding the lifters in position.

NOTE
Do not intermix the lifters when removing them in Step 4. Mark them so you can install them in their original position.

4. Remove the lifters through the bottom of the lifter guide. See **Figure 137**.
5. If you are not going to inspect the lifters as described in the following section, store them in a container filled with new engine oil until installation.
6. Remove the lifter guide gasket.

Disassembly/Inspection

NOTE
Place the lifters on a clean, lint-free cloth when handling and inspecting them in the following steps. When you finish inspecting the lifters, store them in oil as previously described.

1. Clean the lifter guides in solvent and dry thoroughly. Do *not* clean the lifters (**Figure 138**) in solvent.
2. Clean the lifter guide oil passages with compressed air.
3. Check the lifter rollers (**Figure 138**) for pitting, scoring, galling or excessive wear. If the rollers are worn excessively, check the mating cam lobes (**Figure 139**) for the same wear condition.

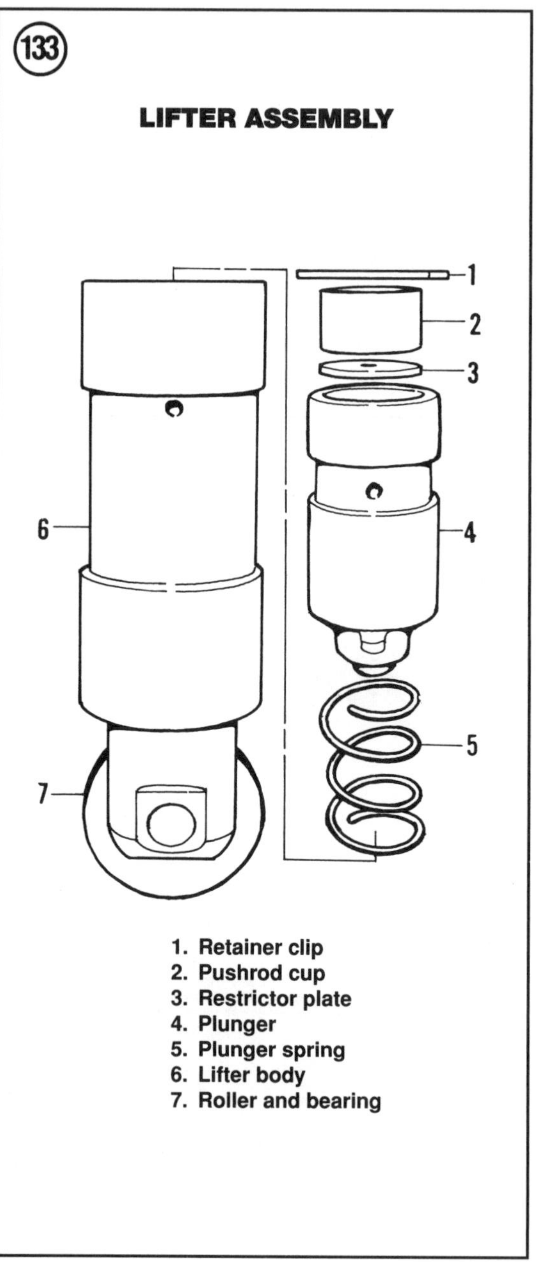

1. Retainer clip
2. Pushrod cup
3. Restrictor plate
4. Plunger
5. Plunger spring
6. Lifter body
7. Roller and bearing

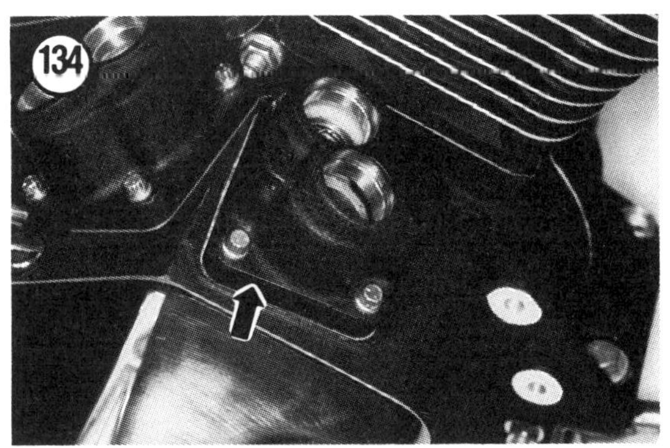

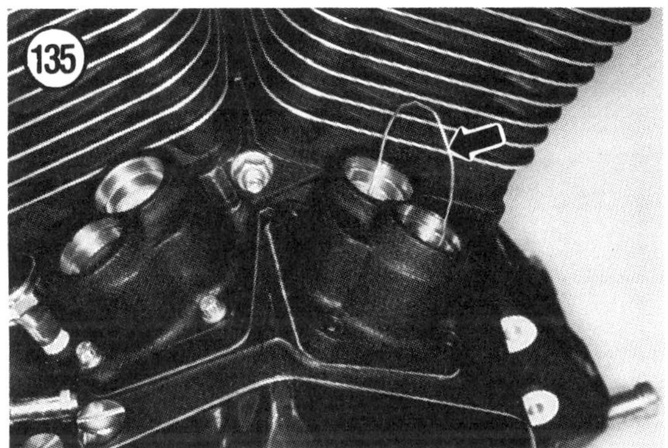

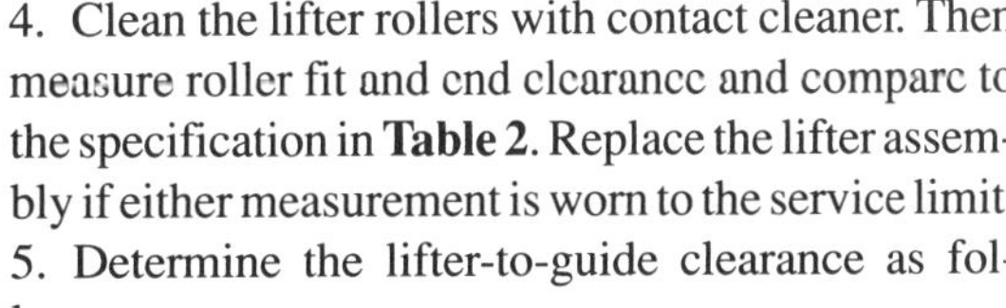

4. Clean the lifter rollers with contact cleaner. Then measure roller fit and cnd clcarancc and comparc to the specification in **Table 2**. Replace the lifter assembly if either measurement is worn to the service limit.
5. Determine the lifter-to-guide clearance as follows:
   a. Measure the lifter guide (A, **Figure 140**) bore inside diameter and record the measurement.
   b. Measure the lifter (**Figure 138**) outside diameter and record the measurement.
   c. Subtract substep b from substep a to determine the lifter-to-guide clearance, then compare the clearance against the service limit in **Table 2**. Replace the lifter or lifter guide if the clearance meets or exceeds the service limit.
6. Determine lifter guide-to-crankcase clearance as follows:
   a. Measure the crankcase lifter bore inside diameter (**Figure 139**) and record the measurement.
   b. Measure the lifter guide outside diameter (**Figure 140**) where it rides in the crankcase. Record the measurement.
   c. Subtract substep b from substep a to determine the lifter guide-to-crankcase clearance, then

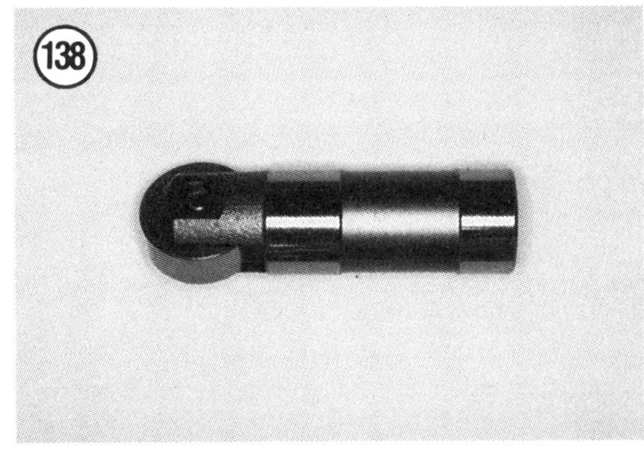

compare the clearance to the specification in **Table 2**. While Harley-Davidson does not list a service limit for this clearance, excessive clearance can cause lifter and guide wear. If the clearance for your model is excessive, refer further inspection to a Harley-Davidson dealership.

7. If a lifter does not show visual damage, but you suspect that it has become contaminated with dirt or has internal damage, replace it. While you can disassemble the lifters (**Figure 141**), replacement parts are not available to rebuild the lifter.

8. After inspecting the lifters, store them in a container filled with new engine oil until installation.

Installation

1. Remove 2 of the lifters from the oil filled container and place them on a clean, lint-free cloth.

NOTE
*You do not have to install the lifters with their oil holes (**Figure 142**) facing in any particular direction.*

2. Install the lifters (**Figure 137**) through the bottom of the lifter guide as shown in **Figure 143**.

NOTE
*The front and rear lifter guides are different. Identify each lifter guide by the word FRONT or REAR cast into the bottom of the guide (B, **Figure 140**).*

3. Install a new lifter guide gasket.

4A. To install the lifter guide and lifters with the gearcase installed on the engine, perform the following:

a. Pour some new engine oil onto the cam lobes (**Figure 139**).
b. Bend a piece of stiff wire into a U-shape, then insert its ends into the holes in the top of each lifter as shown in **Figure 136**.
c. Pull the wire back to bind the lifters in the guide and then install the guide and lifters into the engine at the same time. Remove the wire from the lifters (**Figure 135**).

4B. If the gearcase is removed from the engine, install the lifter guide and lifters as follows:

a. Push the lifters against the side of the lifter guide to hold them in position.

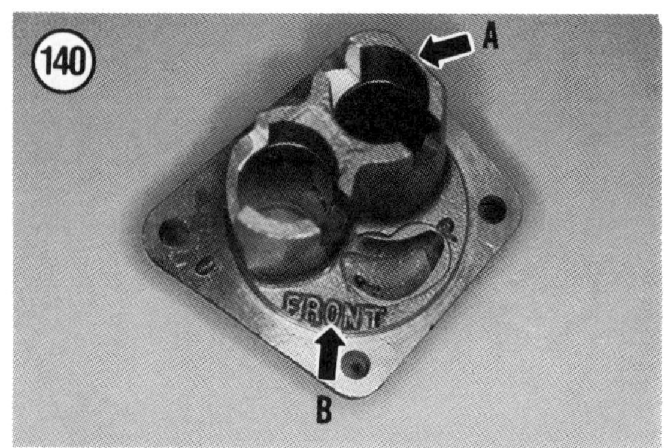

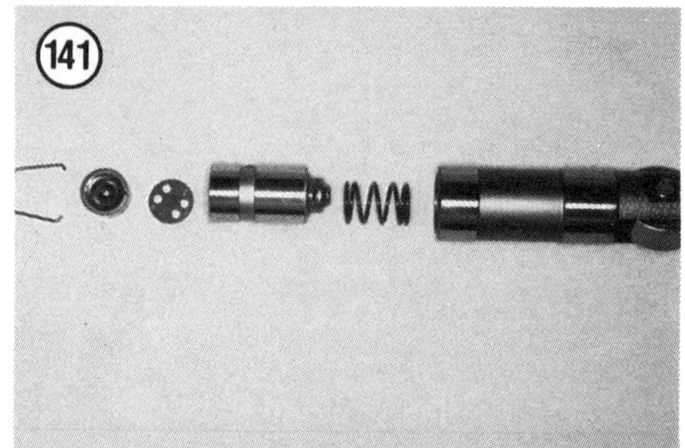

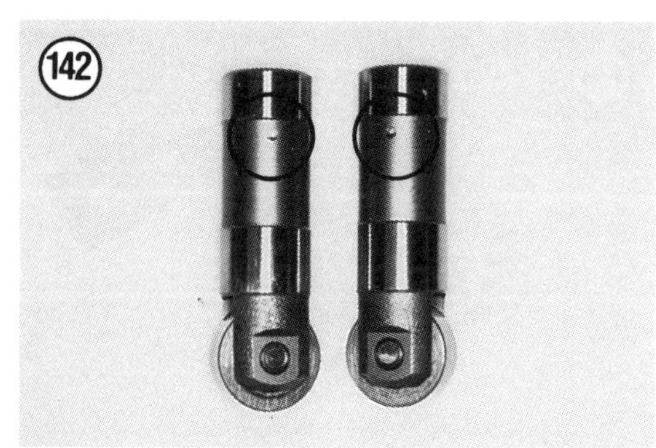

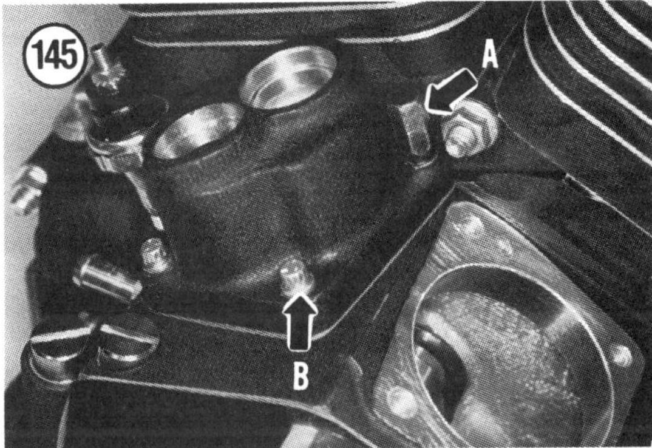

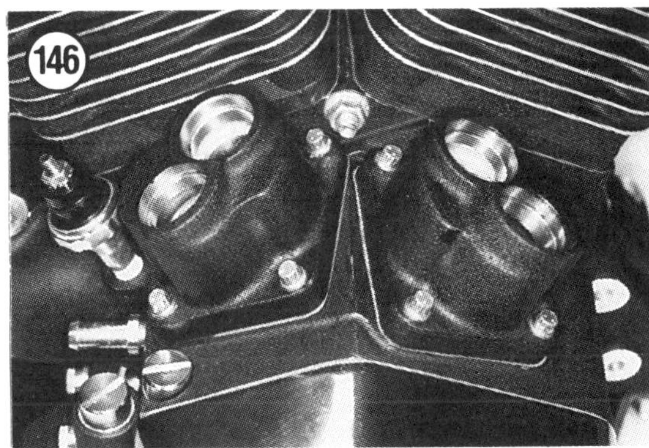

b. Install the lifter guide and lifters into the gearcase. Release the lifters and allow them to contact the cam lobes.

NOTE
***Figure 144** identifies the lifter oil feed hole called out in Step 5.*

5. Screw the Harley-Davidson lifter guide alignment tool (part No. HD-33443) into the lifter guide bolt hole closest to the lifter oil feed hole (A, **Figure 145**). Then install and tighten 3 lifter guide mounting bolts (B, **Figure 145**). Remove the alignment tool and install the remaining lifter guide mounting bolt.
6. Tighten all of the lifter guide mounting bolts to the torque specification in **Table 4**.
7. Repeat Steps 1-6 to install the opposite lifter guide and lifters. See **Figure 146**.
8. Install the pushrods as described under *Rocker Arm Cover and Cylinder Head Installation* in this chapter.

OIL PUMP

The oil pump (**Figure 147**) is mounted behind the gearcase cover. The oil pump consists of 2 sections: a feed pump which supplies oil under pressure to the engine components, and a scavenger pump which returns oil from the engine to the oil tank.

Refer to **Figure 148** when servicing the oil pump in the following sections.

Removal/Disassembly

You can disassemble the oil pump with the gearcase cover installed on the engine and the engine mounted in the frame.

NOTE
Label all gears and Woodruff keys so you can install them into their original mounting positions.

1. Drain the engine oil as described in Chapter Three.
2. If the engine is installed in the frame, perform the following:
   a. If necessary, remove the exhaust system and rear brake pedal assembly to access the oil pump assembly.

(148)

OIL PUMP

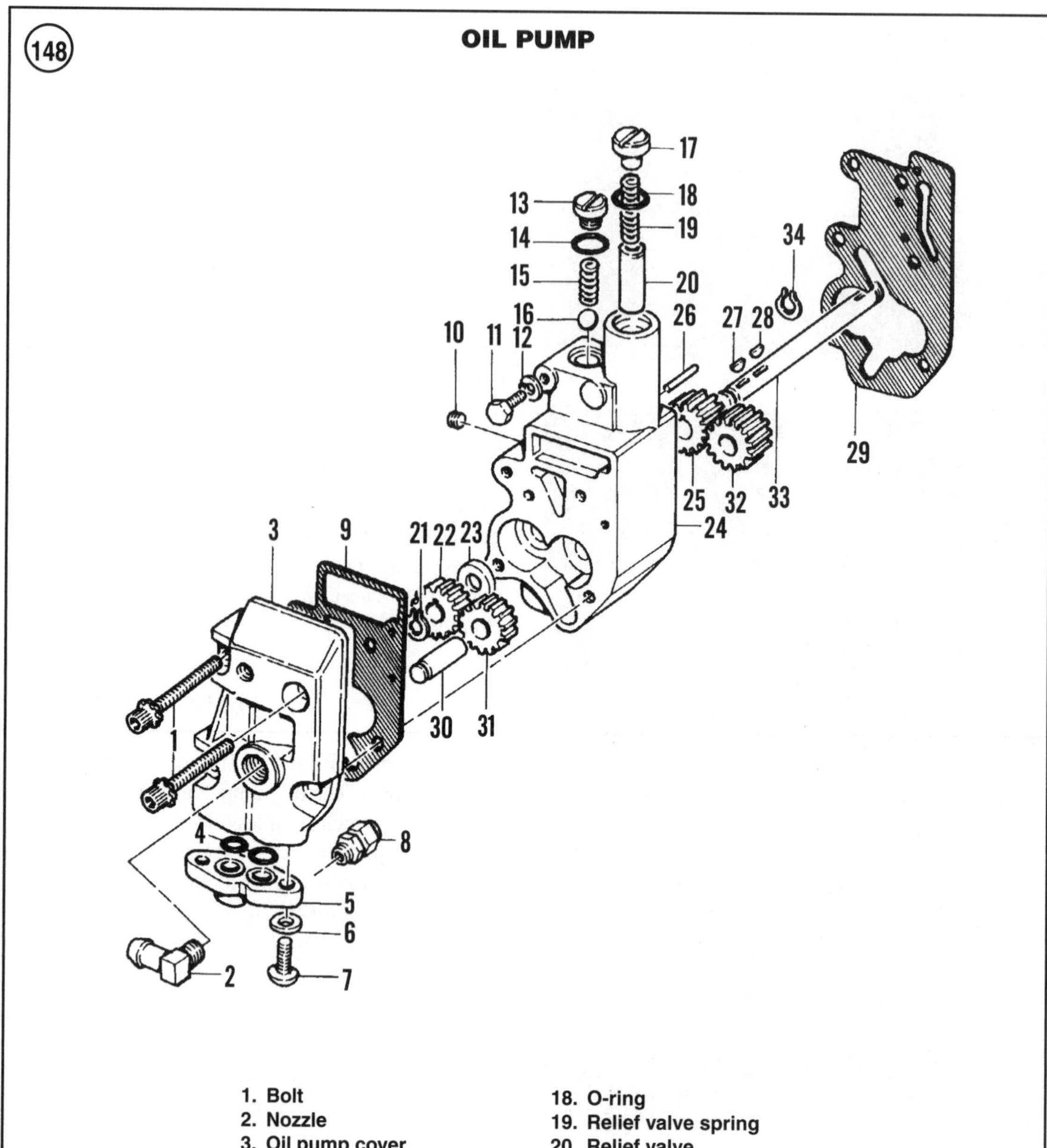

1. Bolt
2. Nozzle
3. Oil pump cover
4. O-rings
5. Manifold
6. Washer
7. Bolt
8. Oil line fitting
9. Gasket
10. Plug
11. Bolt
12. Washer
13. Plug
14. O-ring
15. Check valve spring
16. Check valve ball
17. Plug
18. O-ring
19. Relief valve spring
20. Relief valve
21. Circlip
22. Drive gear (feed gear)
23. Oil seal
24. Housing
25. Drive gear (scavenger gear)
26. Pin
27. Woodruff key
28. Woodruff key
29. Gasket
30. Idler shaft
31. Idler gear (feed gear)
32. Idler gear (scavenger gear)
33. Drive gear shaft
34. Circlip

149

150

151

NOTE
Before disconnecting the oil lines in Step 2, tag each line so that you can reconnect them correctly.

b. On 1991 models, cut the hose clamps securing the oil lines to the oil pump, then disconnect the hoses. Discard the clamps.
c. On 1992 and later models, disconnect the oil hoses from the oil pump as described under *Oil Filter Mount* in this chapter.

NOTE
Plug the end of each hose to prevent oil leakage and hose contamination.

3. Remove the relief valve assembly as follows:
   a. Remove the relief valve plug and O-ring (**Figure 149**).
   b. Remove the spring and relief valve (**Figure 150**).
4. Remove the check valve assembly as follows:
   a. Remove the check valve plug and O-ring (**Figure 151**).
   b. Remove the check valve spring (**Figure 152**).
   c. Remove the check valve ball (**Figure 153**).
5. Remove the oil pump cover mounting bolts and remove the oil pump cover and gasket (**Figure 154**).
6. Remove the drive (A, **Figure 155**) and idler (B, **Figure 155**) feed gears as follows:

NOTE
Do not push the drive gear shaft into the gearcase housing when removing the drive gear in the following steps. This will cause the inner key to fall inside the gearcase housing. If this happens, you will have to remove the gearcase cover to retrieve and install the key.

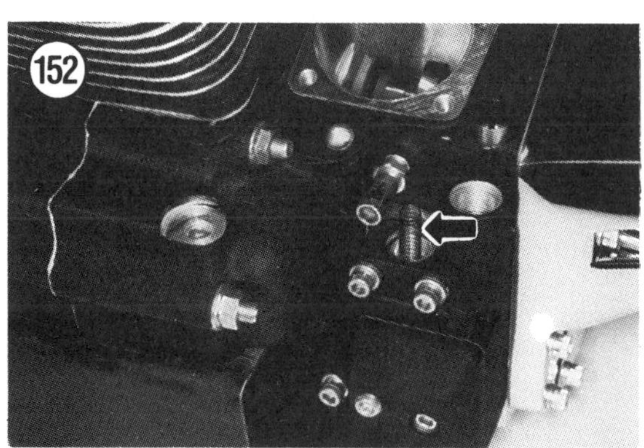
152

153

a. Remove the spiral retaining ring (**Figure 156**) from the groove in the end of drive gear shaft (A, **Figure 155**).

b. Remove the idler (B, **Figure 155**) and drive (A, **Figure 155**) gears.

c. Remove the key (**Figure 157**) from the drive gear shaft keyway.

7. Remove the oil pump housing mounting bolts (A, **Figure 158**).

8. Slide the oil pump housing (B, **Figure 158**) off the drive gear shaft and remove the housing.

9. Remove the scavenger gears as follows:

a. Remove the idler gear (**Figure 159**) from the oil pump housing.

b. Remove the drive gear (**Figure 160**) and key (**Figure 161**) from the drive gear shaft.

10. Remove the oil pump housing gasket.

11. To remove the oil pump drive gear and drive gear shaft, remove the timing gears as described under *Gearcase Cover and Timing Gears* in this chapter.

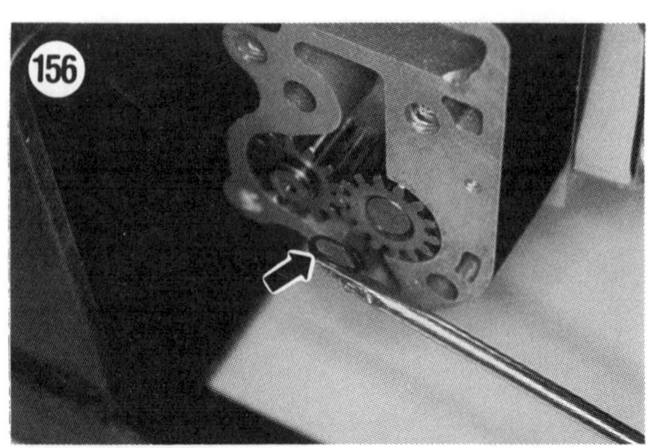

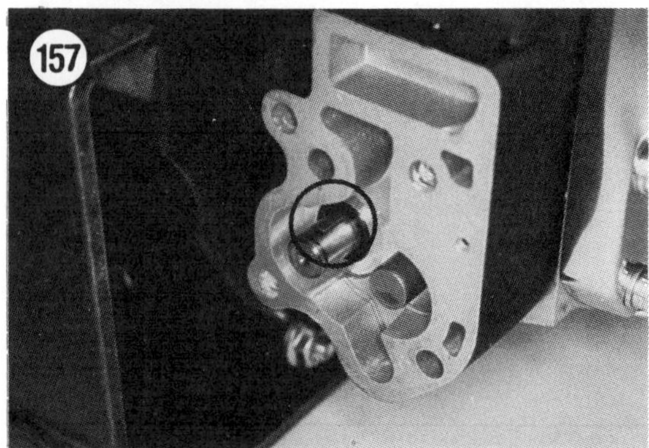

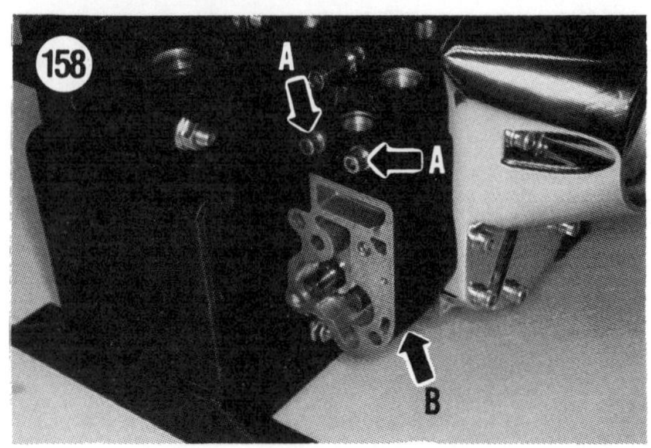

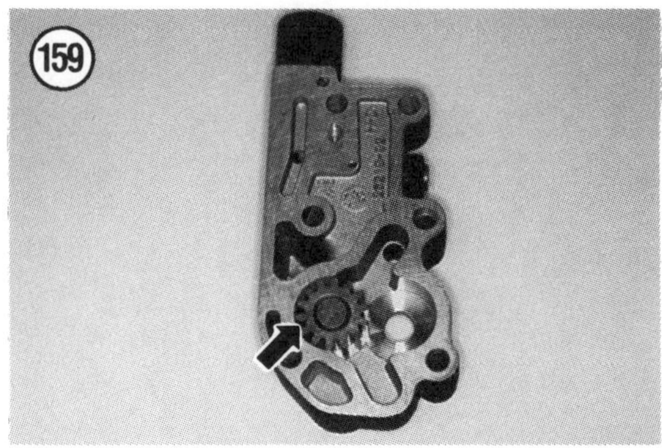

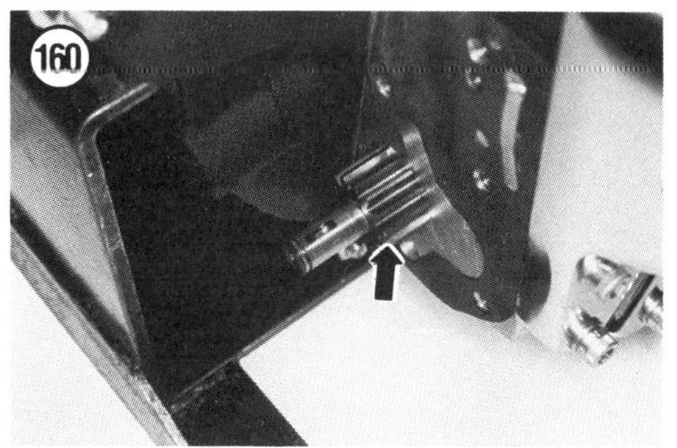
160

161

Inspection

1. Clean all parts thoroughly in solvent and place on a clean, lint-free cloth.
2. Blow compressed air through all of the oil pump cover and housing passages (**Figure 162**).
3. Replace the oil pump housing oil seal (A, **Figure 163**) if worn or damaged. Install the oil seal with its lip facing toward the feed gears.
4. Inspect the idler shaft (B, **Figure 163**) for excessive wear or damage. Replace the idler shaft if necessary.
5. Inspect each gear (**Figure 164**) for chipped teeth, cracks or other damage.
6. Inspect the feed gears and drive gear shaft keyways (**Figure 165**) for damage.
7. Inspect the check valve ball and spring (A, **Figure 166**) for wear or damage. Replace damaged parts.
8. Check the bypass valve plunger and spring (B, **Figure 166**) for wear and damage. Replace the damaged parts.
9. Assemble the scavenger gears into the oil pump housing (**Figure 167**). Lay a straightedge across the

162

164

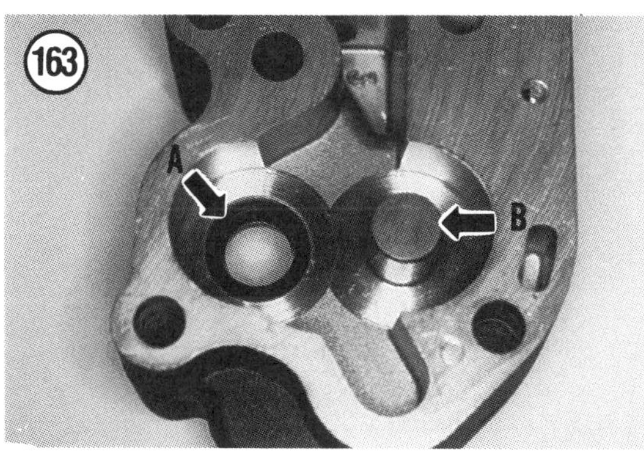

163

165

gears (**Figure 168**) and measure the clearance between the straightedge and the oil pump housing gasket surface with a feeler gauge (**Figure 168**). The correct clearance is 0.003-0.004 in. (0.08-0.10 mm). If the measured clearance is less than 0.003 in. (0.08 mm), replace the oil pump.

10. Repeat Step 9 for the feed gears (**Figure 169**).

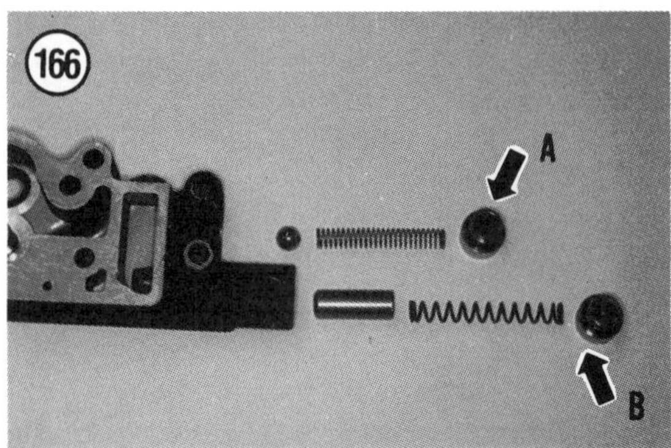

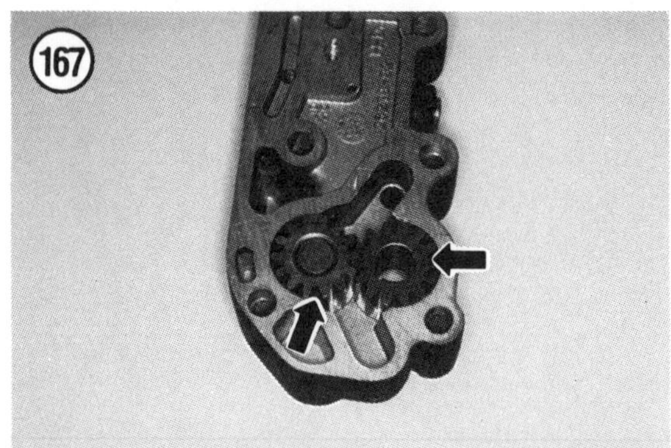

Reassembly/Installation

NOTE

Install all gears and Woodruff keys in their original positions. Refer to your notes made prior to oil pump removal and disassembly.

CAUTION

Never use homemade gaskets to check and reassemble the oil pump. Factory gaskets are made to a specified thickness with holes placed accurately to pass oil through the oil pump. Gaskets of the incorrect thickness can cause loss of oil pressure and severe engine damage.

1. If removed, install the drive gear shaft, oil pump drive gear and timing gears as described under *Gearcase Cover and Timing Gears* in this chapter.
2. Coat all parts with new engine oil prior to installation.
3. Install a new oil pump housing gasket (**Figure 170**).
4. Install the scavenger gears as follows:
   a. Install the key (**Figure 161**) onto the drive gear shaft.
   b. Install the drive gear (**Figure 160**) over the key and seat it against the crankcase.
5. Slide the oil pump housing (B, **Figure 158**) over the drive gear shaft and seat it against the crankcase.
6. Install the oil pump housing mounting bolts and washers (A, **Figure 158**) and tighten to 60-85 in.-lb. (6.8-9.6 N•m).

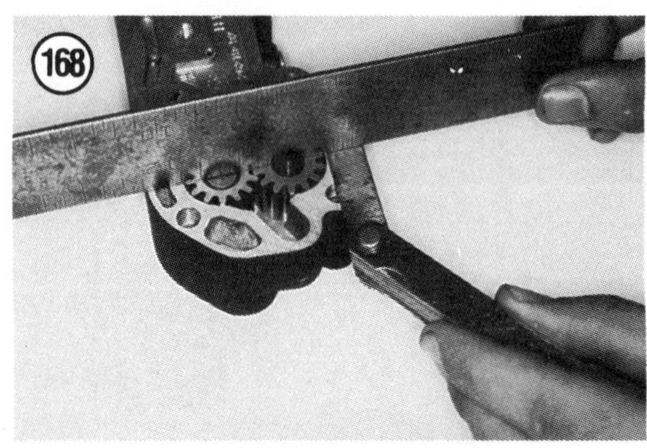

NOTE

Do not push the drive gear shaft into the gearcase housing when installing the drive gear and its spiral retaining ring in the following steps. This will cause the inner key to fall inside the gearcase housing. If this happens, you will have to remove the gearcase cover to retrieve and install the key.

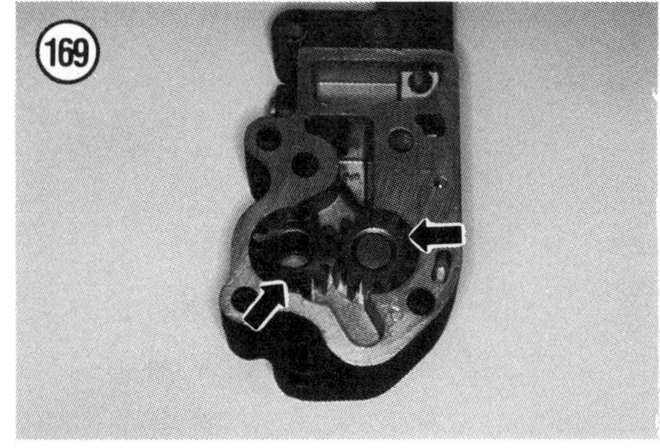

7. Install the feed gears as follows:
   a. Install the key (**Figure 157**) into the drive gear shaft keyway.
   b. Install the drive gear (A, **Figure 155**) over the key and drive gear shaft.
   c. Install the idler gear (B, **Figure 155**) over the idler shaft.
   d. Install a new spiral retaining ring (**Figure 156**) into the groove in the end of the drive gear shaft.

8. Install a new oil pump cover gasket (**Figure 171**) and install the gasket and oil pump cover (**Figure 154**) onto the crankcase.

CAUTION
Do not overtighten the oil pump housing and cover bolts in the following steps. Doing so will decrease pump gear side clearance and cause oil pump seizure.

9. Install the oil pump cover mounting bolts and lockwashers and tighten to the torque specification in **Table 4**.

10. Retighten the 2 oil pump housing mounting bolts (A, **Figure 158**) to 90-110 in.-lb. (10.2-13.6 N•m).

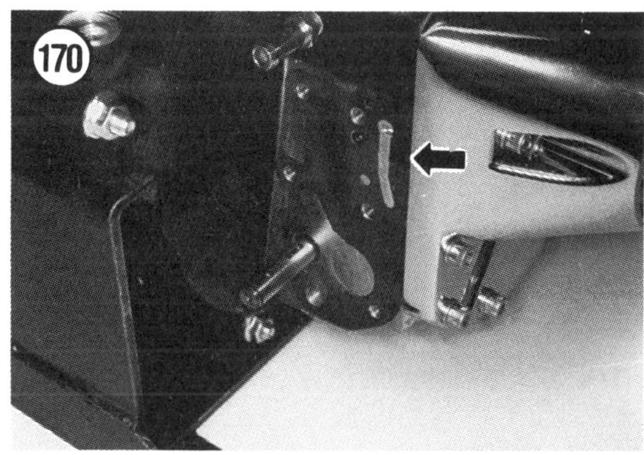

NOTE
If the pump will not turn after tightening the housing and cover mounting bolts, loosen both sets of bolts and reposition the pump to remove binding. Then retighten the upper and lower housing and cover mounting bolts to 115-120 in.-lb. (13.0-13.6 N•m) using an in.-lb. torque wrench only.

11. Install the check valve assembly as follows:
    a. Install the check valve ball (**Figure 153**).
    b. Install the check valve spring (**Figure 152**).
    c. Install the check valve plug and O-ring (**Figure 151**) and tighten securely.

12. Install the relief valve assembly as follows:
    a. Install the relief valve and spring (**Figure 150**).
    b. Install the relief valve plug and O-ring (**Figure 149**) and tighten to 80-110 in.-lb. (9.0-12.4 N•m).

13. Reverse Step 2 to connect the oil lines. On 1991 models, secure the oil lines with new hose clamps.

14. Fill the engine with oil as described in Chapter Three.

OIL FILTER MOUNT (1992-ON)

The oil filter mount (**Figure 172**) is mounted on the front of the engine on the right side.

Refer to **Figure 173** when servicing the oil filter mount in this section.

Removal

1. Park the bike on a level surface.
2. Drain the engine oil and remove the oil filter as described in Chapter Three.
3. Loosen the oil filter line compression nut (9, **Figure 173**) at the oil pump cover manifold until it sets on the oil line.
4. Remove screws and washers securing the oil pump cover manifold to the oil pump. Then remove the manifold and O-rings from the oil pump cover.
5. Remove the oil line clamp nut, washer and spacer.
6. Loosen the oil line compression fittings at the oil filter mount. Then remove the oil lines from the oil filter mount.

4

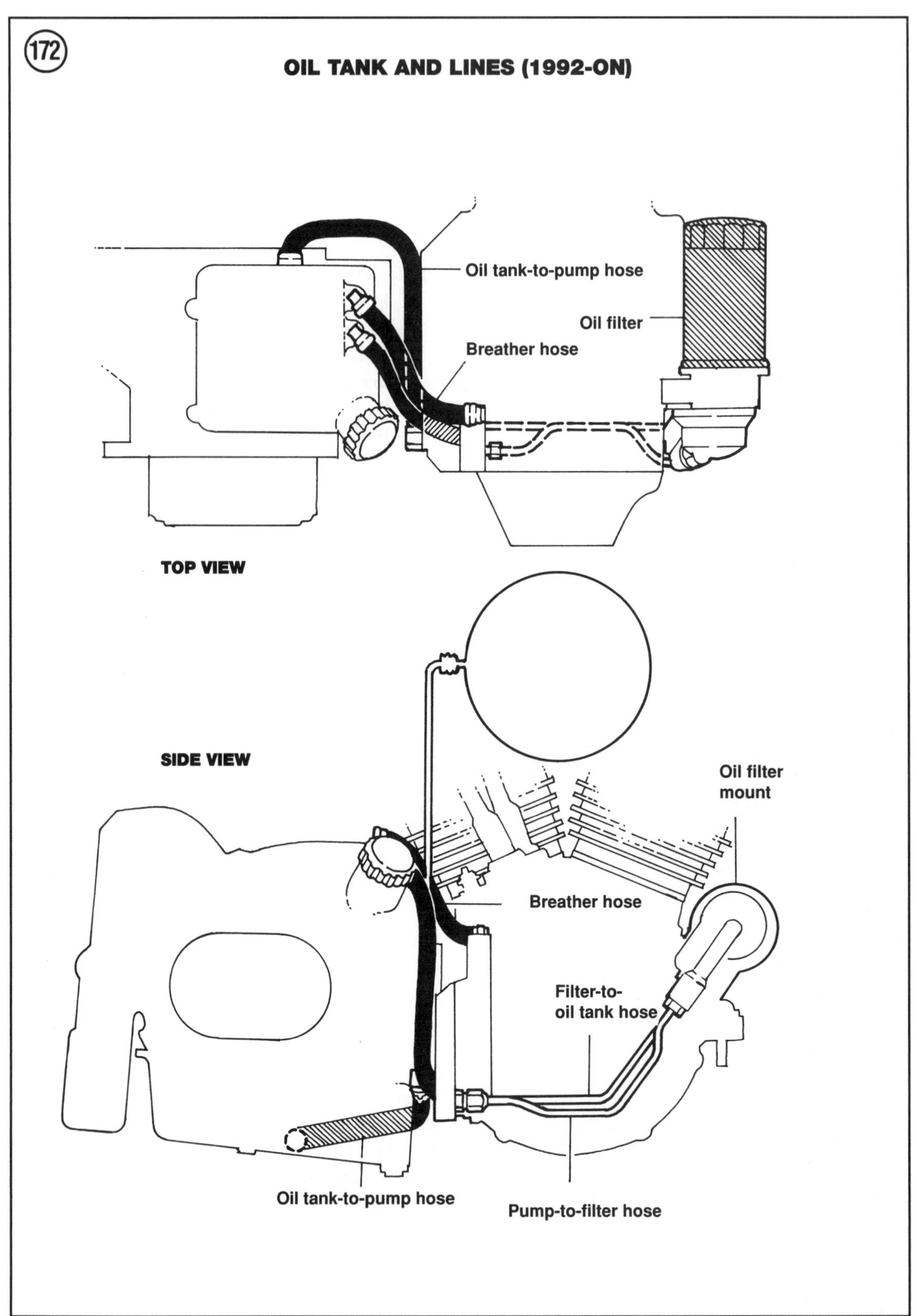
172
OIL TANK AND LINES (1992-ON)
Oil tank-to-pump hose
Oil filter
Breather hose
TOP VIEW
SIDE VIEW
Oil filter
mount
Breather hose
Filter-to-
oil tank hose
Oil tank-to-pump hose
Pump-to-filter hose

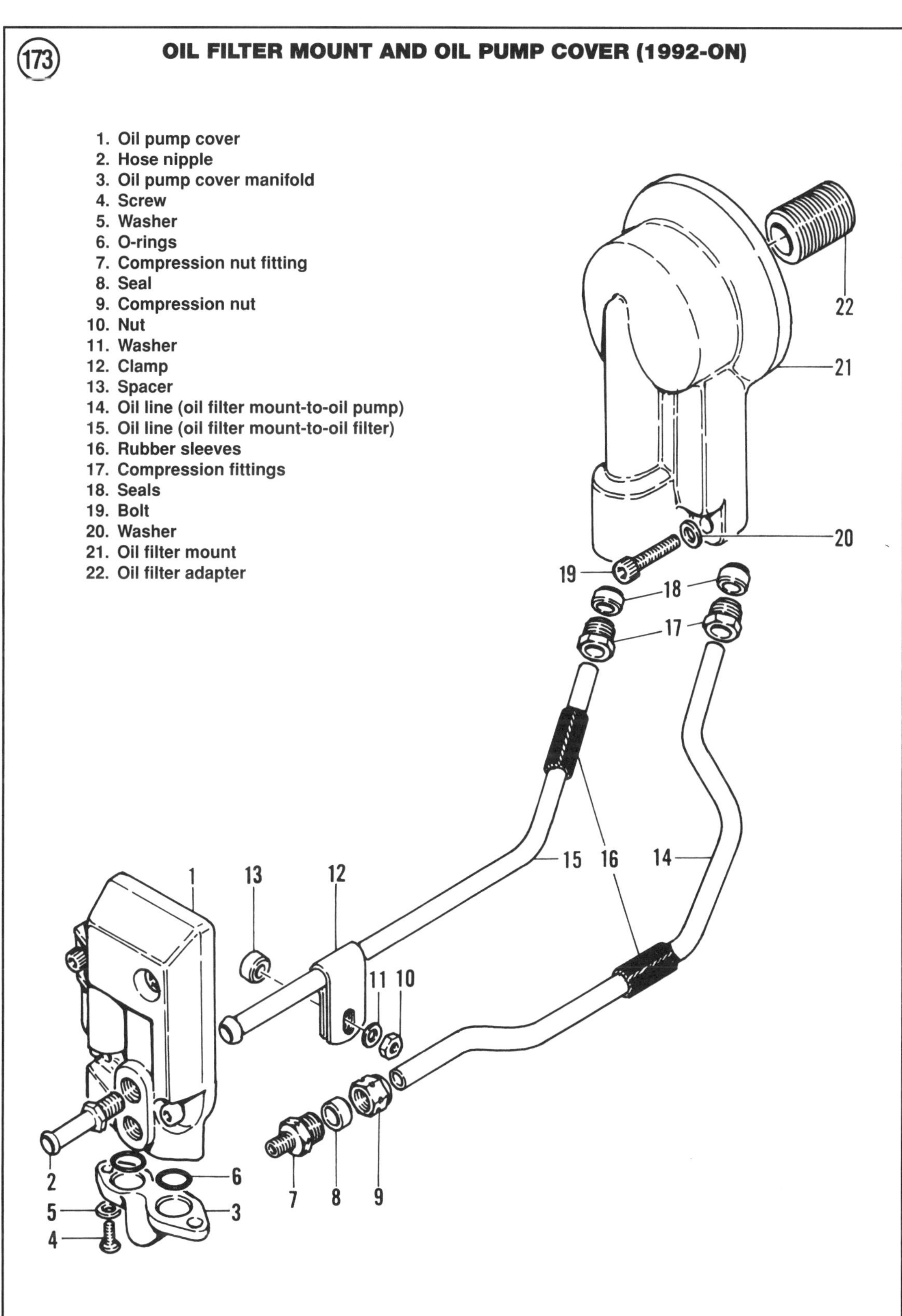
173
OIL FILTER MOUNT AND OIL PUMP COVER (1992-ON)
1. Oil pump cover
2. Hose nipple
3. Oil pump cover manifold
4. Screw
5. Washer
6. O-rings
7. Compression nut fitting
8. Seal
9. Compression nut
10. Nut
11. Washer
12. Clamp
13. Spacer
14. Oil line (oil filter mount-to-oil pump)
15. Oil line (oil filter mount-to-oil filter)
16. Rubber sleeves
17. Compression fittings
18. Seals
19. Bolt
20. Washer
21. Oil filter mount
22. Oil filter adapter
22
21
20
19
18
17
15
16
14
1
13
12
11
10
2
6
5
3
4
7
8
9

7. Remove the screws and washers securing the oil filter mount to the engine and remove the oil filter mount.
8. Remove the upper compression nut seals from the oil lines. If necessary, remove the upper compression nuts.
9. Loosen, then remove the compression nut fitting from the oil pump cover manifold.
10. Remove the lower seal and compression nut from the oil line.
11. If necessary, remove the oil filter adapter from the oil filter mount.
12. If necessary, remove the hose nipple from the oil pump cover.

Inspection

1. Inspect the oil lines for cracks or other damage.
2. If you replace the oil lines, make sure to remove the rubber sleeves from the oil lines and install them on the new lines in the same position.
3. Clean the compression nuts and compression nut fitting in solvent and dry thoroughly.
4. Replace all worn or damaged parts.

Installation

1. Make sure all parts are clean and dry prior to installing them.
2. If removed, install the hose nipple.
3. If removed, install the compression nut fitting (7, **Figure 173**) as follows:
   a. Apply Loctite 242 (blue) to the compression nut fitting threads prior to installation.
   b. Install the compression nut fitting and tighten to the torque specification in **Table 4**.
4. If removed, install the oil filter adapter into the oil filter mount.
5. Install the screws and washers securing the oil filter mount to the engine. Tighten the oil filter mount screws to the torque specification in **Table 4**.
6. Slide the oil line compression nut (9, **Figure 173**) and seal (8, **Figure 173**) onto the oil line.
7. Install the 2 compression fitting oil seals (18, **Figure 173**) into the oil filter mount.
8. Install the upper oil line compression nut fittings (17, **Figure 173**) into the oil filter mount. Tighten the fittings finger-tight only.
9. Insert the oil lines (14 and 15, **Figure 173**) into their respective compression nut fittings until they bottom out.
10. Assemble the oil line clamp, spacer, washer and nut as shown in **Figure 173**; do not tighten the nut at this time.
11. Slide the oil pump manifold compression nut (9, Figure 173) onto the oil line (14, **Figure 173**).
12. Install 2 new O-rings onto the oil pump cover manifold and place the manifold onto the bottom of the oil pump cover. Install the screws and washers securing the manifold to the oil pump and tighten to the torque specification in **Table 4**.
13. Thread the compression nut (9, **Figure 173**) onto the compression nut fitting. Tighten the nut until it bottoms out on the fitting.
14. Tighten the upper oil line compression fittings (17, **Figure 173**) until the hex portion on the fittings seat against the oil filter mount.
15. Tighten the oil line securing nut (10, **Figure 173**) securely.
16. Install the oil filter and fill the engine with oil as described in Chapter Three.
17. Start the engine and check for leaks.

GEARCASE COVER AND TIMING GEARS

Refer to **Figure 174** (1991-1992) or **Figure 175** (1993-on) when servicing the gearcase cover and timing gears in the following sections.

Removal

1. Remove the pushrods, valve lifters and guides as described in this chapter.
2. If necessary, remove the lifter oil screen cap and O-ring. Then remove the spring and screen.
3. Remove the ignition rotor and sensor plate as described in Chapter Nine.
4. Place an oil drain pan underneath the gearcase cover.

NOTE

The gearcase cover uses different length screws. Before you remove these screws, draw an outline of the gearcase cover on cardboard, then punch a hole beside the outline at each screw position. Install each screw into its respective hole.

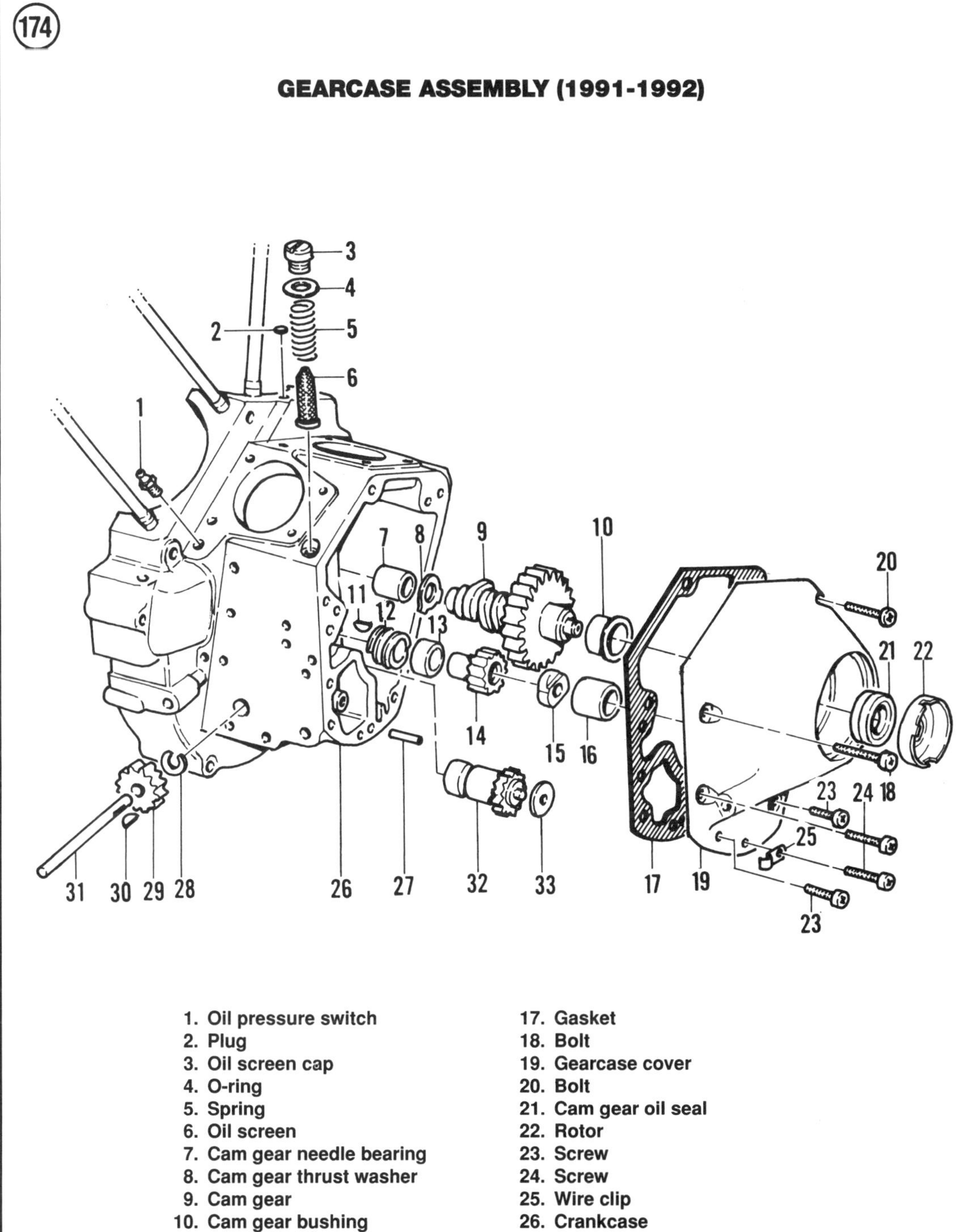

1. Oil pressure switch
2. Plug
3. Oil screen cap
4. O-ring
5. Spring
6. Oil screen
7. Cam gear needle bearing
8. Cam gear thrust washer
9. Cam gear
10. Cam gear bushing
11. Woodruff key
12. Oil pump drive gear
13. Pinion gear spacer
14. Pinion gear
15. Pinion shaft nut
16. Pinion shaft bushing
17. Gasket
18. Bolt
19. Gearcase cover
20. Bolt
21. Cam gear oil seal
22. Rotor
23. Screw
24. Screw
25. Wire clip
26. Crankcase
27. Dowel pin
28. Oil pump drive gear lock ring
29. Oil pump driven gear
30. Woodruff key
31. Oil pump shaft
32. Breather gear
33. Breather gear washer

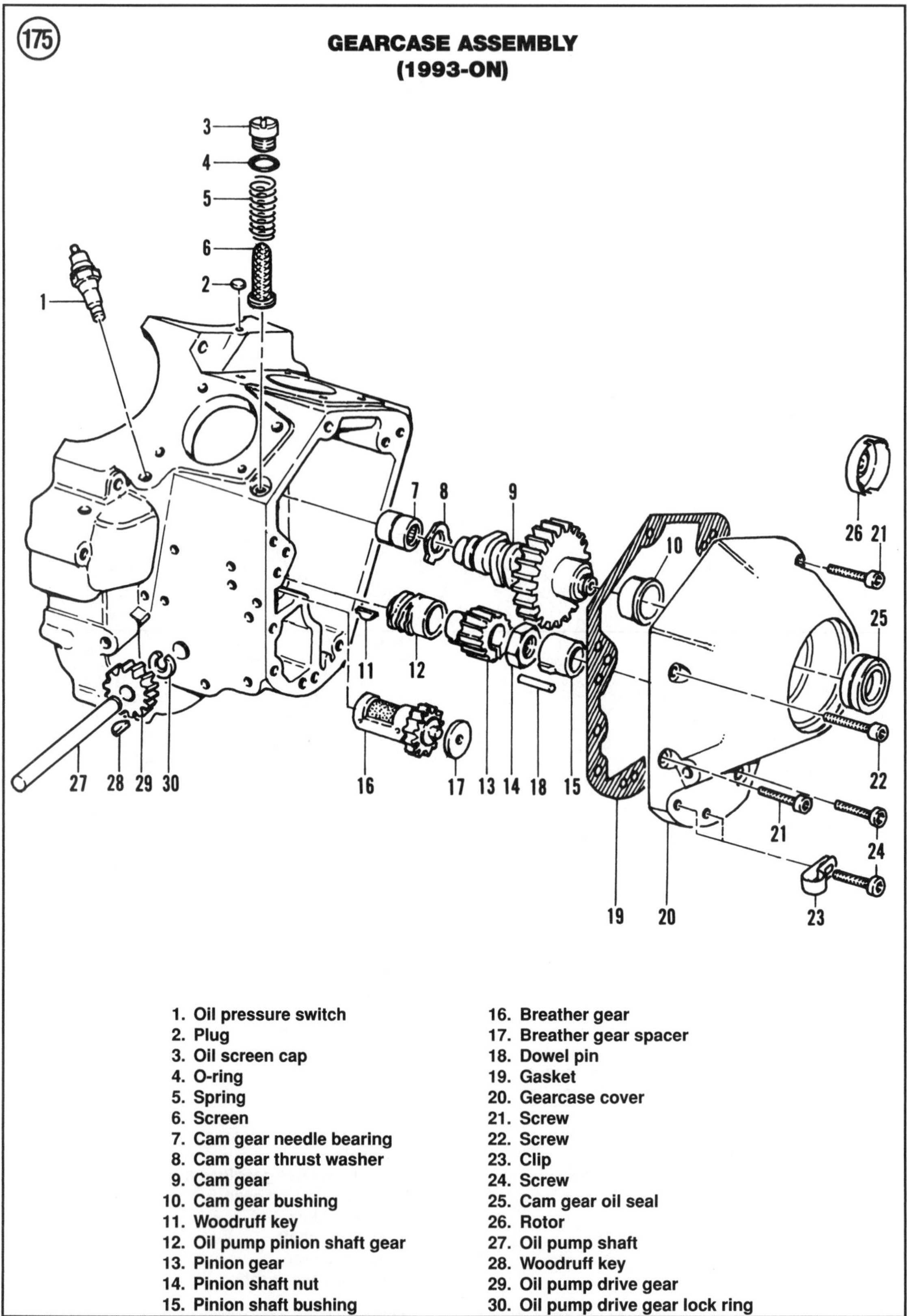

GEARCASE ASSEMBLY (1993-ON)

1. Oil pressure switch
2. Plug
3. Oil screen cap
4. O-ring
5. Spring
6. Screen
7. Cam gear needle bearing
8. Cam gear thrust washer
9. Cam gear
10. Cam gear bushing
11. Woodruff key
12. Oil pump pinion shaft gear
13. Pinion gear
14. Pinion shaft nut
15. Pinion shaft bushing
16. Breather gear
17. Breather gear spacer
18. Dowel pin
19. Gasket
20. Gearcase cover
21. Screw
22. Screw
23. Clip
24. Screw
25. Cam gear oil seal
26. Rotor
27. Oil pump shaft
28. Woodruff key
29. Oil pump drive gear
30. Oil pump drive gear lock ring

5. Loosen and remove the gearcase cover screws.

NOTE

Snug fitting dowel pins locate the gearcase cover. Thus, you must remove the cover carefully in the following steps. Do not try to pry the gearcase cover off with any metal tool. If necessary, tap the cover lightly with a soft-faced hammer at the point where the cover projects beyond the crankcase.

6A. Tap the gearcase cover (**Figure 176**) with a soft-faced hammer and remove the cover and gasket. If you cannot remove the gearcase cover, perform Step 6B.

6B. If you cannot tap the gearcase cover off the crankcase, remove it as follows:

176

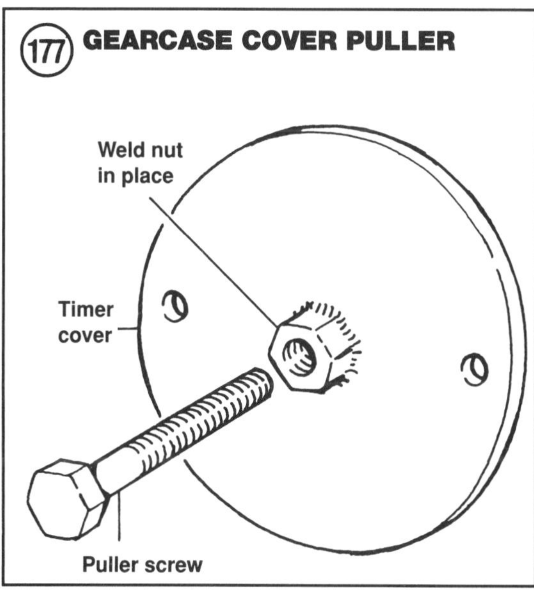

177 GEARCASE COVER PULLER

a. Fabricate the puller shown in **Figure 177**. The pullers outside diameter must be the same size as the ignition sensor plate outside diameter.
b. Mount the puller onto the gearcase cover and secure it with 2 screws (**Figure 178**).
c. Tighten the pullers pressure screw against the crankshaft to force the gearcase cover away from the engine.
d. Remove the gearcase cover and gasket.

7. If necessary, remove the 2 dowel pins (**Figure 179**).
8. Remove the breather gear spacer (**Figure 180**).
9. Remove the breather gear (**Figure 181**).
10. Remove the camshaft (**Figure 182**) and thrust washer. See **Figure 183**.

11A. On 1991-1992 models, remove the pinion gear shaft nut and pinion gear shaft as follows:

NOTE

The pinion gear shaft nut uses left-hand threads. Turn the nut clockwise to remove it.

a. Remove the pinion gear shaft nut using the Harley-Davidson pinion shaft nut socket (part No. HD-94555-55C).
b. Then remove the pinion gear (**Figure 184**) using the Harley-Davidson pinion gear puller (part No. HD-96830-51A).

11B. On 1993-on models, remove the pinion gear shaft nut and pinion gear shaft as follows:

NOTE

On these models, the pinion gear shaft nut uses right-hand threads. Turn the nut counterclockwise to remove it.

a. Loosen and remove the pinion gear shaft nut (A, **Figure 185**).
b. Remove the pinion gear (B, **Figure 185**).

12A. On 1991-1992 models, remove the following parts in order:

a. Pinion gear spacer (**Figure 186**).
b. Oil pump drive gear (**Figure 187**).
c. Woodruff key (**Figure 188**).

12B. On 1993-on models, remove the following parts in order:

a. Oil pump drive gear (**Figure 189**).
b. Woodruff key (**Figure 190**).

13. To remove the oil pump drive gear and drive gear shaft, perform the following:

a. Remove the oil pump as described in this chapter.

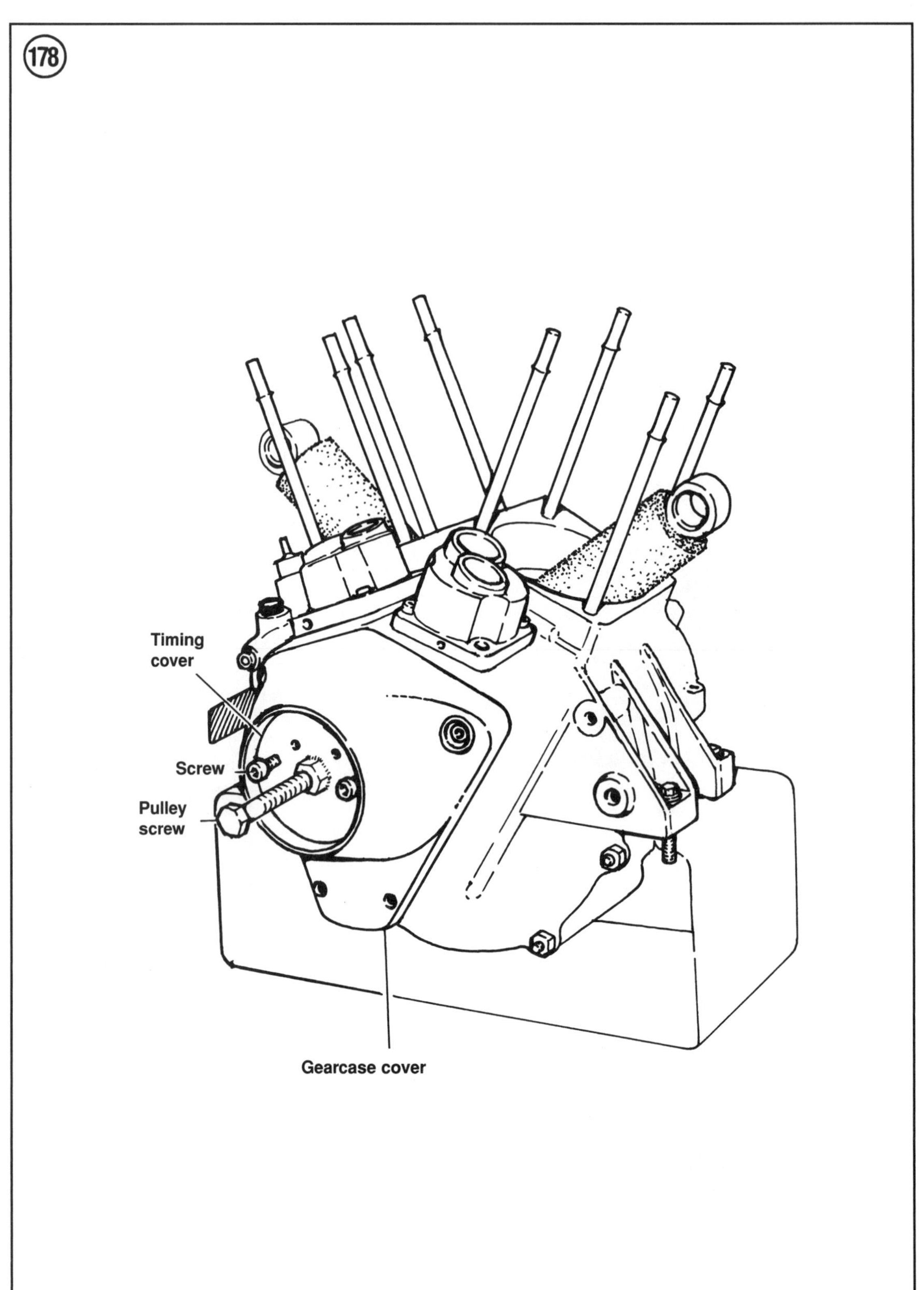
178
Timing cover
Screw
Pulley screw
Gearcase cover

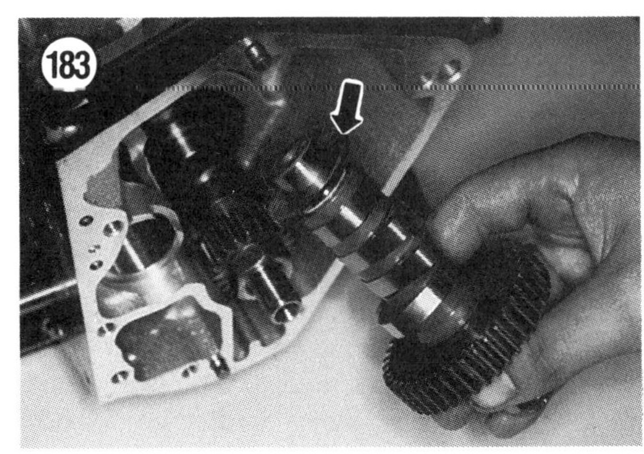

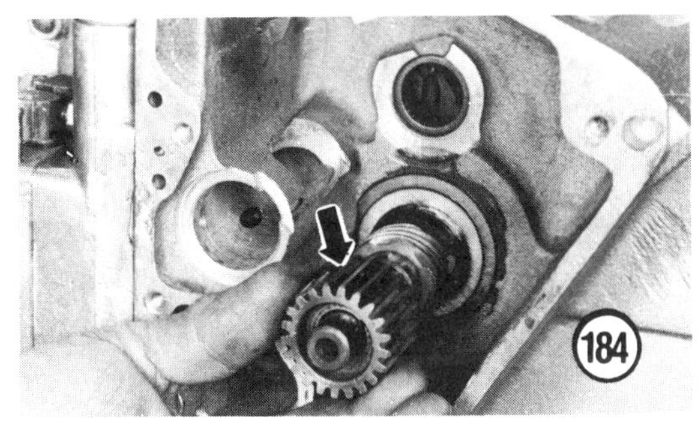

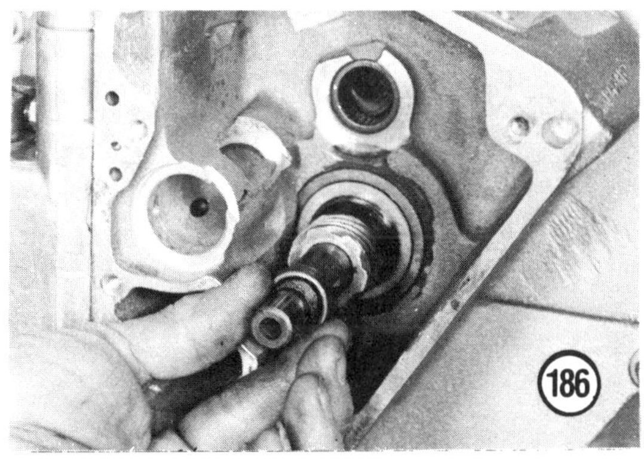

4

b. Remove the oil pump gear circlip (A, **Figure 191**).
c. Remove the oil pump driven gear (B, **Figure 191**).
d. Remove the Woodruff key (**Figure 192**).
e. Remove the driven gear shaft (**Figure 193**).

Inspection

1. Thoroughly clean the gearcase compartment, cover and components with solvent. Blow out all oil passages with compressed air. Make sure that you

190

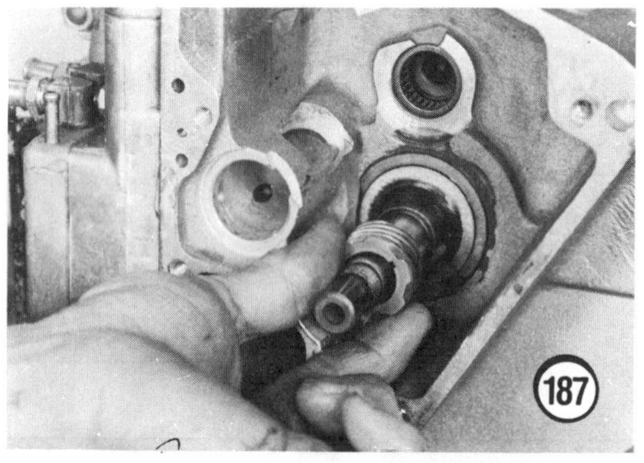
187

191

188

192

189

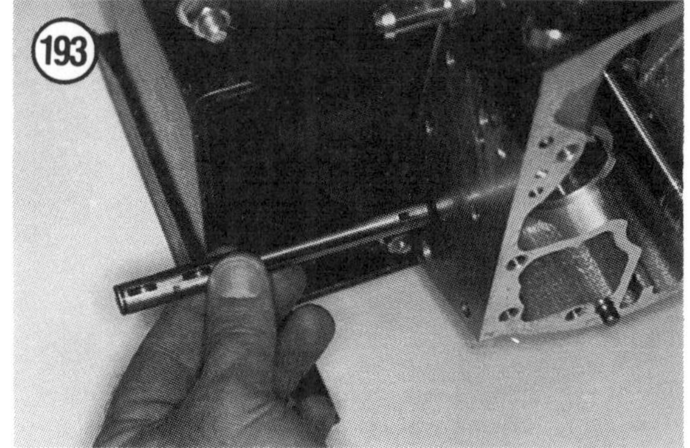
193

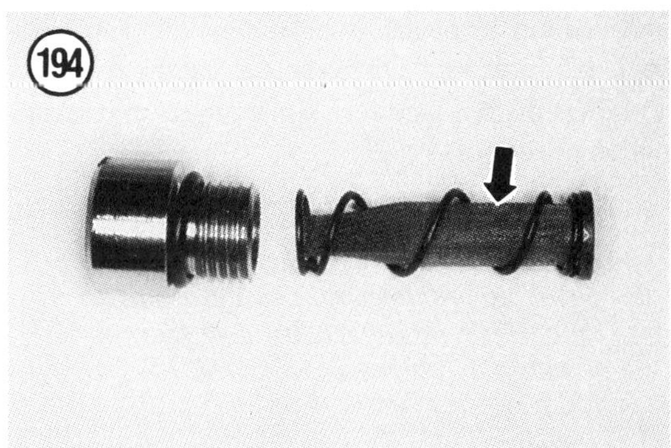

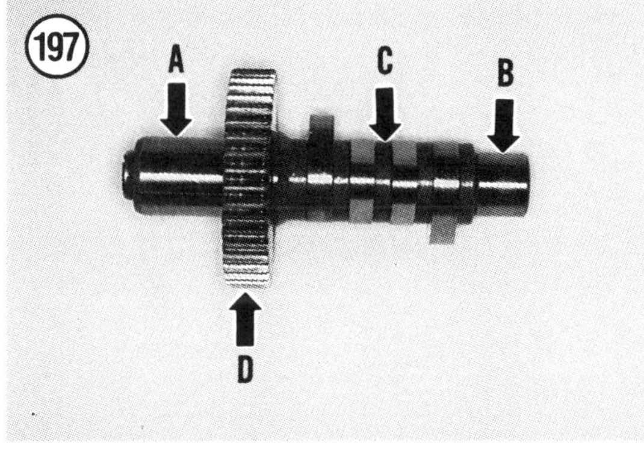

remove all of the gasket residue from the gasket mating surfaces.

2. Check the oil screen (**Figure 194**) for damage or contamination. Test the screen by holding it upside down and filling it with engine oil. Make sure the oil flows evenly through the screen. If not, replace the screen.

3. Check the pinion shaft (A, **Figure 195**) and cam gear (B, **Figure 195**) gearcase cover bushings for grooving, pitting or other wear. If the bushings show visible wear or damage, refer replacement to a Harley-Davidson dealer. If the bushings appear okay, continue with Step 4.

4. Determine the pinion shaft bushing (A, **Figure 195**) clearance as follows:
   a. Measure the pinion shaft bushing inside diameter. Record the measurement.
   b. Measure the pinion shaft (A, **Figure 196**) where it rides in the bushing. Record the measurement.
   c. Subtract sub-step b from substep a to determine pinion shaft bushing clearance. Replace the bushing if the clearance meets or exceeds the service limit in **Table 2**.

5. Determine the cam gear bushing (B, **Figure 195**) clearance as follows:
   a. Measure the cam gear bushing inside diameter. Record the measurement.
   b. Measure the cam gear outside diameter (A, **Figure 197**) where it rides in the bushing. Record the measurement.
   c. Subtract sub-step b from sub-step a to determine cam gear bushing clearance. Replace the bushing if the clearance meets or exceeds the service limit in **Table 2**.

6. Inspect the cam gear needle bearing (B, **Figure 196**) for visible needle wear or damage. If the bearing appears okay, perform Step 7.

7. Measure the cam gear end (B, **Figure 197**) where it rides in the crankcase needle bearing (B, **Figure 196**). Then measure the cam gear end again but closer to the cam lobes where it does not ride in the needle bearing. If the difference between the 2 measurements exceeds 0.003 in. (0.08 in.), replace the cam gear and needle bearing.

8. Measure the camshaft lobes (C, **Figure 197**) with a micrometer and compare with the lobes on a new Evolution cam. If the camshaft lobes are worn more than 0.006 in. (0.15 mm), replace the cam gear.

NOTE

Camshafts used in early V-twin models cannot be used in Evolution engines and vice versa. Do not use a non-Evolution cam when comparing lobe wear in Step 8.

9. Inspect the cam gear (D, **Figure 197**) teeth for excessive wear or damage.
10. Inspect the pinion gear and the oil pump pinion gear shaft for damage.

NOTE

Color codes identify the cam and pinion gear pitch diameters. You must match pitch diameters on replacement gears or abnormal gear noise will result. Refer this service to a Harley-Davidson dealership.

11. Mount a dial indicator to the pinion shaft as shown in **Figure 198**. Turn the crankshaft and measure pinion shaft runout. If the runout exceeds the service limit in **Table 2**, the crankshaft may need retruing or the pinion bearing in the crankcase is worn. Both instances require engine disassembly.
12. Check the cam gear oil seal (**Figure 199**) in the gearcase cover. If worn, carefully pry it out of the case. Install a new seal by driving it into the gearcase cover using a suitable size drift or socket placed on the outside portion of the seal.
13. Inspect the breather gear (**Figure 200**) teeth for damage. Also check the screen for debris or damage and clean with solvent if necessary. Replace the breather gear if necessary.

NOTE

Bushing replacement requires a number of special tools. If any of the bushings described in this section are excessively worn or damaged, refer replacement to a Harley-Davidson dealership.

Cam Gear and Pinion Gear Wear Check

To check cam gear and pinion gear engagement, perform the following:

1. Install the pinion gear and cam gear into the gearcase. Do not install the cam gear spacer.
2. Install the gearcase cover and secure it with a minimum of 3 screws. Tighten the screws securely.
3. Check the gear mesh through the lifter guide hole by hand. Gear mesh is correct when there is no play between the gears and you can move the cam gear back and forth with a noticeable slight drag.
4. If gear mesh is incorrect, replace the cam gear and pinion gear.

NOTE

Color codes identify the cam and pinion gear pitch diameters. You must match pitch diameters on replacement gears or abnormal gear noise will result. Refer this service to a Harley-Davidson dealer.

198

199

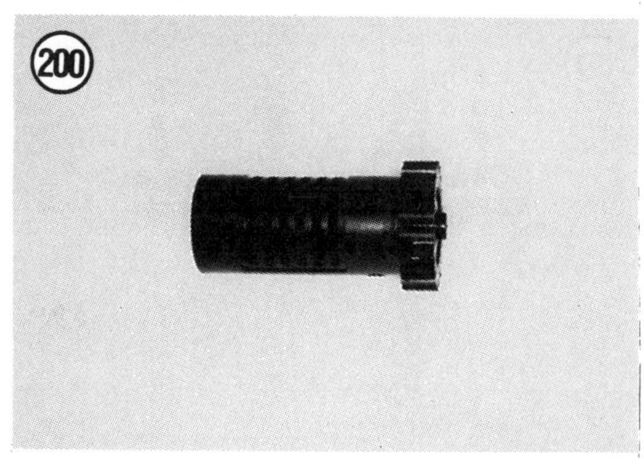

200

Breather Gear End Play Check and Adjustment

Before final assembly of gearcase components, check the breather gear end play as follows:

1. Install the breather gear (A, **Figure 201**) and its spacer (B, **Figure 201**).
2. Install a new cover gasket onto the crankcase gasket surface.
3. Lay a straightedge across the gearcase at the breather gear spacer. Then using a feeler gauge, measure the clearance between the straightedge and the spacer (**Figure 202**).
4. Subtract 0.006 in. (0.15 mm) from the clearance determined in Step 3 to determine breather gear end play. **Table 2** lists the correct breather gear end play specification. Replace the spacer (B, **Figure 201**) to correct the end play. Different thickness spacers are available from a Harley-Davidson dealership.

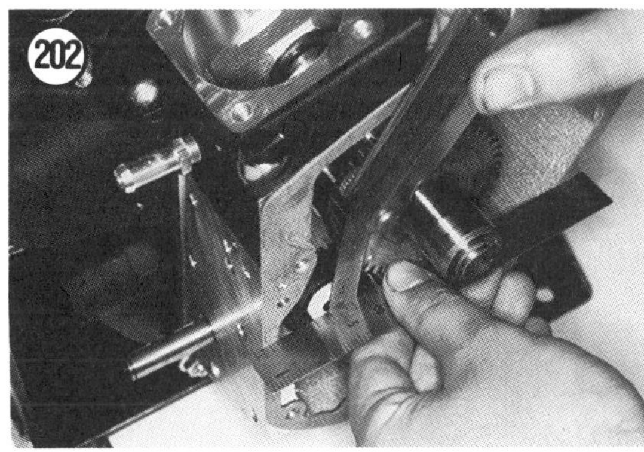

Cam Gear End Play Check and Adjustment

Before final assembly of gearcase components, check the cam gear end play as follows:

1. Install the cam gear thrust washer and the cam gear (**Figure 183**) into the crankcase.
2. Install the gearcase cover and a new gasket. Install a minimum of 4 gearcase cover screws. Tighten the screws securely.
3. Measure the cam gear end play between the gear shaft and the thrust washer with a feeler gauge inserted through the gear case lifter hole (**Figure 203**).
4. **Table 2** lists the correct cam gear end play. If the clearance meets or exceeds the service limit, check for worn or damaged parts. Different thickness thrust washers are not available to adjust end play.

Installation

1. Install the oil pump drive gear shaft and drive gear as follows:
   a. Install the driven gear shaft (**Figure 193**) through the crankcase. The end of the shaft with the 2 keyways must be facing out (away from crankcase).
   b. Install the Woodruff key (**Figure 192**) into the shaft keyway.
   c. Align the oil pump driven gear with the Woodruff key and install the gear onto the shaft (B, **Figure 191**).
   d. Install a new circlip (**Figure 204**) into the groove in the end of the driven gear shaft. See A, **Figure 191**.

NOTE
After installing the oil pump driven gear shaft and driven gear in Step 1, you can install the oil pump now or install it after you install the gearcase assembly.

4

2A. On 1991-1992 models, install the following parts in order:

a. Install the Woodruff key (**Figure 188**) into the pinion shaft keyway.
b. Install the oil pump drive gear (**Figure 187**).
c. Install the pinion gear spacer (**Figure 186**).
d. Install the pinion gear (**Figure 184**).

NOTE
The pinion gear shaft nut on 1991-1992 models uses left-hand threads. Turn the nut counterclockwise to install it.

e. Apply 2 drops of Loctite 262 (red) to the pinion shaft threads and install the pinion gear shaft nut.
f. Tighten the pinion gear shaft nut to the torque specification in **Table 4**.

2B. On 1993-on models, install the following parts in order:

a. Install the Woodruff key (**Figure 205**) into the pinion shaft keyway.
b. Install the oil pump drive gear (**Figure 189**) with its shoulder facing out.
c. Install the pinion gear onto the pinion shaft. Engage the keyway in the gear with the Woodruff key (**Figure 206**).

NOTE
The pinion gear shaft nut on 1993-on models uses right-hand threads. Turn the nut clockwise to tighten it.

d. Apply 2 drops of Loctite 262 (red) onto the pinion shaft threads and install the pinion gear shaft nut (A, **Figure 185**).
e. Tighten the pinion gear shaft nut to the torque specification in **Table 4**.

3. Install the thrust washer onto the cam gear (**Figure 183**).
4. Install the cam gear into the crankcase. Align the index mark on the cam gear with the index mark on the pinion gear. See **Figure 207**.
5. Install the breather gear into the crankcase. Align the index mark on the breather gear with the index mark on the cam gear. See **Figure 208**.

NOTE
Double check that the timing marks in Steps 4 and 5 align.

6. Install the breather gear spacer onto the breather gear (B, **Figure 201**).

204

205

206

207

7. Turn the gear train to make sure all gears rotate freely. Correct any binding before reassembling the engine.

8. If removed, install the 2 gearcase cover dowel pins (**Figure 179**).

9. Install a new gearcase cover gasket.

10. Install the gearcase cover onto the engine (**Figure 176**). Install the gearcase cover screws and tighten to the torque specification in **Table 4**.

11. Pour approximately 1/4 pint of engine oil through the lifter guide hole to provide initial gear train lubrication.

12. Install the electronic ignition sensor plate and rotor as described in Chapter Eight.

13. Install the valve lifters, guides and pushrods as described in this chapter.

14. If removed, install the lifter screen assembly. Tighten the lifter screen plug to the torque specification in **Table 4**.

CRANKCASE AND CRANKSHAFT

Crankshaft End Play Check

Measure crankshaft end play before disassembling the crankcase. Crankshaft end play is a measurement of sprocket shaft bearing wear.

1. Remove the engine from the frame as described in this chapter.
2. Remove the gearcase cover as described in this chapter.
3. Mount the crankcase in an engine stand (**Figure 209**).
4. Install the Harley-Davidson bearing installation tool (part No. HD-97225-55) onto the sprocket shaft to preload the bearing races. See **Figure 210**.
5. Attach a dial indicator so that the probe touches against the end of the crankshaft (**Figure 210**).
6. Turn and pull on the sprocket shaft while noting the end play registering on the dial indicator. If end play exceeds limit in **Table 2**, the bearing inner spacer (4, **Figure 211**) thickness is incorrect. Adjust end play by selecting a different spacer from the chart in **Table 5**.

Disassembly

Refer to **Figure 211** for this procedure.

1. Remove the engine from the frame as described in this chapter.

CAUTION

After removing the cylinders, slip a 1/2 in. diameter rubber hose over each cylinder stud. The hoses will protect the studs during the following service procedures. In addition, do not lift the crankcase assembly by grabbing the cylinder studs. Bent or damaged cylinder studs may cause the engine to leak oil.

2. Remove the following components as described in this chapter:
   a. Pistons.
   b. Pushrods, lifters and lifter guides.
   c. Gearcase and timing gear assembly.
3. Check the crankshaft end play as described in this chapter.

NOTE

When removing the crankcase bolts and studs in Step 4, note that the top center

4

stud and the 2 bottom studs are matched and fitted to the crankcase holes for correct crankcase alignment. Mark these bolts so that you can reinstall them into their original position.

4. See **Figure 212** (1991-1992) or **Figure 213** (1993-on). Remove the crankcase bolts and studs.
5. Lay the crankcase assembly on wooden blocks with the right side facing up.
6. Tap the crankcase with a plastic mallet and remove the right crankcase half (**Figure 214**).
7. Remove the pinion shaft spiral lock ring (**Figure 215**).
8. Remove the needle bearing (**Figure 216**) from the pinion shaft.

WARNING
Wear safety glasses when pressing out the crankshaft in Step 9.

9. Press the crankshaft out of the left crankcase half as follows:
   a. Support the left crankcase half in a press on wooden blocks as shown in **Figure 217**.
   b. Center the press ram with the sprocket shaft, then press the crankshaft out of the left crankcase half. Have an assistant support the crankshaft as it is being pressed out.

CAUTION
Do not remove the crankshaft by driving it out of the crankcase half using a hammer.

10. To remove the outer sprocket shaft bearing assembly, perform the following:
   a. Pry the sprocket shaft spacer (**Figure 218**) out of the oil seal. See **Figure 219**.
   b. Carefully pry the oil seal (**Figure 220**) out of the left crankcase half using a wide-blade screwdriver. Support the screwdriver with a rag to prevent damaging the crankcase. See A, **Figure 221**.
   c. Lift out the outer sprocket shaft bearing half (B, **Figure 221**).

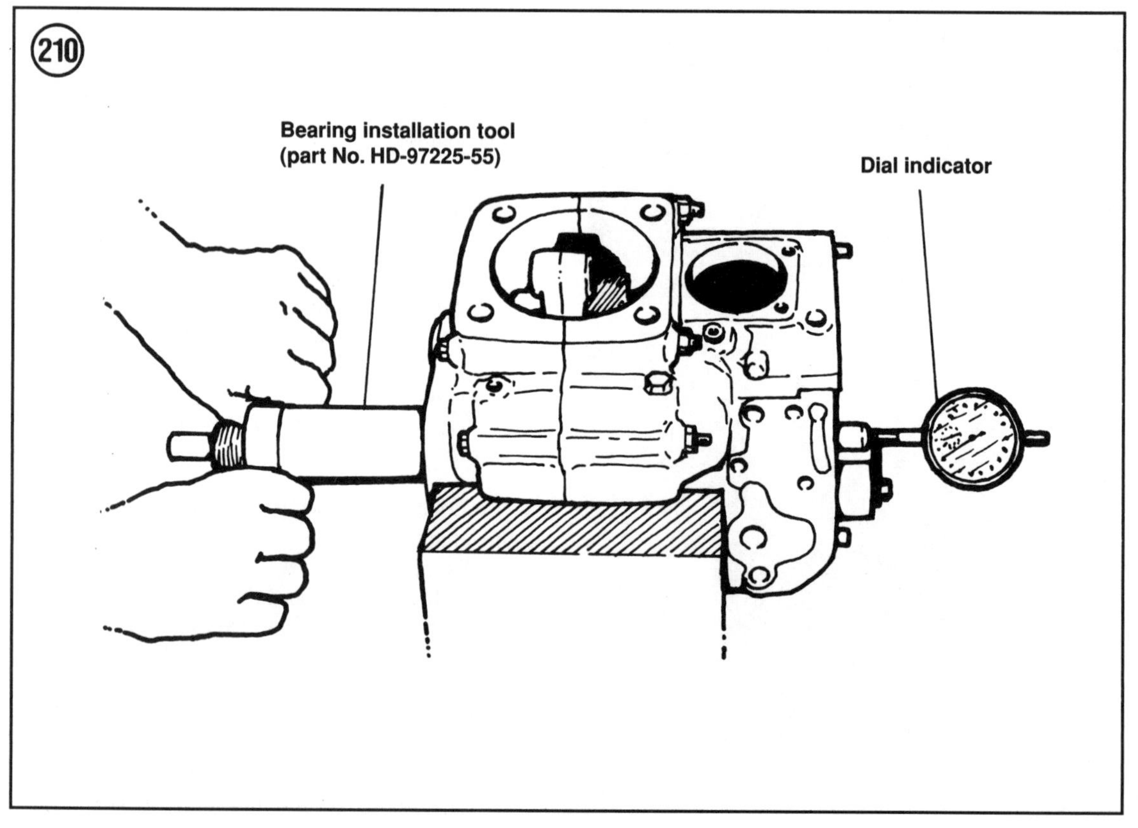

CRANKCASE ASSEMBLY

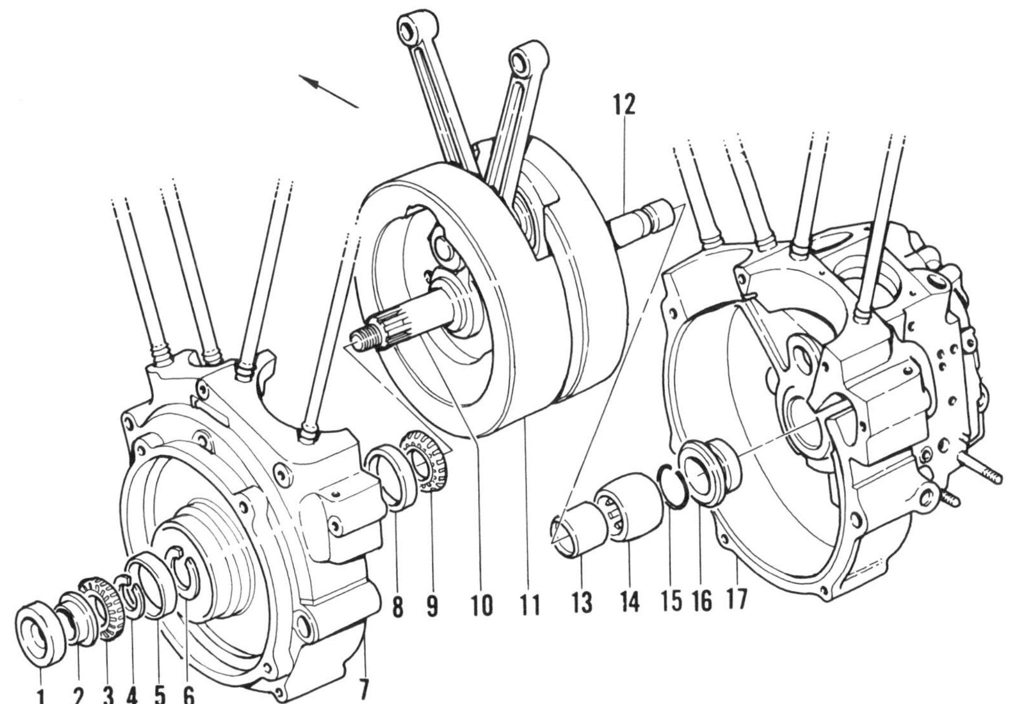

1. Sprocket shaft bearing seal
2. Sprocket shaft spacer
3. Outer sprocket shaft bearing
4. Bearing inner spacer
5. Bearing race
6. Lock ring
7. Left crankcase half
8. Bearing race
9. Inner sprocket shaft bearing
10. Sprocket shaft
11. Crankshaft assembly
12. Pinion shaft
13. Inner race
14. Needle bearing
15. Spiral lock ring
16. Pinion shaft bearing race
17. Right crankcase half

Crankcase Cleaning and Inspection

1. Clean both case halves in solvent and dry with compressed air.
2. Apply a light coat of oil to the races to prevent rust.
3. Inspect the left (**Figure 222**) and right (**Figure 223**) case halves for cracks or other damage.
4. Inspect the case studs for bending, cracks or other damage. Replace studs as described under *Cylinder Stud Replacement* in this chapter.
5. Inspect the left main bearing races (**Figure 222**) and bearings for wear or damage. Replace the bearing assembly as described under *Left Main Bearing Replacement* in this chapter.
6. Inspect the pinion shaft bearing race (A, **Figure 224**) for wear or damage. If you find any damage, check the needle bearing (**Figure 216**) and its inner race (**Figure 225**) for damage. Note the following:
   a. Replace the pinion shaft bearing and both races at the same time.
   b. You need a number of special tools to install, align and lap the pinion shaft bearing assembly. Refer this service to a Harley-Davidson dealer.
7. Inspect the cam gear needle bearing (B, **Figure 224**) in the right crankcase for damage. To replace this bearing, refer to *Cam Gear Needle Bearing Replacement* in this chapter.

Crankshaft and Connecting Rods Cleaning and Inspection

1. Clean the crankshaft (**Figure 226**) in solvent and dry thoroughly.
2. Measure connecting rod side play with a feeler gauge (**Figure 227**) and check against the service limit in **Table 2**. If the end play exceeds the service limit, have a dealer overhaul the crankshaft.
3. Inspect the pinion shaft (A, **Figure 226**) and the sprocket shaft (B, **Figure 226**) for excessive wear or damage. If you find shaft damage, have a dealer overhaul the crankshaft.
4. Support the crankshaft on a truing stand or in a lathe and check runout with a dial indicator. If the runout exceeds the service limit in **Table 2**, have a dealer true or overhaul the crankshaft.

Cam Gear Needle Bearing Replacement

To replace the cam gear needle bearing (B, **Figure 224**), perform the following:

1. Support the right crankcase half in a press and press out the cam gear needle bearing (**Figure 228**).
2. Clean the bearing bore (**Figure 228**) in the crankcase half.

NOTE
*Use a bearing driver like the one shown in **Figure 229** to install the new bearing.*

3. Support the right crankcase half on wooden blocks in a press.
4. Place the new bearing in the crankcase bore (**Figure 230**).

(212) **CRANKCASE STUDS (1991-1992)**

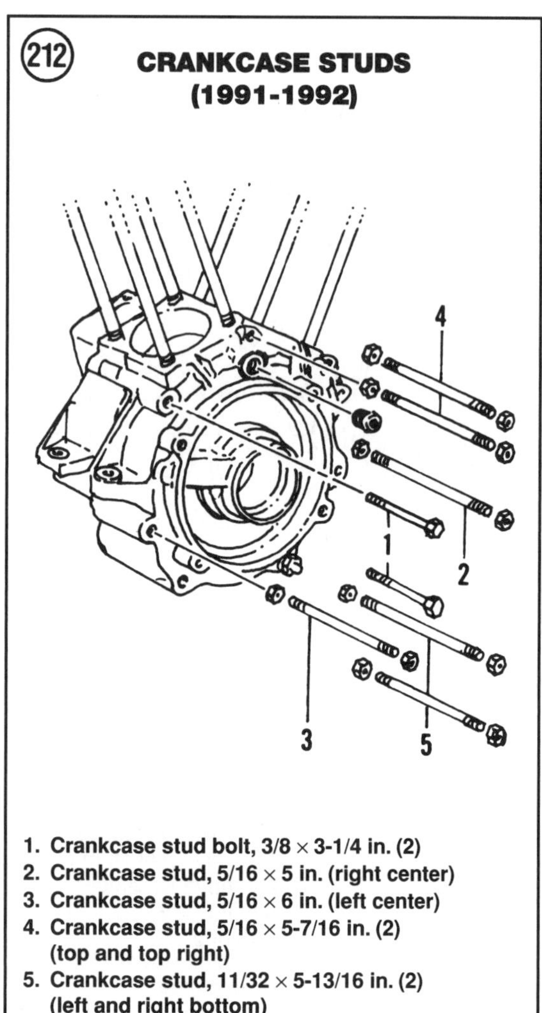

1. Crankcase stud bolt, 3/8 × 3-1/4 in. (2)
2. Crankcase stud, 5/16 × 5 in. (right center)
3. Crankcase stud, 5/16 × 6 in. (left center)
4. Crankcase stud, 5/16 × 5-7/16 in. (2) (top and top right)
5. Crankcase stud, 11/32 × 5-13/16 in. (2) (left and right bottom)

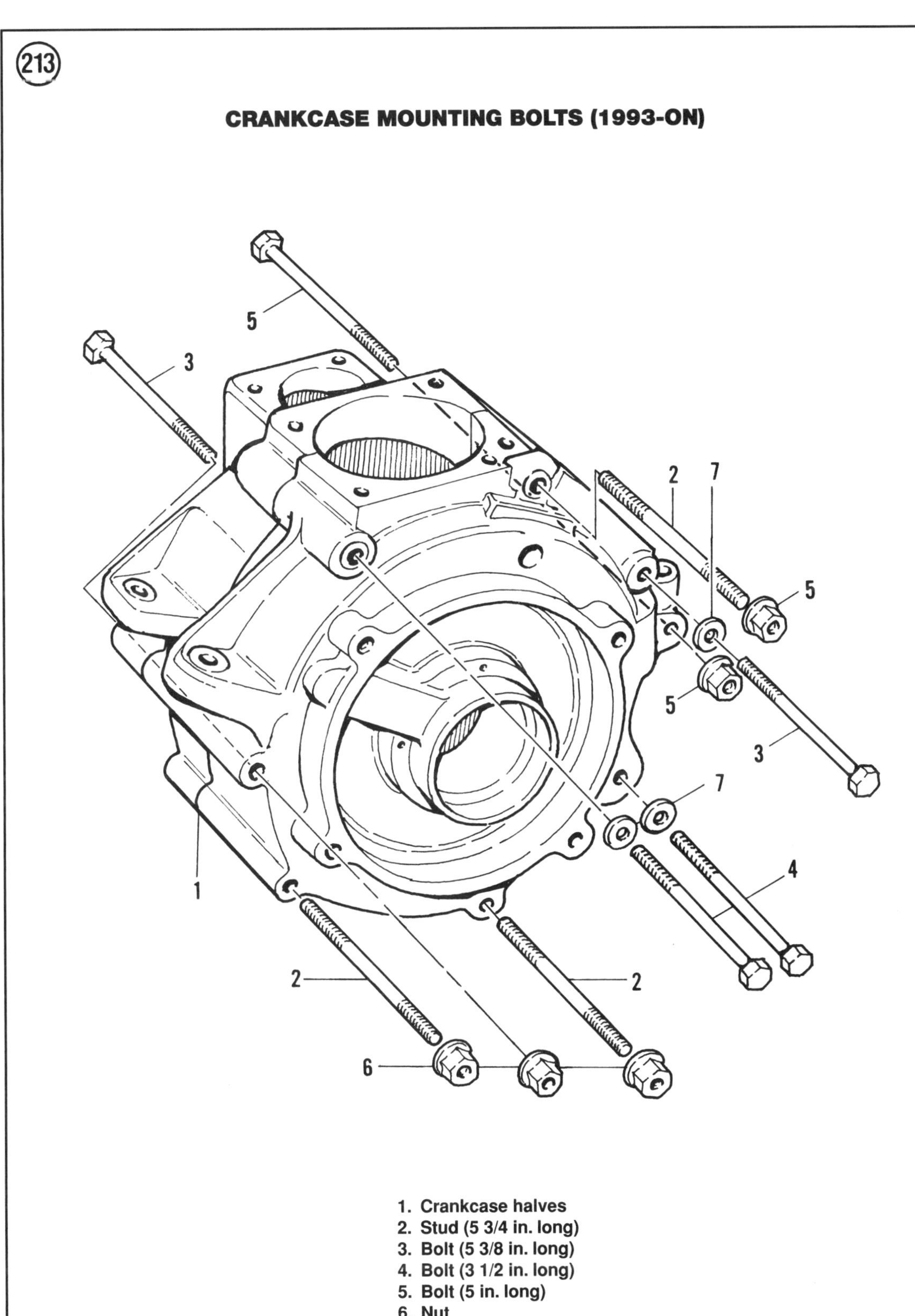

1. Crankcase halves
2. Stud (5 3/4 in. long)
3. Bolt (5 3/8 in. long)
4. Bolt (3 1/2 in. long)
5. Bolt (5 in. long)
6. Nut
7. Washer

214

218

215

219

216

220

217

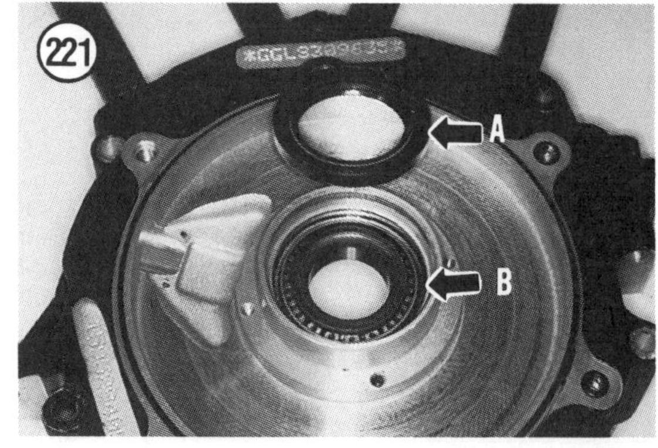
221
A
B

5. Center the bearing driver with the press ram and bearing (**Figure 231**). Then press in the new bearing until it bottoms out against the shoulder in the bearing bore (**Figure 232**).

Left Main Bearing Replacement

You must replace and assemble the left main bearing assembly as a set. If one bearing or race half is damaged, replace the complete inner and outer bearing assembly.

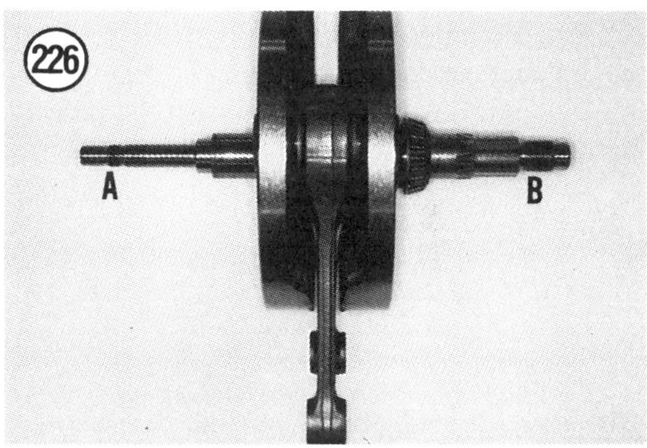

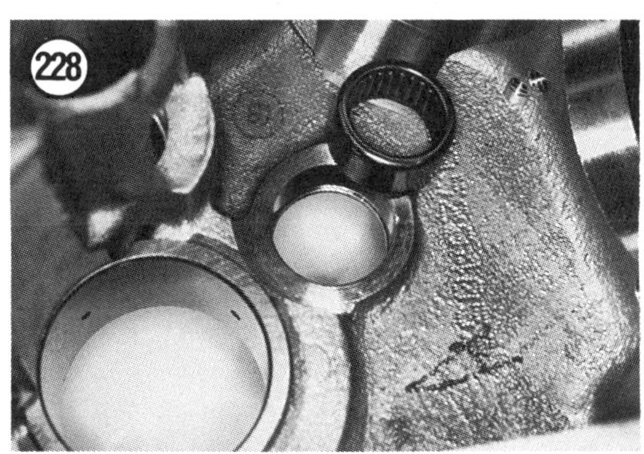

The left main bearing assembly consists of the following components:

a. Outer bearing (3, **Figure 211**).
b. Outer bearing race (5, **Figure 211**).
c. Lock ring (6, **Figure 211**).
d. Inner bearing race (8, **Figure 211**).
e. Inner bearing (9, **Figure 211**).

Inner and outer bearing race replacement

This section describes replacement of the left outer and inner main bearing races.

You need the Harley-Davidson crankshaft bearing removal and installation tool (part No. HD-94547-80) and a press to remove and install the bearing races in the left crankcase half. See **Figure 233**.

NOTE
*When replacing the bearing races in the following steps, do not remove the lock ring (**Figure 234**) installed between the inner and outer bearing races. This ring is under heavy tension and will damage the bearing bore as it passes through it.*

1. Support the left crankcase half on wooden blocks in a press with the inner bearing race facing up (**Figure 235**).
2. Mount the bearing tool onto the outer bearing race as shown in **Figure 235**.
3. Press the outer bearing race (5, **Figure 211**) out of the crankcase half.
4. Turn the crankcase half over and mount the bearing tool onto the inner bearing race as shown in **Figure 236**.
5. Press the inner bearing race (8, **Figure 211**) out of the crankcase.
6. Clean the bearing in solvent and dry thoroughly.
7. Check the lock ring (**Figure 237**) for looseness or damage. If the lock ring is loose or damaged, refer service to a Harley-Davidson dealership.
8. Check the lock ring gap. The gap must be centered with the crankcase oil hole as shown in **Figure 237**.

NOTE
Install both races with their larger diameter side facing out. Install the bearing races with the same tool used to remove the old ones.

229

230

231

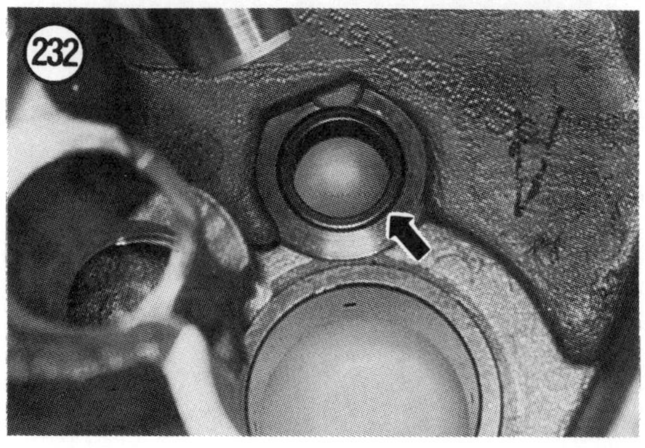
232

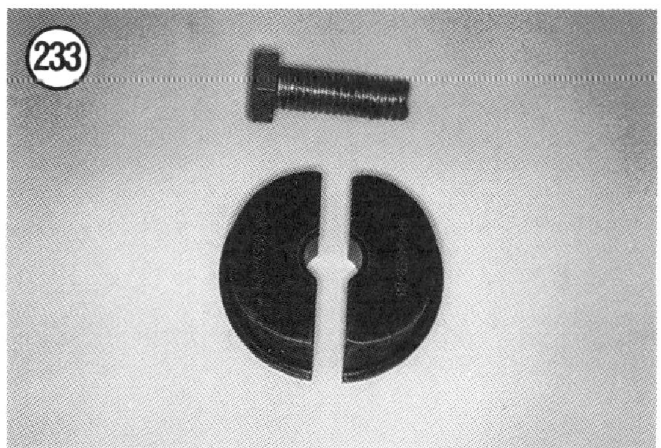

NOTE
*Do not intermix the inner and outer bearings and race sets (**Figure 238**).*

9. Press the inner bearing race into the crankcase half until it bottoms out against the lock ring. Turn the crankcase half over and check that the lock ring gap is centered with the crankcase oil hole (**Figure 239**).

10. Press the outer bearing race into the crankcase half until it bottoms out against the lock ring.

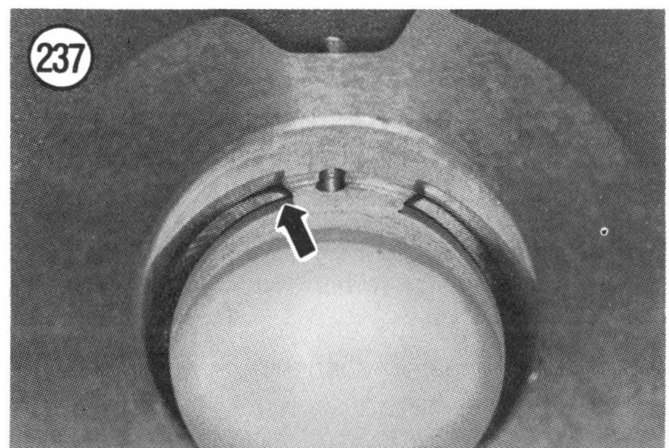

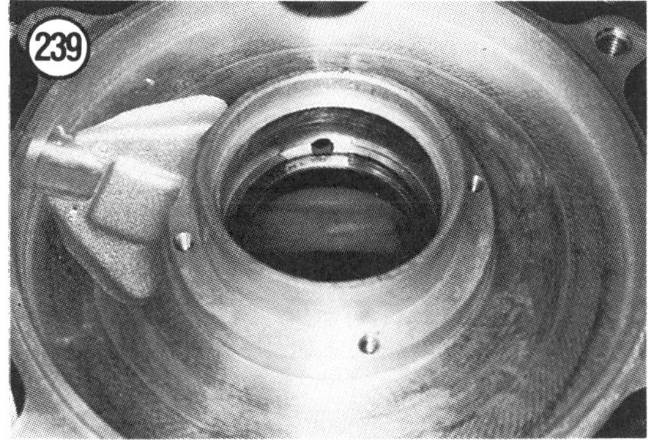

Inner sprocket shaft bearing replacement

This section describes replacement of the inner sprocket shaft bearing (9, **Figure 211**). You removed the outer bearing half (3, **Figure 211**) during crankcase disassembly.

You need a bearing splitter and the Harley-Davidson bearing installation tool (part No. HD-97225-55A) when replacing the inner sprocket shaft bearing.

NOTE
The Harley-Davidson sprocket shaft spacer (part No. HD-24036-70) may be needed with the HD-97225-55A tool.

1. Remove the bearing spacer (**Figure 240**) from the sprocket shaft.
2. Support the crankshaft with the bearing facing up (**Figure 241**).
3. Remove the inner sprocket shaft bearing with a bearing splitter (**Figure 242**).
4. Clean the sprocket shaft with contact cleaner. Check the sprocket shaft (**Figure 243**) for cracks or other damage. If you find any damage, refer service to a Harley-Davidson dealer.
5. Slide the new bearing over the sprocket shaft (**Figure 244**).
6. Install the new bearing with the bearing installation tool (**Figure 245**).
7. Install the inner bearing spacer and seat it against the bearing (**Figure 246**).

Crankcase Assembly

You need the Harley-Davidson bearing installation tool (part No. HD-97225-55A) to assemble the crankcase halves.

Refer to **Figure 211** when assembling the crankcase.

1. Place the left crankcase half over the sprocket shaft as shown in **Figure 247**.
2. Install the outer sprocket shaft bearing over the shaft (**Figure 248**).
3. Install the bearing installation tool onto the end of the crankshaft and tighten until the inner and outer bearings seat tightly against the inner bearing spacer (4, **Figure 211**). Remove the bearing installation tool from the sprocket shaft. **Figure 249** shows the outer bearing properly installed.

240

241

242

243

4. Install the sprocket shaft spacer (A, **Figure 250**) onto a new oil seal (B, **Figure 250**) so that the spacer shoulder seats against the closed side of the oil seal (**Figure 251**).

5. Install the spacer and oil seal into the crankcase half so that the oil seal lip faces out as shown in **Figure 252**.

6. Press the oil seal into the crankshaft with the Harley-Davidson sprocket shaft seal installation tool (part No. HD-39361). See **Figure 253**. **Figure 254** shows the oil seal and spacer properly installed.

7. Support the left crankcase half assembly, on wooden blocks as shown in **Figure 255**.
8. Clean the inner race (**Figure 256**), then coat it with new engine oil.
9. Slide the needle bearing (**Figure 257**) over the inner race.
10. Install a new pinion shaft spiral lock ring (**Figure 258**). Seat the lock ring into the inner race groove.
11. Clean and dry the crankcase gasket surfaces before applying gasket sealer in Step 12.
12. Apply a thin coat of a nonhardening gasket sealer to the crankcase mating surfaces. Use one of the following gasket sealers:
   a. Harley-Davidson crankcase sealant (part No. HD-99650-81).
   b. 3M #800 sealant.
   c. Yamabond No. 4.
   d. ThreeBond Liquid Gasket 1104.
13. Align the crankcase halves and install the right crankcase half (**Figure 259**).
14. Tap the 3 crankcase studs (marked during disassembly) into the crankcase halves. Install the 3 stud nuts and tighten hand-tight. See **Figure 260** (1991-1992) or **Figure 261** (1993-on).
15. Install the remaining crankcase studs, bolts and nuts.
16. Tighten the crankcase fasteners as follows:
   a. Tighten the crankcase fasteners to 10 ft.-lb. (14 N•m) in the order shown in **Figure 262**.
   b. Install the pistons, cylinders and cylinder heads as described in this chapter.
   c. Tighten the crankcase fasteners to 15-17 ft.-lb. (20-35 N•m) in the order shown in **Figure 262**.
17. Recheck flywheel end play as described in this chapter.
18. Install the engine in the frame as described in this chapter.

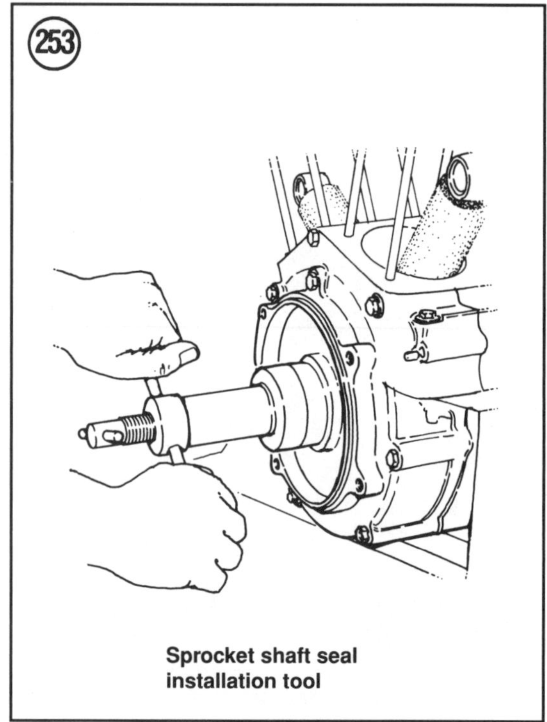

Sprocket shaft seal installation tool

Cylinder Stud Replacement

Replace bent or otherwise damaged cylinder studs (**Figure 263**) to prevent cylinder head leaks. You need the following items to replace the studs:

a. Air or electric impact wrench.
b. 0.313 in. diameter steel ball (Harley-Davidson part No. 8860).
c. Ruler or vernier caliper to measure stud installed height.

1. If the engine bottom end is assembled, block off the lower crankcase opening with clean shop rags.
2. Remove the damaged stud with a stud remover.
3. Clean the crankcase threads with electrical contact cleaner.

NOTE
New studs may have a Loctite patch already applied to the lower stud threads. Do not apply Loctite to these studs.

NOTE
The cylinder studs have a shoulder on one end. Install the stud so that the end with the shoulder faces down.

4. If the new stud does not have the Loctite patch, apply Loctite 271 to the lower stud threads.
5. Drop the 0.313 in. diameter steel ball into a cylinder head bolt, then thread the bolt onto the top of the new stud.

CAUTION
Do not use a breaker bar, ratchet or similar tool to install the studs. These tools may bend the stud and cause the engine to leak oil.

4

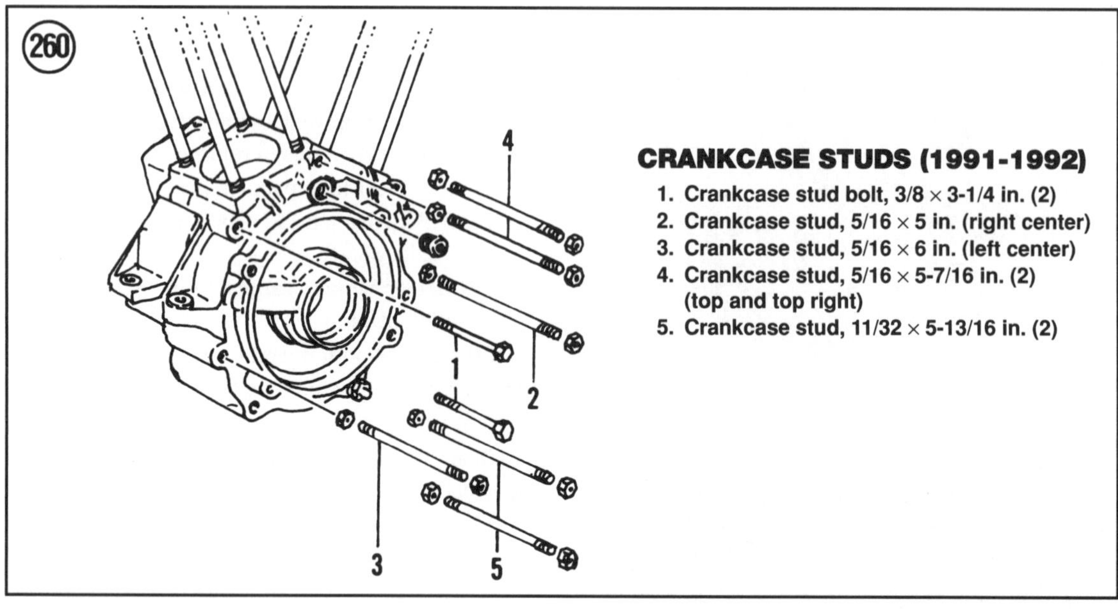

261

CRANKCASE STUDS (1993-ON)

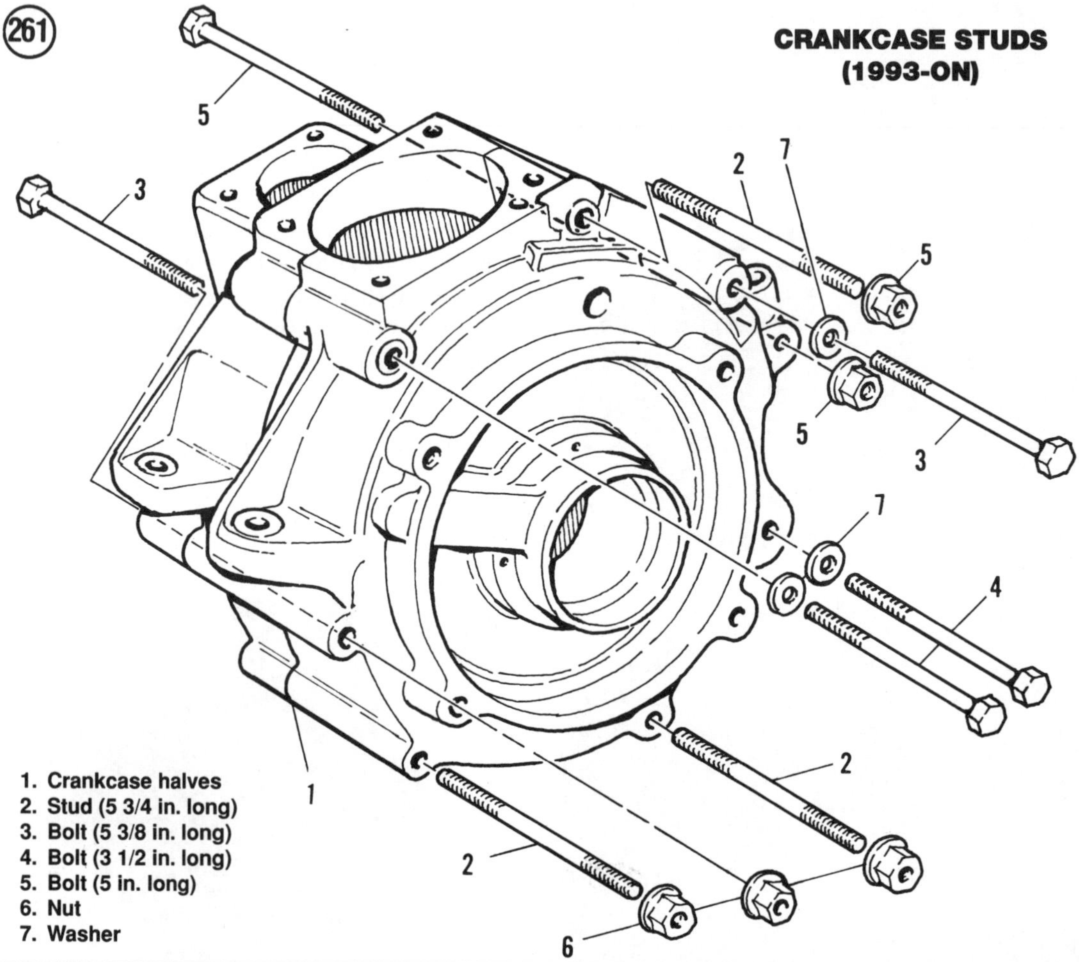

1. Crankcase halves
2. Stud (5 3/4 in. long)
3. Bolt (5 3/8 in. long)
4. Bolt (3 1/2 in. long)
5. Bolt (5 in. long)
6. Nut
7. Washer

6. Hand-thread the new stud into the crankcase, then install it with an impact wrench until the stud measures 5.670-5.770 in. (144.02-146.56 mm) above the crankcase gasket surface.
7. Remove the cylinder head bolt and steel ball from the cylinder stud.
8. Place a 1/2 in. diameter hose over each stud until you assemble the engine.

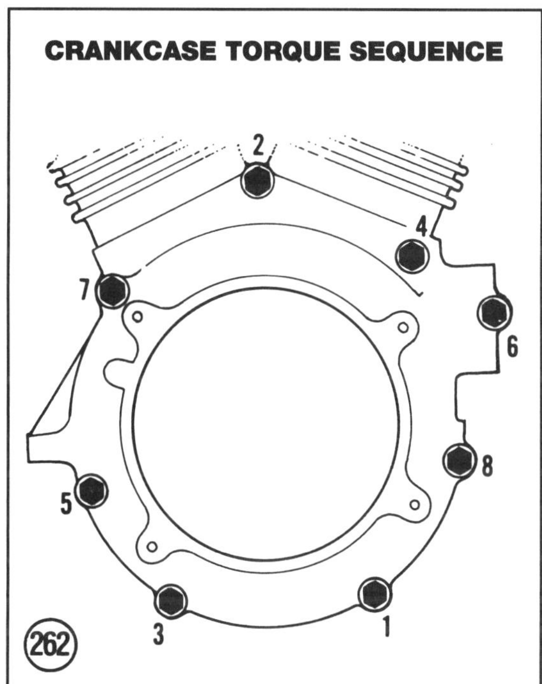

ENGINE BREAK-IN

Following cylinder service (boring, honing, new rings) and major lower end work, the engine must be broken in just as though it were new. The service and performance life of the engine depends on a careful and sensible break-in.

1. For the first 50 mi. (80 km), maintain engine speed below 2,500 rpm in any gear. However, make sure you do not lug the engine. Do not exceed 50 mph during this period.
2. From 50 - 500 mi. (80-804 km) vary the engine speed. Avoid prolonged steady running at one engine speed. During this period, increase engine speed to 3,000 rpm. Do not exceed 55 mph during this period.
3. After the first 500 mi. (804 km), the engine break-in is complete.

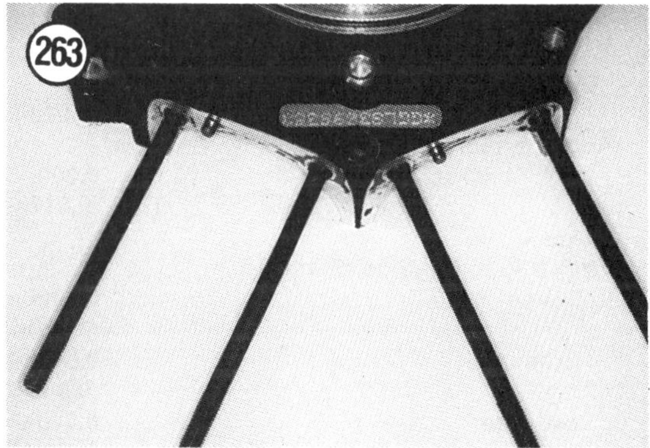

Table 1 GENERAL ENGINE SPECIFICATIONS

Engine	OHV V2 Evolution
Type	4-stroke, 45° V-twin
Bore × stroke	3.498 × 4.250 in. (88.8 × 108.0 mm)
Piston displacement	81.6 cu. in. (1340 cc)
Compression ratio	8.5:1
Horsepower	69 hp (51 kw) @ 5,000 rpm
Torque	82 ft.-lb. (111 N·m) @ 3,600 rpm

Table 2 ENGINE SERVICE SPECIFICATIONS

	New in. (mm)	Service limit in. (mm)
Cylinder head		
Warp limit	–	0.006 (0.15)
Valve guide fit in head	0.0033-0.002 (0.084-0.051)	0.0020 (0.051)
Valve seat fit in head	0.0045-0.0020 (0.114-0.051)	0.0020 (0.051)
Rocker arm		
Shaft fit in rocker cover bushing	0.0007-0.0022 (0.018-0.5)	0.0035 (0.089)
Bushing fit in rocker arm	0.004-0.002 (0.10-0.05)	–
End clearance	0.0003-0.013 (0.008-0.33)	0.025 (0.64)
Rocker arm shaft		
Shaft fit in rocker cover	0.0007-0.0022 (0.018-0.056)	0.0035 (0.089)
Valves		
Valve stem-to-guide clearance		
Intake	0.0008-0.0026 (0.020-0.066)	0.0035 (0.089)
Exhaust	0.0015-0.0033 (0.038-0.084)	0.0040 (0.102)
Seat width	0.040-0.062 (1.02-1.57)	0.090 (2.29)
Valve stem protrusion	1.990-2.024 (50.55-51.41	2.034 (51.66)
Valve springs		
Free length		
Outer	2.105-2.177 (53.47-55.30)	–
Inner	1.926-1.996 (48.92-50.70)	–
Cylinder taper	–	0.002 (0.05)
Cylinder out-of-round	–	0.003 (0.08)
Piston-to-cylinder clearance		
1991-1992		
Mahle piston	0.00055-0.00165 (0.0139-0.0419)	0.0053 (0.135)
KSG piston	0.00075-0.00175 (0.0191-0.0445)	0.0053 (0.135)
1993-on	0.00075-0.00175 (0.0195-0.0445)	0.0053 (0.135)

(continued)

Table 2 ENGINE SERVICE SPECIFICATIONS (continued)

	New in. (mm)	Service limit in. (mm)
Piston pin fit in piston		
1991-1992		
Mahle piston	0.0002-0.0004 (0.0051-0.0102)	0.001 (0.025)
KSG piston	0.0001-0.0004 (0.0025-0.010)	0.001 (0.025)
1993-on	0.0001-0.0004 (0.0025-0.010)	0.001 (0.025)
Piston rings		
Compression ring end gap	0.007-0.020 (0.18-0.51)	0.030 (0.76)
Oil control ring end gap	0.009-0.052 (0.23-0.1.32)	0.065 (1.65)
Compression ring side clearance		
Top ring	0.002-0.0045 (0.05-0.114)	0.006 (0.15)
2nd ring	0.0016-0.0041 (0.041-0.104)	0.006 (0.15)
Oil control ring side clearance	0.0016-0.0076 (0.041-0.193)	0.008 (0.20)
Connecting rod		
Connecting rod-to-crankpin clearance	0.0004-0.0017 (0.010-0.043)	0.002 (0.05)
Piston pin clearance in connecting rod	0.0003-0.0007 (0.008-0.018)	0.001 (0.025)
Connecting rod side play	0.005-0.025 (0.13-0.64)	0.030 (0.76)
Hydraulic lifters		
Fit in guide	0.0008-0.002 (0.020-0.05)	0.003 (0.08)
Lifter guide-to-crankcase clearance	0.000-0.004 (0.00-0.10)	–
Roller fit	–	0.0015 (0.038)
Roller end clearance	–	0.0015 (0.038)
Gearcase		
Breather gear end play	0.001-0.011 (0.025-0.28)	0.016 (0.41)
Cam gear end play	0.001-0.050 (0.025-1.27)	0.050 (1.27)
Cam gear shaft-to-bushing clearance	0.00075-0.00175 (0.0190-0.0445)	0.003 (0.08)
Cam gear shaft-to-bearing clearance	0.0005-0.0025 (0.0127-0.0635)	0.005 (0.13)
Oil pump drive shaft-to-crankcase bushing clearance	0.0004-0.0025 (0.010-0.64)	0.0035 (0.089)
Sprocket shaft bearing		
Cup fit in crankcase	0.003-0.005 (0.08-0.13)	–
Cone fit on shaft	0.0005-0.0015 (0.013-0.038)	–

(continued)

4

Table 2 ENGINE SERVICE SPECIFICATIONS (continued)

	New in. (mm)	Service limit in. (mm)
Pinion shaft and bearings		
Pinion shaft clearance	0.001-0.0025 (0.025-0.64)	0.0035 (0.089)
Pinion shaft runout		
1991-1992	–	
1993-on	0.000-0.0045 (0.000-0.114)	–
Cam gear needle bearing clearance	0.0002-0.0009 (0.005-0.023)	–
Crankshaft end play	0.001-0.005 (0.025-0.13)	0.006 (0.152)
Runout (flywheels @ rim)	0.000-0.010 (0.00-0.25)	0.015 (0.38)
Runout (shaft @ flywheel)	0.000-0.002 (0.00-0.051)	0.003 (0.076)

* See text for measurement procedure.

Table 3 VALVE SPRING COMPRESSION SPECIFICATION

	Compression length* in. (mm)	Pressure lbs.	kg
Outer springs			
Closed	1.282-1.378 (32.56-35.00)	183-207	83-94
Open	1.751-1.848 (44.48-46.94)	72-92	33-42
Inner springs			
Closed	1.107-1.213 (28.12-30.81)	98-112	45-51
Open	1.577-1.683 (40.05-42.75)	38-49	17-22

* A spring compression tool is required; see text for measurement procedure.

Table 4 ENGINE TIGHTENING TORQUES

	ft.-lb.	N•m
Compression nut fitting at oil pump cover manifold (1992-on)	8-12	11-16
Crank pin nut	180-210	244-285
Cylinder head bolts	see text	
Upper engine mounting bracket		
1991-1992	22-28	29-38
1993-on		
At cylinder heads	28-35	38-48
At frame	28-32	38-43
Crankcase fasteners	see text	

(continued)

Table 4 ENGINE TIGHTENING TORQUES (continued)

	ft.-lb.	N•m
Engine mounting bolts		
Front	33-38	45-54
Rear	33-38	45-54
Inner primary housing mounting bolts		
At engine	18-22	24-30
At transmission	18-22	24-30
Pinion gear nut	35-45	47-61
Lifter guide mounting bolts		
1991-1992	12-15	16-20
1993-on	9-12	12-16
Lifter screen plug	7-10	10-14
Oil filter mount bolts		
1991-on	13-17	18-23
Oil pump cover manifold screws		
1992-on	70-80 in.-lb.	7.9-9.0
Oil pump cover bolts	7-10	10.2-13.6
Oil pump housing mounting bolts	60-85 in.-lb.	6.8-9.6
Lower rocker cover bolts		
5/16 in. bolts	15-18	20-24
1/4 in. bolts	10-13	14-18
Gearcase cover screws	7-10	10.2-13.6
Spark plug	18-22	24-30
Tappet screen plug	7-10	10.2-13.6
Timer screws		
Inner cover and sensor plate	15-30 in.-lb.	1.7-3.4
Upper rocker cover mounting bolts	10-13	14-18

Table 5 INNER BEARING SPACER SIZE

	Spacer thickness	
Spacer part No.	**In.**	**mm**
9120	0.0925/0.0915	2.350/2.324
9121	0.0945/0.0935	2.400/2.375
9122	0.0965/0.0955	2.451/2.427
9123	0.0985/0.0975	2.502/2.476
9124	0.1005/0.0995	2.553/2.527
9125	0.1025/0.1015	2.604/2.578
9126	0.1045/0.1035	2.654/2.629
9127	0.1065/0.1055	2.705/2.680
9128	0.1085/0.1075	2.756/2.731
9129	0.1105/0.1095	2.807/2.781
9130	0.1125/0.1115	2.858/2.832
9131	0.1145/0.1135	2.908/2.883
9132	0.1165/0.1155	2.959/2.934
9133	0.1185/0.1175	3.010/2.985
9134	0.1205/0.1195	3.061/3.035

4

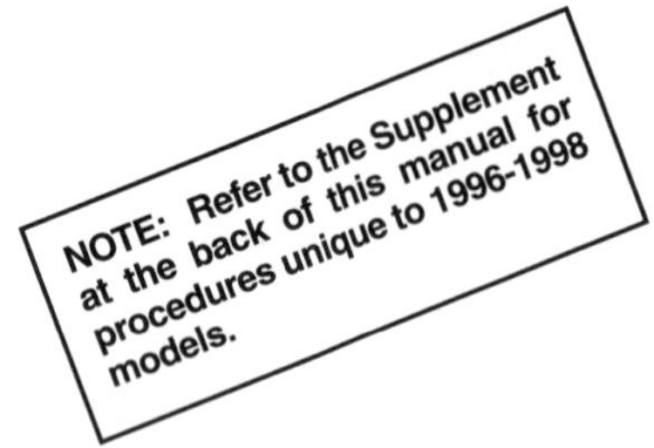

CHAPTER FIVE

CLUTCH AND PRIMARY DRIVE

This chapter describes service procedures for the clutch and primary drive. **Tables 1-4** are at the end of the chapter.

OUTER PRIMARY COVER

Removal

Refer to **Figure 1**.

1. Support the bike on a level surface.
2. Disconnect the negative battery cable from the battery.

WARNING
Disconnect the negative battery cable before working on the clutch or any primary drive component. Otherwise, you may receive a serious personal injury if the starter motor is accidentally activated.

3. Place a drain pan under the primary cover and remove the oil drain plug (**Figure 2**). Allow the oil to drain. Reinstall and tighten the drain plug.
4. Remove the shift lever and the left-hand footpeg assembly (**Figure 3**).
5. Remove the primary chain inspection cover (**Figure 4**) and the gasket.
6. Remove the bolts securing the primary cover (**Figure 5**) to the chaincase and remove the primary cover.
7. On 1995 models, remove the 2 round gaskets (**Figure 6**) installed between the primary cover and chaincase.
8. Remove the dowel pins, if necessary.

Inspection

1. Remove all gasket residue from the primary cover (A, **Figure 7**) and chaincase gasket surfaces.
2. Clean the primary cover in solvent and dry with compressed air.
3. Inspect the starter jackshaft bushing (B, **Figure 7**) for excessive wear, cracks or other damage. To replace the bushing, perform the following:
   a. Remove the bushing with a blind bearing removal tool.
   b. Clean the bushing bore in the housing.

c. Press in the new bushing until its outer surface is flush with the edge of the bushing bore.

Installation

NOTE
The primary cover gasket is large and can be difficult to install flush all the way around the primary cover. To help make gasket installation easier, make a few alignment studs with some threaded bolts that are longer than the original primary cover bolts. To do this, first cut the head off each bolt. Then cut a slot in its place so that you can unscrew the studs using a screwdriver after you install the primary cover. ***Figure 8*** *shows the alignment studs used in the following procedure.*

1. Install the dowel pins, if removed.
2. Thread 3 or 4 alignment studs into the chaincase (**Figure 9**). Then install a new primary cover gasket over the studs and seat it against the gasket surface.

CAUTION
Harley-Davidson specifies installing a new Print-O-Seal gasket between the

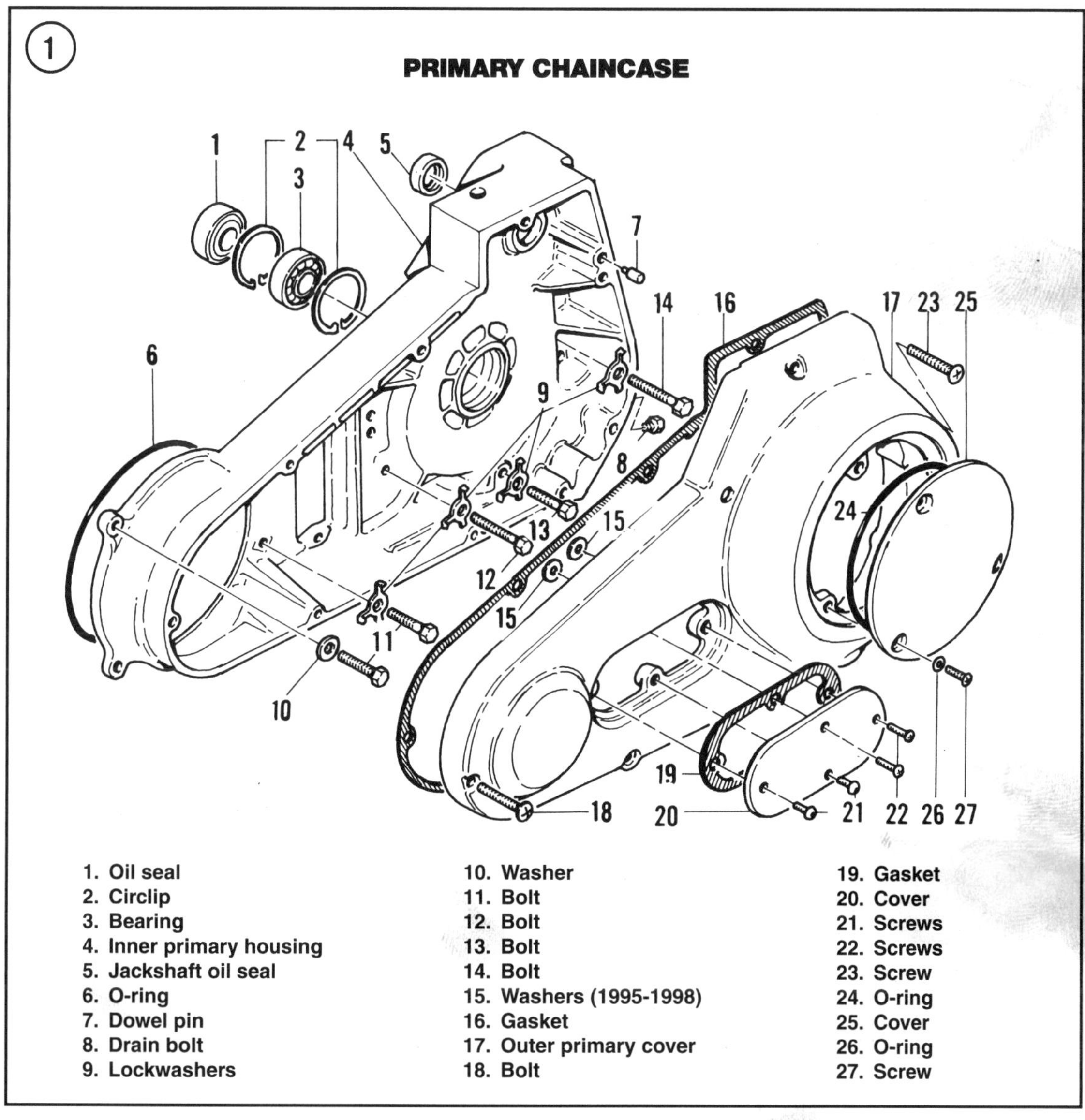

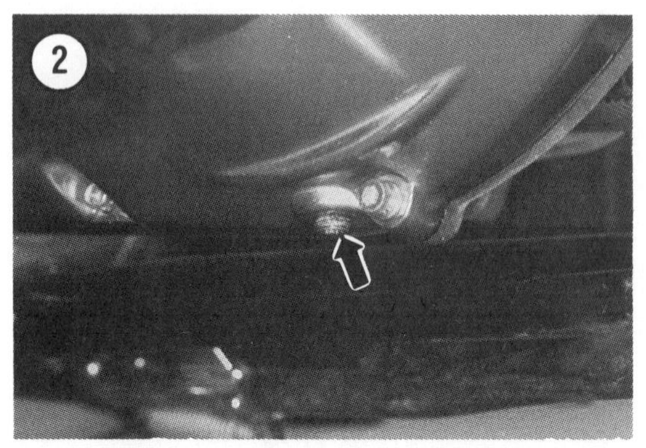
2

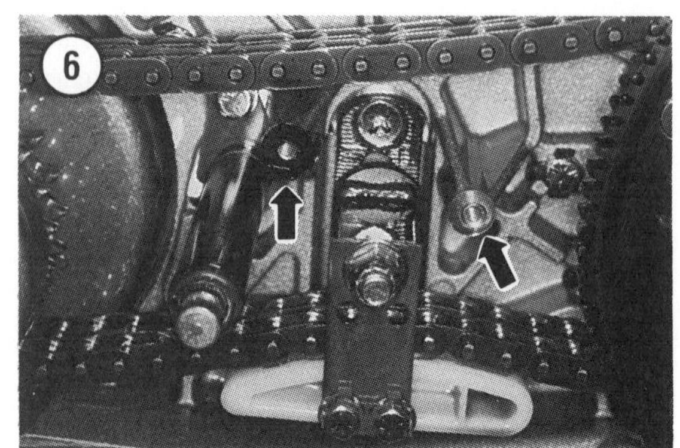
6

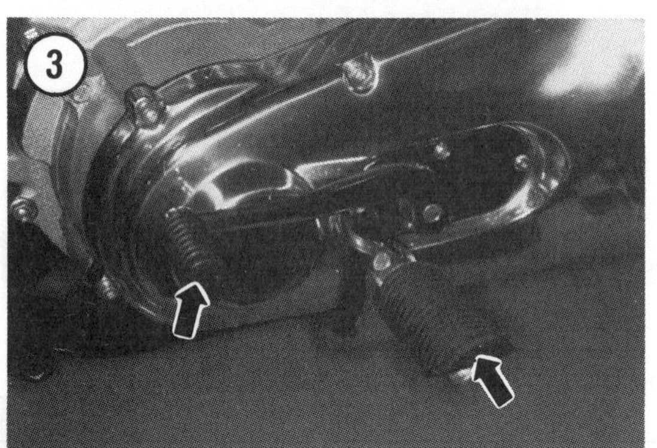
3

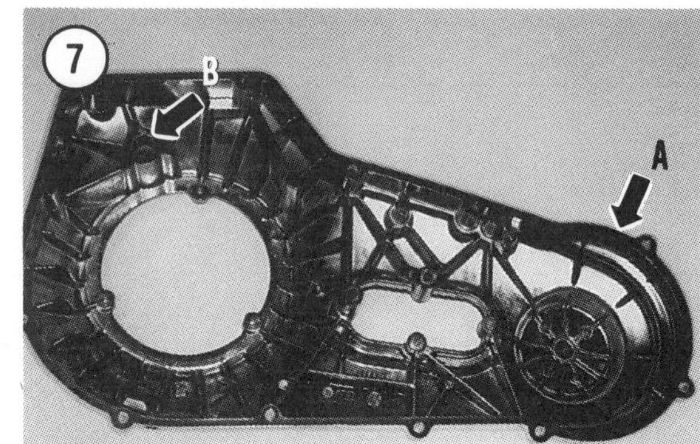
7
B
A

4

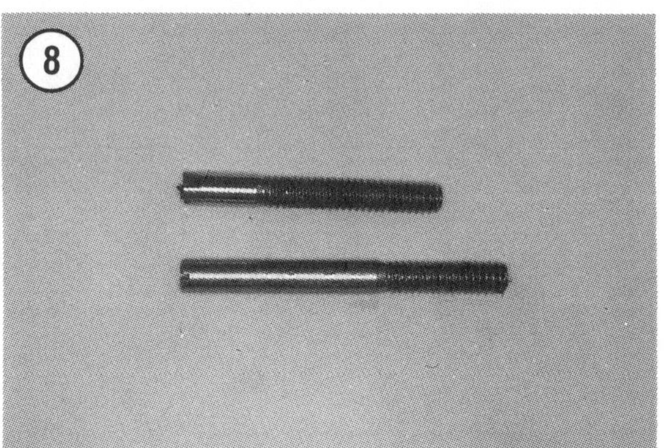
8

5

9

outer primary cover and the inner primary chaincase each time you remove these covers.

3. On 1995 models, install 2 of the studs into the chaincase as shown in A, **Figure 10**, then slide a round gasket over each stud (B, **Figure 10**).
4. Slide the primary cover (**Figure 5**) over the alignment studs and seat flush against the gasket(s).
5. Install the primary cover bolts into the bolt holes that do not have the alignment studs and tighten hand-tight.

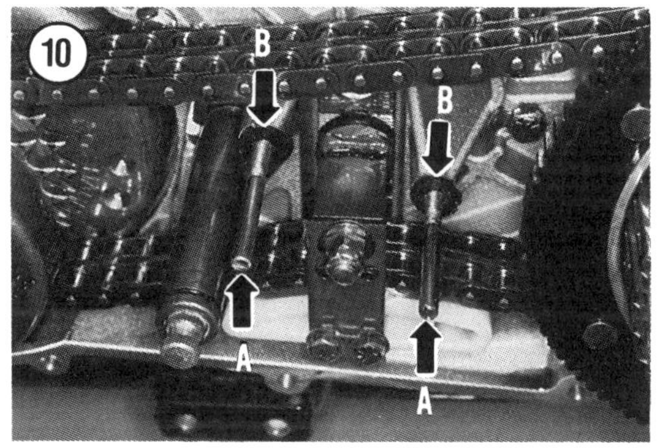

6. Remove the alignment studs and install the remaining primary cover bolts. See **Figure 11** and **Figure 12**, typical.
7. Tighten the primary cover bolts to the torque specification in **Table 4**. Check that the gasket seats flush all the way around the cover.
8. Refill the primary chaincase with the type and quantity oil specified under *Primary Chain Lubrication* in Chapter Three.
9. Install the primary chain inspection cover (**Figure 4**) and a new gasket. Tighten the inspection cover screws to the torque specification in **Table 4**.

NOTE
*On 1995 models, note that **Table 4** specifies 2 different torque specifications for the inspection cover screws: bottom and front bolts and top and rear bolts.*

10. Install the left-hand footpeg and the shift lever (**Figure 3**). Tighten the bolts securely.
11. Reconnect the negative battery cable.

CLUTCH PLATES

This section describes removal, inspection and installation of the clutch plates. If the clutch requires additional service, refer to *Clutch Overhaul* in this chapter.

Refer to **Figure 13** when servicing the clutch.

Special Tools

You need a compression tool when removing and installing the diaphragm spring. You can use the Harley-Davidson Spring Compression tool (part No. HD-3815 [**Figure 14**]) or an equivalent aftermarket tool. **Figure 15** shows an aftermarket tool.

Removal

1. Disconnect the negative battery cable from the battery.
2. Remove the primary cover as described in this chapter.
3. Loosen the clutch cable adjuster (**Figure 16**) to obtain as much cable slack as possible.
4. Loosen the clutch adjusting screw locknut and remove the adjusting screw (**Figure 17**) and locknut.

(13)

WET CLUTCH

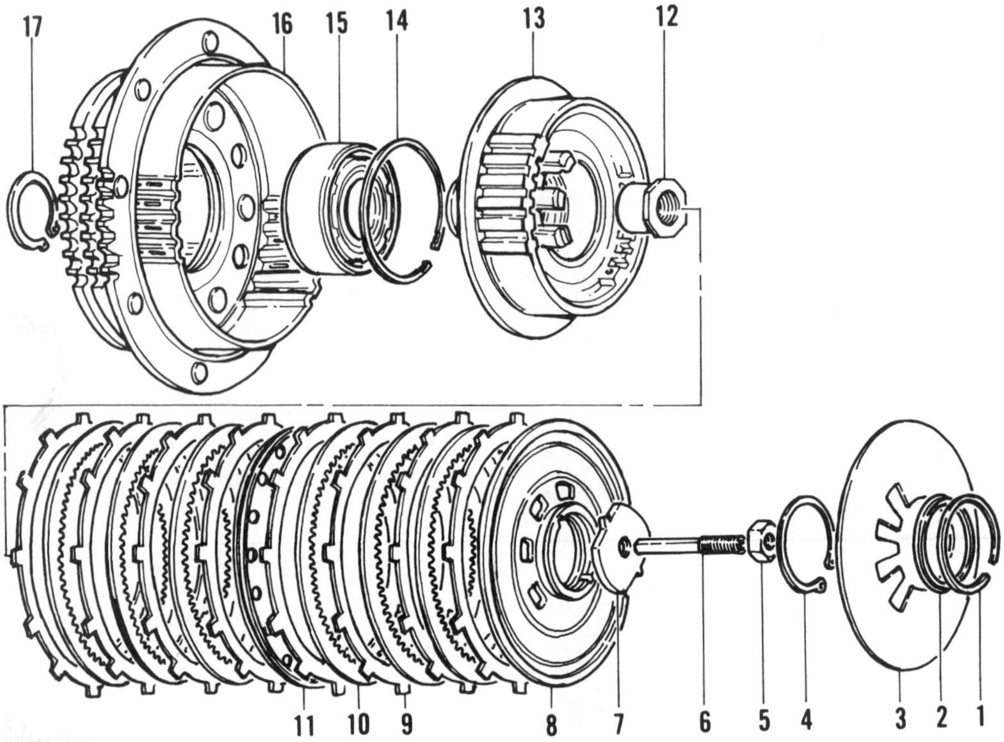

1. Circlip
2. Spring seat
3. Diaphragm spring
4. Circlip
5. Locknut
6. Adjusting screw
7. Release plate
8. Pressure plate
9. Friction plate
10. Steel plate
11. Spring plate
12. Clutch nut
13. Clutch hub
14. Circlip
15. Bearing
16. Clutch shell
17. Circlip

(14)

(15)

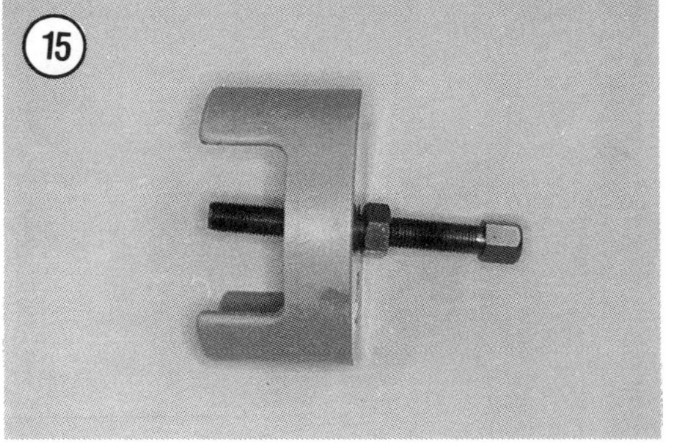

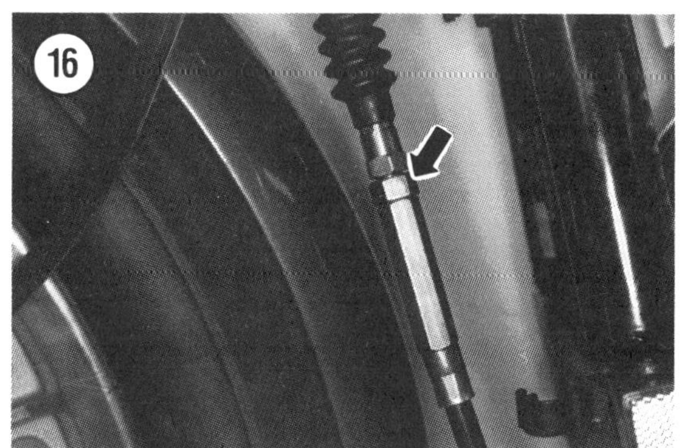

WARNING

Wear safety glasses when compressing the diaphragm spring and removing the circlip in the following steps. The circlip is under high tension and may fly out when you remove it.

5. Center the spring compression tool against the diaphragm spring and thread the tool's pressure bolt into the release plate threads (**Figure 18**). Make sure the pressure bolt engages all of the release plate threads.

NOTE

***Figure 19** shows the Harley-Davidson compression tool.*

WARNING

*The clutch diaphragm spring (3, **Figure 13**) is under extreme pressure. When removing the circlip (1, **Figure 13**) in the following steps, use a spring compression tool to compress the diaphragm spring and remove pressure from the circlip. If you try to remove the circlip without this tool, clutch parts will fly out under great force and cause severe personal injury. If you do not have this tool, stop until you can obtain one or have the clutch plates serviced by a Harley-Davidson mechanic.*

6. Slowly tighten the compression tool to compress the diaphragm spring. When doing so, watch the movement of the diaphragm spring and spring seat (**Figure 20**). If there is any binding, stop and loosen the tool's pressure bolt. If the parts release and move smoothly, continue until the spring seat has moved far enough away from the circlip to allow circlip removal.

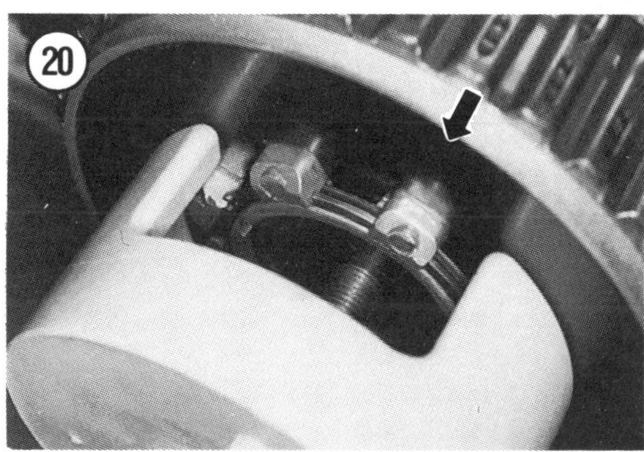

5

CAUTION

*When removing the circlip (1, **Figure 13**) in Step 7, dont try to remove it all at once. Start at one end and work it out of the clutch hub grooves, one groove at a time. If youre not careful, you will snap off one of the clutch hub tabs.*

7. When you have removed all tension from the spring and circlip, carefully pry the circlip (**Figure 21**) out of the clutch hub groove with a small screwdriver or similar tool. When the circlip is free, remove the compression tool with the diaphragm and pressure plate attached (**Figure 22**).
8. Loosen the spring compression tool and remove it.
9. Remove the clutch plates (**Figure 23**) from the clutch shell. Note the spring plate installed between the fourth and fifth friction plate (**Figure 24**).

Clutch Plate Inspection

Refer to **Figure 13** when inspecting the clutch plates.

1. Clean all parts (except friction plates and bearing) in a non-oil based solvent and dry with compressed air. Place all cleaned parts on lint-free paper towels.
2. Check each steel plate (A, **Figure 25**) for cracks or wear grooves. Then place each plate on a surface plate and check for warpage with a feeler gauge. Replace the steel plates as a set if any one plate is warped more than the limit specified in **Table 3**.
3. Inspect each friction plate (B, **Figure 25**) for worn or grooved lining surfaces. Replace the friction plates as a set if any one plate is damaged. If the friction plates do not show visual wear or damage, wipe each plate thoroughly with a lint-free cloth to

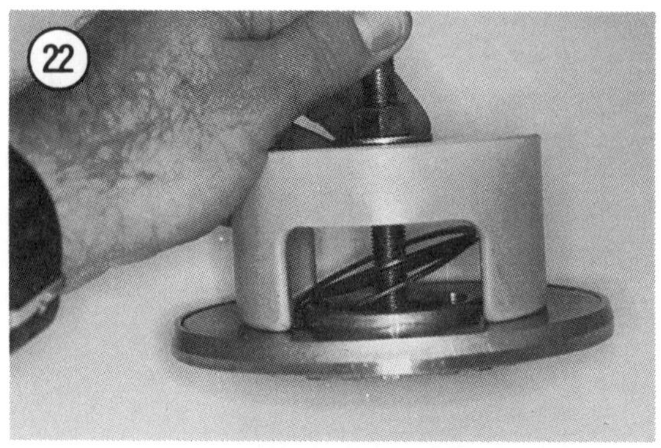

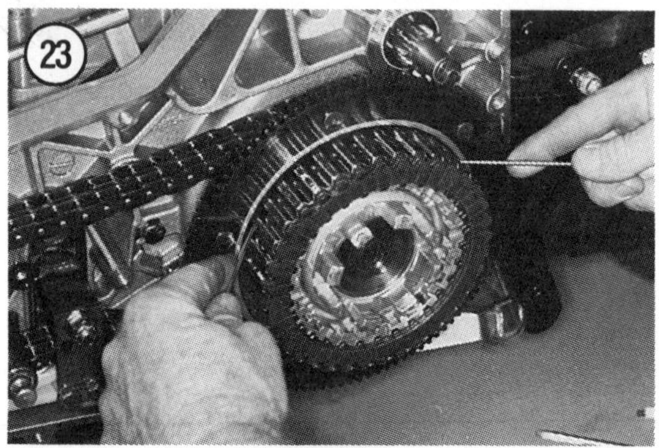

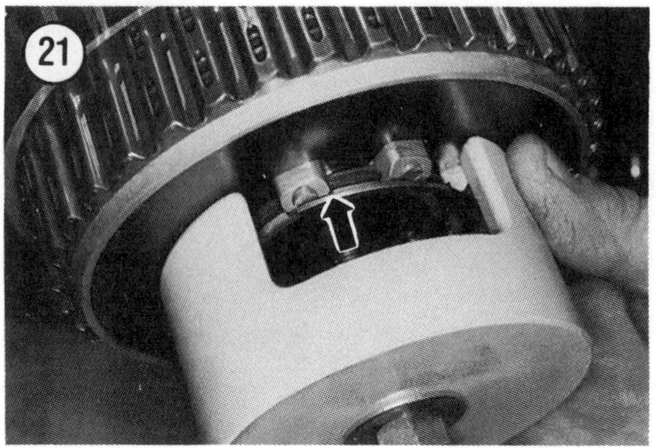

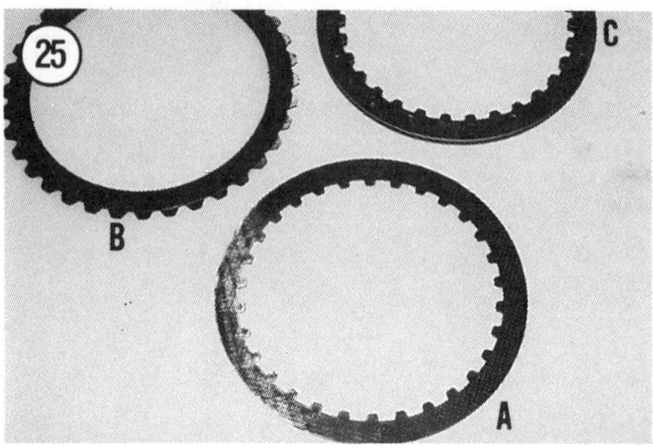

remove as much oil from the plates as possible. Then stack each of the 8 friction plates on top of each other and measure their combined thickness with a vernier caliper (**Figure 26**). Replace the friction plates as an assembly if the combined thickness of the 8 plates is less than the minimum limit specified in **Table 3**.

4. Check the spring plate (C, **Figure 25**) for cracks or damage. Check for loose or damaged rivets (**Figure 27**). Replace the spring plate if necessary.

5. Remove the diaphragm spring (**Figure 28**) from the pressure plate and check it for cracks or damage. Check also for bent or damaged tabs. Replace the diaphragm spring if necessary.

6. Inspect the pressure plate (A, **Figure 29**) for cracks or other damage. Inspect its circlip groove for damage.

7. To remove the release plate (B, **Figure 29**), remove the circlip and release plate. Inspect the release plate and its threads for damage.

8. Replace the spring seat or circlip (**Figure 30**) if damaged.

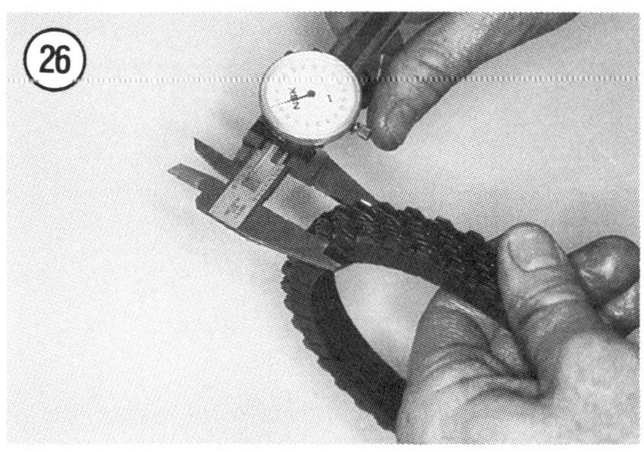

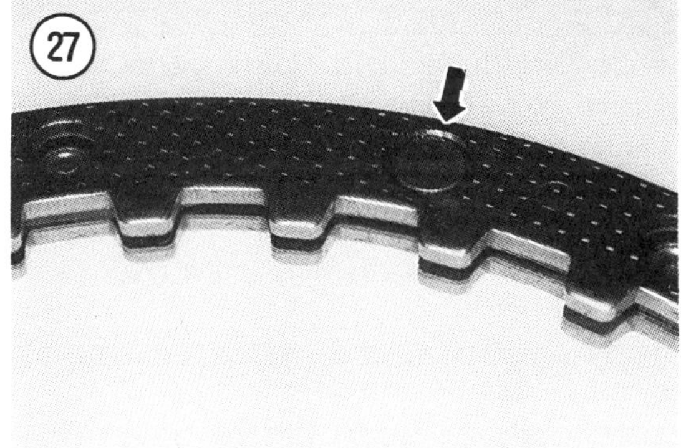

Clutch Plate Installation

1. Soak the clutch plates in new primary drive oil for approximately 5 minutes before installing them.

NOTE

*When installing a stock clutch assembly, count the clutch plates (**Figure 31**). The stock clutch has 8 friction plates, 6 steel plates and 1 spring plate. If you are installing an aftermarket clutch plate assembly, follow its manufacturers instructions for plate alignment and installation.*

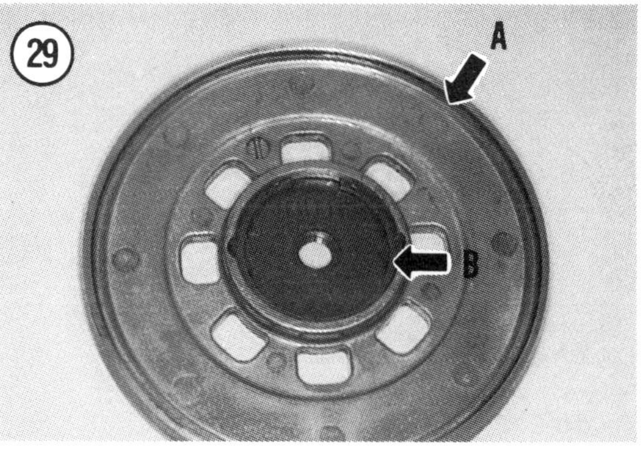

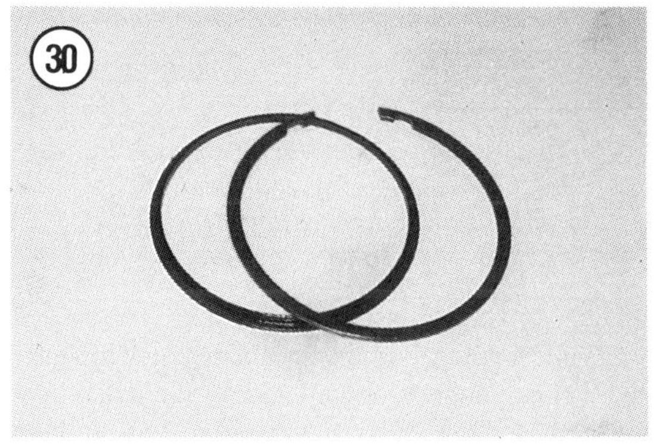

2. Align the tabs on a friction plate with the clutch shell grooves and install the plate. Then align the inner teeth on a steel plate with the clutch hub grooves and install the plate. Repeat until you have installed all of the clutch plates. Install the spring plate (**Figure 24**) between the fourth and fifth friction plates. The last plate installed is a friction plate.
3. If you disassembled the diaphragm spring and pressure plate assembly, reassemble these parts as follows:
   a. Place the pressure plate on your workbench so that its outer side faces up (A, **Figure 29**).
   b. Install the release plate (B, **Figure 29**) into the pressure plate so that the side marked OUT faces out. Align the 2 release plate tabs with the 2 grooves in the pressure plate.
   c. Install the circlip (4, **Figure 13**) to secure the release plate in the pressure plate.
   d. The diaphragm spring (**Figure 28**) is not flat, but instead, has a convex side (side that curves outward). Install the diaphragm spring onto the pressure plate so that the convex side faces *away* from the pressure plate—the convex side must face out.
4. Install the pressure plate against the clutch hub (**Figure 32**). The teeth on the back of the pressure plate must engage the teeth on the clutch hub.
5. Hold the spring seat with its flat, larger outer diameter side facing toward the diaphragm spring. Then hold the circlip against the spring seat. See **Figure 32**.

WARNING
*When you compress the diaphragm spring and install the circlip (1, **Figure 13**) in the following steps, use the same tool that you used during disassembly. For more information, refer to **Clutch Plate Removal** in this section. Severe personal injury can occur if the diaphragm spring flies out while under pressure.*

WARNING
Wear safety glasses when compressing the diaphragm spring and installing the circlip in the following steps. The circlip is under high tension and may fly out during installation.

6. While holding the parts installed in Step 5, center the spring compression tool against the diaphragm spring and thread the tool's pressure bolt into the release plate threads (**Figure 21**). Make sure the pressure bolt engages all of the release plate threads.

CAUTION
Tighten the spring compression tool only the amount required to compress the diaphragm spring and install the circlip. Excessive compression of the diaphragm spring may damage the clutch pressure plate.

7. Install the spring seat and circlip into the groove in the clutch hub.
8. After making sure the circlip is seated completely in the clutch hub groove, slowly loosen the tool pressure bolt while checking that the clutch spring seat lip seats inside the circlip. After you have removed all tension from the tool, remove it from the release plate. See **Figure 33**.
9. Install the clutch adjusting screw and locknut (**Figure 34**).
10. To adjust the clutch, perform the following:

31

32

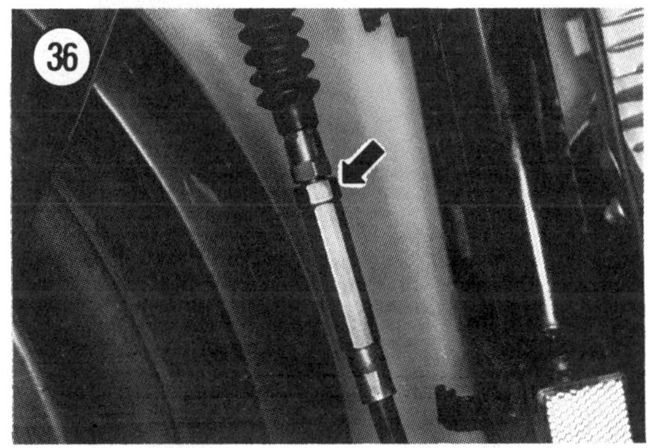

CAUTION

Because the clutch adjuster screw clearance increases with engine temperature, adjust the clutch when the engine is cold (room temperature). Adjusting the clutch on a hot engine may reduce pushrod clearance and cause the clutch to slip.

a. Check that the clutch cable seats squarely in its perch (**Figure 35**) at the handlebar.

b. Check the clutch cable adjuster (**Figure 36**) for cable slack. If there is no cable slack, loosen the locknut and adjuster.

c. Loosen the clutch adjuster locknut (if it is tight), then turn the adjusting screw (**Figure 37**) clockwise (inward) until it is tight.

d. Turn the adjusting screw counterclockwise (outward) 1/2 to 1 turn. Then hold the adjusting screw and tighten the locknut to the torque specification in **Table 4**.

e. Squeeze the clutch lever (**Figure 35**) 3 times maximum to set the clutch ball and ramp release mechanism.

f. Turn the clutch cable adjuster (**Figure 36**) to obtain a 1/16-1/8 in. (1.6-3.2 mm) gap at the clutch lever (**Figure 38**). Pull on the clutch cable sheath (at the clutch lever) when adjusting the cable.

g. When the adjustment is correct, tighten the clutch cable locknut and slide the rubber boot over the cable adjuster.

11. Install the primary cover as described in this chapter.

5

CLUTCH, COMPENSATING SPROCKET AND PRIMARY DRIVE CHAIN REMOVAL AND INSTALLATION

This section describes clutch removal, installation and overhaul. Refer to **Figure 39** and **Figure 40** when servicing the clutch in the following sections.

Special Tools

When removing the clutch, you must remove the compensating sprocket nut and the clutch nut first. These nuts are tightened to high torque specifications and have red Loctite applied to their threads. The easiest way to remove these nuts is with an air

(38)

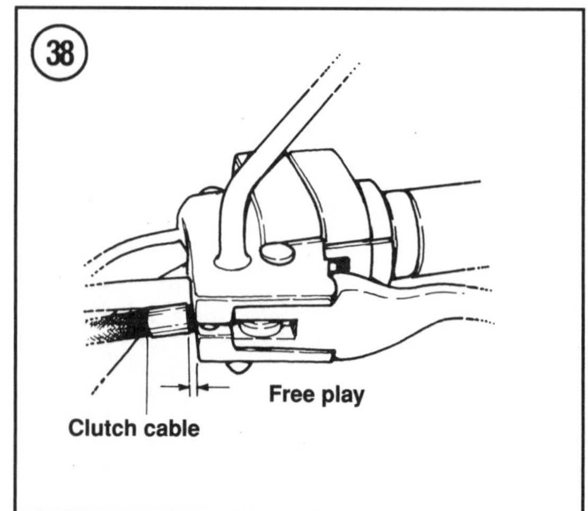

(39)

WET CLUTCH

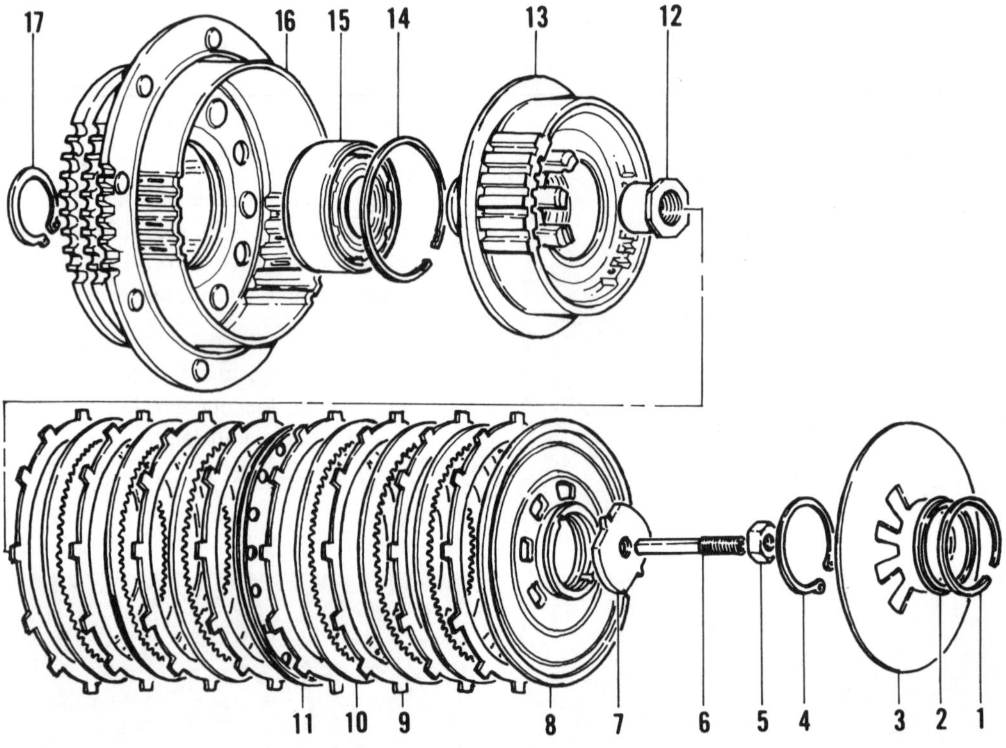

1. Circlip
2. Spring seat
3. Diaphragm spring
4. Circlip
5. Locknut
6. Adjusting screw
7. Release plate
8. Pressure plate
9. Friction plate
10. Steel plate
11. Spring plate
12. Clutch nut
13. Clutch hub
14. Circlip
15. Bearing
16. Clutch shell
17. Circlip

or electric impact wrench. If you do not have one of these tools, rent one before starting the following procedure.

When tightening these 2 nuts, you will first have to lock the engine and transmission assemblies. To do so, use the Harley-Davidson primary drive locking tool (part No. HD-41214) or an equivalent tool. You also need a torque wrench to tighten both nuts accurately.

Removal

This procedure describes removal of the clutch, primary chain and engine sprocket. The diaphragm spring and clutch plates are not removed during this procedure. To service the diaphragm spring and clutch plates, refer to *Clutch Plates* in this chapter. If you are going to service the clutch shell and its bearing, remove the diaphragm spring and clutch plates before removing the clutch assembly; refer to *Clutch Plates* in this chapter.

1. Disconnect the negative battery cable from the battery.
2. Remove the outer primary cover as described in this chapter.
3. Loosen the clutch cable adjuster (**Figure 36**) to obtain as much cable slack as possible.
4. Loosen the clutch adjusting screw locknut and the adjusting screw (**Figure 34**).

NOTE
Use the 2 notches cast in the pressure plate to help pry the circlip out in Step 5.

5. Remove the circlip (4, **Figure 39**) that holds the adjust screw plate in the pressure plate. Then remove the adjust screw plate (**Figure 41**).

NOTE
Read ***Special Tools*** *at the beginning of this section, then continue with Step 6.*

6. Shift the transmission into fifth gear. Have an assistant apply the rear brake.

NOTE
The clutch nut has left-hand threads. Turn the clutch nut clockwise to loosen it.

7. Loosen the compensating sprocket nut (**Figure 42**) and the clutch nut (**Figure 43**) with an impact wrench.

5

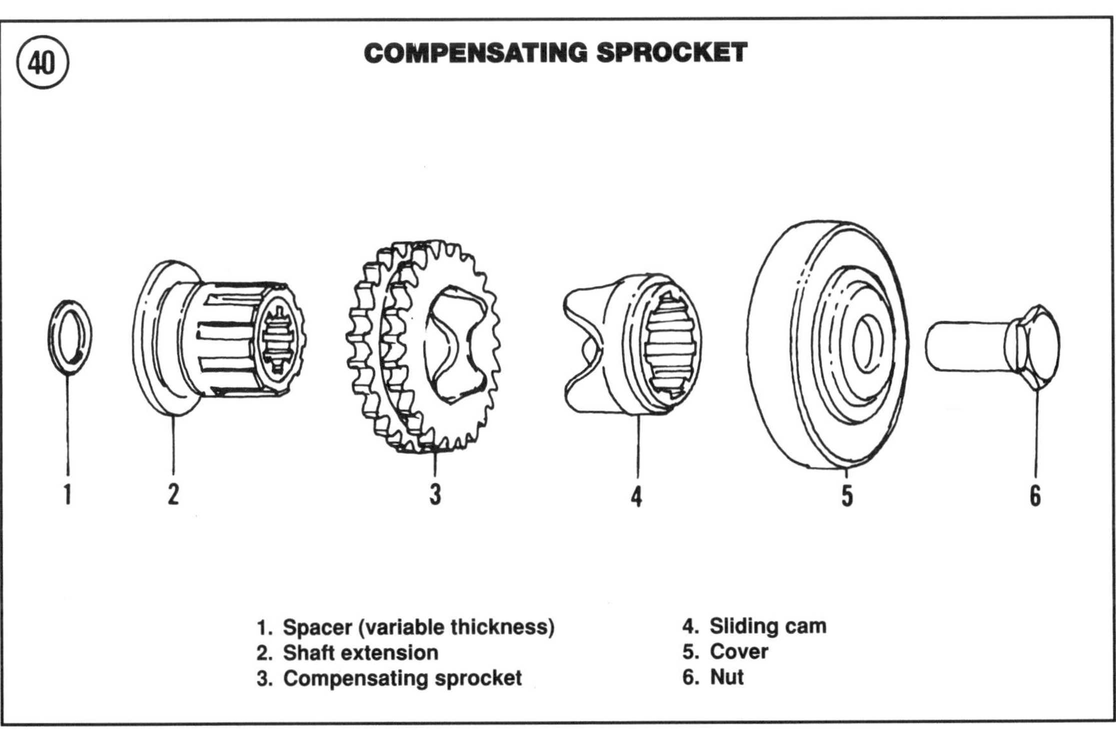

8. Remove the compensating sprocket nut, washer, cover and sliding cam assembly (**Figure 44**).
9. Remove the clutch nut (**Figure 43**).
10. Remove the primary chain shoe adjuster locknut (**Figure 45**).
11. Remove the compensating sprocket, primary chain, chain adjuster and clutch assembly (**Figure 46**) at the same time. See **Figure 47**.
12. To complete compensating sprocket removal, remove the shaft extension (**Figure 48**) and the spacer (**Figure 49**).

48

49

50

51

13. Refer to *Clutch Plates* and *Clutch Overhaul* in this chapter to service the clutch assembly.

14. Refer to *Primary Chain* in this chapter to service the compensating sprocket and primary chain assembly.

Installation

1. Remove all thread sealer residue from the crankshaft and mainshaft threads and from the compensating sprocket and clutch nuts.
2. Remove all gasket residue from the inner primary housing gasket surfaces.
3. Install the spacer (**Figure 49**) and the shaft extension (**Figure 48**) onto the crankshaft.
4. Assemble the compensating sprocket, primary chain, chain adjuster and clutch as shown in **Figure 47**.
5. Install the compensating sprocket, primary chain, chain adjuster and clutch as shown in **Figure 46**. Insert the chain adjuster bolt through the chain adjuster hole as shown in **Figure 50**.
6. Install the remaining compensating sprocket components in the following order (**Figure 44**):
   a. Sliding cam (**Figure 51**).
   b. Cover.
   c. Washer.

NOTE

To prevent the engine and transmission from turning when tightening the compensating sprocket and clutch nuts, lock the engine with the primary drive locking tool (part No. HD-41214). See ***Figure 52****.*

7. Place 2 drops of Loctite 262 (red) on the compensating sprocket nut threads. Then install the nut (**Figure 42**) and tighten to the torque specification in **Table 4**.

NOTE

The clutch nut uses left-hand threads. Turn the nut counterclockwise to tighten it.

8. Place 2 drops of Loctite 262 (red) on the clutch nut threads. Then install the nut (**Figure 43**) and tighten to the torque specification in **Table 4**.
9. Adjust the primary chain as described in Chapter Three.

10. If you removed the clutch plates, refer to *Clutch Plates* in this chapter to install the clutch plates and complete clutch installation. If you did not remove the clutch plates, continue with Step 11.

11. Install the adjust screw plate (**Figure 41**) into the pressure plate. Align the tabs on the adjust screw plate with the 2 notches in the pressure plate. If you removed the adjusting screw and locknut from the plate, install the adjust screw plate so that the side marked OUT faces out.

12. Install the circlip (4, **Figure 39**) into the groove in the pressure plate. Make sure the circlip seats completely in the groove.

13. Adjust the clutch as described under *Clutch Plates, Installation* in this chapter.

14. Reconnect the negative battery cable at the battery.

CLUTCH OVERHAUL

This section describes information on inspecting and servicing the clutch shell, bearing and clutch hub.

Refer to **Figure 39** when performing the following procedures.

Preliminary Inspection

The clutch shell (**Figure 53**) is a subassembly consisting of a bearing (15, **Figure 39**), clutch shell and clutch hub.

1. Remove the clutch as described in this chapter.

2. Hold the clutch hub and rotate the clutch shell by hand. The bearing is damaged if the clutch shell binds or turns roughly.

3. Check the primary chain sprocket and the starter ring gear on the clutch shell for cracks, deep scoring, excessive wear or heat discoloration. If the sprocket or the ring gear is worn or damaged, replace the clutch shell. If the sprocket is worn, also check the primary chain and the compensating sprocket as described in this chapter.

4. If you find clutch hub, shell or bearing damage, replace them as described under *Clutch Hub and Shell Disassembly/Reassembly* in this chapter.

Clutch Hub and Shell Disassembly/Reassembly

Do not separate the clutch hub and shell unless you are going to replace the bearing or one of these parts. Routine disassembly will damage the bearing. Bearing replacement requires a press.

Read this procedure completely through before starting.

1. Remove the clutch as described in this chapter. Slip the clutch shell assembly off the primary drive chain.

2. Remove the circlip (17, **Figure 39**) from the clutch hub groove (**Figure 54**).

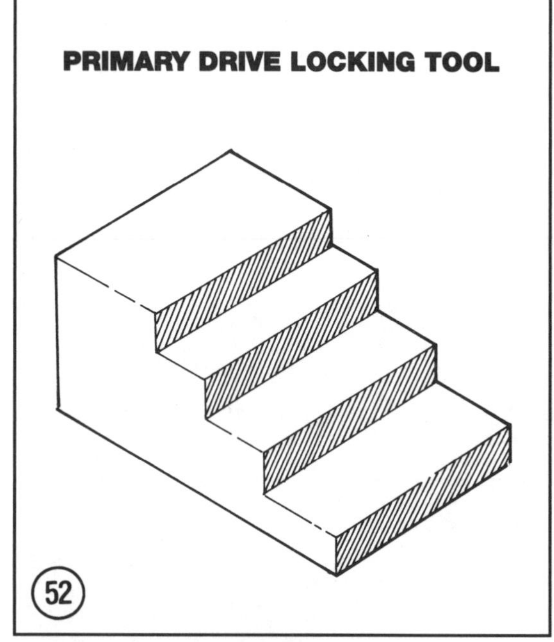

3. Support the clutch hub and clutch shell in a press (**Figure 55**) and press the clutch hub out of the bearing. See **Figure 56**. Remove the clutch shell from the press.

WARNING

*A circlip holds the clutch hub subassembly together (**Figure 57**). The parts comprising the clutch hub are not available separately. If the clutch hub is damaged, replace it as a unit. When handling and servicing the clutch hub, do **not** remove the circlip (**Figure 57**). The clutch hub is under considerable pressure and removal of the circlip will allow the clutch hub to fly apart under extreme force. This could result in severe personal injury.*

NOTE

The circlip called out in Step 4 is not the same circlip referred to in the previous WARNING.

4. Find and remove the circlip (**Figure 58**) in the groove in the middle of the clutch shell. This circlip secures the clutch shell bearing.

NOTE

When removing the bearing in Step 5, remove it through the front of the shell. The clutch shell is manufactured with a shoulder on the rear (primary chain) side.

5. Support the clutch shell in the press and press the bearing out of the shell. Discard the bearing.

6. Discard worn or damaged parts. Clean all parts (except bearing) in solvent and dry thoroughly.

7. Place the clutch shell into the press. Align the bearing with the clutch shell and press the bearing into the clutch shell until the bearing bottoms out against the lower shoulder. When pressing the bearing into the clutch shell, press only on the outer bearing race. Applying force to the bearings inner race will damage the bearing. Refer to *Ball Bearing Replacement* in Chapter One for additional information.

8. Install a new bearing circlip into the clutch shell groove (**Figure 58**). Make sure the circlip seats in the groove completely (**Figure 59**).

9. Press the clutch hub into the clutch shell as follows:

   a. Place the clutch shell in a press. Support the inner bearing race with a sleeve as shown in **Figure 60**.

CAUTION
Failure to support the inner bearing race properly will cause bearing and clutch shell damage. ***Figure 60*** *shows you how to support the inner bearing race.*

   b. Align the clutch hub with the bearing and press the clutch hub into the bearing until the clutch hub shoulder seats against the bearing.
   c. Using circlip pliers, install a new clutch hub circlip (**Figure 54**). Make sure the circlip seats in the clutch hub groove completely.

10. After completing assembly, hold the clutch hub and rotate the clutch shell by hand. The shell must turn smoothly with no roughness or binding. If the clutch shell binds or turns roughly, the bearing may be damaged.

PRIMARY CHAIN AND GUIDE INSPECTION

1. Remove the primary chain (A, **Figure 61**) as described under the *Clutch, Compensating Sprocket and Primary Drive Chain Removal and Installation* procedure in this chapter.

2. Clean the primary chain in solvent and dry thoroughly.

3. Inspect the drive chain for excessive wear, cracks or other damage. If the chain is worn or damaged, check both sprockets for wear and damage.

NOTE
You can gauge primary chain wear by observing how much chain adjustment is available. If the primary chain (A, ***Figure 61****) is near the end of its adjust-*

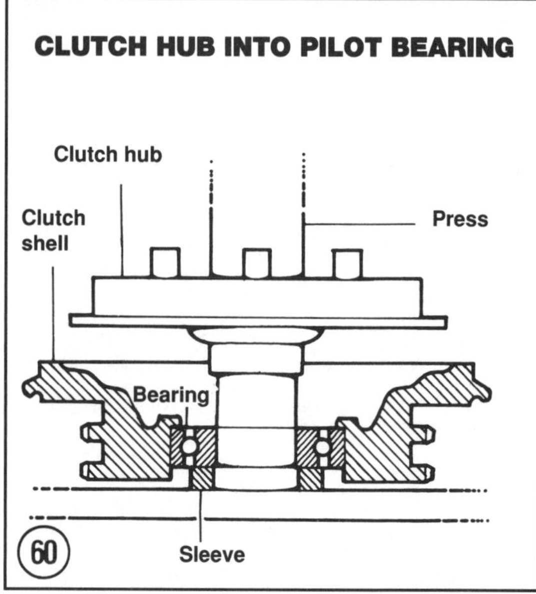

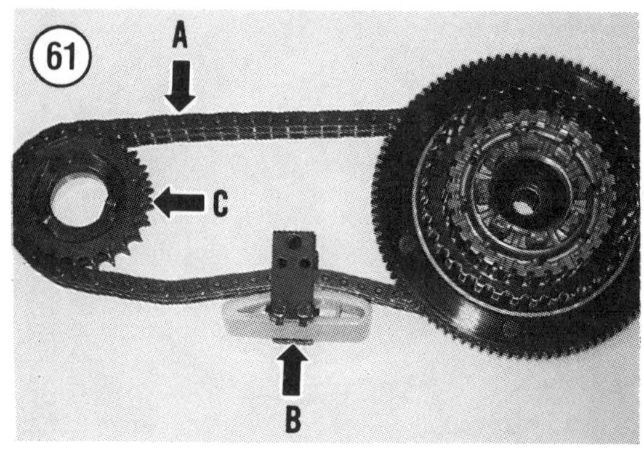

*ment level or if no more adjustment is available, and the adjusting guide (B, **Figure 61**) is not worn or damaged, the primary chain is excessively worn.*

4. Inspect the adjusting guide (B, **Figure 61**) for cracks, severe wear or other damage. Replace the adjusting shoe if necessary.

PRIMARY CHAIN ALIGNMENT

A spacer, installed behind the compensating sprocket (1, **Figure 62**), aligns the compensating and clutch sprockets. Install the original spacer when reinstalling the compensating sprocket, primary chain and clutch assembly. However, if the primary chain is showing wear on one side, or if you installed new components that could affect alignment, perform the following check. You will need a straightedge and vernier caliper for this adjustment.

1. Remove the outer primary cover as described in this chapter.
2. Check and adjust the primary chain tension as described in Chapter Three.
3. Push the primary chain toward the engine and transmission (at both sprockets) as far as it will go.
4. Place a straightedge across the primary chain adjusting shoe outer plate so that one end of the straightedge is as close to the compensating sprocket as possible.
5. Measure the distance from the chain link side plates to the straightedge. Record the measurement.
6. Repeat Steps 4 and 5 with the end of the straightedge as close to the clutch sprocket as possible. Record the measurement.
7. The difference between the 2 measurements must be within 0.030 in. (0.76 mm) of each other. If the difference exceeds this amount, replace the spacer (**Figure 49**) with a suitable size spacer. Spacers are available through Harley-Davidson dealers in the following thicknesses: 0.010 in., 0.020 in., 0.030 in. and 0.060 in.(0.25, 0.51, 0.76 and 1.52 mm).
8. To replace the spacer, perform the *Clutch, Compensating Sprocket and Primary Drive Chain Removal and Installation* procedure in this chapter.

5

COMPENSATING SPROCKET INSPECTION

Refer to **Figure 62** when performing this procedure.

1. Remove the compensating sprocket assembly (C, **Figure 61**) as described under the *Clutch, Compensating Sprocket and Primary Drive Chain Removal and Installation* procedure in this chapter.

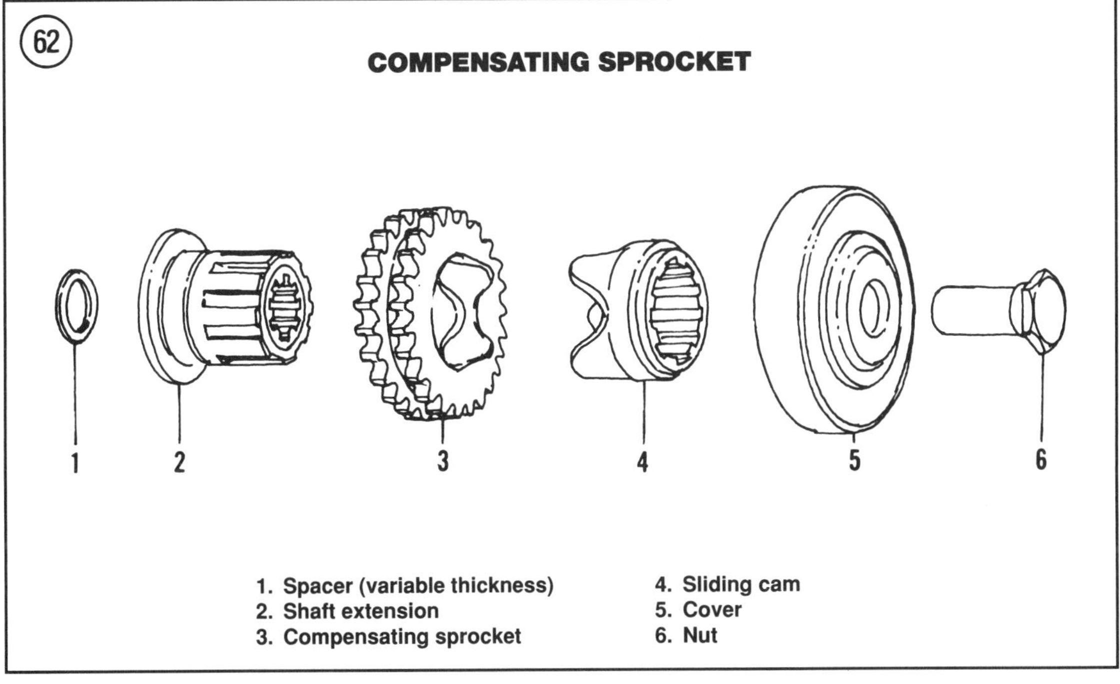

1. Spacer (variable thickness)
2. Shaft extension
3. Compensating sprocket
4. Sliding cam
5. Cover
6. Nut

2. Clean all parts (**Figure 63**) in solvent and dry with compressed air.
3. Check the cam surfaces (A, **Figure 64**) for cracks, deep scoring or excessive wear.
4. Check the compensating sprocket gear teeth (B, **Figure 64**) for cracks or excessive wear.

NOTE
If the compensating sprocket teeth are worn, also check the primary chain and the clutch shell gear teeth for wear.

5. Check the shaft extension splines for wear or galling.
6. Check the cover for damage.
7. Replace all worn or damaged parts.
8. If you replace any component, check the primary chain alignment as described in this chapter.

INNER PRIMARY HOUSING

The inner primary housing is bolted to the engine and transmission. It houses the primary drive assembly, flywheel, starter jackshaft and the mainshaft oil seal and bearing assembly.

Refer to **Figure 65** when performing the following procedure.

NOTE
*You can remove the starter jackshaft without removing the inner primary housing. Refer to **Starter Jackshaft** in this chapter.*

Removal

1. Disconnect the negative battery cable from the battery.
2. Remove the outer primary cover as described in this chapter.
3. Remove the compensating sprocket, primary chain and clutch assembly as described under the *Clutch, Compensating Sprocket and Primary Drive Chain Removal and Installation* procedure in this chapter.
4. Remove the starter motor as described in Chapter Eight.
5. Pry the lockwasher tabs away from the inner primary housing bolts (**Figure 66**, typical).
6. Loosen and then remove all of the inner primary housing-to-engine and transmission mounting bolts and washers.
7. Tap the inner primary housing (**Figure 67**) loose and remove it.
8. Remove the coupling (**Figure 68**) from the starter jackshaft.
9. Remove the starter jackshaft assembly from the inner primary housing.
10. Remove the O-ring from the engine crankcase shoulder (**Figure 69**).

Inspection

1. Remove all gasket residue from the inner primary housing gasket surfaces.
2. Clean the inner primary housing (**Figure 70**) in solvent and dry thoroughly.
3. Check the inner primary housing for cracks or other damage.
4. Check the starter jackshaft oil seal (A, **Figure 71**) for excessive wear or damage. To replace the oil seal, perform the following:

(65)

PRIMARY CHAINCASE

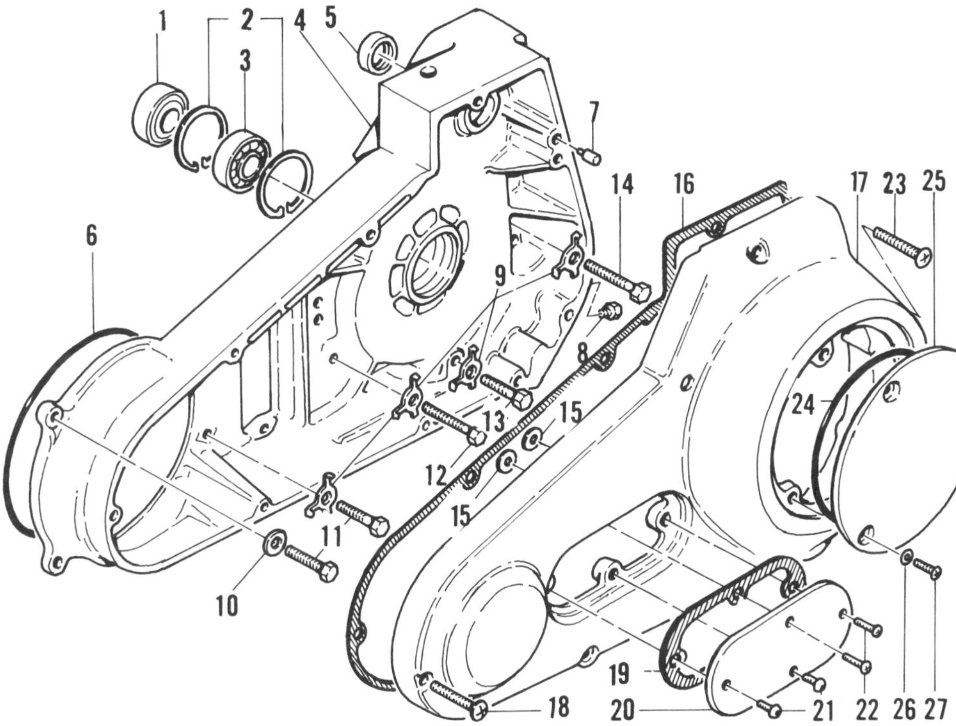

1. Oil seal
2. Circlip
3. Bearing
4. Inner primary housing
5. Jackshaft oil seal
6. O-ring
7. Dowel pin
8. Drain bolt
9. Lockwashers
10. Washer
11. Bolt
12. Bolt
13. Bolt
14. Bolt
15. Washers (1995)
16. Gasket
17. Outer primary cover
18. Bolt
19. Gasket
20. Cover
21. Screws
22. Screws
23. Screw
24. O-ring
25. Cover
26. O-ring
27. Screw

   a. Note the direction in which the oil seal lip is facing in the housing.
   b. Pack the new oil seal lips with grease.
   c. Pry the oil seal out of the inner primary housing.
   d. Carefully drive the new oil seal into the housing until it seats against the housing shoulder (**Figure 72**).

5. Inspect the starter jackshaft bushing (B, **Figure 71**) for excessive wear, cracks or other damage. To replace the bushing, perform the following:
   a. Remove the bushing with a blind bearing removal tool.
   b. Clean the bushing bore in the housing.
   c. Press in the new bushing until its outer surface is flush with the edge of the bushing bore.

6. Turn the inner bearing race (**Figure 73**) by hand. Replace the bearing as follows:
   a. Remove the oil seal as described in Step 7.
   b. Remove the inner and outer bearing circlips (2, **Figure 65**).
   c. Support the inner primary housing and press the bearing out.
   d. Install the outer circlip (clutch side). Make sure you fully seat the circlip in the groove.

68

69

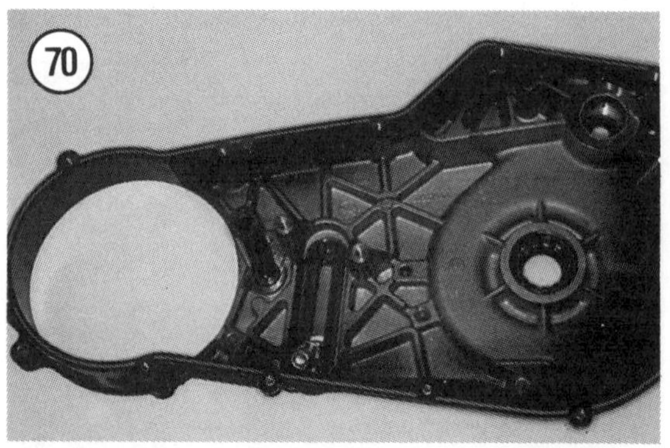
70

71

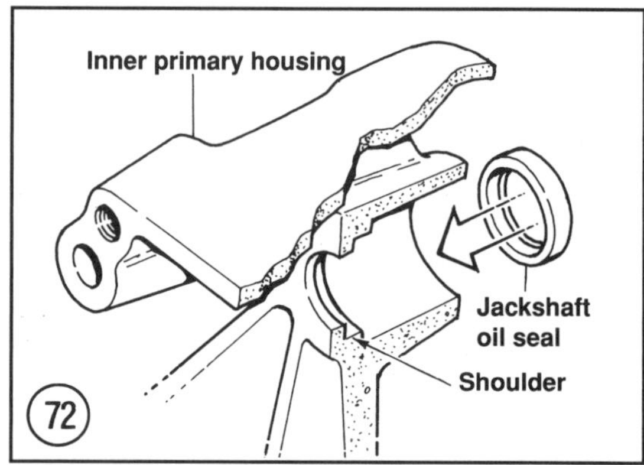

72

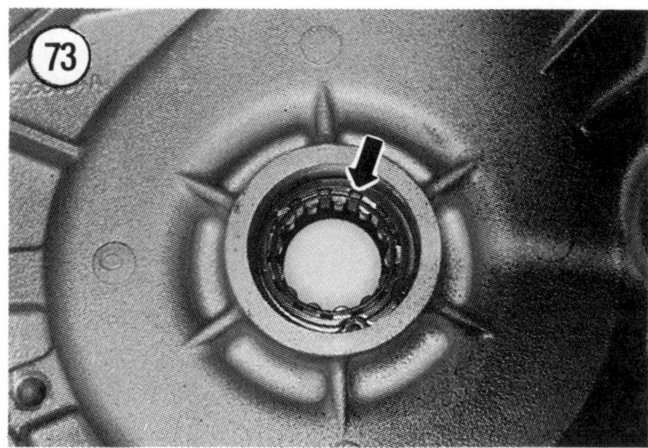
73

CAUTION
When pressing the bearing into the housing, make sure to support the outer circlip. The force required to press the bearing into the inner primary housing may force the circlip out of its groove, damaging the housing.

e. Support the inner primary housing and outer circlip.

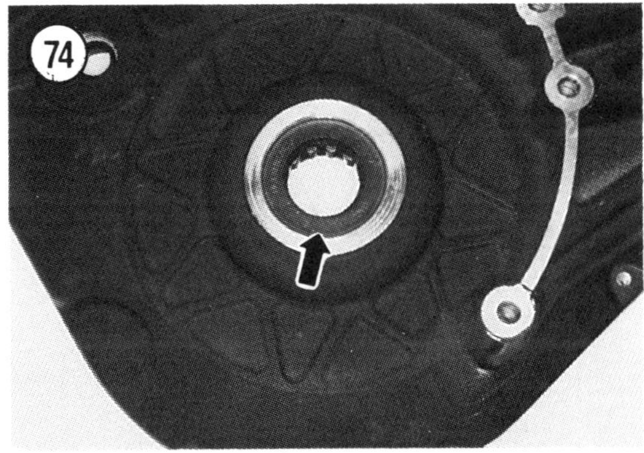

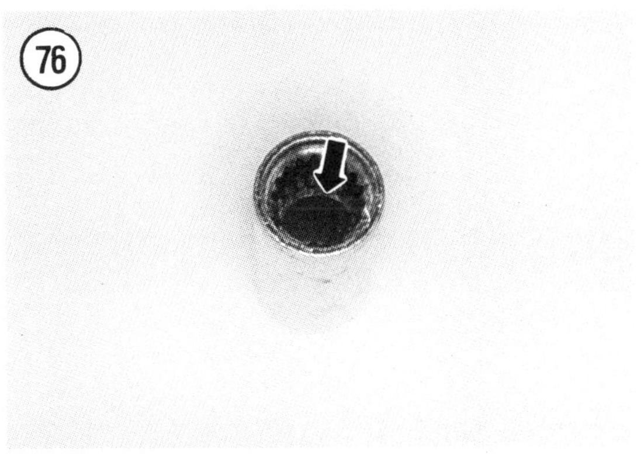

f. Press the bearing into the inner primary housing until it seats against the circlip.

g. Install the inner circlip. Make sure you fully seat the circlip in the groove.

h. Install a new oil seal as described in Step 7.

7. Inspect the inner primary cover oil seal (**Figure 74**) for excessive wear, tearing or other damage. To replace the oil seal, perform the following:

a. Remove the oil seal with a wide-blade screwdriver.

b. Clean the oil seal bore.

c. Pack the oil seal lip with a waterproof bearing grease.

d. Press in the new oil seal until its outer surface is flush with the edge of the bearing bore (**Figure 74**). Install the oil seal with its closed side facing out (**Figure 74**).

8. Check the primary chain adjuster rack screws (**Figure 75**) for looseness. Tighten the screws, if necessary.

9. The inner primary housing mounting bolts use lockwashers. Replace lockwashers that are cracked or have damaged locking tabs.

5

Installation

1. Install the O-ring onto the engine crankcase shoulder (**Figure 69**).

2. Install the starter jackshaft assembly into the inner primary housing as described under *Starter Jackshaft* in this chapter.

NOTE
*Before installing the coupling in Step 2, note the circlip (**Figure 76**) installed inside the coupling. The coupling side with the circlip closest to its end slides over the jackshaft.*

3. Install the coupling (**Figure 68**) onto the end of the starter jackshaft.

4. Wrap the mainshaft splines (**Figure 77**) with tape. This will prevent the splines from damaging the inner primary cover oil seal as it passes over it.

CAUTION
You must perform the following steps in order to ensure correct engine, transmission and inner primary housing alignment. Improper alignment may cause premature primary chain wear and transmission damage.

5. Loosen the engine and transmission frame mounting bolts.

NOTE
If you previously removed the drive belt, install it over the driven sprocket before installing the inner primary housing.

6. Insert the shift shaft (**Figure 78**) through the collar when installing the inner primary housing.
7. Align the inner primary housing with the engine and transmission and install it.
8. Apply a bead of RTV sealant around the 2 bottom inner primary housing bolt holes (**Figure 79**).
9. Install the inner primary housing bolts and washers. Install a lockwasher (**Figure 80**) on each bolt installed inside the housing.
10. Tighten the inner primary housing mounting bolts (at the engine and transmission) to the torque listed in **Table 4**. Bend the lockwasher tabs against the bolt heads.
11. Tighten the engine and transmission frame mounting bolts to the torque specification in **Table 4**.
12. Tighten the engine-to-transmission mounting bolts to the torque specification in **Table 4**.
13. Install the starter motor as described in Chapter Eight.
14. Install the compensating sprocket, primary chain and clutch assembly as described under the *Clutch, Compensating Sprocket and Primary Drive Chain Removal and Installation* procedure in this chapter.
15. Install the outer primary cover as described in this chapter.
16. Reconnect the negative battery cable to the battery.

STARTER JACKSHAFT

Refer to **Figure 81** when servicing the starter jackshaft.

Removal

1. Disconnect the negative battery cable from the battery.
2. Remove the outer primary cover as described in this chapter.

NOTE

If you are only removing parts 1-5 in ***Figure 81****, do not remove the clutch as described in Step 3.*

3. Remove the compensating sprocket, primary chain and clutch assembly as described under the *Clutch, Compensating Sprocket and Primary Drive Chain Removal and Installation* procedure in this chapter.
4. Remove the bolt (A, **Figure 82**), lockplate and thrust washer from the starter jackshaft assembly.
5. Remove the jackshaft assembly (B, **Figure 82**) from the inner primary housing.
6. To remove the coupling (10, **Figure 81**), remove the starter motor as described in Chapter Eight. **Figure 68** shows the coupling with the inner primary cover removed for clarity.

CAUTION

Do not remove the coupling through the oil seal in the inner primary cover or you will damage the oil seal.

Inspection

1. Clean the jackshaft assembly (**Figure 83**) in solvent and dry thoroughly.

5

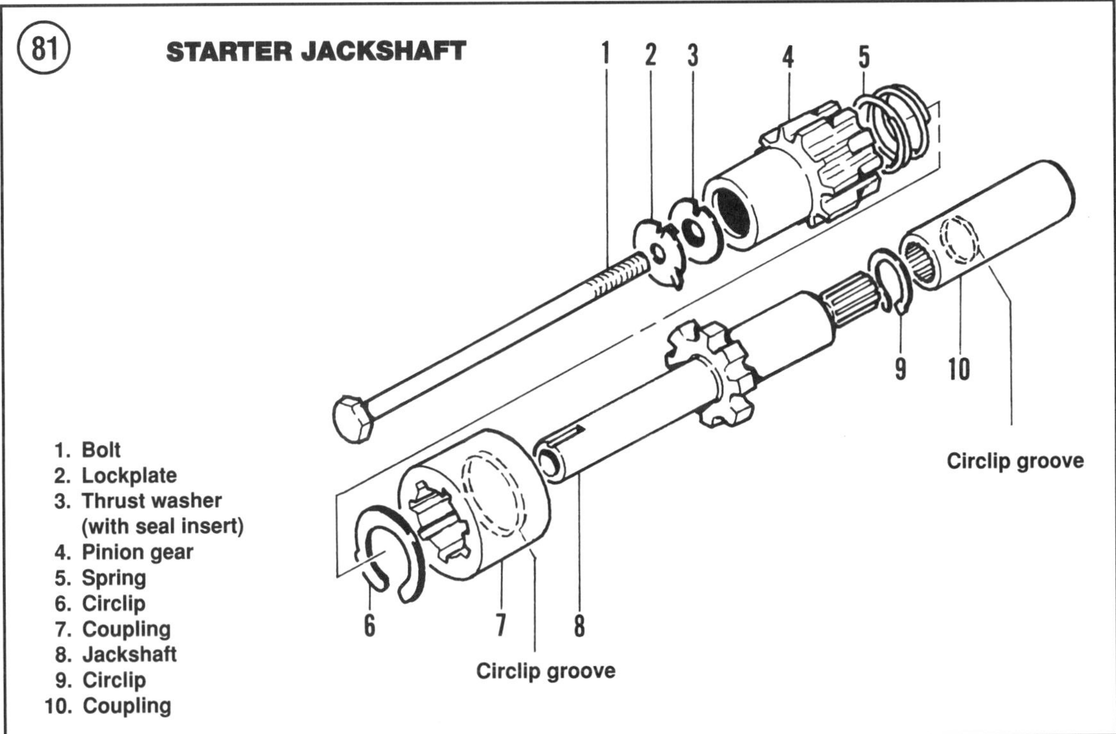

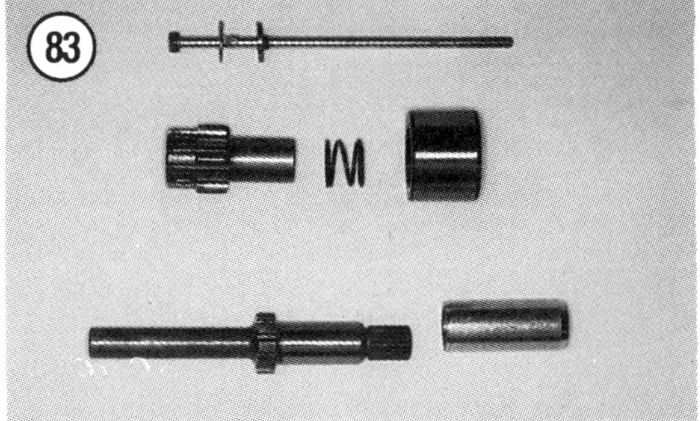

2. Check the circlip installed in each coupling (**Figure 76** and **Figure 84**). Replace any loose or damaged circlips.

3. Replace all worn or damaged parts.

NOTE
*Before installing the coupling in Step 4, note the circlip (**Figure 76**) installed inside the coupling. The coupling side with the circlip closest to its end slides over the jackshaft.*

4. If removed install the coupling (**Figure 68**) and then the starter motor (see Chapter Eight).

5. Install the coupling (A, **Figure 85**) onto the jackshaft (B, **Figure 85**) with the couplings counterbore facing toward the jackshaft. See **Figure 86**.

6. Install the spring (**Figure 87**) inside the coupling. See **Figure 88**.

7. Slide the pinion gear (A, **Figure 89**) into the coupling (B, **Figure 89**).

8. Slide the thrust washer (with the rubber seal) and the lockplate onto the bolt as shown in **Figure 90**.

9. Slide the bolt (A, **Figure 91**) into the jackshaft.

86

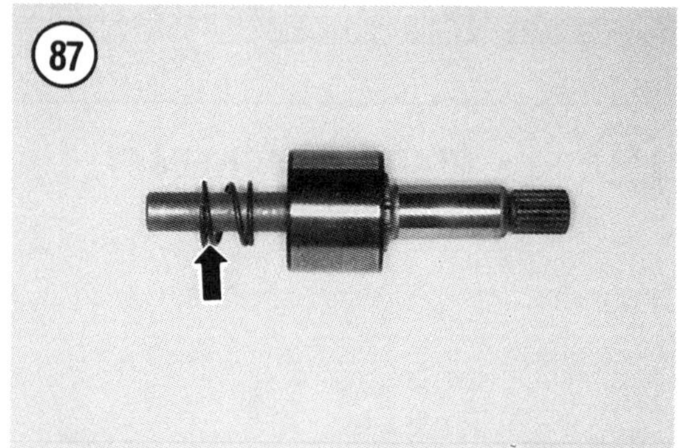
87

84

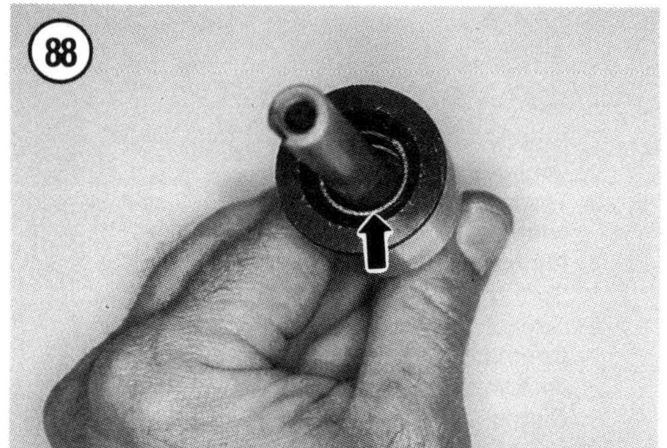
88

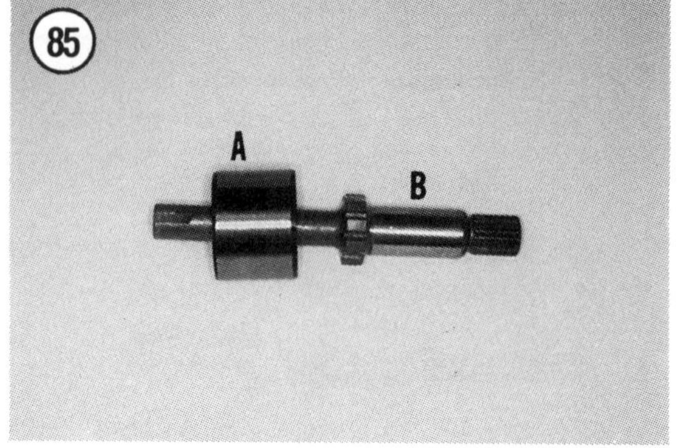

85

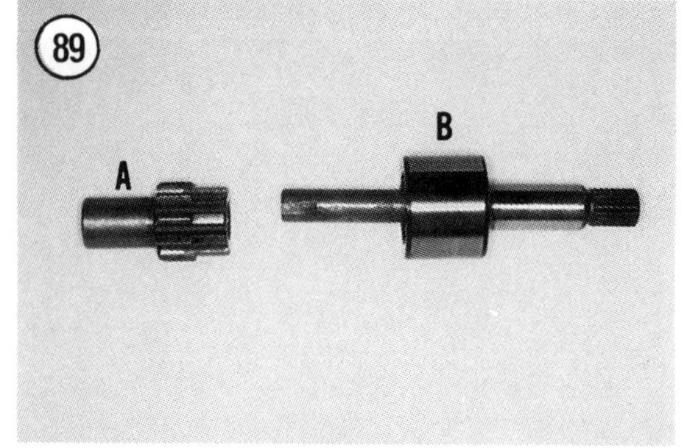

89

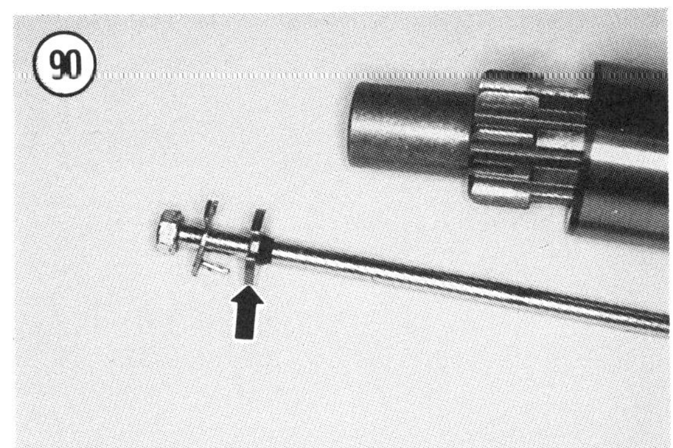
90

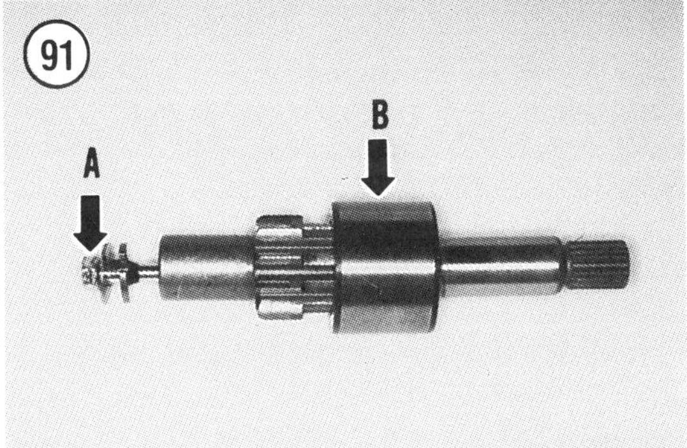

91

92

10. Apply primary chain oil to the coupling (B, **Figure 91**) and install the jackshaft assembly (B, **Figure 82**) into the inner primary housing bushing. Make sure the jackshaft and coupling splines (**Figure 92**) properly engage.

NOTE
***Figure 92** shows the inner primary housing removed for clarity.*

11. Align the lockplate tab (A, **Figure 82**) with its washer, then insert the tab into the notch in the end of the jackshaft. Tighten the jackshaft bolt to the torque specification in **Table 4**. Bend the outer lockplate tab against the bolt head.

12. Install the compensating sprocket, primary chain and clutch assembly as described under the *Clutch, Compensating Sprocket and Primary Drive Chain Removal and Installation* procedure in this chapter.

13. Install the outer primary cover as described in this chapter.

14. Reconnect the negative battery cable at the battery.

CLUTCH CABLE REPLACEMENT

1. Before removing the clutch cable, make a drawing of its routing path from the handlebar to the transmission side door.

2. Disconnect the clutch cable from the clutch release mechanism as described under *Transmission Side Cover* in Chapter Six. See **Figure 93**.

3. Remove the circlip (**Figure 94**) from the clutch lever pivot pin.

4. Remove the pivot pin (**Figure 95**) and slide the clutch lever out its perch.

93

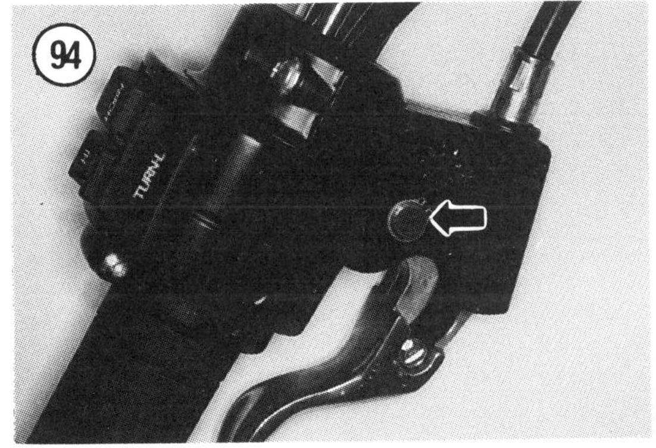

94

5. Remove the plastic anchor pin (**Figure 96**) and disconnect the clutch cable from the lever.
6. Check the clutch lever components (**Figure 97**) for worn or damaged parts.
7. Check that the anti-slack spring screw (**Figure 98**) on the bottom of the clutch lever is tight.
8. Route the new clutch cable from the handlebar to the transmission side cover, following your original drawing.
9. Fit the clutch cable into its lever and secure with the plastic anchor pin (**Figure 96**).
10. Slide the clutch lever into the perch and install the pivot pin (**Figure 95**).
11. Secure the pivot pin with the circlip (**Figure 94**).
12. Reconnect the clutch cable to the clutch release mechanism as described under *Transmission Side Cover* in Chapter Six. See **Figure 93**.
13. Adjust the clutch as described in Chapter Three.

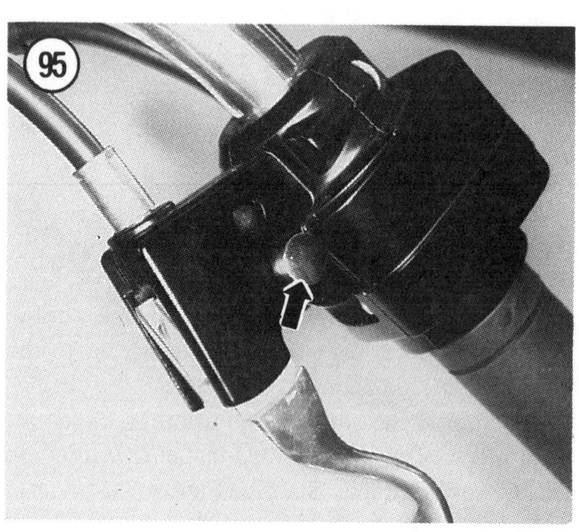

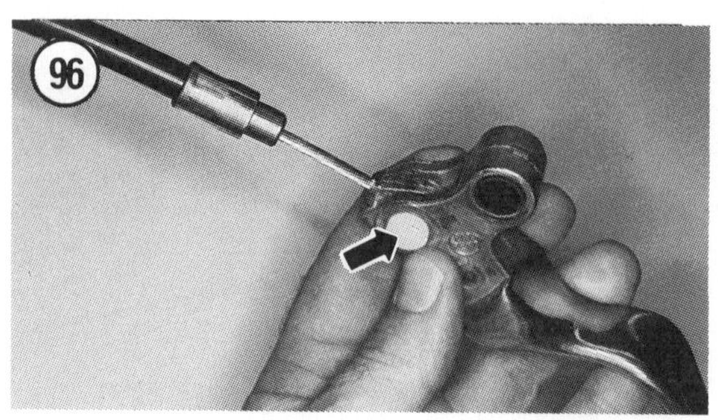

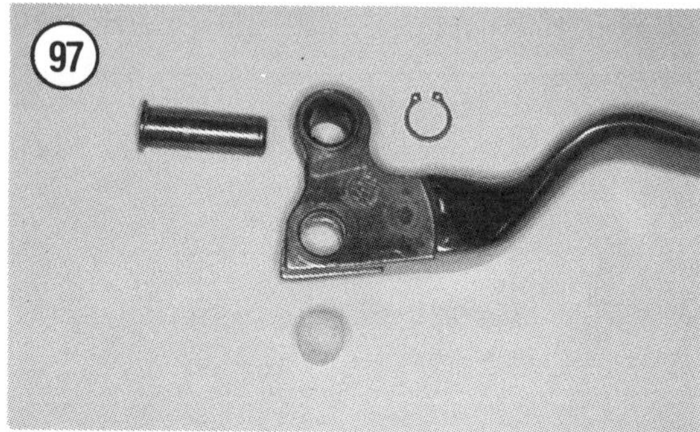

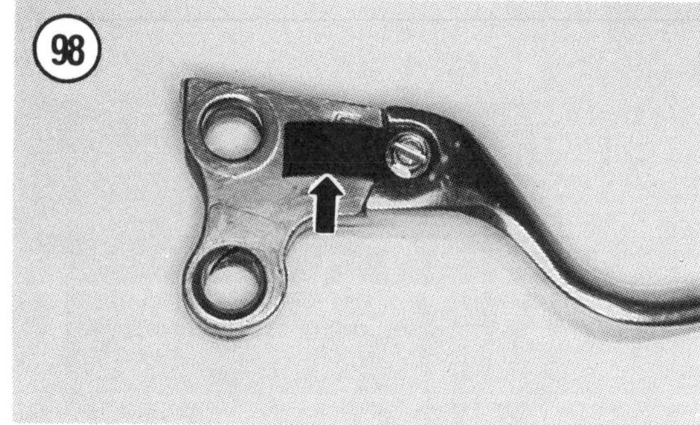

Table 1 CLUTCH GENERAL SPECIFICATIONS

Type	Wet, multiple disc
Capacity (torque)	128 ft.-lb. (174 N·m)
Clutch lever free play	1/16-1/8 in. (1.6-3.2 mm)
Spring pressure (engaged)	374 lb. (170 kg)

Table 2 SPROCKET SIZES

Engine sprocket	
1991-1994	24
1995	25
Clutch sprocket	
1991-1994	37
1995-on	36
Transmission sprocket	32
Rear wheel sprocket	
Domestic	70
Australian	61
International	65

5

Table 3 CLUTCH SERVICE SPECIFICATIONS

Item	in.	mm
Steel plate warpage limit	0.006	0.15
Friction plate assembly		
Minimum lining thickness (assembly)*	0.661	16.79

* See text for procedure on measuring friction plates.

Table 4 CLUTCH TIGHTENING TORQUES

	ft.-lb.	N•m
Clutch adjusting screw locknut	6-10	8-14
Clutch nut	70-80	95-108
Compensating sprocket nut	150-165	203-224
Engine and transmission		
frame mounting bolts	33-38	45-52
Engine-to-transmission mounting bolts	33-38	45-52
Inner primary housing mounting bolts		
At engine	18-22	24-30
At transmission	18-22	24-30
Inspection cover screws		
1991-1994	–	
1995-on		
Bottom and front	70-90 in.-lb.	7.9-10
Top and rear	108-120 in.-lb.	12-13.5
Jackshaft mounting bolt	7-9	9-12
Primary cover mounting bolts	9-10	12-14
Transmission sprocket locking screw		
1991-1992	50-60 in.-lb.	5.7-6.8
1993-on	7-9	9-12
Transmission sprocket nut	110-120	149-163

CHAPTER SIX

TRANSMISSION

All Dyna Glide models are equipped with a 5-speed transmission. The transmission and shifter assemblies are housed in a separate case behind the engine. You can service the transmission and shifter assemblies with the transmission case mounted in the frame. The oil tank mounts to the bottom of the transmission case. Oil tank service is described in this chapter.

An external shift linkage assembly connects the gearshift lever to the transmission. The shift linkage assembly requires adjustment to compensate from normal wear or when reinstalling the transmission case into the frame.

Servicing the transmission and shifter assemblies can be simple or involved, depending on what you are trying to do. When troubleshooting a shifting problem, first determine if the clutch is working correctly, and adjust or service it as necessary. Then check the 2 external shifting adjustments as described under *Shifter Adjustment* in this chapter. If these steps not do solve the problem, then service the shifter and transmission assemblies.

Tables 1-3 list transmission service specifications (end of chapter).

PRODUCTION GEAR CHANGES

Starting with 1994 models, Harley-Davidson produced 2 types of transmission gear sets—domestic gears (U.S., Canada and Japan) and HDI gears (Harley-Davidson International). The center of each domestic gear tooth has a 0.03 in. (0.76 mm) radius groove. Models with the HDI gears have high contact ratio (HCR) gears installed on the mainshaft and countershaft. HDI ratio gears do not have grooved gear teeth.

CAUTION

Do not intermix domestic and HDI gears. Meshing both gear types will cause transmission damage.

SHIFTER ADJUSTMENT

Figure 1 is an exploded view of a typical shifter assembly. The shifter assembly mounts on top of the transmission case, underneath the transmission top cover. You can service the shifter cam with the transmission mounted in the frame.

Your first step in troubleshooting is to determine whether you have a clutch, shifter or transmission problem. Adjusting the clutch can generally fix minor clutch problems (see Chapter Three). If the problem is internal, remove and service the clutch as described in Chapter Five. If the shifter linkage or adjuster is out of adjustment, you can adjust the component as described in this section. Transmission problems, however, require more time and work, so make sure the problem is in the transmission and not in the clutch or shifter.

Shift Linkage Adjustment

The shift linkage assembly (**Figure 2**) consists of the shift linkage rod and 2 ball joints. The shift linkage assembly (**Figure 2**) connects the transmission shifter rod lever to the foot-operated shift lever. The shift linkage adjustment is set at the factory and does not require adjustment unless you replace the shift linkage or the transmission gears do not engage properly.

1. Disconnect the negative battery cable at the battery.
2. Loosen the 2 shift linkage rod locknuts (A, **Figure 2**).
3. Remove the acorn nut, washers and bolt (B, **Figure 2**) securing the shift linkage rod to the shifter rod lever.
4. Turn the shift linkage rod (C, **Figure 2**) as necessary to change the linkage adjustment.
5. Tighten the locknuts and reconnect the shift linkage rod to the shifter rod lever.
6. Recheck the shifting. Readjust if necessary.
7. If you cannot obtain proper shifting by performing this adjustment, check the shift linkage for any interference problems. Then check the shift linkage assembly for worn or damaged parts. Perform the *Gear Engagement Check/Adjustment* procedure if there are no visible interference problems or damage.

Gear Engagement Check/Adjustment

If the transmission gears do not engage properly, check and adjust gear engagement as follows:

1. Make sure the clutch is working properly. Refer to clutch adjustment in Chapter Three. If the clutch is working properly, continue with Step 2.
2. Disconnect the negative battery cable from the battery.
3. Shift the transmission into third gear. Make sure third gear is fully engaged.
4. Remove the transmission top cover as described under *Transmission Top Cover Removal/Installation* in this chapter.
5. Move the shifter shaft lever (**Figure 3**) to check for free play and spring pressure in both directions. Gear engagement is correct if the spring pressure is the same in both directions and with approximately 0.10 in. (0.25 mm) clearance between the shifter pawl arms and the shifter cam pins (**Figure 4**). If necessary, adjust gear engagement as described in Step 6.

NOTE
An incorrectly adjusted shifter pawl adjusting screw causes many shifting related problems.

6. To adjust the gear engagement, follow these steps:
   a. The shifter pawl adjusting screw is mounted on the left-hand side of the transmission case (**Figure 5**). It is between the transmission case and primary chain housing. **Figure 6** shows the shifter pawl adjusting screw and locknut with the inner primary housing removed for clarity.
   b. Use the Harley-Davidson transmission pawl adjuster (part No. HD-39618) to adjust the shifter pawl adjusting screw.
   c. Loosen the adjusting screw locknut (**Figure 6**) and turn the shifter pawl adjusting screw in 1/4 turn (or less) increments (clockwise or counterclockwise) until the shifter lever travel spring pressure is equal on both sides while maintaining a clearance of 0.010 in. (0.25 mm). Tighten the locknut and recheck the adjustment.

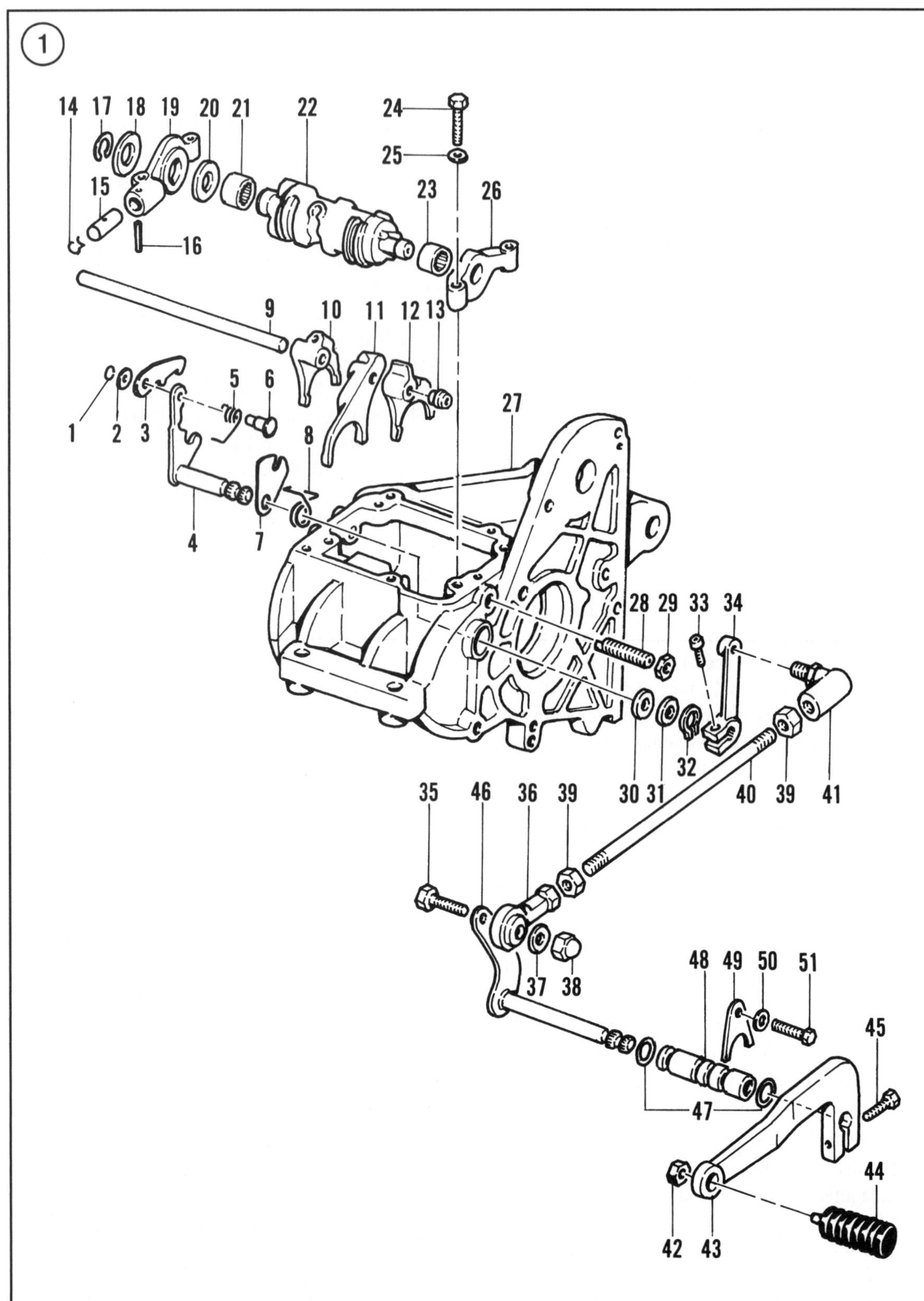
1
14
17
18
19
20
21
22
24
25
15
23
26
16
9
10
11
12
13
5
6
27
1
2
3
8
4
7
28
29
33
34
32
30
31
40
39
41
35
46
36
39
37
38
48
49
50
51
45
47
44
42
43

SHIFTER ASSEMBLY

1. Circlip
2. Washer
3. Shifter pawl
4. Shifter shaft lever
5. Spring
6. Collar
7. Plate
8. Spring
9. Shift fork shaft
10. Shift fork
11. Shift fork
12. Shift fork
13. Set screw
14. Spring
15. Cam follower
16. Roll pin
17. Circlip
18. Outer thrust washer (variable thickness)
19. Right support block
20. Inner thrust washer (1991)
21. Needle bearing
22. Shifter cam
23. Needle bearing
24. Bolt
25. Washer
26. Left support block
27. Transmission case
28. Shifter pawl adjusting screw
29. Nut
30. Oil seal
31. Washer
32. Circlip
33. Screw
34. Shifter rod lever
35. Bolt
36. Shifter rod end
37. Washer
38. Acorn nut
39. Nut
40. Shift linkage rod
41. Ball joint
42. Nut
43. Shift lever
44. Peg
45. Bolt
46. Shift lever
47. O-rings
48. Sleeve
49. Sleeve locator plate
50. Lockwasher
51. Bolt

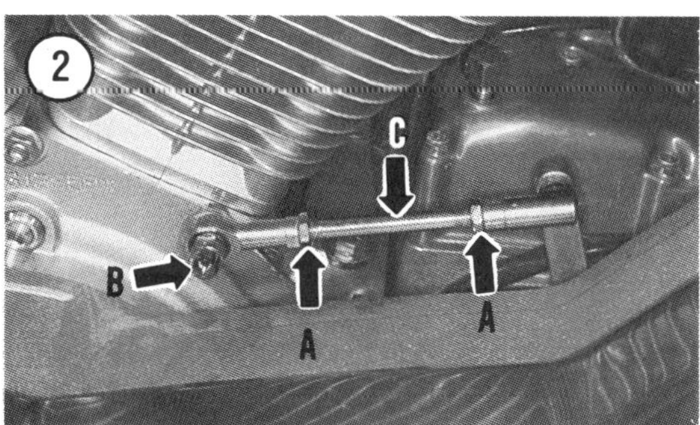

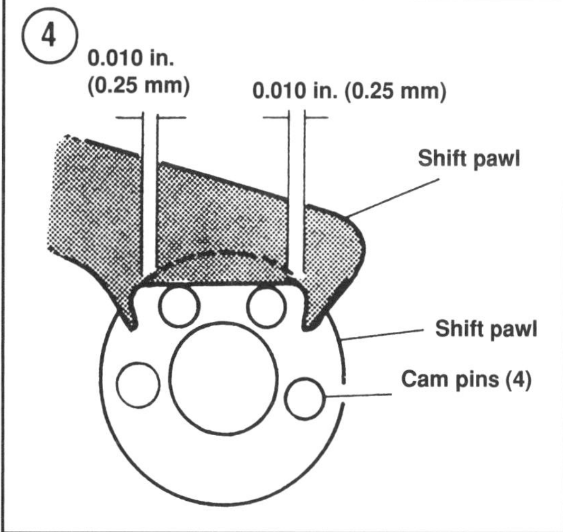

6

7. Reinstall the transmission top cover as described in this chapter.
8. Reconnect the negative battery cable to the battery.

TRANSMISSION TOP COVER

Figure 7 shows the transmission top cover assembly. You can service the transmission top cover assembly with the transmission installed in the frame.

Removal/Installation

1. Remove the battery as described in Chapter Eight.
2. Disconnect the neutral switch wire from the switch (**Figure 8**).
3. Disconnect the 2 hoses (A, **Figure 9**) at the top cover.
4. Remove the dipstick (B, **Figure 9**).
5. Remove the oil fill spout mounting bolts and washers (**Figure 10**). Then lift off and remove the oil fill spout (**Figure 11**).
6. Lift off and remove the dipstick cover (**Figure 12**) and its 2 O-rings. See **Figure 13**.
7. Plug the oil tank opening (**Figure 14**).
8. Remove the bolts securing the transmission cover to the transmission case. Then remove the top cover (**Figure 15**) and the gasket.
9. Inspect the dipstick cover O-rings (**Figure 13**). Replace missing or damaged O-rings.
10. Remove the gasket residue from the transmission cover and case gasket surfaces.
11. Install the transmission top cover by reversing these removal steps. Note the following.
12. Install a new transmission case cover gasket.
13. Apply engine oil to the dipstick cover O-rings (**Figure 13**).

TRANSMISSION CASE ASSEMBLY

1. Dipstick
2. O-ring
3. Oil fill spout
4. Gasket
5. Bolt
6. Washer
7. Bolt
8. Bolt
9. Transmission top cover
10. Dowel pin
11. Hose
12. Hose clamp
13. Hose nozzle
14. Hose nozzle
15. Gasket
16. Transmission case
17 Dowel pin
18. Dowel pin
19. O-ring
20. Dipstick cover
21. O-ring
22. Gasket
23. Oil tank
24. Bolt
25. O-ring
26. Drain plug
27. Hose nozzle
28. Hose
29. Bolt
30. Needle bearing
31. Spacer
32. Bearing
33. Circlip
34. Oil seal

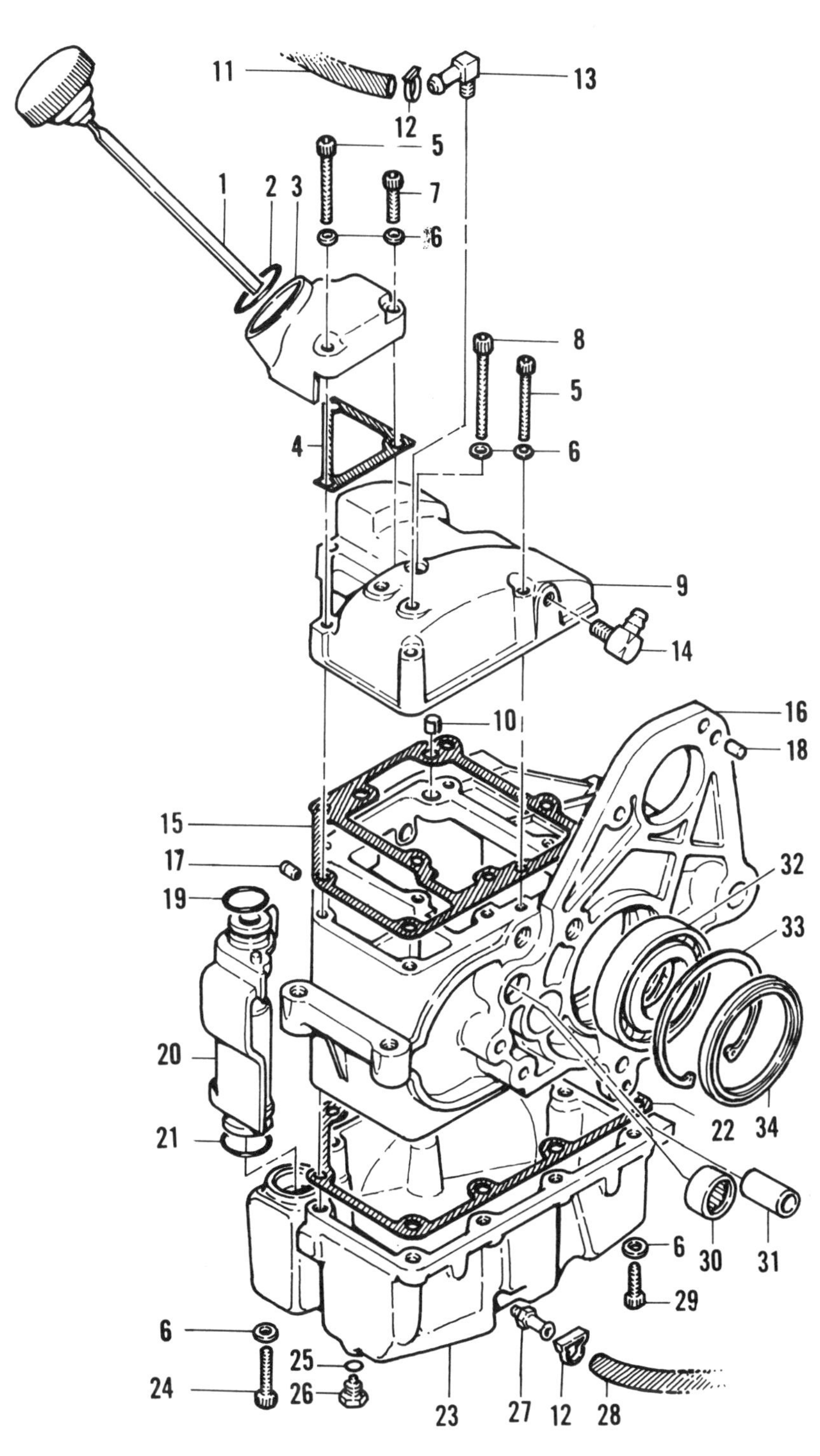
11
12
13
5
7
1
2
3
6
8
5
4
6
9
14
16
10
18
15
17
32
19
33
20
21
22
34
30
31
6
29
6
25
24
26
23
27
12
28

8

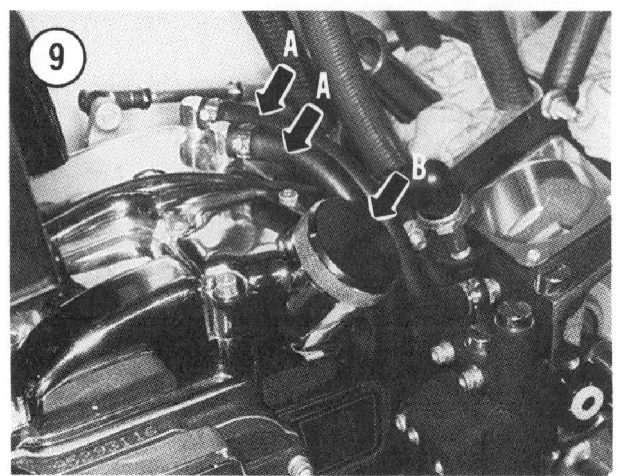
9
A
A
B

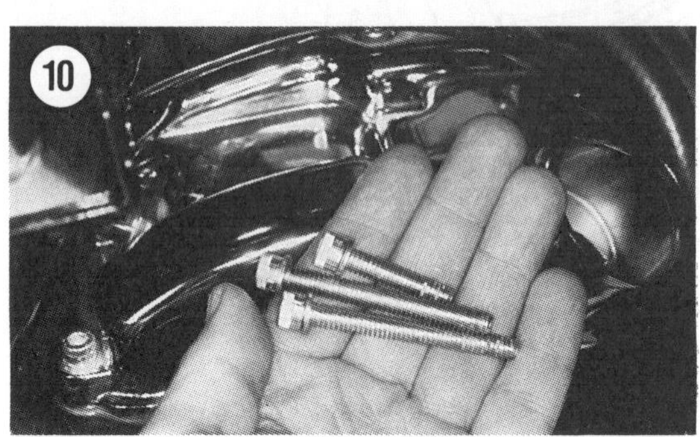
10

11

12

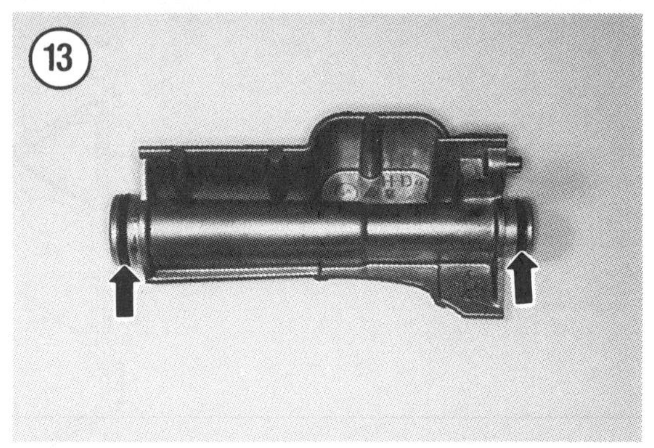
13

14

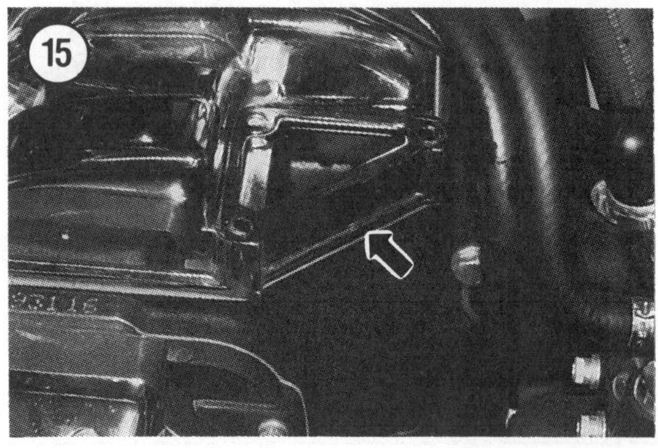
15

14. Secure the 2 hoses (A, **Figure 9**) to the transmission top cover with new hose clamps. To confirm hose routing and connection points, refer to *Oil Tank* in this chapter.

SHIFTER CAM

Figure 16 is an exploded view of the shifter cam assembly. The shifter cam mounts on top of the transmission case, underneath the transmission top cover (**Figure 1**). You can service the shifter cam with the transmission mounted in the frame.

Shifter Cam Design Change

On early 1991 models, a variable thickness thrust washer (11, **Figure 16**) sets the shifter cams position in the transmission case. Late 1991 and later models do not use this washer. Instead, Harley-Davidson machined the shifter cam so that its position is set when you install it in the case. You can identify early and late style shifter cams by its neutral indicator actuator (A, **Figure 17**). Early style shifter cams use a cast neutral indicator actuator. On late style shifter cams, the neutral indicator actuator is a pressed-in pin. On late style shifter cams, 2 dowel pins position the left-hand support block (10, **Figure 16**) in the transmission case.

Removal

1. Remove the transmission top cover as described in this chapter.
2. Remove the shifter cam mounting bolts and lockwashers (**Figure 18**) and lift the shifter cam assembly out of the transmission case.
3. Slide the left side support block (**Figure 19**) off the shifter cam.
4. On late 1991-on models, remove the 2 dowel pins from the transmission case.

NOTE
On early 1991 models, measure and label the inner and outer thrust washers removed in the following steps so you dont mix them up during reassembly.

5. Refer to **Figure 20**. Remove the shifter cam circlip (A) and the outer thrust washer (B).

6

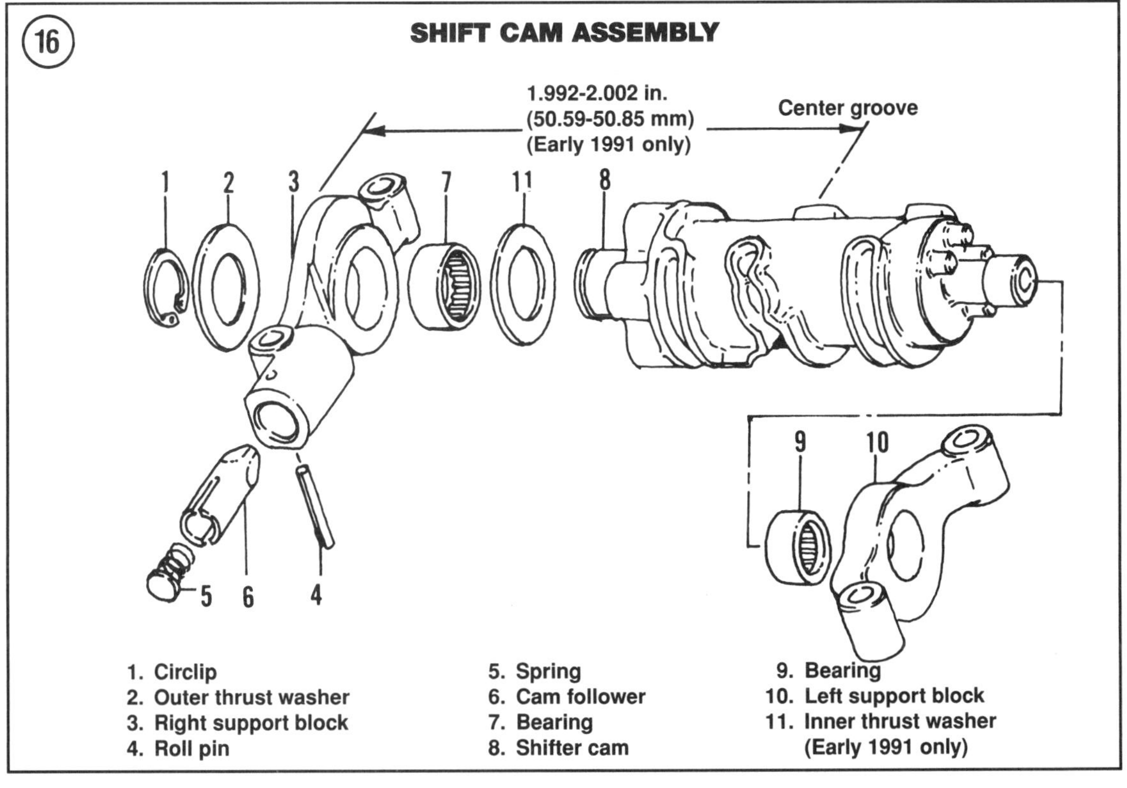

1. Circlip
2. Outer thrust washer
3. Right support block
4. Roll pin
5. Spring
6. Cam follower
7. Bearing
8. Shifter cam
9. Bearing
10. Left support block
11. Inner thrust washer (Early 1991 only)

6. Remove the right side support block (**Figure 21**).
7. On early 1991 models, remove the inner thrust washer (**Figure 22**) from the shifter cam.

Inspection

1. Clean all parts (except support block bearings) in solvent.
2. Check the shifter cam grooves (B, **Figure 17**) for wear or roughness. Replace the shifter cam if the groove profiles show excessive wear or damage.
3. Check the shifter cam ends where the cam rides in the bearings. If the ends show wear or damage, replace the shifter cam and both support block bearings; see *Support Block Bearing Replacement* in this chapter.
4. Check the support block bearings for excessive wear, cracks, or other damage. See **Figure 23** and **Figure 24**. If necessary, refer to *Support Block Bearing Replacement* in this chapter to replace the bearings.
5. Check the support blocks for wear, cracks or other damage. Replace the support blocks if necessary.

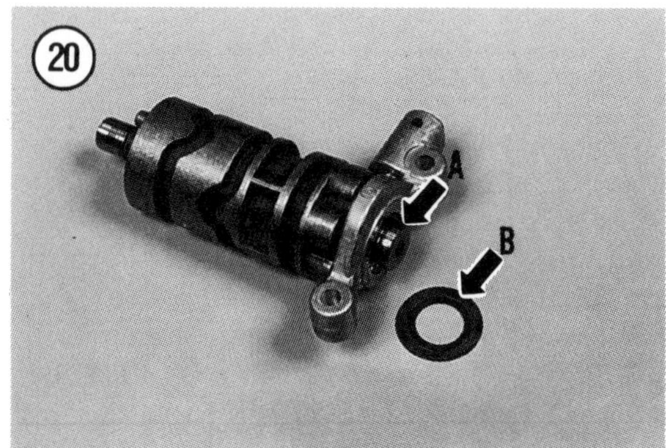

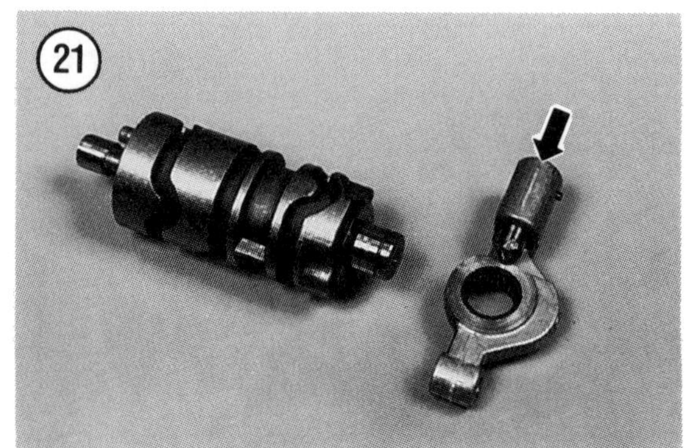

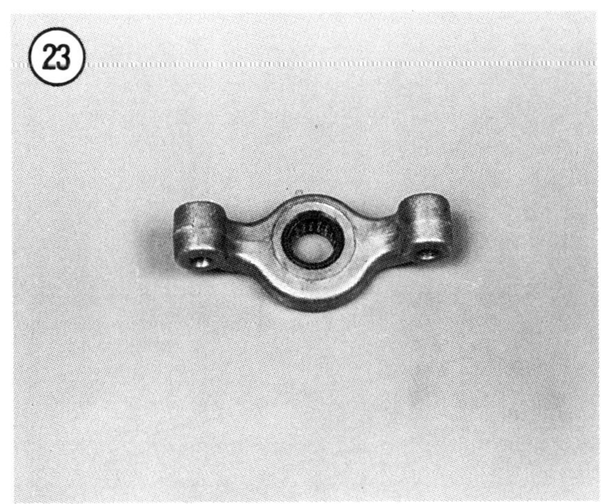
23

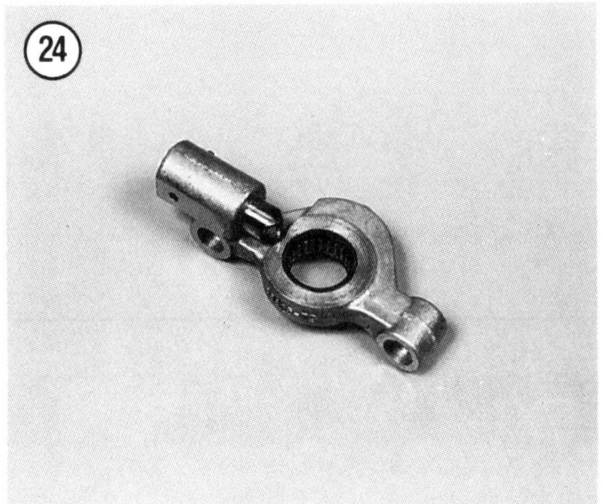
24

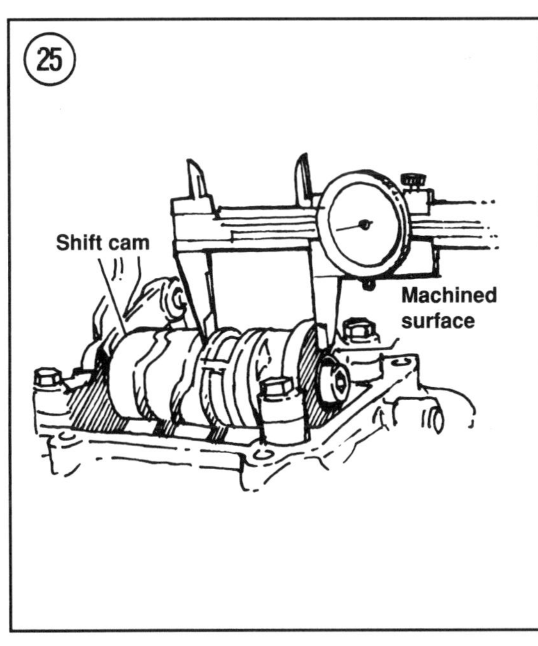

25

Support Block Bearing Replacement

Each support block is equipped with a single needle bearing. See **Figure 23** and **Figure 24**. Replace both bearings at the same time. A press is required to replace the bearings. Refer to *Bearing Replacement* in Chapter One. Before you remove the bearings, record the direction in which the bearing manufacturers marks face for proper installation.

Installation

Refer to **Figure 16** when performing this procedure.

1. Coat all bearing and sliding surfaces with assembly oil.
2. On early 1991 models, install the inner thrust washer (**Figure 22**) on the shifter cam.
3. Install the right support block (**Figure 21**) on the shifter cam.
4. Install the outer thrust washer (B, **Figure 20**) and a new circlip (A, **Figure 20**). Make sure the circlip seats in the shifter cam groove.

NOTE
After installing the circlip, make sure you can rotate the washer(s) by hand.

5. Install the left support block (**Figure 19**) onto the shifter cam.

NOTE
Install the support blocks with their numbered side facing down.

6. On early 1991 models, measure the shifter cam position clearance as follows:
   a. Install the shifter cam/support block assembly onto the transmission case. Align the shift fork pins with the shifter cam slots.
   b. Turn the shifter cam to its neutral position. Use the neutral indicator ramp, mounted on the shifter drum, as a reference point. See **Figure 25**.
   c. Push the shifter cam so that it fits snug against the right support block thrust washer.
   d. Measure from the outer bearing support machined surface to the nearest edge of the center shifter cam groove (**Figure 25**). The correct distance is 1.992-2.002 in. (50.59-50.85 mm).
   e. Replace the inner thrust washer (11, **Figure 16**) if the distance is incorrect.

6

NOTE
Inner and outer thrust washers are available from Harley-Davidson dealers in the following thicknesses: 0.017, 0.020, 0.022, 0.025, 0.028, 0.031, 0.035 and 0.039 in. (0.43, 0.51, 0.56, 0.63, 0.71, 0.79, 0.89 and 0.99 mm).

f. Remove the shifter cam assembly from the transmission case.

7. On late 1991 and later models, install the 2 dowel pins into the transmission case.

8. Measure shifter cam end play as follows:
   a. Install the shifter cam/support block assembly onto the transmission case. Align the shift fork pins with the shifter cam slots.
   b. Measure the clearance between the outer thrust washer and the shifter cam (**Figure 26**) with a feeler gauge. This clearance is shifter cam end play. The correct end play measurement is 0.001-0.004 in. (0.025-0.010 mm).
   c. To correct end play, replace the outer thrust washer (2, **Figure 16**) with a suitable thickness thrust washer.

CAUTION
*On early 1991 models, do not correct shifter cam end play by changing the inner thrust washer (11, **Figure 16**) thickness. This washer sets the shifter cam position only. Late 1991-on models do not use the inner thrust washer.*

NOTE
Inner and outer thrust washers are available from Harley-Davidson dealers in the following thicknesses: 0.017, 0.020, 0.022, 0.025, 0.028, 0.031, 0.035 and 0.039 in. (0.43, 0.51, 0.56, 0.63, 0.71, 0.79, 0.89 and 0.99 mm).

   d. Remove the shifter cam assembly from the transmission case.

9. Apply engine oil to the shifter cam bearing surfaces.

10. Align the shift fork pins with the shifter cam slots and install the shifter cam into position. See **Figure 27**.

11. Engage the shifter pawl with the shifter cam (**Figure 28**).

CAUTION
Overtightening the shifter cam mounting bolts can distort the cam follower

and cause shifting problems. Do not exceed the tightening torque specification in Step 12.

12. Install the shifter cam mounting bolts (**Figure 18**). Tighten in a crisscross pattern to 7-9 ft.-lb. (9-12 N•m).

NOTE
On early 1991 models, make sure the left support block is not binding on its bearing.

13. Perform the *Gear Engagement Check/Adjustment* in this chapter.
14. Install the transmission top cover as described in this chapter.

SHIFT FORKS

The shift forks are installed at the top of the transmission case, underneath the shifter cam (**Figure 1**). You can service the shift forks with the transmission case mounted in the frame.

Removal

Refer to **Figure 29** when performing this procedure.

1. Remove the shifter cam as described in this chapter.
2. Remove the transmission side cover as described under *Transmission Side Cover* in this chapter.

NOTE
*Using a waterproof felt-tip pen, mark the installed position of each shift fork as you remove it. All three shift forks are different (**Figure 29**).*

3. Slide the shift shaft (A, **Figure 30**) out of the transmission case and remove the shift forks (**Figure 31**) from the transmission.

Inspection

1. Inspect each shift fork (**Figure 32**) for excessive wear or damage. Replace worn or damaged shift forks as required.

6

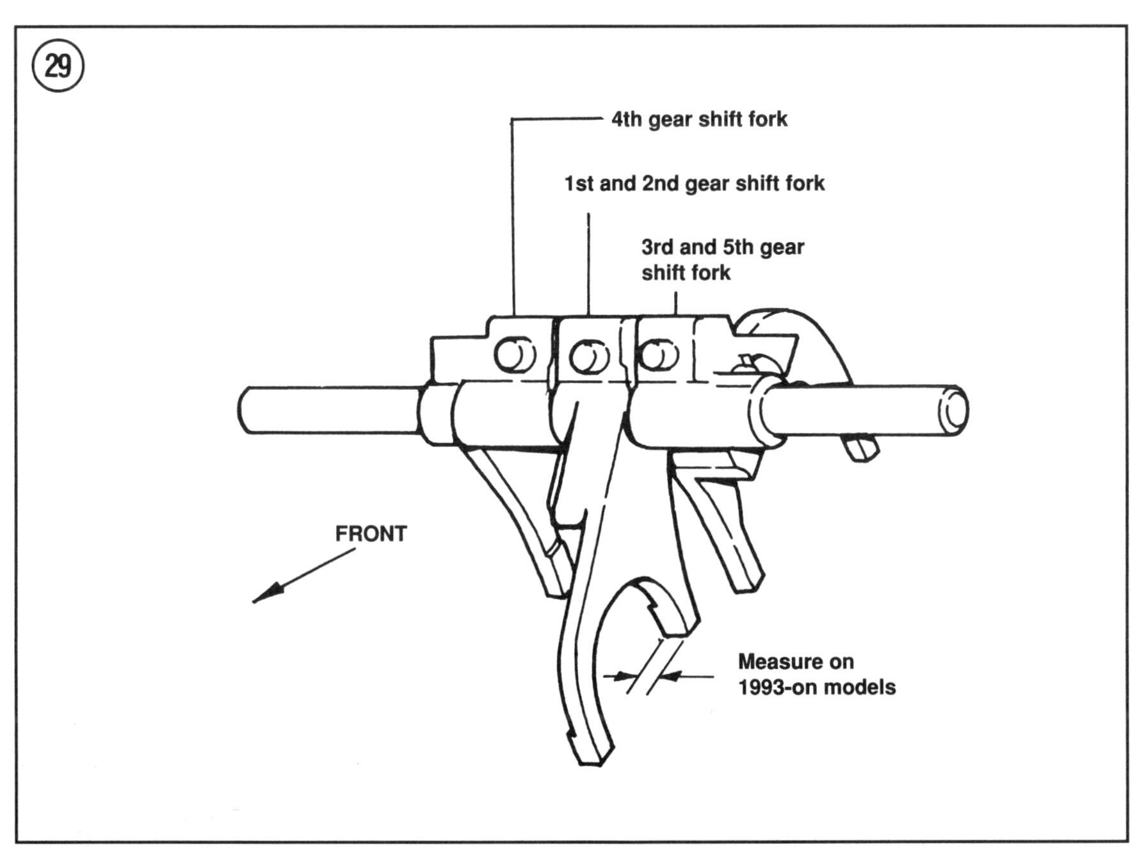

2A. On 1991-1992 models, replace the shift fork fingers (A, **Figure 33**) if excessively worn or damaged.

NOTE
On 1991-1992 models, Harley-Davidson does not specify a thickness measurement for the shift forks. Instead, they specify for you to measure the old shift forks and compare the thickness to that of new shift forks. If the wear difference is equal to or exceeds 0.020 in. (0.51 mm), replace the shift forks.

2B. On 1993-on models, measure the thickness of each shift fork finger where it contacts the sliding gear groove (**Figure 29**). Replace any shift fork with a finger thickness of 0.165 in. (4.19 mm) or less.

3. Check the shift forks for any arc-shaped wear or burn marks at (B, **Figure 33**). Replace damaged shift forks.

4. Roll the shift fork shaft on a flat surface and check for bending. Replace the shaft if bent.

5. Install each shift fork on the shift shaft. The shift fingers must slide smoothly with no binding or roughness.

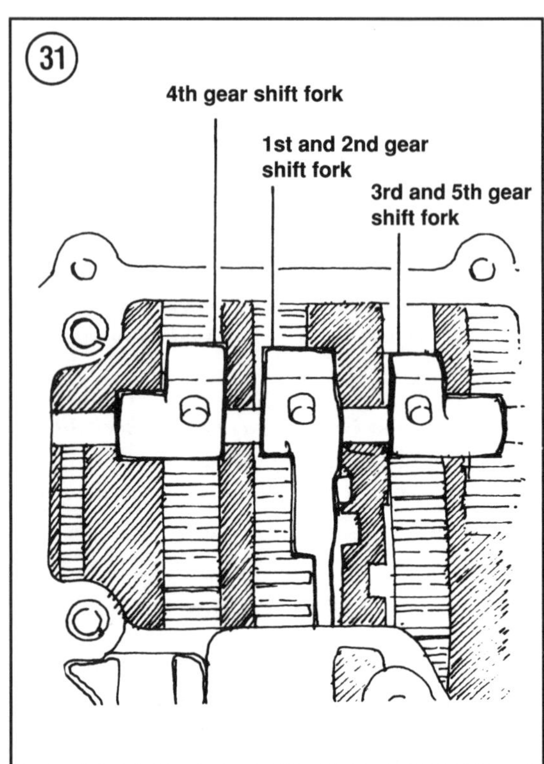

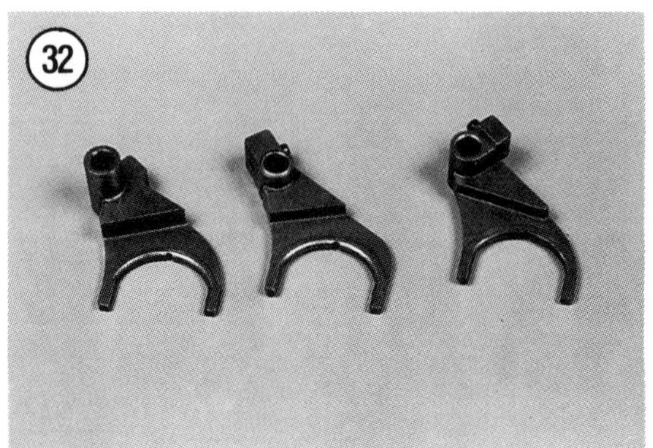

Assembly

1. Coat all bearing and sliding surfaces with assembly oil.

NOTE
***Figure 34** identifies the transmission gears. Refer to this drawing when installing the shift forks in Step 2.*

2. To install the shift forks and shaft, perform the following (**Figure 29**):

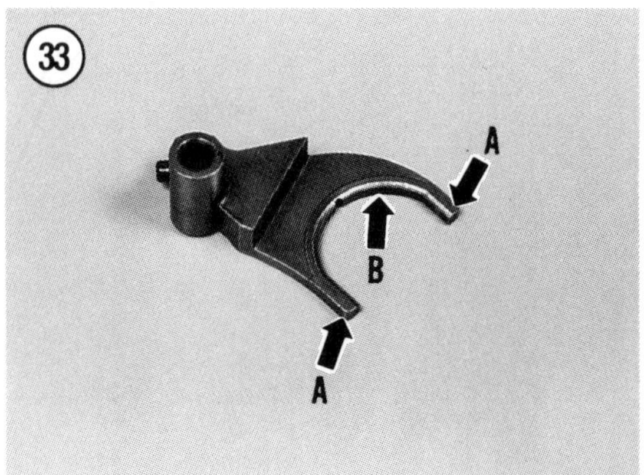

a. Insert the No. 1 shift fork into the mainshaft first gear groove.

b. Install the No. 2 shift fork into the countershaft third gear groove.

c. Install the No. 3 shift fork into the mainshaft second gear groove.

3. Insert the shift shaft through the transmission case (A, **Figure 30**), through each of the three shift forks and into the transmission case.

4. Install the transmission side door as described in this chapter.

5. Check that the shift forks move smoothly when shifting the gears by hand.

6. Install the shifter cam as described in this chapter.

TRANSMISSION SIDE DOOR

You can remove the transmission side door and transmission shafts with the transmission case installed in the frame.

Removal

This section describes removal of the transmission and side door assembly.

1. Remove the exhaust pipes as described in Chapter Seven.
2. Drain the transmission oil as described in Chapter Three.
3. Remove the clutch as described in Chapter Five.
4. Remove the primary chaincase as described in Chapter Five.
5. Remove the shift forks as described in this chapter.

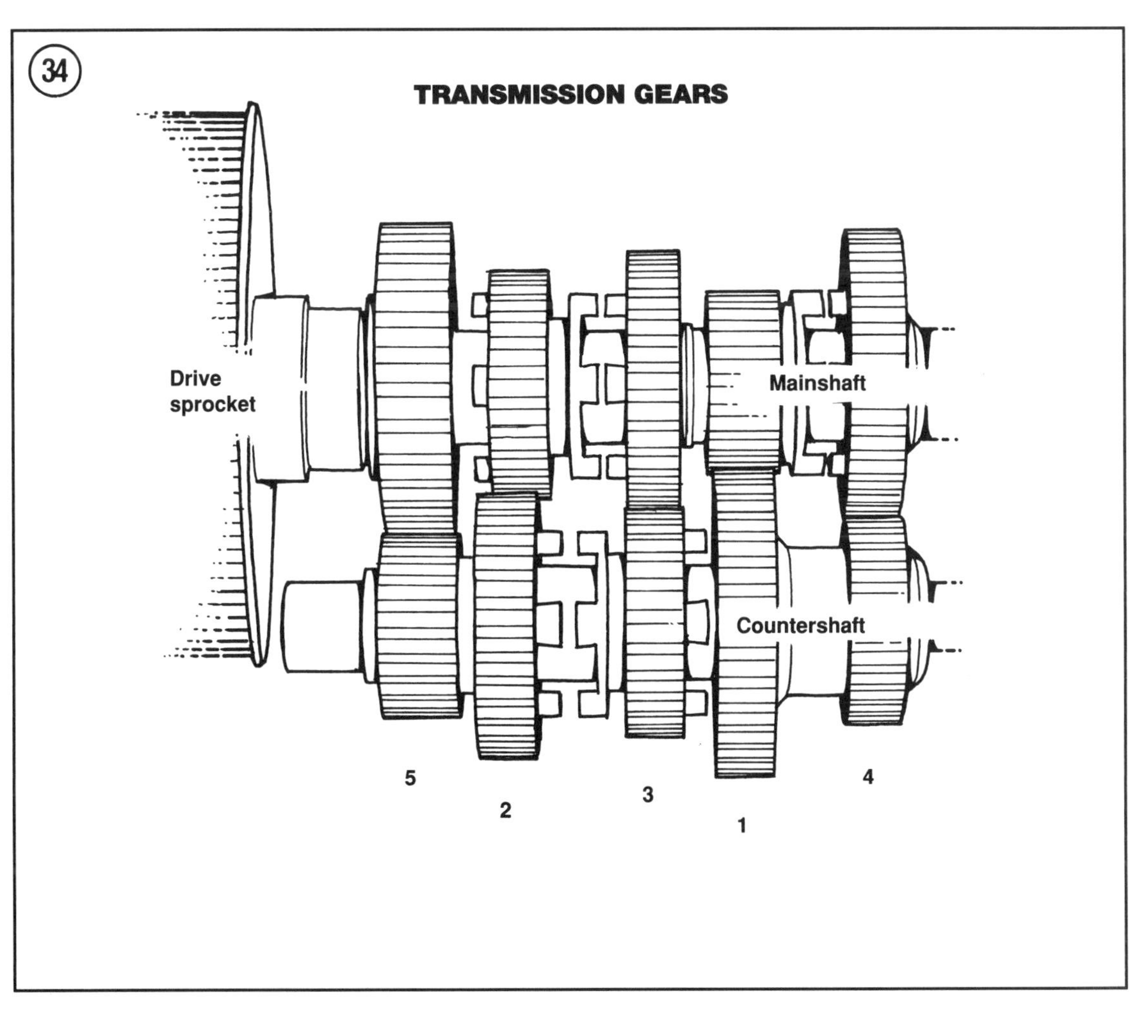

6. Remove the bearing inner race (**Figure 35**) from the mainshaft by performing the following:
   a. Mount the Harley-Davidson bearing race puller and installation tool (part No. HD-34902A) against the inner bearing race. See **Figure 36**.
   b. Operate the puller and pull the race off the mainshaft.
7. Remove the transmission side cover as described in this chapter.
8. Remove the pushrod assembly (B, **Figure 30**).
9. Turn the transmission by hand and shift the transmission into 2 different gear speeds to lock the transmission.
10. Loosen, but do not remove, the countershaft and mainshaft locknuts (**Figure 37**).
11. If you are going to remove the main drive gear, remove the drive sprocket as described under *Drive Sprocket* in Chapter Nine.
12. Remove the bolts securing the transmission side door (**Figure 38**) to the transmission case.

CAUTION

When removing the transmission side door in Step 13, do not tap against the transmission shafts (from the opposite side). Otherwise, you may damage the side door bearings.

13. Tap against the transmission side door to loosen its seal against the transmission case. Then remove the transmission side door (**Figure 39**) along with the transmission assembly. See **Figure 40**.
14. Remove and discard the transmission side door gasket.
15. If necessary, service the side door and transmission assembly as described in this chapter.

36

37

38

35

39

Installation

1. Remove all gasket residue from the side door and transmission case mating surfaces.

2. If you removed the main drive gear, install it as described in this chapter.

3. Install the side door and transmission assembly (**Figure 39**) into the transmission case, using a new gasket. Check that the side door fits flush against the transmission case.

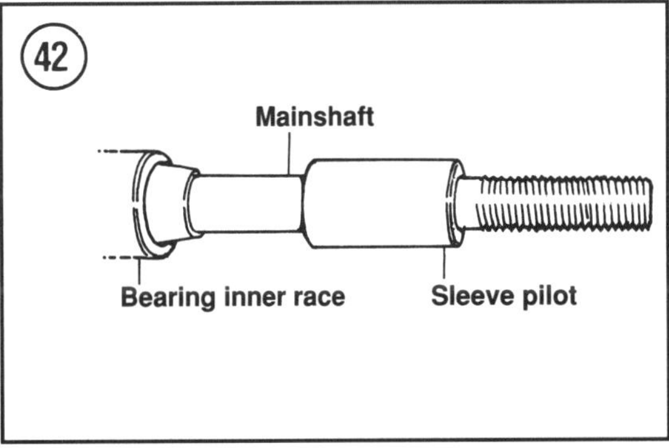

4. Install the transmission side door 5/16 in. and 1/4 in. bolts finger-tight. Then tighten the 5/16 in. bolts then the 1/4 in. bolts to the torque specifications in **Table 3**.

5. Turn the transmission by hand and shift the transmission into 2 different gear speeds to lock the transmission.

6. Tighten the mainshaft and countershaft locknuts (**Figure 37**) to the torque specification in **Table 3**.

7. Perform the following steps to install the bearing inner race onto the mainshaft:

NOTE
*Install the inner bearing race with the sleeve pilot and sleeve (part No. HD-34902A). See **Figure 41**.*

a. The inner bearing race is 0.950-1.000 in. (25.27-25.40 mm) long. When installing a new race, confirm its length by measuring it. Race length determines its final installation position.
b. Slide the bearing inner race—chamfered end first—onto the mainshaft.

NOTE
The mainshaft uses left-hand threads. Turn the sleeve pilot counterclockwise when installing it in sub-step c.

c. Thread the sleeve pilot (**Figure 42**) onto the mainshaft.
d. Slide the sleeve (**Figure 43**) over the sleeve pilot and rest it against the bearing inner race

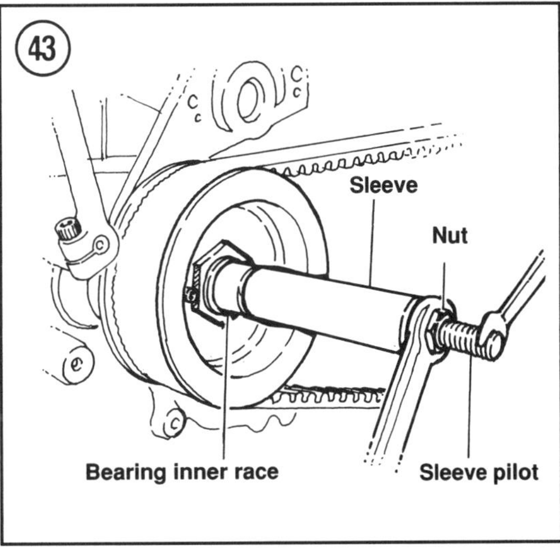

(**Figure 43**). Then install the flat washer and nut onto the sleeve pilot.

CAUTION

Install the inner bearing race to the dimension listed in sub-step e. This will align the race with the bearing outer race installed in the primary chaincase. Installing the wrong race or installing it incorrectly will damage the bearing and race assembly.

e. Hold the sleeve pilot and tighten the nut to press the bearing inner race onto the mainshaft. Install the race so that its inside edge is 0.100 in. (2.54 mm.) away from the main drive gear.

8. Install the pushrod assembly (B, **Figure 30**).
9. Install the transmission side cover as described in this chapter.
10. Install the shift forks, shifter cam and upper transmission cover as described in this chapter.
11. If you removed the transmission drive sprocket, install it as described in Chapter Nine.
12. Install the inner primary chaincase as described in Chapter Six.
13. Install the clutch as described in Chapter Six.
14. Install the drain plug and refill the transmission as described in Chapter Three.

TRANSMISSION

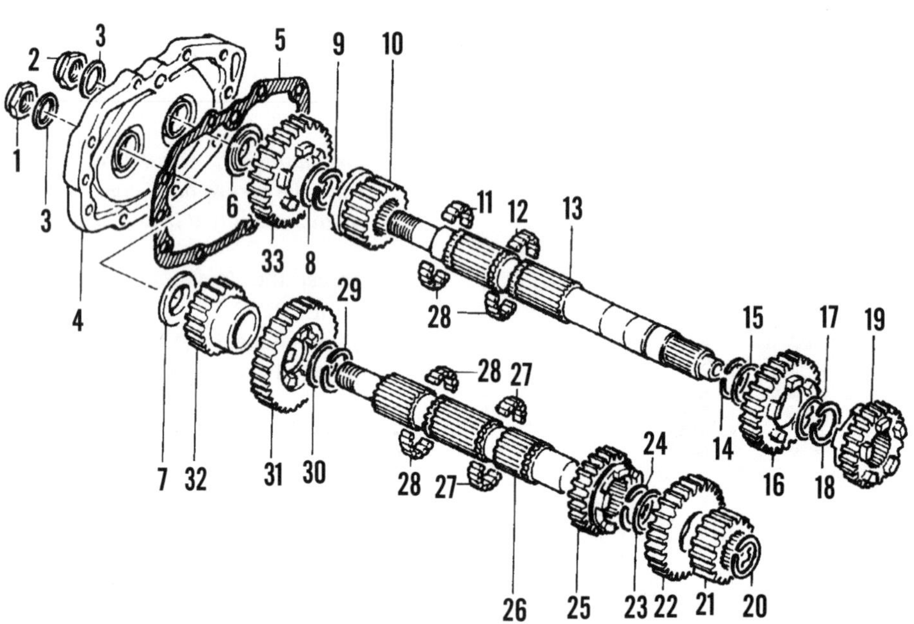

1. Countershaft nut
2. Mainshaft nut
3. Spacer
4. Side boot
5. Gasket
6. Mainshaft spacer
7. Countershaft spacer
8. Thrust washer
9. Circlip
10. Mainshaft 1st gear
11. Bearing
12. Bearing
13. Mainshaft
14. Circlip
15. Thrust washer
16. Mainshaft 3rd gear
17. Thrust washer
18. Circlip
19. Mainshaft 2nd gear
20. Circlip
21. Countershaft 5th gear
22. Countershaft 2nd gear
23. Thrust washer
24. Circlip
25. Countershaft 3rd gear
26. Countershaft
27. Bearing
28. Bearing
29. Circlip
30. Thrust washer
31. Countershaft 1st gear
32. Countershaft 4th gear
33. Mainshaft 4th gear

15. Install the exhaust system as described in Chapter Seven.

TRANSMISSION SHAFTS

This section describes service to the side door and both transmission shafts (**Figure 40**). You need a press to disassemble and reassemble the transmission assembly.

Refer to **Figure 44** and **Figure 45** when performing the following service procedures.

Transmission Disassembly

Refer to **Figures 44 and 45** for this procedure.

1. Remove the transmission side door assembly (**Figure 39**) as described in this chapter.
2. Mount the side door in a vise with soft jaws with the transmission shafts facing up.

NOTE
Label and store all of the transmission gears, circlips, washers and split bearings in their removal order. This will help with inspection and reassembly.

3. Remove the circlip (20, **Figure 44**) from the end of the countershaft (26, **Figure 44**).
4. Remove the countershaft fifth (21, **Figure 44**) and second (22, **Figure 44**) gears.
5. Remove the upper split bearing assembly (27 and 28, **Figure 44**) from the countershaft.
6. Remove the thrust washer (23, **Figure 44**) from the countershaft.
7. Remove the circlip (24, **Figure 44**) from the groove in the countershaft.

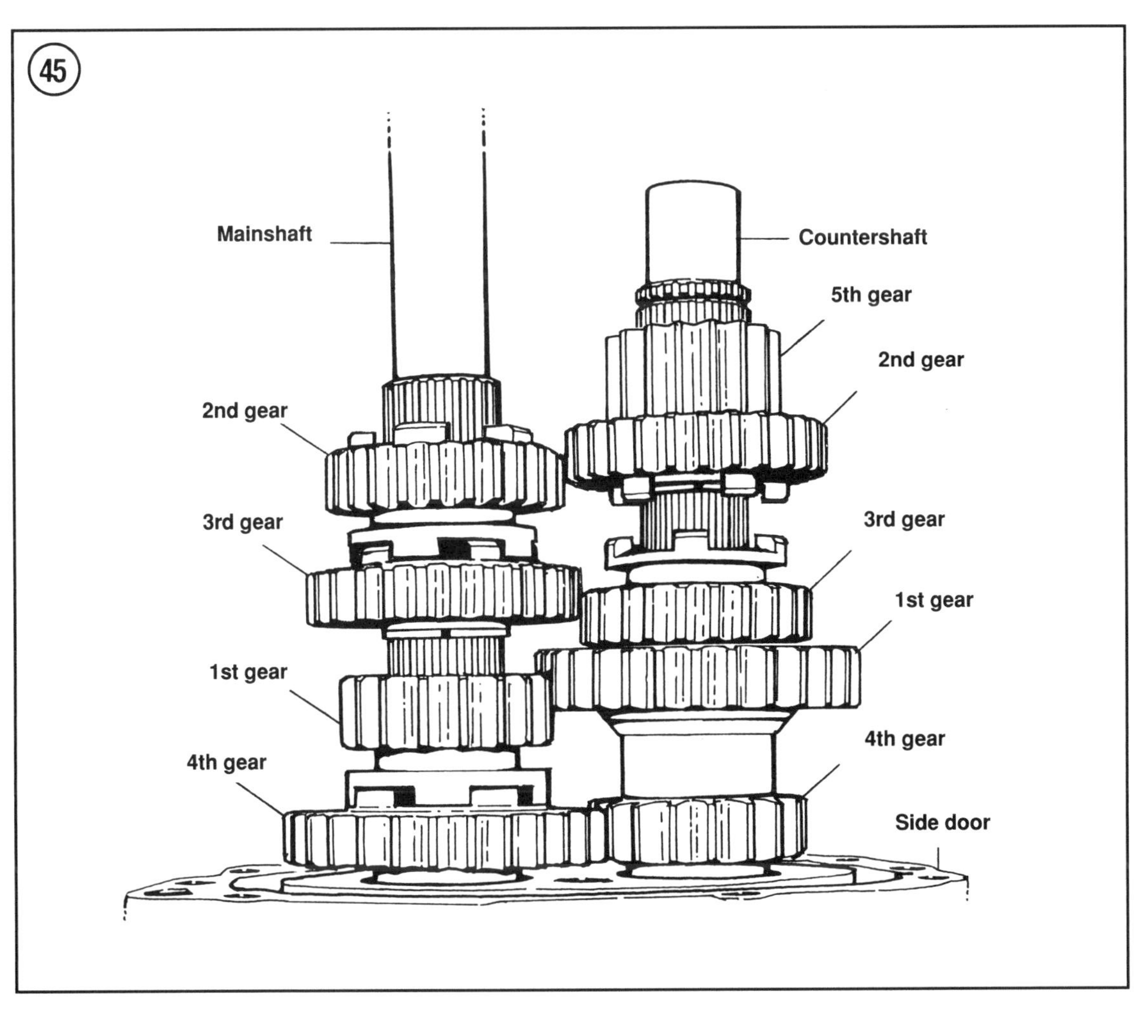

8. Remove countershaft third gear (25, **Figure 44**).
9. Remove mainshaft second gear (19, **Figure 44**).

NOTE
*Before removing the upper circlip (18, **Figure 44**), open the lower circlip (14, **Figure 44**) and slide it out of its groove. This will allow third gear to drop down, accessing the upper circlip. See **Figure 46**.*

10. Carefully pry the circlip (14, **Figure 44**) out of its groove and slide it down the mainshaft, along with third gear (16, **Figure 44**) and both thrust washers (15 and 17, **Figure 44**).
11. Remove the circlip (18, **Figure 44**) from the mainshaft groove.
12. Remove the washer (17, **Figure 44**), third gear (16, **Figure 44**) and the upper split bearing halves (11and 12, **Figure 44**) from the mainshaft.
13. Remove the washer (15, **Figure 44**) and the circlip (14, **Figure 44**) from the mainshaft.
14. Press the countershaft (**Figure 47**) out of its side door bearing as follows:
   a. Remove the side door from the vise.
   b. Remove the locknut (1, **Figure 44**) and spacer (3) from the countershaft.
   c. Support countershaft first gear in a press so that the countershaft can be pressed out without any interference. Center the countershaft under the press ram.
   d. Place a mandrel on top of the countershaft and press the countershaft out of the side door. Catch the countershaft so that it doesnt fall to the floor.
15. Remove the following parts from the countershaft:
   a. Circlip (29, **Figure 44**).
   b. Thrust washer (30, **Figure 44**).
   c. First gear (31, **Figure 44**).
   d. Fourth gear (32, **Figure 44**).
   e. Spacer (7, **Figure 44**).
16. Remove mainshaft first gear (10, **Figure 44**).
17. Press the mainshaft (**Figure 47**) out of its side door bearing as follows:

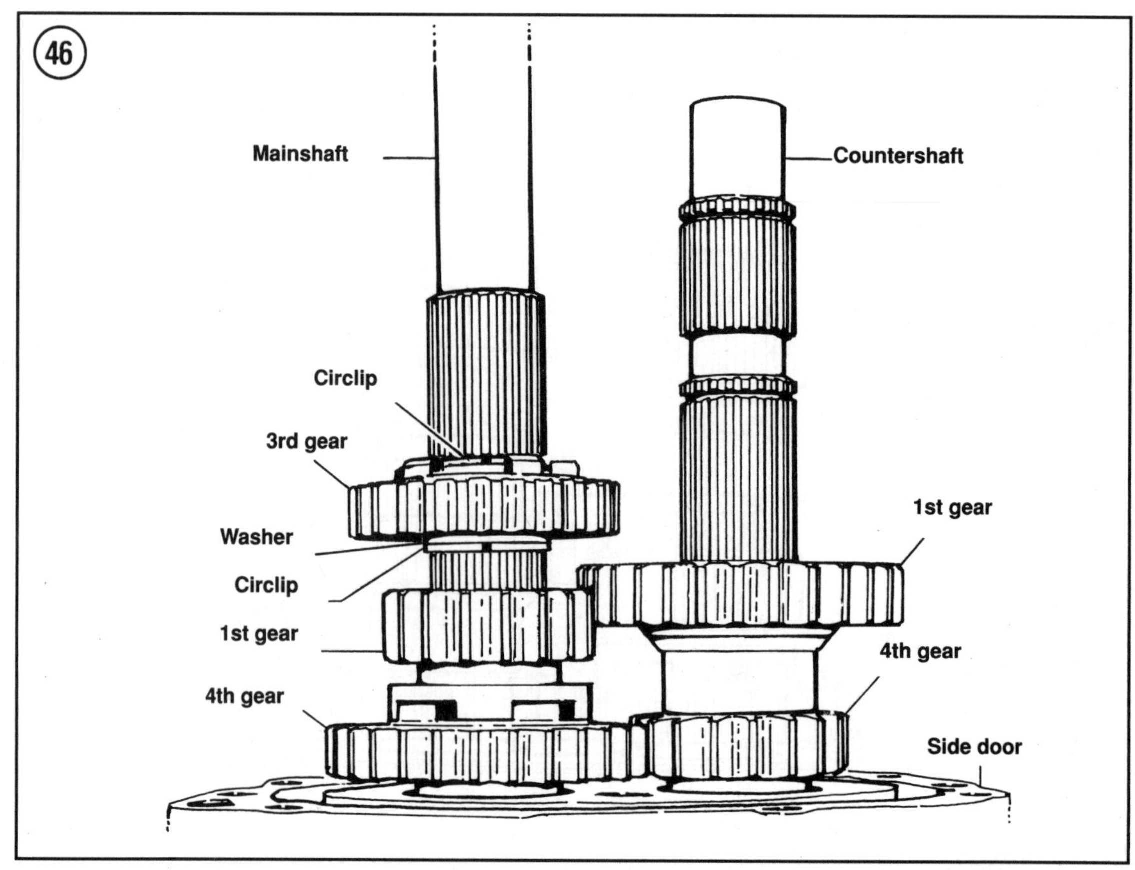

a. Remove the locknut (2, Figure 44) and spacer (3) from the mainshaft.

b. Support mainshaft fourth gear (33, **Figure 44**) in a press so that the mainshaft can be pressed out without any interference. Center the mainshaft under the press ram.

c. Place a mandrel on top of the mainshaft and press the mainshaft out of the side door. Catch the mainshaft so that it doesnt fall to the floor.

18. Remove the following parts from the mainshaft:

a. Fourth gear (33, **Figure 44**).

b. Spacer (6, **Figure 44**).

Transmission Inspection

1. Clean all components in solvent and dry with compressed air, if available.

2. Check each gear tooth for excessive wear, galling and pitting. Check for missing or chipped gear teeth. Check the gear lugs (**Figure 48**) for damage.

3. Install each splined gear (**Figure 49**) on its respective shaft and check for excessive play or binding.

4. Check each freewheeling gear (**Figure 48**) for scoring, galling or seizure marks.

5. Check the shift fork groove in each sliding gear (**Figure 49**). If the groove is worn or damaged, also check the mating shift fork for damage.

NOTE
Always replace defective gears and their mating gear as a set.

6. Check the bearing surfaces (**Figure 50**) on each shaft. These surfaces must be smooth.

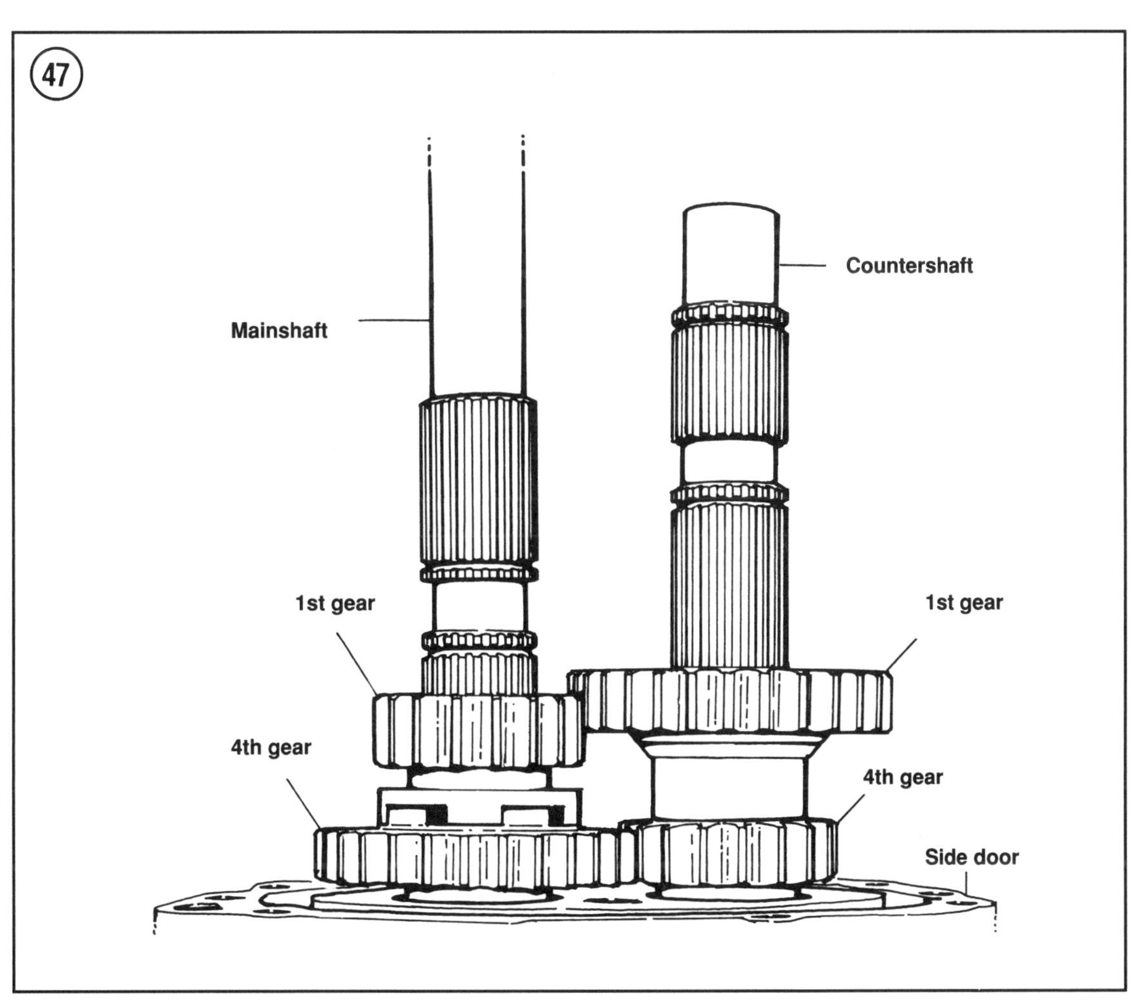

7. Check the shaft splines for excessive wear or damage.
8. Check the mainshaft and countershaft for binding. Mount the shafts between centers and check runout with a dial indicator.
9. Inspect the circlip grooves in each shaft. Each groove must have sharp square shoulders. Replace the shaft if worn or damaged shoulders is noted.
10. Check the split bearings (**Figure 51**) for excessive wear or damage.
11. Check the thrust washers for galling, scoring, cracks or other damage. Replace worn or damaged thrust washers.

Side Door Bearings Inspection and Replacement

You need a press to replace the side door bearings.

1. Clean the side door and bearings in solvent. Dry with compressed air, if available.
2. Turn each bearing inner race (**Figure 52**) by hand. The bearings must turn smoothly with no catching, binding or excessive noise. Continue with Step 3 to replace the bearings.
3. Remove the circlips from the side door cover grooves.
4. Support the side door on the press bed. Then press the bearing out of the side door.
5. Repeat for the opposite bearing.
6. Clean the side door again in solvent and dry thoroughly.
7. Inspect the bearing bores in the side cover for cracks or other damage. Replace the side door if damaged.
8. Inspect the circlips for cracks or other damage. One side of each circlip has a beveled edge. When

49

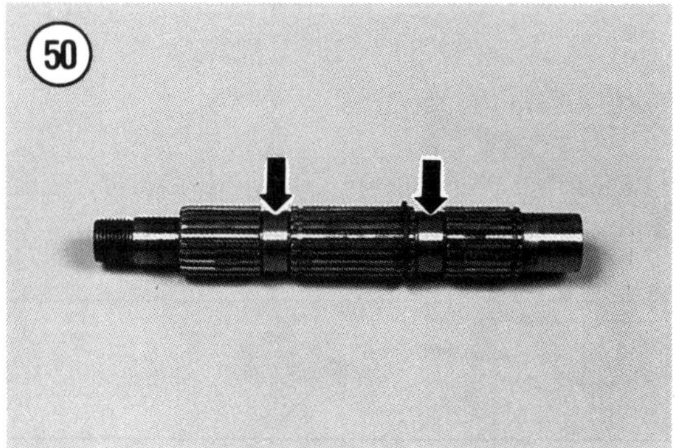
50

51

48

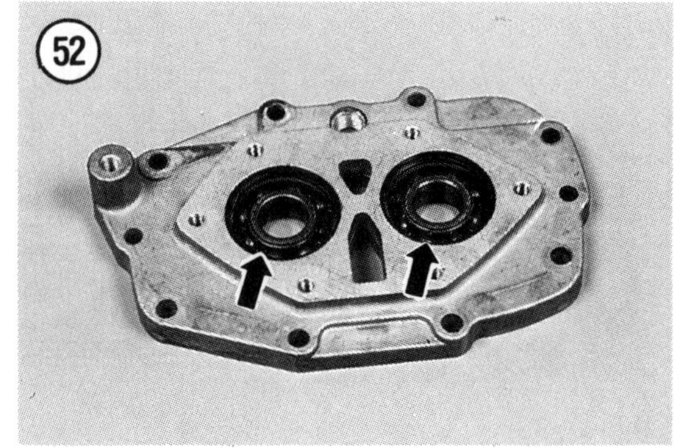
52

replacing the circlips, make sure to purchase the correct type circlip.

NOTE
*Before pressing the bearings into the side door, refer to the information listed under **Bearing Replacement** in Chapter One.*

NOTE
Both side door bearings are identical (same part number).

9. To install the bearings:
   a. Support the side door in a press.
   b. Install bearings with their manufacturer's marks facing out.
   c. Press the bearing into the side door until it bottoms out, using a driver that supports the bearings outer race only.
   d. Repeat for opposite bearing.

NOTE
Both circlips are identical (same part number).

10. Install each of the beveled circlips with their beveled edge facing away from the bearing (toward outside). Make sure each circlips seats in its groove completely.

Transmission Assembly

Refer to **Figure 44** when assembling the transmission.

CAUTION
Never reinstall a circlip you have removed from the transmission. These circlips have become distorted and weakened through use and may fail if reused. Installing new circlips ensures proper gear alignment and engagement.

1. Apply a light coat of clean transmission oil to all mating gear surfaces and to all split bearing halves before reassembly.
2. If removed, install the side door bearings as described in this chapter.
3. Lay out the countershaft and mainshaft assembly in the order shown in **Figure 44**.
4. Install the following parts onto the mainshaft (13, **Figure 44**) as follows:
   a. Install a circlip (9, **Figure 44**) into the outer circlip groove (A, **Figure 53**).
   b. Install a thrust washer next to the circlip as shown in 8, **Figure 44**.
   c. Install the mainshaft fourth gear split bearing (11and 12, **Figure 44**) on the mainshaft and install fourth gear (33, **Figure 44**) over it. The shift dogs on fourth gear must face toward the thrust washer.

NOTE
*The mainshaft (6, **Figure 44**) and countershaft (7, **Figure 44**) spacers are different. The mainshaft spacer has a shoulder while the countershaft spacer does not.*

   d. Install the mainshaft spacer (6, **Figure 44**) with its taper facing away from fourth gear.
   e. Install mainshaft first gear (10, **Figure 44**) with its gear dogs facing toward first gear.
   f. Set the mainshaft assembly aside for now.
5. Install the following parts onto the countershaft (26, **Figure 44**) as follows:
   a. Install a circlip (29, **Figure 44**) into the outer circlip groove (A, **Figure 54**).

6

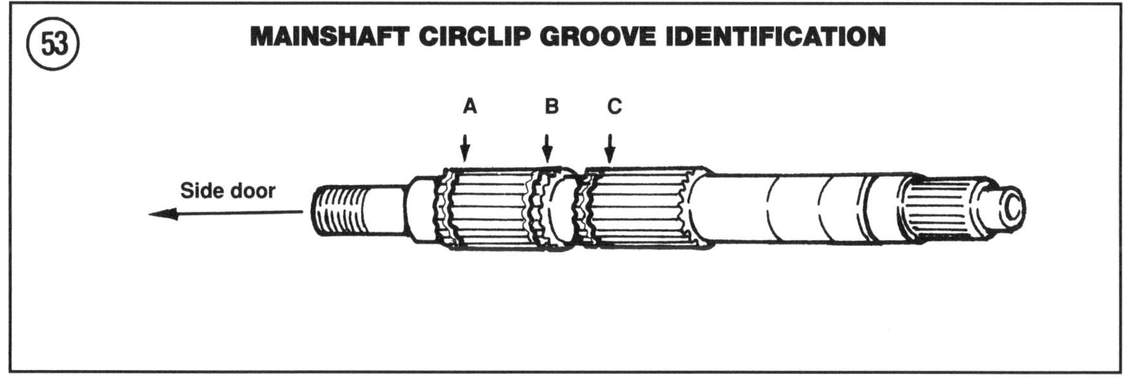

b. Install a thrust washer next to the circlip as shown in 30, **Figure 44**.
c. Install the countershaft first gear split bearing (27 and 28, **Figure 44**) on the countershaft and install first gear (31, **Figure 44**) over it. The shift dogs on first gear must face toward the thrust washer.
d. Install countershaft fourth gear (32, **Figure 44**) so that its shoulder is toward first gear.
e. Install the countershaft spacer (7, **Figure 44**) with its taper facing away from fourth gear.

6. Press the mainshaft into its side door bearing as follows:

CAUTION
When pressing the mainshaft into its side door bearing, support the inner bearing race; otherwise, you will damage the bearing.

a. Place a piece of pipe that matches the mainshaft bearings inner race diameter in the press bed. Then place the inner bearing race on the pipe so that the side door inner surface faces up.
b. Insert the mainshaft into the bearing and center it with the press ram (**Figure 47**).
c. Press the mainshaft into its bearing until its spacer (6, **Figure 44**) bottoms out against the bearing. When you properly install the mainshaft, there will be no spacer end play.

7. Press the countershaft into its side door bearing as follows:

CAUTION
When pressing the countershaft into its side door bearing, support the inner bearing race; otherwise, you will damage the bearing.

a. Place the same piece of pipe used in Step 6 in the press bed. The pipes outer diameter must match the countershaft bearings inner race diameter. Then place the inner bearing race on the pipe.
b. Insert the countershaft into the bearing and center it with the press ram (**Figure 47**). Mesh the mainshaft and countershaft gears so that they do not bind when pressing the countershaft into place.
c. Press the countershaft into its bearing until its spacer (7, **Figure 44**) bottoms out against the bearing. When you properly install the countershaft, there will be no spacer end play.

8. Remove the side door from the press. Then install a spacer and nut onto each shaft. See 1 and 2, **Figure 44**. Tighten the nuts finger-tight only. Final tightening will take place in Step 18.
9. Install a circlip in the mainshaft groove (B, **Figure 53**) above first gear. See 14, **Figure 44**. Then place a thrust washer (15, **Figure 44**) on top of the circlip.
10. Install the mainshaft third gear split bearing (11and 12, **Figure 44**) on the mainshaft and then slide third gear (16, **Figure 44**) over it. The side of third gear that has the shift dogs must face away from first gear (**Figure 46**).
11. Install the thrust washer (17, **Figure 44**) and circlip (18, **Figure 44**) next to third gear. Seat the circlip in mainshaft groove marked C in **Figure 53**.
12. Install mainshaft second gear (19, **Figure 44**). The side of second gear that has the shift fork groove must face toward third gear; see **Figure 55**.
13. Install countershaft third gear (25, **Figure 44**). The shift fork groove in third gear must face away from first gear; see **Figure 56**.
14. Install a circlip (24, **Figure 44**) into the groove above third gear; see **Figure 56**. Then install a thrust washer (23, **Figure 44**) on top of the circlip.
15. Install the countershaft second gear split bearing (27 and 28, **Figure 44**) on the countershaft and then slide second gear (22, **Figure 44**) over it. The side of second gear that has the shift dogs must face toward third gear. See **Figure 45**.
16. Install countershaft fifth gear (21, **Figure 44**).
17. Install a circlip (20, **Figure 44**) in the groove above countershaft fifth gear.
18. To tighten the mainshaft and countershaft locknuts, perform the following:

a. Secure the side door in a vise with soft jaws.

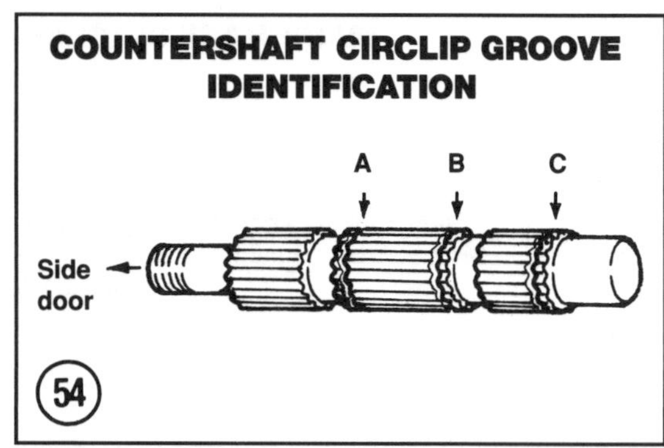

b. Lock the transmission by shifting it into 2 separate gears.

c. Tighten the countershaft and mainshaft locknuts to the torque specification in **Table 3**.

d. Shift the transmission into NEUTRAL.

MAIN DRIVE GEAR

The main drive gear assembly (**Figure 57**) is installed in the transmission case. If you are servicing the main drive gear with the transmission case mounted in the frame, you need the Harley-Davidson main drive gear remover and installer set (part No. HD-35316A). See **Figure 58** and **Figure 59**. If you removed the transmission case from the frame, use a press to remove and install the main drive gear.

Removal

This procedure describes removal of the main drive gear.

1. Remove the transmission assembly as described in this chapter.
2. Remove the spacer from the main drive gear oil seal.
3. Assemble the main drive gear removal tool onto the main drive gear as shown in **Figure 60**. Then tighten the puller and pull the main drive gear from the main drive gear bearing.
4. Drive the main drive gear bearing out of the transmission case, working from inside the transmission case, with a suitable bearing driver. Discard the bearing.

Inspection

1. Clean the main drive gear in solvent and dry with compressed air, if available.

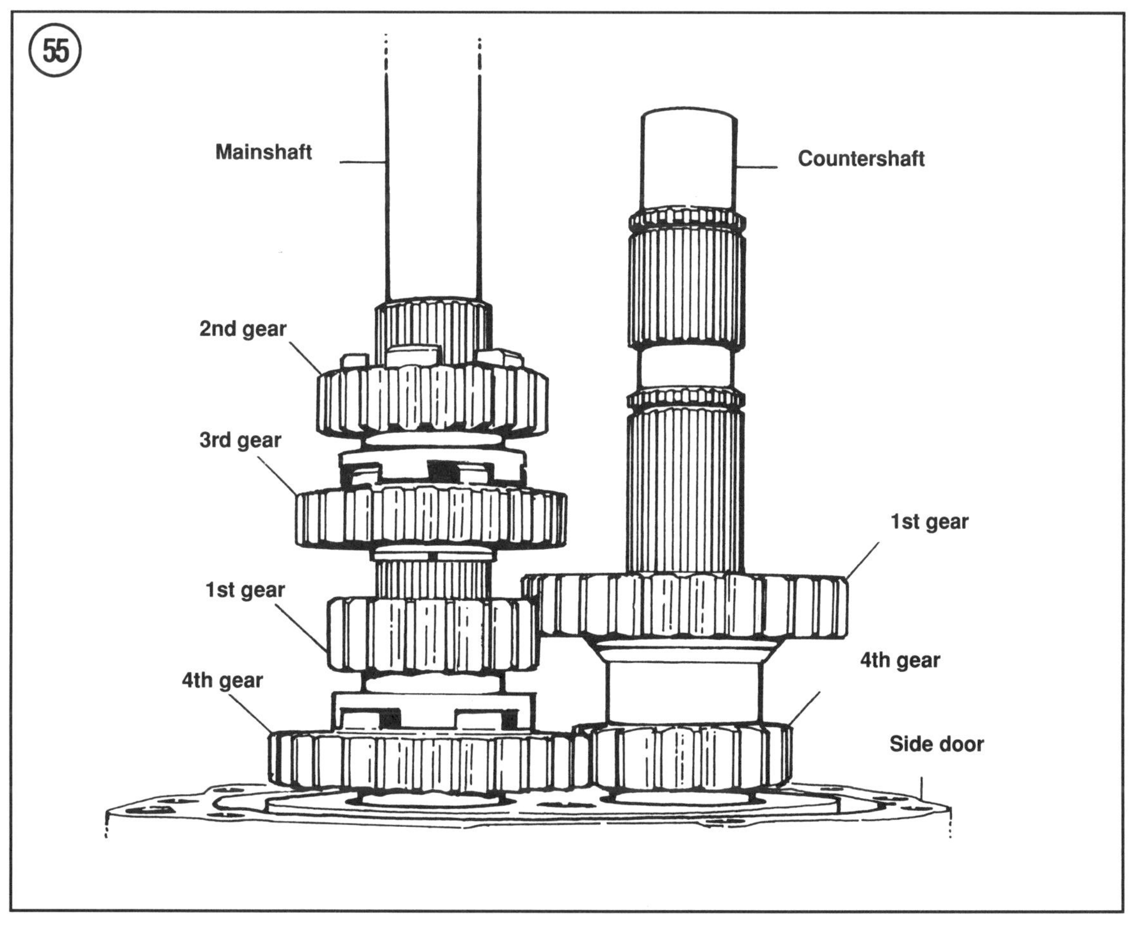

2. Check each gear tooth (**Figure 61**) for excessive wear, burrs, galling and pitting. Check for missing gear teeth.
3. Check the gear splines for excessive wear, galling or other damage.
4. Inspect the 2 main drive gear needle bearings (**Figure 62**) for excessive wear or damage. Insert the mainshaft into the main drive gear to check bearing wear. If necessary, replace the bearings as described in this section.

Main Drive Gear Needle Bearing Replacement

You must install both main drive gear needle bearings (**Figure 57**) to a specific depth. See **Figure 63**. You can do this automatically with the Harley-Davidson main drive gear bearing and oil seal installation tool (part No. HD-37842). If you do not have this tool, measure the depth of the bearings before removing them.

Replace both main drive gear needle bearings at the same time.

CAUTION
Do not reuse a main drive gear needle bearing. Discard the bearings after removing them.

1. Support the main drive gear in a press and press out one needle bearing. Then turn the gear over and press out the opposite bearing. Discard both bearings.
2. Clean the gear and its bearing bore in solvent and dry thoroughly.

NOTE
Install both needle bearings with their manufacturers name and size code facing out.

3. To install the bearings with the Harley-Davidson main drive gear bearing and seal installation tool, perform the following steps:

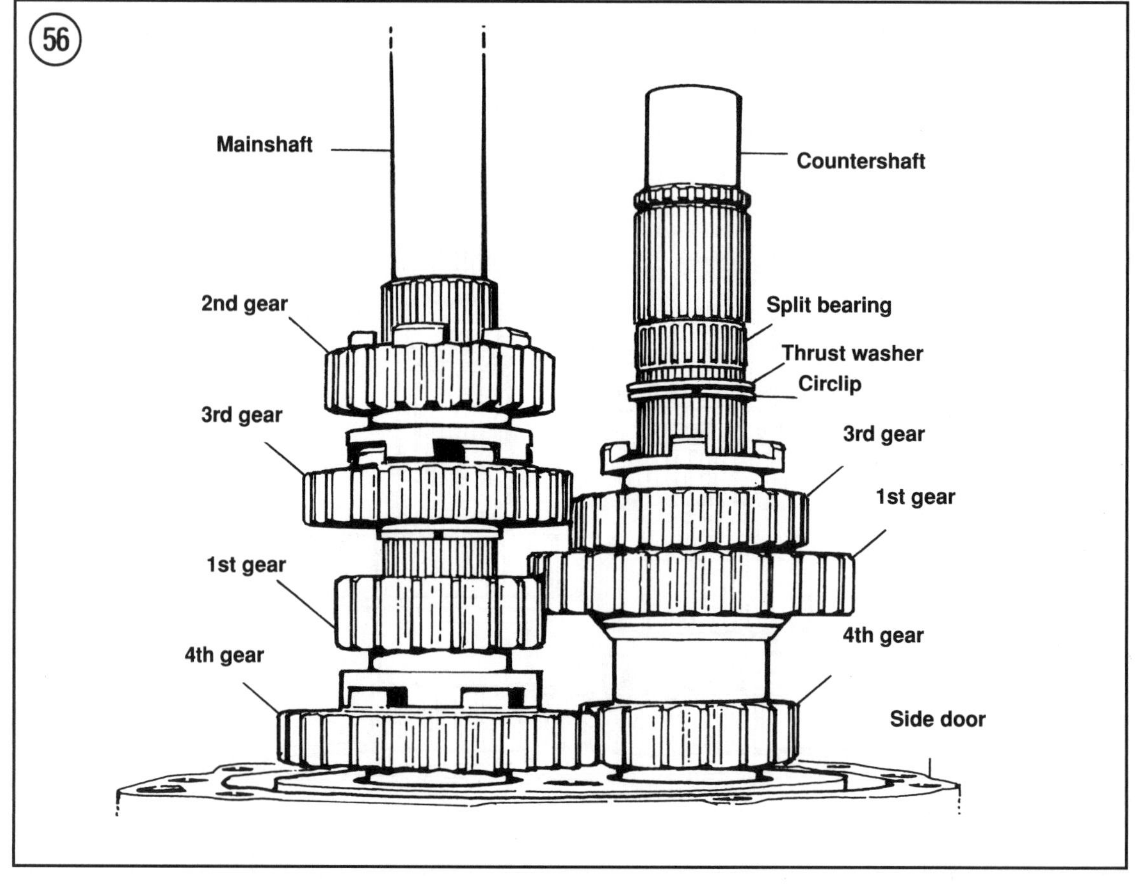

a. Harley-Davidson has stamped the tool with two sets of numbers. The side stamped 0.280 is for pressing in the outer end bearing. The side stamped 0.090 is for pressing in the inner end bearing. **Figure 63** identifies the main drive gear inner and outer ends.

b. Install the main drive gear in a press with the outer end facing up. Align the new bearing with the main drive gear and install the installation tool with the side marked 0.280 inserted into the bearing. Operate the press until the tool bottoms out against the gear.

c. Turn the main drive gear over so that the inner end faces up. Align the new bearing with the main drive gear and install the installation tool with the side marked 0.090 inserted into the bearing. Operate the press until the tool bottoms out against the gear.

3B. If you are installing the bearings without the installation tool, perform the following.

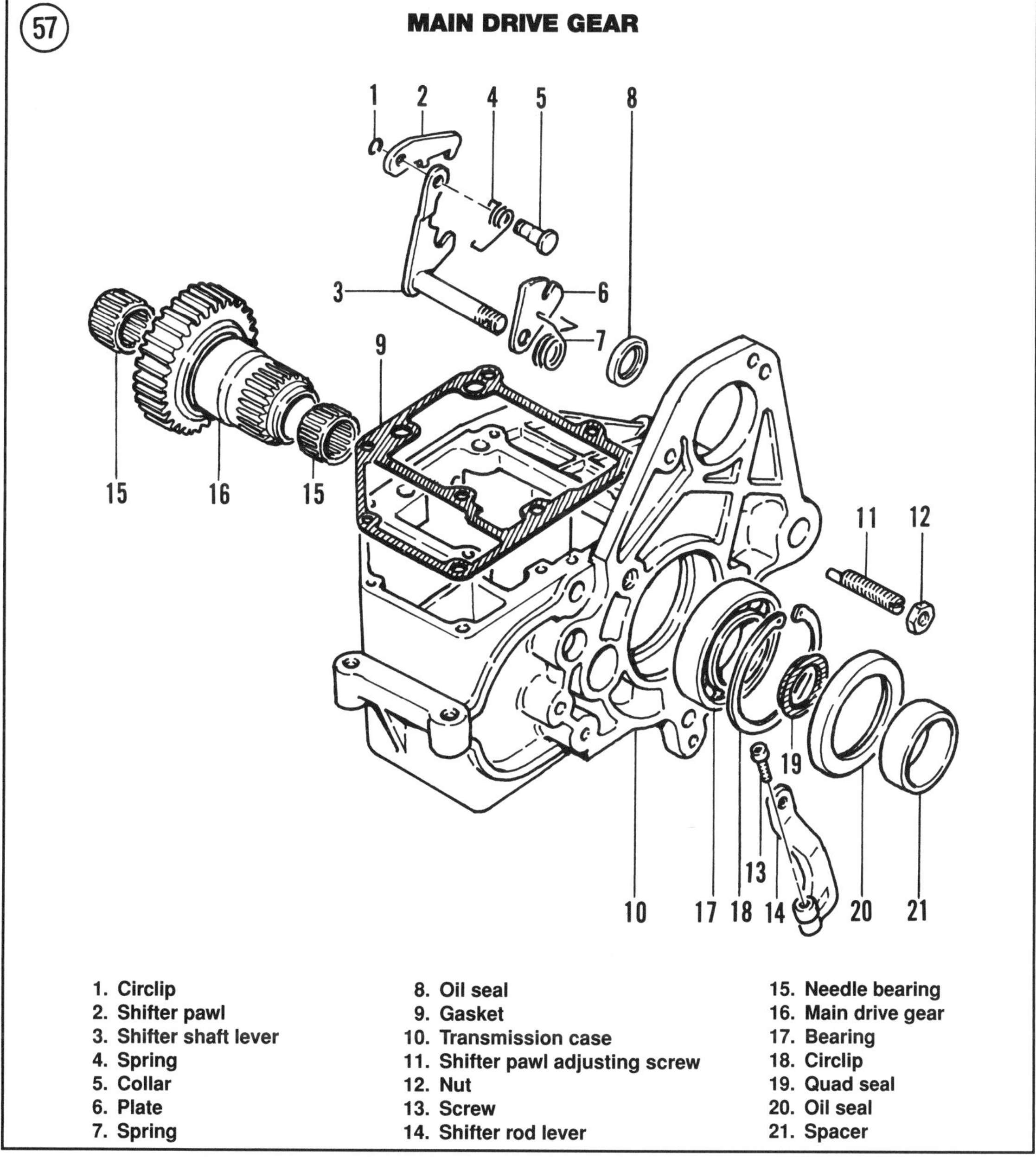

1. Circlip
2. Shifter pawl
3. Shifter shaft lever
4. Spring
5. Collar
6. Plate
7. Spring
8. Oil seal
9. Gasket
10. Transmission case
11. Shifter pawl adjusting screw
12. Nut
13. Screw
14. Shifter rod lever
15. Needle bearing
16. Main drive gear
17. Bearing
18. Circlip
19. Quad seal
20. Oil seal
21. Spacer

a. **Figure 63** identifies the main drive gear inner and outer ends.
b. Using a suitable mandrel, press in the outer end bearing to a depth of 0.280 in. (7.11 mm). See **Figure 63**.
c. Using a suitable mandrel, press in the inner end bearing to a depth of 0.090 in. (2.29 mm). See **Figure 63**.

Main Drive Gear Bearing Replacement

The main drive gear bearing (**Figure 57**) is pressed into the transmission case. When servicing the main drive gear with the transmission case mounted in the frame, use the Harley-Davidson main drive gear remover and installer set (part No. HD-35316A). See **Figure 58** and **Figure 59**. If you removed the transmission case from the frame, replace the main drive gear bearing using a press.

Because the main drive gear bearing (**Figure 57**) is damaged during removal from the main drive gear, do not reuse the bearing. Replace the bearing as described in this section.

1. Pry the main drive gear oil seal out of the transmission case.

NOTE
The circlip removed in Step 2 is mounted behind the main drive gear oil seal.

2. Remove the circlip from the crankcase groove.
3. Drive the main drive gear bearing out of the transmission case, working from inside the transmission case, with a suitable bearing driver. Discard the bearing.
4. Clean the bearing bore and dry with compressed air. Check the bore for nicks or burrs. Check the circlip groove for damage.

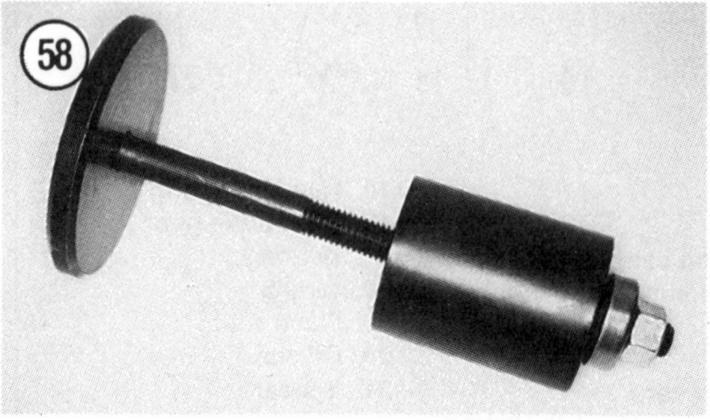
58

59

60

61

62

NOTE

Install the bearing into the transmission case with the bearing manufacturer's name and size code facing out.

5. Install the bearing onto the installation tool and assemble the installation tool and bearing onto the transmission case as shown in **Figure 64**.

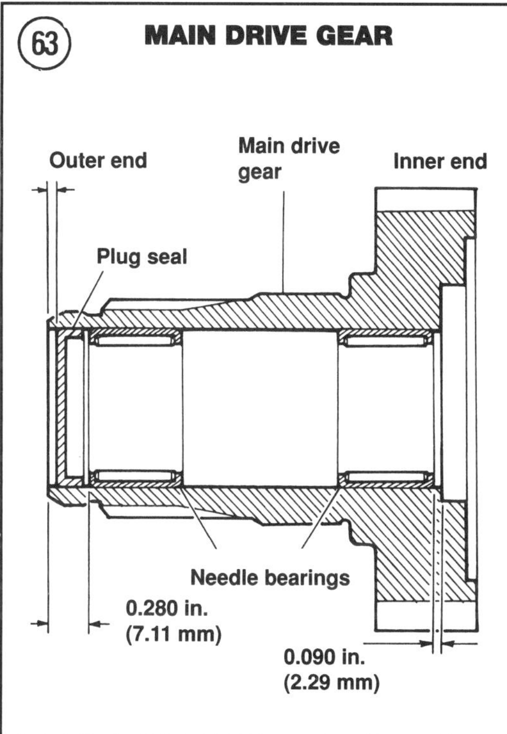

63 MAIN DRIVE GEAR

64 MAINSHAFT BALL BEARING INSTALLATION

6. Tighten the puller nut to pull the bearing into the transmission case. Continue until the bearing bottoms out in the case.

7. Disassemble and remove the installation tool.

8. Install the circlip, with its beveled side facing out, into the crankcase groove. Make sure you fully seat the circlip in the groove.

9. Install the new oil seal into the case so its closed side faces out.

Main Drive Gear Installation

1. Replace the main drive gear bearing and oil seal as described in the previous section.

2. Insert the main drive gear into the main drive gear bearing as far as it will go. Then hold it in place and assemble the Harley-Davidson main drive gear tool onto the main drive gear and transmission case as shown in **Figure 65**.

6

CAUTION

*Note how the installed cup, shown in **Figure 65**, supports the main drive gear bearing inner race. If you are installing the main drive gear with a different tool setup, make sure you support the inner bearing race in the same manner; otherwise; you will damage the bearing when pressing the main drive gear into place.*

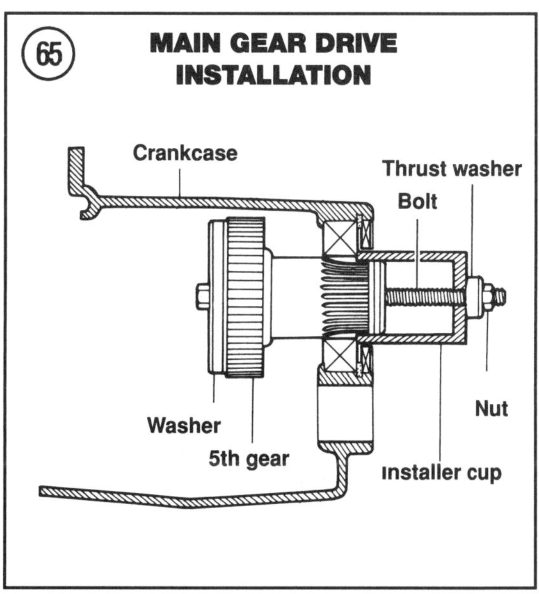

65 MAIN GEAR DRIVE INSTALLATION

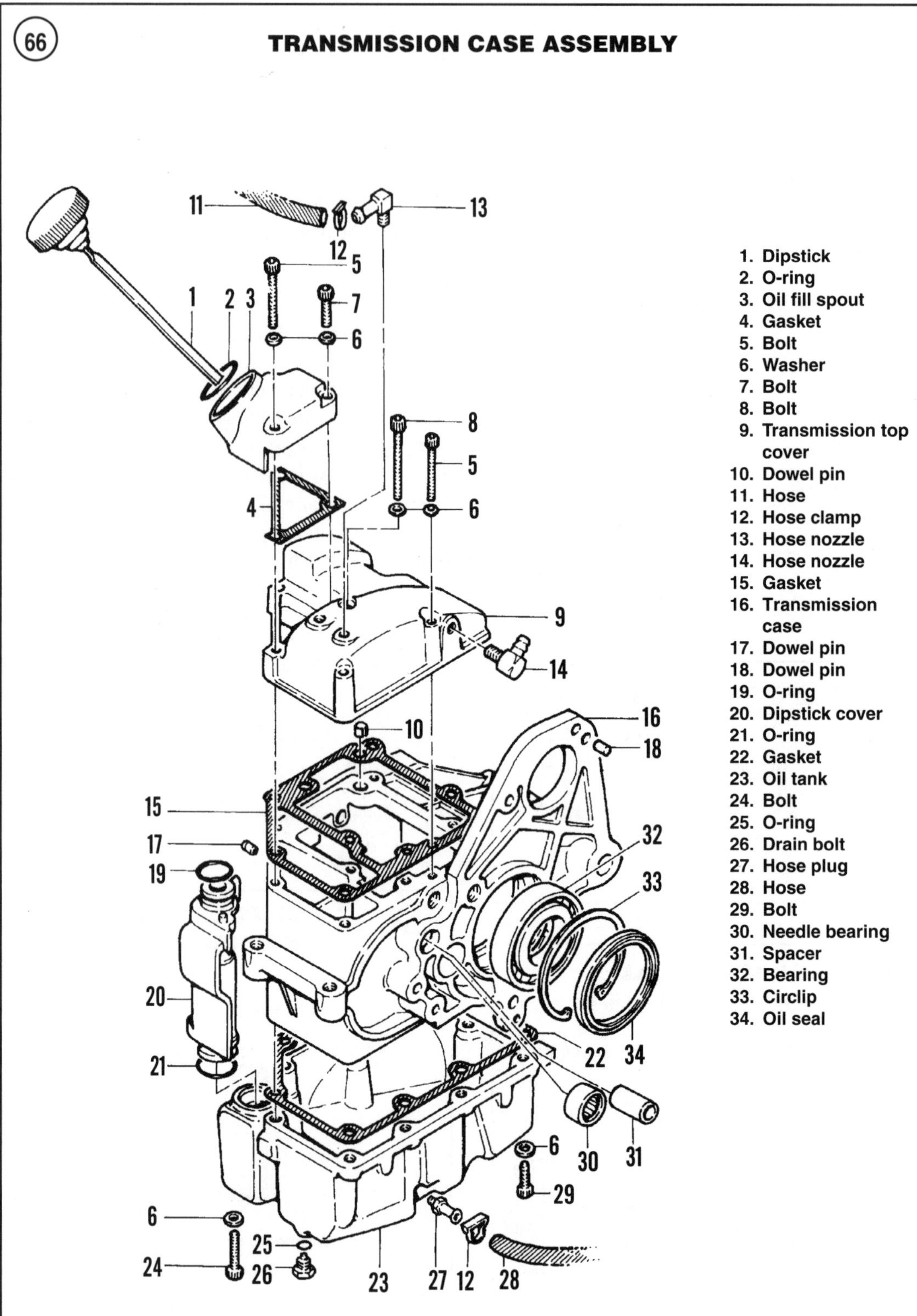
66
TRANSMISSION CASE ASSEMBLY
1. Dipstick
2. O-ring
3. Oil fill spout
4. Gasket
5. Bolt
6. Washer
7. Bolt
8. Bolt
9. Transmission top cover
10. Dowel pin
11. Hose
12. Hose clamp
13. Hose nozzle
14. Hose nozzle
15. Gasket
16. Transmission case
17. Dowel pin
18. Dowel pin
19. O-ring
20. Dipstick cover
21. O-ring
22. Gasket
23. Oil tank
24. Bolt
25. O-ring
26. Drain bolt
27. Hose plug
28. Hose
29. Bolt
30. Needle bearing
31. Spacer
32. Bearing
33. Circlip
34. Oil seal

3. Tighten the puller nut to pull the main drive gear through the bearing. Continue until the gears shoulder bottoms out against the inner bearing race.
4. Disassemble and remove the tool assembly.
5. Tap a new quad seal into the end of the main drive gear.
6. Slide the spacer over the main drive gear and seat it against the bearing.
7. Install the transmission assembly as described in this chapter.

TRANSMISSION CASE

Transmission case (**Figure 66**) removal is only necessary if it requires replacement or when performing extensive frame repair or replacing the frame. **Figure 67** shows the transmission case in the frame with the engine removed for clarity.

67

68

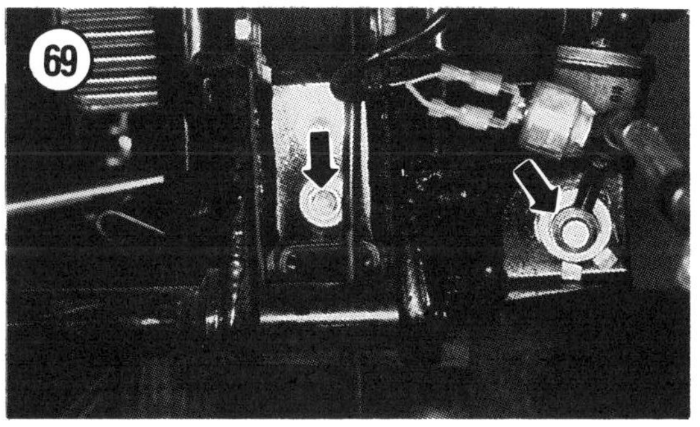
69

Removal/Installation

1. Remove the primary chaincase cover as described in Chapter Five.
2. Remove the starter motor as described in Chapter Eight.
3. Remove the oil tank from the bottom of the transmission case as described in this chapter.
4. If necessary, remove the transmission assembly as described in this chapter.
5. Remove the transmission case-to-engine mounting bolts (**Figure 68**).
6. Remove the rear transmission mounting bolts (**Figure 69**).
7. Remove the transmission case from the frame.
8. Install the transmission case by reversing these removal steps, while noting the following.
9. Tighten the transmission mounting bolts to the torque specification in **Table 3**.

Shift Arm Disassembly/Inspection/Assembly

Refer to **Figure 57** for this procedure.

1. Loosen the shift lever screw at the bottom of the transmission case and slide the shift lever off the shift arm.
2. Loosen the shift lever adjusting screw and turn it counterclockwise until it clears the centering plate. Then pull the shift arm assembly out of the transmission case.
3. Remove the circlip and remove the pawl and spring.
4. Slide the spring and centering plate off the shift arm.
5. The pawl pin is a press fit. If removal is necessary, drive it out with a suitable size punch.
6. Check the shift pawl and centering plate for wear. Replace the pawl if damaged. Replace the centering plate if its adjustment slot is elongated.
7. Check the springs for wear or damage. Assemble the pawl and spring on the shift arm pin. If the spring will not hold the pawl on the cam, replace it.
8. Place the centering plate on the shift lever.
9. Assemble the springs, pin, and pawl. Secure with a new circlip.

10. Install the shift arm assembly into the transmission case.
11. Align the adjusting screw with the centering plate slot.
12. Slide the shift lever on the shift arm. Install the screw, making sure it engages the slot in the shift lever. Then tighten the shift arm screw to the torque specification in **Table 3**.

TRANSMISSION SIDE COVER

Refer to **Figure 70** when servicing the transmission side cover.

Removal

1. Remove the exhaust system.

(70)

TRANSMISSION SIDE COVER AND CLUTCH RELEASE MECHANISM

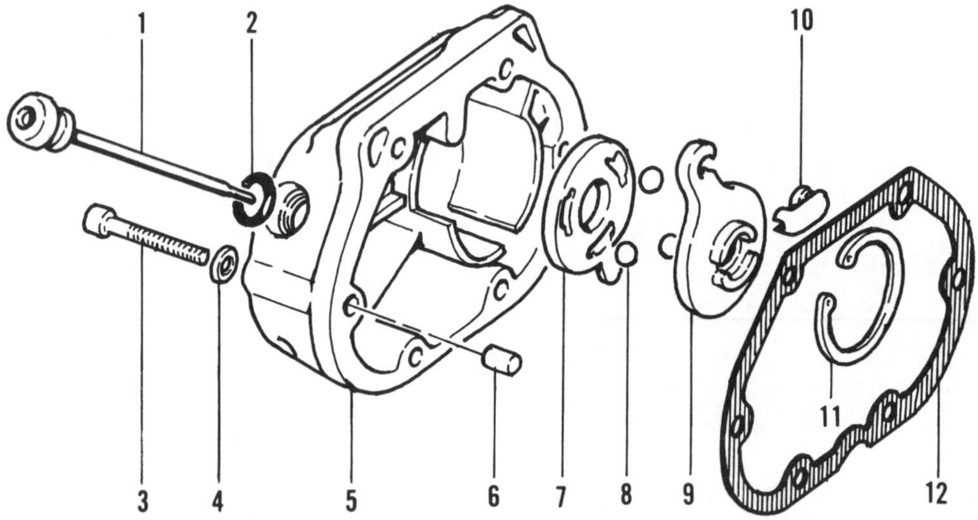

1. Dipstick
2. O-ring
3. Bolt
4. Washer
5. Transmission side cover
6. Dowel pin
7. Outer ramp
8. Balls
9. Inner ramp
10. Coupling
11. Circlip
12. Gasket

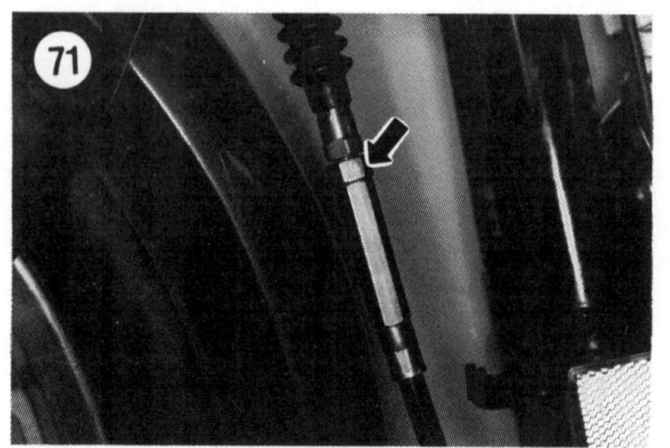

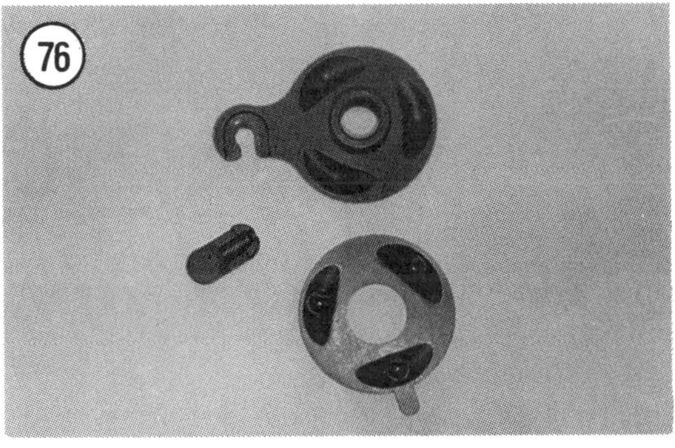

2. Drain the transmission oil as described in Chapter Three.
3. Remove the transmission fill plug/dipstick assembly.
4. Loosen the clutch cable adjuster locknut (**Figure 71**) and turn the adjuster to provide as much slack in the cable as possible.
5. Remove the side cover bolts and remove the side cover (A, **Figure 72**).

Disassembly

NOTE
Before removing the circlip in Step 1, note the position of the circlip opening. You must install the circlip with its opening in the same position.

1. Remove the circlip (**Figure 73**) from the groove in the side cover.
2. Lift the inner ramp (A, **Figure 74**) out of the cover and disconnect it from the clutch cable coupling (B, **Figure 74**).
3. Remove the clutch cable coupling (A, **Figure 75**).
4. Remove the inner ramp and balls (B, **Figure 75**).
5. If necessary, remove the clutch cable from the side cover.

Inspection

1. Wash the side cover and all components thoroughly in solvent and dry thoroughly.
2. Check the release mechanism balls and ramp ball sockets for cracks, deep scoring or excessive wear (**Figure 76**).
3. Check the side cover (**Figure 77**) for cracks or damage. Check the clutch cable threads and the coupling circlip groove for damage. Check the ramp bore in the side cover for excessive wear or lips or grooves that could catch the ramps and bind them sideways, causing improper clutch adjustment.
4. Replace the clutch cable O-ring if missing or damaged.
5. Replace all worn or damaged parts.

Assembly

1. If removed, screw the clutch cable into the side cover. Do not tighten the cable bolt at this time.

2. Install the inner ramp and balls (B, **Figure 75**). Center a ball into each socket.
3. Install the clutch cable coupling onto the clutch cable as shown in A, **Figure 75**.
4. Connect the inner ramp onto the clutch cable coupling (B, **Figure 74**).
5. Align the inner ramp socket with the balls and install the inner ramp as shown in **Figure 78**.
6. Install the circlip (**Figure 73**) into the side cover groove. Position the circlip so that its opening faces to the right of the outer ramp tang slot as shown in **Figure 73**. Make sure the circlip seats in the groove completely.

Installation

1. Install the side cover (A, **Figure 72**) using a new gasket. Install the side cover bolts and tighten to the torque specification in **Table 3**.
2. If you removed the clutch cable or loosened the clutch cable bolt (B, **Figure 72**) at the side cover, tighten the bolt securely.
2. Refill the transmission with oil as described in Chapter Three.
3. Install the exhaust system as described in Chapter Seven.
4. Adjust the clutch as described in Chapter Three.

OIL TANK

The oil tank (**Figure 79**) mounts onto the bottom of the transmission case. You can remove the oil tank with the transmission mounted in the frame.

Refer to **Figure 80** when servicing the oil tank.

Removal

1. Drain the engine oil as described in Chapter Three.
2. Drain the transmission oil as described in Chapter Three.
3. Disconnect the oil hose (**Figure 81**) from the oil tank.
4. Remove the engine oil dipstick (**Figure 82**).
5. Remove the oil fill spout mounting bolts and washers (**Figure 83**). Then lift off and remove the oil fill spout (**Figure 84**) and its gasket.
6. Lift off and remove the dipstick cover (**Figure 85**) and its 2 O-rings. See **Figure 86**.
7. Remove the bolts and washers securing the oil tank to the transmission case. Lower and remove the oil tank and gasket. Discard the gasket.

Installation

1. Remove all gasket residue from the gasket surfaces.
2. Clean the oil tank in solvent and dry thoroughly.
3. Install a new oil tank gasket on the oil tank. Then install the oil tank onto the bottom of the transmission case, using the bolts and washers.
4. Tighten the oil tank mounting bolts to the torque specification in **Table 3**.

77

78

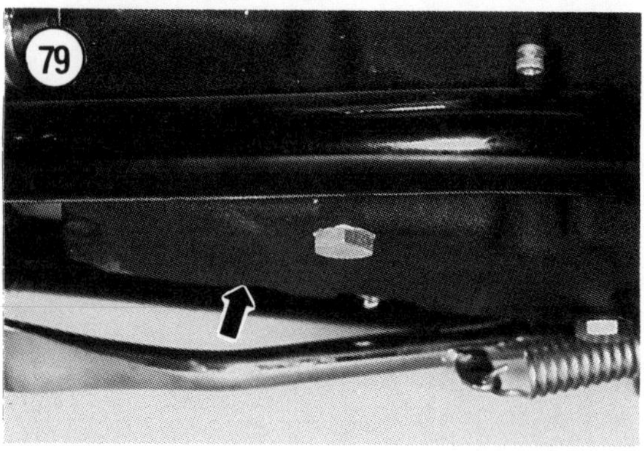
79

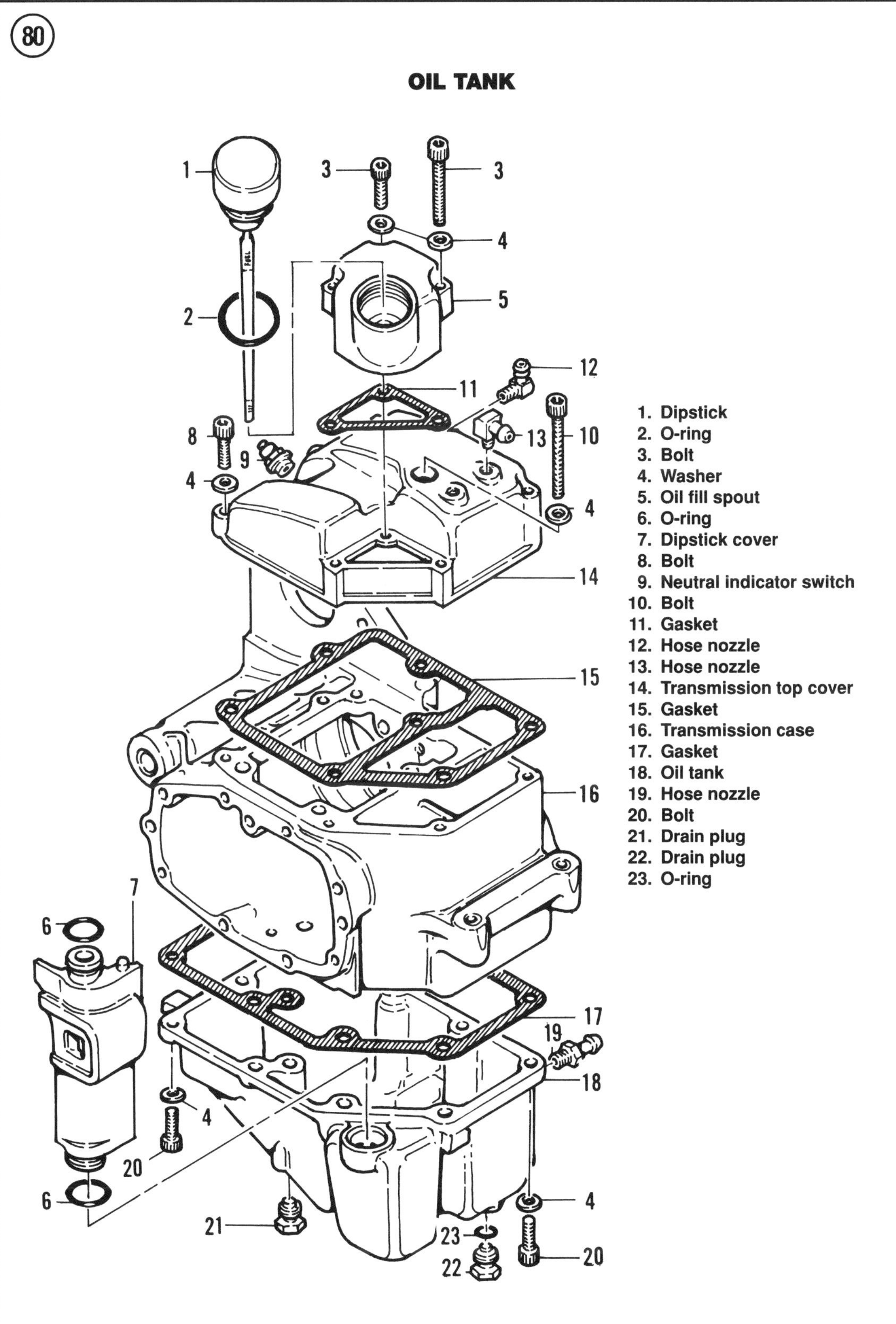
80
OIL TANK
1
2
3
3
4
5
12
11
8
9
13
10
4
4
14
15
16
7
6
17
19
18
4
20
6
21
4
23
22
20
1. Dipstick
2. O-ring
3. Bolt
4. Washer
5. Oil fill spout
6. O-ring
7. Dipstick cover
8. Bolt
9. Neutral indicator switch
10. Bolt
11. Gasket
12. Hose nozzle
13. Hose nozzle
14. Transmission top cover
15. Gasket
16. Transmission case
17. Gasket
18. Oil tank
19. Hose nozzle
20. Bolt
21. Drain plug
22. Drain plug
23. O-ring

5. Reconnect the oil hose (**Figure 81**) and secure with new hose clamps. Tighten the factory hose clamps with the Harley-Davidson hose clamp pliers (part No. HD-97087-65B).
6. Replace the dipstick cover O-rings (**Figure 86**) if worn or damaged.
7. Install the dipstick cover (**Figure 85**) and its O-rings.
8. Install the oil fill spout (**Figure 84**) and a new gasket. Tighten the oil fill spout mounting bolts to the torque specification in **Table 3**.
9. If necessary, replace the engine oil filter as described in Chapter Three.
10. Refill the oil tank with new engine oil as described in Chapter Three.
11. Refill the transmission with new oil as described in Chapter Three.
12. Start the engine and check for leaks.

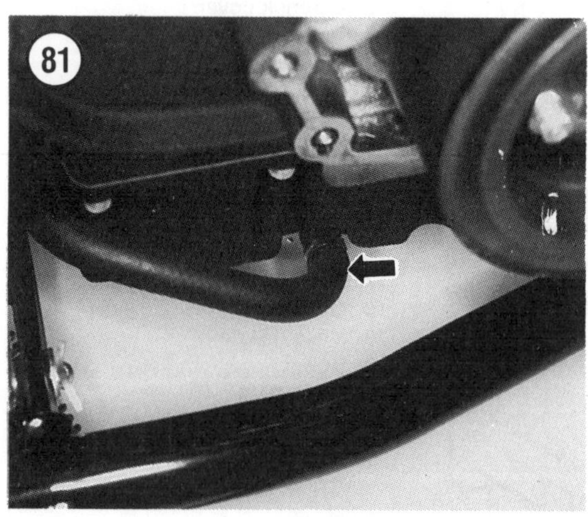
81

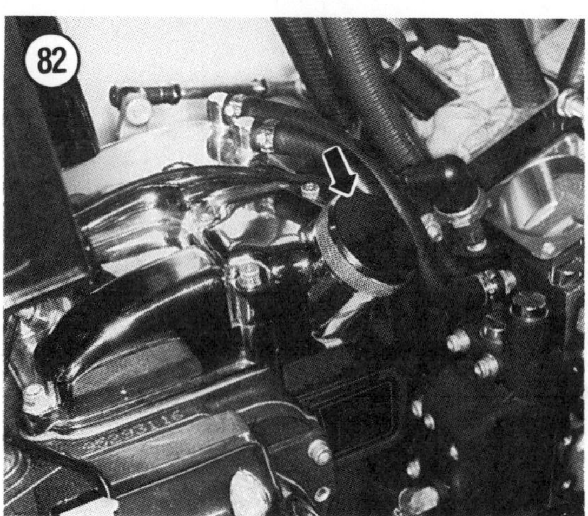
82

83

84

85

86

Table 1 TRANSMISSION SPECIFICATIONS

Transmission type	5-speed, constant mesh
Internal gear ratios	
Domestic models	
1st	3.24
2nd	2.21
3rd	1.60
4th	1.23
5th	1.00
International models	
1st	3.21
2nd	2.21
3rd	1.57
4th	1.23
5th	1.00
Transmission fluid capacity	
1991-1994	16 fl. oz. (473 ml, 16.7 Imp. oz.)
1995-on	20-22 fl. oz. (587-646 ml, 20-23 Imp. oz.)

6

Table 2 TRANSMISSION SERVICE SPECIFICATIONS

	in.	mm
Countershaft		
Runout	0.000-0.003	0.00-0.08
End play	None	
1st gear		
Clearance	0.0003-0.0019	0.008-0.048
End play	0.0039-0.0050	0.099-0.127
2nd gear		
Clearance	0.0003-0.0019	0.008-0.048
End play	0.0050-0.0440	0.127-1.118
3rd gear		
Clearance	0.0000-0.0080	0.000-0.203
4th gear		
Clearance	0.0000-0.0080	0.000-0.203
End play	0.0050-0.0391	0.127-0.991
5th gear		
Clearance	0.0000-0.0080	0.000-0.203
End play	0.0040-0.0050	0.102-0.127
Mainshaft		
Runout	0.000-0.003	0.00-0.08
1st gear clearance	0.0000-0.0080	0.000-0.203
2nd gear clearance	0.0000-0.0800	0.000-2.032
3rd gear		
Clearance	0.0003-0.0019	0.008-0.048
End play	0.0050-0.0420	0.127-1.067
4th gear		
Clearance	0.0003-0.0019	0.008-0.048
End play	0.0050-0.0310	0.127-0.787
Main drive gear		
Bearing fit in transmission case	0.0003-0.0017	0.0076-0.043
End play	None	
Fit in bearing	0.0009	0.023
Fit on mainshaft	0.0001-0.0009	0.0025-0.023
Shifter cam assembly		
Right edge of middle cam groove to right support block distance	1.992-2.002	50.60-50.86
Shifter cam end play	0.0001-0.004	0.0025-0.10

(continued)

Table 2 TRANSMISSION SERVICE SPECIFICATIONS (continued)

	in.	mm
Shifter forks		
Shifter fork-to-cam groove end play	0.0017-0.0019	0.043-0.048
Shifter fork to gear groove end play	0.0010-0.0110	0.025-0.279
Side door bearing		
Fit in side door	0.0014-0.0001	0.036-0.0025
Fit on countershaft		
Tight	0.0007	0.018
Loose	0.0001	0.0025
Fit on mainshaft		
Tight	0.0007	0.018
Loose	0.0001	0.0025

Table 3 TRANSMISSION TIGHTENING TORQUES

	ft.-lb.	N•m
All 1/4 in. fasteners	7-9	9-12
Clutch cable bracket screws	6-8	8-11
Dipstick cover	7-9	9-12
Front mounting bracket bolts	33-38	45-52
Mainshaft and countershaft locknuts (@ side door)	27-33	37-45
Neutral indicator switch	3-5	4-7
Oil tank and fill spoutmounting bolts	7-9	9-12
Rear mounting bracket bolts	13-16	18-22
Shifter arm adjusting screw locknut	20-24	27-33
Shifter arm screw	18-22	24-30
Transmission side door cover mounting bolts		
1/4 in.	7-9	9-12
5/16 in.	13-16	18-22
Support block bolts	7-9	9-12
Top cover mounting bolts	7-9	9-12
Transmission drain plug	14-21	19-28
Transmission mounting bolts	33-38	45-52
Transmission sprocket lockplate screws	7-9	9-12

* Tighten finger tight.

CHAPTER SEVEN

FUEL, EXHAUST AND EMISSION CONTROL SYSTEMS

This chapter includes service procedures for all parts of the fuel, exhaust and emission control systems.

Table 1 lists carburetor jet sizes. **Tables 1-3** are found at the end of the chapter.

AIR FILTER BACKPLATE (All 1991-1995 DOMESTIC AND 1991-1994 INTERNATIONAL MODELS)

Routine air filter service is described in Chapter Three. This section describes service procedures for the air filter backplate assembly.

Refer to **Figure 1** (1991-1992) or **Figure 2** (1993-on).

Removal

1. Remove the cover screw and washer (A, **Figure 3**) and remove the air filter cover (B, **Figure 3**).

2A. On 1991-1992 models, perform the following:

a. Remove the air filter.

b. Disconnect the crankcase breather hose from the backplate.

2B. On 1993-on models, remove the air filter (**Figure 4**) and the breather connectors (**Figure 5**).

3. Remove the bolts and washers (A, **Figure 6**) securing the backplate to the cylinder heads.

CAUTION

*When removing the backplate screws (B, **Figure 6**) in Step 4, loosen each screw a few turns at a time while holding the backplate against the carburetor. This will allow the screw to unthread from the backplate instead of pushing against it. If the screw pushes against the backplate, it may damage the backplate threads.*

4. Remove the backplate screws (B, **Figure 6**). On all 1991 models and 1992-on 49-state models, remove the backplate. On 1992-on California models, perform Step 5.

NOTE

*On 1992-on California models, the backplate is equipped with a solenoid and reed valve assembly (**Figure 7**) that is part of the emission control system.*

5. On 1992-on California models, remove the backplate as follows:
   a. Disconnect the overflow hose from the hose fitting on the backplate.
   b. Disconnect the solenoid harness electrical connector.
   c. Remove the bolt and washers securing the baffle plate and solenoid bracket to the backplate.
   d. Remove the screw securing the solenoid plunger to the butterfly valve assembly and remove the solenoid plunger.
   e. Remove the backplate assembly.

Inspection

1. Inspect the backplate assembly (**Figure 8**) for damage.
2. Replace damaged fasteners.
3. Replace the backplate-to-carburetor gasket (**Figure 9**) if damaged.
4. On 1992-on California, refer to *Emission Control System* in this chapter to inspect or repair the solenoid and reed valve assembly.
5. If necessary, service the air filter as described under *Air Filter Cleaning* in Chapter Three.

Installation

1. On 1992-on California models, perform the following:
   a. Position the backplate and its gasket against the carburetor.
   b. Install the plunger and secure it with its mounting screw.
   c. Install the bolt and washers securing the baffle plate and solenoid bracket to the backplate.

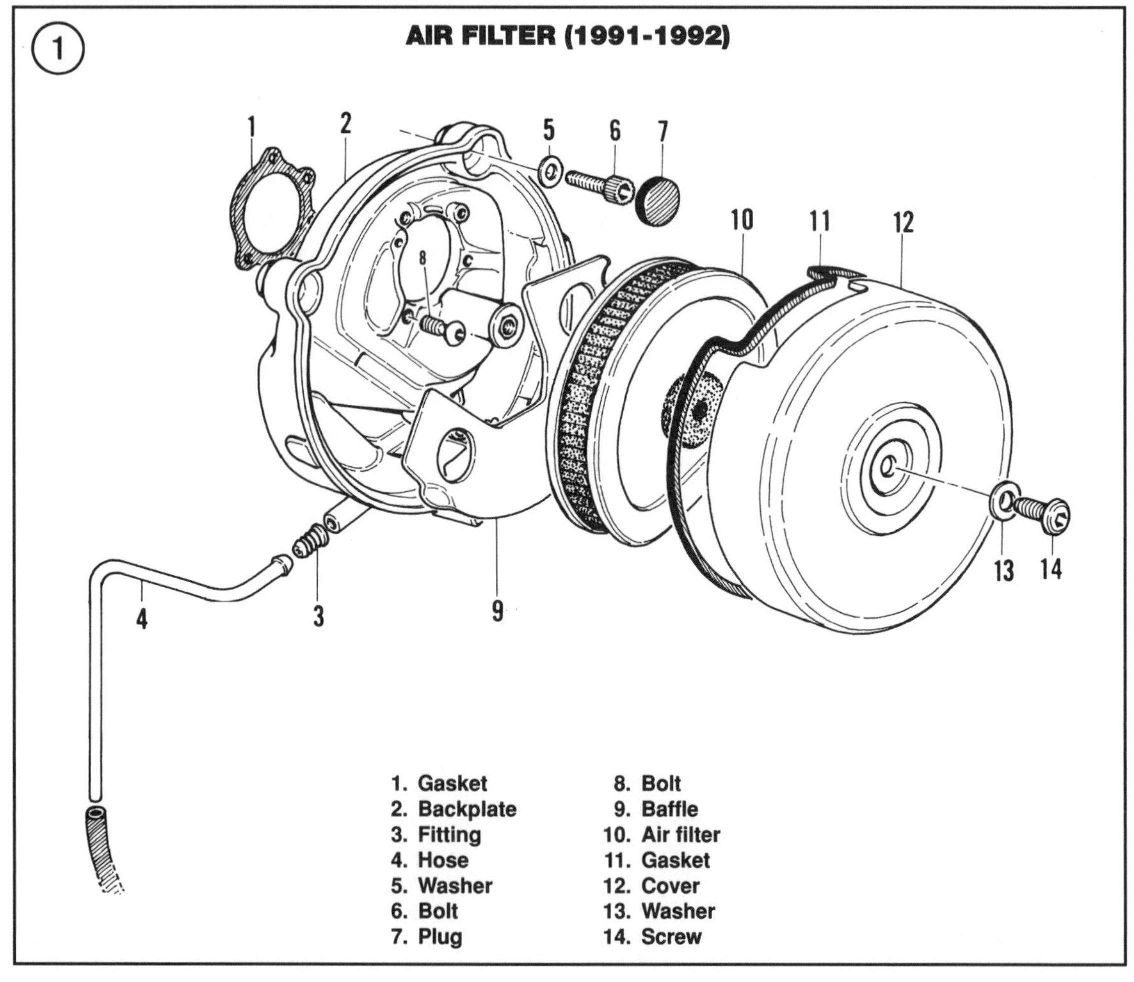

d. Reconnect the solenoid harness electrical connector.

2. Align the backplate and gasket with the carburetor and thread each screw (B, **Figure 6**) into the carburetor. Do not tighten the backplate screws or draw the backplate against the carburetor.

3. Tighten each screw (B, **Figure 6**) a few turns in sequence to draw the backplate evenly, but not tightly, against the carburetor flange. At this point, the backplate will be a loose fit against the carburetor.

4. Apply an antiseize compound to the backplate bolt threads and install the bolts and washers into the cylinder head (A, **Figure 6**). Do not tighten the bolts at this time.

5. Tighten the backplate screws (B, **Figure 6**) to the torque specification in **Table 2**.

6. Tighten the backplate bolts (A, **Figure 6**) to the torque specification in **Table 2**.

7A. On 1991-1992 models, perform the following:

a. Install the rubber plugs (7, **Figure 1**) into the backplate holes.

b. Reconnect the crankcase breather hose to the backplate.

c. Install the air filter.

7B. On 1993-on models, install the air filter (**Figure 4**) and reconnect the breather connectors (**Figure 5**) to the backplate.

8. Install the air filter cover (B, **Figure 3**), washer and cover screw (A, **Figure 3**). Tighten the air filter cover screw to the torque specification in **Table 2**.

AIR FILTER BACKPLATE (1995 INTERNATIONAL MODELS)

Routine air filter service is described in Chapter Three.

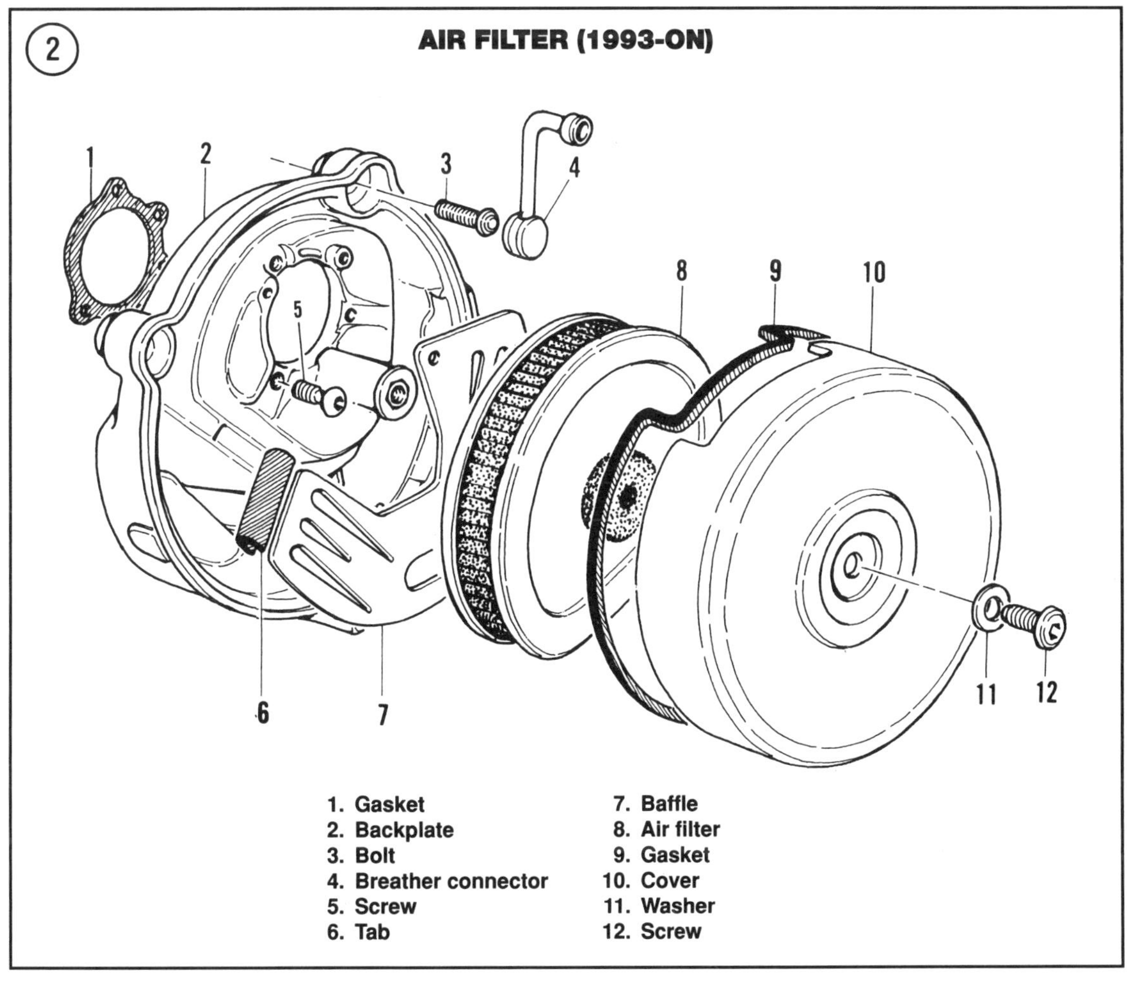

Removal/Installation

Refer to **Figure 10** when servicing the backplate assembly on these models.

CARBURETOR

Carburetor Removal

1. Remove the air filter and backplate as described in this chapter.
2. Disconnect the enrichener cable (**Figure 11**) nut from the mounting bracket. Move the end of the cable out of the mounting bracket.
3. Remove the fuel tank as described in this chapter.
4. Label the 2 cables at the carburetor before disconnecting them. Match the following callouts with the callouts in **Figure 12**:
   a. Throttle cable (A).
   b. Idle cable (B).
5. Disconnect the vacuum hose (C, **Figure 12**) from the carburetor.
6. Twist and then pull the carburetor(**Figure 13**) off the seal ring and intake manifold.
7. Drain the gasoline from the carburetor assembly (**Figure 14**).
8. Inspect the carburetor seal ring (**A, Figure 15**) for excessive wear, hardness, cracks or other damage. Replace the carburetor seal ring if necessary.
9. If necessary, service the intake manifold as described under *Intake Manifold* in this chapter.
10. Plug the intake manifold opening.

Carburetor Installation

1. If removed, seat the seal ring (**A, Figure 15**) onto the intake manifold.
2. Check that the carburetor overflow hose (connected to the float bowl) is unobstructed and mounted onto the float bowl nozzle.
3. Route the enrichener cable between the cylinders and toward its mounting bracket.
4. Slide a new hose clamp over the fuel hose, then connect the fuel hose to the hose nozzle on the carburetor. Do not tighten the clamp at this time.
5. Connect the idle cable (B, **Figure 12**) to the carburetor as follows:
   a. You can identify the idle cable by the small spring on the end of the cable. See **Figure 16**. The throttle cable does not have a spring.

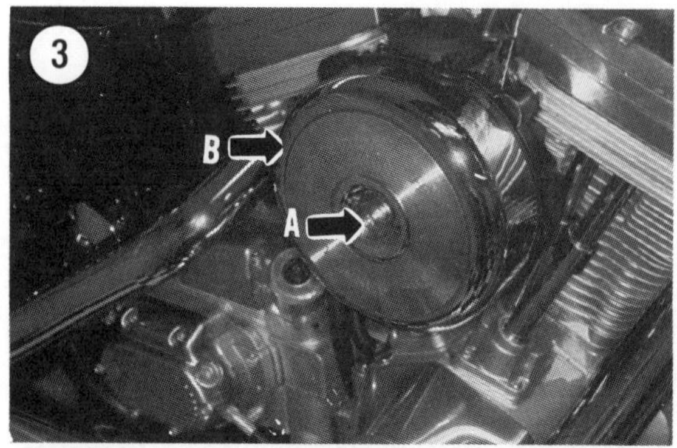

7

SOLENOID-OPERATED BUTTERFLY VALVE (1992-ON CALIFORNIA)

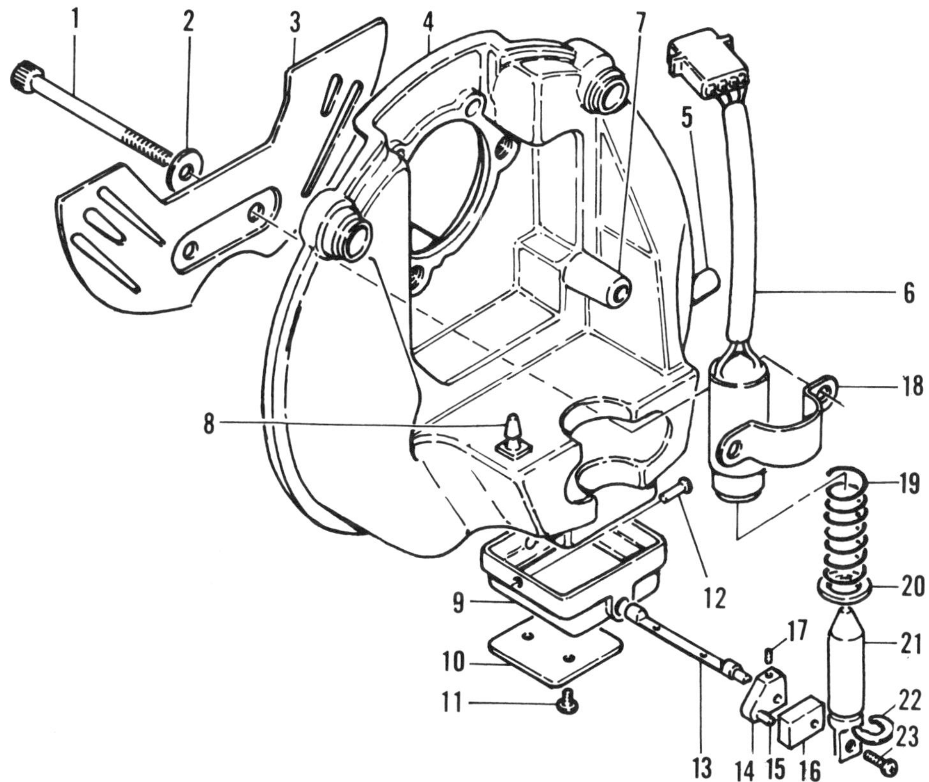

1. Solenoid mounting screws
2. Washer
3. Baffle
4. Backplate
5. Crankcase breather hose nozzle
6. Solenoid
7. Canister inlet hose nozzle
8. Fitting
9. Housing
10. Butterfly valve
11. Screw
12. Rivet
13. Butterfly valve shaft
14. Lever arm
15. Pin
16. Plastic link
17. Set screw
18. Solenoid clamp
19. Spring
20. Plastic washer
21. Plunger
22. E-clip
23. Screw

b. Insert the idle cable sheath into the rear cable bracket guide (installed on the carburetor). See **Figure 17**.
c. Next, fit the end of the idle cable into the carburetor cable plate (A, **Figure 18**).

6. Insert the throttle cable sheath (A, **Figure 12**) into the front cable bracket guide and fit the end of the cable into the carburetor cable plate (B, **Figure 18**).
7. Operate the hand throttle a few times, making sure that the idle (A, **Figure 19**) and the throttle (B,

8

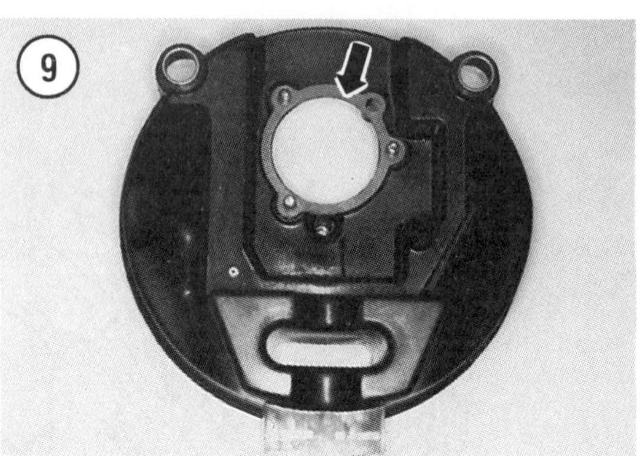

9

10

AIR FILTER HOUSING (1995 INTERNATIONAL MODELS)

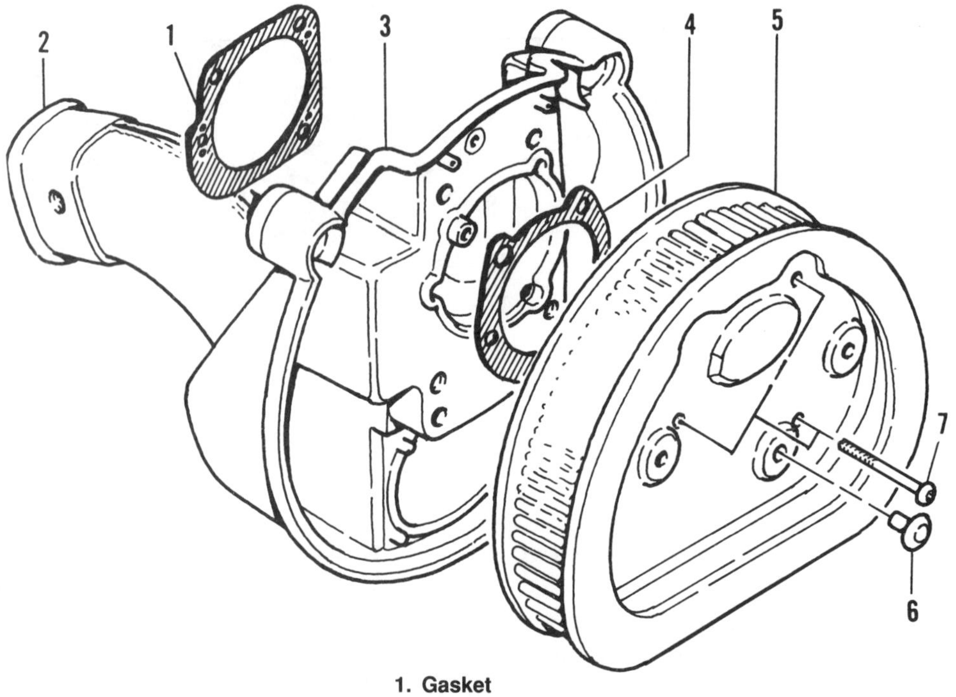

1. Gasket
2. Hose
3. Air filter housing
4. Gasket
5. Air filter
6. Plug
7. Screws

11
CHOKE

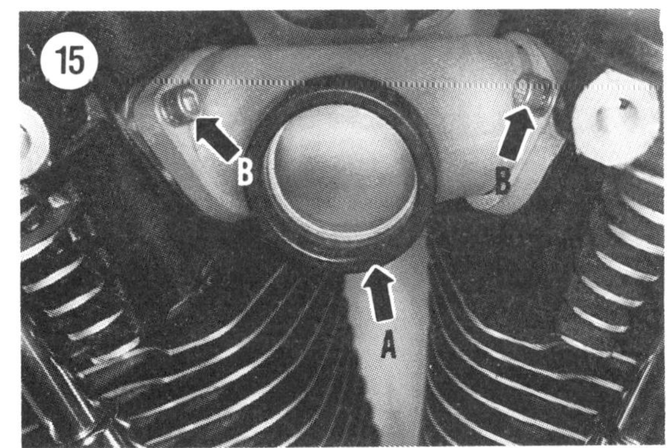
15
B
B
A

12
B
A
C

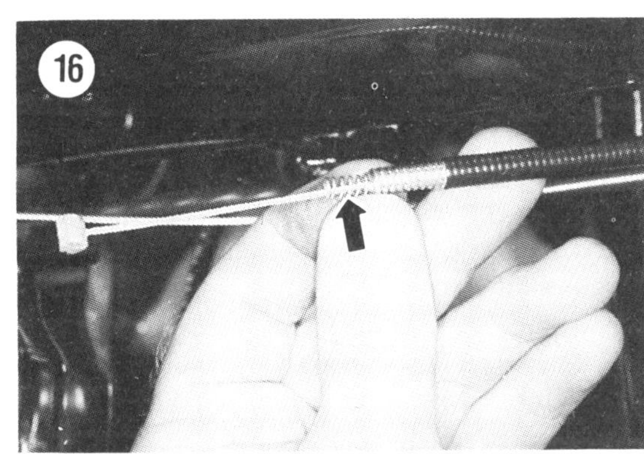
16

13

17

14

18
A
B

Figure 19) cables seat squarely in their cable bracket guides.

8. Align the carburetor squarely with the intake manifold, then push it into the manifold until it bottoms out. Position the carburetor so that it sits square and vertical with the manifold (**Figure 13**).

CAUTION
If the carburetor does not sit squarely in the intake manifold, the misalignment may damage the intake manifold seal ring. This could cause an air leak.

9. Connect the vacuum hose (C, **Figure 12**) to the nozzle on top of the carburetor.
10. Route the carburetor overflow hose between the rear cylinder pushrods, then down between the oil pump cover and crankcase.
11. Secure the enrichener cable to its mounting bracket (**Figure 11**). Adjust the enrichener cable as described in Chapter Three.
12. Before installing the fuel tank, recheck the idle and throttle cable operation. Open and release the hand throttle. Make sure carburetor throttle valve opens and closes smoothly. Check that you routed both cables properly. If necessary, adjust the throttle cables as described in Chapter Three.
13. Tighten the new hose clamp onto the fuel hose at the carburetor.
14. Install the air filter backplate and air filter as described in this chapter.
15. Install the fuel tank as described in this chapter.
16. Start the engine and allow to idle. Check the carburetor overflow hose for leaks.
17. With the engine idling in NEUTRAL, turn the handlebar from side to side. The idle speed must remain the same with no increase in speed. If the idle speed increases while turning the handlebars, the cables are installed incorrectly or damaged. Remove the fuel tank and inspect the cables.

NOTE
*For additional information on the throttle cables, refer to **Throttle and Idle Cable Replacement** in this chapter.*

Intake Manifold Removal/Installation

Refer to **Figure 20** when servicing the intake manifold.

1. Remove the carburetor as described in this chapter.

NOTE
The front and rear intake manifold flanges are different. Label the flanges so that you dont mix them up during reassembly.

2. Remove the Allen bolts and nuts securing the intake manifold (**B, Figure 15**) to the cylinder heads.
3. Remove the intake manifold, flanges and seals (**Figure 21**).

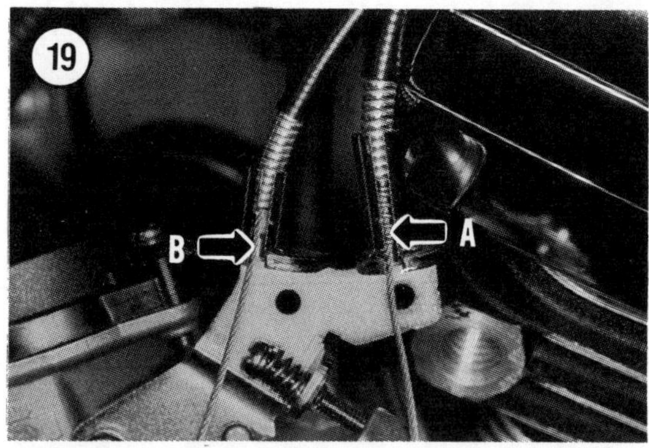

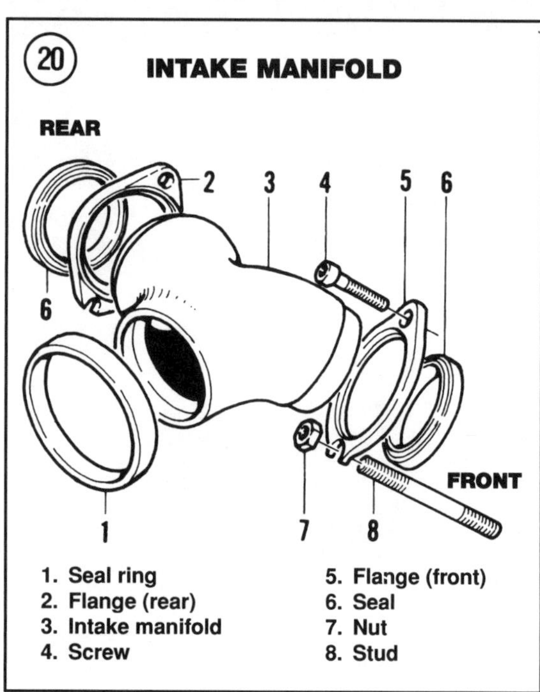

4. Check the intake manifold seals (**Figure 22**) for wear, deterioration or other damage. Replace the seals if necessary.

5. Check the intake manifold seal ring (**Figure 21**) for cracks, flat spots or other damage. Replace if necessary.

6. Install the flanges and seals (**Figure 21**) onto the intake manifold.

7. Install the intake manifold so that the slot in each flange engages with a cylinder head stud. Install the stud nuts, if removed. Do not tighten the nuts at this time.

8. Install the Allen bolts hand-tight.

9. Check that the front and rear seals seat squarely against the cylinder head mating surfaces.

10. Temporarily install the carburetor into the intake manifold.

11. Check that the intake manifold seats squarely against the cylinder heads. Then check that the carburetor seats squarely in the intake manifold. Remove the carburetor.

12. Tighten the intake manifold nuts and Allen bolts to the torque specification listed in **Table 2**.

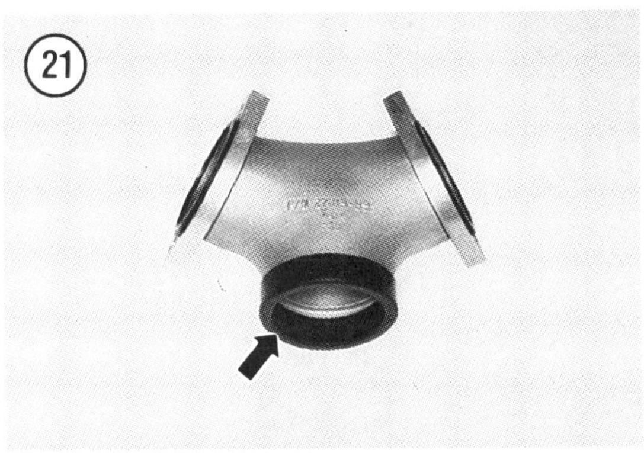

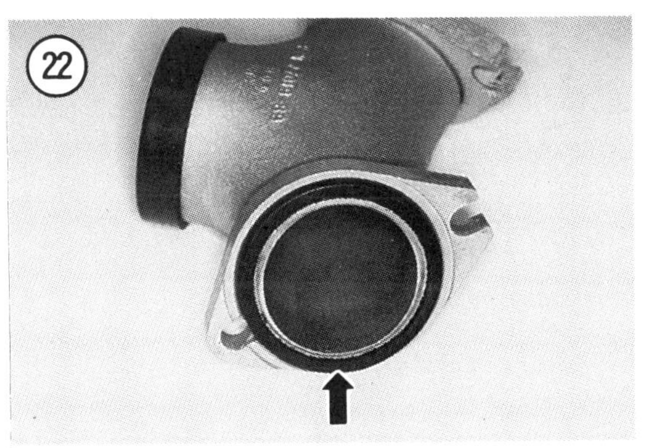

CAUTION
Do not attempt to align the intake manifold after tightening the nuts and bolts. This will damage the seals. Loosen the nuts and bolts, then align the manifold.

13. Install the carburetor as described in this chapter.

Disassembly

Refer to **Figure 23** for this procedure.

1. Disconnect the overflow hose from the float bowl (**Figure 24**).

2. Unscrew and remove the enrichener cable (**Figure 25**).

3. Remove the screws and washers securing the throttle cable bracket to the carburetor. Remove the bracket (**Figure 26**).

4. Remove the remaining cover screws and washers, then remove the cover (**Figure 27**) and spring (**Figure 28**).

5. Remove the vacuum piston (**Figure 29**) from the carburetor housing. Do not damage the jet needle sticking out of the bottom of the vacuum piston.

NOTE
The accelerator pump diaphragm is mounted in a housing on the bottom of the float bowl. The accelerator pump reduces engine hesitation by injecting a fine spray of fuel into the carburetor intake passage during sudden acceleration. Because the pump is synchronized with the throttle valve, note the position of the throttle and pump rods when removing the float bowl in the following steps.

6. Remove the accelerator pump diaphragm as follows:
   a. Remove the screws and lockwashers holding the pump cover (**Figure 30**) to the float bowl and remove the cover.
   b. Remove the small pump cover O-ring (**Figure 31**).
   c. Remove the spring (A, **Figure 32**) and diaphragm (B, **Figure 32**).

7. Remove the float bowl as follows:
   a. Remove the screws and washers securing the float bowl (C, **Figure 32**) to the carburetor. Remove the float bowl body while allowing

7

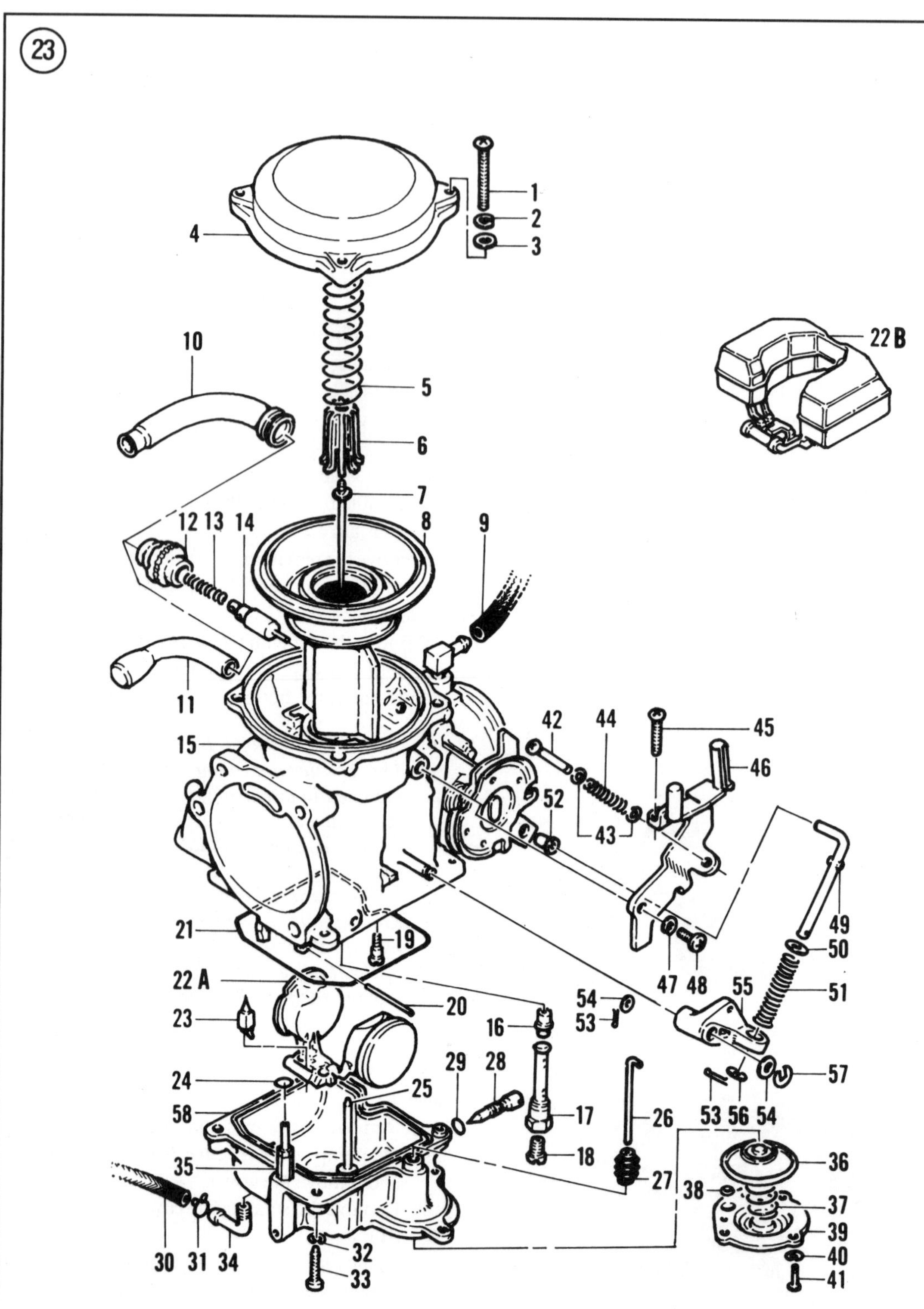
23
1
2
3
4
5
6
7
8
9
10
11
12 13 14
15
16
17
18
19
20
21
22 A
22 B
23
24
25
26
27
28
29
30 31 34
32
33
35
36
37
38
39
40
41
42
43
44
45
46
47 48
49
50
51
52
53
54
55
53 56 54
57
58

CARBURETOR

1. Screw
2. Lockwasher
3. Flat washer
4. Cover
5. Spring
6. Spring seat
7. Jet needle
8. Vacuum piston
9. Vacuum hose
10. Cable guide
11. Starter cap
12. Cable sealing cap
13. Spring
14. Enrichener valve
15. Body
16. Needle jet
17. Needle jet holder
18. Main jet
19. Pilot jet
20. Float pin
21. O-ring

22A. Float (1991)
22B. Float (1992-on)

23. Fuel valve and clip
24. O-ring
25. Overflow pipe
26. Rod
27. Boot
28. Drain screw
29. O-ring
30. Hose
31. Clamp
32. Lockwasher
33. Screw
34. Fitting
35. Accelerator pump nozzle
36. Diaphragm
37. Spring
38. O-ring
39. Cover
40. Lockwasher
41. Screw
42. Idle adjust screw
43. Washer
44. Spring
45. Screw
46. Throttle cable bracket
47. Washer
48. Screw
49. Rod

50 Washer

51. Spring
52. Collar
53. Cotter pin
54. Washer
55. Lever
56. Washer
57. E-clip
58. Float bowl

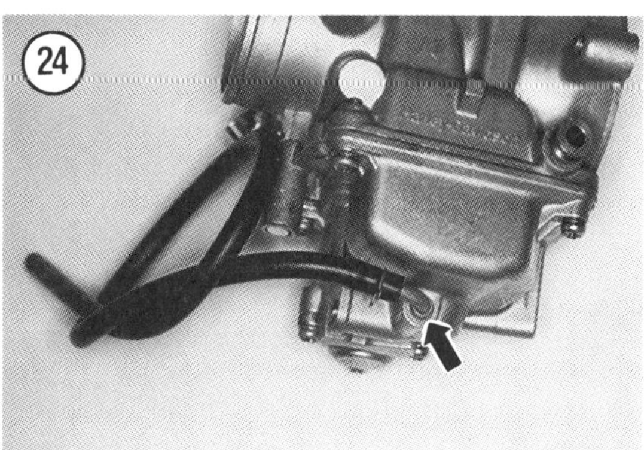

7

the pump rod (**Figure 33**) to withdraw from the boot on the bowl.

b. Disconnect the pump rod from the lever assembly on the carburetor (**Figure 34**).

c. Carefully pull the boot (**Figure 35**) off the float bowl.

8A. On 1991 models, remove the float pin (**Figure 36**) and lift off the float and need valve assembly (**Figure 37**).

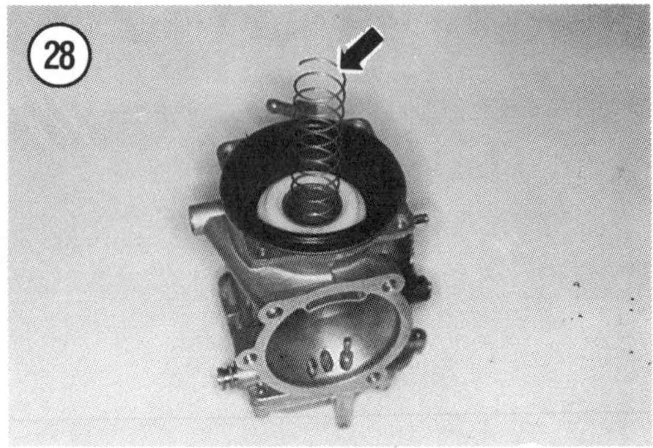

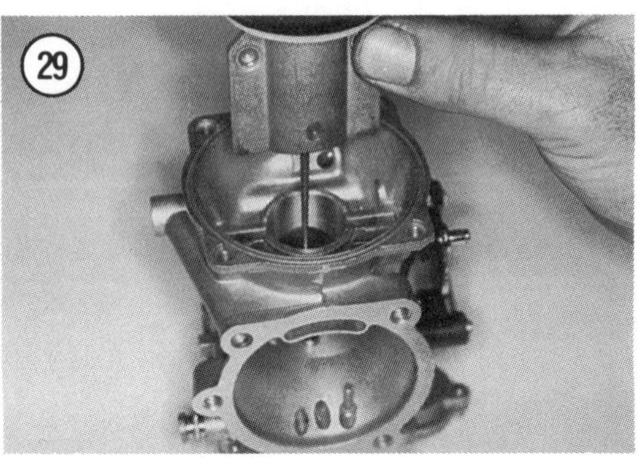

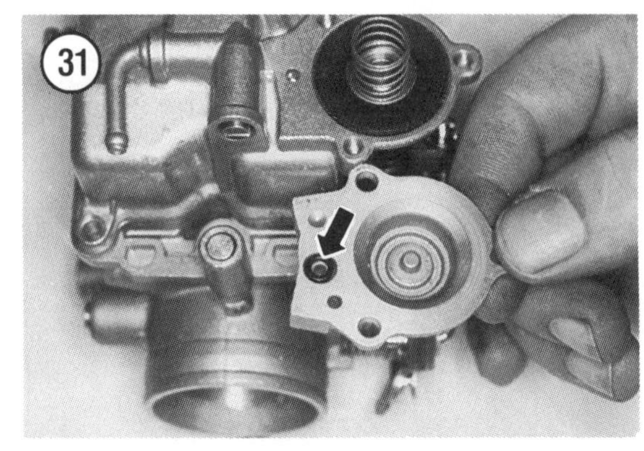

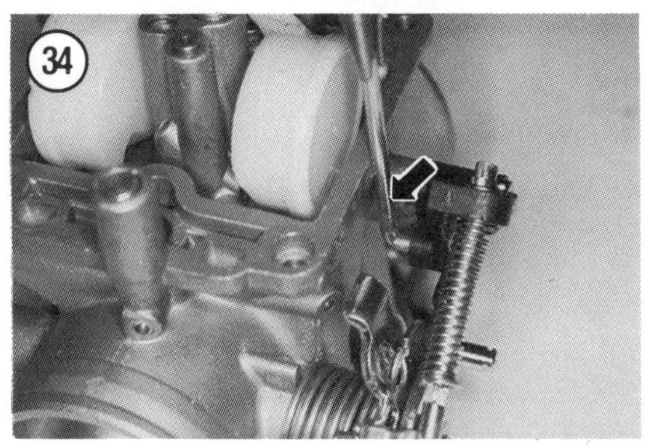

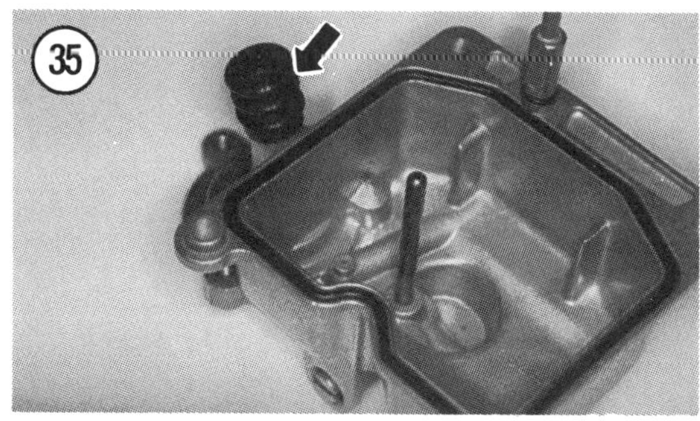

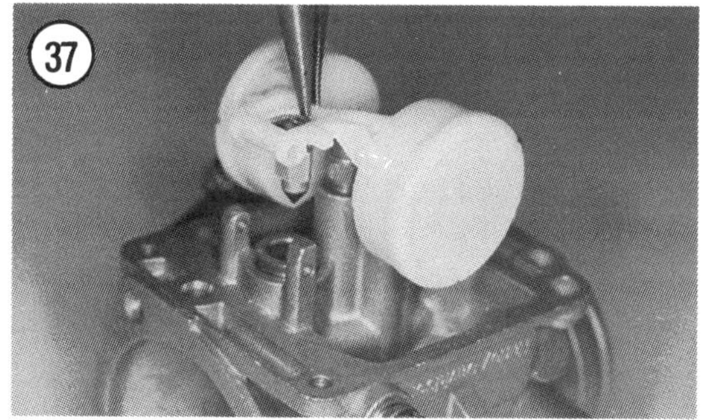

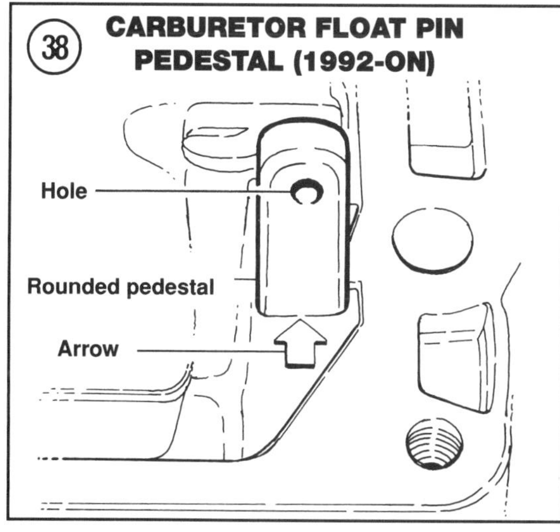

NOTE
*On late model carburetors, one of the float pin pedestals has an interference fit that holds the float pin in place. An arrow, cast into the carburetor, points to this pedestal (**Figure 38**). To remove this float pin, you must tap it out from the interference side (toward the arrow).*

CAUTION
If you remove the float pin from the loose pedestal side (side opposite the arrow), the opposite pedestal may crack or break off. If this happens, you must replace the carburetor.

8B. On 1992 and later models, tap out the float pin (**Figure 39**) and then lift off the float and needle valve assembly (**Figure 40**).

9. Remove the main jet (**Figure 41**) and needle jet (**Figure 42**).

10. Remove the needle jet from the needle jet bore in the carburetor (**Figure 43**).

11. Loosen and remove the pilot jet (**Figure 44**).

NOTE
*Replacement parts are not available for the throttle valve (**Figure 45**) assembly. Do not remove it.*

Inspection

1. Clean all metal parts removed from the carburetor body in a good grade of carburetor cleaner. This solution is available at most automotive supply stores, in a small, resealable tank with a dip basket. Follow its manufacturer's instructions for correct soaking time.

CAUTION
Do not soak the carburetor body in carburetor cleaner. The cleaner can damage the non-removable rubber seals used at the throttle shaft assembly. Likewise, do not place gaskets, plastic, rubber or any other non-metallic part in the carburetor cleaner.

CAUTION
Do not clean the fuel valve in a cold acid dip as the solution may damage the valves alloy surface.

2. Remove all parts from the cleaner and rinse in clear cold water, then dry with compressed air, if available. Blow out the jets (**Figure 46**) with compressed air. *Do not* use a piece of wire to clean them as minor gouges in a jet can alter the flow rate and upset the air/fuel mixture.
3. Make sure the needle jet holder (**Figure 46**) bleed tube orifices are clear.
4. Make sure all fuel and air openings are clear. Blow out with compressed air if necessary.

42

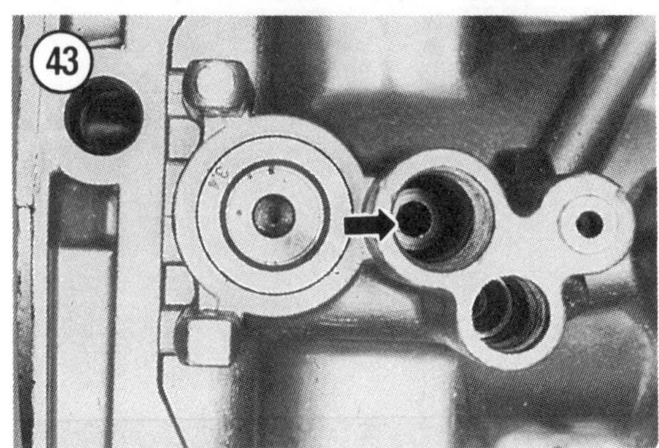
43

44

41

45

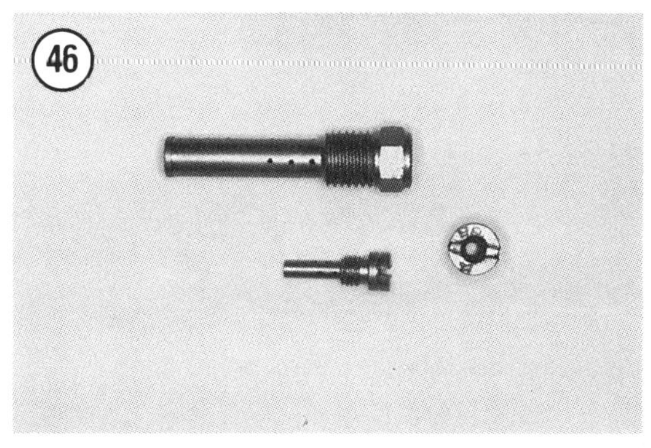

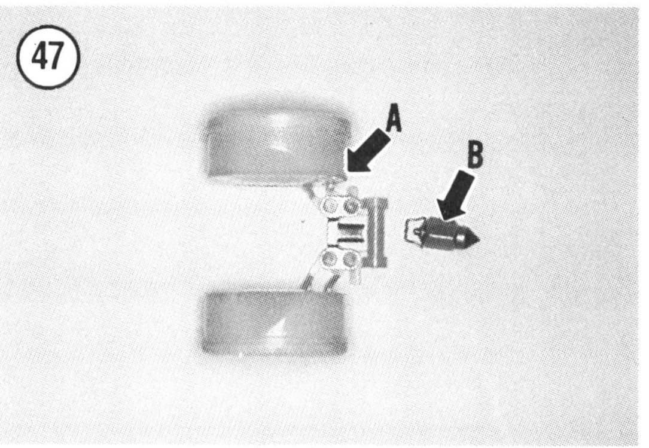

5. Inspect the float for deterioration or damage. See A, **Figure 47** (1991) or **Figure 48** (1992-on). If the float is suspected of leakage, place it in a container of water and push it down. If the float sinks or if bubbles appear (showing a leak), replace the float.

6. Check the fuel valve (B, **Figure 47**) and seat (**Figure 49**) contact areas. Both contact surfaces must appear smooth without any wear or other damage. Replace the fuel valve if damaged. The seat is a permanent part of the carburetor housing; if damaged, replace the housing.

7. A damaged accelerating pump diaphragm (**Figure 50**) will cause poor acceleration. Hold the diaphragm up to a strong light and check the diaphragm for pin holes, cracks or other damage. Replace if necessary.

8. Remove the accelerator pump nozzle and its O-ring (**Figure 51**) from the float bowl. Clean the nozzle with compressed air.

9. Replace the pump rod if bent or worn.

10. O-rings become hardened after prolonged use and lose their ability to seal properly. Inspect all O-rings and replace if necessary. When replacing an

7

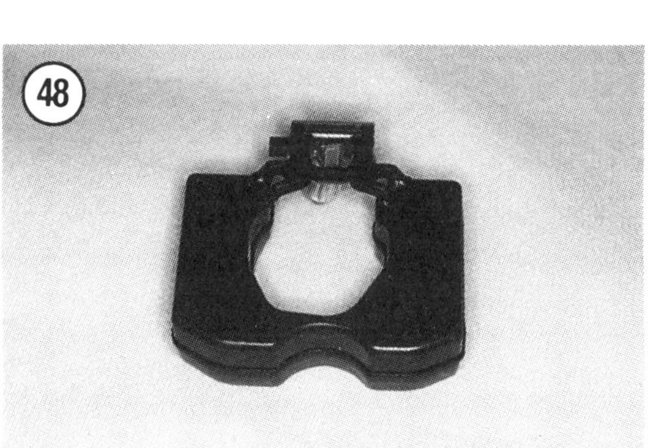

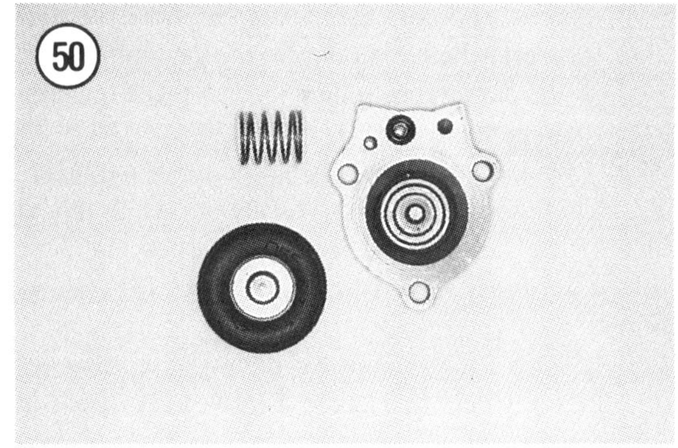

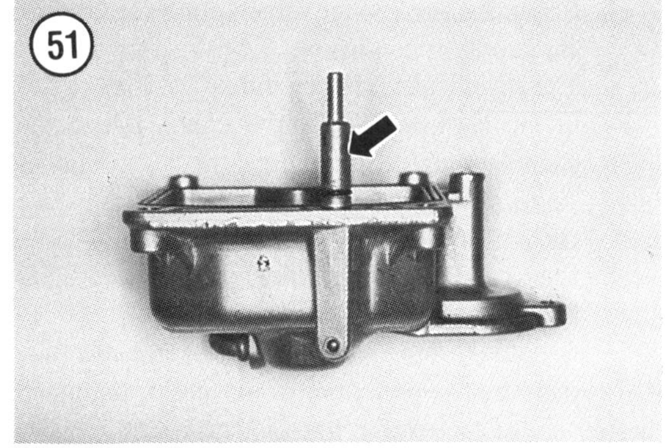

O-ring, make sure the new O-ring fits in its groove properly. See **Figure 52**, typical.

11. Inspect the pilot jet (**Figure 46**) for wear or damage that may have occurred during removal. Check the slot in the top of the jet for cracks or breakage. Do not install a damaged pilot jet.

NOTE

Step 12 describes vacuum piston bench checks. To test the vacuum piston with the engine running, refer to Fuel System in Chapter Two.

12. Check the vacuum piston as follows:
   a. Check the spring (**Figure 53**) for fatigue, stretching, distortion or other damage.
   b. Check the vacuum passage through the bottom of the piston (**Figure 54**) for contamination. Clean the passage if blocked.
   c. Check the piston sides for roughness, nicks, cracks or distortion. If the piston is damaged, check the mating grooves in the carburetor for damage. You can remove minor roughness with emery cloth. However, replace the vacuum piston if damaged.
   d. Hold the vacuum piston up to a light and check the diaphragm for pin holes, tearing, cracks, deterioration or other damage. Check the diaphragm where it mounts to the vacuum piston. If the diaphragm is damaged, replace the vacuum piston.
   e. Check the jet needle for bending or damage.

13. A plugged, improperly seating or contaminated enrichener system will cause hard starting and poor low and high speed performance. Check the following:
   a. Cheek for a rough or damaged enrichener valve. Check the needle (**Figure 55**) on the end of the enrichener valve for bending or contamination.
   b. Check the enrichener valve spring for fatigue, stretching or distortion.
   c. The enrichener valve chamber (A, **Figure 56**) in the carburetor must be clean. Clean the chamber carefully, making sure the enrichener valve air inlet and the air/fuel passages are clear.
   d. Check the enrichener valve cable (**Figure 57**) for kinks or other damage.

14. Check the throttle rod (**Figure 58**) and all external carburetor components for missing or damaged parts.

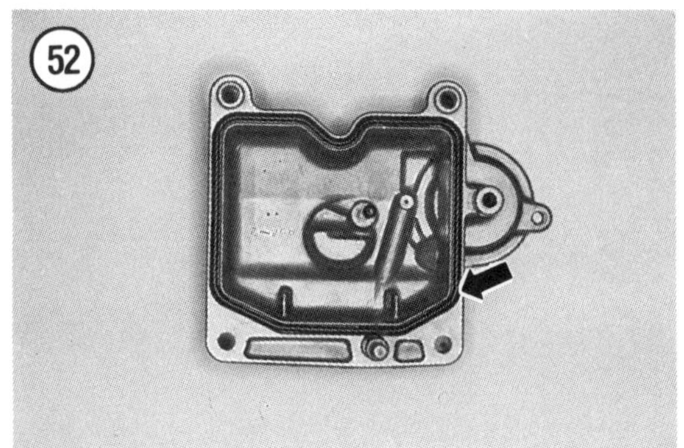

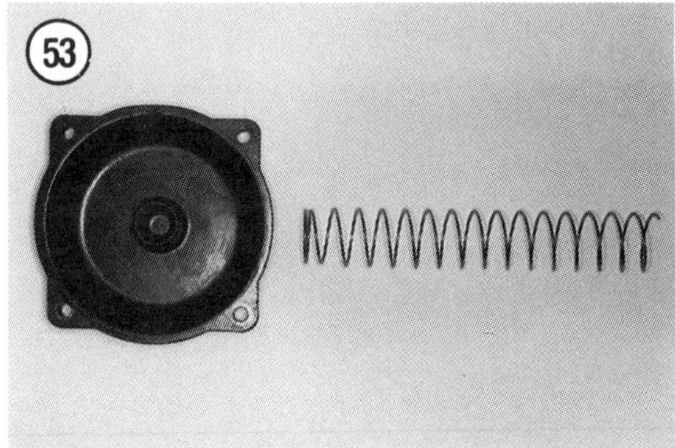

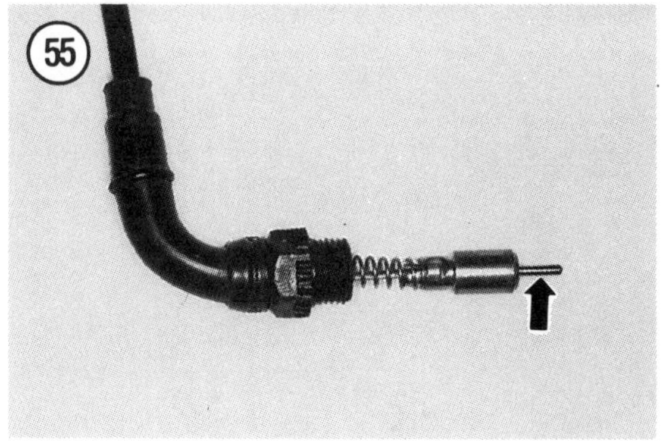

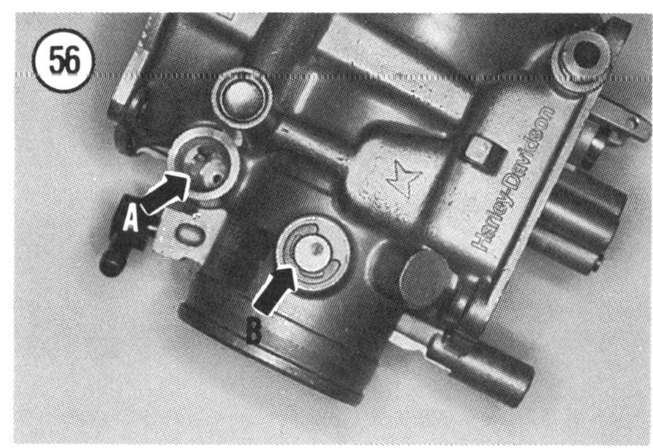

15. Make sure the throttle valve shaft E-clip (B, **Figure 56**) is properly secured in the shaft groove.

Assembly

Refer to **Figure 23** when assembling the carburetor.

1. Clean all parts before assembly.
2. Install and tighten the pilot jet (**Figure 44**).

NOTE
The needle jet has 2 different sides and can be installed incorrectly. Install it as described in Step 3.

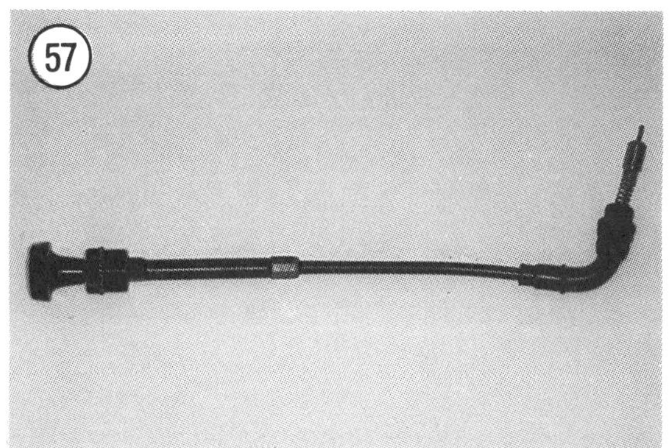

3. Install the needle jet into its passage (**Figure 43**) so that the end with the larger opening faces toward the top of the carburetor.
4. Install the needle jet holder (**Figure 42**) into the main jet passage and tighten securely.
5. Install and tighten the main jet (**Figure 41**).

6A. On 1991 models, install the float as follows:

a. Install the fuel valve onto the float (**Figure 59**) and position the float onto the carburetor so the valve drops into its seat.
b. Align the float pivot pin with the 2 carburetor pedestals and install the pin (**Figure 60**).

NOTE
*On late model carburetors, one of the float pin pedestals has an interference fit that holds the float pin in place. An arrow, cast into the carburetor, points to this pedestal (**Figure 61**). To install the float pin, you must tap it in from the loose pedestal side (opposite the arrow).*

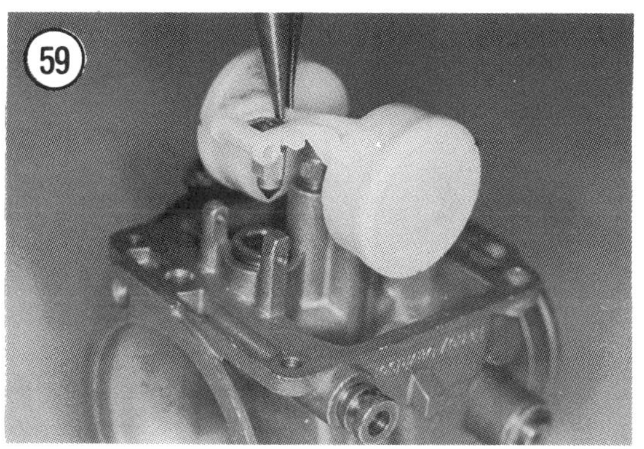

CAUTION
If you install the float pin from the tight pedestal side (side opposite the arrow), the opposite pedestal may crack or break off. If this happens, you must replace the carburetor.

6B. On 1992-on models, install the float as follows:

a. Install the fuel valve onto the float (**Figure 62**) and position the float onto the carburetor so that the valve drops into its seat.
b. Align the float pin with the 2 carburetor pedestals and install the pin (**Figure 63**).

7. Check the float level as described in this chapter.
8. Assemble and install the float bowl as follows:

a. Insert the accelerator pump nozzle into the float bowl. Install the O-ring onto the nozzle. See **Figure 51**.
b. Install the rubber boot (A, **Figure 64**) and O-ring (B, **Figure 64**) onto the float bowl.
c. Connect the pump rod onto the lever assembly on the carburetor (**Figure 65**).
d. Insert the pump rod through the boot on the float bowl and engage the rod with the diaphragm while installing the float bowl (**Figure 66**). The pump rod must still be attached to the lever assembly as shown in **Figure 67**. Check also to see if the pump rod is visible through the hole in the pump chamber in the float bowl (**Figure 68**). If not, remove and reinstall the float bowl and pump rod.
e. Install the float bowl screws and washers and tighten securely in a crisscross pattern.

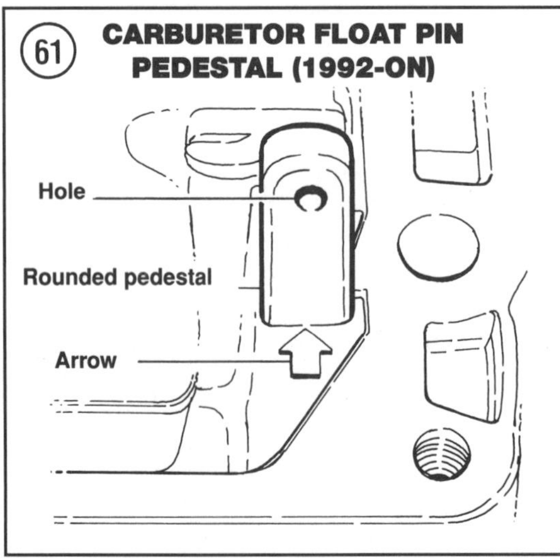

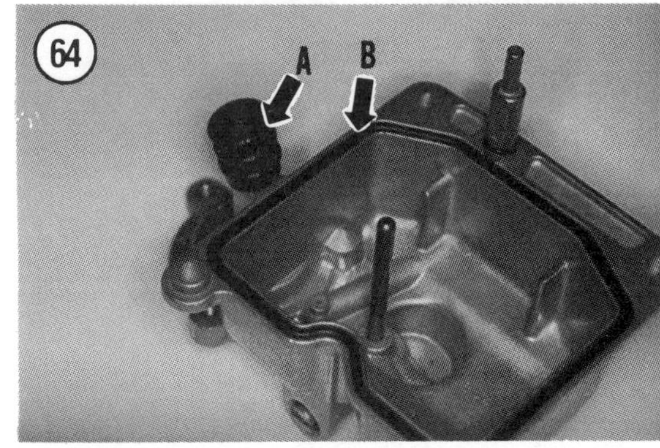

66

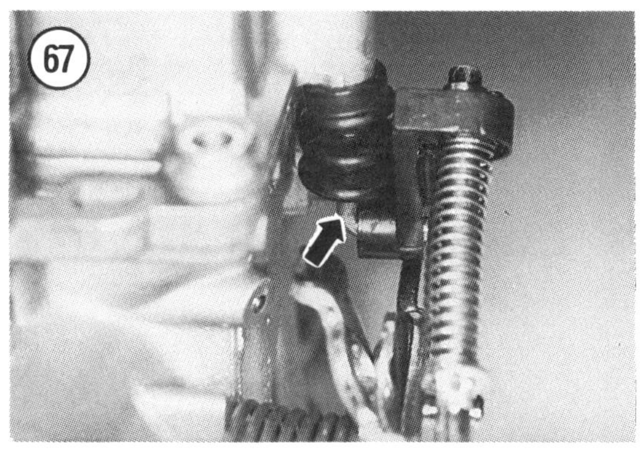
67

9. Install the accelerator pump diaphragm assembly as follows:

   a. Insert the accelerator pump diaphragm into the bottom of the float bowl. Make sure the diaphragm seats around the bowl groove (**Figure 69**).
   b. Install the spring into the center of the accelerator pump diaphragm (**Figure 70**).
   c. Install the O-ring into the cover passageway hole (**Figure 71**).
   d. Align the cover assembly with the diaphragm and bowl and install the cover assembly. Install the screws and lockwashers and tighten securely. See **Figure 72**.

10. Drop the jet needle through the center hole in the vacuum piston. Install the spring seat over the top of the needle to secure it.

11. Align the slides on the vacuum piston with the grooves in the carburetor bore and install the vacuum piston (**Figure 73**). The slides on the piston are offset, so the piston can only be installed one way. When installing the vacuum piston, make sure the jet needle drops through the needle jet.

7

68

70

69

71

12. Seat the outer edge of the vacuum piston into the piston chamber groove.
13. Insert the spring (**Figure 74**) into the vacuum piston so that the end of the spring fits over the spring seat.
14. Align the free end of the spring with the carburetor top and install the top onto the carburetor.
15. Hold the carburetor top in place and lift the vacuum piston with your finger. The piston must move smoothly. If the piston movement is rough or sluggish, the spring is installed incorrectly. Remove the carburetor top and reinstall the spring.
16. Install the 3 carburetor top screws, lockwashers and flat washers finger-tight (**Figure 75**).
17. Install the throttle cable bracket (A, **Figure 76**) onto the carburetor so that the end of the idle speed screw engages the top of the throttle cam stop (B, **Figure 76**). Hold the bracket in place and install the bracket's side mounting screw and washer; tighten the screw securely. Then install the upper bracket mounting screw (**Figure 77**), lockwasher and flat washer finger-tight.
18. Tighten the 4 carburetor cap screws securely in a crisscross pattern.

72

73

74

75

76

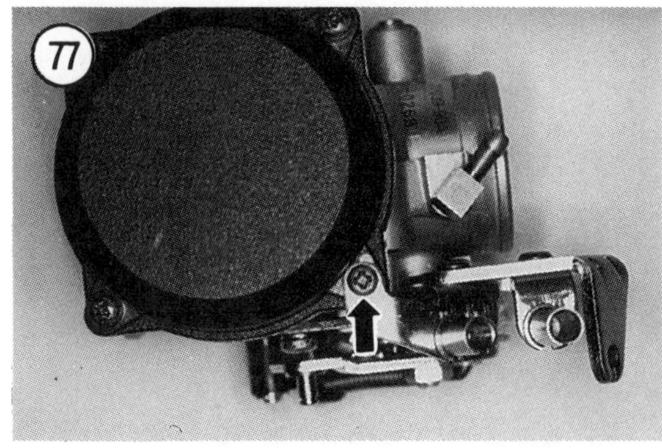
77

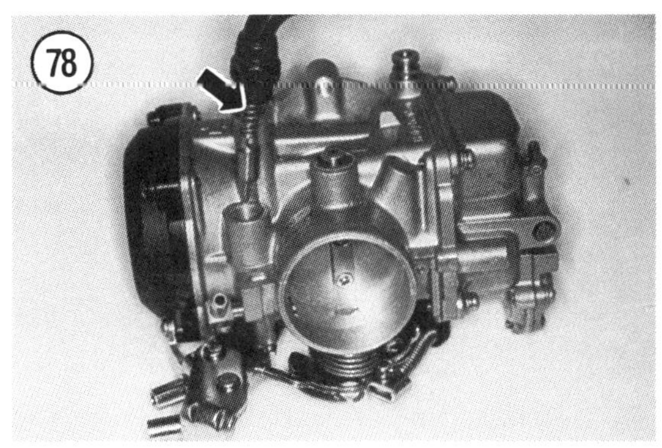

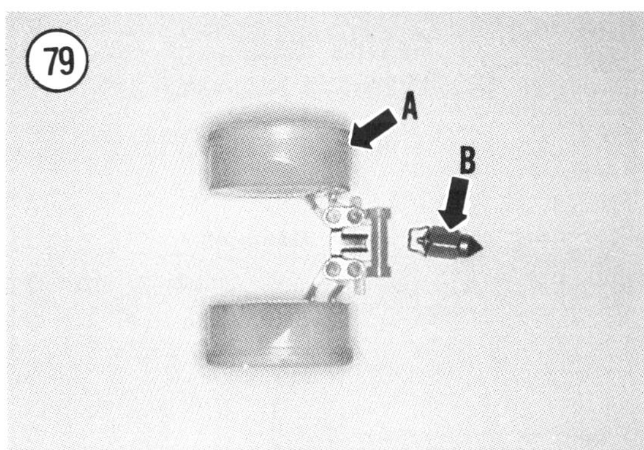

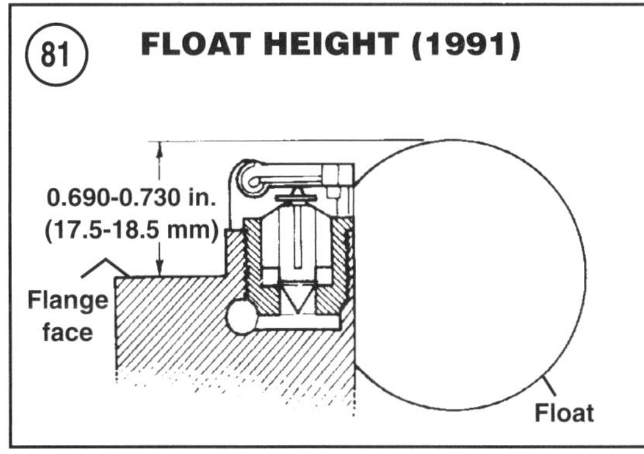

19. Align the enrichener valve needle with the needle passage in the carburetor (**Figure 78**) and install the enrichener valve. Tighten the valve nut securely.

20. Install the float bowl overflow hose and secure it with its clamp.

Float Level Adjustment (1991)

You must remove and partially disassemble the carburetor for this adjustment.

NOTE

*A 3-sided fuel valve (B, **Figure 79**) is installed on all 1991 carburetors. Starting with 1992 models, Harley-Davidson replaced the 3-sided fuel valve with a 4-sided fuel valve. The 4-sided fuel valve is now the replacement fuel valve for all 1991 model carburetors. If your 1991 model carburetor is equipped with a 3-sided fuel valve, service the float level as described in this section. If your 1991 model carburetor is equipped with a 4-sided fuel valve, check and set the float level as described under **Float Level Adjustment (1992-on)** in this chapter.*

1. Remove the carburetor as described in this chapter.
2. Remove the float bowl as described in this chapter.
3. Before checking the float level, check the alignment of the 2 float halves (**Figure 80**). If the float halves do not align with each other, remove the float and check it for damage.
4. Turn the carburetor to position the float bowl as shown in **Figure 81**. Measure the float height from the face of the bowl mounting flange surface to the bottom float surface (**Figure 81**). Do not apply pressure to the float when measuring. The correct float height is 0.690-0.730 in. (17.5-18.5 mm).
5. If the float level is incorrect, remove the float pin and float.
6. Bend the float tang with a screwdriver to adjust.
7. Reinstall the float and the float pin and recheck the float level. Repeat until the float level is correct.
8. Reinstall the float bowl and carburetor as described in this chapter.

Float Adjustment (1992-on)

You must remove and partially disassemble the carburetor for this adjustment.

1. Remove the carburetor as described in this chapter.
2. Remove the float bowl as described in this chapter.
3. Before checking the float level, check the alignment of the 2 float halves (**Figure 82**). If the float halves do not align with each other, remove the float and check it for damage.
4. Place the carburetor intake spigot on a flat surface as shown in **Figure 83**. This is the base position.
5. Tilt the carburetor counterclockwise 15-20° as shown in **Figure 84**. At this position, the float will come to rest without compressing the pin return spring.

NOTE

If you tilt the carburetor less than 15° or more than 20°, the float measurement will be incorrect.

6. Measure from the carburetor flange surface to the top of the float as shown in **Figure 84**. When measuring float level, make sure you do not compress the float. The correct float level measurement is 0.413-0.453 in. (10.5-11.5 mm).
7. If the float level is incorrect, remove the float pin and float. If your carburetor has an arrow pointing toward one of the float pin pedestals (**Figure 85**), remove the float pin as described under *Carburetor Disassembly* in this chapter.
8. Bend the float tang with a screwdriver to adjust.
9. Reinstall the float and the float pin and recheck the float level. If your carburetor has an arrow pointing toward one of the float pin pedestals (**Figure 85**), install the float pin as described under *Carburetor Reassembly* in this chapter.
10. Repeat these steps until the float level is correct.
11. Reinstall the float bowl and carburetor as described in this chapter.

THROTTLE AND IDLE CABLE REPLACEMENT

Figure 86 shows the throttle housing and cable assembly. **Figure 87** and **Figure 88** identify the cables as follows:

82

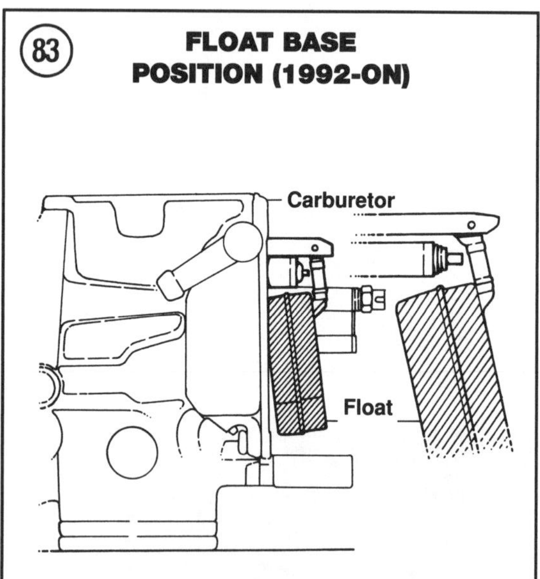

83

FLOAT BASE POSITION (1992-ON)

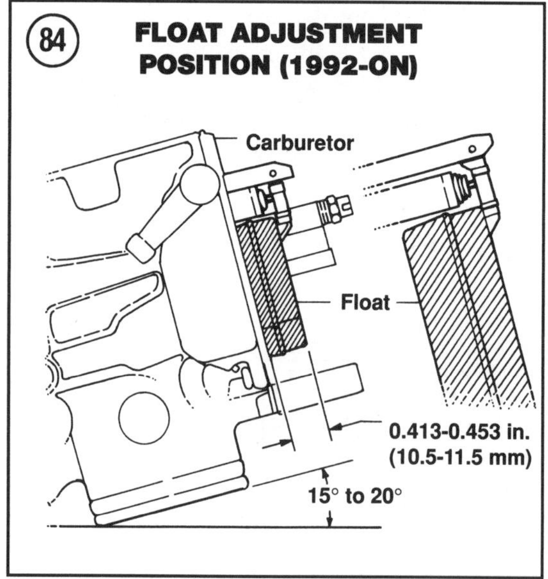

84

FLOAT ADJUSTMENT POSITION (1992-ON)

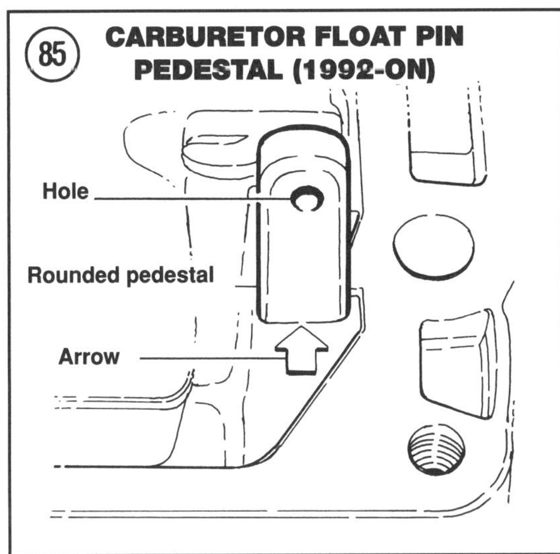

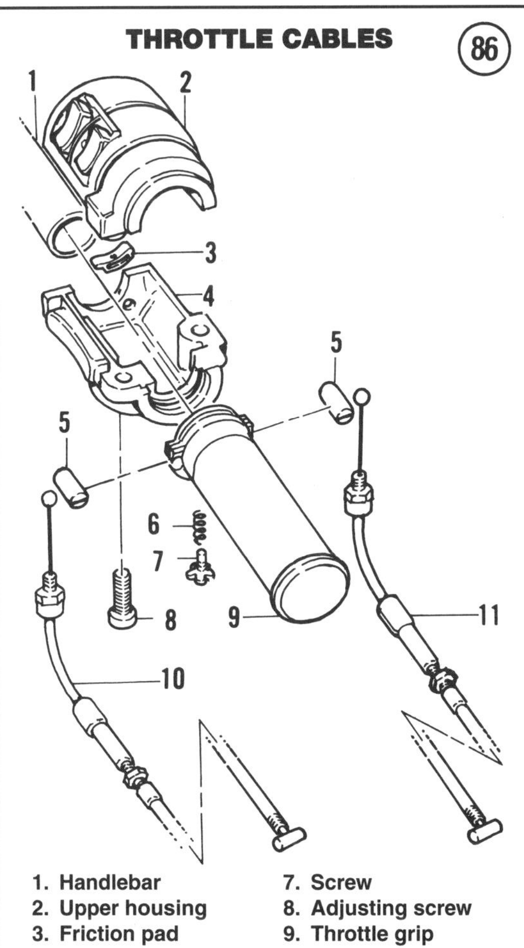

1. Handlebar
2. Upper housing
3. Friction pad
4. Lower housing
5. Ferrule
6. Spring
7. Screw
8. Adjusting screw
9. Throttle grip
10. Idle cable
11. Throttle cable

a. Throttle cable (A, **Figure 87** and A, **Figure 88**).

b. Idle cable (B, **Figure 87** and B, **Figure 88**).

NOTE

You can also identify the throttle and idle cables by checking the size of the threads used on the cables threaded adjusters. The throttle cable uses a 5/16-18 threaded adjuster. The idle cable uses a 1/4-20 threaded adjuster.

1. Remove the fuel tank as described in this chapter.
2. Remove the air filter and backplate as described in this chapter.
3. Draw a diagram of each cable as it is routed from the handlebar to the carburetor.
4. Slide the rubber boot away from each cable adjuster (at the handlebar).

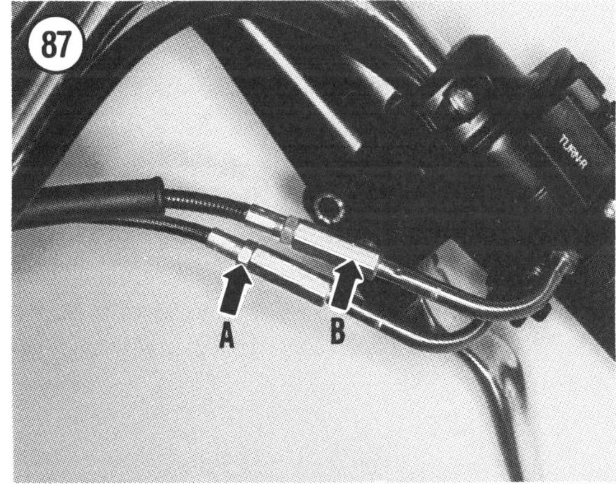

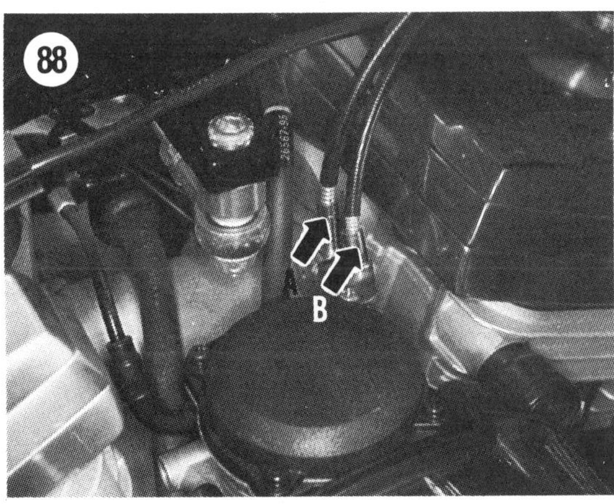

5. Loosen the cable adjust nuts and turn the cable adjusters to obtain as much cable slack as possible. See A and B, **Figure 88**.

6. Loosen the cable jam nuts (A, **Figure 89**) at the throttle housing.

7. Remove the screws (B, **Figure 89**) securing the upper and lower housings to the handlebar, then separate the housings.

8. Remove the friction pad (**Figure 90**) from the lower throttle housing.

9. Unhook the cables (**Figure 91**) from the throttle grip and remove the ferrule from the end of each cable. See **Figure 92**.

10. Unscrew and remove each cable from the lower housing assembly.

11. Disconnect the idle cable (A, **Figure 93**) and throttle cable (B, **Figure 93**) from the carburetor. **Figure 93** shows the cables with the carburetor removed for clarity.

12. Remove the cables from the bike.

13. Clean the throttle grip assembly and dry thoroughly. Check the throttle slots for cracks or other damage. Replace the throttle if necessary.

14. The friction adjust screw is secured to the lower switch housing with a circlip. If necessary, remove the friction spring, circlip, spring and friction adjust screw. Check these parts for wear or damage. Replace damaged parts and reverse to install. Make sure the circlip seats in the friction screw groove completely.

15. Clean the throttle area on the handlebar with solvent or electrical contact cleaner.

16. Apply a light coat of graphite to the housing inside surfaces and to the handlebar.

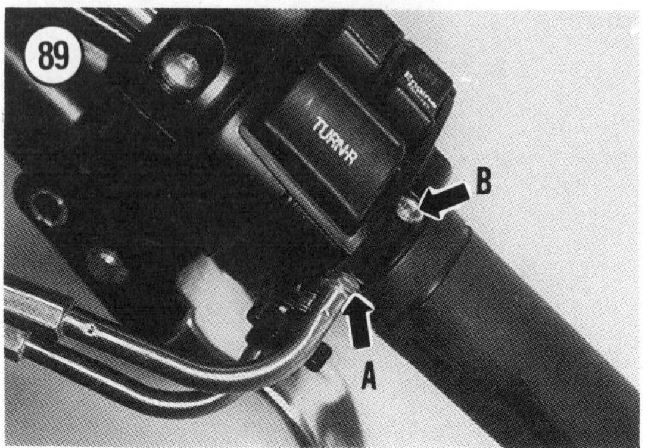

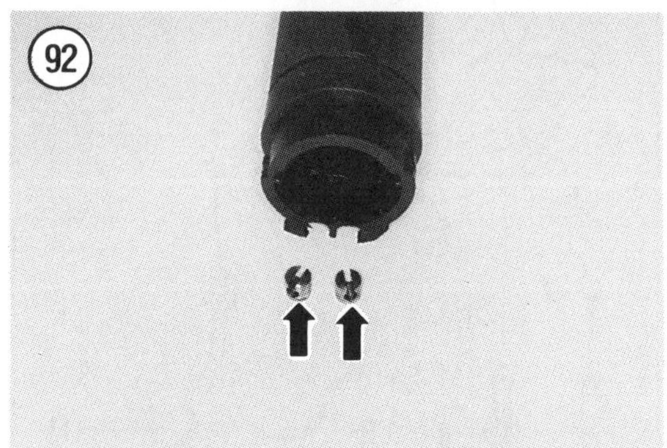

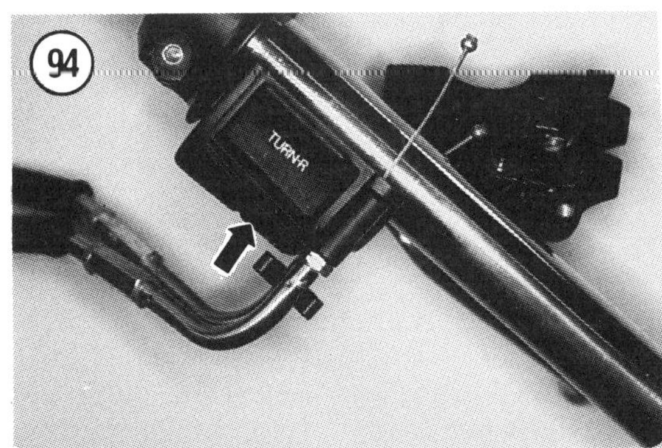

94

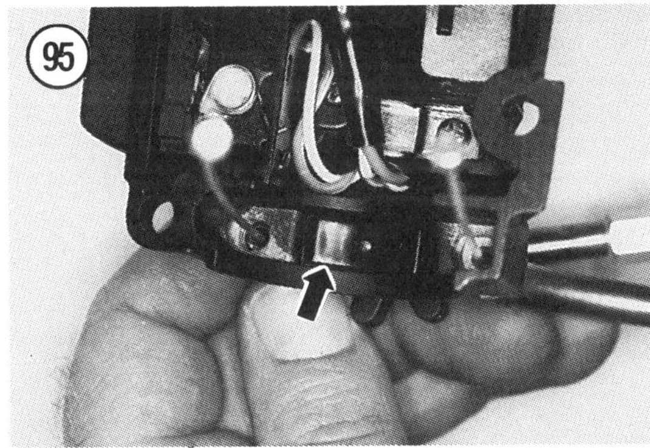

95

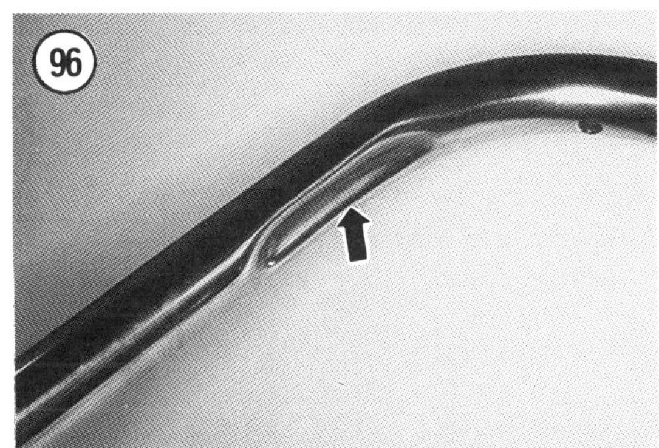

96

NOTE
Refer to the information at the beginning of this procedure to identify the new cables.

17. Reconnect the idle and throttle cables to the lower housing (**Figure 94**). Do not tighten the jam nuts at this time.
18. Install the friction pad (**Figure 90**) into the lower housing; see **Figure 95**. Match the curvature on the friction pad with the handlebar.
19. Install a ferrule (**Figure 92**) onto the end of each cable, then insert the ferrules into the throttle grip slots (**Figure 91**).

NOTE
*If the master cylinder is not mounted on the handlebar, make sure to fit the throttle housing wiring harness into the depression (**Figure 96**) in the bottom of the handlebar.*

20. Assemble the upper and lower switch housings and the throttle grip. Install the lower switch housing screws (B, **Figure 89**) and tighten securely. Operate the throttle and make sure both cables move in and out properly.
21. Route the cables from the handlebar to the carburetor.
22. Connect the idle cable (A, **Figure 93**) to the carburetor as follows:
    a. You can identify the idle cable by the small spring on the end of the cable. See **Figure 97**. The throttle cable does not have a spring.
    b. Insert the idle cable sheath into the rear cable bracket guide (installed on the carburetor). See **Figure 98**.
    c. Next, fit the end of the idle cable into the carburetor cable plate (A, **Figure 93**).

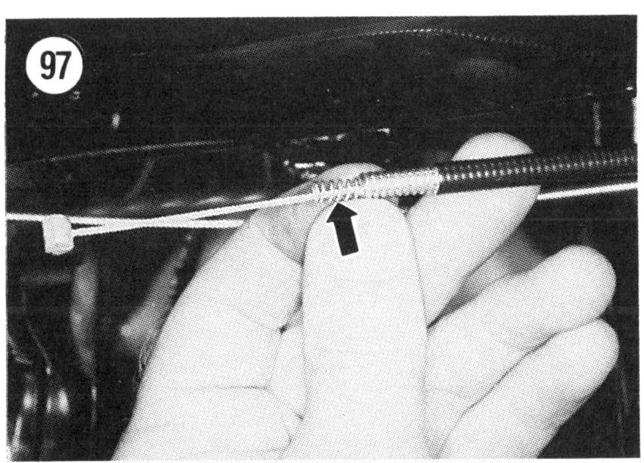

97

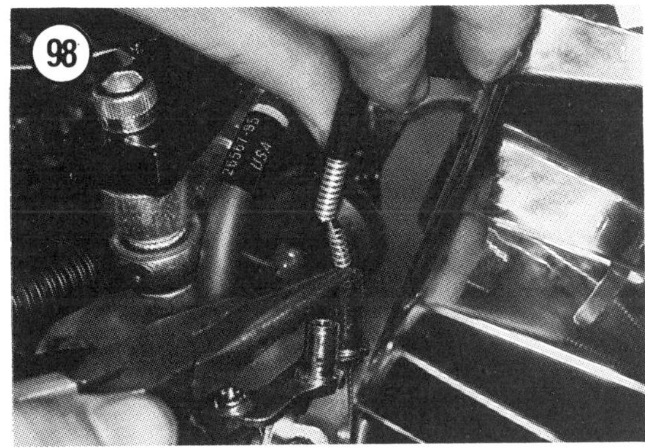

98

23. Insert the throttle cable sheath (B, **Figure 93**) into the front cable bracket guide and fit the end of the cable into the carburetor cable plate.

24. Operate the hand throttle a few times, making sure the idle cable (A, **Figure 99**) and the throttle cable (B, **Figure 99**) seat squarely in their cable bracket guides.

25. Operate the throttle grip and make sure the carburetor throttle linkage is operating correctly. If the throttle operates roughly, first make sure that you installed the cables correctly, then check that there are no tight bends in the cables.

26. Adjust the throttle and idle cables as described in Chapter Three. Make sure you tightened the cable jam nuts (A, **Figure 89**) against the lower housing.

27. Install the air filter backplate and air filter as described in this chapter.

28. Install the fuel tank as described in this chapter.

29. Turn the ignition switch on and operate the front brake lever. The rear brake light must come on. If not, check for a damaged or incorrectly installed front brake light switch. When the brake light and switch operate correctly, continue with Step 30.

30. Start the engine and allow it to idle in NEUTRAL. Then turn the handlebar from side to side. Do not operate the throttle. If the engine speed increases when you turn the handlebar assembly, the throttle cables are routed incorrectly or damaged. Recheck cable routing and adjustment.

WARNING
Do not ride the motorcycle until the throttle cables are properly adjusted. Improper cable routing and adjustment can cause the throttle to stick open. This could cause you to lose control. Recheck your work before riding the bike.

ENRICHENER CABLE REPLACEMENT

The enrichener cable controls the position of the enrichener valve in the carburetor.

1. Remove the air filter and backplate as described in Chapter Three.

2. Note the routing of the enrichener cable from its mounting bracket to the carburetor.

3. Disconnect the enrichener cable (**Figure 100**) nut from the mounting bracket. Move the end of the cable out of the mounting bracket.

4. Unscrew the enrichener cable nut from the carburetor. **Figure 101** shows the enrichener cable with the carburetor removed for clarity.

NOTE
If you cannot unscrew the enrichener cable with the carburetor mounted on the engine, remove the carburetor as described in this chapter.

5. Remove the enrichener cable (**Figure 101**) from the motorcycle.

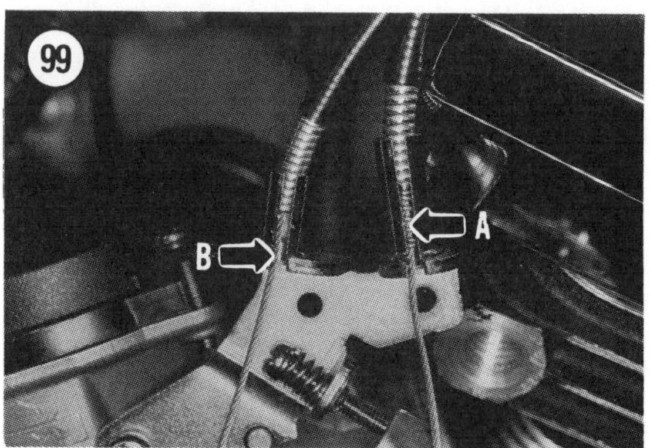

6. Reverse these steps to install the enrichener cable while noting the following.
7. Align the enrichener valve needle(**Figure 102**)with the needle passage in the carburetor and install the enrichener valve. Tighten the valve nut securely.
8. Adjust the enrichener cable as described in Chapter Three.

FUEL TANK

The fuel tank (**Figure 103**) bolts to the upper frame tube. A 3-way fuel valve mounts to the bottom of the tank.

The Dyna Glide fuel tank venting system is described as follows:

a. On 1991 models, the fuel tank vents through the fuel caps.
b. On 1992-on models, the fuel tank vents through a standpipe connected to the inside of the fuel tank. A hose connects the standpipe to a vapor valve (**Figure 104**). On 49-state models, the hose connected to the vapor valve routes along the frame. A vent line connector is connected to the end of the hose. On California models, the vapor valve hose connects the vapor valve to the carbon canister (**Figure 105**).
c. Because of the 2 different venting systems, the fuel tank caps are not interchangeable between 1991 and 1992-on models.

WARNING
Make sure you route the fuel tank vapor hoses so that they cannot contact any hot engine or exhaust component. These hoses contain flammable vapors. If a hose melts from contacting a hot part, leaking vapors may ig fire.

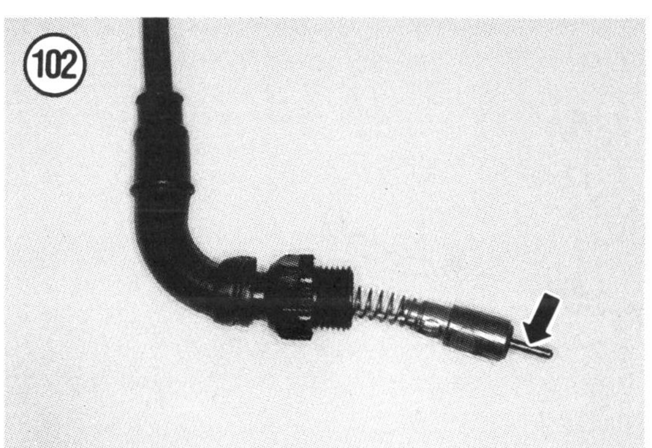

Removal/Installation

When removing the fuel tank in the following procedure, keep track of all fasteners and rubber bushings so that you don't lose or mix them up during installation.

The fuel hose is secured to the fuel tank with a non-reusable clamp. If you are going to reinstall this type of clamp, purchase one before servicing the fuel tank.

Refer to **Figure 103** for this procedure.

WARNING
Gasoline is very volatile and presents an extreme fire hazard. Be sure to work in a well-ventilated area away from any open flames (including pilot lights on household appliances). Do not allow anyone to smoke in the area. Have a fire extinguisher rated for gasoline fires handy.

1. Disconnect the negative battery cable from the battery (**Figure 106**).
2. Turn the fuel valve off. Then cut the factory hose clamp that secures the hose to the valve. Discard the clamp.

NOTE
A crossover tube connects the 2 fuel tanks. Drain the tanks before removing them in the following steps.

WARNING
Make sure there are no open flames in the area when performing Step 3.

3A. On 1991-1994 models, disconnect the fuel supply hose from the fuel valve (**Figure 107**, typical). Connect a longer hose to the fuel valve fitting and place the open end of the hose into a gas can. Turn the fuel valve to RESERVE and drain the fuel into the tank.
3B. On 1995 models, drain the fuel tank as follows:

NOTE
A vacuum operated fuel valve is installed on all 1995 models. You need a hand-operated vacuum pump to drain the fuel tank.

7

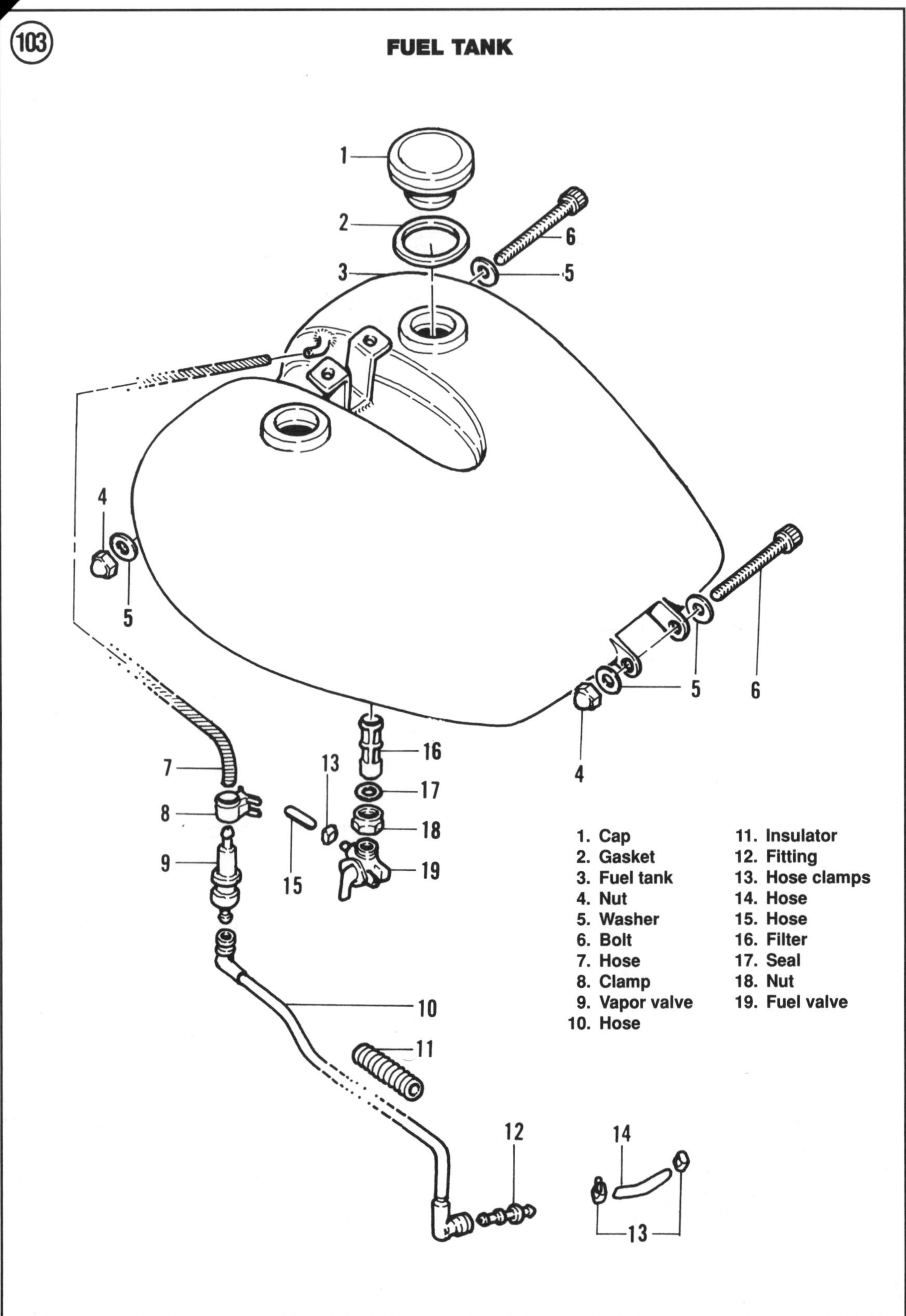
103
FUEL TANK
1
2
3
6
5
4
5
5
6
4
16
13
17
7
18
8
19
9
15
10
11
12
14
13
1. Cap
2. Gasket
3. Fuel tank
4. Nut
5. Washer
6. Bolt
7. Hose
8. Clamp
9. Vapor valve
10. Hose
11. Insulator
12. Fitting
13. Hose clamps
14. Hose
15. Hose
16. Filter
17. Seal
18. Nut
19. Fuel valve

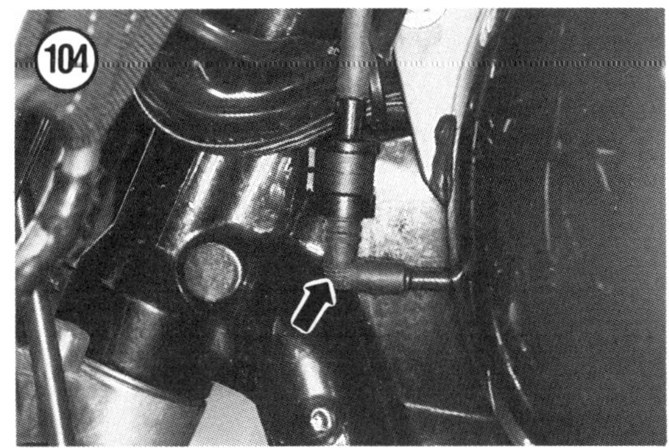

a. Turn the fuel valve off and disconnect the fuel hosc (A, **Figurc 108**) from thc fucl valvc. Plug the open end of the hose.

b. Connect the drain hose (**Figure 109**) to the fuel valve and secure it with a hose clamp. Insert the end of the drain hose into a gas can.

c. Disconnect the vacuum hose (B, **Figure 108**) from the fuel valve.

d. Connect a hand-operated vacuum pump to the fuel valve vacuum hose nozzle (B, **Figure 108**).

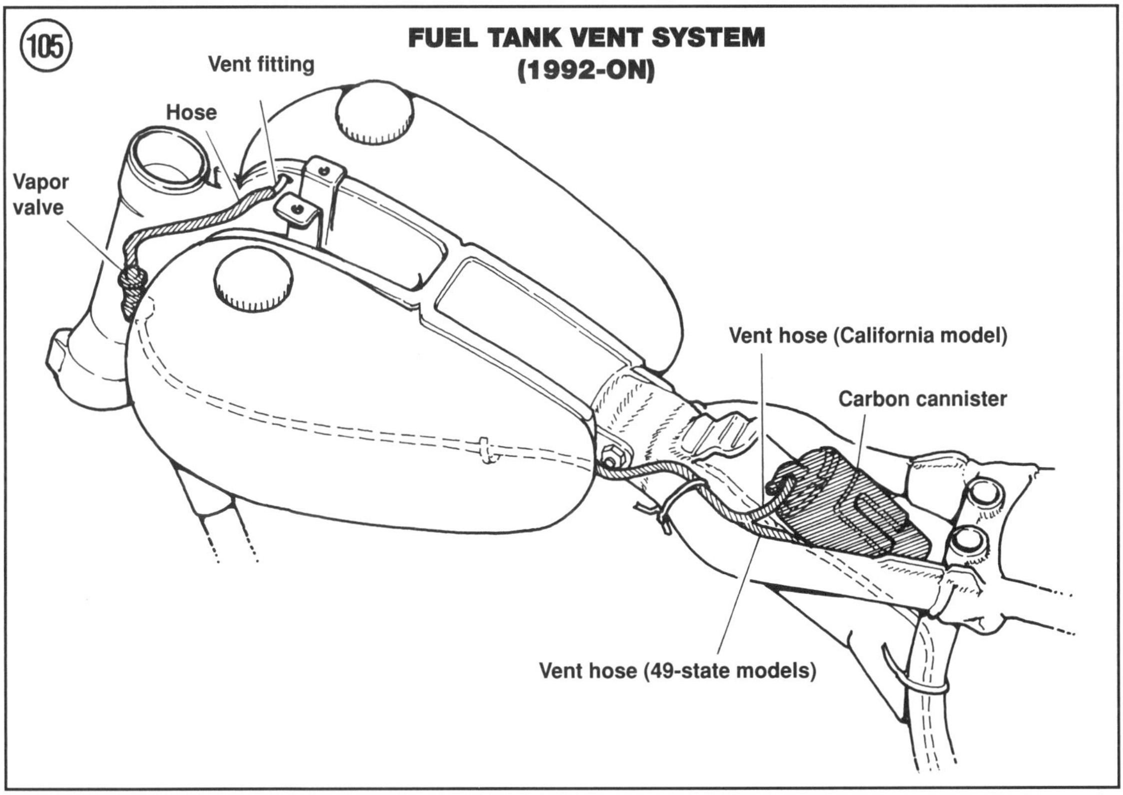

105

FUEL TANK VENT SYSTEM (1992-ON)

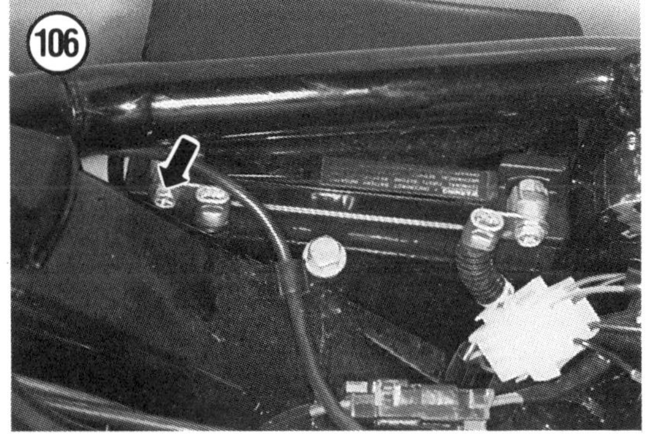

e. Turn the fuel valve (**Figure 108**) to the RES (reserve) position.

CAUTION
In the following step, do not apply more vacuum than 10 in. (254 mm) Hg or you can damage the fuel valve diaphragm.

f. Operate the vacuum pump handle (**Figure 110**) and apply 1-10 in. (25.4-254 mm) Hg of vacuum. When you apply the vacuum, the fuel will start to flow.

g. When fuel stops flowing through the hose, turn the fuel valve off and release the vacuum. Disconnect the vacuum pump and drain hose.

4. On 1992 and later models, disconnect the vent hose from the fuel tank.
5. Disconnect the electrical connectors leading from the gauges mounted on the fuel tank.
6. Disconnect the crossover hose from the fuel tank (**Figure 111**). Plug the hose and tank openings.
7. Remove the nuts, washers and bolts securing the fuel tank to the frame.
8. Lift off and remove the fuel tank.

NOTE
Store the fuel tank in a safe place—away from open flames or objects that could fall and damage it.

9. Drain any remaining fuel left in the tank into a gas can.
10. Installation is the reverse of these steps. Note the following.
11. When installing an aftermarket fuel tank, you must clean and seal the tank before installing it on your bike. See *Installing a New Fuel Tank* in this chapter.
12. Tighten the front and rear bolts and nuts to the torque specification listed in **Table 2**.
13. Make sure you install the insulator tube over the fuel hose.
14. Reconnect the fuel hose to the fuel valve and secure it with a hose clamp. When installing a factory hose clamp, tighten it with the Harley-Davidson hose clamp pliers (part No. HD-97087-66B) or equivalent.
15. Refill the tank and check for leaks.

Inspection

Refer to **Figure 103** for this procedure.

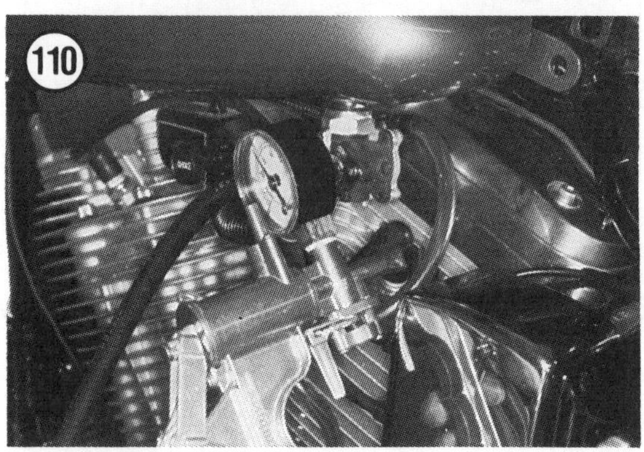

1. Inspect all of the fuel and vent hoses for cracks, deterioration or damage. Replace damaged hoses with the same type and size materials. The fuel line must be flexible and strong enough to withstand engine heat and vibration.
2. Check the fuel line insulator for damage.
3. Check for damaged or missing fuel tank dampers.
4. Remove the filler caps and inspect the tank for rust or contamination. If there is a rust buildup inside the tank, clean and flush the tank as described in this chapter.
5. Inspect the fuel tank for leaks.

Fuel Tank Flushing

The inside surfaces on all factory fuel tanks are treated to resist rusting. However, if you store the motorcycle for long periods, moisture that collects in the tank will eventually cause tank rust to develop. When putting the motorcycle back into service, rust that formed in the tank will break off and contaminate the fuel system. To remove tank rust, perform the following:
1. Remove and drain the fuel tank as described under *Fuel Tank Removal/Installation* in this chapter.
2. Remove the fuel valve as described in this chapter. While the valve is off the tank, clean it as described in this chapter.
3. Plug all of the tank openings.

NOTE
The following steps describe the use of soap and water to clean the tank. If you plan to use a commercial fuel tank cleaning agent, follow the manufacturer's instructions.

4. To help break up the rust buildup, add some nonferrous balls or lead pellets into the tank. Then shake the fuel tank to break the rust loose. Rinse the tank with clear water. Repeat this step as required to remove as much of the loose rust as possible.

WARNING
Do not use metal balls to loosen fuel tank deposits. Metal balls can produce a spark that could ignite fumes trapped in the tank, causing an explosion and serious personal injury.

5. Rinse the tank with a soap and water solution, then pour it out. Inspect the tank again for any rust buildup. If there is still a rust buildup in the tank, you should use a commercial fuel tank cleaning agent to clean the tank thoroughly. The Kreem cleaning kit shown in **Figure 112** is a complete fuel tank cleaning and sealing system available from most motorcycle dealers.

CAUTION
When cleaning and sealing your gas tank with a commercial cleaning and sealing agent, you must protect the outside of the tank as the chemicals are caustic and will destroy its finish. Follow the manufacturers instructions closely.

Repairing Minor Tank Leaks

If the fuel tank is leaking, take it to a dealer for welding and repair. After they repair the tank, take it home and clean and seal it as described in this chapter.

WARNING
Welding a metal gas tank is dangerous as any trace of fuel left in the tank can cause it to explode. If the tank must be welded, refer service to your dealer. Do not attempt this repair at home.

FUEL VALVE

A 3-way fuel valve is mounted to the right-hand fuel tank. A replaceable fuel filter is mounted to the top of the fuel valve. See **Figure 113** (1991-1994) or **Figure 114** (1995). A vacuum operated fuel valve is installed on 1995 models. To troubleshoot this valve, refer to *Vacuum Operated Fuel Valve Testing (1995)* in Chapter Two.

Removal

The fuel filter removes particles which might otherwise enter the carburetor and possibly cause the float to stick open and the carburetor to flood.

WARNING
Gasoline is very volatile and presents an extreme fire hazard. Be sure to work in a well-ventilated area away from any open flames (including pilot lights on household appliances). Do not allow anyone to smoke in the area and have a fire extinguisher rated for gasoline fires nearby.

1. Disconnect the negative battery cable from the battery (**Figure 106**).
2. Turn the fuel valve off.
3. Drain the fuel tank as described under *Fuel Tank Removal/Installation* in this chapter.
4. Loosen the fuel valve fitting and remove the fuel valve from the fuel tank. Catch any gasoline that may leak from the tank after you remove the valve.

Cleaning and Inspection

1. Inspect the filter (16, **Figure 103**) mounted on top of the fuel valve. Remove and clean the filter of all contamination. Replace the filter if damaged.
2. Install a new filter gasket (17, **Figure 103**) before installing the filter onto the fuel valve.

NOTE
*If the filter is contaminated, the fuel tank may require cleaning and flushing. Refer to **Fuel Tank Flushing** in this chapter.*

3. Remove all sealant residue from the fuel tank and fuel valve threads.

Installation

1. If you havent done so, install a new filter gasket (17, **Figure 103**) onto the fuel valve. Then install the filter (16, **Figure 103**).
2. Coat the fuel valve threads (19, **Figure 103**) with Loctite pipe sealant with teflon.

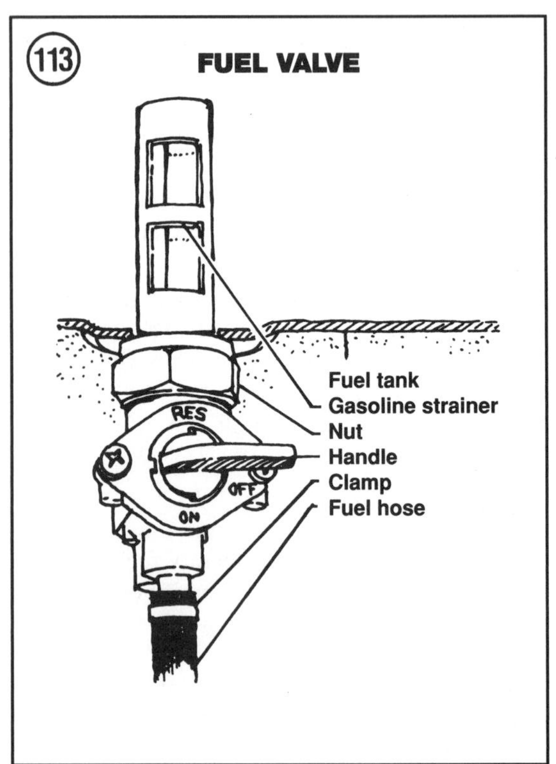

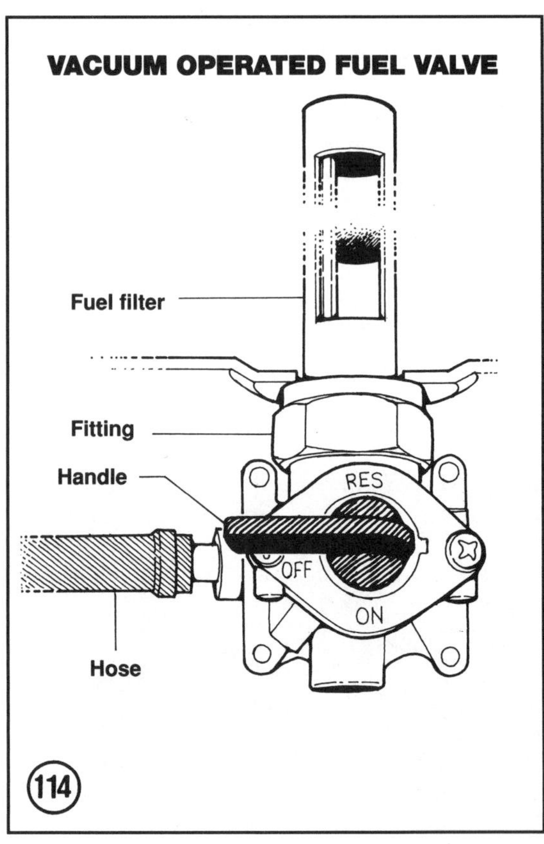

3A. On 1991-1994 models, insert the valve into the tank. Then tighten the valve fitting to secure the valve.

3B. On 1995 models, install the fuel valve as follows:

a. Insert the fuel valve into the tank, then thread the fitting (18, **Figure 103**) onto the fuel tank 2 turns.
b. Hold the fitting and thread the fuel valve (left-hand threads) 2 turns into the fitting.
c. Hold the fuel valve and tighten the fitting to 18 ft.-lb. (24 N•m).

WARNING
If you turn the fitting more than 2 turns on the valve, it may bottom out on the valve and cause a fuel leak. A spark can ignite fuel that leaks from the fuel valve. This could cause an explosion and fire to occur.

4. Install the insulator tube over the fuel hose.
5. Reconnect the fuel hose to the fuel valve and secure it with a hose clamp. When installing a factory hose clamp, tighten it with the Harley-Davidson hose clamp pliers (part No. HD-97087-66B) or equivalent.
6. Refill the fuel tank and check for leaks.

EXHAUST SYSTEM

Figure 115 (1991-1994) and **Figure 116** (1995) shows the factory installed exhaust systems.

Each exhaust pipe clamps to its respective cylinder head exhaust port with a flange plate and 2 nuts. Knitted steel gaskets (**Figure 117**) are placed between the cylinder exhaust pipe and cylinder head to prevent exhaust leakage.

Removal

1. Secure the bike on a workstand.
2. Remove the exhaust pipe heat shields.

3A. On 1991-1994 models, remove the nuts and washers securing the front and rear exhaust pipes to the cylinder heads. See **Figure 118**, typical.

3B. On 1995 models, remove the nuts securing the front and rear exhaust pipes to the cylinder heads. See **Figure 118**, typical.

4. Slide the exhaust flanges (**Figure 119**) off the cylinder head studs. See **Figure 120**.

5A. On 1991-1994 models, remove the nut, washer and bolt securing the front pipe clamp to the gear cover bracket.

5B. On 1995 models, remove the nut and bolt securing the front pipe clamp to the gear cover bracket.

6A. On 1991-1994 models, remove the bolt, washer and nut securing the rear exhaust pipe clamp to the transmission side cover support bracket.

6B. On 1995 models, remove the bolt and washer securing the rear exhaust pipe clamp to the transmission side cover support bracket.

7. Carefully pull the exhaust assembly away from the bike and remove it as an assembly.
8. Remove and discard the exhaust port gaskets (**Figure 121**).
9. Inspect the exhaust system as described in this chapter.

Installation

7

1. Before installing the new exhaust port gaskets, scrape the exhaust port surfaces (**Figure 122**) to remove all carbon residue—removing the carbon will ensure a good gasket fit. Then wipe the port with a rag. Before installing a gasket, note that the inner gasket diameter is tapered. Install the gasket with its wider diameter end facing out (toward exhaust pipe) as shown in **Figure 123**.
2. Before installing the exhaust pipes, check that the retaining rings (**Figure 124**) fit tightly in the upper pipe grooves.
3. Position the exhaust pipe assembly so that the front and rear exhaust pipes fit into the front and rear cylinder head exhaust pipes. Slide the clamps over the mounting studs and install a washer (1991-1994) and nut over each stud (**Figure 118**). Install the nuts finger-tight only.
4. Align the front exhaust pipe clamp with the gear cover bracket, then install the bolt, washer (1991-1994) and nut. Tighten the nut finger-tight only.

5A. On 1991-1994 models, align the rear exhaust pipe clamp with the transmission side cover support bracket. Then install the bolt, washer and nut. Tighten the nut finger-tight only. Be sure to install the support bracket clamp.

5B. On 1995 models, align the rear exhaust pipe clamp with the transmission side cover support bracket. Then install the bolt and nut. Tighten the nut finger-tight only.

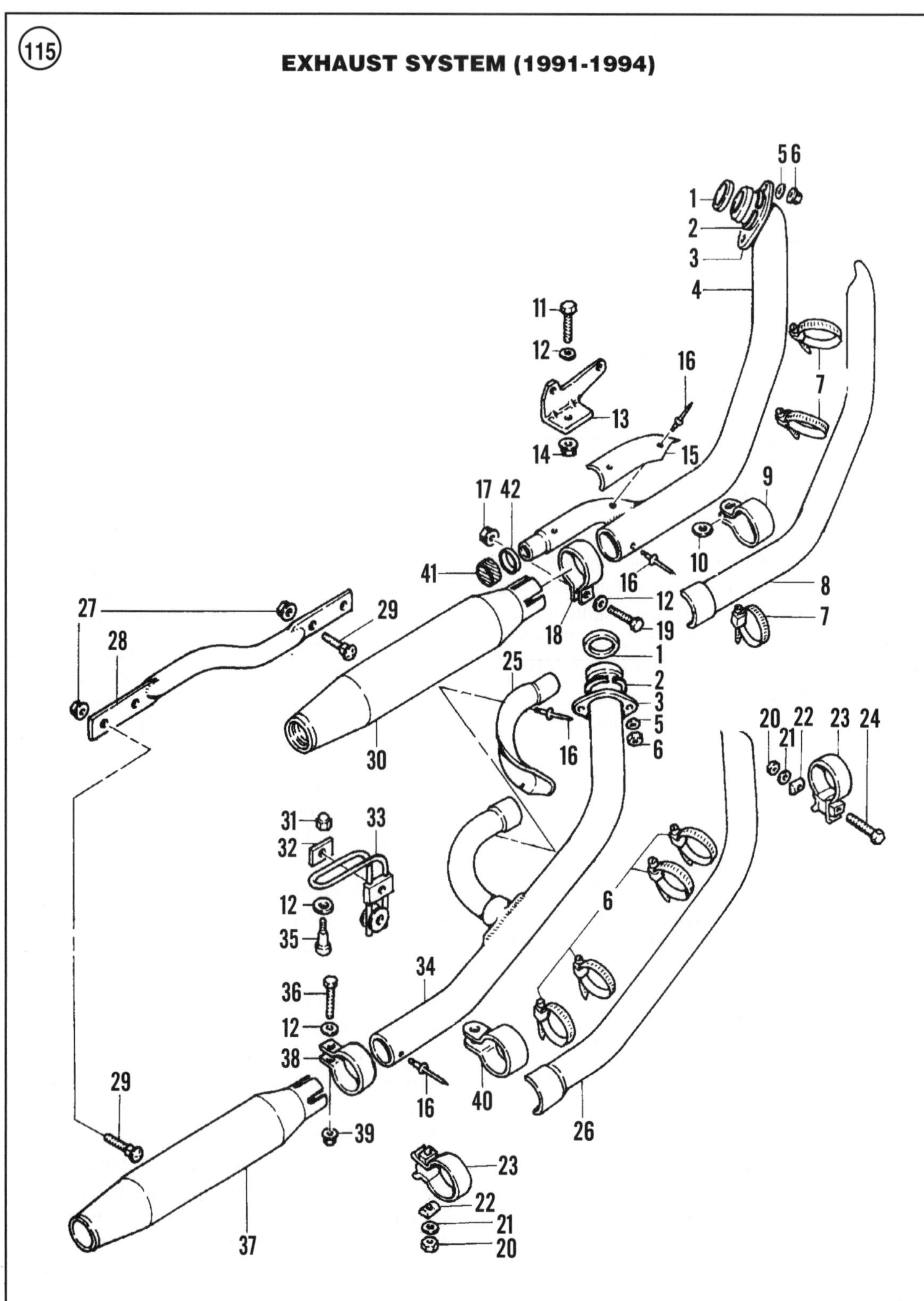
115
EXHAUST SYSTEM (1991-1994)
1
2
3
4
5
6
7
8
9
10
11
12
13
14
15
16
17
18
19
20
21
22
23
24
25
26
27
28
29
30
31
32
33
34
35
36
37
38
39
40
41
42

1. Gasket
2. Retaining ring
3. Exhaust pipe flange
4. Front exhaust pipe
5. Washer
6. Nut
7. Clamp
8. Heat shield
9. Clamp
10. Spacer
11. Bolt
12. Washer
13. Bracket
14. Nut
15. Heat shield
16. Rivet
17. Nut
18. Clamp (1991-1992)
19. Bolt
20. Nut
21. Washer
22. Guide
23. Clamp (1993-1994)
24. Bolt
25. Heat shield
26. Heat shield
27. Nut
28. Bracket
29. Bolt
30. Muffler
31. Nut
32. Clamp
33. Clamp
34. Rear exhaust pipe
35. Bolt
36. Bolt
37. Muffler
38. Clamp
39. Nut
40. Clamp
41. Gasket
42. Washer

6. Check the exhaust assembly alignment, then tighten the cylinder head stud nuts as follows:
   a. Tighten the upper nut to the torque specification in **Table 3**.
   b. Tighten the lower nut to the torque specification in **Table 3**.
7. Tighten the front and then the rear exhaust pipe clamp bolts and/or nuts to the torque specification in **Table 3**.
8. Install the heat shields and tighten the clamps securely.
9. Start the engine and check for leaks.

Inspection

1. Replace rusted or damaged exhaust system components.
2. Remove all rust from pipe and muffler mating surfaces.
3. Check all of the hoses for damage or severe rusting. Clean or repair clamps as required.
4. On 1994 and later models, the muffler clamps are not reusable. Replace the muffler clamps if you remove them.
5. Replace damaged exhaust pipe retaining rings (**Figure 124**).
6. Replace all worn or damaged heat shield clamps as required.
7. Store the exhaust pipes in a safe place until you reinstall them.

7

EVAPORATIVE EMISSION CONTROL SYSTEM (CALIFORNIA MODELS)

An evaporative emission control system is installed on all California models. This system prevents gasoline vapor from escaping into the atmosphere. When the engine is not running, the system routes fuel vapor from the fuel tank through the vapor valve and into the carbon canister. When the engine is running, these vapors are drawn through a purge hose and into the carburetor where they burn in the combustion chambers. The vapor valve also prevents gasoline vapor from escaping from the carbon canister if the bike falls onto its side.

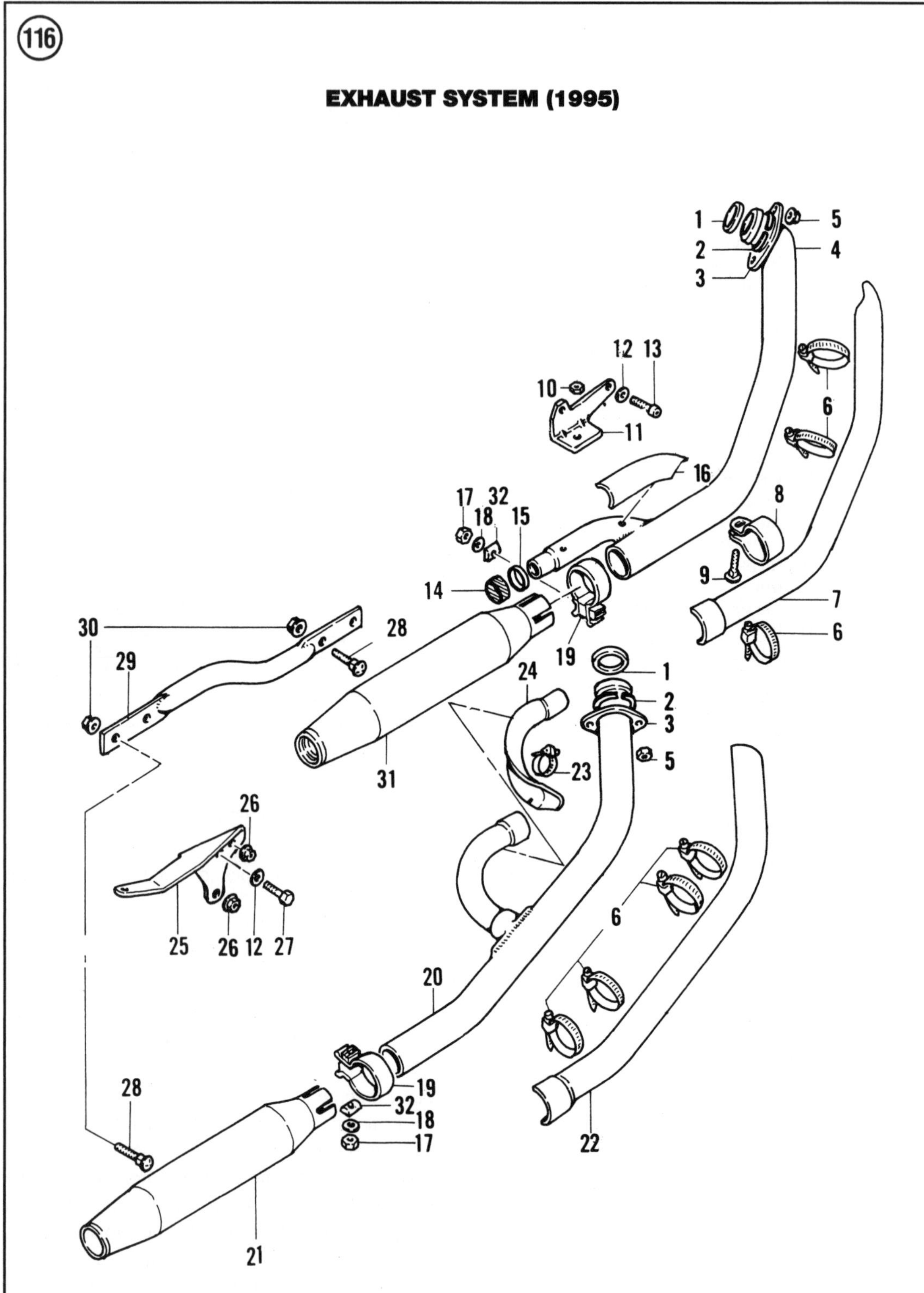
116
EXHAUST SYSTEM (1995)
1
2
3
4
5
6
7
8
9
10
11
12
13
14
15
16
17
18
19
20
21
22
23
24
25
26
27
28
29
30
31
32

1. Gasket
2. Retaining ring
3. Exhaust pipe flange
4. Front exhaust pipe
5. Nut
6. Clamps
7. Heat shield
8. Clamp
9. Bolt
10. Nut
11. Bracket
12. Washer
13. Bolt
14. Gasket
15. Washer
16. Heat shield
17. Nut
18. Washer
19. Clamp
20. Exhaust pipe
21. Muffler
22. Heat shield
23. Clamp
24. Heat shield
25. Bracket
26. Nut
27. Bolt
28. Bolt
29. Bracket
30. Nut
31. Muffler
32. Guide

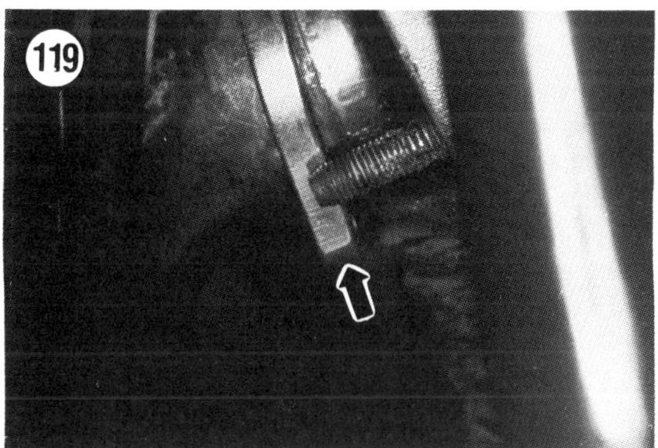

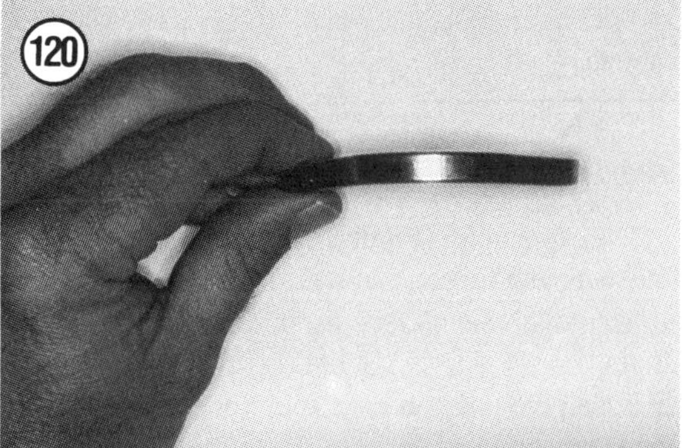

Inspection/Replacement

Refer to **Figure 125** (1991) or **Figure 126** (1992-on) for the components and the hose routing to the various parts. Before removing the hoses from any of the parts, mark the hose and the fitting with a piece of masking tape to identify where the hose goes.

1. Check all emission control lines and hoses to make sure they are correctly routed and connected.

WARNING
Make sure the fuel tank vapor hoses are routed so they cannot contact any hot engine or exhaust component. These hoses contain flammable vapor. If a hose melts from contacting a hot part, leaking vapor may ignite, causing severe bike damage and rider injury.

2. Make sure there are no kinks in the lines or hoses. Also inspect the hose and lines for excessive wear or burning on lines that are routed near engine hot spots.
3. Check the physical condition of all lines and hoses in the system. Check for cuts, tears or loose connections. These lines and hoses are subjected to various temperature and operating conditions and eventually become brittle and crack. Replace damaged lines and hoses.
4. Check all components in the emission control system for damage, such as broken fittings or broken nipples on the component.
5. When replacing one or more lines or hoses, refer to the diagram for your model.

EVAPORATIVE EMISSION CONTROL SYSTEM SERVICE

Refer to **Figure 125** (1991) or **Figure 126** (1992-on) when servicing the evaporative emission control system.

Vapor Valve Replacement

The vapor valve (**Figure 127**) mounts between the fuel tank and carbon canister.

1. Remove the battery as described in Chapter Eight.
2. Label the hoses at the vapor valve, then disconnect them.

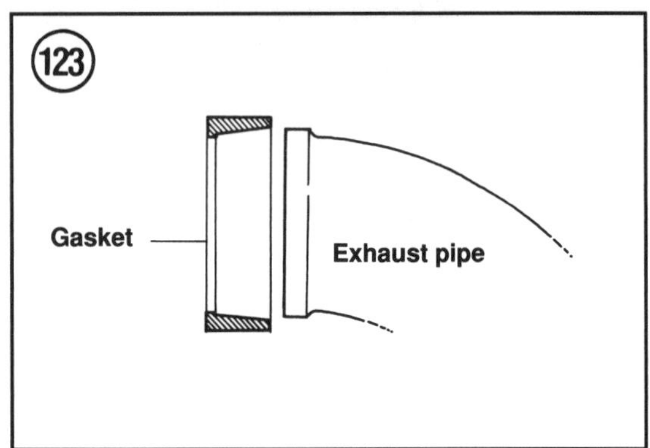

125

EVAPORATIVE EMISSION CONTROL SYSTEM (1991, CALIFORNIA ONLY)

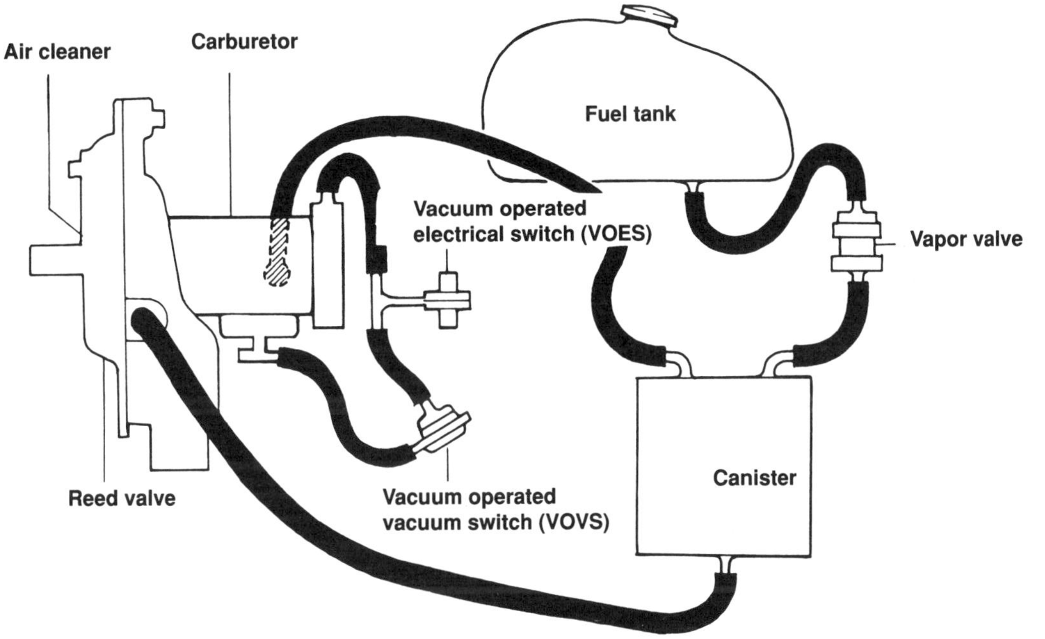

126

EVAPORATIVE EMISSION CONTROL SYSTEM (1992-ON CALIFORNIA MODELS)

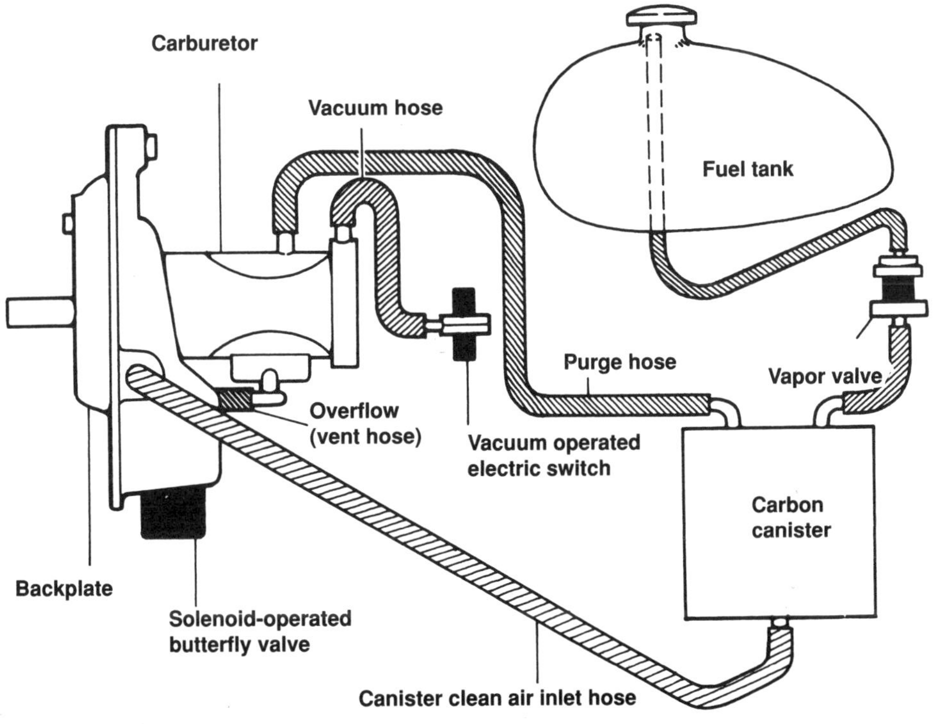

3. Note that one end of the vapor valve is longer than the other end. The longer end must face up when you install the vapor valve on the bike. Remove and replace the vapor valve.

CAUTION
*The vapor valve must be installed in a vertical position with the **longer end** facing up or excessive pressure will build in the fuel tank.*

4. Install the vapor valve by reversing these steps.

Carbon Canister Replacement

1. Find the canister where it mounts on the frame backbone.
2. Label, then disconnect the hoses from the canister. Plug the open end of each hose to prevent contamination.
3. Remove the carbon canister assembly.
4. Install the carbon canister by reversing these steps.

CAUTION
*Do not change the carbon canister's mounting position on the frame. Mount the carbon canister **below** the carburetor.*

Reed Valves (1991)

Whenever you remove the air filter assembly from the bike, check the reed valve assembly for broken reed valves. To replace damaged reed valves, perform the following.

1. Remove the air filter as described in Chapter Three.
2. Refer to **Figure 128**. Remove the screws and washers securing the reed assembly to the backplate. Then remove the reed stop, top reed and bottom reed.
3. Check the reeds for cracks or debris that would prevent the reed from closing. Replace worn or damaged parts as required.
4. Reverse Step 2 to install the reed valve assembly. Tighten the screws securely.
5. Install the air filter as described in Chapter Three.

Vacuum Operated Valve Switch Testing/Replacement (1991)

The vacuum-operated vacuum switch (VOVS) closes off the carburetor's float bowl vent passage when the engine is not running. This prevents fuel vapor from escaping after you turn the engine off.

You need a hand-operated vacuum pump (**Figure 129**) to test the VOVS.

1. Label, then disconnect the hoses from the VOVS. See **Figure 125** and **Figure 130**.

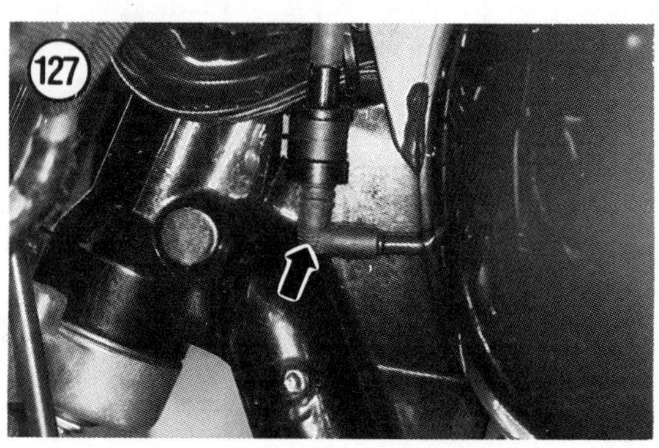

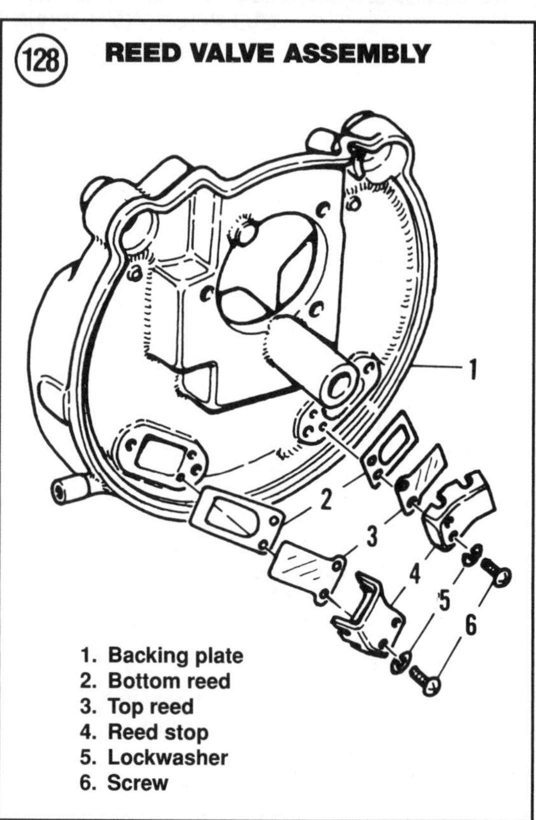

2. Attach a vacuum pump to port A in **Figure 130**.

3. Apply 1-2 in. hg of vacuum to the valve while watching the pump gauge. The vacuum must remain steady. If vacuum reading decreases rapidly, the diaphragm is damaged.

4. If vacuum remains constant (Step 3), blow into port C; air must pass through the VOVS. If air cannot pass through, the VOVS is damaged.

5. Remove the vacuum pump and blow into port B; air must not pass through the VOVS. If air can pass through, the VOVS is damaged.

6. If the VOVS fails to react as described in Steps 3-5, replace it with a new one.

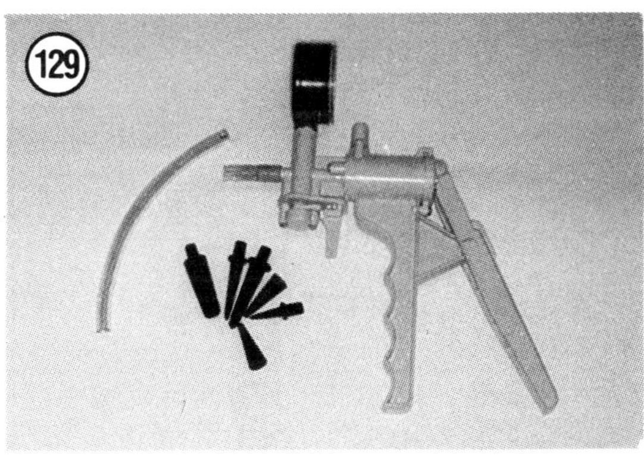

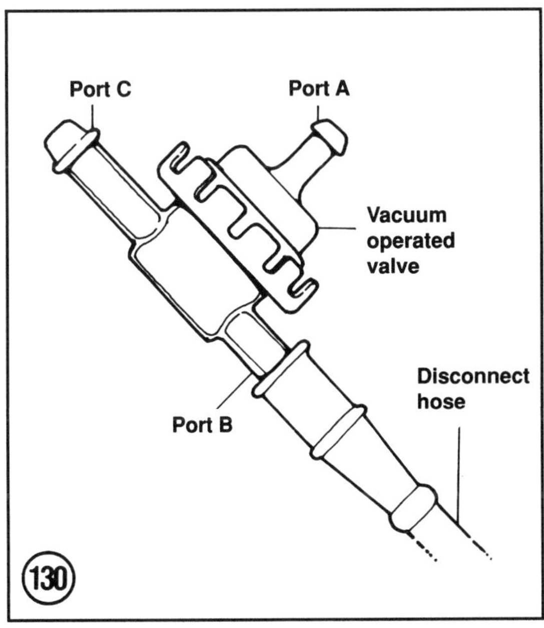

Solenoid-Operated Butterfly Valve Troubleshooting (1992-on)

On 1992-on California models, a solenoid-operated butterfly valve (**Figure 131**) is installed in the air filter backplate. The valve seals the backplate after the ignition switch is turned off, thus preventing fuel vapor from escaping into the atmosphere. Turning the ignition switch to the ON or IGNITION position energize the solenoid hold-in windings. When you operate the start switch, the solenoid pull-in windings are energized. The hold-in windings keep the butterfly valve open until you turn off the ignition switch.

A faulty solenoid-operated butterfly valve assembly (**Figure 131**) can cause the engine to accelerate poorly and reduce top speed. Check the system as follows:

1. First check that all of the hoses are properly connected. See **Figure 126**. If the hoses are okay, continue with Step 2.
2. Then make sure the butterfly valve is not opening due to an electrical malfunction.
   a. Check the solenoid valve electrical connectors for loose or dirty terminals. If the connectors are okay, disconnect the connector and check for dirty or loose-fitting terminals; clean and repair as required. If okay, continue with sub-step b.
   b. Test the solenoid as described under *Solenoid Testing* in this chapter.
3. Next, make sure the butterfly valve is not opening and closing improperly due to mechanical problems:
   a. Check the mechanical linkage assembly (**Figure 131**) for corroded, loose, broken or missing components. Clean the butterfly valve linkage and plunger every 5,000 mi. (8,000 km) as described in this chapter.
   b. Check for a broken solenoid spring (**Figure 131**). If the spring is broken, replace the solenoid assembly. You cannot replace the spring separately. Replace as described in this chapter.

Solenoid Valve Electrical Testing (1992-on)

Prior to testing the solenoid valve, you must fabricate the test harness shown in **Figure 132**. The part

7

(131)

SOLENOID-OPERATED BUTTERFLY VALVE (1992-ON CALIFORNIA)

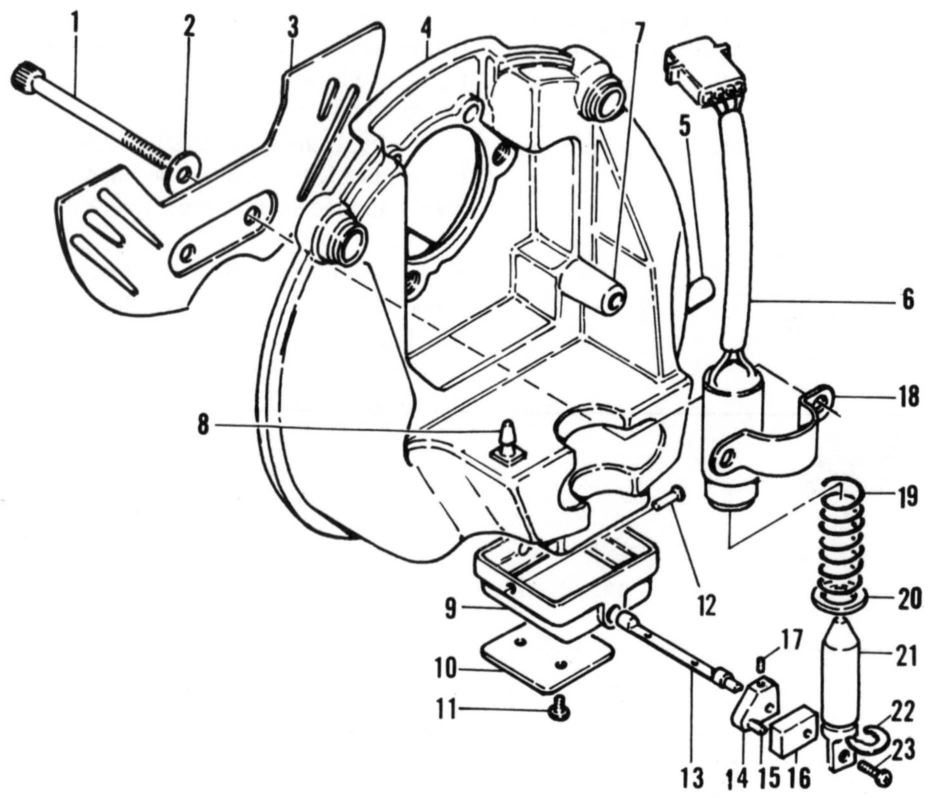

1. Solenoid mounting screws
2. Washer
3. Baffle
4. Backplate
5. Crankcase breather hose nozzle
6. Solenoid
7. Canister inlet hose nozzle
8. Fitting
9. Housing
10. Butterfly valve
11. Screw
12. Rivet
13. Butterfly valve shaft
14. Lever arm
15. Pin
16. Plastic link
17. Set screw
18. Solenoid clamp
19. Spring
20. Plastic washer
21. Plunger
22. E-clip
23. Screw

numbers listed on the drawing are Harley-Davidson part numbers.

Solenoid winding resistance test

1. Remove the air filter and backplate as described in this chapter.
2. Disconnect the solenoid valve 4-prong electrical connector (**Figure 131**).
3. Check for dirty or loose-fitting terminals and connectors.
4. Connect the solenoid test connector to the solenoid connector (**Figure 133**).
5. Refer to **Figure 134** for test connections and values and compare your meter readings to the stated values. If any of the meter readings differ from the stated values, replace the solenoid as described in this chapter.
6. If the resistance readings are correct, continue with thc following test.

Pull-in coil test

This test requires a fully charged 12-volt battery.

1. Remove the air filter and backplate as described in this chapter.
2. Disconnect the solenoid valve 4-prong electrical connector (**Figure 131**).
3. Check for dirty or loose-fitting terminals and connectors.
4. Connect the solenoid test connector to the solenoid connector (**Figure 135**).
5. Connect a 12-volt battery to the 2 solenoid test connector wires shown in **Figure 135**. The butterfly valve must open when you apply battery voltage. Disconnect the battery connections and note the following:

7

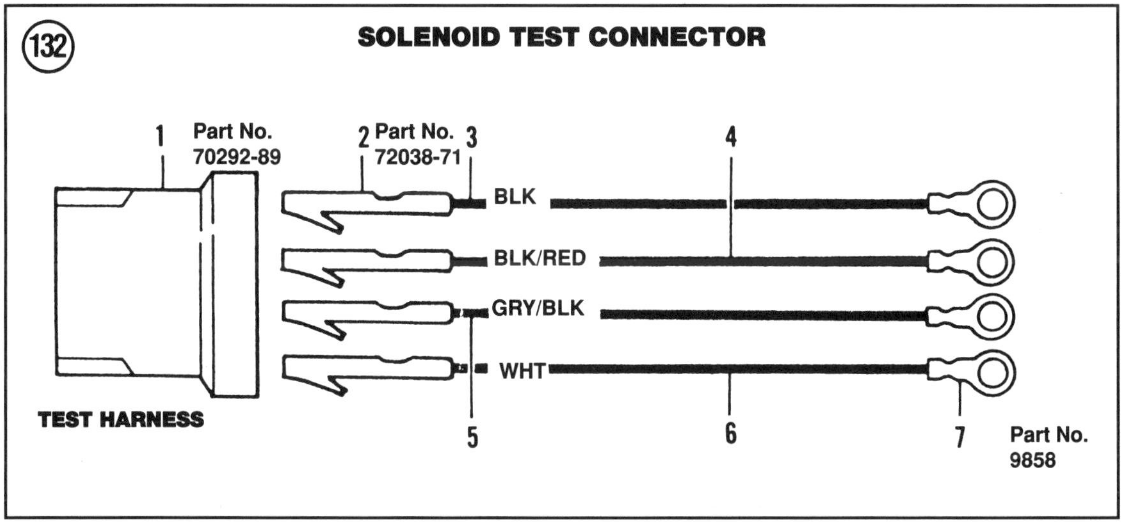

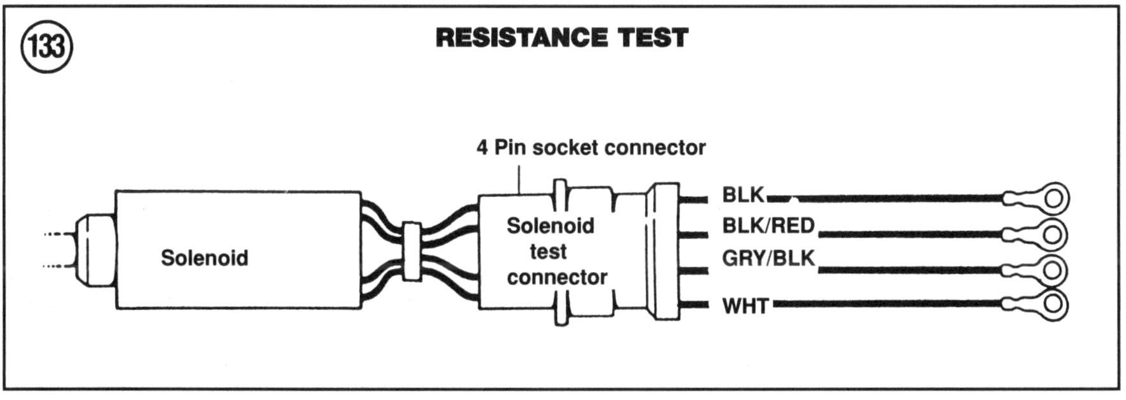

a. If the butterfly valve now opens but did not open when originally connected to the wiring harness, go to Step 6.
b. If the butterfly valve does not open, check the linkage for corroded, missing or damaged parts. If the linkage assembly appears is okay, retest with a new solenoid.

6. Perform the following:
a. Switch an ohmmeter to R × 1, cross the test leads and zero the meter. Then check for a ground at the grey/black connector pin in the solenoid 4-prong connector. The ohmmeter must read 1 ohm or less.
b. Reconnect the solenoid 4-prong connector.
c. Switch a voltmeter to the 12 VDC scale.
d. Connect the positive voltmeter lead to the black/red lead in the 4-prong connector and the negative probe to a good engine ground. Press the start button while reading the voltage showed on the voltmeter. It must be battery voltage.

7. If any of the meter readings differ from those specified in Step 6, look for a problem in the solenoid wiring harness. Use voltage and resistance checks to find the damaged wire(s). After repairing the wire(s), repeat the above checks.

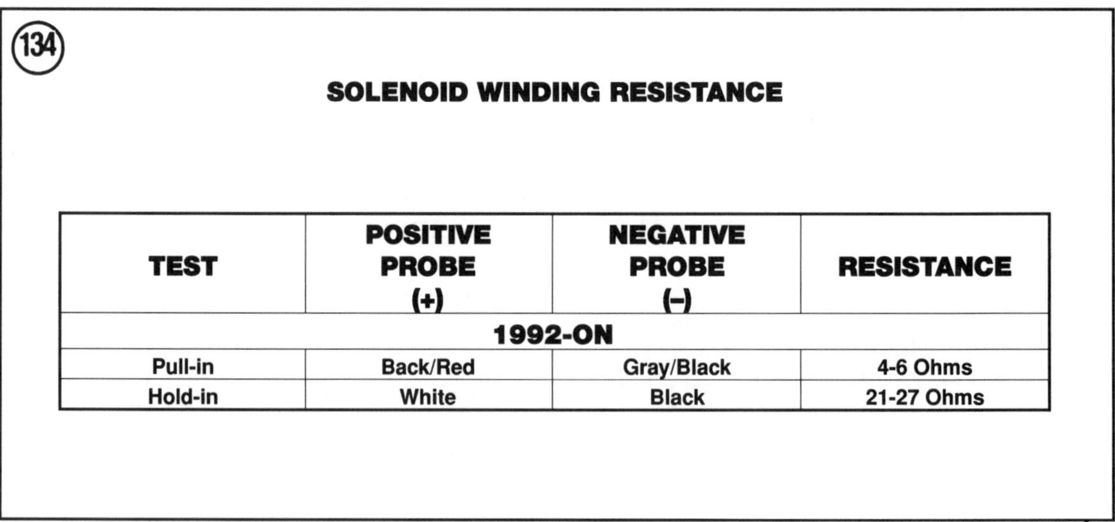

(134)

SOLENOID WINDING RESISTANCE

TEST	POSITIVE PROBE (+)	NEGATIVE PROBE (-)	RESISTANCE
1992-ON			
Pull-in	Back/Red	Gray/Black	4-6 Ohms
Hold-in	White	Black	21-27 Ohms

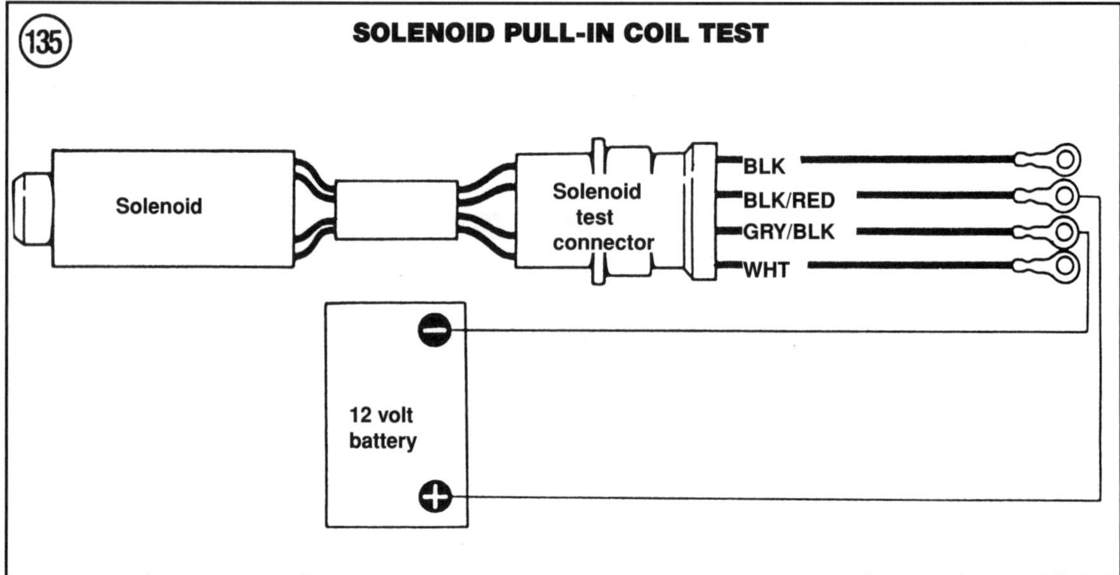

8. If the meter readings are correct as performed in Step 7, perform the following test.

Hold-in coil test

This test requires a fully charged 12-volt battery.

1. Remove the air filter and backplate as described in this chapter.
2. Disconnect the solenoid valve 4-prong electrical connector (**Figure 131**).
3. Check for dirty or loose-fitting terminals and connectors.
4. Connect the solenoid test connector to the solenoid connector (**Figure 136**).
5. Connect a 12-volt battery to the 2 solenoid test connector wires shown in **Figure 136** and perform the following:
   a. Using a screwdriver, carefully push the left-hand side of the butterfly valve up to open it.
   b. Remove the screwdriver. The butterfly valve must remain open when the solenoid hold-in windings are energized.
   c. Disconnect the negative battery cable from the solenoid test connector. The butterfly valve must close.
   d. If the butterfly valve operates as described in sub-steps b and c, the solenoid hold-in windings are operating correctly.
   e. If the butterfly valve fails to operate properly, go to Step 6.
   f. Disconnect the positive battery cable from the solenoid test connector.
6. If the butterfly valve does not remain open in Step 5, sub-step b, perform the following:
   a. Switch an ohmmeter to R × 1, cross the test leads and zero the meter. Then check for ground at the black connector pin in the solenoid 4-prong connector. The ohmmeter must read 1 ohm or less.
   b. Reconnect the solenoid 4-prong connector.
   c. Switch a voltmeter to the 12 VDC scale.
   d. Connect the positive voltmeter lead to the white lead in the 4-prong connector and the negative lead to a good engine ground. Turn the ignition switch to the ON or IGNITION position and read the voltage indicated on the voltmeter. It must be battery voltage.
7. If any of the meter readings differ from those specified in Step 6, look for a problem in the solenoid wiring harness. Use voltage and resistance checks to find the damaged wire(s). After repairing the wire(s), repeat the above checks.
8. If the solenoid test readings are correct but the butterfly valve does not work properly, perform Step 3 under *Solenoid-Operated Butterfly Valve Troubleshooting (1992-on)*.
9. Remove all test equipment and reconnect the solenoid 4-prong connector.

7

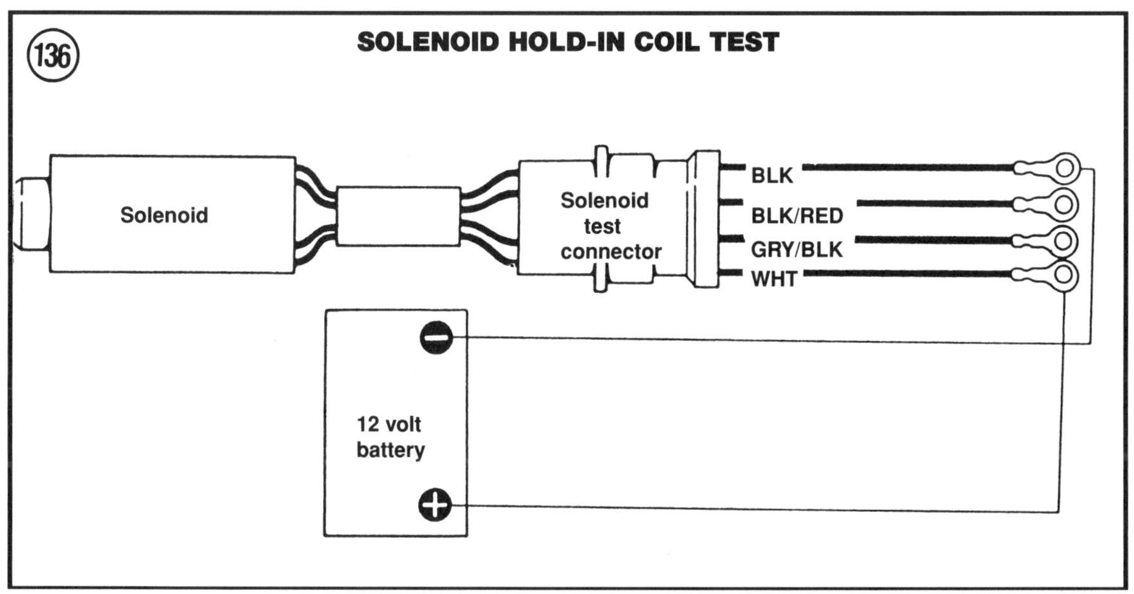

Butterfly Valve and Solenoid Cleaning and Lubrication (1992-on)

Refer to **Figure 131**.

1. Remove the air filter as described in this chapter.
2. At 2,500 mi. (4,022 km) intervals, inspect the butterfly valve and solenoid for proper operation.
3. At 5,000 mi. (8,000 km) intervals, spray the butterfly valve and plunger with carburetor cleaner. Then, after the carburetor cleaner evaporates, lubricate the linkage and plunger with a dry film spray lubricant.
4. Reinstall the air filter as described in this chapter.

Table 1 CARBURETOR JET SIZES

Year and model	Main jet	Pilot jet
1991		
49-state	185	45
California	165	42
1992		
49-state	175	40
California	160	40
1993		
49-state	175	42
California	160	42
International	165	40
1994		
Domestic	165	42
International	165	40
1995		
Domestic	165	42
Swiss	165	40
All other International models	180	40

Table 2 FUEL SYSTEM TIGHTENING TORQUES

	ft.-lb.	N•m
Air filter cover screw	3-5	4-7
Backplate-to-carburetor screws	3-5	4-7
Backplate-to-cylinder head bolts	10-12	14-16
Intake manifold		
Nuts	6-10	8-14
Allen bolts	6-10	8-14
Fuel tank bolts	15-19	20-26

Table 3 EXHAUST SYSTEM TIGHTENING TORQUES

	ft.-lb.	N•m
Cylinder head stud nuts	60-80 in.-lb.	6.8-9.0
Exhaust support tubes-to-frame nuts	19	26
Muffler clamp bolts		
1993	7	9.5
Muffler clamp nuts		
1991-1992	7	9.5
1994-1995	45-60	61-81
Muffler support nuts	19	26

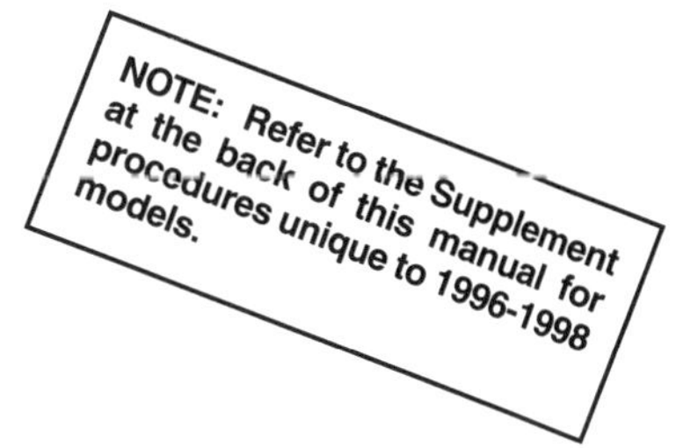

CHAPTER EIGHT

ELECTRICAL SYSTEM

8

This chapter provides service procedures for the battery, charging system, ignition system, starter system, lights, switches and circuit breakers. Chapter Three lists tune-up procedures involving the ignition system.

Tables 1-4 are found at the end of the chapter.

BATTERY

The battery is the single most important component in your motorcycles electrical system. Yet you can trace most electrical system troubles to battery neglect.

To maintain the battery properly, perform the battery cleaning, inspection and charging procedures described in this section. **Table 1** lists the battery capacity for all Dyna Glide models.

Safety Precautions

When working with batteries, use extreme care to avoid spilling or splashing the electrolyte. This solution contains sulfuric acid, which can ruin clothing and cause serious chemical burns. If you spill or splash the electrolyte on your clothing or skin, immediately neutralize the affected area with a solution of baking soda and water. Then flush the area with an abundance of clean water.

WARNING

Electrolyte is extremely harmful when splashed into your eyes or an open cut. You must wear safety glasses and appropriate work clothes when working with batteries. If the electrolyte gets into your eyes, flush the area thoroughly with clean water and get prompt medical attention.

When charging a battery, highly explosive hydrogen gas forms in each cell. Some of this gas escapes through filler cap openings and can form an explosive atmosphere in and around the battery. This condition can persist for several hours. Sparks, an open flame or a lighted cigarette can ignite the gas, causing an internal battery explosion and possible serious personal injury.

When servicing your battery, note the following precautions to prevent an explosion or personal injury:

1. Do not smoke or permit any open flame near any battery being charged or near a recently charged battery.
2. Do not disconnect live circuits from battery terminals since a spark usually occurs when a live circuit is broken.
3. Take care when connecting or disconnecting a battery charger. Be sure its power switch is off before making or breaking connections. Poor connections are a common cause of electrical arcs which cause explosions.
4. Keep all children and pets away from charging equipment and batteries.

Battery Removal

The battery mounts in a battery box (**Figure 1**) on the right side of the motorcycle, behind the rear cylinder head.

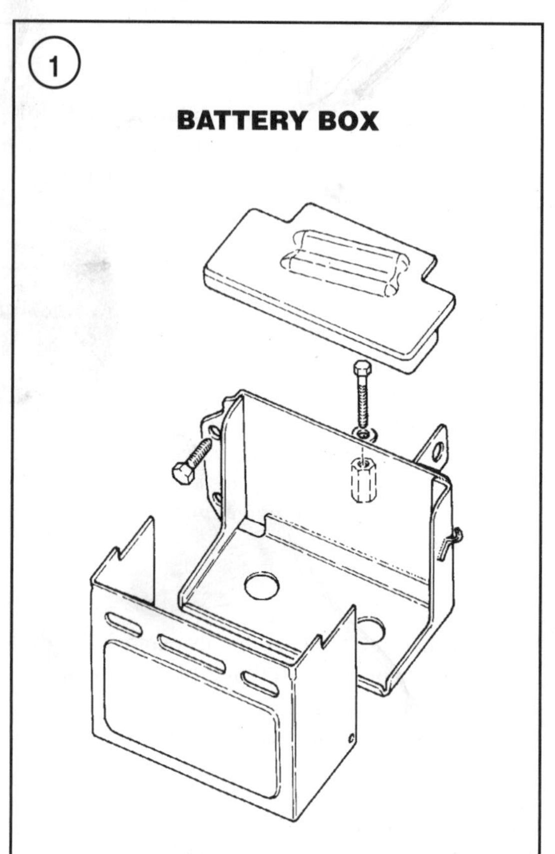

On all models covered in this manual, the negative side is grounded. When removing the battery, disconnect the negative (–) cable first, then the positive (+) cable. This sequence reduces the chance of a tool shorting to ground when disconnecting the "hot" positive cable.

1. Read the information listed under *Service Precautions* in this section, then continue with Step 2.
2. Remove the seat.
3. Disconnect the negative battery cable from the battery (A, **Figure 2**).
4. Remove the positive battery cable bolt, positive battery cable and spacer (B, **Figure 2**) from the battery.
5. Loosen the 2 battery tray mounting bolts (A, **Figure 3**) mounted between the battery tray and the rear fender.
6. Loosen the battery tray bolt (C, **Figure 2**) mounted between the battery tray and frame tube. Then remove the battery top and side (B, **Figure 3**) covers. If you cant remove the covers, loosen the battery tray bolt (C, **Figure 2**) a few more turns.

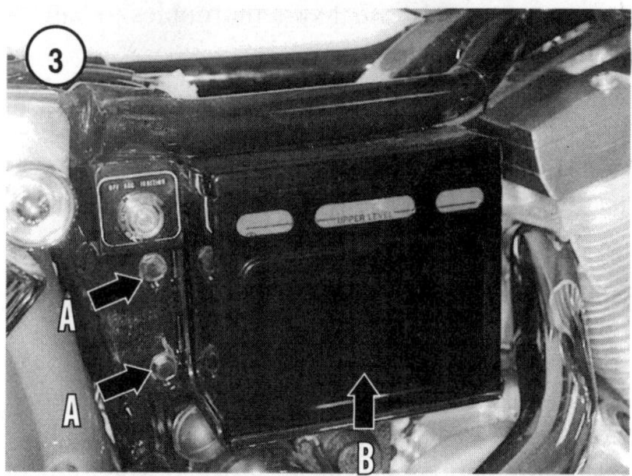

7. Disconnect the vent tube from the battery and remove the battery from the battery box.

CAUTION
Be careful not to spill the electrolyte on painted or polished surfaces. The liquid is highly corrosive and will damage the finish. If you spill it, wash it off immediately with soapy water and thoroughly rinse with clean water.

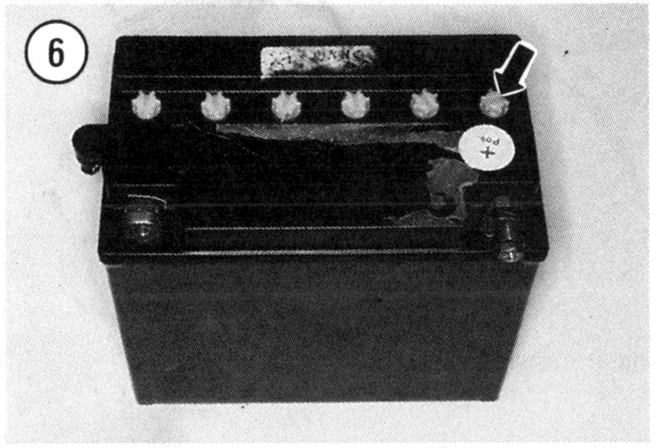

Cleaning and Inspection

For maximum battery life, check it periodically for the correct electrolyte level, state of charge and damage. During hot and cold weather periods, check the battery frequently, even if you are not riding your motorcycle. A battery not in use will discharge about 1 percent of its capacity each day.

If the electrolyte level is below the bottom of the vent well in one or more cells, add distilled water as required. To ensure proper mixing of the water and acid, operate the engine immediately after adding water. *Never* add battery acid to a used battery instead of water. This will shorten the battery's life.

1. Inspect the battery box (**Figure 4**) for contamination or damage. Clean with a solution of baking soda and water.
2. Check the battery case (**Figure 5**) for cracks or other damage. If the battery case is warped, discolored or has a raised top, the battery has been suffering from overcharging or overheating.
3. Check the battery clamps for corrosion and damage. If corrosion is minor, clean the battery cable clamps with a stiff wire brush. Replace severely worn or damaged cables.
4. Check the battery terminal parts—bolts, spacers and nuts—for corrosion or damage. Clean parts thoroughly with a solution of baking soda and water. Replace severely corroded or damaged parts.

NOTE
When cleaning the battery in Step 5, keep the cleaning solution out of the battery cells or it will weaken the electrolyte.

5. Clean the top of the battery with a stiff bristle brush and a baking soda and water solution.

NOTE
Do not overfill the battery cells in Step 6. The electrolyte expands due to heat from charging and will overflow if the level is above the upper level line.

6. Remove the caps (**Figure 6**) from the battery cells and check the electrolyte level. Add distilled water, if necessary, to bring the level between the upper and lower level lines on the battery case (**Figure 6**).

8

Battery Installation

To prevent damage to the battery plates from vibration, install the battery firmly in its battery box.

1. Install the battery into the battery box so that the battery terminals face inward (**Figure 2**). Reconnect the vent tube to the battery.

NOTE
*If you removed the battery vent tube from the bike, refer to **Battery Vent Tube Routing** in this chapter to install the tube.*

2. Install the spacer, positive battery cable and bolt (A, **Figure 2**). Tighten the bolt securely.
3. Install and tighten the negative battery cable (B, **Figure 2**).

CAUTION
Be sure you connect the battery cables to their proper terminals. Connecting the battery terminals backward will reverse the polarity and damage the rectifier and ignition system.

4. Coat the battery connections with dielectric grease or petroleum jelly.
5. Install the battery side cover (B, **Figure 3**). Insert the side covers front bottom edge into the lip in the bottom of the battery box.
6. Install the battery top cover.
7. Tighten the battery tray mounting bolt (C, **Figure 2**) until the battery top cover firmly contacts the upper frame tube.

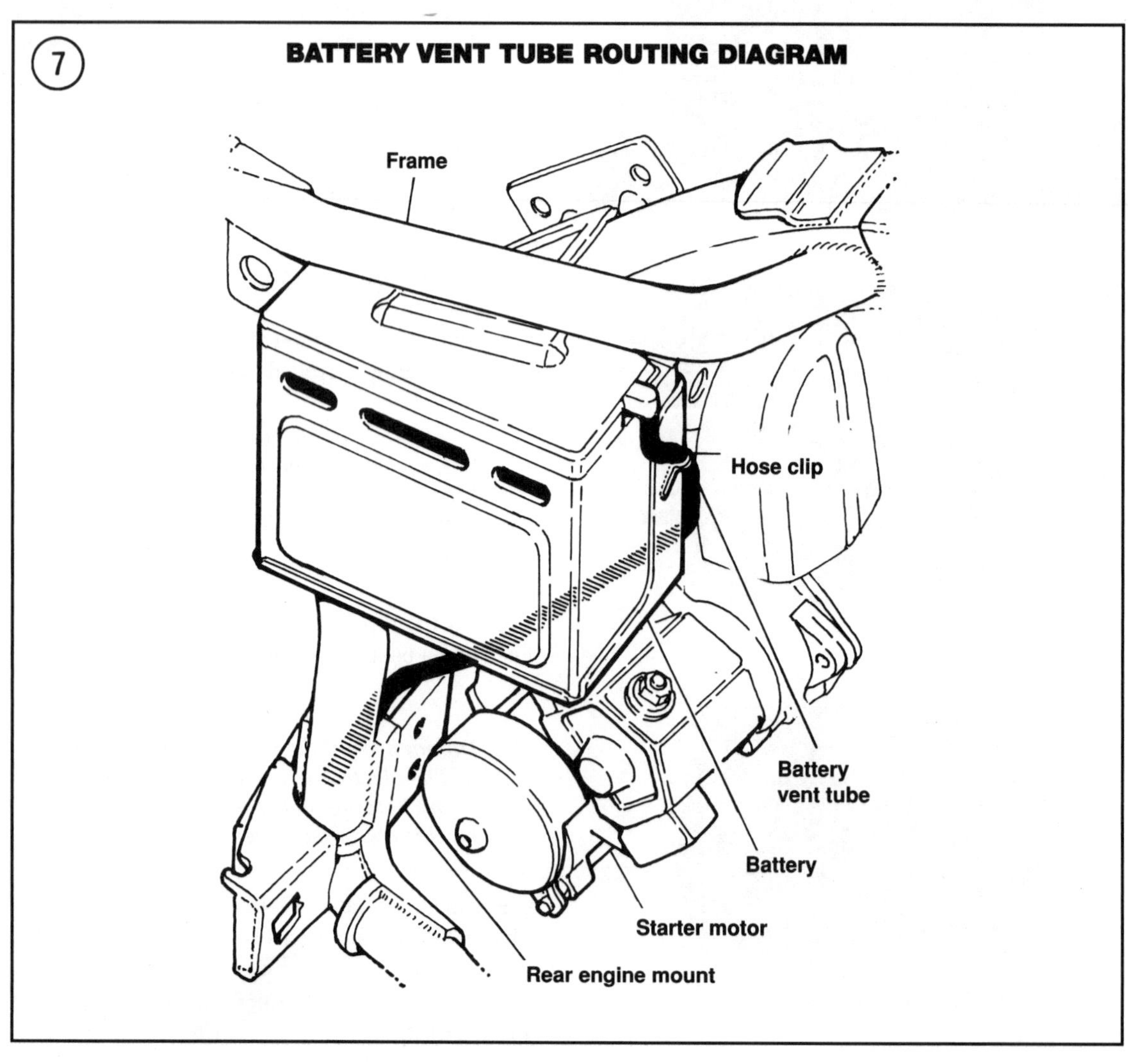

8. Tighten the 2 battery box mounting bolts (A, **Figure 3**) to thc tightcning torque in **Table 4**.

WARNING
After installing the battery, make sure the vent tube is not pinched. A blocked tube will allow high pressure to accumulate in the battery, causing the battery electrolyte to overflow. Replace a plugged or damaged vent tube.

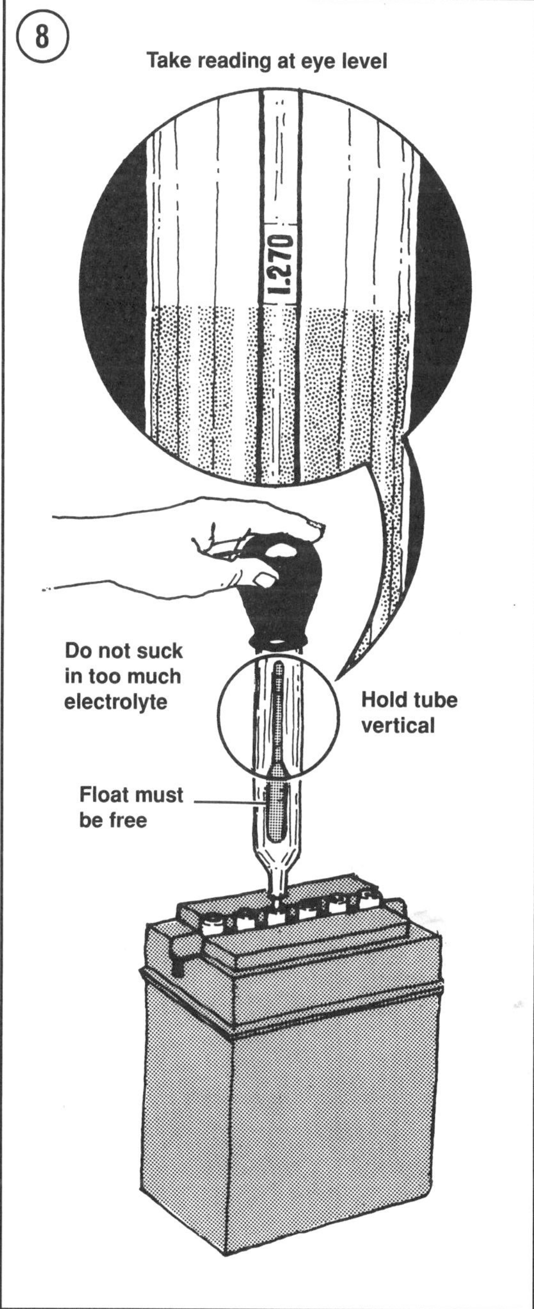

9. Install the seat.

Battery Vent Tube Routing

You must route the battery vent tube properly and so that it is not touching any moving part. Proper routing will ensure that the vent tube outlet (**Figure 7**) is positioned away from all metal components. Replace the vent tube if plugged or damaged.

Connect the vent tube to the battery vent nipple.

Testing

Hydrometer testing is the best way to check battery condition. Use a hydrometer with numbered graduations from 1.100 to 1.300 rather than one with just color-coded bands. To use the hydrometer, squeeze the rubber ball, insert the tip into the cell and release the ball (**Figure 8**).

NOTE
Do not test a battery with a hydrometer immediately after adding water to the cells. Charge the battery for 15-20 minutes at a rate high to cause vigorous gassing and allow the water and electrolyte to mix thoroughly.

Draw enough electrolyte to float the weighted float inside the hydrometer. When using a temperature-compensated hydrometer, release the electrolyte and repeat this process several times to make sure the hydrometer has adjusted to the electrolyte temperature before taking the reading.

Hold the hydrometer vertically and note the number aligned with the surface of the electrolyte (**Figure 9**). This is the specific gravity for this cell. Return the electrolyte to the cell from which it came.

The specific gravity of the electrolyte in each battery cell is an excellent indication of that cell's condition (**Table 2**). A fully charged cell will read 1.275-1.280 while a cell in good condition reads from 1.225-1.250 and anything below 1.225 is dead. Charging is also necessary if the specific gravity varies more than 0.050 from cell to cell.

NOTE
If a temperature-compensated hydrometer is not used, add 0.004 to the

8

specific gravity reading for every 10° above 80° F (25° C). For every 10° below 80° F (25° F), subtract 0.004.

Load Testing

A load test checks the batterys ability to provide current and to maintain a minimum amount of voltage.

You need a battery load tester for this procedure. When using a load tester, follow the manufacturer's instructions. **Figure 10** shows a typical load tester and battery arrangement.

1. Remove the battery from the motorcycle as described in this chapter.
2. This test requires a fully charged battery. Use a hydrometer to check the battery specific gravity as described in this chapter, and bring the battery up to full charge, if required.

WARNING
You must turn the battery load tester OFF prior to connecting or disconnecting the test cables to the battery. Otherwise, a spark could cause the battery to explode, showering the area with sulfuric acid and causing serious injury.

CAUTION
To prevent battery damage during load testing, observe these two requirements: Do not load test a discharged battery and do not load test the battery for more than 20 seconds.

3. Load test the battery as follows:
   a. Connect the load tester cables to the battery following its manufacturer's instructions.
   b. Adjust the load control knob until the ammeter reads 3 times the battery's ampere-hour rating. For example, load your Dyna Glides 19-amp-hour battery to 57 amperes.
   c. Read the voltmeter scale. After 15 seconds, the voltage reading (with the load still applied) must be 9.6 volts or higher. Now quickly remove the load and turn the tester OFF.
4. If the voltage reading is 9.6 volts or higher, the battery output capacity is good. If the reading is below 9.6 volts, the battery is defective.
5. Install the battery as described in this chapter.

Charging

When charging the battery, note the following:

a. During charging, the cells will show signs of gas bubbling. If one cell has no gas bubbles or if its specific gravity is low, the cell is probably defective.
b. A battery is defective if it loses its charge within a week after charging or if the specific

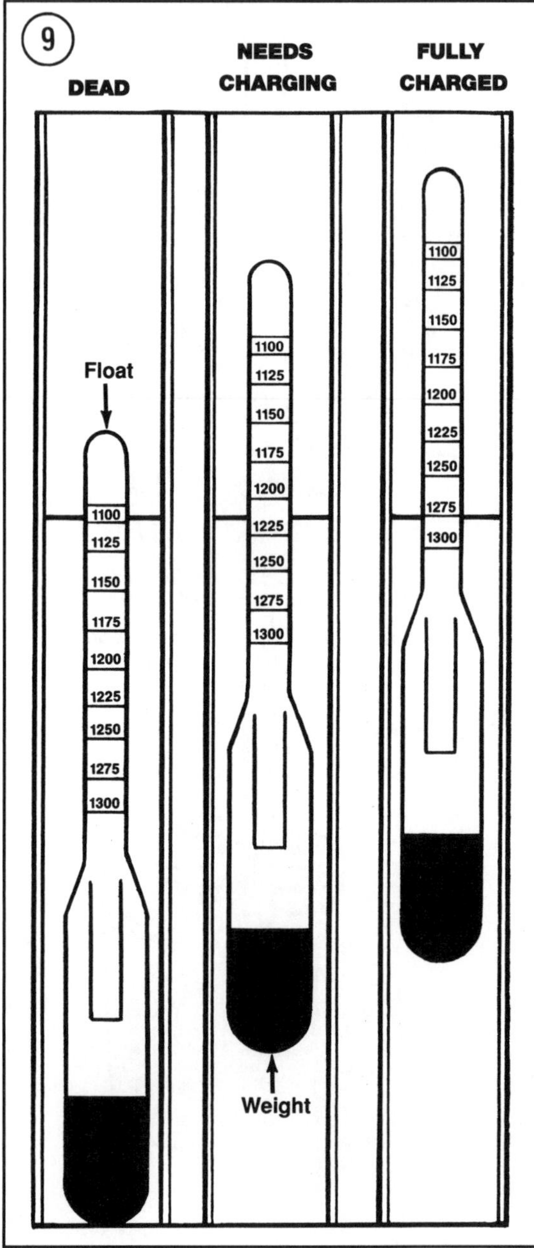

gravity drops quickly. A good battery will self discharge approximately 1% each day.

CAUTION
Always remove the battery from the bike before connecting charging equipment.

WARNING
During charging, the battery releases highly explosive hydrogen gas. Charge the battery in a well-ventilated area, away from all open flames and cigarettes. Never check the charge of the battery by arcing across the terminals; the resulting spark can ignite the hydrogen gas.

1. Remove the battery from the bike as described in this chapter.

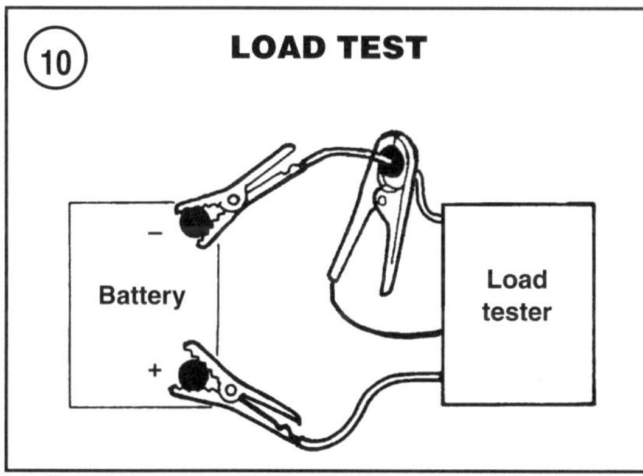

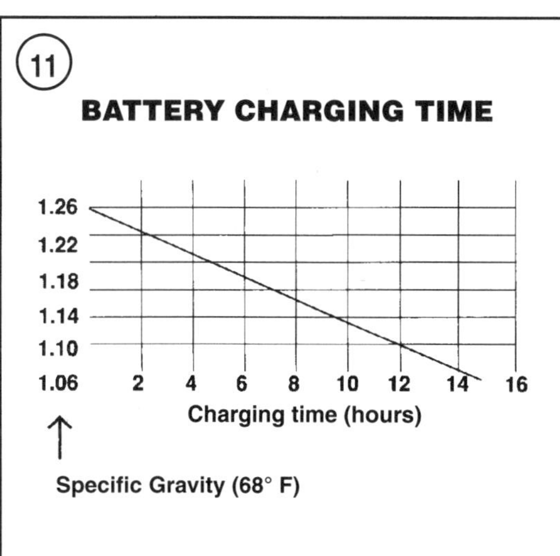

2. Connect the positive (+) charger lead to the positive battery terminal and the negative (–) charger lead to the negative battery terminal.
3. Remove all vent caps (**Figure 6**) from the battery, set the charger at 12 volts, and switch it on. Normally, charge a battery at a slow charge rate of 1/10 its given capacity. See **Table 1** for the battery amp hour rating.

CAUTION
You must maintain the electrolyte level at the upper level during the charging cycle. Refill the battery with distilled water as necessary.

4. The charging time depends on the discharged condition of the battery. You can use the chart in **Figure 11** to determine approximate charging times at different specific gravity readings. For example, if the specific gravity of your battery is 1.180, the approximate charging time is 6 hours.
5. After charging the battery for the required amount of time, turn the charger off, disconnect the leads and check the specific gravity. It must be within the limits specified in **Table 2**. If it is, and remains stable for one hour, the battery is charged.

New Battery Installation

When replacing the old battery with a new one, be sure to charge it completely (specific gravity, 1.260-1.280) before installing it. Failure to do so, or using the battery with a low electrolyte level will permanently damage the battery.

Jump Starting

If the battery is severely discharged, jump start the battery with a separate 12-volt battery. If you do not follow the proper procedure, jump starting can be dangerous. Check the electrolyte level before jump starting any battery. If it is not visible or if it seems frozen, do not attempt to jump start the battery, as the battery may explode or rupture.

A fully charged 12-volt (booster) battery is required for jump starting.

WARNING
To avoid personal injury or vehicle damage, use extreme caution when connecting a booster battery to a dis-

charged battery. Do not lean over the battery when making the connections. Safety glasses must be worn when performing the following procedure.

1. Position the 2 vehicles so that the jumper cables will reach between batteries. The vehicles must not touch during jump starting.
2. Remove the seat to access the dead battery. Remove parts as required to access the booster battery.
3. Turn off all electrical accessories.
4. Connect the jumper cables in the following order (**Figure 12**):
   a. Connect the positive (+) jumper cable between the 2 battery positive terminals.
   b. Connect one end of the negative (–) jumper cable to the booster battery negative terminal. Connect the opposite end to an unpainted engine case bolt on the bike with the dead battery. *Do not* connect the jumper cable to the negative battery terminal on the dead battery.

WARNING
An electrical arc may occur when you make the final connection. This could cause an explosion if it occurs near the battery. Therefore, you must make the final connection to a good ground ***away*** *from the battery and not to the battery itself. This includes keeping the connection away from the battery vent tube.*

NOTE
Do not connect the negative jumper cable to chrome or painted parts or the connection may discolor it.

5. Check that all jumper cables are out of the way of moving parts.

NOTE
When attempting to start the engine in Step 6, do not operate the starter longer than 6 seconds. Excessive starter operation will overheat the starter and cause damage. Allow 15 seconds between starting attempts.

6. Start the engine. Once it starts, run it at a moderate speed.

CAUTION
Racing the engine may cause damage to the electrical system.

7. Remove the jumper cables in the exact reverse order of connection (step 4).

CHARGING SYSTEM

The charging system consists of the battery, alternator, regulator, ignition switch, circuit breaker and connecting wiring. When servicing the charging system, refer to the electrical diagram for your model:

a. 1991-1993 (**Figure 13**).
b. 1994 (**Figure 14**).
c. 1995 (**Figure 15**).

Service Precautions

Before servicing the charging system, observe the following precautions to prevent damage to any charging system component.

1. Never reverse battery connections. Instantaneous damage will occur.
2. Do not short across any connection.
3. Never attempt to polarize an alternator.

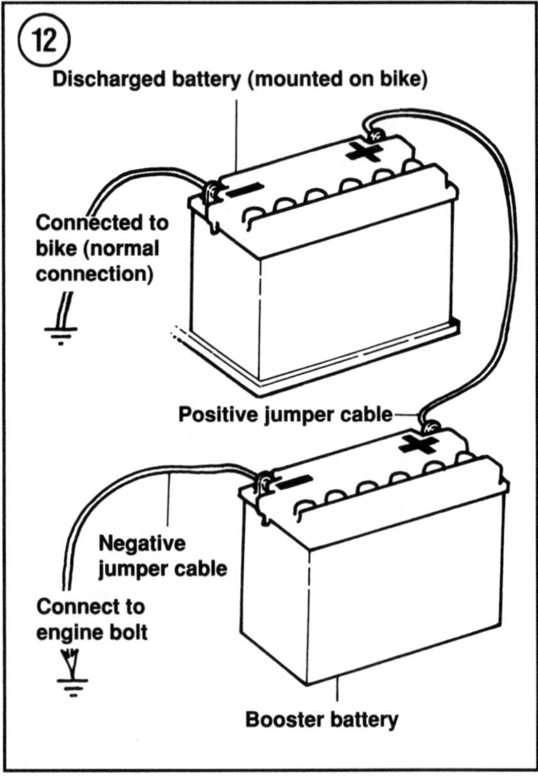

4. Never start the engine with the alternator disconnected from the voltage regulator/rectifier, unless instructed to do so in testing.

5. Never start or run the engine with the battery disconnected.

6. Never attempt to use a high-output battery charger to help start the engine.

7. To charge the battery, refer to *Charging* under *Battery* in this chapter.

8. Never disconnect the voltage regulator connector with the engine running.

9. Do not mount the voltage regulator/rectifier unit at another location.

10. Make sure the battery negative terminal and all ground straps are properly connected.

Testing

A malfunction in the charging system generally causes the battery to remain undercharged. Perform the following visual inspection to determine the cause of the problem. If the visual inspection proves satisfactory, test the charging system as described under *Charging System* in Chapter Two.

1. Make sure the battery cables are connected properly (**Figure 2**). If polarity is reversed, check for a damaged rectifier.

2. Inspect the terminals for loose or corroded connections. Tighten or clean as required.

3. Inspect the physical condition of the battery. Look for bulges or cracks in the case, leaking electrolyte or corrosion build up.

4. Carefully check all connections at the alternator to make sure they are clean and tight.

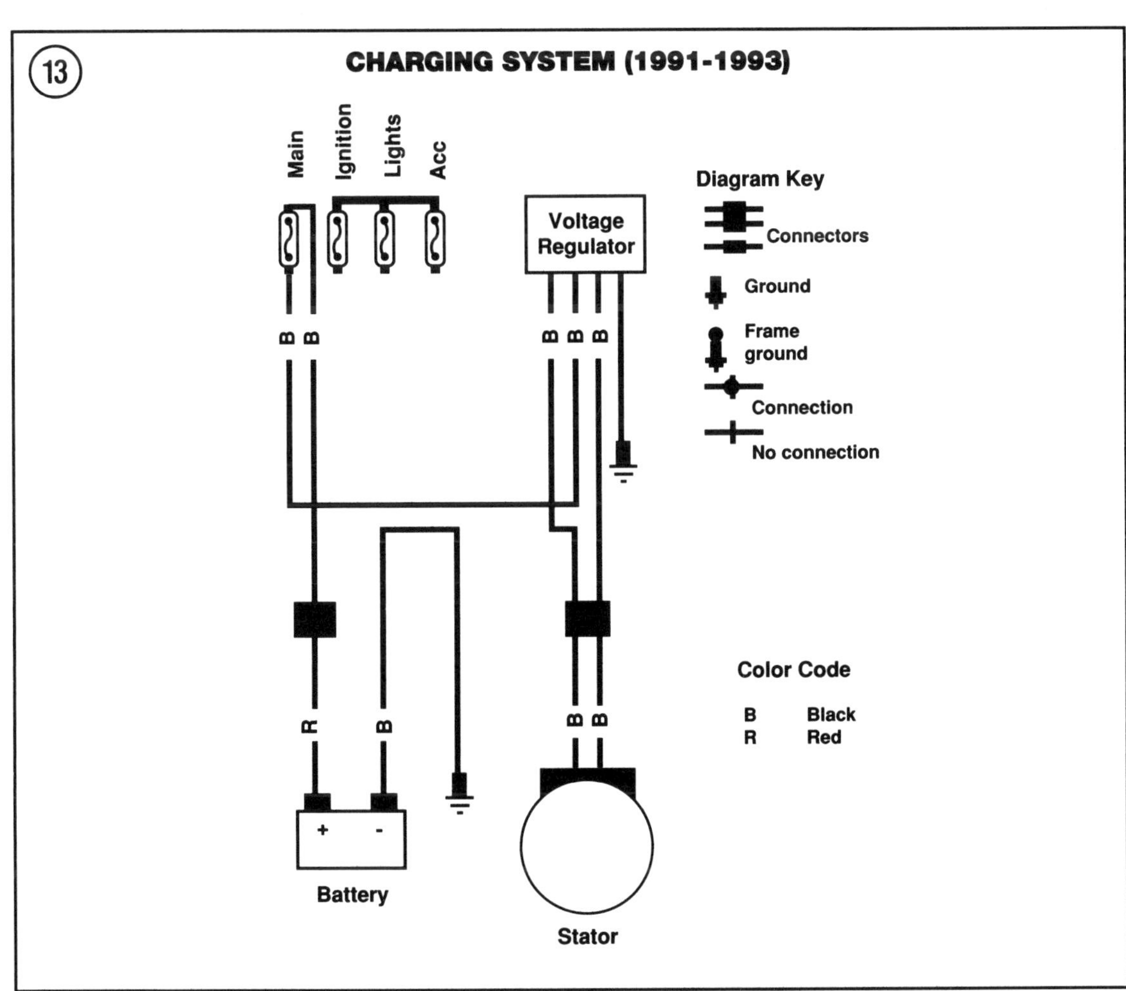

5. Check the circuit wiring for corroded or loose connections. Clean, tighten or connect as required.

Rotor Removal/Installation

The rotor (A, **Figure 16**) mounts behind the compensating sprocket (B, **Figure 16**).

1. Remove the primary chain, engine sprocket and clutch as described in Chapter Five.

2A. To remove the rotor (**Figure 17**) with the inner primary housing installed on the engine, pull the rotor out with 2 pieces of bent wire. Insert the wire hooks into the 2 holes in the face of the rotor.

2B. If you removed the inner primary housing, slide the rotor (**Figure 18**) off the crankshaft.

3. Remove the spacer (**Figure 19**).

4. Install the rotor by reversing these steps, while observing the following *CAUTION*.

CAUTION

*Carefully inspect the rotor magnets (**Figure 20**) for small bolts, washers or other metal debris. These items will damage the stator coils.*

Inspection

1. Check the rotor (**Figure 20**) carefully for cracks or breaks.

WARNING

Replace a cracked or chipped rotor. A damaged rotor may fly apart at high engine speed, throwing metal fragments over a large area. Do not attempt to repair a damaged rotor.

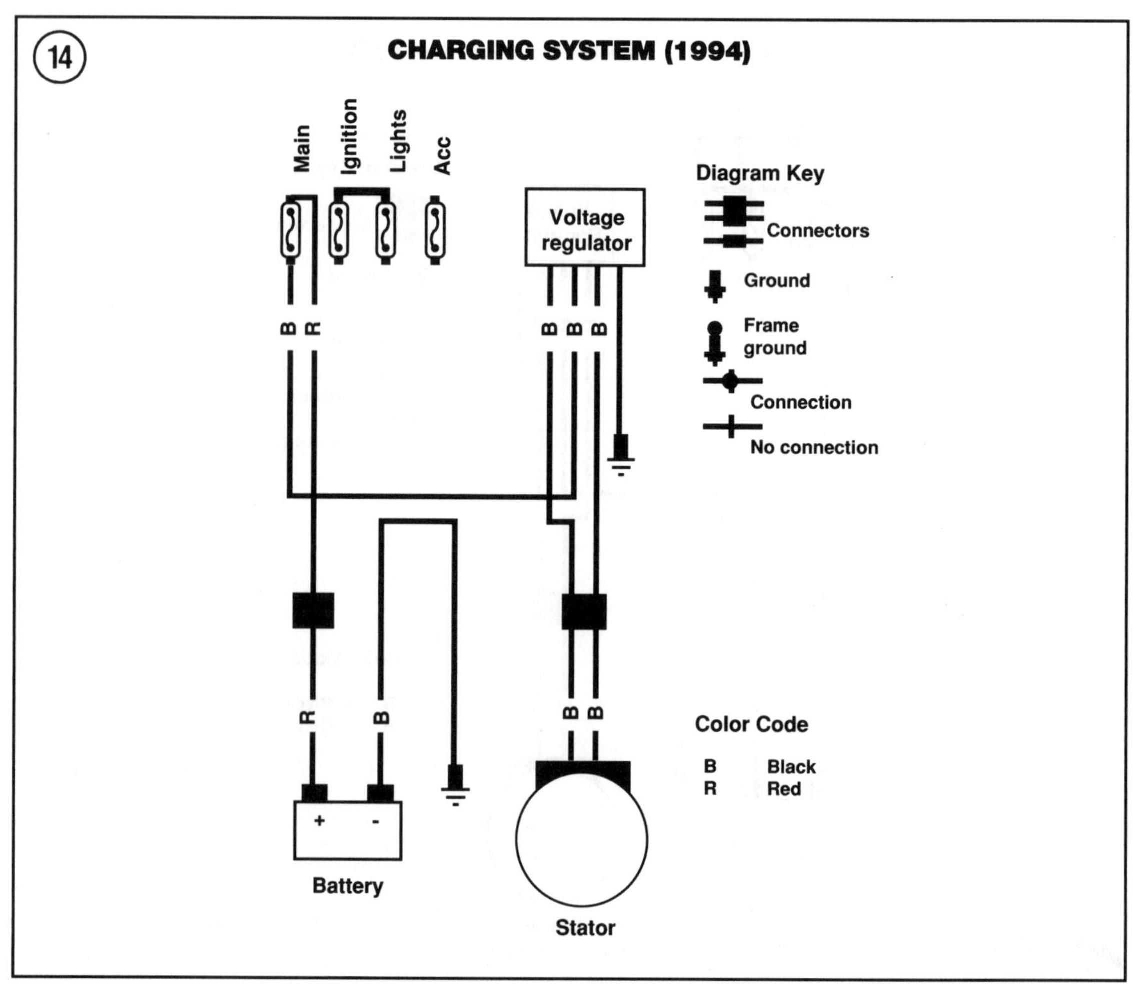

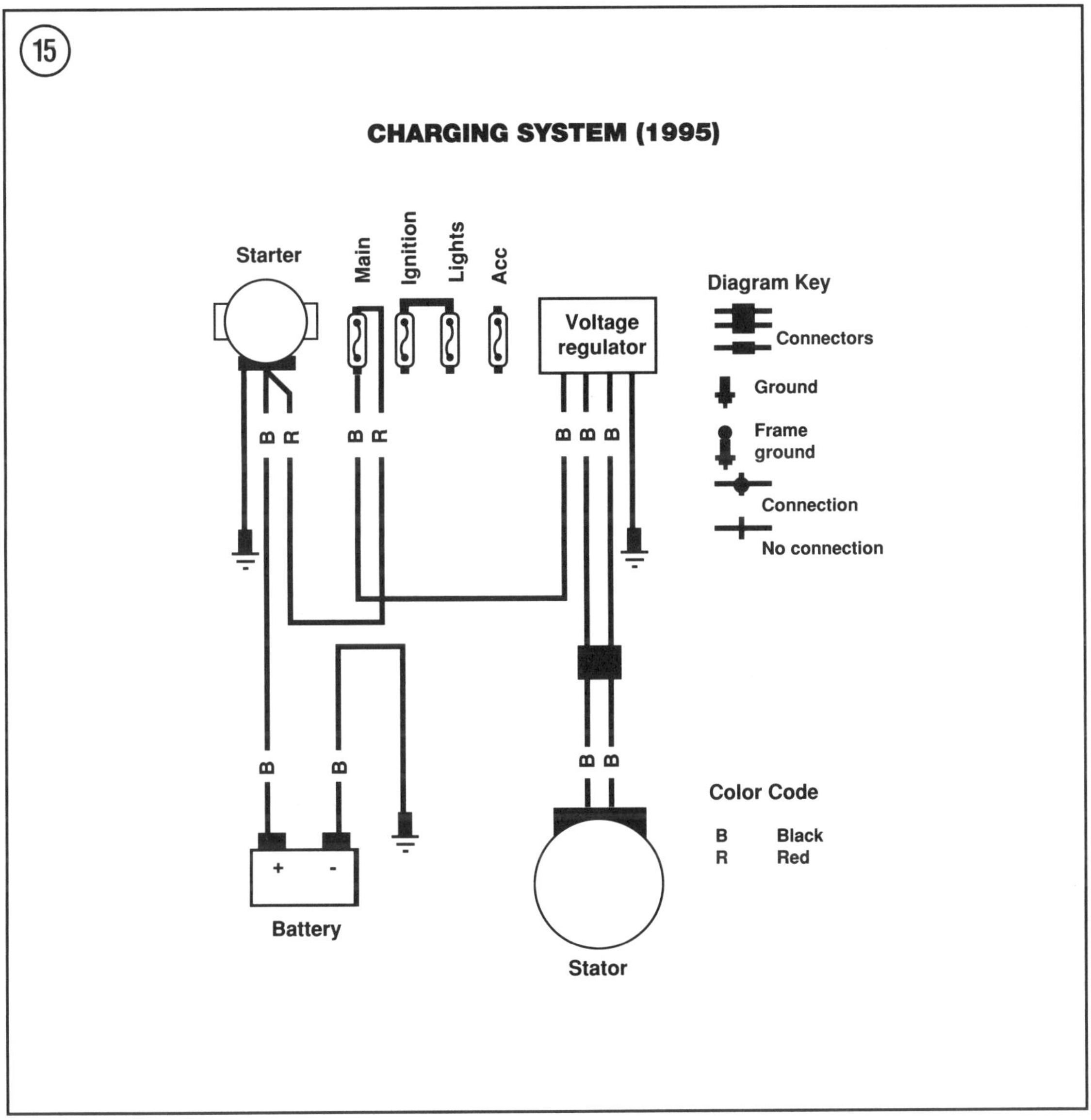

15

CHARGING SYSTEM (1995)

Starter
Main
Ignition
Lights
Acc
Voltage regulator
B R
B R
B B B
B
B
B B
Battery
+
-
Stator

Diagram Key
Connectors
Ground
Frame ground
Connection
No connection

Color Code
B Black
R Red

8

2. Check for damaged or loose rotor magnets (**Figure 20**).

3. Replace the rotor, if necessary.

Stator Removal/Installation

The stator (**Figure 21**) mounts behind the rotor and is bolted to the left-hand crankcase.

1. Remove the rotor as described in this chapter.
2. Disconnect the electrical connector from the stator (**Figure 22**).
3. Remove the retainer plate screws from the retainer plate (**Figure 23**).
4. Remove and discard the stator plate Torx screws (**Figure 24**).
5. Push the stator connector out of the crankcase (**Figure 25**) and remove the stator assembly.
6. Inspect the stator wires (**Figure 26**) for fraying or damage. Check the stator connector pins for looseness or damage. Replace the stator if necessary.
7. Installation is the reverse of these steps. Note the following.

18

19

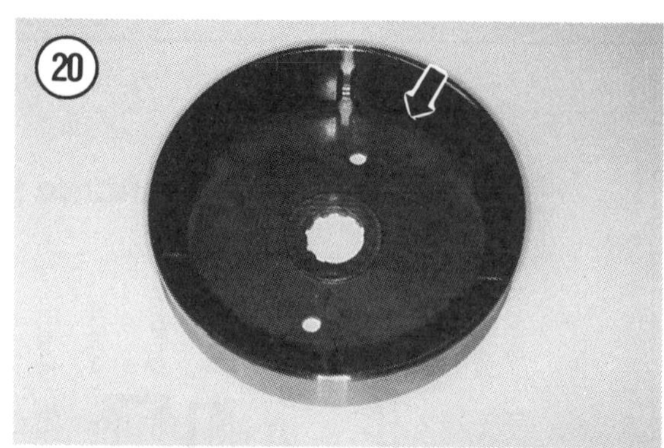

20

21

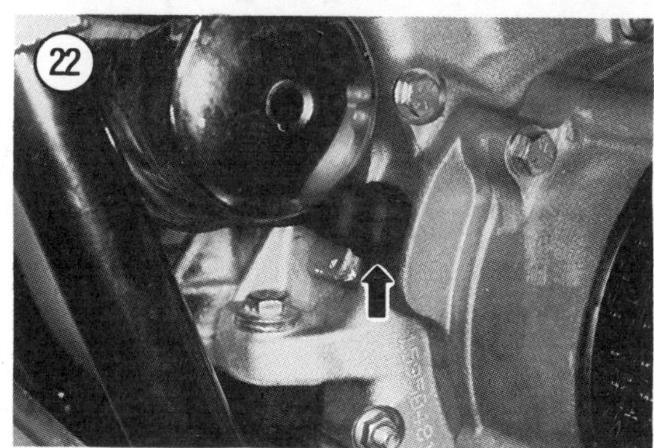

22

23

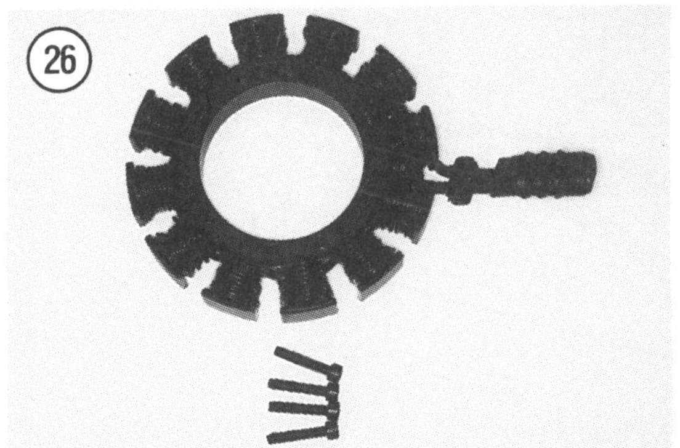

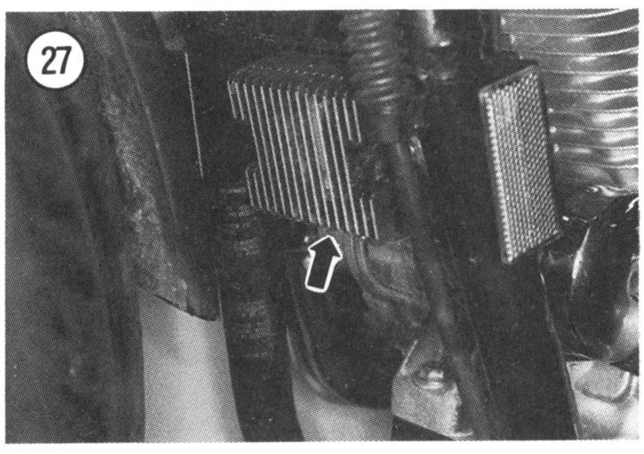

8. Lightly coat the stator connector with engine oil. Then insert the connector (**Figure 25**) into the crankcase.
9. Install *new* stator Torx screws and tighten to the torque specifications in **Table 4**.

CAUTION
As described in Step 9, new Torx screws must be used. The thread locking compound originally applied to the Torx screws is sufficient for one time use only. A loose Torx screw will back out and cause severe alternator damage.

10. Install the rotor as described in this chapter.

Voltage Regulator Removal/Installation

The voltage regulator mounts on the front frame downtubes. See **Figure 27**.
1. Disconnect the negative battery cable as described under *Battery* in this chapter.
2. Remove the electric panel cover (**Figure 28**). Find the main circuit breaker (30 amp) on the back of the electric panel. See **Figure 29** and the charging system diagram for your model (**Figures 13-15**).

8

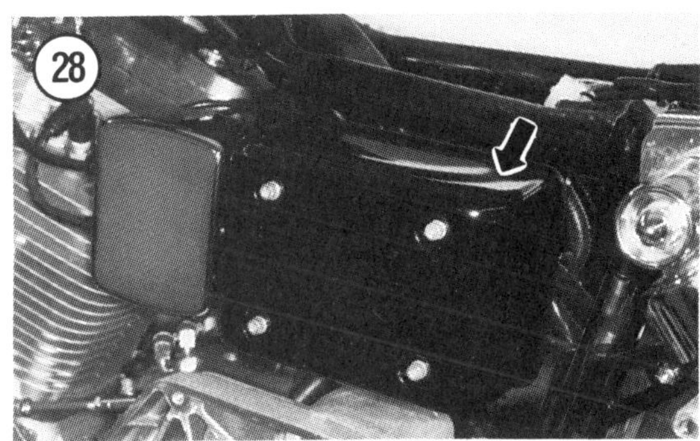

3. Disconnect the voltage regulator wire (**Figure 29**) from the main circuit breaker.

NOTE
Before removing the voltage regulator draw a diagram of its mounting path on a piece of paper.

4. Disconnect and remove any cable straps securing the voltage regulator wiring harness to the frame. Carefully pull the voltage regulator wire away from the frame.
5. Unplug the voltage regulator connector (**Figure 22**) from the crankcase.
6. Remove the voltage regulator mounting fasteners and remove the voltage regulator (**Figure 27**).
7. Install the voltage regulator by reversing these removal steps.

IGNITION SYSTEM

The ignition system (**Figure 30**) consists of a single ignition coil, 2 spark plugs, timing sensor, ignition module and a vacuum operated electric switch (VOES). This system has a full electronic spark advance. The inductive pickup unit is driven by the engine and generates pulses which are routed to the solid-state ignition control module. This control module computes the ignition timing advance and ignition coil dwell time, eliminating the need for mechanical advance and routine ignition service.

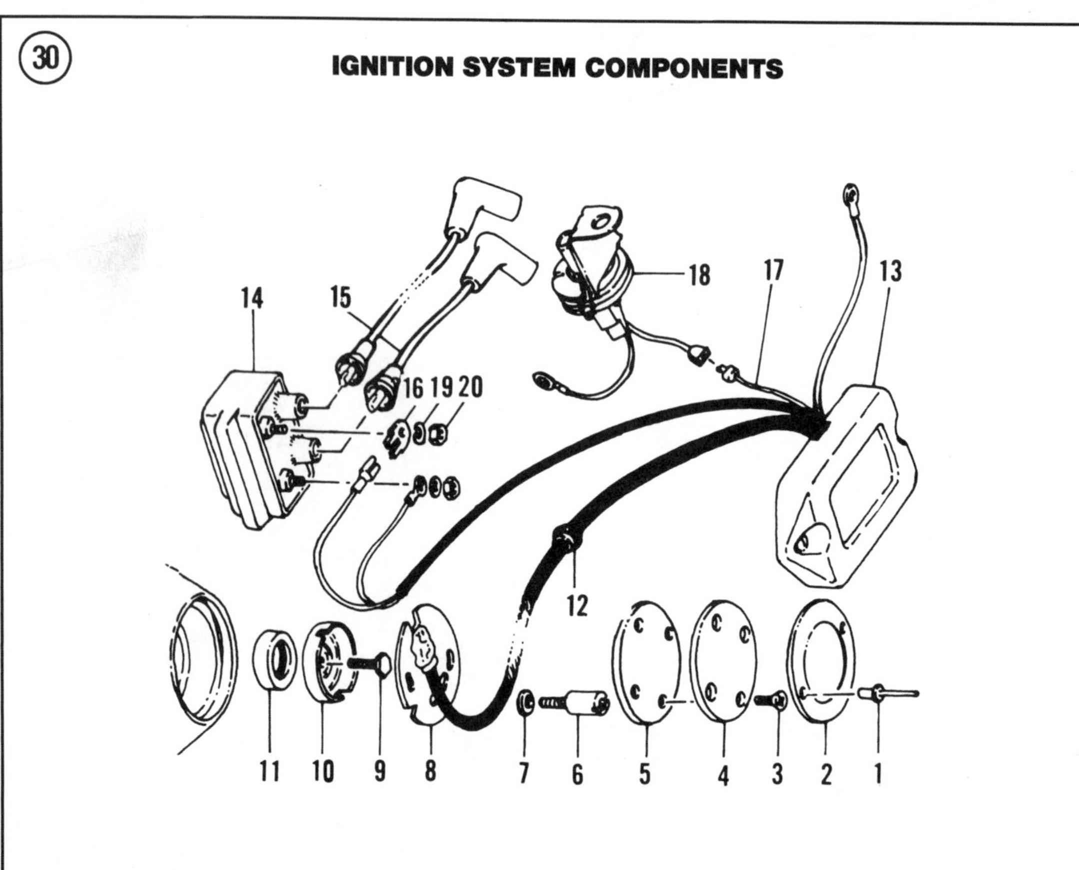

1. Outer cover rivet
2. Outer cover
3. Inner cover screw
4. Inner cover
5. Gasket
6. Sensor plate screw
7. Washer
8. Sensor plate
9. Rotor screw and star washer
10. Rotor
11. Camshaft oil seal
12. Connector
13. Ignition coil module
14. Ignition coil
15. Spark plug cable
16. Ignition coil terminal
17. VOES wire
18. Vacuum operated electric switch (VOES)
19. Washer
20. Nut

The vacuum operated electric switch (VOES) senses intake manifold vacuum through a carburetor body opening. The switch is open when the engine is in low vacuum situations such as acceleration and high loads. The switch is closed when the engine vacuum is high as during a low engine load condition. The VOES allows the ignition system to follow 2 spark advance curves. A maximum spark curve is used during a high-vacuum condition to provide improved fuel economy and performance. During heavy engine load and acceleration (low vacuum) conditions, the spark is retarded to reduce ignition knock and still maintain performance.

The leading and trailing edges of the 2 rotor slots trigger the timing sensor. As rpm increases, the control module steps the timing in three stages of advance.

When servicing the ignition system, refer to the schematic diagram for your model:

a. 1991-1992 models and 1993-1994 FXDL: **Figure 31**.
b. 1993-1994 FXWG: **Figure 32**.
c. 1995: **Figure 33**.

Sensor Plate Removal

Refer to **Figure 30** for this procedure.

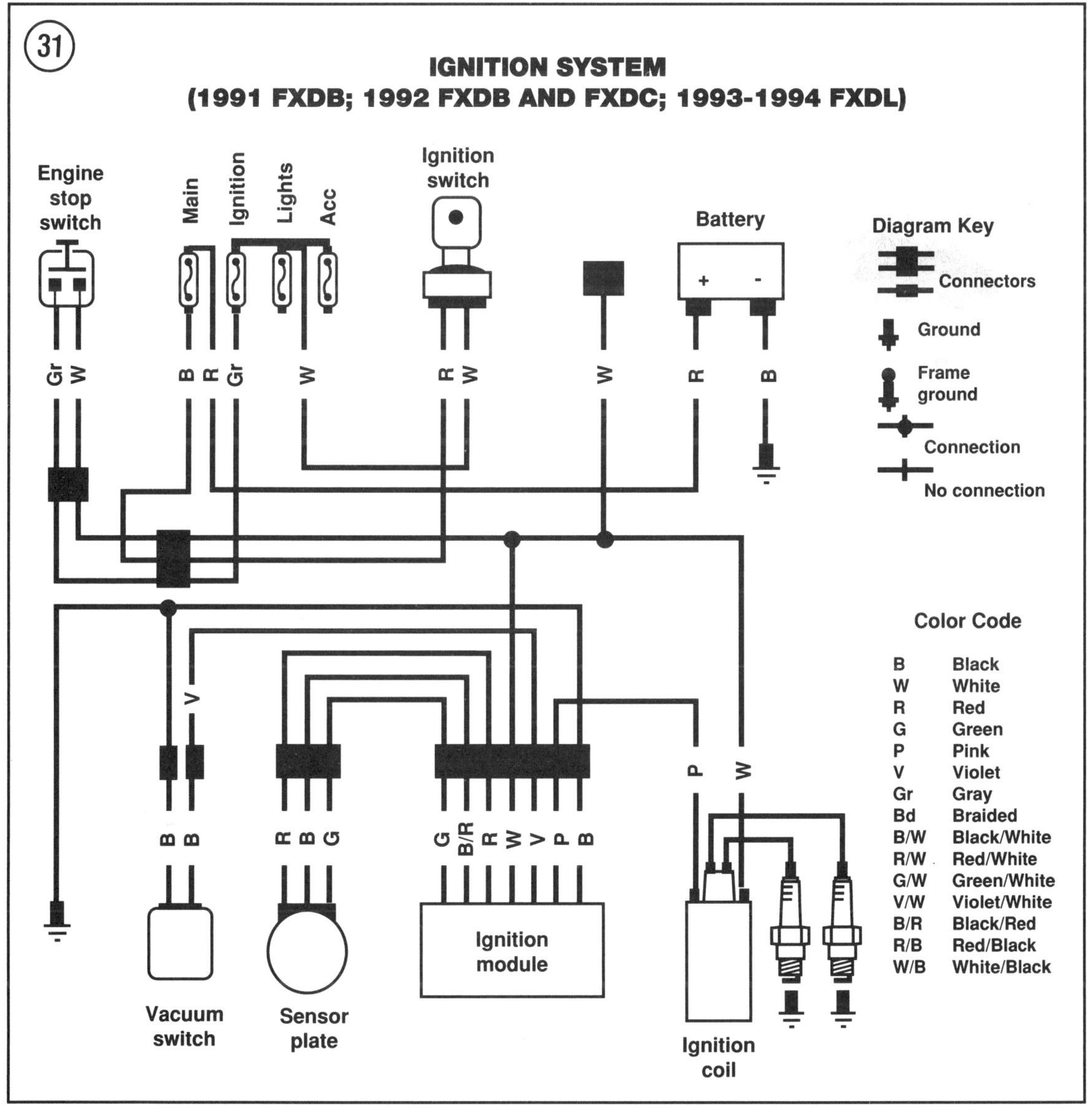

1. Disconnect the negative battery cable as described under *Battery* in this chapter.
2. Drill the heads off the outer cover rivets with a 3/8 in. drill bit (**Figure 34**).
3. Tap the rivets through the outer cover and remove the outer cover (**Figure 35**).
4. Tap the rivets through the inner cover.
5. Remove the inner cover Phillips screws (**Figure 36**). Then remove the cover and gasket (**Figure 37**).
6. Make an alignment mark across the sensor plate mounting screws on the sensor plate so the sensor plate can be reinstalled in its original location.
7. Remove the 2 sensor plate screws (**Figure 38**).

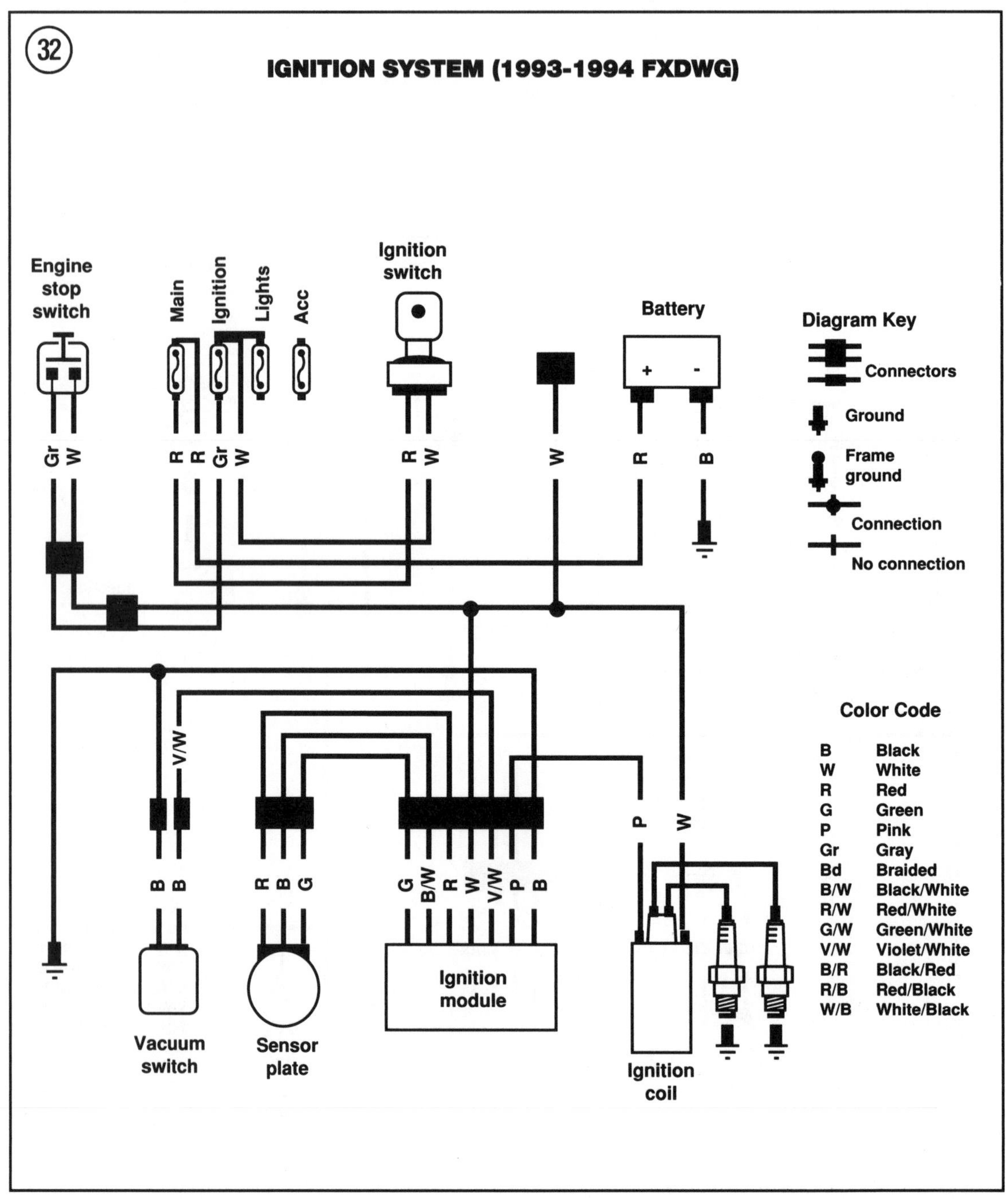

8. Pull the sensor plate away from the rotor. If you are going to remove the sensor plate, perform Step 9. If not, go to Step 10.
9. To remove the sensor plate, perform the following:
   a. Disconnect the sensor plate-to-ignition module electrical connector (**Figure 30**).
   b. Record the position of each sensor plate wiring terminal in the end of the connector (**Figure 39**). See also the ignition system schematic for your model.
   c. Push the terminals from the connector with a small screwdriver or similar tool. See **Figure 40**.
   d. Pull the sensor plate wiring harness out of the gearcase cover (**Figure 41**).
10. Remove the rotor bolt and rotor (**Figure 42**).

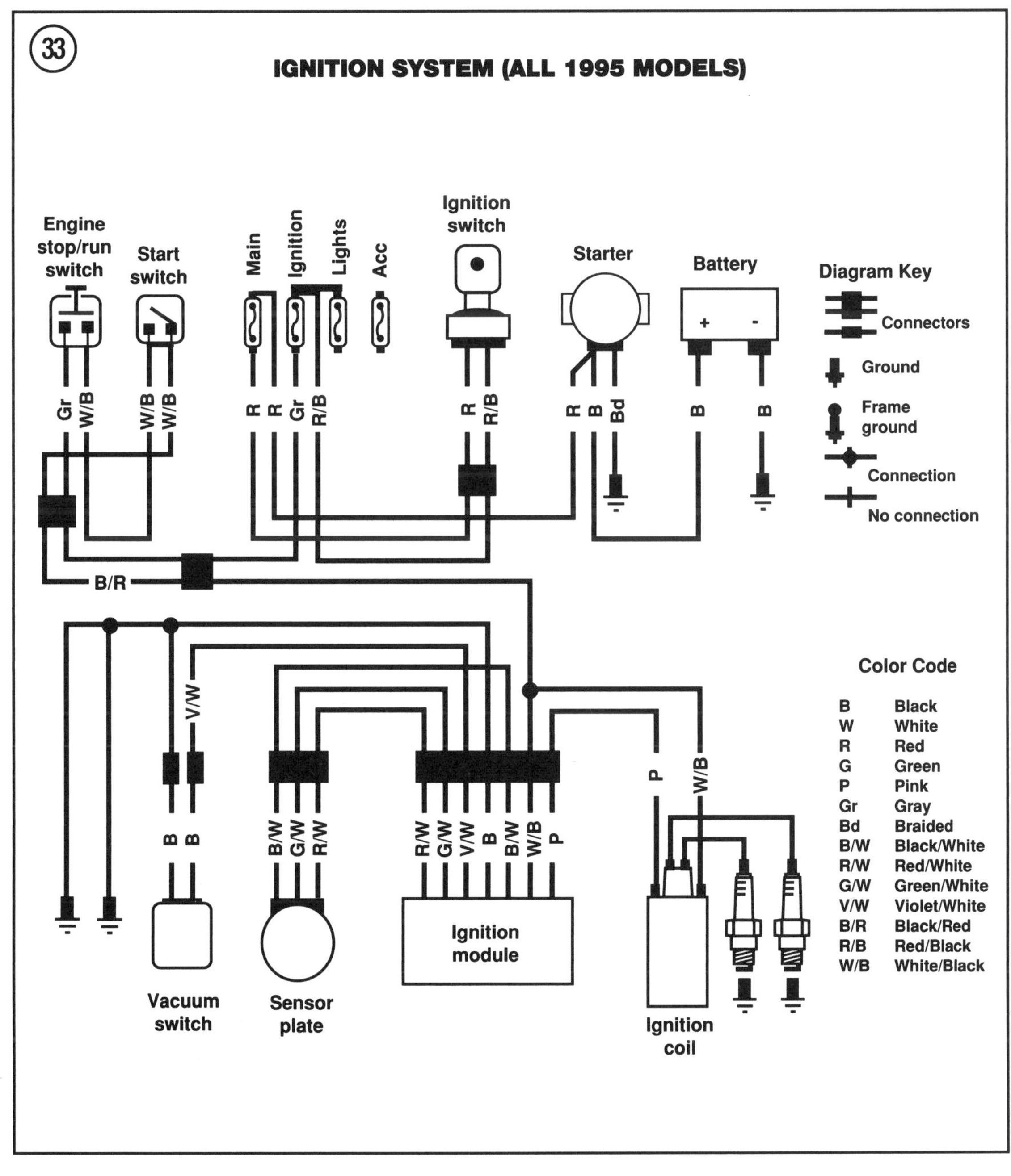

8

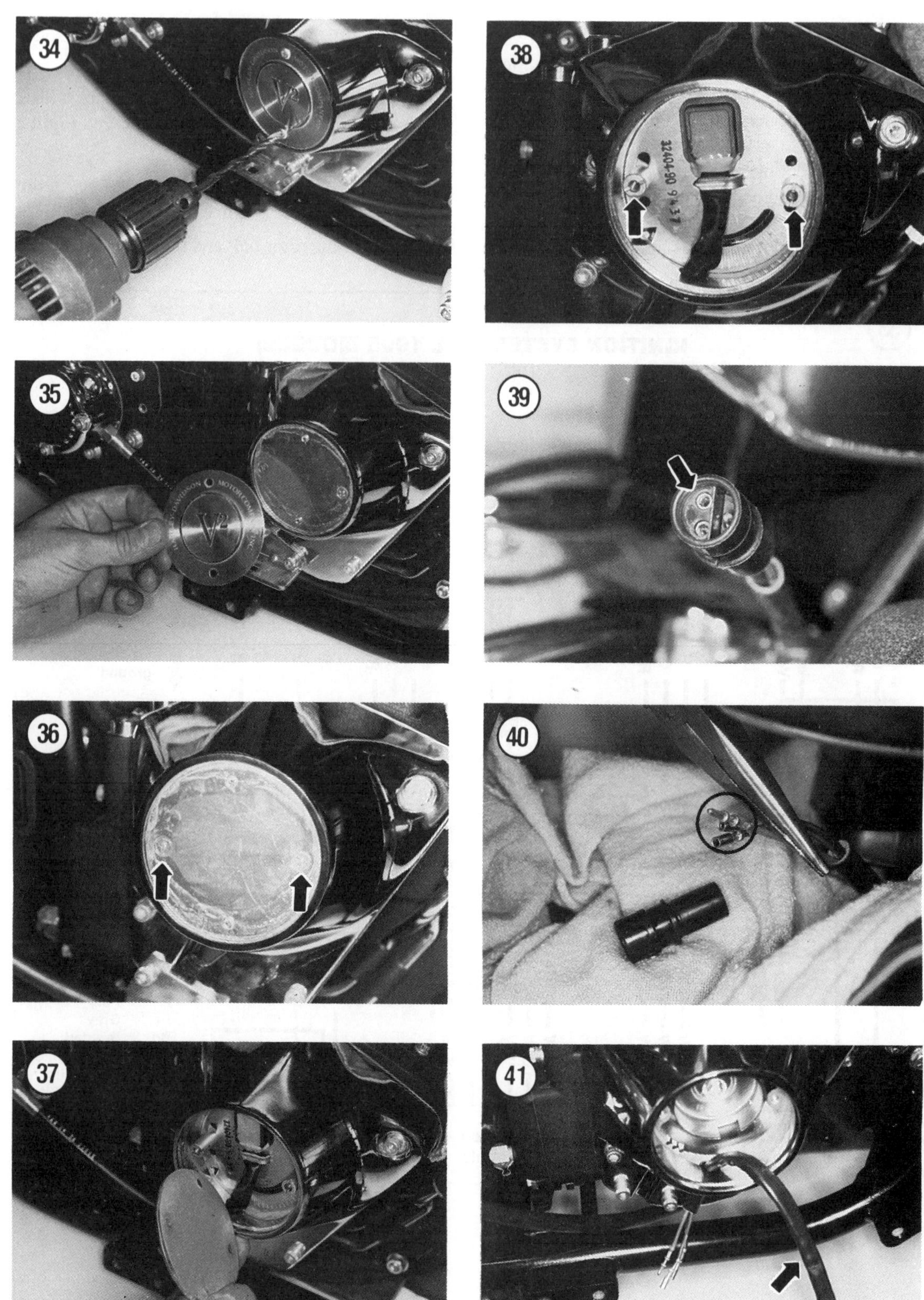
34
38
35
39
36
40
37
41

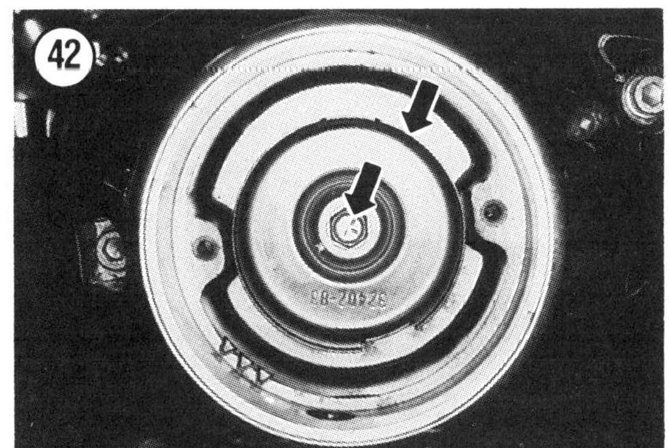

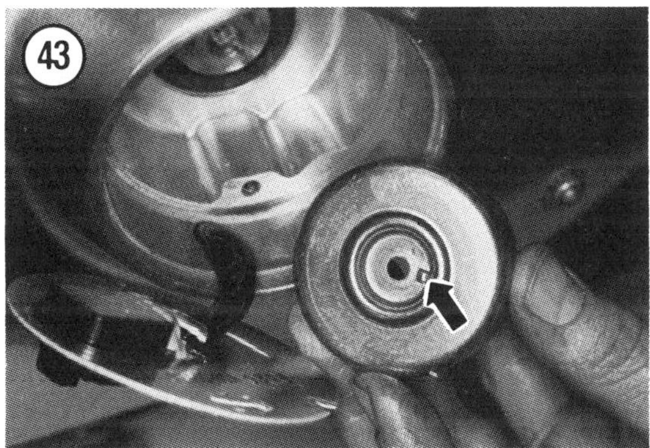

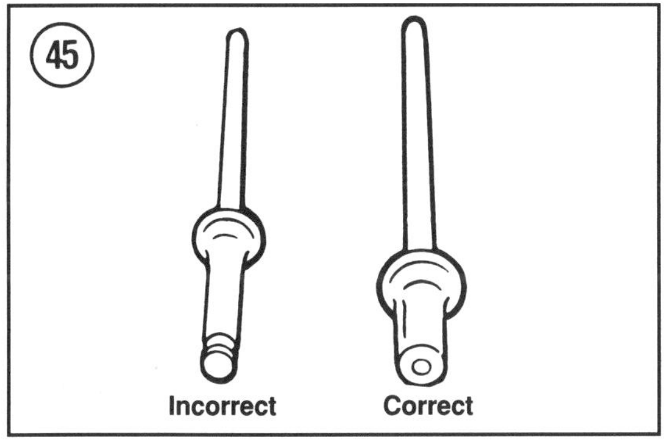

11. Remove the 2 loose rivets from the gearcase cover.

Installation

1. To install the rotor:
   a. Align the tab on the back of the rotor (**Figure 43**) with the notch in the end of the crankshaft (**Figure 44**) and install the rotor. See **Figure 42**.
   b. Apply Loctite 222 (purple) to the rotor bolt (**Figure 42**) and then tighten to the torque specification in **Table 4**.
2. Insert the sensor plate wiring harness through the gearcase cover (**Figure 41**) and route the wiring harness along its original path.
3. Position the sensor plate against the gearcase cover and install the 2 sensor plate screws (**Figure 38**). Align the index marks you made prior to disassembly.
4. To install and reconnect the sensor plate electrical connector, perform the following:
   a. Install the connectors (**Figure 40**) into their respective terminal holes, following your original notes. See **Figure 39**.
   b. Then reconnect the sensor plate-to-ignition module electrical connector.
5. Before riveting the cover in place, check the ignition timing as described in Chapter Three.
6. Install the inner cover and gasket (**Figure 36**). Secure with the 2 mounting screws.

CAUTION
Make sure to use the timing cover rivets specified in Step 7. These rivets do not have ends that fall into the timing compartment when you install them. Loose rivet ends may cause damage to the ignition components inside the gearcase cover.

7. Using Harley-Davidson timing cover rivets (part No. 8699 [**Figure 45**]), rivet the timing cover to the inner cover (**Figure 46**). The rivets must seat flush against the outer cover (**Figure 47**).
8. Reconnect the negative battery cable.

Inspection

1. If necessary, troubleshoot the ignition system as described in Chapter Two.

2. Check the sensor plate and connectors for visible damage (**Figure 48**).
3. Check the ignition compartment for oil leakage. If present, remove the gearcase oil seal (**Figure 44**) by prying it out with a screwdriver or seal remover. Install a new seal by tapping it in place using a suitable size socket. Install the seal until it is flush with the seal bore surface.

Ignition Module Removal/Installation

The ignition module mounts behind the electric panel cover, on the left side of the motorcycle.
1. Disconnect the negative battery cable as described under *Battery* in this chapter.
2. Remove the electric panel cover (A, **Figure 49**).
3. Disconnect the ignition module wires (**Figure 50**) from the ignition coil.
4. Loosen and remove the ignition module ground wire connection from the frame.
5. Remove the nuts securing the electric panel (**Figure 51**) to its mounting studs and carefully pull the panel off its mounting studs. The ignition module (**Figure 52**) mounts on the backside of the electric panel.
6. Disconnect the electrical connector from the ignition module.
7. Remove the nuts, washers and screws securing the ignition module to the electric panel and remove it.
8. Install the ignition module by reversing these steps.

IGNITION COIL

Removal/Installation

The ignition coil (**Figure 50**) mounts on the left side of the motorcycle.
1. Disconnect the negative battery cable as described under *Battery* in this chapter.
2. Remove the ignition coil cover (B, **Figure 49**).

NOTE
Label all wiring connectors prior to disconnecting them in the following steps.

3. Disconnect the ignition module connectors (**Figure 50**) from the ignition coil.

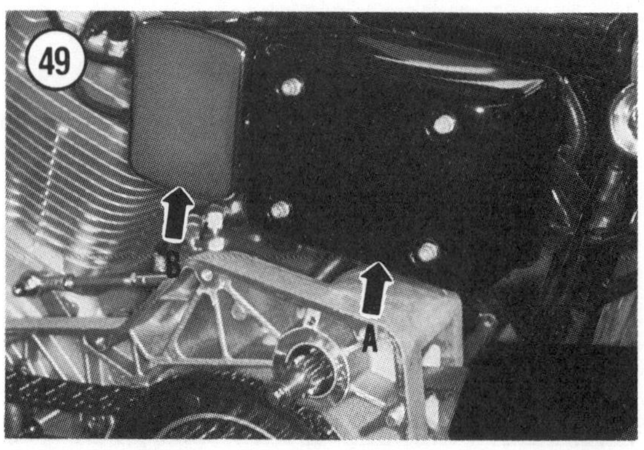

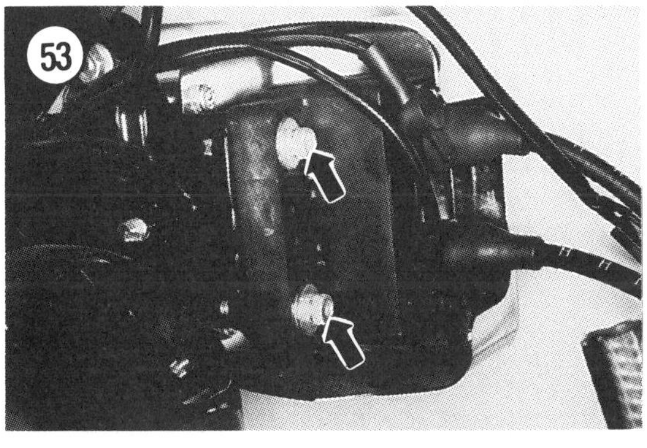

4. Disconnect the spark plug cables from the ignition coil or spark plugs.
5. Remove the bolts and washers (**Figure 53**) securing the ignition coil to the frame and remove the ignition coil.
6. Install the ignition coil by reversing these steps.

VACUUM OPERATED ELECTRIC SWITCH

Removal/Installation

The vacuum operated electric switch (VOES) mounts on the cylinder head mounting bracket.

1. Disconnect the negative battery cable as described under *Battery* in this chapter.
2. Disconnect the ignition module wire from the VOES.
3. Disconnect the VOES ground wire from the engine.
4. Disconnect the vacuum hose from the VOES.
5. Remove the VOES from the mounting bracket.
6. Install the VOES by reversing these steps.

STARTER

When servicing the starting system, refer to the schematic diagram for your model:

a. **Figure 54**: All 1991-1992 and 1993 FXDL.
b. **Figure 55**: 1993 FXDWG.
c. **Figure 56**: 1994 FXDL.
d. **Figure 57**: 1994 FXDWG.
e. **Figure 58**: 1995 FXDL.
f. **Figure 59**: 1995 FXDWG.

CAUTION

Never attempt to operate the starter for more than 5 seconds at a time. If the engine fails to start, wait a minimum of 10 seconds to allow the starter to cool. Otherwise, you can damage the starter.

Removal

1. Disconnect the negative battery cable as described under *Battery* in this chapter.
2. Remove the primary cover as described in Chapter Five.
3. Remove the jackshaft bolt and lockplate (**Figure 60**).

4. Remove the bolt and chrome cover (**Figure 61**) from the end of the starter motor.

5. If necessary, remove the rear exhaust pipe.

6. Disconnect the electrical connectors from the starter motor.

7. Remove the starter motor mounting bolts and washers and remove the starter motor from the right-hand side.

8. If necessary, service the starter motor as described in this chapter.

Installation

1. Install the starter motor from the right-hand side, engaging the starter motor shaft with the jackshaft coupling.

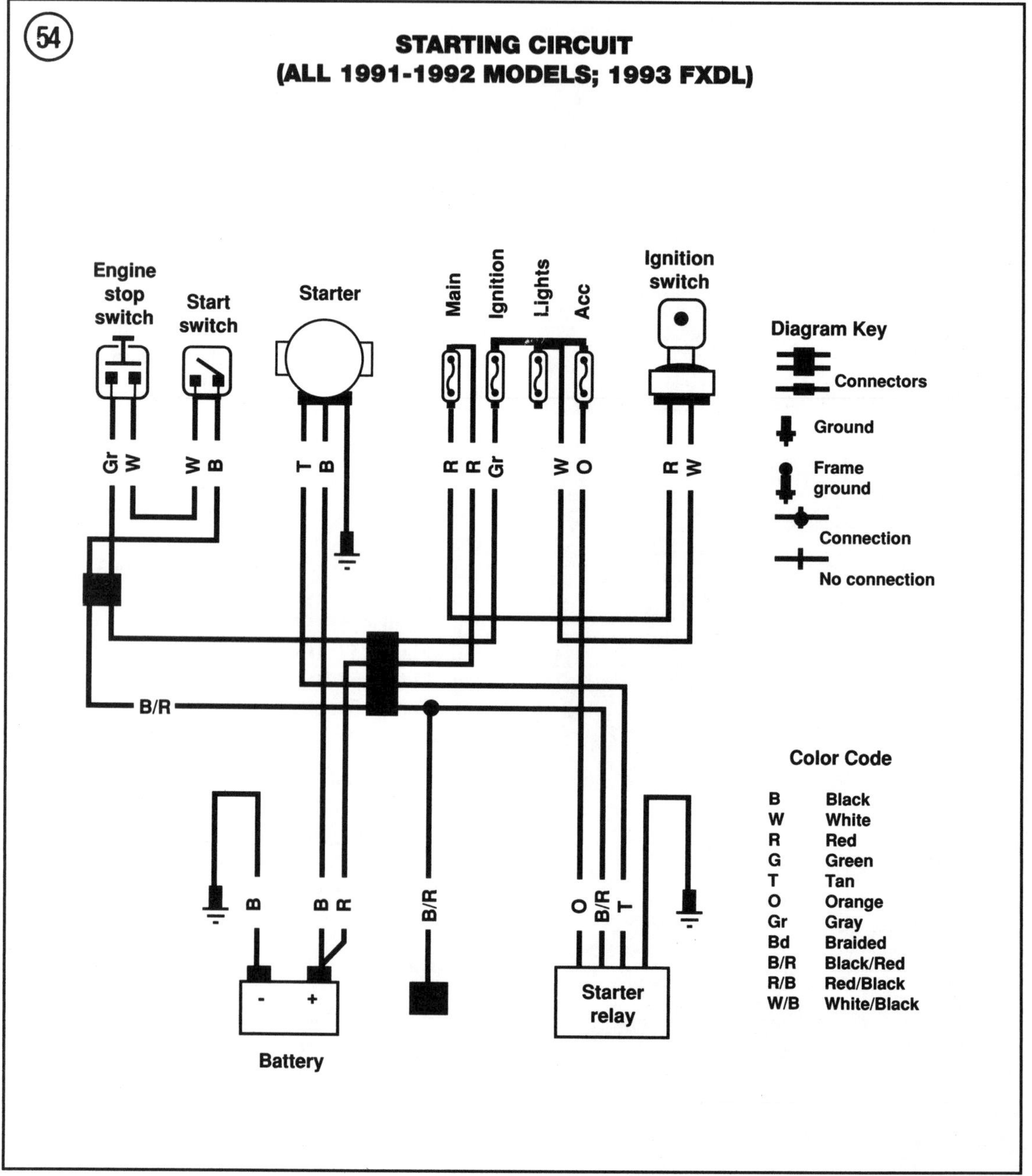

NOTE

*If you removed the jackshaft coupling (**Figure 62**) or if it fell off after removing the starter motor, slide the coupling onto the jackshaft before installing the starter motor. However, before installing the coupling, note the circlip (**Figure 63**) installed inside the coupling. The coupling side with the circlip closest to its end slides over the jackshaft. **Figure 62** shows the jackshaft coupling with the inner primary housing removed for clarity.*

2. Reconnect the electrical connectors from the starter motor.

3. Install the starter mounting bolts and washers and tighten to the torque specification in **Table 4**.

4. Install the jackshaft bolt (**Figure 60**) and lockplate. Align the lockplate tab (**Figure 64**) with its washer, then insert the tab into the notch in the end of the jackshaft. Tighten the jackshaft bolt to the torque specification in **Table 4**. Bend the outer lockplate tab against the bolt head.

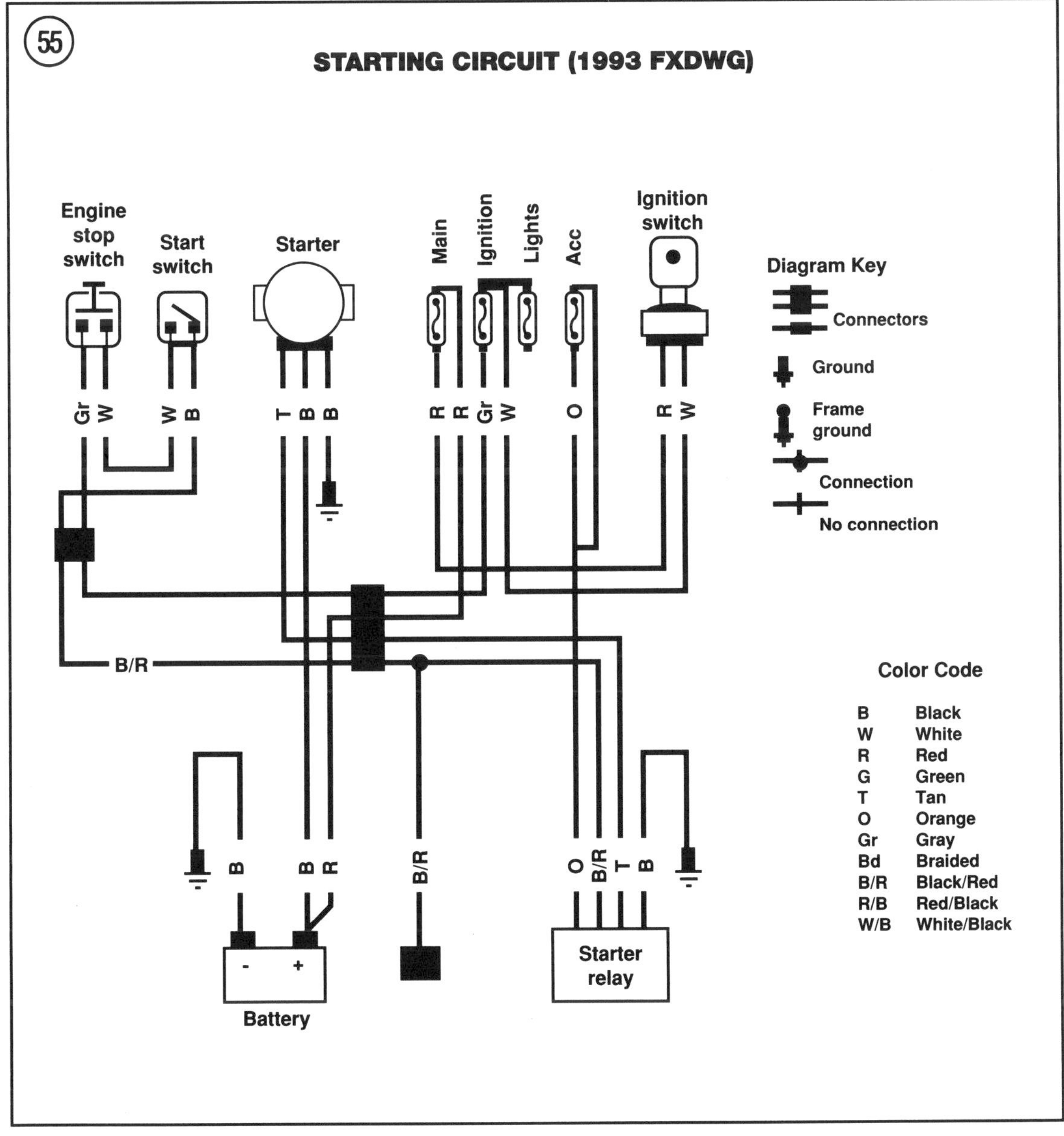

8

5. Install the primary cover as described in Chapter Five.

6. Install the starter chrome cover and its mounting screw.

7. Install the rear exhaust pipe, if removed.

8. Reconnect the negative battery cable to the battery.

Disassembly

Refer to **Figure 65** for this procedure.

Figure 66 identifies the 3 main starter housing subassemblies:

a. Drive housing (A, **Figure 66**).
b. Solenoid housing (B, **Figure 66**).
c. Field coil (C, **Figure 66**).

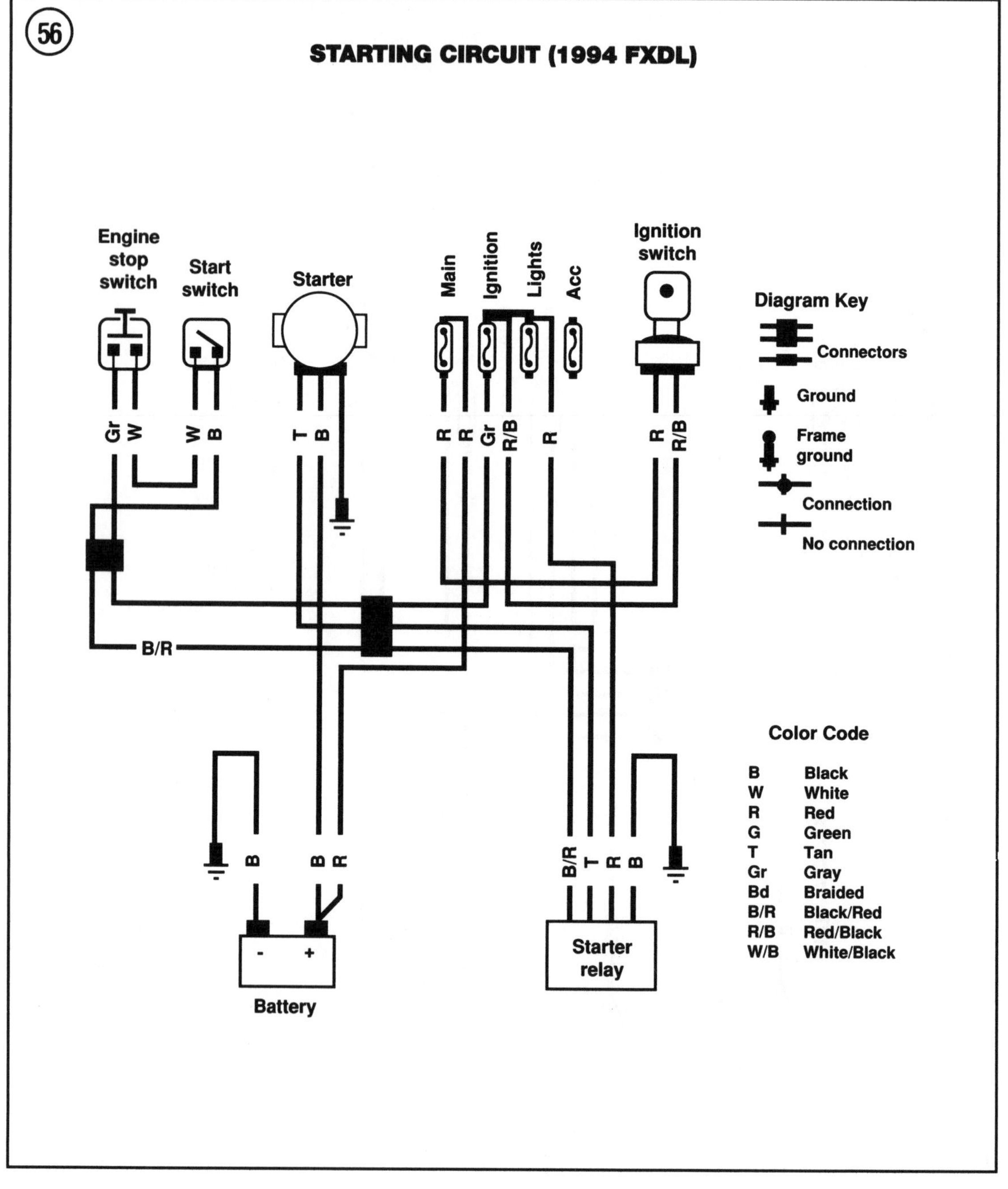

NOTE
*If you only need to service the solenoid assembly (B, **Figure 66**), refer to **Solenoid Housing** in this chapter.*

1. Clean all grease, dirt and carbon from the case and end covers.

2. Remove the 2 through bolts (**Figure 67**).

3. Remove the 2 drive housing screws (**Figure 68**) and lockwashers.

3. Tap the drive housing and remove it from the starter assembly (**Figure 69**).

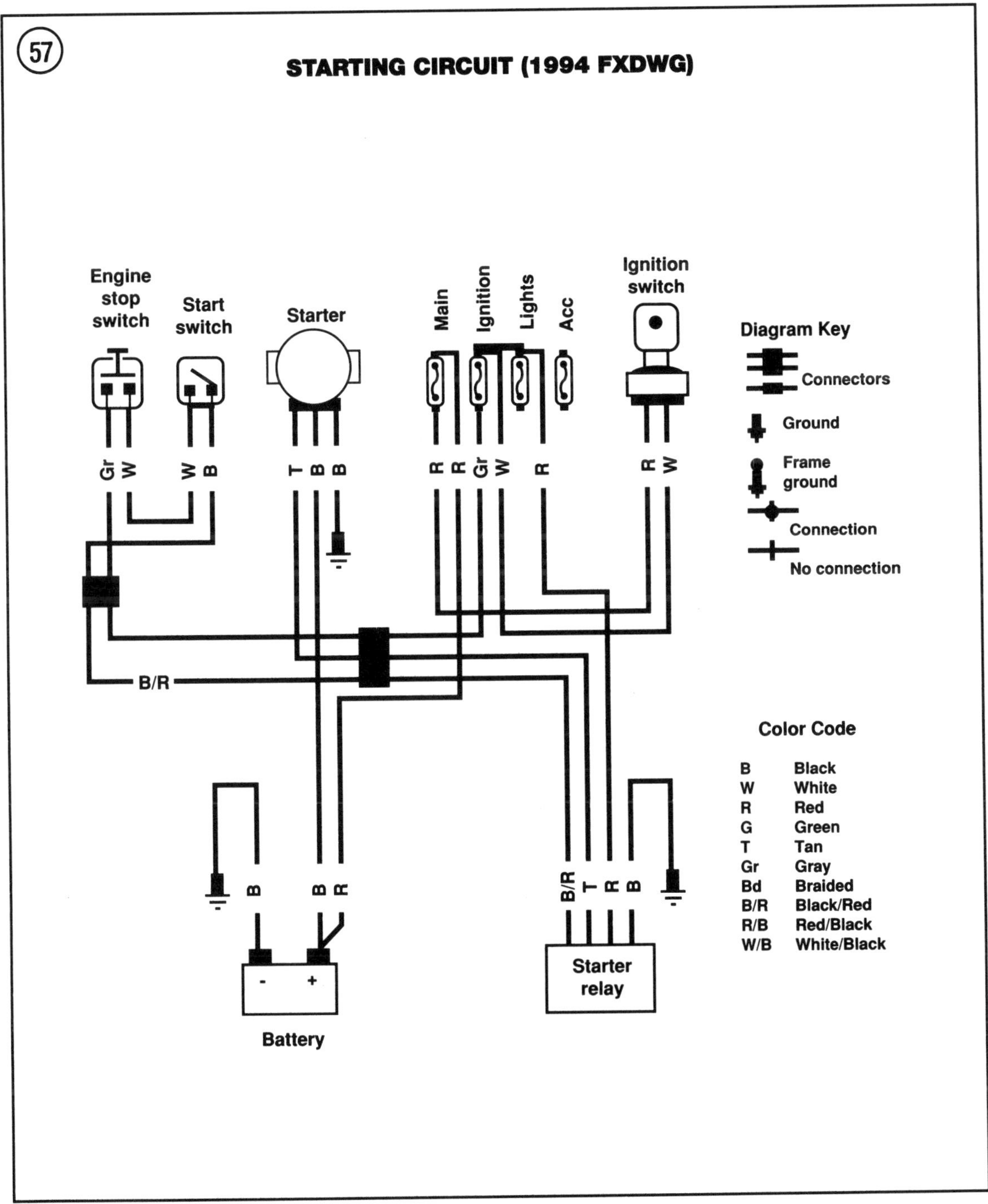

4. Disconnect the C terminal field wire (A, **Figure 70**) from the solenoid housing.

5. Separate the field coil (B, **Figure 70**) from the solenoid housing (C, **Figure 70**). **Figure 71** shows the field coil.

6. Remove the end cap screws, washers and O-rings (A, **Figure 72**). Then remove the end cap (B, **Figure 72**).

7. Pull the brush plate (A, **Figure 73**) away from the commutator and remove the armature (B, **Figure 73**) from the field coil assembly.

8. Remove the 2 field coil brushes from the brush plate (**Figure 74**).

9. To service the drive housing assembly, refer to *Drive Housing Inspection* in this chapter.

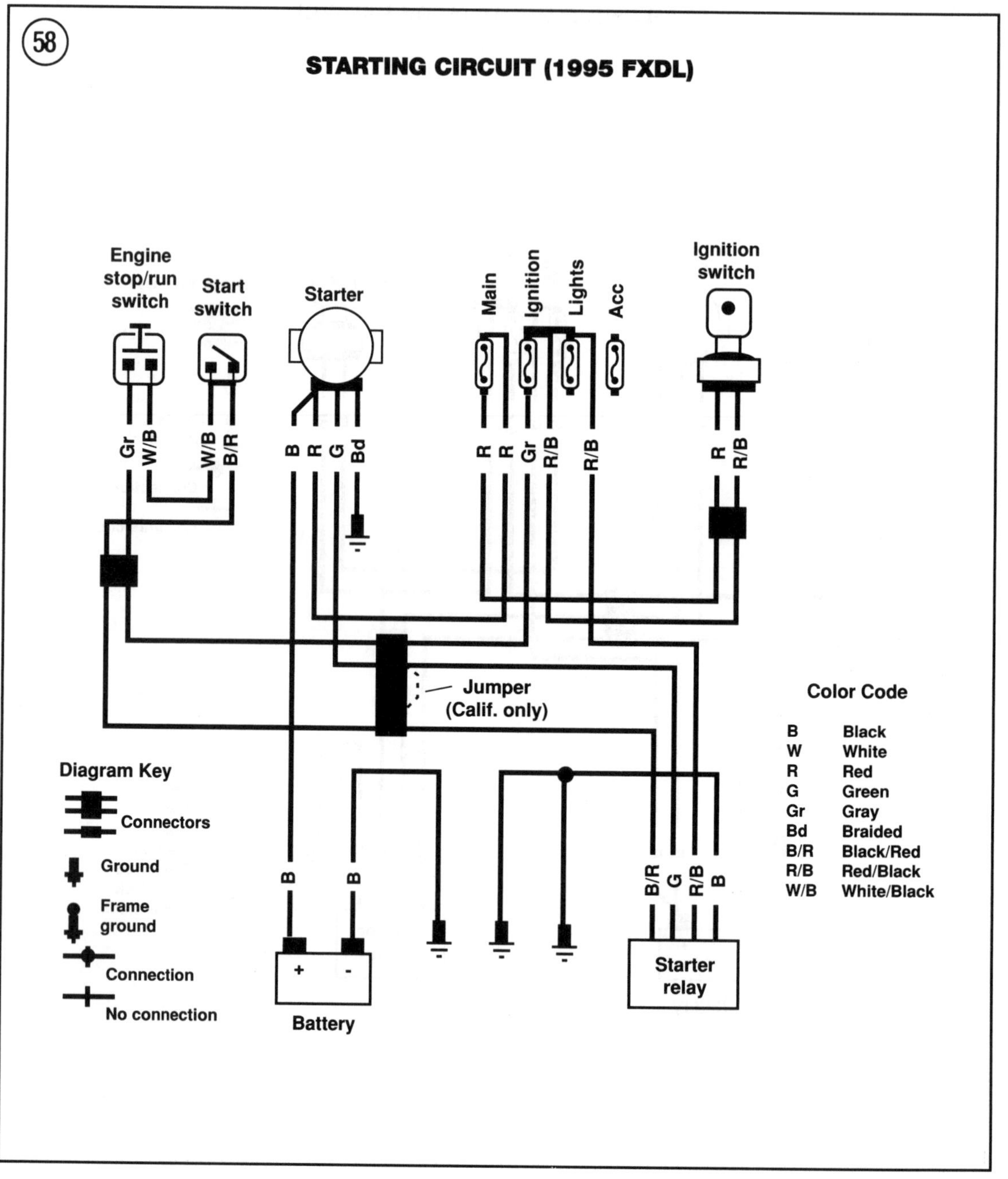

10. To service the solenoid housing, refer to *Solenoid Housing Inspection* in this chapter.

Inspection

CAUTION

In Step 1, do not clean the field coils or armature in any cleaning solution that could damage their insulation surfaces. Wipe these parts off with a clean rag. Likewise, do not soak the overrunning clutch in any cleaning solution as the chemicals could dissolve the lubrication within the clutch and ruin it.

1. Clean and dry the starter components.

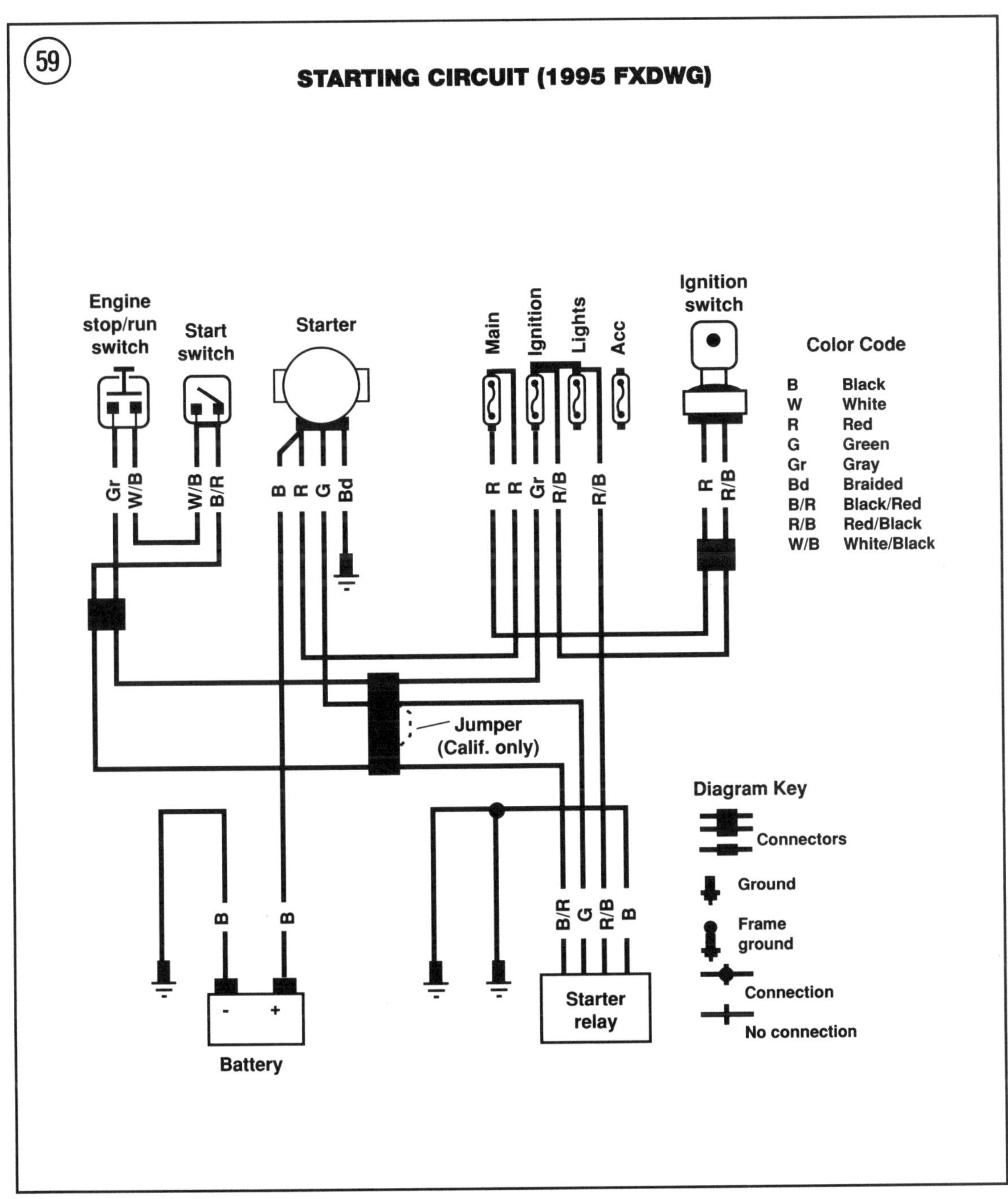

59 **STARTING CIRCUIT (1995 FXDWG)**

2. Measure the length of each brush with a vernier caliper (**Figure 75**). If the length is less than the minimum specified in **Table 3**, replace all of the brushes as a set. See **Figure 76** (field coil) and **Figure 77** (brush holder).

NOTE

*The field coil brushes (**Figure 76**) are soldered in position. To replace, unsolder the brushes by heating their joints with a soldering gun or iron, then pull them out with a pair of pliers. Position the new brushes and solder in place with rosin core solder—do not use acid core solder.*

3. Inspect the condition of the commutator (A, **Figure 78**). If the mica undercut is less than 0.008 in. (0.20 mm), undercut it with a hacksaw blade to a depth of 1/32 in. (0.79 mm). A dealer or automotive specialist with an undercutting machine can also perform this procedure. When undercutting mica, each groove must form a right angle. Do not cut the mica so that a thin edge is left next to the commutator segment. **Figure 79** shows the proper angle. After undercutting the mica, remove burrs by sanding the commutator lightly with crocus cloth.

4. Inspect the commutator copper bars for discoloration. If you find a pair of discolored bars, the armature coils are grounded.

5. Check the armature winding for shorts with a growler (**Figure 80**). Refer this test to a Harley-Davidson dealership or automotive electrical specialist.

6. Place the armature in a lathe or between crankshaft centers and check commutator runout with a dial indicator. If runout exceeds 0.016 in. (0.41 mm), true the commutator on a lathe. When truing the

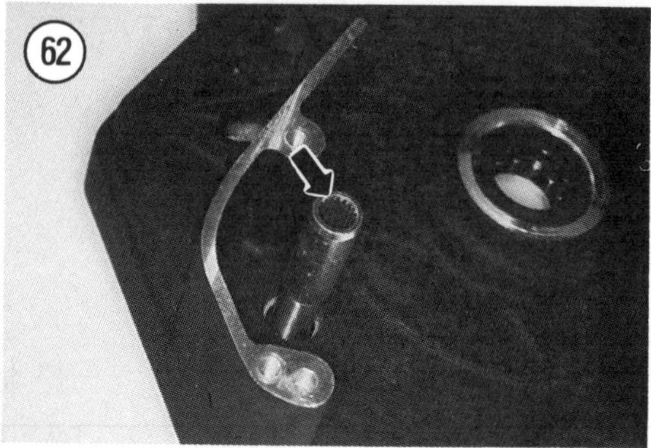

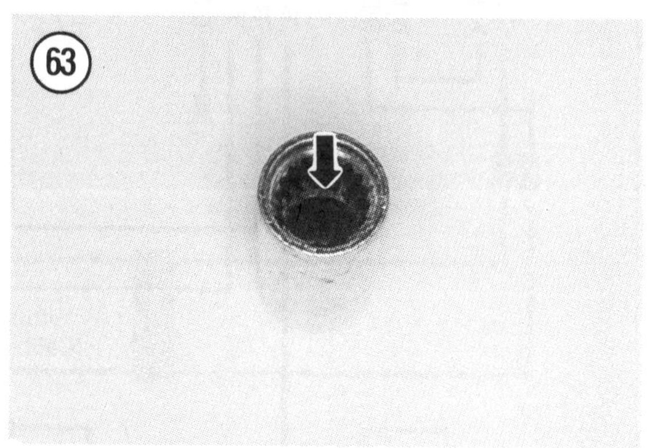

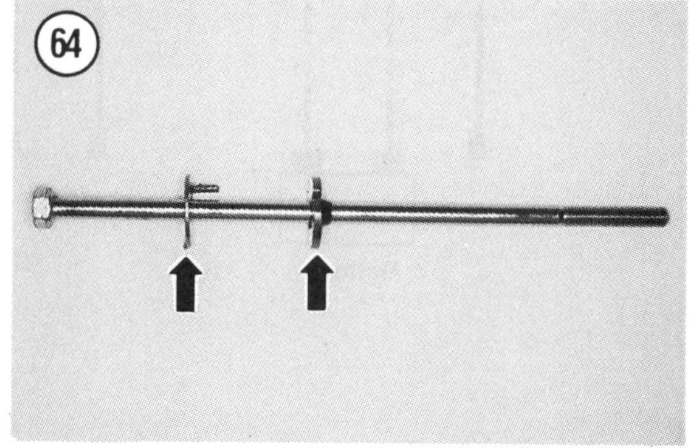

65

STARTER MOTOR

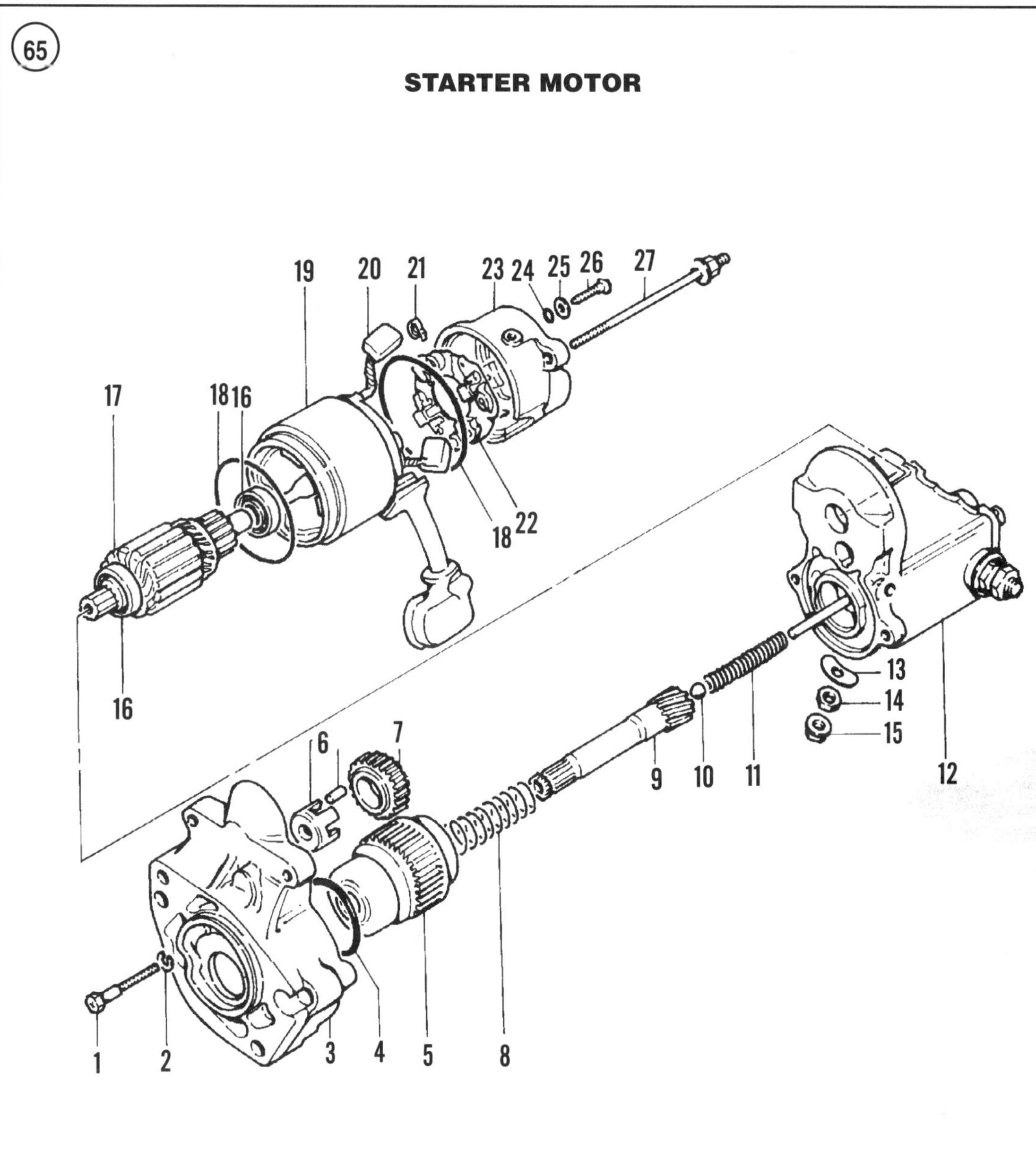

1. Screw
2. Lockwasher
3. Drive housing
4. O-ring
5. Drive assembly
6. Idler gear bearing
7. Idler gear
8. Drive spring
9. Clutch shaft
10. Ball
11. Return spring
12. Solenoid housing
13. Tab
14. Nut
15. Nut
16. Bearing
17. Armature
18. O-ring
19. Field coil assembly
20. Brushes
21. Brush springs
22. Brush holder
23. End cap
24. O-ring
25. Washer
26. Screw
27. Through bolt

66
D
C
A
B

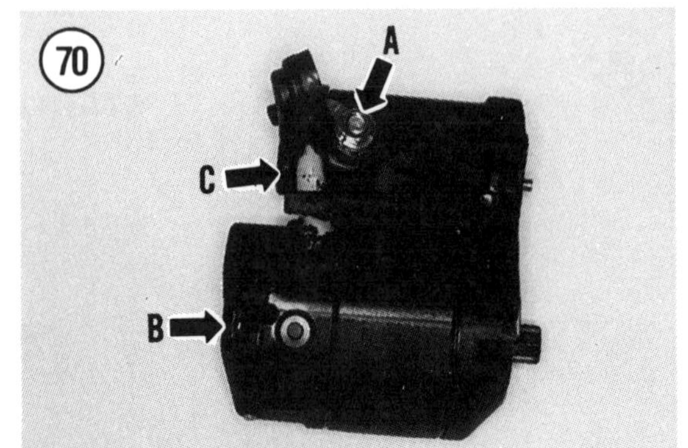
70
A
C
B

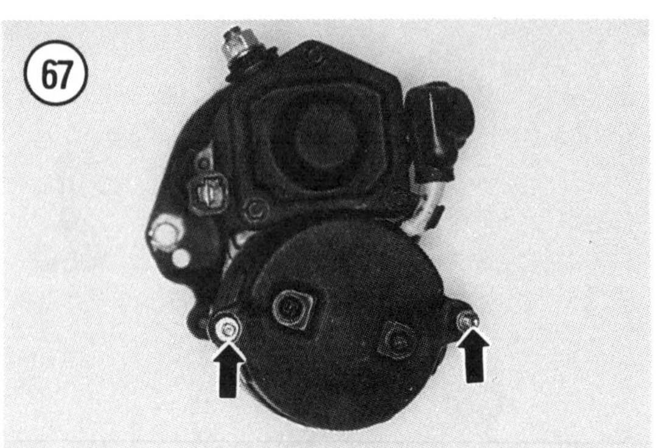
67

71

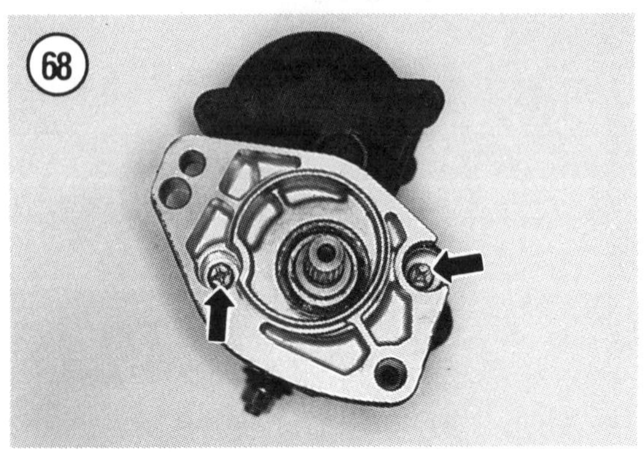
68

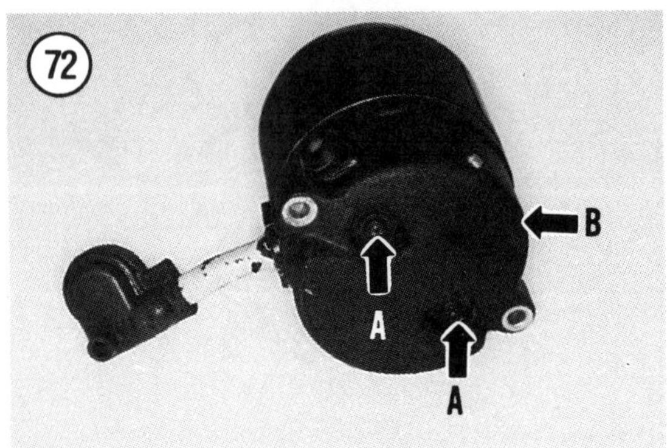
72
B
A
A

69

73
A
B

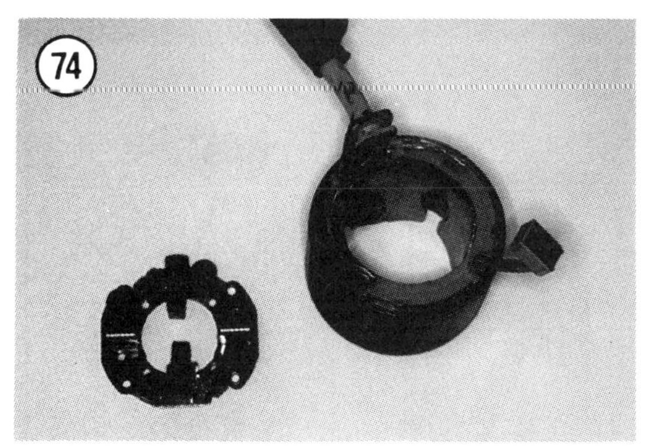
74

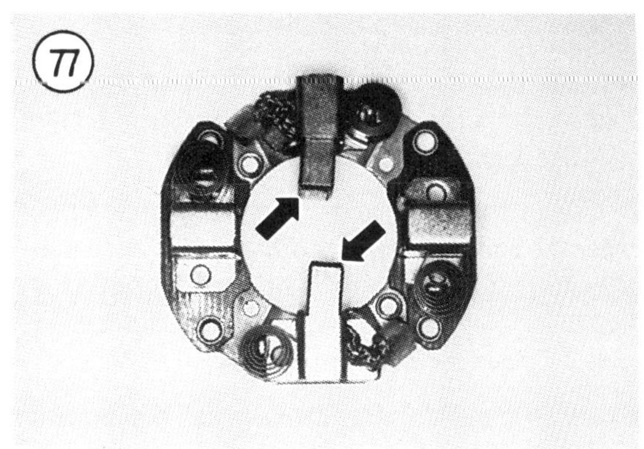
77

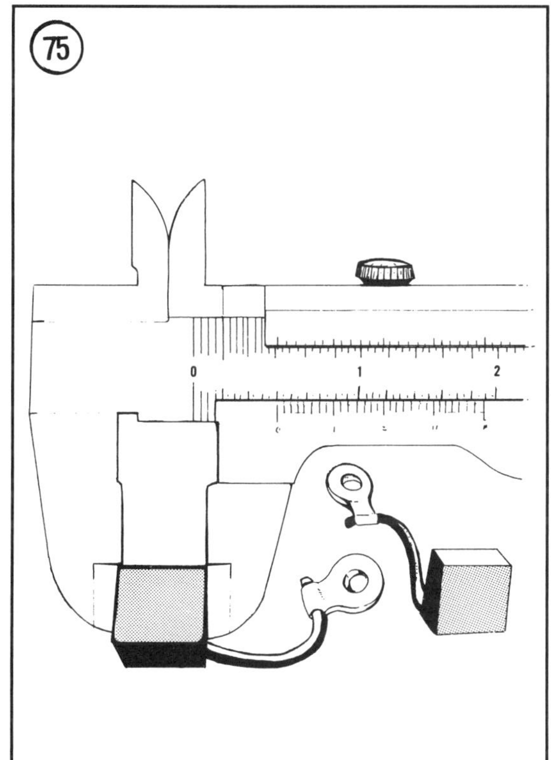
75
0
1
2

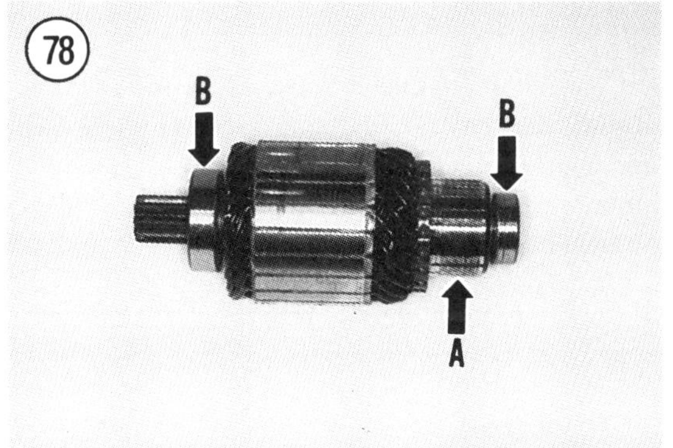
78
B
B
A

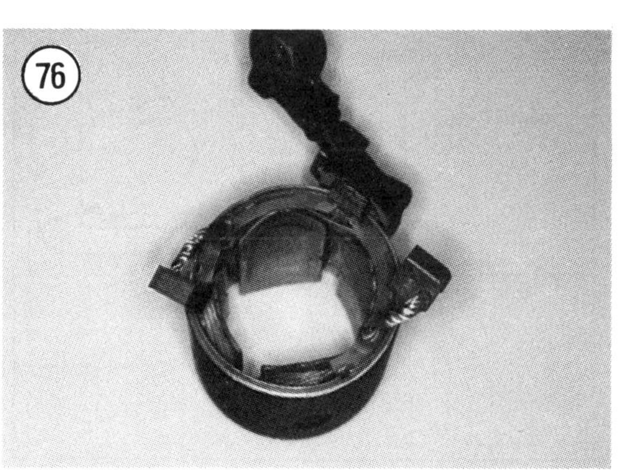
76

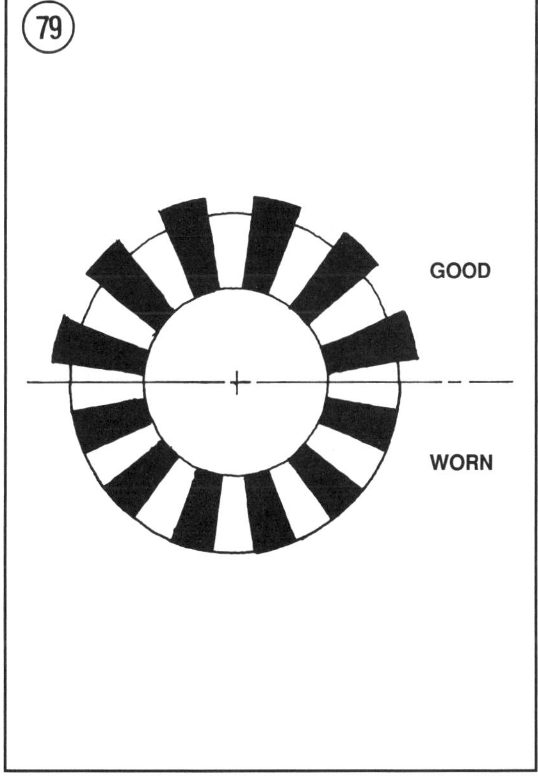
79
GOOD
WORN

commutator on a lathe, make the cuts as light as possible. Replace the armature if the commutator outer diameter (**Figure 81**) is less than the minimum diameter listed in **Table 3**.

7. Use an ohmmeter and check for continuity between the commutator bars (**Figure 82**); there must be continuity between pairs of bars. If there is no continuity between pairs of bars, the armature is open. Replace the armature.

8. Connect an ohmmeter between any commutator bar and the armature core (**Figure 83**); there must be no continuity. If there is continuity, the armature is grounded. Replace the armature.

9. Connect an ohmmeter between the starter cable terminal and each field frame brush (**Figure 84**); there must be continuity. If there is no continuity at either brush, the field windings are open. Replace the field frame assembly.

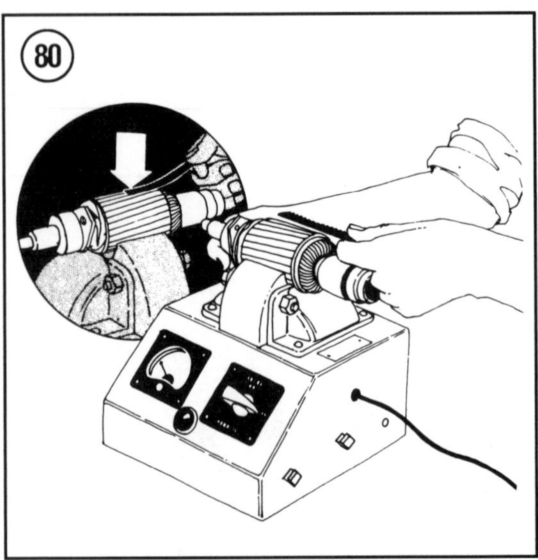

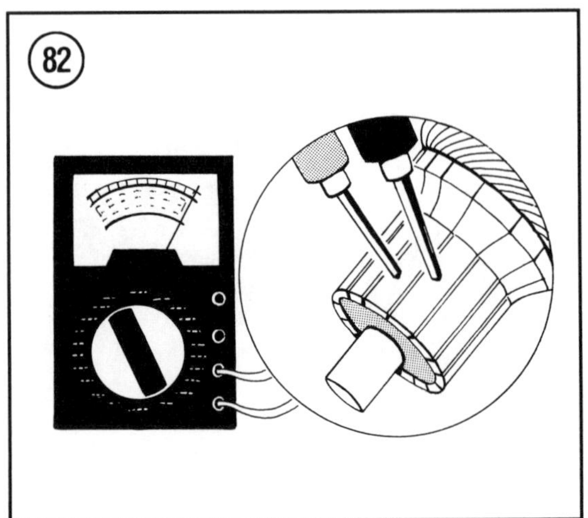

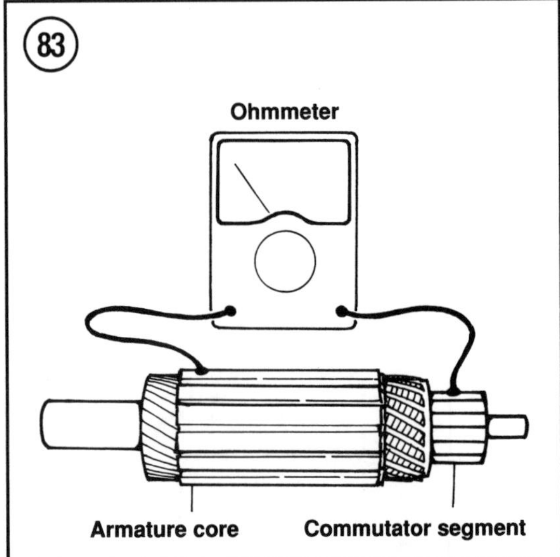

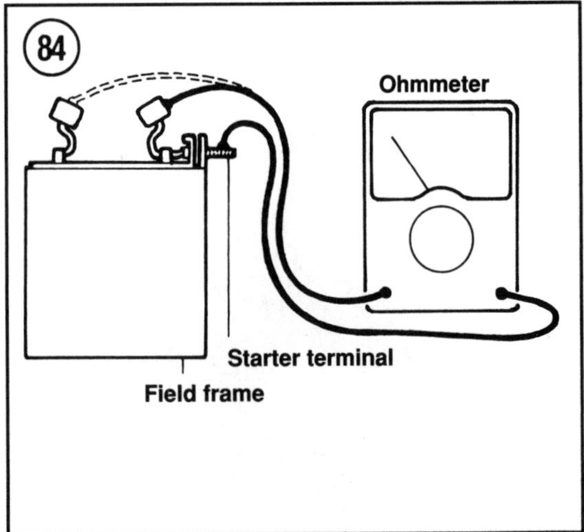

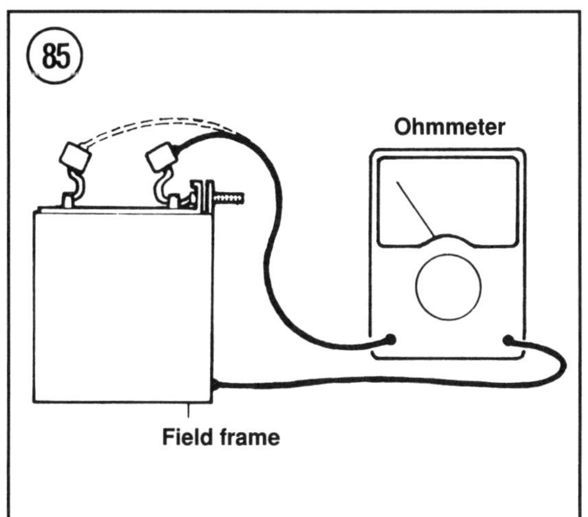

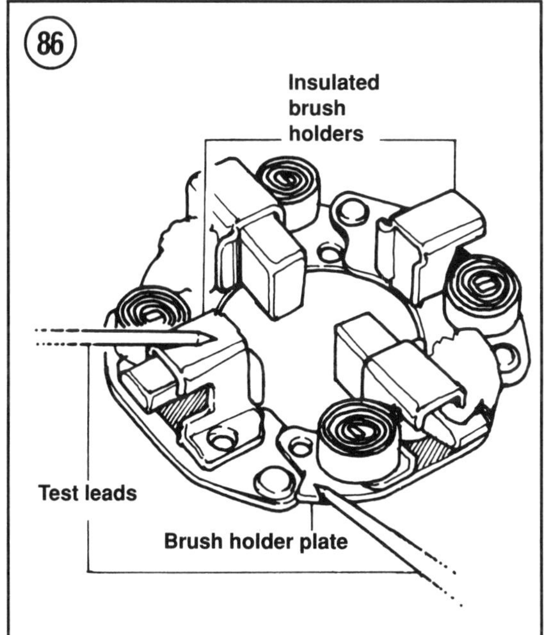

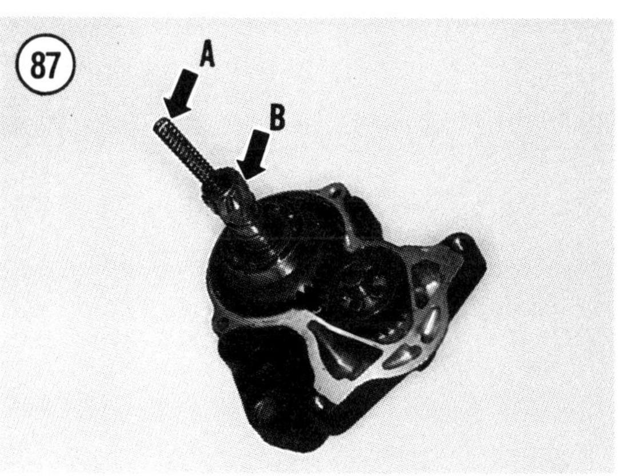

10. Connect an ohmmeter between the field frame housing and each field frame brush (**Figure 85**); there must be no continuity. If there is continuity at either brush, the field windings are grounded. Replace the field frame assembly.

11. Connect an ohmmeter between the brush holder plate and each brush holder (**Figure 86**); there must be no continuity. If there is continuity between a brush holderand brush holder plate, the brush holder or plate is damaged. Replace the brush holder plate.

12. Service the armature bearings as follows:

   a. Check the bearings (B, **Figure 78**) on the armature shaft. Replace worn or damaged bearings.

   NOTE
   The 2 bearings installed on the armature shaft have different part numbers. Identify the old bearings before removing them.

   b. Check the bearing bores in the end cover and solenoid housing. Replace the cover or housing if the area is worn or cracked.

8

Drive Housing Inspection

You removed the drive housing during starter disassembly. To service and inspect the drive housing assembly, perform the following:

1. Remove the return spring (A, **Figure 87**), ball, clutch shaft (B, **Figure 87**), and drive spring from the drive assembly. **Figure 88** shows the drive spring.

2. Remove the idler gear (**Figure 89**) from the drive housing.

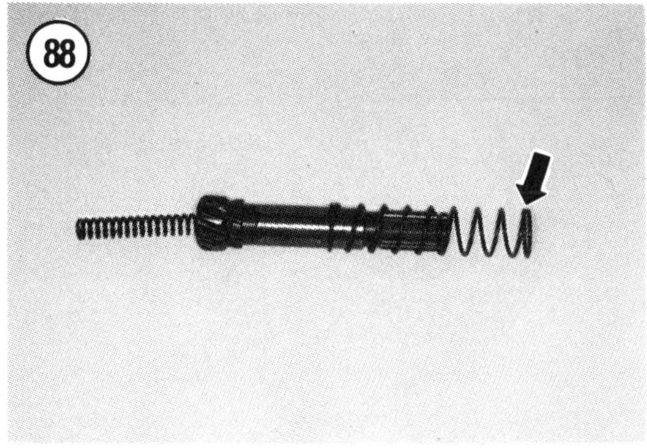

3. Remove the idler gear bearing and cage assembly (A, **Figure 90**). There are 5 individual bearing rollers (**Figure 91**).
4. Remove the drive assembly (B, **Figure 90**).
5. Replace the drive housing O-ring (**Figure 92**) if worn or damaged. Lubricate the O-ring with high temperature grease.
6. Inspect the idler gear bearing and cage assembly (**Figure 91**) for worn or damaged parts.

CAUTION
*The drive assembly (**Figure 92**) is a sealed unit. Do not clean or soak it in any type of solvent.*

7. Inspect the drive assembly and its bearings (**Figure 92**) for worn or damaged parts. If the bearings are worn or damaged, replace the drive assembly and bearings as a set.
8. Assemble the drive housing by reversing these steps, while noting the following.
9. Lubricate the following components with high temperature grease:
   a. Idler gear bearing and cage assembly (**Figure 91**).
   b. Drive housing O-ring and shaft (**Figure 92**).
   c. Drive assembly (**Figure 93**).
   d. Clutch shaft, drive spring, return spring, and ball.
10. Install the idler gear bearing and cage assembly so that the open side of the cage (A, **Figure 90**) faces toward the solenoid housing.

Solenoid Housing Inspection

You removed the solenoid housing (**Figure 94**) during starter disassembly. To service and inspect the solenoid housing assembly, perform the following:

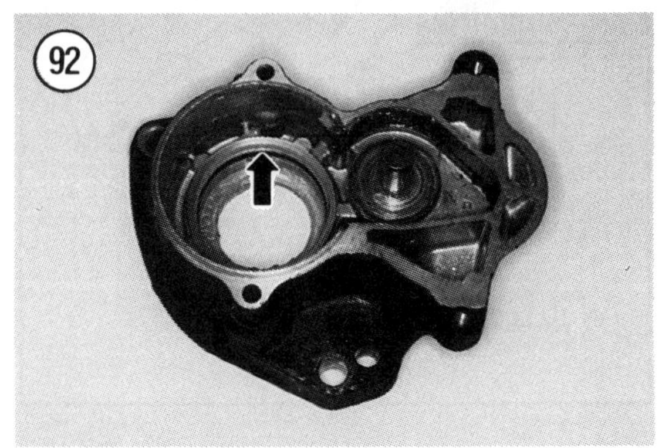

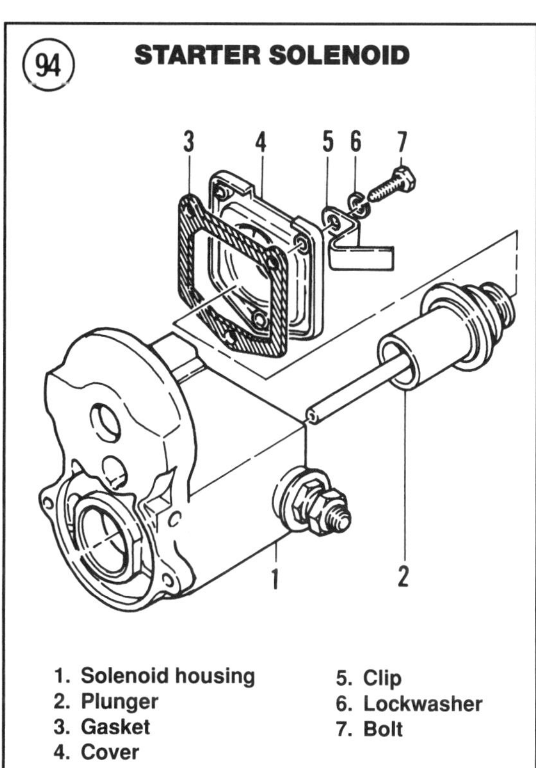

1. Remove the screws, washers and clip securing the end cover to the solenoid housing. Then remove the end cover (**Figure 95**) and the gasket.
2. Remove the plunger assembly (**Figure 96**).
3. Inspect the plunger (**Figure 97**) for scoring, deep wear marks or other damage.
4. Inspect the solenoid housing (**Figure 98**) for wear, cracks or other damage.
5. The solenoid housing is a separate assembly. If any one part of the solenoid is damaged, you must replace the solenoid housing as an assembly.
6. Assemble the solenoid housing by reversing these steps, while noting the following.
7. Lubricate the solenoid plunger with high temperature grease.

Assembly

Refer to **Figure 65** for this procedure.

1. Assemble the drive housing as described in this chapter.
2. Assemble the solenoid housing as described in this chapter.
3. Lubricate the armature bearings (B, **Figure 78**) with high-temperature grease.

4. Install the 2 O-rings onto the field coil shoulders (**Figure 99**).
5. Install the 2 field coil brushes into the brush plate holders (**Figure 100**).
6. Install the armature partway through the field coil as shown in **Figure 73**. Then pull the brushes back and push the armature forward so that when released, all of the brushes contact the commutator. See **Figure 101** and **Figure 102**.
7. Install the end cap (**Figure 103**) and secure with the 2 screws, washers and O-rings.
8. Align the field coil (A, **Figure 104**) with the solenoid housing (B, **Figure 104**) and assemble both

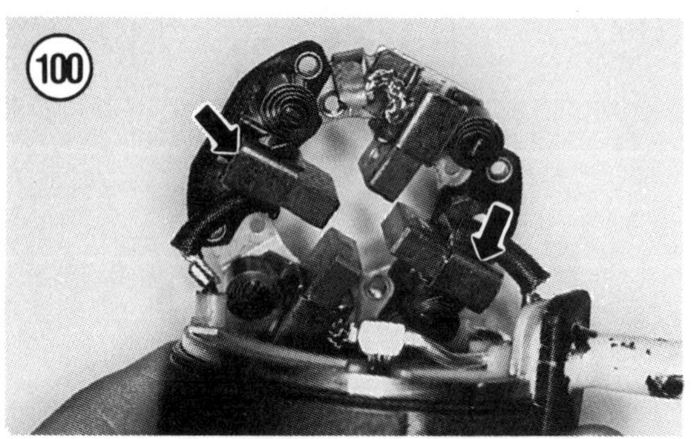

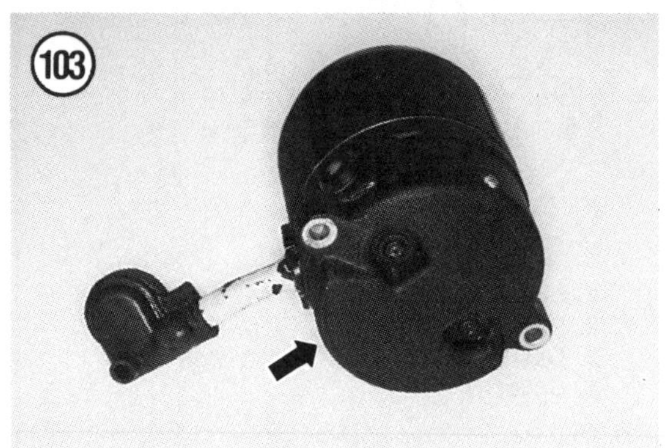

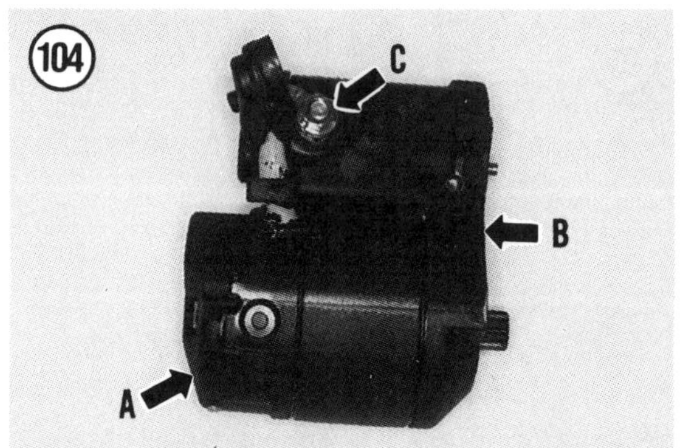

housings. Hold the assembly together while you install the drive housing in Step 9.

9. Align the drive housing (**Figure 105**) with the field coil and solenoid housing assembly and install it. Then install the 2 drive housing screws and lockwashers (**Figure 106**) and tighten securely.

10. Install the 2 through bolts, washes and O-rings (**Figure 107**) and tighten securely.

11. Reconnect the C terminal field wire (C, **Figure 104**) at the solenoid housing.

LIGHTING SYSTEM

The lighting system consists of a headlight, taillight/brake light combination and turn signals. The indicator and speedometer illumination lights are covered in a separate section later in this chapter.

Always use the correct wattage bulb. Harley-Davidson lists bulb sizes by part number. The use of a larger wattage bulb will give a dim light and a smaller wattage bulb will burn out prematurely. You can replace blown bulbs through Harley-Davidson dealers by part number or by reading the number off the defective bulb and cross-referencing it with another supplier.

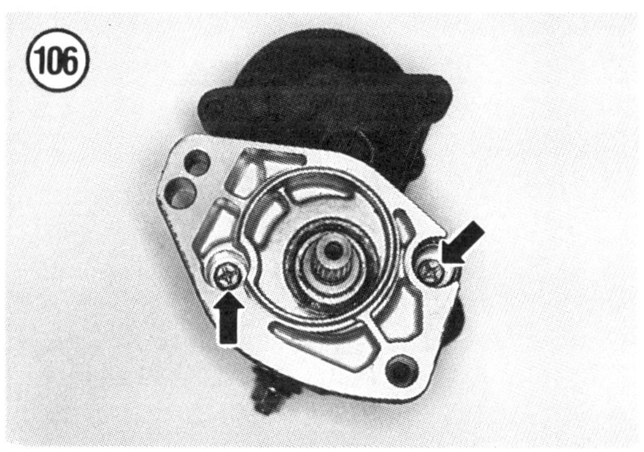

Headlight (Sealed Beam Replacement) (1991)

The 1991 FXDB model is equipped with a sealed beam headlight unit (**Figure 108**).

WARNING
*If the headlight has just burned out or turned off it will be **Hot**! Don't touch the sealed beam until it cools off.*

1. Remove the molding ring screw and remove the front molding ring.
2. Remove the sealed beam from the rubber ring, then disconnect the sealed beam from its connector and remove it.
3. Check the connector contacts for corrosion or damage.
4. Plug the connector into the new sealed beam and position the sealed beam in the rubber ring in the headlight housing.
5. Install the front molding ring and secure it with its screw.
6. Check headlight adjustment as described in this chapter.

Headlight (Bulb Replacement) (1992-on)

Refer to **Figure 109** for this procedure.

WARNING
*If the headlight has just burned out or turned off it will be **Hot**! Don't touch the bulb until it cools off.*

1. Remove the outer molding ring pinch screw (A, **Figure 110**) and remove the outer molding ring (B, **Figure 110**).

2A. On 1992-1994 models, carefully pry the headlight lens assembly (**Figure 111**) from the rubber gasket.

2B. On 1995 models, remove the headlight lens from the headlight housing (**Figure 112**).

3. Unplug the connector from the bulb (**Figure 113**) and remove the headlight assembly.

4. Remove the socket cover (A, **Figure 114**) from the back of the headlight lens assembly.
5. Depress the ends of the bulb retaining clip and unhook the clip from the headlight assembly slots (A, **Figure 115**). Pivot the retaining clip away from the bulb.

CAUTION
*A quartz halogen bulb (**Figure 116**) is used on these models. Do not touch the bulb glass with your fingers because traces of oil on the bulb will create temperature variances in the glass when the bulb is on; this may cause the bulb to fracture or will drastically reduce the life of the bulb. Clean traces of oil from the bulb glass with an alcohol or lacquer thinner moistened cloth. When handling the bulb, touch only the metal base or terminals.*

6. Lift the bulb (B, **Figure 115**) out of the headlight lens assembly.
7. Replace the retaining clip (A, **Figure 115**) if cracked or otherwise damaged.
8. Install the bulb by reversing these steps while noting the following:
9. Read the previous CAUTION prior to handling the replacement bulb.
10. When installing the bulb, the projections on the bulb must mesh with the slots in the lens assembly; see B, **Figure 115**.
11. Position the socket cover with its TOP mark facing up; see B, **Figure 114**.
12. Make sure the electrical connector (**Figure 113**) is free of corrosion and that all of the wiring in the headlight housing is pushed aside.
13. Push the connector halves together tightly (**Figure 112**).
14. On 1995 models, align the tab on the lens assembly with the notch in the retaining ring (**Figure 117**).
15. Check headlight adjustment as described in this chapter.

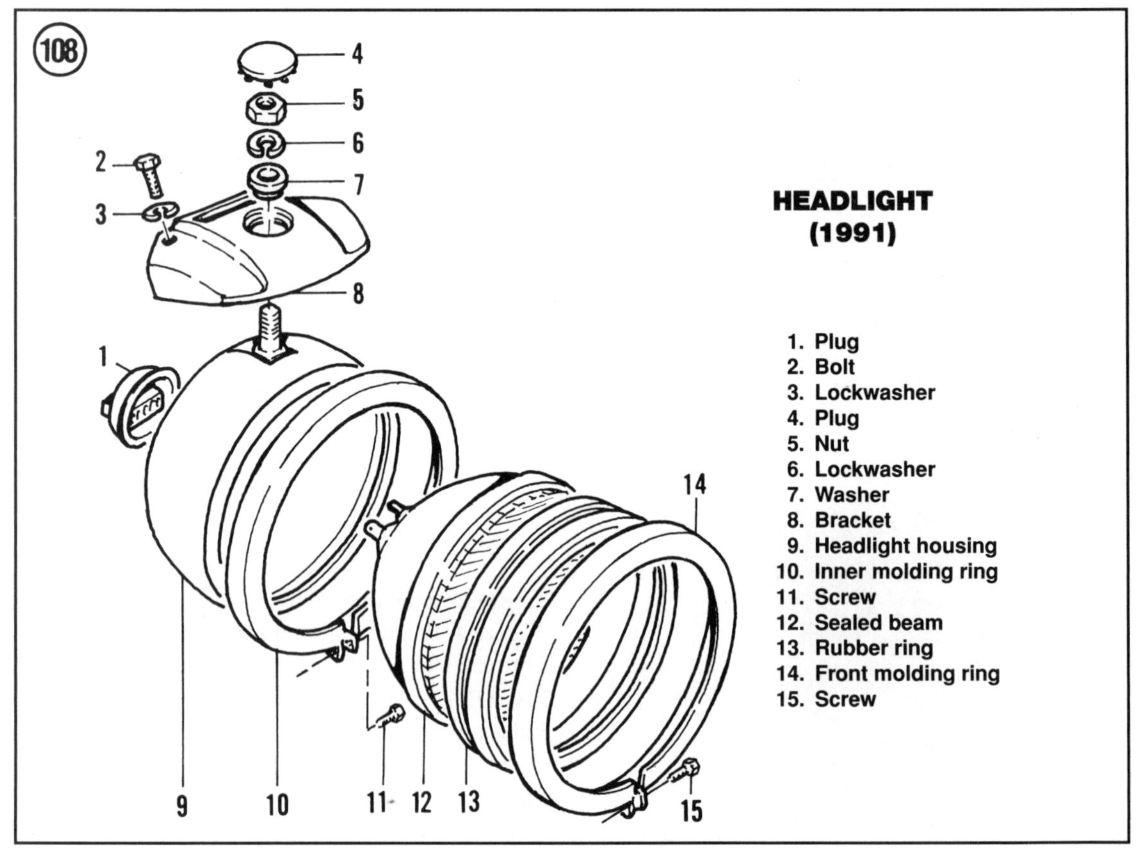

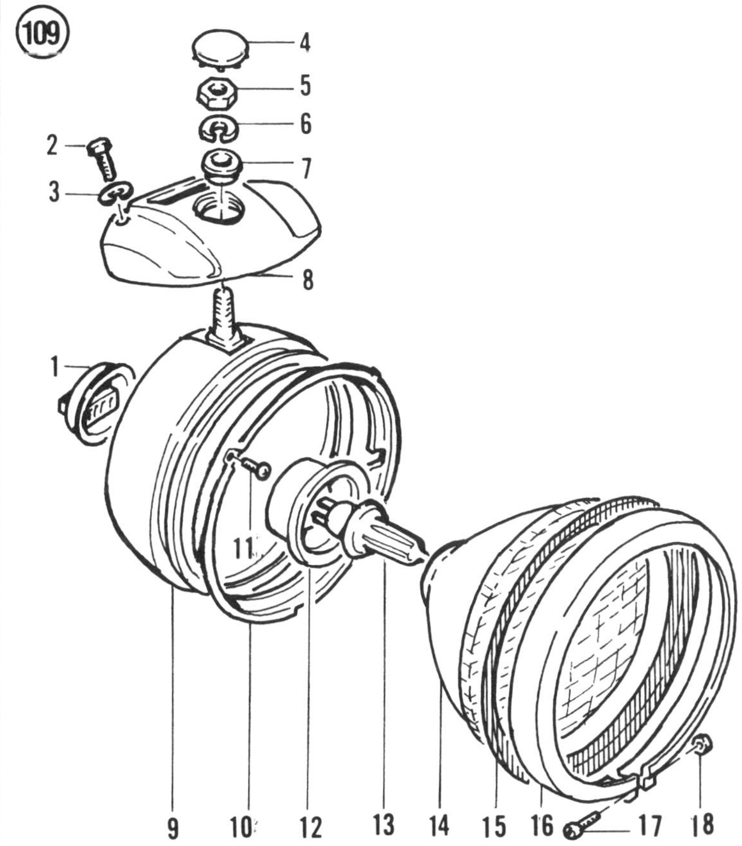

109

HEADLIGHT (1992-ON)

1. Plug
2. Bolt
3. Washer
4. Plug
5. Nut
6. Lockwasher
7. Washer
8. Bracket
9. Headlight housing
10. Retaining ring
11. Screw
12. Boot
13. Bulb
14. Lens
15. Gasket
16. Outer mounting ring
17. Screw
18. Nut

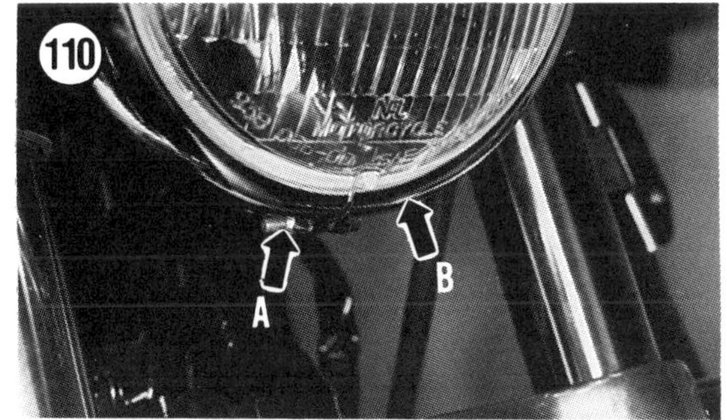

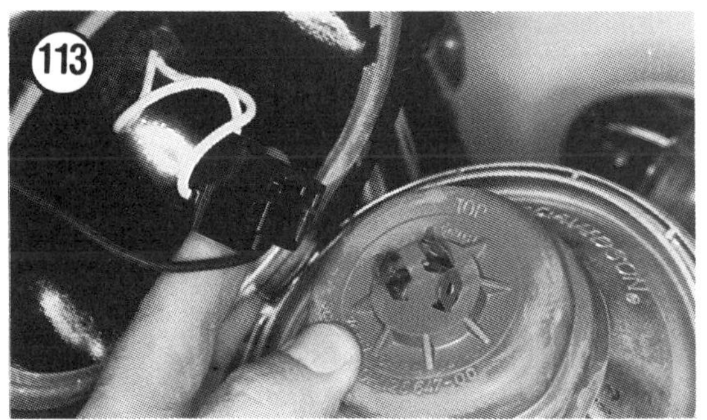

Headlight Adjustment

1. Park the motorcycle on a level surface approximately 25 ft. (7.6 m) from the wall (test pattern). Have a rider sit on the seat. Inflate the tires to the correct tire pressure. See **Figure 118**.
2. Draw a horizontal line on the wall that is 35 in. (889 mm) above the floor.
3. Aim the headlight at the wall and turn on the headlight. Switch the headlight to the high beam. The front wheel must be pointing straight ahead.
4. Check the headlight beam alignment. The broad, flat pattern of light (main beam of light) must be centered on the horizontal line (equal area of light above and below line).
5. Now check the headlight beam lateral alignment. With the headlight beam pointed straight ahead (centered), there must be an equal area of light to the left and right of center.
6. If the beam is incorrect as described in Step 4 or Step 5, adjust as follows.
   a. Remove the plug from the top of the headlight housing.
   b. Loosen the headlight clamp nut (**Figure 119**).
   c. Using your hands, tilt the headlight assembly up or down to adjust the beam vertically while turning the assembly to the left or right sides to adjust the beam horizontally.
   d. When the beam is properly adjusted both horizontally and vertically, tighten the headlight adjust nut (**Figure 119**) securely.
   e. Push the plug into the headlight housing.

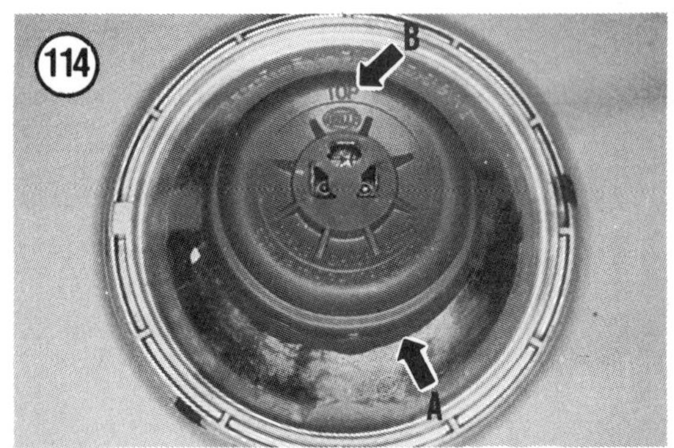

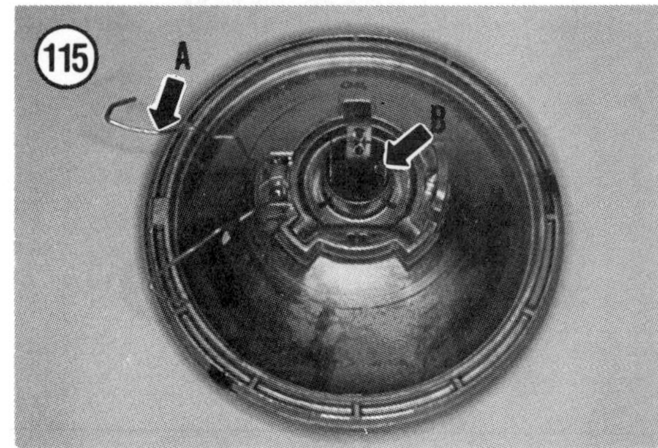

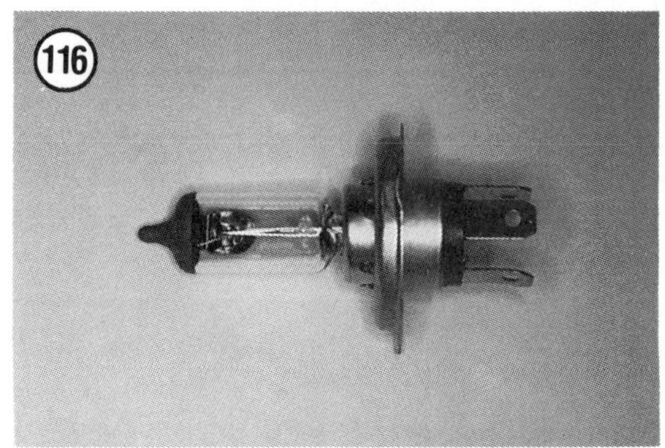

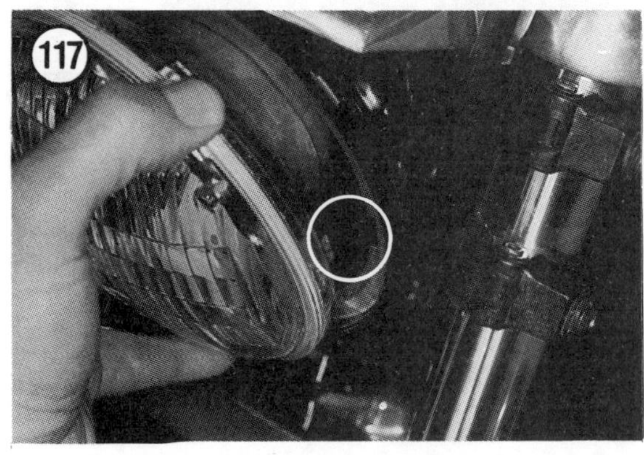

Taillight/Brake Light Replacement

1. Remove the rear lens and its gasket (**Figure 120**).
2. Push in on the bulb (**Figure 121**) and remove it.
3. Replace the lens gasket if torn or otherwise damaged.
4. Replace the bulb and install the lens.

Turn Signal Light Replacement

1. Remove the turn signal lens (**Figure 122**).
2. Push in on the bulb (**Figure 123**) and remove it.
3. Replace the bulb and install the lens.

SWITCHES

Test switches using an ohmmeter (see Chapter One) connected to the switch connectors by operating the switch in each of its operating positions. Then compare the test results with the switch operation. When testing switches, consider the following:

a. First check the circuit breaker.
b. Check the battery as described in this chapter and charge the battery, if required.

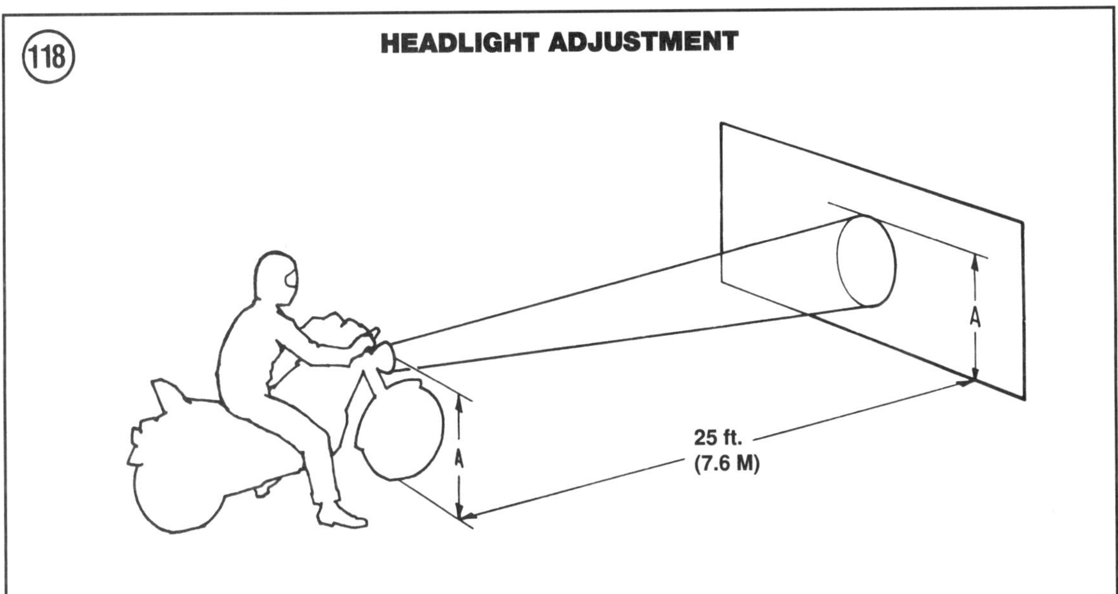

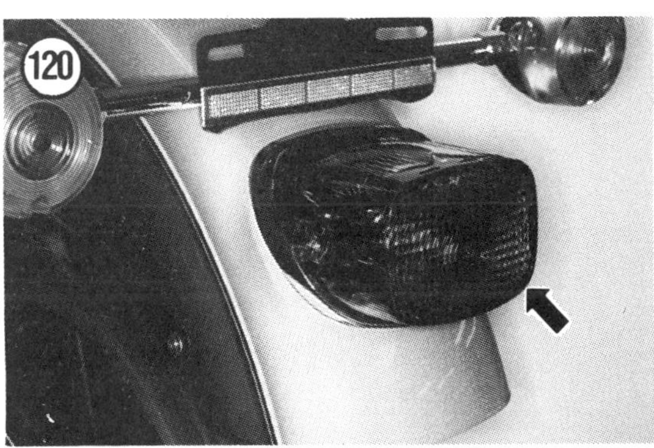

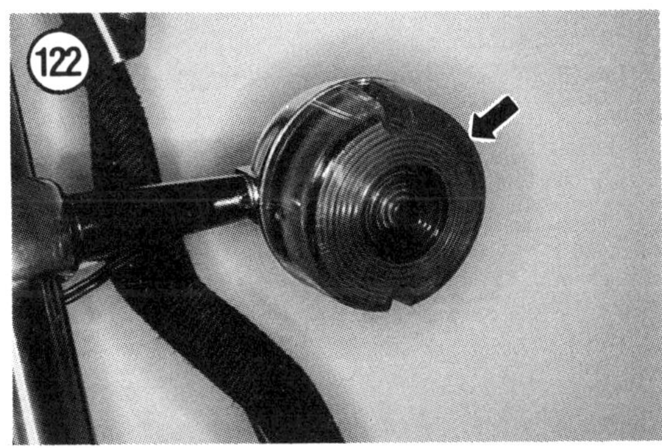

8

c. When separating 2 connectors, pull on the connector housings and not the wires.
d. After finding a defective circuit, check the connectors to make sure they are clean and properly connected. Check all wires going into a connector housing to make sure each wire is properly positioned and that the wire terminal is tight.
e. Push the connectors together until they click firmly into place.

Handlebar Switch Replacement

The left-hand handlebar switch housing (**Figure 124**) is equipped with the following switches:

a. Headlight HI-LO beam.
b. Horn.
c. Left-hand turn signal.

The right-hand handlebar switch housing (**Figure 125**) is equipped with the following switches:

a. RUN-OFF.
b. Starter.
c. Right-hand turn signal.
d. Front brake light.

1A. Remove the screws securing the left-hand switch housing (**Figure 126**) to the handlebar. Then carefully separate the switch housing to access the defective switch. The switches are identified in the following photographs:

a. Headlight switch (A, **Figure 127**).
b. Horn switch (B, **Figure 127**).
c. Left-hand turn signal (**Figure 128**).

1B. Remove the screws securing the right-hand switch housing (**Figure 129**) to the handlebar. Then carefully separate the switch housing to see the defective switch. The switches are identified in the following photographs:

a. RUN-OFF switch (A, **Figure 130**).

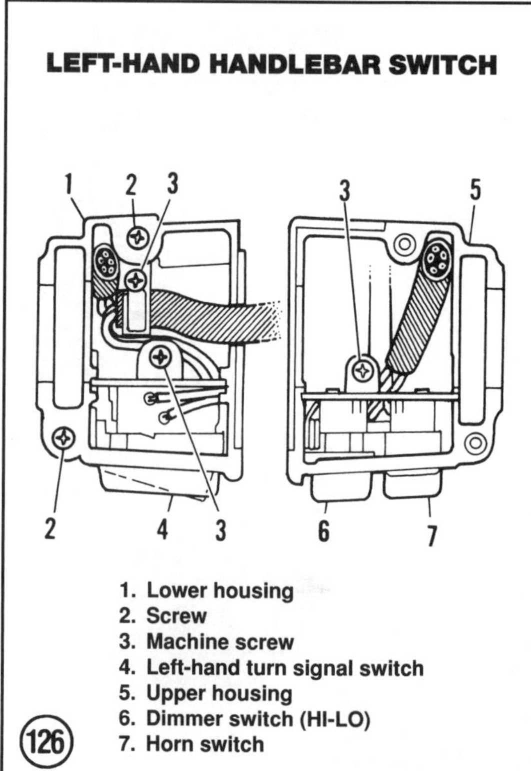

1. Lower housing
2. Screw
3. Machine screw
4. Left-hand turn signal switch
5. Upper housing
6. Dimmer switch (HI-LO)
7. Horn switch

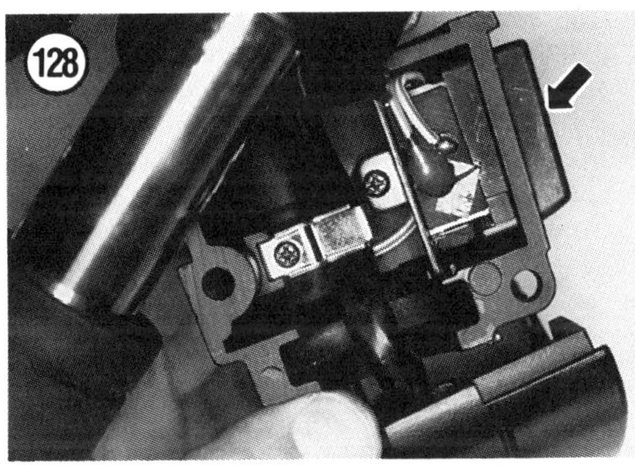

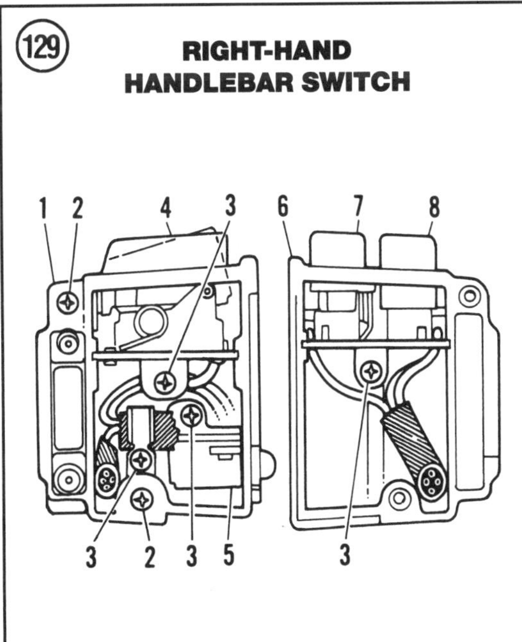

b. Starter (B, **Figure 130**).
c. Right-hand turn signal (A, **Figure 131**).
d. Front brake light (B, **Figure 131**).

NOTE
To service the front brake light switch, refer to ***Front Brake Light Switch Replacement*** *in this chapter.*

2. Replace the defective switch by removing its mounting screw. Then pull the switch out of the housing.
3. Cut the switch wire(s) from the defective switch.
4. Slip a piece of heat shrink tubing over each wire cut in Step 2.
5. Solder the wire end(s) to the new switch. Then shrink the tubing over the wire(s).
6. Install the switch by reversing these steps, plus the following.
7. When clamping the switch housing onto the handlebar, check the wiring harness routing position to make sure it is not pinched between the housing and handlebar.

8

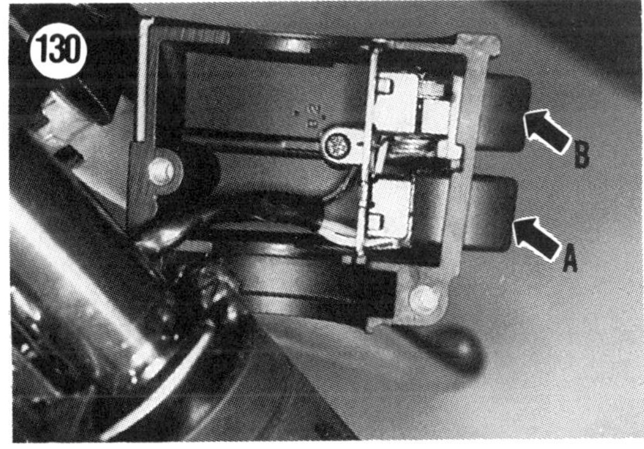

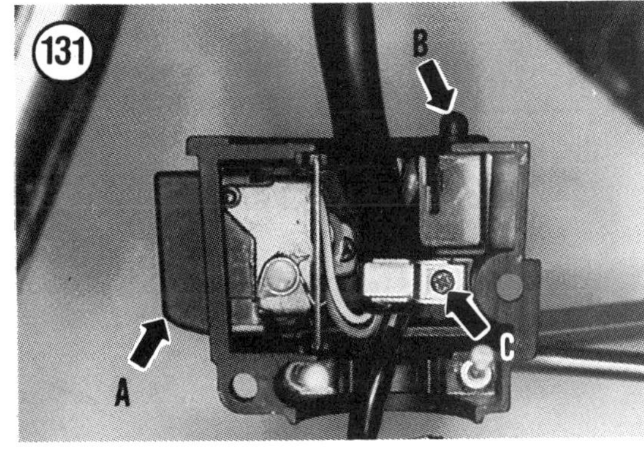

8. To install the right-hand switch housing, refer to *Throttle and Idle Cable Replacement* in Chapter Seven.

WARNING

Do not ride the motorcycle until the throttle cables are properly adjusted. Also, the cables must not catch or pull when you turn the handlebars. Improper cable routing and adjustment can cause the throttle to stick open. This could cause you to lose control. Recheck your work before riding the bike.

Front Brake Light Switch Replacement

The front brake light switch (B, **Figure 131**) is mounted in the right-hand switch housing.

1. Separate the right-hand switch housing as described under *Handlebar Switch Replacement* in this chapter.
2. Remove the wire clamp screw and clamp (C, **Figure 131**).
3. Push the switch button and slide the switch out of the housing (**Figure 132**).
4. Scrape the silicone off the red/yellow wire connection (A, **Figure 133**) at the switch.
5. Heat the 2 wire solder connections and pull the wires away from the switch, then discard the switch.

NOTE

There must be no exposed wire after you solder the wires to the new switch. If you had to strip some wire, slide heat shrink tubing over the wire ends before soldering them to the new switch.

6. Using rosin core solder, solder the red/yellow (A, **Figure 133**) and orange/white (B, **Figure 133**) wires to the new switch.
7. Allow the solder connections to cool completely, then apply a dab of silicone to the red/yellow wire connection at the switch (A, **Figure 133**).

NOTE

Allow the silicone to dry before reassembling the switch halves onto the handlebar.

8. Push the switch button and slide the switch into the housing as shown in **Figure 131**.
9. Route the brake switch wires through the half-moon guide in the bottom of the switch housing. Then install the wire clamp and screw (**Figure 131**).
10. When clamping the switch housing onto the handlebar, check the wiring harness routing position to make sure it is not pinched between the housing and handlebar.
11. To install the right-hand switch housing and check the brake light switch operation, refer *Throttle and Idle Cable Replacement* in Chapter Seven.

WARNING

Do not ride the motorcycle until you properly adjust the throttle cables. Likewise, the cables must not catch or pull when you turn the handlebars. Improper cable routing and adjustment can cause the throttle to stick open. This could cause you to lose control. Recheck your work before riding the bike.

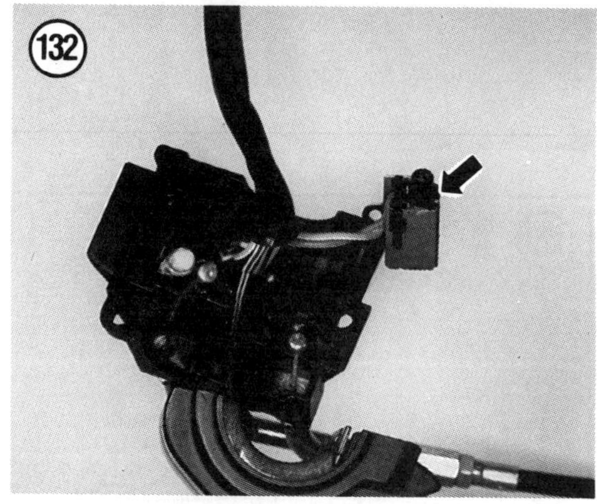

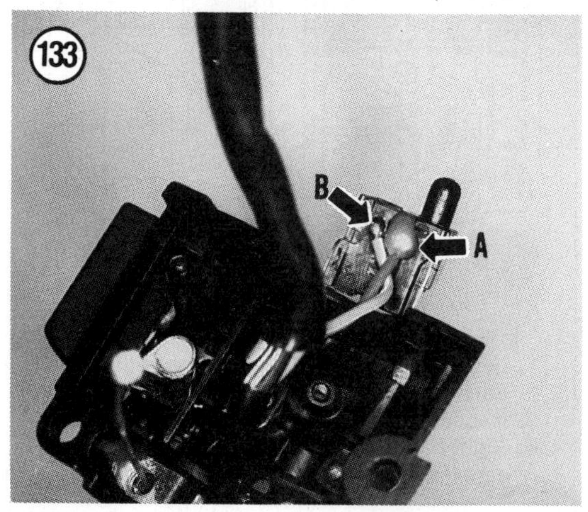

134

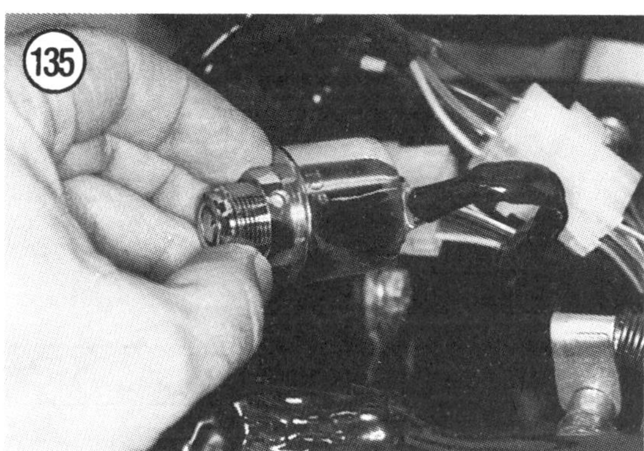
135

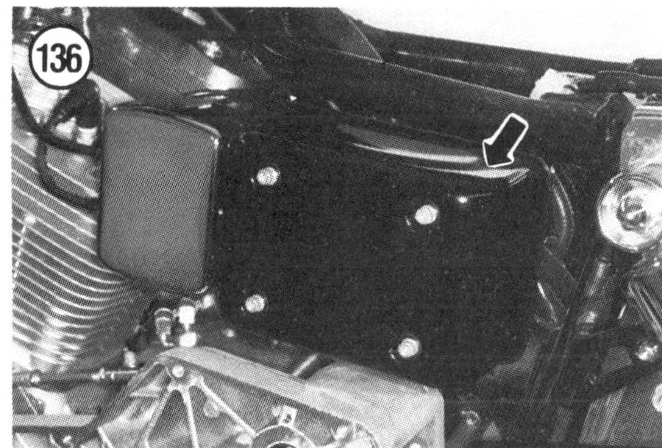
136

137

Ignition/Light Switch Removal/Installation

The ignition/light switch is not serviceable. If the switch is faulty, replace it as follows.

1991-1994 side mounted switch

1. Disconnect the negative battery cable as described under *Battery* in this chapter.
2. Turn the ignition switch off and remove the ignition key.
3. Loosen and remove the outer chrome nut securing the ignition switch to the mounting plate (**Figure 134**).
4. Push the ignition switch through the cover (toward inside) and remove it from the mounting plate (**Figure 135**).
5. Remove the electric panel cover (**Figure 136**).
6. Find the main and ignition circuit breakers on the back of the electric panel. See **Figure 137** and the ignition system wiring diagram for your model. The ignition switch is wired into these 2 circuit breakers.

NOTE
Before disconnecting the wires in Step 7, confirm the wire colors from the switch to the circuit breakers. Use the wiring diagram for your model.

7. Disconnect the ignition switch wires from the main and ignition circuit breakers.

NOTE
Before removing the ignition switch, trace its path on a piece of paper from the voltage regulator to the main circuit breaker.

8. Disconnect and remove any cable straps securing the ignition switch wiring harness to the frame. Then remove the ignition switch.
9. Reverse these steps to install the new switch.
10. Check the switch in each of its operating positions.

1995 side mounted switch

1. Disconnect the negative battery cable as described under *Battery* in this chapter.
2. Turn the ignition switch off and remove the ignition key.

3. Loosen and remove the outer chrome nut securing the ignition switch to the mounting plate (**Figure 134**).
4. Push the ignition switch through the cover (toward inside) and remove it from the mounting plate (**Figure 135**).
5. Remove the ignition switch harness cover and cut the switch wires 3 in. (76.2 mm) from the switch.
6. To reconnect the new ignition switch:
   a. Slide the replacement conduit onto the wiring harness.
   b. Match the ignition switch and wiring harness color codes, install new butt connectors to the wiring harness and ignition switch wires. Seal the butt splice connectors as shown in **Figure 138**.
7. Install the ignition switch into the hole in the switch cover so that the TOP mark stamped on the switch body faces up (toward the switch position decal).
8. Tighten the ignition switch locknut securely.

138

SEALED BUTT CONNECTOR INSTALLATION

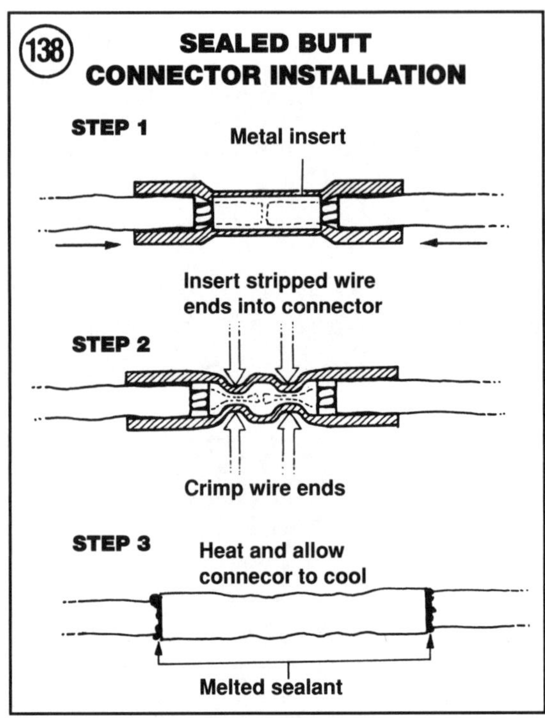

139

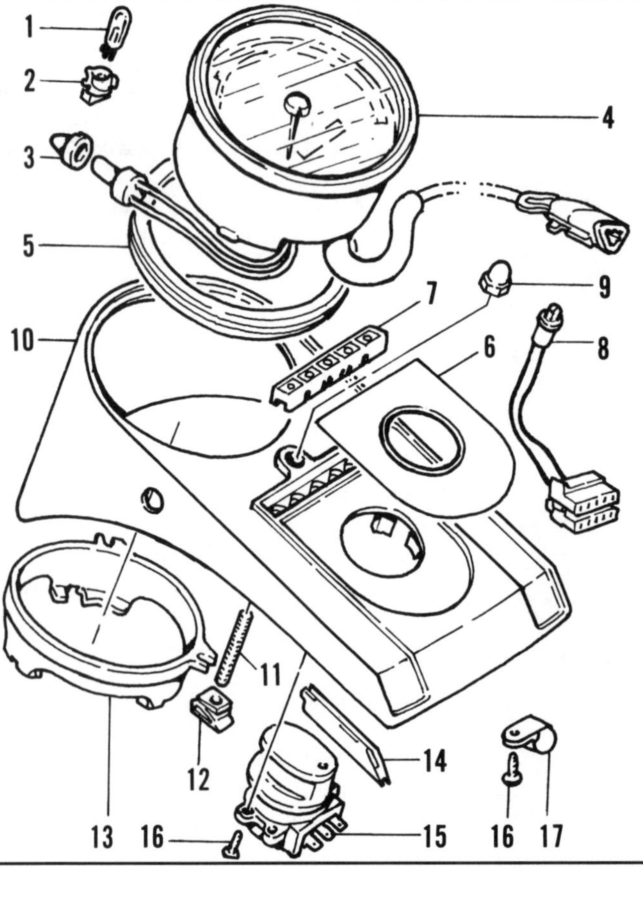

INSTRUMENTS

1. Bulb
2. Connector
3. Boot
4. Speedometer
5. Ring
6. Cover
7. Indicator lens
8. Bulb and socket
9. Nut
10. Cover
11. Stud
12. Nut
13. Clamp
14. Trim
15. Ignition switch
16. Screw
17. Clamp

9. Check the switch operation in each of its operating positions.

Fuel tank mounted switch

Refer to **Figure 139** when performing this procedure.

1. Disconnect the negative battery cable as described under *Battery* in this chapter.
2. Turn the ignition switch off and remove the ignition key.
3. Remove the acorn nut from the instrument panel on the fuel tank.
4. Lift the instrument panel up and then turn it over. Place a heavy cloth under the instrument panel to avoid scratching the fuel tank.

NOTE
Before disconnecting the wires in Step 5, confirm the wire color connections at the ignition switch with the wiring diagram for your model.

5. Disconnect the ignition switch wires from the ignition switch.

140

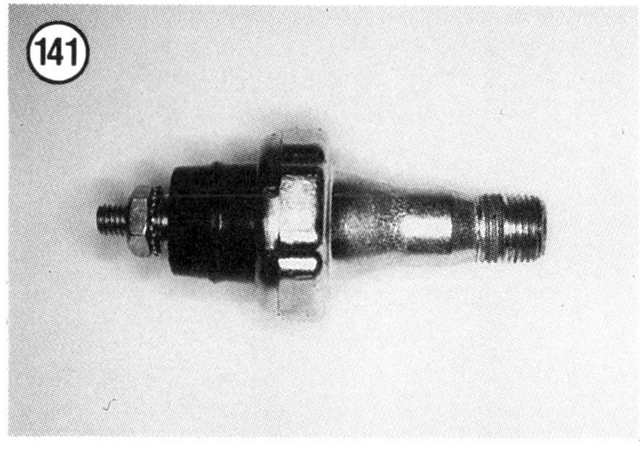

141

6. Remove the ignition switch screws. Then remove the ignition switch.
7. Reverse these steps to install the new ignition switch.
8. Check the switch in each of its operating positions.

Oil Pressure Switch Testing/Replacement

The oil pressure switch (**Figure 140**) mounts in the right crankcase, next to the rear tappet guide. **Figure 141** shows the oil pressure switch removed from the engine.

A pressure-actuated diaphragm-type oil pressure switch is used. When the oil pressure is low or when oil is not circulating through a running engine, spring tension inside the switch holds the switch contacts closed. This completes the signal light circuit and causes the oil pressure indicator lamp to light.

The oil pressure signal light must turn on when:

a. The ignition switch is turned on prior to starting the engine.
b. The engine idle is below 1,000 rpm.
c. The engine is operating with low oil pressure.
d. Oil is not circulating through the running engine.

The oil pressure signal light must turn off when:

a. The engine has sufficient oil pressure.
b. Engine rpm is 1,000 rpm or higher.

NOTE
The oil pressure signal light may not come on when the ignition switch is turned off and then back on immediately. This is due to the oil pressure retained in the oil filter housing.

The following steps test the electrical part of the oil pressure switch. If the oil pressure switch, indicator lamp and related wiring are okay, inspect the lubrication system as described in Chapter Two.

1. Remove the rubber boot and disconnect the electrical connector from the switch.
2. Turn the ignition switch ON.
3. Ground the switch wire to the engine.
4. The oil pressure indicator lamp on the instrument panel must light.

8

5. If the signal indicator lamp does not light, check for a defective indicator lamp and inspect all wiring between the switch and the indicator lamp.
6A. If the oil pressure warning light operates properly, you solved the problem in Steps 3-5, attach the electrical connector to the pressure switch. Make sure the connection is tight and free from oil. Slide the rubber boot back into position.
6B. If the warning light remains ON when the engine is running, shut the engine off. Check the engine lubrication system as described in Chapter Two.
7. To replace the switch, unscrew it from the engine and install a new one. Test the new switch as described in Steps 1-4.

Neutral Indicator Switch Testing/Replacement

The neutral indicator switch mounts in the transmission top cover (**Figure 142**). The neutral indicator light on the instrument panel must light when the ignition is turned ON and the transmission is in NEUTRAL.

1. Disconnect the electrical connector from the neutral indicator switch (**Figure 142**).
2. Turn the ignition switch on.
3. Ground the neutral indicator switch wire to the transmission or to any other suitable ground.
4. If the neutral indicator lamp lights, the neutral switch if faulty. Replace the neutral indicator switch and retest.
5. If the neutral indicator lamp does not light, check for a defective indicator lamp, faulty wiring or a loose or corroded connection.
6A. If you solved the problem in Steps 3-5, attach the electrical connector to the neutral switch. Make sure the connection is tight and free from oil.
6B. If you did not solve the problem in Steps 3-5, replace the neutral indicator switch.
7. Remove and discard the old switch.
8. Install the new switch. Coat the switch threads with Loctite Pipe Sealant With Teflon. Tighten the neutral indicator switch to the torque specification in **Table 4**.

Rear Brake Light Switch Testing/Replacement

A hydraulic, normally-open rear brake light switch is used on all models. The rear brake light switch mounts in the rear brake caliper brake hose (**Figure 143**).

When you turn on the ignition switch and release the brake pedal, the brake switch contacts are open and the rear brake light is off. When you apply the rear brake pedal, hydraulic pressure closes the switch contacts, providing a ground path so the rear brake lamp comes on.

If the rear brake lamp does not come on, perform the following.

1. Turn the ignition switch off.
2. Use an ohmmeter and check for continuity between the 2 terminals on the brake light switch connector. There must be no continuity (infinite resistance) with the rear brake pedal released. With the rear brake pedal applied there must be continuity (low resistance). If the rear brake switch fails either of these tests, replace the switch as follows:
3. Disconnect the electrical wires from the bottom of the switch body.
4. Loosen and remove the switch (**Figure 143**) from the tee nut on the rear brake line.
5. Thread the new switch into the tee nut and tighten securely.

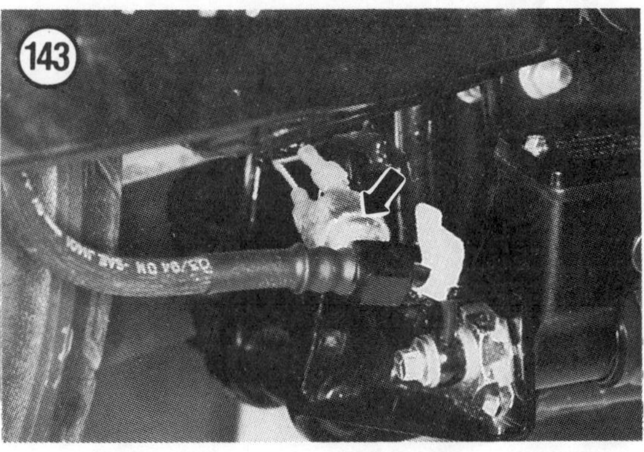

6. Reconnect the switch electrical connectors.
7. Bleed the rear brake as described in Chapter Twelve.
8. Check the rear brake light with the ignition switch turned on and the rear brake applied.

WARNING
Do not ride the motorcycle until the brakes are working properly.

HORN

The horn is an important safety device. Replace a weak or damaged horn.

If the horn fails to blow properly, check for broken or frayed horn wires. Also, check the battery as described in this chapter.

Testing/Replacement

The horn (**Figure 144**) mounts to the back of the battery box.

1. Remove those items necessary to access the horn.
2. If the horn loudness is weak or if it doesnt sound at all, perform the following:

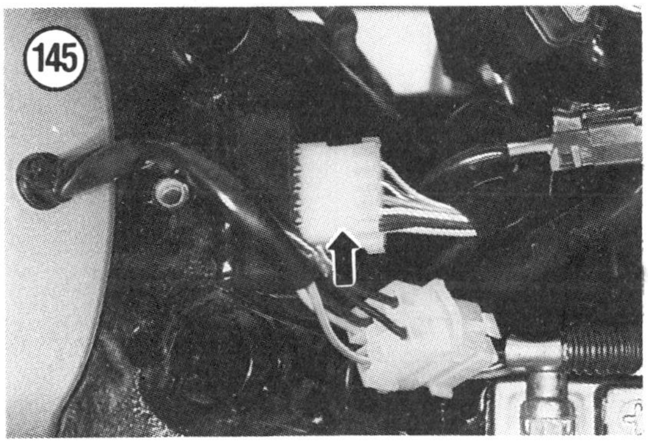

   a. First check the horn wires for loose or damaged connectors or frayed wiring.
   b. If the wiring is okay, locate the adjust screw in the center backside of the horn. Turn the adjust screw clockwise until the horn makes a single click. Then turn the adjuster screw counterclockwise until the horn sounds with its best tone.
   c. If you cant get the horn to work properly by adjusting the adjust screw, replace the horn.
3. Label, then disconnect the horn electrical connectors from the horn spade terminals.
4. Remove the nuts and lockwashers securing the horn to its mounting bracket. Remove the horn.
5. Install the horn by reversing these removal steps. Note the following.
   a. Make sure the electrical connectors and horn spade terminals are free of corrosion.
   b. Check that the horn operates correctly.

TURN SIGNAL MODULE

The turn signal module is an electronic microprocessor that controls the turn signals and the 4-way hazard flasher. The turn signal module receives its information from the speedometer and turn signal switches.

The turn signal module mounts underneath the rear seat on the rear frame tubes (**Figure 145**).

Performance Test

If the turn signals do not work properly, perform the following performance test. This test requires a jumper wire, ohmmeter and voltmeter.

1. Disconnect the connector from the module (**Figure 145**). Then identify the socket connector and module pin connectors using the diagram in **Figure 146**.
2. With the ignition switch turned off, check for ground at the No. 1 socket connector pin.

NOTE
Perform the following tests with the ignition switch turned on.

3. Turn the ignition switch on.
4. Check for voltage at the No. 2 socket connector pin. Battery voltage be present.

5. Connect a jumper wire between the No. 2 and No. 4 socket connector pins. The right-hand front and rear turn signal lights must illuminate.

6. Connect a jumper wire between the No. 2 and No. 6 socket connector pins. The left-hand front and rear turn signal lights must illuminate.

7. Connect a jumper wire between the No. 4 and No. 8 socket connector pins and depress the right-hand turn signal switch button. The right-hand front and rear turn signal lights must illuminate.

8. Connect a jumper wire between the No. 6 and No. 10 socket connector pins and depress the left-hand turn signal switch button. The left-hand front and rear turn signal lights must illuminate.

9. Turn the ignition switch off and remove the jumper wire.

10. If the module passes all 6 tests, install the module as described in this chapter. If the module fails one or more tests, refer to *Troubleshooting* in this section.

Troubleshooting

The following troubleshooting procedures will help isolate some specific turn signal module problems. To access the turn signal module, remove it as described in this chapter.

Refer to **Figure 146** for socket and module pin connector identification.

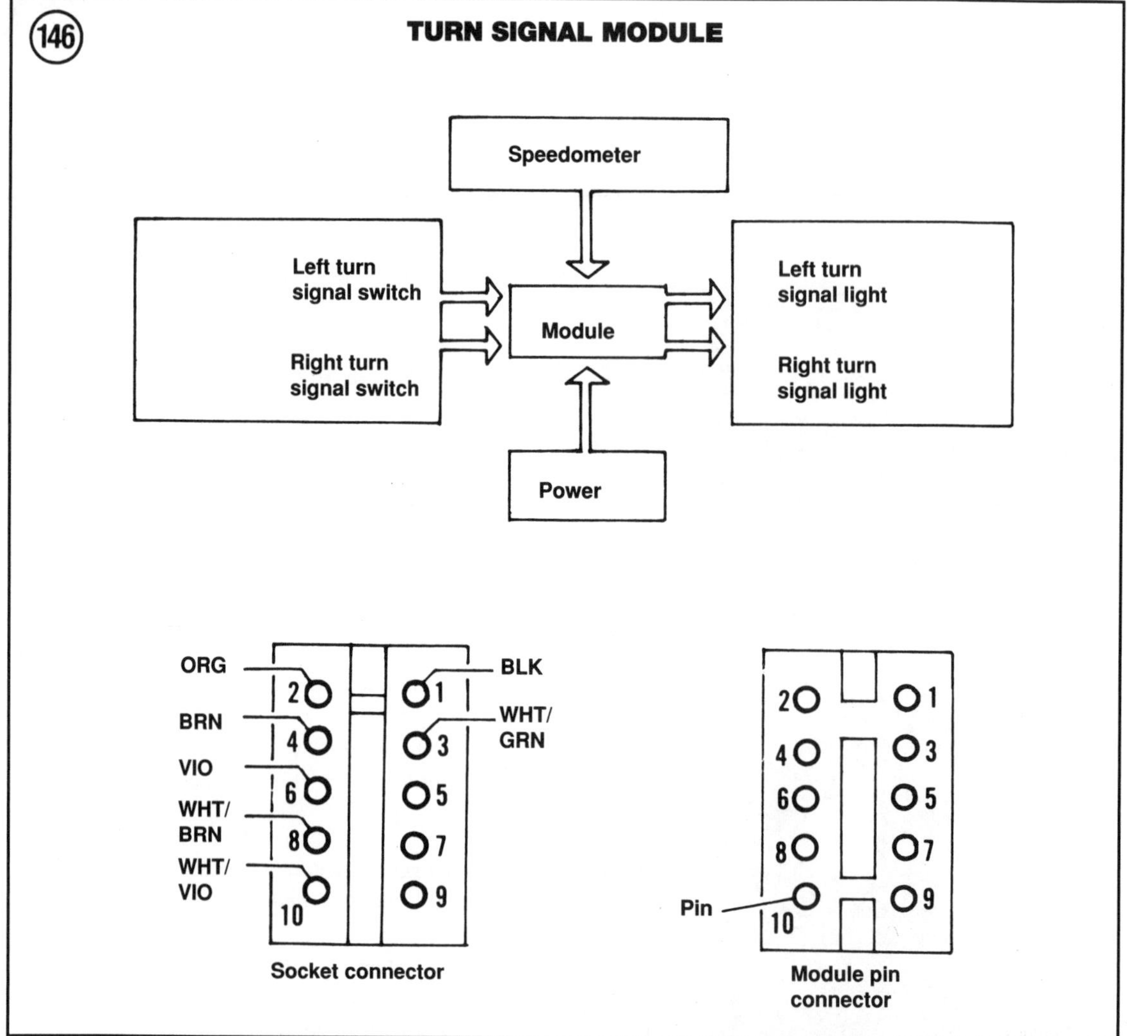

One or both turn signals do not flash. Light on front or rear sides is lit, but does not flash

1. Remove the lens and check for a defective bulb. Replace the bulb if necessary.
2. If the bulb is okay, check for one of the following problems:
   a. Check the bulb socket contacts for corrosion. Clean the contacts and recheck. If you have a problem with corrosion building on the contacts, wipe the contacts with a dielectric grease before installing the bulb.
   b. Check for a broken bulb wire. Repair the wire or connector.
   c. Check for a loose bulb socket where it is staked to the housing. If the bulb socket is loose, replace the light assembly.
   d. Check for a poor ground connection. If the ground is poor, scrape the ground mounting area or replace damaged ground wire(s), as required.

Turn signals do not operate on one side

1. Perform the checks listed under *One or both turn signals do not flash. Light on front or rear sides is lit, but does not flash.* If these checks do not find the problem, continue with Step 2.
2. Check for inoperative handlebar directional switch. Perform the following:
   a. Turn the ignition switch ON.
   b. Disconnect the turn signal module electrical connector.
   c. Find the No. 8 or No. 10 socket connector pin.
   d. With a voltmeter set on the DC scale, connect the negative lead to a good ground and the positive lead to one of the pin numbers specified in sub-step c for your model. Then press the turn signal switch. The voltmeter must read battery voltage when the switch is pressed in.
   e. If battery voltage is present, continue with Step 3.
   f. If there is no voltage reading, go to Step 4.
3. Check for an inoperative module. If the voltmeter recorded battery voltage in Step 2, and the lights and connecting wires are in good condition, the module may be damaged. Replace the module and retest.
4. Check for damaged directional switch wire circuits. If the no voltage is present in Step 2, check the handlebar switch and related wiring for damage.
5. Reconnect the turn signal module electrical connector.

Turn signals/hazard lights do not operate on both sides

1. If none of the turn signals or hazard flashers operate, check the module for a proper ground using an ohmmeter. Using the wiring diagram for your model at the end of this book, trace the ground connection from the module to the frame tab. If a ground is not present, remove the ground wire from the frame and scrape the frame and clean the connector. Check the ground wire for breaks. Repair as required. If a ground is present, perform Step 2.

CAUTION
Do not operate the module without the No. 1 pin grounded; otherwise, the module will be damaged.

2. Refer to the wiring diagram for your model and find the accessory circuit breaker. Turn the ignition switch ON and measure voltage on the hot or load side of the circuit breaker with a voltmeter. If there is no voltage, check the following components:
   a. Accessory circuit breaker.
   b. Main circuit breaker.
   c. Starter relay.
   d. Ignition switch.
   e. Circuit wiring.

8

Turn signals do not cancel

1. Support the bike so that the front wheel clears the ground.
2. Connect an ohmmeter to the speedometer white/green wire and ground. Spin the front wheel and watch the ohmmeter scale. The ohmmeter must alternate between 0 ohms and infinity.
   a. If the ohmmeter reading is correct, disconnect the module connector. With a voltmeter set on the DC scale, connect the negative lead to a good ground and the positive lead to the No. 3 pin connector. The voltmeter must indicate battery voltage. If ohm and volt readings are correct, the module is damaged.
   b. If the ohmmeter reading is incorrect, check for damaged wiring from the speedometer white/green wire to the module. If the wiring

is okay, the speedometer reed switch may be damaged.

Turn Signal Module Removal/Installation

1. Remove the seat.
2. Turn the ignition switch off.
3. Disconnect the harness connector from the module (**Figure 146**).
4. Remove the module bolt, rubber washer and steel washer. Then remove the module.
5. Install the module by reversing these removal steps while noting the following:
6. Make sure the electrical connectors are free of moisture.
7. Tighten the screw securely.
8. Check that the turn signal and flasher systems work properly.

SPEEDOMETER SPEED SENSOR (1995)

All 1995 models are equipped with an electronic speedometer assembly that consists of the speedometer, speed sensor and function switch. **Figure 147** shows a schematic of the electronic speedometer circuit.

The speed sensor (**Figure 148**) mounts inside the transmission housing, directly over fourth gear.

Performance Check

Harley-Davidson specifies using a speedometer tester to verify speedometer calibration, sweep action and operation. To have this test performed to your Dyna Glide, see your local Harley-Davidson dealership.

Speedometer Speed Sensor Removal/Installation

The speedometer speed sensor (**Figure 148**) mounts on top of the transmission housing.

1. Disconnect the negative battery cable as described under *Battery* in this chapter.
2. Disconnect the speed sensor 3-prong connector (**Figure 149**) found underneath the seat.
3. Cut or disconnect any tie straps or clamps holding the speed sensor wiring harness to the frame.
4. Remove the speed sensor mounting screw and lift the sensor (**Figure 148**) from the transmission housing.

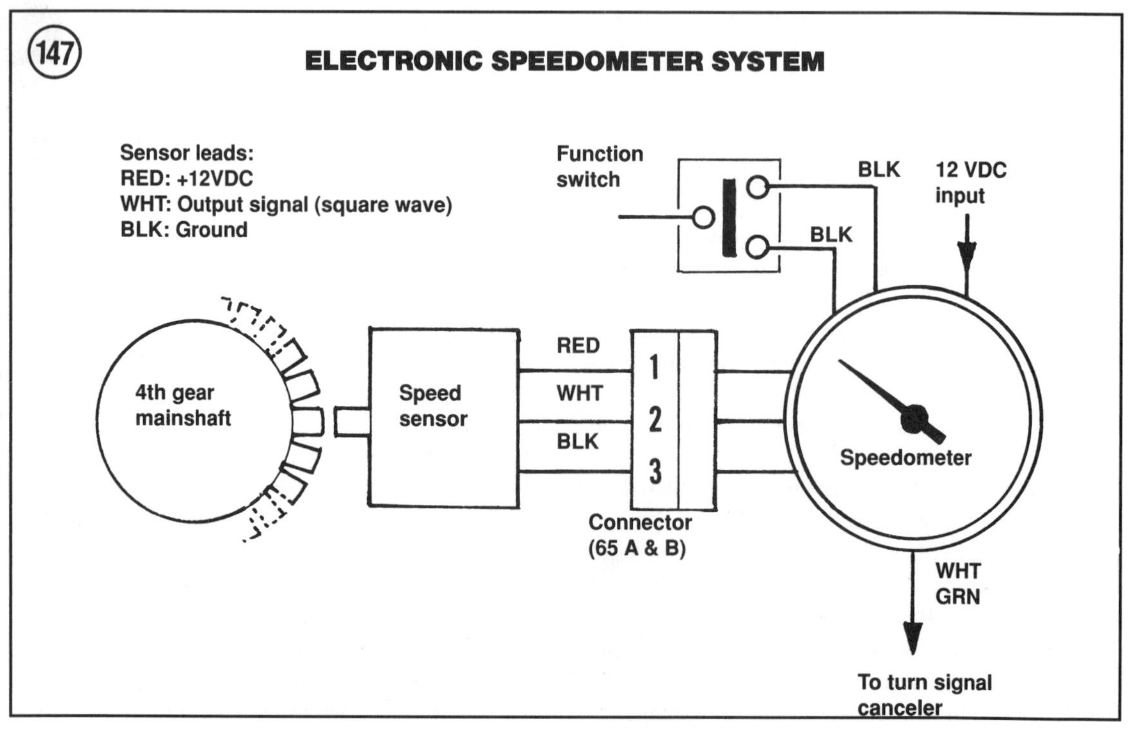

148

149

150

151

5. Remove the speed sensor and its wiring harness from the left hand side of the motorcycle.

6. Reverse these steps to install a new speed sensor. Tighten the speed sensor mounting bolt to the torque specification in **Table 4**.

INDICATOR LIGHTS

Indicator lights monitor most functions, depending on model and year. When replacing a defective bulb, refer to **Figure 139** or to **Figure 150**. When assembling the handlebar type indicator panel, make sure to position the bulb lens plate (**Figure 151**) over the bulbs.

ELECTRIC PANEL

The electric panel assembly mounts on the left side of the motorcycle. The panel assembly houses the circuit breakers, ignition module, starter relay and the main wiring harness connector.

To access the items installed in the electric panel, perform the following:

1. Disconnect the negative battery cable as described under *Battery* in this chapter.

2. Remove the electric panel cover (**Figure 136**).

3. Remove the nuts securing the outer panel (**Figure 152**) to the mounting studs, then carefully pull the panel off its mounting studs. See **Figure 153**.

4. Reverse these steps to install the outer panel and its cover.

152

STARTER RELAY SWITCH REPLACEMENT

The starter relay switch mounts inside the electrical panel.

1. Remove the electric panel cover as described under *Electric Panel* in this chapter.
2. Unplug the starter relay switch (**Figure 154**) and remove its mounting bolt. Then remove the switch.
3. To test the switch, refer to *Starter Relay Testing* under *Electric Starting System* in Chapter Two.
4. Install by reversing these steps.

CIRCUIT BREAKERS

All models use circuit breakers to protect the electrical circuits. **Table 1** lists the circuit breaker ratings for the different circuits.

Whenever a failure occurs in any part of the electrical system, each circuit breaker is self-resetting and will automatically return power to the circuit when the electrical fault is found and corrected.

CAUTION

If the electrical fault is not found and corrected, the circuit breaker will cycle on and off continuously. This will cause the motorcycle to run erratically.

Usually you can trace the trouble to a short circuit in the wiring connected to the circuit breaker. By following the wiring diagrams at the end of the book, you can determine the circuits protected by each circuit breaker.

You must treat a tripped circuit breaker as more than a minor annoyance; it must serve also as a warning that something is wrong in the electrical system.

Replacement

The circuit breakers are installed inside the electrical panel.

1. Disconnect the negative battery cable as described under *Battery* in this chapter.
2. Remove the electric panel cover as described under *Electric Panel* in this chapter.
3. Find the circuit breakers on the back of the electrical panel. See **Figure 155** and the wiring diagram for your model (end of book). Compare the wiring arrangement on the diagram with the actual wiring connections on your Dyna Glide.
4. Remove the nuts and wire connections at the circuit breaker. Then remove the circuit breaker.
5. Install the circuit breaker by reversing these steps.

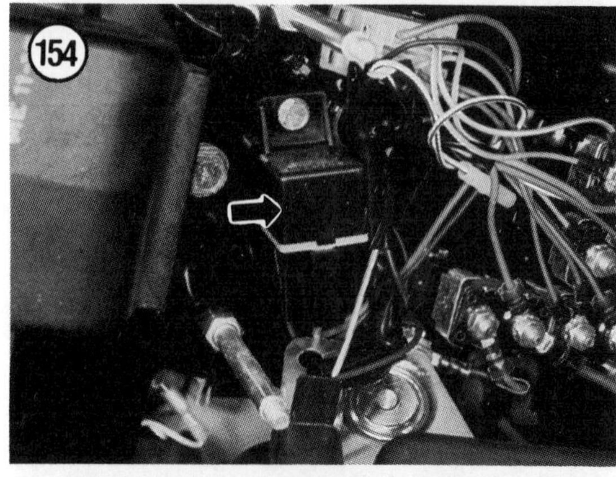

Table 1 ELECTRICAL SPECIFICATIONS

Battery	12 volt, 19 amp-hours
Circuit breakers	
Main	30 amp
Accessory	15 amp
Ignition	15 amp
Lights	15 amp

Table 2 BATTERY STATE OF CHARGE

1.110-1.130	Discharged
1.140-1.160	Almost discharged
1.170-1.190	One-quarter charged
1.200-1.220	One-half charged
1.230-1.250	Three-quarters charged
1.260-1.280	Fully charged

Table 3 ELECTRIC STARTER SPECIFICATIONS

Minimum free speed @ 11.5 volts	3,000 rpm
Maximum free current @ 11.5 volts	90 amps
Cranking current	200 amps maximum @ 68° F
Brush length (minimum)	0.433 in. (11 mm)
Commutator diameter (minimum)	1.141 in. (28.98 mm)

Table 4 TIGHTENING TORQUES

	in.-lb.	ft.-lb.	N•m
Battery box mounting bolts	–	12	16
Cable terminal nuts	65-80	–	7.3-9.0
End cover center screw	90-110	–	10.2-12.4
Jackshaft bolt	80-106	–	9-12
Neutral indicator switch	35-62	–	4-7
Rotor bolt	75-80	–	8.5-9.0
Spark plug	–	18-22	24-30
Speedometer speed sensor mounting bolt			
1995	80-106	–	9.5-12
Starter end cover mounting bracket	50-60		5.6-6.8
Starter mounting bolts	–	13-20	18-27
Starter through bolts	39-65	–	4.4-7.3
Stator Torx screws	30-40	–	3.5-4.5

CHAPTER NINE

WHEELS, HUBS AND TIRES

This chapter describes disassembly and repair of the front and rear wheels, hubs and tire service. For routine maintenance, see Chapter Three.

Models are equipped with either wire spoke or cast wheels. Make sure you use the procedure and illustrations applicable to your bike.

Tire service is a critical aspect to the overall operation and safety of your motorcycle. Tires must be properly mounted, balanced and maintained while in service.

Tables 1-4 are found at the end of the chapter.

FRONT WHEEL

Proper front wheel maintenance and inspection is critical to the safe operation of your motorcycle. The following section describes complete service to the front wheel. Service to the front hub and bearings is described later in this chapter.

Removal

1. Support the bike with the front wheel off the ground.
2. Loosen the upper brake caliper mounting screw (A, **Figure 1**) and the lower mounting pin (B, **Figure 1**). Remove the mounting upper screw and washer and the lower mounting pin.
3. Slide the brake caliper off the brake disc and wedge a wooden or plastic spacer block between the

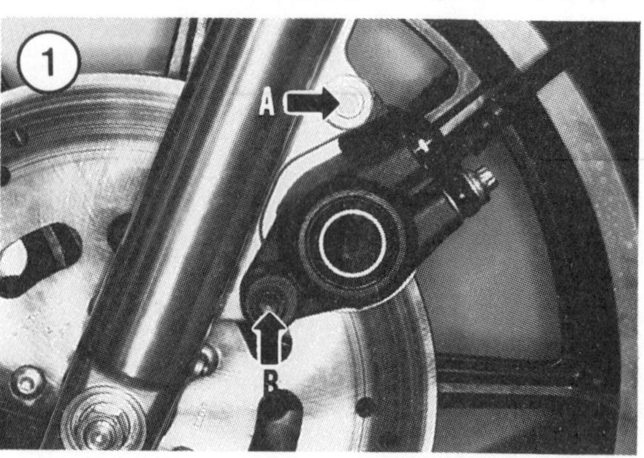

2

3

4

5

brake pads (**Figure 2**). Support the brake caliper(s) with a heavy wire hook

NOTE

Squeezing the brake lever with the caliper removed from the brake disc will force the caliper piston out of its bore. If the piston is forced out, you must disassemble the caliper to reseat the piston.

4. Remove the axle nut (**Figure 3**), lockwasher and flat washer.

5A. On cast wheels, loosen the front axle pinch bolt (A, **Figure 4**).

5B. On laced wheels, loosen the fork slider cap nuts.

NOTE

Before removing the front axle from your bike, note its installation position, as it may differ from the axle arrangement shown in the text photographs.

6. Tap the end of the axle (B, **Figure 4**) with a soft-faced mallet and remove it from the wheel. If the axle is tight, tap the end of the axle with a brass or aluminum drift.

7A. On 1991-1994 models, pull the wheel away from the fork sliders and remove the speedometer drive gear (**Figure 5**). Note the right-hand axle spacer (**Figure 6**).

NOTE

All 1995 models are equipped with an electronic speedometer unit installed in the transmission housing. This assembly replaces the speedometer cable and drive unit used on earlier models. A spacer, installed in the left-hand side of the wheel, takes up space previously used by the speedometer drive unit.

6

7B. On 1995 models, pull the wheel away from the fork sliders and remove it. Note the position of the left-hand (**Figure 7**) and right-hand (**Figure 8**) axle spacers.

CAUTION
Do not set the wheel down on the disc surface, as it may be scratched or warped. Either lean the wheel against a wall or place it on a couple of wooden blocks.

8. Inspect the front wheel assembly as described in this chapter.

Installation

1. Clean the axle in solvent and dry thoroughly. Make sure the axle bearing surfaces on both fork sliders and the axle are free of burrs and nicks.
2. Apply an antiseize lubricant to the axle shaft prior to installation.
3. If you replaced the oil seals or bearings, confirm front axle spacer alignment as described under *Front Hub* in this chapter.
4A. On 1991-1994 models, install the wheel as follows:
  a. Install the spacer (**Figure 6**) in the right-hand side of the wheel.
  b. Install the rubber washer-type seal on the speedometer drive (**Figure 5**).
  c. Align the speedometer drive dogs with the wheel gear case notches and install the speedometer drive into the wheel.
  d. Hold the speedometer drive in position and install the wheel between the fork tubes.
  e. Insert the axle through the front forks and wheel from the same side recorded prior to removal. Then install the flat washer, lockwasher and axle nut (B, **Figure 4**). Check that you positioned the axle spacer correctly.

4B. On 1995 models, install the wheel as follows:
  a. Install the left (**Figure 7**) and right axle spacers in the wheel. The left side axle spacer (**Figure 7**) is longer than the right side.
  b. Install the wheel between the fork tubes and install the axle from the same side recorded prior to removal. Then install the flat washer, lockwasher and axle nut (B, **Figure 4**) finger tight. Check that you positioned both axle spacers correctly.

5A. On cast wheels, tighten the pinch bolt (A, **Figure 4**) securely to prevent the axle from turning, then tighten the axle nut (B, **Figure 4**) to the torque specification in **Table 4**. Loosen the pinch bolt and then retighten to the torque specification in **Table 4**.

5B. On laced wheels, tighten the slider cap nuts securely to prevent the axle from turning, then tighten the axle nut to the torque specification in **Table 4**. Loosen the slider cap nuts and then retighten to the torque specification in **Table 4**. Then check the gap between the fork slider and slider cap. The gap must be equal on both sides.

6. Check that the front wheel is centered between the fork tubes. If not, check the position of the left and right axle spacers.

7. Perform the *Front Axle End Play Check* in this chapter.

8. Install the brake caliper(s) as follows:
  a. Remove the spacer block from between the brake pads. Then *carefully* insert the pads over the disc when installing the brake caliper. Be careful not to damage the leading edge of the brake pads when installing the brake disc.

b. Align the 2 mounting holes in the caliper with the fork tube mounting lugs. Then install the screw and mounting pin as follows:
c. Install a washer onto the upper mounting screw and insert the screw through the slider lug and then thread into the caliper bushing (A, **Figure 1**). Install the screw finger-tight.
d. Insert the lower mounting pin (B, **Figure 1**) through the caliper and then thread into the slider lug. Tighten the mounting pin finger-tight.
e. Tighten the lower mounting pin to the torque specification in **Table 4**.
f. Tighten the upper mounting screw to the torque specification in **Table 4**.

9. While the bike is stationary with the engine off, squeeze the front brake lever several times to seat the pads against the disc.

WARNING
Do not ride the motorcycle until you are sure the brakes are operating correctly with full hydraulic advantage. If necessary, bleed the brake system as described in this chapter.

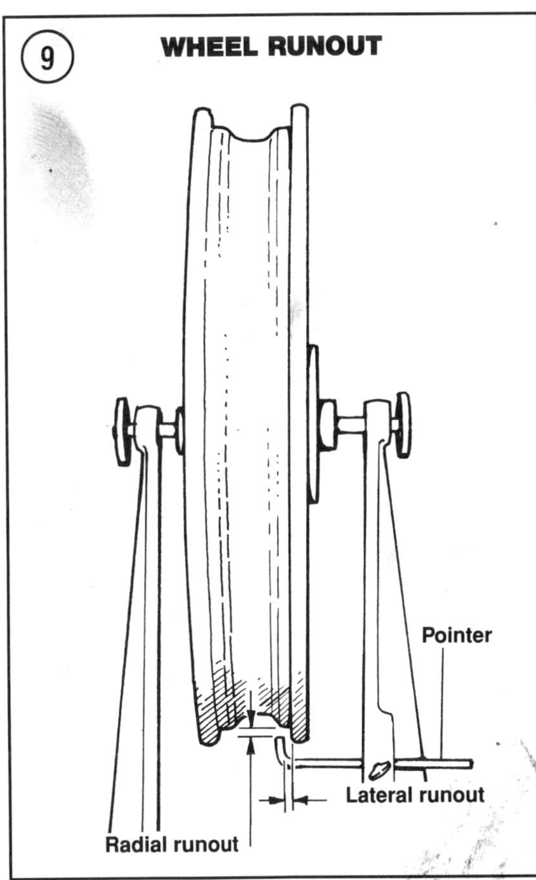

10. Remove the stand and lower the front wheel onto the ground.

Inspection

1. Remove any rust or corrosion from the front axle.
2. Install the wheel in a wheel truing stand and check the wheel for excessive wobble or runout. If the wheel is not running true, remove the tire from the rim as described later in this chapter. Then remount the wheel into the truing stand and measure axial and lateral runout (**Figure 9**) with a pointer or dial indicator. Compare actual runout readings with the service limit specification listed in **Table 1**. Note the following:
   a. *Cast wheels*: If the runout meets or exceeds the service limit (**Table 1**), check the wheel bearings as described under *Front Hub* in this chapter. If the wheel bearings are okay, you must replace the cast wheel as it cannot be serviced. Inspect the wheel for cracks, fractures, dents or bends. Replace a damaged wheel.

   WARNING
   Do not try to repair any damage to a cast wheel as it will result in an unsafe riding condition.

   b. *Laced wheels*: If the wheel bearings, spokes, hub and rim assembly are not damaged, you can remove the runout by truing the wheel. Refer to *Spoke Adjustment* in this chapter. If the rim is dented or damaged in any way, the rim must be replaced and the wheel rebuilt by a Harley-Davidson dealership.
3. While the wheel is off, check the brake disc and its mounting bolts as described in Chapter Twelve.

Front Wheel Bearing End Play Check

Front wheel bearing end play establishes the amount of axial (lengthwise) movement between the left and right bearings. **Table 1** lists the correct end play specification. Excessive end play can cause bearing side loading. If the end play is too tight, bearing seizure could result. Check end play each time you install the front wheel.

On 1991 models, the length of the spacer sleeve controls end play (**Figure 10**) between the bearings. On 1992 and later models, the thickness of the spacer shim controls end play between the spacer sleeve and washer; see **Figure 11** or **Figure 12**.

Measure end play with a dial indicator as follows:

1. Support the bike on a stand so that the front wheel is off the ground.
2. Tighten the front axle to the tightening torque listed in **Table 4**.
3. Mount a dial indicator securely on the brake disc and center its stem against the end of the axle (**Figure 13**). Then zero the dial gauge. Grasp the tire and move it (with the axle) in and out along the axle center line and note the indicator reading. The total indicator reading is axle end play.

4A. On 1991 models, note the following:
  a. If there is not enough end play, install a shorter spacer sleeve (7, **Figure 10**).
  b. If the end play is excessive, install a longer spacer sleeve (7, **Figure 10**).
  c. **Table 2** lists the different spacer sleeve lengths available from Harley-Davidson dealers.

4B. On 1992 and later models, note the following:
  a. If there is not enough end play, install a thinner spacer shim. See **Figure 11** or **Figure 12**.
  b. If the end play is excessive, install a thicker spacer shim; see **Figure 11** or **Figure 12**.
  c. **Table 3** lists the different spacer shim thickness available from a Harley-Davidson dealership.

5. To replace a spacer sleeve (1991) or spacer shim (1992-on), disassemble the front hub as described under *Front Hub* in this chapter.

FRONT HUB

Tapered roller bearings are installed on each side of the hub. Oil seals are installed on the outside of each bearing to protect them from dirt and other contaminants. You can remove the bearings from the hub after removing the outer oil seals. The bearing races are pressed into the hub. Do not remove the bearing races unless they require replacement.

Disassembly/Inspection/Reassembly

Refer to the following for your model when performing this procedure:

  a. 1991 models: **Figure 10**.
  b. 1992-on cast wheels: **Figure 11**.

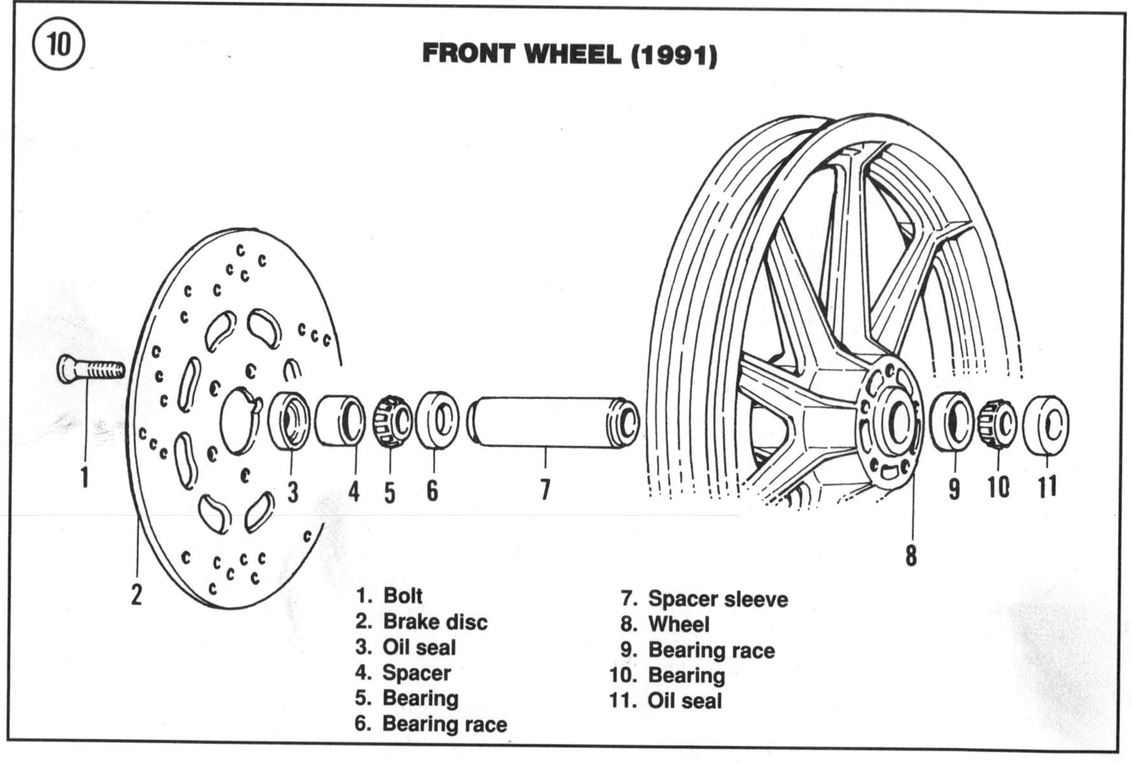

(11)

CAST FRONT WHEEL (1992-ON)

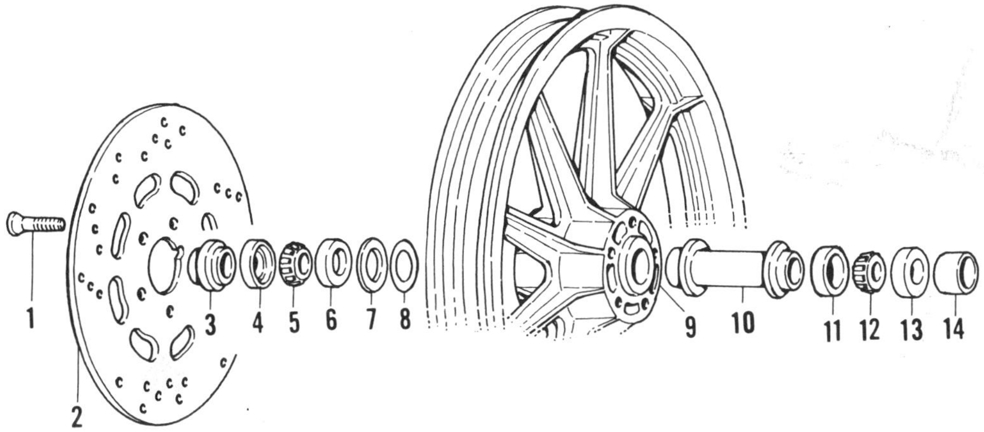

1. Bolt
2. Brake disc
3. Spacer
4. Oil seal
5. Bearing
6. Bearing race
7. Washer
8. Spacer shim
9. Wheel
10. Spacer sleeve
11. Bearing race
12. Bearing
13. Oil seal
14. Spacer

(12)

LACED FRONT WHEEL (1992-ON)

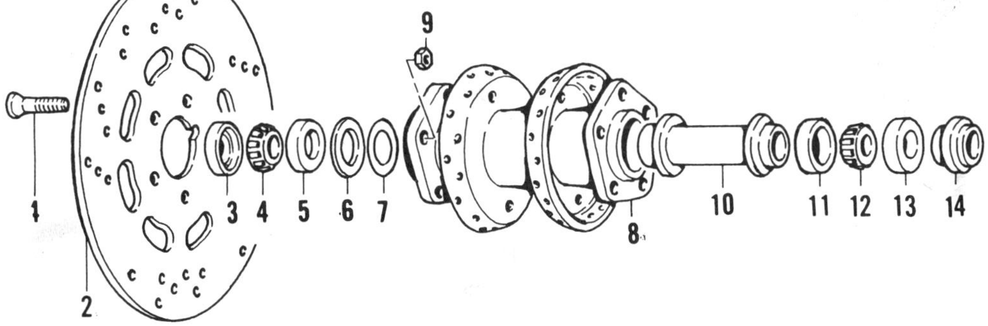

1. Bolt
2. Brake disc
3. Oil seal
4. Bearing
5. Bearing race
6. Washer
7. Spacer
8. Hub
9. Nut
10. Spacer sleeve
11. Bearing race
12. Bearing
13. Oil seal
14. Spacer shim

c. 1992-on laced wheels: **Figure 12**.

NOTE
The bearings and races are matched pairs. Label all parts so that you may return them to their original positions.

1. Remove the front wheel as described in this chapter.
2. If necessary, remove the brake disc as described in Chapter Twelve.

NOTE
The length of the outer axle spacers on some models may be different. Identify each spacer so you don't mix them up during reassembly.

3. Remove the outer spacer(s) from the hub.
4. Pry one of the oil seals out of the hub (**Figure 14**) and remove the bearing (**Figure 15**) and spacer sleeve (**Figure 16**). Turn the wheel over and remove the opposite oil seal and bearing. On 1992 and later models, remove the washer and spacer shim.
5. Wash the bearings in clean solvent and dry with compressed air. Wipe the bearing races off with a clean rag dipped in solvent.
6. Check the roller bearings and races (**Figure 17**) for wear, pitting or excessive heat (a bluish tint). Replace the bearings and races as a complete set (both sides). Perform Step 7 to replace the bearing races. If the bearings and races do not require replacement, go to Step 8. If you are going to reuse the original bearings, pack the bearings with grease and then wrap in a clean, lint-free cloth or wax paper

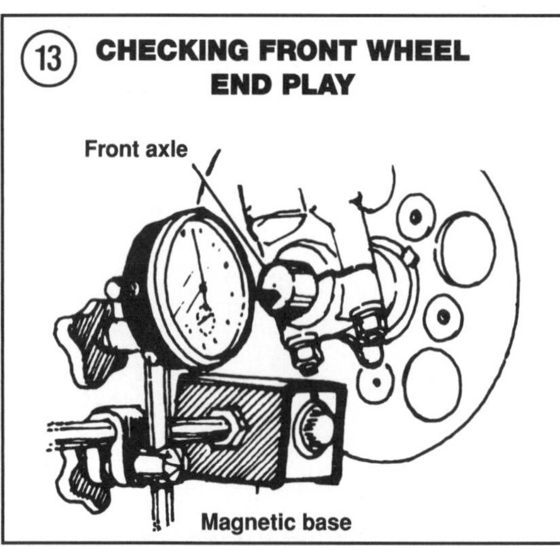

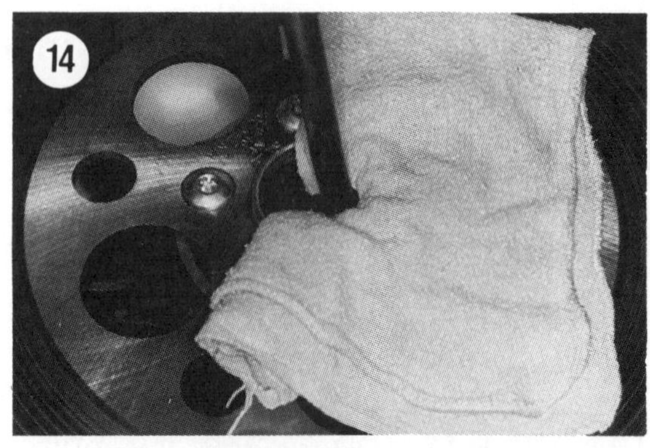

until reassembly. Apply a film of grease across the bearing race (**Figure 17**).

NOTE
You must apply grease to the bearings and races after cleaning them; otherwise, both parts will begin to rust.

7. Replace the bearing races (Figure 17) as follows:
   a. To protect the hub from damage, remove the bearing races with the Harley-Davidson wheel bearing race remover and installer tool (part No. HD-33071) shown in **Figure 18**. If this tool is unavailable, insert a drift punch through the hub and drive the race out of the hub. Tap on alternate sides of the race to drive it squarely out of the hub. If the race binds in the hub bore, level it by tapping it from its opposite side (Figure 17).

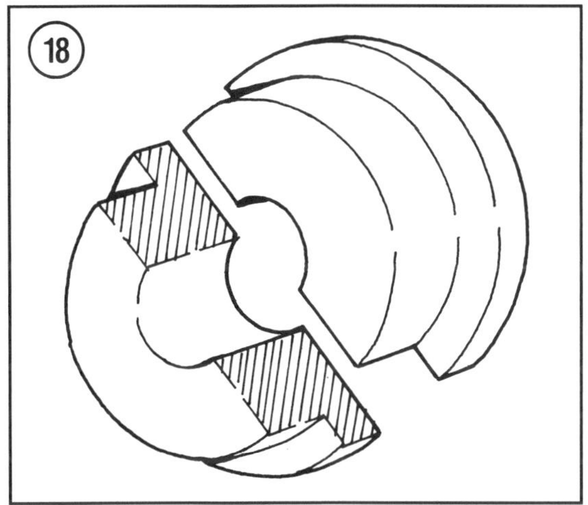
18

19

20

If you drive the race out at an angle, severe damage to the hubs race bore can occur.
   b. Clean the hub with solvent. Dry with compressed air.
   c. Wipe the outside of the new race with oil and align it with its bore in the hub. Install the race with the Harley-Davidson tool (part No. HD-33071) or a bearing driver or socket. Drive the race into the hub until it bottoms on the hub shoulder.

NOTE
When installing the race, stop and check your work often, making sure the race is square with the hub bore. Do not allow the race to bind during installation or you may damage the race bore in the hub.

NOTE
If you do not have the proper size tools, refer this service to a Harley-Davidson dealer.

8. Blow any dirt or foreign matter out of the hub.
9. Wipe each bearing race (**Figure 17**) with grease.
10. Pack each seal lip with grease, then set aside until reassembly.
11. Pack the bearings with grease, then place them on a clean, lint-free cloth until you are ready to install them. When installing used bearings, install them in their original mounting position.
12. When installing the oil seals in Step 12, use a bearing driver or socket with an outer diameter smaller than the oil seal (**Figure 19**).

13A. On 1991 models, assemble the front hub in the order shown in **Figure 10**, while noting the following:
   a. If you are changing the wheel bearing end play, make sure to install the correct length spacer sleeve.
   b. After installing the bearings (**Figure 20**), pack the area between the bearings and oil seals with grease.
   c. Install both oil seals so that they are flush with the outer hub surface.

13B. On 1992-on models with cast wheels, assemble the front hub in the order shown in **Figure 11**, while noting the following:

a. Apply grease to both ends of the spacer sleeve.
b. Install the spacer washer (7, **Figure 11**) with its shoulder (smaller diameter) facing toward its adjacent bearing.

CAUTION
*If you install the spacer washer (7, **Figure 11**) with its larger diameter side toward the bearing, the spacer washer could contact the bearing cage and damage it.*

c. After installing the bearings (**Figure 20**), pack the area between the bearings and oil seals with grease.
d. Install the oil seals until they are flush with the hub or recessed 0.04 in. (1.0 mm) below the hub surface. See **Figure 21**.
e. Install the spacer (3, **Figure 11**) so that its large chamfered end faces toward the bearing on the valve stem hole side of the wheel.

13C. On 1992-on models with laced wheels, assemble the front hub in the order shown in **Figure 12**, while noting the following:

a. Apply grease to both ends of the spacer sleeve.
b. Install the spacer washer (7, **Figure 12**) with its shoulder (smaller diameter) facing toward its adjacent bearing.

CAUTION
*If you install the spacer washer (7, **Figure 12**) with its larger diameter side toward the bearing, the spacer washer could contact the bearing cage and damage it.*

c. After installing the bearings (**Figure 20**), pack the area between the bearings and oil seals with grease.
d. Install the oil seals until they are flush with the hub or recessed 0.02 in. (0.51 mm) below the hub surface. See **Figure 21**.
e. Install the spacer (3, **Figure 11**) so that its large chamfered end faces toward the bearing on the valve stem hole side of the wheel.

14. If removed, install the brake disc as described in Chapter Twelve.
15. After you install the wheel and tighten the front axle, check bearing end play as described in this chapter.

REAR WHEEL

Removal

1. Support the bike with the rear wheel off the ground.
2. Remove the rear muffler if it interferes with rear wheel removal.

NOTE
*If you can't lift the rear wheel high enough off the ground, you may have to remove the belt guard (A, **Figure 22**) and the debris deflector (B, **Figure 22**) from the swing arm. Because the rear wheel is heavy and awkward to remove by yourself, check the tire-to-ground clearance before removing the rear axle.*

3. Remove the cotter pin from the rear axle. Discard the cotter pin as you must install a new one.
4. Loosen and remove the axle nut (A, **Figure 23**) and washer.

5. Slide the axle out of the wheel and allow the wheel to drop to the ground.

6. Remove the outer left-hand axle spacer (B, **Figure 23**).

7. Lift the belt off the sprocket and remove the rear wheel.

8. Note the position of the 2 inner axle spacers (**Figure 24**, typical) installed in the oil seals.

9. Wedge a wooden or plastic spacer block between the brake pads.

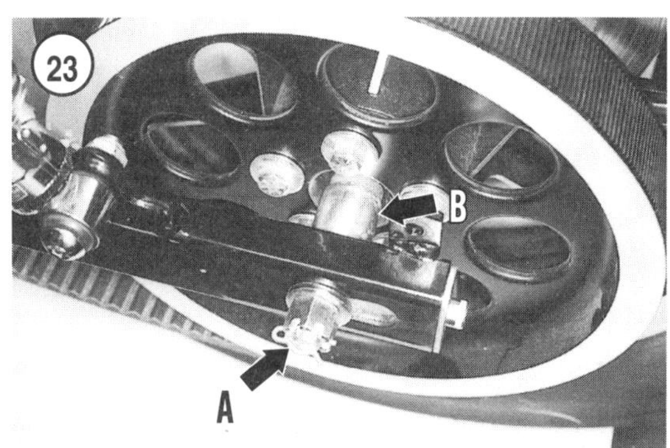

NOTE

Pressing the rear brake lever with the brake disc removed from the caliper will force the caliper piston out of its bore. If the piston is forced out, you must disassemble the caliper to reseat the piston.

CAUTION

Do not set the wheel down on the disc surface. Either lean the wheel against a wall or place it on a couple of wooden blocks.

10. Inspect the rear wheel as described in this chapter.

Installation

1. Clean the axle in solvent and dry thoroughly. Make sure the bearing surfaces on the axle are free from burrs and nicks.
2. Apply an antiseize lubricant to the axle shaft prior to installation.
3. Install the left and right spacers into the rear wheel oil seals (**Figure 24**, typical), if removed.
4. Remove the spacer block from between the brake pads.

CAUTION

When installing the rear wheel in the following steps, carefully insert the brake disc between the brake pads in the caliper assembly. Do not force the brake disc as it can damage the leading edge of both brake pads.

5. Position the rear wheel between the swing arm sides and place the drive belt on the sprocket.
6. Lift the rear wheel and install the rear axle from the right-hand side. Install the axle through the swing arm and the rear brake caliper mounting bracket. Then position the left-hand axle spacer (B, **Figure 23**) between the wheel and swing arm and slide the axle (**Figure 25**) through it.
7. Install the washer and axle nut (A, **Figure 23**). Tighten the axle nut to the torque specification in **Table 4**.
8. Perform the *Rear Axle End Play Check* in this chapter. When the rear axle end play is correct, continue with Step 9.
9. Check drive belt tension and alignment as described in Chapter Three.

10. If necessary, retighten the axle nut (A, **Figure 23**) to the torque specification in **Table 4**.
11. Tighten the axle nut, if necessary, to align the cotter pin hole with the nut slot. Then install a new cotter pin through the rear axle and bend its arms over to lock it (**Figure 26**).
12. Install the debris deflector and belt guard, if removed.
13. Install the muffler, if removed.
14. Rotate the wheel several times to make sure it rotates freely. Then press the rear brake pedal several times to seat the pads against the disc.

WARNING
Do not ride the motorcycle until the rear brake is working properly.

15. Remove the stand and lower the rear wheel to the ground.

Inspection

1. Remove any rust or corrosion on the rear axle.
2. Install the wheel in a wheel truing stand and visually check the wheel for excessive wobble or runout. If it appears that the wheel is not running true, remove the tire from the rim as described later in this chapter. Then remount the wheel into the truing stand and measure axial and lateral runout (**Figure 27**) with a pointer or dial indicator. Compare actual runout readings with the service limit specifications listed in **Table 1**. Note the following:
   a. *Cast wheels*: If the runout meets or exceeds the service limit (**Table 1**), check the wheel bearings as described under *Rear Hub* in this chapter. If the wheel bearings are okay, replace the cast wheel. Inspect the wheel for signs of cracks, fractures, dents or bends. Replace a damaged wheel.

   WARNING
   Do not try to repair any damage to a cast wheel as it will result in an unsafe riding condition.

   b. *Laced wheel*: If the wheel bearings, spokes, hub and rim assembly are not damaged, you can remove runout by truing the wheel. Refer to *Spoke Adjustment* in this chapter. If the rim is dented or damaged in any way, the rim must be replaced and the wheel respoked and trued by a Harley-Davidson dealership.
3. While the wheel is off, check the brake disc and its mounting bolts as described in Chapter Twelve.

Rear Wheel Bearing End Play Check

Rear wheel bearing end play establishes the amount of axial (lengthwise) movement between the left and right bearings. **Table 1** lists the correct end play specifications. Excessive end play can cause bearing side loading. If the end play is too tight,

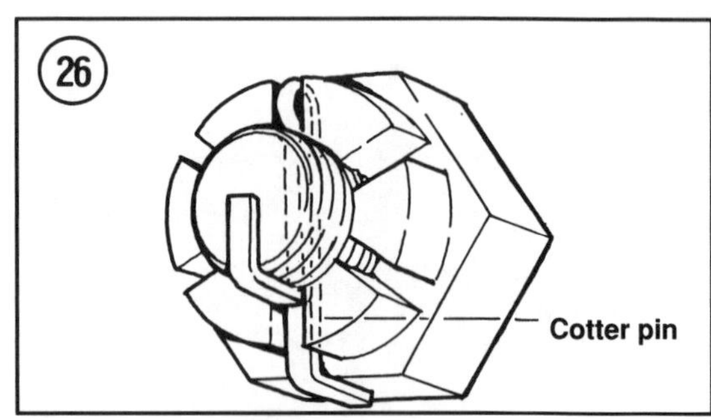

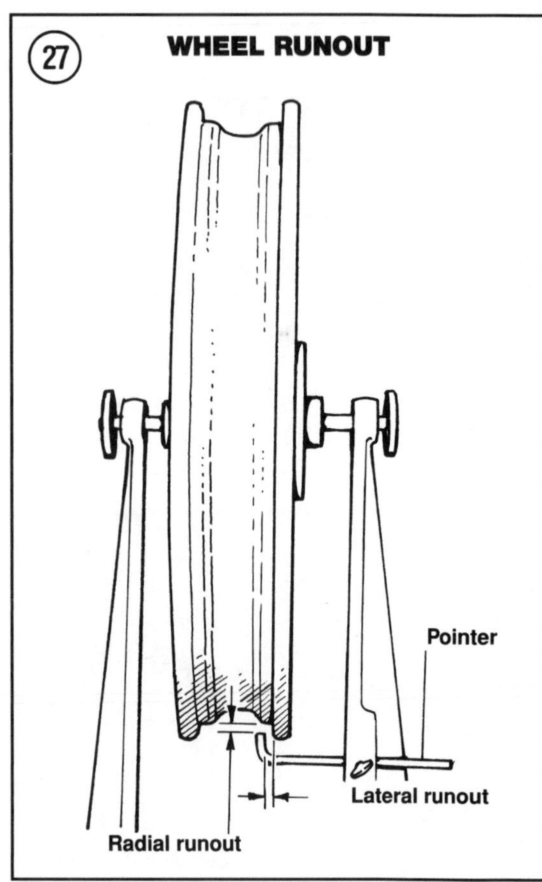

bearing seizure could result. Check end play each time you install the rear wheel.

On 1991 models, the length of the spacer sleeve (8, **Figure 28**) controls end play between the bearings. On 1992 and later models, the thickness of the spacer shim (8, **Figure 29**) controls end play between the spacer sleeve and spacer washer.

Measure end play with a dial indicator as follows:

1. Support the bike on a stand so that the rear wheel is off the ground.

2. Remove and discard the rear axle cotter pin.

3. Tighten the rear axle to the tightening torque listed in **Table 4**.

4. Mount a dial indicator securely on the brake disc and center its stem against the end of the axle (**Figure 13**). Then zero the dial gauge. Grasp the tire and move it (with the axle) in and out along the axle center line and note the indicator reading. The total indicator reading is axle end play.

5A. On 1991 models, note the following:
   a. If there is not enough end play, install a shorter spacer sleeve (8, **Figure 28**).
   b. If the end play is excessive, install a longer spacer sleeve (8, **Figure 28**).
   c. **Table 2** lists the different spacer sleeve lengths available from Harley-Davidson dealers.

5B. On 1992 and later models, note the following:
   a. If there is not enough end play, install a thinner spacer shim (8, **Figure 29**).
   b. If the end play is excessive, install a thicker spacer shim (8, **Figure 29**).
   c. **Table 3** lists the different shim thickness available from Harley-Davidson dealers.

6. To replace a spacer sleeve (1991) or spacer shim (1992-on), disassemble the rear hub as described under *Rear Hub* in this chapter.

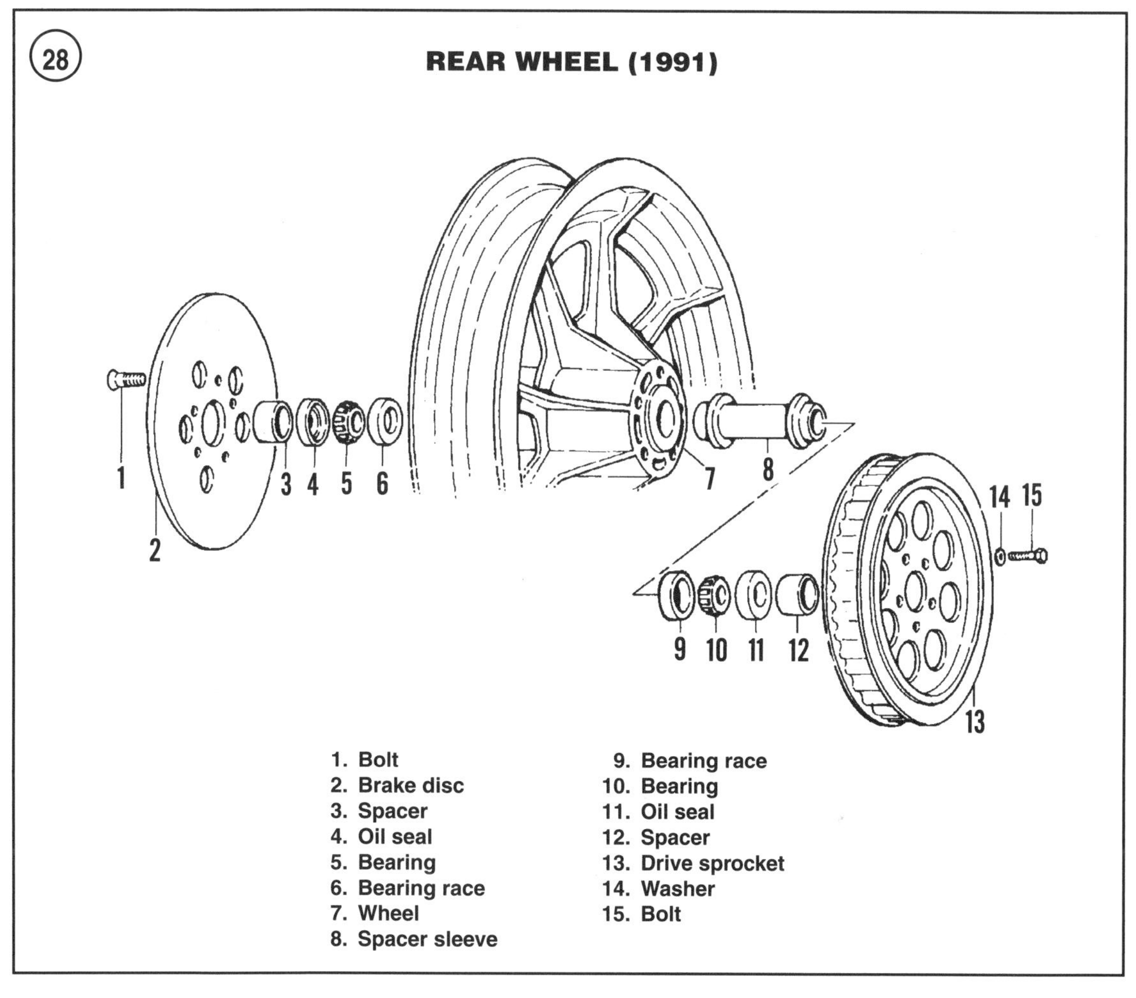

1. Bolt
2. Brake disc
3. Spacer
4. Oil seal
5. Bearing
6. Bearing race
7. Wheel
8. Spacer sleeve
9. Bearing race
10. Bearing
11. Oil seal
12. Spacer
13. Drive sprocket
14. Washer
15. Bolt

REAR HUB

Tapered roller bearings are installed in each side of the hub. Oil seals are installed on the outside of each bearing to protect them from dirt and other contaminants. You can remove the bearings from the hub after removing the outer oil seals. The bearing races are pressed into the hub. Do not remove the races unless they require replacement.

Disassembly/Inspection/Reassembly

Refer to the figure for your model when performing this procedure:

a. **Figure 28**: 1991 models.

b. **Figure 29**: 1992-on models.

NOTE
*The bearings and races are matched pairs (**Figure 30**). Label all parts so that*

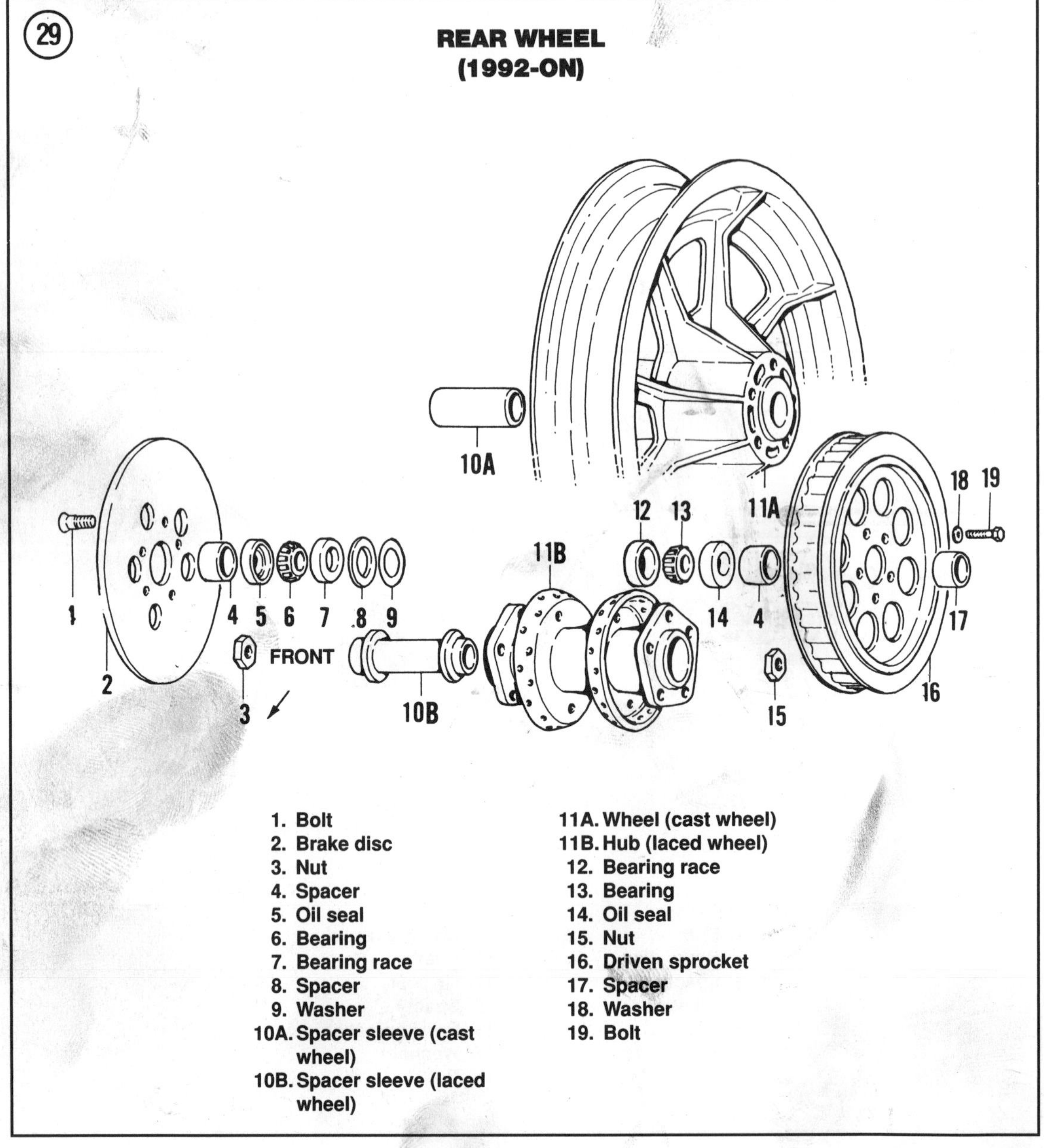

1. Bolt
2. Brake disc
3. Nut
4. Spacer
5. Oil seal
6. Bearing
7. Bearing race
8. Spacer
9. Washer

10A. Spacer sleeve (cast wheel)
10B. Spacer sleeve (laced wheel)
11A. Wheel (cast wheel)
11B. Hub (laced wheel)

12. Bearing race
13. Bearing
14. Oil seal
15. Nut
16. Driven sprocket
17. Spacer
18. Washer
19. Bolt

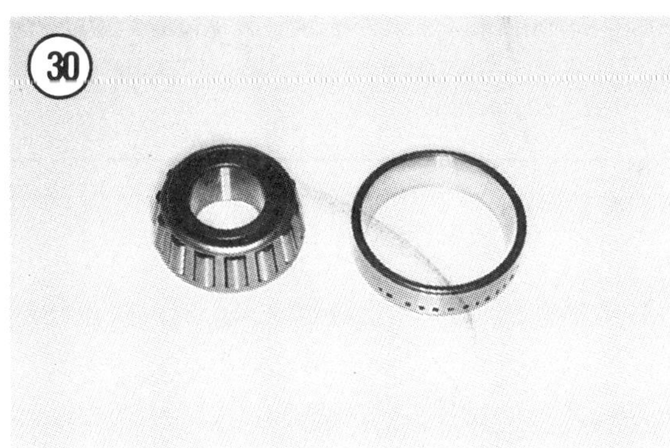

you reinstall them in the sitions.

1. Remove the rear wheel as described in this chapter.
2. If necessary, remove the brake disc as described in Chapter Twelve.
3. Remove the spacers (**Figure 24**) from the hub.
4. Pry an oil seal out of the hub (**Figure 31**), then remove the bearing (**Figure 32**) and spacer sleeve (**Figure 33**). Turn the wheel over and remove the opposite oil seal and bearing. On 1992 and later models, remove the washer and spacer shim.
5. Wash the bearings thoroughly in clean solvent and dry with compressed air. Wipe the bearing races off with a clean rag dipped in solvent.
6. Check the roller bearings and races (**Figure 34**) for wear, pitting or excessive heat (a bluish tint). Replace the bearings and races as a complete set (both sides). Perform Step 7 to replace the bearing races. If the bearings and races do not require replacement, go to Step 8. If you are going to reuse the original bearings, pack the bearings with grease and then wrap in a clean, lint-free cloth or wax paper until reassembly. Apply a film of grease across the bearing race (**Figure 34**).
7. Replace the bearing races (**Figure 34**) as follows:
   a. To protect the hub from damage, remove the bearing races with the Harley-Davidson wheel bearing race remover and installer tool (part No. HD-33071) shown in **Figure 35**. If this tool is unavailable, insert a drift punch through the hub and drive the race out of the hub. If the race binds in the hub bore, level it by tapping it from its opposite side.
   b. Clean the hub with solvent. Dry with compressed air.

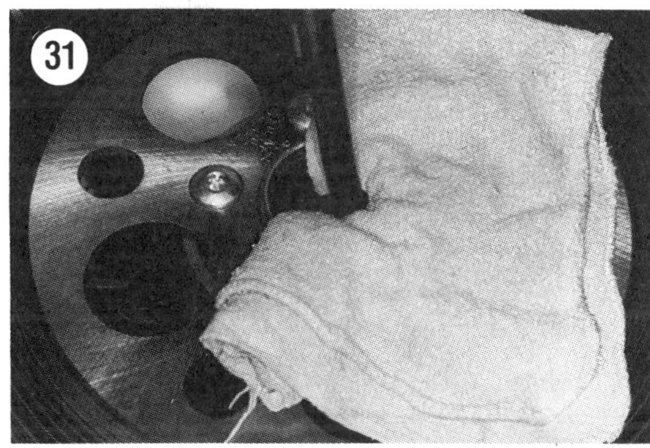

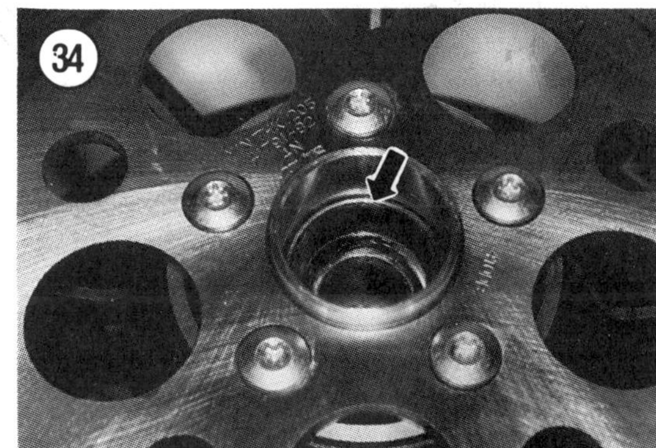

9

c. Wipe the outside of the new race with oil and align it with the hub. Install the race with the Harley-Davidson tool (part No. HD-33071) or a bearing driver or socket. Drive the race into the hub until it bottoms on the hub shoulder.

NOTE
When installing the race, stop and check your work often, making sure the race is square with the hub bore. Do not allow the race to bind during installation or you may damage the race bore in the hub.

NOTE
If you do not have the proper size tools, have the race installed by a Harley-Davidson dealership.

8. Blow any dirt or foreign matter out of the hub prior to installing the bearings.
9. Wipe each bearing race (**Figure 34**) with grease.
10. Pack the seal lip cavity of each seal with grease, then set aside until reassembly.
11. Pack the bearings with grease, then place them on a clean, lint-free cloth until you are ready to install them. When installing used bearings, install them in their original position.

Note:
*When installing the oil seals in Step 13, use a bearing driver or socket with an outer diameter smaller than the oil seal (**Figure 36**).*

12A. On 1991 models, assemble the rear hub assembly in the order shown in **Figure 28**, while noting the following:

a. When changing the wheel bearing end play, make sure to install the correct length spacer sleeve.
b. After installing the bearings (**Figure 37**), pack the area between the bearings and oil seals with grease.
c. Install both oil seals so that they are 0.29-0.31 in. (7.5-7.9 mm) below the outer hub surface.

12B. On 1992-on models with cast wheels, assemble the rear hub in the order shown in **Figure 29**, while noting the following:

a. Apply grease onto both ends of the spacer sleeve prior to installation.
b. Install the spacer washer (8, **Figure 29**) with its shoulder (smaller diameter) facing toward its adjacent bearing.

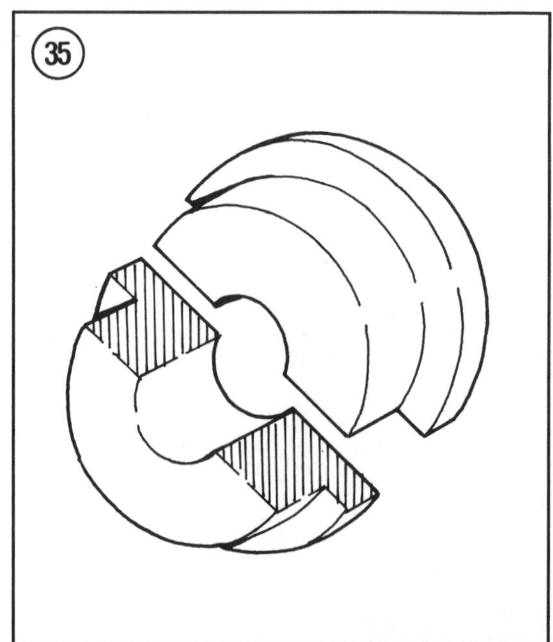
35

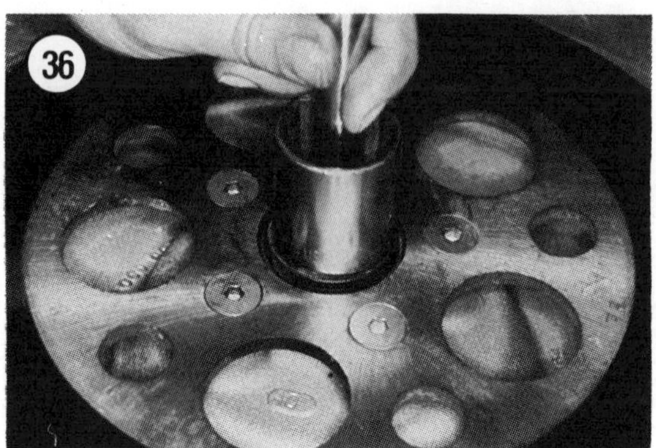
36

37

CAUTION

*If you install the spacer washer (8, **Figure 29**) with its larger diameter side toward the bearing, the spacer washer could contact the bearing cage and damage it.*

c. After installing the bearings (**Figure 37**), pack the area between the bearings and oil seals with grease.

d. Install the right-hand oil seal (brake disc side) so that it is flush with the outer hub surface.

e. Install the left-hand oil seal (sprocket side) so that it is 0.31 in. (7.9 mm) below the outer hub surface.

f. Install the spacers (4, **Figure 29**) with their large chamfered end facing toward their adjacent bearing.

12C. On 1992-on models with laced wheels, assemble the rear hub in the order shown in **Figure 29**, while noting the following:

a. Apply grease onto both ends of the spacer sleeve prior to installation.

38

39

b. Install the washer (8, **Figure 29**) with its shoulder (smaller diameter) facing toward its adjacent bearing.

CAUTION

*If you install the spacer washer (8, **Figure 29**) with its larger diameter side toward the bearing, the spacer washer could contact the bearing cage and damage it.*

c. After installing the bearings (**Figure 37**), pack the area between the bearings and oil seals with grease.

d. Install both oil seals so that they are 0.26-0.28 in. (6.6-7.1 mm) below the outer hub surface.

e. Install the spacers (4, **Figure 29**) with their large chamfered end facing toward their adjacent bearing.

13. If removed, install the brake disc as described in Chapter Twelve.

14. After you install the rear wheel and tighten the rear axle, check bearing end play as described in this chapter.

DRIVEN SPROCKET ASSEMBLY

Removal/Installation

1. Remove the rear wheel as described in this chapter.
2. Remove the bolts, washers and nuts (if used) securing the sprocket to the hub and remove the sprocket. See **Figure 38**, typical.
3. Installation is the reverse of these steps. Tighten the sprocket bolts to specifications in **Table 4**.

Inspection

Inspect the sprocket teeth (**Figure 39**). If the teeth are visibly worn, replace the drive belt and both sprockets.

SECONDARY DRIVE BELT

CAUTION

When handling a new or used drive belt, never wrap the belt in a loop that is smaller than 5 in. (130 mm) or bend it sharply in any direction. This will weaken or break the belt fibers and cause premature belt failure.

Removal/Installation

1. Remove the rear wheel as described in this chapter.
2. Remove the compensating sprocket and clutch as described in Chapter Five.
3. Remove the primary housing as described in Chapter Five.

NOTE
You must install a used drive belt so that it runs in its original direction. Before removing a used belt, draw an arrow on the belt facing forward.

4. Remove the drive belt (**Figure 40**) from the sprocket.
5. Installation is the reverse of these steps. Adjust the drive belt tension as described in Chapter Three.

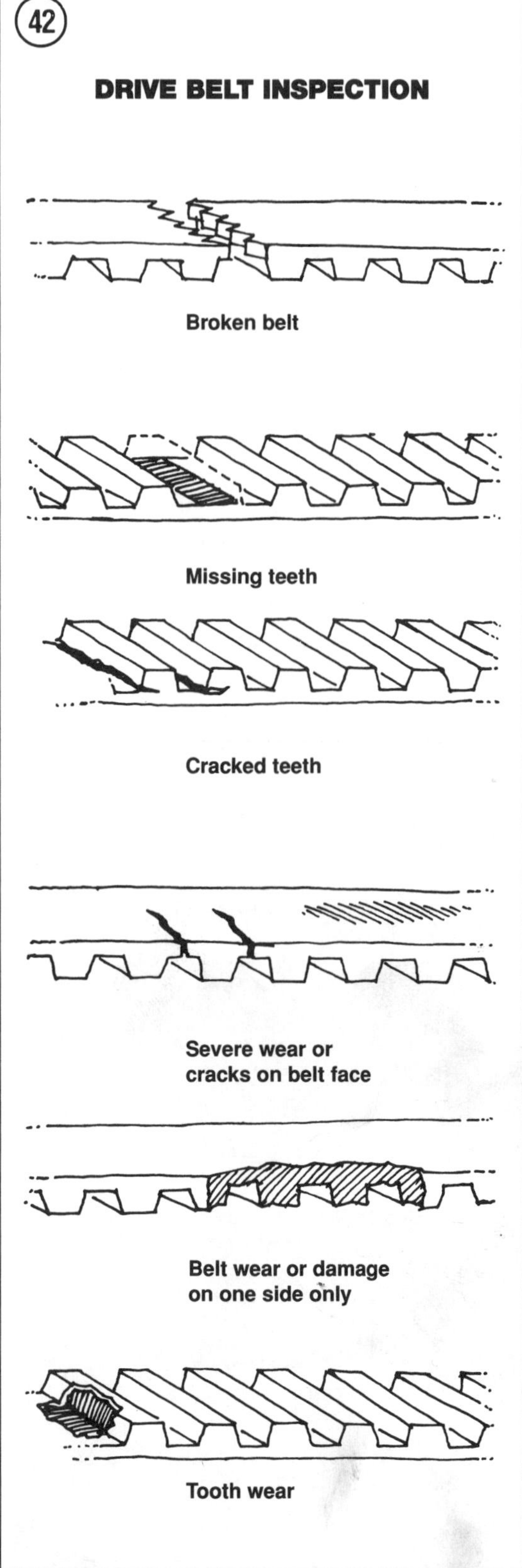

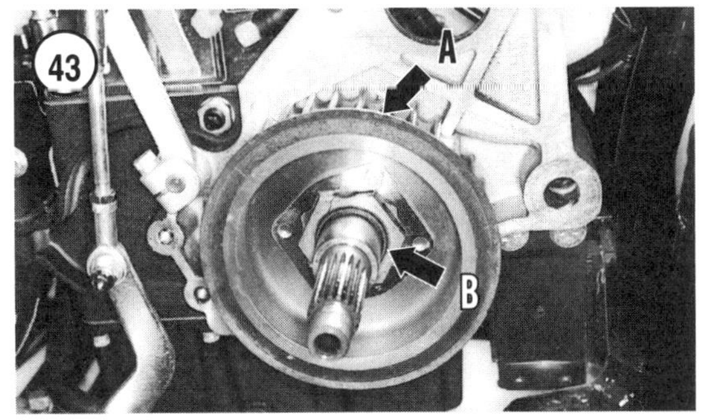

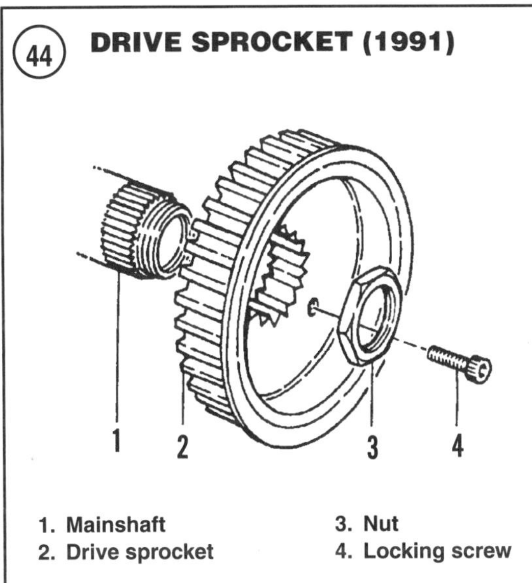

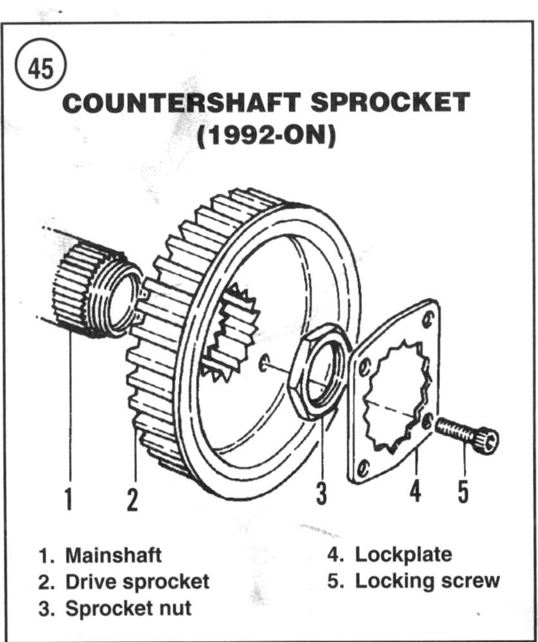

Inspection

Do not apply any type of lubricant to the drive belt. Inspect the drive belt and teeth (**Figure 41**) for severe wear, damage or oil contamination. **Figure 42** shows typical belt wear and damage signs.

Replace the drive belt if severely worn or damaged.

DRIVE SPROCKET

The drive sprocket (A, **Figure 43**) is mounted on the main drive gear and is located behind the primary chain housing. Depending on the model year, 2 different locking designs have been used to secure the drive sprocket to the main drive gear. Make sure to follow your models service and tightening torque procedures when removing and installing the drive sprocket.

Special Tools

The Harley-Davidson mainshaft locknut wrench (part No. HD-94660-37A) or an equivalent deep size socket is required to loosen and tighten the sprocket nut.

Removal

1. Remove the inner primary housing as described in Chapter Five.

NOTE
You do not have to remove the bearing race (B, ***Figure 43****) before removing the drive sprocket.*

CAUTION
Along with the external lockplate and locking screw, red Loctite and a high torque installation are used to keep the sprocket nut tight on the mainshaft. If you do not have access to the special tools described in the following steps, have a dealership or service shop remove the drive sprocket nut for you.

2A. On 1991 models, remove the sprocket nut locking screw (**Figure 44**).
2B. On 1992 and later models, remove the 2 locking screws and lockplate (**Figure 45**).
3. Have an assistant apply the rear brake.

9

NOTE
The sprocket nut uses left-hand threads. Turn the nut clockwise to remove it.

4. Loosen and remove the sprocket nut.
5. Support the bike on a stand so that the rear wheel clears the ground.
6. Loosen the rear axle nut. Then loosen the drive belt adjusters (**Figure 46**) and push the rear wheel forward to obtain as much belt slack as possible.
7. Push the drive belt forward and remove the drive sprocket.

Inspection

1. Clean the drive sprocket in solvent and dry with compressed air, if available.
2. Remove all sealer residue from the sprocket locking screw(s), drive sprocket, sprocket nut and main drive gear threads.
3. Inspect the drive sprocket for the following conditions:
   a. Cracks or other damage.
   b. Worn sprocket teeth.
4. A damaged or worn drive sprocket will increase drive belt wear. Replace the sprocket if necessary.

Installation

1. Slide the drive sprocket onto the main drive gear threads. Fit the drive belt around the sprocket.

NOTE
The sprocket nut uses left-hand threads. Turn the sprocket nut counterclockwise when installing and tightening it in the following steps.

2A. On 1991 models, install and tighten the sprocket nut (**Figure 44**) as follows:
   a. Apply Loctite 262 (red) to the sprocket nut and thread it onto the main drive gear.
   b. Have an assistant apply the rear brake.
   c. Tighten the sprocket nut to the torque specification in **Table 4**.
   d. Find a locking screw hole in the drive sprocket that most closely matches the alignment shown in **Figure 47**. If none of the screw holes align, tighten the sprocket nut to align the screw holes. Do not loosen the nut to align the holes. Apply Loctite 242 (blue) to the locking screw threads and thread the screw into the sprocket. Tighten the lockscrew to the torque specification in **Table 4**.

NOTE
Do not exceed 150 ft.-lb. (203 N•m) when aligning the sprocket nut and screw hole.

2B. On 1992-1994 models, install and tighten the sprocket nut (**Figure 45**) as follows:
   a. Apply Loctite 262 (red) to the sprocket nut and thread it onto the main drive gear.
   b. Have an assistant apply the rear brake.
   c. Tighten the sprocket nut to the torque specification in **Table 4**.
   d. Install the lockplate and align 2 diagonally opposite lockplate holes with 2 tapped sprocket holes (**Figure 48**). If none of the holes align, tighten the sprocket nut counterclockwise to align the screw holes. Do not loosen the nut to align the holes.

46

47

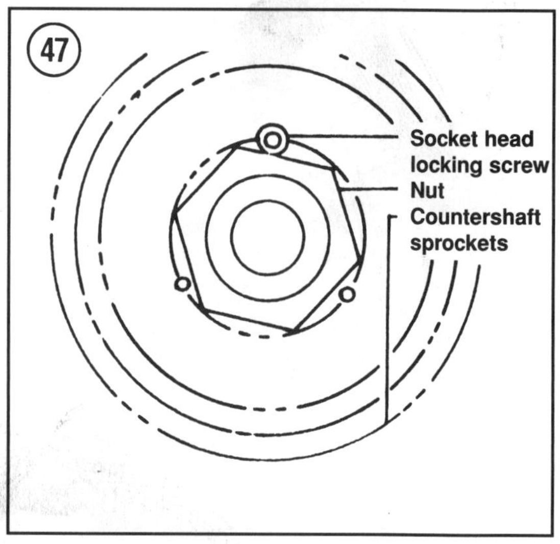

NOTE
Loctite patches are applied to the locking screw threads. These screws can be used 3 to 5 times. Then, either replace the screws or apply Loctite 242 (blue) to them.

e. Install the 2 locking screws and tighten to the torque specification in **Table 4**. If necessary, apply Loctite 242 (blue) to the locking screw threads before installing them.

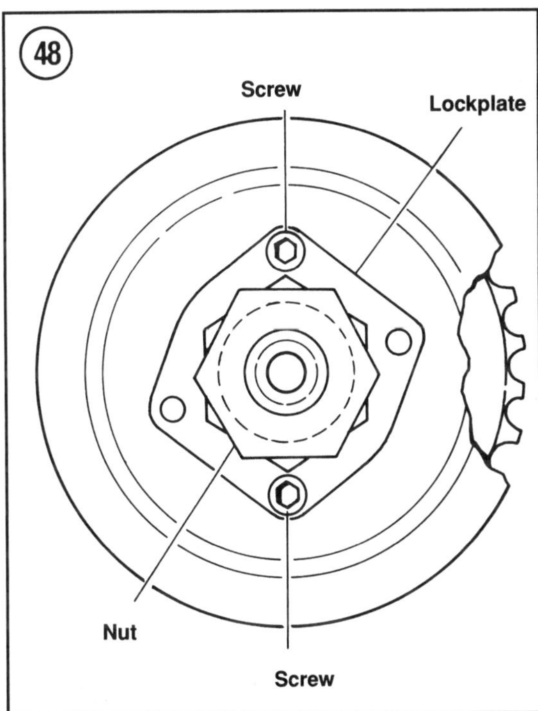

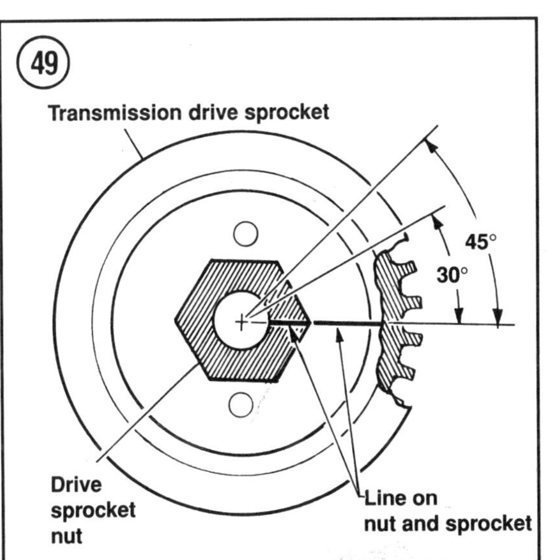

NOTE
Always use 2 locking screws to secure the lockplate.

2C. On 1995 models, install and tighten the sprocket nut (**Figure 45**) as follows:

a. Apply Loctite 262 (red) to the sprocket nut. Then install the sprocket nut with its flanged side facing the drive sprocket.
b. Have an assistant apply the rear brake.
c. Tighten the sprocket nut to 50 ft.-lb. (67.8 N•m).
d. Scribe a line across the sprocket nut and drive sprocket as shown in **Figure 49**. Then tighten the sprocket nut an additional 30-40° (**Figure 49**).
e. Install the lockplate and align 2 diagonally opposite lockplate holes with 2 tapped sprocket holes (**Figure 48**). If none of the holes align, tighten the sprocket nut to align the screw holes—do not exceed 45° when tightening the sprocket nut. Do not loosen the sprocket nut to align the holes.

NOTE
Loctite patches are applied to the locking screw threads. These screws can be used 3 to 5 times. Then, either replace the screws or apply Loctite 242 (blue) to them.

f. Install the 2 locking screws and tighten to the torque specification in **Table 4**. If necessary, apply Loctite 242 (blue) to the locking screw threads before installing them.

NOTE
Always use 2 locking screws to secure the lockplate.

3. Install the primary chaincase as described in Chapter Five.
4. Recheck belt alignment and tension as described in Chapter Three. Tighten the rear axle nut to the torque specification in **Table 4**.

WIRE SPOKE WHEELS

Loose or improperly tightened spokes can cause hub damage and overall handling problems. Check the wheels for looseness, missing or damaged spokes, rim damage, runout and balance at the maintenance intervals listed in Chapter Three. Wheel bearing service is described in this chapter.

Inspection and Replacement

1. Support the bike with the wheel off the ground.
2. Check the rim for dents, cracks or other damage. Severe rim damaged is easily detected, though most small dents are discovered while the rim is spinning on a stand.
3. Check the hub for cracks or damage. Check closely where the spokes seat into the hub.
4. Check for bending, loose or broken spokes. Replace damaged spokes when you detect them. Replace a damaged spoke as follows:

CAUTION

Do not bend a new spoke in order to install it in the wheel. Because these wheels are laced to a specific offset dimension, refer wheel service to a dealer.

a. Remove the brake disc or rear sprocket if required.
b. Unscrew the nipple from the spoke and depress the nipple into the rim far enough to free the end of the spoke; take care not to push the nipple all the way in. Remove the damaged spoke from the hub and use it to match a new spoke of identical length.

NOTE

Spokes differ in length, size, head angle and spoke throat length. Compare the used and replacement spokes carefully.

c. If necessary, trim the new spoke to match the original and dress the end of the thread with a thread die. Install the new spoke in the hub and screw on the nipple; tighten it until the spoke's tone is similar to the tone of the other spokes in the wheel. After installing the spokes, seat the spokes into the hub as described in this chapter. Periodically check the tightness of the new spokes. New spokes stretch and you may have to retighten them before they take a final set.

NOTE

If a replacement spoke requires more than 2 turns to tighten it, the end of the spoke may protrude through the end of the nipple and puncture the tube. If necessary, remove the spoke and grind the end to a suitable length. To make sure that the spoke is not too long, remove the tire and tube and check the end of the spoke.

5. Spokes loosen with use and must be checked periodically. The "tuning fork" method for checking spoke tightness is simple and works well. Tap the center of each spoke with a spoke wrench or screwdriver (**Figure 50**) and listen for a tone. A tightened spoke will emit a clear, ringing tone and a loose spoke will sound flat or dull. All the spokes in a correctly tightened wheel will emit tones of similar pitch but not necessarily the same precise tone. Spoke tension does not determine wheel balance.

Spoke Adjustment

This section describes minor spoke adjustment. If a few spokes are loose, you can tighten the spokes with a spoke wrench. If more than a few spokes are loose or if the wheel is out of true, have the wheel serviced at a Harley-Davidson dealership. These wheels are laced to a specific offset dimension. This dimension must be adjusted, if required, when truing the wheel.

Initially, check runout with the wheel mounted on the bike. One way to check rim runout is to mount a

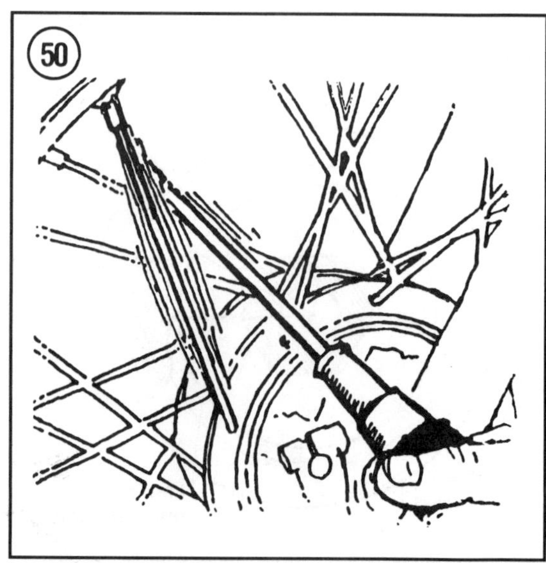

dial indicator on the front fork or swing arm, so that it bears against the rim.

If you don't have a dial indicator, improvise one as shown in **Figure 51**. Adjust the position of the bolt until it just clears the rim. Rotate the rim and note whether the clearance increases or decreases. Place a mark at areas that produce significantly large or small clearances. Clearance must not change by more than 1/32 in. (0.79 mm).

To pull the rim out, tighten spokes which terminate on the same side of the hub and loosen spokes which terminate on the opposite side (**Figure 52**). In most cases, only a slight amount of adjustment is necessary to true a rim. After adjustment, rotate the rim and make sure another area has not been pulled out of true. Continue adjustment and checking until runout is less than 1/32 in. (0.79 mm).

CAUTION
Overtightening the spokes can cause spoke and nipple damage.

Spoke Seating

When spokes loosen or when installing new spokes, the head of the spoke must be checked for seating in the wheel. If the spoke is not seated correctly, it can loosen and result in wheel hub damage.

If one or more spokes require reseating, tap the head of the spoke with a punch and hammer. Make sure the head of the spoke is seated squarely in the hub.

True the wheel as described under *Spoke Adjustment* in this chapter.

Rim Replacement

If the rim becomes bent or damaged, replace it. A bent or distorted rim can cause serious handling problems.

CAST WHEELS

Cast wheels (**Figure 38**) consists of a single assembly equipped with bearings, oil seals and a spacer sleeve.

While these wheels are virtually maintenance free, they must be checked for damage at the maintenance intervals listed in Chapter Three. Wheel bearing service is described in this chapter.

To check these wheels, refer to *Inspection* under *Front Wheel* and *Rear Wheel* in this chapter.

WARNING
Do not try to repair any damage to a cast wheel as it will result in an unsafe riding condition.

9

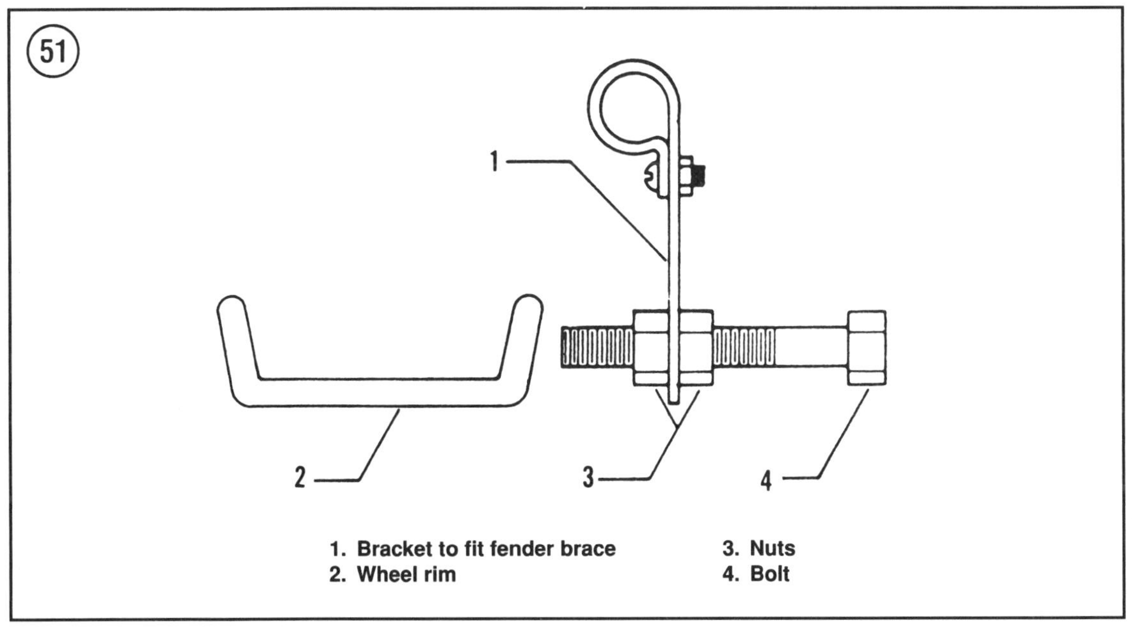

1. Bracket to fit fender brace
2. Wheel rim
3. Nuts
4. Bolt

WHEEL BALANCE

An unbalanced wheel is unsafe and causes premature tire wear. Depending on the degree of unbalance and the speed of the motorcycle, the rider may experience anything from a mild vibration to a violent shimmy which may result in loss of control.

This procedure covers static balancing, which requires a wheel stand in which the wheel can be rotated. Dynamic balancing requires the use of a machine that spins the wheel. For dynamic wheel balancing, take the wheels to a motorcycle dealership.

On alloy wheels, weights are attached to the flat surface on the rim (**Figure 53**). On wire spoke wheels, the weights are attached to the spoke nipples (**Figure 54**).

Before you attempt to balance the wheel, check to be sure that the wheel bearings are in good condition and properly lubricated. The wheel must rotate freely. Refer to *Front Wheel* or *Rear Wheel* in this chapter.

1. Remove the wheel to be balanced.
2. Mount the wheel on a fixture such as the one in **Figure 55** so it can rotate freely.
3. Give the wheel a spin and let it coast to a stop. Mark the tire at the lowest point.
4. Spin the wheel several more times. If the wheel keeps coming to rest at the same point, it is out of balance.

5A. *Alloy wheels*: Tape a test weight to the upper (or light) side of the wheel (**Figure 53**).

5B. *Wire spoke wheels*: Attach a weight to the upper or light side of the wheel on the spoke (**Figure 54**).

6. Experiment with different weights until the wheel, when spun, comes to rest at a different position each time.
7. Remove the test weight and install the correct size weight.
   a. Attach the weights to the flat surface on the rim (**Figure 53**). Clean the rim of all road residue before installing the weights; otherwise, the weights may fall off.
   b. Add weights in 1/4 oz. (7g) increments. If 1 oz. (28 g) or more must be added to one location, apply half the amount to each side of the rim.
   c. To apply Harley-Davidson wheel weights, remove the paper backing from the weight and apply 3 drops of Loctite 420 (Superbonder) to the bottom of the weight. Position the weight on the rim, press it down, and hold in position for 10 seconds. To allow the adhesive to cure properly, do not use the wheel for 8 hours.
8. When fitting weights on wire spoke wheels for the final time, crimp the weights onto the spoke with slip-joint pliers.

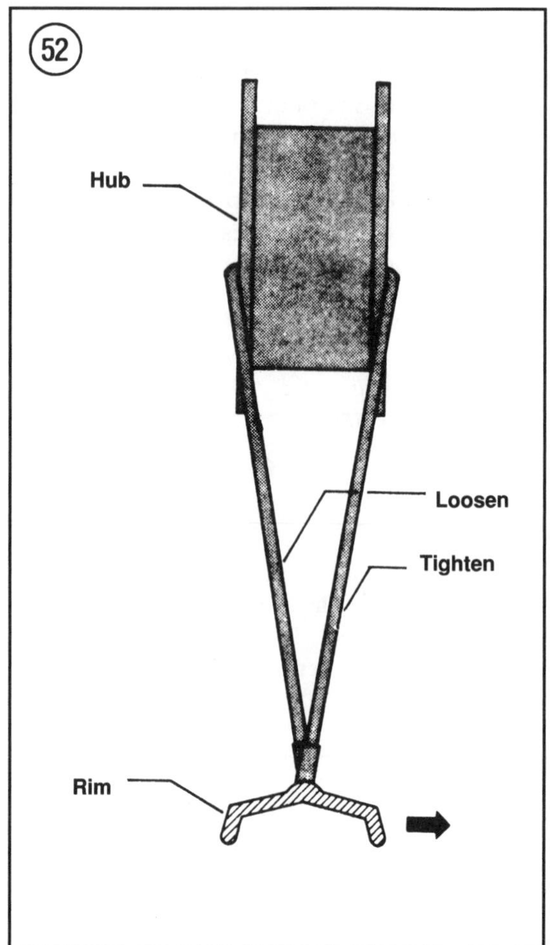

TIRES

Proper tire service includes frequent inflation checks and adjustment as well as tire inspection, removal, repair and installation. By maintaining a routine tire maintenance schedule, you can find tire damage or other abnormal conditions and repair them before they affect the motorcycle's operation and handling. Refer to Chapter Three for general tire inspection and inflation procedures.

Inspection

Visually inspect the tires for tread wear, cracks, cuts, aging and other damage. Check the tire for torn or damaged tread. Improper inflation pressure, vehicle overloading or an unbalanced tire will cause uneven tread wear.

Run your hand along the sidewall and check for bulges or knots. If you note a bulge, mark the area with chalk, then remove the tire from the rim; check both sides of the tire carefully, looking for broken or separated plies. This condition can cause the tire to blow out. Likewise, if a tire is damaged on the outside, remove the tire from the rim and examine for broken or separated plies or other damage.

WARNING
Tires exhibiting bulges or other questionable damage must be inspected by a motorcycle technician before the tire is put back into use. A damaged or deformed tire can fail suddenly and cause you to lose control.

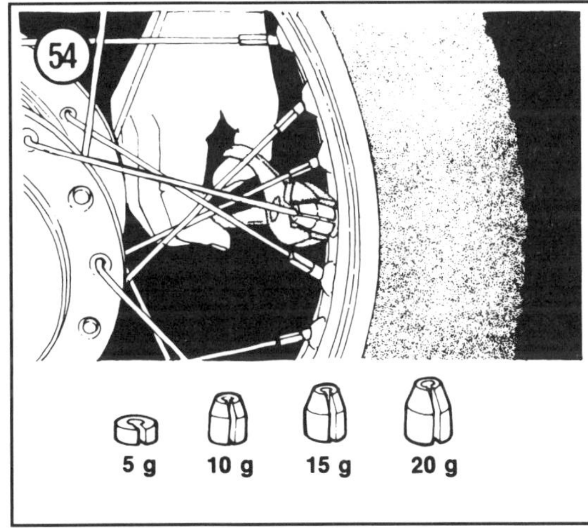

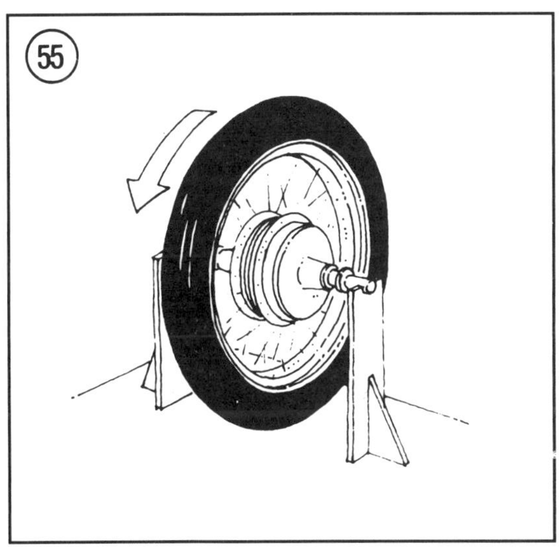

Service Notes

Before changing tires, note the following:

1. You must only undertake tire changing if you have access to the proper tools:
   a. At least 2 motorcycle tire irons.
   b. Rim protectors (part No. HD-01289 or equivalent) or scrap pieces of leather.
   c. A bead breaker is required when breaking tires from alloy rims and may be required on wire spoke wheels.
   d. Accurate tire gauge.
   e. Water and liquid soap solution or a special tire mounting lubricant.
   f. Talcum powder for tube tires.
2. The alloy wheels can be easily damaged. Special care must be taken with tire irons when changing a tire to avoid scratches and gouges to the outer rim surface. Insert rim protectors between the tire iron and the rim to protect the rim from damage.
3. When removing tubeless tires, take care not to damage the tire beads, inner liner of the tire or the wheel rim flange. Use tire levers or flat handled tire irons with rounded ends—do not use screwdrivers or similar tools to remove tires.

9

Removal

1. Remove the wheel and place it on a suitable stand or surface.
2. If you are going to reuse the tire, place a chalk mark on the tire aligning the tire with the valve stem

(**Figure 56**). This helps to maintain tire and wheel balance during reassembly.

3. Remove the valve cap and unscrew the valve core to deflate the tire or tube. Block the valve core with your hand to keep it from flying out.

4. Press the entire bead on both sides of the tire into the center of the rim. If the bead is tight, use a bead breaker (**Figure 57**).

CAUTION

*Do **not** attempt to insert the tire irons between the tire bead and rim flange to break the bead. This can permanently damage both the tire and rim.*

5. Lubricate the beads with a tire lubricant or soapy water.

6. Place rim protectors (**Figure 58**) along the rim near the valve stem and insert the tire iron under the bead next to the valve, making sure the tire iron contacts the rim protectors and not the rim. Step on the side of the tire opposite the valve stem with your knee and pry the bead over the rim with the tire iron.

CAUTION

Do not use excessive force when prying the tire over the rim or you may stretch or break the bead wires in the tire. If the tire is difficult to pry over the rim, lubricate it with the tire lubricant or soapy water.

7. Insert a second tire iron next to the first to hold the bead over the rim. Then work around the tire with the first tool prying the bead over the rim (**Figure 59**). On tube-type tires, be careful not to pinch the inner tube with the tools.

NOTE

If you are repairing a flat tire on a tube-type tire, mark the tube after removing it from the tire. This will help you to find the puncture hole in the tire.

8. On tube-type tires, use your thumb and push the valve from its hole in the rim to the inside of the tire. Carefully pull the tube out of the tire and lay it aside.

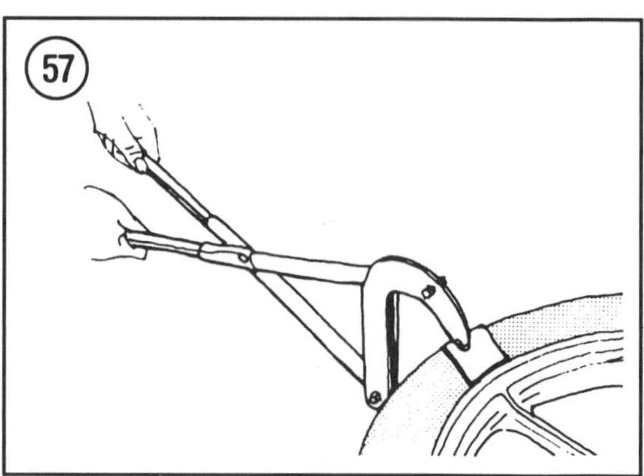

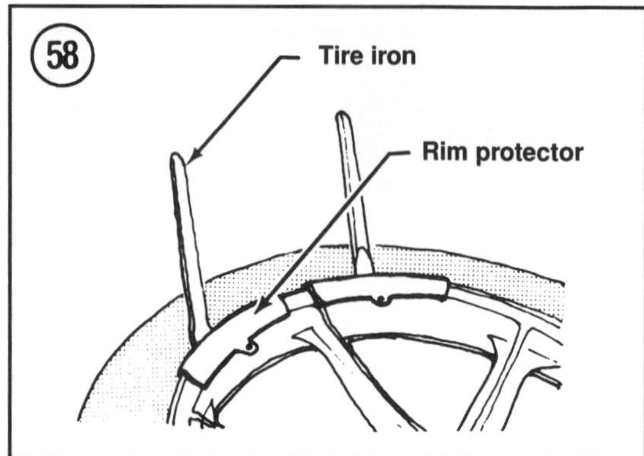

NOTE
Step 9 is required only if removing the tire from the rim is necessary.

9. You can generally remove the second bead from the rim without tire irons. Lubricate the second bead thoroughly and stand the wheel upright. Grasp the wheel at the top with one hand to steady it and then lift and pull the second bead over the top of the rim at the top of the wheel and remove the tire. If you can't remove the tire, insert a tire tool between the second bed and the same side of the rim that the first bead was pried over (**Figure 60**). Force the bead on the opposite side from the tool into the center of the rim. Pry the second bead off the rim, working around the wheel with 2 tire irons as with the first. Remove the rim band on laced wheels.

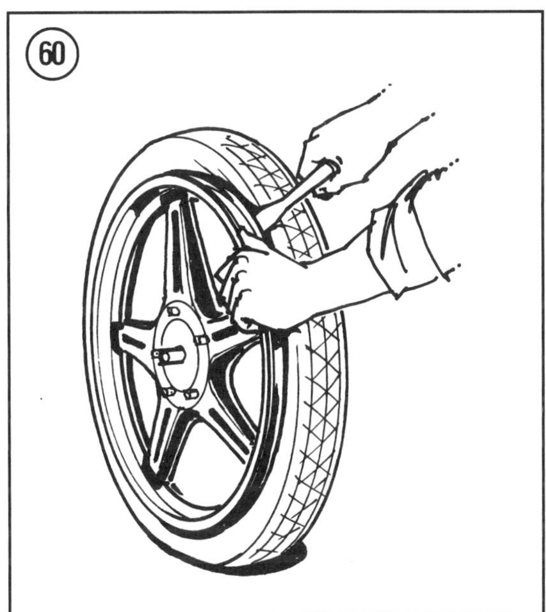

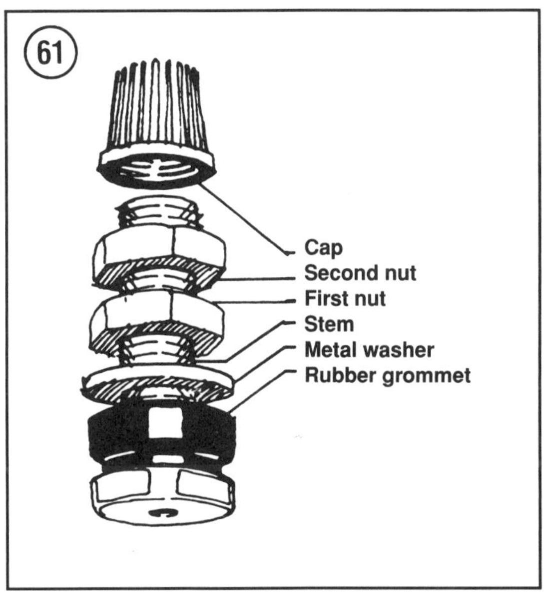

Inspection

1. *Tubeless tires*: Alloy wheels use a bolt-in type valve stem (**Figure 61**, typical). Inspect the rubber grommet where it seats against the inner surface of the wheel. Replace the valve stem if it has started to deteriorate or has lost its resiliency.

NOTE
Because of weight and design configurations, replace bolt-in valve stems with O.E.M. Harley-Davidson valve stems. In addition, the bolt-in valve stems used on 16 in. and 19 in. wheels are different. Make sure to purchase the correct valve stem for your wheel. See your Harley-Davidson dealership for further information.

2. To replace bolt-in valve stems, perform the following:
   a. Loosen and remove the 2 valve stem nuts.
   b. Remove the valve stem from the wheel, with its washer and rubber grommet.
   c. Remove all rubber residue from the wheel left by the previous rubber grommet.
   d. Before installing the new valve stem, remove the valve cap, 2 nuts and washer from the stem.
   e. Slide the rubber grommet down onto the valve stem so that the shoulder on the grommet seats into the valve stem head recess.
   f. Insert the valve stem into the rim and hold it in position, making sure the rubber grommet seats against the wheel. Then slide the washer onto the valve stem so that the side of the washer with the raised center faces away from the rim.
   g. Install the first valve stem nut and tighten to 20-25 in.-lb. (2.3-2.8 N•m).
   h. Hold the first valve stem nut with a wrench, then install and tighten the second nut to 40-60 in.-lb. (4.0-4.5 N•m).

3. Clean the rim thoroughly to remove all residue. Use steel wool, a stiff wire brush or sandpaper to remove rust from wire wheels.

CAUTION
Work carefully when removing burrs or other rough spots from the rim flange on alloy wheels; otherwise, you may damage the sealing surface, requiring replacement of the wheel.

4. Mount the wheel on a truing stand (if available) and check the rim-to-tire mating surface for dents, burrs or other rough spots. Use emery cloth to remove burrs on alloy wheels. Use a file or sandpaper to remove burrs on wire spoke wheels.

5. Check the wheel for dents or other damage. On wire spoke wheels, the rim can be replaced by a qualified mechanic. On cast wheels, the entire wheel assembly must be replaced.

6. Check wheel runout as described in this chapter. Check for protruding spokes on wire wheels. File or grind the end of the spokes as required.

7. Blow out the inside tire casing to remove all dust and dirt. Run your hand along the tire casing and check for small nails, cracks or other damage.

8. If a tire has been punctured, refer to *Tire Repairs* in this chapter.

9. *Tube-type tires*: Inspect the rim band for tearing or excessive wear. Replace the rim band if necessary. Install the valve core into the tube, then fill the tube with air. Check the tube for leaks. If the tube holds air, check the base of the valve stem for tearing or other signs of wear that may cause the tube to fail later.

Installation

1. A new tire may have balancing rubbers inside. These are not patches and must not be disturbed. A colored spot near the bead shows a lighter point on the tire. Place this spot next to the valve stem (**Figure 62**).

2. Install the rim band over the wheel (wire spoke wheels) and align the hole in the rim band with the hole in the rim.

3. Align the tire with the rim so that the directional arrows molded in the tire's side wall face in the normal rotation position.

NOTE
On some tires, the rotation arrow may have to be reversed, depending on whether the tire is mounted on the front or rear wheel. Follow the tire manufacturer's instructions.

4. Lubricate both beads of the tire with soapy water.

5. With the tire properly aligned with the wheel, press the first bead over the rim, working around the tire in both directions with your hands only (**Figure 63**). If necessary, use a tire iron (with rim protectors) for the last few inches of bead (**Figure 64**).

6. On tube-type tires, inflate the tube just enough to round it out. Too much air will make installation difficult. Wipe the outside of the tube with talcum powder to help reduce friction between the tire and tube during operation. Place the tube on top of the tire, aligning the valve stem with the matching hole

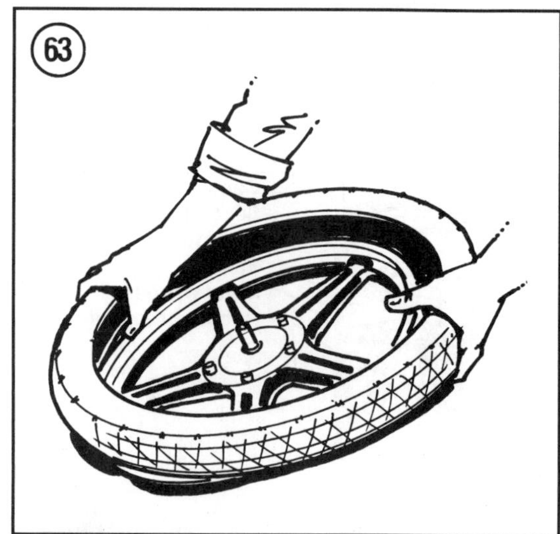

in the rim. Then insert the tube into the tire. Lift the upper tire bead away from the rim with your hand and insert the tubes valve stem through the rim hole. Check the tube to make sure that the valve stem is straight up (90°) and not turned to one side.

7. Lubricate the upper bead.

8. Starting 180° away from the valve stem, press the upper bead into the rim. Using tire tools and rim protectors, work around the rim to the valve. On tube-type tires, the last few inches will offer you the most difficulty and the greatest chance of pinching the tube. Work the tire tools carefully to prevent pinching the tube.

9. On tube-type tires, the valve stem must point straight up (90°). If the valve is turned to one side, align the tube by sliding the tire along the rim either way while holding the rim securely. When the valve stem is straight up, screw the valve nut onto the valve, but do not tighten it against the rim.

10. Check the bead on both sides of the tire for an even fit around the rim.

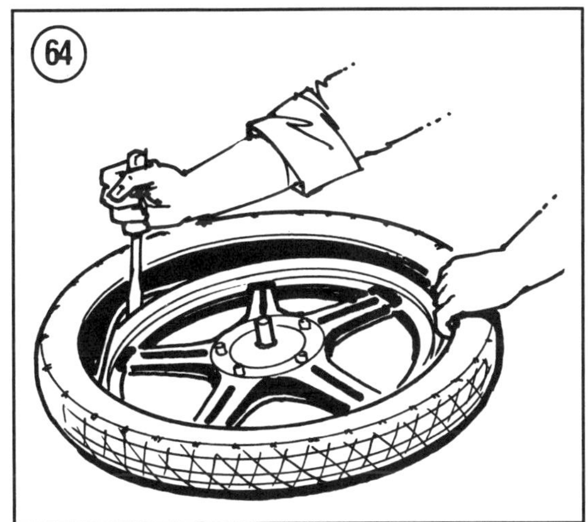

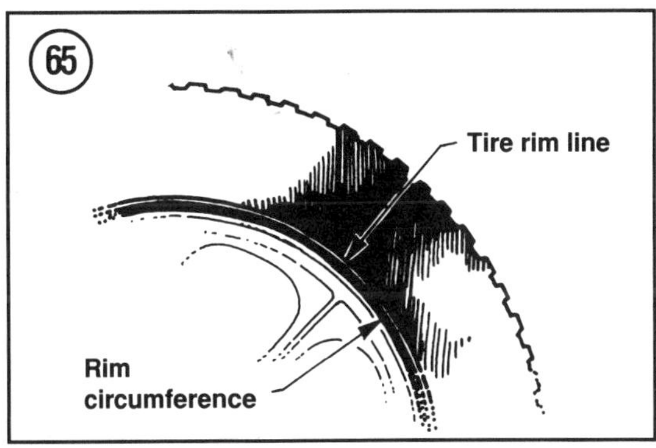

11. Lubricate both tire beads.

WARNING

When seating the tire beads in Step 12, never inflate the tire beyond the tire manufacturer's maximum pressure specification listed on the tire's side wall. Exceeding this pressure could cause the tire or rim to burst, causing severe personal injury. If the beads fail to seat properly, deflate the tire and lubricate the beads. Never stand directly over a tire while inflating it.

12A. *Tube-type tires*: Inflate the tube to its maximum tire pressure to seat the beads in the rim. If the tire beads do not seat, release all air pressure from the tire and lubricate the tire beads. The tire is properly seated when the wheel rim and tire side wall lines are parallel (**Figure 65**). When the tire has seated properly on both sides, remove the valve core to deflate the tube; this allows the tube to straighten out, then reinstall the valve core and inflate the tire to pressure reading listed in Chapter Three. Tighten the valve stem nuts and screw on the valve cap.

12B. *Tubeless tires*: Place an inflatable band around the circumference of the tire. Slowly inflate the band until the tire beads are pressed against the rim. Inflate the tire enough to seat it, deflate the band and remove it. The tire is properly seated when the wheel rim and tire side wall lines are parallel (**Figure 65**). Inflate the tire to the tire pressure listed in Chapter Three. Screw on the valve cap.

13. Check tire runout as described in this chapter.

14. Balance the wheel assembly as described in this chapter.

Tire Runout

Check the tires for excessive lateral and radial runout after wheel mounting or if the motorcycle developed a wobble that you cannot trace to another component. Mount the wheels on their axles when making the following checks.

1. *Lateral runout*: This procedure will check the tire for excessive side-to-side play. Perform the following:

   a. Position a fixed pointer next to the tire side wall as shown in **Figure 66**. Position the pointer tip so that it is not directly in line with the molded tire logo or any other raised surface.

b. Rotate the tire and measure lateral runout.

c. The lateral runout must not exceed 0.080 in. (2.03 mm). If runout is excessive, remove the tire from the wheel and recheck the wheel's lateral runout as described in this chapter. If the runout is excessive, the wheel must be trued (laced wheels) or replaced (alloy wheels). If wheel runout is correct, the tire runout is excessive and the tire must be replaced.

2. *Radial runout*: This procedure will check the tire for excessive up-and-down play. Perform the following:

a. Position a fixed pointer at the center bottom of the tire tread as shown in **Figure 67**.

b. Rotate the tire and measure the amount of radial runout.

c. The radial runout must not exceed 0.090 in. (2.29 mm). If runout is excessive, remove the tire from the wheel and recheck the wheels radial runout as described in this chapter. If the runout is excessive, true or replace the wheel. If wheel runout is correct, the tire runout is excessive and the tire must be replaced.

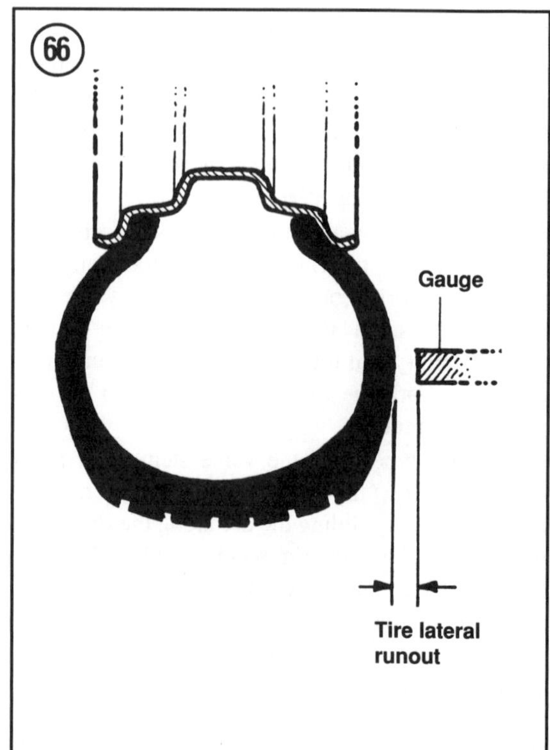

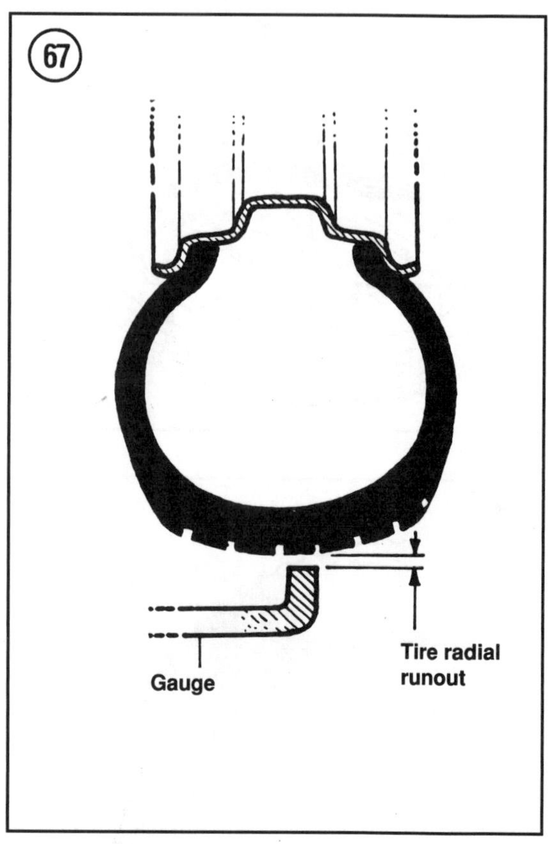

TIRE REPAIRS (TUBE-TYPE TIRES)

Every rider will eventually experience trouble with a tire or tube. Repair and replacement are simple.

Patching a motorcycle tube is only a temporary fix. A motorcycle tire flexes too much and the patch could rub off.

Tube Repair Kits

You can purchase repair kits from motorcycle dealers and auto supply stores. When buying, specify that the kit you want is for motorcycles.

There are 2 types of tube repair kits:

a. Hot patch.

b. Cold patch.

Hot patches are stronger because they vulcanize to the tube, becoming part of it. However, they are far too bulky to carry for roadside repairs and the strength is unnecessary for a temporary repair.

Cold patches do not vulcanize to the tube; you simply glue them to it. Though not as strong as hot patches, cold patches are still very durable. Cold patch kits are less bulky than hot patches and more easily applied under adverse conditions. A cold patch kit contains everything necessary and easily tucks in with your emergency tool kit.

Tube Inspection

1. Remove the inner tube as described in this chapter.
2. Install the valve core into the valve stem and inflate the tube slightly. Do not overinflate.
3. Immerse the tube in water a section at a time. Look carefully for bubbles showing a hole. Mark each hole and continue checking until you are certain that you found and marked all holes. Also make sure that the valve core is not leaking; tighten it if necessary.

NOTE

If you do not have enough water to immerse sections of the tube, try running your hand over the tube slowly and very close to the surface. If your hand is damp, it works even better. If you suspect a hole, apply some water to the area to verify it.

4. Apply a cold patch according to its manufacturer's instructions.
5. Dust the patch area with talcum powder to prevent it from sticking to the tire.
6. Carefully check the inside of the tire casing for small rocks or sand which may have damaged the tube. If the inside of the tire is split, apply a patch to the area to prevent it from pinching and damaging the tube again.
7. Check the inside of the rim.
8. Deflate the tube prior to installation in the tire.

TIRE REPAIRS (TUBELESS TYPE)

Patching a tubeless tire on the road is very difficult. If both beads are still in place against the rim, a pressurized tire sealant may inflate the tire and seal the hole. The beads must be against the wheel for this method to work. Because an incorrectly patched tire might blow out and cause an accident, note the following:

a. Due to the variations of material supplied with different tubeless tire repair kits, follow the instructions and recommendations supplied with the repair kit.
b. The tire industry recommends to patch tubeless tires from the inside of the tire. Therefore, do not patch the tire with an external type plug. If you find an external patch on a tire, reinforce it from the inside or discard it.
c. Do not patch tires which have a tread depth of less than 1/16 in. (1.6 mm).
d. Do not patch a tire in which the puncture hole is larger than 1/4 in. (6.4 mm).
e. Apply patches to puncture holes in the tread area. Do not apply patches to holes in a tire's side wall.

VEHICLE ALIGNMENT

This procedure checks the alignment of the rear axle with the swing arm pivot shaft. It also checks the engine stabilizer adjustment that aligns the engine in the frame. These checks determine the condition and alignment of the components that hold the motorcycle together: steering stem, front axle, engine, swing arm pivot shaft and rear axle. If any of these items are out of alignment, the motorcycle will not handle properly. Bad handling will increase the motorcycles vibration level while reducing its overall performance and driveability.

9

Preliminary Inspection

Before checking vehicle alignment, make the following checks to spot problems caused from normal wear. Adjust, repair or replace any component as required.

1. The engine stabilizer (**Figure 68**), mounted between the cylinder heads and upper frame tube, aligns the engine in the frame. Check the engine stabilizer every 5,000 miles (8,000 km) for loose or damaged parts. To service or replace the engine stabilizer, refer to Chapter Four. To adjust the engine stabilizer, perform the *Alignment* procedure in this section.
2. Check the steering head bearing adjustment as described under *Steering Play Adjustment* in Chapter Ten.

3. Check the runout of each wheel as described in this chapter.

Special Tools

You need the following tools to check vehicle alignment:

1. An inclinometer (**Figure 69**) checks the vertical position (angle) of the brake discs when checking engine alignment. This tool, which has a magnetic base and a 360-degree dial, can be purchased from most tool and hardware stores.
2. The tool shown in **Figure 70** checks rear axle alignment. Using a piece of 1/8 in. (3.2 mm) welding rod 11 in. (280 mm) long, make the alignment tool to the dimensions shown in **Figure 71**. You can purchase grommets from electronic supply and hardware stores. To use this tool accurately, the grommet must be a snug fit on the tool.

Alignment

Each alignment step (check and adjustment) affects the next one. Work carefully and accurately when performing the following steps.

1. Perform all of the checks listed under *Preliminary Inspection* in this section. When all of the checks are within factory specifications, continue with Step 2. If your Dyna Glide has been involved in a crash, refer frame alignment to a dealership or motorcycle frame alignment specialist.
2. The exhaust system must be installed on the bike when performing the following steps.
3. Support the bike with the rear wheel off the ground.
4. Insert the alignment tool into one of the swing arm index holes. Then hold it parallel with the rear axle and slide the grommet along the tool until it is centered with the axle (**Figure 72**).
5. Without repositioning the grommet, remove the tool and repeat for the opposite swing arm side, comparing this position with the first measurement. For the swing arm alignment to be correct, the axle measurements must be equal to 1/32 in. (0.8 mm) on both sides.
6. If the alignment is incorrect, perform the *Final Drive Belt Adjustment* procedure in Chapter Three. When the belt adjustment is correct, continue with Step 7.

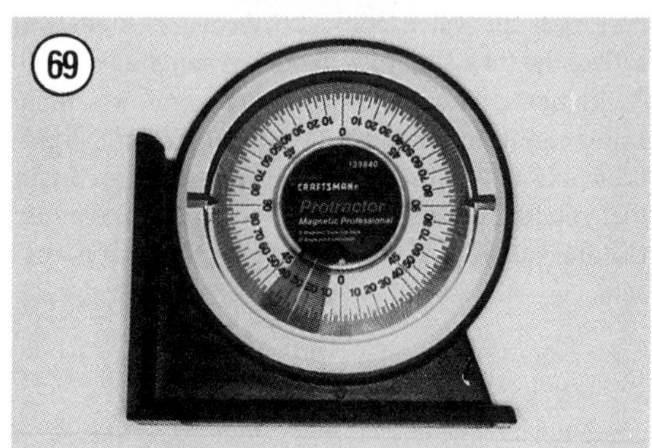

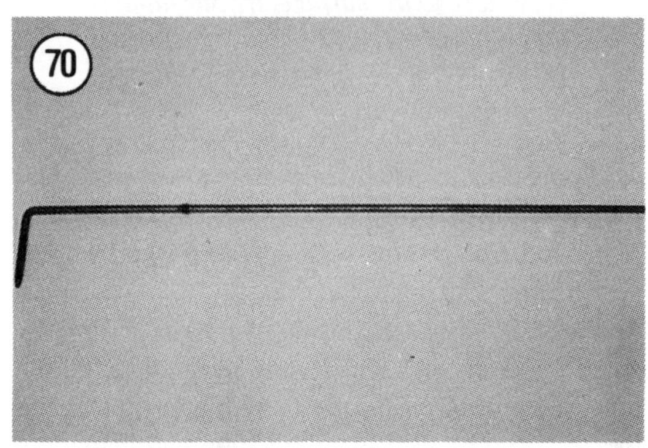

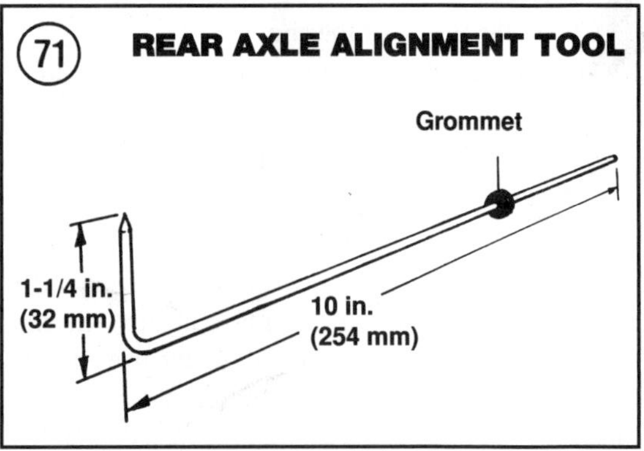

NOTE
You must perform the following steps with the rear wheel off the ground.

7. Remove the bolt (**Figure 73**) securing the stabilizer link to the engine mounting bracket. Do not remove the bolt securing the stabilizer link to the frame.
8. Place the inclinometer on the front brake disc. Position the front wheel so that the brake disc is vertical (90°). You must maintain this position when performing Steps 9 and 10.
9. Align the stabilizer link hole with the engine mounting bracket and install the stabilizer link bolt (**Figure 73**). Do not force the bolt into position. Note the following:
   a. If the holes do not align, adjust the stabilizer, starting with Step 10.
   b. If the holes align, go to Step 14.

NOTE
A redesigned stabilizer unit is installed on 1995 models. When adjusting this stabilizer in Step 10, adjust on the end that has the threads showing. Do not loosen or adjust the opposite end.

10. Loosen the stabilizer locknut. Then adjust the stabilizer link until you can install the bolt (**Figure 73**) without moving the engine. Tighten the locknut when the adjustment is correct.
11. Now put the inclinometer on the rear brake disc and compare its position with the front brake disc. If the readings are not within 1° of each other, continue with Step 12.
12. Readjust the stabilizer link (Step 10) until the rear brake disc is within 1° of the front brake disc. Note the following:
   a. If you cannot adjust the brake discs to within 1° of each other, inspect the swing arm, frame, steering head and front forks for damage. If necessary, take your bike to a Harley-Davidson dealership for further inspection.
   b. If you can adjust the brake disc angle to within 1°, but it takes more than 5 turns of the stabilizer link to do so, perform the chassis inspections described in sub-step a. If you cannot find a problem with a chassis component, go to Step 13.
   c. If you can adjust the brake disc angle to within 1° and it takes less than 5 turns of the stabilizer link, tighten the stabilizer locknut and go to Step 14.
13. These steps center the frame and engine mounts. Perform this procedure if it takes more than 5 turns to align the brake discs. Read through and then follow these steps:
   a. Loosen, but do not remove, the front and rear engine isolator mounting bolts.
   b. Lower the bike so that both wheels are on the ground.
   c. With the transmission in NEUTRAL, start the bike and idle it for approximately 5 seconds. Then shut the engine off.
   d. Tighten all of the isolator mounting bolts to 25 ft.-lb. (34 N•m).
14. Tighten the stabilizer link-to-engine mounting bracket bolt (**Figure 73**) securely.

9

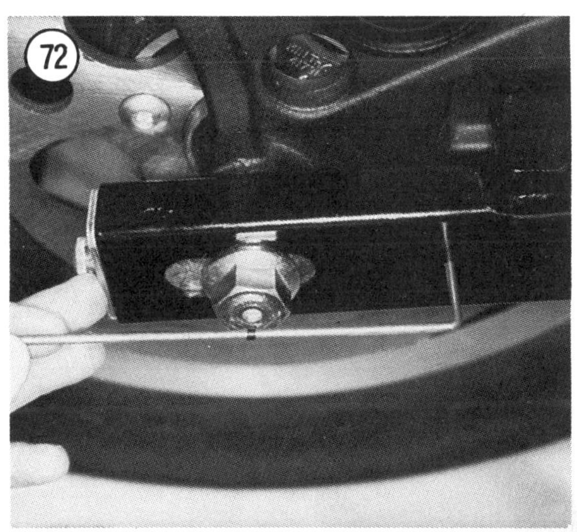

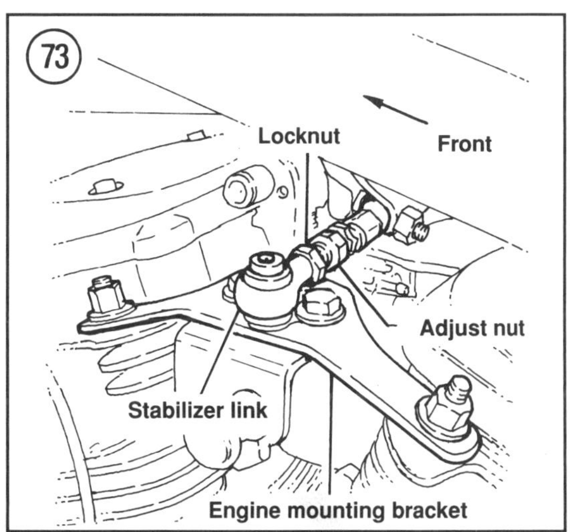

Table 1 WHEEL SPECIFICATIONS

	in.	mm
Front and rear wheel bearing end play		
1991	0.004-0.018	0.10-0.45
1992-on	0.002-0.006	0.05-0.15
Wheel runout (maximum)		
Laced wheels		
Lateral and axial	0.031	0.79
Cast wheels		
Lateral	0.040	1.02
Axial	0.030	0.76

Table 2 FRONT AND REAR WHEEL BEARING SPACER SLEEVES (1991)

Part number	Length in. (mm)	Color code
43623-78	2.564 (65.12)	Violet
43624-78	2.550 (64.77)	Pink
43625-78	2.536 (64.41)	Gold

Table 3 FRONT AND REAR WHEEL BEARING SPACER SHIMS (1992-ON)

Part number	Thickness in. (mm)
43290-82	0.030-0.033 (0.76-0.84)
43291-82	0.015-0.017 (0.38-0.43)
43292-82	0.0075-0.0085 (0.190-0.216)
43293-82	0.0035-0.0045 (0.089-0.114)
43294-82	0.0015-0.0025 (0.038-0.064)

Table 4 TIGHTENING TORQUES

	ft.-lb.	N•m
Front axle nut		
Cast wheel	50-55	68-75
Laced wheel	50	68
Front axle pinch bolt	21-27	28-37
Front axle slider cap nuts	11	15
Front brake caliper		
Upper mounting screw	25-30	34-41
Lower mounting pin	25-30	34-41
Rear axle nut	60-65	81-88
Rear wheel sprocket bolts		
1991-1992	65-70	88-95
1993-on		
Cast wheel	55-65	75-88
Laced wheel	45-55	61-75
Drive sprocket nut		
1991-1994	110-120	149-163
1995	*	
Drive sprocket lockscrew		
1991	50-60 in.-lb.	5-6.7
1992-on	7-9	9-12

*See text for initial torque specification and final tightening procedure.

CHAPTER TEN

FRONT SUSPENSION AND STEERING

This chapter covers the handlebar, steering head and front fork assemblies.

Table 1 and **Table 2** are at the end of the chapter.

HANDLEBAR

The handlebar mounts to the upper triple clamp with a single clamp (**Figure 1**). Rubber bushings are used between the handlebar holders and the upper triple clamp to help reduce vibration. The handlebar is knurled where it fits between the clamp and holders; this machining process is used to provide additional gripping power.

Handlebars are an important part in the overall comfort and safety of your motorcycle. Inspect the handlebars at regular intervals for loose mounting bolts or damage. Check the controls, master cylinder and turn signals frequently for loose or missing fasteners.

Replace the handlebars if bent or damaged. Never try to heat, bend or weld handlebars. These efforts will seriously weaken the bar and may cause it to break.

If replacing the handlebar, you can order an exact replacement through a Harley-Davidson dealership, or you can order bars through an accessory manufacturer. When ordering accessory bars, you must know the handlebar's outside diameter, width, bar height and sweep (**Figure 2**). When changing handlebars, make sure the new bar has enough room to mount the controls, brake master cylinder, etc., without excessive crowding and that the controls feel comfortable when you turn the handlebar. In addition, if the new handlebar is higher, make sure the stock cables and switch wiring harnesses are long enough.

Removal/Installation

1. Park the bike on a stand.
2. Unscrew and remove the mirrors.

NOTE
Cover the fuel tank with a heavy cloth or plastic tarp to protect it from accidental scratches or dents when removing the handlebar.

NOTE
Make a drawing of the clutch and throttle cable routing before removing them.

3. Remove the bolts securing the master cylinder (A, **Figure 3**). Do not disconnect the hydraulic brake line.
4. Loosen the throttle housing (B, **Figure 3**) screws. This will allow you to slide the housing off the handlebar (without disassembling it) later in this procedure.
5. Remove the left-hand switch housing (A, **Figure 4**) screws and separate the housing halves (**Figure 5**).
6. Remove the clutch lever clamp mounting screws (B, **Figure 4**) and separate the clamp halves.
7. Disconnect or remove any wiring harness clamps at the handlebar.
8. Remove the 2 front handlebar clamp bolts and washers or collars (**Figure 6**). Then set the instrument housing forward (A, **Figure 7**) so it does not scratch the handlebar clamp.
9. Remove the 2 rear clamp bolts, then remove the holder (B, **Figure 7**) and handlebars.
10. Install the handlebar by reversing these steps. Note the following.
11. Check the knurled rings on the handlebar for galling and bits of aluminum blocking up the rings. Clean the knurled section with a wire brush.
12. Check the handlebar for cracks, bends or other damage. Replace the handlebar if necessary. Do not attempt to repair it.
13. Clean the clamp halves thoroughly of all residues before installing the handlebar.
14. After installing the handlebar, cap, bolts and nuts, reposition the handlebar while sitting on the

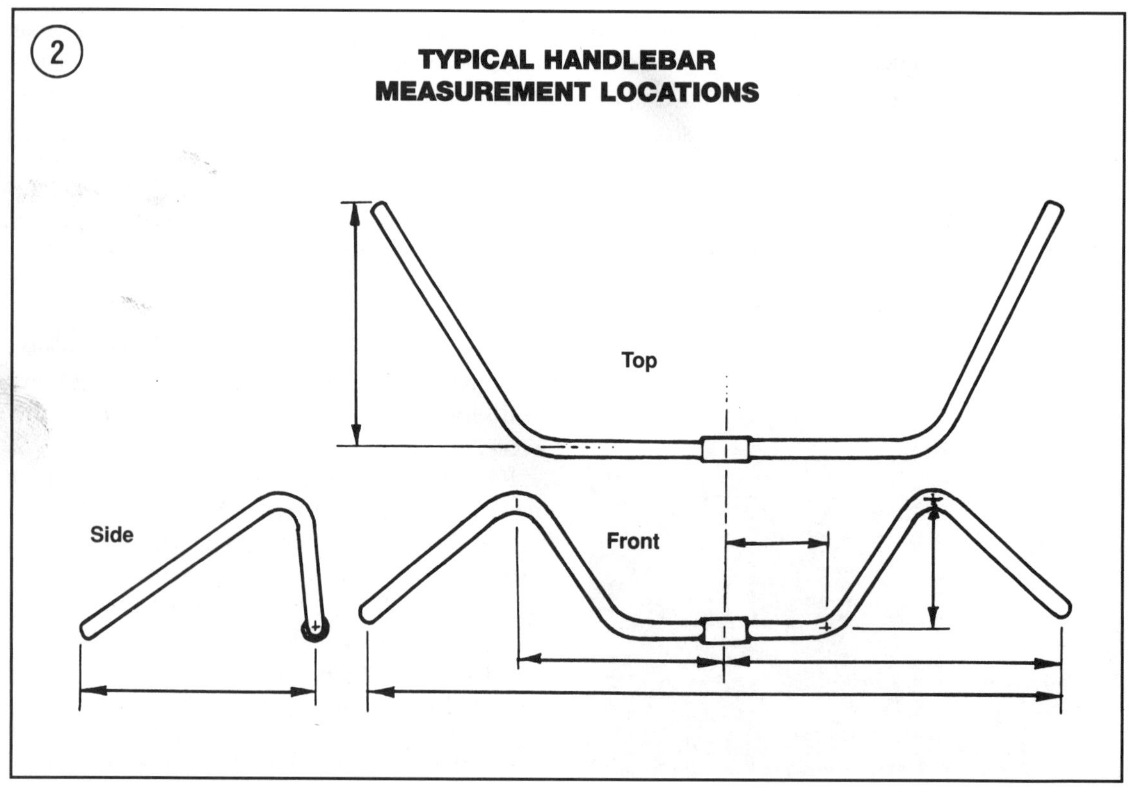

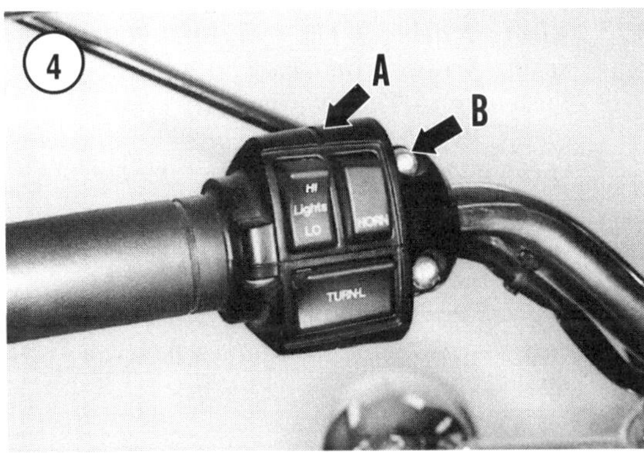

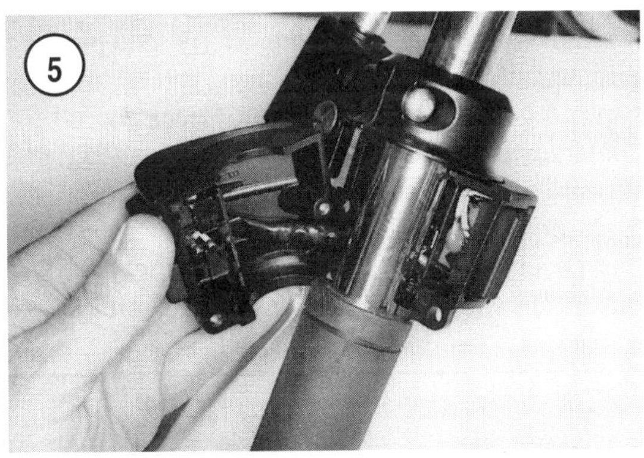

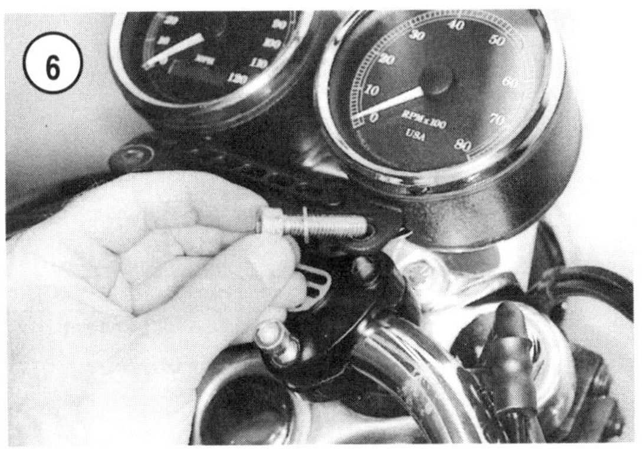

bike. Push it forward and backward to best suit your riding style. Make sure, before tightening the cap bolts, that you align the knurled sections at the base of the handlebar with the clamp halves.

15. Tighten the handlebar clamp bolts securely.

FRONT FORKS

You can overhaul the fork tubes with basic hand tools. However, you need an oil seal driver to install the oil seals without damaging them.

Removal

1. Support the bike with the front wheel off the ground.
2. Remove the front wheel as described in Chapter Nine.
3. Remove the front fender bolts and locknuts and remove the front fender.
4. Remove the windshield and its mounting clamps, if so equipped.
5. On FXDWG models, remove the fork tube cap, washer and oil seal from the top of one fork tube.
6. Loosen the upper fork bracket pinch bolt (A, **Figure 8**).

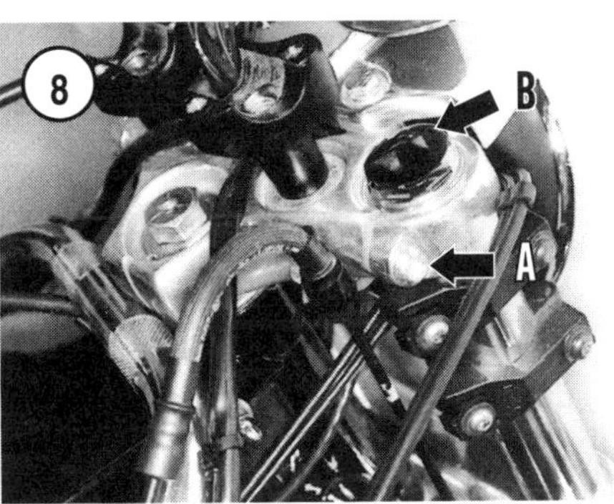

7. If you are going to disassemble the fork tubes, loosen the fork cap (B, **Figure 8**).

NOTE
Identify the fork tubes so that you can install them on their correct side.

8. Loosen the lower fork bracket pinch bolt and slide the fork tube out of the fork brackets.
9. If the forks require service, refer to *Disassembly* in this chapter.

Installation

1. Clean off any corrosion or dirt on the upper and lower fork bracket receptacles.
2A. On all models except FXDWG, install each fork tube so that the tube extends 0.42-0.50 in. (10.7-12.7 mm) above the upper fork bracket as shown in **Figure 9**.
2B. On FXDWG models, install a fork tube through the fork brackets. Then position the fork tube so that one flat on the fork tube cap faces toward the inside of the fork. Hold the fork in this position and install the oil seal, washer and the fork tube cap. Repeat for the other fork tube.
3. Tighten the lower fork bracket pinch bolt to the torque specification in **Table 1**.
4. If loose, tighten the fork cap (B, **Figure 8**) securely.
5. Tighten the upper fork bracket pinch bolt (A, **Figure 8**) to the torque specification in **Table 1**.
6. On FXDWG models, tighten the fork tube cap securely.
7. Install the front fender and its mounting bolts and locknuts. Tighten the front fender bolts to the torque specification in **Table 1**.
8. Install the front wheel as described in Chapter Nine.
9. Apply the front brake and pump the front forks several times to seat the forks and front wheel.

Disassembly/Reassembly

Refer to **Figure 10** or **Figure 11** for this procedure.

1. Using the front axle boss at the bottom of the fork tube, clamp the slider in a vise with soft jaws. Do *not* clamp the slider at any point above the fork axle boss in a vise.

NOTE
Loosen the bottom Allen bolt before removing the fork cap and spring. Leaving the cap on provides spring tension against the damper rod. This prevents the damper rod from turning when loosening the Allen bolt.

2. Loosen, but do not remove, the Allen bolt from the bottom of the slider. See 19, **Figure 10** or 20, **Figure 11**.

WARNING
Keep your face away from the fork cap when removing it. The fork cap is under spring pressure and may fly off when loosening it. This is especially critical on FXDWG fork tubes because the fork springs are preloaded. Extend the fork tubes fully before removing the fork cap. If the forks are damaged or stuck in a compressed position, refer fork service to a dealership. The fork cap and spring may fly out of the fork tube when you remove the cap.

3. Remove the fork cap from the top of the fork tube. Then pull the spring out of the fork tube.
4. Remove the fork tube from the vise and pour the oil into a drain pan. Pump the fork several times by hand to get most of the oil out. Check the oil for contamination, indicating worn or damaged parts. Discard the oil after examining it.
5. Insert a small flat-tipped screwdriver under the dust cover (9, **Figure 10**) and carefully pry the cover out of the slider and remove it. Be careful not to

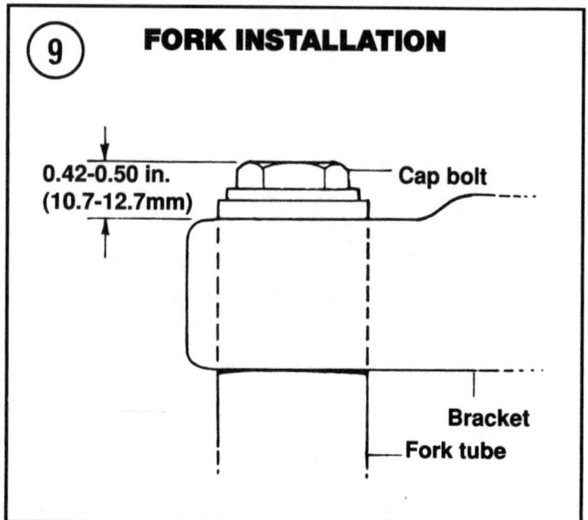

damage the slider surface. Remove the cover (9, **Figure 10**) from the slider, if so equipped.

6. Insert a small flat-tipped screwdriver under the dust seal (**Figure 12**)and carefully pry the seal out of the slider and remove it . Be careful not to damage the slider surface.

7. Pry the retaining ring (**Figure 13**) out of the groove in the slider and remove it. See **Figure 14**.

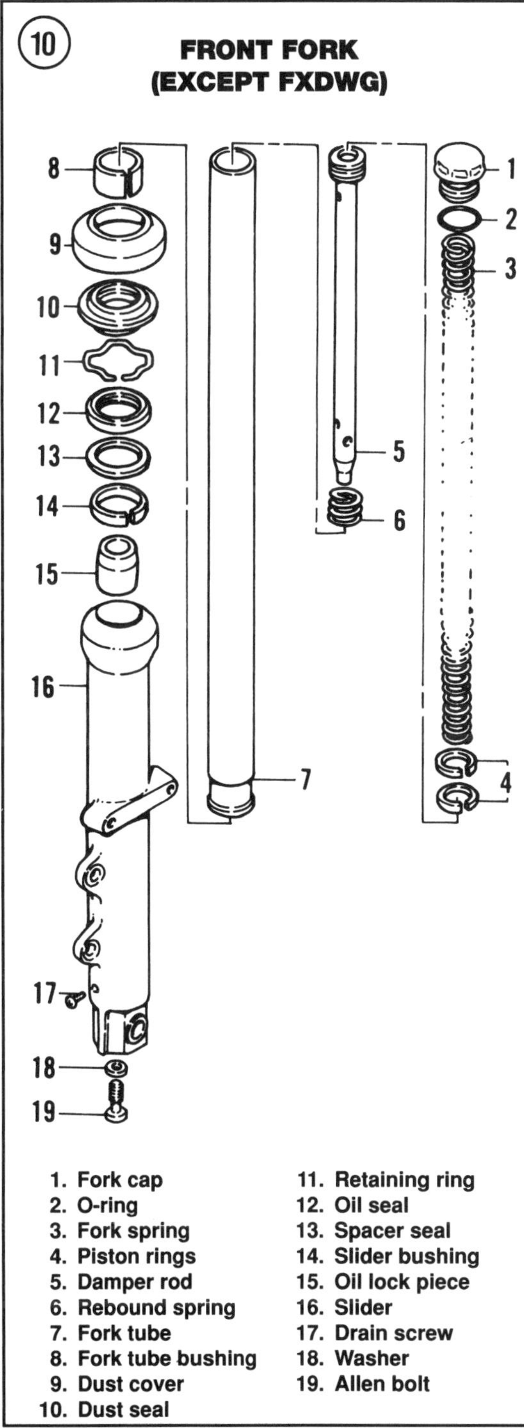

1. Fork cap
2. O-ring
3. Fork spring
4. Piston rings
5. Damper rod
6. Rebound spring
7. Fork tube
8. Fork tube bushing
9. Dust cover
10. Dust seal
11. Retaining ring
12. Oil seal
13. Spacer seal
14. Slider bushing
15. Oil lock piece
16. Slider
17. Drain screw
18. Washer
19. Allen bolt

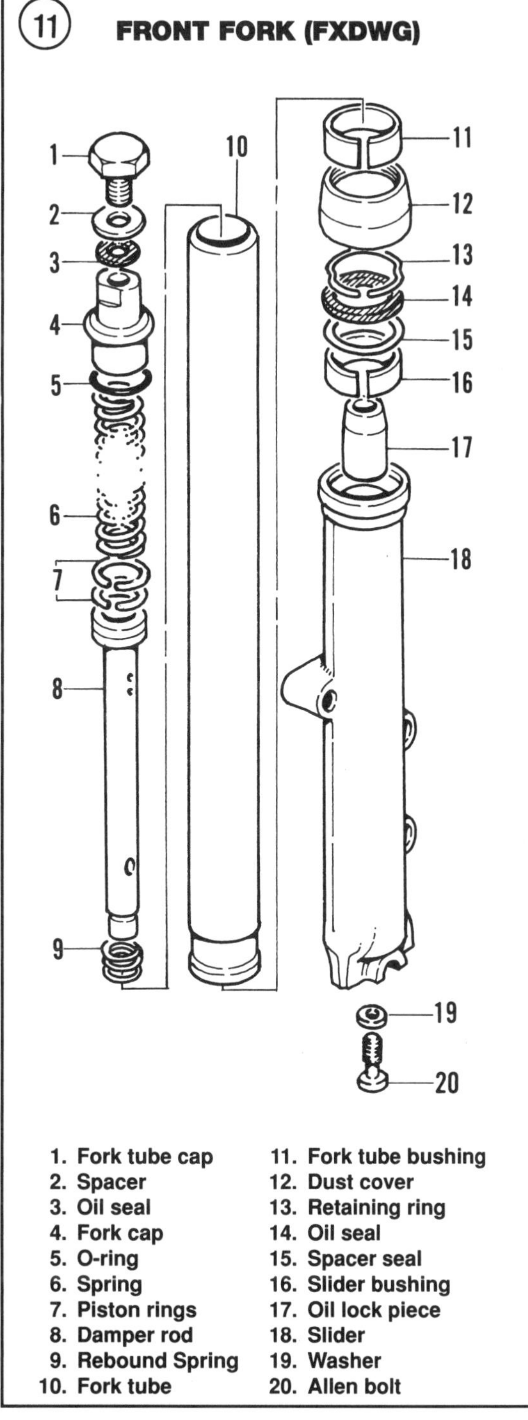

1. Fork tube cap
2. Spacer
3. Oil seal
4. Fork cap
5. O-ring
6. Spring
7. Piston rings
8. Damper rod
9. Rebound Spring
10. Fork tube
11. Fork tube bushing
12. Dust cover
13. Retaining ring
14. Oil seal
15. Spacer seal
16. Slider bushing
17. Oil lock piece
18. Slider
19. Washer
20. Allen bolt

8. Remove the Allen bolt and washer (**Figure 15**) at the bottom of the slider.

NOTE
The slider bushing is installed with an interference fit. When separating the fork tube and slider, you will remove the slider bushing, spacer seal and oil seal at the same time.

9. Hold the fork tube in one hand and pull the slider downward repeatedly with your other hand, knocking the slider bushing against the fork tube bushing (**Figure 16**). As you knock out the slider bushing, it will push the oil seal and spacer seal out of the slider. Continue until these components are forced out of the slider.
10. Remove the oil lock piece (**Figure 17**) from the damper rod.
11. Remove the damper rod and rebound spring (**Figure 18**) from the fork tube.

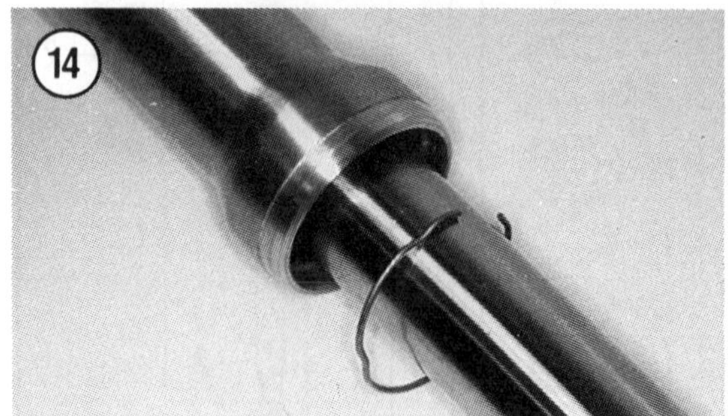

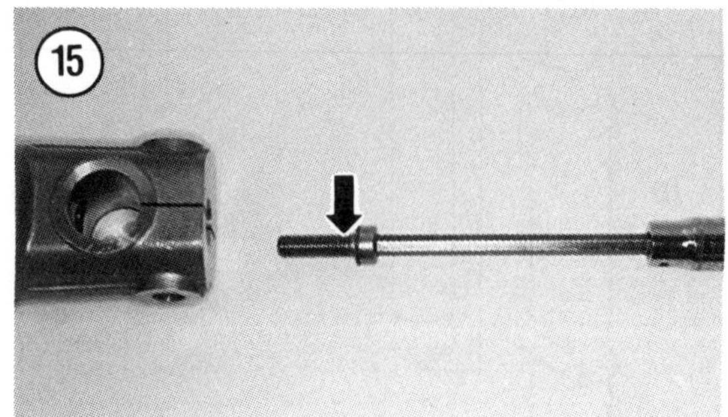

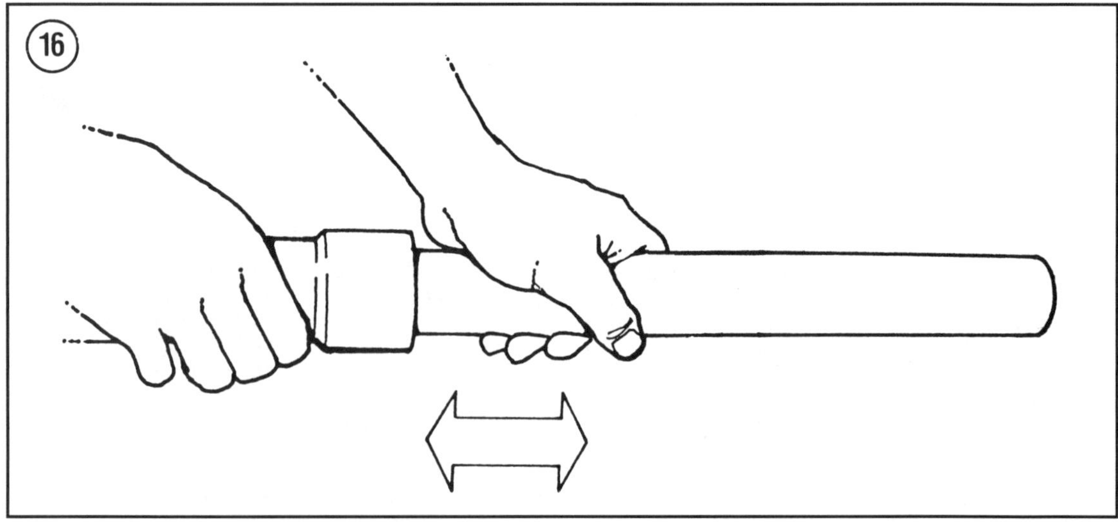

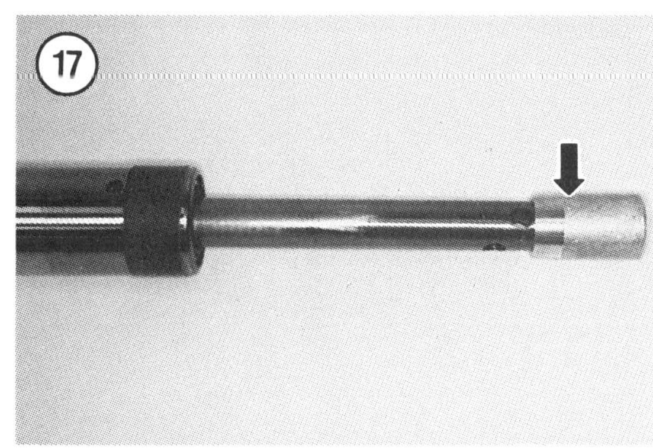

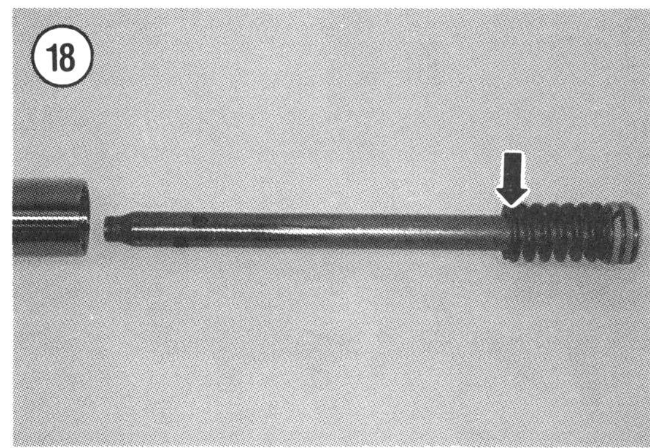

Inspection

NOTE
*Handle the guide bushings (**Figure 19**) carefully to prevent scratching them or removing any of their coating material. If there is any metal powder clinging to the guide bushings, clean them with new fork oil and a nylon brush.*

1. Clean and dry the fork components.
2. Check the fork tube (A, **Figure 20**) for bending, nicks, rust or other damage. Place the fork tube on a set of V-blocks and check runout with a dial indicator. If you do not have these tools, roll the fork tube on a large plate glass or other flat surface. Harley-Davidson does not provide service specifications for runout. If a fork tube is slightly bent, it may be straightened with a press and special blocks; see your dealer. Replace the fork tube if it is creased or wrinkled.
3. Check the slider (B, **Figure 20**) for dents or other exterior damage. Check the retaining ring groove (**Figure 21**) in the top of the slider for cracks or other damage. Replace the slider if the groove is cracked or damaged.
4. Check the slider and fork tube bushings (**Figure 19**) for excessive wear, cracks or damage. You removed the slider bushing with the oil seal. To replace the fork tube bushing, perform the following:
   a. Expand the bushing slit (**Figure 22**) with a screwdriver and then slide the bushing off the fork tube.
   b. Coat the new bushing with new fork oil.
   c. Install the new bushing by expanding the slit with a screwdriver.
   d. Seat the new bushing (**Figure 22**) into the fork tube groove.

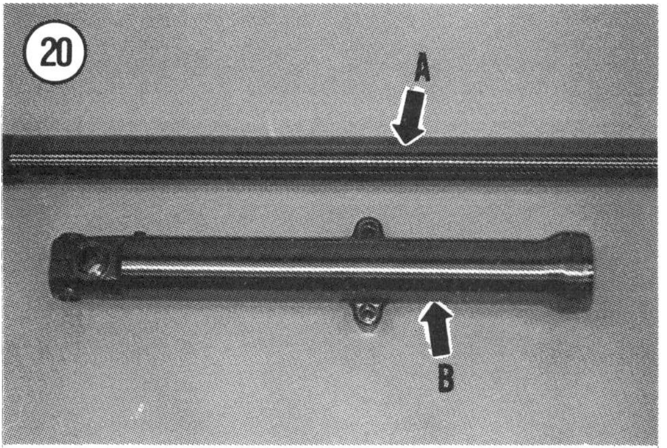

5. Replace damaged drain screw and Allen bolt washers.
6. Check the damper rod piston rings (**Figure 23**) for excessive wear, cracks or other damage. If necessary, replace both rings as a set.
7. Check the damper rod for straightness with a set of V-blocks and a dial indicator (**Figure 24**) or by rolling it on a piece of place glass. Harley-Davidson does not provide a service limit specification for runout. If the damper rod is not straight, replace it.
8. Make sure the oil passage holes in the damper rod (**Figure 25**) are open. If clogged, flush with solvent and dry with compressed air.
9. Check the threads in the bottom of the damper rod for stripping, cross-threading or sealer residue. Use a tap to true up the threads and to remove sealer deposits.
10. Check the damper rod rebound spring and the fork spring for wear or damage. Harley-Davidson does not provide a service limit specification for spring free length.
11. Replace the oil seals (A, **Figure 26**) whenever you remove them. Always replace both oil seals as a set.
12. Inspect the outer dust seals (B, **Figure 26**) for cracks, deterioration or other damage. A damaged dust seal will allow dirt to pass through and damage the oil seal.
13. Replace the fork cap O-ring if leaking or if wear or damage is apparent.
14. Replace worn or damaged parts. When replacing fork springs, replace both springs as a set; do not replace only one spring.

Assembly

Refer to **Figure 10** or **Figure 11** for this procedure.

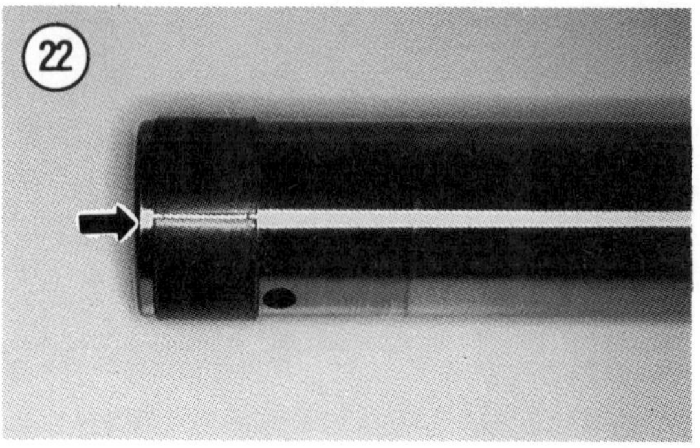

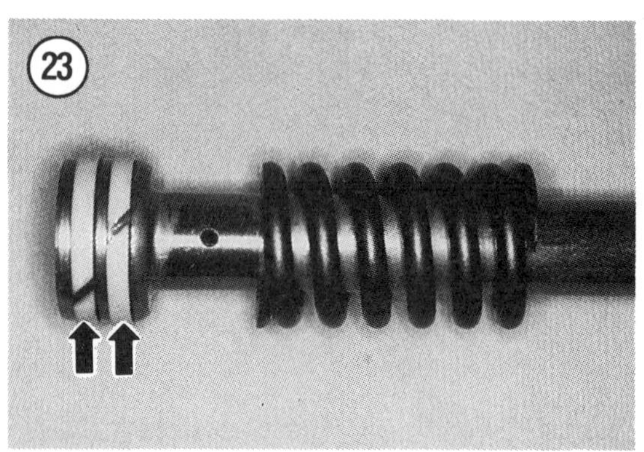

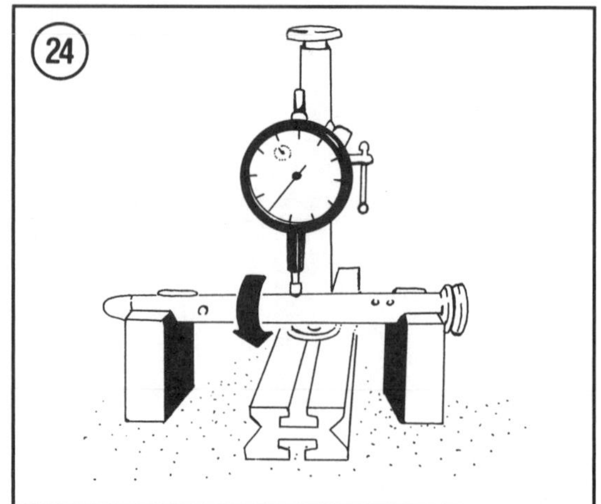

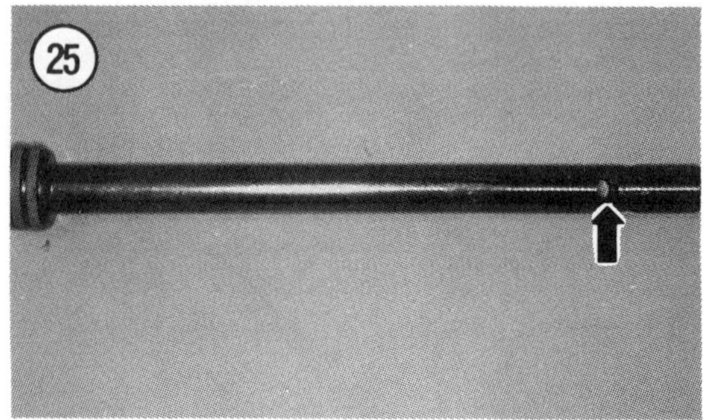

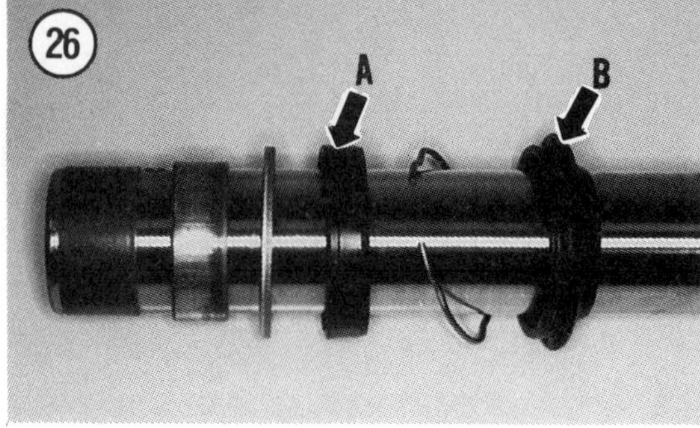

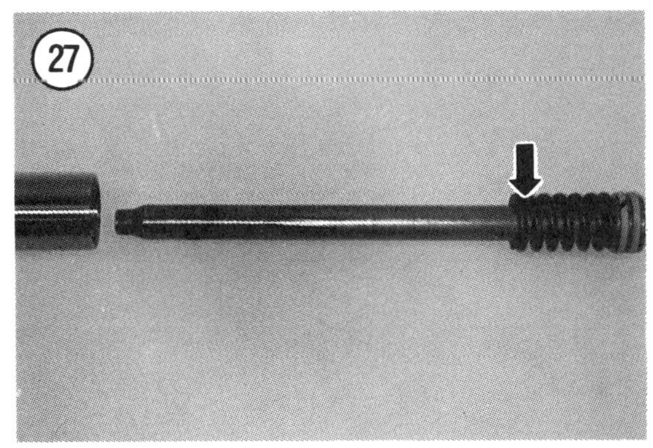

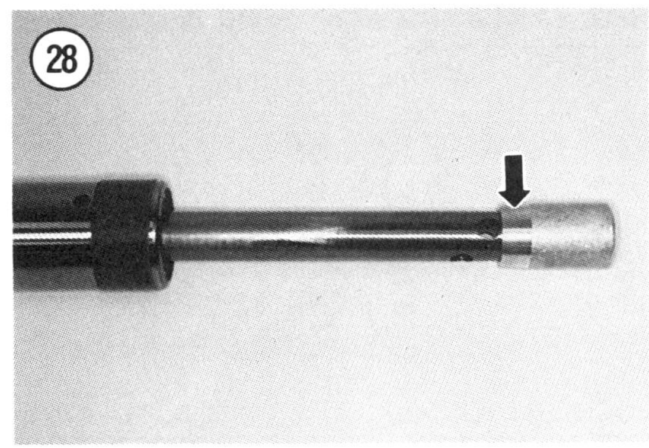

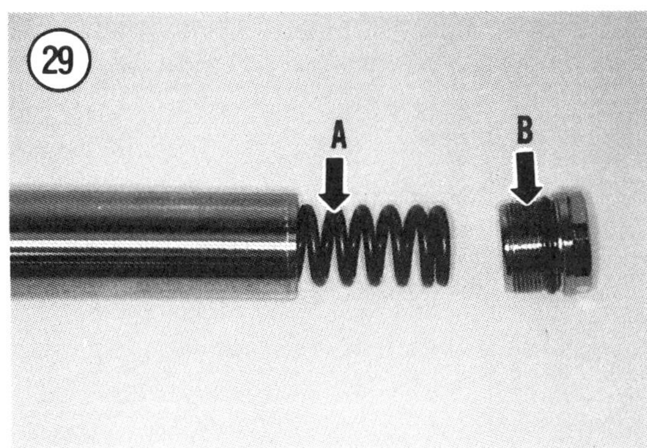

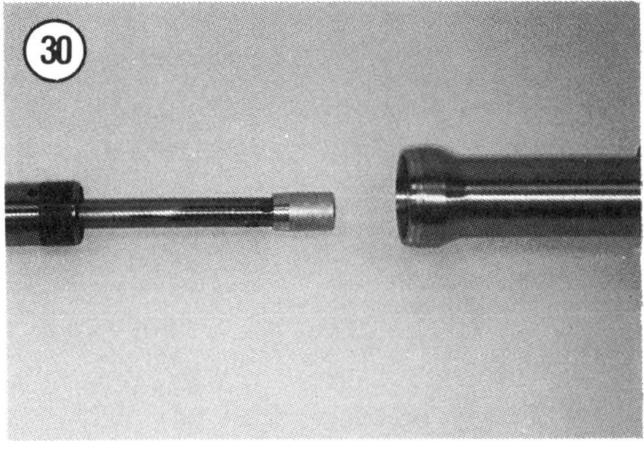

1. Prior to assembly, perform the *Inspection* procedure to make sure all worn or defective parts have been repaired or replaced. Clean parts before assembly.
2. Coat all parts with Harley-Davidson Type E Fork Oil or an equivalent fork oil before assembly.
3. Install the rebound spring onto the damper rod (**Figure 27**) and slide the rod into the fork tube until it extends out the end of the tube.
4. Install the oil lock piece (**Figure 28**) onto the end of the damper rod.
5. Insert the fork spring (A, **Figure 29**) into the fork tube so that the tapered side of the spring faces down (toward the damper rod). Install the fork cap (B, **Figure 29**) to tension the spring and hold the damper rod in place.
6. Install the slider over the damper rod (**Figure 30**) and into the fork tube until it bottoms out. Make sure the oil lock piece is mounted on the end of the damper rod.
7. Install the gasket onto the damper rod Allen bolt.
8. Apply a non-permanent thread locking compound to the damper rod Allen bolt threads prior to installation. Insert the Allen bolt (**Figure 31**) through the lower end of the slider and thread it into the damper rod. Tighten the bolt securely.
9. Remove the fork cap and fork spring (**Figure 29**).

NOTE

The slider bushing, spacer seal, and oil seal are installed into the slider with a driver placed over the fork tube and against the oil seal. Use the Harley-Davidson fork seal driver (part No. HD-36583) or an aftermarket driver. A piece of pipe can also be used to drive the parts into the slider. When using a piece of pipe or similar tool, you must take care to prevent damaging the slider, oil

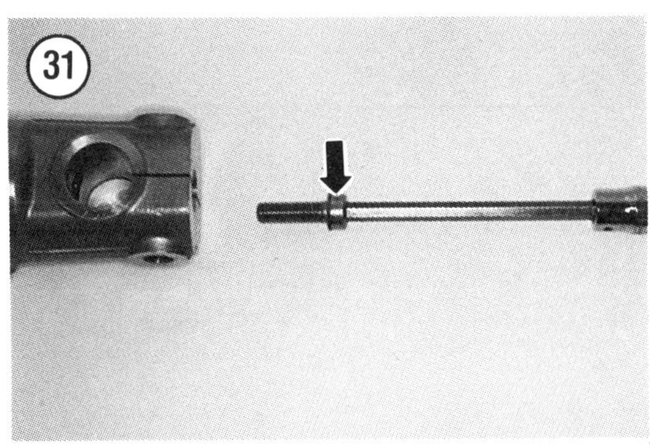

seal or fork tube. Wrap both ends of the pipe or tool with duct tape to prevent it from scratching the fork tube and tearing the oil seal.

10. To install the slider bushing, spacer seal and oil seal, perform the following:
   a. Coat the slider bushing (A, **Figure 32**) with fork oil and slide it down the fork tube, resting it against the slider bore.
   b. Install the spacer seal (B, **Figure 32**) over the fork tube (dished or concave side facing downward) and rest it on top of the slider bushing.

NOTE
Because the top fork tube edges are sharp, they can cut the oil and dust seal lips as you install them over the top of the tube. To protect the oil and dust seal lips, place a thin plastic bag on top of the fork tube. Before installing the seals in the following steps, lightly coat the bag and the seal lips with fork oil.

   c. Slide a new oil (C, **Figure 32**) seal over the fork tube (lettered side facing up). Rest the oil seal on the seal spacer.
   d. Slide the fork seal driver (**Figure 33**) down the fork tube.
   e. Using the driver, knock the bushing, spacer seal and oil seal into the slider until you can see the retaining ring groove in the slider above the oil seal.
   f. Remove the fork seal driver tool.

11. Install the retaining ring (**Figure 34**) into the slider groove. Make sure the retaining ring seats in the groove.
12. Slide the dust seal (**Figure 35**) down the fork tube and seat it into the top of the slider.
13. Install the dust cover (**Figure 36**) as follows:

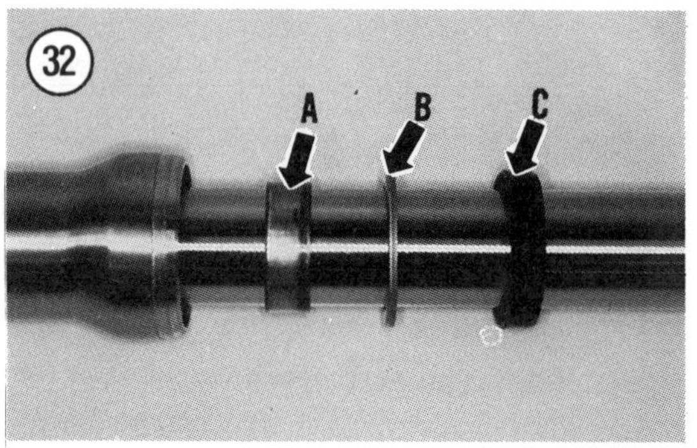

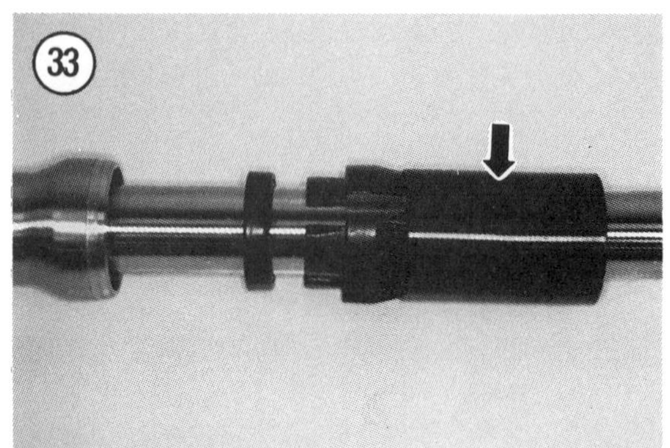

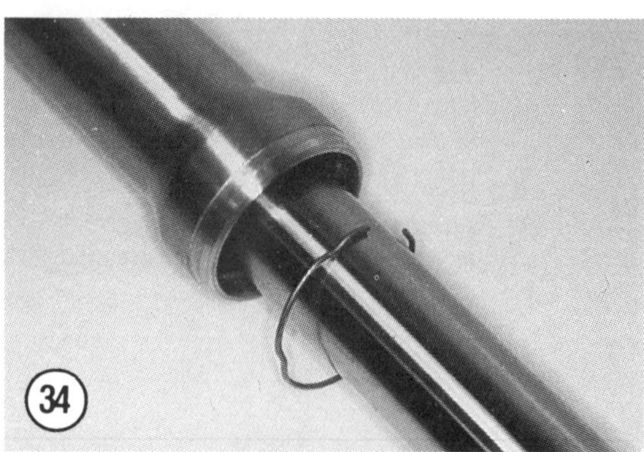

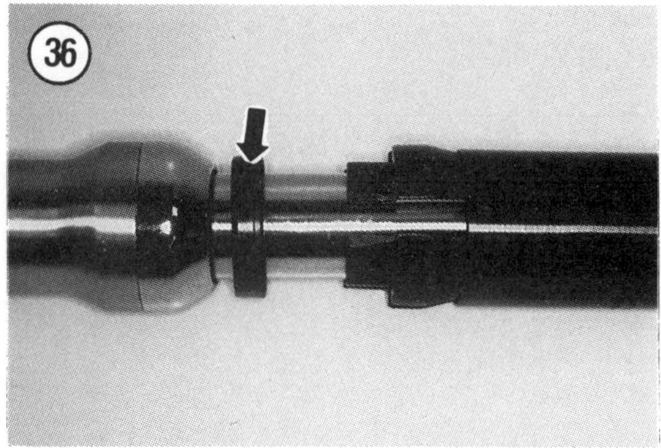

a. Slide the dust cover down the fork tube and rest it against the top of the slider. Remove the plastic bag, if used.
b. Slide one of the discarded oil seals down the fork tube and rest it against the dust cover (**Figure 36**).
c. Use the fork seal driver (**Figure 36**) and carefully tap the dust cover onto the top of the slider.
d. Remove the seal driver and oil seal.

14. Fill the fork tube with the correct quantity of Harley-Davidson Type E Fork Oil listed in **Table 2**.
15. The fork spring is tapered at one end. Install the spring (A, **Figure 29**) with the tapered end facing down (toward the damper rod).
16. Wipe the fork cap O-ring and threads with fork oil.
17. Align the fork cap (B, **Figure 29**) with the spring and push down on the cap to compress the spring. Start the cap slowly, making sure you do not cross thread it.
18. Place the slider in a vise with soft jaws and tighten the fork cap securely.
19. Install the fork tube as described in this chapter.

STEERING HEAD AND STEM

The fork stem mounts onto the lower triple clamp. A dust shield and a tapered bearing are installed onto the bottom of the fork stem. The fork stem is inserted through the steering head where another bearing is installed at the top of the steering head. Both bearings seat against races pressed into the steering head. Dust covers protect bearings from dust and other contaminants.

Removal (All Models Except FXDWG)

Refer to **Figure 37** for this procedure.

1. Remove the front wheel as described in Chapter Nine.
2. Remove the fuel tank as described in Chapter Eight.
3. Remove the brake hose union from the bottom of the lower fork bracket (**Figure 38**). Do not disconnect the brake hose connection.
4. Remove the headlight mounting bracket bolt and remove the bracket (**Figure 39**) from the upper fork bracket.
5. Remove the 2 front handlebar clamp bolts and washers or collars. Then set the instrument housing forward (A, **Figure 40**) so that it doesnt scratch the handlebar clamp.
6. Remove the 2 rear clamp bolts, then remove the holder (B, **Figure 40**) and handlebars.
7. Unscrew and remove the cap (C, **Figure 40**) from the steering stem bolt
8. Remove the front forks (A, **Figure 41**) as described in this chapter.
9. Loosen the steering stem pinch bolt (B, **Figure 41**).

NOTE
Hold or secure the steering stem to keep it from falling after removing the steering stem bolt in Step 10.

10. Remove the steering stem bolt (C, **Figure 41**) and washer. The lift the upper fork bracket off the steering stem and lower the steering stem out of the frame and remove it.
11. Remove the upper dust shield and bearing.
12. Inspect the steering stem and bearing assembly as described under *Inspection* in this section.

10

Installation (All Models Except FXDWG)

1. Make sure you seat the steering head bearing races in the frame.
2. Wipe the bearing races with a clean lint-free cloth. Then lubricate each race with bearing grease.
3. Pack the upper and lower bearings with bearing grease. Install the lower bearing and lower dust shield on the steering stem before installing the steering stem in the frame. If necessary, install the lower bearing as described in this chapter.
4. Insert the steering stem into the frame steering head and hold it firmly in place.
5. Install the upper bearing (7, **Figure 37**) over the fork stem and seat it into to the upper race. Install the upper dust shield (6, **Figure 37**).
6. Install the upper fork bracket (4, **Figure 37**) over the steering stem.
7. Install the washer and the steering stem bolt (C, **Figure 41**). Tighten the bolt hand-tight only.
8. Install the front forks as described in this chapter.

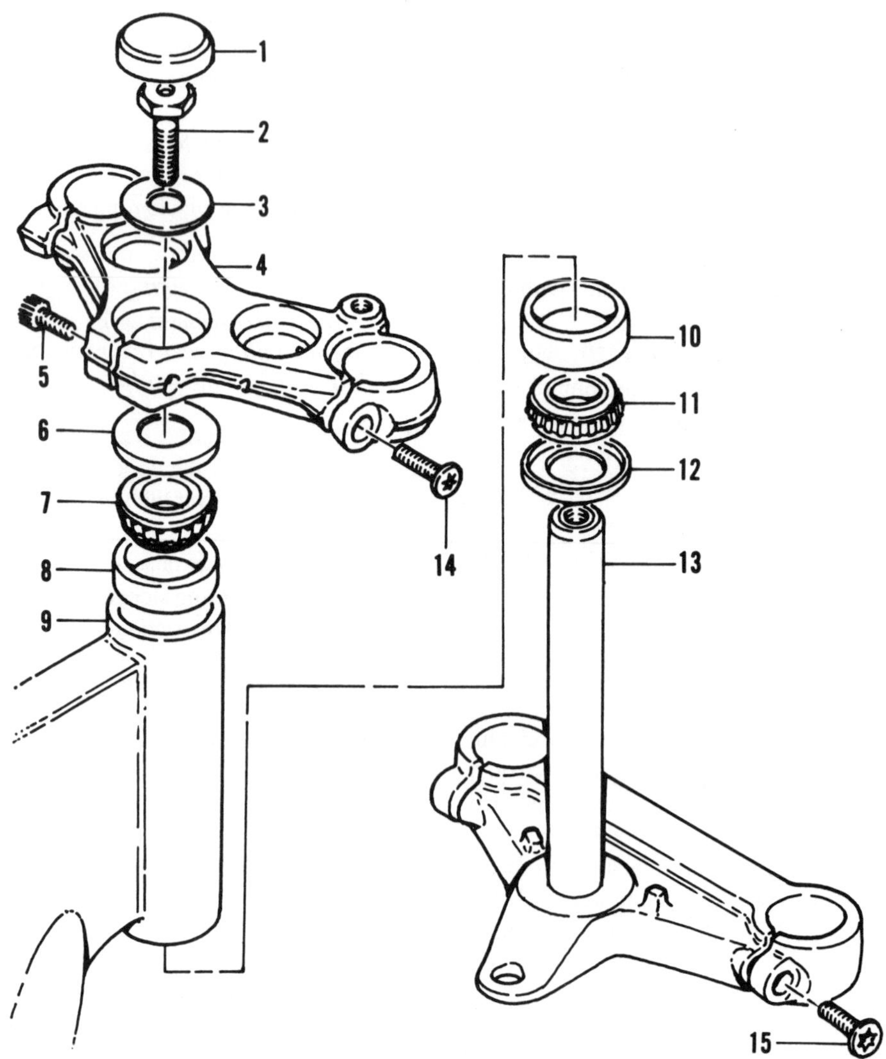

1. Cap
2. Steering stem bolt
3. Washer
4. Upper fork bracket
5. Pinch bolt
6. Dust shield
7. Upper bearing
8. Upper bearing race
9. Frame neck
10. Lower bearing race
11. Lower bearing
12. Dust shield
13. Steering stem/lower fork bracket
14. Upper fork tube pinch bolt
15. Lower fork tube pinch bolt

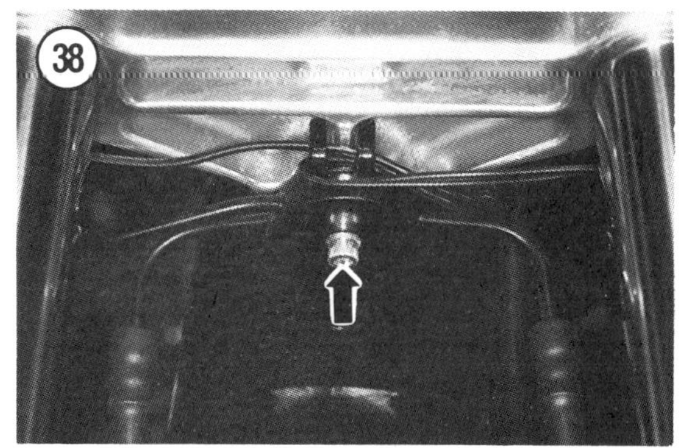

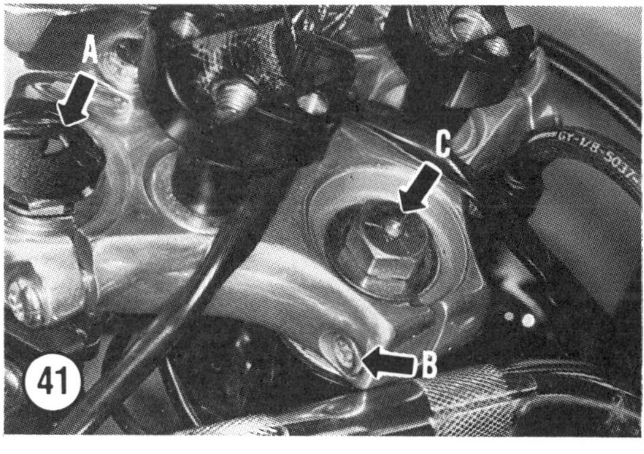

CAUTION

Do not overtighten the steering stem bolt in Step 9 or you can damage the bearings and races. Final adjustment of the fork stem will take place after you have installed the front wheel on the bike.

9. Tighten the steering stem bolt (C, **Figure 41**) until you can turn the steering stem from side to side with no noticeable axial or lateral play. When the play feels correct, tighten the steering stem pinch bolt (B, **Figure 41**) to the torque specification in **Table 1**.
10. Install the handlebar and tighten the clamp bolts as described under *Handlebar Removal/Installation* in this chapter.
11. Install the headlight mounting bracket (**Figure 39**) onto the upper fork bracket. Tighten the mounting bolts securely.
12. Install the brake hose union onto the bottom of the lower fork bracket (**Figure 38**). Tighten the bolt securely.
13. Install the front wheel as described in Chapter Nine.
14. Adjust the steering play as described under *Steering Play Adjustment* in this chapter.

10

Removal (FXDWG)

Refer to **Figure 42** for this procedure.

1. Remove the front wheel as described in Chapter Nine.
2. Remove the fuel tank as described in Chapter Eight.
3. Remove the brake hose union from the bottom of the lower fork bracket. Do not disconnect the brake hose connection.
4. Remove the headlight mounting bracket bolt and remove the bracket from the fork bracket.
5. Remove the 2 front handlebar clamp bolts and washers or collars. Then set the instrument housing forward so that it doesnt scratch the handlebar clamp.
6. Remove the 2 rear clamp bolts, then remove the holder and handlebar.
7. Unscrew and remove the cap (1, **Figure 42**) from the steering stem nut.
8. Remove the front forks as described in this chapter.

9. Bend the lockwasher tab away from the steering stem nut, then remove the nut and lockwasher.
10. Lift the upper fork bracket (4, **Figure 42**) off the steering stem and remove it.

NOTE
Hold or secure the steering stem/lower fork bracket. This will prevent it from falling after you remove the steering stem adjust nut in Step 11.

11. Loosen and remove the adjust nut (6, **Figure 42**). Then lower the steering stem assembly out of the frame and remove it.
12. Remove the upper dust shield and bearing.
13. Inspect the steering stem and bearing assembly as described under *Inspection* in this section.

Installation (FXDWG)

1. Make sure you seat the steering head bearing races in the frame.
2. Wipe the bearing races with a clean lint-free cloth. Then lubricate each race with bearing grease.
3. Pack the upper and lower bearings with bearing grease. Install the lower bearing (11, **Figure 42**) and the lower dust shield onto the steering stem before you install the steering stem in the frame. If necessary, install the lower bearing as described in this chapter.
4. Insert the steering stem into the frame and hold it firmly in place.
5. Install the upper bearing (8, **Figure 42**) over the fork stem and seat it into to the upper race. Install the upper dust shield (7, **Figure 42**).

CAUTION
Do not overtighten the adjust nut in Step 6 or you can damage the bearings and races. Final adjustment of the fork stem will take place after you have installed the front wheel on the bike.

6. Thread the adjust nut (6, **Figure 42**) onto the steering stem. Tighten the adjust nut until you can turn the steering stem from side to side with no noticeable axial or lateral play. The steering stem must turn with no binding or roughness.
7. Install the upper fork bracket (4, **Figure 42**) over the steering stem.

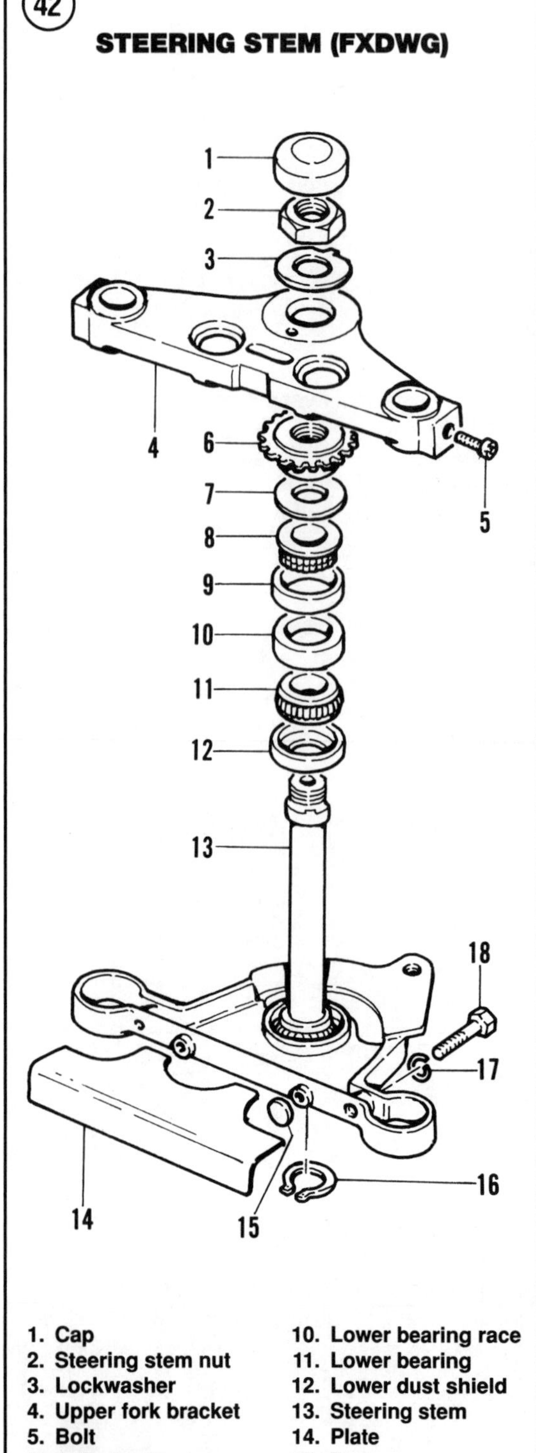

1. Cap
2. Steering stem nut
3. Lockwasher
4. Upper fork bracket
5. Bolt
6. Adjust nut
7. Upper dust shield
8. Upper bearing
9. Upper bearing race
10. Lower bearing race
11. Lower bearing
12. Lower dust shield
13. Steering stem
14. Plate
15. Pad
16. Circlip
17. Lockwasher
18. Bolt

8. Install a new lockwasher (3, **Figure 42**) over the steering stem. Engage the lockwasher pin into the hole in the upper fork bracket. Then install the steering stem nut (2, **Figure 42**). Tighten the steering stem nut securely.
9. Install the front forks as described in this chapter.
10. nstall the handlebar and tighten the clamp bolts as described under *Handlebar Removal/Installation* in this chapter.
11. Install the headlight mounting bracket onto the fork bracket. Tighten the mounting bolts securely.
12. Install the brake hose bracket onto the bottom of the lower fork bracket. Tighten the brake hose bracket bolt to the torque specification in **Table 1**.
13. Install the front wheel as described in Chapter Nine.
14. Adjust the steering play as described under *Steering Play Adjustment* in this chapter.
15. Tighten the steering stem nut (2, **Figure 42**) to the torque specification in **Table 1**. Bend the lockwasher tab (3, **Figure 42**) against one nut flat.
16. Install the cap (1, **Figure 42**) onto the steering stem nut.

Inspection (All Models)

The bearing races (8 and 10, **Figure 37** or 9 and 10, **Figure 42**) are pressed into the steering head.

Pack the bearings and races with wheel bearing grease in the following steps.

1. Wipe the bearing races with a solvent soaked rag and then dry with compressed air or a lint-free cloth. Check the races in the steering head for pitting, scratches, galling or excessive wear. If any of these conditions exist, replace the races as described in this chapter. If the races are okay, wipe each race with grease.
2. Clean the bearings in solvent to remove all of the old grease. Blow the bearing dry with compressed air, making sure not to allow the air jet to spin the bearing. Do not remove the lower bearing from the fork stem unless you must replace it. Clean the bearing while installed in the steering stem.
3. After the bearings are dry, hold the inner race with one hand and turn the outer race with your other hand. Turn the bearing slowly, checking for roughness, looseness, trapped dirt or grit. Visually check the bearing for pitting, scratches or visible damage. If the bearings are worn, check the dust covers for wear or damage or for improper bearing lubrication. Replace the bearing if necessary. If you can reuse the bearing, pack it with grease and wrap it with wax paper or some other type of lint-free material until you can reinstall it. Do not store the bearings for any length of time without lubricating them or they will rust.
4. Check the steering stem for cracks or damage. Check the threads at the top of the stem for damage. Check the steering stem bolt by threading it into the steering stem; make sure the bolt threads easily with no roughness.
5. Replace all worn or damaged parts. Replace bearing races as described in this chapter.
6. Replace the lower steering stem bearing (11, **Figure 37** or 11, **Figure 42**) and the dust shield as described in this chapter.
7. Check for broken welds on the frame around the steering head. If any are found, have them repaired by a competent frame shop or welding service familiar with motorcycle frame repair.

STEERING HEAD BEARING RACE

Upper and Lower Bearing Race Replacement

10

The upper and lower bearing races (8 and 10, **Figure 37** or 9 and 10, **Figure 42**) are pressed into the frame. Do not remove the bearing races unless replacement is necessary. Both races are identical (same part number) and can be purchased separately from the bearing. If you are replacing the bearing, purchase the bearing and race as a set.

1. To remove a race, insert an aluminum or brass rod into the steering head and carefully tap the race out from the inside (**Figure 43**). Tap all around the race so that neither the race nor the steering head is bent.
2. Clean the steering head with solvent and dry thoroughly.

NOTE

Install the bearing races with the Harley-Davidson head bearing race installation tool (part No. HD-39301). If you do not have this tool, perform Step 3.

3. Install the bearing races as follows:
   a. Clean the race thoroughly before installing it.

b. Align the upper race with the frame steering head and tap it slowly and squarely in place. Make sure you do not contact the bearing race surfaces. See **Figure 44**. If you saved an old race, grind its outside rim so that it is a slip fit in the steering head, then use it to drive the new race into place. Drive the race into the steering head until it bottoms out on the bore shoulder.

c. Repeat to install the lower race into the steering head.

4. Apply bearing grease to the face of each race.

Fork Stem Lower Bearing Replacement

Do not remove the fork stem lower bearing (**Figure 45**) unless you are going to replace the bearing and its race. When replacing the lower bearing, install a new lower dust shield. See 12, **Figure 37** or 12, **Figure 42**.

WARNING
Safety glasses and insulated gloves must be worn when removing the inner race in Step 1.

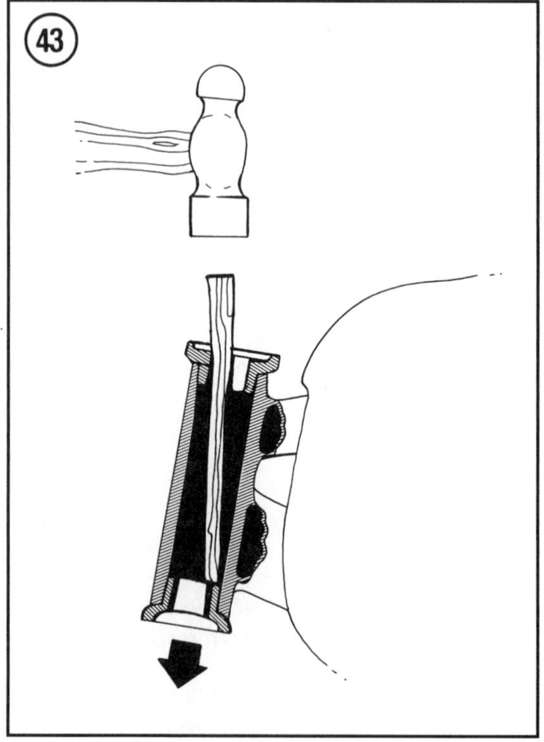

1. Using a chisel, break the bearing cage and rollers from the inner race. To remove the inner race, heat the race with a torch until it expands enough to slide or drop off the fork stem. Remove and discard the dust shield after removing the bearing.

2. Clean the fork stem with solvent and dry thoroughly.

3. Pack the new bearing with grease before installing it.

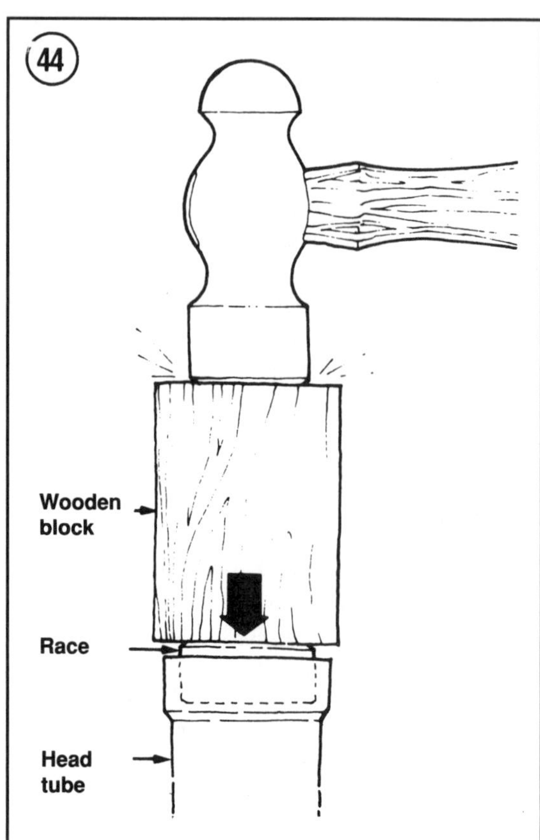

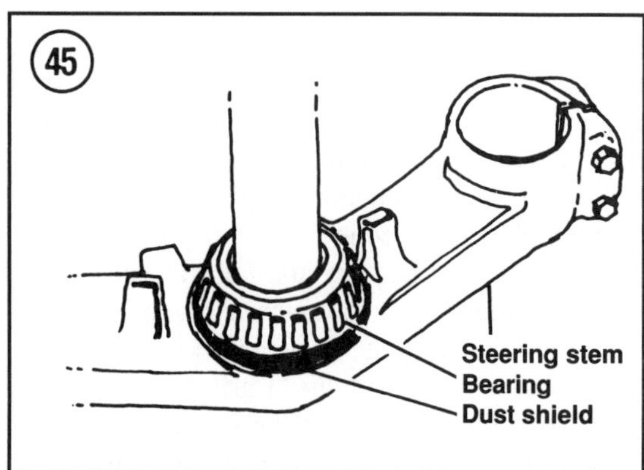

4. Slide a new dust cover over the fork stem until it bottoms out on the lower bracket.

5. Align the new bearing with the fork stem and press or drive it onto the fork stem until it bottoms out.

Install the new bearing with a bearing driver placed against the inner bearing race (**Figure 46**). Do *not* install the bearing by driving against the outer bearing race.

STEERING PLAY ADJUSTMENT

1. Support the bike with the front wheel off the ground.

2. Remove the windshield (if used) and all other accessory weight from the handlebar and front forks that could affect this adjustment.

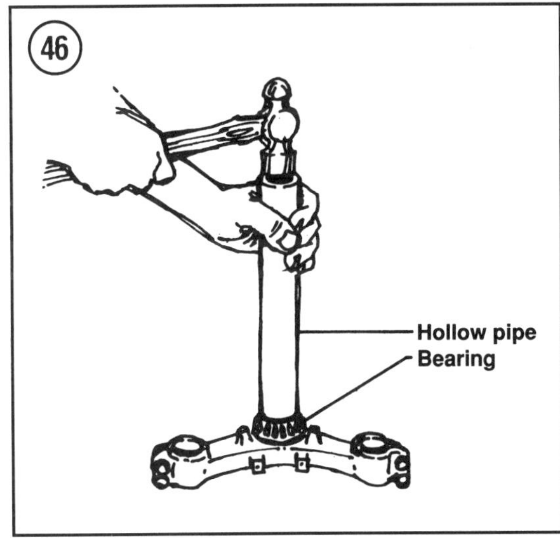

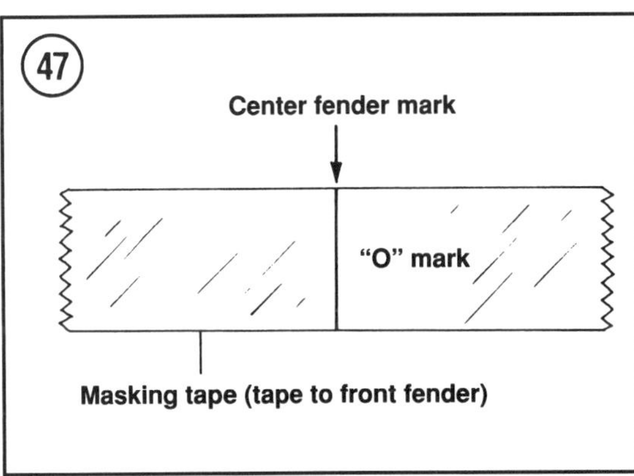

NOTE

If a control cable affects handlebar movement, disconnect it.

3. Apply a strip of masking tape across the front end of the front fender. Draw a vertical line across the tape at the center of the fender. Then draw a line on each side of the center line, 1 in. (25.4 mm) apart from each other. See **Figure 47**.
4. Turn the handlebar so that the front wheel faces straight ahead.
5. Place a pointer on a stand above the tape marks. Then center the pointer so that its tip points to the center of the fender (tape marks) when the wheel is facing straight ahead.
6. Lightly push the fender toward the right side until the front end starts to turn by itself. Mark this point on the tape.
7. Repeat Step 6 for the left side.
8. Measure the distance between the 2 marks on the tape. The correct distance is 1-2 in. (25-50 mm). If the distance is incorrect, perform Step 9.

9A. On all models except FXDWG, adjust steering play as follows:

a. Loosen the lower fork bracket pinch bolts (15, **Figure 37**).
b. Unscrew and remove the bolt cap (1, **Figure 37**).
c. Loosen the fork stem pinch bolt (5, **Figure 37**).
d. If the distance is less than 1 in. (25 mm), tighten the steering stem bolt (2, **Figure 37**).
e. If the distance is more than 2 in. (50 mm), loosen the steering stem bolt (2, **Figure 37**).
f. Repeat Steps 6-8 to measure steering play. Continue until the distance is within 1-2 in. (25-50 mm).
g. When the steering play adjustment is correct, continue with sub-step h.
h. Tighten the steering stem pinch bolt (5, **Figure 37**) to the torque specification in **Table 1**.
i. Tighten the lower fork bracket pinch bolt (15, **Figure 37**) to the torque specification in **Table 1**.
j. Install and tighten the bolt cap (1, **Figure 37**) securely.

9B. On FXDWG models, adjust steering play as follows:

a. Loosen the lower fork bracket pinch bolts (18, **Figure 42**).
b. Remove the cap (1, **Figure 42**).

c. Bend the lockwasher tab away from the steering stem nut, then loosen the nut (2, **Figure 42**).

d. If the distance (step 8) is less than 1 in. (25 mm), tighten the adjust nut (6, **Figure 42**).

e. If the distance is more than 2 in. (50 mm), loosen the adjust nut (6, **Figure 42**).

f. Repeat Steps 6-8 to measure steering play. Continue until the adjustment is within 1-2 in. (25-50 mm).

g. When the steering play adjustment is correct, continue with sub-step h.

h. Tighten the steering stem nut (2, **Figure 42**) to the torque specification in **Table 1**. Then bend the lockwasher tab against one nut flat.

i. Tighten the lower fork bracket pinch bolt (18, **Figure 42**) to the torque specification in **Table 1**.

j. Install the cap (1, **Figure 42**).

10. Reinstall all parts previously removed.

Table 1 FRONT SUSPENSION TIGHTENING TORQUES

	ft.-lb.	N•m
Upper and lower fork bracket pinch bolts		
FXDWG	30-35	41-47
All other models	25-30	34-41
Steering stem nut (FXDWG)	35-40	47-54
Steering stem bolt (all other models)	see text	
Steering stem pinch bolt		
(all models except FXDWG)	21-27	28-37
Brake hose bracket bolt (FXDWG)	11	15
Front fender mounting bolts	16-20	22-27

Table 2 FRONT FORK OIL CAPACITY

	Wet		Dry	
	fl. oz.	mL	fl. oz.	mL
1991-1992	9.2	272	10.2	302
1993-1994				
FXDL	9.2	272	10.2	302
FXDWG	10.2	302	11.2	331
1995				
FXDWG	10.2	302	11.2	331
All other models	9.2	272	10.2	302

CHAPTER ELEVEN

REAR SUSPENSION

This chapter covers service related to the rear shock absorbers and rear swing arm. **Table 1** is at the end of the chapter.

SHOCK ABSORBERS

The rear shocks are spring controlled and hydraulically damped. Spring preload is adjustable on all models.

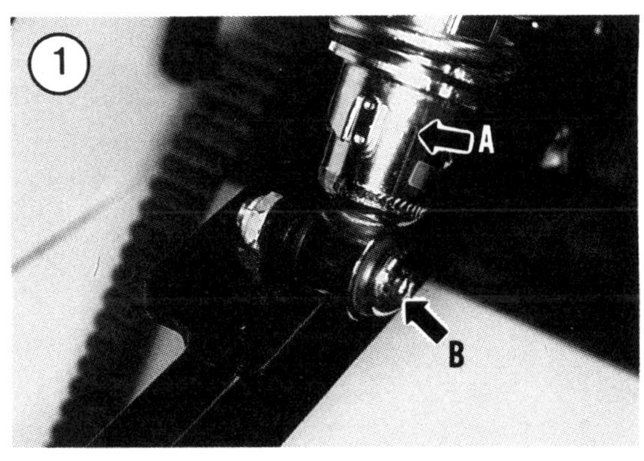

Spring Preload Adjustment

You can change the ride height (height of a motorcycle at rest with no rider or passenger) by adjusting the cam preload adjuster at the base of each shock spring. Turning the cam adjuster moves the cam ramps up or down (compressing or extending the spring). Increasing the cam angle increases the spring load and raises the ride height.

Each shock absorber has a cam type preload adjuster that changes the length of the installed shock spring and its preload adjustment. Spring preload controls how far the shock absorber compresses under the weight of the bike and rider. The adjuster assembly consists of a cam with five different recessed steps. As you turn the cam, it indexes with a bracket fixed to the damper housing.

The cam positions range from No. 1 (a rider with no luggage) to No. 5 (maximum loads). Select the position that best suits the vehicle load requirements.

Rotate the cam (A, **Figure 1**) to compress the spring (heavy loads) or extend the spring (light loads). Rotate the cam with a spanner wrench (**Figure 2**). Set both cams to the same preload position.

Removal/Installation

When servicing the rear shocks, remove one shock at a time. If it is necessary to remove both shocks, support the bike with the rear wheel off the ground.

Refer to **Figure 3**, typical.

1. Support the bike with the rear wheel off the ground.
2. Remove the upper shock absorber nut and washer (**Figure 4**).
3. Remove the lower shock absorber nut, washer and bolt. See B, **Figure 1**, typical.
4. Remove the shock absorber.
5. Check the upper shock stud (**Figure 5**) for looseness. Tighten if necessary.
6. Install the shocks by reversing these removal steps, noting the following.
7. Apply Loctite 242 (blue) to the shock stud and bolt threads. Then install the washers and nuts and tighten to the torque specification in **Table 1**.

Inspection

1. Remove the shock absorber as described in this chapter.
2. Inspect both shock bushings (A, **Figure 6**). Replace worn or damaged bushings.
3. Inspect the shock absorber (**Figure 7**). If the damper housing is leaking, bent, or in any way damaged, replace the shock absorber.
4. Inspect the shock spring, spring retainer, cover and cam for cracks or damage. If necessary, remove the shock spring as described in this section and replace the damaged part.

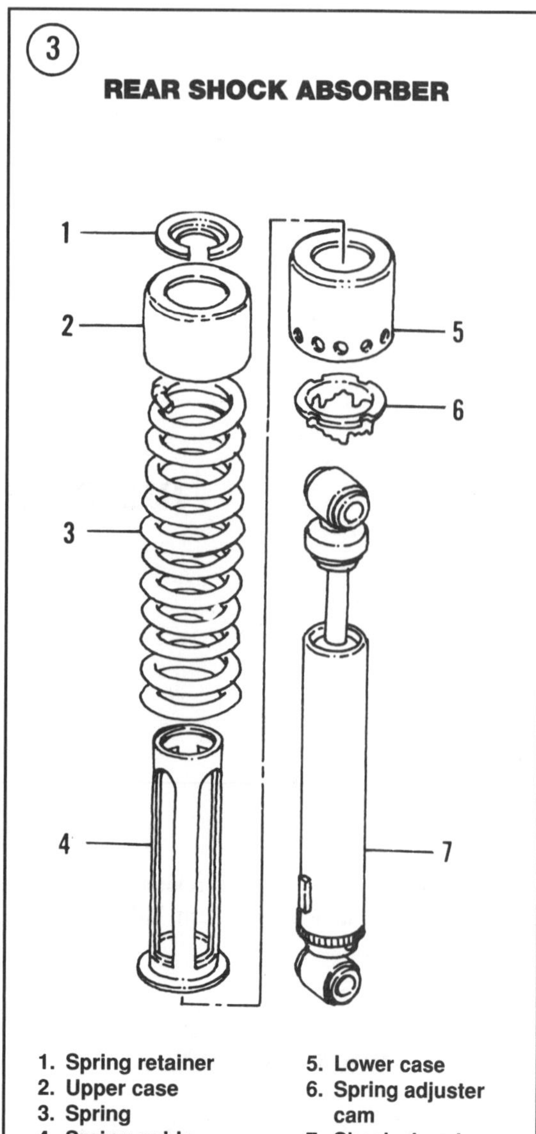

1. Spring retainer
2. Upper case
3. Spring
4. Spring guide
5. Lower case
6. Spring adjuster cam
7. Shock absorber

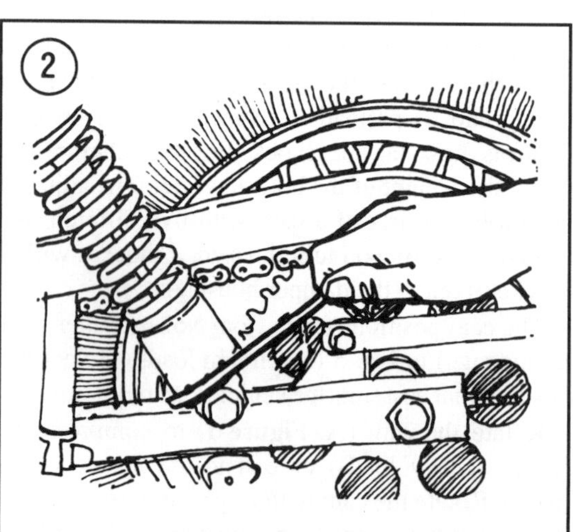

Shock Bushing Inspection and Replacement

Refer to **Figure 3** and A, **Figure 6**. Replace both bushings at the same time.

1. Remove the shock absorber as described in this chapter.

CAUTION
When supporting the shock absorbers in a press (Step 2), position the press blocks or other equipment so that they do not dent or otherwise damage the damper body.

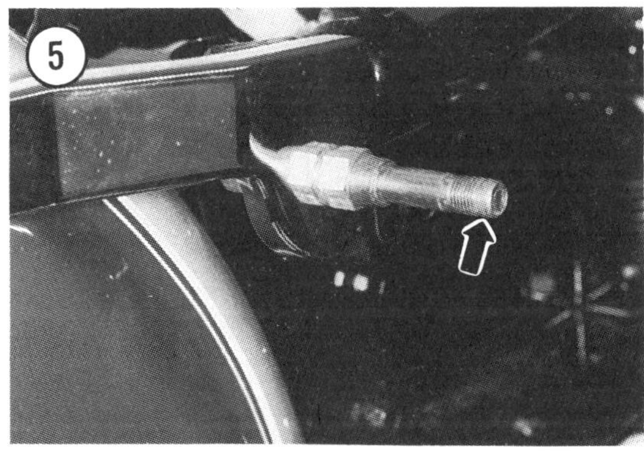

2. Support the shock absorber in a press and press out the first bushing. Then press out the second bushing.
3. Clean the shock eyelets of all rust and rubber residue. Then check the eyelets for cracks, dents and other problems. Replace the shock absorber if damaged.

NOTE
The upper and lower shock bushings are identical.

4. Align the new bushing with the shock eyelet and start it into place. Then support the shock absorber in a press and press the bushing into place, centering it in the shock eyelet. Repeat for the second bushing.

Spring Removal/Installation

You need a spring compressor to remove and install the shock springs. When servicing aftermarket shocks, follow the manufacturers instructions.

Refer to **Figure 3**.

1. Remove the shock absorber as described in this chapter.
2. Mount the shock absorber in a spring compressor tool. See **Figure 8**, typical.

WARNING
Do not attempt to remove the spring from the shock absorber without some type of spring compressor tool. Because the spring is under considerable pressure, using makeshift tools or incorrect procedures may allow the spring retainer to fly off, causing severe personal injury.

3. Compress the spring and remove the spring retainer. Then release spring tension and remove the shock absorber from the tool. Complete disassembly by removing the parts in the order shown in **Figure 3**.
4. Harley-Davidson does not list a spring free length specification. If you feel that a spring has sagged, you may want to remove the other shock spring and compare the length of both springs. Replace both springs if there is any appreciable difference.

5. Inspect the spring adjuster for cracks, excessive wear or other damage.
6. Reverse these steps to assemble the shock absorber. Make sure the spring retainer (**Figure 9**) seats in the cover before you remove the shock from the spring tool.

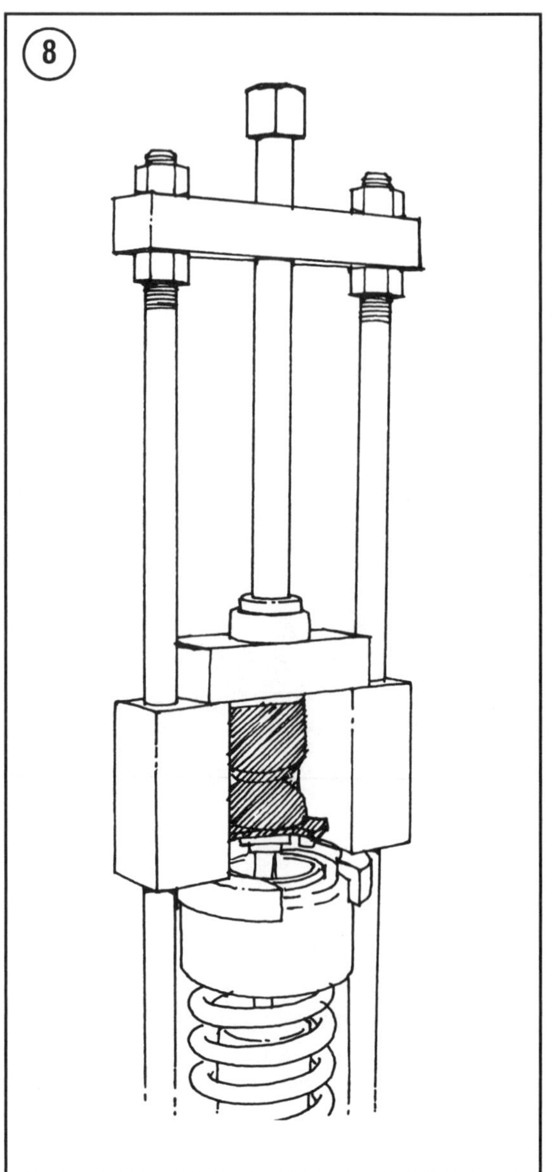

REAR SWING ARM

Refer to **Figure 10** when servicing the swing arm in the following sections.

Rear Swing Arm Bearing Check

The swing arm pivots on a combination bushing and bearing assembly. Because Harley-Davidson does not list a service limit specification for the bushing and bearing assemblies, check for wear or damage with the swing arm mounted on the frame.

1. Remove the rear wheel as described in this chapter.
2. Remove the shock absorber nuts and bolts at the swing arm.
3. Check that the swing arm pivot shaft bolt is tight.

CAUTION
Make sure you securely support the bike before performing Step 4.

4. Grasp the back of the swing arm and try to move it from side to side. Any play (movement) between the swing arm and transmission may suggest worn or damaged swing arm bearings (and bushing). If you note any play, remove the swing arm and inspect the bushing and bearing assemblies.
5. Reverse Steps 1 and 2, or continue with the following procedure.

Swing Arm Removal

1. Remove the left-rear footpeg mounting bracket (**Figure 11**).
2. Remove the upper (A, **Figure 12**) and lower (B, **Figure 12**) belt guards.
3. Remove the rear wheel as described in Chapter Nine.
4. Remove the brake hose bolt and clamp from the swing arm.
5. Remove the rear brake caliper mounting bracket (**Figure 13**) from the swing arm.

6. Remove both shock absorber mounting bolts from the swing arm.

NOTE
*Check the condition of the swing arm bearings as described under **Rear Swing Arm Bearing Check** in the previous section.*

7. Pry the pivot shaft plug (**Figure 14**) from the right-hand side of the swing arm.
8. Remove the cotter pin from the end of the pivot shaft (**Figure 15**). Discard the cotter pin.

9. Hold the nut and loosen the pivot shaft (**Figure 16**) from thc right-hand side. Then pull the shaft out slightly and remove the nut.

10. Support the swing arm and remove the pivot shaft (**Figure 16**). Remove the swing arm (**Figure 17**).

11. Clean and lubricate the swing arm assembly as described in the following procedure. If you are going to replace the swing arm bushing and bearings, refer to *Swing Arm Overhaul* in this section.

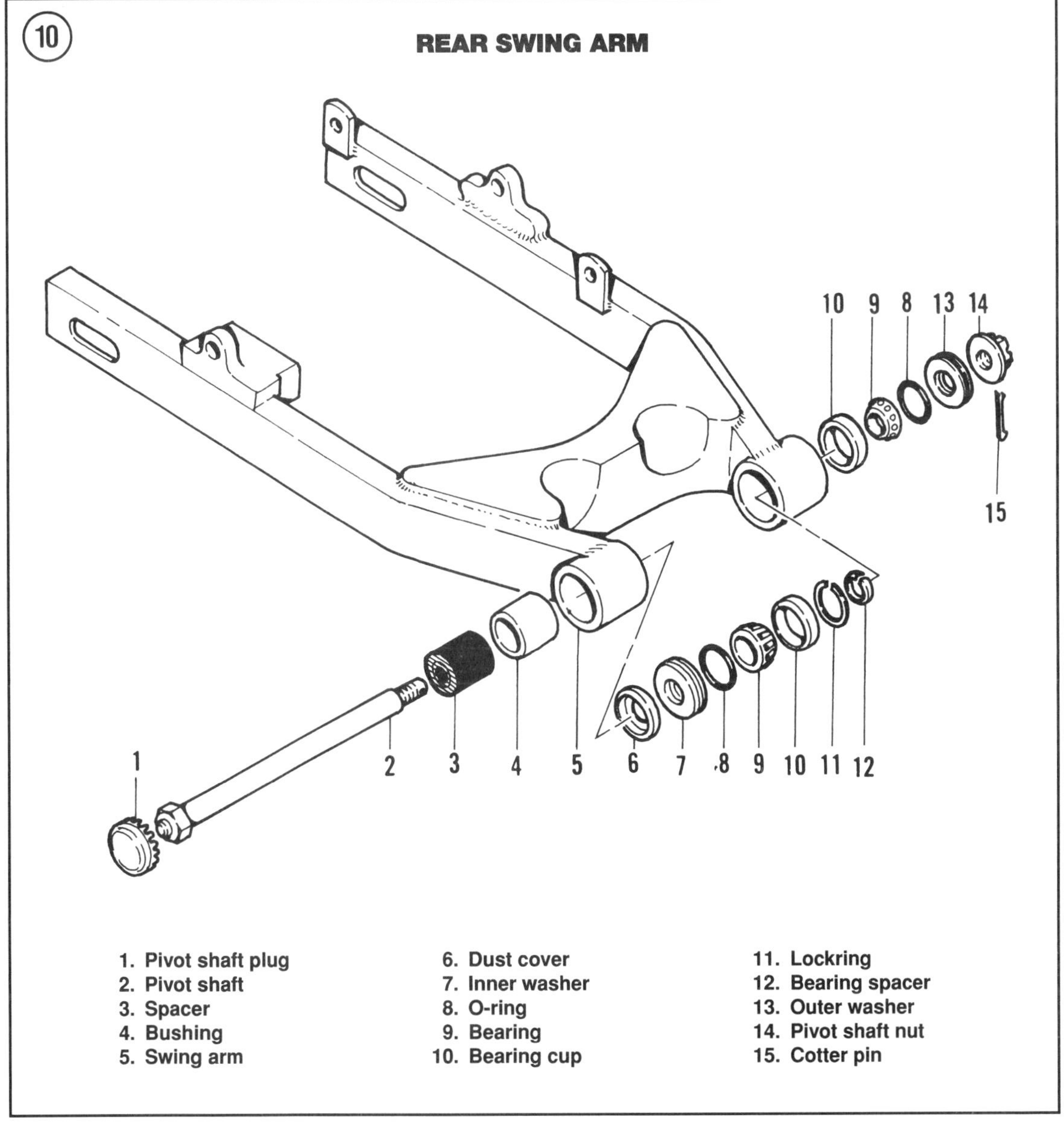

1. Pivot shaft plug
2. Pivot shaft
3. Spacer
4. Bushing
5. Swing arm
6. Dust cover
7. Inner washer
8. O-ring
9. Bearing
10. Bearing cup
11. Lockring
12. Bearing spacer
13. Outer washer
14. Pivot shaft nut
15. Cotter pin

Swing Arm
Bushing and Bearing Lubrication

While Harley-Davidson does not specify a regular maintenance interval for lubricating the swing arm bushing and bearing assemblies, you must clean and lubricate them at least once a year.

Refer to **Figure 10** for this procedure.

1. Remove the right-hand spacer and dust cover (**Figure 18**).

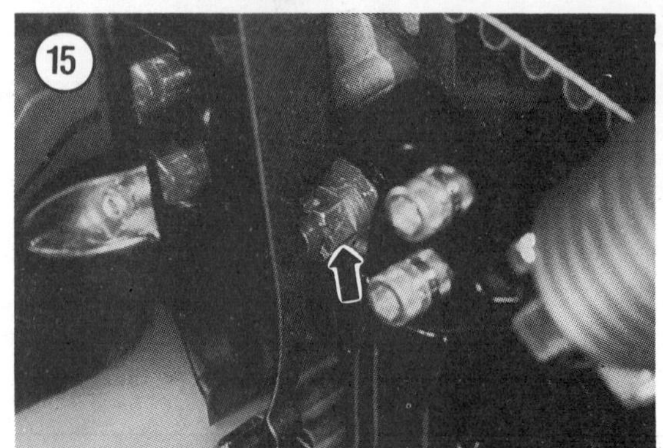

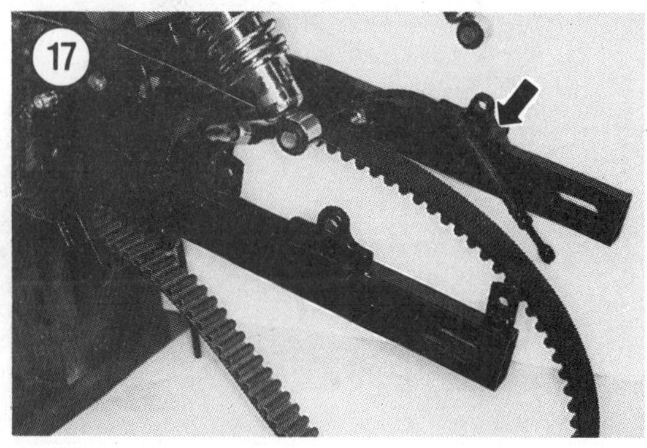

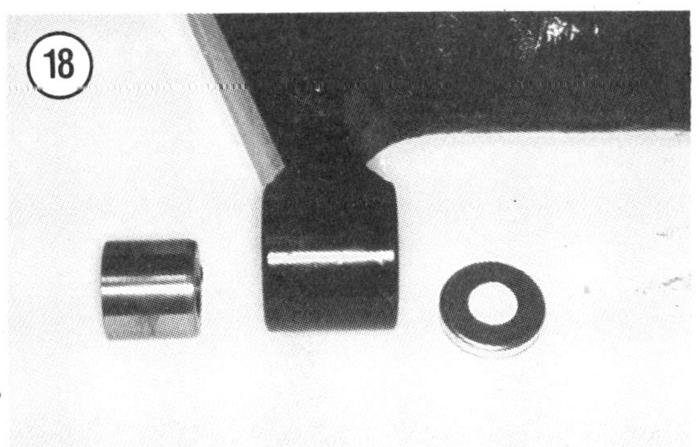

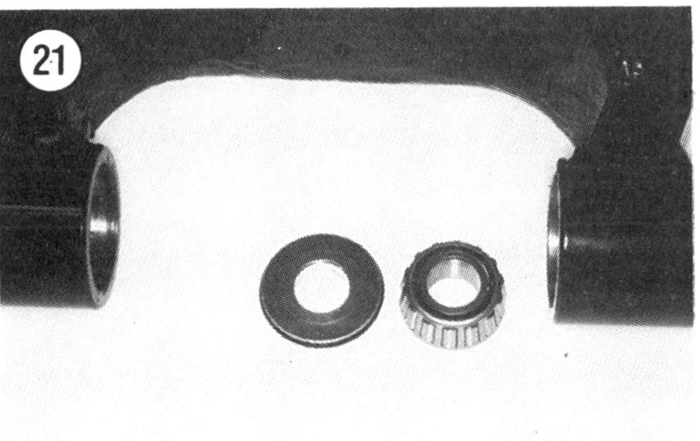

2. From the left-hand side of the swing arm, remove the following:

NOTE

If reusing the roller bearings, install them in their original operating positions. Wear patterns have developed on the individual bearing and cup assemblies and rapid wear could occur if you intermix the bearings. Likewise, the 2 washers installed on the outside of each bearing are different—the outer washer is thicker.

a. Remove the outer washer and bearing (**Figure 19**).
b. Remove the bearing spacer (**Figure 20**).
c. Remove the inner washer and bearing (**Figure 21**).

NOTE

Do not remove the swing arm bushing and bearing cups unless you are going to replace them. Refer to the ***Swing Arm Overhaul*** *in this section.*

3. Clean the pivot shaft, spacer, bushing, bearing cups, and washers in solvent and dry with compressed air, if available.
4. Inspect the O-rings installed in the outer edge of each washer (**Figure 22**). Replace worn or damaged O-rings.
5. Wipe off all excess grease from one roller bearing and then soak it in a container filled with kerosene. Brush the bearing with a soft nylon brush and then blow with compressed air to remove as much of the old grease as possible. Repeat until the bearing is clean with none of the old grease visible. When the bearing is clean, dip it in a container of new kerosene, then remove and blow it off. Wrap the bearing

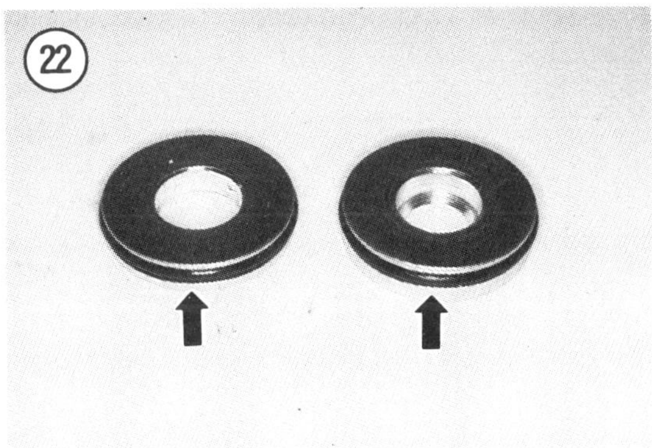

in a piece of wax paper or other lint-free material until reassembly. Repeat for the opposite bearing.

6. To assemble the roller bearing into the left-hand side of the swing arm, perform the following:
   a. Apply wheel bearing grease to each cup (**Figure 23**) installed in the swing arm.
   b. Pack the bearing with wheel bearing grease. If you dont have a bearing packer, take your time and work the grease into the bearing until it is fully packed.
   c. Repeat to lubricate the opposite bearing.

NOTE
*When installing the washers (**Figure 22**) in the following steps, note that the washers are different. Install the washer with the smaller hole diameter into the outside of the swing arm. The pivot shaft will not pass through this washer if it is installed on the inside of the swing arm.* **Figure 24** *shows the pivot shaft and outer washer.*

   d. Apply grease to each of the washer O-rings (**Figure 22**).
   e. Install the outer bearing and washer (**Figure 19**) into the swing arm. Install the outer washer with its wider edge (**Figure 25**) facing out. Make sure the washer is flush with the swing arm as shown in **Figure 26**.
   f. Grease the bearing spacer (**Figure 20**) and install it against the outer bearing.

CAUTION
Install the bearing spacer between the bearing races; otherwise, the bearings may fail during operation.

   g. Install the inner bearing and washer (**Figure 21**) into the swing arm. Install the inner washer with its wider edge (**Figure 27**) facing out.

23

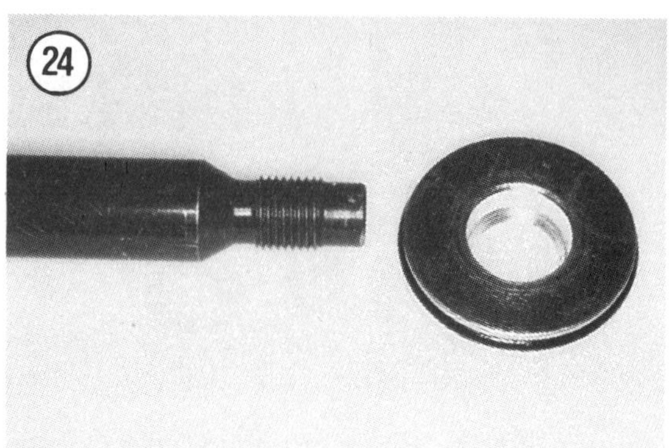
24

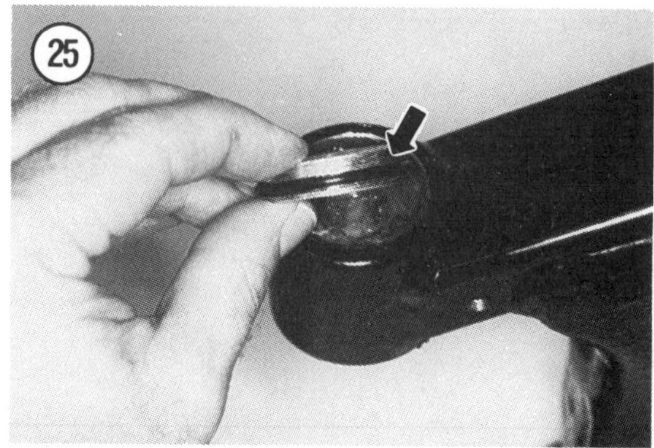
25

26

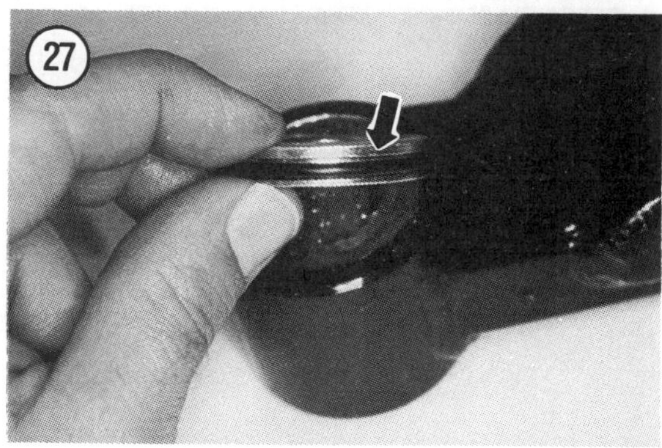
27

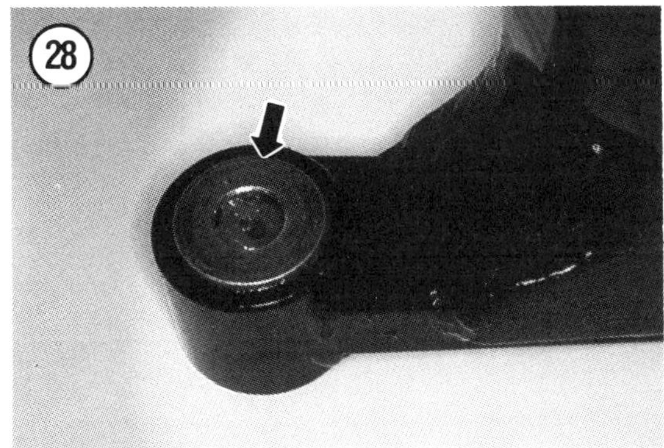

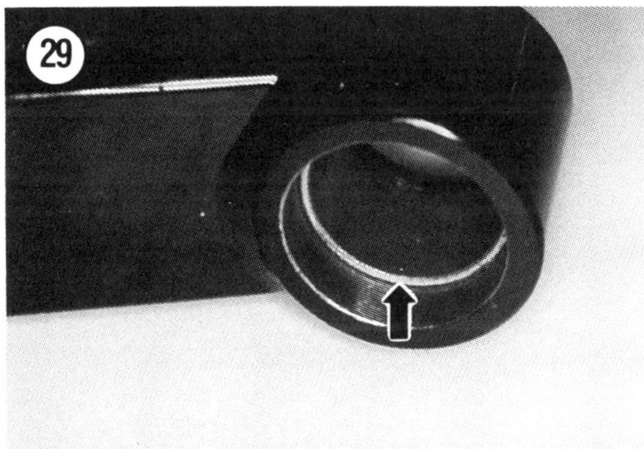

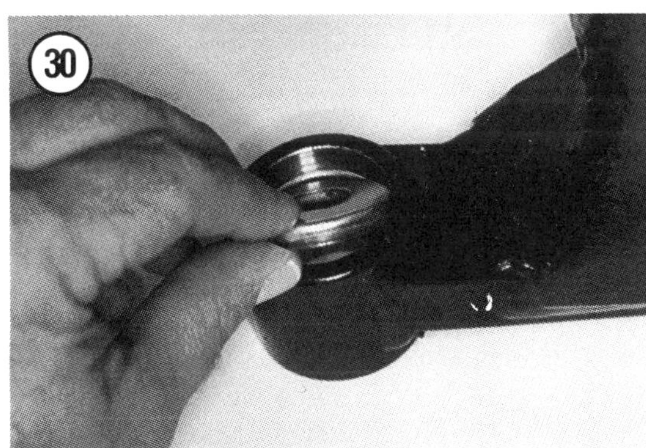

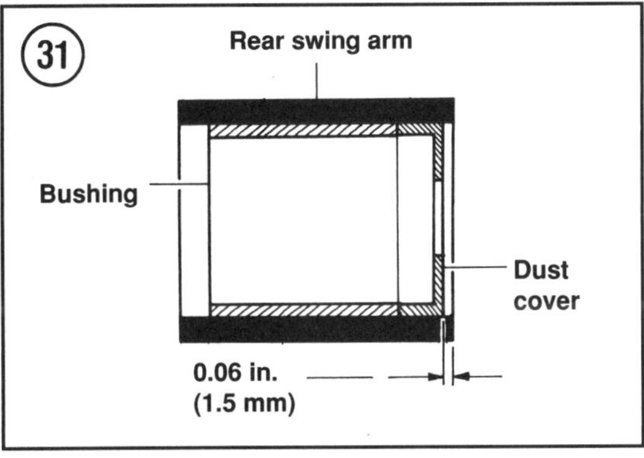

Make sure the washer is flush with the swing arm as shown in **Figure 28**.

7. To install the right-hand spacer and dust cover, perform the following:
   a. Lubricate the spacer and bushing (**Figure 29**) with wheel bearing grease.
   b. Install the dust cover (**Figure 30**) into the swing arm and seat it against the bushing. The dust cover must seat flush with or be recessed 0.06 in. (1.5 mm) from the edge of the swing arm. See **Figure 31**.
   c. Install the spacer (**Figure 18**) through the bushing and seat it against the dust cover.
8. Install the rear swing arm as described in this chapter.

Swing Arm Overhaul

This procedure describes how to replace the swing arm bushing and bearing cup assemblies.

1. Remove the spacer and roller bearing assemblies as described under *Swing Arm Bushing and Bearing Lubrication* in this chapter.
2. To replace the bushing (**Figure 29**), perform the following:
   a. Before removing the bushing (**Figure 29**), measure its installed position from the inside edge of the swing arm to the bushing edge.
   b. Using an expandable puller or a press, remove the bushing (**Figure 29**) from the swing arm.
   c. Clean the swing arm bushing bore with solvent and dry with compressed air, if available.
   d. Align the new bushing with the spring arm and press it into the swing arm.
3. To remove the bearing cups (**Figure 23**), perform the following:
   a. **Figure 32** shows a complete roller bearing assembly. Do not intermix the bearing assemblies.
   b. Remove the inner and outer bearing cups (**Figure 23**) from the swing arm with a puller. Discard the bearing assembly. See **Figure 33**.
4. To replace the lock ring (**Figure 34**), perform the following:

NOTE

*The lock ring (**Figure 34**) seats in a groove inside the swing arm. Because the lock ring is under tension, prying it out of the swing arm will damage the* *bearing bore. The following steps describe how to remove the lock ring.*

a. Insert a fine tooth hacksaw blade (24 or 32 teeth per in.) through the swing arm bearing bore and mount it onto a hacksaw (**Figure 35**). Then, starting at the center of the lock ring, cut the ring down to the swing arm. Do *not* cut into the swing arm.
b. Make a second and third cut close to the original cut. These cuts help weaken the lock ring.
c. Then, using a screwdriver at one end of the lock ring, carefully pry it up and out of the swing arm groove. If the lock ring is still under sufficient tension, try to remove it at the other end. Remove and discard the lock ring.
d. Clean the lock ring groove.

WARNING
Wear safety glasses when installing the lock ring.

e. To install the new lock ring (**Figure 36**), first lubricate the swing arm bore with oil. This helps the ring slide through the bore without damaging it. The lock ring is compressed when installing it in the swing arm. To do this, tap the lock ring into the swing arm with a hammer (**Figure 37**). When the ring is in the bore, turn it so that it is parallel with the groove. Then drive or press it into the groove with a suitable bearing driver. Check that the lock ring (**Figure 34**)seats in the groove.

5. Press the inner and outer bearing cups (**Figure 33**) into the swing arm (**Figure 23**). Seat both bearings against the lock ring.
6. Install the spacer and roller bearing assemblies as described under *Swing Arm Bushing and Bearing Lubrication* in this chapter.

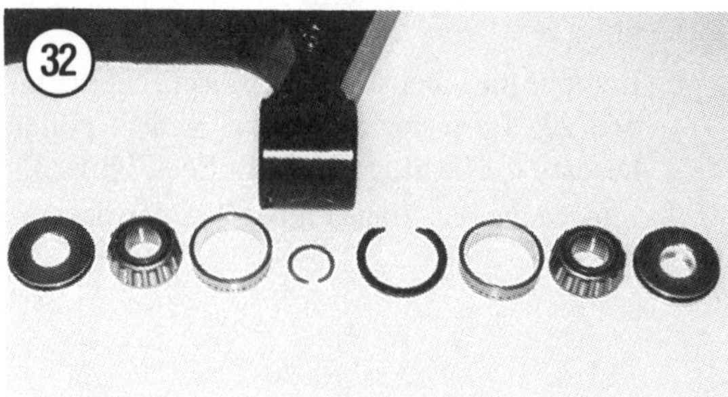

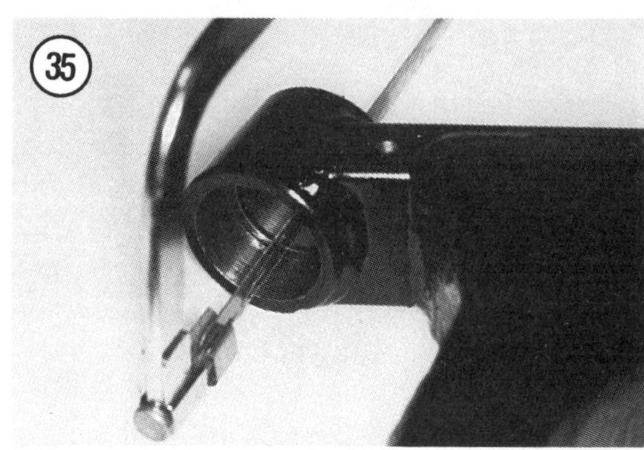

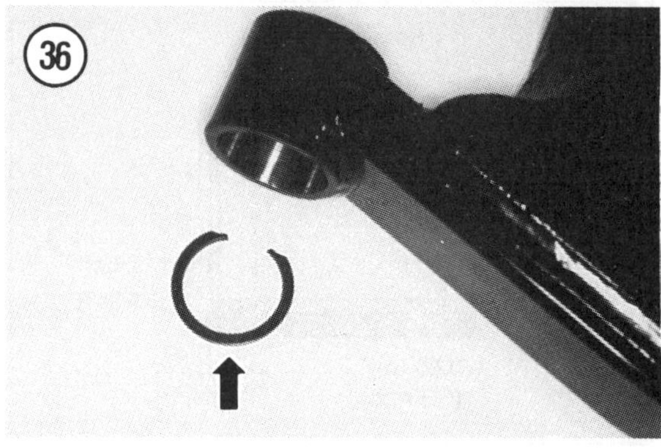

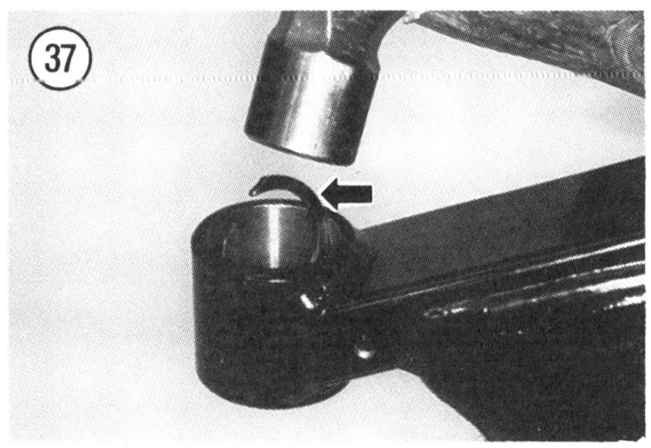
37

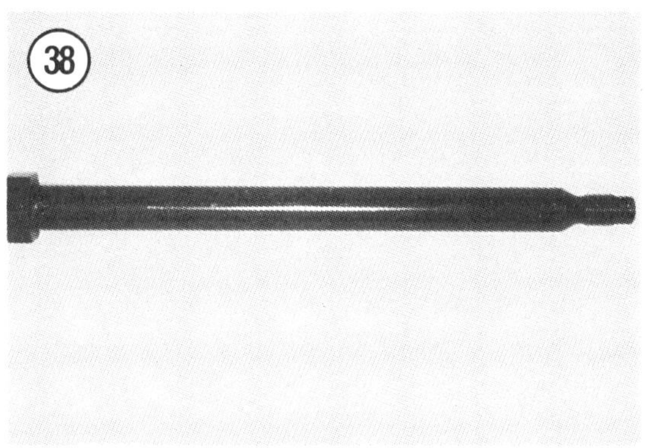
38

39

40

Swing Arm Installation

1. Lubricate the pivot shaft (**Figure 38**) with wheel bearing grease.
2. If removed, install the spacer, roller bearings and washers as described under *Swing Arm Bushing and Bearing Lubrication* in this chapter.
3. Slide the swing arm onto the transmission housing mounting boss. Make sure you install and position the drive belt toward the swing arm. See **Figure 39**.
4. Install the pivot shaft through the frame and swing arm from the right-hand side (**Figure 40**).
5. Install the pivot shaft nut (**Figure 41**). Then tighten the pivot shaft to the torque specification in **Table 1**.
6. Install a *new* cotter pin through the pivot shaft and nut.
7. Grasp the swing arm with your hand and swing it up and down. The swing arm must move without binding or excessive bearing play.
8. Install the pivot shaft plug (**Figure 42**) into the right-hand side of the swing arm.
9. Install and tighten both shock absorber bolts and nuts at the swing arm. Tighten the nuts to the torque specification in **Table 1**.

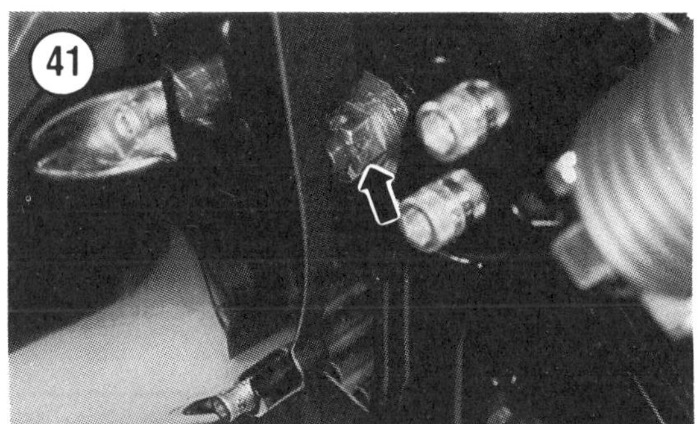
41

42

10. Route the rear brake hose along the inside of the swing arm and secure it with its clamp and bolt. See **Figure 43**.
11. Install the rear brake caliper mounting bracket (**Figure 44**) onto the swing arm.
12. If removed, install the chain adjusters (**Figure 45**) into the end of the swing arm.
13. Install the rear wheel as described in Chapter Nine.
14. Install the upper (A, **Figure 46**) and lower (B, **Figure 46**) belt guards.
15. If removed, install the left-rear footpeg mounting bracket (**Figure 47**). Tighten the bolts securely.

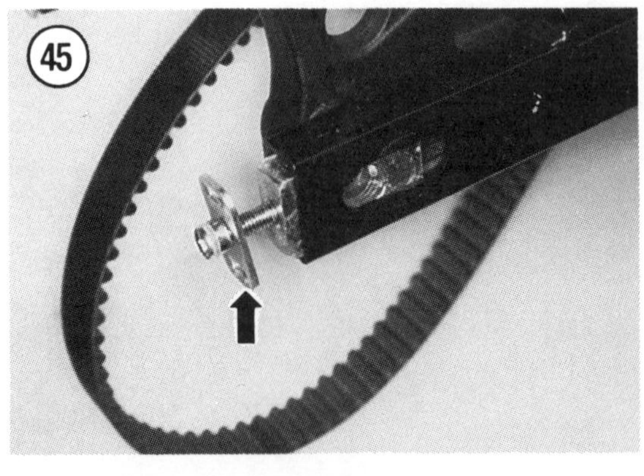

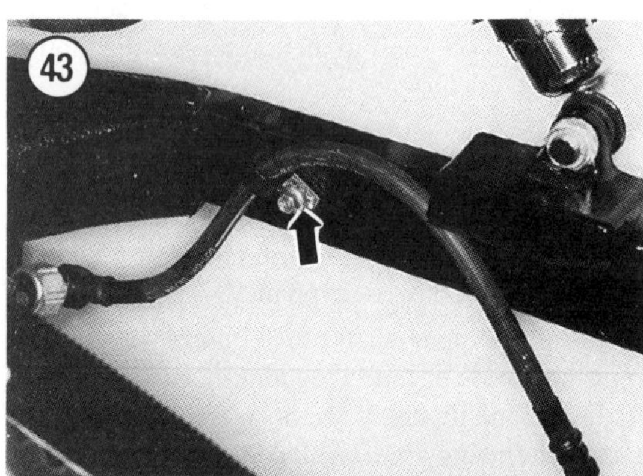

Table 1 REAR SUSPENSION TIGHTENING TORQUES

	ft.-lb.	N•m
Rear shock absorbers		
Upper stud Acorn nut	25-40	34-54
Bottom bolt	25-40	34-54
Swing arm pivot shaft	70	95

CHAPTER TWELVE

BRAKES

This chapter describes repair and replacement procedure for all brake components.
Table 1 and **Table 2** are at the end of the chapter.

Brake Fluid

The brake system is designed to use *silicone-base DOT 5 brake fluid*. DOT 3, DOT 4 and DOT 5.1 brake fluids are not silicone-based brake fluid and must *not* be used in your Dyna Glide. Use of non-silicone-based brake fluid in your Dyna Glide can cause brake failure. If a nonsilicone-based brake fluid is used, the system is contaminated and you must overhaul and flush the brake system. You will have to replace all of the rubber hoses and seals in the hydraulic system.

Disc Brake System Service Hints

Consider the following before servicing the front and rear disc brake systems.

1. Disc brake components rarely require disassembly, so do not disassemble them unless necessary.
2. When adding brake fluid, use DOT 5 silicone-based brake fluid. See *Brake Fluid* in this chapter for additional information.
3. Keep the master cylinder reservoir covers closed to prevent contamination.
4. Use only DOT 5 silicone-based brake fluid to wash parts. Never clean any internal brake component with solvent. Solvents will cause the seals to swell and distort and require replacement.
5. Whenever you disconnect *any* brake line, the system is considered "opened." After opening the system, you must bleed the line to remove air bubbles. Also, if the brake feels "spongy," this usually means air is in the system. For safe brake operation, refer to *Bleeding the System* in this chapter for complete details.
6. When working on hydraulic brake systems, keep the work area and all tools clean. Any tiny particles of foreign matter or grit on the caliper assembly or the master cylinder can damage the components. Also, do not use sharp tools inside the caliper or on the caliper piston.

7. If there is any doubt about your ability to carry out major service on the brake components correctly and safely, refer the job to a Harley-Davidson dealership.

FRONT BRAKE PADS

There is no recommended mileage interval for changing the friction pads in the disc brake. Pad wear depends greatly on riding habits and conditions. Check the pads for wear at the intervals listed in Chapter Three and replace when the lining thickness reaches 1/16 in. (1.6 mm) or less. To maintain an even brake pressure on the disc, replace both (or all 4) pads at the same time.

Replacement

Refer to **Figure 1** for this procedure.

1. Park the bike on a level surface.
2. Loosen the upper brake caliper mounting screw (A, **Figure 2**) and the lower mounting pin (B, **Figure 2**). Remove the upper screw and washer and the mounting pin.
3. Slide the brake caliper (**Figure 3**) off the brake disc.

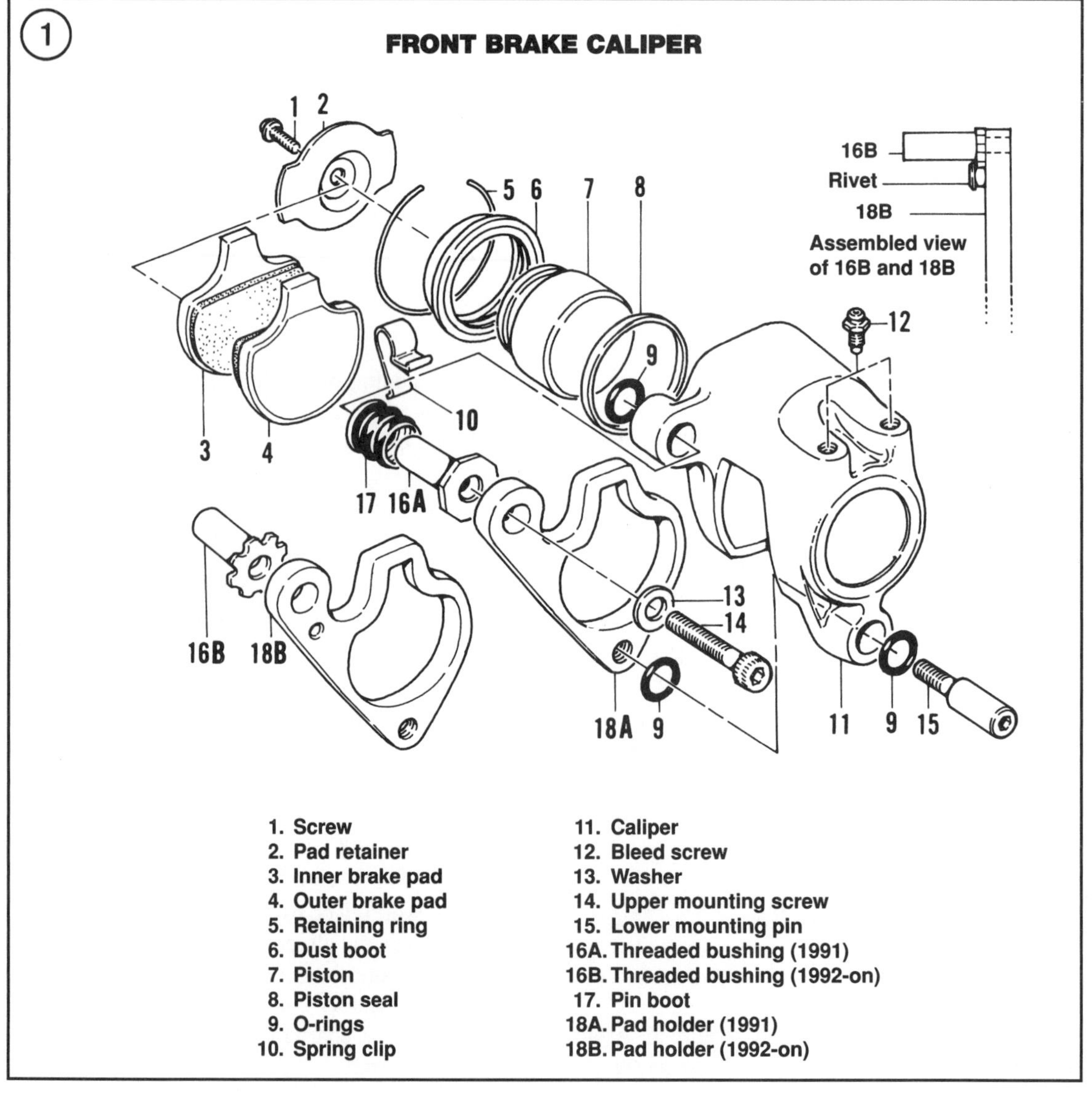

1. Screw
2. Pad retainer
3. Inner brake pad
4. Outer brake pad
5. Retaining ring
6. Dust boot
7. Piston
8. Piston seal
9. O-rings
10. Spring clip
11. Caliper
12. Bleed screw
13. Washer
14. Upper mounting screw
15. Lower mounting pin
16A. Threaded bushing (1991)
16B. Threaded bushing (1992-on)
17. Pin boot
18A. Pad holder (1991)
18B. Pad holder (1992-on)

NOTE
If you intend to reuse the brake pads, mark them so that you can reinstall them in their original mounting position.

4. Remove the outer pad, pad holder and spring clip as an assembly (**Figure 4**).

5. Remove the screw (A, **Figure 5**), pad retainer (B, **Figure 5**) and inner pad (**Figure 6**).

6. Push the outer pad (A, **Figure 7**) free of the spring clip (B, **Figure 7**) and remove it. See **Figure 8**.

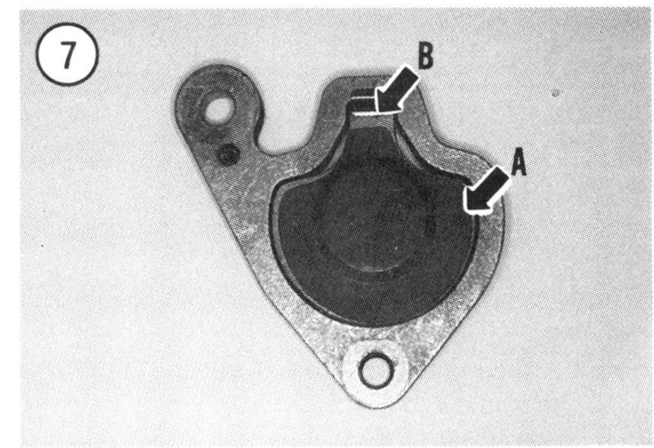

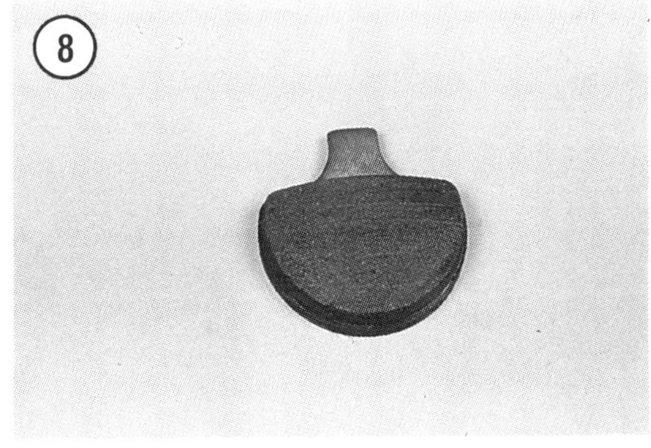

7. Check the brake pads (**Figure 8**) for wear or damage. Measure the thickness of the brake pad friction material (**Figure 9**). Replace the brake pads if they are worn to 1/16 in. (1.6 mm) or less. Replace both pad sets (left and right calipers) at the same time.

8. Inspect the upper mounting screw and the lower-mounting pin (**Figure 10**). Replace if damaged or badly corroded.

9. Replace the pad retainer (**Figure 11**) if damaged.

10. Check the piston dust boot (**Figure 12**) in the caliper. Remove and overhaul the caliper if the boot is swollen or damaged, or if brake fluid is leaking from the caliper. Refer to *Front Brake Caliper* in this chapter.

11. Remove all corrosion from the pad holder.

12. Replace the spring clip (10, **Figure 1**) if damaged or badly corroded.

13. Check the brake disc for wear as described under *Brake Disc* in this chapter. Service the brake disc if necessary.

14. Assemble the pad holder, spring clip and outer brake pad as follows:

a. Lay the pad holder on a workbench so that the upper mounting screw hole is positioned at the upper right as shown in A, **Figure 13**.
b. Install the spring clip (B, **Figure 13**) at the top of the pad holder so that the spring loop faces in the direction shown in **Figure 14**.
c. The outer brake pad has an insulator pad mounted on its backside (A, **Figure 7**).
d. Center the outer brake pad into the pad holder so that the lower end of the pad rests inside the pad holder. Then push firmly on the upper end of the brake pad, past the spring clip and into the holder. See **Figure 13**.

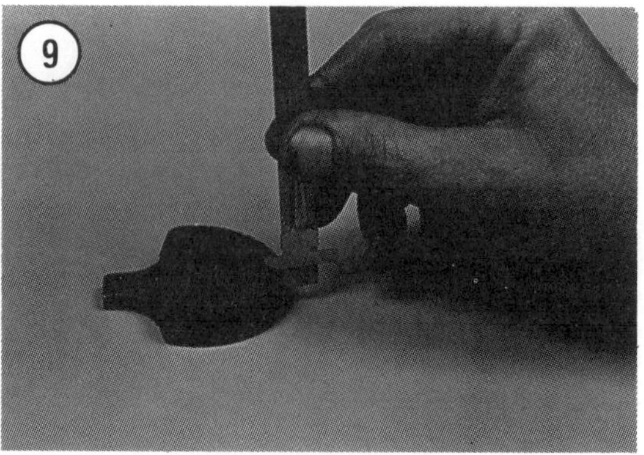

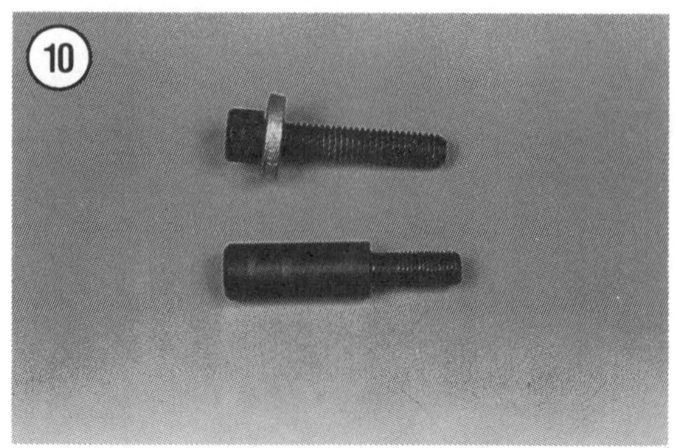

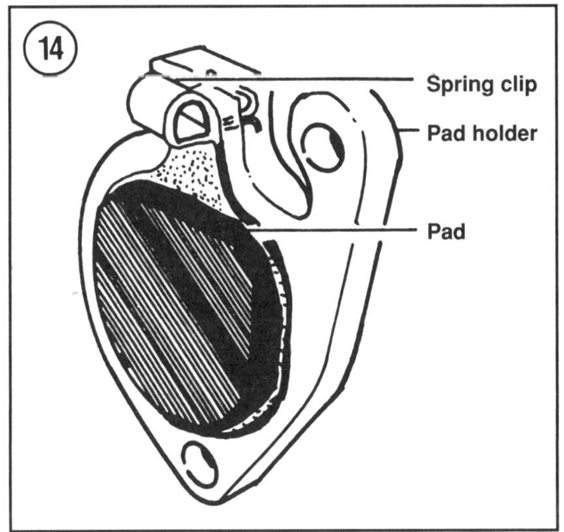

NOTE

*After installing new brake pads, you must push the caliper piston back into the caliper before installing the caliper over the brake disc. While this step makes room for the new pads, doing so will force brake fluid to back up into the master cylinder reservoir. To prevent the reservoir from overflowing, first remove the reservoir cover (**Figure 15**) and diaphragm. Then watch the brake fluid level as you reposition the piston in Step 15.*

15. Hold the caliper with both hands and push the piston (**Figure 12**) into the cylinder with your fingers. Reinstall the master cylinder diaphragm and cover (**Figure 15**) but do not install the cover screws.
16. Install the inner brake pad (without the insulator backing) in the caliper's recessed seat (**Figure 6**).
17. Insert the pad retainer (B, **Figure 5**) in the caliper counterbore. Install the pad retainer screw (A, **Figure 5**) through the pad retainer and thread it into the brake pad. Tighten the screw to the torque specification in **Table 2**.

WARNING

The caliper bushings locate the brake caliper on the fork tube in relation to the brake disc. Do not install the caliper without the bushings in place (Step 18); otherwise, the brake may lockup when applied and cause you to lose control.

18. If removed, install the caliper bushings into the fork tube lugs as shown in **Figure 16**.
19. To install the outer brake pad/pad holder assembly (**Figure 4**), note the following:

WARNING

The spring clip loop and the brake pad friction material must face away from the piston when you install the pad holder in the caliper. Brake failure will occur if you assemble the brake pads incorrectly.

a. Insert the outer brake pad/pad holder assembly into the caliper so that the brake pad insulator backing faces against the piston.
b. Position the threaded bushing flange (**Figure 17**) so that its shoulder is installed between the pad holder and its rivet head as shown in **Figure 1**. If the threaded bushing shoulder is

machined with a series of U-shaped notches, position the bushing so that one notch engages the rivet (**Figure 18**).

CAUTION
*The brake caliper threaded bushing shoulder (**Figure 17**) must be positioned as described in Step 19. Otherwise, the pad holder rivet and bushing will be damaged when you tighten the caliper mounting screw and pin.*

20. Install the caliper over the brake disc, making sure the friction surface on each pad faces against the disc.

21. Coat the lower mounting pin shoulder (**Figure 19**) with Dow Corning Moly 44 grease.

22. Align the 2 mounting holes in the caliper with the fork tube mounting lugs. Then install the screw and mounting pin as follows:

   a. Install a washer onto the upper mounting screw and insert the screw through the slider lug and then thread into the caliper bushing (A, **Figure 2**). Install the screw finger-tight.
   b. Insert the lower mounting pin (B, **Figure 2**) through the caliper and then thread into the slider lug. Tighten mounting pin finger-tight.
   c. Tighten the lower mounting pin to the torque specification in **Table 2**.
   d. Tighten the upper mounting screw to the torque specification in **Table 2**.

23. Repeat Steps 2-22 to replace the brake shoes in the opposite brake caliper.

24. Refill the master cylinder reservoir with DOT 5 silicone-based brake fluid, if necessary, to maintain the correct fluid level. Install the diaphragm and top cap (**Figure 15**).

25. Squeeze the front brake lever several times to seat the pads against the disc.

WARNING
Do not ride the motorcycle until you are sure the brakes are operating correctly with full hydraulic advantage. If necessary, bleed the brake system as described in this chapter.

FRONT BRAKE CALIPER

Removal/Installation (Caliper Will Not Be Disassembled)

To remove the brake caliper without disassembling it, perform this procedure. If you are going to disassemble the brake caliper, go to the *Caliper Removal/Piston Removal* procedure in this section.

1A. To remove the brake caliper from the bike, perform the following:

   a. Loosen and remove the banjo bolt at the caliper (A, **Figure 20**). Remove the bolt and the 2 washers.
   b. Remove the upper mounting screw and washer (B, **Figure 20**) and the lower mounting pin (C, **Figure 20**).
   c. Lift the brake caliper off the brake disc and remove it.

1B. To remove the brake caliper partially from the bike (brake hose will not be disconnected), perform the following:

18

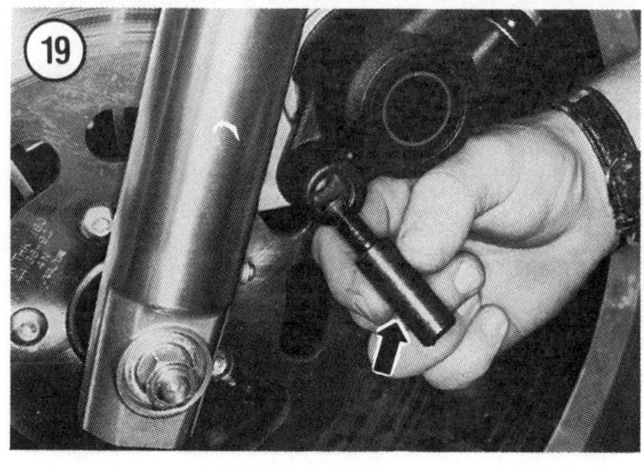
19

a. Remove the upper mounting screw and washer (B, **Figure 20**) and the lower mounting pin (C, **Figure 20**).
b. Lift the brake caliper off the brake disc.
c. Insert a wooden or plastic spacer block between the brake pads (**Figure 21**) in the caliper.

NOTE
Squeezing the brake lever with the caliper removed from the brake disc will force the piston out of its bore. Using the spacer block as mentioned in the previous step can prevent this from happening.

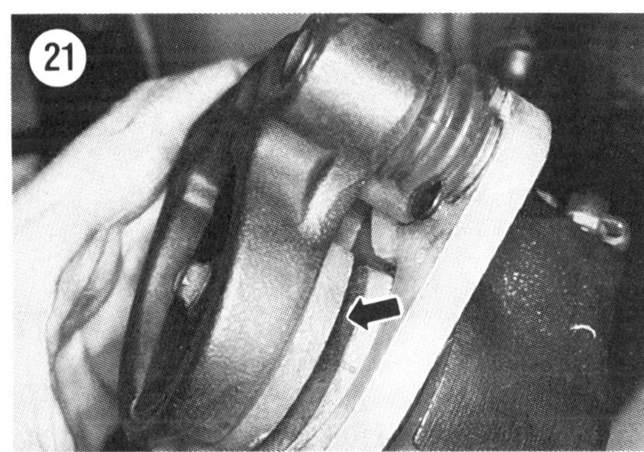

d. Support the caliper with a piece of heavy wire.

2. Install the brake caliper by reversing these steps, while noting the following.

WARNING
The caliper bushings locate the brake caliper on the fork tube in relation to the brake disc. Do not install the caliper without the bushings in place (Step 3); otherwise, the brake may lockup when applied and cause you to lose control.

3. If removed, install the caliper bushings into the fork tube lugs as shown in **Figure 16**.
4. If removed, install the brake pads as described in this chapter.
5. Install the caliper over the brake disc, making sure the friction surface on each pad faces against the disc.
6. Coat the lower mounting pin (**Figure 19**) with Dow Corning Moly 44 grease.
7. Align the 2 mounting holes in the caliper with the slider mounting lugs.
8. Align the 2 mounting holes in the caliper with the fork tube mounting lugs. Then install the screw and mounting pin as follows:
   a. Install a washer onto the upper mounting screw and insert the screw through the slider lug and then thread into the caliper bushing (B, **Figure 20**). Install the screw finger-tight.
   b. Insert the lower mounting pin (C, **Figure 20**) through the caliper and then thread into the slider lug. Tighten mounting pin finger-tight.
   c. Tighten the lower mounting pin to the torque specification in **Table 2**.
   d. Tighten the upper mounting screw to the torque specification in **Table 2**.
9. Tighten the bleed screw.

NOTE
*Install **new** steel/rubber banjo bolt washers (**Figure 22**) when performing Step 10.*

10. If removed, assemble the brake line onto the caliper by placing a new washer on both sides of the brake line fitting, then secure the fitting to the caliper with the banjo bolt (A, **Figure 20**). Tighten the banjo bolt to the torque specification in **Table 2**. Make sure

the fitting seats against the caliper as shown in A, **Figure 20**.

11. If necessary, refill the system and bleed the brake as described in this chapter.

12. Squeeze the front brake lever several times to seat the pads against the disc.

WARNING
Do not ride the motorcycle until you are sure the brakes are operating properly.

Caliper Removal/Piston Removal (Caliper Will Be Disassembled)

If disassembling the brake caliper, the piston must be forced out of the caliper bore. To do this, you can use hydraulic pressure in the brake system or compressed air. When using the system's hydraulic pressure, you must do so prior to disconnecting the brake hose from the caliper. This procedure describes how to remove the piston with the caliper mounted on the bike.

1. Remove the brake pads as described in this chapter.
2. Insert a small screwdriver into the notched groove machined in the bottom of the piston bore. Then pry the retaining ring (5, **Figure 23**) out of the caliper body.
3. To remove the piston, perform the following:
   a. Wrap a large cloth around the brake caliper.
   b. Hold the caliper with your hand and fingers placed away from the piston/brake pad area.

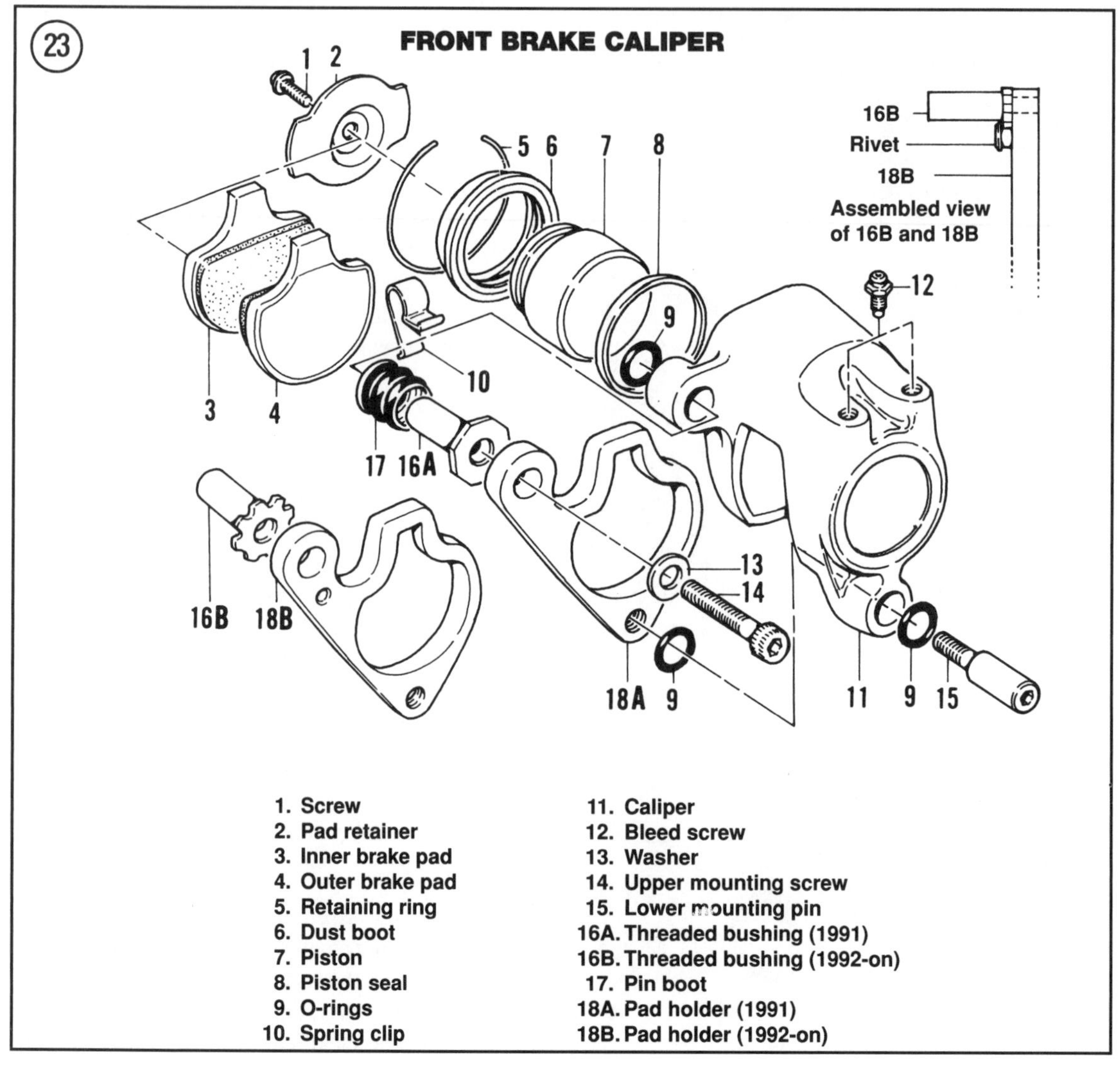

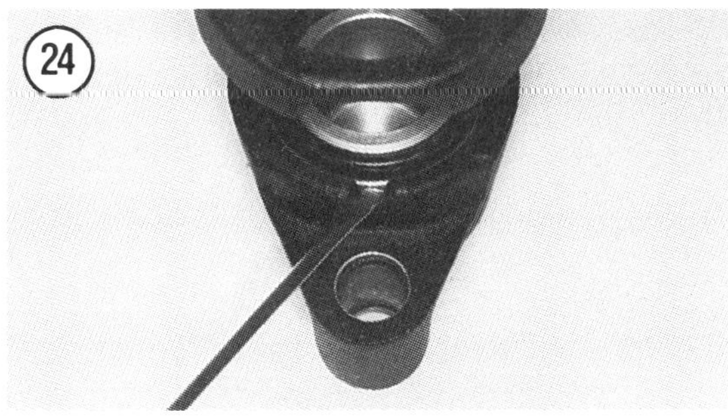

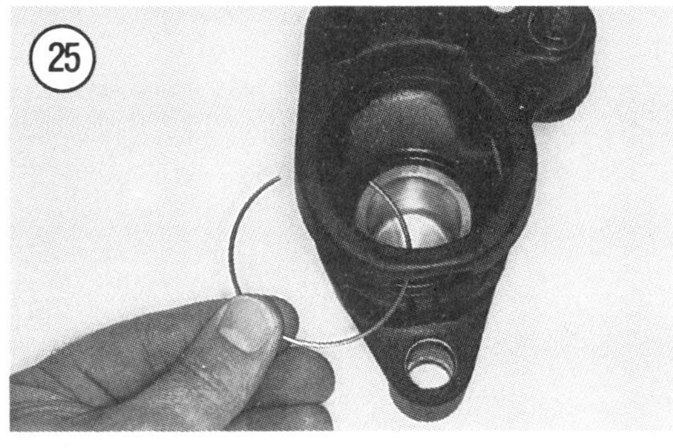

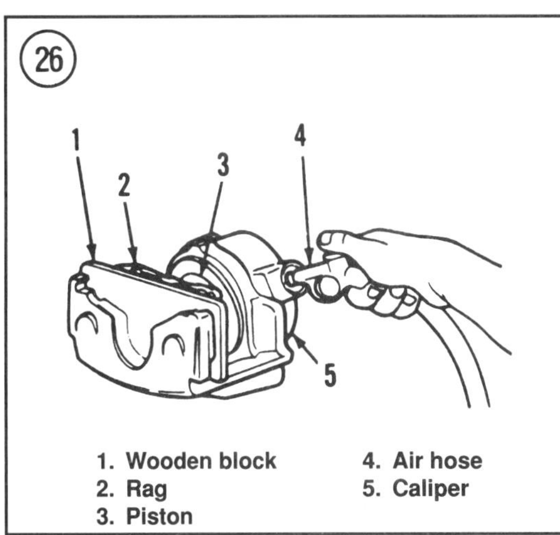

1. Wooden block
2. Rag
3. Piston
4. Air hose
5. Caliper

c. Operate the front brake lever to force the piston out of the caliper. Remove the piston and dust seal.

NOTE
If the piston did not come out in Step 3, use compressed air to remove it. Refer to ***Disassembly*** *in this section.*

4. Remove the caliper banjo bolt (A, **Figure 20**) and washers. Plug the brake hose to prevent leakage and to keep out dirt.

Disassembly

Harley-Davidson does not provide service specifications on any of the front caliper components (except brake pads). Replace any worn, damaged or questionable part.

Refer to **Figure 23** for this procedure.

1. Remove the brake pads as described in this chapter.

NOTE
If you previously removed the piston, go to Step 5.

2. Insert a small screwdriver into the piston bore notched groove (**Figure 24**) and pry the retaining ring out of the groove (**Figure 25**).

WARNING
When performing Step 3, the piston can shoot out of the caliper like a bullet. Keep your hand and fingers out of the way. Wear shop gloves and apply compressed air gradually.

3. Place a rag or piece of wood in the piston's path (**Figure 26**). Then apply compressed air to the hydraulic hose opening and blow the piston out.
4. Remove the piston and dust boot assembly (**Figure 27**).
5. Remove the piston seal (**Figure 28**) from the groove in the caliper body.
6. Pull the threaded bushing out of the caliper, then remove the pin boot. See **Figure 29**.
7. Remove the 3 O-rings from the caliper body. See **Figure 30**, typical.

Inspection

1. Inspect the caliper for damage. Do not hone or bore the piston bore.
2. Inspect the hydraulic fluid passageway in the cylinder bore. Make sure it is clean and open. Apply compressed air to the opening and make sure it is clear. Clean out, if necessary, with fresh brake fluid.
3. Inspect the piston and cylinder bore (**Figure 31**) for scratches, scoring or other damage. Replace worn, corroded or damaged parts.
4. Inspect the banjo bolt and bleed valve threads in the caliper body. If damaged, repair the threads with the proper size thread tap. If the threads are worn or damaged beyond repair, replace the caliper body.
5. Make sure the hole in the bleed valve screw is clean and open. Clean with compressed air.
6. Check the threaded bushing, upper mounting screw and the lower mounting pin for thread damage. Repair threads or replace damaged parts as required. Check the mounting pin shoulder for deep scoring or excessive wear.
7. Check the pad retainer for cracks or damage.
8. Check the brake pads (**Figure 8**) for wear or damage. Measure the thickness of the brake pad friction material (**Figure 9**). Replace the brake pads if they are worn to 1/16 in. (1.6 mm) or less. Replace both pad sets (left and right calipers) at the same time.
9. Check all of the rubber parts (dust boot, O-rings, piston seal and hoses.) for cracks, wear or deterioration. Because very minor damage or deterioration can make these parts useless, replace questionable parts. If you plan to reuse a rubber part, clean the part thoroughly in new brake fluid and place on a lint-free cloth until reassembly.
10. Clean all serviceable metal parts with rubbing alcohol.

Assembly

1. The parts equipped in a factory rebuild kit are identified in **Figure 32**. After replacing all worn or damaged parts, coat the following parts with new DOT 5 brake fluid. To prevent contamination, place the parts on a clean lint-free cloth.
   a. Piston.
   b. Piston seal.
2. Make sure the retaining ring, piston and caliper bore are thoroughly clean.

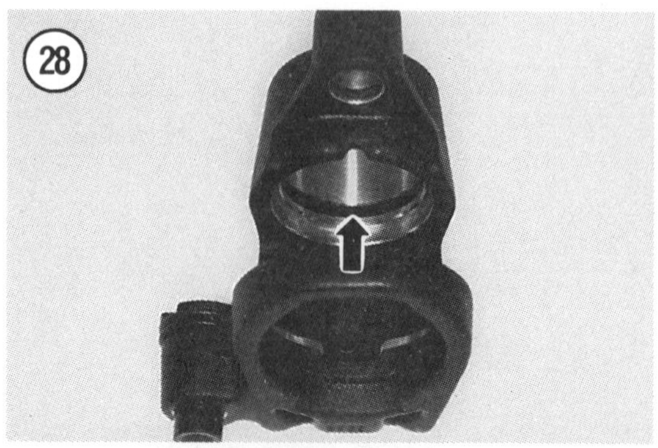
28

29

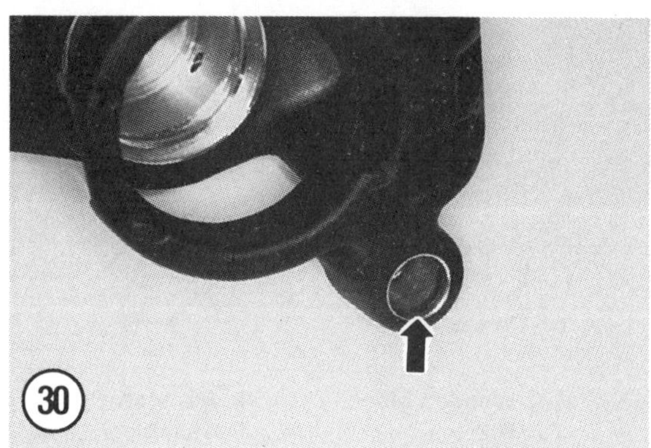
30

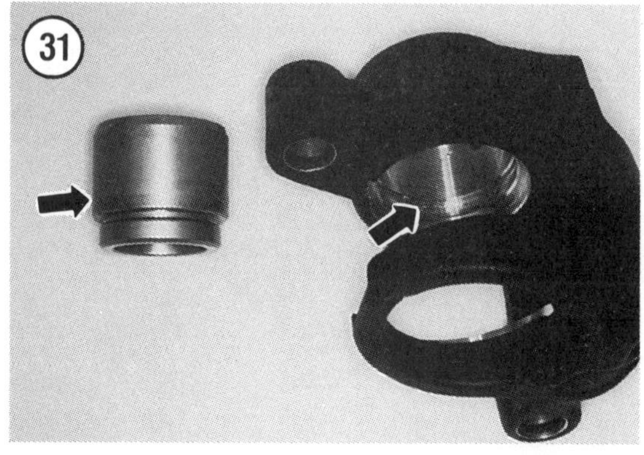
31

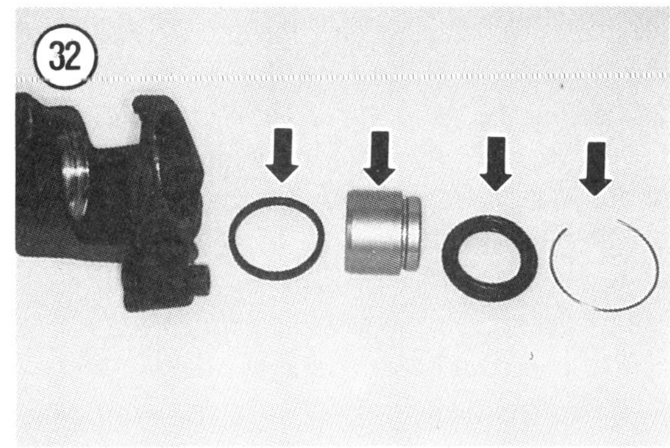

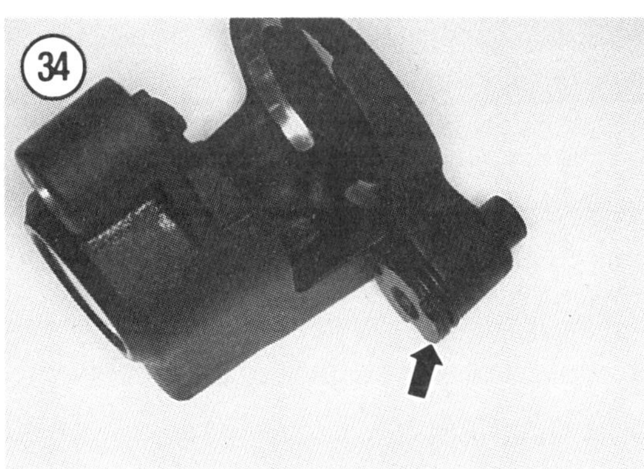

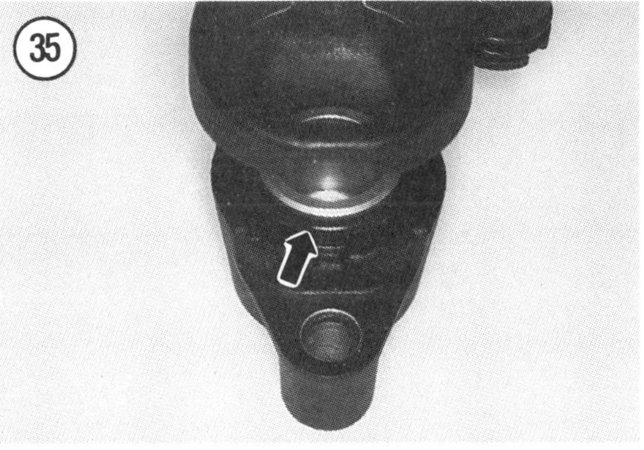

3. Install the piston seal (**Figure 28**) into the caliper body groove.
4. Install the 3 O-rings into the caliber grooves. See **Figure 23**.
5. Wipe the inside of the pin boot with Dow Corning MOLY 44 grease. Then insert the boot into the bushing bore with the boots flange end seating in the bore groove (**Figure 33**).
6. Insert the threaded bushing into the boot (**Figure 34**).
7. Install the piston dust boot on the piston *before* the piston is installed in the caliper bore. Perform the following:
   a. Place the piston on your workbench with its open side facing up.
   b. Align the piston dust boot with the piston so that the shoulder on the dust boot faces up.
   c. Slide the piston dust boot onto the piston until the inner lip on the dust boot seats in the piston groove (**Figure 27**).
8. Coat the piston and the caliper bore with DOT 5 brake fluid.
9. Align the piston with the caliper bore so that its open end faces out (**Figure 27**). Then push the piston in until it bottoms out.
10. Seat the piston dust boot (**Figure 35**) into the caliper bore.
11. Find the retaining ring groove in the end of the caliper bore. Then align the retaining (**Figure 25**) ring so that its gap (**Figure 36**) is at the top of the caliper bore. Then install the ring into the ring groove. Make sure you correctly seat the retaining ring in the groove.

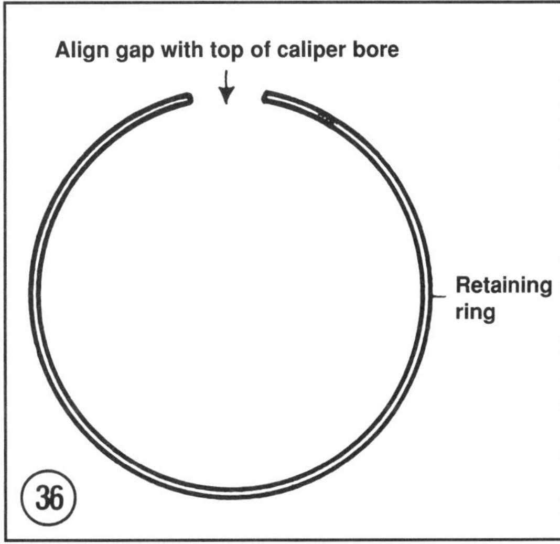

12. Wipe the caliper mounting lug bores with Dow Corning MOLY 44 grease.
13. Install the brake pads as described in this chapter.

FRONT MASTER CYLINDER

Removal/Installation

Refer to **Figure 37** for this procedure.

1. Insert a hose onto the end of the bleeder valve (**Figure 38**). Insert the open end of the hose into a container. Open the front bleeder valve and operate the hand lever to drain the brake fluid from the front brake assembly. Remove the hose and close the bleeder valve after draining the assembly. Discard the brake fluid.
2. Remove the banjo bolt and washers securing the brake hose to the master cylinder (A, **Figure 39**).
3. Remove the master cylinder screws (B, **Figure 39**) from the handlebar.
4. Install the master cylinder by reversing these removal steps, while noting the following.
5. Clean the handlebar of all brake fluid residue.
6. Clean the banjo bolt (**Figure 40**) with compressed air.
7. Check the clamp for cracks or damage. Replace the clamp if necessary.
8. Position the master cylinder and clamp onto the handlebar and secure with the 2 screws (B, **Figure**

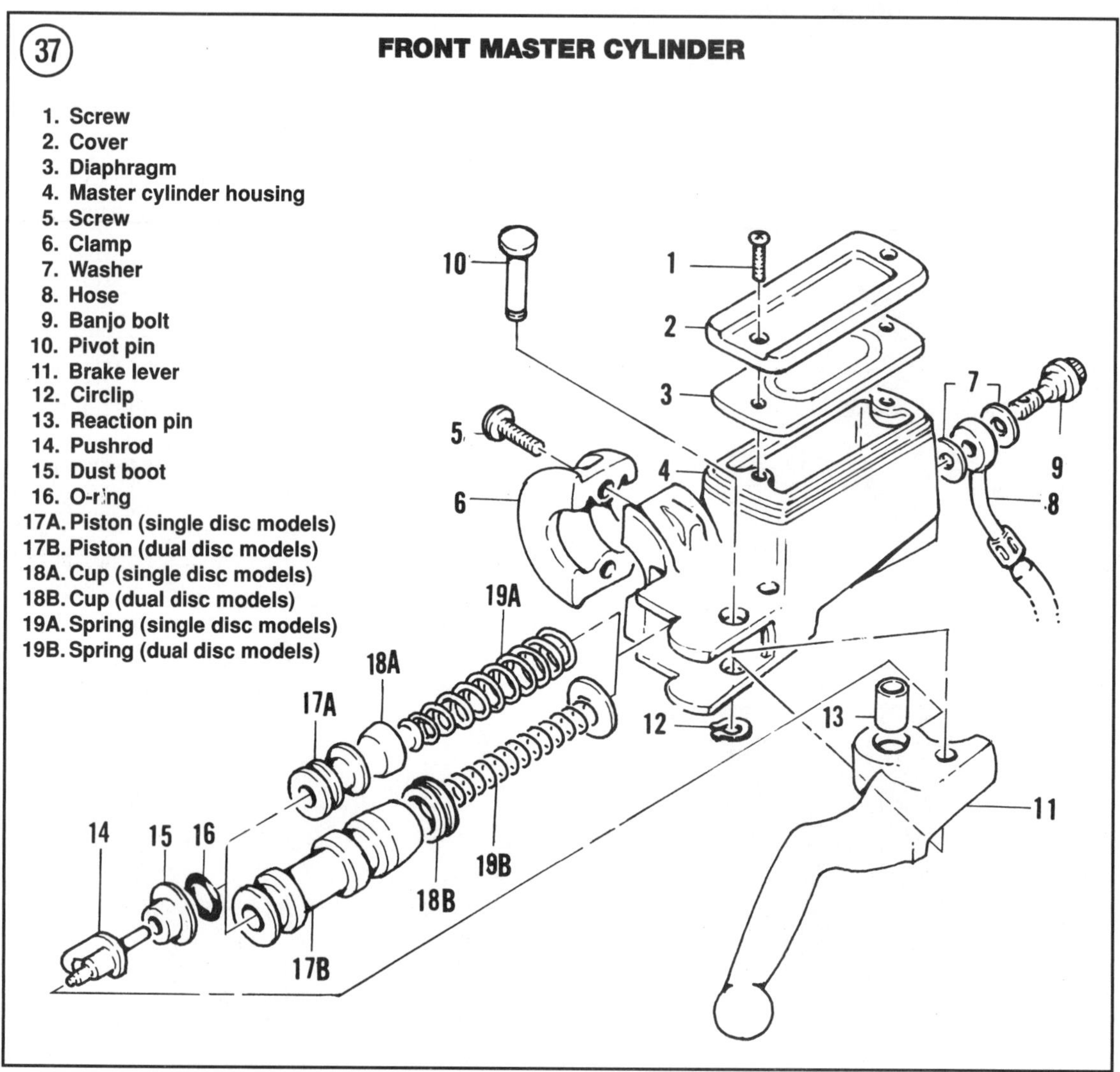

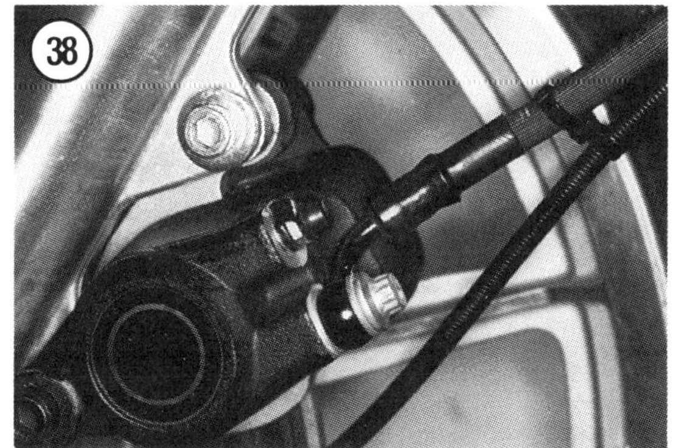

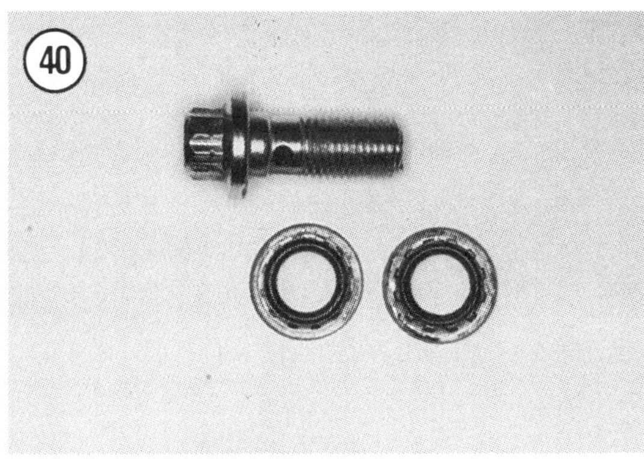

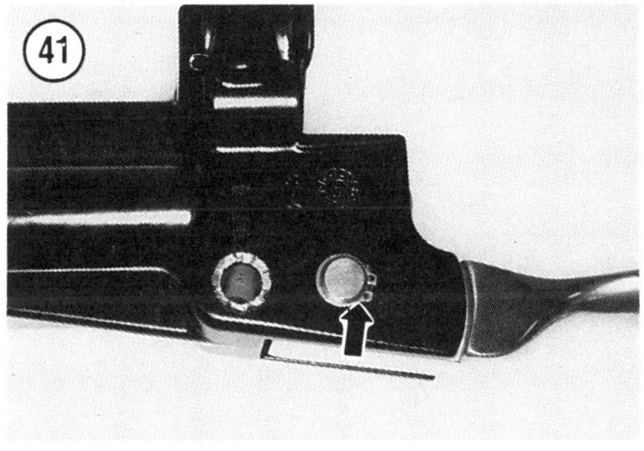

39). Tighten the screws to the torque specification in **Table** 2.

NOTE
*Install **new** steel/rubber banjo bolt washers (**Figure 40**) when performing Step 9.*

9. Place a new washer on each side of the hose fitting (A, **Figure 39**) and install the banjo bolt through the washers and hose fitting. Tighten the banjo bolt to the torque specification listed in **Table 2**.
10. Fill the master cylinder with new DOT 5 brake fluid. Bleed the brake system as described in this chapter.

NOTE
When actuating the brake lever in Step 10, look for a small spurt of fluid breaking through the fluid surface in the master cylinder. This indicates that the internal master cylinder components are working properly.

11. Install the master cylinder diaphragm and cover after bleeding the brakes.

WARNING
Do not ride the motorcycle until you are sure the brakes are working properly.

Disassembly

Refer to **Figure 37** when performing this procedure.

1. Drain and remove the master cylinder as described in this chapter.
2. Remove the screws securing the top cover and remove the cover and diaphragm.
3. To remove the brake lever assembly:
   a. Remove the pivot pin circlip (**Figure 41**).
   b. Push out the pivot pin (A, **Figure 42**) and remove the brake lever (B, **Figure 42**) assembly.
   c. Remove the reaction pin (A, **Figure 43**) from the brake lever.
   d. Remove the pushrod (B, **Figure 43**) from the piston assembly.
4. Remove the piston assembly as follows:
   a. Remove the dust boot (**A, Figure 44**).
   b. Remove the piston and spring assembly (**B, Figure 44**).

5. If damaged, remove the grommet and sight glass from the rear side of the master cylinder housing.

Inspection

Harley-Davidson does not provide service specifications for any of the master cylinder components. Replace any part that appears worn or damaged.

1. Clean all parts in denatured alcohol or fresh DOT 5 brake fluid. Then place parts on a clean lint-free cloth until reassembly.
2. The piston assembly consists of the dust boot, O-ring, piston, cup and spring (**Figure 45**). Inspect the rubber parts (**Figure 46**) for wear, cracks, swelling or other damage. Check the piston for wear or damage. Check the spring for fatigue or breakage. If any one part of the piston assembly is damaged, replace the piston assembly.
3. Inspect the master cylinder bore for scratches or wear grooves.
4. Clean the vent hole in the cover if plugged.
5. Inspect the piston bore in the master cylinder for wear, corrosion or damage. Replace the master cylinder if necessary.
6. Make sure the banjo bolt passage hole is clear.
7. Check the reaction pin and pivot pin (**Figure 47**) holes in the brake lever for cracks, spreading or other damage. Check the lever for cracks or damage.
8. Check the reaction pin, pivot pin and pushrod (**Figure 47**) for severe wear or damage. Check the fit of each pin in the brake lever. Replace worn or damaged parts as required.
9. Replace the pivot pin circlip (**Figure 47**) if weak or damaged.

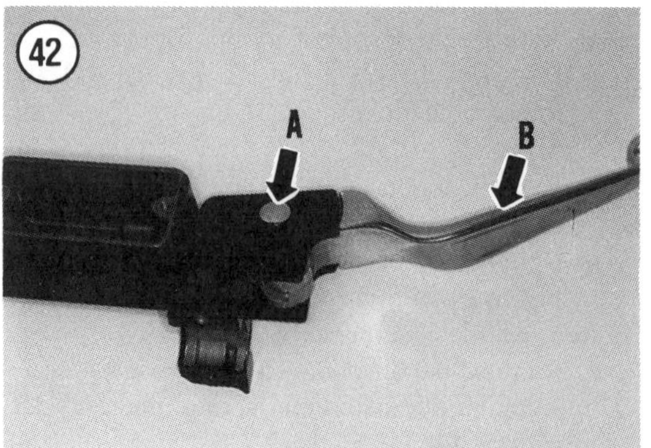

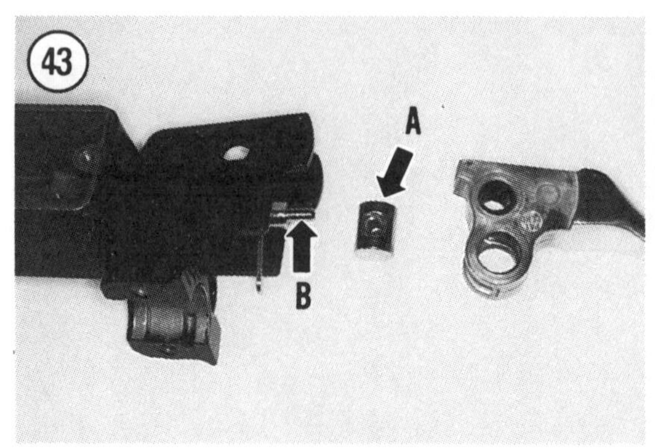

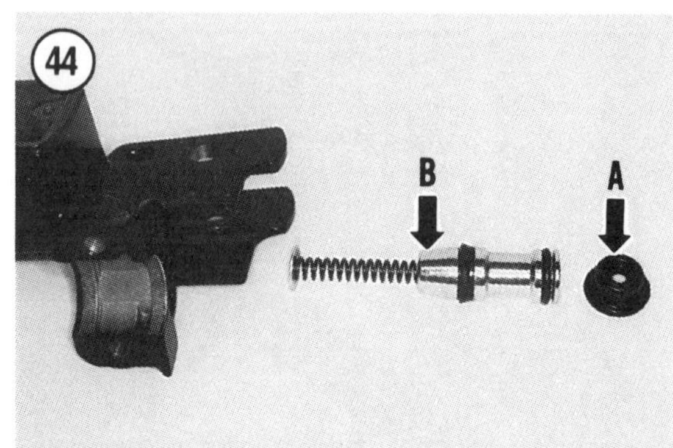

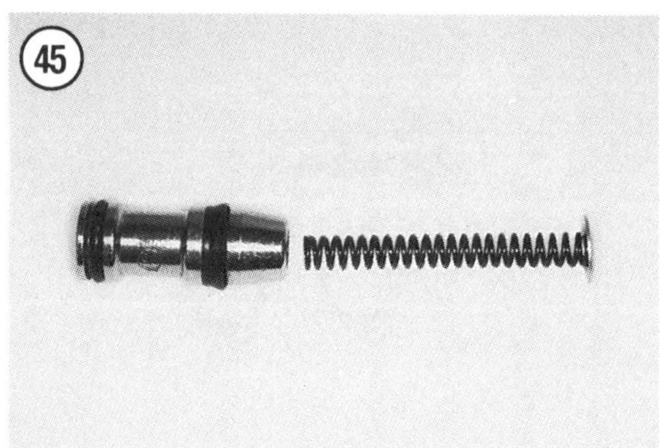

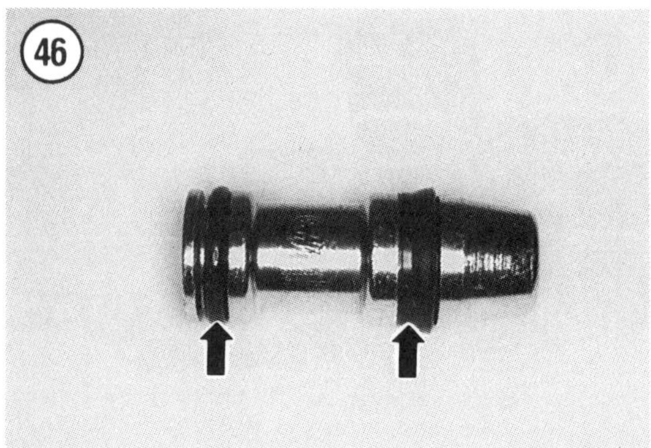

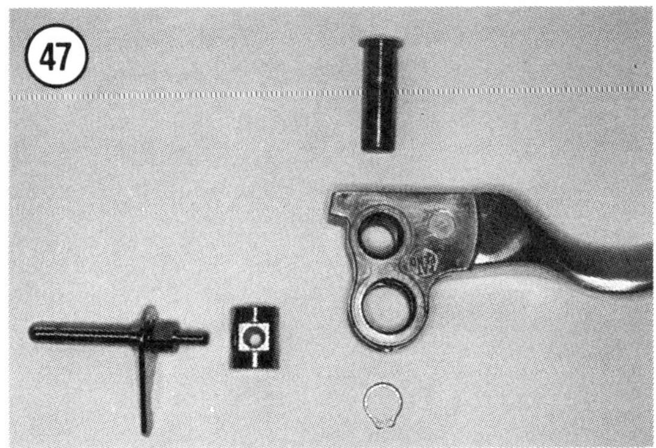
47

48

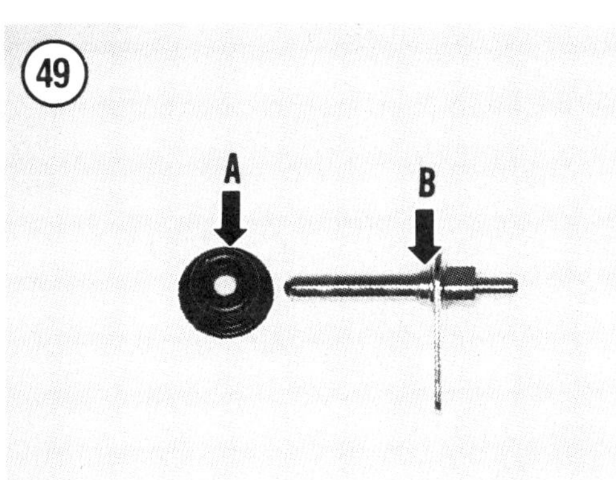

49

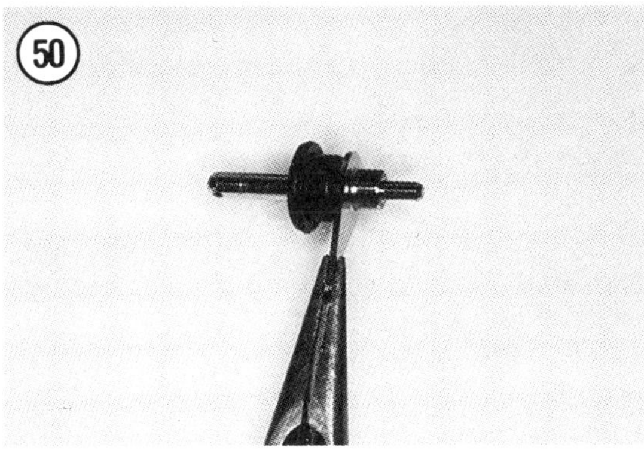
50

Assembly

The piston assemblies installed in single disc and dual disc master cylinders are different. See **Figure 37** for a drawing of each piston assembly.

1A. If you are installing a factory master cylinder rebuild kit, coat the master cylinder bore and all of the piston components with the lubricant supplied in the rebuild kit.

1B. If you are not installing a factory master cylinder rebuild kit, soak the piston O-ring and cup in fresh DOT 5 brake fluid prior to installation. Apply a thin coat of brake fluid to the cylinder bore prior to assembly.

2. Install the master cylinder grommet and sight glass if removed.

3A. On single disc models, assemble the piston assembly as follows:

 a. Install the cup onto the narrow end of the spring.
 b. Install the O-ring onto the piston.

3B. On dual disc models, assemble the piston assembly as follows:

 a. Install the O-ring and cup onto the piston as shown in **Figure 46**.
 b. Make sure the small plate is installed onto the piston spring as shown in **Figure 37** and **Figure 45**.

4A. On single disc models, install the piston assembly (**Figure 37**) as follows:

 a. Insert the spring—wide end first—into the master cylinder.
 b. Install the piston—O-ring side facing out—into the master cylinder.

4B. On dual disc models, install the piston assembly as follows:

 a. Install the spring into the piston (**Figure 44**). The plate mounted on end of the spring must be facing out.
 b. Install the spring and piston into the master cylinder (**Figure 48**).

5. Slide the dust boot (A, **Figure 49**) onto the pushrod (B, **Figure 49**). See **Figure 50**.

6. To assemble the brake lever assembly (**Figure 47**), perform the following:

 a. Slide the long end of the pushrod into the piston (**Figure 51**). The dust boot must face toward the piston. Then turn the pushrod so that its arm faces toward the master cylinder as shown in **Figure 51**.

NOTE
Do not seat the dust boot into the master cylinder at this time.

b. Lightly coat the reaction pin (A, **Figure 52**) with Loctite antiseize compound.
c. Install the reaction pin (A, **Figure 52**) into the brake lever (B, **Figure 52**) with the pins square hole facing out. See **Figure 53**.
d. Slide the brake lever into the master cylinder while seating the end of the pushrod into the reaction pin hole (**Figure 54**). Hold the brake lever in this position. Install the pushrod arm into the cutout in the master cylinder.
e. Slide the pivot pin (A, **Figure 42**) through the master cylinder and brake lever pivot holes.
f. Turn the master cylinder over and install the circlip (**Figure 41**) into the pivot pin groove.
g. Pump the brake lever once to seat the dust seal into the master cylinder bore (**Figure 55**).

7. Pump the brake lever several times. There must be no binding or excessive free play. Check that the pushrod seats in the reaction pin hole (**Figure 55**). If the brake lever does not operate correctly, disassemble the parts and reassemble them correctly.

WARNING
An incorrectly assembled pushrod and reaction pin assembly will cause the front master cylinder to become inoperable. This will cause the front brake to lockup or result in complete loss of the front brake.

REAR BRAKE PADS

There is no recommended mileage interval for changing the friction pads in the disc brake. Pad wear depends greatly on riding habits and conditions.

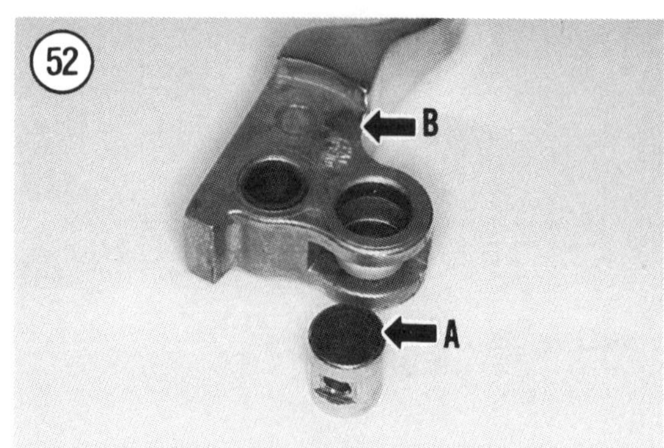

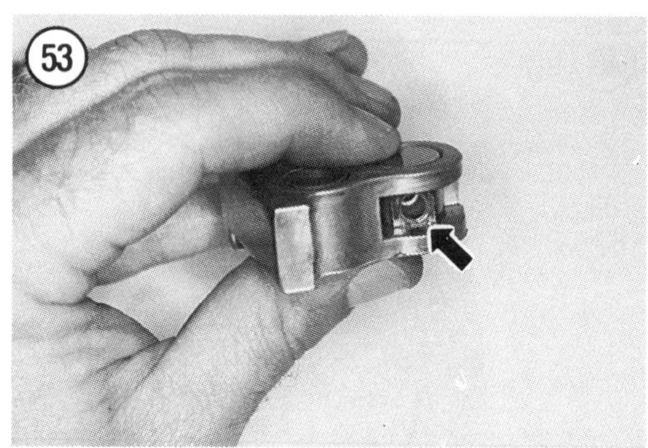

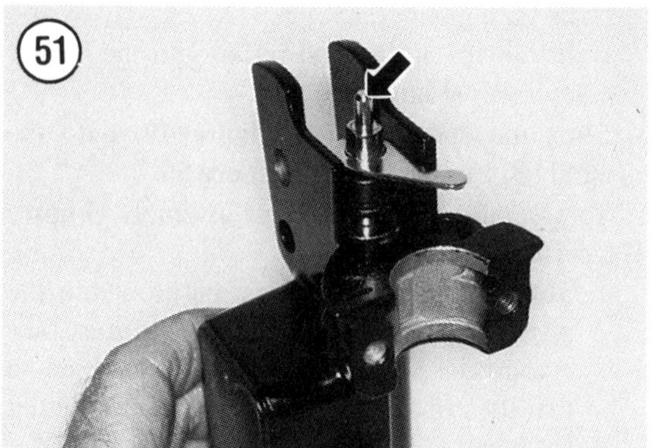

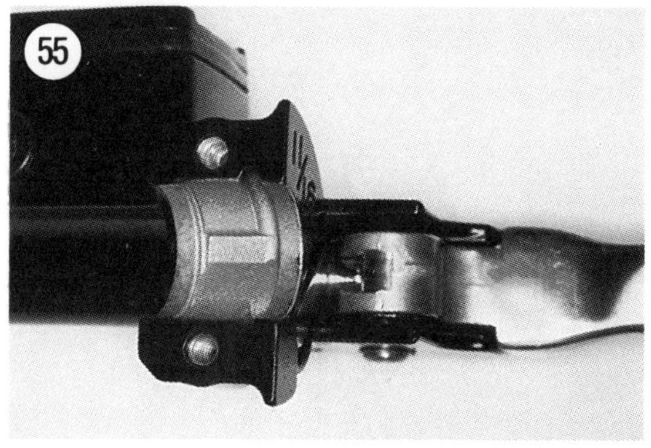

Check the pads for wear at the intervals listed in Chapter Three and replace when the lining thickness reaches 1/16 in. (1.6 mm) or less. To maintain an even brake pressure on the disc always replace both pads in the caliper at the same time.

Brake Pad/Pad Shim Identification

Harley-Davidson made a design change between early 1991 and late 1991 and later models regarding the brake pads and pad shims (**Figure 56**). When purchasing replacement parts, note the following while referring to the brake pad and shim drawings in **Figure 57** (early 1991) or **Figure 58** (late 1991-on):

a. Early 1991 pad shim thickness is 0.015 in. (0.38 mm).
b. Late 1991-on pad shim thickness is 0.030 in. (0.76 mm).
c. Early 1991 pad shims have a tab in the middle of each long side.
d. Late 1991-on pad shims have an open loop at one end of the shim.
e. Early 1991 brake pads measure approximately 3.44 in. (87.4 mm) between the "V" notches as shown in **Figure 57**. Late 1991-on brake pads measure approximately 3.39 in. (86.1 mm) as shown in **Figure 58**.
f. Early 1991 outboard brake pads have an angle-cut, half-size insulator mounted on the

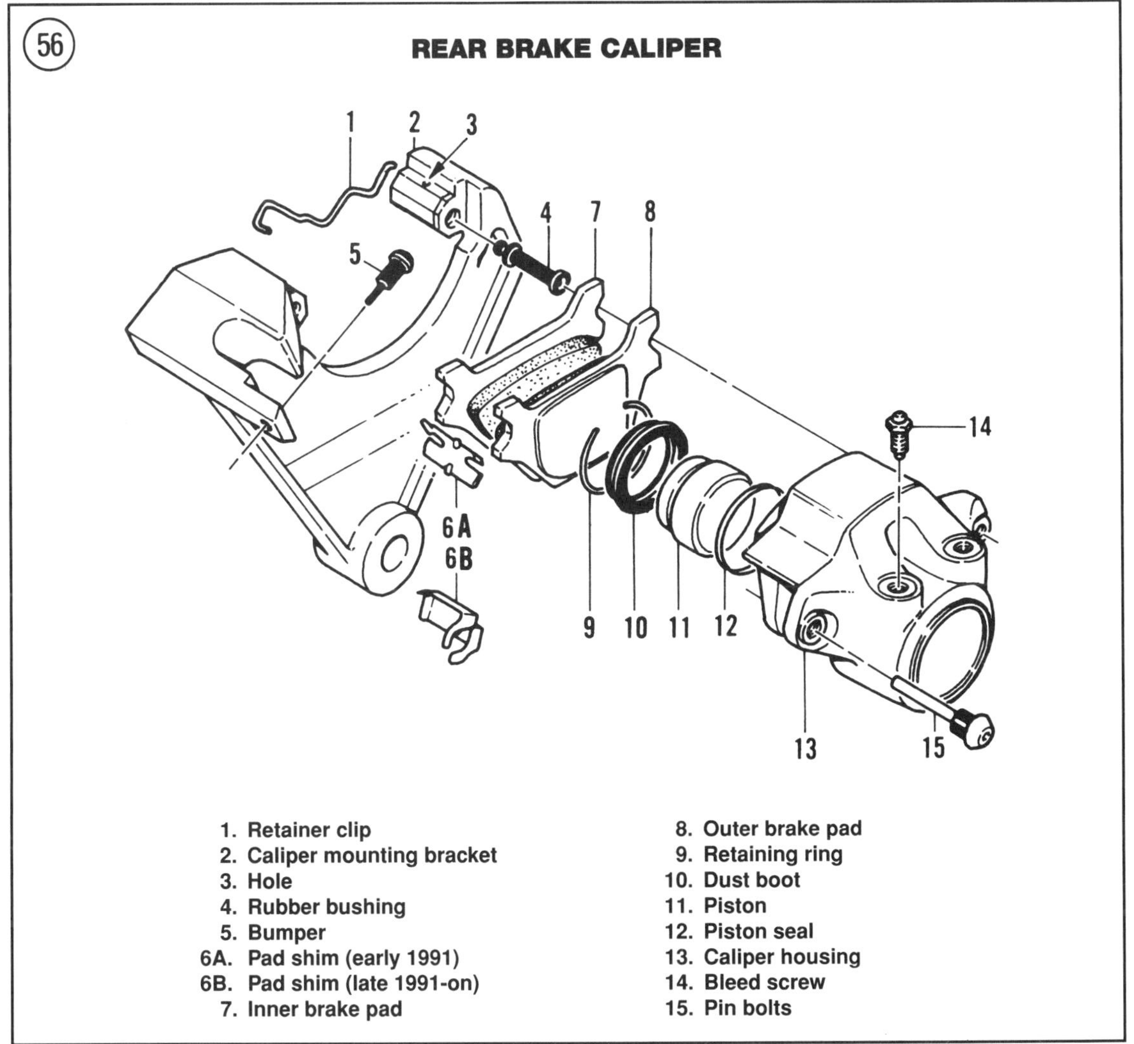

56

REAR BRAKE CALIPER

1. Retainer clip
2. Caliper mounting bracket
3. Hole
4. Rubber bushing
5. Bumper
6A. Pad shim (early 1991)
6B. Pad shim (late 1991-on)
7. Inner brake pad
8. Outer brake pad
9. Retaining ring
10. Dust boot
11. Piston
12. Piston seal
13. Caliper housing
14. Bleed screw
15. Pin bolts

back of the pad. The inboard brake pad has a full-size insulator.

g. Late 1991-on brake pads have full-size insulators mounted on the back of each pad.

WARNING
When replacing brake pads, do not intermix early 1991 and late 1991-on brake pads and pad shims. Otherwise, improper rear brake operation will occur. This may cause brake failure and loss of control, resulting in personal injury. When purchasing new brake pads for a 1991 model, take your frames serial number and the used brake parts to the dealer and have them verify your model as an early or late model.

Replacement

Refer to **Figure 56** for this procedure.

1. Support the bike on a flat surface.

2. Remove the 2 caliper pin bolts (A, **Figure 59**) and lift the caliper (B, **Figure 59**) off the mounting bracket. Do not disconnect the brake hose from the caliper. Support the caliper with a piece of heavy wire.

3. Lift and then pull the retainer clip (**Figure 60**) over the mounting bracket and remove it.

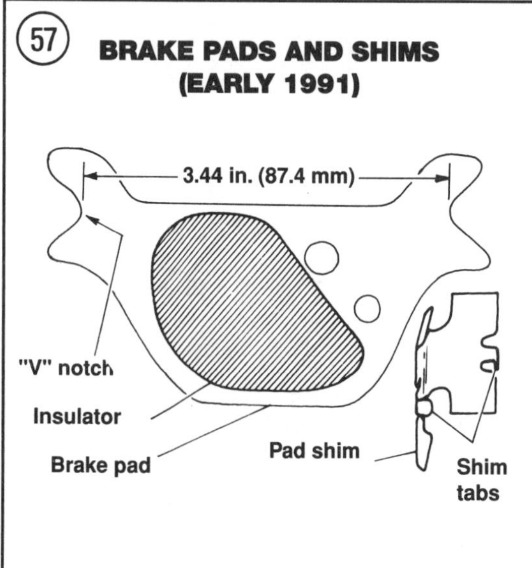

NOTE
If you intend to reuse the brake pads, mark them so that you can reinstall them in their original mounting position.

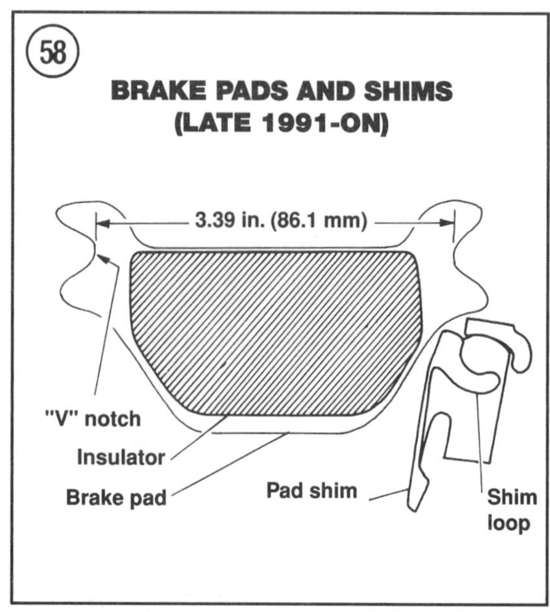

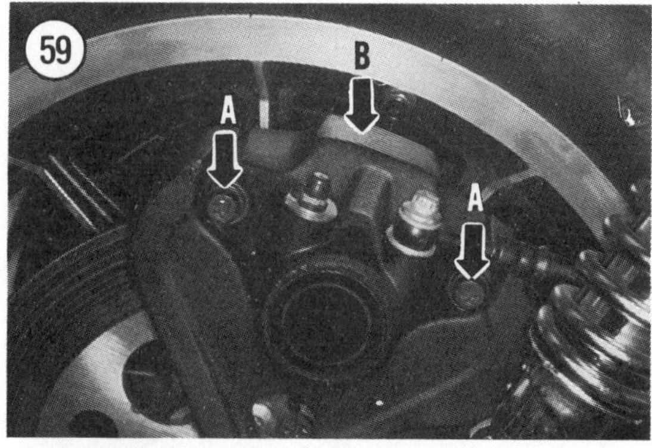

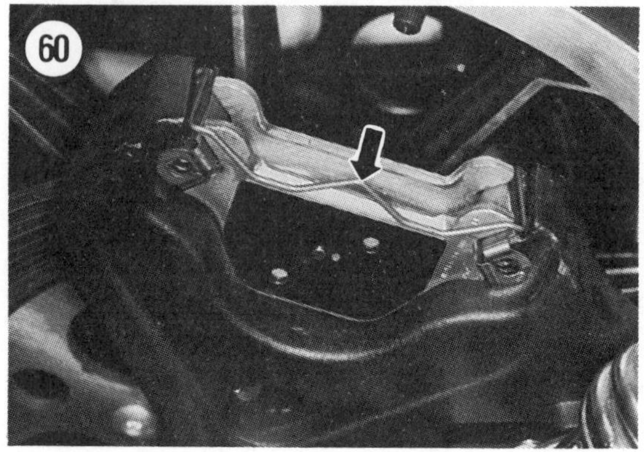

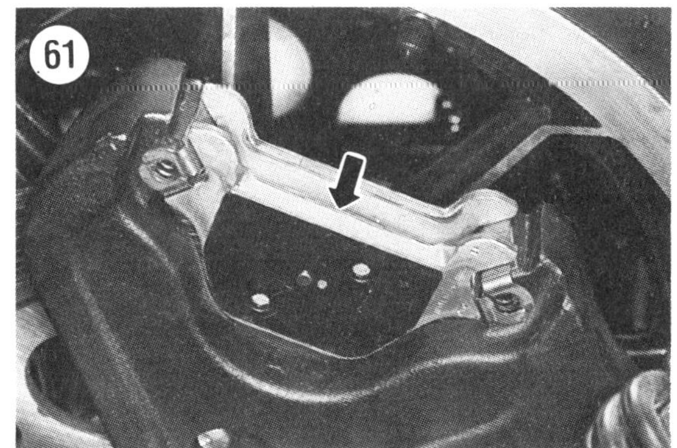

4. Slide the outer brake pad (**Figure 61**) off the mounting bracket.
5. Slide the inner brake pad toward the wheel and off the mounting bracket.
6. Remove the 2 pad shims (**Figure 62**) from the mounting bracket. Refer to **Figure 56** for a comparison of the early 1991 and late 1991-on pad shims.
7. Check the brake pads (**Figure 63**) for wear or damage. Measure the thickness of the brake pad friction material (**Figure 64**). Replace the brake pads if they are worn to 1/16 in. (1.6 mm) or less. Replace both pads as a set. **Figure 65** shows a brake pad worn down to the metal backing plate.
8. Clean the pad shims and check for cracks or damage. Replace if necessary.
9. Clean the pad shim mounting areas on the mounting bracket.
10. Check the retainer clip for rust, cracks or other damage. Replace if necessary.
11. Inspect the caliper pin bolts (**Figure 66**) for cracks, corrosion or other damage. Replace if necessary.
12. Check the piston dust boot (**Figure 67**) for damage. Remove and overhaul the caliper if the boot

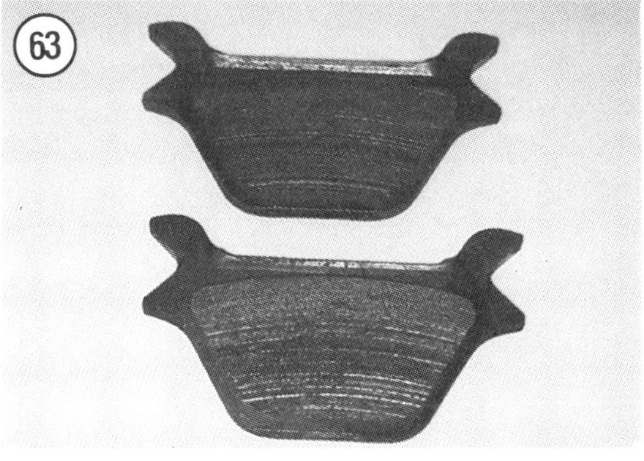

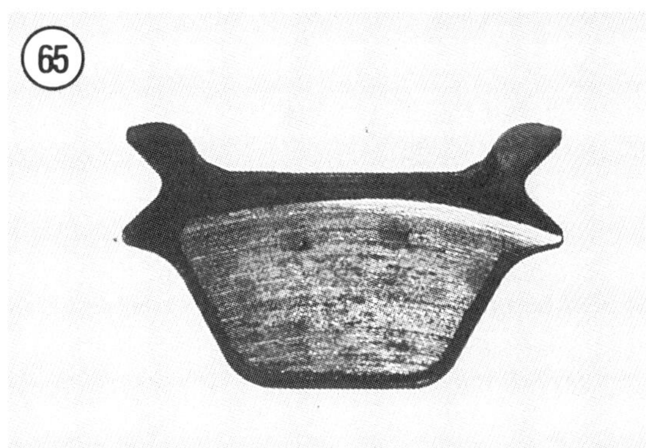

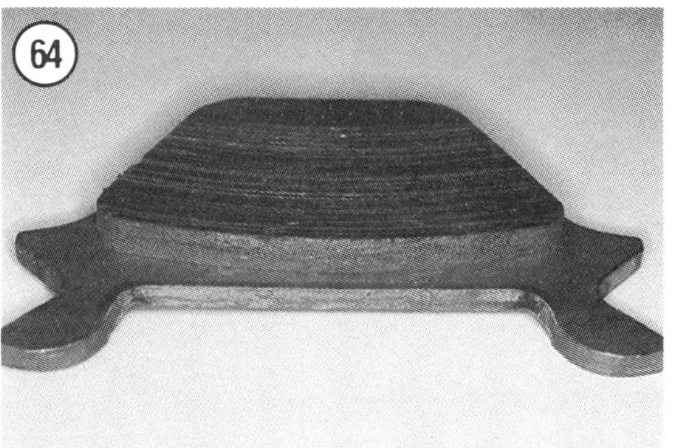

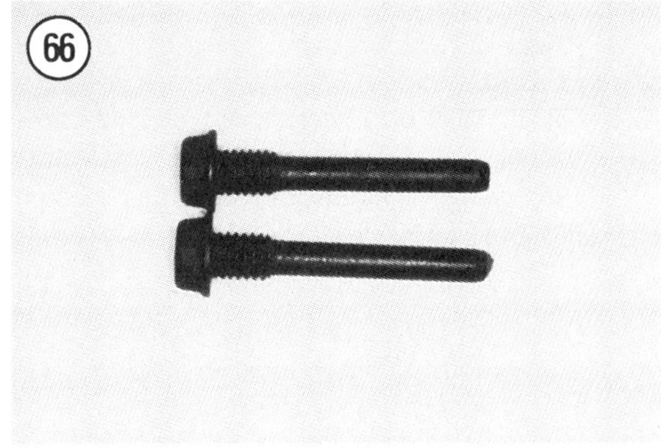

is swollen or damaged or if brake fluid is leaking from the caliper. Refer to *Rear Brake Caliper* in this chapter.

13. Check the brake disc for wear as described under *Brake Disc* in this chapter. Service the brake disc if necessary.

NOTE
*After installing new brake pads, you must push the caliper piston (**Figure 67**) into the caliper before installing the caliper over the brake pads and brake disc. While this step makes room for the new pads, doing so will force brake fluid to back up into the master cylinder reservoir. To prevent the reservoir from overflowing, first remove the reservoir cover (**Figure 68**) and diaphragm. Then watch the brake fluid level as you reposition the piston in Step 15.*

14. Hold the caliper with both hands and push the piston (**Figure 67**) into the cylinder with your fingers.

NOTE
The piston must move freely. If not, remove the caliper and service it as described in this chapter.

15. Reinstall the master cylinder diaphragm and cover but do not install the cover screws.

NOTE
*When replacing the brake pads and pad shims, refer to **Brake Pad/Pad Shim Identification** in this chapter. Confirm that you have the correct brake pads and shims for your model.*

16. Install the pad shims onto the caliper mounting bracket rails as follows:
   a. On early 1991 models, insert the pad shim tabs (**Figure 57**) into the caliper bracket shim holes (3, **Figure 56**).
   b. On late 1991-on models, install the pad shims so that their retaining loops face against the outer caliper mounting bracket rails as shown in **Figure 62**.

NOTE
*On early 1991 models, the outboard brake pad is different from the inboard brake pad. The outboard brake pad (piston side) has an angle-cut, half-size insulator mounted on the back of the pad (**Figure 57**). The inboard brake pad has a full-size insulator.*

17. Slide the outboard brake pad (**Figure 69**) over the pad shims and against the outer brake disc surface.

18. Slide the inboard brake pad (**Figure 70**) over the pad shims and against the inner brake disc surface.

19. Check that the pad shims did not move out of position (**Figure 61**).

NOTE
***Figure 71** shows the caliper mounting bracket removed from the swing arm for clarity.*

19. Insert the retainer clip into the 2 large holes (**Figure 71**) in the back of the caliper mounting bracket. Then swing the retainer clip over the top of the brake pads and snap it in place against the outer brake pad (**Figure 60**).

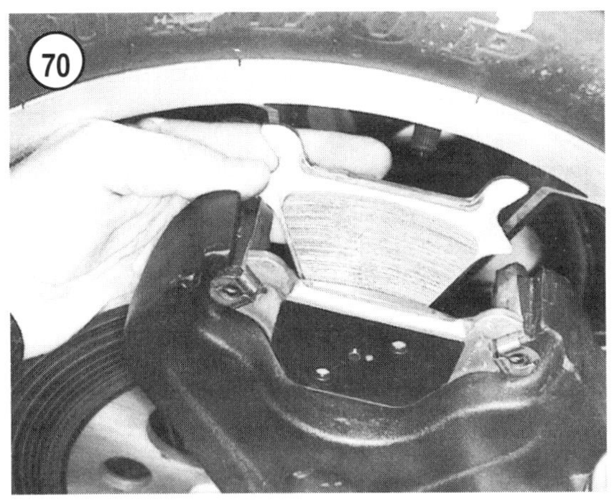

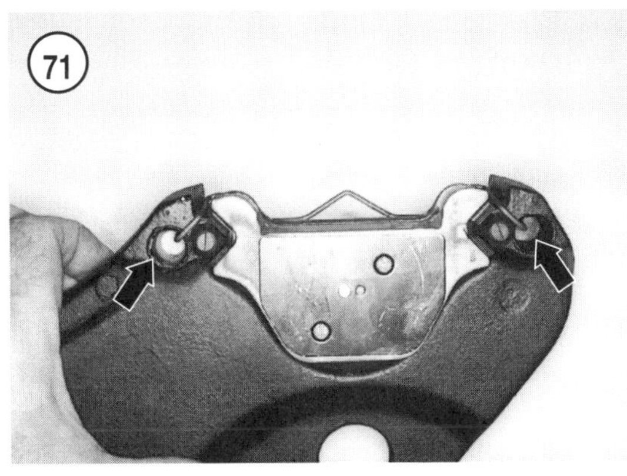

CAUTION
*The brake pads must seat against the 2 pad shims evenly (**Figure 60**). If not, the rear brake will drag, causing uneven pad wear and caliper bracket damage.*

NOTE
When installing the caliper over the brake pads, do not dislodge the brake pads and pad shims.

20. Slide the caliper over the brake pads (B, **Figure 59**). Install the 2 pin bolts (A, **Figure 59**) and tighten to the torque specification in **Table 2**.
21. Refill the master cylinder reservoir, if necessary, to maintain the correct fluid level. Install the diaphragm and top cap.

WARNING
Use brake fluid clearly marked DOT 5 from a sealed container. Other types may vaporize and cause brake failure. Always use the same brand name; do not intermix as many brands are not compatible.

22. Press the rear brake pedal several times to seat the pads against the disc.

WARNING
Do not ride the motorcycle until you are sure the brakes are operating correctly with full hydraulic advantage. If necessary, bleed the brake system as described in this chapter.

12

REAR BRAKE CALIPER

Removal/Installation (Caliper Will Not Be Disassembled)

To remove the brake caliper without disassembling it, perform this procedure. If you are going to disassemble the brake caliper, go to the *Caliper Removal/Piston Removal* procedure in this section.
1A. To remove the brake caliper from the bike, perform the following:

a. Loosen the banjo bolt at the caliper (A, **Figure 72**). Remove the bolt and the 2 washers.
b. Remove the 2 brake caliper pin bolts (B, **Figure 72**).
c. Lift the brake caliper off the brake disc and remove it.

1B. To remove the brake caliper partially from the bike (brake hose will not be disconnected), perform the following:

a. Remove the 2 brake caliper pin bolts (B, **Figure 72**).
b. Lift the brake caliper off the brake disc.
c. Insert a wooden or plastic spacer block between the piston and the opposite side of the caliper.

NOTE
Operating the brake pedal with the caliper removed from the brake disc will force the piston out of the caliper. Using the spacer block as mentioned in the previous step can prevent this from happening.

d. Support the caliper with a piece of heavy wire.

2. Install the brake caliper by reversing these steps, while noting the following.
3. If removed, install the brake pads as described in this chapter.

NOTE
When installing the caliper, do not knock the brake pads and dislodge the pad shims.

4. Slide the caliper over the brake pads. Install the 2 pin bolts (B, **Figure 72**) and tighten to the torque specification in **Table 2**.
5. Tighten the bleed screw.

NOTE
*Install **new** steel/rubber banjo bolt washers (**Figure 73**) when performing Step 7.*

6. If removed, assemble the brake line onto the caliper. Install a new washer on both sides of the brake line fitting, then secure the fitting to the caliper with the banjo bolt (A, **Figure 72**). Tighten the banjo bolt to the torque specification in **Table 2**. Make sure the fitting seats against the caliper as shown in A, **Figure 72**.
7. If necessary, add Dot 5 brake fluid and bleed the system as described in this chapter.
8. Operate the front brake pedal several times to seat the pads against the disc.

WARNING
Do not ride the motorcycle until you are sure the brakes are operating properly.

Caliper Removal/Piston Removal (Caliper Will Be Disassembled)

If disassembling the brake caliper, the piston must be forced out of the caliper bore. To do this, you can use hydraulic pressure in the brake system or compressed air. When using the system's hydraulic pressure, you must do so prior to disconnecting the brake hose from the caliper. This procedure describes how to remove the piston with the caliper mounted on the bike.

1. Remove the brake pads as described in this chapter.
2. Insert a small screwdriver into the notched groove machined in the bottom of the piston bore. Then pry the retaining ring (**Figure 67**) out of the caliper body.
3. Remove the piston dust boot from the groove at the top of the piston.
4. To remove the piston, perform the following:

a. Wrap a large cloth around the brake caliper.
b. Hold the caliper with your hand and fingers placed away from the piston/brake pad area.
c. Operate the rear brake pedal to force the piston out of the caliper cylinder. Remove the piston and dust seal.

NOTE
*If the piston did not come out in Step 4, use compressed air to remove it. Refer to **Disassembly** in this section.*

5. Remove the brake caliper banjo bolt (A, **Figure 72**) and washers. Plug the brake hose to prevent leakage and to keep out dirt.

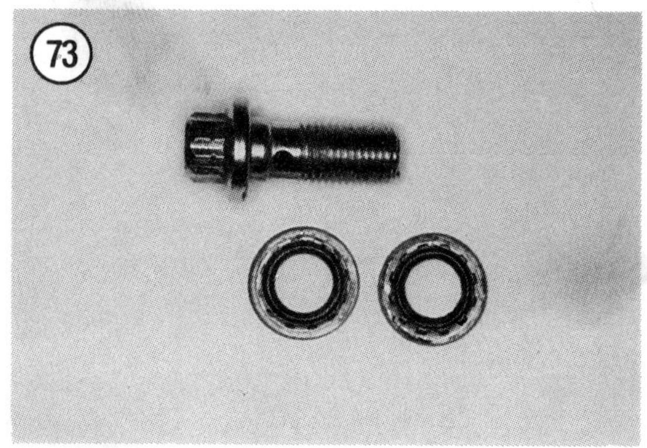
73

Disassembly

Harley-Davidson does not provide service specifications for any of the caliper components (except brake pads). Replace any worn or damaged or questionable part.

Refer to **Figure 74** for this procedure.

1. Remove the brake caliper as described in this chapter.

NOTE

If you have previously removed the piston, go to Step 5.

2. Insert a screwdriver into the caliper body notched groove (A, **Figure 75**) and pry the retaining ring out of the groove (**Figure 76**).

WARNING

When performing Step 3, the piston can shoot out of the caliper like a bullet. Keep your hand and fingers out of the way. Wear shop gloves and apply compressed air gradually.

3. Place a rag or piece of wood in the pistons path (**Figure 77**). Then apply compressed air to the hydraulic hose opening and blow the piston out.

4. Remove the piston and dust boot assembly (**Figure 78**).

5. Remove the piston seal (**Figure 79**) from the groove in the caliper body.

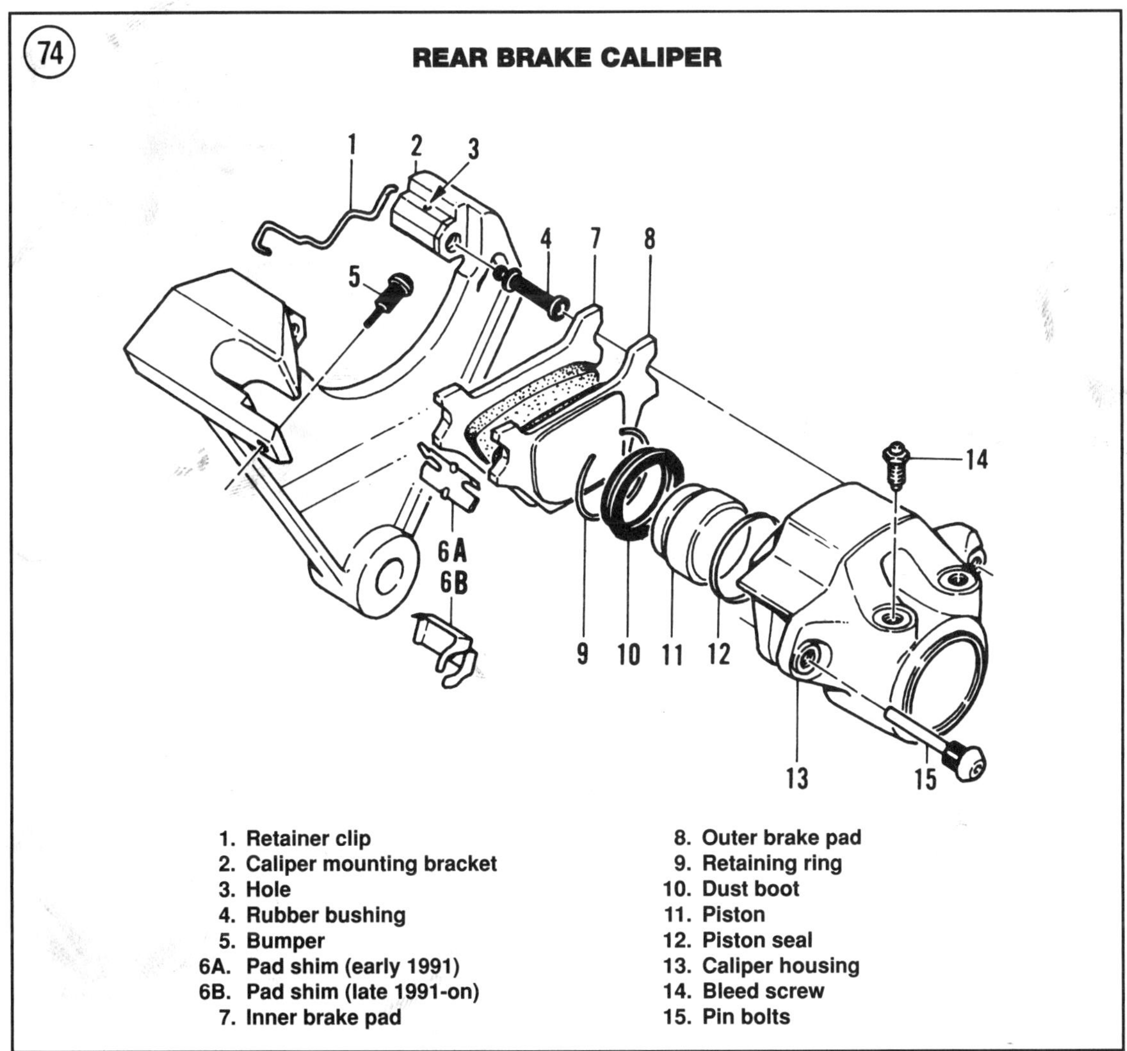

(74) **REAR BRAKE CALIPER**

1. Retainer clip
2. Caliper mounting bracket
3. Hole
4. Rubber bushing
5. Bumper

6A. Pad shim (early 1991)

6B. Pad shim (late 1991-on)

7. Inner brake pad
8. Outer brake pad
9. Retaining ring
10. Dust boot
11. Piston
12. Piston seal
13. Caliper housing
14. Bleed screw
15. Pin bolts

Inspection

1. Inspect the caliper for damage. Do not hone or bore the caliper bore. Clean the caliper with rubbing alcohol.

2. Inspect the hydraulic fluid passageway in the cylinder bore. Make sure it is clean and open. Clean with compressed air.

3. Inspect the piston and cylinder bore (**Figure 80**) wall for scratches, scoring or other damage. Replace worn, corroded or damaged parts.

4. Make sure the hole in the bleed valve screw (**Figure 81**) is clean and open. Clean with compressed air.

5. Check the pin bolts for wear or damage. Replace if necessary.

6. Replace the pad shims if corroded or damaged.

7. Check the brake pads (**Figure 82**) for excessive wear or damage. Measure the thickness of the brake pad friction material. Replace the brake pads if they are worn to 1/16 in. (1.6 mm) or less. Replace both pads as a set.

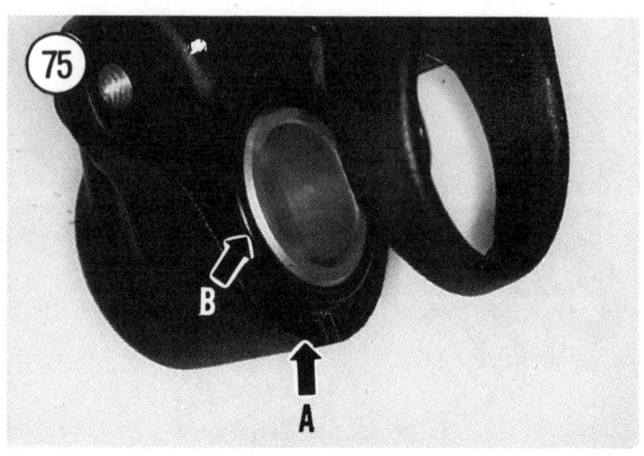

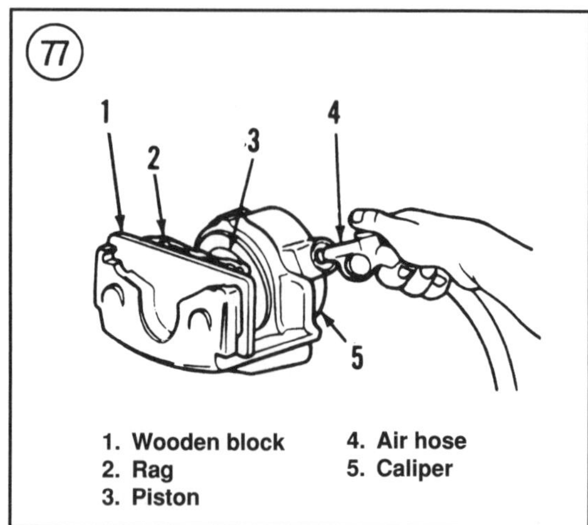

1. Wooden block
2. Rag
3. Piston
4. Air hose
5. Caliper

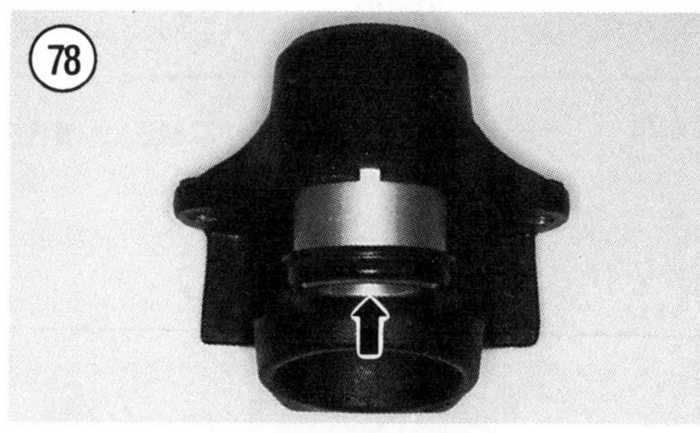

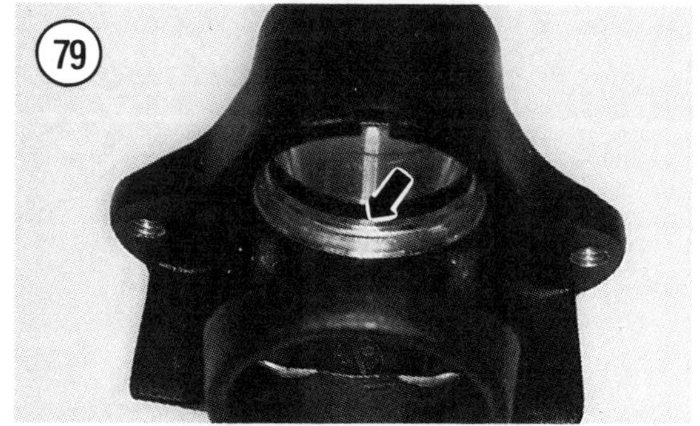

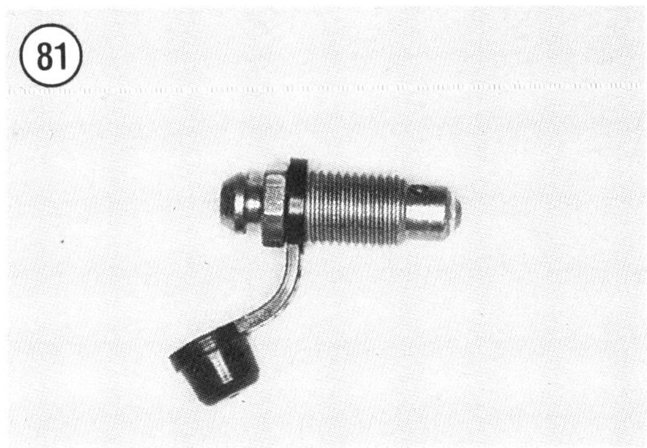

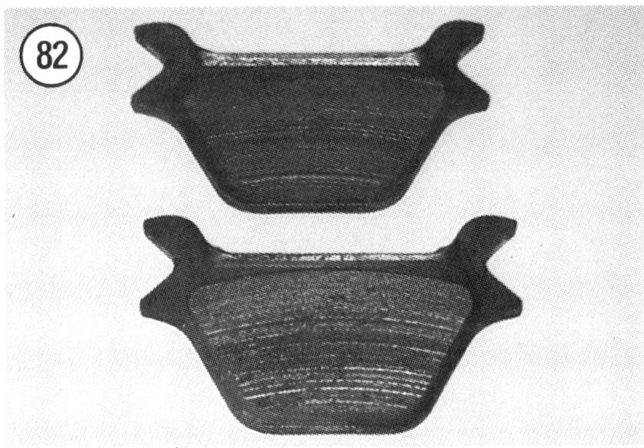

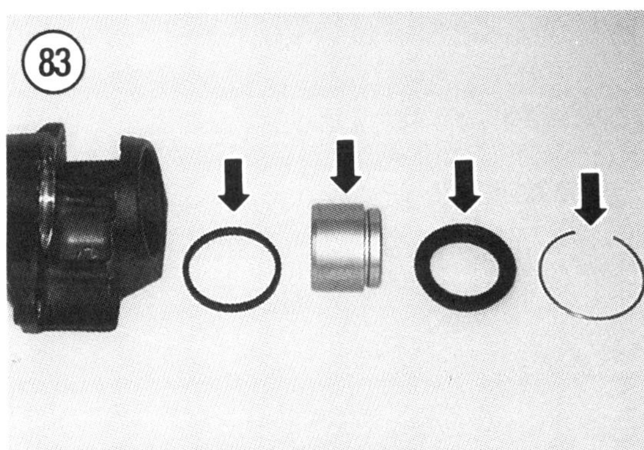

8. Check all of the rubber parts (dust boot, piston seal, bumper and bushings) for cracks, wear or deterioration.

Assembly

1. The parts in a factory rebuild kit are identified in **Figure 83**. After replacing all worn or damaged parts, coat the following parts with new DOT 5 silicone-based brake fluid. To prevent contamination, place the parts on a clean lint-free cloth.
   a. Piston.
   b. Piston seal.
2. Make sure the retaining ring, piston and caliper bore are thoroughly clean.
3. Install the piston seal (**Figure 79**) into the caliper body groove.
4. Install the piston dust boot on the piston *before* installing the piston in the caliper bore. Perform the following:
   a. Place the piston on your workbench with its open side facing up.
   b. Align the piston dust boot with the piston so that the shoulder on the dust boot faces up.
   c. Slide the dust boot over the piston until the inner lip on the dust boot seats in the piston groove (**Figure 84**).
5. Coat the piston and caliper bore with DOT 5 brake fluid.
6. Align the piston with the caliper bore so that its open end faces out (**Figure 85**), then push the piston in until it bottoms out.
7. Seat the piston dust boot (B, **Figure 75**) into the caliper bore.
8. Find the retaining ring groove in the end of the caliper bore. Then install the retaining ring (**Figure 76**) so that the gap in the ring (**Figure 86**) is at the

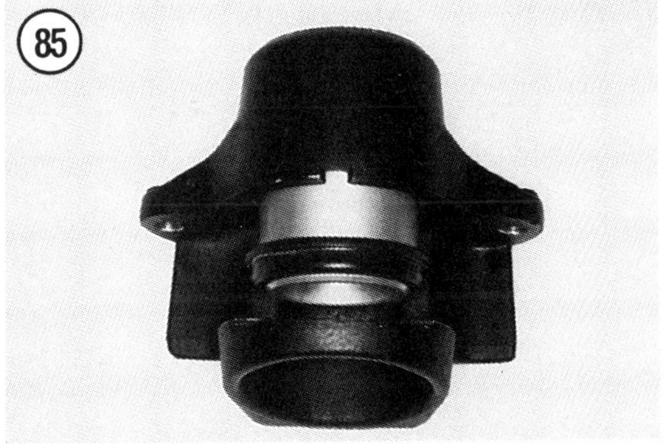

top of the caliper bore. Make sure the retaining ring seats in the groove and pushes against the piston dust boot.

9. Install the brake pads as described in this chapter.

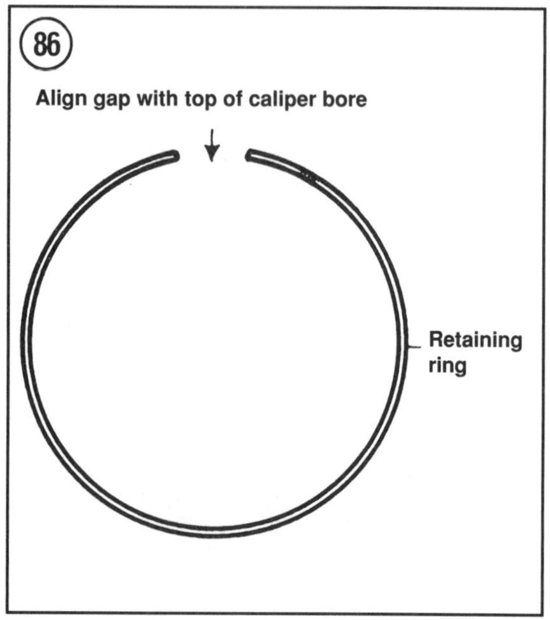

REAR MASTER CYLINDER

Removal/Installation

Refer to **Figure 87** for this procedure.

1. Insert a hose onto the end of the bleed valve (**Figure 88**). Insert the open end of the hose into a container. Open the bleeder valve and operate the rear brake pedal to drain the brake fluid. Remove the hose and close the bleeder valve after draining the assembly. Discard the brake fluid.
2. Remove the banjo bolt (**Figure 89**) and washers securing the brake hose to the master cylinder.

(87)

REAR MASTER CYLINDER

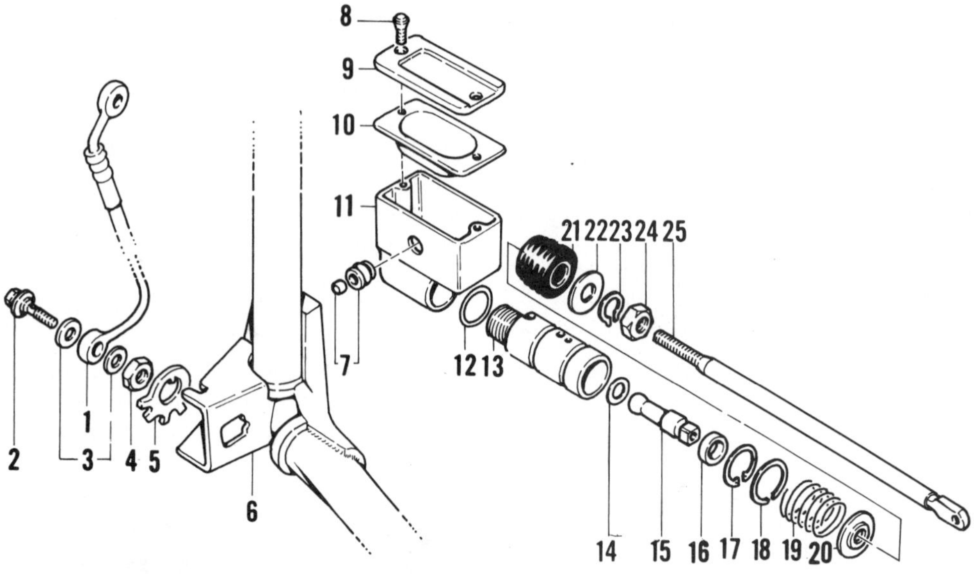

1. Rear brake hose
2. Banjo bolt
3. Washer
4. Nut
5. Lockwasher
6. Frame
7. Sight glass
8. Screw
9. Cover
10. Diaphragm
11. Reservoir
12. O-ring
13. Cartridge body
14. O-ring
15. Pushrod
16. Washer
17. Circlip
18. Circlip
19. Spring
20. Retainer
21. Boot
22. Washer
23. Circlip
24. Nut
25. Pushrod

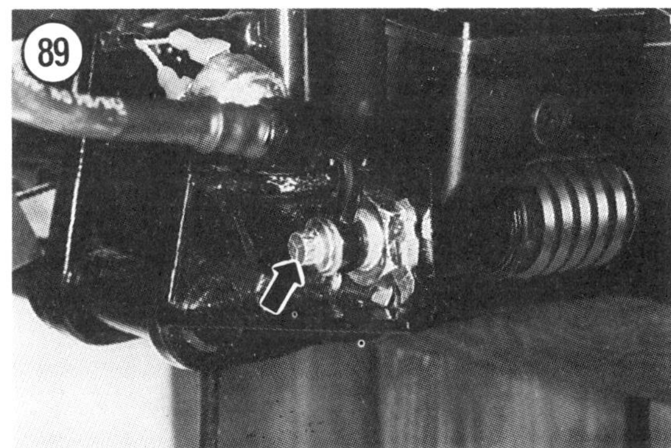

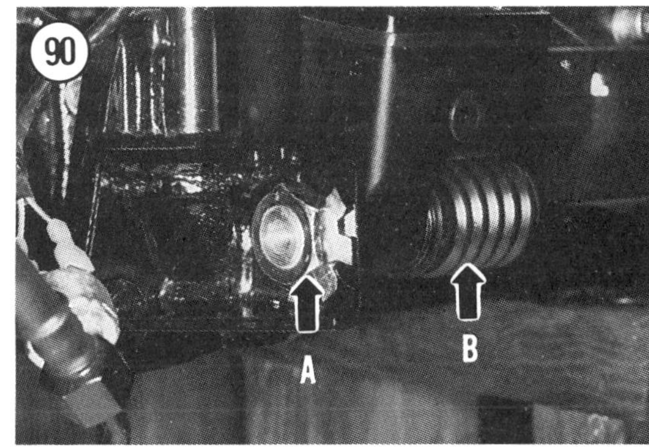

3. Pry the lockwasher tab away from the rear master cylinder nut (A, **Figure 90**). Then loosen and remove the nut (**A, Figure 90**) and lockwasher.

4. Loosen the brake rod locknut (24, **Figure 87**) at the master cylinder.

5. Lift the brake pedal and slide the master cylinder out of the frame bracket.

6. Unscrew the pushrod from the brake rod, then remove the master cylinder (**Figure 91**).

7. Service the master cylinder as described in this chapter.

8. Insert the master cylinder cartridge body threads (B, **Figure 90**) through the square hole in the frame bracket.

9. Fit the lockwasher tab into the hole in the frame bracket and thread the rear master cylinder nut (A, **Figure 90**) onto the cartridge body threads. Tighten the nut to the torque specification in **Table 2**. Bend the lockwasher tabs over the nut flats.

10. Thread the brake pushrod (25, **Figure 87**) into the pushrod. Do not tighten the locknut (24, **Figure 87**) at this time.

NOTE
Tighten the brake rod locknut after you adjust the rear brake pedal. This step is performed in Step 12 of this procedure.

11. Install a new steel/rubber washer (**Figure 92**) on each side of the brake hose banjo fitting. Insert the banjo bolt through the washers and banjo fitting and thread into the cartridge (**Figure 89**). Then tighten the banjo bolt to the torque specification in **Table 2**.

12. Adjust the rear brake as described in Chapter Three.

13. Bleed the rear brake as described in this chapter.

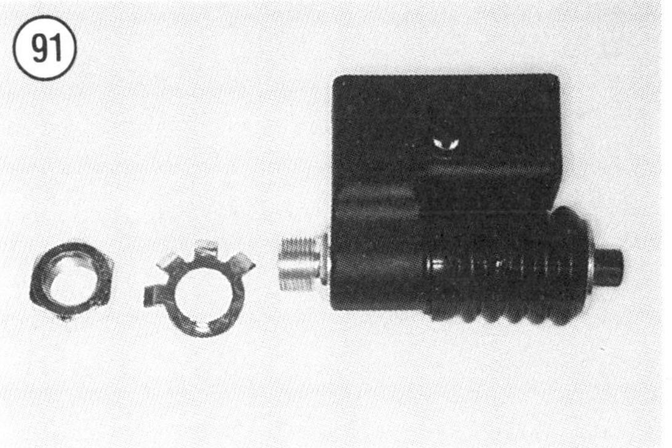

WARNING
Do not ride the motorcycle until you are sure the brakes are working properly.

Disassembly

If overhauling the master cylinder, use all of the parts included in the repair kit.

Refer to **Figure 87** for this procedure.

1. Clean the exterior master cylinder housing with rubbing alcohol.
2. Remove the master cylinder cover and diaphragm.
3. Thread the banjo bolt (A, **Figure 93**) into the cartridge body.

NOTE
The banjo bolt helps to protect the cartridge body during disassembly.

4. Remove the boot (B, **Figure 93**) from the reservoir groove.

CAUTION
If you are going to reuse the cartridge body, handle it carefully during the following steps, making sure to protect it from oil, grease and dirt. The piston assembly installed inside the cartridge body is not available as a separate item. Replace the cartridge body if damaged or if brake fluid leaks past the piston seals.

5. Set the master cylinder on the banjo bolt, then push the reservoir housing down and slide off the cartridge body (**Figure 94**).
6. Remove the circlip (**Figure 95**) from the pushrod groove. Then remove the large washer, rubber boot, retainer (inside boot) and spring (**Figure 96**) from the cartridge body.
7. Push the pushrod in, then remove the circlip (**Figure 97**), pushrod and washer. Discard the circlip.

NOTE
Do not remove the piston assembly unless visual inspection of the cartridge bore and piston assembly is required.

8. Withdraw the piston and spring assembly (**Figure 98**) from the cartridge body.

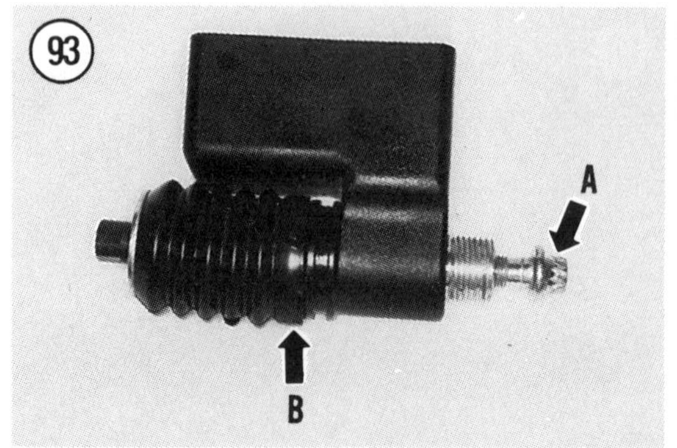

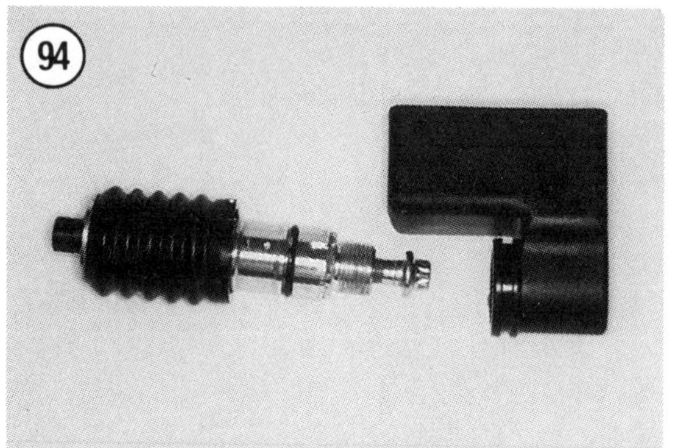

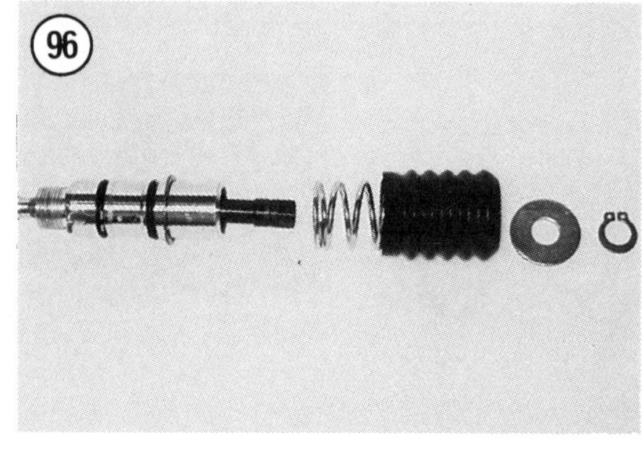

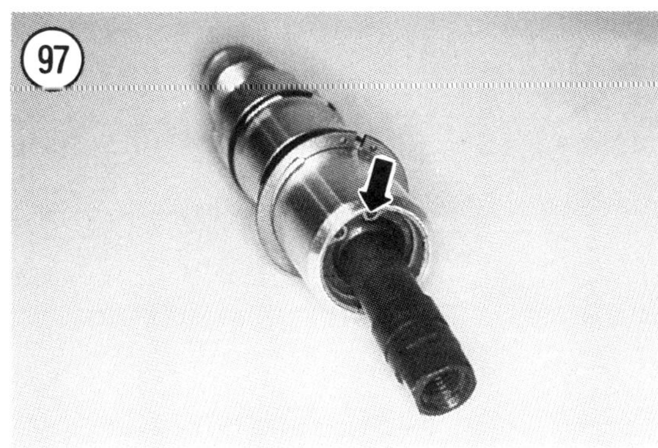

97

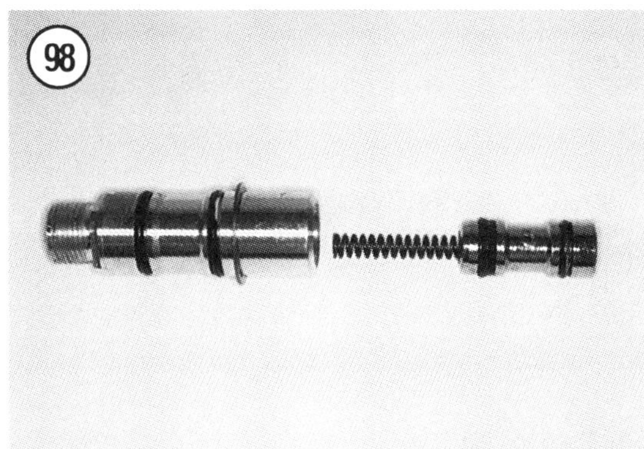

98

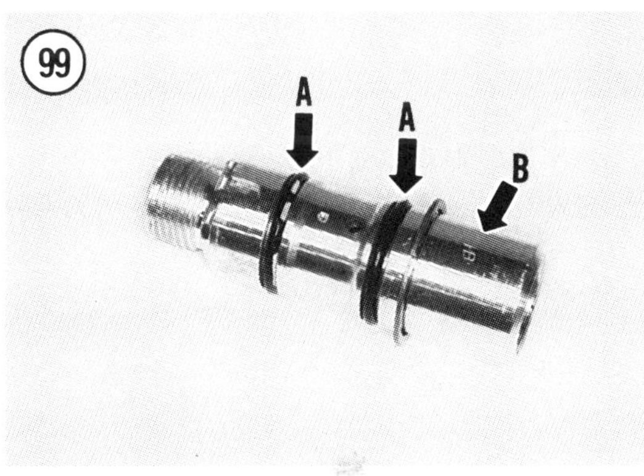

99

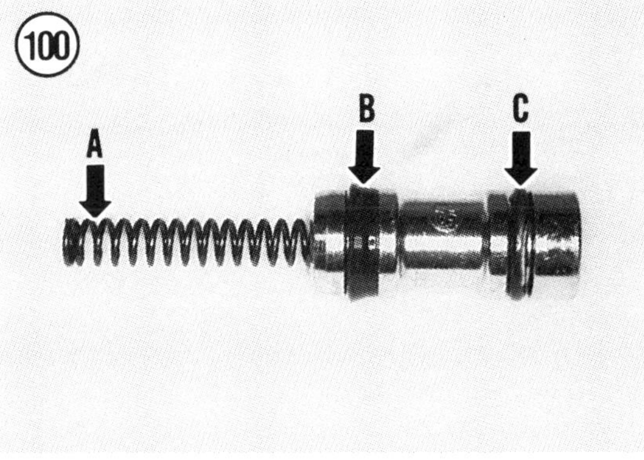

100

Inspection

NOTE

The 2 cartridge body O-rings (A, ***Figure 99****) are not available separately. Handle them carefully in the following steps.*

1. Remove the 2 O-rings (A, **Figure 99**) from the cartridge body grooves.
2. Clean the master cylinder assembly in new DOT 5 brake fluid. Make sure to remove all dirt and other foreign matter from the O-ring grooves in the cartridge body. Make sure the reservoir vent hole is clear. Place parts on a clean, lint-free towel.

WARNING

Never wash brake parts with gasoline or any type of mineral- or petroleum-based solvents. These chemicals will cause the rubber parts in the brake system to deteriorate. Continued deterioration will eventually cause brake system failure.

3. Inspect the cartridge body O-rings (A, **Figure 99**) for deterioration, cracks or other damage. Replace the cartridge body if the O-rings are damaged.
4. Inspect the cartridge body. If the O-ring grooves or threads are damaged, replace the cartridge body assembly.
5. Inspect the cartridge body bore (B, **Figure 99**). If the bore is cracked, corroded, or in any way damaged, replace the cartridge body assembly. Do not hone the cartridge bore to clean or repair it.
6. This piston assembly consists of the spring, piston cup, O-ring and piston body. Inspect the piston assembly as follows:

CAUTION

Because the piston cup and O-ring are not available separately, do not remove them from the piston. If damaged, you must replace the cartridge body.

a. Check the spring (A, **Figure 100**) for bending, unequally spaced coils or corrosion.
b. Check the piston cup (B, **Figure 100**) and O-ring (C, **Figure 100**) for tearing, deterioration or other damage.
c. Check the piston body for corrosion or other damage.
d. If corrosion, wear, or any damage is present, replace the cartridge body assembly.

7. Replace the pushrod (**Figure 101**) if bent or damaged.
8. Check the reservoir housing, reservoir cap and diaphragm. Replace all worn or damaged parts.

Assembly

Refer to **Figure 87** for this procedure.

1. If you are installing a repair kit, open it and place all of the parts on a clean, lint-free cloth. Wash these parts in new DOT 5 brake fluid. Clean the cartridge body O-ring grooves with a soft brush.
2. If you removed the piston assembly, install it as follows:
   a. Lubricate the spring, piston, piston cup and O-ring with DOT 5 brake fluid.
   b. Lubricate the cartridge body bore with DOT 5 brake fluid.
   c. Check that there is no foreign matter on the piston assembly or in the cartridge body bore.
   d. Install the piston assembly—spring side first—into the cartridge body bore (**Figure 98**). When installing the assembly, make sure the piston cup does not tear as it passes through the bore entrance. See **Figure 102**.

3. Assemble and install the pushrod assembly as follows:
   a. If removed, install the washer (**Figure 101**) onto the pushrod.
   b. Install a new circlip over the end of the pushrod (**Figure 101**).
   c. Place the pushrod ball end against the piston, then push the pushrod in and slide the washer into the cartridge bore groove. Using circlip pliers, install the circlip (**Figure 97**) into the cartridge bore groove.
   d. Release the pushrod, making sure the circlip is fully seated in the groove. Check that the pushrod rotates freely.

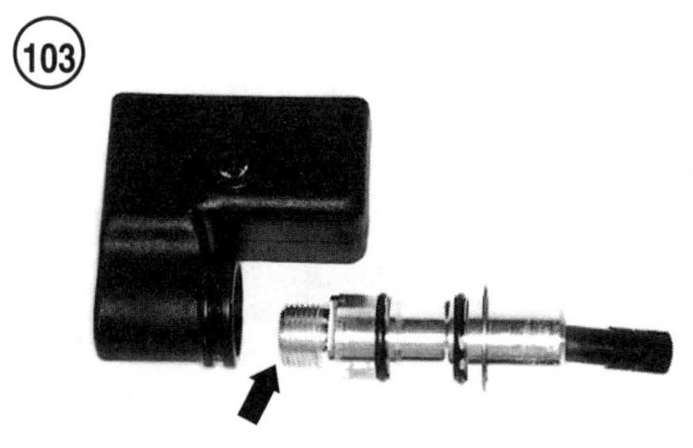

4. Coat the cartridge body O-rings with DOT 5 brake fluid, then install them in the cartridge body O-ring grooves.
5. Lightly coat the cartridge body with DOT 5 brake fluid. Then insert the cartridge body (**Figure 103**) into the reservoir bore-threaded end first. Align the slot on the cartridge body with the key in the reservoir (**Figure 104**) and push the cartridge body until it bottoms. See **Figure 105**.
6. If removed, install the spring retainer and spring into the rubber boot (**Figure 106**). Install the spring

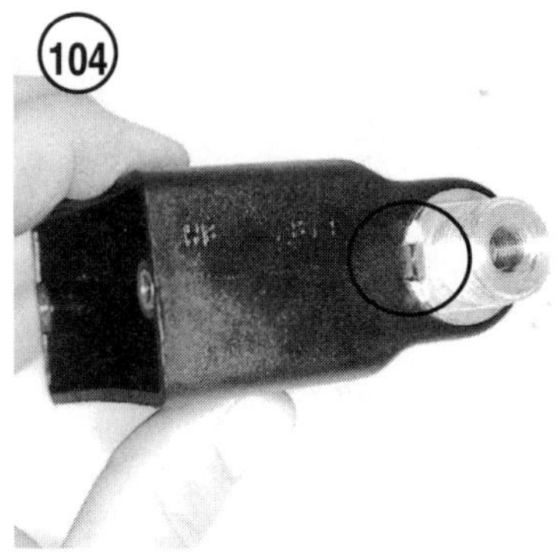

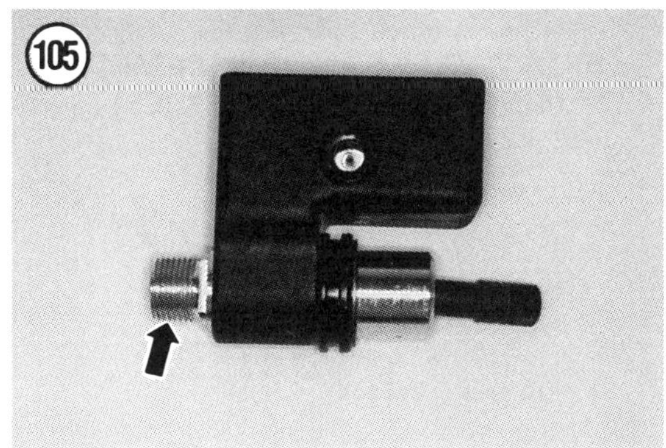

retainer so that its large cup side faces toward the boot.

7. Install the spring, boot and flat washer over the pushrod (**Figure 107**). Turn the boot so that its drain faces down.
8. Compress the washer and boot, then install the circlip into the pushrod groove. Make sure the circlip is fully seated in the groove.
9. Seat the boot (**Figure 108**) into the groove in the reservoir housing.
10. Install the diaphragm and reservoir cover.
11. Install the master cylinder as described in this chapter.

WARNING
Do not ride the motorcycle until you are sure the brakes are working properly.

BRAKE HOSE AND LINE REPLACEMENT

A combination of steel and flexible brake lines connect the master cylinder to its brake caliper(s). Banjo fittings and bolts connect brake hoses to the master cylinder and brake caliper(s). Steel/rubber washers seal the banjo fittings.

Replace a hose if the flexible portion shows swelling, cracking or other damage. Likewise, replace the brake hose if the metal portion leaks or if there are dents or cracks.

Front Brake Hose Removal/Installation

A combination steel/flexible brake hose (**Figure 109** or **Figure 110**) connects the front master cylinder to the front brake caliper(s). When purchasing a new hose, compare it to the old hose to make sure that the length and angle of the steel hose portion are correct. Install new banjo bolt washers (**Figure 111**) at both ends.

1. Drain the front brake system as follows:
   a. Connect a hose over the bleed valve.
   b. Insert the loose end of the hose in a container to catch the brake fluid.
   c. Open the bleed valve and apply the front brake lever to pump the fluid out of the master cylinder and brake line. Continue until you have removed all of the fluid.
   d. Close the bleed valve and disconnect the hose.

e. On models with dual front brakes, repeat for the opposite side.

f. Dispose of this brake fluid—*never* reuse brake fluid. Contaminated brake fluid will cause brake failure.

2. Before removing the brake line, note the brake line routing from the master cylinder to the caliper. In addition, note the number and position of the metal hose clamps and plastic ties used to hold the brake line in place. Install the brake hose along its original path. You can reuse the metal clamps. However, you must install new plastic ties.

3. Cut the plastic ties and discard them.

4. On dual disc models, remove the bolt and lockwasher (**Figure 112**) securing the brake hose union to the lower steering stem.

5. Remove the screw or nut securing the metal clamps around the brake line. Spread the clamp and remove it from the brake line.

6. Remove the banjo bolt and washers securing the hose to the brake caliper(s). See **Figure 113**.

7. Remove the banjo bolt and washers securing the hose to the master cylinder. See **Figure 114**.

8. Cover the ends of the brake hose(s) to prevent brake fluid from dripping onto the motorcycle when removing the cable assembly.

9. Remove the brake hose from the motorcycle.

10. If you intend to reuse the brake hose assembly, inspect it as follows:

a. Check the metal pipe where it enters and exits at the flexible hose. Check the crimped clamp for looseness or damage.

b. Check the flexible hose portion for swelling, cracks or other damage.

c. If any wear or damage is found, replace the brake hose.

11. Install the brake hose, washers (**Figure 111**) and banjo bolts in the reverse order of removal. Install a washer against the side of each hose fitting (**Figure 115**).

12. Carefully install the clips and guides to hold the brake hose in place.

13. Tighten the banjo bolts to the torque specification listed in **Table 2**.

14. Refill the master cylinder with fresh brake fluid clearly marked DOT 5. Bleed the front brake system as described in this chapter.

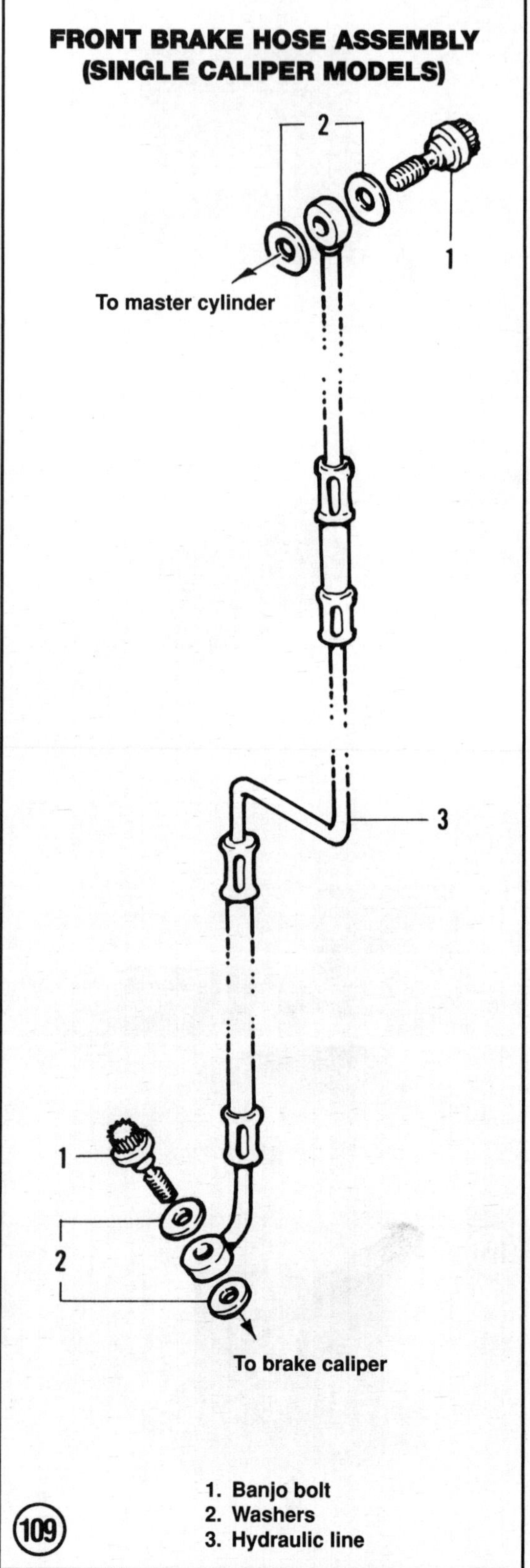

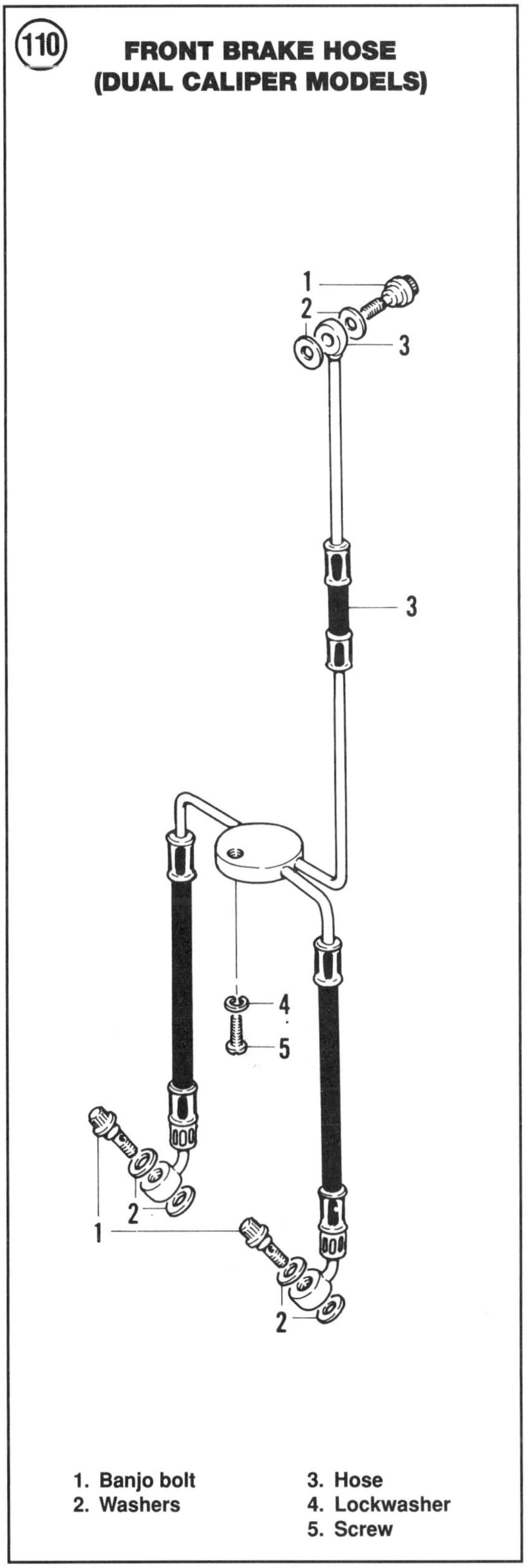

110
FRONT BRAKE HOSE
(DUAL CALIPER MODELS)
1
2
3
3
4
5
1
2
1
2
1. Banjo bolt
2. Washers
3. Hose
4. Lockwasher
5. Screw

111

112

113

114

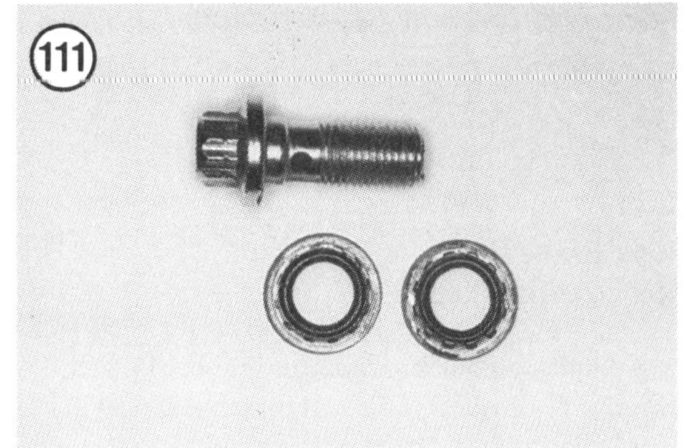

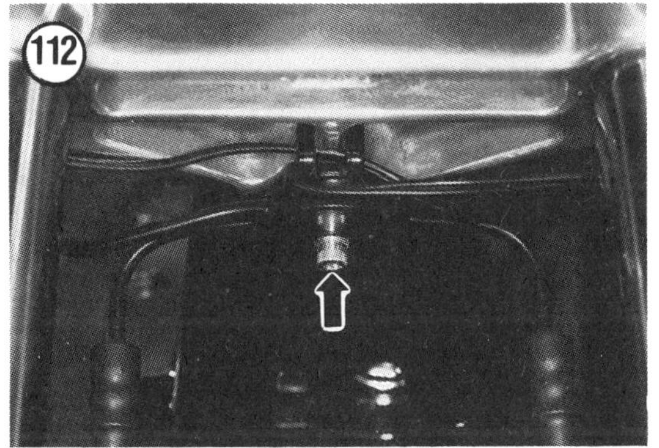

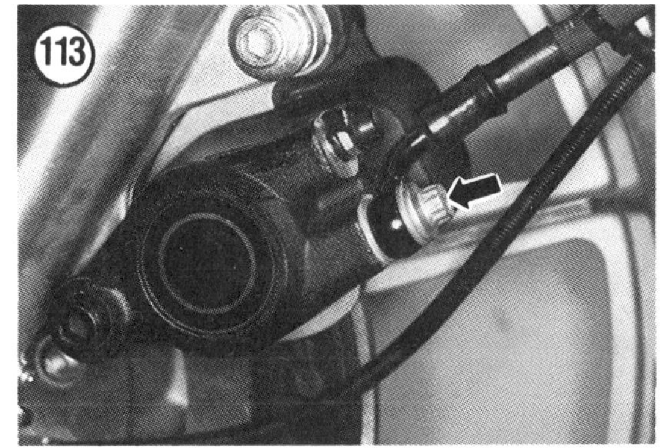

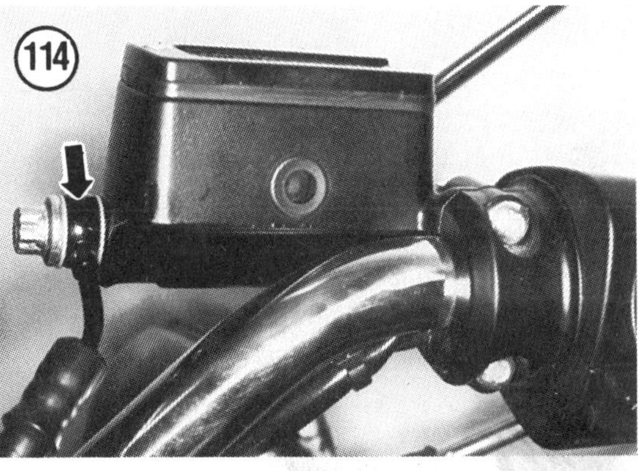

WARNING
Do not ride the motorcycle until you are sure that the brakes are operating properly.

Rear Brake Hose Removal/Installation

A single combination steel and rubber brake hose (**Figure 116**) connects the rear master cylinder to the rear brake caliper. The rear brake switch is installed in the rear brake hose.

When buying a new hose, compare it to the old hose. Make sure the length and angle of the steel hose portion is correct. Install new banjo bolt washers (**Figure 111**) at both hose ends.

1. Drain the hydraulic brake fluid from the front brake system as follows:
   a. Connect a hose to the bleed valve (A, **Figure 117**).
   b. Insert the loose end of the hose in a container to catch the brake fluid.
   c. Open the caliper bleed valve and operate the rear brake pedal to pump the fluid out of the master cylinder and brake line. Continue until you have removed all of the fluid.
   d. Close the bleed valve and disconnect the hose.
   e. Dispose of this brake fluid—*never* reuse brake fluid. Contaminated brake fluid will cause brake failure.
2. Before removing the brake line, note the brake line routing from the master cylinder to the caliper. In addition, note the number and position of the metal hose clamps and plastic ties used to hold the brake line in place. Install the brake hose along its original path. You can reuse the metal clamps. However, new plastic ties will have to be installed.
3. Cut the plastic ties and discard them.
4. Remove the bolt and clamp securing the brake hose to the rear swing arm (**Figure 118**).
5. Disconnect the 2 electrical connectors (A, **Figure 119**) from the rear brake switch.
6. Remove the banjo bolt and washers securing the hose to the brake caliper (B, **Figure 117**).
7. Remove the banjo bolt and washers securing the hose to the master cylinder (B, **Figure 119**).
8. Remove the brake hose from the motorcycle.
9. If you intend to reuse the brake hose assembly, inspect it as follows:
   a. Check the metal pipe where it enters and exits the flexible hose. Check the crimped clamp for looseness or damage.
   b. Check the flexible hose portion for swelling, cracks or other damage.
   c. If any wear or damage is found, replace the brake hose.
10. If necessary, remove the stoplight switch (**A, Figure 119**) from the rear brake hose fitting. Reverse to install the switch. Tighten the switch securely.
11. Install the brake hose in the reverse order of removal. Install new banjo bolt washers on both sides of each hose fitting. Tighten the banjo bolts to the torque specification in **Table 2**.
12. Refill the master cylinder with fresh brake fluid clearly marked DOT 5. Bleed the rear brake system as described in this chapter.

WARNING
Do not ride the motorcycle until you are sure that the brakes are operating properly.

BRAKE DISC (FRONT AND REAR)

The front wheel is equipped with either a single or dual disc brake assembly. The rear wheel is equipped with a single brake disc assembly. Periodically, measure the thickness of each brake disc. Harley-Davidson stamps the minimum disc thickness on each disc (A, **Figure 120**). See **Table 1** for disc thickness specifications.

Removal/Installation

1. Remove the front or rear wheel as described in Chapter Nine.

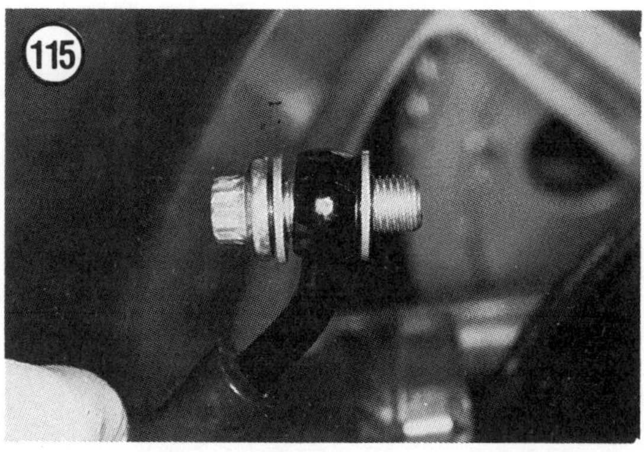

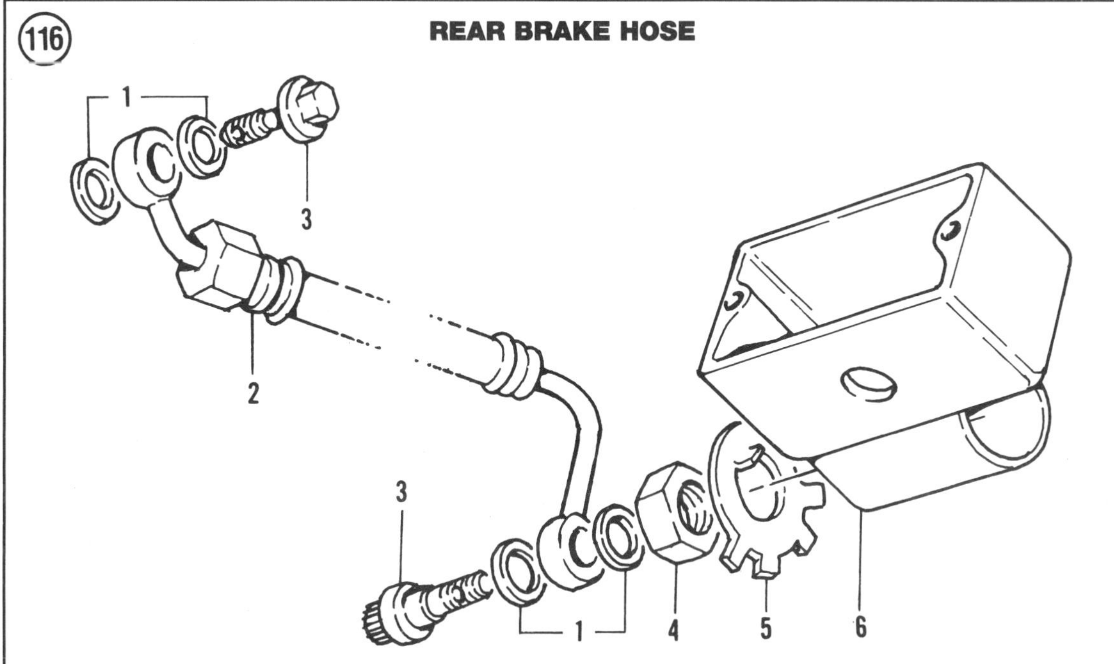

116

REAR BRAKE HOSE

1. Washer
2. Hose
3. Banjo bolt
4. Nut
5. Lockwasher
6. Master cylinder housing

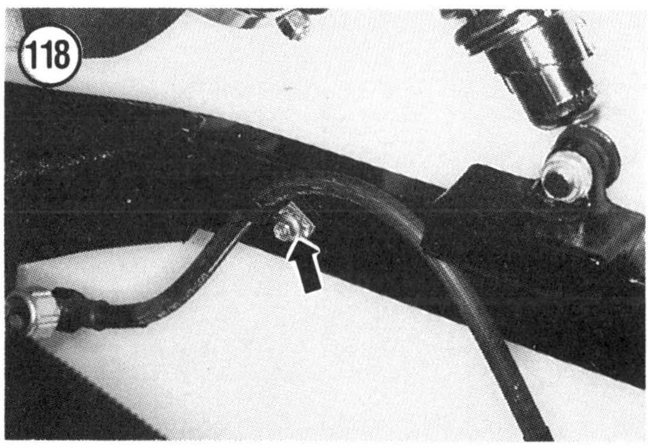

2. Remove the bolts (and locknuts) securing the brake disc to the hub and remove the disc. See B, **Figure 120**, typical.
3. Install the brake disc by reversing these removal steps, noting the following.
4. Check the brake disc bolts (and locknuts) for thread damage. Replace worn or damaged fasteners.
5. Clean the disc and the disc mounting surface thoroughly with brake cleaner or contact cleaner. Allow the surfaces to dry before installation.
6. To install the front brake disc(s):
   a. To install the disc, align the notch in the brake disc with the 1/4 in. (6.3 mm) blind hole in the hub; see **Figure 121**.

CAUTION
If you do not align the notch and blind hole, the speedometer drive tang will not seat against the disc when you install the speedometer drive unit. This may damage the speedometer drive unit.

   b. Install *new Torx bolts and nuts and tighten to the torque specification in* **Table 2**.
7. To install the rear brake disc:
   a. Install new bolts.
   b. Install new nuts, if used.
   c. On models with bolts only, apply a drop of Loctite 242 (blue) to each bolt.
   d. Tighten the bolts (and nuts) to the torque specification in **Table 2**.

Inspection

You can inspect each brake disc while it is mounted on its wheel.

1. Inspect the brake disc. If the disc is cracked, has deep scratches, warped, or in any way damaged, replace it.
2. Measure the thickness around the disc at several locations with a vernier caliper or micrometer (**Figure 122**). Replace the disc if the thickness at any point is less than the minimum thickness stamped on the disc (A, **Figure 120**).

NOTE
Use the disc specifications listed in ***Table 1*** *if the stamping mark on the disc is unclear.*

3. Clean the disc of any rust or corrosion and wipe clean with lacquer thinner. Never use an oil-based solvent that may leave an oil residue on the disc.

BLEEDING THE SYSTEM

If air enters the brake system, the brake will feel soft or spongy, greatly reducing braking pressure. If this happens, you must bleed the system to remove the air. Air can enter the system if there is a leak in the system, the brake fluid level in a master cylinder runs low, if opening a brake line, or if replacing the brake fluid.

When bleeding the brakes, you can use one of two methods—with a brake bleeder or manually. This section describes both procedures separately.

Before bleeding the brake system, observe the following conditions:

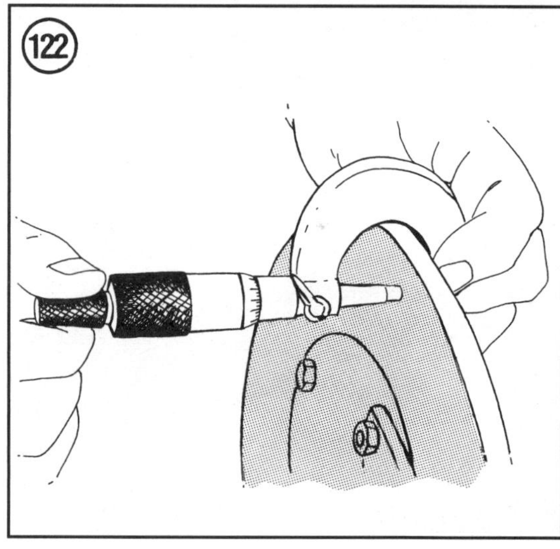

a. Check the brake lines to make sure that all fittings are tight.
b. Check that the caliper piston does not stick or bind in its bore.
c. Check piston movement in each master cylinder. Operate the lever or brake pedal, making sure there is no binding or other abnormal conditions present.

Bleeding the Brake with a Brake Bleeder

This procedure uses the Mityvac hydraulic brake bleeding kit (**Figure 123**). This tool is available from automotive supply stores.

1. Remove the dust cap from the caliper bleed valve (A, **Figure 117**).
2. Assemble the Mityvac tool according to its manufacturers instructions. Secure it to the caliper bleed valve (**Figure 124**).
3. Clean the top of the master cylinder of all dirt and foreign matter.
4. Remove the screws securing the master cylinder top cover and remove the cover and rubber diaphragm.

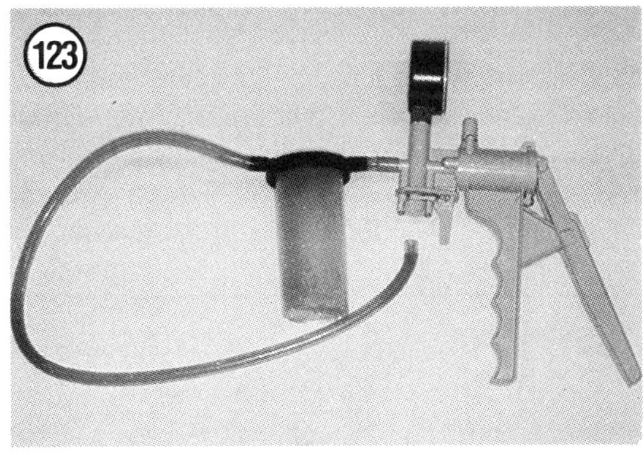

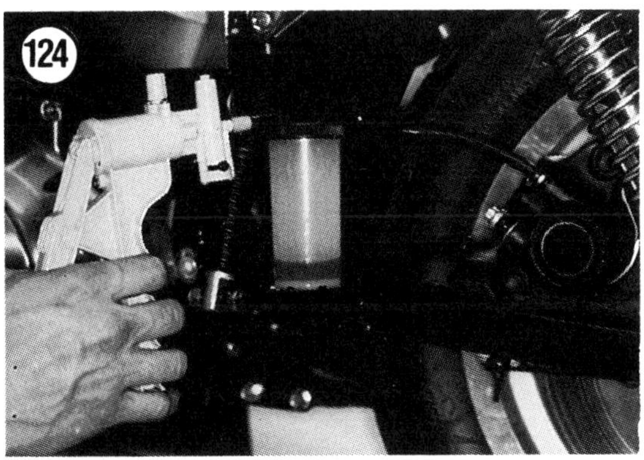

5. Fill the reservoir almost to the top with DOT 5 brake fluid and reinstall the diaphragm and cover. Leave the cover in place during this procedure to prevent the entry of dirt.

WARNING
Do not intermix brake fluid. Harley-Davidson installed DOT 5 brake fluid at the time of manufacture. Do not install DOT 3, DOT 4 or DOT 5.1 brake fluid as it can lead to brake system failure.

6. Operate the pump several times to create a vacuum in the line. Then open the bleed screw approximately 1/2 turn. Brake fluid will quickly draw from the caliper into the pumps reservoir. Tighten the caliper bleed screw before the fluid stops flowing through the hose. To prevent air from being drawn through the master cylinder, add fluid to maintain its level at the top of the reservoir.

NOTE
Do not allow the master cylinder reservoir to empty during the bleeding operation or more air will enter the system. If this occurs, you must repeat the procedure.

7. Continue the bleeding process until the fluid drawn from the caliper is bubble free. If bubbles are withdrawn with the brake fluid, more air is trapped in the line. Repeat Step 6, making sure to refill the master cylinder to prevent air from being drawn into the system.
8. When the brake fluid is free of bubbles, tighten the bleed valve and remove the brake bleeder assembly. Reinstall the bleed valve dust cap.

NOTE
Do not reuse the brake fluid from the tools reservoir.

9. If necessary, add fluid to correct the level in the master cylinder reservoir. When topping off the front master cylinder, turn the handlebar until the reservoir is level; add fluid until it is level with the reservoir gasket surface. The fluid level in the rear master cylinder must be slightly below the upper gasket surface.
10. Reinstall the reservoir diaphragm and cap. Secure the cap with its 2 screws.
11. Test the feel of the brake lever or pedal. It must be firm and offer the same resistance each time it's

operated. If it feels spongy, it is likely that there is still air in the system and you must bleed it again. After bleeding the system, check for leaks and tighten all fittings and connections as necessary.

WARNING
Before riding the bike, make certain that the brake is operating correctly by operating the lever or pedal several times.

12. Test ride the bike slowly at first to make sure that the brakes are operating properly.

Bleeding the Brake Manually

When bleeding the brake system manually, you need a clean jar, a suitable length of clear hose and the correct wrench.

NOTE
Before bleeding the brake, check that all brake hoses and lines are tight.

1. Connect a length of clear tubing to the bleeder valve on the caliper. Place the other end of the tube into a clean container. Fill the container with enough fresh DOT 5 brake fluid to keep the end of the tube submerged. The tube must be long enough so that you can make a loop higher than the bleeder valve to prevent air from being drawn into the caliper during bleeding. See **Figure 125**, typical.
2. Clean the top of the master cylinder of all dirt and foreign matter.
3. Remove the screws securing the master cylinder top cover and remove the cover and rubber diaphragm.
4. Fill the reservoir almost to the top with DOT 5 brake fluid and reinstall the diaphragm and cover. Leave the cover in place during this procedure to prevent the entry of dirt.

WARNING
Do not intermix brake fluid. Harley-Davidson installed DOT 5 brake fluid at the time of manufacture. Do not install DOT 3, DOT 4 or DOT 5.1 brake fluid as it will lead to brake system failure.

NOTE
During this procedure, it is important to check the fluid level in the master cylinder reservoir often. If the reservoir runs dry, more air will enter the system.

5. Slowly apply the brake lever several times. Hold the lever in the applied position and open the bleed screw about 1/2 turn. Allow the lever to travel to its limit. When you reach this limit, tighten the bleed screw, then release the brake lever. As the brake fluid enters the system, the level will drop in the master cylinder reservoir. Maintain the level at the top of the reservoir to prevent air from being drawn into the system.
6. Continue the bleeding process until the fluid emerging from the hose is completely free of air bubbles. If you are replacing the fluid, continue until the fluid emerging from the hose is clean.

NOTE
If bleeding is difficult, allowing the fluid to stabilize for a few hours. Repeat the bleeding procedure when the tiny bubbles in the system settle out.

7. Hold the lever in the applied position and tighten the bleeder valve. Remove the bleeder tube and install the bleeder valve dust cap.

NOTE
Do not reuse the brake fluid forced into the jar.

8. If necessary, add fluid to correct the level in the master cylinder reservoir. When topping off the front master cylinder, turn the handlebar until the reservoir is level; add fluid until it is level with the reservoir gasket surface. The fluid level in the rear master

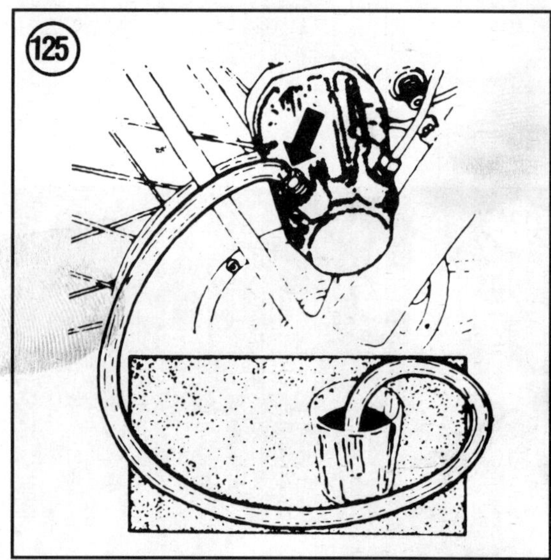

cylinder must be slightly below the upper gasket surface.

9. Install the cap and diaphragm and tighten the screws securely.

10. Test the feel of the brake lever or pedal. It must be firm and offer the same resistance each time it's operated. If it feels spongy, it is likely that there is still air in the system and you must bleed it again.

After bleeding the system check for leaks and tighten all fittings and connections as necessary.

WARNING
Before riding the bike, make certain that the brake is operating correctly by operating the lever or pedal several times.

11. Test ride the bike slowly at first to make sure that the brakes are operating properly.

Table 1 BRAKE SPECIFICATIONS

Brake fluid	DOT 5 silicone-based
Disc pad thickness (minimum)	0.062 in. (1.57 mm)
Brake disc thickness	0.205 in. (5.21 mm) or specification stamped on disc.

Table 2 BRAKE TIGHTENING TORQUES

	ft.-lb.	N•m
Brake bleeder nipples	32-48 in.-lb.	3.6-5.4
Brake line banjo bolts	17-22	23-30
Front brake caliper		
Pad retainer screw		
1991-1992	15-20 in.-lb.	1.7-2.3
1993-on	40-50 in.-lb.	4.5-5.6
Upper mounting screw	25-30	34-41
Lower mounting pin	25-30	34-41
Front master cylinder mounting screws	70-80 in.-lb.	7.9-9.0
Front brake disc mounting bolts	16-18	22-24
Rear brake pad pin bolts	15-20	20-27
Rear brake caliper mounting bolts	15-20	20-27
Rear brake disc mounting bolts		
1991-1992	23-27	31-37
1993-on		
Allen bolts	23-27	31-37
Torx bolts	30-45	41-61
Rear master cylinder mounting nut	30-40	41-54

SUPPLEMENT

1996-1998 SERVICE INFORMATION

This Supplement contains all procedures and specifications unique to the 1996-1998 Dyna Glide models. If a specific procedure is not included, refer to the procedure in the prior chapter in the main body of this manual.

This Supplement is divided into sections that correspond to those in the other chapters of this manual.

CHAPTER TWO

TROUBLESHOOTING

Refer to the wiring diagrams at the end of the manual for 1996-1998 models:

CHAPTER THREE

LUBRICATION, MAINTENANCE AND TUNE-UP

PERIODIC LUBRICATION

Primary Chaincase Oil Level Check (1998 Model)

The primary chaincase oil lubricates the clutch, primary chain and sprockets. **Table 1** in Chapter Three lists the chaincase oil level check intervals. When checking the primary chaincase oil level, do not allow any dirt or foreign matter to enter the housing.

1. Park the bike on a level surface and support it so that it is standing straight up. Do not support it on its jiffy stand.

CAUTION
Do not check the oil level with the motorcycle supported on its jiffy stand or the reading will be incorrect.

2. Remove the screws securing the clutch inspection cover (**Figure 1**) and O-ring. Remove the cover.
3. The oil level is correct if it is even with the bottom of the clutch opening or at the bottom of the clutch diaphragm spring (**Figure 2**).

CAUTION
Do not add engine oil. Add only the recommended primary chaincase lubricant.

13

4. If necessary, add Harley-Davidson Primary Chaincase Lubricant (**Figure 3**), or equivalent, through the opening (**Figure 4**) to correct the level.
5. Install the clutch inspection cover O-ring (**Figure 5**) onto the primary chain case cover.
6. Install the clutch inspection cover and tighten the screws to 50-70 in.-lbs. (6-8 N·m).

Primary Chaincase Oil Replacement (1998 Model)

Table 1 in Chapter Three lists the factory-recommended primary chaincase lubricant replacement intervals. To change the primary chaincase lubricant, the following items are required:

a. Drain pan.
b. Wrench for drain plug.
c. Primary chaincase oil; 26 oz. (770 ml).

1. Ride the bike for approximately 10 minutes and shift through all five gears until the transmission oil has reached normal operating temperature. Turn off the engine and allow the oil to settle. Park the bike on a level surface and have an assistant support it so that it is standing straight up. Do not support it with its jiffy stand.
2. Place a drain pan under the chaincase and remove the drain plug (**Figure 6**).
3. Allow the oil to drain for at least 10 minutes.
4. The drain plug is magnetic. Check the plug for metal debris that may suggest primary drive component or clutch damage, then wipe the plug off. Replace the plug if damaged.
5. Reinstall the drain plug and tighten securely.
6. Remove the screws securing the clutch inspection cover (**Figure 1**) and O-ring. Remove the cover.

CAUTION
*Do not add engine oil. Add only the recommended primary chaincase lubricant (**Figure 3**).*

7. Refill the primary chaincase through the clutch opening (**Figure 4**) with the recommended quantity and type primary chaincase oil. Do not overfill. The oil level must be even with the bottom of the clutch opening or at the bottom of the clutch diaphragm spring (**Figure 2**).
8. Install the clutch inspection cover O-ring (**Figure 5**) onto the primary chain case cover.
9. Install the clutch inspection cover and tighten the screws to 50-70 in.-lbs. (5-8 N·m).
10. Ride the bike until the primary chaincase oil reaches normal operating temperature. Then shut the engine off.
11. Check the primary chaincase drain plug for leaks.

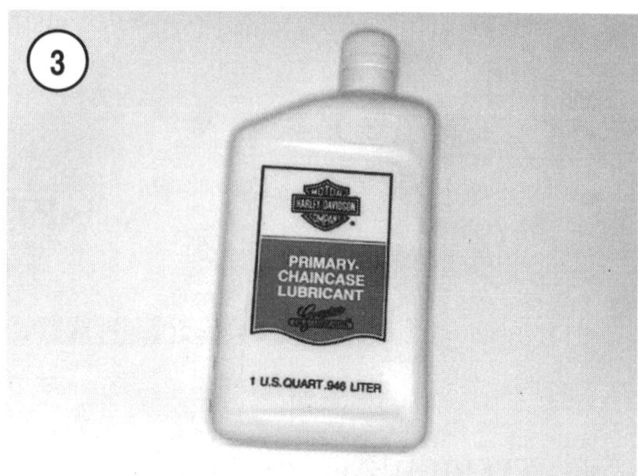

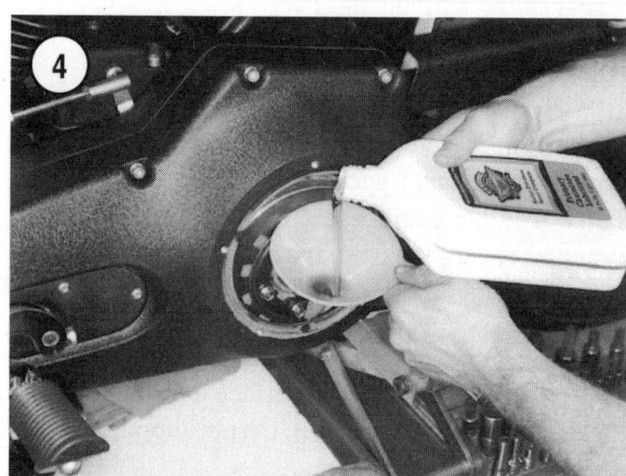

PERIODIC MAINTENANCE

Front Disc Brake Fluid Level

1. To check the front master cylinder, perform the following:
   a. Turn the handlebar so the master cylinder is level.
   b. Observe the brake fluid level by looking at the sight glass (A, **Figure 7**) on the master cylinder reservoir top cover. If the fluid level is correct, the sight glass will appear dark purple, if the level is low the sight glass will have lightened or will appear clear.

WARNING
*A different non-silicone based brake fluid is available that is labeled **DOT5.1**. This is glycol based and **is not compatible** with the silicone based DOT5. DOT5 brake fluid is purple in color while the DOT5.1 is amber/clear color. Do not intermix these two completely different based brake fluids as this will lead to brake component damage and possible brake failure.*

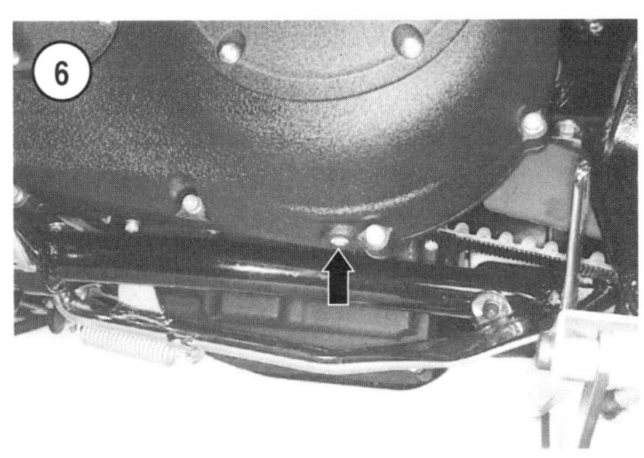

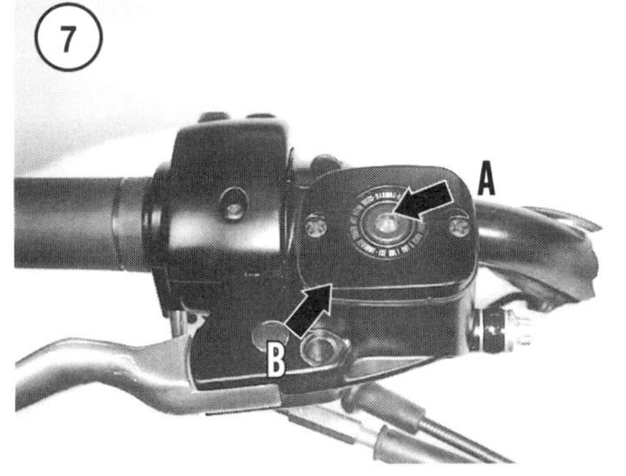

WARNING
Only use brake fluid clearly marked DOT 5 and specified for disc brakes. Others may vaporize and cause brake failure.

CAUTION
Be careful when handling brake fluid. Do not spill it on painted or plastic surfaces, as it damages them. Wash the area immediately with soap and water and thoroughly rinse it.

NOTE
To control the flow of brake fluid, punch a small hole in the seal of a new container of brake fluid nest to the edge of the pour spout. This helps eliminate the fluid spillage, especially while adding fluid to the small reservoir.

2. If the brake fluid level is low, perform the following:
   a. Clean any dirt from the master cylinder cover prior to removing it.
   b. Remove the top cover (B, **Figure 7**) and lift the diaphragm out of the reservoir.
   c. Add fresh DOT 5 brake fluid to correct the level.
   d. Reinstall the diaphragm and top cover. Tighten the screws securely.

NOTE
If the brake fluid level is low enough to allow air in the hydraulic system, bleed the brakes as described in Chapter Twelve.

Clutch Adjustment (1998 Model)

CAUTION
Because the clutch cable adjuster clearance increases with engine temperature, adjust the clutch when the engine is cold. If the clutch is adjusted when the engine is hot, insufficient pushrod clearance can cause the clutch to slip.

1. Remove the clutch mechanism inspection cover (**Figure 1**) and O-ring.

2. Slide the rubber boot off the clutch in-line cable adjuster.

3. Loosen the adjuster locknut (**Figure 8**) and turn the adjuster to provide maximum cable slack.

4. Check that the clutch cable seats squarely in its perch (**Figure 9**) at the handlebar.

5. At the clutch mechanism, loosen the clutch adjusting screw locknut (A, **Figure 10**) and turn the adjusting screw (B) *clockwise* until it is lightly seated.

6. Squeeze the clutch lever three times to verify the clutch balls are seated in the ramp release mechanism located behind the transmission side cover.

7. Back out the adjusting screw (B, **Figure 10**) *counterclockwise* 1/2 to 1 turn. Then hold the adjusting screw (A, **Figure 11**) and tighten the locknut (B) to 70-120 in.-lbs. (8-14 N·m).

8. Once again, squeeze the clutch lever to its maximum limit three times to set the clutch ball and ramp release mechanism.

9. Check the free play as follows:

   a. At the in-line cable adjuster, turn the adjuster away from the locknut until slack is eliminated at the clutch hand lever.

   b. Pull on the clutch cable sheath away from the clutch lever, then turn the clutch cable ad-

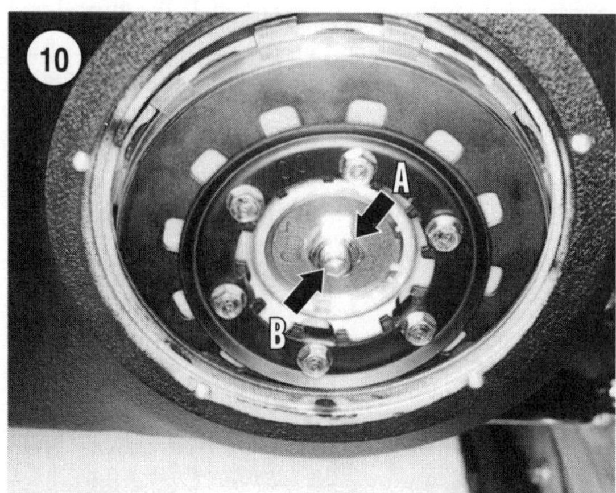

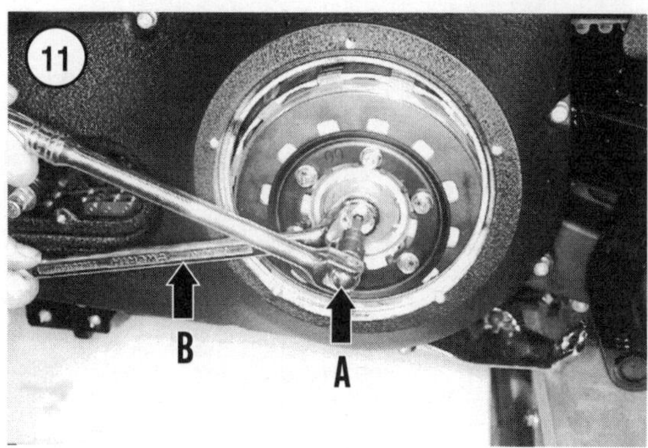

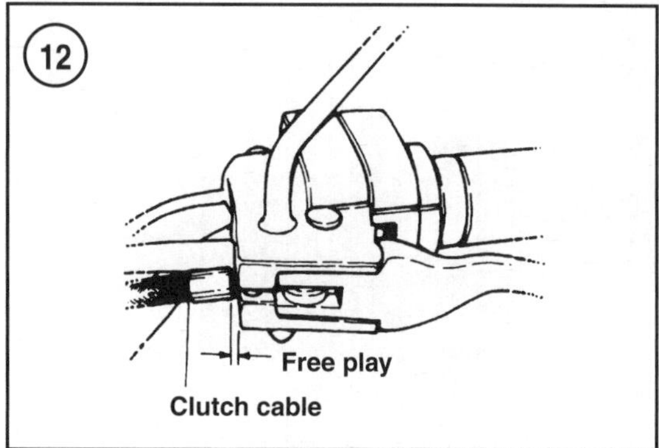

juster to obtain the specified free play (**Figure 12**) of 1/16-1/8 in. (1.6-3.2 mm).

c. When the adjustment is correct, tighten the clutch in-line cable locknut (**Figure 8**) and slide the rubber boot over the cable adjuster.

10. Install the clutch inspection cover O-ring (**Figure 5**) onto the primary chain case cover.
11. Install the clutch inspection cover and tighten the screws to 50-70 in.-lbs. (6-8 N·m).

IGNITION SERVICE

Ignition Timing Inspection and Adjustment

The ignition timing inspection and adjustment is the same as on prior years with the exception of the engine speed. Start the engine and allow it to run at 1050-1500 rpm. If necessary, adjust the engine speed as described in Chapter Three.

CHAPTER FIVE

CLUTCH AND PRIMARY DRIVE

CLUTCH PLATES (1998 MODEL)

This section describes removal, inspection and installation of the clutch plates. If the clutch requires additional service, refer to *Clutch Overhaul* in this section.

Refer to **Figure 13**.

Removal

1. Disconnect the battery negative lead.
2. Remove the clutch mechanism inspection cover (**Figure 14**) and O-ring.
3. At the clutch mechanism, loosen the clutch adjusting screw locknut (A, **Figure 15**) and turn the adjusting screw (B) *counterclockwise* to allow slack against the diaphragm spring.
4. Remove the primary chaincase outer cover as described in Chapter Five.
5. Loosen the bolts securing the diaphragm spring retainer (A, **Figure 16**) in a crisscross pattern. Remove the bolts and the retainer and diaphragm spring (B, **Figure 16**).
6. Remove the pressure plate (**Figure 17**).
7. Remove the clutch plates and friction discs from the clutch shell. After the first six clutch plates and friction discs are removed, carefully remove the remaining ones with a pick tool.
8. Remove the damper spring and damper spring seat from the clutch shell. Keep all parts in order as shown in **Figure 18**.

Inspection

When measuring the clutch components, compare the actual measurements to the specifications in **Table 1**. Replace parts that are out of specification or show damage as described in this section.

1. Clean all parts in solvent and thoroughly dry with compressed air.
2. Inspect the friction discs as follows:

NOTE

If any friction disc is damaged or out of specification as described in the following steps, replace all of the friction discs as a set. Never replace only 1 or 2 discs.

a. The friction material used on the friction discs (**Figure 19**) is bonded onto an aluminum plate for warp resistance and durability. Inspect the friction material for excessive or uneven wear, cracks and other damage. Check the disc tangs

(13)

CLUTCH ASSEMBLY

1. Snap ring
2. Clutch shell and sprocket
3. Bearing
4. Snap ring
5. Clutch hub
6. Clutch nut
7. Diaphragm spring seat
8. Diaphragm spring
9. Friction disc B
10. Clutch plates
11. Friction disc A
12. Pressure plate
13. Diaphragm spring
14. Diaphragm spring retainer
15. Bolt
16. Release plate
17. Snap ring
18. Snap ring
19. Thrust washer
20. Radial bearing
21. Oil slinger
22. Pushrod (right side)
23. Pushrod (right side)
24. Push rod (left side)
25. Locknut

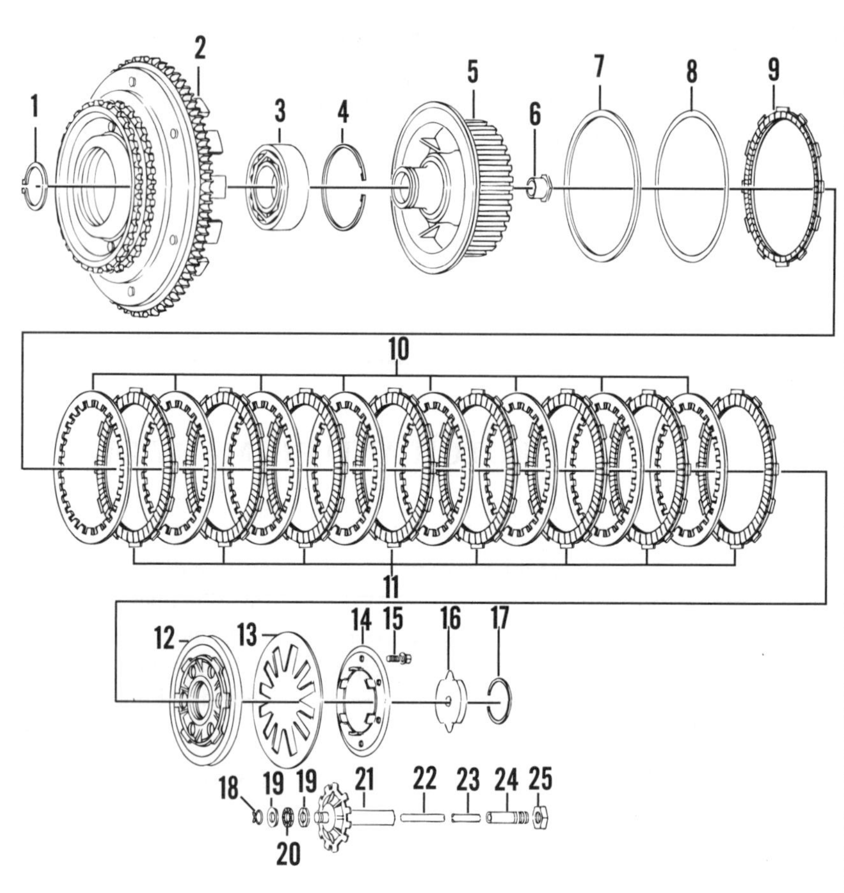

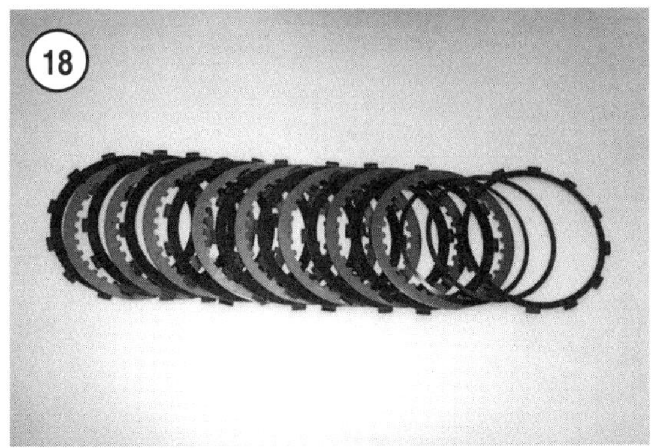

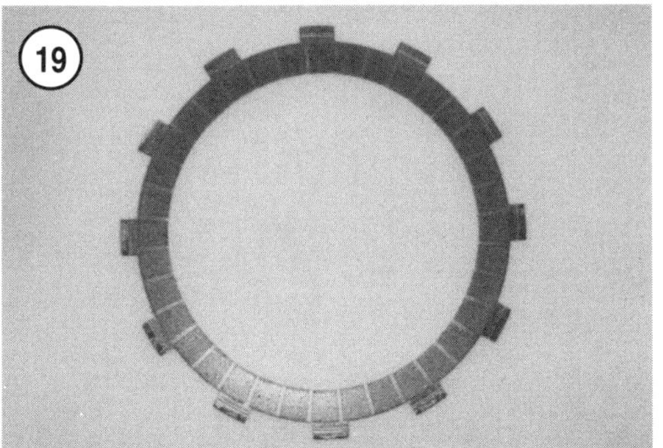

for surface damage. The sides of the disc tangs where they contact the clutch shell fingers must be smooth; otherwise, the discs cannot engage and disengage correctly.

NOTE
If the disc tangs are damaged, inspect the clutch shell fingers carefully as described later in this section.

b. Measure the thickness of each friction disc with a vernier caliper (**Figure 20**). Measure at several places around the disc.

3. Inspect the clutch plates (**Figure 21**) as follows:

a. Inspect the clutch plates for cracks, damage or color change. Overheated clutch plates will have a blue discoloration.

b. Check the clutch plates for an oil glaze buildup. Remove by lightly sanding both sides of each plate with 400 grit sandpaper placed on a surface plate or piece of glass.

c. Place each clutch plate on a flat surface and check warpage with a feeler gauge (**Figure 22**).

d. The clutch plate inner teeth mesh with the clutch hub splines. Check the clutch plate teeth for any roughness or damage. The teeth contact surfaces must be smooth; otherwise, the plates cannot engage and disengage correctly.

NOTE
If the clutch plate teeth are damaged, inspect the clutch hub splines carefully as described later in this section.

4. Inspect the diaphragm spring (**Figure 23**) for cracks or damage.

13

5. Inspect the diaphragm spring retainer for cracks or damage. Check also for bent or damaged tabs (**Figure 24**).

6. Inspect the pressure plate contact surface (**Figure 25**) for cracks or other damage.

7. If necessary, disassemble the pressure plate as follows:

   a. Remove the snap ring and remove the release plate, left side pushrod and locknut (**Figure 26**) from the pressure plate.
   b. Inspect the release plate, left side pushrod and locknut for wear or damage.
   c. Inspect its snapring groove for damage.
   d. Position the release plate with the OUT mark facing out (**Figure 27**) and install the assembly into the pressure plate.
   e. Install the snap ring and make sure it is correctly seated in the pressure plate groove.

Installation

NOTE

The clutch assembly has nine friction plates, eight steel plates, one damper spring and one damper spring seat. Make sure each one is installed and in the correct order.

If installing an aftermarket clutch plate assembly, follow the manufacturer's instructions for plate quantity, alignment and installation sequence.

1. Soak the clutch friction disc and clutch plates in new primary drive oil for approximately 5 minutes before installing them.

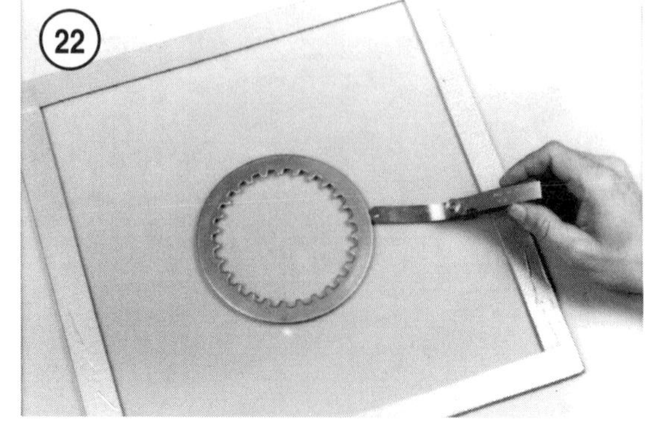

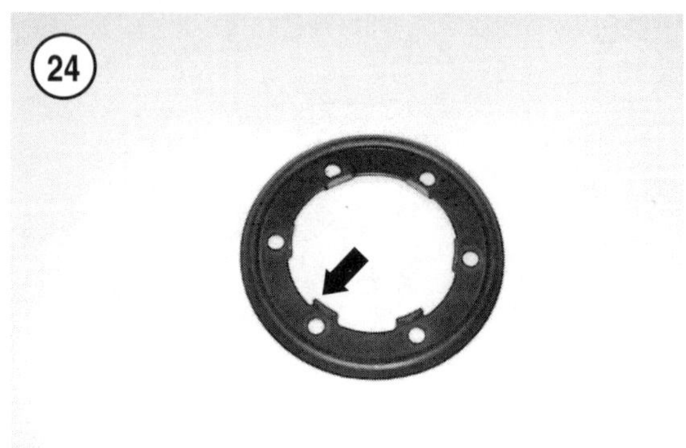

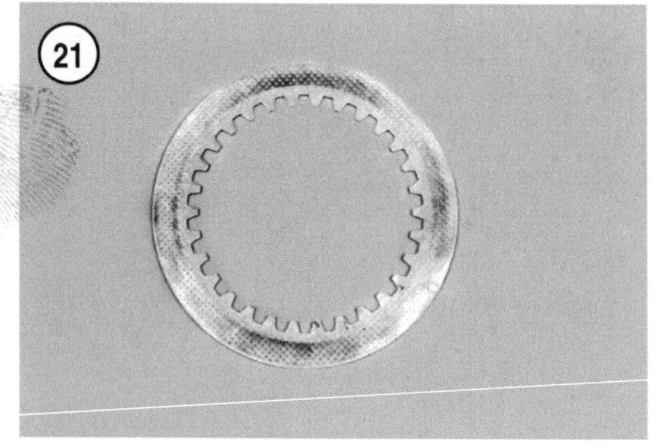

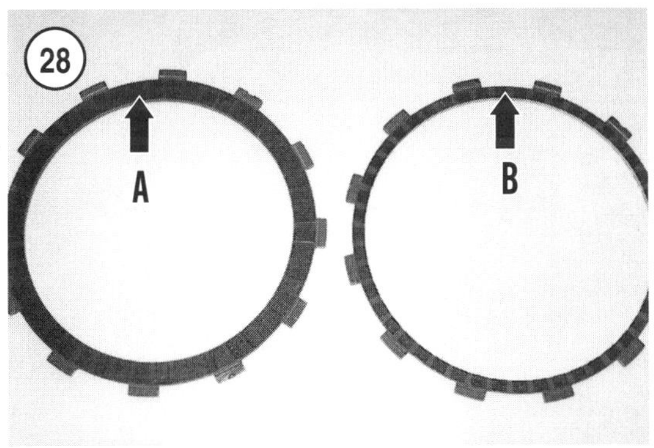

NOTE

*There are two different types of clutch friction discs (**Figure 28**). The wider friction disc A is the normal width disc while the narrow width friction disc B is installed first as it works in conjunction with the damper spring and damper spring seat.*

2. Install the clutch friction disc B (**Figure 29**) onto the clutch shell and clutch hub. Push it on all the way until it bottoms within the clutch hub.
3. Install the damper spring seat (**Figure 30**) onto the clutch hub and push it in until it is seats within the clutch friction disc B.
4. Position the damper spring (**Figure 31**) with the dished side facing out and install it onto the clutch hub against the damper spring seat (**Figure 32**).
5. Install a clutch plate (**Figure 33**) then a friction disc A (**Figure 34**). Continue to alternately install the clutch plates and friction discs. The last part installed is a friction disc A (**Figure 35**).
6. Make sure the oil slinger assembly (**Figure 36**) is in place in the pressure plate. Install the pressure plate onto the clutch hub (**Figure 37**).
7. Position the diaphragm spring with the dished side facing out (**Figure 38**) and install it onto the pressure plate (**Figure 39**). Hold the pressure plate in place.
8. Position the diaphragm spring retainer with the finger side (**Figure 40**) facing in toward the diaphragm spring (B, **Figure 16**). Install the diaphragm spring retainer (A, **Figure 16**) and bolts.
9. Tighten the bolts in a crisscross pattern to 90-110 in.-lbs. (10-12 N·m).
10. Install the primary chaincase outer cover as described in Chapter Five

13

11. Install the clutch mechanism inspection cover and O-ring (**Figure 14**).
12. Connect the battery negative lead.

CLUTCH OVERHAUL

Inspection

The clutch shell is a subassembly consisting of the clutch shell, the clutch hub, the bearing and two snap rings.

1. Remove the clutch shell as described in this section.
2. Hold the clutch shell and rotate the clutch hub by hand. The bearing is damaged if the clutch hub binds or turns roughly.
3. Check the sprocket (A, **Figure 41**) and the starter ring gear (B) on the clutch shell for cracks, deep scoring, excessive wear or heat discoloration.
4. If the sprocket or the ring gear are worn or damaged, replace the clutch shell. If the primary chain sprocket is worn, also check the primary chain and the compensating sprocket as described in Chapter Five.
5. Inspect the clutch hub for the following conditions:

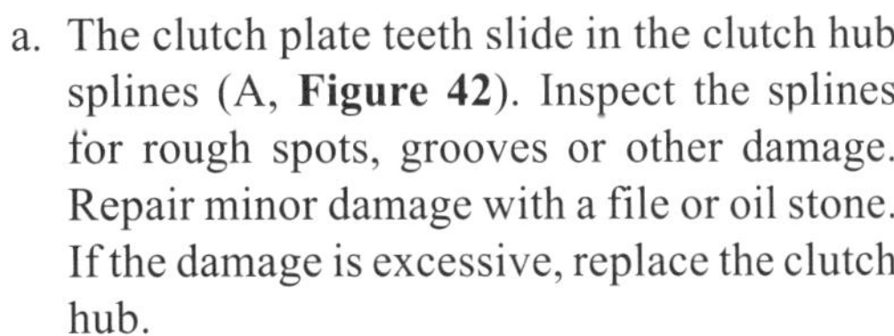

a. The clutch plate teeth slide in the clutch hub splines (A, **Figure 42**). Inspect the splines for rough spots, grooves or other damage. Repair minor damage with a file or oil stone. If the damage is excessive, replace the clutch hub.

b. Inspect the clutch hub inner splines (**Figure 43**) for galling, severe wear or other damage. Repair minor damage with a fine cut file. If damage is severe, replace the clutch hub.

c. Inspect the bolt towers and threads (B, **Figure 42**) for thread damage or cracks at the base of the tower. Repair thread damage with correct size metric tap. If the tower(s) is cracked or damaged, replace the clutch hub.

6. Check the clutch shell. The friction disc tangs slide in the clutch housing grooves (C, **Figure 42**). Inspect the grooves for cracks or galling. Repair minor damage with a file. If the damage is excessive, replace the clutch housing.

7. If the clutch hub, the clutch shell or the bearing is damage, replace them as described in the following procedure.

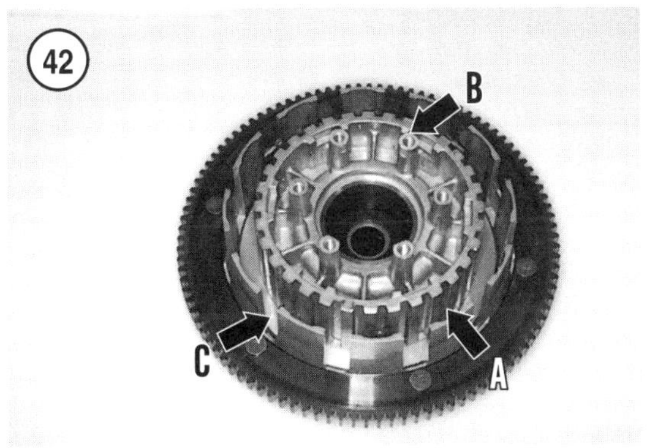

Disassembly/Assembly

Do not separate the clutch hub and shell unless the bearing or either part is going to be replaced. If the two parts are separated the bearing will be damaged.

Removal and installation of the bearing requires the use of a hydraulic press.

Refer to **Figure 44**.

1. Remove the clutch as described in this section. Remove the clutch shell assembly from the primary drive chain.

44

CLUTCH ASSEMBLY

1. Snap ring
2. Clutch shell and sprocket
3. Bearing
4. Snap ring
5. Clutch hub
6. Clutch nut
7. Diaphragm spring seat
8. Diaphragm spring
9. Friction disc B
10. Clutch plates
11. Friction disc A
12. Pressure plate
13. Diaphragm spring
14. Diaphragm spring retainer
15. Bolt
16. Release plate
17. Snap ring
18. Snap ring
19. Thrust washer
20. Radial bearing
21. Oil slinger
22. Pushrod (right side)
23. Pushrod (right side)
24. Push rod (left side)
25. Locknut

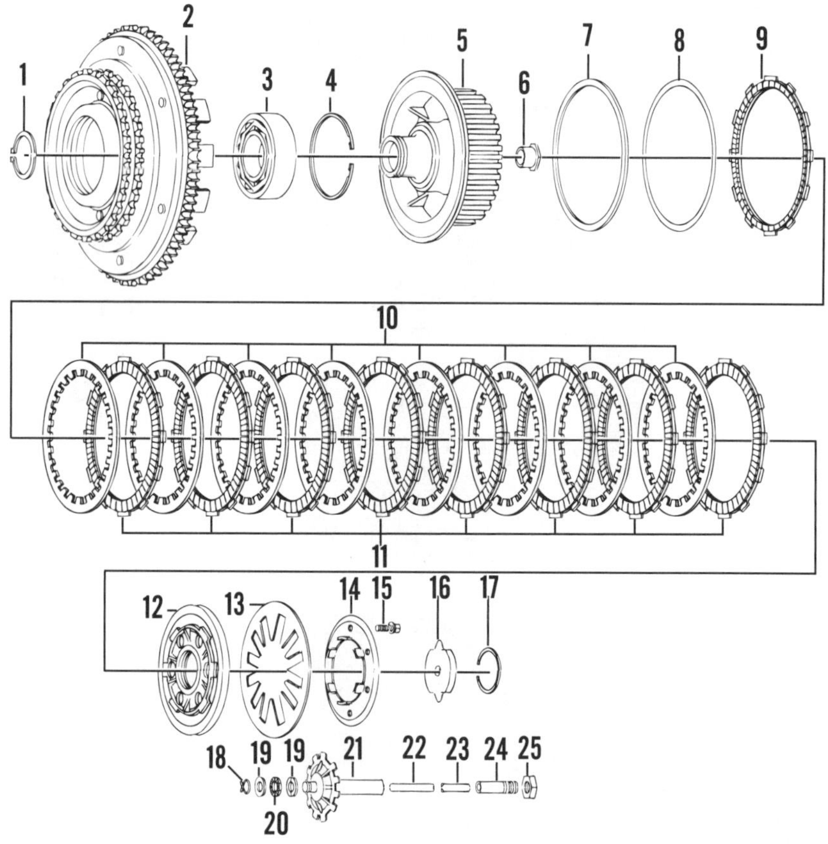

1 2 3 4 5 6 7 8 9
10
11
12 13 14 15 16 17
18 19 19 21 22 23 24 25
20

2. Remove the snap ring (**Figure 45**) from the clutch hub groove.
3. Position the clutch hub and shell with the primary chain sprocket side facing up.
4. Support the clutch hub and clutch shell in a press (**Figure 46**).
5. Place a suitable size arbor in the clutch hub surface and press the clutch hub (A, **Figure 47**) out of the bearing.
6. Remove the clutch shell from the press (B, **Figure 48**).

7. On the inner surface of the clutch shell, remove the bearing retaining snap ring (**Figure 49**) from the groove in the middle of the clutch shell.

CAUTION
Press the bearing out from the primary chain sprocket side of the clutch shell. The bearing bore has a shoulder on the primary chain side.

8. Support the clutch shell in the press with the primary chain sprocket side *facing up*.
9. Place a suitable size arbor on the bearing inner race and press the bearing out of the clutch shell (**Figure 49**).
10. Thoroughly clean the clutch hub and shell in solvent and dry with compressed air.
11. Inspect the bearing bore in the clutch shell for damage or burrs. Clean off any burrs that would interfere with new bearing installation.
12. Support the clutch shell in the press with the primary chain sprocket side *facing down*.
13. Apply chaincase lubricant to the clutch shell bearing receptacle and to the outer surface of the bearing.
14. Align the bearing with the clutch shell receptacle.
15. Place a suitable size arbor on the bearing outer race and slowly press the bearing into the clutch shell until it bottoms on the lower shoulder. Press only on the outer bearing race. Applying force to the bearings inner race will damage the bearing. Refer to *Ball Bearing Replacement* in Chapter One for additional information.

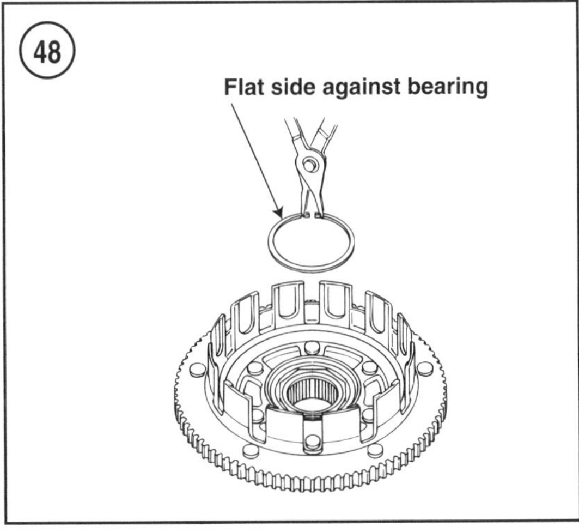

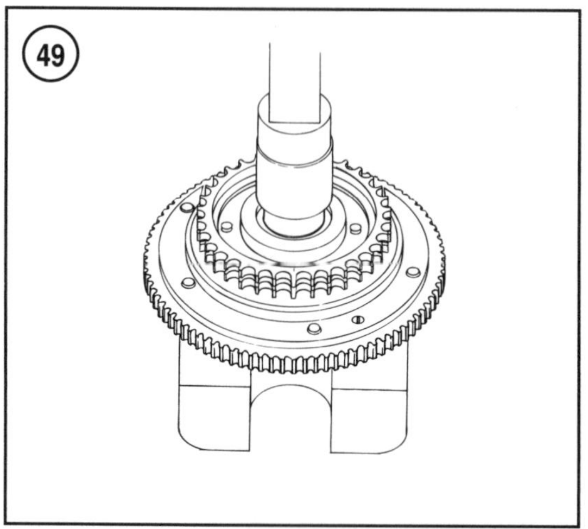

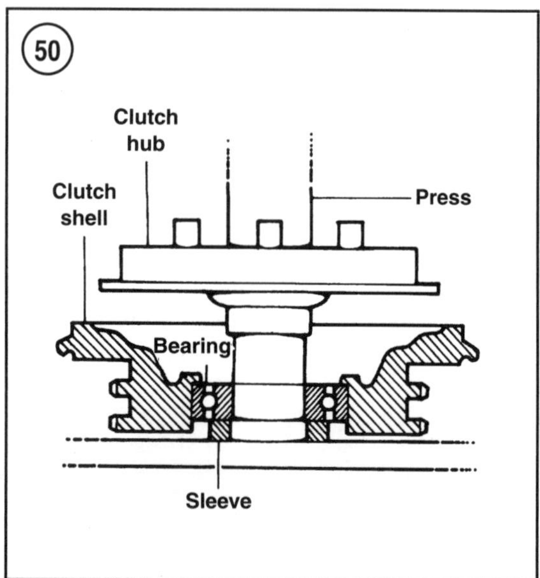

16. Position the *new* snap ring with the flat side against the bearing and install the snap ring into the clutch shell groove (**Figure 48**). Make sure the snap ring is seated correctly in the clutch shell groove.

17. Press the clutch hub into the clutch shell as follows:

CAUTION
Failure to support the inner bearing race properly will cause bearing and clutch shell damage.

a. Place the clutch shell in a press. Support the inner bearing race with a sleeve as shown in **Figure 50**.

b. Align the clutch hub with the bearing and slowly press the clutch hub into the bearing until the clutch hub shoulder seats against the bearing inner race.

c. Install a *new* snap ring (**Figure 45**) into the clutch hub. Make sure the snap ring is seated correctly in the clutch hub groove.

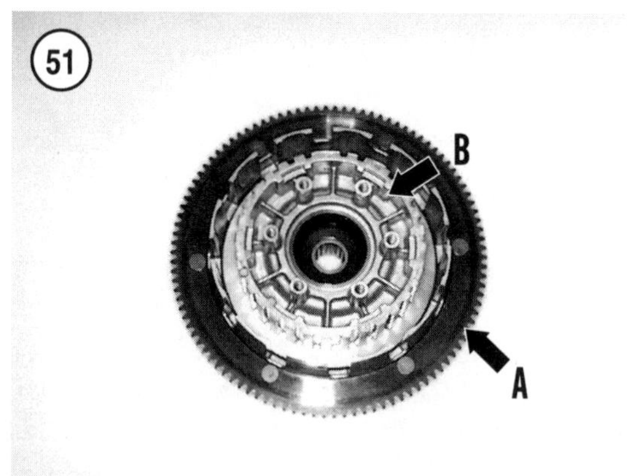

18. After completing assembly, hold the clutch shell (A, **Figure 51**) and rotate the clutch hub (B) by hand. The shell must turn smoothly with no roughness or binding. If the clutch shell binds or turns roughly, the bearing was installed incorrectly. Repeat this procedure until this problem is corrected.

Table 1 CLUTCH SPECIFICATIONS

Item	in.	mm
Clutch lever free play	1/16-1/8	1.6-3.2
Clutch friction disc thickness		
Service limit	0.143	3.63
Clutch plate warpage		
Service limit	0.006	0.15

CHAPTER EIGHT

ELECTRICAL SYSTEM

BATTERY

Negative Cable

Some of the component replacement procedures and some of the test procedures in this chapter require disconnecting the negative cable from the battery as a safety precaution.

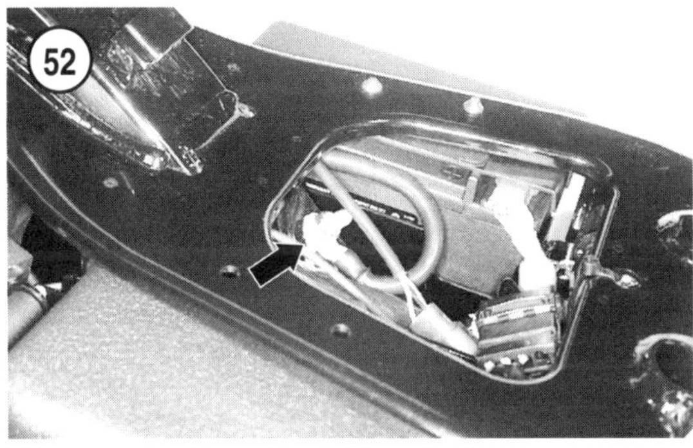

52

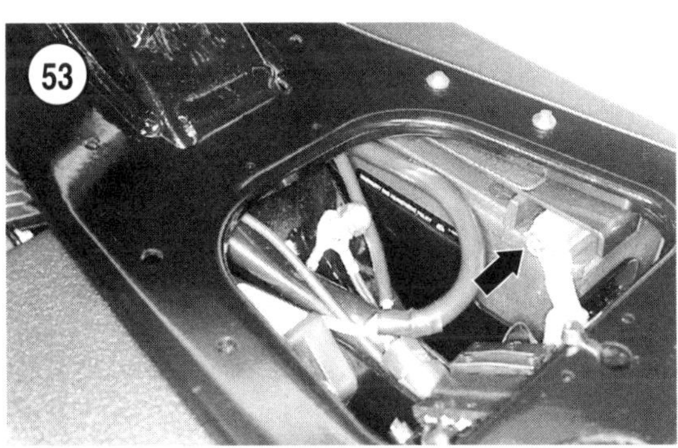

53

54

1. Remove the seat.
2. Remove the nut (**Figure 52**) securing the negative cable to the frame. Move the cable away from the battery to avoid making accidental contact with the battery post.
3. Connect the negative cable onto the frame post, reinstall the nut (**Figure 52**) and tighten securely.
4. After connecting the electrical cables, apply a light coating of dielectric grease to the electrical terminals of the battery to retard corrosion and decomposition of the terminals.
5. Install the seat.

Battery and Tray Removal/Installation

1. Remove the seat.
2. Remove the nut (**Figure 52**) securing the negative cable to the frame.
3. Disconnect the negative cable from the frame post and reinstall the nut to avoid misplacing it.
4. Remove the bolt (**Figure 53**) securing the positive cable to the battery. Disconnect the cable.
5. Remove the bolt (**Figure 54**), at the rear of the battery case, securing the battery tray to the chassis.
6. Carefully tilt the battery and tray down and remove the top cover (**Figure 55**).
7. Remove the battery (**Figure 56**) from the tray and frame.
8. If necessary, unhook the tab on the backside of the battery tray (A, **Figure 57**) from the frame

55

mount and remove the battery tray (B) from the frame.

9. Inspect the battery tray for corrosion or damage. Replace if necessary.

10. If removed, hook the front of the battery tray onto the frame mount (**Figure 58**) and install the battery tray (B, **Figure 57**) onto the frame. Correctly locate the battery positive cable (C, **Figure 57**) behind the battery tray.

11. If removed, install the negative cable onto the battery negative terminal as shown in A, **Figure 59**. Do not wait until the battery is installed since there is limited working room after the battery is installed.

12. Position the battery with the cable terminal side going in first.

13. Reinstall the battery onto the battery tray in the frame (**Figure 56**). Direct the negative cable through the frame and into position on the frame mount.

14. Install the battery top cover (**Figure 55**).

15. Install the bolt (**Figure 54**) securing the battery tray to the chassis and tighten securely.

16. Connect the positive cable (**Figure 53**) to the battery. Tighten the bolt securely.

17. Connect the negative cable onto the frame post, reinstall the nut (**Figure 52**) and tighten securely.

18. After connecting the electrical cables, apply a light coating of dielectric grease to the electrical terminals of the battery to retard corrosion and decomposition of the terminals.

19. Install the seat.

Inspection and Testing

The battery electrolyte level cannot be serviced. *Never* attempt to remove the sealing bar cap (B, **Figure 59**) from the top of the battery. This bar cap was removed for the initial filling of electrolyte prior to delivery of the motorcycle, or the installation of a new battery, and is not to be removed thereafter. The battery does not require periodic electrolyte inspection or water refilling. Refer to the label (**Figure 60**) on top of the battery.

Even though the battery is a sealed type, protect eyes, skin and clothing; electrolyte may have spilled out and is very corrosive and can cause severe chemical skin burns and permanent injury. The battery case may be cracked and leaking electrolyte. If any electrolyte is spilled or splashed on clothing or skin, immediately neutralize with a solution of baking soda and water, then flush with an abundance of clean water.

WARNING

Electrolyte splashed into the eyes is extremely harmful. Always wear safety glasses while working with a battery. If electrolyte gets into the eyes, call a physician immediately and force the eyes open and flood them with cool, clean water for approximately 15 minutes.

1. Remove the battery as described in this section. Do not clean the battery while it is mounted in the framc.
2. Set the battery on a stack of newspapers or shop cloths to protect the surface of the workbench.
3. Check the entire battery case (A, **Figure 61**) for cracks or other damage. If the battery case is warped, discolored or has a raised top, the battery has been suffering from overcharging or overheating.
4. Check the battery terminal bolts, spacers and nuts (B, **Figure 61**) for corrosion or damage. Clean parts thoroughly with a solution of baking soda and water. Replace corroded or damaged parts.
5. If corroded, clean the top of the battery with a stiff bristle brush using the baking soda and water solution.
6. Check the battery cable ends (C, **Figure 61**) for corrosion and damage. If corrosion is minor, clean the battery cable ends with a stiff wire brush. Replace worn or damaged cables.
7. Connect a digital voltmeter between the battery negative and positive leads. Note the following:
   a. If the battery voltage is 12.6 volts (at 68° F [20° C]), or greater, the battery is fully charged
   b. If the battery voltage is 12.0 to 12.5 volts (at 68° F [20° C]), or lower, the battery is undercharged and requires charging.
8. If the battery is undercharged, recharge it as described in this section. Then test the charging system as described in Chapter Two.
9. Inspect the battery case for contamination or damage. Clean with a solution of baking soda and water.

59

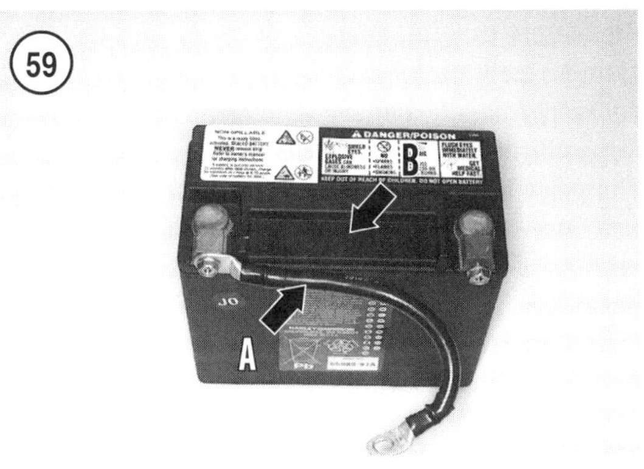

60

61

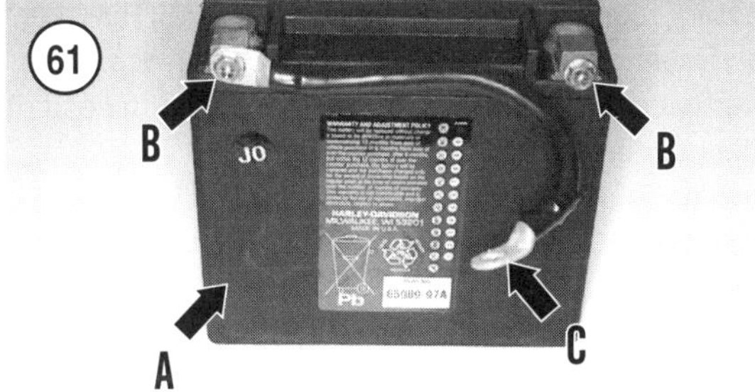

Charging

Refer to *Battery Initialization* in this section if the battery is new.

If recharging is required on the maintenance free battery, a digital voltmeter and a charger with an adjustable amperage output are required. If this equipment is not available, it is recommended that battery charging be entrusted to a shop with the proper equipment. Excessive voltage and amperage from an unregulated charger can damage the battery and shorten service life.

The battery should only self-discharge approximately one percent each day. If a battery not in use, with no loads connected, loses its charge within a week after charging, the battery is defective.

If the motorcycle is not used for long periods of time, an automatic battery charger with variable voltage outputs is recommended for optimum battery service life.

WARNING

During charging, highly explosive hydrogen gas is released from the battery. The battery should be charged only in a well-ventilated area away from open flames (including pilot

13

lights on some gas home appliances). Do not allow any smoking in the area. Never check the charge of the battery by arcing across the terminals; the resulting spark can ignite the hydrogen gas.

CAUTION

Always disconnect the battery cables from the battery. If the cables are left connected during the charging procedure the charger may destroy the diodes within the voltage regulator/ rectifier.

1. Remove the battery from the motorcycle as described in this section.
2. Set the battery on a stack of newspapers or shop cloths to protect the surface of the workbench.
3. Make sure the battery charger is turned to the OFF position, prior to attaching the charger leads to the battery.
4. Connect the charger red positive lead to the positive (+) battery terminal and the black negative charger lead to the negative battery terminal.
5. Set the charger at 12 volts. If the output of the charger is variable, it is best to select the low setting.
6. The charging time depends on the discharged condition of the battery. Refer to **Table 2** for the suggested charging length of time. Normally, a battery should be charged at a slow charge rate of 1/10th its given capacity.

CAUTION

If the battery emits an excessive amount of gas during the charging cycle, decrease the charge rate. If the battery becomes hotter than 110° F (43° C) during the charging cycle, turn the charger to the OFF position and allow the battery to cool. After cooling down, continue with a reduced charging rate and continue to monitor the battery temperature.

7. Turn the charger to the ON position.
8. After the battery has been charged for the pre-determined time, turn the charger to the OFF position, disconnect the leads and measure the battery voltage. Refer to the following:
   a. If the battery voltage is 12.6 volts (at 68° F [20° C]), or greater, the battery is fully charged
   b. If the battery voltage is 2.5 volts (at 68° F [20° C]), or lower, the battery is undercharged and requires additional charging time.
9. If the battery remains stable for one hour, the battery is charged.
10. Install the battery into the bike as described in this section.

Battery Initialization

A new battery must be *fully* charged to a specific gravity of 1.260-1.280 before installation. To bring the battery to a full charge, give it an initial charge. Using a new battery without an initial charge will cause permanent battery damage. That is, the battery will never be able to hold more than an 80% charge. Charging a new battery after it has been used will not bring its charge to 100%. When purchasing a new battery, verify its charge status. If necessary, have the parts supplier perform the initial charge to bring the battery up to 100% charge prior to picking up the battery.

NOTE

***Recycle the old battery**. When a new battery is purchased, turn in the old one for recycling. Most motorcycle dealerships will accept the old battery in trade when purchasing a new one. Never place an old battery in the household trash since it is illegal, in most states, to place any acid or lead (heavy metal) contents in landfills.*

CHARGING SYSTEM

The charging system consists of the battery, alternator, regulator, ignition switch, circuit breakers and connecting wiring. When servicing the charging system, refer to the wiring diagram at the end of the manual for 1996-1998 models.

IGNITION SYSTEM

The ignition system consists of a single ignition coil, 2 spark plugs, timing sensor, ignition module and a vacuum operated electric switch (VOES). When servicing the ignition system, refer to the wiring diagrams at the end of the manual for 1997-1998 models.

STARTER

When servicing the ignition system, refer to the wiring diagrams at the end of the manual for 1997-1998 models

SWITCHES

Testing

Test switches for continuity using an ohmmeter (see Chapter One) or a self-powered test light at the switch connector plug, operating the switch in each of its operating positions and compare results with its switch operating diagram. For *example*, **Figure 62** shows a continuity diagram for the ignition switch. It shows which terminals should show continuity when the switch is in a given position.

When the ignition switch is in the IGNITION position, there should be continuity between the red/black, the red and red/gray terminals. The line on the continuity diagram indicates this. An ohmmeter connected between these three terminals should indicate little or no resistance, or a test light should light. When the starter switch is OFF, there should be no continuity between the same terminals.

When testing the switches, note the following:

1. Check the battery as described under *Battery Testing* in this section; if necessary, charge or replace the battery.
2. Disconnect the battery negative cable from the battery (see this section) before checking the continuity of any switch.
3. Detach all connectors located between the switch and the electrical circuit.

CAUTION
Do not attempt to start the engine with the battery disconnected.

4. When separating two connectors, pull on the connector housings and not the wires.
5. After locating a defective circuit, check the connectors to make sure they are clean and properly connected. Check all wires going into a connector housing to make sure each wire is positioned properly and that the wire end is not loose.
6. To reconnect connectors properly, push them together until they click or snap into place.

If the switch or button does not perform properly, replace it.

Handlebar Switch Replacement

The left side handlebar switch housing (**Figure 63**) is equipped with the following switches:

a. Headlight HI-LO beam.
b. Horn.
c. Left side turn signal.

The right side handlebar switch housing (**Figure 64**) is equipped with the following switches:

a. Engine stop/run.
b. Starter.
c. Right side turn signal.
d. Front brake light.

1. Remove the screws securing the left side switch housing to the handlebar. Then carefully separate

13

(62)

Position \ Switch	Red/Black	Red	Red/Gray
Off			
Acc.		●	●
Ignition	●	●	●

63

64

65

LEFT SIDE HANDLEBAR SWITCH

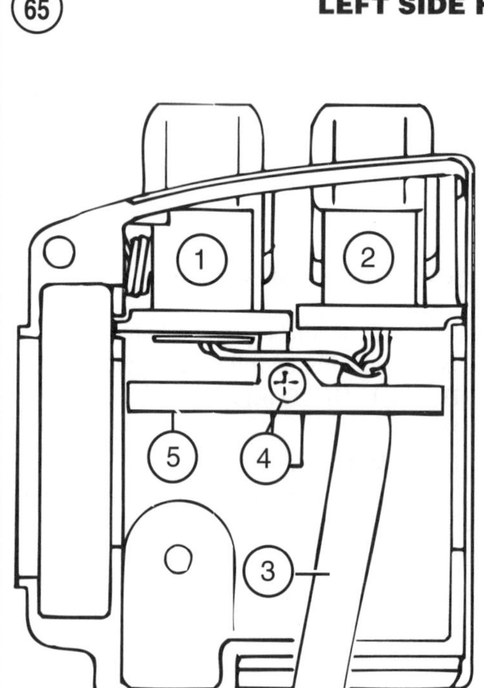

Upper housing without splices

1. **Horn switch**
2. **Headlight high/low beam switch**
3. **Conduit**
4. **Phillps screw and washer**
5. **Bracket**

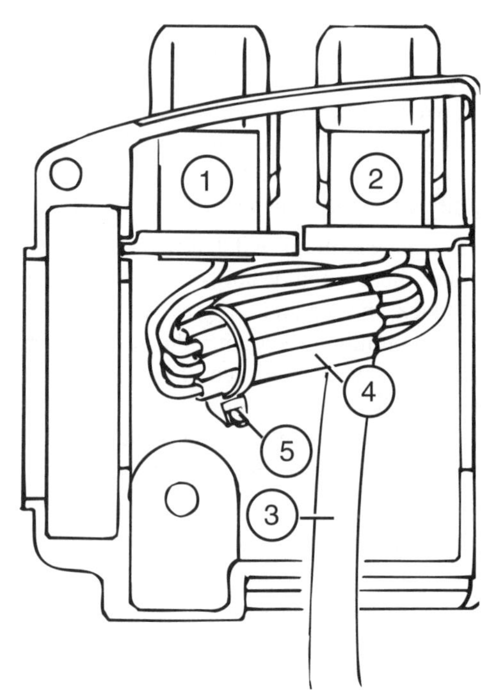

Upper housing with splices

1. **Horn switch**
2. **Headlight high/low beam switch**
3. **Conduit or splices**
4. **Splices**
5. **Cable strap**

the switch housing to access the defective switch (**Figure 65**).

2. Remove the screws securing the right side switch housing to the handlebar. Then carefully separate the switch housing to see the defective switch (**Figure 66**).

NOTE
To service the front brake light switch, refer to ***Front Brake Light Switch Replacement*** *in Chapter Eight.*

3A. On models without splices, remove the screw and bracket.

3B. On models with splices, remove the cable strap.

4. Pull the switch(s) out of the housing.

5. Cut the switch wire(s) from the defective switch(s).

6. Slip a piece of heat shrink tubing over each wire cut in Step 2.

7. Solder the wire end(s) to the new switch. Then shrink the tubing over the wire(s).

8. Install the switch by reversing these steps, plus the following.

   a. When clamping the switch housing onto the handlebar, check the wiring harness routing position to make sure it is not pinched between the housing and handlebar.

   b. To install the right side switch housing, refer to *Throttle and Idle Cable Replacement* in Chapter Seven.

WARNING
Do not ride the motorcycle until the throttle cables are properly adjusted. Also, the cables must not catch or pull when the handlebars are turned. Improper cable routing and adjustment can cause the throttle to stick open. This could cause lose of control. Recheck all work before riding the motorcycle.

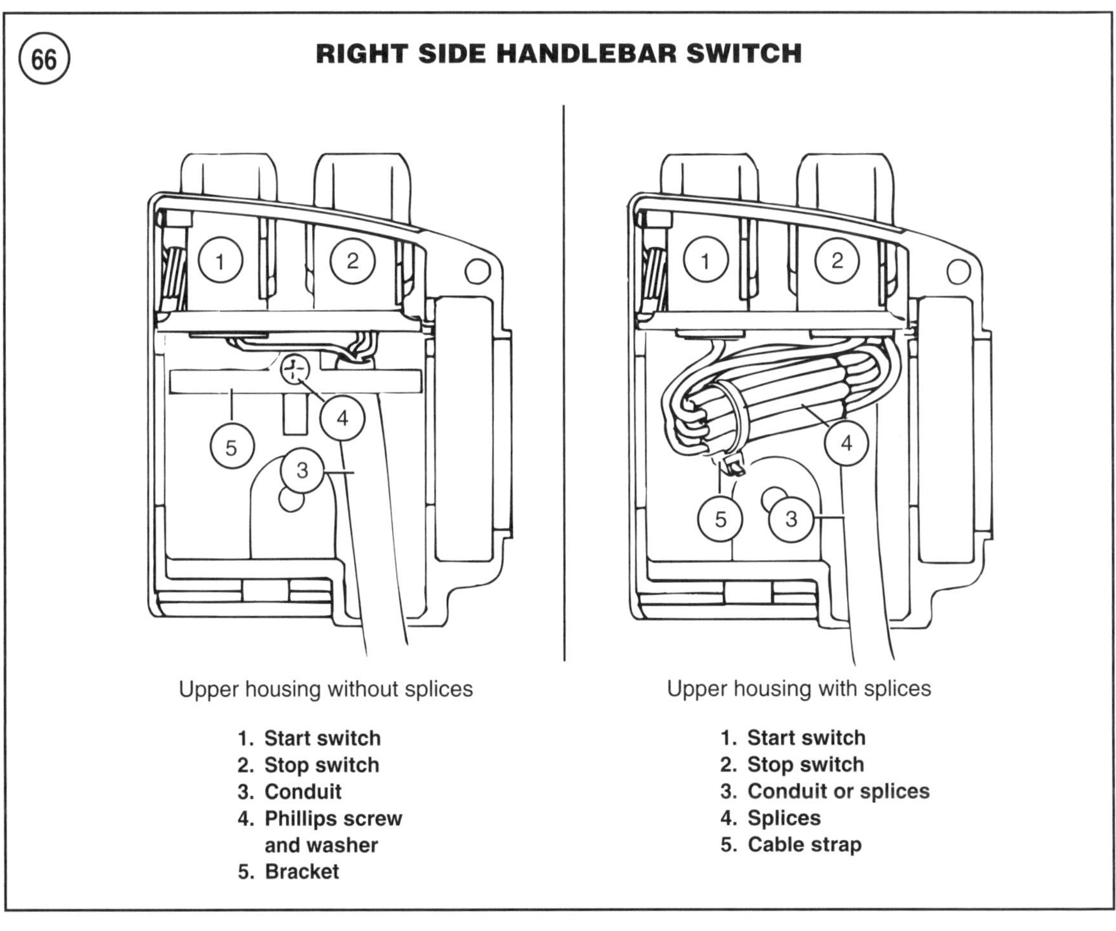

66 **RIGHT SIDE HANDLEBAR SWITCH**

Upper housing without splices

1. **Start switch**
2. **Stop switch**
3. **Conduit**
4. **Phillips screw and washer**
5. **Bracket**

Upper housing with splices

1. **Start switch**
2. **Stop switch**
3. **Conduit or splices**
4. **Splices**
5. **Cable strap**

Table 2 BATTERY CHARGING RATES/TIMES (APPROXIMATE)

Voltage	% of charge	3 amp charger	6 amp charger	10 amp charger	20 amp charger
12.8	100%	–	–	–	–
12.6	75%	1.75 hours	50 minutes	30 minutes	15 minutes
12.3	50%	3.5 hours	1.75 hours	1 hour	30 minutes
12.0	25%	5 hours	2.5 hours	1.5 hours	45 minutes
11.8	0%	6 hours and 40 minutes	3 hours and 20 minutes	2 hours	1 hour

CHAPTER TWELVE

BRAKES

FRONT MASTER CYLINDER

Removal

CAUTION
Cover the fuel tank with a heavy cloth or plastic tarp to protect it from accidental brake fluid spills. Wash brake fluid off any painted, plated or plastic surfaces or plastic parts immediately, as it will destroy most surfaces it contacts. Use soapy water and rinse completely.

1. Clean the top of the master cylinder of all debris.
2. Remove the screws (A, **Figure 67**) securing the top cover.
3. Remove the top cover (B, **Figure 67**) and diaphragm from the master cylinder reservoir.
4. Use a shop syringe and draw all of the brake fluid out of the master cylinder reservoir. Temporarily reinstall the diaphragm and the cover. Tighten the screws finger tight.
5. On models so equipped, remove the windshield.
6. Loosen and remove the mirror (A, **Figure 68**) from the master cylinder.
7. On models so equipped, remove the front turn signal assembly (B, **Figure 68**) from the master cylinder.

CAUTION
Failure to install the spacer in Step 8 will result in damage to the rubber

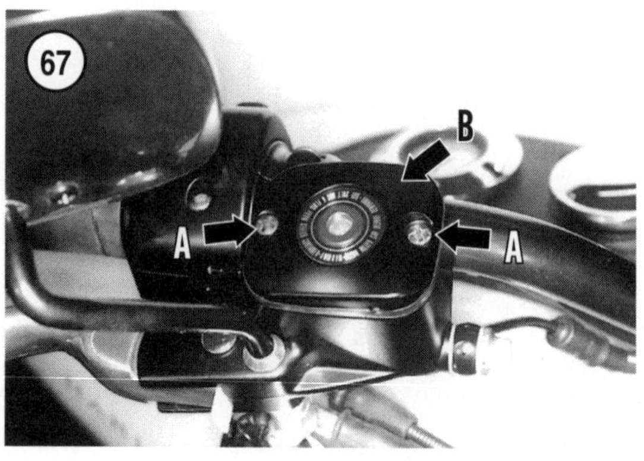

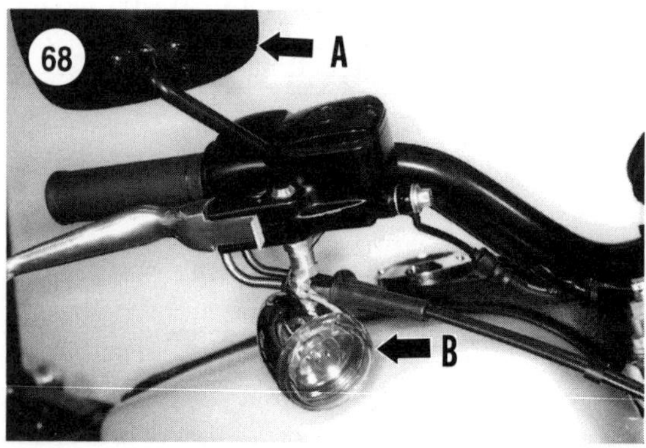

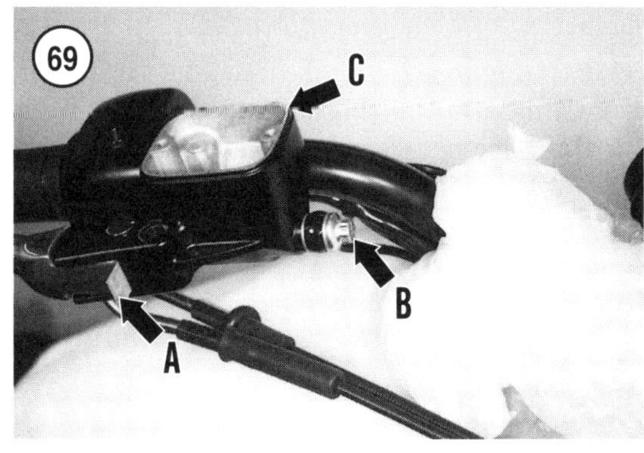

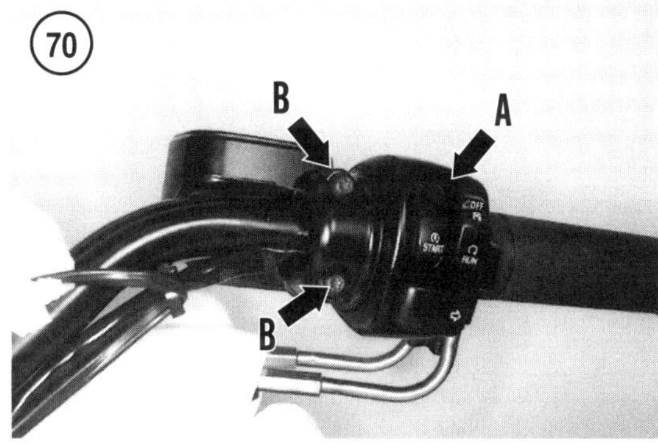

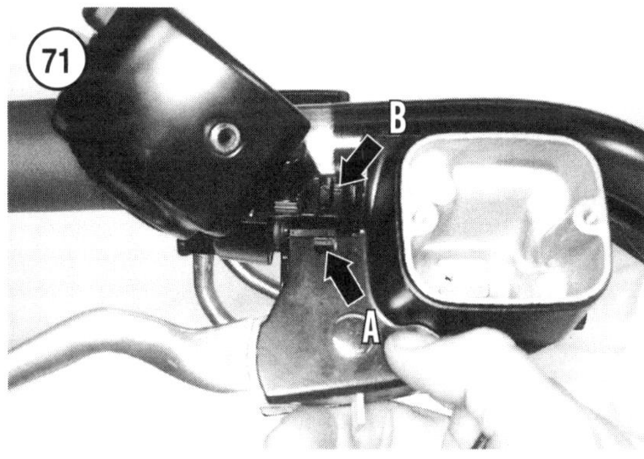

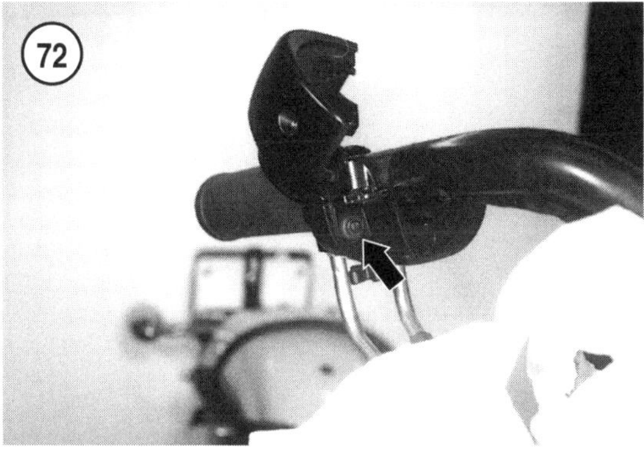

boot and plunger on the front brake switch.

8. Insert a 5/32 in. (4 mm) thick spacer (A, **Figure 69**) between the brake lever and lever bracket. Make sure the spacer stays in place during the following steps.
9. Remove the banjo bolt and sealing washers (B, **Figure 69**) securing the brake hose to the master cylinder.
10. Place the loose end of the brake hose in a reclosable plastic bag to prevent the entry of moisture and foreign matter. Tie the loose end of the hose up to the handlebar
11. Remove the screw securing the right side switch together and separate the switch (A, **Figure 70**).
12. Remove the T27 Torx screws and washers (B, **Figure 70**) securing the clamp and master cylinder to the handlebar.
13. Remove the master cylinder assembly (C, **Figure 69**) from the handlebar.
14. Drain any residual brake fluid from the master cylinder and dispose of properly.
15. If the master cylinder assembly is not going to be serviced; reinstall the clamp and Torx bolts to the master cylinder. Place the assembly in a reclosable plastic bag to protect it from foreign matter.

Installation

1. If not in place, insert the 5/32 in. (4 mm) thick spacer (A, **Figure 69**) between the brake lever and lever bracket. Make sure the spacer stays in place during the following steps.
2. Position the front master cylinder onto the handlebar. Align the master cylinder notch (A, **Figure 71**) with the locating tab (B, **Figure 71**) on the lower portion of the right side switch.

CAUTION
*Do not damage the front brake light switch and rubber boot (**Figure 72**) when installing the master cylinder in Step 3.*

3. Push the master cylinder all the way onto the handlebar (A, **Figure 73**), hold it in this position and install the upper portion of the right side switch (B, **Figure 73**) into place. Install the switch's clamping screw and tighten securely.

4. Position the clamp and install the clamping Torx screws and washers (B, **Figure 70**). Tighten the upper mounting bolt first, then the lower bolt. Tighten the bolts to 70-80 in.-lbs. (8-9 N·m).

5. Apply fresh DOT 5 brake fluid to the rubber portions of the *new* sealing washers prior to installation.

6. Install *new* sealing washers and the banjo bolt (B, **Figure 69**) securing the brake hose to the master cylinder. Tighten the banjo bolt to 17-22 ft.-lbs. (23-30 N·m).

7. Remove the spacer (A, **Figure 69**) from the brake lever.

8. On models so equipped, install the front turn signal assembly (B, **Figure 68**) onto the master cylinder. Aim the lens in the same direction as the one on the left side.

9. Install the mirror (A, **Figure 68**) onto the master cylinder. Correctly adjust the mirror.

10. On models so equipped, install the windshield or front fairing.

11. Temporarily install the diaphragm and top cover (B, **Figure 67**) onto the reservoir. Tighten the screws finger-tight at this time.

12. Refill the master cylinder reservoir and bleed the brake system as described under *Bleeding the System* in Chapter Twelve.

Disassembly

Refer to **Figure 74**.

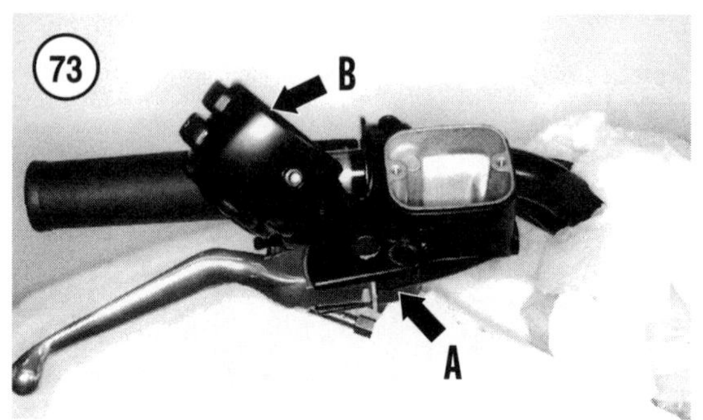

(74)

FRONT MASTER CYLINDER

1. Screw
2. Sight glass
3. Top cover
4. Diaphragm
5. Pivot pin
6. T27 Torx screw
7. Washer
8. Clamp
9. Body
10. Piston assembly
11. Bushing
12. Hand lever
13. Snap ring
14. Washer
15. Acorn nut

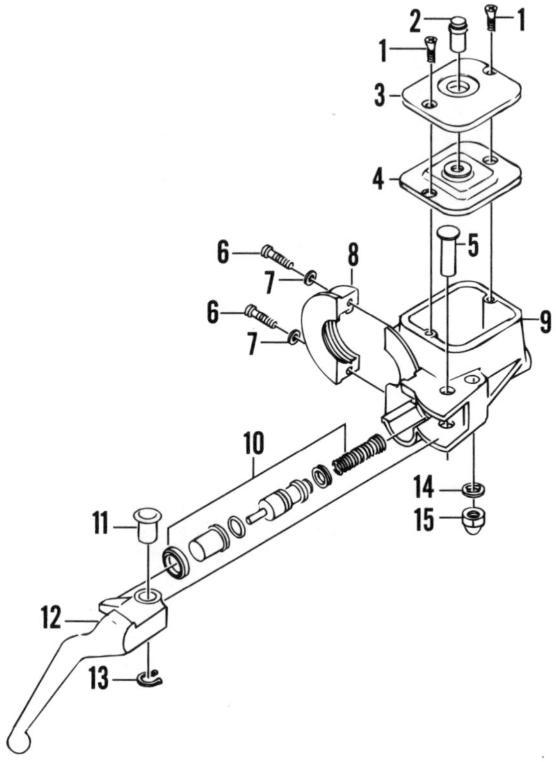

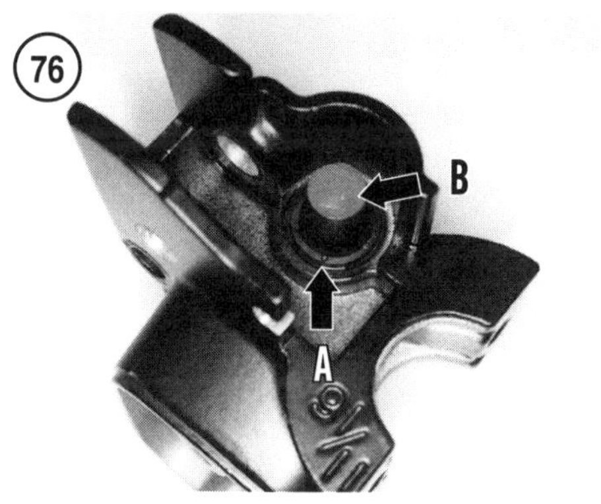

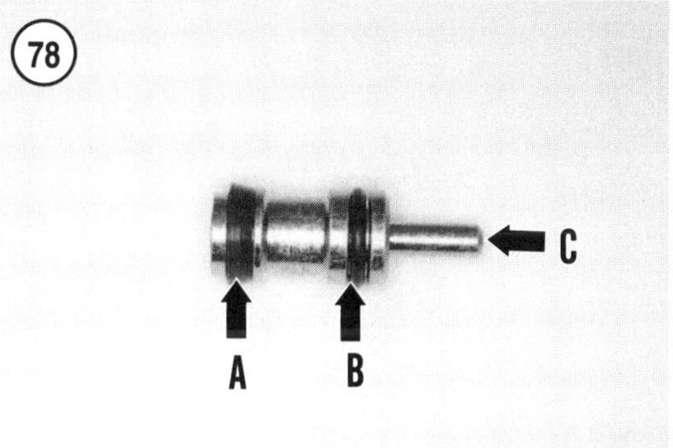

1. Store the master cylinder components in a divided container such as a restaurant-size egg carton to help maintain their correct alignment position.
2. If still in place, remove the screws securing the top cover. Remove the top cover and the diaphragm from the master cylinder.
3. Remove the master cylinder assembly as described in this chapter.
4. Remove the snap ring (A, **Figure 75**) and pivot pin securing the hand lever to the master cylinder. Remove the hand lever (B).
5. Remove the retainer (A, **Figure 76**) and the rubber boot (B) from the area where the hand lever actuates the piston assembly.
6. Remove the piston assembly (**Figure 77**) and the spring.
7. Inspect all parts as described in this section.

Inspection

Replace worn or damage parts as described in this section. It is recommended that a new piston kit assembly be installed every time the master cylinder is disassembled.

1. Clean all parts in isopropyl alcohol or fresh DOT5 brake fluid. Inspect the body cylinder bore surface for signs of wear and damage. If less than perfect, replace the master cylinder assembly. The body cannot be replaced separately.
2. Inspect the piston cup (A, **Figure 78**) and O-ring (B) for signs of wear and damage.
3. Make sure the fluid passage (**Figure 79**) in the bottom of the master cylinder reservoir is clear. Clean out if necessary.
4. Inspect the piston contact surface for signs of wear and damage.

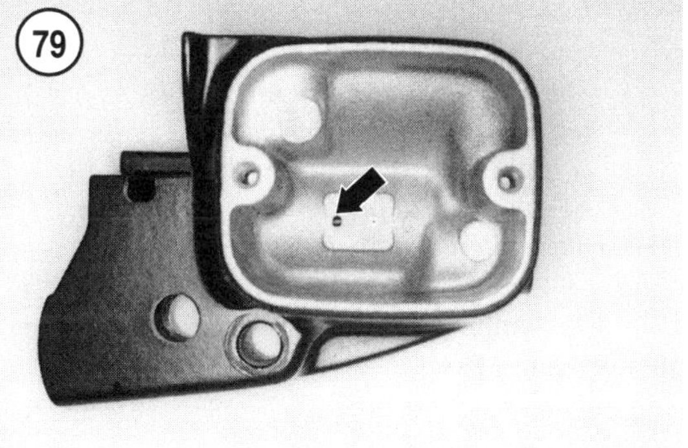

5. Check the end of the piston (C, **Figure 78**) for wear caused by the hand lever.
6. Check the hand lever pivot lugs in the master cylinder body for cracks or elongation.
7. Inspect the hand lever pivot hole and bushing (A, **Figure 80**) and the pivot pin (B) for wear, cracks or elongation.
8. Inspect the piston cap and retainer (**Figure 81**) for wear or damage.
9. Inspect the threads in the bore for the banjo bolt. If worn or damaged, clean out with a thread tap or replace the master cylinder assembly.
10. Check the top cover and diaphragm for damage and deterioration.
11. If necessary, separate the cover from the diaphragm as follows:
   a. Pull straight up on the sight glass (**Figure 82**) and remove it from the cover and diaphragm.
   b. Separate the diaphragm from the cover.
   c. The trim plate may separate from the cover.

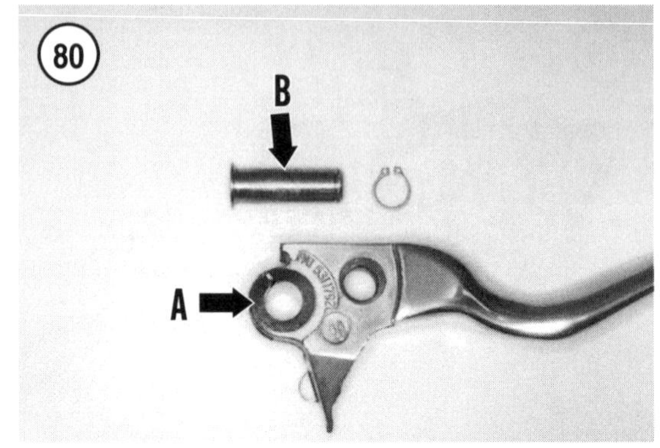

Assembly

NOTE
If installing a new piston assembly, coat all parts with the lubricant provided in the new H-D parts kit instead of using DOT5 brake fluid. If installing existing parts, coat them with DOT5 brake fluid.

NOTE
Be sure to purchase the correct new piston parts kit for the specific bike being worked on. The piston bore diameter is larger on models equipped with dual front discs. The parts for the two different master cylinders are not interchangeable.

NOTE
The cover and diaphragm must be assembled as follows. If the sight glass is not installed correctly through the cover and diaphragm neck, brake fluid will leak past these components.

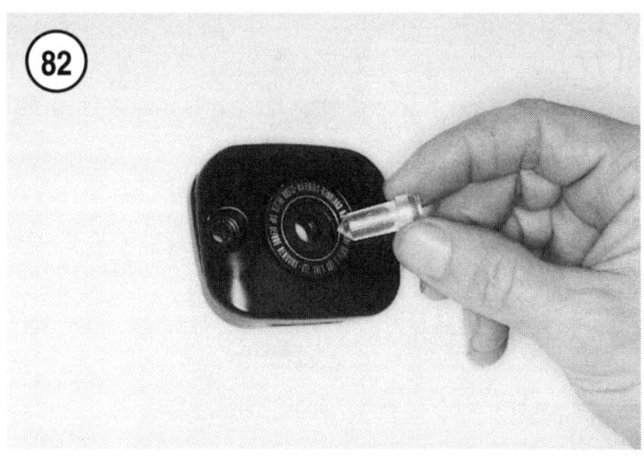

1. If disassembled, assemble the cover and the diaphragm as follows:
   a. If removed, install the trim plate (**Figure 83**) onto the cover.

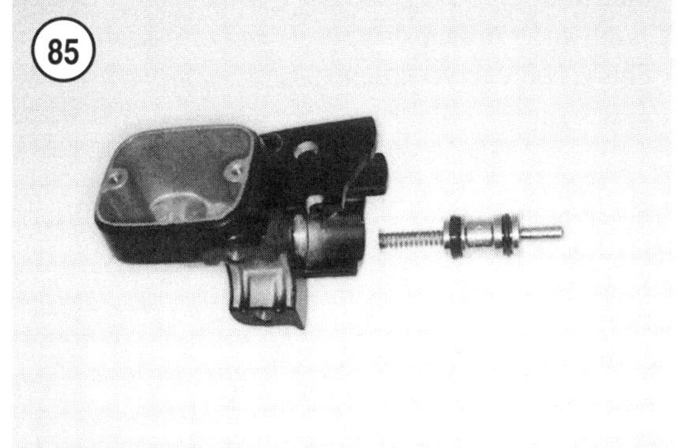

b. Insert the neck of the diaphragm into the cover. Press it in until it seats correctly and the outer edges are aligned with the cover.

c. Push the sight glass (**Figure 82**) straight down through the cover and the neck of the diaphragm (**Figure 84**) until it snaps into place. The sight glass must lock these two parts together to avoid a brake fluid leak.

2. Soak the new cup and O-ring and piston assembly in fresh DOT5 brake fluid for at least 15 minutes to make them pliable. Coat the inside of the cylinder bore with fresh brake fluid prior to the assembly of parts.

CAUTION

When installing the piston assembly, do not allow the cup to turn inside out as it will be damaged and allow brake fluid leakage within the cylinder bore.

3. Position the flared end of the going into the master cylinder first.

4. Install the spring and piston assembly into the cylinder (**Figure 85**). Push them in until they bottom in the cylinder.

5. Position the retainer with the flat side going on first and install the piston cap and retainer onto the piston end.

6. Push on the piston cap down (**Figure 86**), hold it there and press the retainer down until it correctly seats in the cylinder groove (A, **Figure 76**).

7. Make sure the bushing is in place in the hand lever pivot area.

8. Install the hand lever (B, **Figure 75**) into the master cylinder, install the pivot pin and secure it with the circlip. Make sure the circlip is correctly seated in the pivot pin groove (A, **Figure 75**).

9. Slowly apply the lever to make sure it pivots freely.

10. Install the master cylinder as described in this chapter.

INDEX

F

G

H

I

L

14

V

W

1991 FXD

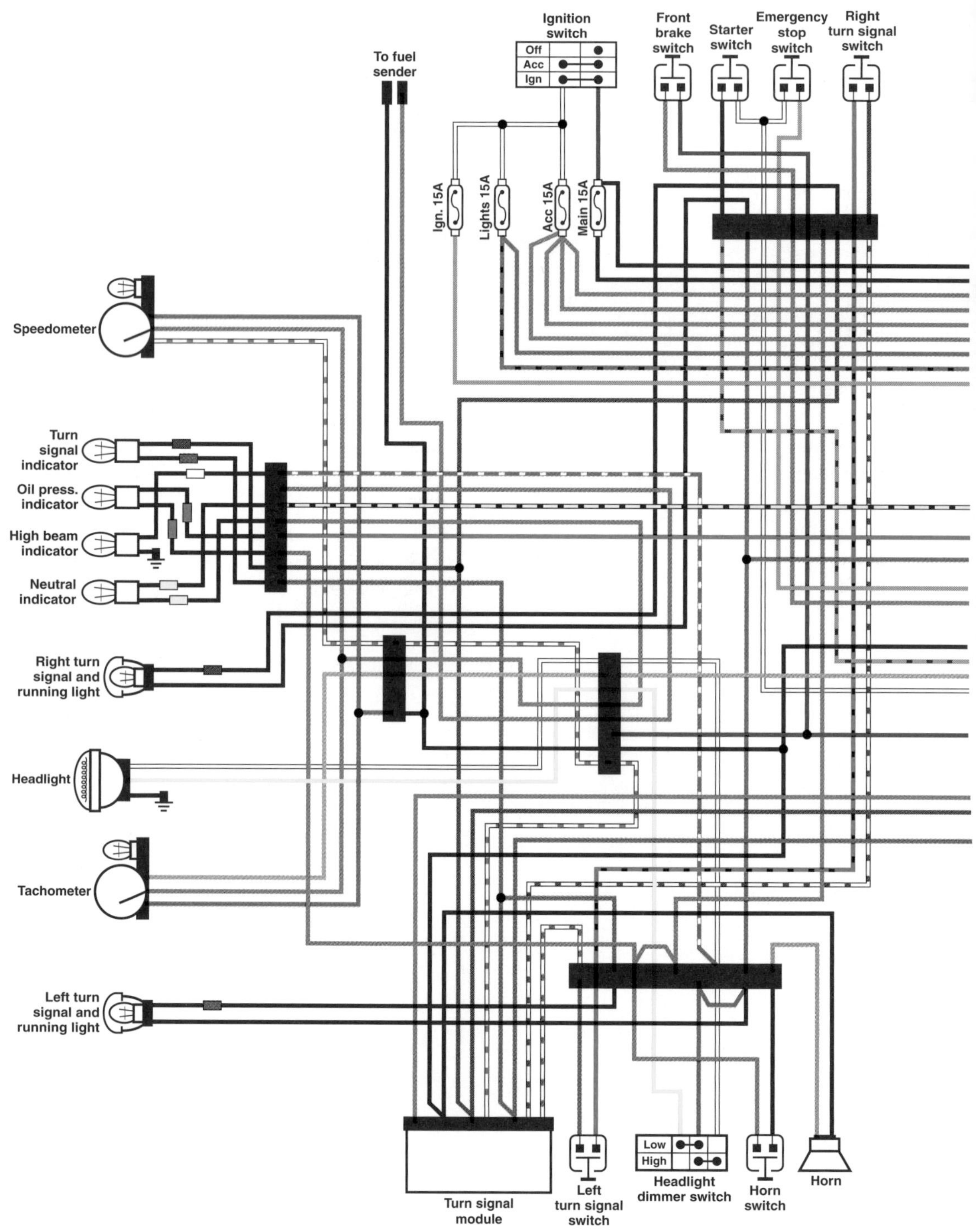

To fuel sender
Ignition switch
Off
Acc
Ign
Front brake switch
Starter switch
Emergency stop switch
Right turn signal switch
Ign. 15A
Lights 15A
Acc 15A
Main 15A
Speedometer
Turn signal indicator
Oil press. indicator
High beam indicator
Neutral indicator
Right turn signal and running light
Headlight
Tachometer
Left turn signal and running light
Turn signal module
Left turn signal switch
Low
High
Headlight dimmer switch
Horn switch
Horn

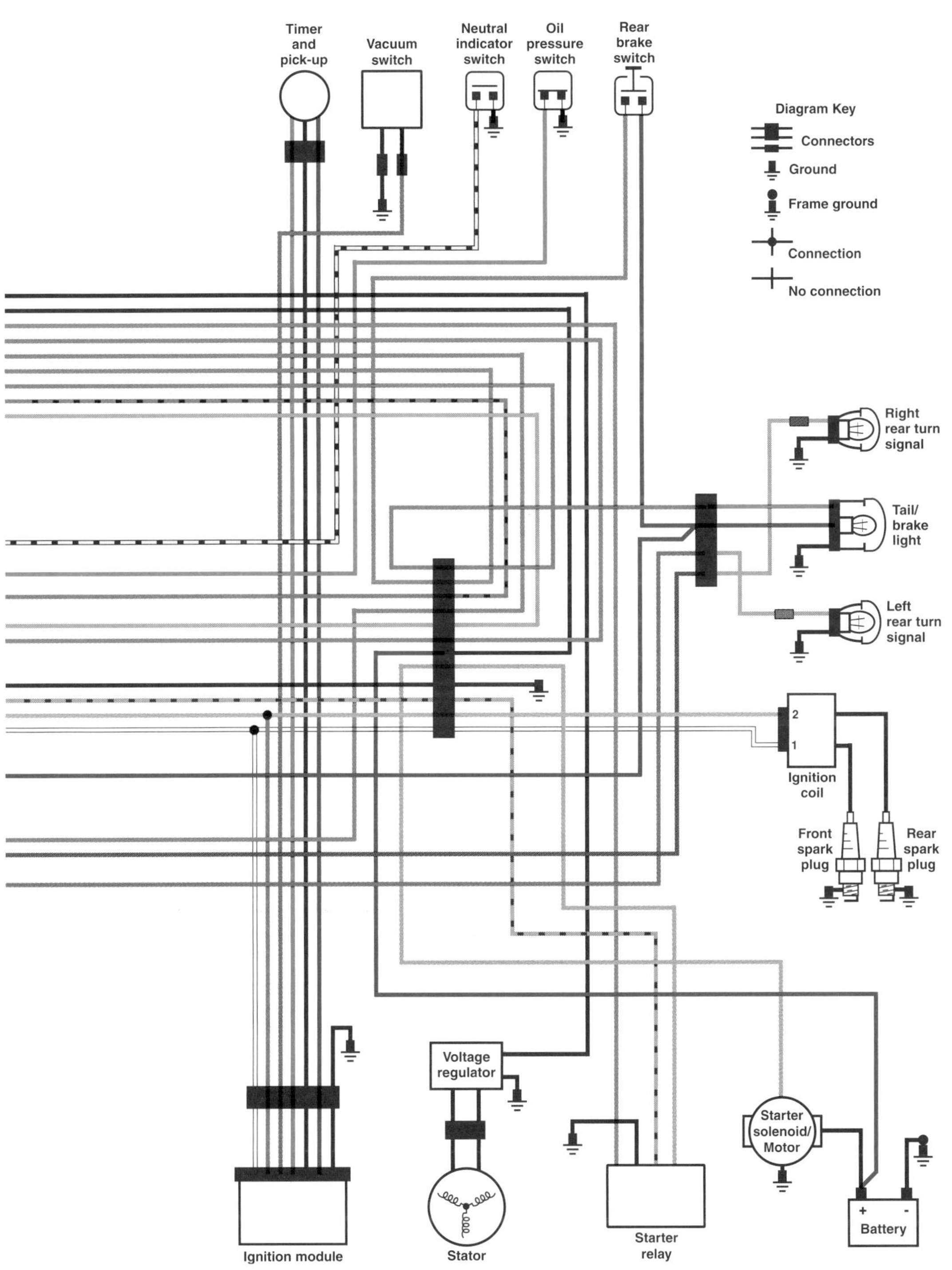
Timer and pick-up
Vacuum switch
Neutral indicator switch
Oil pressure switch
Rear brake switch
Diagram Key
Connectors
Ground
Frame ground
Connection
No connection
Right rear turn signal
Tail/ brake light
Left rear turn signal
2
1
Ignition coil
Front spark plug
Rear spark plug
Voltage regulator
Starter solenoid/ Motor
+
-
Battery
Ignition module
Stator
Starter relay

1992 FXD

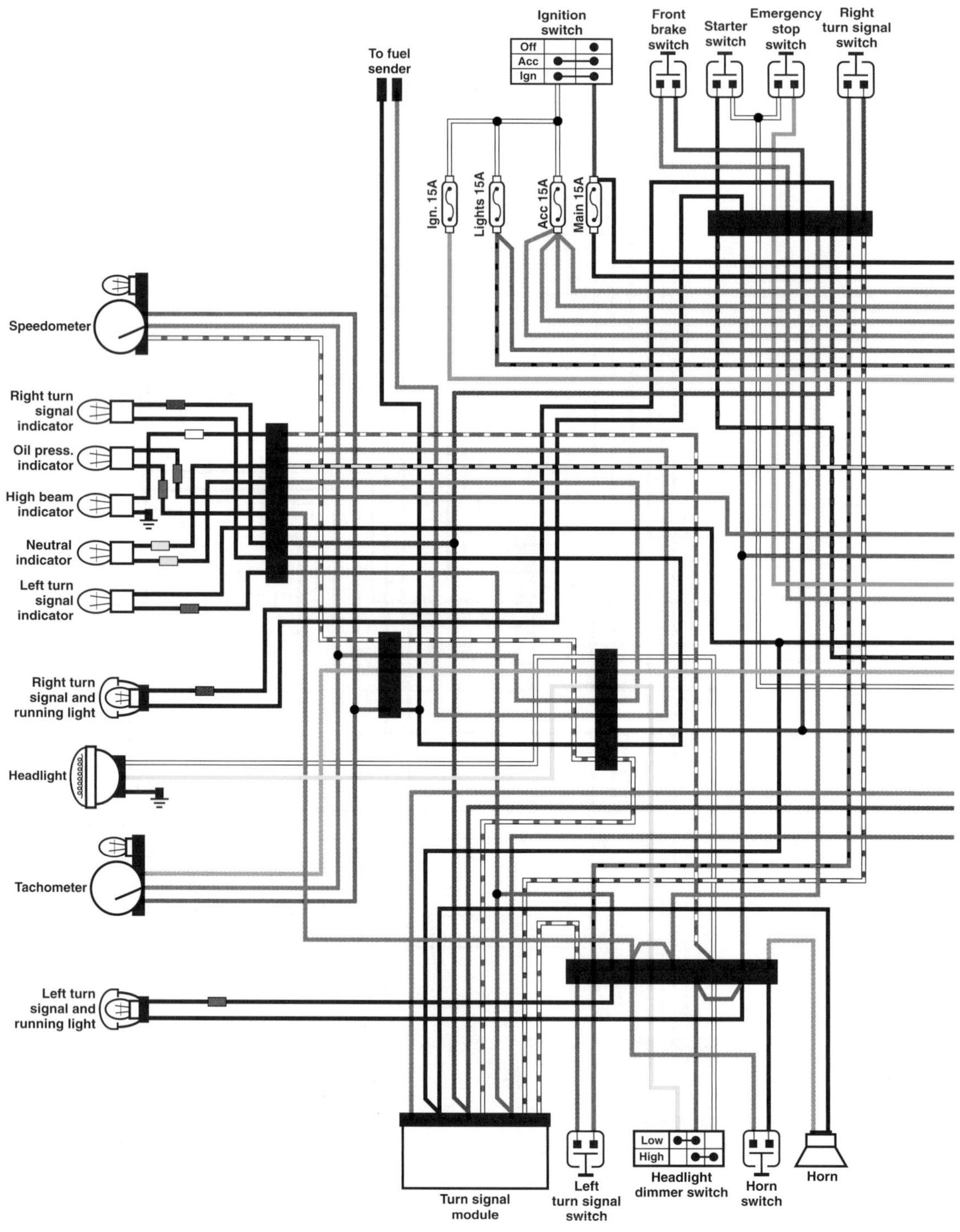

Ignition switch
Off
Acc
Ign
Front brake switch
Starter switch
Emergency stop switch
Right turn signal switch
To fuel sender
Ign. 15A
Lights 15A
Acc 15A
Main 15A
Speedometer
Right turn signal indicator
Oil press. indicator
High beam indicator
Neutral indicator
Left turn signal indicator
Right turn signal and running light
Headlight
Tachometer
Left turn signal and running light
Turn signal module
Left turn signal switch
Low
High
Headlight dimmer switch
Horn switch
Horn

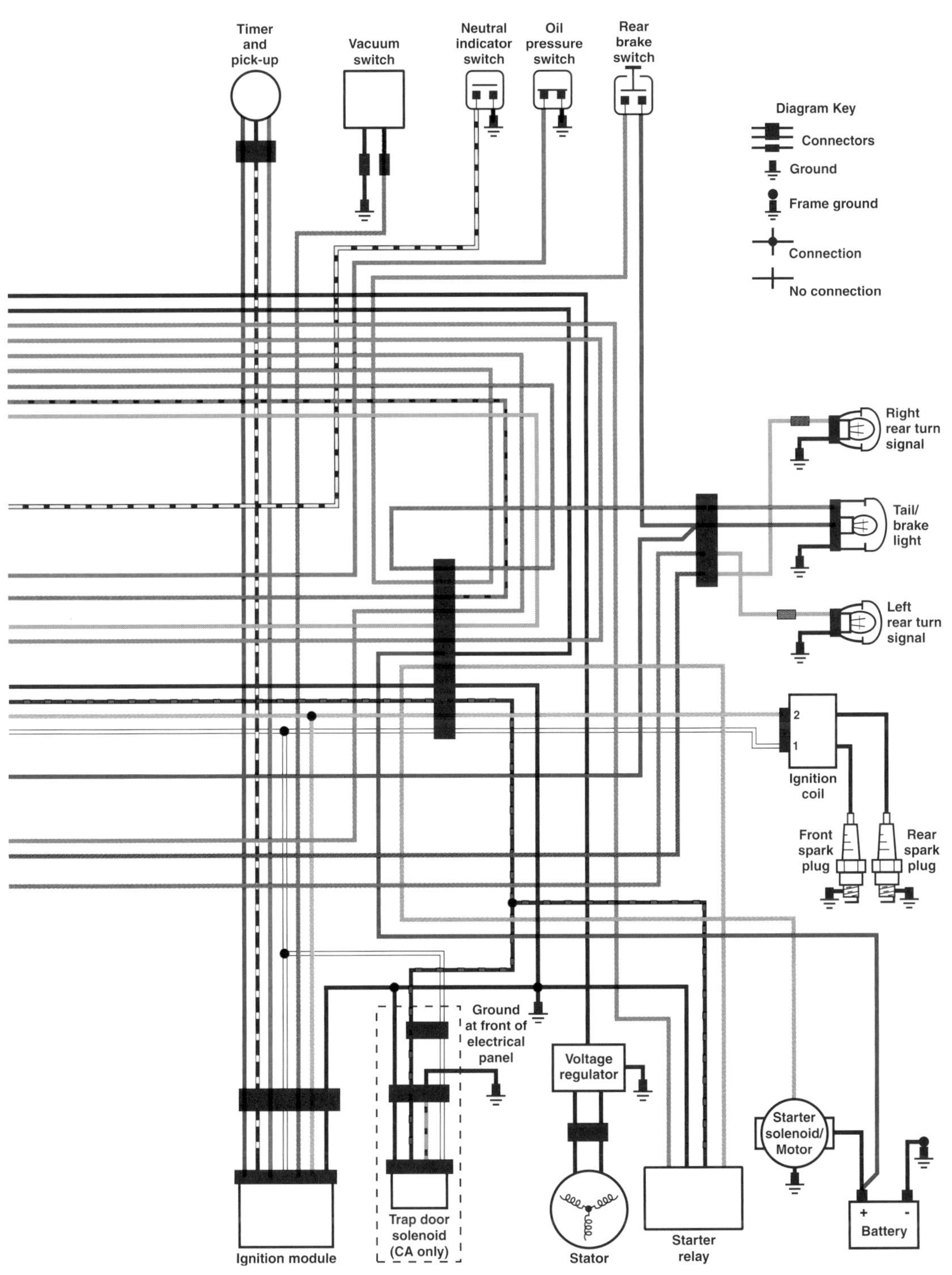
Timer
and
pick-up
Vacuum
switch
Neutral
indicator
switch
Oil
pressure
switch
Rear
brake
switch
Diagram Key
Connectors
Ground
Frame ground
Connection
No connection
Right
rear turn
signal
Tail/
brake
light
Left
rear turn
signal
2
1
Ignition
coil
Front
spark
plug
Rear
spark
plug
Ground
at front of
electrical
panel
Voltage
regulator
Starter
solenoid/
Motor
+
-
Battery
Ignition module
Trap door
solenoid
(CA only)
Stator
Starter
relay

15

1993 FXDL

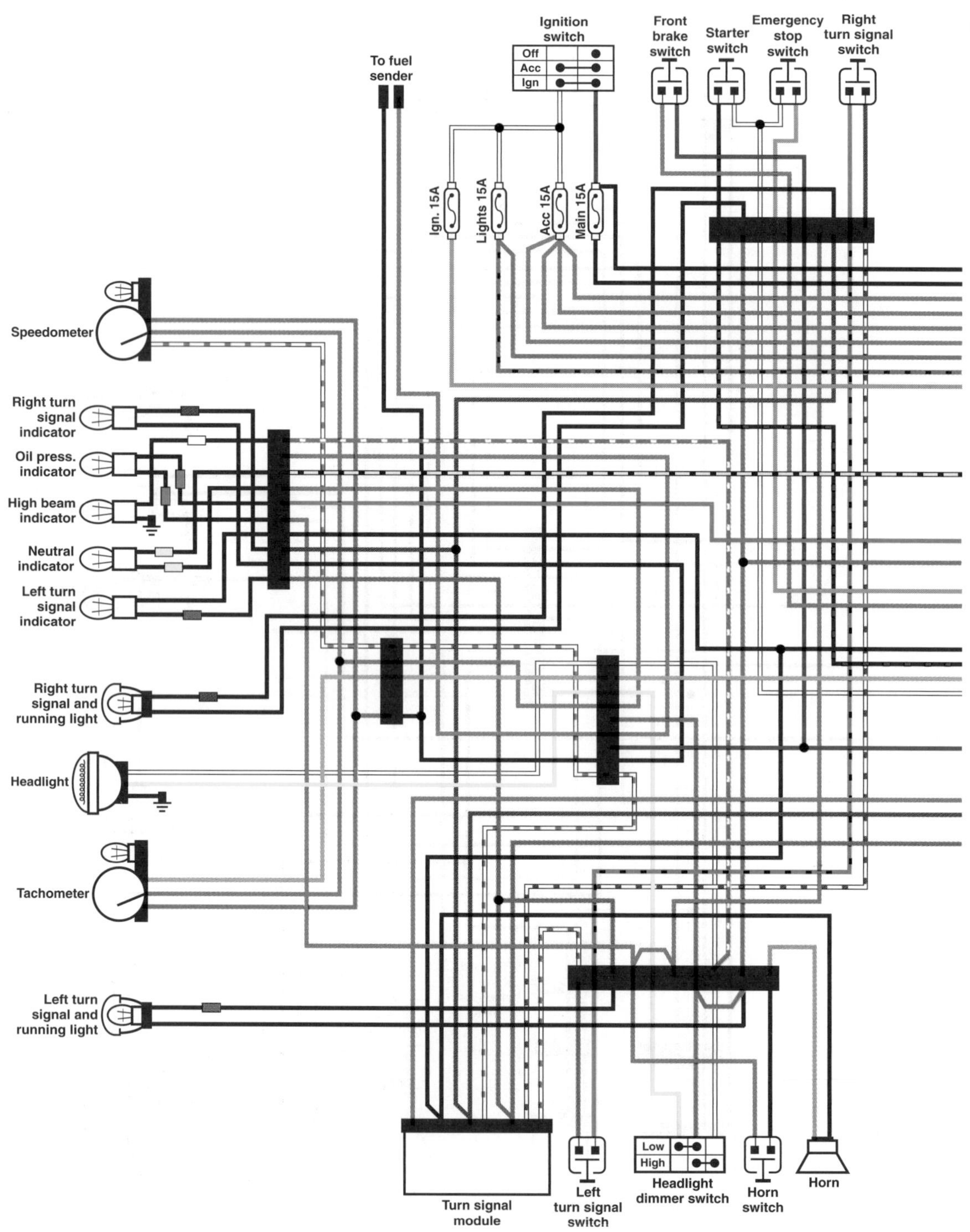

Ignition switch
Off
Acc
Ign
To fuel sender
Front brake switch
Starter switch
Emergency stop switch
Right turn signal switch
Ign. 15A
Lights 15A
Acc 15A
Main 15A
Speedometer
Right turn signal indicator
Oil press. indicator
High beam indicator
Neutral indicator
Left turn signal indicator
Right turn signal and running light
Headlight
Tachometer
Left turn signal and running light
Turn signal module
Left turn signal switch
Low
High
Headlight dimmer switch
Horn switch
Horn

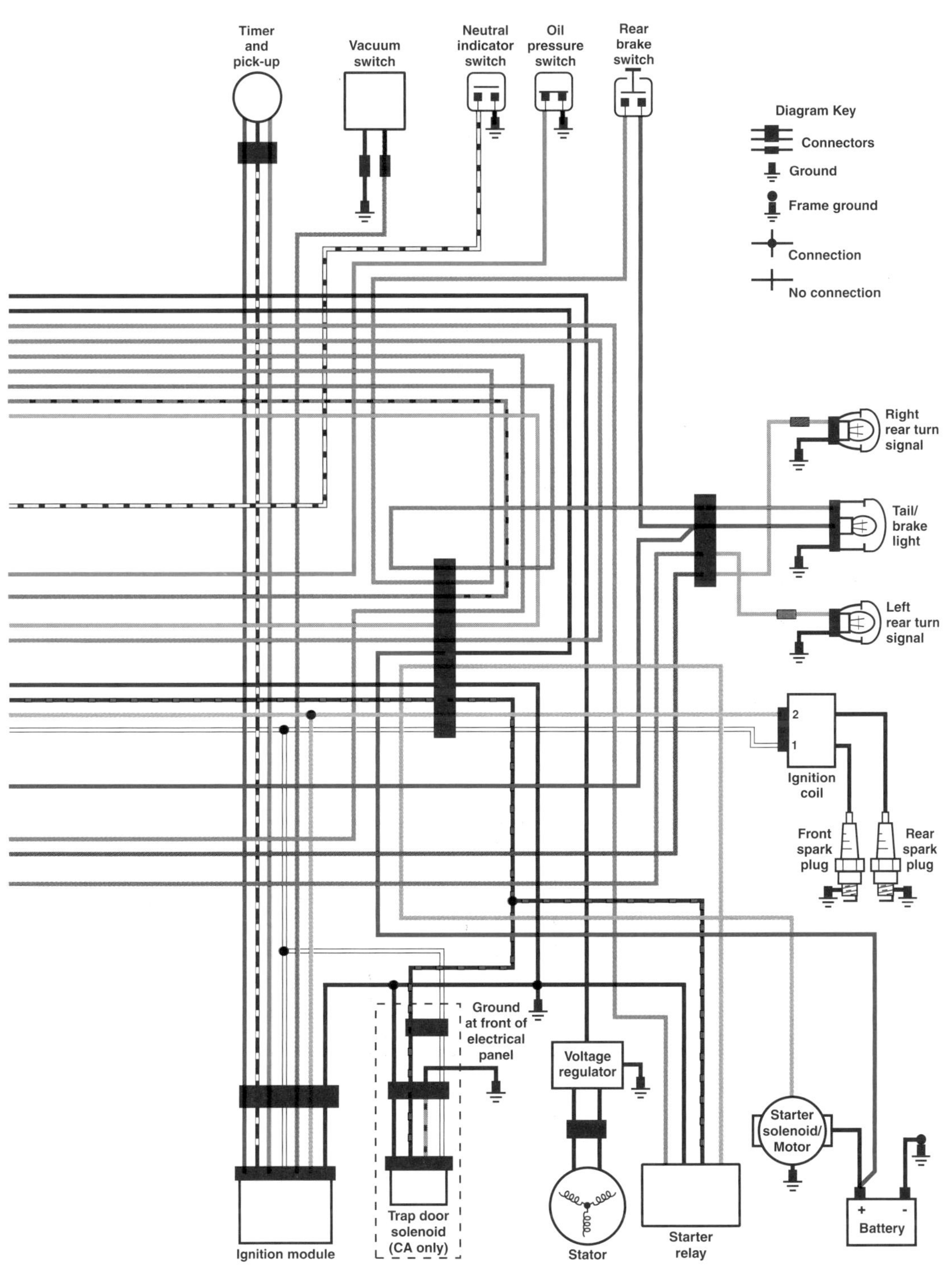
Timer and pick-up
Vacuum switch
Neutral indicator switch
Oil pressure switch
Rear brake switch
Diagram Key
Connectors
Ground
Frame ground
Connection
No connection
Right rear turn signal
Tail/ brake light
Left rear turn signal
2
1
Ignition coil
Front spark plug
Rear spark plug
Ground at front of electrical panel
Voltage regulator
Starter solenoid/ Motor
+
-
Battery
Ignition module
Trap door solenoid (CA only)
Stator
Starter relay

15

1993 FXDWG

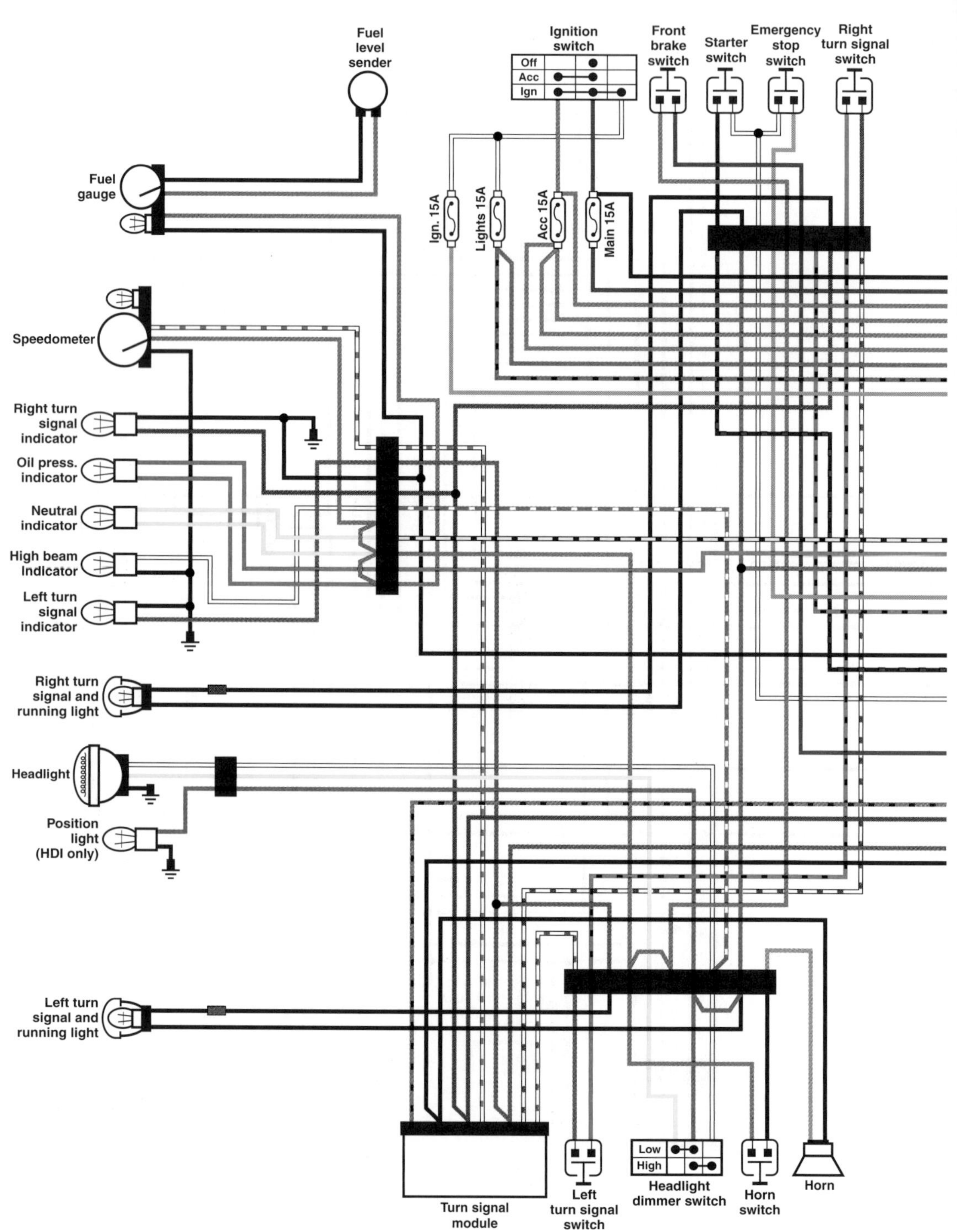
Fuel
level
sender
Ignition
switch
Off
Acc
Ign
Front
brake
switch
Starter
switch
Emergency
stop
switch
Right
turn signal
switch
Fuel
gauge
Ign. 15A
Lights 15A
Acc 15A
Main 15A
Speedometer
Right turn
signal
indicator
Oil press.
indicator
Neutral
indicator
High beam
Indicator
Left turn
signal
indicator
Right turn
signal and
running light
Headlight
Position
light
(HDI only)
Left turn
signal and
running light
Turn signal
module
Left
turn signal
switch
Low
High
Headlight
dimmer switch
Horn
switch
Horn

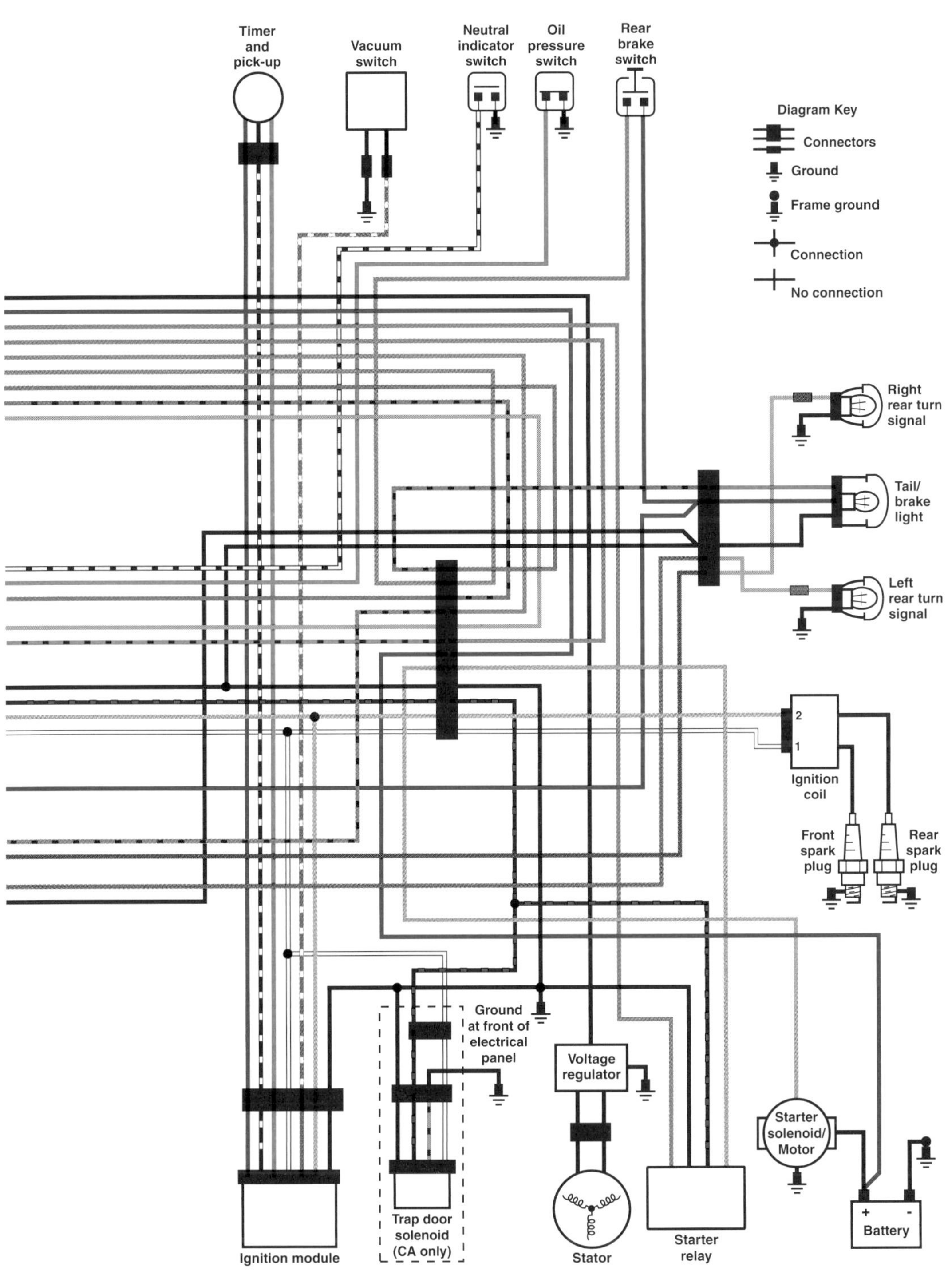
Timer
and
pick-up
Vacuum
switch
Neutral
indicator
switch
Oil
pressure
switch
Rear
brake
switch
Diagram Key
Connectors
Ground
Frame ground
Connection
No connection
Right
rear turn
signal
Tail/
brake
light
Left
rear turn
signal
2
1
Ignition
coil
Front
spark
plug
Rear
spark
plug
Ground
at front of
electrical
panel
Voltage
regulator
Starter
solenoid/
Motor
+
-
Battery
Ignition module
Trap door
solenoid
(CA only)
Stator
Starter
relay

1994 FXDL

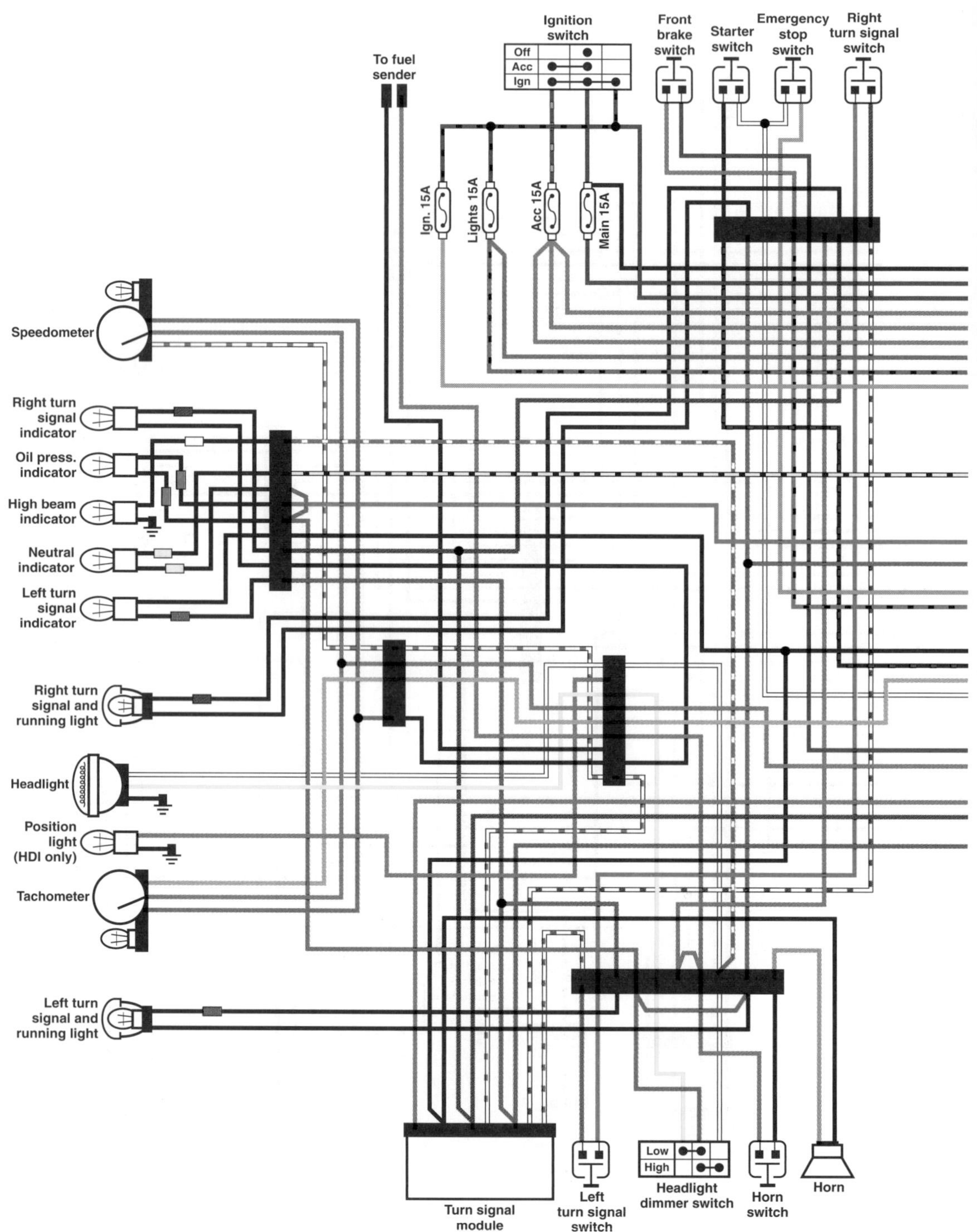

To fuel sender
Ignition switch
Off
Acc
Ign
Front brake switch
Starter switch
Emergency stop switch
Right turn signal switch
Ign. 15A
Lights 15A
Acc 15A
Main 15A
Speedometer
Right turn signal indicator
Oil press. indicator
High beam indicator
Neutral indicator
Left turn signal indicator
Right turn signal and running light
Headlight
Position light (HDI only)
Tachometer
Left turn signal and running light
Turn signal module
Left turn signal switch
Low
High
Headlight dimmer switch
Horn switch
Horn

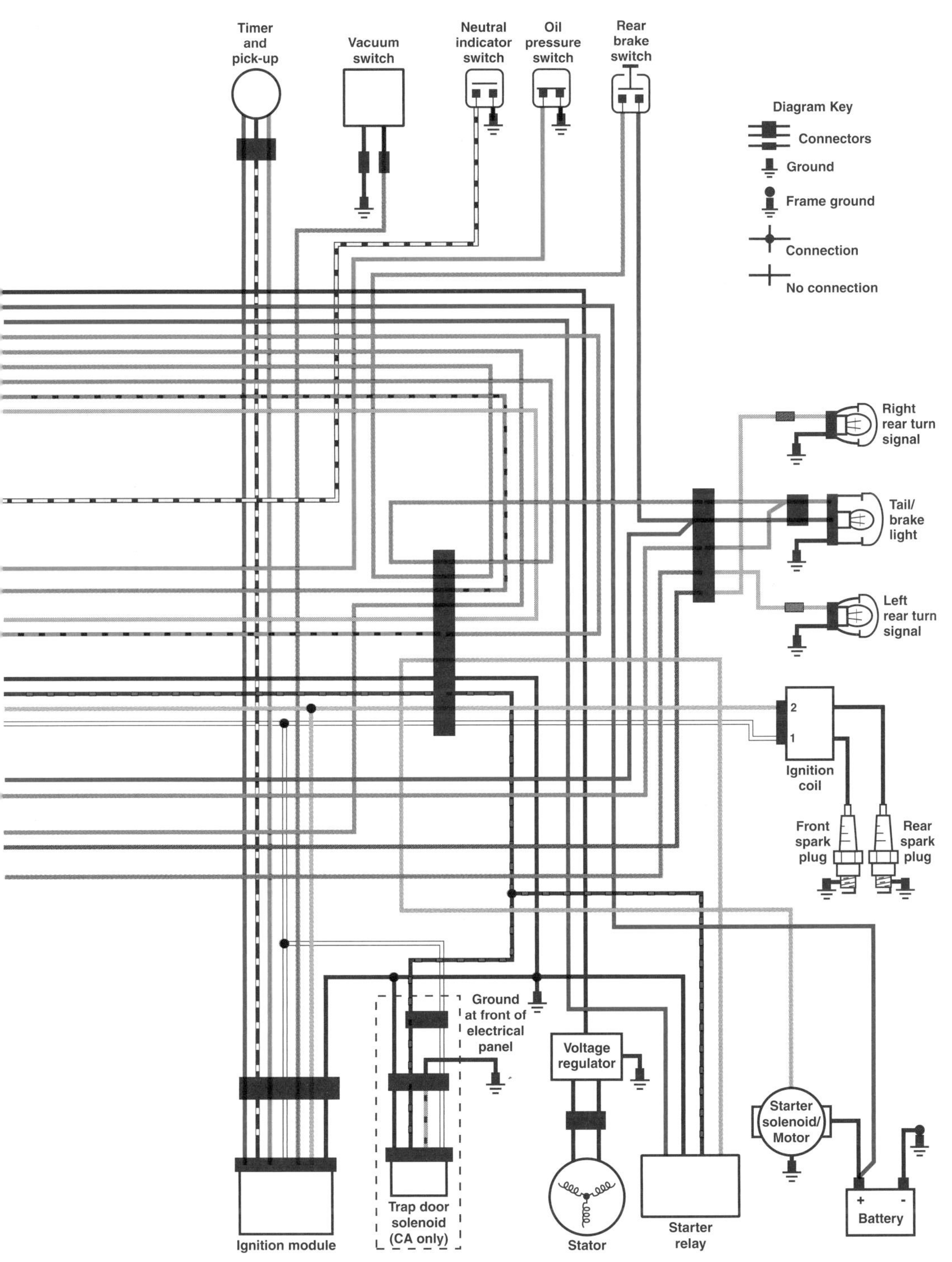
Timer and pick-up
Vacuum switch
Neutral indicator switch
Oil pressure switch
Rear brake switch
Diagram Key
Connectors
Ground
Frame ground
Connection
No connection
Right rear turn signal
Tail/ brake light
Left rear turn signal
2
1
Ignition coil
Front spark plug
Rear spark plug
Ground at front of electrical panel
Voltage regulator
Starter solenoid/ Motor
+
-
Battery
Ignition module
Trap door solenoid (CA only)
Stator
Starter relay

1994 FXDWG

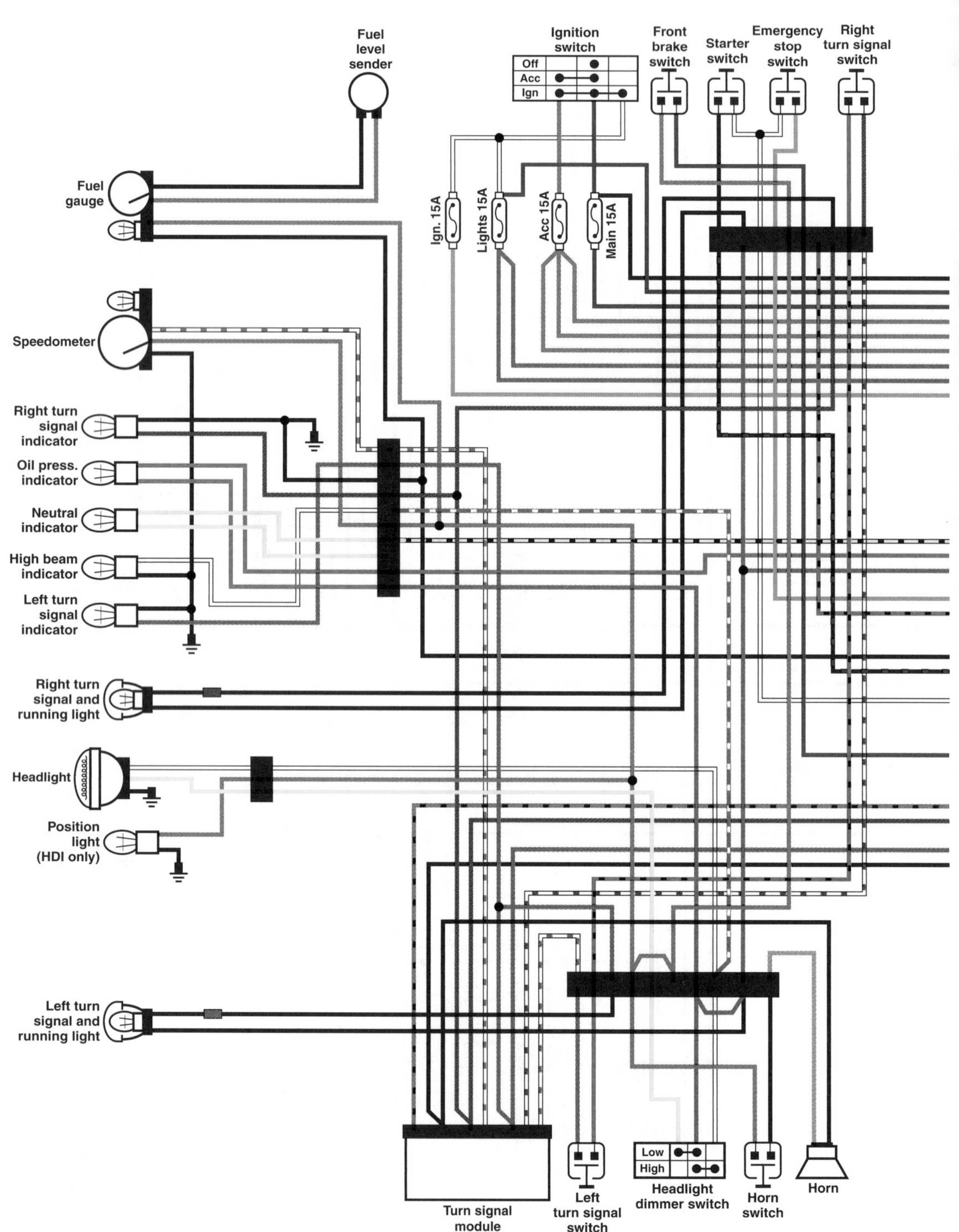

Fuel level sender
Ignition switch
Off
Acc
Ign
Front brake switch
Starter switch
Emergency stop switch
Right turn signal switch
Fuel gauge
Ign. 15A
Lights 15A
Acc 15A
Main 15A
Speedometer
Right turn signal indicator
Oil press. indicator
Neutral indicator
High beam indicator
Left turn signal indicator
Right turn signal and running light
Headlight
Position light (HDI only)
Left turn signal and running light
Turn signal module
Left turn signal switch
Low
High
Headlight dimmer switch
Horn switch
Horn

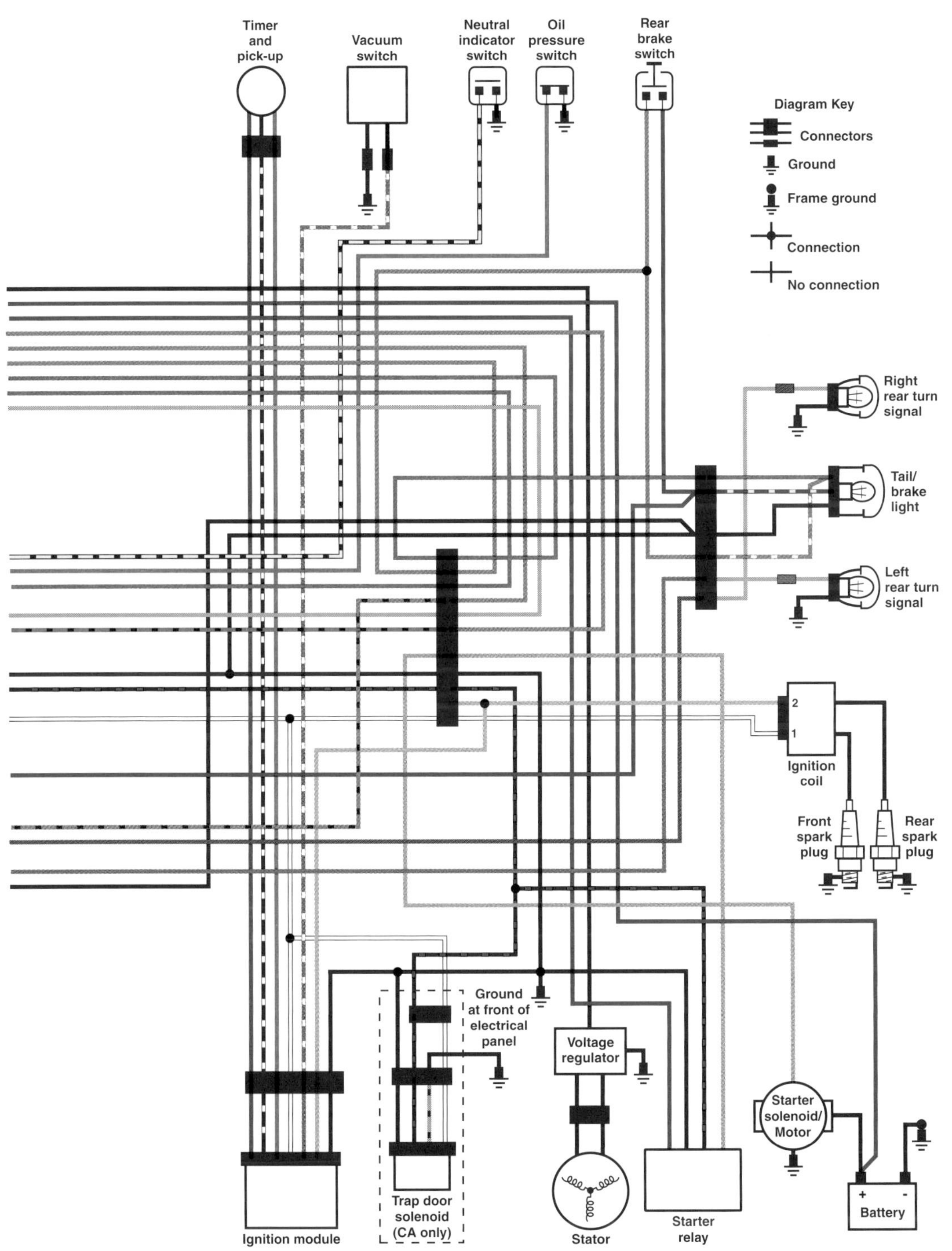
Timer and pick-up
Vacuum switch
Neutral indicator switch
Oil pressure switch
Rear brake switch
Diagram Key
Connectors
Ground
Frame ground
Connection
No connection
Right rear turn signal
Tail/ brake light
Left rear turn signal
2
1
Ignition coil
Front spark plug
Rear spark plug
Ground at front of electrical panel
Voltage regulator
Starter solenoid/ Motor
+
-
Battery
Ignition module
Trap door solenoid (CA only)
Stator
Starter relay

1995 FXDL

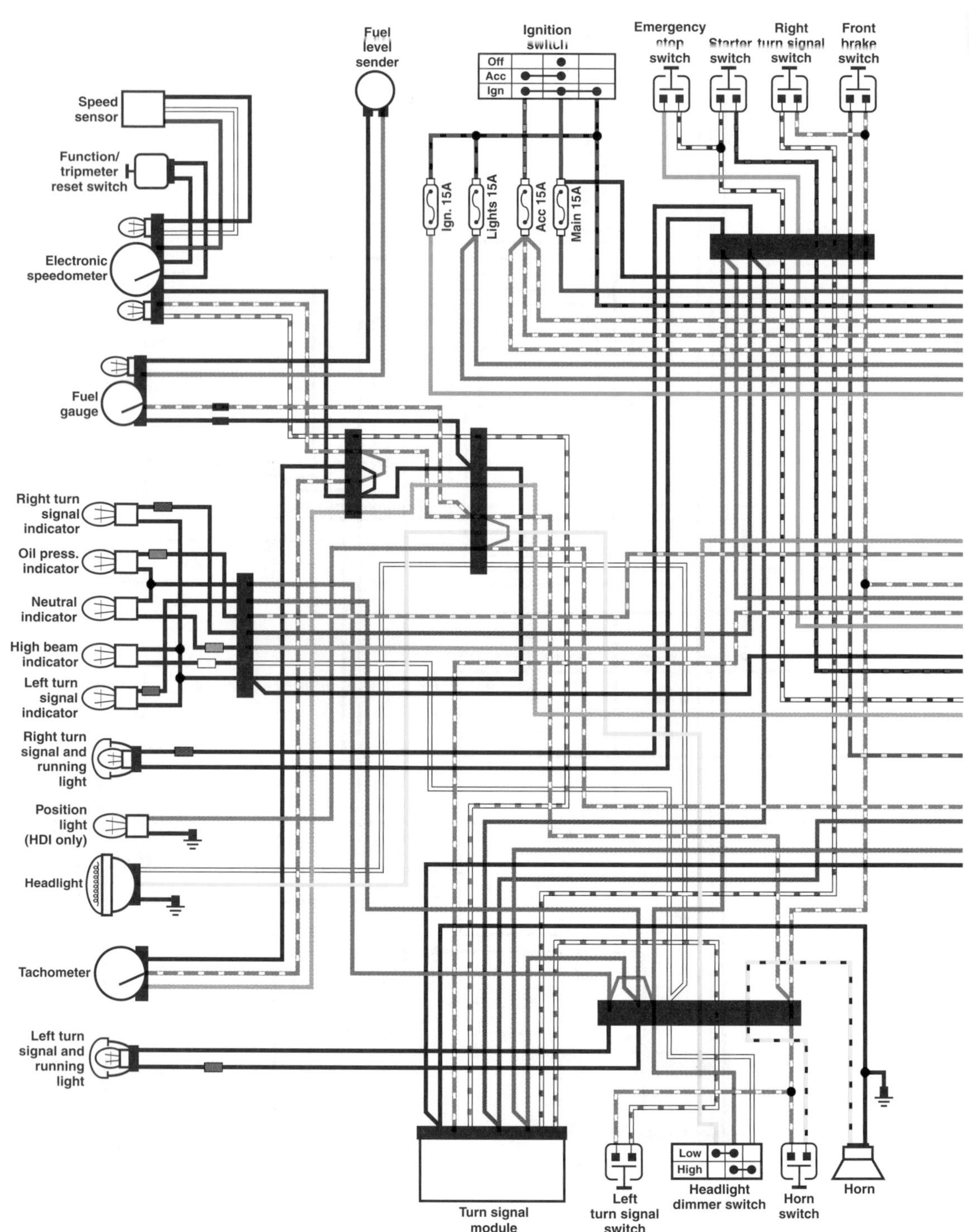

Fuel level sender
Ignition switch
Off
Acc
Ign
Emergency stop switch
Starter switch
Right turn signal switch
Front brake switch
Speed sensor
Function/ tripmeter reset switch
Electronic speedometer
Ign. 15A
Lights 15A
Acc 15A
Main 15A
Fuel gauge
Right turn signal indicator
Oil press. indicator
Neutral indicator
High beam indicator
Left turn signal indicator
Right turn signal and running light
Position light (HDI only)
Headlight
Tachometer
Left turn signal and running light
Turn signal module
Left turn signal switch
Low
High
Headlight dimmer switch
Horn switch
Horn

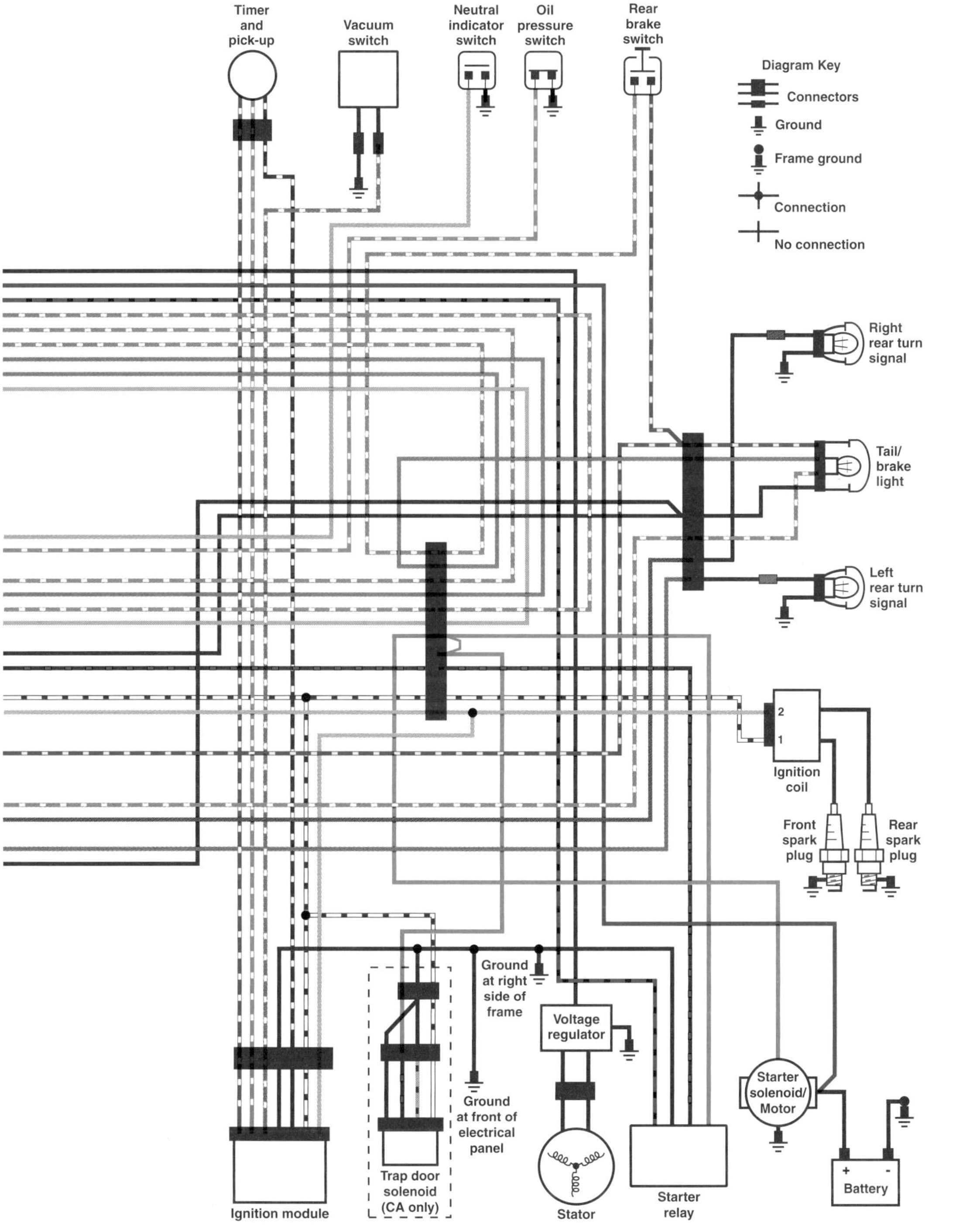

Timer and pick-up
Vacuum switch
Neutral indicator switch
Oil pressure switch
Rear brake switch
Diagram Key
Connectors
Ground
Frame ground
Connection
No connection
Right rear turn signal
Tail/ brake light
Left rear turn signal
2
1
Ignition coil
Front spark plug
Rear spark plug
Ground at right side of frame
Voltage regulator
Ground at front of electrical panel
Starter solenoid/ Motor
+
-
Battery
Ignition module
Trap door solenoid (CA only)
Stator
Starter relay

1995 FXD AND FXDS-CONV

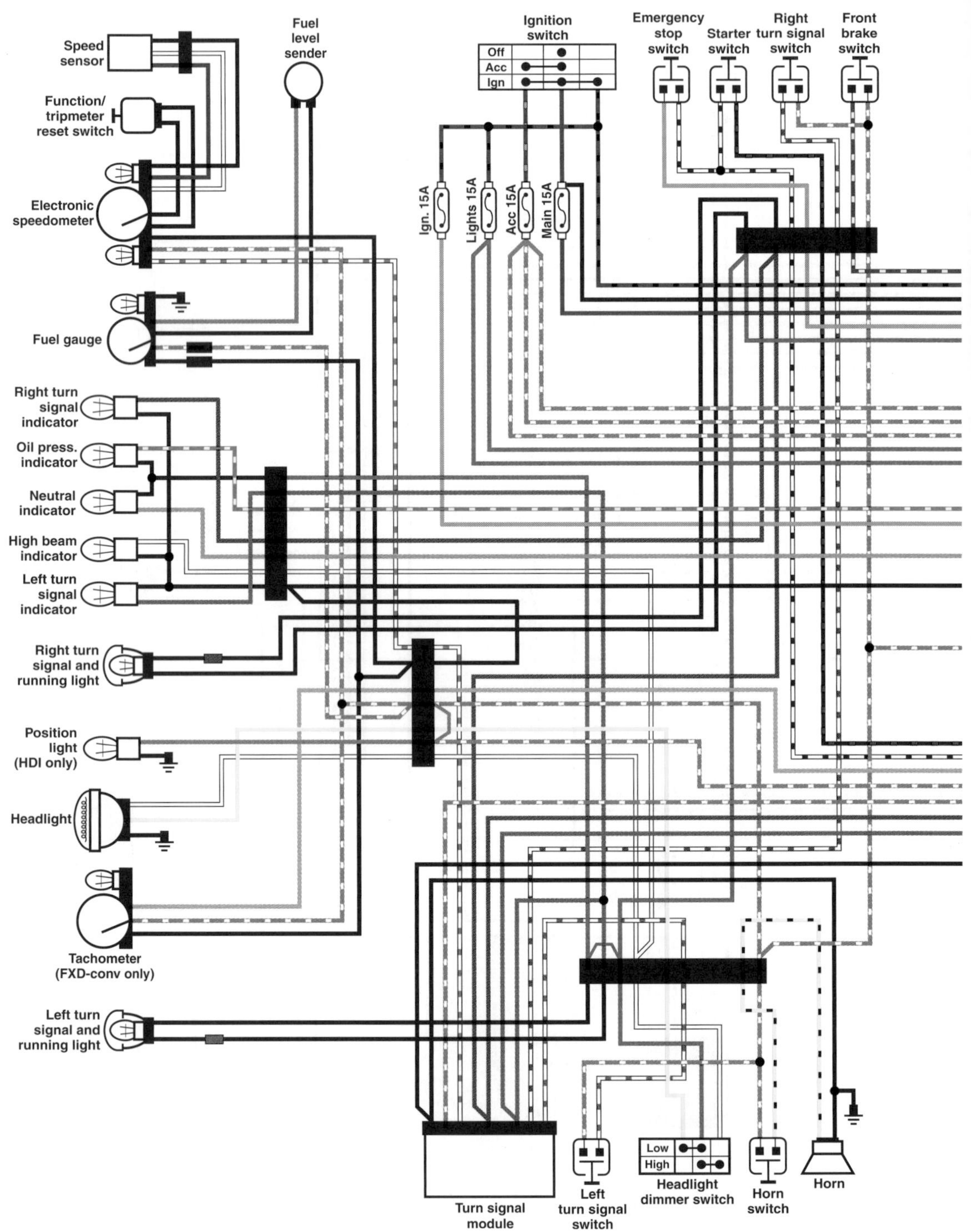

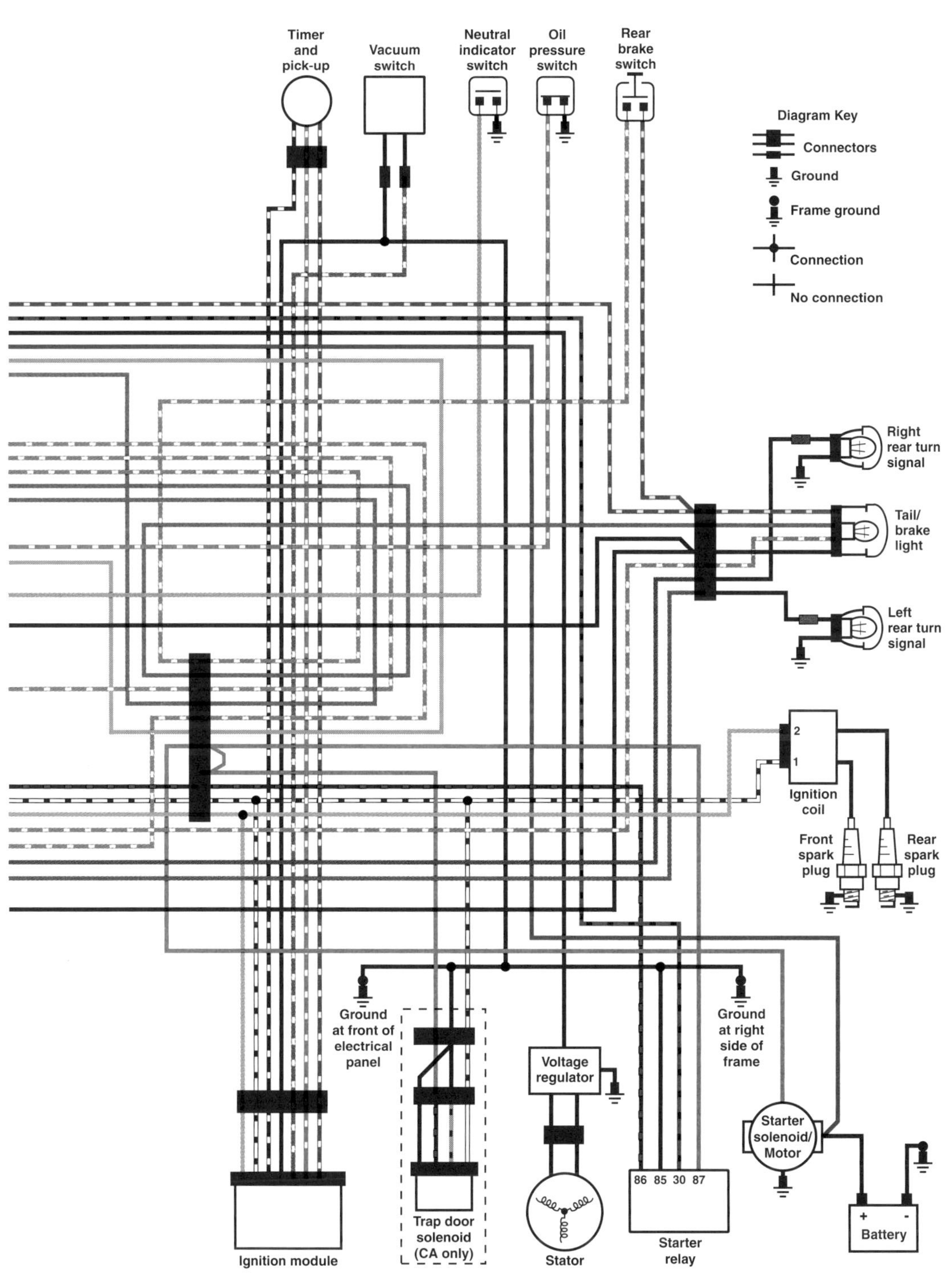
Timer and pick-up
Vacuum switch
Neutral indicator switch
Oil pressure switch
Rear brake switch
Diagram Key
Connectors
Ground
Frame ground
Connection
No connection
Right rear turn signal
Tail/ brake light
Left rear turn signal
2
1
Ignition coil
Front spark plug
Rear spark plug
Ground at front of electrical panel
Ground at right side of frame
Voltage regulator
Starter solenoid/ Motor
86 85 30 87
Starter relay
+
-
Battery
Ignition module
Trap door solenoid (CA only)
Stator

1995 FXDWG

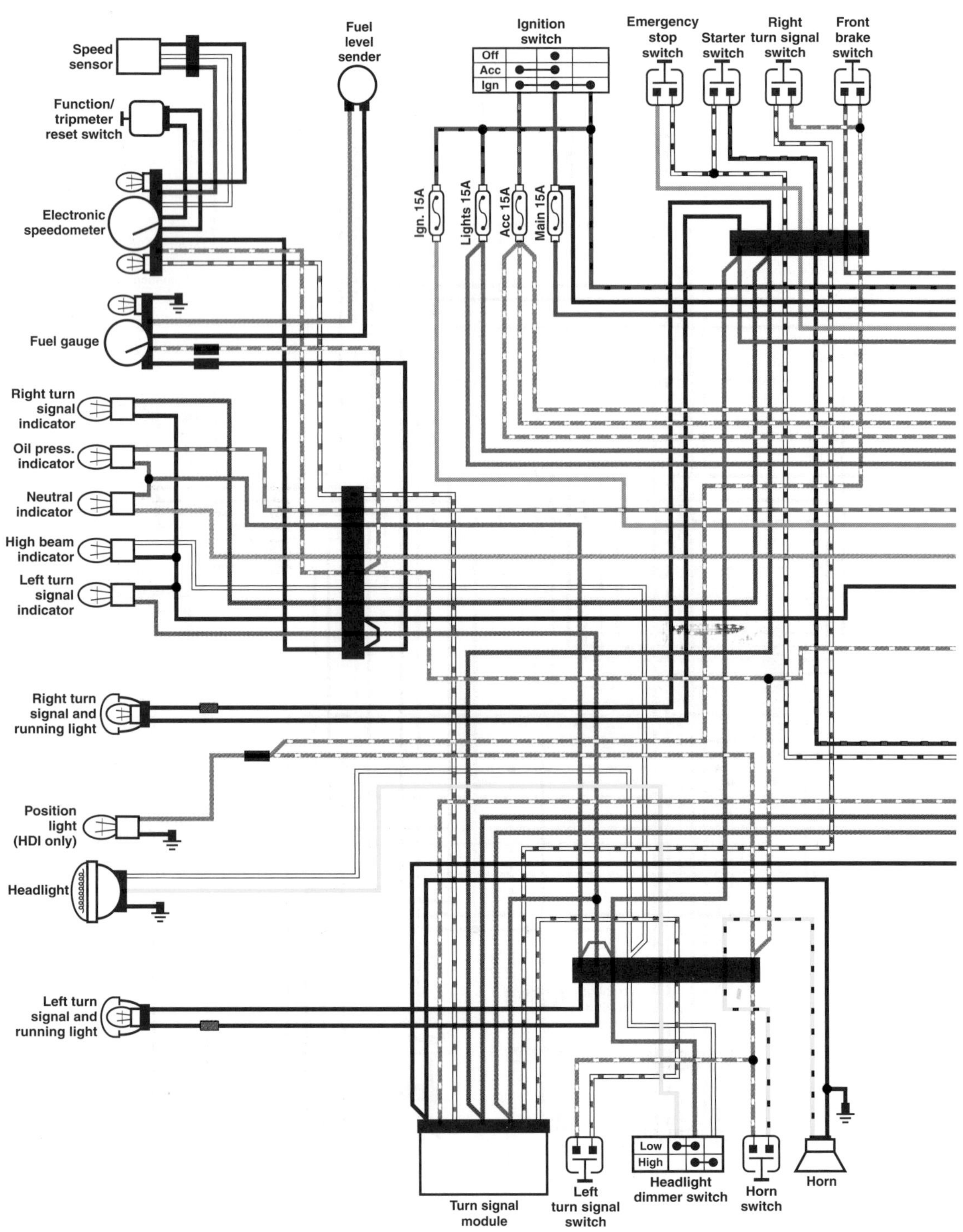

Speed sensor
Function/ tripmeter reset switch
Electronic speedometer
Fuel gauge
Right turn signal indicator
Oil press. indicator
Neutral indicator
High beam indicator
Left turn signal indicator
Right turn signal and running light
Position light (HDI only)
Headlight
Left turn signal and running light
Fuel level sender
Ignition switch
Off
Acc
Ign
Ign. 15A
Lights 15A
Acc 15A
Main 15A
Emergency stop switch
Starter switch
Right turn signal switch
Front brake switch
Turn signal module
Left turn signal switch
Low
High
Headlight dimmer switch
Horn switch
Horn

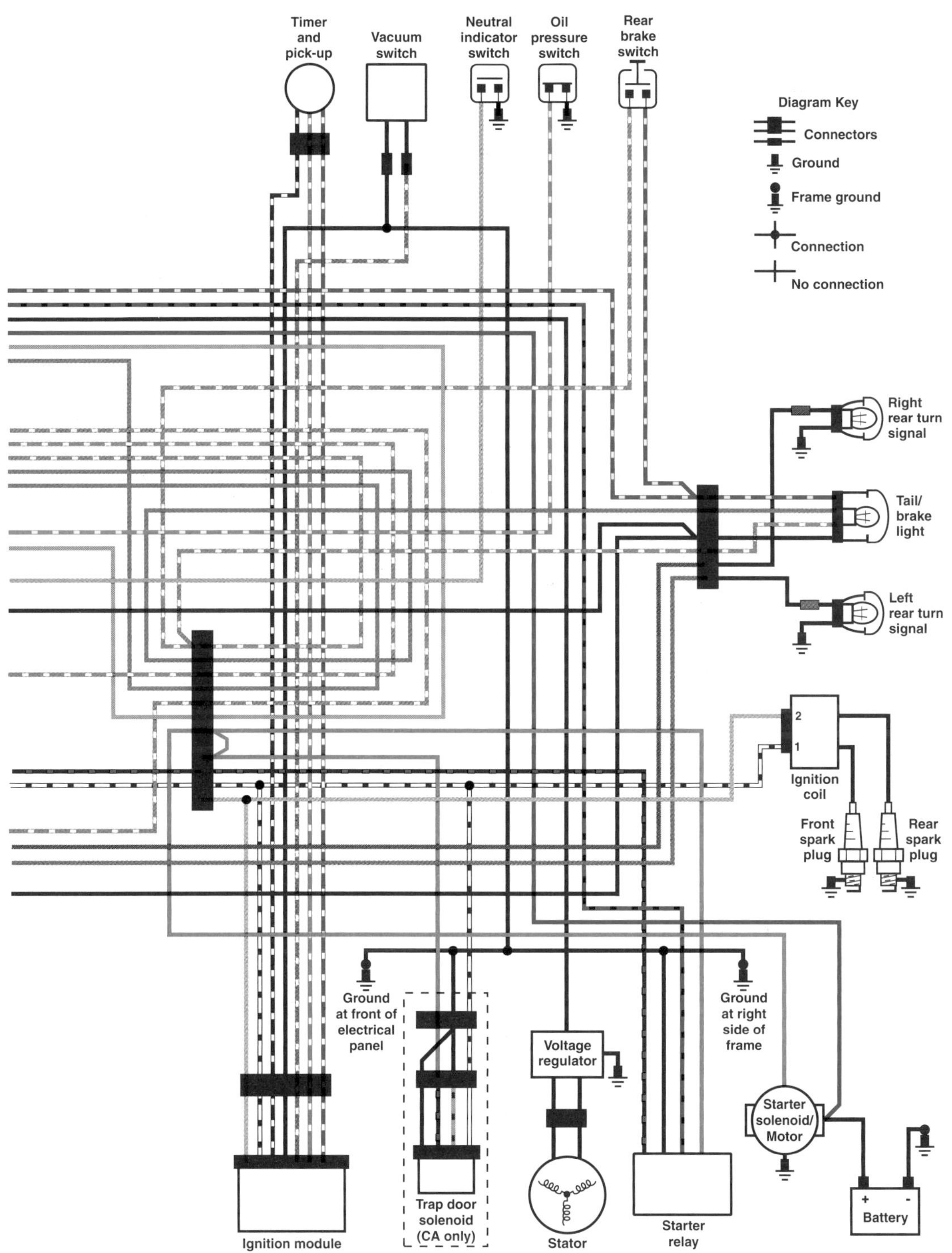
Timer and pick-up
Vacuum switch
Neutral indicator switch
Oil pressure switch
Rear brake switch
Diagram Key
Connectors
Ground
Frame ground
Connection
No connection
Right rear turn signal
Tail/ brake light
Left rear turn signal
2
1
Ignition coil
Front spark plug
Rear spark plug
Ground at front of electrical panel
Ground at right side of frame
Voltage regulator
Starter solenoid/ Motor
+
-
Battery
Ignition module
Trap door solenoid (CA only)
Stator
Starter relay

1996 ALL FXD

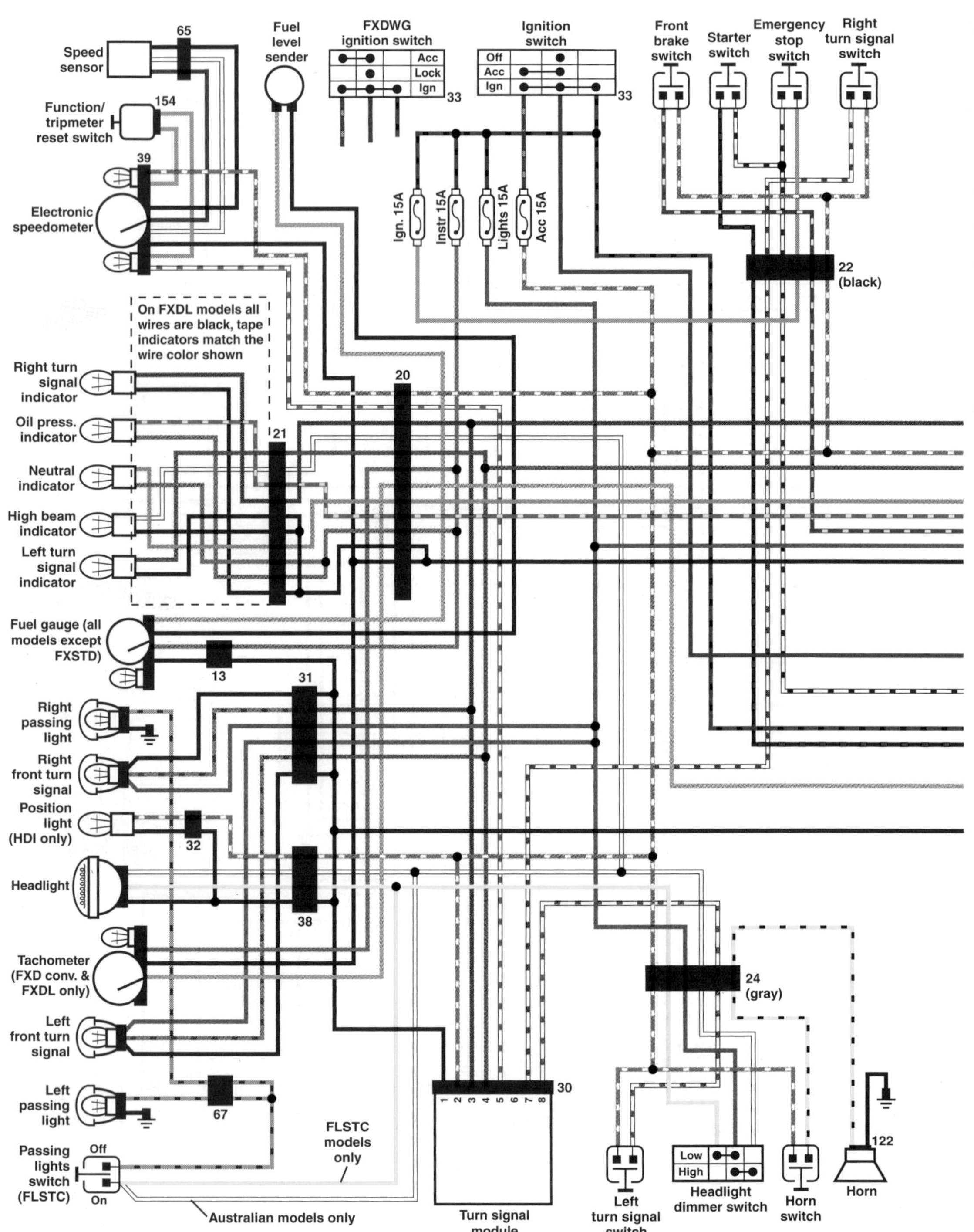
Speed sensor
65
Function/ tripmeter reset switch
154
39
Electronic speedometer
Fuel level sender
FXDWG ignition switch
Acc
Lock
Ign
33
Ignition switch
Off
Acc
Ign
33
Ign. 15A
Instr 15A
Lights 15A
Acc 15A
Front brake switch
Starter switch
Emergency stop switch
Right turn signal switch
22 (black)
On FXDL models all wires are black, tape indicators match the wire color shown
Right turn signal indicator
Oil press. indicator
Neutral indicator
High beam indicator
Left turn signal indicator
21
20
Fuel gauge (all models except FXSTD)
13
31
Right passing light
Right front turn signal
Position light (HDI only)
32
Headlight
38
Tachometer (FXD conv. & FXDL only)
Left front turn signal
Left passing light
67
Passing lights switch (FLSTC)
Off
On
FLSTC models only
Australian models only
30
1 2 3 4 5 6 7 8
Turn signal module
24 (gray)
Left turn signal switch
Low
High
Headlight dimmer switch
Horn switch
122
Horn

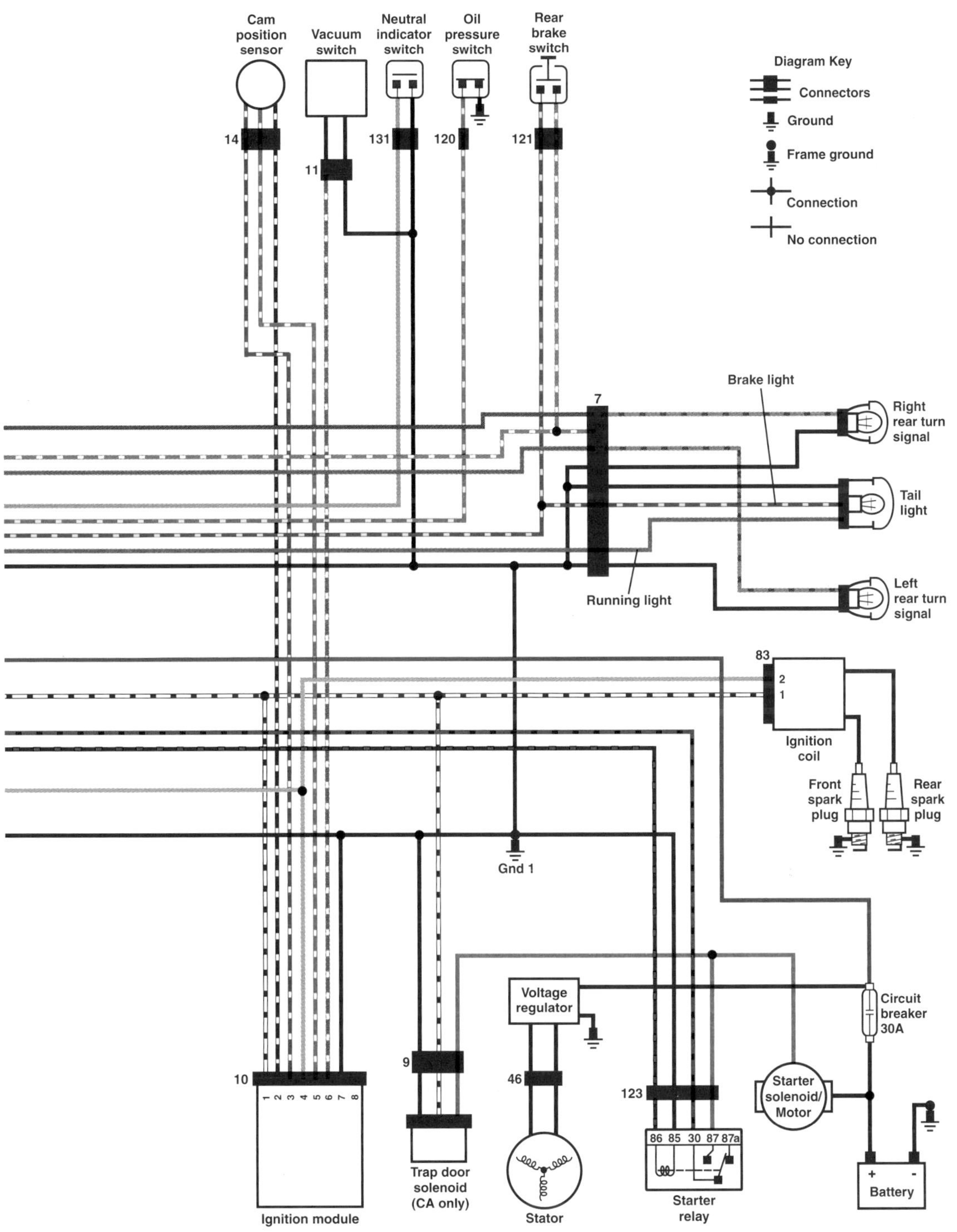
Cam position sensor
Vacuum switch
Neutral indicator switch
Oil pressure switch
Rear brake switch
Diagram Key
Connectors
Ground
Frame ground
Connection
No connection
14
11
131
120
121
7
Brake light
Right rear turn signal
Tail light
Left rear turn signal
Running light
83
2
1
Ignition coil
Front spark plug
Rear spark plug
Gnd 1
Voltage regulator
Circuit breaker 30A
10
1 2 3 4 5 6 7 8
Ignition module
9
Trap door solenoid (CA only)
46
Stator
123
86 85 30 87 87a
Starter relay
Starter solenoid/ Motor
+ -
Battery

1997 ALL FXD

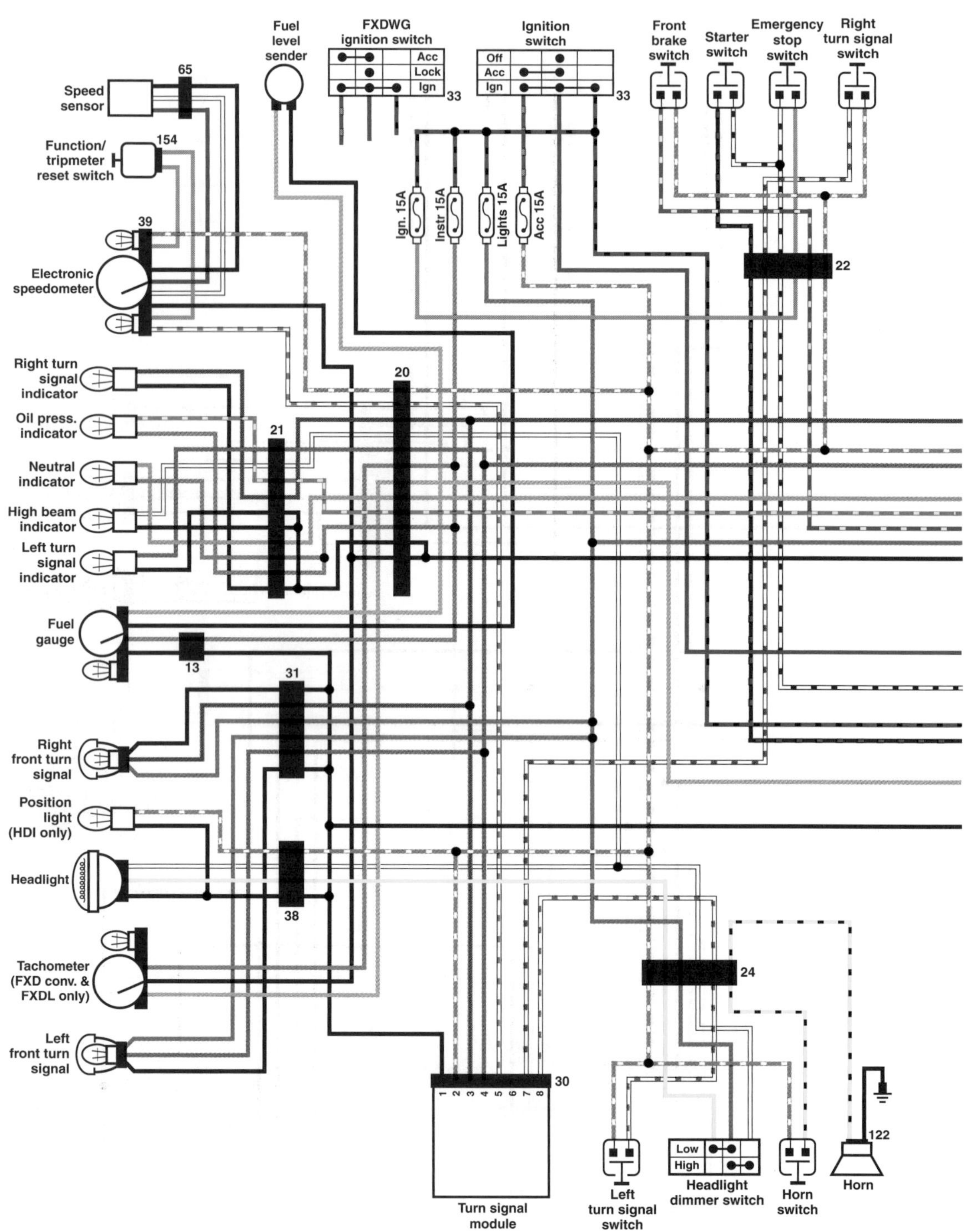

Speed sensor
65
Function/ tripmeter reset switch
154
39
Electronic speedometer
Fuel level sender
FXDWG ignition switch
Acc
Lock
Ign
33
Ignition switch
Off
Acc
Ign
33
Ign. 15A
Instr 15A
Lights 15A
Acc 15A
Front brake switch
Starter switch
Emergency stop switch
Right turn signal switch
22
Right turn signal indicator
Oil press. indicator
Neutral indicator
High beam indicator
Left turn signal indicator
21
20
Fuel gauge
13
31
Right front turn signal
Position light (HDI only)
Headlight
38
Tachometer (FXD conv. & FXDL only)
Left front turn signal
30
1 2 3 4 5 6 7 8
Turn signal module
24
Left turn signal switch
Low
High
Headlight dimmer switch
Horn switch
122
Horn

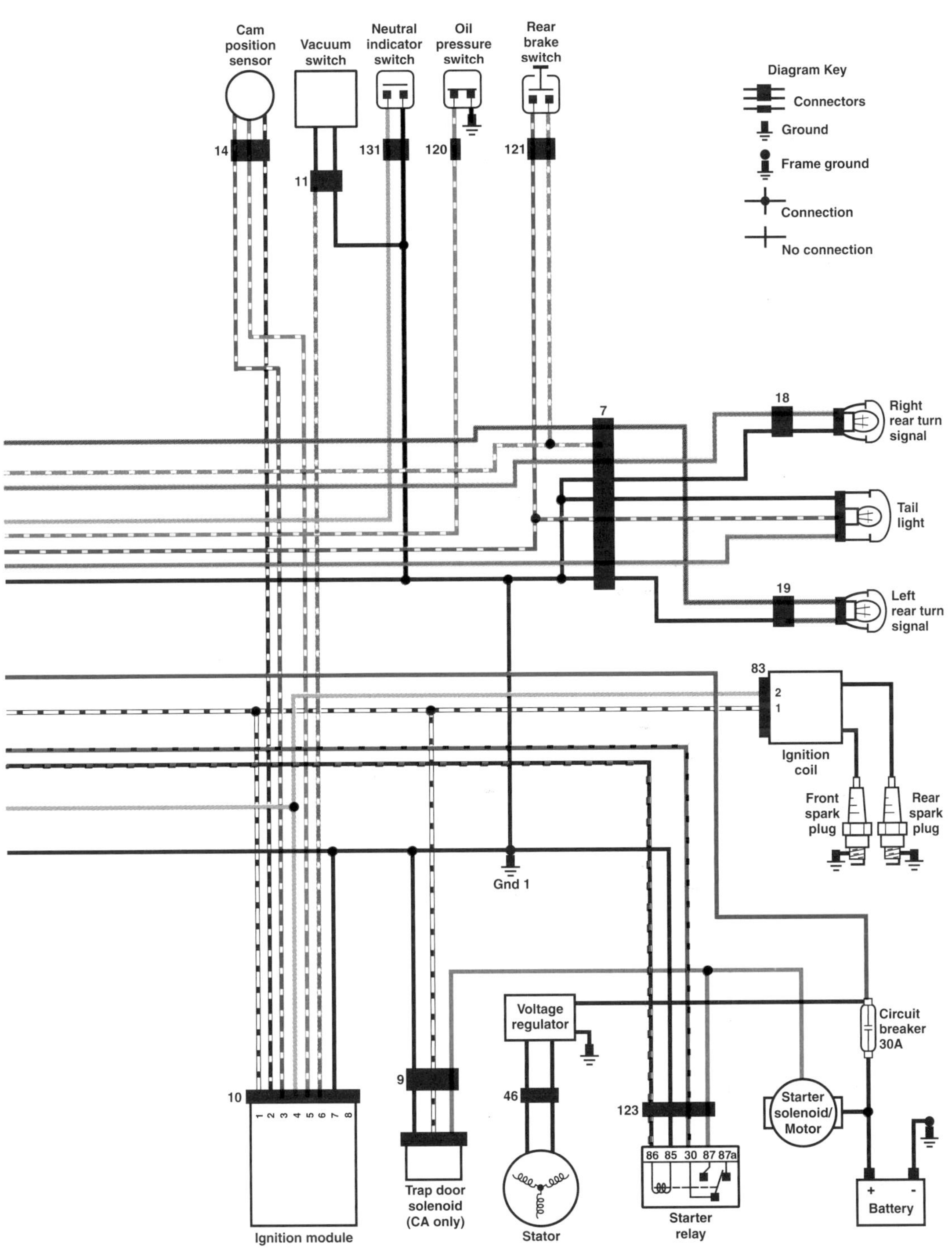
Cam position sensor
Vacuum switch
Neutral indicator switch
Oil pressure switch
Rear brake switch
Diagram Key
Connectors
Ground
Frame ground
Connection
No connection
14
11
131
120
121
7
18
Right rear turn signal
Tail light
19
Left rear turn signal
83
2
1
Ignition coil
Front spark plug
Rear spark plug
Gnd 1
Voltage regulator
Circuit breaker 30A
10
1 2 3 4 5 6 7 8
Ignition module
9
Trap door solenoid (CA only)
46
Stator
123
86 85 30 87 87a
Starter relay
Starter solenoid/ Motor
+ -
Battery
15

1998 ALL FXD

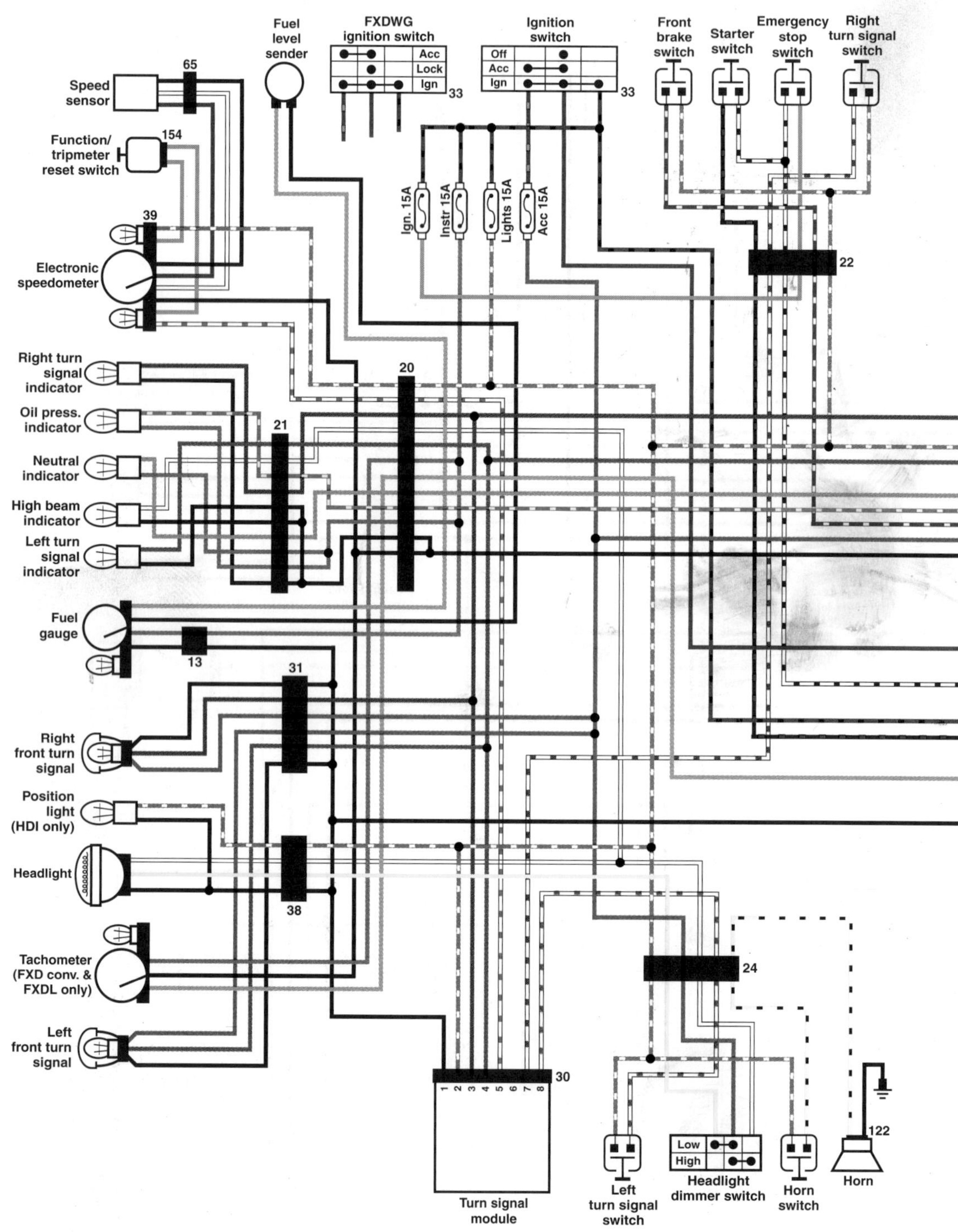

Speed sensor
65
Function/ tripmeter reset switch
154
39
Electronic speedometer
Fuel level sender
FXDWG ignition switch
Acc
Lock
Ign
33
Ignition switch
Off
Acc
Ign
33
Front brake switch
Starter switch
Emergency stop switch
Right turn signal switch
Ign. 15A
Instr 15A
Lights 15A
Acc 15A
22
Right turn signal indicator
Oil press. indicator
Neutral indicator
High beam indicator
Left turn signal indicator
21
20
Fuel gauge
13
31
Right front turn signal
Position light (HDI only)
Headlight
38
Tachometer (FXD conv. & FXDL only)
Left front turn signal
24
30
1 2 3 4 5 6 7 8
Turn signal module
Left turn signal switch
Low
High
Headlight dimmer switch
Horn switch
122
Horn

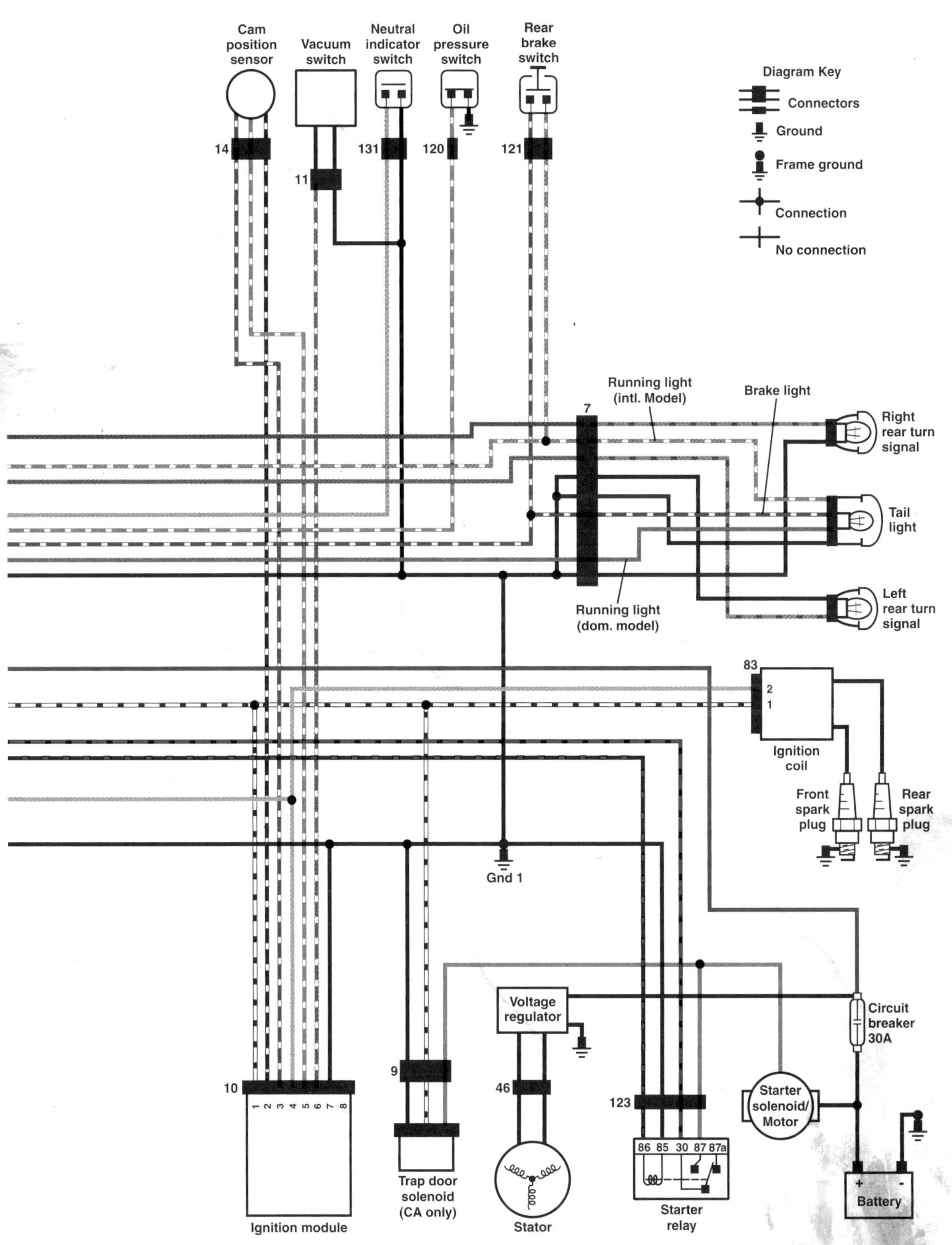
Cam position sensor
Vacuum switch
Neutral indicator switch
Oil pressure switch
Rear brake switch
Diagram Key
Connectors
Ground
Frame ground
Connection
No connection
14
11
131
120
121
7
Running light (intl. Model)
Brake light
Right rear turn signal
Tail light
Left rear turn signal
Running light (dom. model)
83
2
1
Ignition coil
Front spark plug
Rear spark plug
Gnd 1
Voltage regulator
Circuit breaker 30A
Starter solenoid/ Motor
Battery
10
1 2 3 4 5 6 7 8
Ignition module
9
Trap door solenoid (CA only)
46
Stator
123
86 85 30 87 87a
Starter relay

NOTES

NOTES

NOTES

NOTES

NOTES

MAINTENANCE LOG

Date	Miles	Type of Service

Check out *clymer.com* for our full line of powersport repair manuals.

BMW

- M308 500 & 600cc Twins, 55-69
- M502-3 BMW R50/5-R100GS PD, 70-96
- M500-3 BMW K-Series, 85-97
- M501-3 K1200RS, GT & LT, 98-10
- M503-3 R850, R1100, R1150 & R1200C, 93-05
- M309 F650, 1994-2000

HARLEY-DAVIDSON

- M419 Sportsters, 59-85
- M429-5 XL/XLH Sportster, 86-03
- M427-4 XL Sportster, 04-13
- M418 Panheads, 48-65
- M420 Shovelheads,66-84
- M421-3 FLS/FXS Evolution,84-99
- M423-2 FLS/FXS Twin Cam, 00-05
- M250 FLS/FXS/FXC Softail, 06-09
- M422-3 FLH/FLT/FXR Evolution, 84-98
- M430-4 FLH/FLT Twin Cam, 99-05
- M252 FLH/FLT, 06-09
- M426 VRSC Series, 02-07
- M424-2 FXD Evolution, 91-98
- M425-3 FXD Twin Cam, 99-05
- M254 Dyna Series, 06-11

HONDA

ATVs

- M316 Odyssey FL250, 77-84
- M311 ATC, TRX & Fourtrax 70-125, 70-87
- M433 Fourtrax 90, 93-00
- M326 ATC185 & 200, 80-86
- M347 ATC200X & Fourtrax 200SX, 86-88
- M455 ATC250 & Fourtrax 200/250, 84-87
- M342 ATC250R, 81-84
- M348 TRX250R/Fourtrax 250R & ATC250R, 85-89
- M456-4 TRX250X 87-92; TRX300EX 93-06
- M446-3 TRX250 Recon & Recon ES, 97-07
- M215-2 TTRX250EX Sportrax and TRX250X, 01-12
- M346-3 TRX300/Fourtrax 300 & TRX300FW/Fourtrax 4x4, 88-00
- M200-2 TRX350 Rancher, 00-06
- M459-3 TRX400 Foreman 95-03
- M454-5 TRX400EX Fourtrax & Sportrax 99-13
- M201 TRX450R & TRX450ER, 04-09
- M205 TRX450 Foreman, 98-04
- M210 TRX500 Rubicon, 01-04
- M206 TRX500 Foreman, 05-11

Singles

- M310-13 50-110cc OHC Singles, 65-99
- M315 100-350cc OHC, 69-82
- M317 125-250cc Elsinore, 73-80
- M442 CR60-125R Pro-Link, 81-88
- M431-2 CR80R, 89-95, CR125R, 89-91
- M435 CR80R &CR80RB, 96-02
- M457-2 CR125R, 92-97; CR250R, 92-96
- M464 CR125R, 1998-2002
- M443 CR250R-500R Pro-Link, 81-87
- M432-3 CR250R, 88-91 & CR500R, 88-01
- M437 CR250R, 97-01
- M352 CRF250R, CRF250X, CRF450R & CRF450X, 02-05
- M319-3 XR50R, CRF50F, XR70R & CRF70F, 97-09
- M312-14 XL/XR75-100, 75-91
- M222 XR80R, CRF80F, XR100R, & CRF100F, 92-09
- M318-4 XL/XR/TLR 125-200, 79-03
- M328-4 XL/XR250, 78-00; XL/XR350R 83-85; XR200R, 84-85; XR250L, 91-96
- M320-2 XR400R, 96-04
- M221 XR600R, 91-07; XR650L, 93-07
- M339-8 XL/XR 500-600, 79-90
- M225 XR650R, 00-07

Twins

- M321 125-200cc Twins, 65-78
- M322 250-350cc Twins, 64-74
- M323 250-360cc Twins, 74-77
- M324-5 Twinstar, Rebel 250 & Nighthawk 250, 78-03
- M334 400-450cc Twins, 78-87
- M333 450 & 500cc Twins, 65-76
- M335 CX & GL500/650, 78-83
- M344 VT500, 83-88
- M313 VT700 & 750, 83-87
- M314-3 VT750 Shadow Chain Drive, 98-06
- M440 VT1100C Shadow, 85-96
- M460-4 VT1100 Series, 95-07
- M230 VTX1800 Series, 02-08
- M231 VTX1300 Series, 03-09

Fours

- M332 CB350-550, SOHC, 71-78
- M345 CB550 & 650, 83-85
- M336 CB650,79-82
- M341 CB750 SOHC, 69-78
- M337 CB750 DOHC, 79-82
- M436 CB750 Nighthawk, 91-93 & 95-99
- M325 CB900, 1000 & 1100, 80-83
- M439 600 Hurricane, 87-90
- M441-2 CBR600F2 & F3, 91-98
- M445-2 CBR600F4, 99-06
- M220 CBR600RR, 03-06
- M434-2 CBR900RR Fireblade, 93-99
- M329 500cc V-Fours, 84-86
- M349 700-1000cc Interceptor, 83-85
- M458-2 VFR700F-750F, 86-97
- M438 VFR800FI Interceptor, 98-00
- M327 700-1100cc V-Fours, 82-88
- M508 ST1100/Pan European, 90-02
- M340 GL1000 & 1100, 75-83
- M504 GL1200, 84-87

Sixes

- M505 GL1500 Gold Wing, 88-92
- M506-2 GL1500 Gold Wing, 93-00
- M507-3 GL1800 Gold Wing, 01-10
- M462-2 GL1500C Valkyrie, 97-03

KAWASAKI

ATVs

- M465-3 Bayou KLF220 & KLF250, 88-10
- M466-4 Bayou KLF300, 86-04
- M467 Bayou KLF400, 93-99
- M470 Lakota KEF300, 95-99
- M385-2 Mojave KSF250, 87-04

Singles

- M350-9 80-350cc Rotary Valve, 66-01
- M444-2 KX60, 83-02; KX80 83-90
- M448-2 KX80, 91-00; KX85, 01-10 & KX100, 89-09
- M351 KDX200, 83-88
- M447-3 KX125 & KX250, 82-91; KX500, 83-04
- M472-2 KX125, 92-00
- M473-2 KX250, 92-00
- M474-3 KLR650, 87-07
- M240-2 KLR650, 08-12

Twins

- M355 KZ400, KZ/Z440, EN450 & EN500, 74-95
- M241 Ninja 250R (EX250), 88-12
- M360-3 EX500, GPZ500S, & Ninja 500R, 87-02
- M356-5 Vulcan 700 & 750, 85-06
- M354-3 Vulcan 800, 95-05
- M246 Vulcan 900, 06-12
- M357-2 Vulcan 1500, 87-99
- M471-3 Vulcan 1500 Series, 96-08
- M245 Vulcan 1600 Series, 03-08

Fours

- M449 KZ500/550 & ZX550, 79-85
- M450 KZ, Z & ZX750, 80-85
- M358 KZ650, 77-83
- M359-3 Z & KZ 900-1000cc, 73-81
- M451-3 KZ, ZX & ZN 1000 &1100cc, 81-02
- M452-3 ZX500 & Ninja ZX600, 85-97
- M468-2 Ninja ZX-6, 90-04
- M469 Ninja ZX-7, ZX7R & ZX7RR, 91-98
- M453-3 Ninja ZX900, ZX1000 & ZX1100, 84-01
- M409-2 Concours, 86-06

POLARIS

ATVs

- M496 3-, 4- and 6-Wheel Models w/250-425cc Engines, 85-95
- M362-2 Magnum & Big Boss, 96-99
- M363 Scrambler 500 4X4, 97-00
- M365-5 Sportsman/Xplorer, 96-13
- M366 Sportsman 600/700/800 Twins, 02-10
- M367 Predator 500, 03-07

SUZUKI

ATVs

- M381 ALT/LT 125 & 185, 83-87
- M475 LT230 & LT250, 85-90
- M380-2 LT250R Quad Racer, 85-92
- M483-2 LT-4WD, LT-F4WDX & LT-F250, 87-98
- M270-2 LT-Z400, 03-08
- M343-2 LT-F500F Quadrunner, 98-02

Singles

- M369 125-400cc, 64-81
- M371 RM50-400 Twin Shock, 75-81
- M379 RM125-500 Single Shock, 81-88
- M386 RM80-250, 89-95
- M400 RM125, 96-00
- M401 RM250, 96-02
- M476 DR250-350, 90-94
- M477-4 DR-Z400E, S & SM, 00-12
- M272 DR650, 96-12
- M384-5 LS650 Savage/S40, 86-12

Twins

- M372 GS400-450 Chain Drive, 77-87
- M484-3 GS500E Twins, 89-02
- M361 SV650, 1999-2002
- M481-6 VS700-800 Intruder/S50, 85-09
- M261-2 1500 Intruder/C90, 98-09
- M260-3 Volusia/Boulevard C50, 01-11
- M482-3 VS1400 Intruder/S83, 87-07

Triple

- M368 GT380, 550 & 750, 72-77

Fours

- M373 GS550, 77-86
- M364 GS650, 81-83
- M370 GS750, 77-82
- M376 GS850-1100 Shaft Drive, 79-84
- M378 GS1100 Chain Drive, 80-81
- M383-3 Katana 600, 88-96 GSX-R750-1100, 86-87
- M331 GSX-R600, 97-00
- M264 GSX-R600, 01-05
- M478-2 GSX-R750, 88-92; GSX750F Katana, 89-96
- M485 GSX-R750, 96-99
- M377 GSX-R1000, 01-04
- M266 GSX-R1000, 05-06
- M265 GSX1300R Hayabusa, 99-07
- M338 Bandit 600, 95-00
- M353 GSF1200 Bandit, 96-03

YAMAHA

ATVs

- M499-2 YFM80 Moto-4, Badger & Raptor, 85-08
- M394 YTM200, 225 & YFM200, 83-86
- M488-5 Blaster, 88-05
- M489-2 Timberwolf, 89-00
- M487-5 Warrior, 87-04
- M486-6 Banshee, 87-06
- M490-3 Moto-4 & Big Bear, 87-04
- M493 Kodiak, 93-98
- M287-2 YFZ450, 04-13
- M285-2 Grizzly 660, 02-08
- M280-2 Raptor 660R, 01-05
- M290 Raptor 700R, 06-09
- M291 Rhino 700, 2008-2012

Singles

- M492-2 PW50 & 80 Y-Zinger & BW80 Big Wheel 80, 81-02
- M410 80-175 Piston Port, 68-76
- M415 250-400 Piston Port, 68-76
- M412 DT & MX Series, 77-83
- M414 IT125-490, 76-86
- M393 YZ50-80 Monoshock, 78-90
- M413 YZ100-490 Monoshock, 76-84
- M390 YZ125-250, 85-87 YZ490, 85-90
- M391 YZ125-250, 88-93 & WR250Z, 91-93
- M497-2 YZ125, 94-01
- M498 YZ250, 94-98; WR250Z, 94-97
- M406 YZ250F & WR250F, 01-03
- M491-2 YZ400F, 98-99 & 426F, 00-02; WR400F, 98-00 & 426F, 00-01
- M417 XT125-250, 80-84
- M480-3 XT350, 85-00; TT350, 86-87
- M405 XT/TT 500, 76-81
- M416 XT/TT 600, 83-89

Twins

- M403 650cc Twins, 70-82
- M395-10 XV535-1100 Virago, 81-03
- M495-7 V-Star 650, 98-11
- M284 V-Star 950, 09-12
- M281-4 V-Star 1100, 99-09
- M283 V-Star 1300, 07-10
- M282-2 Road Star, 99-07

Triple

- M404 XS750 & XS850, 77-81

Fours

- M387 XJ550, XJ600 & FJ600, 81-92
- M494 XJ600 Seca II/Diversion, 92-98
- M388 YX600 Radian & FZ600, 86-90
- M396 FZR600, 89-93
- M392 FZ700-750 & Fazer, 85-87
- M411 XS1100, 78-81
- M461 YZF-R6, 99-04
- M398 YZF-R1, 98-03
- M399 FZ1, 01-05
- M397 FJ1100 & 1200, 84-93
- M375-2 V-Max, 85-07
- M374-2 Royal Star, 96-10

VINTAGE MOTORCYCLES

Clymer® Collection Series

- M330 Vintage British Street Bikes, BSA 500–650cc Unit Twins; Norton 750 & 850cc Commandos; Triumph 500-750cc Twins
- M300 Vintage Dirt Bikes, V. 1 Bultaco, 125-370cc Singles; Montesa, 123-360cc Singles; Ossa, 125-250cc Singles
- M305 Vintage Japanese Street Bikes Honda, 250 & 305cc Twins; Kawasaki, 250-750cc Triples; Kawasaki, 900 & 1000cc Fours